PHILOSOPHY OF LAW

Sixth Edition

Edited by

Joel Feinberg
University of Arizona

Jules Coleman
Yale Law School

Australia • Canada • Denmark • Japan • Mexico • New Zealand • Philippines • Puerto Rico
Singapore • South Africa • Spain • United Kingdom • United States

Philosophy Editor: Peter Adams
Assistant Editor: Kerri Abdinoor
Editorial Assistant: Mindy Newfarmer
Marketing Manager: Dave Garrison
Print Buyer: Stacey Weinberger
Permissions Editor: Robert Kauser

Production: Matrix Productions
Copyeditor: Mimi Kusch
Cover Design: Harry Voigt
Compositor: Thompson Type
Printer: R. R. Donnelley & Sons

For permission to use material from this text, contact us:
web   www.thomsonrights.com
fax   1-800-730-2215
phone   1-800-730-2214

Printed in the United States of America
2 3 4 5 6 03 02 01

Wadsworth/Thompson Learning
10 Davis Drive
Belmont, CA 94002-3098
USA
www.wadsworth.com

International Headquarters
Thompson Learning
290 Harbor Drive, 2nd Floor
Stamford, CT 06902-7477
USA

UK/Europe/Middle East
Thompson Learning
Berkshire House
168-173 High Holborn
London WCIV7AA
United Kingdom

Asia
Thompson Learning
60 Albert Street #15-01
Albert Complex
Singapore 189969

Canada
Nelson/Thompson Learning
1120 Birchmount Road
Scarborough, Ontario M1K 5G4
Canada

Library of Congress Cataloging-in-Publication Data

Philosophy of law / edited by Joel Feinberg, Jules Coleman.—6th ed.
        p.   cm.
    ISBN 0-534-52497–4
    1. Law—Philosophy. 2. Law and ethics. 3. Law—United States—Philosophy
    4. Law—United States—Moral and ethical aspects.
  I. Feinberg, Joel, 1926–   . II. Coleman, Jules L.
  K231.P47   1999   99-12973
  340'.1—dc21

DEDICATION

For Joel Feinberg
my teacher and friend

CONTENTS

PART FOUR: RESPONSIBILITY   549

Responsibility for Results   554

Responsibility for Nonintervention   623

Some Criminal Defenses   646

PART FIVE: PUNISHMENT 683

PREFACE

There is currently a widespread and truly philosophical perplexity about law. That perplexity is occasioned by the events of the day and the legal proceedings to which they give rise. Increasing numbers of students have been attracted to courses in philosophy of law and social philosophy offered by philosophy departments, and law students, constantly challenged by the theoretical dimensions of law school subjects, are prompted more than ever to enroll in jurisprudence courses. These students often are disappointed by what seems to them an excessively abstract approach. Portentous terms such as *law, morality*, and *justice* are manipulated like counters in an uncertain game, and hoary figures from the past are marched by, each with a distinctive dogmatic pronouncement and a curious technical vocabulary. No wonder traditional jurisprudence often seems among the driest and most remote of academic subjects.

We have tried in this volume to relate the traditional themes of legal philosophy to the live concerns of modern society in a way that invigorates one and illuminates the other. The volume begins with essays by classic and contemporary figures on the essential nature of law and on the relation of law to morality or to other sources of principle outside the legal system. No attempt is made to give contending doctrines equal time or even to give them all a day in court. We have passed over much excellent material that might have been included, though this is sure to cause some displeasure in an area of

jurisprudential concern that is so marked by doctrinal partisanship. Our endeavor is not to represent every important point of view, or to represent any in a truly comprehensive way, but instead to offer a series of selections that raise sharply the most important issues. Many of these philosophical issues debated in the first part recur later in the book, where authors take up specific problems about liberty, justice, responsibility, and punishment.

This sixth edition represents an extensive and substantial revision. While it largely follows the fifth in its organization of materials, nineteen of the seventy-nine selections included here are new ones. The new selections include works by Brian Bix, Jules Coleman and Arthur Ripstein, Susan Dimock, Ronald Dworkin, Joel Feinberg, Leslie Green, Mark Kelman, Anthony T. Kronman, David Luban, Toni M. Massaro, Stephen Perry, Plato, Russ Shafer-Landau, and Ernest J. Weinrib.

We have benefited from the advice of many professors who used some or all of the earlier editions of this book. We especially wish to thank those who agreed to write formal reviews: Jerome Falmouth, Colgate University; Kenneth Baynes, SUNY-Stony Brook; Susan J. Brison, Dartmouth College; Douglas Husak, Rutgers University; and Berleigh T. Wilkins, UC Santa Barbara.

We appreciate also the helpful work of research assistants Jennifer Ryan, a graduate student in philosophy at the University of Arizona, and Eric Cavallero, a graduate student in philosophy at Yale.

PART ONE

Law

The question "What is law?" seems at first glance hardly to deserve a philosopher's attention. Ask a lawyer about the law: if he or she is unable to give an answer on the spot, such a professional knows where to look it up or at least where to get the ingredients for a reliable opinion. Statutes, judicial opinions, administrative regulations, and constitutional provisions are all official pronouncements of law. When these texts leave the matter ambiguous, a lawyer knows the appropriate techniques to resolve the ambiguity, and in aid of that consults scholarly works of interpretation and other sources of authoritative opinion. The question "What is law?" then seems simply a request for a general definition that covers all those, and only those, items of official pronouncement that lawyers finally treat as law. It is true that even the best dictionary may leave us unsatisfied, for something more informative than a mere guide for word use is wanted. Still, at first sight nothing in the question appears to need the fine grinding of the philosopher's mill, and we conclude that we are adequately acquainted with the notion of something as familiar as law, with only the details remaining to be filled in.

Our simple belief is shattered not only by philosophical reflection but also by the common experience of those who use and are subject to the law. The late Professor H. L. A. Hart, whose work has dominated Anglo-American legal philosophy, has described this illusion of understanding with these words:

> The same predicament was expressed by some famous words of St. Augustine about the notion of time. "What then is time? If no one asks me I know: if I wish to explain it to

one that asks I know not." It is in this way that even skilled lawyers have felt that, though they know the law, there is much about law and its relations to other things that they cannot explain and do not fully understand. Like a person who can get from one point to another in a familiar town but cannot explain or show others how to do it, those who press for a definition need a map exhibiting clearly the relationships dimly felt to exist between the law they know and other things.[1]

The articles in Part One present important theories about the nature of law. The articles are arranged in four subsections:

- Natural Law Theory
- The Challenge of Legal Positivism
- Law from the Perspective of the Judge
- The Moral Obligation to Obey the Law

This introduction to Part One will acquaint you with the subject matter of each section and, in many cases, discuss how particular articles have influenced the theory and practice of law.

Natural Law Theory

Any philosopher who constructs a theory about the nature of law is likely to express that theory in the form of a definition of the word *law* or, when that definition seems ambiguous, a definition of each important sense. In the long history of this subject there have been two main types of definition. The first, chronologically speaking, goes with the natural law theory that prevailed from the time of the ancient Stoic philosophers and Roman lawyers, through the age of the medieval schoolmen, to the seventeenth- and eighteenth-century revolutionaries. The formal definition of *law* proposed by St. Thomas Aquinas in the thirteenth century is typical of definitions of this class: "Law is nothing else than an ordinance of reason for the promotion of the common good, made by him who has the care of the community, and promulgated." The second type of definition is that associated with the theory called legal positivism, of which John Austin's definition in the nineteenth century is typical:

> A valid law [that is, one that exists and is in effect in a given legal jurisdiction] is a command, that is (1) an expression of a general desire that others act or forbear in certain ways (2) together with a threat of evil for noncompliance (a sanction), (3) together with the power to enforce compliance, (4) emanating from a person (or group of persons) who alone is (or are) habitually obeyed by the bulk of the society and who habitually obey no one else (that person or persons is the sovereign in that society).

There are several important differences between these classes of definitions: The natural law definitions are *normative*. They do not attempt to eliminate such terms as *rational, common good,* and *properly possessing authority*. Instead they employ these terms, using their own standards of application. The positivists, on the other hand, think of themselves as more "scientific." They are sympathetic to efforts to eliminate normative terms by defining them in turn in nonnormative terms. The positivists' key terms are words like *command, threat, power, habit,* and *obedience,* which they regard as empirical notions capable of empirical apprehension, confirmation, and even measurement. The positivists' account of law is intended to be entirely neutral in respect to moral-political controversies. The natural law theory denies that a conceptual analysis of law *can* be neutral, since some minimal principles, at least, of morality and justice are built in to the very concept of law. Moreover, the natural law theorists' definition is avowedly of the kind called functional or teleological. Like definitions of organs that function within larger organisms; and component parts of machines; and tools and instruments, jobs and professions, so-called

functional terms must be defined by reference to their *telos:* what they are *for*. Legal positivists, on the other hand, seek to define *law* in terms that describe its actual functioning and structure. They will insist that as "analytic jurisprudents," they are more interested in what law *is* than in what law *ought to be*. Positivists reject the natural law theorists' claim that reference to morality (or to that part of morality called justice) is an essential part of any account of what law is. But positivists insist that their theory does not preclude them from advocating changes in an existing legal code that will make it more like what it ought to be—more just, reasonable, and humane—or from evaluating existing laws and systems as good or bad, better or worse, fair or unfair, etc.

Legal positivists, moreover, are likely to distinguish two senses of morality: (1) the conventional morality of a given community at some particular time and place (there are better and worse moralities in this sense, and some moralities that are actually immoral!) and (2) rational, critical, or "true" morality, which can be used as a standard for judging conventional moralities. The most important of the questions that divide the schools of natural law and legal positivism is the following: "Is reference to critical, rational, or true morality—as opposed to merely conventional morality—an essential part of any adequate account of what law is?"

Legal positivism answers this question categorically and negatively. It holds that law is one thing and morality another and that neither can be reduced to the other. Positivists happily concede that it is a good idea for law to conform to morality—that is, to be fair and humane—but an unfair rule is still a valid law provided only that it is made in accordance with accepted lawmaking rules of an existing legal system. As the positivist H. L. A. Hart was wont to say, there is a content-neutral test for determining (a) whether a legal system exists in a given community and (b) whether a given rule is a valid law within that system. The validity of a particular rule is determined by its *pedigree* (how it was made), not by its *content* (what it says).

Natural law theorists, as we have already seen, give an affirmative answer to our question. Morality is not simply a desirable feature to import into law, but rather an essential part of law as it really is. No adequate test of the validity of a legal rule, or the existence of a legal system, could possibly be content neutral, since it is usually the content of a rule that determines whether it is fair or unfair, reasonable or unreasonable. That is, simply to pronounce the obvious truth of whether or not a given rule is (say) fair, depends at least in part on what sort of conduct it requires, permits, or prohibits, or in other words on its *content*.

Thomas Aquinas is certainly the most influential writer in the natural law tradition. However, his writings are difficult to penetrate and can prove frustrating for beginning students. In the first selection of this part, "Natural Law Theory," Brian Bix gives us a broad historical overview of the natural law tradition. Starting with Cicero and the Stoics, Bix traces the tradition through the contribution of Aquinas and on to the present day. Two of the modern natural law theorists he discusses—Lon Fuller and Ronald Dworkin —are represented elsewhere in this volume, and Bix's contribution is especially helpful in situating these modern natural law theorists in a long tradition of legal scholarship. In "The Natural Law Theory of St. Thomas Aquinas," the second selection in Part One, Susan Dimock provides an excellent commentary on the key portions of Aquinas's writings on natural law. Dimock's approach, which incorporates large portions of Aquinas's own text, yields an accessible yet rigorous introduction to Aquinas's legal theory.

The topic of natural law theory figures prominently in the third section of Part One as well. In "The Dilemmas of Judges Who Must interpret 'Immoral Laws'," Joel Feinberg considers the consequences of the positivism-natural law debate for conflicts in the political arena. He uses, as his chief example, the conflict among American abolitionist judges over the Fugitive Slave Acts of 1793 and 1850—unjust enactments if ever there were any. This article also draws on the Hart-Fuller debate, represented in the second section of Part One.

The Challenge of Legal Positivism

John Austin's *The Province of Jurisprudence Determined* was published in England in 1832, and it has long been regarded in the Anglo-American tradition as the leading work in opposition to natural law theory. It is an exceedingly careful work of great range and refinement. The portions reprinted here set forth only the essentials of Austin's views about the nature of law. His theory has been one of the first to be studied by English-speaking students for over a century and a half now, so it is no wonder that it has called forth more abundant criticism than any other theory.

A consensus has formed over the difficulties encountered by Austin's sort of positivism, the most authoritative statement of which is that of the leading twentieth-century positivist, H. L. A. Hart, in his seminal work, *The Concept of Law,* published in 1961. In our selection from that work, Hart analyzes the concept of a legal system as a union of two kinds of rules. The first, like an ordinary criminal statute, prohibits, requires, or permits specific kinds of conduct. The second type of rule confers powers on persons to create, to revise, or to terminate specific legal relationships (for example, creditor-debtor, husband-wife, seller-buyer). The full statement of a power-conferring rule will function in a way similar to that of a recipe: The rule is a set of directions for changing our legal status in some respects, and doing so voluntarily. Such rules tell us how to get married, how to get divorced, how to make out a will, etc. Of prime interest among these secondary rules, as Hart calls them, are those telling us how to make, revise, or revoke primary rules. Late in the selection, Hart addresses the concept of legal validity and develops a much more subtle account than Austin's of a "rule of recognition" that enables judges to distinguish legitimate from spurious claims of legality, and to do so in a "content-neutral" way.

Various kinds of controversy over theories about the nature and validity of law are possible, but most of them are of the kind we have already anticipated: controversies over the relationship between law and morality. Those who are spoken of as positivists tend to view a legal system as having its own criteria for valid laws, and so tend to regard moral judgments about laws as important in deciding what the law *should be* (a question for legislators and voters), yet not relevant in deciding what the law *is*. Hart's famous Holmes Lecture at the Harvard Law School, "Positivism and the Separation of Law and Morals," was published in the *Harvard Law Review* about three years before Hart's book. We publish it here for the new light it shed at the time on its subject, and partly because a reply to it was published in the next issue of the *Harvard Law Review* by America's most distinguished legal philosopher at the time, Lon L. Fuller, of Harvard. (Hart spent almost thirty years as professor of jurisprudence at Oxford.) In "Positivism and Fidelity to Law," Fuller found much to admire in Hart's lecture, but as a kind of natural law theorist himself, he was in basic disagreement with Hart's position. Fuller's natural law theory was as imaginative and original a departure from the more traditional natural law theories as

Hart's theory was from the earlier forms of positivism. The debate between these towering figures was a great event in the history of legal philosophy in the twentieth century.

Among the more interesting of Fuller's innovations were his effort to construct a natural law theory without a theological foundation and his argument that morality provides criteria for the (continued) existence of a whole system of rules, not criteria for the validity of a single rule or statute. It is possible then, according to Fuller, for an unjust law to be a valid law, but if the whole network of rules and rule-making powers, or a substantial subsection thereof, is antithetical to morality (as in Nazi Germany, where a genuine legal system was corrupted and undermined), then it is no longer a functioning legal system but, at best, another method of social control—one based on arbitrary power.

Another innovation in Fuller's theory was his novel insistence that the morality that is essential to law is what he called "the internal morality of law" or "the morality that makes law possible," not the more usual prohibition of immoral *content* in rules. The internal morality of law is summed up in a handful of procedural rules requiring promulgation and understandability, and invalidating retroactivity, contradiction, and constant change. He discusses eight of these "ways" in "Eight Ways to Fail to Make Law," a chapter of his book *The Morality of Law*. That chapter is reprinted here.

One of the most important questions in jurisprudence is Can we—and if so, how—explain the possibility of legal authority without invoking the notion of legal authority itself? In "Negative and Positive Positivism," Jules Coleman argues that legal authority is made possible by a social convention among relevant officials: a decision by those individuals to have their behavior guided by a rule setting out conditions of legality. (Hart himself, in the recently published postscript to *The Concept of Law,* came to accept this line of argument and to regard it as the proper interpretation of his own position.) Coleman argues that his social convention account can meet Dworkin's complaint (in "The Model of Rules," reprinted in section three of Part One) that some legal norms cannot derive their authority from the master social convention. Coleman (like Hart to follow) claims that such norms can be conventional if the rule of recognition allows that the moral merits of a principle can be a condition of its legality. Against this view, which he calls "soft conventionalism," Dworkin has objected that the controversiality

of moral principles is incompatible with the claim that their authority could rest on a convention. By drawing a distinction between disagreement in content and disagreement in application or implementation, Coleman meets this objection of Dworkin's. (While Coleman's essay properly belongs in this subsection on legal positivism, it may be helpful to read it after Dworkin's "Model of Rules.")

Law from the Perspective of the Judge

Since the retirement of Professor Hart, the person who has probably had the greatest impact on the philosophy of law in our time is Hart's successor at University College, Oxford, Ronald Dworkin, an American. (Dworkin has also been a regular faculty member for many years at the College of Law of New York University.) Even when legal positivism was riding high at Oxford, partly because of Hart's influence, Dworkin was publishing articles meant to expose its defects. In "The Model of Rules," reprinted here, he argues that there is much more to a system of law than mere rules, even when primary rules are supplemented by secondary ones. Any full-fledged system of law will also contain what Dworkin calls principles, a miscellany that includes in its precise and narrow sense such moral precepts as "No man may profit by his own wrong." The latter principle was a part of the law, Dworkin argues, that was violated when a trial court permitted Elmer Palmer to inherit money from his grandfather, even though Elmer had been convicted of murdering the testator (before he could change his mind). Needless to say, the will was invalidated through a civil suit brought by two daughters of the testator, even though no rule (in Hart's sense) seemed to be violated. Even the dissenting opinion in this case seemed to invoke a Dworkinian principle, namely that courts have no warrant, in the absence of explicit legislative authorization, to "add to the respondent's penalties by depriving him of property." The formerly obscure case of *Riggs v. Palmer* has, since Dworkin's article, become quite famous. *Riggs v. Palmer* is summarized in an article in this section.

The other selection from Dworkin, "Law as Integrity," is an excerpt from Dworkin's book *Law's Empire* and develops in outline Dworkin's full theory of the nature of law. He argues first that every theory of law must be understood as an interpretive theory, that is, as a theory about the meaning of meaning in legal discourse. Meaning for Dworkin contains two elements: fit and value. A theory of law must take seriously all previous legal pronouncements in a way that makes them cohere with one another. In addition, it must see the law, so conceived, in its best light. This last idea is that the law must be understood so as to make the coercive exercise of the state's power at least plausibly justified. In answering the question What is the law on a particular matter? the judge must construct a theory of law. That theory must respect the past political decisions, and thus the judge can be seen as authoring the latest chapter in what we might think of as a "chain novel." Each chapter requires respecting that which came before—suitably purged of its mistaken chapters—and only in the light of a sense of the kind of book one is writing could one fashion the current chapter. In this sense, the judge looks both to the past and to the future. It is noteworthy how much more inclusive and subtle Dworkin's theory is than those of typical (pre-Hart) positivists (one must also exclude Hart's brilliant student, Joseph Raz) and how much less vague than the typical natural law theorist at least before Fuller and, more recently, John Finnis (*Natural Law and Natural Rights, 1980*).

But if Dworkin's theory isn't exactly like traditional natural law and positivist theories, then J. L. Mackie was entirely justified in baptizing it "the third theory of law," giving it its own precise set of defining arguments and then formulating his own distinctive polemical arguments to match them. In philosophy, the more original a given set of arguments are, the more original an inevitable set of counterarguments are likely to be. In "The Third Theory of Law," Mackie effectively voices his doubts that Herculean judicial labor would produce the decision that Dworkin would prefer at least in one class of cases, the Fugitive Slave Acts cases discussed by Feinberg in his earlier essay in Part One. Mackie also concludes his discussions with some important observations about the likely effects of Dworkin's theory if it were adopted explicitly as a guide to adjudication in hard cases.

A disproportionate number of the contributors to Part One of this collection are British. But Americans too have made important contributions to the philosophy of law. No single essay in Anglo-American jurisprudence has received more attention than Oliver Wendell Holmes's "The Path of the Law," first published in 1897. His famous declaration that "The prophecies of what the courts will do in fact,

and nothing more pretentious, are what I mean by the law" became the cornerstone of legal realism in America. How such prophecies are best made is a matter that occupies much of Holmes's attention in the selection that is included here.

The brief selection that follows next is from the writings of another distinguished American judge, Jerome Frank. Here one sees how the law appears to those who wish to use it and not simply make it the subject of a body of theory. A legal saga unfolds as the affairs of the Joneses and the Williamses are put in the hands of their lawyers, and the conception of law that emerges gives weight to Holmes's opening remark: "When we study law we are not studying a mystery but a well known profession." Read together, these two selections lead us to concentrate on the question that perhaps must precede all others in this branch of the philosophy of law: "What, exactly, is its proper subject matter?"

The tradition of legal realism represented here in the selections from Holmes and Frank has in recent years been revived and radicalized in the theoretical movement known as "critical legal studies." In what amounts to a skeptical attack on the entire mainstream of Anglo-American jurisprudence, critical legal theorists have argued that judges are inevitably and unconsciously guided in their decisions by a variety of ideological forces. The last essay in this section, "Interpretive Construction in the Substantive Criminal Law," exemplifies this critical approach. Focusing his attention on the substantive criminal law, Mark Kelman details a significant but largely unexamined feature of legal argument, namely the process by which the legally relevant facts of a concrete situation are selected and organized. Only after this often-unconscious process of "interpretive construction" has occurred can the more familiar forms of legal argumentation begin.

The Moral Obligation to Obey the Law

Most positivists agree with their natural-law rivals that citizens in a democracy have a *moral* obligation—parallel to their moral obligations to keep promises, tell the truth, oppose injustice, and so on—to obey the valid laws of their country. One might similarly affirm that any individual judge in a functioning democracy whose institutions are more or less just has a moral obligation of fidelity to the law that he or she is sworn to apply impartially to others. Each standard theory then must give some account of the basis for this moral obligation (if there is one) and some explanation of how it can fail to apply—as when, for example, *disobedience* (or judicial nullification) is morally justified.

There are three articles in this section of Part One. It begins with Plato's dialogue, *The Crito*. Here Socrates—condemned to death by the council of Athens—explains his decision to submit to that judgment. Despite his confident belief that the death sentence passed upon him is wrong, and despite the ready option of an escape aided by his friends, Socrates argues that he has a moral duty to obey the laws of the city. The powerfully eloquent "Letter from Birmingham Jail" by Martin Luther King, Jr. is another classic in the history of political action and theory, philosophy, and legal theory. King justifies his resistance even to "legal" racial segregation by appealing to a "high-law" version of natural law theory. King is the model civil disobedient. The final selection in this section, "Difference Made Legal: The Court and Dr. King," is both a defense of King and an appraisal of the role of narrative in legal argument. By contrasting the "Letter from Birmingham Jail" with the *Walker* decision (which sustained King's conviction), David Luban seeks to illustrate his contention that legal argument is often "a struggle for the privilege of recounting the past." While critical of both texts, Luban seeks ultimately to vindicate King's argument by grounding its narrative elements in the egalitarian promise of American political traditions.

---

1. H. .L. A. Hart, *The Concept of Law* (Oxford University Press, 1961), pp. 13–14.

Natural Law Theory

NATURAL LAW THEORY*

Brian Bix

Natural law theory has a long and distinguished history, encompassing many and varied theories and theorists—though there are probably no points of belief or methodology common to all of them. In legal theory, most of the approaches dubbed "natural law" can be placed into one of two broad groups, which I call "traditional" and "modern" natural law theory, and will consider in turn below. Some modern natural law theorists who do not fit comfortably into either group will be noted in summary at the end.

Traditional Natural Law Theory

We take it for granted that the laws and legal system under which we live can be criticized on moral grounds: that there are standards against which legal norms can be compared and sometimes found wanting. The standards against which law is judged have sometimes been described as "a (the) higher law." For some, this is meant literally: that there are law-like standards that have been stated in or can be derived from divine revelation, religious texts, a careful study of human nature, or consideration of nature. For others, the reference to "higher law" is meant metaphorically, in which case it at least reflects our mixed intuitions about the moral status of law: on

the one hand, that not everything properly enacted as law is binding morally; on the other hand, that the law, as law, does have moral weight. (If it did not, we would not need to point to a "higher law" as a justification for ignoring the requirements of our society's laws.)

"Traditional" natural law theory offers arguments for the existence of a "higher law", elaborations of its content, and analyses of what consequences follow from the existence of a "higher law" (in particular, what response citizens should have to situations where the positive law—the law enacted within particular societies—conflicts with the "higher law").

Cicero

While one can locate a number of passages in ancient Greek writers that express what appear to be natural law positions, including passages in Plato (*Laws, Statesman, Republic*) and Aristotle (*Politics, Nicomachean Ethics*), as well as Sophocles' *Antigone*, the best known ancient formulation of a Natural Law position was offered by the Roman orator Cicero.

Cicero (*Laws, Republic*), wrote in the first century bc, and was strongly influenced (as were many Roman writers on law) by the works of the Greek Stoic philosophers (some would go so far as to say

*From Dennis Patterson, ed., *A Companion to Philosophy of Law and Legal Theory* (Oxford: Blackwell Publishers, Ltd. 1996), pp. 223–40.

that Cicero merely offered an elegant restatement of already established Stoic views). Cicero offered the following characterization of "natural law":

> True law is right reason in agreement with nature; it is of universal application, unchanging and everlasting; it summons to duty by its commands, and averts from wrongdoing by its prohibitions. And it does not lay its commands or prohibitions upon good men in vain, though neither have any effect on the wicked. It is a sin to try to alter this law, nor is it allowable to attempt to repeal any part of it, and it is impossible to abolish it entirely. We cannot be freed from its obligations by senate or people, and we need not look outside ourselves for an expounder or interpreter of it. And there will not be different laws at Rome and at Athens, or different laws now and in the future, but one eternal and unchangeable law will be valid for all nations and all times, and there will be one master and ruler, that is, God, over us all, for he is the author of this law, its promulgator, and its enforcing judge. Whoever is disobedient is fleeing from himself and denying his human nature, and by reason of this very fact he will suffer the worst penalties, even if he escapes what is common-ly considered punishment.

In Cicero's discussions of law, we come across most of the themes traditionally associated with traditional natural law theory (though, as might be expected in the first major treatment of a subject, some of the analysis is not always as systematic or as precise as one might want): natural law is unchanging over time and does not differ in different societies; every person has access to the standards of this higher law by use of reason; and only just laws "really deserve [the] name" law, and "in the very definition of the term 'law' there inheres the idea and principle of choosing what is just and true."

Within Cicero's work, and the related remarks of earlier Greek and Roman writers, there was often a certain ambiguity regarding the reference of "natural" in "natural law": it was not always clear whether the standards were "natural" because they derived from "human nature" (our "essence" or "purpose"), because they were accessible by our natural faculties (that is, by human reason or conscience), because they derived from or were expressed in nature, that is, in the physical world about us, or some combination of all three.

As one moves from the classical writers on natural law to the early Church writers, aspects of the theory necessarily change and therefore raise different issues within this approach to morality and law. For example, with classical writers, the source of the higher standards is said to be (or implied as being) inherent in the nature of things. With the early Church writers, there is a divine being who actively intervenes in human affairs and lays down express commands for all mankind—though this contrast overstates matters somewhat, as the classical writers referred to a (relatively passive) God, and the early Church writers would sometimes refer to rules of nature which express divine will. To the extent that the natural law theorists of the early Church continued to speak of higher standards inherent in human nature or in the nature of things, they also had to face the question of the connection between these standards and divine commands: for example, whether God can change natural law or order something which is contrary to it, a question considered by Ambrose and Augustine (among others) in the time of the early Church and by Francisco Suarez more than a thousand years later.

Aquinas

The most influential writer within the traditional approach to natural law is undoubtedly Thomas Aquinas (*Summa Theologiae*), who wrote in the thirteenth century. The context of Aquinas's approach to law, its occurrence within a larger theological project that offered a systematic moral system, should be kept in mind when comparing his work with more recent theorists.

Aquinas identified four different kinds of law: the eternal law, the natural law, the divine law, and human (positive) law. For present purposes, the important categories are natural law and positive law.

According to Aquinas, (genuine or just) positive law is derived from natural law. This derivation has different aspects. Sometimes natural law dictates what the positive law should be: for example, natural law both requires that there be a prohibition of murder and settles what its content will be. At other times, natural law leaves room for human choice (based on local customs or policy choices). Thus while natural law would probably require regulation of automobile traffic for the safety of others, the choice of whether driving should be on the left or the right side of the road, and whether the speed limit should be set at 55 miles per hour or 65, are matters for which either choice would probably be compatible with the requirements of natural law. The first form of derivation is like logical deduction; the second Aquinas refers to as the "determination" of general principles ("determination" not in the sense of "finding out," but rather in the sense of making specific or concrete). The theme of different ways in which human (positive) law derives from natural law is carried by later writers, including Sir William Blackstone (*Commentaries on the Laws of England*, Vol. I [1765]), and, in modern times, John Finnis (discussed below).

As for citizens, the question is what their obligations are regarding just and unjust laws. According to Aquinas, positive laws which are just "have the power of binding in conscience." A just law is one which is consistent with the requirements of natural law—that is, it is "ordered to the common good," the law-giver has not exceeded its authority, and the law's burdens are imposed on citizens fairly. Failure with respect to any of those three criteria, Aquinas asserts, makes a law unjust; but what is the citizen's obligation in regard to an unjust law? The short answer is that there is no obligation to obey that law. However, a longer answer is warranted, given the amount of attention this question usually gets in discussions of natural law theory in general and of Aquinas in particular.

The phrase *lex iniusta non est lex* ("an unjust law is not law") is often ascribed to Aquinas, and is sometimes given as a summation of his position and the (traditional) natural law position in general. While Aquinas never used the exact phrase above, one can find similar expressions: "every human law has just so much of the nature of law, as it is derived from the law of nature. But if in any point it deflects from the law of nature, it is no longer a law but a perversion of law"; and "[unjust laws] are acts of violence rather than laws; because, as Augustine says, a law that is not just, seems to be no law at all." (One also finds similar statements by Plato, Aristotle, Cicero, and Augustine—though, with the exception of Cicero's, these statements are not part of a systematic discussion of the nature of law.)

Questions have been raised regarding the significance of the phrase. What does it mean to say that an apparently valid law is "not law," "a perversion of law" or "an act of violence rather than a law"? Statements of this form have been offered and interpreted in one of two ways. First, one can mean that an immoral law is not valid law at all. The *nineteenth-century* English jurist John Austin (*The Province of Jurisprudence Determined* [1832]) interpreted state-

ments by Sir William Blackstone (for example, "no human laws are of any validity, if con- trary to [the law of nature]") in this manner, and pointed out that such analyses of validity are of little value. Austin wrote,

> Suppose an act innocuous, or positively beneficial, be prohibited by the sovereign under the penalty of death; if I commit this act, I shall be tried and condemned, and if I object to the sentence, that it is contrary to the law of God . . . the Court of Justice will demonstrate the inconclusiveness of my reasoning by hanging me up, in pursuance of the law of which I have impugned the validity.

Though one must add that we should not conflate questions of power with questions of validity—for a corrupt legal system might punish someone even if shown that the putative law was invalid under the system's own procedural requirements—we understand the distinction between validity under the system's rules and the moral worth of the enactment in question.

A more reasonable interpretation of statements like "an unjust law is no law at all" is that unjust laws are not laws "in the fullest sense." As we might say of some professional, who had the necessary degrees and credentials, but seemed nonetheless to lack the necessary ability or judgment: "she's no lawyer" or "he's no doctor." This only indicates that we do not think that the title in this case carries with it all the implications it usually does. Similarly, to say that an unjust law is "not really law" may only be to point out that it does not carry the same moral force or offer the same reasons for action as laws consistent with "higher law." This is almost certainly the sense in which Aquinas made his remarks, and the probable interpretation for nearly all proponents of the position. However, this interpretation leaves the statement as clearly right as under the prior (Austinian) interpretation it was clearly wrong. One wonders why such declarations have, historically, been so controversial.

To say that an unjust law is not law in the fullest sense is usually intended not as a simple declaration, but as the first step of a further argument. For example: "this law is unjust; it is not law in the fullest sense, and therefore citizens can in good conscience act as if it was never enacted; that is, they should feel free to disobey it." This is a common understanding of the idea that an unjust law is no law at all, but it expresses a conclusion that is controversial.

There are often moral reasons for obeying even an unjust law: for example, if the law is part of a generally just legal system, and public disobedience of the law might undermine the system, there is a moral reason for at least minimal, public obedience to the unjust law. This is Aquinas's position (he stated that a citizen is not bound to obey "a law which imposes an unjust burden on its subjects" if the law "can be resisted without scandal or greater harm"), and it has been articulated at greater length by later natural law theorists (for example, by John Finnis).

Finally, it should be noted that the proper interpretation of certain basic aspects of Aquinas's work remains in dispute. For example, there is debate within the modern literature regarding whether Aquinas believed moral norms could be derived directly from knowledge of human nature or experience of natural inclinations, or whether they are the product of practical understanding and reasoning by way of reflection on one's experience and observations.

Natural Law in Early Modern Europe

In the period of the Renaissance and beyond, discussions about natural law were tied in with other issues: assertions about natural law were often the basis of or part of the argument for individual rights and limitations on government; and such discussions were also often the groundwork offered for principles of international law. Hugo Grotius and Samuel Pufendorf (writing in the early and late seventeenth century, respectively) were prominent examples of theorists whose writings on natural law had significance in both debates. (Grotius and Pufendorf, along with other prominent seventeenth-century theorists, Francisco Suarez, Thomas Hobbes, and John Locke, were also central in developing the concept of individual rights in the modern sense of that term.)

A further significance of Grotius' work was its express assertion that natural law, the higher law against which the actions of nations, law-makers and citizens could be judged, did not require the existence of God for its validity. (However, one can find hints of such a separation of natural law from a divine being at least as far back as the fourteenth-century writings of Gregory of Rimini.) From that time to the present, an increasingly large portion of the writing on questions of natural law (and the related idea of "natural rights") was secular in tone and purpose, usually referring to "the requirements of reason" rather than divine command, purpose, will, or wisdom.

Perspective

It is normally a mistake to try to evaluate the discussions of writers from distant times with the perspective of modern analytical jurisprudence.

Cicero and Aquinas and Grotius were not concerned with a social–scientific-style analysis of law, as the modern advocates of legal positivism could be said to be. These theorists were concerned with what legislators and citizens and governments ought to do, or could do in good conscience. It is not that these writers (and their followers) never asked questions like "what is law?" However, they were asking the questions as a starting point for an ethical inquiry, and therefore one should not be too quick in comparing their answers with those in similar-sounding discussions by recent writers, who see themselves as participating in a conceptual or sociological task.

Natural law has, from time to time and with varying degrees of importance, escaped the confines of theory to influence directly the standards created and applied by officials. For example, natural law (or standards and reasoning that appear similar to natural law, but which are characterized as "substantive due process", "natural justice" or simply "reason") has been offered as the source of legal standards for international law, centuries of development in the English common law, and certain aspects of United States constitutional law. Natural law also appears to have played a significant role in American history, where its reasoning, or at least its rhetoric, has been prominent (among other places) in the Declaration of Independence, the Abolition (anti-slavery) movement, and parts of the modern Civil Rights movement.

John Finnis

In modern times, the traditional approach to natural law has been advocated by a number of theorists, most of whom were self-consciously writing in the tradition of Aquinas. For example, the French writer Jacques Maritain (*Man and the State* [1951]) has had significant influence in the area. Among the English-language writers, the most prominent advocate of the traditional approach is arguably John Finnis (*Natural Law and Natural Rights* [1980]).

Finnis's work is an explication and application of Aquinas's views (at least, of one reading of Aquinas, a reading advocated by Germain Grisez, among others): an application to ethical questions, but with special attention to the problems of social theory in general and analytical jurisprudence in particular.

Finnis's ethical theory has a number of levels. The foundation is the claim that there are a number of distinct but equally valuable intrinsic goods (that is, things one values for their own sake), which he calls "basic goods." In *Natural Law and Natural Rights*, Finnis lists the following as basic goods: life (and health), knowledge, play, aesthetic experience, sociability (friendship), practical reasonableness, and religion (Finnis's list of basic goods changes somewhat in later articles). These are "intrinsic" goods in the following sense: one can value, for example, health for its own sake, but medical treatment only as a means to health. If someone stated that she was buying medicine, not because she or someone she knew was sick or might become sick, and not because it was part of some study or some business, but simply because she liked acquiring medicines and having a lot of them around, one might rightly begin to question her sanity.

However, the difference between right and wrong cannot be drawn at the level of basic goods. At this level, one can only distinguish the intelligible from the unintelligible. We *understand* the person who is materialistic, greedy, malicious or unfair, however much we disapprove of such attitudes and actions. The greedy person is seeking the same basic goods as we, though in a way we would consider out of balance (and thus wrong).

Finnis describes the basic goods he identifies, and other principles identified in his moral theory, as "self-evident," but he does not mean this in the sense that the truth of these propositions would be immediately obvious to all competent thinkers. For Finnis, what it means for a (true) proposition to be "self-evident" is that it cannot be derived from some more foundational proposition; thus, "self-evident" is here the opposite of syllogistically demonstrable. (However, while these propositions cannot be thus demonstrated, they can be supported by consistent data of experience and by dialectical arguments, for example, from consis- tency.) Nor does the claim about "self-evidence" suggest that everyone will be equally adept at reaching these propositions. People of substantial experience, who are able and willing to inquire and reflect deeply may be better able to discover the "self-evident" truths than would others (Aquinas wrote that some propositions, including the first principles of practical reason and natural law, were only self-evident to the wise).

Much of what is conventionally considered to be ethics and morality occurs at a second level in Finnis's theory. Because there are a variety of basic goods, with no hierarchy or priority among them, there must be principles to guide choice when alternative courses of conduct promote different goods. (This is one basis for contrasting Finnis's position with utilitarian moral theories, under which all goods can be compared according to their value in a single unit, for example, promoting happiness.) On a simple level, we face such choices when we consider whether to spend the afternoon playing soccer (the value of play) or studying history (the value of knowledge). The choice is presented in a sharper form when someone (say, a medical researcher) must choose whether to kill (choosing against the basic good of life), in a situation where the person believes that doing so would lead to some significant benefit (perhaps saving more lives at some future time) or avoid a greater evil. Morality offers a basis for rejecting certain available choices, but there will often remain more than one equally legitimate choice (again, there is a contrast with most utilitarian theories, under which there would always be a "best" choice).

For Finnis, the move from the basic goods to moral choices occurs through a series of intermediate principles, which Finnis calls "the basic requirements of practical reasonableness." Among the most significant, and most controversial, is the prescription that one may never choose to destroy, damage or impede a basic good regardless of the benefit one believes will come from doing so. In other words, the end never justifies the means where the chosen means entails intending to harm a basic good.

Other intermediate principles listed in *Natural Law and Natural Rights* (the list changes somewhat in Finnis's later writings) include that one should form a rational plan of life; have no arbitrary preferences among persons; foster the common good of the community; and have no arbitrary preferences among the basic goods.

Law enters the picture as a way of effecting some goods—social goods which require the co-ordination of many people—that could not be effected (easily or at all) without law, and it also enters as a way of making it easier to obtain other goods. Thus, the suggestions Finnis makes about law and about legal theory are derivative from the ethical code which is, in a sense, his primary concern. As to questions regarding the obligation to obey the law, Finnis follows Aquinas: one has an obligation to obey just laws; laws which are unjust are not "law" in the fullest sense of the term, and one has an obligation to comply with their requirements only to the extent that this is compatible with moral norms and necessary to uphold otherwise just institutions.

Even though Finnis's theory might be seen as primarily a prescriptive account—a theory of how we should live our lives—the analysis also has implications for descriptive theory, including a descriptive theory of law. Finnis argues that a proper ethical theory is necessary for doing descriptive theory well because evaluation is a necessary and integral part of theory formation. For example, while he agrees with the legal positivist H. L. A. Hart that a descriptive theory of a social practice like law should be constructed around the viewpoint of a participant in the practice, Finnis proposes a significant amendment to Hart's approach. He argues that, when doing legal theory, one should not take the perspective of those who merely accept the law as valid (Hart would include those who accept the law as valid for a variety of reasons, including prudential ones); rather, the theory should assume the perspective of those who accept the law as binding *because* they believe that valid legal rules (presumptively) create moral obligations. The difference may seem minor, but it means crossing a theoretically significant dividing line: between the legal positivist's insistence on doing theory in a morally neutral way and the Natural Law theorist's assertion that moral evaluation is an integral part of proper description and analysis.

Modern Natural Law Theory

As has been noted, the concept of "natural law" or the "natural law approach" to analyzing law has deep historical roots. It is fair to speak of the "natural law tradition," but the meaning and significance of the earlier works are sufficiently ambiguous that many different perspectives have claimed to be part of that tradition. What criteria should be used in identifying a theorist's affiliation, and which theorists one includes under a particular label, will generally not be important, as long as one understands the moral or analytical problems to which the various theorists were responding, and the answers the theories are proposing.

While it may not be useful to try to adopt the role of gatekeeper, saying which theories are prop-

erly called "natural law theories" and which are not, there may be some point, for the purpose of greater understanding, to identify similarities among those theorists who have defined themselves (or have been defined by later commentators) with that label. One such division is as follows: there are two broadly different groups of approaches that carry the label "natural law" theory. The first group includes the theorists already discussed: Cicero, Aquinas, Grotius, Pufendorf, and Finnis, among many others. The second group reflects debates of a different kind and a more recent origin; the second approach focusses more narrowly on the proper understanding of law as a social institution or a social practice. (The two types of approaches are by no means contradictory or inconsistent, but they reflect sets of theoretical concerns sufficiently different that it is rare to find writers contributing to both.)

The second (or "modern") set of approaches to natural law arises as responses to legal positivism, and the way legal positivists portrayed (and sometimes caricatured) traditional natural law positions. While attacks on the merits of natural law theory can be found in the works of John Austin, O. W. Holmes, and Hans Kelsen, a large portion of the recent discussions of "natural law theory" derive from the 1958 "Hart-Fuller Debate" in the *Harvard Law Review*. In this exchange, H. L. A. Hart laid the groundwork for a restatement of legal positivism (which he more fully articulated in *The Concept of Law* [1961]). Part of his defense and restatement involved demarcating legal positivism from natural law theory, and the demarcation point offered was the conceptual separation of law and morality. Lon Fuller argued against a sharp separation of law and morality, but the position he defended under the rubric of "natural law theory" was quite different from the traditional natural law theories of Cicero and Aquinas (as will be discussed in detail below).

In part, because of responses to legal positivists like Hart, a category of "natural law theories" has arisen which is best understood by its contrast to legal positivism, rather than by its connection with the traditional natural law theories of Cicero and Aquinas. While the traditional theories were generally taking a particular position on the status of morality (that true moral beliefs are based in or derived from human nature or the natural world, that they are not relative, that they are accessible to human reason, and so on), a position which then had some implications for how legislators, judges, and citizens should act (as well as for all other aspects of living a good life); this second category of "natural law theories" contains theories specifically about law, which hold that moral evaluation of some sort is required in describing law in general, particular legal systems, or the legal validity of individual laws.

Lon Fuller

Lon Fuller (*The Morality of Law* [1964]) rejected what he saw as legal positivism's distorted view of law as a "one-way projection of authority": the government gives orders and the citizens obey. Fuller believed that this approach missed the need for co-operation and reciprocal obligations between officials and citizens for a legal system to work.

Fuller described law as "the enterprise of subjecting human conduct to the governance of rules." Law is a form of guiding people, to be contrasted with other forms of guidance, for example, managerial direction. Law is a particular means to an end, a particular kind of tool, if you will. With that in mind, one can better understand the claim that rules must meet certain criteria relating to that means, to that function, if they are to warrant the title "law." If we defined "knife" as something that cuts, something which failed to cut would not warrant the label, however much it might superficially resemble true knives. Similarly, if we define law as a particular way of guiding and co-ordinating human behavior, if a system's rules are so badly constructed that they cannot succeed in effectively guiding behavior, then we are justified in withholding the label "law" from them.

Fuller offered, in place of legal positivism's analysis of law based on power, orders, and obedience, an analysis based on the "internal morality" of law. Like traditional natural law theorists, he wrote of there being a threshold that must be met (or, to change the metaphor, a test that must be passed) before something could properly (or in the fullest sense) be called "law." Unlike traditional natural law theorists, however, the test Fuller applies is one of function rather than strictly one of moral content; though, as will be noted, for Fuller these questions of procedure or function have moral implications.

The internal morality of law consists of a series of requirements which Fuller asserted that a system of rules must meet—or at least substantially meet—if that system was to be called "law." (At the same time, Fuller wrote of systems being "legal" to different degrees, and he held that a system which partly but not fully met his requirements would be "partly legal" and could be said to have "displayed a greater respect for the principles of legality" than systems which did not meet the requirements.)

The eight requirements were:

1. laws should be general;
2. they should be promulgated, that citizens might know the standards to which they are being held;
3. retroactive rule-making and application should be minimized;
4. laws should be understandable;
5. they should not be contradictory;
6. laws should not require conduct beyond the abilities of those affected;
7. they should remain relatively constant through time; and
8. there should be a congruence between the laws as announced and their actual administration.

Fuller's approach is often contrasted with that of traditional natural law positions. Fuller at one point tried to show a connection, writing that "Aquinas in some measure recognized and dealt with all eight of the principles of legality." On the other hand, Fuller also realized that there were significant differences: he once referred to his theory as "a procedural, as distinguished from a substantive natural law." However, he chafed at the dismissal of his set of requirements as "merely procedural": an argument frequently made by critics that his "principles of legality" were amoral solutions to problems of efficiency, such that one could just as easily speak of "the internal morality of poisoning." Such criticisms misunderstand the extent to which our perceptions of justice incorporate procedural matters. This is a matter Fuller himself brought up through an example from the former Soviet Union. In that system, there was once an attempt to increase the sentence for robbery, an increase also to be applied retroactively to those convicted of that crime in the past. Even in the Soviet legal system, not known for its adherence to the rule of law, there was a strong reaction against this attempt to increase sentences retroactively. It is a matter of procedure only, but still it seemed to them—and it would seem to us—a matter of justice. Following the rules laid down (just one example of procedural justice) is a good thing, and it is not stretching matters to characterize it as a moral matter and a matter of justice.

On the other hand, there were times when Fuller overstated the importance of his "principles of legality." When critics argued that a regime could follow those principles and still enact wicked laws,

Fuller stated that he "could not believe" that adherence to the internal requirements of law was as consistent with a bad legal system as they were with a good legal system. There are various ways that this "faith" can be understood. One argument could be that a government which is just and good will likely also do well on procedural matters. Additionally, when proper procedures are followed (for example the requirement that reasons publicly be given for judicial decisions), some officials might be less willing to act in corrupt ways. The contrary claim, that governments which are evil will be likely to ignore the procedural requirements, also has some initial plausibility. There have been regimes so evil that they have not even bothered with any of the legal niceties, with establishing even the pretense of legality, and to some extent Nazi Germany is an example. However, there have also been regimes, generally condemned as evil, which have at least at times been quite meticulous about legal procedures (South Africa before the fall of apartheid or East Germany before the fall of Communism may be examples). Since the principles of legality can be understood as guidelines for making the legal system more effective in guiding citizen behavior, wicked regimes would have reason to follow them.

Thus, on the one hand, one might say: first, that following the principles of legality is itself a moral good; second, the fact that a government follows those principles may indicate that it is committed to morally good actions; and third, that following such principles may hinder or restrict base actions. On the other hand, it is probably claiming too much for those principles to say that following them would guarantee a substantively just system. However, one should not conclude, as some critics have, that the evaluation of Fuller's entire approach to law should turn on the empirical question of whether there have ever been (or ever could be) wicked governments which, for whatever reason, followed the rules of procedural justice. (Like the question of whether there can ever be, over the long term, "honor among thieves", the ability to maintain procedural fairness amidst significant iniquities, is an interesting topic for speculation, but little more.) The main points of Fuller's position—that a value judgment about the system described is part of the way we use the word "law"; and that there is analytic value to seeing law as a particular kind of social guidance, which is to be contrasted with other forms of social guidance, and which can be more or less effective according to how well it meets certain criteria—would not be undermined by pointing out legal systems which were substantively unjust but which seemed to do well on questions of procedural justice.

Those who approach natural law through the Hart-Fuller debate sometimes overemphasize the question of when a rule or a system of social control merits the label "law" or "legal." There is a danger with such a focus, in that debates about proper labeling (not just whether something is "law" or not, but also whether an object is "art" or not, whether a particular form of government is "democratic" or not, and so forth) often smother real moral, sociological, or conceptual arguments beneath line-drawing exercises. It is always open to theorists to stipulate the meaning of the terms they use, even for the limited purpose of a single discussion. To say that it is important that the products of a wicked regime be called "law" or not indicates that there is something further at stake (for example, whether and when citizens have a moral obligation to obey the law, and whether punishment is ever warranted for people who had been acting in accord with what the law at the time required or permitted), but the burden must be on the advocate to clarify what the further point is. It is probably preferable to bypass questions of labeling and line-drawing, to face directly whatever further substantive issues may be present.

Ronald Dworkin

Ronald Dworkin is probably the most influential English-language legal theorist now writing. Over the course of thirty years, he has developed a sophisticated alternative to legal positivism. Though his theory has little resemblance to the traditional natural law theories of Aquinas and his followers, Dworkin has occasionally referred to his approach as a natural law theory, and it is clearly on the natural law side of the theoretical divide set by the Hart-Fuller debate.

In Dworkin's early writings (collected in *Taking Rights Seriously* [1978]), he challenged a particular view of legal positivism, a view which saw law as being comprised entirely of rules, and judges as having discretion in their decision making where the dispute before them was not covered by any existing rule. Dworkin offered an alternative vision of law, in which the resources for resolving disputes "according to law" were more numerous and varied, and the process of determining what the law required in a particular case more subtle.

Dworkin argues that along with rules, legal systems also contain principles. As contrasted with rules, principles do not act in an all-or-nothing fashion. Rather, principles (for example, "one should not be able to profit from one's own wrong" and "one is held to intend all the foreseeable consequences of one's actions") have "weight," they favor one result or another; there can be—and often are—principles favoring contrary results on a single legal question. Legal principles are moral propositions that are grounded (exemplified, quoted or somehow supported by) past official acts (for example, the text of statutes, judicial decisions, or constitutions). There is still a legal positivist-like separation of law and morality in this view of law, in that judges are told to decide cases based not on whatever principles (critical) morality might require, but rather based on a different and perhaps inconsistent set of principles: those cited in, or implicit in, past official actions.

Dworkin argued for the existence of legal principles (principles which are part of the legal system, which judges are bound to consider where appropriate) by reference to legal practice (in the United States and England). Particularly telling for Dworkin's argument are those "landmark" judicial decisions where the outcome appears to be contrary to the relevant precedent, but the courts still held that they were following the "real meaning" or "true spirit" of the law; and also, more mundane cases where judges have cited principles as the justification for modifying, creating exceptions in, or overturning, legal rules.

With the conclusion that there were legal principles as well as legal rules, it would seem to follow that there are fewer occasions than previously thought where judges have discretion because there are "gaps" in the law (that is, places where there is no relevant law on the subject). However, now the likely problem was not the absence of law on a question, but its abundance; where legal principles could be found to support a variety of different results, how is the judge to make a decision? Dworkin's answer is that judges should consider a variety of views of what the law requires in the area in question, rejecting those (for example, "in tort cases, the richer party should lose") which do not adequately "fit" past official actions (statutes, precedent, constitutions). Among the theories of what the law requires that adequately fit the relevant legal materials, the judge would then choose that theory which was morally best, which made the law the best it could be. This final stage of judicial decision making is where moral (or partly moral, partly political—the characterization is neither obvious nor crucial) factors take a central

role in Dworkin's view of how judges do (and should) decide cases. Two tenets of Dworkin's early writings were thus related: that law contained principles as well as rules; and that for nearly all legal questions, there was a unique right answer.

In his later writings, Dworkin (*Law's Empire* [1986]) offered what he called "an interpretive approach" to law. (While Dworkin has said little about the relationship between his earlier writings and his later work, the later work is probably best seen as a reworking of earlier themes within a philosophically more sophisticated analysis.) He argued that "legal claims are interpretive judgments and therefore combine backward- and forward-looking elements; they interpret contemporary legal practice as an unfolding narrative."

According to Dworkin, both law (as a practice) and legal theory are best understood as processes of "constructive interpretation." (He believes that constructive interpretation is also the proper approach to artistic and literary works, and his writings frequently compare the role of a judge with that of a literary critic. Both the applicability of constructive interpretation to art and literature and the treatment of legal interpretation as analogous to artistic or literary interpretation, are controversial claims.) One can think of constructive interpretation as being similar to the way people have looked at collections of stars and seen there pictures of mythic figures, or the way modern statistical methods can analyze points on a graph (representing data), and determine what line (representing a mathematical equation, and thus a correlation of some form between variables) best explains that data. Constructive interpretation is both an imposition of form upon the object being interpreted (in the sense that the form is not immediately apparent in the object) and a derivation of form from it (in the sense that the interpreter is constrained by the object of interpretation, and not free to impose any form she might choose). Dworkin also described the concept of "Integrity": the argument that judges should decide cases in a way which makes the law more coherent, preferring interpretations which make the law more like the product of a single moral vision.

For Dworkin, the past actions of legal officials, whether judges deciding cases and giving reasons for their decisions or legislators passing statutes, are data to be explained. In some areas, there will be little doubt as to the correct theory, the correct "picture." The answer seems easy because only one theory shows adequate "fit."

Often, however, there will be alternative theories, each with adequate "fit." Among these, some will do better on "fit," others on moral value. In making comparisons among alternative theories, the relative weighting of "fit" and moral value will itself be an interpretive question, and will vary from one legal area to another (for example, protecting expectations—having new decisions "fit" as well as possible with older ones—may be more important regarding estate or property law, while moral value may be more important than "fit" for civil liberties questions). The evaluation of theories thus takes into account (directly and indirectly) a view about the purpose of law in general, and a view about the objectives of the particular area of law in which the question falls. Dworkin wrote, "Judges who accept the interpretive ideal of integrity decide hard cases by trying to find, in some coherent set of principles about people's rights and duties, the best constructive interpretation of the political structure and legal doctrine of their community."

Dworkin's writings (both earlier and later) can be seen as attempts to come to terms with aspects of legal practice that are not easily explained within the confines of legal positivism. For example:

1. the fact that participants in the legal system (regularly, if not frequently) argue over even basic aspects of the way the system works (for example, the correct way to interpret ambiguous statutes, and how one should apply constitutional provisions to new legal questions), not just over peripheral matters or the application of rules to borderline cases;

2. even in the hardest of hard cases, lawyers and judges speak as if there were a unique correct answer which the judge has a duty to discover; and

3. in landmark cases, where the law seems on the surface to have changed radically, both the judges and commentators often speak of the new rule having "already been present" or "the law working itself pure."

A standard response to Dworkin's work (both to his early writings and to the later "interpretative" work) is that judges and legal theorists should not look at law through "rose-colored glasses," making it "the best it can be"; rather, they should describe law "as it is." The key to understanding Dworkin, in particular his later work, is to understand his response to this kind of comment: that there is no simple description of law "as it is"; or, more accurately, describing law "as it is" necessarily involves an interpretative process, which in turn requires determining what is the best interpretation of past official actions. Law "as it is," law as objective or non-controversial, is only the collection of past official decisions by judges and legislators (which Dworkin refers to as the "pre-interpretive data," that which is subject to the process of constructive interpretation). However, even collectively, these individual decisions and actions cannot offer an answer to a current legal question until some order is imposed upon them. And the ordering involves a choice, a moral-political choice among tenable interpretations of those past decisions and actions.

Dworkin, like Fuller, is a natural law theorist in the modern rather than traditional sense of that label, in that he denies the conceptual separation of law and morality, and asserts instead that moral evaluation is integral to the description and understanding of law.

General Considerations

Within this second type of natural law debate, as exemplified by the works of Fuller and Dworkin (and their critics), it is not always immediately clear what the nature or status is of the claims being made. Some of them could be merely sociological or lexicographical: that is, statements about the way we actually use the label "law." For example, one could plausibly interpret Fuller as arguing that, for better or worse, the way most people use the word "law" includes a moral claim (in other words, that we tend to withhold the label from wicked laws or wicked regimes).

At other times, for example, with some of Dworkin's arguments, the claims regard the best description of our practices, but not merely our linguistic practices in how we use terms like "law," but also our practices in how we act within or react to the legal system. In a different sense, Dworkin's theory also (tacitly) presents a normative claim: that law and legal theory seen as Dworkin would have us see them are (morally) better than the same practices as viewed through the alternative characterizations of other theories.

A different set of problems arises when students of legal theory try to understand traditional natural law theories (such as the works of Aquinas and Finnis). The difficulties come because the issues central to many of these theorists (for example, the extent to which moral truths are "self-evident"; the extent to which various goods, claims, or arguments are incommensurable; whether a moral theory can be constructed or defended independent of a belief in God; and the like) bear little resemblance to what normally passes for legal theory. This, of course, is not a criticism of the traditional natural law theorists; if anything, it is a criticism of the way such material is often presented to a general audience, glossing over the differences in concern and focus between traditional natural law theorists and (many) modern analytical legal theorists.

Other Modern Writers

A number of other modern writers have written works offered as "natural law" theories, some of which do not fit comfortably in either of the two broad subcategories considered above.

Michael Moore has discussed various aspects of law in the light of a Platonist (metaphysically realist) approach to language, morality, and legal concepts. Moore's analysis might be best understood as responding to the question: how do we determine the meanings of legal terms like "valid contract," "criminal malice," and "due process"? On one extreme is the ("conventionalist") response that like all language, the terms mean whatever we want them to mean, or whatever meaning they have gained from our practices and conventions over generations. Moore's response is at the opposite extreme: simple descriptive terms ("bird", "tree"), legal terms ("malice," "valid contract"), and moral concepts ("due process," "equal treatment") all have meanings determined by the way the world is, not by our changing, and often erroneous beliefs about those objects. Moore has shown how this approach to metaphysics (and language) has numerous repercussions for the way we should interpret constitutions and statutes and analyze problems of the common law and precedent.

Lloyd Weinreb (*Natural Law and Justice* [1987]) has offered an interesting characterization of the natural law tradition (that is, the tradition of Cicero and Aquinas) that varies from the way it is seen by most commentators and advocates today. In particular, Weinreb sees the works of the ancient classical theorists and Aquinas (among others) as having been concerned, each in his own way, with the problem of explaining the possibility of human moral freedom in a world that otherwise appears determined by fate or fortune (in classical thinking) or by divine providence (in the view of the early Church). In Weinreb's view, recent natural law writers like Finnis and Fuller are missing the basic point of natural law theory when they try to distance their claims from earlier arguments about normative natural order, which can now be understood as addressing generally the problem of the ontology, or reality, of morality.

Ernest Weinrib sees law as having an "immanent moral rationality." For Weinrib, one can speak of the essence or the nature of law, of various parts of the law (for example, tort law) and of doctrines within the law. This view of law is contrasted with approaches which assert or assume that law is basically a kind of politics, or that it is a means of maximizing some value (for example, utility or wealth). In Weinrib's words, "legal ordering is not the collective pursuit of a desirable purpose. Instead, it is the specification of the norms and principles immanent to juridically intelligible relationships." The essence of law can be worked out to particular normative propositions, and therefore what the law requires is not merely identical with the rules legislatures (and judges) promulgate. While Weinrib generally does not use the label "natural law" for his approach (provocatively choosing instead "legal formalism," a label modern theorists usually apply pejoratively), he has noted the overlap of his arguments with those put forward by Aquinas and other traditional natural law theorists.

Deryck Beyleveld and Roger Brownsword (*Law as a Moral Judgment* [1986]) have constructed an approach to legal theory around Alan Gewirth's argument for objective moral principles. Gewirth's argument states that engaging in practical reasoning itself presupposed a commitment to a number of moral principles. Beyleveld and Brownsword use this analysis to argue against value-free social theory; in the context of legal theory, they argue that Gewirth's analysis requires a rejection of legal positivism in favor of an equation of law with morally legitimate power.

Conclusion

A diverse family of theories carries the label "natural law." Within legal theory, there are two well-known groupings which cover most (but not all) of the writing that has carried the label "natural law": (1) "traditional natural law theory" sets out a moral theory (or an approach to moral theory) in which one can better analyze how to think about and act on legal matters; and (2) "modern natural law theory" argues that one cannot properly understand or describe the law without moral evaluation.

References

Aquinas, T.
1993:   *The Treatise on Law*, ed. R. J. Henle, Notre Dame, Indiana: University of Notre Dame Press (text of Summa Theologiae, I–II, pp. 90–7, with translation, commentary and introduction).

Blackstone, Sir W.
1765:   Commentaries on the Laws of England, Volume I: *Of the Rights of Persons*. Oxford: Clarendon Press.

Cicero, Marcus Tullius
1988:   De Re Publica; De Legibus, tr. C. W. Keyes, Cambridge, Mass.: Harvard University Press.

Dworkin, R.
1978:   *Taking Rights Seriously*. London: Duckworth (the 1978 edition contains as an appendix "A reply to critics").
1986:   *Law's Empire*. Cambridge, Mass.: Harvard University Press.

Finnis, J.
1980:   *Natural Law and Natural Rights*. Oxford: Clarendon Press.

Finnis, J. (ed.)
1991:   Natural Law, 2 vols. New York: New York University Press (a wide-ranging collection of law review articles on natural law theory).

Fuller, L.
1958:   Positivism and fidelity to law—a response to Professor Hart. Harvard Law Review, 71, 630–72.
1969:   *The Morality of Law*. New Haven: Yale University Press, rev. edn (the revised edition contains a helpful reply to critics).

George, R. (ed.)
1992:   *Natural Law Theory*. Oxford: Clarendon Press (a collection of relatively recent articles on natural law theory).

Grotius, H.
1925:   *De Jure Belli ac Pacis Libri Tres*, tr. F. Kelsen, Oxford: Clarendon Press.

Hart, H. L. A.
1958:   *Positivism and the separation of law and morals.* Harvard Law Review, 71, 593–629.

Kelly, J. M.
1992:   *A Short History of Western Legal Theory*. Oxford: Clarendon Press.

Moore, M.
1985:   A natural law theory of interpretation. *Southern California Law Review*, 58, 277–398.

Pufendorf, S.
1991:   *On the Duty of Man and Citizen according to Natural Law*, ed. J. Tully, tr. M. Silverthorne. Cambridge: Cambridge University Press.

Weinreb, L.
1987:   *Natural Law and Justice*. Cambridge, Mass.: Harvard University Press.

THE NATURAL LAW THEORY OF ST. THOMAS AQUINAS*

Susan Dimock

Introduction

In this essay I present the core of St. Thomas Aquinas's theory of law. The aim is to introduce students both to the details of Aquinas's particular theory of law, as well as to the features of his view that define what has come to be known as "the natural law" conception of law more generally. Though the essay is for the most part exegetical, some of the more important implications of the natural law position are raised for further thought and to pave the way for the study of alternative views that have been developed in the subsequent history of the philosophy of law.

One brief note about the structure of the essay will complete my introductory remarks: The essay tries as far as possible to present Aquinas's theory in his own words. Material taken directly from Aquinas appears in italic type throughout, with the origin of the quotation given in parentheses following the text. All of the material is taken from Aquinas's *Summa Theologica*; the translation from Latin is that of the Fathers of the English Dominican Province.[1]

I. Of the Essence of Law

Aquinas begins his discussion of law with a consideration of the nature or essence of law in general. In this way he sets the tone and task of future jurisprudence or philosophy of law. What makes a particular rule or directive a law? What is it that all laws have in common and which gives them the force of law? This is the search for the nature of law as law. In the course of his discussion of this matter Aquinas offers the following "definition of law": law *is nothing else than an ordinance of reason for the common good, made by him who has the care of the community, and promulgated* (Question 90: Of the Essence of Law, Article 4 "Whether Promulgation is Essential to a Law?"). We shall do well to begin our discussion of Aquinas's philosophy of law with an explication of each of the four component parts of this definition.

I.1 Law Is an Ordinance of Reason:

> Law is a rule and measure of acts whereby man is induced to act or is restrained from acting; for lex (law) is derived from ligare (to bind), because it binds one to act. Now the rule and measure of human acts is the reason, which is the first principle of human acts . . . since it belongs to the reason to direct to the end, which is the first principle in all matters of action, according to the Philosopher [Aristotle]. . . . Consequently it follows that the law is something pertaining to reason (Q.90, Article 1 "Whether Law Is Something Pertaining to Reason?").

In arguing that law is an ordinance of reason, Aquinas is appealing to "practical reason", which provides practical directions concerning how one ought to act, rather than to "speculative reason", which provides us with propositional knowledge of the way things are. Since law aims to direct actions, and practical reason governs how we ought to act, law falls within the scope of reason.

To understand how practical reason directs us to action, however, we must be able to specify an "end" at which our action aims (a goal or objective that we hope to achieve). Reason then directs us to take those steps that are necessary to the achievement of our end. Thus, to say that law is an ordinance of practical reason is to say that there must be some end at which is it is directed. Aquinas identifies that end as "the common good".

I.2 Law Has As Its End the Common Good:

> [T]he law belongs to that which is a principle of human acts, because it is their rule and measure. Now as reason is a principle of human acts, so in reason itself there is something which is the principle in respect of all the rest; wherefore to this principle chiefly and mainly law must needs be referred. Now the first principle in practical matters, which are the object of the practical reason, is the last end; and the last end of human life is bliss or happiness . . . Consequently the law must needs regard principally the relationship to happiness. Moreover, since every part is ordained to the whole, as perfect to imperfect; and since one man is a part of the perfect community, the law must needs regard properly the relationship to universal happiness. Wherefore the Philosopher . . . says that we call those legal matters just, "which are adapted to produce and preserve happiness and its parts for the body politic," since the state is a perfect community, as he says in Politics i, I.[2]
>
> . . . Consequently, since the law is chiefly ordained to the common good, any other precept in regard to some individual work must needs be devoid of the nature of law, save in so far as it regards the common good. Therefore every law is ordained to the common good (Q.90, Article 2 "Whether Law Is Always Directed to the Common Good?").

In this article Aquinas makes clear his belief that happiness is the final end of human action and the first principle of practical reason. In other words, the end of all we do, when we act in accordance with reason, is happiness. In so far as law is an ordinance of reason, it too must aim at happiness. But the happiness at which the law must be directed is not the happiness of any particular individual or privileged group (such as the rulers), but the happiness of the whole as the perfect community.

The insistence that law must be aimed at the common good serves a number of purposes in Aquinas's theory of law. Together with the insistence that law is an ordinance of reason, the requirement that law serve the common good denies the truth of a widely held maxim which had been adopted from the Roman jurists: "Whatever pleases the sovereign, has the force of law" [Ulpian, *Digest* i, ff.]. This maxim had not only been accepted by subsequent philosophers, but by the Christian church as well. Yet it seems to imply that the will of the sovereign, however arbitrary, is sufficient to make law. Thus, the aim of law might simply be the sovereign's personal good. This Aquinas denies. He argues that in making law the sovereign (of whom we will say more shortly) must aim not merely at his own good, but at the good of all.

The good of all, however, should not be understood to mean the individual good of those subject to the law aggregated in some way. It is not just any individual interests that the sovereign may seek to serve in making law, even if those interests are shared by the majority or even all of the subjects. Rather, to say that the law must serve the common good is to say that it must serve the interests that all have *as members of* the perfect community or body politic. To understand which interests these are, some brief comment on what Aquinas means by the perfect community is needed.

Drawing both on Aristotelian philosophy and Christian theology, Aquinas holds that only within political society can human beings achieve the happiness that is appropriate to them. This is so for a number of reasons. First, human beings are born without the natural advantages that brute animals have with respect to satisfying their physical needs. In order to live, a multitude of individuals is needed, each performing different tasks according to a division of labour and in keeping with their varying skills and talents. This diversity must be brought into unity or order through law, which governs economic activity within society. Moreover, human beings require political society not only to meet their biological needs, but also to satisfy their uniquely human intellectual and spiritual needs. For Aquinas believes that, just as we seek our own biological preservation and the success of our offspring, so too do we seek knowledge, culture and religious enlightenment. These goods are attainable only through the order that political society makes possible. The conditions of an orderly society, in so far as they make possible the fulfillment of our needs and the highest happiness we can achieve on earth, are thus goods that are truly common to all members of the community. It is the aim of law to secure these goods.

I.3 Law Is Made by Him Who Has the Care of the Community:

> A law, properly speaking, regards first and foremost the order of the common good. Now to order anything to the common good belongs either to the whole people or to someone who is the viceregent of the whole people. And therefore the making of a law belongs either to the whole people or to a public personage who has the care of the whole people, since in all other matters the directing of anything to the end concerns him to whom the end belongs (Q.90, Article 3 "Whether the Reason of Any Man Is Competent to Make Laws?").

There are a number of issues raised in this article, which concerns who is authorized to make laws. The obvious answer from the text quoted is that, because the laws are to govern the whole people, they must be made by the whole people or by their representatives. Thus it may seem that Aquinas is committed either to democratic or representative government. This conclusion would be premature, however.

Rather, following both Aristotle and St. Augustine, Aquinas believes that the relationship of political authority, between the ruler and the ruled, is natural. There are some who are naturally fit to rule, and others who are naturally fit to follow the ruler's commands. Those who are most fit to rule are those in whom virtue is most perfect. They are to rule with the goal of providing the unity and order necessary for those ruled to achieve material, intellectual and moral/spiritual well-being.

Moreover, Aquinas believes that these natural political relations must contain a coercive component. Before the Fall, when all desired what was truly good, the ruler had only to lead by example and instruction; after the Fall, however, men could no longer be trusted to seek the true good or to pursue that good voluntarily. Thus, there came to be added to the ruler's authority the coercive power of making laws and compelling obedience through the threat of penalties for those who transgress the law. The power to punish—to deprive others of their life, liberty or property—was thus annexed to political rulers, and it

was so, on Aquinas's view, by divine authorization. Indeed, within canon law it was held that "All power comes from God" (St. Paul's Epistle to the Romans).

That Aquinas is not an advocate of democratic governance may also be seen in his political writings[3], where he makes it clear that the form of legitimate government may be monarchical (rule by one), aristocratic or oligarchic (rule by a few), or timocratic or democratic (rule by the many or all). The modern notion that all legitimate government derives in some way from the will or consent of the governed is foreign to him. Indeed, for the most part Aquinas favours monarchy—though he recognizes that what form of government is best for a given political community depends upon the material circumstances and cultural/moral development of the community in question.

I.4 Law Must Be Promulgated:

> [A] law is imposed on others by way of a rule and measure. Now a rule or measure is imposed by being applied to those who are to be ruled and measured by it. Wherefore, in order that a law obtain the binding force which is proper to a law, it must needs be applied to the men who have to be ruled by it. Such application is made by its being notified to them by promulgation. Wherefore promulgation is necessary for the law to obtain its force (Q.90, Article 4 "Whether Promulgation Is Essential to a Law?").

In this article Aquinas is making the seemingly common-sense observation that laws must be made public. According to this requirement, a secret law, or a law willed only in the heart of the ruler, would fail to be law. And one reason for this requirement is quite simple: People can use the law as a rule and measure for their conduct only if they know what the law enjoins or forbids them to do.

There is another reason to insist upon promulgation, however, which is normative rather than pragmatic. Aquinas believes (as we shall see) that there is a general obligation to obey just laws and that individuals may be punished for disobedience. This is the normative sense of "the binding force which is proper to a law". But both the obligation to obey the law and the permissibility of punishing those who violate it presuppose that the laws which people have an obligation to conform to can be known by them. It would surely be morally wrong to hold people responsible and punishable for violating laws they could not be aware of.

I.5 The Validity Conditions for Law:

Question 90, which we have been considering, lays out Aquinas's answer to the question: what is the essence of law? What must be true of any rule or directive if it is to be law? One way of thinking about this is to say that Aquinas has provided *validity conditions* for law. In order to be valid law, a practical directive must be an ordinance of reason; it must be issued by the person or group who holds law-making authority within the community; it must be directed toward the common good; and it must be promulgated. Any directive which fails to meet one or more of these conditions thereby fails to be valid law. . . .

II. Of The Various Kinds of Law

In Question 91 Aquinas identifies four kinds of laws that are of interest to us. To fully understand Aquinas's theory of law, it is necessary to understand not only the essence of each kind of law here identified, but also the relations between them. One way of working through this somewhat difficult discussion of the various kinds of law is to ask the following five questions of each kind: (1) by whom is it made? (2) to whom is it directed, or whom does it bind? (3) to what end is it directed? (4) how is it promulgated? (5) is it a dictate of reason? In this way we can apply the conditions for valid law which Aquinas laid out in the previous question to better understand why the various kinds of law here discussed are, in fact, laws.

II.1 Eternal Law:

[A] law is nothing else but a dictate of practical reason emanating from the ruler who governs the perfect community. Now it is evident, granted that the world is ruled by divine providence . . . that the whole community of the universe is governed by divine reason. Wherefore the very Idea of the government of things in God the Ruler of the universe has the nature of a law. And since the divine reason's conception of things is not subject to time but is eternal, according to Proverbs viii. 23, therefore it is that this kind of law must be
called eternal (Question 91: Of the Various Kinds of Law, Article 1 "Whether There Is an Eternal Law?"). . . .

It is sufficient, for those who do not accept the theological underpinnings of Aquinas's view, to think of eternal law as comprising all those scientific (physical, chemical, biological, psychological, etc.) "laws" by which the universe is ordered. It must be kept in mind by those who wish to take this route, however, that what we call scientific laws could not properly be considered laws by Aquinas were they not also expressions of the divine will. This is because for Aquinas a law must necessarily have a law-maker.

II.2 Natural Law:

[L]aw, being a rule and measure, can be in a person in two ways: in one way, as in him that rules and measures; in another way, as in that which is ruled and measured, since a thing is ruled and measured in so far as it partakes of the rule or measure. Wherefore, since all things subject to divine providence are ruled and measured by the eternal law . . . it is evident that all things partake somewhat of the eternal law, in so far as, namely, from its being imprinted on them, they derive their respective inclinations to their proper acts and ends. Now among all others the rational creature is subject to divine providence in the most excellent way, in so far as it partakes of a share of providence, by being provident both for itself and others. Wherefore it has a share of the eternal reason, whereby it has a natural inclination to its proper act and end: and this participation of the eternal law in the rational creature is called the natural law. . . . [T]he light of natural reason, whereby we discern what is good and what is evil, which is the function of the natural law, is nothing else than an imprint on us of the divine light. It is therefore evident that the natural law is nothing else than the rational creature's partici- pation of the eternal law (Q.91, Article 2 "Whether There Is in Us a Natural Law?").

This is a crucial article for understanding Aquinas's theory of law. Though God is once again the legislator of this law, and the natural law is a proper subset of the eternal law, it differs from the eternal law as binding only rational creatures. The idea is that, in virtue of having reason and free will, rational creatures are not bound merely to obey eternal law through instinct or inclination, as irrational creatures are bound, but may participate more fully and more perfectly in the law. Through "natural reason", which we have through divine creation, we are able to distinguish right from wrong. Through free will, we are able to choose what is right. In so far as we do so, we participate more fully in eternal law: rather than merely being led blindly to our proper end, we are able to choose that end and so make our compliance with the eternal law an act of self-direction as well. In this way the law comes to be in us as a rule and measure; it is no longer merely a rule and measure imposed upon us from an external source. "Although [the Gentiles] have no written law, yet they have the natural law, whereby each one knows, and is conscious of, what is good and what is evil" [Romans ii. 14]. When we order our own actions in accordance with what is good and shun what is evil, we follow the natural law and participate in the eternal law rather than being merely acted upon by that law. . . .

We turn now to the all-important question of the end to which natural law directs rational creatures. Aquinas provides the following discussion of this matter.

> *[The precepts of the natural law are the self-evident first principles of practical reason.] Now . . . "good" is the first thing that falls under the apprehension of the practical reason, which is directed to action, since every agent acts for an end under the aspect of good. Consequently the first principle in the practical reason is one founded on the notion of good, viz., that* good is that which all things seek after. *Hence this is the first precept of law, that* good is to be done and ensued, and evil is to be avoided. *All other precepts of the natural law are based upon this, so that whatever the practical reason naturally apprehends as man's good (or evil) belongs to the precepts of the natural law as something to be done or avoided.*
>
> *Since, however, good has the nature of an end, and evil the nature of a contrary, hence it is that all those things to which man has a natural inclination are naturally apprehended by reason as being good and, consequently, as objects of pursuit, and their*

> *contraries as evil and objects of avoidance. Wherefore the order of the precepts of the natural law is according to the order of the natural inclinations. Because in man there is first of all an inclination to good in accor-dance with the nature which he has in common with all substances, inasmuch as every substance seeks the preservation of its own being, according to its nature; and by reason of this inclination, whatever is a means of preserving human life and of warding off its obstacles belongs to the natural law. Secondly, there is in man an inclination to things that pertain to him more specifically, according to that nature which he has in common with other animals; and in virtue of this inclination, those things are said to belong to natural law "which nature has taught to all animals," [Justinian, Digest I, tit.i] such as sexual intercourse, education of offspring, and so forth. Thirdly, there is in man an inclination to good, according to the nature of his reason, which nature is proper to him: thus man has a natural inclination to know the truth about God and to live in society; and in this respect, whatever pertains to this inclination belongs to the natural law, for instance, to shun ignorance, to avoid offending those among whom one has to live, and other such things regarding the above inclination (Question 94: Of The Natural Law, Article 2 "Whether the Natural Law Contains Several Precepts, or Only One?").*

There is a great deal that requires comment upon in this passage. The first is the understanding of practical reason upon which Aquinas is relying. At the basis of this form of reasoning are indemonstrable first principles. These are definitions, which are self-evident in the sense that if a person knows the meaning of the terms then they must immediately recognize the truth of the principle. The first principle of practical reason is: "Good is that which all things seek after." The first precept of natural law, drawn from this principle as a conclusion is: "Good is to be done, evil avoided." In this case it is an action-guiding principle, and the conclusion of reasoning from it will be a directive about what action one ought to take.

Before we can draw any conclusions about which specific actions we ought to undertake from our first principle, however, we need an intermediate proposition concerning what is good or evil. Thus we need something like "The education of offspring is good, because it satisfies our natural inclination to procreate and to live together in on-going societies." The conclusion is "Therefore, we ought to perform those actions necessary for the education of our children." In this way we proceed from the first precept of the natural law to specific conclusions about what we ought to do or what the natural law directs us to do.

This means that, in order to understand what the natural law demands of us, we must be able to identify what is good and what is evil, so that the former may be pursued and the latter avoided. Aquinas thinks that we can do this by examining human nature. In taking this tack Aquinas is adopting an "essentialist" view of human nature, claiming that there are some characteristics or inclinations which are essential to human beings, and that our good consists in acting in accordance with those characteristics and inclinations. He identifies in the passage quoted three principal sets of interests which are essential to our nature in the relevant sense: those we have as living creatures, such as the interest in self preservation; those we have as animals, such as the interest in procreation; and those we have as rational creatures, such as the interest in living in society and exercising our intellectual and spiritual capacities in the pursuit of knowledge. Once we have filled out such a view of what is essential to human flourishing, based on our fundamental nature, we can determine by practical reason what is good for us and what bad. In this way natural law is an ordinance of reason.

This kind of essentialism about human nature, which implies that our most important ends are predetermined and that at base we all have common interests, has come into disfavour in contemporary philosophy. But it is important to note that, even if one rejects this foundation for determining what is good, as a natural law theorist one must provide an alternative which has the following characteristic: it must provide an "objective" conception of the good. That is, whatever the good is, it must be good independently of our believing it is good. We shall return to this idea later.

This discussion provides the basis of an answer to the question: What is the end toward which the natural law directs us? The natural law directs us to the good, as determined by those interests which we all share in virtue of our nature as human beings, and away from evil, which are those things that are incompatible with human flourishing. Thus we might think of the natural law as containing the basic precepts of the correct moral code.

The natural law is known to men innately: in creating men as rational creatures God has implanted within them knowledge of the first principles of the natural law. Thus *we must say that the natural law, as to general principles, is the same for all, both as to rectitude [validity] and as to knowledge* (Q.94, Article 4 "Whether the Natural Law Is the Same in All Men?"). Both through natural inclinations and the divine light we are informed of our proper acts and ends.

But if the natural law directs us to our common good, to those things which allow us to flourish in accordance with our nature, and all action aims at what is good; and if, furthermore, all men know what the natural law commands, and are naturally inclined to follow it, how is it that we sometimes pursue evil? How is it that human societies differ as greatly in their basic organizations as they do around the world and at different times? And why is natural law alone not enough to govern human behavior: why do we need human laws as well? Aquinas recognizes that his account raises these and related questions, and he provides the following answer.

> *[T]o the natural law belongs [sic] those things to which a man is inclined naturally; and among these it is proper to man to be inclined to act according to reason. Now the process of reason is from the common [general] to the proper [specific], as stated in* Physics i *[Aristotle]. The speculative reason, however, is differently situated in this matter, from the prac- tical reason. For, since the speculative reason is busied chiefly with necessary things, which cannot be otherwise than they are, its proper conclusion, like the universal principles, contain the truth without fail. The practical reason, on the other hand, is busied with contingent matters, about which human actions are concerned; and consequently, although there is necessity in the general principles, the more we descend to matters of detail, the more frequently we encounter defects. . . . [I]n matters of action, truth or practical rectitude is not the same for all, as to matters of detail but only as to general principles; and where there is the same rectitude in matters of detail, it is not equally known to all.*
> *. . . Thus it is right and true for all to act according to reason: and from this principle*

it follows as a proper conclusion, that goods entrusted to another should be restored to their owner. Now this is true for the majority of cases: but it may happen in a particular case that it would be injurious, and therefore unreasonable, to restore goods held in trust; for instance if they are claimed for the purpose of fighting against one's country. And this principle will be found to fail the more, according as we descend further into detail, e.g., if one were to say that goods held in trust should be restored with such and such a guarantee, or in such and such a way; because the greater the number of conditions added, the greater the number of ways in which the principle may fail, so that it is not right to restore or not to restore.

Consequently we must say that the natural law, as to general principles, is the same for all, both as to rectitude and as to knowledge. But as to certain matters of details, which are conclusions, as it were, of those general principles, it is the same for all in the majority of cases, both as to rectitude and as to knowledge; and yet in some few cases it may fail, both as to rectitude, by reason of certain obstacles . . . and as to knowledge, since in some the reason is perverted by passion, or evil habit, or an evil disposition of nature; thus formerly theft, although it is expressly contrary to the natural law, was not considered wrong among the Germans, as Julius Caesar relates [De bello Gallico] *(Q.94, Article 4).*

Here Aquinas offers three different reasons why human beings may fail to act according to the natural law, and why they might disagree about what is good (he will offer more reasons in what follows). The first two might be considered to arise from the same source, namely, the very general and indeterminate nature of natural law when it is applied to specific matters of human action. The first difficulty that the general nature of natural law creates is that the conclusions which are drawn from it using practical reason are not universally valid. For instance, even though the natural law clearly proscribes violence, there are exceptions to this rule: in the case of self-defense, for example, or a just war, violence may be justified. Thus as we attempt to deduce more specific rules from the natural law, exceptions arise, general rules have to be modified to

fit exceptional circumstances, and so on. Secondly, because natural law provides only very general rules, which must be applied to specific cases by fallible human beings, error is possible concerning the exact content of the natural law, even when it is being interpreted by good people. Finally, though the most basic demands of natural law are known to all through natural reason, reason is sometimes perverted or overwhelmed by passion and bad habits, as the example of the Germans sanctioning theft illustrates. Thus although it is our nature to follow reason, we sometimes are led to vice by impulses which run contrary to reason. Human law remedies these defects by giving determinate content to the law and by providing an additional motive to obey it: the fear of punishment.

II.3 Human Law:

[A] law is a dictate of the practical reason. . . . [I]t is from the precepts of the natural law, as from general and indemonstrable principles, that the human reason needs to proceed to the more particular determination of certain matters. These particular determinations, devised by human reason, are called human laws, provided the other essential conditions of law be observed, as stated above (Q.90, Articles 2, 3 and 4). Wherefore Cicero says in his Rhetoric *that "justice has its source in nature; thence certain things came into custom by reason of their utility; afterward these things which emanated from nature and were approved by custom were sanctioned by fear and reverence for the law"* [Cicero, De inventione rhetorica, ii] *(Q.91, Article 3 "Whether There Is a Human Law?").*

Here the purpose of human law is to render determinate the precepts of the natural law, and make it known what is required in particular cases in light of a society's specific circumstances. Human law is needed to clarify the demands of natural law, not only because the natural law's generality and human moral failings give rise to problems in our knowing and applying the natural law, but also because the natural law is sometimes *underdetermined*; it can be fulfilled in a variety of ways, all equally good. Aquinas stresses this issue of underdetermination in the following passage.

But it must be noted that something may be derived from the natural law in two ways: first, as a conclusion from premises; secondly, by way of determination of certain generalities. The first way is like to that by which, in the sciences, demonstrated conclusions are drawn from the principles, while the second mode is likened to that whereby, in the arts, general forms are particularized as to details: thus the craftsman needs to determine the general form of a house to some particular shape. Some things are therefore derived from the general principles of the natural law by way of conclusions, e.g., that "one must not kill" may be derived as a conclusion from the principle that "one should do harm to no man"; while some are derived therefrom by way of determination, e.g., the law of nature has it that the evildoer should be punished; but that he be punished in this or that way is not directly by natural law but is a derived determination of it.

Accordingly, both modes of derivation are found in the human law. But those things which are derived in the first way are contained in human law, not as emanating therefrom exclusively, but having some force from the natural law also. But those things which are derived in the second way have no other force than that of human law (Q.95, Article 2 "Whether Every Human Law Is Derived from the Natural Law?").

This discussion indicates that the underdetermined nature of the natural law leaves open room for variations within legal codes in different communities. For while the most basic principles of all human legal codes must be derived deductively from natural law "as conclusions", and so must be the same for all communities, those human laws which are derived "by determination" allow societies to tailor their legal codes to fit their particular circumstances and needs. Thus we can have a diversity of positive (human) laws in different communities: when human laws are enacted as particularizations from general principles, it is sometimes possible that different communities will choose different particular laws to give content to the general principles, just as different communities will give different particular shapes to their houses, despite the fact that houses have a general form (walls and a roof designed to provide shelter from the elements).

In drawing this distinction between those human laws that are derived deductively from natural law, on the one hand, and those which are mere determinations, on the other, Aquinas marks an important division within the category of human laws. For those laws that fall into the first group have not only the status of human law but also of the natural law. As such, they must direct behaviour in accordance with the correct moral code. This has the implication that any violation of such laws is not only a legal offense but also an offense against morality, i.e., a sin or vice. Such offenses, we say, are *mala in se*, for they involve actions that would be wrong independently of and prior to being made illegal. Murder is a *mala in se* offense, for it is morally wrong quite independently of being legally prohibited. Those laws which are derived from natural law in the second way, however, and which have only the force of human law, lack this independent moral status. When the human law prohibits actions that are not themselves morally wrong, we call such offenses *mala prohibita*. They are legal offenses, but not moral offenses, and one who commits them is guilty of legal wrongdoing but not also of an independent sin or vice. Thus, for example, in many jurisdictions there is a legal prohibition against persons under a certain age driving a car. Let's suppose the age is 16 years. Now, no one would want to say that driving when under the age of 16 is independently immoral or vicious, though it is equally clearly illegal. And this law may well be justified as a law derived in the second way from natural law: for having such restrictions on the use of dangerous machines like cars serves the common good. Thus while *mala in se* offenses are universally and invariably wrong, their wrongness being deductively derived from natural law, the class of *mala prohibita* offenses contains room for considerable variation across different communities.

Let us return now to our more immediate topic, which concerns the many reasons why we need human law. As we saw in our previous discussion, it is not only the generality and underdetermined nature of the natural law that explains why it must be supplemented with human law. A different reason is to be found in the moral failings of human beings: for we sometimes fail to willingly follow the dictates of natural law.

[M]an has a natural aptitude for virtue, but the perfection of virtue must be acquired by man by means of some kind of training. . . . Now it is difficult to see how man could suffice

for himself in the matter of this training, since the perfection of virtue consists chiefly in withdrawing man from undue pleasures, to which above all man is inclined, and especially the young, who are more capable of being trained. Consequently a man needs to receive this training from another, whereby to arrive at the perfection of virtue. And as to those young people who are inclined to acts of virtue, by their good natural disposition, or by custom, or rather by the gift of God, paternal training suffices, which is by admonitions. But since some are found to be depraved and prone to vice, and not easily amenable to words, it was necessary for such to be restrained from evil by force and fear, in order that, at least, they might desist from evil-doing and leave others in peace, and that they themselves, by being habituated in this way, might be brought to do willingly what hitherto they did from fear, and thus become virtuous. Now this kind of training which compels through fear of punishment is the discipline of laws. Therefore, in order that man might have peace and virtue, it is necessary for laws to be framed . . . (Question 95: Of Human Law, Article 1 "Whether It Was Useful for Laws to be Framed by Men?").

Aquinas speaks here of two additional reasons why human laws are needed. First, they provide an educative effect upon those who do not pursue virtue willingly. In this way they promote virtue. But they do so by coercion, by threat of force (punishment) and the fear that threat engenders. This may itself lead to virtue, for what one does in the beginning out of fear can become habitual; when one habitually refrains from evil and does as virtue requires, then one has become virtuous. And this leads to the second role for human law, especially as backed up by the threat of coercive sanctions: it deters those who would do evil from actually doing it, and thus serves the goals of peace, security and order. . . .

Despite the fact that human law is needed for these reasons as a supplement to the natural law, Aquinas believes that valid human law is derived from the natural law. This is so because he believes that human law must meet one further validity condition to be genuine law: it must be just. Now this requirement is really only relevant to human law, since the law given by God cannot be unjust. But because human law is made by people, who are fal-

lible as well as susceptible to vice, it is possible that a law-maker might try to make laws which are unjust. Aquinas denies that such are valid laws, on the grounds that human law must be derived from natural law (as an ordinance of reason), and so it cannot be unjust. Rules only have the binding force appropriate to law if they are just.

As Augustine says, "that which is not just seems to be no law at all" [De libero arbitrio]; wherefore the force of law depends on the extent of its justice. Now in human affairs a thing is said to be just from being right according to the rule of reason. But the first rule of reason is the law of nature . . . Consequently, every human law has just so much of the nature of law as it is derived from the law of nature. But if in any point it deflects from the law of nature, it is no longer a law but a perversion of law (Q.95, Article 2 "Whether Every Human Law Is Derived from the Natural Law?").

What are we to say of Aquinas's insistence that human laws have the binding force of law only if they are just? This seems, in some ways, an extraordinary claim, given that we are all familiar with things that seem to be human laws but which are clearly unjust, e.g., the slave laws of the United States before the Civil War, or the Nazi laws in Germany which sent millions of Jews to the death camps. Aquinas does not deny that such directives have the form of law, but he insists nonetheless that they fail to be genuine laws, that they fail to have the binding force of law. They lack that force, and the status of law, because they fail to conform with the dictates of justice which are contained within the natural law which is an ordinance of right reason.

Human law has the nature of law in so far as it partakes of right reason; and it is clear that, in this respect, it is derived from the eternal law. But in so far as it deviates from reason, it is called an unjust law and has the nature, not of law, but of violence. Nevertheless even an unjust law, in so far as it retains some appearance of law, through being framed by one who is in power, is derived from the eternal law, since all power is from the Lord God, according to Romans xiii. I (Question 93, Article 3 "Whether Every Law Is Derived from the Eternal Law?").

To say that "unjust laws" fail to have the binding force of law we must consider briefly what Aquinas calls the power of law "to bind a man in conscience". This is the power of law to impose a moral obligation of obedience upon those to whom the law applies. In discussing this question, Aquinas directly deals with this obligation, as well as specifies in more detail his conception of justice.

> Laws framed by man are either just or unjust. If they be just, they have the power of binding in conscience, from the eternal law whence they are derived, according to Proverbs viii. 15: "By Me kings reign, and lawgivers decree just things." Now laws are said to be just—from the end, when, to wit, they are ordained to the common good—and from their author, that is to say, when the law that is made does not exceed the power of the lawgiver—and from their form, when, to wit, burdens are laid on the subjects, according to an equality of proportion and with a view to the common good. For, since one man is a part of the community, each man, in all that he is and has, belongs to the community, just as a part, in all that it is, belongs to the whole; wherefore nature inflicts a loss on the part in order to save the whole, so that on this account such laws as these which impose proportionate burdens are just and binding in conscience and are legal laws.
>
> On the other hand, laws may be unjust in two ways: first, by being contrary to human good, through being opposed to the things mentioned above—either in respect of the end, as when an authority imposes on his subjects burdensome laws, conducive, not to the common good, but rather to his own cupidity or vainglory; or in respect of the author, as when a man makes a law that goes beyond the power committed to him; or in the respect of form, as when burdens are imposed unequally on the community, although with a view to the common good. The like are acts of violence rather than laws, because, as Augustine says, "A law that is not just seems to be no law at all." Wherefore such laws do not bind in conscience, except perhaps in order to avoid scandal or disturbance, for which cause a man should even yield his right . . .
>
> Secondly, laws may be unjust through being opposed to the divine good: such are the laws of tyrants inducing to idolatry or to anything else contrary to the divine law; and laws

> of this kind must nowise be observed because, as stated in Acts v.29, "we ought to obey God rather than men" (Q.95, Article 4 "Whether Human Law Binds a Man in Conscience?"). . . .

. . . [Here] Aquinas gives some content to his conception of justice and its relation to law. He outlines various ways in which a law may fail to be just: it may aim at the good of the lawgiver only, rather than at the common good; it may exceed the authority of the lawgiver; it may impose disproportionate burdens upon some of the people; it may be contrary in its directives to the divine law as known through revelation. In each of these cases, the law denies to those who are governed what they are due. Thus they can demand as their due that the ruler make laws which are directed to the common good rather than to his personal glory; that they be allowed to worship God; that they be ruled only within the limits of proper authority; and that the ruler not impose disproportionate burdens upon some for the benefit of others. This last requirement may lend itself to misunderstanding, however, in light of Aquinas's insistence that justice concerns the relations between persons and demands an equality of some kind. For Aquinas is not advocating an egalitarian society or insisting that the benefits and burdens of society be distributed equally. Indeed, he believes that class divisions and even slavery are natural relations. But he does insist that justice demands that the burdens and benefits of society be distributed proportionately and in the service of the common good. This allows that unequal burdens can be placed upon some, when that is needed for the good of the whole. Thus, for example, we can demand that the young and strong provide military service in defense of the society, and in so doing impose a heavy burden upon them that is not shared by all, provided that it be necessary for the common good and they receive compensatory benefits from society in other areas.

In all of the cases of unjust laws that he considers, Aquinas declares that such laws lose their binding force. In all but the last case, we may disobey such laws, though we must not do so at the risk of causing "scandal and disturbance". Scandal and disturbance signify a break-down of the order which is the foundation of human society, a loss of peace and security, as would be found in a situation of massive civil unrest or civil war. This should not be risked, even if that requires obeying laws which are unjust in terms of the end, author or form. The final case, however, involving laws which are contrary to divine law, such as a law requiring that everyone abstain from Christian worship would be, is different: we must not obey such laws, regardless of the consequences. . . .

To say that we all have an obligation to obey (just) laws raises a different question, however: does it require that in every instance we must obey the letter of the law, even if doing so would be ruinous or cause great hardship to the common good? This issue was thought by Aquinas to raise the question of whether those who are subject to law are competent to interpret it and perhaps decide, in a given case, that the real intentions of the lawgiver would be better served by an action which is contrary to the letter of the law. He answers that it is sometimes permissible for those subject to the law to interpret the intentions of the lawmaker and decide not to obey the letter of the law.

[E]very law is directed to the common weal of men and derives the force and nature of law accordingly. Hence the Jurist says: "By no reason of law or favor of equity is it allowable for us to interpret harshly and render burdensome those useful measures which have been enacted for the welfare of man" [Ulpian, Digest i. 3]. Now it happens often that the observance of some point of law conduces to the common weal in the majority of instances, and yet, in some cases, is very hurtful. Since, then, the lawgiver cannot have in view every single case, he shapes the law according to what happens most frequently, by directing his attention to the common good. Wherefore, if a case arises wherein the observance of that law would be hurtful to the general welfare, it should not be observed. For instance, suppose that in a besieged city it is an established law that the gates of the city are to be kept closed, this is good for public welfare as a general rule, but if it were to happen that the enemy are in pursuit of certain citizens who are defenders of the city, it would be a great loss to the city if the gates were not opened to them; and so in that case the gates ought to be opened, contrary to the letter of the law, in order to maintain the common weal, which the lawgiver had in view.

Nevertheless it must be noted that if the observance of the law according to the letter does not involve any sudden risk needing instance

remedy, it is not competent for everyone to expound what is useful and what is not useful to the state; those alone can do this who are in authority and who, on account of suchlike cases, have the power to dispense from the laws. If, however, the peril be so sudden as not to allow of the delay involved by referring the matter to authority, the mere necessity brings with it a dispensation, since necessity knows no law (Q.96, Article 6 "Whether He Who Is Under a Law May Act Beside the Letter of the Law?").

Thus we find Aquinas recognizing that blind obedience to the letter of the law is not desirable. While we must avoid a situation wherein every person feels competent to judge the law and decide he shall obey it only as it serves his own interests, we must equally avoid the situation wherein great harm is done to the common good out of servile obedience to the law. In his example of the besieged city, Aquinas notes one case in which the law ought not to be obeyed. But there are others, readily imaginable: in case of a fire within the city, for example, the law also ought not to be obeyed. These are exceptions to the general rule, but they cannot themselves be written into the law, both because they are too numerous and too unforeseeable. To attempt to write all the possible exceptions into the law would make the law too complex to be useful as a general rule and measure for human action. Thus we must be content to use general laws, while recognizing that exceptional cases may arise in which obedience to the letter of the law must give way to the spirit of the law, which aims always at the common good.

As these articles make clear, Aquinas believes that one important purpose of human laws is to make men virtuous. . . .

Human law is limited, however, in the extent to which it can aim to make men fully virtuous. In the first place, there are many forms of vice that do not fall within the prohibitions of human law.

Now human law is framed for a number of human beings, the majority of whom are not perfect in virtue. Wherefore human laws do not forbid all vices from which the virtuous abstain, but only the more grievous vices from which it is possible for the majority to abstain; and chiefly those that are to the hurt of others, without the prohibition of which human society could not be maintained: thus human law prohibits murder, theft, and suchlike (Q.96,

Article 2 "Whether it Belongs to Human Law to Repress All Vices?").

Likewise, human law does not proscribe all virtues, but only those which are ordainable to the common good (Q.96, Article 3 "Whether Human Law Prescribes Acts of All the Virtues?"). This defect in human law is rectified, however, with the addition of the final type of law: divine law.

II.4 Divine Law:

Besides the natural and the human law it was necessary for the directing of human conduct to have a divine law. And this for four reasons. First, because it is by law that man is directed how to perform his proper acts in view of his last end. And indeed, if man were ordained to no other end than that which is proportionate to his natural faculty, there would be no need for man to have any further direction on the part of his reason besides the natural law and human law which is derived from it. But since man is ordained to an end of eternal happiness which is inproportionate to man's natural faculty . . . therefore it was necessary that, besides the natural and the human law, man should be directed to his end by a law given by God.

Secondly, because, on account of the uncertainty of human judgment, especially on contingent and particular matters, different people form different judgments on human acts; whence also different and contrary laws result. In order, therefore, that man may know without any doubt what he ought to do and what he ought to avoid, it was necessary for man to be directed in his proper acts by a law given by God, for it is certain that such a law cannot err.

Thirdly, because man can make laws in those matters of which he is competent to judge. But man is not competent to judge of interior movements that are hidden, but only of exterior acts which appear; and yet for the perfection of virtue it is necessary for man to conduct himself aright in both kinds of acts. Consequently human law could not sufficiently curb and direct interior acts, and it was necessary for this purpose that a divine law should supervene.

Fourthly, because, as Augustine says, human law cannot punish or forbid all evil deeds; since while aiming at doing away with all evils, it would do away with many good things, and would hinder the advance of the common good, which is necessary for human intercourse [De libero arbitrio i, 5, 6]. In order, therefore, that no evil might remain unforbidden and unpunished, it was necessary for the divine law to supervene, whereby all sins are forbidden (Q.91, Article 3 "Whether There Was Any Need for a Divine Law?").

Divine law is directed to the common good of mankind as beings capable of salvation and eternal happiness. That is its end. It is promulgated in the words of divine revelation and the pronouncements of the Pope. Because men cannot know, by natural reason unassisted by divine revelation, what God demands of them in order to be worthy of eternal happiness, divine law is needed in addition to natural and human law. It is also needed because human law must confine its attentions to the actions of persons; since having good motives and not merely doing the right thing is also part of virtue, and law aims to make men virtuous, human law must be supplemented with divine law. Moreover, as Aquinas points out, if human law were to attempt to prohibit and punish all vices, many good things would become exceedingly difficult or impossible to achieve. For instance, suppose that the human law attempted to forbid backbiting gossip, on the grounds that it is vicious; in order to enforce such a law, the privacy and trust which is necessary between spouses, friends, co-workers and others would have to be severely restricted. Given that the price of enforcing such a law would certainly outweigh the benefits of it, such a sin as gossiping ought not to be made an object of human law but must be left to God to judge of and punish.

Natural Law Theory: Aquinas's Legacy

Although Aquinas developed his theory of law within the context of a Christian world-view, much of what he says remains relevant within modern secular societies. And in many ways the issues he raised continue yet to dominate the philosophy of law. Furthermore, the natural law theory of which he is taken to be the founder still attracts thoughtful adherents today, both Thomistic and secular. What, then, is the natural law theory?

Though there are many differences dividing natural law theorists on a myriad of issues, the following is meant to capture the central tenets of the natural law position. First, natural law theorists typically accept from Aquinas some version of the claim that law is a rule and measure. In more modern parlance, law is a system of rules by which human beings are to direct their behavior. But they also accept from Aquinas the view that the system of rules is supposed to direct human behavior *aright*. What is distinctive to the natural law position is the insistence that the direction provided by the law must be toward ends that are rationally defensible or objectively good; law must direct behaviour toward the common good. It is this requirement, that all genuine law aims at what is truly good, not just for the ruler but also for the ruled, that sets natural law theory apart from a great many others.

The insistence that law has as its end the common good makes natural law theory teleological. Teleology is the view that some things (perhaps all) have an end or function proper to them, and that they cannot be fully understood without reference to that end or function. So, for example, we cannot fully understand the essence of a knife without reference to its end, which is to cut things. Now one need not be a teleologist about everything in order to be a natural law theorist. But one must be a teleologist about law itself. That is, one must believe that law has an end, which is truly good, and that all genuine law aims at that end; there is some end which law must serve, *qua* law. Stated in terms of functions, the natural law theorist is committed to the view that law has some function, which is objectively good, and we cannot fully understand law independently of that function. Now there have been many functions proposed as essential to law: the preservation of order, to assist us in achieving the good appropriate to our nature, to make us virtuous, and so on. It is important to keep in mind, however, that it is not only natural law theorists who may attribute an essential function to law; one might think that the purpose of law is just to ensure obedience to the sovereign, and yet not be a natural law theorist. One will only be offering a natural law position if the end or func-tion claimed to be essential to law must be objectively good. The important point to all of this is that if one does offer such a position then one makes moral conditions validity conditions of law.

To say that valid law must have a certain moral content in order to be valid is to say that we cannot identify something as genuine law by its form or structure alone; we must look also to its content to determine whether it is law. For Aquinas and most natural law theorists who have followed him, this requirement takes the form of providing necessary conditions of law: it is necessary, though not sufficient, for something to be a human or positive law that it be aimed at the common good and that it be just. That is, it is enough to make a law invalid that it aim at something which is contrary to the common good or that is unjust. Thus "an unjust law is no law at all" has come to be one of the defining tenets of the natural law position.

Because there is a necessary connection between genuine law and morality, one further conclusion is licensed. Not only do we have a prudential reason to obey the law namely to avoid punishment; but we also have a moral obligation to obey the law, which derives from its independent justification or objective rightness. While the former may hold even with respect to "unjust laws", the latter holds only because the law, as genuine law, enjoins what we already morally ought to do. This is so directly in the case of *mala in se* offenses, which we ought to refrain from because they are both immoral and illegal, and indirectly in the case of *mala prohibita* offenses, which we ought to refrain from because doing so serves the common good. As Aquinas makes clear, however, the moral obligation binds us to the spirit of the law and not merely to its letter.

This conception of crime as being not only illegal but also immoral leads us to the final noteworthy feature common amongst natural law theorists: they have usually been committed to a retributivist theory of punishment. Though the natural lawyer's defense of retributivism cannot be fully explained or justified here, it typically consists of a defense of the following claims. Because those who break the law thereby also commit a sin, they deserve punishment. Their moral culpability makes them fit subjects of retribution. This is in keeping with justice, moreover, because it is just that those who do wrong suffer harm: for due equality is served when good is returned for good, and evil for evil. Whether the natural law theorist must adopt a retributive theory of punishment is an interesting question that we cannot explore here; we must be content with simply noting that Aquinas himself accepted the connection between his theory of law and retributivism in punishment.

This concludes our brief discussion of natural law theory. Though I have attempted to identify those tenets that are most common to the natural law tradition, this account must surely be deemed inadequate even for that purpose: for the natural law tradition embodies a diversity and richness of views that make it impossible to capture in an essay such as this. I shall be content, however, if I have suc-ceeded it presenting and explicating Aquinas's particular brand of natural law theory in sufficient detail to enable those who may be interested to pursue the many controversies which surround it. I have not been able to enter into those controversies here, nor have I been able to critically assess the many tenets

---

that I have just sketched. I leave such commentary and criticism to the history of jurisprudence.[4]

1. Published by Burns, Oates and Washbourne, Ltd., London, Publishers to the Holy See; 22 volumes, 1912–36.
2. When Aquinas refers to the "perfect community" he does not mean some ideal or utopian state, but rather he means only the whole community of individuals united in a particular way. A perfect community is one in which a multiplicity of individuals are brought together, their diverse activities coordinated and directed to the attainment of their common end.
3. See especially St. Thomas Aquinas, *De Regimine (On Kingship)* trans. G. B. Phelan and I. T. Eschmann (Toronto: PIMS, 1949).
4. I would like to thank David Braybrooke, who many years ago taught me that Aquinas has much to say even to a secular society. I would also like to thank Eric Cavallero for his many helpful comments on an earlier draft of this essay.

The Challenge of Legal Positivism

A Positivist Conception of Law*

John Austin

Lecture I

The matter of jurisprudence is positive law: law, simply and strictly so called: or law set by political superiors to political inferiors. But positive law (or law, simply and strictly so called) is often confounded with objects to which it is related by *resemblance,* and with objects to which it is related in the way of *analogy:* with objects which are *also* signified, *properly* and *improperly,* by the large and vague expression *law.* To obviate the difficulties springing from that confusion, I begin my projected Course with determining the province of jurisprudence, or with distinguishing the matter of jurisprudence from those various related objects: trying to define the subject of which I intend to treat, before I endeavour to analyse its numerous and complicated parts.

A law, in the most general and comprehensive acceptation in which the term, in its literal meaning, is employed, may be said to be a rule laid down for the guidance of an intelligent being by an intelligent being having power over him. Under this definition are concluded, and without impropriety, several species. It is necessary to define accurately the line of demarcation which separates these species from one another, as much mistiness and intricacy has been infused into the science of jurisprudence by their being confounded or not clearly distinguished. In the comprehensive sense above indicated, or in the largest meaning which it has, without extension

by metaphor or analogy, the term *law* embraces the following objects:—Laws set by God to his human creatures, and laws set by men to men.

The whole or a portion of the laws set by God to men is frequently styled the law of nature, or natural law: being, in truth, the only natural law of which it is possible to speak without a metaphor, or without a blending of objects which ought to be distinguished broadly. But, rejecting the appellation Law of Nature as ambiguous and misleading, I name those laws or rules, as considered collectively or in a mass, the *Divine law,* or the *law of God.*

Laws set by men to men are of two leading or principal classes: classes which are often blended, although they differ extremely; and which, for that reason, should be severed precisely, and opposed distinctly and conspicuously.

Of the laws or rules set by men to men, some are established by *political* superiors, sovereign and subject: by persons exercising supreme and subordinate *government,* in independent nations, or independent political societies. The aggregate of the rules thus established, or some aggregate forming a portion of that aggregate, is the appropriate matter of jurisprudence, general or particular. To the aggregate of the rules thus established, or to some aggregate forming a portion of that aggregate, the term *law,* as used simply and strictly, is exclusively applied. But, as contradistinguished to *natural* law, or to the law of *nature* (meaning, by those expressions,

*From *The Province of Jurisprudence Determined,* selections from Lectures I and VI. First published in 1832.

the law of God), the aggregate of the rules, established by political superiors, is frequently styled *positive* law, or law existing *by position*. As contradistinguished to the rules which I style *positive morality,* and on which I shall touch immediately, the aggregate of the rules, established by political superiors, may also be marked commodiously with the name of *positive law*. For the sake, then, of getting a name brief and distinctive at once, and agreeable to frequent usage, I style that aggregate of rules, or any portion of that aggregate, *positive law:* though rules, which are *not* established by political superiors are also *positive,* or exist *by position,* if they be rules or laws, in the proper signification of the term.

Though *some* of the laws or rules, which are set by men to men, are established by political superiors, *others* are *not* established by political superiors, or are *not* established by political superiors, in that capacity or character.

Closely analogous to human laws of this second class, are a set of objects frequently but *improperly* termed *laws,* being rules set and enforced by *mere opinion,* that is, by the opinions or sentiments held or felt by an indeterminate body of men in regard to human conduct. Instances of such a use of the term *law* are the expressions—"The law of honour"; "The law set by fashion"; and rules of this species constitute much of what is usually termed "International law."

The aggregate of human laws properly so called belonging to the second of the classes above mentioned, with the aggregate of objects *improperly* but by *close analogy* termed laws, I place together in a common class, and denote them by the term *positive morality*. The name *morality* severs them from *positive law,* while the epithet *positive* disjoins them from the *law of God*. And to the end of obviating confusion, it is necessary or expedient that they *should* be disjoined from the latter by that distinguishing epithet. For the name *morality* (or *morals*), when standing unqualified or alone, denotes indifferently either of the following objects: namely, positive morality *as it is,* or without regard to its merits; and positive morality *as it would be,* if it conformed to the law of God, and were, therefore, deserving of *approbation.*

Besides the various sorts of rules which are included in the literal acceptation of the term law, and those which are by a close and striking analogy, though improperly, termed laws, there are numerous applications of the term law, which rest upon a slender analogy and are merely metaphorical or figurative. Such is the case when we talk of *laws* observed by the lower animals; of *laws* regulating the growth or decay of vegetables; of *laws* determining the movements of inanimate bodies or masses. For where *intelligence* is not, or where it is too bounded to take the name of *reason,* and, therefore, is too bounded to conceive the purpose of a law, there is not the *will* which law can work on, or which duty can incite or restrain. Yet through these misapplications of a *name,* flagrant as the metaphor is, has the field of jurisprudence and morals been deluged with muddy speculation.

Having suggested the *purpose* of my attempt to determine the province of jurisprudence: to distinguish positive law, the appropriate matter of jurisprudence, from the various objects to which it is related by resemblance, and to which it is related, nearly or remotely, by a strong or slender analogy: I shall now state the essentials of a *law* or *rule* (taken with the largest signification which can be given to the term *properly*).

Every *law* or *rule* (taken with the largest signification which can be given to the term *properly*) is a *command*. Or, rather, laws or rules, properly so called, are a *species* of commands.

Now, since the term *command* comprises the term *law,* the first is the simpler as well as the larger of the two. But, simple as it is, it admits of explanation. And, since it is the *key* to the sciences of jurisprudence and morals, its meaning should be analysed with precision.

Accordingly, I shall endeavour, in the first instance, to analyse the meaning of *'command'*: an analysis which I fear, will task the patience of my hearers, but which they will bear with cheerfulness, or, at least, with resignation, if they consider the difficulty of performing it. The elements of a science are precisely the parts of it which are explained least easily. Terms that are the largest, and, therefore, the simplest of a series, are without equivalent expressions into which we can resolve them *concisely*. And when we endeavour to *define* them, or to translate them into terms which we suppose are better understood, we are forced upon awkward and tedious circumlocutions.

If you express or intimate a wish that I shall do or forbear from some act, and if you will visit me with an evil in case I comply not with your wish, the *expression* or *intimation* of your wish is a *command*. A command is distinguished from other significations of desire, not by the style in which the desire is signified, but by the power and the purpose of the party commanding to inflict an evil or pain in case the desire be disregarded. If you cannot or will not harm me in case I comply not with your wish, the expression of your wish is not a command, although you utter your wish in imperative phrase. If you are able and willing to harm me in case I comply not with your wish, the expression of your wish amounts to a command, although you are prompted by a spirit of courtesy to utter it in the shape of a request. *"Preces* erant, sed *quibus contradici non posset."* Such is the language of Tacitus, when speaking of a petition by the soldiery to a son and lieutenant of Vespasian.

A command, then, is a signification of desire. But a command is distinguished from other significations of desire by this peculiarity: that the party to whom it is directed is liable to evil from the other, in case he comply not with the desire.

Being liable to evil from you if I comply not with a wish which you signify, I am *bound* or *obliged* by your command, or I lie under a *duty* to obey it. If, in spite of that evil in prospect, I comply not with the wish which you signify, I am said to disobey your command, or to violate the duty which it imposes.

Command and duty are, therefore, correlative terms: the meaning denoted by each being implied or supposed by the other. Or (changing the expression) wherever a duty lies, a command has been signified; and whenever a command is signified, a duty is imposed.

Concisely expressed, the meaning of the correlative expressions is this: He who will inflict an evil in case his desire be disregarded, utters a command by expressing or intimating his desire. He who is liable to the evil in case he disregard the desire, is bound or obliged by the command.

The evil which will probably be incurred in case a command be disobeyed or (to use an equivalent expression) in case a duty be broken, is frequently called a *sanction,* or an *enforcement of obedience.* Or (varying the phrase) the command or the duty is said to be *sanctioned* or *enforced* by the chance of incurring the evil.

Considered as thus abstracted from the command and the duty which it enforces, the evil to be incurred by disobedience is frequently styled a *punishment.* But, as punishments, strictly so called, are only a *class* of sanctions, the term is too narrow to express the meaning adequately.

I observe that Dr. Paley, in his analysis of the term *obligation,* lays much stress upon the *violence*

of the motive to compliance. In so far as I can gather a meaning from his loose and inconsistent statement, his meaning appears to be this: that unless the motive to compliance be *violent* or *intense,* the expression or intimation of a wish is not a *command,* nor does the party to whom it is directed lie under a *duty* to regard it.

If he means, by a *violent* motive, a motive operating with certainty, his proposition is manifestly false. The greater the evil to be incurred in case the wish be disregarded, and the greater the chance of incurring it on that same event, the greater, no doubt, is the *chance* that the wish will *not* be disregarded. But no conceivable motive will *certainly* determine to compliance, or no conceivable motive will render obedience inevitable. If Paley's proposition be true, in the sense which I have now ascribed to it, commands and duties are simply impossible. Or, reducing his proposition to absurdity by a consequence as manifestly false, commands and duties are possible, but are never disobeyed or broken.

If he means by a *violent* motive, an evil which inspires fear, his meaning is simply this: that the party bound by a command is bound by the prospect of an evil. For that which is not feared is not apprehended as an evil: or (changing the shape of the expression) is not an evil in prospect.

The truth is, that the magnitude of the eventual evil, and the magnitude of the chance of incurring it, are foreign to the matter in question. The greater the eventual evil, and the greater the chance of incurring it, the greater is the efficacy of the command, and the greater is the strength of the obligation: Or (substituting expressions exactly equivalent), the greater is the *chance* that the command will be obeyed, and that the duty will not be broken. But where there is the smallest chance of incurring the smallest evil, the expression of a wish amounts to a command, and, therefore, imposes a duty. The sanction, if you will, is feeble or insufficient; but still there *is* a sanction, and, therefore, a duty and a command.

By some celebrated writers (by Locke, Bentham, and I think, Paley), the term *sanction,* or *enforcement of obedience,* is applied to conditional good as well as to conditional evil: to reward as to punishment. But, with all my habitual veneration for the names of Locke and Bentham, I think that this extension of the term is pregnant with confusion and perplexity.

Rewards are, indisputably, *motives* to comply with the wishes of others. But to talk of commands and duties as *sanctioned* or *enforced* by rewards, or to talk of rewards as *obliging* or *constraining* to obedience, is surely a wide departure from the established meaning of the terms.

If *you* expressed a desire that *I* should render a service, and if you proffered a reward as the motive or inducement to render it, *you* would scarcely be said to *command* the service, nor should I, in ordinary language, be *obliged* to render it. In ordinary language, *you* would *promise* me a reward, on condition of my rendering the service, whilst *I* might be *incited* or *persuaded* to render it by the hope of obtaining the reward.

Again: If a law holds out a *reward* as an inducement to do some act, an eventual *right* is conferred, and not an *obligation* imposed, upon those who shall act accordingly: The *imperative* part of the law being addressed or directed to the party whom it requires to *render* the reward.

In short, I am determined or inclined to comply with the wish of another, by the fear of disadvantage or evil. I am also determined or inclined to comply with the wish of another, by the hope of advantage or good. But it is only by the chance of incurring *evil*, that I am *bound* or *obliged* to compliance. It is only by conditional *evil*, that duties are *sanctioned* or *enforced*. It is the power and the purpose of inflicting eventual *evil*, and *not* the power and the purpose of imparting eventual *good*, which gives to the expression of a wish the name of a *command*.

If we put *reward* into the import of the term *sanction*, we must engage in a toilsome struggle with the current of ordinary speech; and shall often slide unconsciously, notwithstanding our efforts to the contrary, into the narrower and customary meaning.

It appears, then, from what has been premised, that the ideas or notions comprehended by the term *command* are the following. 1. A wish or desire conceived by a rational being, that another rational being shall do or forbear. 2. An evil to proceed from the former, and to be incurred by the latter, in case the latter comply not with the wish. 3. An expression or intimation of the wish by words or other signs.

It also appears from what has been premised, that *command*, *duty*, and *sanction* are inseparably connected terms: that each embraces the same ideas as the others, though each denotes those ideas in a peculiar order or series.

"A wish conceived by one, and expressed or intimated to another, with an evil to be inflicted and incurred in case the wish be disregarded," are signified directly and indirectly by each of the three expressions. Each is the name of the same complex notion.

But when I am talking *directly* of the expression or intimation of the wish, I employ the term *command:* The expression or intimation of the wish being presented *prominently* to my hearer; whilst the evil to be incurred, with the chance of incurring it, are kept (if I may so express myself) in the background of my picture.

When I am talking *directly* of the chance of incurring the evil, or (changing the expression) of the liability or obnoxiousness to the evil, I employ the term *duty*, or the term *obligation:* The liability or obnoxiousness to the evil being put foremost, and the rest of the complex notion being signified implicitly.

When I am talking *immediately* of the evil itself, I employ the term *sanction*, or a term of the like import: The evil to be incurred being signified directly; whilst the obnoxiousness to that evil, with the expression or intimation of the wish, are indicated indirectly or obliquely.

To those who are familiar with the language of logicians (language unrivalled for brevity, distinctness, and precision), I can express my meaning accurately in a breath:—Each of the three terms *signifies* the same notion; but each *denotes* a different part of that notion, and *connotes* the residue.

Commands are of two species. Some are *laws* or *rules*. The others have not acquired an appropriate name, nor does language afford an expression which will mark them briefly and precisely. I must, therefore, note them as well as I can by the ambiguous and inexpressive name of "*occasional* or *particular* commands."

The term *laws* or *rules* being not unfrequently applied to occasional or particular commands, it is hardly possible to describe a line of separation which shall consist in every respect with established forms of speech. But the distinction between laws and particular commands may, I think, be stated in the following manner.

By every command, the party to whom it is directed is obliged to do or to forbear.

Now where it obliges *generally* to acts or forbearances of a *class*, a command is a law or rule. But where it obliges to a *specific* act or forbearance, or to acts or forbearances which it determines *specifically* or *individually*, a command is occasional or particular. In other words, a class or description of acts is determined by a law or rule, and acts of that class or description are enjoined or forbidden generally. But where a command is occasional or particular, the act or acts, which the command enjoins or forbids, are assigned or determined by their specific or individual natures as well as by the class or description to which they belong.

The statement which I have given in abstract expressions I will now endeavour to illustrate by apt examples.

If you command your servant to go on a given errand, or *not* to leave your house on a given evening, or to rise at such an hour on such a morning, or to rise at that hour during the next week or month, the command is occasional or particular. For the act or acts enjoined or forbidden are specially determined or assigned.

But if you command him *simply* to rise at that hour, or to rise at that hour *always,* or to rise at that hour *till further orders,* it may be said, with propriety, that you lay down a *rule* for the guidance of your servant's conduct. For no specific act is assigned by the command, but the command obliges him generally to acts of a determined class.

If a regiment be ordered to attack or defend a post, or to quell a riot, or to march from their present quarters, the command is occasional or particular. But an order to exercise daily till further orders shall be given would be called a *general* order, and *might* be called a *rule.*

If Parliament prohibited simply the exportation of corn, either for a given period or indefinitely, it would establish a law or rule: a *kind* or *sort* of acts being determined by the command, and acts of that kind or sort being *generally* forbidden. But an order issued by Parliament to meet an impending scarcity, and stopping the exportation of corn *then shipped and in port,* would not be a law or rule, though issued by the sovereign legislature. The order regarding exclusively a specified quantity of corn, the negative acts or forbearances, enjoined by the command, would be determined specifically or individually by the determinate nature of their subject.

As issued by a sovereign legislature, and as wearing the form of a law, the order which I have now imagined would probably be *called* a law. And hence the difficulty of drawing a distinct boundary between laws and occasional commands.

Again: An act which is not an offence, according to the existing law, moves the sovereign to displeasure: and, though the authors of the act are legally innocent or unoffending, the sovereign commands that they shall be punished. As enjoining a

specific punishment in that specific case, and as not enjoining generally acts or forbearances of a class, the order uttered by the sovereign is not a law or rule.

Whether such an order would be *called* a law, seems to depend upon circumstances which are purely immaterial: immaterial, that is, with reference to the present purpose, though material with reference to others. If made by a sovereign assembly deliberately, and with the forms of legislation, it would probably be called a law. If uttered by an absolute monarch, without deliberation or ceremony, it would scarcely be confounded with acts of legislation, and would be styled an arbitrary command. Yet, on either of these suppositions, its nature would be the same. It would not be a law or rule, but an occasional or particular command of the sovereign One or Number.

To conclude with an example which best illustrates the distinction, and which shows the importance of the distinction most conspicuously, *judicial commands* are commonly occasional or particular, although the commands which they are calculated to enforce are commonly laws or rules.

For instance, the lawgiver commands that thieves shall be hanged. A specific theft and a specified thief being given, the judge commands that the thief shall be hanged, agreeably to the command of the lawgiver.

Now the lawgiver determines a class or description of acts; prohibits acts of the class generally and indefinitely; and commands, with the like generality, that punishment shall follow transgression. The command of the lawgiver is, therefore, a law or rule. But the command of the judge is occasional or particular. For he orders a specific punishment, as the consequence of a specific offence.

According to the line of separation which I have now attempted to describe, a law and a particular command are distinguished thus:—Acts of forbearances of a *class* are enjoined *generally* by the former. Acts *determined specifically* are enjoined or forbidden by the latter.

A different line of separation has been drawn by Blackstone and others. According to Blackstone and others, a law and a particular command are distinguished in the following manner:—A law obliges *generally* the members of the given community, or a law obliges *generally* persons of a given class. A particular command obliges a *single* person, or persons whom it determines *individually.*

That laws and particular commands are not to be distinguished thus, will appear on a moment's reflection.

For, *first,* commands which oblige generally the members of the given community, or commands which oblige generally persons of given classes, are not always laws or rules.

Thus, in the case already supposed; that in which the sovereign commands that all corn actually shipped for exportation be stopped and detained; the command is obligatory upon the whole community, but as it obliges them only to a set of acts individually assigned, it is not a law. Again, suppose the sovereign to issue an order, enforced by penalties, for a general mourning, on occasion of a public calamity. Now, though it is addressed to the community at large, the order is scarcely a rule, in the usual acceptation of the term. For, though it obliges generally the members of the entire community, it obliges to acts which it assigns specifically, instead of obliging generally to acts or forbearances of a class. If the sovereign commanded that *black* should be the dress of his subjects, his command would amount to a law. But if he commanded them to wear it on a specified occasion, his command would be merely particular.

And, *secondly,* a command which obliges exclusively persons individually determined, may amount, notwithstanding, to a law or a rule.

For example, A father may set a *rule* to his child or children: a guardian, to his ward: a master, to his slave or servant. And certain of God's *laws* were as binding on the first man, as they are binding at this hour on the millions who have sprung from his loins.

Most, indeed, of the laws which are established by political superiors, or most of the laws which are simply and strictly so called, oblige generally the members of the political community, or oblige generally persons of a class. To frame a system of duties for every individual of the community, were simply impossible: and if it were possible, it were utterly useless. Most of the laws established by political superiors are, therefore, *general* in a twofold manner: as enjoining or forbidding generally acts of kinds or sorts; and as binding the whole community, or, at least, whole classes of its members.

But if we suppose that Parliament creates and grants an office, and that Parliament binds the grantee to services of a given description, we suppose a law established by political superiors, and yet exclusively binding a specified or determinate person.

Laws established by political superiors, and

exclusively binding specified or determinate persons, are styled, in the language of the Roman jurists, *privilegia.* Though that, indeed, is a name which will hardly denote them distinctly: for, like most of the leading terms in actual systems of law, it is not the name of a definite class of objects, but a heap of heterogeneous objects.[1]

It appears, from what has been premised, that a law, properly so called, may be defined in the following manner.

A law is a command which obliges a person or persons.

But, as contradistinguished or opposed to an occasional or particular command, a law is a command which obliges a person or persons, and obliges *generally* to acts or forbearances of a class.

In language more popular but less distinct and precise, a law is a command which obliges a person or persons to a *course* of conduct.

Laws and other commands are said to proceed from *superiors,* and to bind or oblige *inferiors.* I will, therefore, analyse the meaning of those correlative expressions; and will try to strip them of a certain mystery, by which that simple meaning appears to be obscured.

Superiority is often synonymous with *precedence* or *excellence.* We talk of superiors in rank; of superiors in wealth; of superiors in virtue: comparing certain persons with certain other persons; and meaning that the former precede or excel the latter in rank, in wealth, or in virtue.

But, taken with the meaning wherein I here understand it, the term *superiority* signifies *might:* the power of affecting others with evil or pain, and of forcing them, through fear of that evil, to fashion their conduct to one's wishes.

For example, God is emphatically the *superior* of Man. For his power of affecting us with pain, and of forcing us to comply with his will, is unbounded and resistless.

To a limited extent, the sovereign One or Number is the superior of the subject or citizen: the master, of the slave or servant: the father, of the child.

In short, whoever can *oblige* another to comply with his wishes, is the *superior* of that other, so far as the ability reaches: The party who is obnoxious to the impending evil, being, to that same extent, the *inferior.*

The might or superiority of God, is simple or absolute. But in all or most cases of human superiority, the relation of superior and inferior, and the relation of inferior and superior, are reciprocal. Or (changing the expression) the party who is the superior as viewed from one aspect, is the inferior as viewed from another.

For example, to an indefinite, though limited extent, the monarch is the superior of the governed: his power being commonly sufficient to enforce compliance with his will. But the governed, collectively or in mass, are also the superior of the monarch: who is checked in the abuse of his might by his fear of exciting their anger; and of rousing to active resistance the might which slumbers in the multitude.

A member of a sovereign assembly is the superior of the judge: the judge being bound by the law which proceeds from that sovereign body. But, in his character of citizen or subject, he is the inferior of the judge: the judge being the minister of the law, and armed with the power of enforcing it.

It appears, then, that the term *superiority* (like the terms *duty* and *sanction*) is implied by the term *command*. For superiority is the power of enforcing compliance with a wish: and the expression or intimation of a wish, with the power and the purpose of enforcing it, are the constituent elements of a command.

"That *laws* emanate from *superiors*" is, therefore, an identical proposition. For the meaning which it affects to impart is contained in its subject. If I mark the peculiar source of a given law, or if I mark the peculiar source of laws of a given class, it is possible that I am saying something which may instruct the hearer. But to affirm of laws universally "that they flow from *superiors*," or to affirm of laws universally "that *inferiors* are bound to obey them," is the merest tautology and trifling.

Like most of the leading terms in the sciences of jurisprudence and morals, the term *laws* is extremely ambiguous. Taken with the largest signification which can be given to the term properly, *laws* are a species of *commands*. But the term is improperly applied to various objects which have nothing of the imperative character: to objects which are *not* commands; and which, therefore, are *not* laws, properly so called.

Accordingly, the proposition "that laws are commands" must be taken with limitations. Or, rather, we must distinguish the various meanings of the term *laws;* and must restrict the proposition to that class of objects which is embraced by the largest signification that can be given to the term properly.

I have already indicated, and shall hereafter more fully describe, the objects improperly termed laws, which are *not* within the province of jurisprudence (being either rules enforced by opinion and closely analogous to laws properly so called, or being laws so called by a metaphorical application of the term merely). There are other objects improperly termed laws (not being commands) which yet may properly be included within the province of jurisprudence. These I shall endeavour to particularise:—

1. Acts on the part of legislatures to *explain* positive law, can scarcely be called laws, in the proper signification of the term. Working no change in the actual duties of the governed, but simply declaring what those duties are, they properly *are* acts of *interpretation* by legislative authority. Or, to borrow an expression from the writers on the Roman Law, they are acts of *authentic* interpretation.

    But, this notwithstanding, they are frequently styled laws; *declaratory* laws, or declaratory statutes. They must, therefore, be noted as forming an exception to the proposition "that laws are a species of commands."

    It often, indeed, happens (as I shall show in the proper place), that laws declaratory in name are imperative in effect: Legislative, like judicial interpretation, being frequently deceptive; and establishing new law, under guise of expounding the old.

2. Laws to repeal laws, and to release from existing duties, must also be excepted from the proposition "that laws are a species of commands." In so far as they release from duties imposed by existing laws, they are not commands, but revocations of commands. They authorise or permit the parties, to whom the repeal extends, to do or to forbear from acts which they were commanded to forbear from or to do. And, considered with regard to *this*, their immediate or direct purpose, they are often named *permissive laws*, or, more briefly and more properly, *permissions*.

    Remotely and indirectly, indeed, permissive laws are often or always imperative. For the parties released from duties are restored to liberties or rights: and duties answering those rights are, therefore, created or revived.

    But this is a matter which I shall examine with exactness, when I analyse the expressions "legal right," "permission by the sovereign or state," and "civil or political liberty."

3. Imperfect laws, or laws of imperfect obligation, must also be excepted from the proposition "that laws are a species of commands."

An imperfect law (with the sense wherein the term is used by the Roman jurists) is a law which wants a sanction, and which, therefore, is not binding. A law declaring that certain acts are crimes, but annexing no punishment to the commission of acts of the class, is the simplest and most obvious example.

Though the author of an imperfect law signifies a desire, he manifests no purpose of enforcing compliance with the desire. But where there is not a purpose of enforcing compliance with the desire, the expression of a desire is not a command. Consequently, an imperfect law is not so properly a law, as counsel, or exhortation, addressed by a superior to inferiors.

Examples of imperfect laws are cited by the Roman jurists. But with us in England, laws professedly imperative are always (I believe) perfect or obligatory. Where the English legislature affects to command, the English tribunals not unreasonably presume that the legislature exacts obedience. And, if no specific sanction be annexed to a given law, a sanction is supplied by the courts of justice, agreeably to a general maxim which obtains in cases of the kind.

The imperfect laws, of which I am now speaking, are laws which are imperfect, in the sense of *the Roman jurists:* that is to say, laws which speak the desires of political superiors, but which their authors (by oversight or design) have not provided with sanctions. Many of the writers on *morals,* and on the so called *law of nature,* have annexed a different meaning to the term *imperfect.* Speaking of imperfect obligations, they commonly mean duties which are *not legal:* duties imposed by commands of God, or duties imposed by positive morality, as contradistinguished to duties imposed by positive law. An imperfect obligation, in the sense of the Roman jurists, is exactly equivalent to no obligation at all. For the term *imperfect* denotes simply, that the law wants the sanction appropriate to laws of the kind. An imperfect obligation, in the other meaning of the expression, is a religious or a moral obligation. The term *imperfect* does not denote that the law imposing the duty wants the appropriate sanction. It denotes that the law imposing the duty is *not* a law established by a political superior: that it wants that *perfect,* or that surer or more cogent sanction, which is imparted by the sovereign or state.

I believe that I have now reviewed all the classes of objects, to which the term *laws* is improperly applied. The laws (improperly so called) which I have here lastly enumerated, are (I think) the only laws which are not commands, and which yet may be properly included within the province of jurisprudence. But though these, with the so called laws set by opinion and the objects metaphorically termed laws, are the only laws which *really* are not commands, there are certain laws (properly so called) which may *seem* not imperative. Accordingly, I will subjoin a few remarks upon laws of this dubious character.

1. There are laws, it may be said, which *merely* create *rights*: And, seeing that every command imposes a *duty,* laws of this nature are not imperative.

But, as I have intimated already, and shall show completely hereafter, there are no laws *merely* creating *rights.* There are laws, it is true, which *merely* create *duties:* duties not correlating with correlating rights, and which, therefore may be styled *absolute.* But every law, really conferring a right, imposes expressly or tacitly a *relative* duty, or a duty correlating with the right. If it specify the remedy to be given, in case the right shall be infringed, it imposes the relative duty expressly. If the remedy to be given be not specified, it refers tacitly to pre-existing law, and clothes the right which it purports to create with a remedy provided by that law. Every law, really conferring a right is, therefore, imperative: as imperative, as if its only purpose were the creation of a duty, or as if the relative duty, which it inevitably imposes, were merely absolute.

The meanings of the term *right,* are various and perplexed; taken with its proper meaning, it comprises ideas which are numerous and complicated; and the searching and extensive analysis, which the term, therefore, requires, would occupy more room than could be given to it in the present lecture. It is not, however, necessary, that the analysis should be performed here. I purpose, in my earlier lectures, to determine the province of jurisprudence; or to distinguish the laws established by political superiors, from the various laws, proper and improper, with which they are frequently confounded. And this I may accomplish exactly enough, without a nice inquiry into the import of the term *right.*

2. According to an opinion which I must notice *incidentally here,* though the subject to which it

relates will be treated directly hereafter, *customary* laws must be excepted from the proposition "that laws are a species of command."

By many of the admirers of customary laws (and, especially, of their German admirers), they are thought to oblige legally (independently of the sovereign or state), *because* the citizens or subjects have observed or kept them. Agreeably to this opinion, they are not the *creatures* of the sovereign or state, although the sovereign or state may abolish them at pleasure. Agreeably to this opinion, they are positive law (or law, strictly so called), inasmuch as they are enforced by the courts of justice: But, that notwithstanding, they exist as *positive law* by the spontaneous adoption of the governed, and not by position or establishment on the part of political superiors. Consequently, customary laws, considered as positive law, are not commands. And, consequently, customary laws, considered as positive law, are not laws or rules properly so called.

An opinion less mysterious, but somewhat allied to this, is not uncommonly held by the adverse party: by the party which is strongly opposed to customary law; and to all law made judicially, or in the way of judicial legislation. According to the latter opinion, all judge-made law, or all judge-made law established by *subject* judges, is purely the creature of the judges by whom it is established immediately. To impute it to the sovereign legislature, or to suppose that it speaks the will of the sovereign legislature, is one of the foolish or knavish *fictions* with which lawyers, in every age and nation, have perplexed and darkened the simplest and clearest truths.

I think it will appear, on a moment's reflection, that each of these opinions is groundless: that customary law is *imperative,* in the proper signification of the term; and that all judge-made law is the creature of the sovereign or state.

At its origin, a custom is a rule of conduct which the governed observe spontaneously, or not in pursuance of a law set by a political superior. The custom is transmuted into positive law, when it is adopted as such by the courts of justice, and when the judicial decisions fashioned upon it are enforced by the power of the state. But before it is adopted by the courts, and clothed with the legal sanction, it is merely a rule of positive morality: a rule generally observed by the citizens or subjects; but deriving the only force, which it can be said to possess, from the general disapprobation falling on those who transgress it.

Now when judges transmute a custom into a legal rule (or make a legal rule not suggested by a custom), the legal rule which they establish is established by the sovereign legislature. A subordinate or subject judge is merely a minister. The portion of the sovereign power which lies at his disposition is merely delegated. The rules which he makes derive their legal force from authority given by the state: an authority which the state may confer expressly, but which it commonly imparts in the way of acquiescence. For, since the state may reverse the rules which he makes, and yet permits him to enforce them by the power of the political community, its sovereign will "that his rules shall obtain as law" is clearly evinced by its conduct, though not by its express declaration.

The admirers of customary law love to trick out their idol with mysterious and imposing attributes. But to those who can see the difference between positive law and morality, there is nothing of mystery about it. Considered as rules of positive morality, customary laws arise from the consent of the governed, and not from the position or establishment of political superiors. But, considered as moral rules turned into positive laws, customary laws are established by the state: established by the state directly, when the customs are promulgated in its statutes; established by the state circuitously, when the customs are adopted by its tribunals.

The opinion of the party which abhors judge-made laws, springs from their inadequate conception of the nature of commands.

Like other significations of desire, a command is express or tacit. If the desire be signified by *words* (written or spoken), the command is express. If the desire be signified by conduct (or by any signs of desire which are *not* words), the command is tacit.

Now when customs are turned into legal rules by decisions of subject judges, the legal rules which emerge from the customs are *tacit* commands of the sovereign legislature. The state, which is able to abolish, permits its ministers to enforce them: and it, therefore, signifies its pleasure, by that its voluntary acquiescence, "that they shall serve as a law to the governed."

My present purpose is merely this: to prove that the positive law styled *customary* (and all positive law made judicially) is established by the state directly or circuitously, and, therefore, is *imperative.* I am far from disputing, that law made judicially (or in the way of improper legislation) and law made by statute (or in the properly legislative manner) are distinguished by weighty differences. I shall inquire, in future lectures, what those differences are; and why subject judges, who are properly ministers of the law, have commonly shared with the sovereign in the business of making it.

I assume, then, that the only laws which are not imperative, and which belong to the subject-matter of jurisprudence, are the following:

1. Declaratory laws, or laws explaining the import of existing positive law.
2. Laws abrogating or repealing existing positive law.
3. Imperfect laws, or laws of imperfect obligation (with the sense wherein the expression is used by the Roman jurists).

But the space occupied in the science by these improper laws is comparatively narrow and insignificant. Accordingly, although I shall take them into account so often as I refer to them directly, I shall throw them out of account on other occasions. Or (changing the expression) I shall limit the term *law* to laws which are imperative, unless I extend it expressly to laws which are not.

Lecture VI

. . . The superiority which is styled sovereignty, and the independent political society which sovereignty implies, is distinguished from other superiority, and from other society, by the following marks or characters:—1. The *bulk* of the given society are in a *habit* of obedience or submission to a *determinate* and *common* superior: let that common superior be a certain individual person or a certain body or aggregate of individual persons. 2. That certain individual, or that certain body of individuals, is *not* in a habit of obedience to a determinate human superior. Laws (improperly so called) which opinion sets or imposes, may permanently affect the conduct of that certain individual or body. To express or tacit commands of other determinate parties, that certain individual or body may yield occasional submission. But there is no determinate person, or determinate aggregate of persons, to whose commands, express or tacit, that certain individual or body renders habitual obedience.

Or the notions of sovereignty and independent political society may be expressed concisely thus.—If a *determinate* human superior, *not* in a habit of obedience to a like superior, receive *habitual* obedience from the *bulk* of a given society, that determinate superior is sovereign in that society, and the society (including the superior) is a society political and independent.

To that determinate superior, the other members of the society are *subject:* or on that determinate superior, to other members of the society are *dependent*. The position of its other members towards that determinate superior, is *a state of subjection,* or *a state of dependence*. The mutual relation which subsists between that superior and them, may be styled *the relation of sovereign and subject, or the relation of sovereignty and subjection*.

Hence it follows, that it is only through an ellipsis, or an abridged form of expression, that the *society* is styled *independent*. The party truly independent (independent, that is to say, of a determinate human superior), is not the society, but the sovereign portion of the society: that a certain member of the society, or that certain body of its members, to whose commands, expressed or intimated, the generality or bulk of its members render habitual obedience. Upon that certain person, or certain body of persons, the other members of the society are *dependent:* or to that certain person, or certain body of persons, the other members of the society are *subject*. By "an independent political society," or "an independent and sovereign nation," we mean a political society consisting of a sovereign and subjects, as opposed to a political society which is merely subordinate: that is to say, which is merely a limb or member of another political society, and which therefore consists entirely of persons in a state of subjection.

In order that a given society may form a society political and independent, the two distinguishing marks which I have mentioned above must unite. The *generality* of the given society must be in the *habit* of obedience to a *determinate* and *common* superior: whilst that determinate persons, or determinate body of persons must *not* be habitually obedient to a determinate person or body. It is the union of that positive, with this negative mark, which renders that given society (including that certain superior) a society political and independent.

To show that the union of those marks renders a given society a society political and independent, I call your attention to the following positions and examples.

1. In order that a given society may form a society political, the generality or bulk of its members must be in a *habit* of obedience to a determinate and common superior.

In case the generality of its members obey a determinate superior, but the obedience be rare or transient and not habitual or permanent, the relation of sovereignty and subjection is not created thereby between that certain superior and the members of that given society. In other words, that determinate superior and the members of that given society do not become thereby an independent political society. Whether that given society be political and independent or not, it is not an independent political society whereof that certain superior is the sovereign portion.

For example: In 1815 the allied armies occupied France; and so long as the allied armies occupied France, the commands of the allied sovereigns were obeyed by the French government, and, through the French government, by the French people generally. But since the commands and the obedience were comparatively rare and transient, they were not sufficient to constitute the relation of sovereignty and subjection between the allied sovereigns and the members of the invaded nation. In spite of those commands, and in spite of that obedience, the French government was sovereign or independent. Or in spite of those commands, and in spite of that obedience, the French government and its subjects were an independent political society whereof the allied sovereigns were not the sovereign portion.

Now if the French nation, before the obedience to those sovereigns, had been an independent society in a state of nature or anarchy, it would not have been changed by the obedience into a society political. And it would not have been changed by the obedience into a society political, because the obedience was not habitual. For, inasmuch as the obedience was not habitual, it was not changed by the obedience from a society political and independent, into a society political but subordinate.—A given society, therefore, is not a society political, unless the generality of its members be in a *habit* of obedience to a determinate and common superior.

Again: A feeble state holds its independence precariously, or at the will of the powerful states to whose aggressions it is obnoxious. And since it is obnoxious to their aggressions, it and the bulk of its subjects render obedience to commands which they occasionally express or intimate. Such, for instance, is the position of the Saxon government and its subjects in respect of the conspiring sovereigns who form the Holy Alliance. But since the commands and the obedience are comparatively few and rare, they are not sufficient to constitute the relation of sovereignty and subjection between the powerful states and the feeble state with its subjects. In spite of those commands, and in spite of that obedience, the feeble state is sovereign or independent. Or in spite of those commands, and in spite of that obedience, the feeble state and its subjects are an independent political society whereof the powerful states are not the sovereign portion. Although the powerful states are permanently *superior,* and although the feeble state is permanently *inferior,* there is neither a *habit* of command on the part of the former, nor a *habit* of obedience on the part of the latter. Although the latter is unable to defend and maintain its independence, the latter is independent of the former in fact or practice.

From the example now adduced, as from the example adduced before, we may draw the following inference: that a given society is not a society political, unless the generality of its members be in a *habit* of obedience to a determinate and common superior.—By the obedience to the powerful states, the feeble state and its subjects are not changed from an independent, into a subordinate political society. And they are not changed by the obedience into a subordinate political society, because the obedience is not habitual. Consequently, if they were a natural society (setting that obedience aside), they would not be changed by that obedience into a society political.

2. In order that a given society may form a society political, habitual obedience must be rendered, by the *generality* or *bulk* of its members, to a determinate and *common* superior. In other words, habitual obedience must be rendered, by the *generality* or *bulk* of its members, to *one and the same* determinate person, or determinate body of persons.

Unless habitual obedience be rendered by the *bulk* of its members, and be rendered by the bulk of its members to *one and the same* superior, the given society is either in a state of nature, or is split into two or more independent political societies.

For example: In case a given society be torn by intestine war, and in case the conflicting parties be nearly balanced, the given society is in one of the two positions which I have now supposed.—As there is no common superior to which the bulk of its members render habitual obedience, it is not a political society single or undivided.—If the bulk of each of the parties be in a habit of obedience to its head, the given society is broken into two or more societies, which, perhaps, may be styled independent political societies.—If the bulk of each of the parties be not in that habit of obedience, the given society is simply or absolutely in a state of nature or anarchy. It is either resolved or broken into its individual elements, or into numerous societies of an extremely limited size: of a size so extremely limited, that they could hardly be styled societies independent and *political.* For, as I shall show hereafter, a given independent society would hardly be styled *political,* in case it fell short of a *number* which cannot be fixed with precision, but which may be called considerable, or not extremely minute.

3. In order that a given society may form a society political, the generality or bulk of its members must habitually obey a superior *determinate* as well as common.

On this position I shall not insist here. For I have shown sufficiently in my fifth lecture, that no indeterminate party can command expressly or tacitly, or can receive obedience or submission: that no indeterminate body is capable of corporate conduct, or is capable, as a body, of positive or negative deportment.

4. It appears from what has preceded, that, in order that a given society may form a society political, the bulk of its members must be in a habit of obedience to a certain and common superior. But, in order that the given society may form a

society political and independent, that certain superior must *not* be habitually obedient to a determinate human superior.

The given society may form a society political and independent, although that certain superior be habitually affected by laws which opinion sets or imposes. The given society may form a society political and independent, although that certain superior render occasional submission to commands of determinate parties. But the society is not independent, although it may be political, in case that certain superior habitually obey the commands of a certain person or body.

Let us suppose, for example, that a viceroy obeys habitually the author of his delegated powers. And, to render the example complete, let us suppose that the viceroy receives habitual obedience from the generality or bulk of the persons who inhabit his province.—Now though he commands habitually within the limits of his province, and receives habitual obedience from the generality or bulk of its inhabitants, the viceroy is not sovereign within the limits of his province, nor are he and its inhabitants an independent political society. The viceroy, and (through the viceroy) the generality or bulk of its inhabitants, are habitually obedient or submissive to the sovereign of a larger society. He and the inhabitants of his province are therefore in a state of subjection to the sovereign of that larger society. He and

---

1. Where a *privilegium* merely imposes a duty, it exclusively obliges a determinate person or persons. But where a *privilegium* confers a right, and the right conferred *avails against the world at large,* the law is *privilegium* as viewed from a certain aspect, but is also a *general law* as viewed from another aspect. In respect of the right conferred, the law exclusively regards a determinate person, and, therefore, is *privilegium.* In respect of

the duty imposed, and corresponding to the right conferred, the law regards generally the members of the entire community.

This I shall explain particularly at a subsequent point of my Course, when I consider the peculiar nature of so-called *privilegia,* or of so-called *private laws.*

A MORE RECENT POSITIVIST CONCEPTION OF LAW*

H. L. A. Hart

Law as the Union of Primary and Secondary Rules

A Fresh Start

[As I have discussed elsewhere] at various crucial points, the simple model of law as the sovereign's coercive orders failed to reproduce some of the salient features of a legal system. To demonstrate this, we did not find it necessary to invoke (as earlier critics have done) international law or primitive law which some may regard as disputable or borderline examples of law; instead we pointed to certain familiar features of municipal law in a modern state, and showed that these were either distorted or altogether unrepresented in this over-simple theory.

The main ways in which the theory failed are instructive enough to merit a second summary. First, it became clear that though of all the varieties of law, a criminal statute, forbidding or enjoining certain actions under penalty, most resembles orders backed by threats given by one person to others, such a statute nonetheless differs from such orders in the important respect that it commonly applies to those who enact it and not merely to others. Secondly, there are other varieties of law, notably those conferring legal powers to adjudicate or legislate (public powers) or to create or vary legal relations (private powers) which cannot, without absurdity, be construed as orders backed by threats. Thirdly, there are legal rules which differ from orders in their mode of origin, because they are not brought into being by anything analogous to explicit prescription. Finally, the analysis of law in terms of the sovereign, habitually obeyed and necessarily exempt from all legal limitation, failed to account for the continuity of legislative authority characteristic of a modern legal system, and the sovereign, person or persons could not be identified with either the electorate or the legislature of a modern state.

It will be recalled that in thus criticizing the conception of law as the sovereign's coercive orders we considered also a number of ancillary devices which were brought in at the cost of corrupting the primitive simplicity of the theory to rescue it from its difficulties. But these too failed. One device, the notion of a *tacit* order, seemed to have no application to the complex actualities of a modern legal system, but only to very much simpler situations like that of a general who deliberately refrains from interfering with orders given by his subordinates. Other devices, such as that of treating power-conferring rules as mere fragments of rules imposing duties, or treating all rules as directed only to officials, distort the ways in which these are spoken of, thought of, and actually used in social life. This had no better claim to our assent than the theory that all the rules of a game are "really" directions to the umpire and the scorer. The device, designed to reconcile the self-binding character of legislation with the theory that a statute is an order given to *others*, was to distinguish the legislators acting in their official capacity, as *one* person ordering *others* who include themselves in their private capacities. This device, impeccable in itself, involved supplementing the theory with something it does not contain: this is the notion of a rule defining what must be done to legislate; for it is only in conforming with such a rule that legislators have an official capacity and a separate personality to be contrasted with themselves as private individuals.

[My previous discussions] are therefore the record of a failure and there is plainly need for a fresh start. Yet the failure is an instructive one, worth the detailed consideration we have given it, because at each point where the theory failed to fit the facts it was possible to see at least in outline why it was bound to fail and what is required for a better account. The root cause of failure is that the elements out of which the theory was constructed, viz. the ideas of orders, obedience, habits, and threats, do not include, and cannot by their combination yield, the idea of a rule, without which we cannot hope to elucidate even the most elementary forms of law. It is true that the idea of a rule is by no means a simple one: we have already seen in [a previous discussion] the need, if we are to do justice to the complexity of a legal system, to discriminate between two different though related types. Under rules of the one type, which may well be considered the basic or primary type, human beings are required to do or abstain from certain actions, whether they wish to or not. Rules of the other type are in a sense parasitic upon or secondary to the first; for they provide that human beings may be doing or saying certain things that introduce new rules of the primary type, extinguish or modify old ones, or in various ways determine their incidence or control their operations. Rules of the first type impose duties; rules of the second type confer powers, public or private. Rules of the first type concern actions involving physical movement or changes; rules of the second type provide for operations which lead not merely to physical movement or change, but to the creation or variation of duties or obligations.

We have already given some preliminary analysis of what is involved in the assertion that rules of these two types exist among a given social group, and in this chapter we shall not only carry this analysis a little farther but we shall make the general claim that in the combination of these two types of rule there lies what Austin wrongly claimed to have found in the notion of coercive orders, namely, "the key to the science of jurisprudence." We shall not indeed claim that wherever the word "law" is "properly" used this combination of primary and secondary rules is to be found; for it is clear that the diverse range of cases of which the word "law" is used are not linked by any such simple uniformity, but by less direct relations—often of analogy of either form or content to a central case. What we shall attempt to show, in this and the succeeding chapters, is that most of the features of law which have

proved most perplexing and have both provoked and eluded the search for definition can best be rendered clear, if these two types of rule and the interplay between them are understood. We accord this union of elements a central place because of their explanatory power in elucidating the concepts that constitute the framework of legal thought. The justification for the use of the word "law" for a range of apparently heterogeneous cases is a secondary matter which can be undertaken when the central elements have been grasped.

The Idea of Obligation

It will be recalled that the theory of law as coercive orders, notwithstanding its errors, started from the perfectly correct appreciation of the fact that where there is law, there human conduct is made in some sense non-optional or obligatory. In choosing this starting-point the theory was well inspired, and in building up a new account of law in terms of the interplay of primary and secondary rules we too shall start from the same idea. It is, however, here, at this crucial first step, that we have perhaps most to learn from the theory's errors.

Let us recall the gunman situation. A orders B to hand over his money and threatens to shoot him if he does not comply. According to the theory of coercive orders this situation illustrates the notion of obligation or duty in general. Legal obligation is to be found in this situation writ large; A must be the sovereign habitually obeyed and the orders must be general, prescribing courses of conduct not single actions. The plausibility of the claim that the gunman situation displays the meaning of obligation lies in the fact that it is certainly one in which we would say that B, if he obeyed, was "obliged" to hand over his money. It is, however, equally certain that we should misdescribe the situation if we said, on these facts, that B "had an obligation" or a "duty" to hand over the money. So from the start it is clear that we need something else for an understanding of the idea of obligation. There is a difference, yet to be explained, between the assertion that someone *was obliged* to do something and the assertion that he *had an obligation* to do it. The first is often a statement about the beliefs and motives with which an action is done: B was obliged to hand over his money may simply mean, as it does in the gunman case, that he believed that some harm or other unpleasant consequences would befall him if he did not hand it over and he handed it over to avoid those consequences. In such cases the prospect of what would happen to the agent if he disobeyed has rendered something he would otherwise have preferred to have done (keep the money) less eligible.

Two further elements slightly complicate the elucidation of the notion of being obliged to do something. It seems clear that we should not think of B as obliged to hand over the money if the threatened harm was, according to common judgments, trivial in comparison with the disadvantage or serious consequences, either for B or for others, of complying with the orders, as it would be, for example, if A merely threatened to pinch B. Nor perhaps should we say that B was obliged, if there were no reasonable grounds for thinking that A could or would probably implement his threat of relatively serious harm. Yet, though such references to common judgments of comparative harm and reasonable estimates of likelihood, are implicit in this notion, the statement that a person was obliged to obey someone is, in the main, a psychological one referring to the beliefs and motives with which an action was done. But the statement that someone *had an obligation* to do something is of a very different type and there are many signs of this difference. Thus not only is it the case that the facts about B's action and his beliefs and motives in the gunman case, though sufficient to warrant the statement that B was obliged to hand over his purse, are *not sufficient* to warrant the statement that he had an obligation to do this; it is also the case that facts of this sort, i.e. facts about beliefs and motives, are *not necessary* for the truth of a statement that a person had an obligation to do something. Thus the statement that a person had an obligation, e.g. to tell the truth or report for military service, remains true even if he believed (reasonably or unreasonably) that he would never be found out and had nothing to fear from disobedience. Moreover, whereas the statement that he had this obligation is quite independent of the question whether or not he in fact reported for service, the statement that someone was obliged to do something, normally carries the implication that he actually did it.

Some theorists, Austin among them, seeing perhaps the general irrelevance of the person's beliefs, fears, and motives to the question whether he had an obligation to do something, have defined this notion not in terms of these subjective facts, but in terms of the *chance* or *likelihood* that the person having the obligation will suffer a punishment or "evil" at the hands of others in the event of disobedience. This, in effect, treats statements of obligation not as psychological statements but as predictions or assessments of chances of incurring punishment or "evil." To many later theorists this has appeared as a revelation, bringing down to earth an elusive notion and restating it in the same clear, hard, empirical terms as are used in science. It has, indeed, been accepted sometimes as the only alternative to metaphysical conceptions of obligation or duty as invisible objects mysteriously existing "above" or "behind" the world of ordinary, observable facts. But there are many reasons for rejecting this interpretation of statements of obligation as predictions, and it is not, in fact, the only alternative to obscure metaphysics.

The fundamental objection is that the predictive interpretation obscures the fact that, where rules exist, deviations from them are not merely grounds for a prediction that hostile reactions will follow or that a court will apply sanctions to those who break them, but are also a reason or justification for such reaction and for applying the sanctions. We have already drawn attention in [a previous discussion] to this neglect of the internal aspect of rules and we shall elaborate on it later in this chapter.

There is, however, a second, simpler, objection to the predictive interpretation of obligation. If it were true that the statement that a person had an obligation meant that *he* was likely to suffer in the event of disobedience, it would be a contradiction to say that he had an obligation, e.g. to report for military service but that, owing to the fact that he had escaped from the jurisdiction, or had successfully bribed the police or the court, there was not the slightest chance of his being caught or made to suffer. In fact, there is no contradiction in saying this, and such statements are often made and understood.

It is, of course, true that in a normal legal system, where sanctions are exacted for a high proportion of offences, an offender usually runs a risk of punishment; so, usually the statement that a person has an obligation and the statement that he is likely to suffer for disobedience will both be true together. Indeed, the connexion between these two statements is somewhat stronger than this: at least in a municipal system it may well be true that, unless *in general* sanctions were likely to be exacted from offenders, there would be little or no point in making particular statements about a person's obligations. In this sense, such statements may be said to presuppose belief in the continued normal operation of the system of sanctions much as the statement "he is out" in cricket presupposes, though it does not assert, that players, umpire, and scorer will probably take the usual steps.

Nonetheless, it is crucial for the understanding of the idea of obligation to see that in individual cases the statement that a person has an obligation under some rule and the prediction that he is likely to suffer for disobedience may diverge.

It is clear that obligation is not to be found in the gunman situation, though the simpler notion of being obliged to do something may well be defined in the elements present there. To understand the general idea of obligation as a necessary preliminary to understanding it in its legal form, we must turn to a different social situation which, unlike the gunman situation, includes the existence of social rules; for this situation contributes to the meaning of the statement that a person has an obligation in two ways. First, the existence of such rules, making certain types of behaviour a standard, is the normal, though unstated, background or proper context for such a statement; and, secondly, the distinctive function of such statement is to apply such a general rule to a particular person by calling attention to the fact that his case falls under it. We have already seen in [a previous discussion] that there is involved in the existence of any social rules a combination of regular conduct with a distinctive attitude to that conduct as a standard. We have also seen the main ways in which these differ from mere social habits, and how the varied normative vocabulary ("ought," "must," "should") is used to draw attention to the standard and to deviations from it, and to formulate the demands, criticisms, or acknowledgments which may be based on it. Of this class of normative words the words "obligation" and "duty" form an important sub-class, carrying with them certain implications not usually present in the others. Hence, though a grasp of the elements generally differentiating social rules from mere habits is certainly indispensable for understanding the notion of obligation or duty, it is not sufficient by itself.

The statement that someone has or is under an obligation does indeed imply the existence of a rule; yet it is not always the case that where rules exist the standard of behaviour required by them is conceived of in terms of obligation. "He ought to have" and "He had an obligation to" are not always interchangeable expressions, even though they are alike in carrying an implicit reference to existing standards of conduct or are used in drawing conclusions in particular cases from a general rule. Rules of etiquette or correct speech are certainly rules: they are more than convergent habits or regularities of behaviour; they are taught and efforts are made to maintain them; they are used in criticizing our own and other people's behaviour in the characteristic normative vocabulary. "You ought to take your hat off," "It is wrong to say 'you was.'" But to use in connexion with rules of this kind the words "obligation" or "duty" would be misleading and not merely stylistically odd. It would misdescribe a social situation; for though the line separating rules of obligation from others is at points a vague one, yet the main rationale of the distinction is fairly clear.

Rules are conceived and spoken of as imposing obligations when the general demand for conformity is insistent and the social pressure brought to bear upon those who deviate or threaten to deviate is great. Such rules may be wholly customary in origin: there may be no centrally organized system of punishments for breach of the rules; the social pressure may take only the form of a general diffused hostile or critical reaction which may stop short of physical sanctions. It may be limited to verbal manifestations of disapproval or of appeals to the individuals' respect for the rule violated; it may depend heavily on the operation of feelings of shame, remorse, and guilt. When the pressure is of this last-mentioned kind we may be inclined to classify the rules as part of the morality of the social group and the obligation under the rules as moral obligation. Conversely, when physical sanctions are prominent or usual among the forms of pressure, even though these are neither closely defined nor administered by officials but are left to the community at large, we shall be inclined to classify the rules as a primitive or rudimentary form of law. We may, of course, find both these types of serious social pressure behind what is, in an obvious sense, the same rule of conduct; sometimes this may occur with no indication that one of them is peculiarly appropriate as primary and the other secondary, and then the question whether we are confronted with a rule of morality or rudimentary law may not be susceptible of an answer. But for the moment the possibility of drawing the line between law and morals need not detain us. What is important is that the insistence on importance or *seriousness* of social pressure behind the rules is the primary factor determining whether they are thought of as giving rise to obligations.

Two other characteristics of obligation go naturally together with this primary one. The rules supported by this serious pressure are thought important because they are believed to be necessary to the maintenance of social life or some highly prized feature of it. Characteristically, rules so obviously essential as those which restrict the free use of violence are thought of in terms of obligation. So too rules which require honesty or truth or require the keeping of promises, or specify what is to be done by one who performs a distinctive role or function in the social group are thought of in terms of either "obligation" or perhaps more often "duty." Secondly, it is generally recognized that the conduct required by these rules may, while benefitting others, conflict with what the person who owes the duty may wish to do. Hence obligations and duties are thought of as characteristically involving sacrifice or renunciation, and the standing possibility of conflict between obligation or duty and interest is, in all societies, among the truisms of both the lawyer and the moralist.

The figure of a *bond* binding the person obligated, which is buried in the word "obligation," and the similar notion of a debt latent in the word "duty" are explicable in terms of these three factors, which distinguish rules of obligation or duty from other rules. In this figure, which haunts much legal thought, the social pressure appears as a chain binding those who have obligations so that they are not free to do what they want. The other end of the chain is sometimes held by the group or their official representatives, who insist on performance or exact the penalty: sometimes it is entrusted by the group to a private individual who may choose whether or not to insist on performance or its equivalent in value to him. The first situation typifies the duties or obligations of criminal law and the second those of civil law where we think of private individuals having rights correlative to the obligations.

Natural and perhaps illuminating though these figures or metaphors are, we must not allow them to trap us into a misleading conception of obligation as essentially consisting in some feeling of pressure or compulsion experienced by those who have obligations. The fact that rules of obligation are generally supported by serious social pressure does not entail that to have an obligation under the rules is to experience feelings of compulsion or pressure. Hence there is no contradiction in saying of some hardened swindler, and it may often be true, that he had an obligation to pay the rent but felt no pressure to pay when he made off without doing so. To *feel* obliged and to have an obligation are different though frequently concomitant things. To identify them would be one way of misinterpreting, in terms of psychological feelings, the important internal aspect of rules to which we drew attention in [a previous discussion].

Indeed, the internal aspect of rules is something to which we must again refer before we can

dispose finally of the claims of the predictive theory. For an advocate of that theory may well ask why, if social pressure is so important a feature of rules of obligation, we are yet so concerned to stress the inadequacies of the predictive theory; for it gives this very feature a central place by defining obligation in terms of the likelihood that threatened punishment or hostile reaction will follow deviation from certain lines of conduct. The difference may seem slight between the analysis of a statement of obligation as a prediction, or assessment of the chances, of hostile reaction to deviation, and our own contention that though this statement presupposes a background in which deviations from rules are generally met by hostile reactions, yet its characteristic use is not to predict this but to say that a person's case falls under such a rule. In fact, however, this difference is not a slight one. Indeed, until its importance is grasped, we cannot properly understand the whole distinctive style of human thought, speech, and action which is involved in the existence of rules and which constitutes the normative structure of society.

The following contrast again in terms of the "internal" and "external" aspect of rules may serve to mark what gives this distinction its great importance for the understanding not only of law but of the structure of any society. When a social group has certain rules of conduct, this fact affords an opportunity for many closely related yet different kinds of assertion; for it is possible to be concerned with the rules, either merely as an observer who does not himself accept them, or as a member of the group which accepts and uses them as guides to conduct. We may call these respectively the "external" and the "internal points of view." Statements made from the external point of view may themselves be of different kinds. For the observer may, without accepting the rules himself, assert that the group accepts the rules, and thus may from outside refer to the way in which *they* are concerned with them from the internal point of view. But whatever the rules are, whether they are those of games, like chess or cricket, or moral or legal rules, we can if we choose occupy the position of an observer who does not even refer in this way to the internal point of view of the group. Such an observer is content merely to record the regularities of observable behaviour in which conformity with the rules partly consists and those further regularities, in the form of the hostile reaction, reproofs, or punishments, with which deviations from the rules are met. After a time the external observer may, on the basis of the regularities observed, correlate deviation with hostile reaction, and be able to predict with a fair measure of success, and to assess the chances that a deviation from the group's normal behaviour will meet with hostile reaction or punishment. Such knowledge may not only reveal much about the group, but might enable him to live among them without unpleasant consequences which would attend one who attempted to do so without such knowledge.

If, however, the observer really keeps austerely to this extreme external point of view and does not give any account of the manner in which members of the group who accept the rules view their own regular behaviour, his description of their life cannot be in terms of rules at all, and so not in the terms of the rule-dependent notions of obligation or duty. Instead, it will be in terms of observable regularities of conduct, predictions, probabilities, and signs. For such an observer, deviations by a member of the group from normal conduct will be a sign that hostile reaction is likely to follow, and nothing more. His view will be like the view of one who, having observed the working of a traffic signal in a busy street for some time, limits himself to saying that when the light turns red there is a high probability that the traffic will stop. He treats the light merely as a natural *sign that* people will behave in certain ways, as clouds are a *sign that* rain will come. In so doing he will miss out on a whole dimension of the social life of those whom he is watching, since for them the red light is not merely a sign that others will stop: they look upon it as a *signal for* them to stop, and so a reason for stopping in conformity to rules which make stopping when the light is red a standard of behaviour and an obligation. To mention this is to bring into account the way in which the group regards its own behaviour. It is to refer to the internal aspect of rules seen from their internal point of view.

The external point of view may very nearly reproduce the way in which the rules function in the lives of certain members of the group, namely those who reject its rules and are only concerned with them when and because they judge that unpleasant consequences are likely to follow violation. Their point of view will need for its expression, "I was obliged to do it," "I am likely to suffer for it if . . . ," "You will probably suffer for it if . . . ," "They will do that to you if. . . ." But they will not need forms of expression like "I had an obligation" or "You have an obligation" for these are required only by those who see their own and other persons' conduct from the internal point of view. What the external point

of view, which limits itself to the observable regularities of behaviour, cannot reproduce is the way in which the rules function as rules in the lives of those who normally are the majority of society. These are the officials, lawyers, or private persons who use them, in one situation after another, as guides to the conduct of social life, as the basis for claims, demands, admissions, criticism, or punishment, viz., in all the familiar transactions of life according to rules. For them the violation of a rule is not merely a basis for the prediction that a hostile reaction will follow but a *reason* for hostility.

At any given moment the life of any society which lives by rules, legal or not, is likely to consist in a tension between those who, on the one hand, accept and voluntarily co-operate in maintaining the rules, and so see their own and other persons' behaviour in terms of the rules, and those who, on the other hand, reject the rules and attend to them only from the external point of view as a sign of possible punishment. One of the difficulties facing any legal theory anxious to do justice to the complexity of the facts is to remember the presence of both these points of view and not to define one of them out of existence. Perhaps all our criticisms of the predictive theory of obligation may be best summarized as the accusation that this is what it does to the internal aspect of obligatory rules.

The Elements of Law

It is, of course, possible to imagine a society without a legislature, courts or officials of any kind. Indeed, there are many studies of primitive communities which not only claim that this possibility is realized but depict in detail the life of a society where the only means of social control is that general attitude of the group towards its own standard modes of behaviour in terms of which we have characterized rules of obligation. A social structure of this kind is often referred to as one of "custom"; but we shall not use this term, because it often implies that the customary rules are very old and supported with less social pressure than other rules. To avoid these implications we shall refer to such a social structure as one of primary rules of obligation. If a society is to live by such primary rules alone, there are certain conditions which, granted a few of the most obvious truisms about human nature and the world we live in, must clearly be satisfied. The first of these conditions is that the rules must contain in some form restrictions on the free use of violence, theft, and deception to which human beings are tempted but which they must, in general, repress, if they are to coexist in close proximity to each other. Such rules are in fact always found in the primitive societies of which we have knowledge, together with a variety of others imposing on individuals various positive duties to perform services or make contributions to the common life. Secondly, though such a society may exhibit the tension, already described, between those who accept the rules and those who reject the rules except where fear of social pressure induces them to conform, it is plain that the latter cannot be more than a minority, if so loosely organized a society of persons, approximately equal in physical strength, is to endure: for otherwise those who reject the rules would have too little social pressure to fear. This too is confirmed by what we know of primitive communities where, though there are dissidents and malefactors, the majority live by the rules seen from the internal point of view.

More important for our present purpose is the following consideration. It is plain that only a small community closely knit by ties of kinship, common sentiment, and belief, and placed in a stable environment, could live successfully by such a régime of unofficial rules. In any other conditions such a simple form of social control must prove defective and will require supplementation in different ways. In the first place, the rules by which the group lives will not form a system, but will simply be a set of separate standards, without any identifying or common mark, except of course that they are the rules which a particular group of human beings accepts. They will in this respect resemble our own rules of etiquette. Hence if doubts arise as to what the rules are or as to the precise scope of some given rule, there will be no procedure for settling this doubt, either by reference to an authoritative text or to an official whose declarations on this point are authoritative. For, plainly, such a procedure and the acknowledgement of either authoritative text or persons involve the existence of rules of a type different from the rules of obligation or duty which *ex hypothesi* are all that the group has. This defect in the simple social structure of primary rules we may call its *uncertainty*.

A second defect is the *static* character of the rules. The only mode of change in the rules known to such a society will be the slow process of growth, whereby courses of conduct once thought optional become first habitual or usual, and then obligatory, and the converse process of decay, when devia-

tions, once severely dealt with, are first tolerated and then pass unnoticed. There will be no means, in such a society, of deliberately adapting the rules to changing circumstances, either by eliminating old rules or introducing new ones: for, again, the possibility of doing this presupposes the existence of rules of a different type from the primary rules of obligation by which alone the society lives. In an extreme case the rules may be static in a more drastic sense. This, though never perhaps fully realized in any actual community, is worth considering because the remedy for it is something very characteristic of law. In this extreme case, not only would there be no way of deliberately changing the general rules, but the obligations which arise under the rules in particular cases could not be varied or modified by the deliberate choice of any individual. Each individual would simply have fixed obligations or duties to do or abstain from doing certain things. It might indeed very often be the case that others would benefit from the performance of these obligations; yet if there are only primary rules of obligation they would have no power to release those bound from performance or to transfer to others the benefits which would accrue from performance. For such operations of release or transfer create changes in the initial positions of individuals under the primary rules of obligation, and for these operations to be possible there must be rules of a sort different from the primary rules.

The third defect of this simple form of social life is the *inefficiency* of the diffuse social pressure by which the rules are maintained. Disputes as to whether an admitted rule has or has not been violated will always occur and will, in any but the smallest societies, continue interminably, if there is no agency specially empowered to ascertain finally, and authoritatively, the fact of violation. Lack of such final and authoritative determinations is to be distinguished from another weakness associated with it. This is the fact that punishments for violations of the rules, and other forms of social pressure involving physical effort or the use of force, are not administered by a special agency but are left to the individuals affected or to the group at large. It is obvious that the waste of time involved in the group's unorganized efforts to catch and punish offenders, and the smouldering vendettas which may result from self help in the absence of an official monopoly of "sanctions," may be serious. The history of law does, however, strongly suggest that the lack of official agencies to determine authoritatively the fact of violation of the rules is a much more serious defect; for many societies have remedies for this defect long before the other.

The remedy for each of these three main defects in this simplest form of social structure consists in supplementing the *primary* rules of obligation with *secondary* rules which are rules of a different kind. The introduction of the remedy for each defect might, in itself, be considered a step from the pre-legal into the legal world; since each remedy brings with it many elements that permeate law: certainly all three remedies together are enough to convert the régime of primary rules into what is indisputably a legal system. We shall consider in turn each of these remedies and show why law may most illuminatingly be characterized as a union of primary rules of obligation with such secondary rules. Before we do this, however, the following general points should be noted. Though the remedies consist in the introduction of rules which are certainly different from each other, as well as from the primary rules of obligation which they supplement, they have important features in common and are connected in various ways. Thus they may all be said to be on a different level from the primary rules, for they are all *about* such rules; in the sense that while primary rules are concerned with the actions that individuals must or must not do, these secondary rules are all concerned with the primary rules themselves. They specify the ways in which the primary rules may be conclusively ascertained, introduced, eliminated, varied, and the fact of their violation conclusively determined.

The simplest form of remedy for the *uncertainty* of the régime of primary rules is the intro- duction of what we shall call a "rule of recognition." This will specify some feature or features possession of which by a suggested rule is taken as a conclusive affirmative indication that it is a rule of the group to be supported by the social pressure it exerts. The existence of such a rule of recognition may take any of a huge variety of forms, simple or complex. It may, as in the early law of many societies, be no more than that an authoritative list or text of the rules is to be found in a written document or carved on some public monument. No doubt as a matter of history this step from the pre-legal to the legal may be accomplished in distinguishable stages, of which the first is the mere reduction to writing of hitherto unwritten rules. This is not itself the crucial step, though it is a very important one: what is crucial is the acknowledgement of reference to the writing or inscription as *authoritative,* i.e. as the *proper* way of disposing of

doubts as to the existence of the rule. Where there is such an acknowledgement there is a very simple form of secondary rule: a rule for conclusive identification of the primary rules of obligation.

In a developed legal system the rules of recognition are of course more complex; instead of identifying rules exclusively by reference to a text or list they do so by reference to some general characteristic possessed by the primary rules. This may be the fact of their having been enacted by a specific body, or their long customary practice, or their relation to judicial decisions. Moreover, where more than one of such general characteristics are treated as identifying criteria, provision may be made for their possible conflict by their arrangement in an order of superiority, as by the common subordination of custom or precedent to statute, the latter being a "superior source" of law. Such complexity may make the rules of recognition in a modern legal system seem very different from the simple acceptance of an authoritative text: yet even in this simplest form, such a rule brings with it many elements distinctive of law. By providing an authoritative mark it introduces, although in embryonic form, the idea of a legal system: for the rules are now not just a discrete unconnected set but are, in a simple way, unified. Further, in the simple operation of identifying a given rule as possessing the required feature of being an item on an authoritative list of rules we have the germ of the idea of legal validity.

The remedy for the *static* quality of the régime of primary rules consists in the introduction of what we shall call "rules of change." The simplest form of such a rule is that which empowers an individual or body of persons to introduce new primary rules for the conduct of the life of the group, or of some class within it, and to eliminate old rules. As we have already argued in [a previous discussion] it is in terms of such a rule, and not in terms of orders backed by threats, that the ideas of legislative enactment and repeal are to be understood. Such rules of change may be very simple or very complex: the powers conferred may be unrestricted or limited in various ways: and the rules may, besides specifying the persons who are to legislate, define in more or less rigid terms the procedure to be followed in legislation. Plainly, there will be a very close connexion between the rules of change and the rules of recognition: for where the former exists the latter will necessarily incorporate a reference to legislation as an identifying feature of the rules, though it need not refer to all the details of procedure involved in legislation. Usually some official certificate or official copy will, under the rules of recognition, be taken as a sufficient proof of due enactment. Of course if there is a social structure so simple that the only "source of law" is legislation, the rule of recognition will simply specify enactment as the unique identifying mark or criterion of validity of the rules. This will be the case for example in the imaginary kingdom of Rex I depicted in [a previous discussion]: there the rule of recognition would simply be that whatever Rex I enacts is law.

We have already described in some detail the rules which confer on individuals power to vary their initial positions under the primary rules. Without such private power-conferring rules society would lack some of the chief amenities which law confers upon it. For the operations which these rules make possible are the making of wills, contracts, transfers of property, and many other voluntarily created structures of rights and duties which typify life under law, though of course an elementary form of power-conferring rule also underlies the moral institution of a promise. The kinship of these rules with the rules of change involved in the notion of legislation is clear, and as recent theory such as Kelsen's has shown, many of the features which puzzle us in the institutions of contract or property are clarified by thinking of the operations of making a contract or transferring property as the exercise of limited legislative powers by individuals.

The third supplement to the simple régime of primary rules, intended to remedy the *inefficiency* of its diffused social pressure, consists of secondary rules empowering individuals to make authoritative determinations of the question whether, on a particular occasion, a primary rule has been broken. The minimal form of adjudication consists in such determinations, and we shall call the secondary rules which confer the power to make them "rules of adjudication." Besides identifying the individuals who are to adjudicate, such rules will also define the procedure to be followed. Like the other secondary rules these are on a different level from the primary rules: though they may be reinforced by further rules imposing duties on judges to adjudicate, they do not impose duties but confer judicial powers and a special status on judicial declarations about the breach of obligations. Again these rules, like the other secondary rules, define a group of important legal concepts: in this case the concepts of judge or court, jurisdiction and judgment. Besides these resemblances to the other secondary rules,

rules of adjudication have intimate connexions with them. Indeed, a system which has rules of adjudication is necessarily also committed to a rule of recognition of an elementary and imperfect sort. This is so because, if courts are empowered to make authoritative determinations of the fact that a rule has been broken, these cannot avoid being taken as authoritative determinations of what the rules are. So the rule which confers jurisdiction will also be a rule of recognition, identifying the primary rules through the judgments of the courts and these judgments will become a "source" of law. It is true that this form of rule of recognition, inseparable from the minimum form of jurisdiction, will be very imperfect. Unlike an authoritative text or a statute book, judgments may not be couched in general terms and their use as authoritative guides to the rules depends on a somewhat shaky inference from particular decisions, and the reliability of this must fluctuate both with the skill of the interpreter and the consistency of the judges.

It need hardly be said that in few legal systems are judicial powers confined to authoritative determinations of the fact of violation of the primary rules. Most systems have, after some delay, seen the advantages of further centralization of social pressure; and have partially prohibited the use of physical punishments or violent self help by private individuals. Instead they have supplemented the primary rules of obligation by further secondary rules, specifying or at least limiting the penalties for violation, and have conferred upon judges, where they have ascertained the fact of violation, the exclusive power to direct the application of penalties by other officials. These secondary rules provide the centralized official "sanctions" of the system.

If we stand back and consider the structure which has resulted from the combination of primary rules of obligation with the secondary rules of recognition, change and adjudication, it is plain that we have here not only the heart of a legal system, but a most powerful tool for the analysis of much that has puzzled both the jurist and the political theorist.

Not only are the specifically legal concepts with which the lawyer is professionally concerned, such as those of obligation and rights, validity and source of law, legislation and jurisdiction, and sanction, best elucidated in terms of this combination of elements. The concepts (which bestride both law and political theory) of the state, of authority, and of an official require a similar analysis if the obscurity which still lingers about them is to be dissipated.

The reason why an analysis in these terms of primary and secondary rules has this explanatory power is not far to seek. Most of the obscurities and distortions surrounding legal and political concepts arise from the fact that these essentially involve reference to what we have called the internal point of view: the view of those who do not merely record and predict behaviour conforming to rules, but *use* the rules as standards for the appraisal of their own and others' behaviour. This requires more detailed attention in the analysis of legal and political concepts then it has usually received. Under the simple régime of primary rules the internal point of view is manifested in its simplest form, in the use of those rules as the basis of criticism, and as the justification of demands for conformity, social pressure, and punishment. Reference to this most elementary manifestation of the internal point of view is required for the analysis of the basic concepts of obligation and duty. With the addition to the system of secondary rules, the range of what is said and done from the internal point of view is much extended and diversified. With this extension comes a whole set of new concepts and they demand a reference to the internal point of view for their analysis. These include the notions of legislation, jurisdiction, validity and, generally, of legal powers, private and public. There is a constant pull towards an analysis of these in the terms of ordinary or "scientific," fact-stating or predictive discourse. But this can only reproduce their external aspect: to do justice to their distinctive, internal aspect we need to see the different ways in which the law-making operations of the legislator, the adjudication of a court, the exercise of private or official powers, and other "acts-in-the-law" are related to secondary rules.

In [a subsequent discussion] we shall show how the ideas of the validity of law and sources of law, and the truths latent among the errors of the doctrines of sovereignty may be rephrased and clarified in terms of rules of recognition. But we shall conclude this chapter with a warning: though the combination of primary and secondary rules merits, because it explains many aspects of law, the central place assigned to it, this cannot by itself illuminate every problem. The union of primary and secondary rules is at the centre of a legal system; but it is not the whole, and as we move away from the centre we shall have to accommodate, in ways indicated in later chapters, elements of a different character.

The Foundations of a Legal System

Rule of Recognition and Legal Validity

According to the theory criticized in [a previous discussion] the foundations of a legal system consist of the situation in which the majority of a social group habitually obey the orders backed by threats of the sovereign person or persons, who themselves habitually obey no one. This social situation is, for this theory, both a necessary and a sufficient condition of the existence of law. We have already exhibited in some detail the incapacity of this theory to account for some of the salient features of a modern municipal legal system: yet nonetheless, as its hold over the minds of many thinkers suggests, it does contain, though in a blurred and misleading form, certain truths about certain important aspects of law. These truths can, however, only be clearly presented, and their importance rightly assessed, in terms of the more complex social situation where a secondary rule of recognition is accepted and used for the identification of primary rules of obligation. It is this situation which deserves, if anything does, to be called the foundations of a legal system. In this chapter we shall discuss various elements of this situation which have received only partial or misleading expression in the theory of sovereignty and elsewhere.

Wherever such a rule of recognition is accepted, both private persons and officials are provided with authoritative criteria for identifying primary rules of obligation. The criteria so provided may, as we have seen, take any one or more of a variety of forms: these include reference to an authoritative text; to legislative enactment; to customary practice; to general declarations of specified persons, or to past judicial decisions in particular cases. In a very simple system like the world of Rex I depicted in [a previous discussion], where only what he enacts is law and no legal limitations upon his legislative power are imposed by customary rule or constitutional document, the sole criterion for identifying the law will be a simple reference to fact of enactment by Rex I. The existence of this simple form of rule of recognition will be manifest in the general practice, on the part of officials or private persons, of identifying the rules by this criterion. In a modern legal system where there are a variety of "sources" of law, the rule of recognition is correspondingly more complex: the criteria for identifying the law are multiple and commonly include a written constitution, enactment by a legislature, and judicial precedents. In most cases, provision is made for possible conflict by ranking these criteria in an order of relative subordination and primacy. It is in this way that in our system "common law" is subordinate to "statute."

It is important to distinguish this relative *subordination* of one criterion to another from *derivation,* since some spurious support for the view that all law is essentially or "really" (even if only "tacitly") the product of legislation, has been gained from confusion of these two ideas. In our own system, custom and precedent are subordinate to legislation since customary and common law rules may be deprived of their status as law by statute. Yet they owe their status of law, precarious as this may be, not to a "tacit" exercise of legislative power but to the acceptance of a rule of recognition which accords them this independent though subordinate place. Again, as in the simple case, the existence of such a complex rule of recognition with this hierarchical ordering of distinct criteria is manifested in the general practice of identifying the rules by such criteria.

In the day-to-day life of a legal system its rule of recognition is very seldom expressly formulated as a rule; though occasionally, courts in England may announce in general terms the relative place of one criterion of law in relation to another, as when they assert the supremacy of Acts of Parliament over other sources or suggested sources of law. For the most part the rule of recognition is not stated, but its existence is *shown* in the way in which particular rules are identified, either by courts or other officials or private persons or their advisers. There is, of course, a difference in the use made by courts of the criteria provided by the rule and the use of them by others: for when courts reach a particular conclusion on the footing that a particular rule has been correctly identified as law, what they say has a special authoritative status conferred on it by other rules. In this respect, as in many others, the rule of recognition of a legal system is like the scoring rule of a game. In the course of the game the general rule defining the activities which constitute scoring (runs, goals, &c.) is seldom formulated; instead it is *used* by officials and players in identifying the particular phases which count towards winning. Here too, the declarations of officials (umpire or scorer) have a special authoritative status attributed to them by other rules. Further, in both cases there is the possibility of a conflict between these authoritative applications of the rule and the general understanding of what the rule plainly requires according to its terms. This, as we shall see later, is a complication which must be catered for in any account of what it is for a system of rules of this sort to exist.

The use of unstated rules of recognition, by courts and others, in identifying particular rules of the system is characteristic of the internal point of view. Those who use them in this way thereby manifest their own acceptance of them as guiding rules and with this attitude there goes a characteristic vocabulary different from the natural expressions of the external point of view. Perhaps the simplest of these is the expression, "It is the law that . . . ," which we may find on the lips not only of judges, but of ordinary men living under a legal system, when they identify a given rule of the system. This, like the expression "Out" or "Goal," is the language of one assessing a situation by reference to rules which he in common with others acknowledges as appropriate for this purpose. This attitude of shared acceptance of rules is to be contrasted with that of an observer who records *ab extra* the fact that a social group accepts such rules but does not himself accept them. The natural expression of this external point of view is not "It is the law that . . ." but "In England they recognize as law . . . whatever the Queen in Parliament enacts. . . ." The first of these forms of expression we shall call an *internal statement* because it manifests the internal point of view and is naturally used by one who, accepting the rule of recognition and without stating the fact that it is accepted, applies the rule in recognizing some particular rule of the system as valid. The second form of expression we shall call an *external statement* because it is the natural language of an external observer of the system who, without himself accepting its rule of recognition, states the fact that others accept it.

If this use of an accepted rule of recognition in making internal statements is understood and carefully distinguished from an external statement of fact that the rule is accepted, many obscurities concerning the notion of legal "validity" disappear. For the word "valid" is most frequently, though not always, used, in just such internal statements, applying to a particular rule of a legal system, an unstated but accepted rule of recognition. To say that a given rule is valid is to recognize it as passing all the tests provided by the rule of recognition and so as a rule of the system. We can indeed simply say that the statement that a particular rule is valid means that it satisfies all the criteria provided by the rule of recognition. This is incorrect only to the extent that it might obscure the internal character of such statements; for, like the cricketers' "Out," these statements of validity normally apply to a particular case a rule of recognition accepted by the speaker and others, rather than expressly state that the rule is satisfied.

Some of the puzzles connected with the idea of legal validity are said to concern the relation between the validity and the "efficacy" of law. If by "efficacy" is meant that the fact that a rule of law which requires certain behaviour is obeyed more often than not, it is plain that there is no necessary connexion between the validity of any particular rule and *its* efficacy, unless the rule of recognition of the system includes among its criteria, as some do, the provision (sometimes referred to as a rule of obsolescence) that no rule is to count as a rule of the system if it has long ceased to be efficacious.

From the inefficacy of a particular rule, which may or may not count against its validity, we must distinguish a general disregard of the rules of the system. This may be so complete in character and so protracted that we should say, in the case of a new system, that it had never established itself as the legal system of a given group, or, in the case of a once-established system, that it had ceased to be the legal system of the group. In either case, the normal context or background for making any internal statement in terms of the rules of the system is absent. In such cases it would be generally *pointless* either to assess the rights and duties of particular persons by reference to the primary rules of a system or to access the validity of any of its rules by reference to its rules of recognition. To insist on applying a system of rules which had either never actually been effective or had been discarded would, except in special circumstances mentioned below, be as futile as to assess the progress of a game by reference to a scoring rule which had never been accepted or had been discarded.

One who makes an internal statement concerning the validity of a particular rule of a system may be said to *presuppose* the truth of the external statement of fact that the system is generally efficacious. For the normal use of internal statements is in such a context of general efficacy. It would however be wrong to say that statements of validity "mean" that the system is generally efficacious. For though it is normally pointless or idle to talk of the validity of a rule of a system which has never established itself or has been discarded, none the less it is not meaningless nor is it always pointless. One vivid way of teaching Roman Law is to speak *as if* the system were efficacious still and to discuss the validity of particular rules and solve problems in their terms; and one way of nursing hopes for the restoration of an old social order destroyed by revolution, and rejecting the new, is to cling to the criteria of legal validity of the old régime. This is implicitly done by the White Russian who still claims property under some rule of descent which was a valid rule of Tsarist Russia.

A grasp of the normal contextual connexion between the internal statement that a given rule of a system is valid and the external statement of fact that the system is generally efficacious, will help us see in its proper perspective the common theory that to assert the validity of a rule is to predict that it will be enforced by courts or some other official action taken. In many ways this theory is similar to the predictive analysis of obligation which we considered and rejected in [a previous discussion]. In both cases alike the motive for advancing this predictive theory is the conviction that only thus can metaphysical interpretations be avoided: that either a statement that a rule is valid must ascribe some mysterious property which cannot be detected by empirical means or it must be a prediction of future behaviour of officials. In both cases also the plausibility of the theory is due to the same important fact: that the truth of the external statement of fact, which an observer might record, that the system is generally efficacious and likely to continue so, is normally presupposed by anyone who accepts the rules and makes an internal statement of obligation or validity. The two are certainly very closely associated. Finally, in both cases alike the mistake of the theory is the same: it consists in neglecting the special character of the internal statement and treating it as an external statement about official action.

This mistake becomes immediately apparent when we consider how the judge's own statement that a particular rule is valid functions in judicial decision; for, though here too, in making such a statement, the judge presupposes but does not state the general efficacy of the system, he plainly is not concerned to predict his own or others' official action. His statement that a rule is valid is an internal statement recognizing that the rule satisfies the tests for identifying what is to count as law in his court, and constitutes not a prophecy of but part of the *reason* for his decision. There is indeed a more plausible case for saying that a statement that a rule is valid is a prediction when such a statement is made by a private person; for in the case of conflict between unofficial statements of validity or invalidity and that of a court in deciding a case, there is often good sense in saying that the former must then be withdrawn. Yet even here, as we shall see when we come . . . to investigate the significance of such conflicts between official declarations and the plain requirements of the rules, it may be dogmatic to assume that it is withdrawn as a statement now shown to be *wrong,* because it has falsely *predicted* what a court would say. For there are more reasons for withdrawing statements than the fact that they are wrong, and also more ways of being wrong than this allows.

The rule of recognition providing the criteria by which the validity of other rules of the system is assessed is in an important sense, which we shall try to clarify, an *ultimate* rule: and where, as is usual, there are several criteria ranked in order of relative subordination and primacy one of them is *supreme.* These ideas of the ultimacy of the rule of recognition and the supremacy of one of its criteria merit some attention. It is important to disentangle them from the theory, which we have rejected, that somewhere in every legal system, even though it lurks behind legal forms, there must be a sovereign legislative power which is legally unlimited.

Of these two ideas, supreme criterion and ultimate rule, the first is the easiest to define. We may say that a criterion of legal validity or source of law is supreme if rules identified by reference to it are still recognized as rules of the system, even if they conflict with rules identified by reference to the other criteria, whereas rules identified by reference to the latter are not so recognized if they conflict with the rules identified by reference to the supreme criterion. A similar explanation in comparative terms can be given of the notions of "superior" and "subordinate" criteria which we have already used. It is plain that the notions of a superior and a supreme criterion merely refer to a *relative* place on a scale and do not import any notion of legally *unlimited* legislative power. Yet "supreme" and "unlimited" are easy to confuse—at least in legal theory. One reason for this is that in the simpler forms of legal system the ideas of ultimate rule of recognition, supreme criterion, and legally unlimited legislature seem to converge. For where there is a legislature subject to no constitutional limitations and competent by its enactment

to deprive all other rules of law emanating from other sources of their status as law, it is part of the rule of recognition in such a system that enactment by that legislature is the supreme criterion of validity. This is, according to constitutional theory, the position in the United Kingdom. But even systems like that of the United States in which there is no such legally unlimited legislature may perfectly well contain an ultimate rule of recognition which provides a set of criteria of validity, one of which is supreme. This will be so, where the legislative competence of the ordinary legislature is limited by a constitution which contains no amending power, or places some clauses outside the scope of that power. Here there is no legally unlimited legislature, even in the widest interpretation of "legislature"; but the system of course contains an ultimate rule of recognition and, in the clauses of its constitution, a supreme criterion of validity.

The sense in which the rule of recognition is the *ultimate* rule of a system is best understood if we pursue a very familiar chain of legal reasoning. If the question is raised whether some suggested rule is legally valid, we must, in order to answer the question, use a criterion of validity provided by some other rule. Is this purported by-law of the Oxfordshire County Council valid? Yes: because it was made in exercise of the powers conferred, and in accordance with the procedure specified, by a statutory order made by the Minister of Health. At this first stage the statutory order provides the criteria in terms of which the validity of the by-law is assessed. There may be no practical need to go farther; but there is a standing possibility of doing so. We may query the validity of the statutory order and assess its validity in terms of the statute empowering the minister to make such orders. Finally when the validity of the statute has been queried and assessed by reference to the rule that what the Queen in Parliament enacts is law, we are brought to a stop in inquiries concerning validity: for we have reached a rule which, like the intermediate statutory order and statute, provides criteria for the assessment of the validity of other rules; but it is also unlike them in that there is no rule providing criteria for the assessment of its own legal validity.

There are, indeed, many questions which we can raise about this ultimate rule. We can ask whether it is the practice of courts, legislatures, officials, or private citizens in England actually to use this rule as an ultimate rule of recognition. Or has our process of legal reasoning been an idle game with the criteria of validity of a system now discarded? We can ask whether it is a satisfactory form of legal system which has such a rule at its root. Does it produce more good than evil? Are there prudential reasons for supporting it? Is there a moral obligation to do so? These are plainly very important questions; but, equally plainly, when we ask them about the rule of recognition, we are no longer attempting to answer the same kind of question about it as those which we answered about other rules with its aid. When we move from saying that a particular enactment is valid, because it satisfies the rule that what the Queen in Parliament enacts is law, to saying that in England this last rule is used by courts, officials, and private persons as the ultimate rule of recognition, we have moved from an internal statement of law asserting the validity of a rule of the system to an external statement of fact which an observer of the system might make even if he did not accept it. So too when we move from the statement that a particular enactment is valid, to the statement that the rule of recognition of the system is an excellent one and the system based on it is one worthy of support, we have moved from a statement of legal validity to a statement of value.

Some writers, who have emphasized the legal ultimacy of the rule of recognition, have expressed this by saying that, whereas the legal validity of other rules of the system can be demonstrated by reference to it, its own validity cannot be demonstrated but is "assumed" or "postulated" or is a "hypothesis." This may, however, be seriously misleading. Statements of legal validity made about particular rules in the day-to-day life of a legal system whether by judges, lawyers, or ordinary citizens do indeed carry with them certain presuppositions. They are internal statements of law expressing the point of view of those who accept the rule of recognition of the system and, as such, leave unstated much that could be stated in external statements of fact about the system. What is thus left unstated forms the normal background or context of statements of legal validity and is thus said to be "presupposed" by them. But it is important to see precisely what these presupposed matters are, and not to obscure their character. They consist of two things. First, a person who seriously asserts the validity of some given rule of law, say a particular statute, himself makes use of a rule of recognition which he accepts as appropriate for identifying the law. Secondly, it is the case that this rule of recognition, in terms of which he assesses the validity of a particular statute, is not only accepted by him but is the rule of recognition actually accepted and employed in the general operation of

the system. If the truth of this presupposition were doubted, it could be established by reference to actual practice: to the way in which courts identify what is to count as law, and to the general acceptance of or acquiescence in these identifications.

Neither of these two presuppositions are well described as "assumptions" of a "validity" which cannot be demonstrated. We only need the word "validity," and commonly only use it, to answer questions which arise *within* a system of rules where the status of a rule as a member of the system depends on its satisfying certain criteria provided by the rule of recognition. No such question can arise as to the validity of the very rule of recognition which provides the criteria; it can neither be valid nor invalid but is simply accepted as appropriate for use in this way. To express this simple fact by saying darkly that its validity is "assumed but cannot be demonstrated," is like saying that we assume, but can never demonstrate, that the standard metre bar in Paris which is the ultimate test of the correctness of all measurement in metres, is itself correct.

A more serious objection is that talk of the "assumption" that the ultimate rule of recognition is valid conceals the essentially factual character of the second presupposition which lies behind the lawyers' statements of validity. No doubt the practice of judges, officials, and others, in which the actual existence of a rule of recognition consists, is a complex matter. As we shall see later, there are certainly situations in which questions as to the precise content and scope of this kind of rule, and even as to its existence, may not admit of a clear or determinate answer. None the less it is important to distinguish "assuming the validity" from "presupposing the existence" of such a rule; if only because failure to do this obscures what is meant by the assertion that such a rule *exists*.

In the simple system of primary rules of obligation sketched in the last chapter, the assertion that a given rule existed could only be an external statement of fact such as an observer who did not accept the rules might make and verify by ascertaining whether or not, as a matter of fact, a given mode of behaviour was generally accepted as a standard and was accompanied by those features which, as we have seen, distinguish a social rule from mere convergent habits. It is in this way also that we should now interpret and verify the assertion that in England a rule—though not a legal one—exists that we must bare the head on entering a church. If such rules as these are found to exist in the actual practice of a social group, there is no separate question of their validity to be discussed, though of course their value or desirability is open to question. Once their existence has been established as a fact we should only confuse matters by affirming or denying that they were valid or by saying that "we assumed" but could not show their validity. Where, on the other hand, as in a mature legal system, we have a system of rules which includes a rule of recognition so that the status of a rule as a member of the system now depends on whether it satisfies certain criteria provided by the rule of recognition, this brings with it a new application of the word "exist." The statement that a rule exists may now no longer be what it was in the simple case of customary rules—an external statement of the *fact* that a certain mode of behaviour was generally accepted as a standard in practice. It may now be an internal statement applying an accepted but unstated rule of recognition and meaning (roughly) no more than "valid given the systems criteria of validity." In this respect, however, as in others a rule of recognition is unlike other rules of the system. The assertion that it exists can only be an external statement of fact. For whereas a subordinate rule of a system may be valid and in that sense "exist" even if it is generally disregarded, the rule of recognition exists only as a complex, but normally concordant, practice of the courts, officials, and private persons in identifying the law by reference to certain criteria. Its existence is a matter of fact.

POSITIVISM AND THE SEPARATION OF LAW AND MORALS*

H. L. A. Hart

In this article I shall discuss and attempt to defend a view which Mr. Justice Holmes, among others, held and for which he and they have been much criticized. But I wish first to say why I think that Holmes, whatever the vicissitudes of his American reputation may be, will always remain for Englishmen a heroic figure in jurisprudence. This will be so because he magically combined two qualities: One of them is imaginative power, which English legal thinking has often lacked; the other is clarity, which English legal thinking usually possesses. The English lawyer who turns to read Holmes is made to see that what he had taken to be settled and stable is really always on the move. To make this discovery with Holmes is to be with a guide whose words may leave you unconvinced, sometimes even repelled, but never mystified. Like our own Austin, with whom Holmes shared many ideals and thoughts, Holmes was sometimes clearly wrong; but again like Austin, when this was so he was always wrong clearly. This surely is a sovereign virtue in jurisprudence. Clarity I know is said not to be enough; this may be true, but there are still questions in jurisprudence where the issues are confused because they are discussed in a style which Holmes would have spurned for its obscurity. Perhaps this is inevitable: Jurisprudence trembles so uncertainly on the margin of many subjects that there will always be need for someone, in Bentham's phrase, "to pluck the mask of Mystery" from its face. This is true, to a pre-eminent degree, of the subject of this article. Contemporary voices tell us we must recognize something obscured by the legal "positivists" whose day is now over: that there is a "point of intersection between law and morals," or that what is and what ought to be are somehow indissolubly fused or inseparable, though the positivists denied it. What do these phrases mean?

*From 71 *Harvard Law Review* 593 (1958). Copyright © 1958 by The Harvard Law Review Association. Reprinted by permission of the author and the publisher. Footnotes have been edited and renumbered.

Or rather which of the many things that they could mean, do they mean? Which of them do "positivists" deny and why is it wrong to do so?

I

I shall present the subject as part of the history of an idea. At the close of the eighteenth century and the beginning of the nineteenth the most earnest thinkers in England about legal and social problems and the architects of great reforms were the great utilitarians. Two of them, Bentham and Austin, constantly insisted on the need to distinguish, firmly and with the maximum of clarity, law as it is from law as it ought to be. This theme haunts their work, and they condemned the natural-law thinkers precisely because they had blurred this apparently simple but vital distinction. By contrast, at the present time in this country and to a lesser extent in England, this separation between law and morals is held to be superficial and wrong. Some critics have thought that it blinds men to the true nature of law and its roots in social life. Others have thought it not only intellectually misleading but corrupting in practice, at its worst apt to weaken resistance to state tyranny or absolutism, and at its best apt to bring law into disrespect. The nonpejorative name "legal positivism," like most terms which are used as missiles in intellectual battles, has come to stand for a baffling multitude of different sins. One of them is the sin, real or alleged, of insisting, as Austin and Bentham did, on the separation of law as it is and law as it ought to be.

How then has this reversal of the wheel come about? What are the theoretical errors in this distinction? Have the practical consequences of stressing the distinction as Bentham and Austin did been bad? Should we now reject it or keep it? In considering these questions we should recall the social philosophy which went along with the utilitarians' insistence on this distinction. They stood firmly but on their own utilitarian ground for all the principles of liberalism in law and government. No one has ever combined, with such even-minded sanity as the utilitarians, the passion for reform with respect for law together with a due recognition of the need to control the abuse of power even when power is in the hands of reformers. One by one in Bentham's works you can identify the elements of the *Rechtstaat* and all the principles for the defense of which the terminology of natural law has in our day been revived. Here are liberty of speech, and of press, the right of association, the need

that laws should be published and made widely known before they are enforced, the need to control administrative agencies, the insistence that there should be no criminal liability without fault, and the importance of the principle of legality, *nulla poena sine lege*. Some, I know, find the political and moral insight of the utilitarians a very simple one, but we should not mistake this simplicity for superficiality nor forget how favorably their simplicities compare with the profundities of other thinkers. Take only one example: Bentham on slavery. He says the question at issue is not whether those who are held as slaves can reason, but simply whether they suffer. Does this not compare well with the discussion of the question in terms of whether or not there are some men whom Nature has fitted only to be the living instruments of others? We owe it to Bentham more than anyone else that we have stopped discussing this and similar questions of social policy in that form.

So Bentham and Austin were not dry analysts fiddling with verbal distinctions while cities burned, but were the vanguard of a movement which laboured with passionate intensity and much success to bring about a better society and better laws. Why then did they insist on the separation of law as it is and law as it ought to be? What did they mean? Let us first see what they said. Austin formulated the doctrine:

> The existence of law is one thing; its merit or demerit is another. Whether it be or be not is one enquiry; whether it be or be not conformable to an assumed standard, is a different enquiry. A law, which actually exists, is a law, though we happen to dislike it, or though it vary from the text, by which we regulate our approbation and disapprobation. This truth, when formally announced as an abstract proposition, is so simple and glaring that it seems idle to insist upon it. But simple and glaring as it is, when enunciated in abstract expressions the enumeration of the instances in which it has been forgotten would fill a volume.
>
> Sir William Blackstone, for example, says in his "Commentaries," that the laws of God are superior in obligation to all other laws; that no human laws should be suffered to contradict them; that human laws are of no validity if contrary to them; and that all valid laws derive their force from that Divine original.
>
> Now he may mean that all human laws ought to conform to the Divine laws. If this

be his meaning, I assent to it without hesitation. . . . Perhaps, again, he means that human lawgivers are themselves obliged by the Divine laws to fashion the laws which they impose by that ultimate standard, because if they do not, God will punish them. To this also I entirely assent. . . .

But the meaning of this passage of Blackstone, if it has a meaning, seems rather to be this: that no human law which conflicts with the Divine law is obligatory or binding; in other words, that no human law which conflicts with the Divine law is a law. . . .

Austin's protest against blurring the distinction between what law is and what it ought to be is quite general: it is a mistake, whatever our standard of what ought to be, whatever "the text by which we regulate our approbation or disapprobation." His examples, however, are always a confusion between law as it is and law as morality would require it to be. For him, it must be remembered, the fundamental principles of morality were God's commands, to which utility was an "index": besides this there was the actual accepted morality of a social group or "positive" morality.

Bentham insisted on this distinction without characterizing morality by reference to God but only, of course, by reference to the principles of utility. Both thinkers' prime reason for this insistence was to enable men to see steadily the precise issues posed by the existence of morally bad laws, and to understand the specific character of the authority of a legal order. Bentham's general recipe for life under the government of laws was simple: it was "*to obey punctually; to censure freely.*" But Bentham was especially aware, as an anxious spectator of the French revolution, that this was not enough: the time might come in any society when the law's commands were so evil that the question of resistance had to be faced, and it was then essential that the issues at stake at this point should neither be oversimplified nor obscured.[1] Yet, this was precisely what the confusion between law and morals had done and Bentham found that the confusion had spread symmetrically in two different directions. On the one hand Bentham had in mind the anarchist who argues thus: "This ought not to be the law, therefore it is not and I am free not merely to censure but to disregard it." On the other hand he thought of the reactionary who argues: "This is the law, therefore it is what it ought to be," and thus stifles criticism at its birth. Both errors, Bentham thought, were to be found in Blackstone: there was his incautious statement that

human laws were invalid if contrary to the law of God,[2] and "that spirit of obsequious *quietism* that seems constitutional in our Author" which "will scarce ever let him recognise a difference" between what is and what ought to be. This indeed was for Bentham the occupational disease of lawyers: "[I]n the eyes of lawyers—not to speak of their dupes—that is to say, as yet, the generality of non-lawyers—the *is* and *ought to be*. . . were one and indivisible." There are therefore two dangers between which insistence on this distinction will help us to steer: the danger that law and its authority may be dissolved in man's conceptions of what law ought to be and the danger that the existing law may supplant morality as a final test of conduct and so escape criticism.

In view of later criticisms it is also important to distinguish several things that the utilitarians did not mean by insisting on their separation of law and morals. They certainly accepted many of the things that might be called "the intersection of law and morals." First, they never denied that, as a matter of historical fact, the development of legal systems had been powerfully influenced by moral opinion, and, conversely, that moral standards had been profoundly influenced by law, so that the content of many legal rules mirrored moral rules or principles. It is not in fact always easy to trace this historical causal connection, but Bentham was certainly ready to admit its existence; so too Austin spoke of the "frequent coincidence" of positive law and morality and attributed the confusion of what law is with what law ought to be to this very fact.

Secondly, neither Bentham nor his followers denied that by explicit legal provisions moral principles might at different points be brought into a legal system and form part of its rules, or that courts might be legally bound to decide in accordance with what they thought just or best. Bentham indeed recognized, as Austin did not, that even the supreme legislative power might be subjected to legal restraints by a constitution and would not have denied that moral principles, like those of the Fifth Amendment, might form the content of such legal constitutional restraints. Austin differed in thinking that restraints on the supreme legislative power could not have the force of law, but would remain merely political or moral checks; but of course he would have recognized that a statute, for example, might confer a delegated legislative power and restrict the area of its exercise by reference to moral principles.

What both Bentham and Austin were anxious to assert were the following two simple things: first, in the absence of an expressed constitutional or legal provision, it could not follow from the mere fact that a rule violated standards of morality that it was not a rule of law; and, conversely, it could not follow from the mere fact that a rule was morally desirable that it was a rule of law.

The history of this simple doctrine in the nineteenth century is too long and too intricate to trace here. Let me summarize it by saying that after it was propounded to the world by Austin it dominated English jurisprudence and constitutes part of the framework of most of those curiously English and perhaps unsatisfactory productions—the omnibus surveys of the whole field of jurisprudence. A succession of these were published after a full text of Austin's lectures finally appeared in 1863. In each of them the utilitarian separation of law and morals is treated as something that enables lawyers to attain a new clarity. Austin was said by one of his English successors, Amos, "to have delivered the law from the dead body of morality that still clung to it"; and even Maine, who was critical of Austin at many points, did not question this part of his doctrine. In the United States men like N. St. John Green, Gray, and Holmes considered that insistence on this distinction had enabled the understanding of law as a means of social control to get off to a fruitful new start; they welcomed it both as self-evident and as illuminating—as a revealing tautology. This distinction is, of course, one of the main themes of Holmes' most famous essay "The Path of the Law," but the place it had in the estimation of these American writers is best seen in what Gray wrote at the turn of the century in *The Nature and Sources of the Law*. He said:

> The great gain in its fundamental conceptions which Jurisprudence made during the last century was the recognition of the truth that the Law of a State . . . is not an ideal, but something which actually exists. . . . [It] is not that which ought to be, but that which is. To fix this definitely in the Jurisprudence of the Common Law, is the feat that Austin accomplished.

II

So much for the doctrine in the heyday of its success. Let us turn now to some of the criticisms. Undoubtedly, when Bentham and Austin insisted on the distinction between law as it is and as it ought to be,

they had in mind *particular* laws the meanings of which were clear and so not in dispute, and they were concerned to argue that such laws, even if morally outrageous, were still laws. It is, however, necessary, in considering the criticisms which later developed, to consider more than those criticisms which were directed to this particular point if we are to get at the root of the dissatisfaction felt; we must also take account of the objection that, even if what the utilitarians said on this particular point were true, their insistence on it, in a terminology suggesting a general cleavage between what is and ought to be law, obscured the fact that at other points there is an essential point of contact between the two. So in what follows I shall consider not only criticisms of the particular point which the utilitarians had in mind, but also the claim that an essential connection between law and morals emerges if we examine how laws, the meanings of which are in dispute, are interpreted and applied in concrete cases; and that this connection emerges again if we widen our point of view and ask, not whether every particular rule of law must satisfy a moral minimum in order to be a law, but whether a system of rules which altogether failed to do this could be a legal system.

There is, however, one major initial complexity by which criticism has been much confused. We must remember that the utilitarians combined with their insistence on the separation of law and morals two other equally famous but distinct doctrines. One was the important truth that a purely analytical study of legal concepts, a study of the meaning of the distinctive vocabulary of the law, was as vital to our understanding of the nature of law as historical or sociological studies, though of course it could not supplant them. The other doctrine was the famous imperative theory of law—that law is essentially a command.

These three doctrines constitute the utilitarian tradition in jurisprudence; yet they are distinct doctrines. It is possible to endorse the separation between law and morals and to value analytical inquiries into the meaning of legal concepts and yet think it wrong to conceive of law as essentially a command. One source of great confusion in the criticism of the separation of law and morals was the belief that the falsity of any one of these three doctrines in the utilitarian tradition showed the other two to be false; what was worse was the failure to see that there were three quite separate doctrines in this tradition. The indiscriminate use of the label "positivism" to designate ambiguously each one of these three separate doctrines (together with some others which the utilitarians never professed) has perhaps confused the issue more than any other single factor.[3] Some of the early American critics of the Austinian doctrine were, however, admirably clear on just this matter. Gray, for example, added at the end of the tribute to Austin, which I have already quoted, the words, "He may have been wrong in treating the Law of the State as being the command of the sovereign" and he touched shrewdly on many points where the command theory is defective. But other critics have been less clearheaded and have thought that the inadequacies of the command theory which gradually came to light were sufficient to demonstrate the falsity of the separation of law and morals.

This was a mistake, but a natural one. To see how natural it was we must look a little more closely at the command idea. The famous theory that law is a command was a part of a wider and more ambitious claim. Austin said that the notion of a command was "the key to the sciences of jurisprudence and morals," and contemporary attempts to elucidate moral judgments in terms of "imperative" or "prescriptive" utterances echo this ambitious claim. But the command theory, viewed as an effort to identify even the quintessence of law, let alone the quintessence of morals, seems breathtaking in its simplicity and quite inadequate. There is much, even in the simplest legal system, that is distorted if presented as a command. Yet the utilitarians thought that the essence of a legal system could be conveyed if the notion of a command were supplemented by that of a habit of obedience. The simple scheme was this: What is a command? It is simply an expression by one person of the desire that another person should do or abstain from some action, accompanied by a threat of punishment which is likely to follow disobedience. Commands are laws if two conditions are satisfied: First, they must be general; second, they must be commanded by what (as both Bentham and Austin claimed) exists in every political society whatever its constitutional form, namely, a person or a group of persons who are in receipt of habitual obedience from most of the society but pay no such obedience to others. These persons are its sovereign. Thus law is the command of the uncommanded commanders of society—the creation of the legally untrammelled will of the sovereign who is by definition outside the law.

It is easy to see that this account of a legal system is threadbare. One can also see why it might seem that its inadequacy is due to the omission of some essential connection with morality. The situation which the simple trilogy of command, sanction, and sovereign avails to describe, if you take these notions at all precisely, is like that of a gunman saying to his victim, "Give me your money or your life." The only difference is that in the case of a legal system the gunman says it to a large number of people who are accustomed to the racket and habitually surrender to it. Law surely is not the gunman situation writ large, and legal order is surely not to be thus simply identified with compulsion.

This scheme, despite the points of obvious analogy between a statute and a command, omits some of the most characteristic elements of law. Let me cite a few. It is wrong to think of a legislature (and a fortiori an electorate) with a changing membership, as a group of persons habitually obeyed: this simple idea is suited only to a monarch sufficiently long-lived for a "habit" to grow up. Even if we waive this point, nothing which legislators do makes law unless they comply with fundamental accepted rules specifying the essential lawmaking procedures. This is true even in a system having a simple unitary constitution like the British. These fundamental accepted rules specifying what the legislature must do to legislate are not commands habitually obeyed, nor can they be expressed as habits of obedience to persons. They lie at the root of a legal system, and what is most missing in the utilitarian scheme is an analysis of what it is for a social group and its officials to accept such rules. This notion, not that of a command as Austin claimed, is the "key to the science of jurisprudence," or at least one of the keys.

Again, Austin, in the case of a democracy, looked past the legislators to the electorate as "the sovereign" (or in England as part of it). He thought that in the United States the mass of the electors to the state and federal legislatures were the sovereign whose commands, given by their "agents" in the legislatures, were law. But on this footing the whole notion of the sovereign outside the law being "habitually obeyed" by the "bulk" of the population must go: for in this case the "bulk" obeys the bulk, that is, it obeys itself. Plainly the general acceptance of the authority of a lawmaking procedure, irrespective of the changing individuals who operate it from time to time, can be only distorted by an analysis in terms of mass habitual obedience to certain persons who are by definition outside the law, just as the cognate but much simpler phenomenon of the general social acceptance of a rule, say of taking off the hat when entering a church, would be distorted if represented as habitual obedience by the mass to specific persons.

Other critics dimly sensed a further and more important defect in the command theory, yet blurred the edge of an important criticism by assuming that the defect was due to the failure to insist upon some important connection between law and morals. This more radical defect is as follows. The picture that the command theory draws of life under law is essentially a simple relationship of the commander to the commanded, of superior to inferior, of top to bottom; the relationship is vertical between the commanders or authors of the law conceived of as essentially outside the law and those who are commanded and subject to the law. In this picture no place, or only an accidental or subordinate place, is afforded for a distinction between types of legal rules which are in fact radically different. Some laws require men to act in certain ways or to abstain from acting whether they wish to or not. The criminal law consists largely of rules of this sort: like commands they are simply "obeyed" or "disobeyed." But other legal rules are presented to society in quite different ways and have quite different functions. They provide facilities more or less elaborate for individuals to create structures of rights and duties for the conduct of life within the coercive framework of the law. Such are the rules enabling individuals to make contracts, wills, and trusts, and generally to mould their legal relations with others. Such rules, unlike the criminal law, are not factors designed to obstruct wishes and choices of an antisocial sort. On the contrary, these rules provide facilities for the realization of wishes and choices. They do not say (like commands) "do this whether you wish it or not," but rather "if you wish to do this, here is the way to do it." Under these rules we exercise powers, make claims, and assert rights. These phrases mark off characteristic features of laws that confer rights and powers; they are laws which are, so to speak, put at the disposition of individuals in a way in which the criminal law is not. Much ingenuity has gone into the task of "reducing" laws of this second sort to some complex variant of laws of the first sort. The effort to show that laws conferring rights are "really" only conditional stipulations of sanctions to be exacted from the person ultimately under a legal duty characterizes much of Kelsen's work. Yet to urge this is really just to exhibit dogmatic determination to suppress one aspect of the legal system in order to maintain the theory that the stipulation of a sanction, like Austin's command, represents the quintessence of law. One might as well urge that the rules of baseball were "really" only complex conditional directions to the scorer and that this showed their real or "essential" nature.

One of the first jurists in England to break with the Austinian tradition, Salmond, complained that the analysis in terms of commands left the notion of a right unprovided with a place. But he confused the point. He argued first, and correctly, that if laws are merely commands it is inexplicable that we should have come to speak of legal rights and powers as conferred or arising under them, but then wrongly concluded that the rules of a legal system must necessarily be connected with moral rules or principles of justice and that only on this footing could the phenomenon of legal rights be explained. Otherwise, Salmond thought, we would have to say that a mere "verbal coincidence" connects the concepts of legal and moral right. Similarly, continental critics of the utilitarians, always alive to the complexity of the notion of a subjective right, insisted that the command theory gave it no place. Hägerström insisted that if laws were merely commands the notion of an individual's right was really inexplicable, for commands are, as he said, something which we either obey or we do not obey; they do not confer rights. But he, too, concluded that moral, or, as he put it, commonsense, notions of justice must therefore be necessarily involved in the analysis of any legal structure elaborate enough to confer rights.

Yet, surely these arguments are confused. Rules that confer rights, though distinct from commands, need not be moral rules or coincide with them. Rights, after all, exist under the rules of ceremonies, games, and in many other spheres regulated by rules which are irrelevant to the question of justice or what the law ought to be. Nor need rules which confer rights be just or morally good rules. The rights of a master over his slaves show us that. "Their merit or demerit," as Austin termed it, depends on how rights are distributed in society and over whom or what they are exercised. These critics indeed revealed the inadequacy of the simple notions of command and habit for the analysis of law; at many points it is apparent that the social acceptance of a rule or standard of authority (even if it is motivated only by fear or superstition or rests on inertia) must be brought into the analysis and cannot itself be reduced to the two simple terms. Yet nothing in this showed the utilitarian insistence on the distinction between the existence of law and its "merits" to be wrong.

III

I now turn to a distinctively American criticism of the separation of the law that is from the law that ought to be. It emerged from the critical study of the judicial process with which American jurisprudence has been on the whole so beneficially occupied. The most skeptical of these critics—the loosely named "Realists" of the 1930s—perhaps too naïvely accepted the conceptual framework of the natural sciences as adequate for the characterization of law and for the analysis of rule-guided action of which a living system of law at least partly consists. But they opened men's eyes to what actually goes on when courts decide cases, and the contrast they drew between the actual facts of judicial decision and the traditional terminology for describing it as if it were a wholly logical operation was usually illuminating; for in spite of some exaggeration the "Realists" made us acutely conscious of one cardinal feature of human language and human thought, emphasis on which is vital not only for the understanding of law but in areas of philosophy far beyond the confines of jurisprudence. The insight of this school may be presented in the following example. A legal rule forbids you to take a vehicle into the public park. Plainly this forbids an automobile, but what about bicycles, roller skates, toy automobiles? What about airplanes? Are these, as we say, to be called "vehicles" for the purpose of the rule or not? If we are to communicate with each other at all, and if, as in the most elementary form of law, we are to express our intentions that a certain type of behavior be regulated by rules, then the general words we use—like "vehicle" in the case I consider—must have some standard instance in which no doubts are felt about its application. There must be a core of settled meaning, but there will be, as well, a penumbra of debatable cases in which words are neither obviously applicable nor obviously ruled out. These cases will each have some features in common with the standard case; they will lack others or be accompanied by features not present in the standard case. Human invention and natural processes continually throw up such variants on the familiar, and if we are to say that these ranges of facts do or do not fall under existing rules, then the classifier must make a decision which is not dictated to him, for the facts and phenomena to which we fit our words and apply our rules are as it were *dumb*. The toy automobile cannot speak up and say, "I am a vehicle for the purpose of this legal rule," nor can the roller skates chorus, "We are not a vehicle." Fact situations do not await us neatly labeled, creased, and folded, nor is their legal classification written on them to be simply read off by the judge. Instead, in applying legal rules, someone must take the responsibility of deciding that words do or do not cover some case in hand with all the practical consequences involved in this decision.

We may call the problems which arise outside the hard core of standard instances or settled meaning "problems of the penumbra"; they are always with us whether in relation to such trivial things as the regulation of the use of the public park or in relation to the multidimensional generalities of a constitution. If a penumbra of uncertainty must surround all legal rules, then their application to specific cases in the penumbral area cannot be a matter of logical deduction, and so deductive reasoning, which for generations has been cherished as the very perfection of human reasoning, cannot serve as a model for what judges, or indeed anyone, should do in bringing particular cases under general rules. In this area men cannot live by deduction alone. And it follows that if legal arguments and legal decisions of penumbral questions are to be rational, their rationality must lie in something other than a logical relation to premises. So if it is rational or "sound" to argue and to decide that for the purposes of this rule an airplane is not a vehicle, this argument must be sound or rational without being logically conclusive. What is it then that makes such decisions correct or at least better than alternative decisions? Again, it seems true to say that the criterion which makes a decision sound in such cases is some concept of what the law ought to be; it is easy to slide from that into saying that it must be a moral judgment about what law ought to be. So here we touch upon a point of necessary "intersection between law and morals" which demonstrates the falsity or, at any rate, the misleading character of the utilitarians' emphatic insistence on the separation of law as it is and ought to be. Surely, Bentham and Austin could only have written as they did because they misunderstood or neglected this aspect of the judicial process, because they ignored the problems of the penumbra.

The misconception of the judicial process which ignores the problems of the penumbra and which views the process as consisting preeminently in deductive reasoning is often stigmatized as the error of "formalism" or "literalism." My question now is, how and to what extent does the demonstration of this error show the utilitarian distinction to be wrong or misleading? Here there are many issues which have been confused, but I can only disentangle some. The charge of formalism has been leveled both at the "positivist" legal theorist and at the courts, but of course it must be a very different charge in each case. Leveled at the legal theorist, the charge means that he has made a theoretical mistake about the character of legal decision; he has thought of the reasoning involved as consisting in deduction from premises in which the judges' practical choices or decision play no part. It would be easy to show that Austin was guiltless of this error; only an entire misconception of what analytical jurisprudence is and why he thought it important has led to the view that he, or any other analyst, believed that the law was a closed logical system in which judges deduced their decisions from premises. On the contrary, he was very much alive to the character of language, to its vagueness or open character; he thought that in the penumbral situation judges must necessarily legislate, and, in accents that sometimes recall those of the late Judge Jerome Frank, he berated the common-law judges for legislating feebly and timidly and for blindly relying on real or fancied analogies with past cases instead of adapting their decisions to the growing needs of society as revealed by the moral standard of utility. The villains of this piece, responsible for the conception of the judge as an automaton, are not the utilitarian thinkers. The responsibility, if it is to be laid at the door of any theorist, is with thinkers like Blackstone and, at an earlier stage, Montesquieu. The root of this evil is preoccupation with the separation of powers and Blackstone's "childish fiction" (as Austin termed it) that judges only "find," never "make," law.

But we are concerned with "formalism" as a vice not of jurists but of judges. What precisely is it for a judge to commit this error, to be a "formalist," "automatic," a "slot machine"? Curiously enough the literature which is full of the denunciation of these vices never makes this clear in concrete terms; instead we have only descriptions which cannot mean what they appear to say: it is said that in the formalist error courts make an excessive use of logic, take a thing to "a dryly logical extreme," or make an excessive use of analytical methods. But just how in being a formalist does a judge make an excessive use of logic? It is clear that the essence of his error is to give some general term an interpretation which is blind to social values and consequences (or which is in some other way stupid or perhaps merely disliked by critics). But logic does not prescribe interpretation of terms; it dictates neither the stupid nor intelligent interpretation of any expression. Logic only tells you hypothetically that if you give a certain term a certain interpretation then a certain conclusion follows. Logic is silent on how to classify particulars— and this is the heart of a judicial decision. So this reference to logic and to logical extremes is a mis-

nomer for something else, which must be this. A judge has to apply a rule to a concrete case—perhaps the rule that one may not take a stolen "vehicle" across state lines, and in this case an airplane has been taken. He either does not see or pretends not to see that the general terms of this rule are susceptible of different interpretations and that he has a choice left open uncontrolled by linguistic conventions. He ignores, or is blind to, the fact that he is in the area of the penumbra and is not dealing with a standard case. Instead of choosing in the light of social aims, the judge fixes the meaning in a different way. He either takes the meaning that the word most obviously suggests in its ordinary nonlegal context to ordinary men, or one which the word has been given in some other legal context, or, still worse, he thinks of a standard case and then arbitrarily identifies certain features in it—for example, in the case of a vehicle, (1) normally used on land, (2) capable of carrying a human person, (3) capable of being self-propelled—and treats these three as always necessary and always sufficient conditions for the use in all contexts of the word "vehicle," irrespective of the social consequences of giving it this interpretation. This choice, not "logic," would force the judge to include a toy motor car (if electrically propelled) and to exclude bicycles and the airplane. In all this there is possibly great stupidity but no more "logic," and no less, than in cases in which the interpretation given to a general term and the consequent application of some general rule to a particular case is consciously controlled by some identified social aim.

Decisions made in a fashion as blind as this would scarcely deserve the name of decisions; we might as well toss a penny in applying a rule of law. But it is at least doubtful whether any judicial decisions (even in England) have been quite as automatic as this. Rather either the interpretations stigmatized as automatic have resulted from the conviction that it is fairer in a criminal statute to take a meaning which would jump to the mind of the ordinary man at the cost even of defeating other values, and this itself is a social policy (though possibly a bad one); or much more frequently, what is stigmatized as "mechanical" and "automatic" is a determined choice made indeed in the light of a social aim but of a conservative social aim. Certainly many of the Supreme Court decisions at the turn of the century which have been so stigmatized represent clear choices in the penumbral area to give effect to a policy of a conservative type. This is peculiarly true of Mr. Justice Peckham's opinions defining the spheres of police power and due process.

But how does the wrongness of deciding cases in an automatic and mechanical way and the rightness of deciding cases by reference to social purposes show that the utilitarian insistence on the distinction between what the law is and what it ought to be is wrong? I take it that no one who wished to use these vices of formalism as proof that the distinction between what is and what ought to be is mistaken would deny that the decisions stigmatized as automatic are law; nor would he deny that the system in which such automatic decisions are made is a legal system. Surely he would say that they are law, but they are bad law, they ought not to be law. But this would be to use the distinction, not to refute it; and of course both Bentham and Austin used it to attack judges for failing to decide penumbral cases in accordance with the growing needs of society.

Clearly, if the demonstration of the errors of formalism is to show the utilitarian distinction to be wrong, the point must be drastically restated. The point must be not merely that a judicial decision to be rational must be made in the light of some conception of what ought to be, but that the aims, the social policies and purposes to which judges should appeal if their decisions are to be rational, are themselves to be considered as part of the law in some suitably wide sense of "law" which is held to be more illuminating than that used by the utilitarians. This restatement of the point would have the following consequence: Instead of saying that the recurrence of penumbral questions shows us that legal rules are essentially incomplete, and that, when they fail to determine decisions, judges must legislate and so exercise a creative choice between alternatives, we shall say that the social policies which guide the judges' choice are in a sense there for them to discover; the judges are only "drawing out" of the rule what, if it is properly understood, is "latent" within it. To call this judicial legislation is to obscure some essential continuity between the clear cases of the rule's application and the penumbral decisions. I shall question later whether this way of talking is salutory, but I wish at this time to point out something obvious, but likely, if not stated, to tangle the issues. It does not follow that, because the opposite of a decision reached blindly in the formalist or literalist manner is a decision intelligently reached by reference to some conception of what ought to be, we have a junction of law and morals. We must, I think, beware of thinking in a too simple-minded fashion about the word "ought." This is not because there is no distinction to be made between law as it is and ought to be. Far from it. It is because the distinction should be between what is and what from many different points of view ought to be. The word "ought" merely reflects the presence of some standard of criticism; one of these standards is a moral standard but not all standards are moral. We say to our neighbour, "You ought not to lie," and that may certainly be a moral judgment, but we should remember that the baffled poisoner may say, "I ought to have given her a second dose." The point here is that intelligent decisions which we oppose to mechanical or formal decisions are not necessarily identical with decisions defensible on moral grounds. We may say of many a decision: "Yes, that is right; that is as it ought to be," and we may mean only that some accepted purpose or policy has been thereby advanced; we may not mean to endorse the moral propriety of the policy or the decision. So the contrast between the mechanical decision and the intelligent one can be reproduced inside a system dedicated to the pursuit of the most evil aims. It does not exist as a contrast to be found only in legal systems which, like our own, widely recognize principles of justice and moral claims of individuals.

An example may make this point plainer. With us the task of sentencing in criminal cases is the one that seems most obviously to demand from the judge the exercise of moral judgment. Here the factors to be weighed seem clearly to be moral factors: society must not be exposed to wanton attack; too much misery must not be inflicted on either the victim or his dependents; efforts must be made to enable him to lead a better life and regain a position in the society whose laws he has violated. To a judge striking the balance among these claims, with all the discretion and perplexities involved, his task seems as plain an example of the exercise of moral judgment as could be; and it seems to be the polar opposite of some mechanical application of a tariff of penalties fixing a sentence careless of the moral claims which in our system have to be weighed. So here intelligent and rational decision is guided however uncertainly by moral aims. But we have only to vary the example to see that this need not necessarily be so and surely, if it need not necessarily be so, the utilitarian point remains unshaken. Under the Nazi regime men were sentenced by courts for criticism of the regime. Here the choice of sentence might be guided exclusively by consideration of what was needed to maintain the state's tyranny effectively. What sentence would both terrorize the public at large and keep the friends and family of the prisoner in suspense so that both hope and fear would cooperate as factors making for subservience? The prisoner of such a system would be regarded simply as an object to be used in pursuit of these aims. Yet, in contrast with a mechanical decision, decision on these grounds would be intelligent and purposive, and from one point of view the decision would be as it ought to be. Of course, I am not unaware that a whole philosophical tradition has sought to demonstrate the fact that we cannot correctly call decisions or behavior truly rational unless they are in conformity with moral aims and principles. But the example I have used seems to me to serve at least as a warning that we cannot use the errors of formalism as something which per se demonstrates the falsity of the utilitarian insistence on the distinction between law as it is and law as *morally* it ought to be.

We can now return to the main point. If it is true that the intelligent decision of penumbral questions is one made not mechanically but in the light of aims, purposes, and policies, though not necessarily in the light of anything we would call moral principles, is it wise to express this important fact by saying that the firm utilitarian distinction between what the law is and what it ought to be should be dropped? Perhaps the claim that it is wise cannot be theoretically refuted for it is, in effect, an *invitation* to revise our conception of what a legal rule is. We are invited to include in the "rule" the various aims and policies in the light of which its penumbral cases are decided on the ground that these aims have, because of their importance, as much right to be called law as the core of legal rules whose meaning is settled. But though an invitation cannot be refuted, it may be refused and I would proffer two reasons for refusing this invitation. First, everything we have learned about the judicial process can be expressed in other less mysterious ways. We can say laws are incurably incomplete and we must decide the penumbral cases rationally by reference to social aims. I think Holmes, who had such a vivid appreciation of the fact that "general propositions do not decide concrete cases," would have put it that way. Second, to insist on the utilitarian distinction is to emphasize that the hard core of settled meaning is law in some centrally important sense and that even if there are borderlines, there must first be lines. If this were not so the notion of rules controlling courts' decisions would be senseless as some of the "Realists"—in their most extreme moods, and, I think, on bad grounds—claimed.

By contrast, to soften the distinction, to assert mysteriously that there is some fused identity between law as it is and as it ought to be, is to suggest that all legal questions are fundamentally like those of the penumbra. It is to assert that there is no central element of actual law to be seen in the core of central meaning which rules have, that there is nothing in the nature of a legal rule inconsistent with *all* questions being open to reconsideration in the light of social policy. Of course, it is good to be occupied with the penumbra. Its problems are rightly the daily diet of the law schools. But to be occupied with the penumbra is one thing, to be preoccupied with it another. And preoccupation with the penumbra is, if I may say so, as rich a source of confusion in the American legal tradition as formalism in the English. Of course we might abandon the notion that rules have authority; we might cease to attach force or even meaning to an argument that a case falls clearly within a rule and the scope of a precedent. We might call all such reasoning "automatic" or "mechanical," which is already the routine invective of the courts. But until we decide that this *is* what we want; we should not encourage it by obliterating the utilitarian distinction.

IV

The third criticism of the separation of law and morals is of a very different character; it certainly is less an intellectual argument against the utilitarian distinction than a passionate appeal supported not by detailed reasoning but by reminders of a terrible experience. For it consists of the testimony of those who have descended into Hell, and, like Ulysses or Dante, brought back a message for human beings. Only in this case the Hell was not beneath or beyond earth, but on it; it was a Hell created on earth by men for other men.

This appeal comes from those German thinkers who lived through the Nazi regime and reflected upon its evil manifestations in the legal system. One of these thinkers, Gustav Radbruch, had himself shared the "positivist" doctrine until the Nazi tyranny, but he was converted by this experience and so his appeal to other men to discard the doctrine of the separation of law and morals has the special poignancy of a recantation. What is important about this criticism is that it really does confront the particular point which Bentham and Austin had in mind in urging the separation of law as it is and as it ought to be. These German thinkers put their insistence on the need to join together what the utilitarians separated just where this separation was of most importance in the eyes of the utilitarians; for they were concerned with the problem posed by the existence of morally evil laws.

Before his conversion Radbruch held that resistance to law was a matter for the personal conscience, to be thought out by the individual as a moral problem, and the validity of a law could not be disproved by showing that the effect of compliance with the law would be more evil than the effect of disobedience. Austin, it may be recalled, was emphatic in condemning those who said that if human laws conflicted with the fundamental principles of morality then they cease to be [laws. He said they were] talking "stark nonsense."

> The most pernicious laws, and therefore those which are most opposed to the will of God, have been and are continually enforced as laws by judicial tribunals. Suppose an act innocuous, or positively beneficial, be prohibited by the sovereign under the penalty of death; if I commit this act, I shall be tried and condemned, and if I object to the sentence, that it is contrary to the law of God . . . the court of justice will demonstrate the inconclusiveness of my reasoning by hanging me up, in pursuance of the law of which I have impugned the validity. An exception, demurrer, or plea, founded on the law of God was never heard in a Court of Justice, from the creation of the world down to the present moment.

These are strong, indeed brutal words, but we must remember that they went along—in the case of Austin and, of course, Bentham—with the conviction that if laws reached a certain degree of iniquity then there would be a plain moral obligation to resist them and to withhold obedience. We shall see, when we consider the alternatives, that this simple presentation of the human dilemma which may arise has much to be said for it.

Radbruch, however, had concluded from the ease with which the Nazi regime had exploited subservience to mere law—or expressed, as he thought, in the "positivist" slogan "law is law" (*Gesetz als Gesetz*)—and from the failure of the German legal profession to protest against the enormities which they were required to perpetrate in the name of law, that "positivism" (meaning here the insistence on the separation of law as it is from law as it ought to be) had powerfully contributed to the horrors. His considered reflections led him to the doctrine that the fundamental principles of humanitarian morality were part of the very concept of *Recht* or Legality and that no positive enactment or statute, however clearly it was expressed and however clearly it conformed with the formal criteria of validity of a given legal system, could be valid if it contravened basic principles of morality. This doctrine can be appreciated fully only if the nuances imported by the German word *Recht* are grasped. But it is clear that the doctrine meant that every lawyer and judge should denounce statutes that transgressed the fundamental principles not as merely immoral or wrong but as having no legal character, and enactments which on this ground lack the quality of law should not be taken into account in working out the legal position of any given individual in particular circumstances. The striking recantation of his previous doctrine is unfortunately omitted from the translation of his works, but it should be read by all who wish to think afresh on the question of the interconnection of law and morals.

It is impossible to read without sympathy Radbruch's passionate demand that the German legal conscience should be open to the demands of morality and his complaint that this has been too little the case in the German tradition. On the other hand there is an extraordinary naïveté in the view that insensitiveness to the demands of morality and subservience to state power in a people like the Germans should have arisen from the belief that law might be law though it failed to conform with the minimum requirements of morality. Rather this terrible history prompts inquiry into why emphasis on the slogan "law is law," and the distinction between law and morals, acquired a sinister character in Germany, but elsewhere, as with the utilitarians themselves, went along with the most enlightened liberal attitudes. But something more disturbing than naïveté is latent in Radbruch's whole presentation of the issues to which the existence of morally iniquitous laws give rise. It is not, I think, uncharitable to say that we can see in his argument that he has only half digested the spiritual message of liberalism which he is seeking to convey to the legal profession. For everything that he says is really dependent upon an enormous overvaluation of the importance of the bare fact that a rule may be said to be a valid rule of law, as if this, once declared, was conclusive of the final moral question: "Ought this rule of law to be obeyed?" Surely the truly liberal answer to any sinister use of the slogan "law is law" or of the distinction between law and morals is, "Very well, but that does not conclude the question. Law is not morality; do not let it supplant morality."

However, we are not left to a mere academic discussion in order to evaluate the plea which Radbruch made for the revision of the distinction between law and morals. After the war Radbruch's conception of law as containing in itself the essential moral principle of humanitarianism was applied in practice by German courts in certain cases in which local war criminals, spies, and informers under the Nazi regime were punished. The special importance of these cases is that the persons accused of these crimes claimed that what they had done was not illegal under the laws of the regime in force at the time these actions were performed. This plea was met with the reply that the laws upon which they relied were invalid as contravening the fundamental principles of morality. Let me cite briefly one of these cases.

In 1944 a woman, wishing to be rid of her husband, denounced him to the authorities for insulting remarks he had made about Hitler while home on leave from the German army. The wife was under no legal duty to report his acts, though what he had said was apparently in violation of statutes making it illegal to make statements detrimental to the government of the Third Reich or to impair by any means the military defense of the German people. The husband was arrested and sentenced to death, apparently pursuant to these statutes, though he was not executed but was sent to the front. In 1949 the wife was prosecuted in a West German court for an offense which we would describe as illegally depriving a person of his freedom (*rechtswidrige Freiheitsberaubung*). This was punishable as a crime under the German Criminal Code of 1871 which had remained in force continuously since its enactment. The wife pleaded that her husband's imprisonment was pursuant to the Nazi statutes and hence that she had committed no crime. The court of appeal to which the case ultimately came held that the wife was guilty of procuring the deprivation of her husband's liberty by denouncing him to the German courts, even though he had been sentenced by a court for having violated a statute, since, to quote the words of the court, the statute "was contrary to the sound conscience and sense of justice of all decent human beings." This reasoning was followed in many cases which have been hailed as a triumph of the doctrines of natural law and as signaling the overthrow of positivism. The unqualified satisfaction with this result seems to me to be hysteria. Many of us might applaud the objective—that of punishing a woman for an outrageously immoral act—but this was secured only by declaring a statute established since 1934 not to have the force of law, and at least

the wisdom of this course must be doubted. There were, of course, two other choices. One was to let the woman go unpunished; one can sympathize with and endorse the view that this might have been a bad thing to do. The other was to face the fact that if the woman were to be punished it must be pursuant to the introduction of a frankly retrospective law and with a full consciousness of what was sacrificed in securing her punishment in this way. Odious as retrospective criminal legislation and punishment may be, to have pursued it openly in this case would at least have had the merits of candour. It would have made plain that in punishing the woman a choice had to be made between two evils, that of leaving her unpunished and that of sacrificing a very precious principle of morality endorsed by most legal systems. Surely if we have learned anything from the history of morals it is that the thing to do with a moral quandary is not to hide it. Like nettles, the occasions when life forces us to choose between the lesser of two evils must be grasped with the consciousness that they are what they are. The vice of this use of the principle that, at certain limiting points, what is utterly immoral cannot be law or lawful is that it will serve to cloak the true nature of the problems with which we are faced and will encourage the romantic optimism that all the values we cherish ultimately will fit into a single system, that no one of them has to be sacrificed or compromised to accommodate another.

All Discord Harmony not Understood
All Partial Evil Universal Good

This is surely untrue and there is an insincerity in any formulation of our problem which allows us to describe the treatment of the dilemma as if it were the disposition of the ordinary case.

It may seem perhaps to make too much of forms, even perhaps of words, to emphasize one way of disposing of this difficult case as compared with another which might have led, so far as the woman was concerned, to exactly the same result. Why should we dramatize the difference between them? We might punish the woman under a new retrospective law and declare overtly that we were doing something inconsistent with our principles as the lesser of two evils; or we might allow the case to pass as one in which we do not point out precisely where we sacrifice such a principle. But candour is not just one among many minor virtues of the administration of law, just as it is not merely a minor virtue of morality. For if we adopt Radbruch's view, and with him the German courts make our protest against evil law in the form of an assertion that certain rules cannot be law because of their moral iniquity, we confuse one of the most powerful, because it is the simplest, forms of moral criticism. If with the utilitarians we speak plainly, we say that laws may be law but too evil to be obeyed. This is a moral condemnation which everyone can understand and it makes an immediate and obvious claim to moral attention. If, on the other hand, we formulate our objection as an assertion that these evil things are not law, here is an assertion which many people do not believe, and if they are disposed to consider it at all, it would seem to raise a whole host of philosophical issues before it can be accepted. So perhaps the most important single lesson to be learned from this form of the denial of the utilitarian distinction is the one that the utilitarians were most concerned to teach: when we have the ample resources of plain speech we must not present the moral criticism of institutions as propositions of a disputable philosophy.

V

I have endeavored to show that, in spite of all that has been learned and experienced since the utilitarians wrote, and in spite of the defects of other parts of their doctrine, their protest against the confusion of what is and what ought to be law has a moral as well as an intellectual value. Yet it may well be said that, though this distinction is valid and important if applied to any particular law of a system, it is at least misleading if we attempt to apply it to "law," that is, to the notion of a legal system, and that if we insist, as I have, on the narrower truth (or truism), we obscure a wider (or deeper) truth. After all, it may be urged, we have learned that there are many things which are untrue of laws taken separately, but which are true and important in a legal system considered as a whole. For example, the connection between law and sanctions and between the existence of law and its "efficacy" must be understood in this more general way. It is surely not arguable (without some desperate extension of the word "sanction" or artificial narrowing of the word "law") that every law in a municipal legal system must have a sanction, yet it is at least plausible to argue that a legal system must, to be a legal system, provide sanctions for certain of its rules. So too, a rule of law may be said to exist though enforced or obeyed in only a minority of cases, but this could not be said of a legal system as

a whole. Perhaps the differences with respect to laws taken separately and a legal system as a whole are also true of the connection between moral (or some other) conceptions of what law ought to be and law in this wider sense.

This line of argument, found (at least in embryo form) in Austin, where he draws attention to the fact that every developed legal system contains certain fundamental notions which are "necessary" and "bottomed in the common nature of man," is worth pursuing—up to a point—and I shall say briefly why and how far this is so.

We must avoid, if we can, the arid wastes of inappropriate definition, for, in relation to a concept as many-sided and vague as that of a legal system, disputes about the "essential" character, or necessity to the whole, of any single element soon begin to look like disputes about whether chess could be "chess" if played with pawns. There is a wish, which may be understandable, to cut straight through the question whether a legal system, to be a legal system, must measure up to some moral or other standard with simple statements of fact: for example, that no system which utterly failed in this respect has ever existed or could endure; that the normally fulfilled assumption that a legal system aims at some form of justice colours the whole way in which we interpret specific rules in particular cases, and if this normally fulfilled assumption were not fulfilled no one would have any reason to obey except fear (and probably not that) and still less, of course, any moral obligation to obey. The connection between law and moral standards and principles of justice is therefore as little arbitrary and as "necessary" as the connection between law and sanctions, and the pursuit of the question whether this necessity is logical (part of the "meaning" of law) or merely factual or causal can safely be left as an innocent pastime for philosophers.

Yet in two respects I should wish to go further (even though this involves the use of a philosophical fantasy) and show what could intelligibly be meant by the claim that certain provisions in a legal system are "necessary." The world in which we live, and we who live in it, may one day change in many different ways; and if this change were radical enough not only would certain statements of fact now true be false and vice versa, but whole ways of thinking and talking which constitute our present conceptual apparatus, through which we see the world and each other, would lapse. We have only to consider how the whole of our social, moral, and legal life, as we understand it now, depends on the contingent fact that though our bodies do change in shape, size, and other physical properties they do not do this so drastically nor with such quicksilver rapidity and irregularity that we cannot identify each other as the same persistent individual over considerable spans of time. Though this is but a contingent fact which may one day be different, on it at present rest huge structures of our thought and principles of action and social life. Similarly, consider the following possibility (not because it is more than a possibility but because it reveals why we think certain things necessary in a legal system and what we mean by this): suppose that men were to become invulnerable to attack by each other, were clad perhaps like giant land crabs with an impenetrable carapace, and could extract the food they needed from the air by some internal chemical process. In such circumstances (the details of which can be left to science fiction) rules forbidding the free use of violence and rules constituting the minimum form of property—with its rights and duties sufficient to enable food to grow and be retained until eaten— would not have the necessary nonarbitrary status which they have for us, constituted as we are in a world like ours. At present, and until such radical changes supervene, such rules are so fundamental that if a legal system did not have them there would be no point in having any other rules at all. Such rules overlap with basic moral principles vetoing murder, violence, and theft; and so we can add to the factual statement that all legal systems in fact coincide with morality at such vital points, the statement that this is, in this sense, necessarily so. And why not call it a "natural" necessity?

Of course even this much depends on the fact that in asking what content a legal system must have we take this question to be worth asking only if we who consider it cherish the humble aim of survival in close proximity to our fellows. Natural-law theory, however, in all its protean guises, attempts to push the argument much further and to assert that human beings are equally devoted to and united in their conception of aims (the pursuit of knowledge, justice to their fellow men) other than that of survival, and these dictate a further necessary content to a legal system (over and above my humble minimum) without which it would be pointless. Of course we must be careful not to exaggerate the differences among human beings, but it seems to me that above this minimum the purposes men have for living in society are too conflicting and varying to make possible much extension of the argument that some fuller overlap of legal rules and moral standards is

"necessary" in this sense.

Another aspect of the matter deserves attention. If we attach to a legal system the minimum meaning that it must consist of general rules—general both in the sense that they refer to courses of action, not single actions, and to multiplicities of men, not single individuals—this meaning connotes the principle of treating like cases alike, though the criteria of when cases are alike will be, so far, only the general elements specified in the rules. It is, however, true that *one* essential element of the concept of justice is the principle of treating like cases alike. This is justice in the administration of the law, not justice of the law. So there is, in the very notion of law consisting of general rules, something which prevents us from treating it as if morally it is utterly neutral, without any necessary contact with moral principles. Natural procedural justice consists therefore of those principles of objectivity and impartiality in the administration of the law which implement just this aspect of law and which are designed to ensure that rules are applied only to what are genuinely cases of the rule or at least to minimize the risks of inequalities in this sense.

These two reasons (or excuses) for talking of a certain overlap between legal and moral standards as necessary and natural, of course, should not satisfy anyone who is really disturbed by the utilitarian or "positivist" insistence that law and morality are distinct. This is so because a legal system that satisfied these minimum requirements might apply, with the most pedantic impartiality as between the persons affected, laws which were hideously oppressive, and might deny to a vast rightless slave population the minimum benefits of protection from violence and theft. The stink of such societies is, after all, still in our nostrils and to argue that they have (or had) no legal system would only involve the repetition of the argument. Only if the rules failed to provide these essential benefits and protection for anyone—even for a slave-owning group—would the minimum be unsatisfied and the system sink to the status of a set of meaningless taboos. Of course no one denied those benefits would have any reason to obey except fear and would have every moral reason to revolt.

VI

I should be less than candid if I did not, in conclusion, consider something which, I suspect, most troubles those who react strongly against "legal positivism." Emphasis on the distinction between law as it is and law as it ought to be may be taken to depend upon and to entail what are called "subjectivist" and "relativist" or "noncognitive" theories concerning the very nature of moral judgments, moral distinctions, or "values." Of course the utilitarians themselves (as distinct from later positivists like Kelsen) did not countenance any such theories, however unsatisfactory their moral philosophy may appear to us now. Austin thought ultimate moral principles were the commands of God, known to us by revelation or through the "index" of utility, and Bentham thought they were verifiable propositions about utility. Nonetheless I think (though I cannot prove) that insistence upon the distinction between law as it is and ought to be has been, under the general head of "positivism," confused with a moral theory according to which statements of what is the case ("statements of fact") belong to a category or type radically different from statements of what ought to be ("value statements"). It may therefore be well to dispel this source of confusion.

There are many contemporary variants of this type of moral theory: according to some, judgments of what ought to be, or ought to be done, either are or include as essential elements expression of "feeling," "emotion," or "attitudes" or "subjective preferences"; in others such judgments both express feelings or emotions or attitudes and enjoin others to share them. In other variants such judgments indicate that a particular case falls under a general principle or policy of action which the speaker has "chosen" or to which he is "committed" and which is itself not a recognition of what is the case but analogous to a general "imperative" or command addressed to all including the speaker himself. Common to all these variants is the insistence that judgments of what ought to be done, because they contain such "non-cognitive" elements, cannot be argued for or established by rational methods as statements of fact can be, and cannot be shown to follow from any statement of fact but only from other judgments of what ought to be done in conjunction with some statement of fact. We cannot, on such a theory, demonstrate, for example, that an action was wrong, ought not to have been done, merely by showing that it consisted of the deliberate infliction of pain solely for the gratification of the agent. We only show it to be wrong if we add to those verifiable "cognitive" statements of fact a general principle not itself verifiable or "cognitive" that the infliction of pain in such circumstances is wrong,

ought not to be done. Together with this general distinction between statements of what is and what ought to be go sharp parallel distinctions between statements about means and statements of moral ends. We can rationally discover and debate what are appropriate means to given ends, but ends are not rationally discoverable or debatable; they are "fiats of the will," expression of "emotions," "preferences," or "attitudes."

Against all such views (which are of course far subtler than this crude survey can convey) others urge that all these sharp distinctions between is and ought, fact and value, means and ends, cognitive and noncognitive, are wrong. In acknowledging ultimate ends or moral values we are recognizing something as much imposed upon us by the character of the world in which we live, as little a matter of choice, attitude, feeling, emotion as the truth of factual judgments about what is the case. The characteristic moral argument is not one in which the parties are reduced to expressing or kindling feelings or emotions or issuing exhortations or commands to each other but one by which parties come to acknowledge after closer examination and reflection that an initially disputed case falls within the ambit of a vaguely apprehended principle (itself no more "subjective," no more a "fiat of our will" than any other principle of classification) and this has as much title to be called "cognitive" or "rational" as any other initially disputed classification of particulars.

Let us now suppose that we accept this rejection of "noncognitive" theories of morality and this denial of the drastic distinction in type between statements of what is and what ought to be, and that moral judgments are as rationally defensible as any other kind of judgments. What would follow from this as to the nature of the connection between law as it is and law as it ought to be? Surely, from this alone, nothing. Laws, however morally iniquitous, would still (so far as this point is concerned) be laws. The only difference which the acceptance of this view of the nature of moral judgments would make would be that the moral iniquity of such laws would be something that could be demonstrated; it would surely follow merely from a statement of what the rule required to be done that the rule was morally wrong and so ought not to be law or conversely that it was morally desirable and ought to be law. But the demonstration of this would not show the rule not to be (or to be) law. Proof that the principles by which we evaluate or condemn laws are rationally discoverable, and not mere "fiats of the will," leaves untouched the fact that there are laws which may have any degree of iniquity or stupidity and still be laws. And conversely there are rules that have every moral qualification to be laws and yet are not laws.

Surely something further or more specific must be said if disproof of "noncognitivism" or kindred theories in ethics is to be relevant to the distinction between law as it is and law as it ought to be, and to lead to the abandonment at some point or some softening of this distinction. No one has done more than Professor Lon Fuller of the Harvard Law School in his various writings to make clear such a line of argument and I will end by criticising what I take to be its central point. It is a point which again emerges when we consider not those legal rules or parts of legal rules the meanings of which are clear and excite no debate but the interpretation of rules in concrete cases where doubts are initially felt and argument develops about their meaning. In no legal system is the scope of legal rules restricted to the range of concrete instances which were present or are believed to have been present in the minds of legislators; this indeed is one of the important differences between a legal rule and a command. Yet, when rules are recognized as applying to instances beyond any that legislators did or could have considered, their extension to such new cases often presents itself not as a deliberate choice or fiat on the part of those who so interpret the rule. It appears neither as a decision to give the rule a new or extended meaning nor as a guess as to what legislators, dead perhaps in the eighteenth century, would have said had they been alive in the twentieth century. Rather, the inclusion of the new case under the rule takes its place as a natural elaboration of the rule, as something implementing a "purpose" which it seems natural to attribute (in some sense) to the rule itself rather than to any particular person dead or alive. The utilitarian description of such interpretative extension of old rules to new cases as judicial legislation fails to do justice to this phenomenon; it gives no hint of the differences between a deliberate fiat or decision to treat the new case in the same way as past cases and a recognition (in which there is little that is deliberate or even voluntary) that inclusion of the new case under the rule will implement or articulate a continuing and identical purpose, hitherto less specifically apprehended.

Perhaps many lawyers and judges will see in this language something that precisely fits their experience; others may think it a romantic gloss on facts better stated in the utilitarian language of judi-cial "legislation" or in the modern American terminology of "creative choice."

To make the point clear Professor Fuller uses a nonlegal example from the philosopher Wittgenstein which is, I think, illuminating.[4]

> Someone says to me: "Show the children a game." I teach them gaming with dice and the other says "I did not mean that sort of game." Must the exclusion of the game with dice have come before his mind when he gave me the order?

Something important does seem to me to be touched on in this example. Perhaps there are the following (distinguishable) points. First, we normally do interpret not only what people are trying to do but what they say in the light of assumed common human objectives so that unless the contrary were expressly indicated we would not interpret an instruction to show a young child a game as a mandate to introduce him to gambling even though in other contexts the word "game" would be naturally so interpreted. Second, very often, the speaker whose words are thus interpreted might say: "Yes, that's what I mean [or "that's what I meant all along"] though I never thought of it until you put this particular case to me." Third, when we thus recognize, perhaps after argument or consultation with others, a particular case not specifically envisaged beforehand as falling within the ambit of some vaguely expressed instruction, we may find this experience falsified by description of it as a mere decision on our part so to treat the particular case, and that we can only describe this faithfully as coming to realize and to articulate what we "really" want or our "true purpose"—phrases which Professor Fuller uses later in the same article.[5]

I am sure that many philosophical discussions of the character of moral argument would benefit from attention to cases of the sort instanced by Professor Fuller. Such attention would help to provide a corrective to the view that there is a sharp separation between "ends" and "means" and that in debating "ends" we can only work on each other nonrationally, and that rational argument is reserved for discussion of "means." But I think the relevance of his point to the issue whether it is correct or wise to insist on the distinction between law as it is and law as it ought to be is very small indeed. Its net effect is that in interpreting legal rules there are some cases which we find after reflection to be so natural an elaboration or articulation of the rule that to think of and refer to this as "legislation," "making law," or a "fiat" on our part would be misleading. So, the argument must be, it would be misleading to distinguish in such cases between what the rule is and what it ought to be—at least in some sense of ought. We think it ought to include the new case and come to see after reflection that it really does. But even if this way of presenting a recognizable experience as an example of a fusion between is and ought to be is admitted, two caveats must be borne in mind. The first is that "ought" in this case need have nothing to do with morals for the reasons explained already in section III: there may be just the same sense that a new case will implement and articulate the purpose of a rule in interpreting the rules of a game or some hideously immoral code of oppression whose immorality is appreciated by those called in to interpret it. They too can see what the "spirit" of the game they are playing requires in previously unenvisaged cases. More important is this: After all is said and done we must remember how rare in the law is the phenomenon held to justify this way of talking, how exceptional is this feeling that one way of deciding a case is imposed upon us as the only nat-

ural or rational elaboration of some rule. Surely it cannot be doubted that, for most cases of interpretation, the language of choice between alternatives, "judicial legislation" or even "fiat" (though not arbitrary fiat), better conveys the realities of the situation.

Within the framework of relatively well-settled law there jostle too many alternatives too nearly equal in attraction between which judge and lawyer must uncertainly pick their way to make appropriate here language which may well describe those experiences which we have in interpreting our own or others' principles of conduct, intention, or wishes, when we are not conscious of exercising a deliberate choice, but rather of recognizing something awaiting recognition. To use in the description of the interpretation of laws the suggested terminology of a fusion of inability to separate what is law and ought to be will serve (like earlier stories that judges only find, never make, law) only to conceal the facts, that here if anywhere we live among uncertainties between which we have to choose, and that the existing law imposes only limits on our choice and not the choice itself.

---

1. See Bentham, *Principles of Legislation*, in The Theory of Legislation 1, 65 n.* (Ogden ed. 1931) (c. XII, 2d para. n.*).

    Here we touch upon the most difficult of questions. If the law is not what it ought to be; if it openly combats the principle of utility; ought we to obey it? Ought we to violate it? Ought we to remain neuter between the law which commands an evil, and morality which forbids it? See also Bentham, *A Fragment on Government*, in 1 Works 221, 287–88 (Bowring ed. 1859) (c. iv, 20th–25th paras.).

2. 1 Blackstone, Commentaries *41. Bentham criticized "this dangerous maxim," saying "the natural tendency of such a doctrine is to impel a man, by the force of conscience, to rise up in arms against any law whatever that he happens not to like. *Bentham, A Fragment on Government*, in 1 Works 221, 287 (Bowring ed. 1859) (c. IV, 19th para.). See also *Bentham, A Comment on the Commentaries* 49 (1928) (c. III). For an expression of a fear lest anarchy result from such a doctrine, combined with a recognition that resistance may be justified on grounds of utility, see Austin, The Province of Jurisprudence Determined, 186 (Library of Ideas ed. 1954).

3. It may help to identify five (there may be more) meanings of "positivism" bandied about in contemporary jurisprudence:

    (1) the contention that laws are commands of human beings.

    (2) the contention that there is no necessary connection between law and morals or law as it is and ought to be.

    (3) the contention that the analysis (or study of the meaning of legal concepts) is (a) worth pursuing and (b) to be distinguished from historical inquiries into the causes or origins of laws, from sociological inquiries into the relation of law and other social phenomena, and from the criticism or appraisal of law whether in terms of morals, social aims, "functions," or otherwise.

    (4) the contention that a legal system is a "closed logical system" in which correct legal decisions can be deduced by logical means from predetermined legal rules without reference to social aims, policies, moral standards.

    (5) the contention that moral judgments cannot be established or defended, as statements of facts can, by rational argument, evidence, or proof ("noncognitivism" in ethics).

    Bentham and Austin held the views described in (1), (2), and (3) but not those in (4) and (5). Opinion (4) is often ascribed to analytical jurists, but I know of no "analyst" who held this view.

4. Fuller, *Human Purpose and Natural Law*, 53 J. Philos. 697, 700 (1956).

5. *Id*. at 701, 702

POSITIVISM AND FIDELITY TO LAW— A REPLY TO PROFESSOR HART*

Lon L. Fuller

I. The Definition of Law

Throughout his essay Professor Hart aligns himself with a general position which he associates with the names of Bentham, Austin, Gray, and Holmes. He recognizes, of course, that the conceptions of these men as to "what law is" vary considerably, but this diversity he apparently considers irrelevant in his defense of their general school of thought.

If the only issue were that of stipulating a meaning for the word "law" that would be conducive to intellectual clarity, there might be much justification for treating all of these men as working in the same direction. Austin, for example, defines law as the command of the highest legislative power, called the sovereign. For Gray, on the other hand, law consists in the rules laid down by judges. A statute is, for Gray, not a law, but only a source of law, which becomes law only after it has been interpreted and applied by a court. Now if our only object were to obtain that clarity which comes from making our definitions explicit and then adhering strictly to those definitions, one could argue plausibly that either conception of the meaning of "law" will do. Both conceptions appear to avoid a confusion of morals and law, and both writers let the reader know what meaning they propose to attribute to the word "law."

The matter assumes a very different aspect, however, if our interest lies in the ideal of fidelity to law, for then it may become a matter of capital importance what position is assigned to the judiciary in the general frame of government. Confirmation for this observation may be found in the slight rumbling of constitutional crisis to be heard in this country today. During the past year readers of newspapers have been writing to their editors urging solemnly, and even apparently with sincerity, that we should abolish the Supreme Court as a first step toward a restoration of the rule of law. It is unlikely that this remedy for our governmental ills derives from any deep study of Austin or Gray, but surely those who propose it could hardly be expected to view with indifference the divergent definitions of law offered by those two jurists. If it be said that it is a perversion of Gray's meaning to extract from his writings any moral for present controversies about the role of the Supreme Court, then it seems to me there is equal reason for treating what he wrote as irrelevant to the issue of fidelity of law generally.

Another difference of opinion among the writers defended by Professor Hart concerns Bentham and Austin and their views on constitutional limitations on the power of the sovereign. Bentham considered that a constitution might preclude the highest legislative power from issuing certain kinds of laws. For Austin, on the other hand, any legal limit on the highest lawmaking power was an absurdity and an impossibility. What guide to conscience would be offered by these two writers in a crisis that might some day arise out of the provision of our constitution to the effect that the amending power can never be used to deprive any state without its consent of its equal representation in the Senate? Surely it is not only in the affairs of everyday life that we need clarity about the obligation of fidelity to law, but most particularly and urgently in times of trouble. If all the positivist school has to offer in such times is the observation that, however you may choose to define law, it is always something different from morals, its teachings are not of much use to us.

---

*From 71 *Harvard Law Review* 630 (1958). Copyright © 1958 by The Harvard Law Review Association. Reprinted by permission of the publisher. Footnotes deleted.

I suggest, then, that Professor Hart's thesis as it now stands is essentially incomplete and that before he can attain the goals he seeks he will have to concern himself more closely with a definition of law that will make meaningful the obligation of fidelity to law.

II. The Definition of Morality

It is characteristic of those sharing the point of view of Professor Hart that their primary concern is to preserve the integrity of the concept of law. Accordingly, they have generally sought a precise definition of law, but have not been at pains to state just what it is they mean to exclude by their definitions. They are like men building a wall for the defense of a village, who must know what it is they wish to protect, but who need not, and indeed cannot, know what invading forces those walls may have to turn back.

When Austin and Gray distinguish law from morality, the word "morality" stands indiscriminately for almost every conceivable standard by which human conduct may be judged that is not itself law. The inner voice of conscience, notions of right and wrong based on religious belief, common conceptions of decency and fair play, culturally conditioned prejudices—all of these are grouped together under the heading of "morality" and are excluded from the domain of law. For the most part Professor Hart follows in the tradition of his predecessors. When he speaks of morality he seems generally to have in mind all sorts of extra-legal notions about "what ought to be," regardless of their sources, pretensions, or intrinsic worth. This is particularly apparent in his treatment of the problem of interpretation, where uncodified notions of what ought to be are viewed as affecting only the penumbra of law, leaving its hard core untouched.

Toward the end of the essay, however, Professor Hart's argument takes a turn that seems to depart from the prevailing tenor of his thought. This consists in reminding us that there is such a thing as an immoral morality and that there are many standards of "what ought to be" that can hardly be called moral. Let us grant, he says, that the judge may properly and inevitably legislate in the penumbra of a legal enactment, and that this legislation (in default of any other standard) must be guided by the judge's notions of what ought to be. Still, this would be true even in a society devoted to the most evil

ends, where the judge would supply the insufficiencies of the statute with the iniquity that seemed to him most apt for the occasion. Let us also grant, says Professor Hart toward the end of his essay, that there is at times even something that looks like discovery in the judicial process, when a judge by restating a principle seems to bring more clearly to light what was really sought from the beginning. Again, he reminds us, this could happen in a society devoted to the highest refinements of sin, where the implicit demands of an evil rule might be a matter for discovery when the rule was applied to a situation not consciously considered when it was formulated.

I take it that this is to be a warning addressed to those who wish "to infuse more morality into the law." Professor Hart is reminding them that if their program is adopted the morality that actually gets infused may not be to their liking. If this is his point it is certainly a valid one, though one wishes it had been made more explicitly, for it raises much the most fundamental issue of his whole argument. Since the point is made obliquely, and I may have misinterpreted it, in commenting I shall have to content myself with a few summary observations and questions.

First, Professor Hart seems to assume that evil aims may have as much coherence and inner logic as good ones. I, for one, refuse to accept that assumption. I realize that I am here raising, or perhaps dodging, questions that lead into the most difficult problems of the epistemology of ethics. Even if I were competent to undertake an excursus in that direction, this is not the place for it. I shall have to rest on the assertion of a belief that may seem naive, namely, that coherence and goodness have more affinity than coherence and evil. Accepting this belief, I also believe that when men are compelled to explain and justify their decisions, the effect will generally be to pull those decisions toward goodness, by whatever standards of ultimate goodness there are. Accepting these beliefs, I find a considerable incongruity in any conception that envisages a possible future in which the common law would "work itself pure from case to case" toward a more perfect realization of iniquity.

Second, if there is a serious danger in our society that a weakening of the partition between law and morality would permit an infusion of "immoral morality," the question remains, what is the most effective protection against this danger? I cannot myself believe it is to be found in the positivist position espoused by Austin, Gray, Holmes, and Hart. For those writers seem to me to falsify the problem into a specious simplicity which leaves untouched the difficult issues where real dangers lie.

Third, let us suppose a judge bent on realizing through his decisions an objective that most ordinary citizens would regard as mistaken or evil. Would such a judge be likely to suspend the letter of the statute by openly invoking a "higher law"? Or would he be more likely to take refuge behind the maxim that "law is law" and explain his decision in such a way that it would appear to be demanded by the law itself?

Fourth, neither Professor Hart nor I belong to anything that could be said in a significant sense to be a "minority group" in our respective countries. This has its advantages and disadvantages to one aspiring to a philosophic view of law and government. But suppose we were both transported to a country where our beliefs were anathemas, and where we, in turn, regarded the prevailing morality as thoroughly evil. No doubt in this situation we would have reason to fear that the law might be covertly manipulated to our disadvantage; I doubt if either of us would be apprehensive that its injunctions would be set aside by an appeal to a morality higher than law. If we felt that the law itself was our safest refuge, would it not be because even in the most perverted regimes there is a certain hesitancy about writing cruelties, intolerances, and inhumanities into law? And is it not clear that this hesitancy itself derives, not from a separation of law and morals, but precisely from an identification of law with those demands of morality that are the most urgent and the most obviously justifiable, which no man need be ashamed to profess?

Fifth, over great areas where the judicial process functions, the danger of an infusion of immoral, or at least unwelcome, morality does not, I suggest, present a real issue. Here the danger is precisely the opposite. For example, in the field of commercial law the British courts in recent years have, if I may say so, fallen into a "law-is-law" formalism that constitutes a kind of belated counterrevolution against all that was accomplished by Mansfield. The matter has reached a stage approaching crisis as commercial cases are increasingly being taken to arbitration. The chief reason for this development is that arbitrators are willing to take into account the needs of commerce and ordinary standards of commercial fairness. I realize that Professor Hart repudiates "formalism," but I shall try to show later why I think his theory necessarily leads in that direction.

Sixth, in the thinking of many there is one question that predominates in any discussion of the relation of law and morals, to the point of coloring everything that is said or heard on the subject. I refer to the kind of question raised by the Pope's pronouncement concerning the duty of Catholic judges in divorce actions. This pronouncement does indeed raise grave issues. But it does not present a problem of the relation between law, on the one hand, and, on the other, generally shared views of right conduct that have grown spontaneously through experience and discussion. The issue is rather that of a conflict between two pronouncements, both of which claim to be authoritative; if you will, it is one kind of law against another. When this kind of issue is taken as the key to the whole problem of law and morality, the discussion is so denatured and distorted that profitable exchange becomes impossible. In mentioning this last aspect of the dispute about "positivism," I do not mean to intimate that Professor Hart's own discussion is dominated by any *arrière-pensée;* I know it is not. At the same time I am quite sure that I have indicated accurately the issue that will be uppermost in the minds of many as they read his essay.

In resting content with these scant remarks, I do not want to seem to simplify the problem in a direction opposite to that taken by Professor Hart. The questions raised by "immoral morality" deserve a more careful exploration than either Professor Hart or I have offered in these pages.

III. The Moral Foundations of a Legal Order

Professor Hart emphatically rejects "the command theory of law," according to which law is simply a command backed by a force sufficient to make it effective. He observes that such a command can be given by a man with a loaded gun, and "law surely is not the gunman situation writ large." There is no need to dwell here on the inadequacies of the command theory, since Professor Hart has already revealed its defects more clearly and succinctly than I could. His conclusion is that the foundation of a legal system is not coercive power, but certain "fundamental accepted rules specifying the essential lawmaking procedures."

When I reached this point in his essay, I felt certain that Professor Hart was about to acknowledge an important qualification on his thesis. I confidently expected that he would go on to say something like this: I have insisted throughout on the importance of keeping sharp the distinction between law and morality. The question may now be raised, therefore, as to the nature of these fundamental rules that furnish the framework within which the making of law takes place. On the one hand, they seem to be rules, not of law, but of morality. They derive their efficacy from a general acceptance, which in turn rests ultimately on a perception that they are right and necessary. They can hardly be said to be law in the sense of an authoritative pronouncement, since their function is to state when a pronouncement is authoritative. On the other hand, in the daily functioning of the legal system they are often treated and applied much as ordinary rules of law are. Here, then, we must confess there is something that can be called a "merger" of law and morality, and to which the term "intersection" is scarcely appropriate.

Instead of pursuing some such course of thought, to my surprise I found Professor Hart leaving completely untouched the nature of the fundamental rules that make law itself possible, and turning his attention instead to what he considers a confusion of thought on the part of the critics of positivism. Leaving out of account his discussion of analytical jurisprudence, his argument runs something as follows: Two views are associated with the names of Bentham and Austin. One is the command theory of law, the other is an insistence on the separation of law and morality. Critics of these writers came in time to perceive— "dimly," Professor Hart says—that the command theory is untenable. By a loose association of ideas they wrongly supposed that in advancing reasons for rejecting the command theory they had also refuted the view that law and morality must be sharply separated. This was a "natural mistake," but plainly a mistake just the same.

I do not think any mistake is committed in believing that Bentham and Austin's error in formulating improperly and too simply the problem of the relation of law and morals was part of a larger error that led to the command theory of law. I think the connection between these two errors can be made clear if we ask ourselves what would have happened to Austin's system of thought if he had abandoned the command theory.

One who reads Austin's Lectures V and VI cannot help being impressed by the way he hangs doggedly to the command theory, in spite of the fact that every pull of his own keen mind was toward abandoning it. In the case of a sovereign monarch, law is what the monarch commands. But what shall we say of the "laws" of succession which tell who the "lawful" monarch is? It is of the essence of a command that it be addressed by a superior to an inferior, yet in the case of a "sovereign many," say, a parliament, the sovereign seems to command itself since a member of parliament may be convicted under a law he himself drafted and voted for. The sovereign must be unlimited in legal power, for who could adjudicate the legal bounds of a supreme lawmaking power? Yet a "sovereign many" must accept the limitation of rules before it can make law at all. Such a body can gain the power to issue commands only by acting in a "corporate capacity"; this it can do only by proceeding "agreeably to the modes and forms" established and accepted for the making of law. Judges exercise a power delegated to them by the supreme lawmaking power, and are commissioned to carry out its "direct or circuitous commands." Yet in a federal system it is the courts which must resolve conflicts of competence between the federation and its components.

All of these problems Austin sees with varying degrees of explicitness, and he struggles mightily with them. Over and over again he teeters on the edge of an abandonment of the command theory in favor of what Professor Hart has described as a view that discerns the foundations of a legal order in "certain fundamental accepted rules specifying the essential lawmaking procedures." Yet he never takes the plunge. He does not take it because he had a sure insight that it would forfeit the black-and-white distinction between law and morality that was the whole object of his Lectures—indeed, one may say, the enduring object of a dedicated life. For if law is made possible by "fundamental accepted rules"—which for Austin must be rules, not of law, but of positive morality—what are we to say of the rules that the lawmaking power enacts to regulate its own lawmaking? We have election laws, laws allocating legislative representation to specific geographic areas, rules of parliamentary procedure, rules for the qualification of voters, and many other laws and rules of similar nature. These do not remain fixed, and all of them shape in varying degrees the lawmaking process. Yet how are we to distinguish between those basic rules that owe their validity to acceptance, and those which are properly rules of law, valid even when men generally consider them to be evil or ill-advised? In other words, how are we to define the words "fundamental" and "essential" in Professor Hart's own formulation: "certain fundamental accepted rules specifying the essential lawmaking procedure"?

The solution for this problem in Kelsen's theory is instructive. Kelsen does in fact take the plunge over which Austin hesitated too long. Kelsen realizes that before we can distinguish between what is law and what is not, there must be an acceptance of some basic procedure by which law is made. In any legal system there must be some fundamental rule that points unambiguously to the source from which laws must come in order to be laws. This rule Kelsen called "the basic norm." In his own words,

> The basic norm is not valid because it has been created in a certain way, but its validity is assumed by virtue of its content. It is valid, then, like a norm of natural law. . . . The idea of a pure positive law, like that of natural law, has its limitations.

It will be noted that Kelsen speaks, not as Professor Hart does, of "fundamental rules" that regulate the making of law, but of a single rule or norm. Of course, there is no such single rule in any modern society. The notion of the basic norm is admittedly a symbol, not a fact. It is a symbol that embodies the positivist quest for some clear and unambiguous test of law, for some clean, sharp line that will divide the rules which owe their validity to acceptance and intrinsic appeal. The difficulties Austin avoided by sticking with the command theory, Kelsen avoids by a fiction which simplifies reality into a form that can be absorbed by positivism.

A full exploration of all the problems that result when we recognize that law becomes possible only by virtue of rules that are not law, would require drawing into consideration the effect of the presence or absence of a written constitution. Such a constitution in some ways simplifies the problems I have been discussing, and in some ways complicates them. In so far as a written constitution defines basic lawmaking procedure, it may remove the perplexities that arise when a parliament in effect defines itself. At the same time, a legislature operating under a written constitution may enact statutes that profoundly affect the lawmaking procedure and its predictable outcome. If these statutes are drafted with sufficient cunning, they may remain within the frame of the constitution and yet undermine the institutions it was intended to establish. If the "court-packing" proposal of the thirties does not illustrate

this danger unequivocally, it at least suggests that the fear of it is not fanciful. No written constitution can be self-executing. To be effective it requires not merely the respectful deference we show for ordinary legal enactments, but that willing convergence of effort we give to moral principles in which we have an active belief. One may properly work to amend a constitution, but so long as it remains unamended one must work with it, not against it or around it. All this amounts to saying that to be effective a written constitution must be accepted, at least provisionally, not just as law, but as good law.

What have these considerations to do with the ideal of fidelity to law? I think they have a great deal to do with it, and that they reveal the essential incapacity of the positivistic view to serve that ideal effectively. For I believe that a realization of this ideal is something for which we must plan, and that is precisely what positivism refuses to do.

Let me illustrate what I mean by planning for a realization of the ideal of fidelity to law. Suppose we are drafting a written constitution for a country just emerging from a period of violence and disorder in which any thread of legal continuity with previous governments has been broken. Obviously such a constitution cannot lift itself unaided into legality; it cannot be law simply because it says it is. We should keep in mind that the efficacy of our work will depend upon general acceptance and that to make this acceptance secure there must be a general belief that the constitution itself is necessary, right, and good. The provisions of the constitution should, therefore, be kept simple and understandable, not only in language, but also in purpose. Preambles and other explanations of what is being sought, which would be objectionable in an ordinary statute, may find an appropriate place in our constitution. We should think of our constitution as establishing a basic procedural framework for future governmental action in the enactment and administration of laws. Substantive limitations on the power of government should be kept to a minimum and should generally be confined to those for which a need can be generally appreciated. In so far as possible, substantive aims should be achieved procedurally, on the principle that if men are compelled to act in the right way, they will generally do the right things.

These considerations seem to have been widely ignored in the constitutions that have come into existence since World War II. Not uncommonly these constitutions incorporate a host of economic and political measures of the type one would ordinarily associate with statutory law. It is hardly likely that these measures have been written into the constitution because they represent aims that are generally shared. One suspects that the reason for their inclusion is precisely the opposite, namely, a fear that they would not be able to survive the vicissitudes of an ordinary exercise of parliamentary power. Thus, the divisions of opinion that are a normal accompaniment of lawmaking are written into the document that makes law itself possible. This is obviously a procedure that contains serious dangers for a future realization of the ideal of fidelity to law.

I have ventured these remarks on the making of constitutions not because I think they can claim any special profundity, but because I wished to illustrate what I mean by planning the conditions that will make it possible to realize the ideal of fidelity to law. Even within the limits of my modest purpose, what I have said may be clearly wrong. If so, it would not be for me to say whether I am also wrong clearly. I will, however, venture to assert that if I am wrong, I am wrong significantly. What disturbs me about the school of legal positivism is that it not only refuses to deal with problems of the sort I have just discussed, but bans them on principle from the province of legal philosophy. In its concern to assign the right labels to the things men do, this school seems to lose all interest in asking whether men are doing the right things.

IV. The Morality of Law Itself

Most of the issues raised by Professor Hart's essay can be restated in terms of the distinction between order and good order. Law may be said to represent order *simpliciter*. Good order is law that corresponds to the demands of justice, or morality, or men's notions of what ought to be. This rephrasing of the issue is useful in bringing to light the ambitious nature of Professor Hart's undertaking, for surely we would all agree that it is no easy thing to distinguish order from good order. When it is said, for example, that law simply represents that public order which obtains under all governments—democratic, Fascist, or Communist—the order intended is certainly not that of a morgue or cemetery. We must mean a functioning order, and such an order has to be at least good enough to be considered as functioning by some standard or other. A reminder that workable order usually requires some play in the joints, and

therefore cannot be too orderly, is enough to suggest some of the complexities that would be involved in any attempt to draw a sharp distinction between order and good order.

For the time being, however, let us suppose we can in fact clearly separate the concept of order from that of good order. Even in this unreal and abstract form the notion of order itself contains what may be called a moral element. Let me illustrate this "morality of order" in its crudest and most elementary form. Let us suppose an absolute monarch, whose word is the only law known to his subjects. We may further suppose him to be utterly selfish and to seek in his relations with his subjects solely his own advantage. This monarch from time to time issues commands, promising rewards for compliance and threatening punishment for disobedience. He is, however, a dissolute and forgetful fellow, who never makes the slightest attempt to ascertain who have in fact followed his directions and who have not. As a result he habitually punishes loyalty and rewards disobedience. It is apparent that this monarch will never achieve even his own selfish aims until he is ready to accept that minimum self-restraint that will create a meaningful connection between his words and his actions.

Let us now suppose that our monarch undergoes a change of heart and begins to pay some attention to what he said yesterday when, today, he has occasion to distribute bounty or to order the chopping off of heads. Under the strain of this new responsibility, however, our monarch relaxes his attention in other directions and becomes hopelessly slothful in the phrasing of his commands. His orders become so ambiguous and are uttered in so inaudible a tone that his subjects never have any clear idea what he wants them to do. Here, again, it is apparent that if our monarch for his own selfish advantage wants to create in his realm anything like a system of law he will have to pull himself together and assume still another responsibility. Law, considered merely as order, contains, then, its own implicit morality. This morality of order must be respected if we are to create anything that can be called law, even bad law. Law by itself is powerless to bring this morality into existence. Until our monarch is really ready to face the responsibilities of his position, it will do no good for him to issue still another futile command, this time self-addressed and threatening himself with punishment if he does not mend his ways.

There is a twofold sense in which it is true that law cannot be built on law. First of all, the authority to make law must be supported by moral attitudes that accord to it the competency it claims. Here we are dealing with a morality external to law, which makes law possible. But this alone is not enough. We may stipulate that in our monarchy the accepted "basic norm" designates the monarch himself as the only possible source of law. We still cannot have law until our monarch is ready to accept the internal morality of law itself.

In the life of a nation these external and internal moralities of law reciprocally influence one another; a deterioration of the one will almost inevitably produce a deterioration in the other. So closely related are they that when the anthropologist Lowie speaks of "the generally accepted ethical postulates underlying our . . . legal institutions as their ultimate sanction and guaranteeing their smooth functioning," he may be presumed to have both of them in mind.

What I have called "the internal morality of law" seems to be almost completely neglected by Professor Hart. He does make brief mention of "justice in the administration of the law," which consists in the like treatment of like cases, by whatever elevated or perverted standards the word "like" may be defined. But he quickly dismisses this aspect of law as having no special relevance to his main enterprise.

In this I believe he is profoundly mistaken. It is his neglect to analyze the demands of a morality of order that leads him throughout his essay to treat law as a datum projecting itself into human striving. When we realize that order itself is something that must be worked for, it becomes apparent that the existence of a legal system, even a bad or evil legal system, is always a matter of degree. When we recognize this simple fact of everyday legal experience, it becomes impossible to dismiss the problems presented by the Nazi regime with a simple assertion: "Under the Nazis there was law, even if it was bad law." We have instead to inquire how much of a legal system survived the general debasement and perversion of all forms of social order that occurred under the Nazi rule, and what moral implications this mutilated system had for the conscientious citizen forced to live under it.

It is not necessary, however, to dwell on such moral upheavals as the Nazi regime to see how completely incapable the positivistic philosophy is of serving the one high moral ideal it professes, that of fidelity to law. Its default in serving this ideal actually becomes most apparent, I believe, in the everyday problems that confront those who are earnestly desirous of meeting the moral demands of a legal order, but who have responsible functions to discharge in the very order toward which loyalty is due.

Let us suppose the case of a trial judge who has had an extensive experience in commercial matters and before whom a great many commercial disputes are tried. As a subordinate in a judicial hierarchy, our judge has of course the duty to follow the law laid down by his supreme court. Our imaginary Scrutton has the misfortune, however, to live under a supreme court which he considers woefully ignorant of the ways and needs of commerce. To his mind, many of this court's decisions in the field of commercial law simply do not make sense. If a conscientious judge caught in this dilemma were to turn to the positivistic philosophy what succor could he expect? It will certainly do no good to remind him that he has an obligation of fidelity to law. He is aware of this already and painfully so, since it is the source of his predicament. Nor will it help to say that if he legislates, it must be "interstitially," or that his contributions must be "confined from molar to molecular motions." This mode of statement may be congenial to those who like to think of law, not as a purposive thing, but as an expression of the dimensions and directions of state power. But I cannot believe that the essentially trite idea behind this advice can be lifted by literary eloquence to the point where it will offer any real help to our judge; for one thing, it may be impossible for him to know whether his supreme court would regard any particular contribution of his as being wide or narrow.

Nor is it likely that a distinction between core and penumbra would be helpful. The predicament of our judge may well derive, not from particular precedents, but from a mistaken conception of the nature of commerce which extends over many decisions and penetrates them in varying degrees. So far as his problem arises from the use of particular words, he may well find that the supreme court often uses the ordinary terms of commerce in senses foreign to actual business dealings. If he interprets those words as a business executive or accountant would, he may well reduce the precedents he is bound to apply to a logical shambles. On the other hand, he may find great difficulty in discerning the exact sense in which the supreme court used those words, since in his mind that sense is itself the product of a confusion.

Is it not clear that it is precisely positivism's insistence on a rigid separation of law as it is from law as it ought to be that renders the positivistic philosophy incapable of aiding our judge? Is it not also clear that our judge can never achieve a satisfactory resolution of his dilemma unless he views his duty of fidelity to law in a context which also embraces his responsibility for making law what it ought to be?

The case I have supposed may seem extreme, but the problem it suggests pervades our whole legal system. If the divergence of views between our judge and his supreme court were less drastic, it would be more difficult to present his predicament graphically, but the perplexity of his position might actually increase. Perplexities of this sort are a normal accompaniment of the discharge of any adjudicative function; they perhaps reach their most poignant intensity in the field of administrative law.

One can imagine a case—surely not likely in Professor Hart's country or mine—where a judge might hold profound moral convictions that were exactly the opposite of those held, with equal attachment, by his supreme court. He might also be convinced that the precedents he was bound to apply were the direct product of a morality he considered abhorrent. If such a judge did not find the solution for his dilemma in surrendering his office, he might well be driven to a wooden and literal application of precedents which he could not otherwise apply because he was incapable of understanding the philosophy that animated them. But I doubt that a judge in this situation would need the help of legal positivism to find these melancholy escapes from his predicament. Nor do I think that such a predicament is likely to arise within a nation where both law and good law are regarded as collaborative human achievements in need of constant renewal, and where lawyers are still at least as interested in asking "What is good law?" as they are in asking "What is law?"

V. The Problem of Restoring Respect for Law and Justice After the Collapse of a Regime That Respected Neither

After the collapse of the Nazi regime the German courts were faced with a truly frightful predicament. It was impossible for them to declare the whole dictatorship illegal or to treat as void every decision and legal enactment that had emanated from Hitler's government. Intolerable dislocations would have resulted from any such wholesale outlawing of all that occurred over a span of twelve years. On the other

hand, it was equally impossible to carry forward into the new government the effects of every Nazi perversity that had been committed in the name of law; any such course would have tainted an indefinite future with the poisons of Nazism.

This predicament—which was, indeed, a pervasive one, affecting all branches of law—came to a dramatic head in a series of cases involving informers who had taken advantage of the Nazi terror to get rid of personal enemies or unwanted spouses. If all Nazi statutes and judicial decisions were indiscriminately "law," then these despicable creatures were guiltless, since they had turned their victims over to processes which the Nazis themselves knew by the name of law. Yet it was intolerable, especially for the surviving relatives and friends of the victims, that these people should go about unpunished, while the objects of their spite were dead, or were just being released after years of imprisonment, or, more painful still, simply remained unaccounted for.

The urgency of this situation does not by any means escape Professor Hart. Indeed, he is moved to recommend an expedient that is surely not lacking itself in a certain air of desperation. He suggests that a retroactive criminal statute would have been the least objectionable solution to the problem. This statute would have punished the informer, and branded him as a criminal, for an act which Professor Hart regards as having been perfectly legal when he committed it. On the other hand, Professor Hart condemns without qualification those judicial decisions in which the courts themselves undertook to declare void certain of the Nazi statutes under which the informer's victims had been convicted. One cannot help raising at this point the question whether the issue as presented by Professor Hart himself is truly that of fidelity to law. Surely it would be a necessary implication of a retroactive criminal statute against informers that, for purposes of that statute at least, the Nazi laws as applied to the informers or their victims were to be regarded as void. With this turn the question seems no longer to be whether what was once law can now be declared not to have been law, but rather who should do the dirty work, the courts or the legislature.

But, as Professor Hart himself suggests, the issues at stake are much too serious to risk losing them in a semantic tangle. Even if the whole question were one of words, we should remind ourselves that we are in an area where words have a powerful effect on human attitudes. I should like, therefore, to undertake a defense of the German courts, and to advance reasons why, in my opinion, their decisions do not represent the abandonment of legal principle that Professor Hart sees in them. In order to understand the background of those decisions we shall have to move a little closer, within smelling distance of the witches' caldron, than we have been brought so far by Professor Hart. We shall have also to consider an aspect of the problem ignored in his essay, namely, the degree to which the Nazis observed what I have called the inner morality of law itself.

Throughout his discussion Professor Hart seems to assume that the only difference between Nazi law and, say, English law is that the Nazis used their laws to achieve ends that are odious to an Englishman. This assumption is, I think, seriously mistaken, and Professor Hart's acceptance of it seems to me to render his discussion unresponsive to the problem it purports to address.

Throughout their period of control the Nazis took generous advantage of a device not wholly unknown to American legislatures, the retroactive statute curing past legal irregularities. The most dramatic use of the curative powers of such a statute occurred on July 3, 1934, after the "Roehm purge." When this intraparty shooting affair was over and more than seventy Nazis had been—one can hardly avoid saying— "rubbed out," Hitler returned to Berlin and procured from his cabinet a law ratifying and confirming the measures taken between June 30, and July 1, 1934, without mentioning the names of those who were now considered to have been lawfully executed. Some time later Hitler declared that during the Roehm purge "the supreme court of the German people . . . consisted of myself," surely not an overstatement of the capacity in which he acted if one takes seriously the enactment conferring retroactive legality on "the measures taken."

Now in England and America it would never occur to anyone to say that "it is in the nature of law that it cannot be retroactive," although, of course, constitutional inhibitions may prohibit certain kinds of retroactivity. We would say it is normal for a law to operate prospectively, and that it may be arguable that it ought never operate otherwise, but there would be a certain occult unpersuasiveness in any assertion that retroactivity violates the very nature of law itself. Yet we have only to imagine a country in which all laws are retroactive in order to see that retroactivity presents a real problem for the internal morality of law. If we suppose an absolute monarch who allows his realm to exist in a constant state of anarchy, we

would hardly say that he could create a regime of law simply by enacting a curative statute conferring legality on everything that had happened up to its date and by announcing an intention to enact similar statutes every six months in the future.

A general increase in the resort to statutes curative of past legal irregularities represents a deterioration in that form of legal morality without which law itself cannot exist. The threat of such statutes hangs over the whole legal system, and robs every law on the books of some of its significance. And surely a general threat of this sort is implied when a government is willing to use such a statute to transform into lawful execution what was simple murder when it happened.

During the Nazi regime there were repeated rumors of "secret laws." In the article criticized by Professor Hart, Radbruch mentions a report that the wholesale killings in concentration camps were made "lawful" by a secret enactment. Now surely there can be no greater legal monstrosity than a secret statute. Would anyone seriously recommend that following the war the German courts should have searched for unpublished laws among the files left by Hitler's government so that citizens' rights could be determined by a reference to these laws?

The extent of the legislator's obligation to make his laws known to his subjects is, of course, a problem of legal morality that has been under active discussion at least since the Secession of the Plebs. There is probably no modern state that has not been plagued by this problem in one form or another. It is most likely to arise in modern societies with respect to unpublished administrative directions. Often these are regarded in quite good faith by those who issue them as affecting only matters of internal organization. But since the procedures followed by an administrative agency, even in its "internal" actions, may seriously affect the rights and interests of the citizen, these unpublished, or "secret," regulations are often a subject for complaint.

But as with retroactivity, what in most societies is kept under control by the tacit restraints of legal decency broke out in monstrous form under Hitler. Indeed, so loose was the whole Nazi morality of law that it is not easy to know just what should be regarded as an unpublished or secret law. Since unpublished instructions to those administering the law could destroy the letter of any published law by imposing on it an outrageous interpretation, there was a sense in which the meaning of every law was "secret." Even a verbal order from Hitler that a thousand prisoners in concentration camps be put to death was at once an administrative direction and a validation of everything done under it as being "lawful."

But the most important affronts to the morality of law by Hitler's government took no such subtle forms as those exemplified in the bizarre outcroppings I have just discussed. In the first place, when legal forms became inconvenient, it was always possible for the Nazis to bypass them entirely and "to act through the party in the streets." There was no one who dared bring them to account for whatever outrages might thus be committed. In the second place, the Nazi-dominated courts were always ready to disregard any statute, even those enacted by the Nazis themselves, if this suited their convenience or if they feared that a lawyer-like interpretation might incur displeasure "above."

This complete willingness of the Nazis to disregard even their own enactments was an important factor leading Radbruch to take the position he did in the articles so severely criticized by Professor Hart. I do not believe that any fair appraisal of the action of the postwar German courts is possible unless we take this factor into account, as Professor Hart fails completely to do.

These remarks may seem inconclusive in their generality and to rest more on assertion than evidentiary fact. Let us turn at once, then, to the actual case discussed by Professor Hart.

In 1944 a German soldier paid a short visit to his wife while under travel orders on a reassignment. During the single day he was home, he conveyed privately to his wife something of his opinion of the Hitler government. He expressed disapproval of (sich abfällig geäussert über) Hitler and other leading personalities of the Nazi party. He also said it was too bad Hitler had not met his end in the assassination attempt that had occurred on July 20th of that year. Shortly after his departure, his wife, who during his long absence on military duty "had turned to other men" and who wished to get rid of him reported his remarks to the local leader of the Nazi party, observing that "a man who would say a thing like that does not deserve to live." The result was a trial of the husband by a military tribunal and a sentence of death. After a short period of imprisonment, instead of being executed, he was sent to the front again. After the collapse of the Nazi regime, the wife was brought to trial for having procured the imprisonment of her husband. Her defense rested on the ground that her husband's statements to her about Hitler and the Nazis constituted a crime under the

laws then in force. Accordingly, when she informed on her husband she was simply bringing a criminal to justice.

This defense rested on two statutes, one passed in 1934, the other in 1938. Let us first consider the second of these enactments, which was part of a more comprehensive legislation creating a whole series of special wartime criminal offenses. I reproduce below a translation of the only pertinent section:

> The following persons are guilty of destroying the national power of resistance and shall be punished by death: Whoever publicly solicits or incites a refusal to fulfill the obligations of service in the armed forces of Germany, or in armed forces allied with Germany, or who otherwise publicly seeks to injure or destroy the will of the German people or an allied people to assert themselves stalwartly against their enemies.

It is almost inconceivable that a court of present-day Germany would hold the husband's remarks to his wife, who was barred from military duty by her sex, to be a violation of the final catch-all provision of this statute, particularly when it is recalled that the test reproduced above was part of a more comprehensive enactment dealing with such things as harboring deserters, escaping military duty by self-inflicted injuries, and the like. The question arises, then, as to the extent to which the interpretive principles applied by the courts of Hitler's government should be accepted in determining whether the husband's remarks were indeed unlawful.

This question becomes acute when we note that the act applies only to *public* acts or utterances, whereas the husband's remarks were in the privacy of his own home. Now it appears that the Nazi courts (and it should be noted we are dealing with a special military court) quite generally disregarded this limitation and extended the act to all utterances, private or public. Is Professor Hart prepared to say that the legal meaning of this statute is to be determined in the light of this apparently uniform principle of judicial interpretation?

Let us turn now to the other statute upon which Professor Hart relies in assuming that the husband's utterance was unlawful. This is the act of 1934, the relevant portions of which are translated below:

> (1) Whoever publicly makes spiteful or provocative statements directed against, or statements which disclose a base disposition

toward, the leading personalities of the nation or of the National Socialist German Workers' Party, or toward measures taken or institutions established by them, and of such a nature as to undermine the people's confidence in their political leadership, shall be punished by imprisonment.

(2) Malicious utterances not made in public shall be treated in the same manner as public utterances when the person making them realized or should have realized they would reach the public.

(3) Prosecution for such utterances shall be only on the order of the National Minister of Justice; in case the utterance was directed against a leading personality of the National Socialist German Workers' Party, the Minister of Justice shall order prosecution only with the advice and consent of the Representative of the Leader.

(4) The National Minister of Justice shall, with the advice and consent of the Representative of the Leader, determine who shall belong to the class of leading personalities for purposes of Section 1 above.

Extended comment on this legislative monstrosity is scarcely called for, overlarded and undermined as it is by uncontrolled administrative discretion. We may note only: first, that it offers no justification whatever for the death penalty actually imposed on the husband, though never carried out; second, that if the wife's act in informing on her husband made his remarks "public," there is no such thing as a private utterance under this statute. I should like to ask the reader whether he can actually share Professor Hart's indignation that, in the perplexities of the postwar reconstruction, the German courts saw fit to declare this thing not a law. Can it be argued seriously that it would have been more beseeming to the judicial process if the postwar courts had undertaken a study of "the interpretative principles" in force during Hitler's rule and had than solemnly applied those "principles" to ascertain the meaning of this statute? On the other hand, would the courts really have been showing respect for Nazi law if they had construed the Nazi statutes by their own, quite different, standards of interpretation? Professor Hart castigates the German courts and Radbruch, not so much for what they believed had to be done, but because they failed to see that they were confronted by a moral dilemma of a

sort that would have been immediately apparent to Bentham and Austin. By the simple dodge of saying, "When a statute is sufficiently evil it ceases to be law," they ran away from the problem they should have faced.

This criticism is, I believe, without justification. So far as the courts are concerned, matters certainly would not have been helped if, instead of saying, "This is not law," they had said, "This is law but it is so evil we will refuse to apply it." Surely moral confusion reaches its height when a court refuses to apply something it admits to be law, and Professor Hart does not recommend any such "facing of the true issue" by the courts themselves. He would have preferred a retroactive statute. Curiously, this was also the preference of Radbruch. But unlike Professor Hart, the German courts and Gustav Radbruch were living participants in a situation of drastic emergency. The informer problem was a pressing one, and if legal institutions were to be rehabilitated in Germany it would not do to allow the people to begin taking the law into their own hands, as might have occurred while the courts were waiting for a statute.

As for Gustav Radbruch, it is, I believe, wholly unjust to say that he did not know he was faced with a moral dilemma. His postwar writings repeatedly stress the antinomies confronted in the effort to rebuild decent and orderly government in Germany. As for the ideal of fidelity to law, I shall let Radbruch's own words state his position:

> We must not conceal from ourselves— especially not in the light of our experiences during the twelve-year dictatorship—what frightful dangers for the rule of law can be contained in the notion of "statutory lawlessness" and in refusing the quality of law to duly enacted statutes.

The situation is not that legal positivism enables a man to know when he faces a difficult problem of choice, while Radbruch's beliefs deceive him into thinking there is no problem to face. The real issue dividing Professor Hart and Radbruch is: How shall we state the problem? What is the nature of the dilemma in which we are caught?

I hope I am not being unjust to Professor Hart when I say that I can find no way of describing the dilemma as he sees it but to use some such words as the following: On the one hand, we have an amoral datum called law, which has the peculiar quality of creating a moral duty to obey it. On the other hand, we have a moral duty to do what we think is right and decent. When we are confronted by a statute we believe to be thoroughly evil, we have to choose between those two duties.

If this is the positivist position, then I have no hesitancy in rejecting it. The "dilemma" it states has the verbal formulation of a problem, but the problem it states makes no sense. It is like saying I have to choose between giving food to a starving man and being mimsy with the borogoves. I do not think it is unfair to the positivistic philosophy to say that it never gives any coherent meaning to the moral obligation of fidelity to law. This obligation seems to be conceived as sui generis, wholly unrelated to any of the ordinary, extralegal ends of human life. The fundamental postulate of positivism—that law must be strictly severed from morality—seems to deny the possibility of any bridge between the obligation to obey law and other moral obligations. No mediating principle can measure their respective demands on conscience, for they exist in wholly separate worlds.

While I would not subscribe to all of Radbruch's postwar views—especially those relating to "higher law"—I think he saw, much more clearly than does Professor Hart, the true nature of the dilemma confronted by Germany in seeking to rebuild her shattered legal institutions. Germany had to restore both respect for law and respect for justice. Though neither of these could be restored without the other, painful antinomies were encountered in attempting to restore both at once, as Radbruch saw all too clearly. Essentially Radbruch saw the dilemma as that of meeting the demands of order, on the one hand, and those of good order, on the other. Of course no pat formula can be derived from this phrasing of the problem. But, unlike legal positivism, it does not present us with opposing demands that have no living contact with one another, that simply shout their contradictions across a vacuum. As we seek order, we can meaningfully remind ourselves that order itself will do us no good unless it is good for something. As we seek to make our order good, we can remind ourselves that justice itself is impossible without order, and that we must not lose order itself in the attempt to make it good.

VI. The Moral Implications of Legal Positivism

We now reach the question whether there is any ground for Gustav Radbruch's belief that a general acceptance of the positivistic philosophy in pre-Nazi Germany made smoother the route to dictatorship. Understandably, Professor Hart regards this as the most outrageous of all charges against positivism.

Here indeed we enter upon a hazardous area of controversy, where ugly words and ugly charges have become commonplace. During the last half century in this country no issue of legal philosophy has caused more spilling of ink and adrenalin than the assertion that there are "totalitarian" implications in the views of Oliver Wendell Holmes, Jr. Even the most cautiously phrased criticisms of that grand old figure from the age of Darwin, Huxley, and Haeckel seem to stir the reader's mind with the memory of past acerbities. It does no good to suggest that perhaps Holmes did not perceive all the implications of his own philosophy, for this is merely to substitute one insult for another. Nor does it help much to recall the dictum of one of the closest companions of Holmes' youth—surely no imperceptive observer—that Holmes was "composed of at least two and a half different people rolled into one, and the way he keeps them together in one tight skin, without quarreling any more than they do, is remarkable."

In the venturing upon these roughest of all jurisprudential waters, one is not reassured to see even so moderate a man as Professor Hart indulging in some pretty broad stokes of the oar. Radbruch disclosed "an extraordinary naivete" in assessing the temper of his own profession in Germany and in supposing that its adherence to positivism helped the Nazis to power. His judgment on this and other matters shows that he had "only half-digested" the spiritual message of liberalism he mistakenly thought he was conveying to his countrymen. A state of "hysteria" is revealed by those who see a wholesome reorientation of German legal thinking in such judicial decisions as were rendered in the informer cases.

Let us put aside at least the blunter tools of invective and address ourselves as calmly as we can to the question whether legal positivism, as practiced and preached in Germany, had, or could have had, any causal connection with Hitler's ascent to power. It should be recalled that in the seventy-five years before the Nazi regime the positivistic philosophy had achieved in Germany a standing such as it enjoyed in no other country. Austin praised a German scholar for bringing international law within the clarity-producing restraints of positivism. Gray reported with pleasure that the "abler" German jurists of his time were "abjuring all '*nicht positivisches Recht*,'" and cited Bergbohm as an example. This is an illuminating example, for

Bergbohm was a scholar whose ambition was to make German positivism live up to its own pretensions. He was distressed to encounter vestigial traces of natural law thinking in writings claiming to be positivistic. In particular, he was disturbed by the frequent recurrence of such notions as that law owes its efficacy to a perceived moral need for order, or that it is in the nature of man that he requires a legal order, etc. Bergbohm announced a program, never realized, to drive from positivistic thinking these last miasmas from the swamp of natural law. German jurists generally tended to regard the Anglo-American common law as a messy and unprincipled conglomerate of law and morals. Positivism was the only theory of law that could claim to be "scientific" in an Age of Science. Dissenters from this view were characterized by positivists with that epithet modern man fears above all others: "naive." The result was that it could be reported by 1927 that "to be found guilty of adherence to natural law theories is a kind of social disgrace."

To this background we must add the observation that the Germans seem never to have achieved that curious ability possessed by the British, and to some extent by the Americans, of holding their logic on short leash. When a German defines law, he means his definition to be taken seriously. If a German writer had hit upon the slogan of American legal realism, "Law is simply the behavior patterns of judges and other state officials," he would not have regarded this as an interesting little conversation-starter. He would have believed it and acted on it.

German legal positivism not only banned from legal science any consideration of the moral ends of law, but it was also indifferent to what I have called the inner morality of law itself. The German lawyer was therefore peculiarly prepared to accept as "law" anything that called itself by that name, was printed at government expense, and seemed to come *"von oben herab."*

In the light of these considerations I cannot see either absurdity or perversity in the suggestion that the attitudes prevailing in the German legal profession were helpful to the Nazis. Hitler did not come to power by a violent revolution. He was Chancellor before he became the Leader. The exploitation of legal forms started cautiously and became bolder as power was consolidated. The first attacks on the established order were on ramparts which, if they were manned by anyone, were manned by lawyers and judges. These ramparts fell almost without a struggle.

Professor Hart and others have been understandably distressed by references to a "higher law" in some of the decisions concerning informers and in Radbruch's postwar writings. I suggest that if German jurisprudence had concerned itself more with the inner morality of law, it would not have been necessary to invoke any notion of this sort in declaring void the more outrageous Nazi statutes.

To me there is nothing shocking in saying that a dictatorship which clothes itself with a tinsel of legal form can so far depart from the morality of order, from the inner morality of law itself, that it ceases to be a legal system. When a system calling itself law is predicated upon a general disregard by judges of the terms of the laws they purport to enforce, when this system habitually cures its legal irregularities, even the grossest, by retroactive statutes, when it has only to resort to forays of terror in the streets, which no one dares challenge, in order to escape even those scant restraints imposed by the pretence of legality—when all these things have become true of a dictatorship, it is not hard for me, at least, to deny to it the name of law.

I believe that the invalidity of the statutes involved in the informer cases could have been grounded on considerations such as I have just outlined. But if you were raised with a generation that said "law is law" and meant it, you may feel the only way you can escape one law is to set another off against it, and this perforce must be a "higher law." Hence these notions of "higher law," which are a justifiable cause for alarm, may themselves be a belated fruit of German legal positivism.

It should be remarked at this point that it is chiefly in Roman Catholic writings that the theory of natural law is considered, not simply as a search for those principles that will enable men to live together successfully, but as a quest for something that can be called "a higher law." This identification of natural law with a law that is above human laws seems in fact to be demanded by any doctrine that asserts the possibility of an authoritative pronouncement of the demands of natural law. In those areas affected by such pronouncements as have so far been issued, the conflict between Roman Catholic doctrine and opposing views seems to me to be a conflict between two forms of positivism. Fortunately, over most of the area with which lawyers are concerned, no such pronouncements exist. In these areas I think those of us who are not adherents of its faith can be grateful to the Catholic Church for having kept alive the rationalistic tradition in ethics.

I do not assert that the solution I have suggested for the informer cases would not have entailed its own difficulties, particularly the familiar one of knowing where to stop. But I think it demonstrable that the most serious deterioration in legal morality under Hitler took place in branches of the law like those involved in the informer cases; no comparable deterioration was to be observed in the ordinary branches of private law. It was in those areas where the ends of law were most odious by ordinary standards of decency that the morality of law itself was most flagrantly disregarded. In other words, where one would have been most tempted to say, "This is so evil it cannot be a law," one could usually have said instead, "This thing is the product of a system so oblivious to the morality of law that it is not entitled to be called a law." I think there is something more than accident here, for the overlapping suggests that legal morality cannot live when it is severed from a striving toward justice and decency.

But as an actual solution for the informer cases, I, like Professors Hart and Radbruch, would have preferred a retroactive statute. My reason for this preference is not that this is the most nearly lawful way of making unlawful what was once law. Rather I would see such a statute as a way of symbolizing a sharp break with the past, as a means of isolating a kind of cleanup operation from the normal functioning of the judicial process. By this isolation it would become possible for the judiciary to return more rapidly to a condition in which the demands of legal morality could be given proper respect. In other words, it would make it possible to plan more effectively to regain for the ideal of fidelity to law its normal meaning.

VII. The Problem of Interpretation: The Core and the Penumbra

It is essential that we be just as clear as we can be about the meaning of Professor Hart's doctrine of "the core and the penumbra," because I believe the casual reader is likely to misinterpret what he has to say. Such a reader is apt to suppose that Professor Hart is merely describing something that is a matter of everyday experience for the lawyer, namely, that in the interpretation of legal rules it is typically the case (though not universally so) that there are some situations which will seem to fall rather clearly within the rule, while others will be more doubtful. Professor Hart's thesis takes no such jejune form. His extended discussion of the core and the penumbra is not just a complicated way of recognizing that some cases are hard, while others are easy. Instead, on the basis of a theory about language meaning generally, he is proposing a theory of judicial interpretation which is, I believe, wholly novel. Certainly it has never been put forward in so uncompromising a form before.

As I understand Professor Hart's thesis (if we add some tacit assumptions implied by it, as well as some qualifications he would no doubt wish his readers to supply) a full statement would run something as follows: The task of interpretation is commonly that of determining the meaning of the individual words of a legal rule, like "vehicle" in a rule excluding vehicles from a park. More particularly, the task of interpretation is to determine the range of reference of such a word, or the aggregate of things to which it points. Communication is possible only because words have a "standard instance," or a "core of meaning" that remains relatively constant, whatever the context in which the word may appear. Except in unusual circumstances, it will always be proper to regard a word like "vehicle" as embracing its "standard instance," that is, that aggregate of things it would include in all ordinary contexts, within or without the law. This meaning the word will have in any legal rule, whatever its purpose. In applying the word to its "standard instance," no creative role is assumed by the judge. He is simply applying the law "as it is."

In addition to a constant core, however, words also have a penumbra of meaning which, unlike the core, will vary from context to context. When the object in question (say, a tricycle) falls within this penumbral area, the judge is forced to assume a more creative role. He must now undertake, for the first time, an interpretation of the rule in the light of its purpose or aim. Having in mind what was sought by the regulation concerning parks, ought it to be considered as barring tricycles? When questions of this sort are decided there is at least an "intersection" of "is" and "ought," since the judge, in deciding what the rule "is," does so in the light of his notions of what "it ought to be" in order to carry out its purpose.

If I have properly interpreted Professor Hart's theory as it affects the "hard core," then I think it is quite untenable. The most obvious defect of his theory lies in its assumption that problems of interpretation typically turn on the meaning of individual words. Surely no judge applying a rule of the common law ever followed any such procedure as that described (and, I take it, prescribed) by Professor Hart; indeed, we do not normally even think of his problem as being one of "interpretation." Even in the case of statutes, we commonly have to assign meaning, not to a single word, but to a sentence, a paragraph, or a whole page or more of text. Surely a paragraph does not have a "standard instance" that remains constant whatever the context in which it appears. If a statute seems to have a kind of "core meaning" that we can apply without a too precise inquiry into its exact purpose, this is because we can see that, however one might formulate the precise objective of the statute, *this* case would still come within it.

Even in situations where our interpretive difficulties seem to head up in a single word, Professor Hart's analysis seems to me to give no real account of what does or should happen. In his illustration of the "vehicle," although he tells us this word has a core of meaning that in all contexts defines unequivocally a range of objects embraced by it, he never tells us what these objects might be. If the rule excluding vehicles from parks seems easy to apply in some cases, I submit this is because we can see clearly enough what the rule "is aiming at in general" so that we know there is no need to worry about the difference between Fords and Cadillacs. If in some cases we seem to be able to apply the rule without asking what its purpose is, this is not because we can treat a directive arrangement as if it had no purpose. It is rather because, for example, whether the rule be intended to preserve quiet in the park, or to save carefree strollers from injury, we know, "without thinking," that a noisy automobile must be excluded.

What would Professor Hart say if some local patriots wanted to mount on a pedestal in the park a truck used in World War II, while other citizens, regarding the proposed memorial as an eyesore, support their stand by the "no vehicle" rule? Does this truck, in perfect working order, fall within the core or the penumbra?

Professor Hart seems to assert that unless words have "standard instances" that remain constant regardless of context, effective communication would break down and it would become impossible to construct a system of "rules which have authority." If in every context words took on a unique meaning, peculiar to that context, the whole process of interpretation would become so uncertain and subjective that

the ideal of a rule of law would lose its meaning. In other words, Professor Hart seems to be saying that unless we are prepared to accept his analysis of interpretation, we must surrender all hope of giving an effective meaning to the ideal of fidelity to law. This presents a very dark prospect indeed, if one believes, as I do, that we cannot accept his theory of interpretation. I do not take so gloomy a view of the future of the ideal of fidelity to law.

An illustration will help to test, not only Professor Hart's theory of the core and the penumbra, but its relevance to the ideal of fidelity to law as well. Let us suppose that in leafing through the statutes, we come upon the following enactment: "It shall be a misdemeanor, punishable by a fine of five dollars, to sleep in any railway station." We have no trouble in perceiving the general nature of the target toward which this state is aimed. Indeed, we are likely at once to call to mind the picture of a disheveled tramp, spread out in an ungainly fashion on one of the benches of the station, keeping weary passengers on their feet and filling their ears with raucous and alcoholic snores. This vision may fairly be said to represent the "obvious instance" contemplated by the statute, though certainly it is far from being the "standard instance" of the physiological state called "sleep."

Now let us see how this example bears on the ideal of fidelity to law. Suppose I am a judge, and that two men are brought before me for violating this statute. This first is a passenger who was waiting at 3 A.M. for a delayed train. When he was arrested he was sitting upright in an orderly fashion, but was heard by the arresting officer to be gently snoring. The second is a man who had brought a blanket and pillow to the station and had obviously settled himself down for the night. He was arrested, however, before he had a chance to go to sleep. Which of these cases presents the "standard instance" of the word "sleep"? If I disregard that question, and decide to fine the second man and set free the first, have I violated a duty of fidelity to law? Have I violated that duty if I interpret the word "sleep" as used in this statute to mean something like "to spread oneself out on a bench or floor to spend the night, or as if to spend the night"? . . .

EIGHT WAYS TO FAIL TO MAKE LAW*

Lon L. Fuller

This chapter will begin with a fairly lengthy allegory. It concerns the unhappy reign of a monarch who bore the convenient, but not very imaginative and not even very regal sounding name of Rex. . . .

Rex came to the throne filled with the zeal of a reformer. He considered that the greatest failure of his predecessors had been in the field of law. For generations the legal system had known nothing like a basic reform. Procedures of trial were cumbersome, the rules of law spoke in the archaic tongue of another age, justice was expensive, the judges were slovenly and sometimes corrupt. Rex was resolved to remedy all this and to make his name in history as a great lawgiver. It was his unhappy fate to fail in this ambition. Indeed, he failed spectacularly, since not only did he not succeed in introducing the needed reforms, but he never even succeeded in creating any law at all, good or bad.

His first official act was, however, dramatic and propitious. Since he needed a clean slate on which to write, he announced to his subjects the immediate repeal of all existing law, of whatever kind. He then set about drafting a new code. Unfortunately, trained as a lonely prince, his education had been very defective. In particular he found himself incapable of making even the simplest generalizations. Though not lacking in confidence when it came to deciding specific controversies, the effort to give articulate reasons for any conclusion strained his capacities to the breaking point.

Becoming aware of his limitations, Rex gave up the project of a code and announced to his subjects that henceforth he would act as a judge in any disputes that might arise among them. In this way under the stimulus of a variety of cases he hoped that his latent powers of generalization might develop and, proceeding case by case, he would gradually work out a system of rules that could be incorporated in a code.

Unfortunately the defects in his education were more deep-seated than he had supposed. The venture failed completely. After he had handed down literally hundreds of decisions neither he nor his subjects could detect in those decisions any pattern whatsoever. Such tentatives toward generalization as were to be found in his opinions only compounded the confusion, for they gave false leads to his subjects and threw his own meager powers of judgment off balance in the decision of later cases.

After this fiasco Rex realized it was necessary to take a fresh start. His first move was to subscribe to a course of lessons in generalization. With his intellectual powers thus fortified, he resumed the project of a code and, after many hours of solitary labor, succeeded in preparing a fairly lengthy document. He was still not confident, however, that he had fully overcome his previous defects. Accordingly, he announced to his subjects that he had written out a code and would henceforth be governed by it in deciding cases, but that for an indefinite future the contents of the code would remain an official state secret, known only to him and his scrivener. To Rex's surprise this sensible plan was deeply resented by his subjects. They declared it was very unpleasant to have one's case decided by rules when there was no way of knowing what those rules were.

Stunned by this rejection Rex undertook an earnest inventory of his personal strengths and weaknesses. He decided that life had taught him one clear lesson, namely, that it is easier to decide things with the aid of hindsight than it is to attempt to foresee and control the future. Not only did hindsight make it easier to decide cases, but—and this was of supreme importance to Rex—it made it easier to give reasons. Deciding to capitalize on this insight, Rex hit on the following plan. At the beginning of each calendar year he would decide all the controversies

---

that had arisen among his subjects during the preceding year. He would accompany his decisions with a full statement of reasons. Naturally, the reasons thus given would be understood as not controlling decisions in future years, for that would be to defeat the whole purpose of the new arrangement, which was to gain the advantages of hindsight. Rex confidently announced the new plan to his subjects, observing that he was going to publish the full text of his judgments with the rules applied by him, thus meeting the chief objection to the old plan. Rex's subjects received this announcement in silence, then quietly explained through their leaders that when they said they needed to know the rules, they meant they needed to know them *in advance* so they could act on them. Rex muttered something to the effect that they might have made that point a little clearer, but said he would see what could be done.

Rex now realized that there was no escape from a published code declaring the rules to be applied in future disputes. Continuing his lessons in generalization, Rex worked diligently on a revised code, and finally announced that it would shortly be published. This announcement was received with universal gratification. The dismay of Rex's subjects was all the more intense, therefore, when his code became available and it was discovered that it was truly a masterpiece of obscurity. Legal experts who studied it declared that there was not a single sentence in it that could be understood either by an ordinary citizen or by a trained lawyer. Indignation became general and soon a picket appeared before the royal palace carrying a sign that read, "How can anybody follow a rule that nobody can understand?"

The code was quickly withdrawn. Recognizing for the first time that he needed assistance, Rex put a staff of experts to work on a revision. He instructed them to leave the substance untouched, but to clarify the expression throughout. The resulting code was a model of clarity, but as it was studied it became apparent that its new clarity had merely brought to light that it was honeycombed with contradictions. It was reliably reported that there was not a single provision in the code that was not nullified by another provision inconsistent with it. A picket again appeared before the royal residence carrying a sign that read, "This time the king made himself clear—in both directions."

Once again the code was withdrawn for revision. By now, however, Rex had lost his patience with his subjects and the negative attitude they seemed to adopt toward everything he tried to do for them. He decided to teach them a lesson and put an end to their carping. He instructed his experts to purge the code of contradictions, but at the same time to stiffen drastically every requirement contained in it and to add a long list of new crimes. Thus, where before the citizen summoned to the throne was given ten days in which to report, in the revision the time was cut to ten seconds. It was made a crime, punishable by ten years' imprisonment, to cough, sneeze, hiccough, faint or fall down in the presence of the king. It was made treason not to understand, believe in, and correctly profess the doctrine of evolutionary, democratic redemption.

When the new code was published a near revolution resulted. Leading citizens declared their intention to flout its provisions. Someone discovered in an ancient author a passage that seemed apt: "To command what cannot be done is not to make law; it is to unmake law, for a command that cannot be obeyed serves no end but confusion, fear and chaos." Soon this passage was being quoted in a hundred petitions to the king.

The code was again withdrawn and a staff of experts charged with the task of revision. Rex's instructions to the experts were that whenever they encountered a rule requiring an impossibility, it should be revised to make compliance possible. It turned out that to accomplish this result every provision in the code had to be substantially rewritten. The final result was, however, a triumph of draftsmanship. It was clear, consistent with itself, and demanded nothing of the subject that did not lie easily within his powers. It was printed and distributed free of charge on every street corner.

However, before the effective date for the new code had arrived, it was discovered that so much time had been spent in successive revisions of Rex's original draft, that the substance of the code had been seriously overtaken by events. Ever since Rex assumed the throne there had been a suspension of ordinary legal processes and this had brought about important economic and institutional changes within the country. Accommodation to these altered conditions required many changes of substance in the law. Accordingly as soon as the new code became legally effective, it was subjected to a daily stream of amendments. Again popular discontent mounted; an anonymous pamphlet appeared on the streets carrying scurrilous cartoons of the king and a leading article with the title: "A law that changes every day is worse than no law at all."

Within a short time this source of discontent began to cure itself as the pace of amendment gradually slackened. Before this had occurred to any noticeable degree, however, Rex announced an important decision. Reflecting on the misadventures of his reign, he concluded that much of the trouble lay in bad advice he had received from experts. He accordingly declared he was reassuming the judicial power in his own person. In this way he could directly control the application of the new code and insure his country against another crisis. He began to spend practically all of his time hearing and deciding cases arising under the new code.

As the king proceeded with this task, it seemed to bring to a belated blossoming his long dormant powers of generalization. His opinions began, indeed, to reveal a confident and almost exuberant virtuosity as he deftly distinguished his own previous decisions, exposed the principles on which he acted, and laid down guide lines for the disposition of future controversies. For Rex's subjects a new day seemed about to dawn when they could finally conform their conduct to a coherent body of rules.

This hope was, however, soon shattered. As the bound volumes of Rex's judgments became available and were subjected to closer study, his subjects were appalled to discover that there existed no discernible relation between those judgments and the code they purported to apply. Insofar as it found expression in the actual disposition of controversies, the new code might just as well not have existed at all. Yet in virtually every one of his decisions Rex declared and redeclared the code to be the basic law of his kingdom. Leading citizens began to hold private meetings to discuss what measures, short of open revolt, could be taken to get the king away from the bench and back on the throne. While these discussions were going on Rex suddenly died, old before his time and deeply disillusioned with his subjects.

The first act of his successor, Rex II, was to announce that he was taking the powers of government away from the lawyers and placing them in the hands of psychiatrists and experts in public relations. This way, he explained, people could be made happy without rules.

The Consequences of Failure

Rex's bungling career as legislator and judge illustrates that the attempt to create and maintain a system of legal rules may miscarry in at least eight ways; there are in this enterprise, if you will, eight distinct routes to disaster. The first and most obvious lies in a failure to achieve rules at all, so that every issue must be decided on an ad hoc basis. The other routes are: (2) a failure to publicize, or at least to make available to the affected party, the rules he is expected to observe; (3) the abuse of retroactive legislation, which not only cannot itself guide action, but undercuts the integrity of rules prospective in effect, since it puts them under the threat of retrospective change; (4) a failure to make rules understandable; (5) the enactment of contradictory rules or (6) rules that require conduct beyond the powers of the affected party; (7) introducing such frequent changes in the rules that the subject cannot orient his action by them; and, finally, (8) a failure of congruence between the rules as announced and their actual administration.

A total failure in any one of these eight directions does not simply result in a bad system of law; it results in something that is not properly called a legal system at all, except perhaps in the Pickwickian sense in which a void contract can still be said to be one kind of contract. Certainly there can be no rational ground for asserting that a man can have a moral obligation to obey a legal rule that does not exist, or is kept secret from him, or that came into existence only after he had acted, or was unintelligible, or was contradicted by another rule of the same system, or commanded the impossible, or changed every minute. It may not be impossible for a man to obey a rule that is disregarded by those charged with its administration, but at some point obedience becomes futile—as futile, in fact, as casting a vote that will never be counted. As the sociologist Simmel has observed, there is a kind of reciprocity between government and the citizen with respect to the observance of rules.[1] Government says to the citizen in effect, "These are the rules we expect you to follow. If you follow them, you have our assurance that they are the rules that will be applied to your conduct." When this bond of reciprocity is finally and completely ruptured by government, nothing is left on which to ground the citizen's duty to observe the rules.

The citizen's predicament becomes more difficult when, though there is no total failure in any direction, there is a general and drastic deterioration in legality, such as occurred in Germany under Hitler.[2] A situation begins to develop, for example, in which though some laws are published, others, including the most important, are not. Though most laws are prospective in effect, so free a use is made of retrospective legislation that no law is immune to change ex post facto if it suits the convenience of those in power. For the trial of criminal cases concerned with loyalty to the regime, special military tribunals are established and these tribunals disregard, whenever it suits their convenience, the rules that are supposed to control their decisions. Increasingly the principal object of government seems to be, not that of giving the citizen rules by which to shape his conduct, but to frighten him into impotence. As such a situation develops, the problem faced by the citizen is not so simple as that of a voter who knows with certainty that his ballot will not be counted. It is more like that of the voter who knows that the odds are against his ballot being counted at all, and that if it is counted, there is a good chance that it will be counted for the side against which he actually voted. A citizen in this predicament has to decide for himself whether to stay with the system and cast his ballot as a kind of symbolic act expressing the hope of a better day. So it was with the German citizen under Hitler faced with deciding whether he had an obligation to obey such portions of the laws as the Nazi terror had left intact.

In situations like these there can be no simple principle by which to test the citizen's obligation of fidelity to law, any more than there can be such a principle for testing his right to engage in a general revolution. One thing is, however, clear. A mere respect for constituted authority must not be confused with fidelity to law. Rex's subjects, for example, remained faithful to him as king throughout his long and inept reign. They were not faithful to his law, for he never made any.

---

1. *The Sociology of Georg Simmel* (1950), trans. Wolff, § 4, "Interaction in the Idea of 'Law,'" pp. 186–89; see also Chapter 4, "Subordination under a Principle," pp. 250–67. Simmel's discussion is worthy of study by those concerned with defining the conditions under which the ideal of "the rule of law" can be realized.
2. I have discussed some of the features of this deterioration in my article. "Positivism and Fidelity to Law," 71 *Harvard Law Review* 630, 648–57 (1958). This article makes no attempt at a comprehensive survey of all the postwar judicial decisions in Germany concerned with events occurring during the Hitler regime. Some of the later decisions rested the nullity of judgments rendered by the courts under Hitler not on the ground that the statutes applied were void, but on the ground that the Nazi judges misinterpreted the statutes of their own government. See Pappe, "On the Validity of Judicial Decisions in the Nazi Era," 23 *Modern Law Review* 260–74 (1960). Dr. Pappe makes more of this distinction than seems to me appropriate. After all, the meaning of a statute depends in part on accepted modes of interpretation. Can it be said that the postwar German courts gave full effect to Nazi laws when they interpreted them by their own standards instead of the quite different standards current during the Nazi regime? Moreover, with statutes of the kind involved, filled as they were with vague phrases and unrestricted delegations of power, it seems a little out of place to strain over questions of their proper interpretation.

NEGATIVE AND POSITIVE POSITIVISM*

Jules Coleman

1. Introduction

Every theory about the nature or essence of law purports to provide a standard, usually in the form of a statement of necessary and sufficient conditions, for determining which of a community's norms constitute its law. For example, the naive version of legal realism maintains that the law of a community is constituted by the official pronouncements of judges. For the early positivists like Austin, law consists in the commands of a sovereign, properly so called. For substantive natural law theory, in every conceivable legal system, being a true principle of morality is a necessary condition of legality for at least some norms. Legal positivism of the sort associated with H. L. A. Hart maintains that, in every community where law exists, there exists a standard that determines which of the community's norms are legal ones. Following Hart, this standard is usually referred to as a rule of recognition. If all that positivism meant by a rule of recognition were "the standard in every community by which a community's legal norms were made determinate," every theory of law would be reducible to one or another version of positivism. Which form of positivism each would take would depend on the particular substantive conditions of legality that each theory set out. Legal positivism would be true analytically, since it would be impossible to conceive of a theory of law that did not satisfy the minimal condition for a rule of recognition. Unfortunately, the sort of truth legal positivism would then reveal would be an uninteresting one.

In order to distinguish a rule of recognition in the positivist sense from other statements of the conditions of legality, and therefore to distinguish positivism from alternative jurisprudential theses, additional constraints must be placed on the rule of recognition. Candidates for these constraints fall into two categories: (1) restrictions on the conditions of legality set out in a rule of recognition and (2) constraints on the possible sources of authority (or normativity) of the rule of recognition.

An example of the first sort of constraint is expressed by the requirement that in every community the conditions of legality must be ones of pedigree or form, not substance or content. Accordingly, for a rule specifying the conditions of legality in any society to constitute a rule of recognition in the positivist sense, legal normativity under it must be determined, for example, by a norm's being enacted in the requisite fashion by a proper authority.

The claim that the authority of the rule of recognition is a matter of its acceptance by officials rather than its truth as a normative principle, and the related claim that judicial duty under a rule of recognition is one of conventional practice rather than critical morality, express constraints of the second sort.

Ronald Dworkin expresses this second constraint as the claim that a rule of recognition in the positivist sense must be a social, rather than a normative, rule. A social rule is one whose authority is a matter of convention; the nature and scope of the duty it imposes are specified or constituted by an existing, convergent social practice. In contrast, a normative rule may impose an obligation or confer a right in the absence of the relevant practice or in the face of a contrary one. If a normative rule imposes an obligation, it does so because it is a correct principle of morality, not, *ex hypothesi*, because it corresponds to an accepted practice.

Dworkin, for one, conceives of the rule of recognition as subject to constraints of both sorts. His view is that only pedigree standards of legality can constitute rules of recognition, and that a rule of recognition must be a social rule.[1] Is legal positivism committed to either or both of these constraints on the rule of recognition?

---

*From *The Journal of Legal Studies* v. 11 (Jan. 1982) 139–64. Endnotes have been edited and renumbered.

2. Negative Positivism

Candidates for constraints on the rule of recognition are motivated by the need to distinguish legal positivism from other jurisprudential theses: in particular, natural law theory. Positivism denies what natural law theory asserts, namely, a necessary connection between law and morality. I refer to the denial of a necessary or constitutive relationship between law and morality as the separability thesis. One way of asking whether positivism is committed to any particular kind of constraint on the rule of recognition is simply to ask whether any constraints on the rule are required by commitment to the separability thesis.

To answer this question we have to make some preliminary remarks concerning how we are to understand both the rule of recognition and the separability thesis. The notion of a rule of recognition is ambiguous; it has both an epistemic and a semantic sense. In one sense, the rule of recognition is a standard that one can use to identify, validate or discover a community's law. In another sense, the rule of recognition specifies the conditions a norm must satisfy to constitute part of a community's law. The same rule may or may not be a rule of recognition in both senses, since the rule one employs to determine the law need not be the same rule as the one that makes law determinate. This ambiguity between the epistemic and semantic interpretations of the rule of recognition pervades the literature and is responsible for a good deal of confusion about the essential claims of legal positivism. In my view, legal positivism is committed to the rule of recognition in the semantic sense at least; whether it is committed to the rule of recognition as a standard for identifying law (epistemic sense) is a question to which we shall return later.[2]

In the language that is fashionable in formal semantics, to say that the rule of recognition is a semantic rule is to say that is specifies the truth conditions for singular propositions of law of the form "It is the law in *C* that *P*," where *C* is a particular community and *P* a putative statement of law. The question whether the separability thesis imposes substantive constraints on the rule of recognition is just the question whether the separability thesis restricts the conditions of legality for norms or the truth conditions for propositions of law.

The separability thesis is the claim that there exists at least one conceivable rule of recognition (and therefore one possible legal system) that does not specify truth as a moral principle among the truth conditions for any proposition of law.[3] Consequently, a particular rule of recognition may specify truth as a moral principle as a truth condition for some or all propositions of law without violating the separability thesis, since it does not follow from the fact that in one community in order to be law a norm must be a principle of morality that being a true principle of morality is a necessary condition of legality in all possible legal systems. . . .

The form of positivism generated by commitment to the rule of recognition as constrained by the separability thesis I call negative positivism to draw attention to both the character and the weakness of the claim it makes.[4] Because negative positivism is essentially a negative thesis, it cannot be undermined by counterexamples, any one of which would show only that, in some community or other, morality is a condition of legality at least for some norms.

3. Positive Positivism: Law as Hard Facts

In Model of Rules I (MOR-I), Dworkin persuasively argues that in some communities moral principles have the force of law, though what makes them law is their truth or their acceptance as appropriate to the resolution of controversial disputes rather than their having been enacted in the appropriate way by the relevant authorities. These arguments would suffice to undermine positivism were it committed to the claim that truth as a moral principle could never constitute a truth condition for a proposition of law under any rule of recognition. The arguments are inadequate to undermine the separability thesis, however, because the separability thesis makes no claim about the truth conditions of any particular proposition of law in any particular community. The arguments in MOR-I, therefore, are inadequate to undermine negative positivism.

However, Dworkin's target in MOR-I is not really negative positivism; it is that version of positivism one would get by conjoining the rule of recognition with the requirement that the truth conditions for any proposition of law could not include reference to the morality of a norm. Moreover, in fairness to Dworkin, one has to evaluate his arguments in a broader context. In MOR-I Dworkin is anxious to demonstrate not only the inadequacy of the separability thesis, but that of other essential tenets of positivism—or at least what Dworkin takes to be essential features of positivism—as well.

The fact that moral principles have the force of law, because they are appropriate, true or accepted even though they are not formally enacted, establishes for Dworkin that (1) the positivist's conception of law as rules must be abandoned; as must (2) the claim that judges exercise discretion—the authority to extend beyond the law to appeal to moral principles—to resolve controversial cases; and (3) the view that the law of every community can be identified by use of a noncontroversial or pedigree test of legality.

The first claim of positivism must be abandoned because principles, as well as rules, constitute legal norms; the second because, while positivists conceive of judges as exercising discretion by appealing to moral principles, Dworkin rightly characterizes them as appealing to moral principles, which, though they are not rules, nevertheless may be binding legal standards. The third tenet of positivism must be abandoned because the rule of recognition in Dworkin's view must be one of pedigree, that is, it cannot make reference to the content or truth of a norm as a condition of its legality; and any legal system that includes moral principles among its legal standards cannot have as its standard of authority a pedigree criterion.[5]

The question, of course, is whether positivism is committed to judicial discretion, to the model of rules or to a pedigree or uncontroversial standard of legality. We know at least that it is committed to the separability thesis, from which only negative positivism appears to follow. Negative positivism is committed to none of these claims. Is there another form of positivism that is so committed?

Much of the debate between the positivists and Dworkin appears rather foolish, unless there is a version of positivism that makes Dworkin's criticism, if not compelling, at least relevant. That version of positivism, whatever it is, cannot be motivated by the separability thesis alone. The question, then, is what other than its denial of the central tenet of natural law theory motivates positivism? . . .

Certainly one reason some positivists have insisted upon the distinction between law and morality is the following: While both law and morality provide standards by which the affairs of people are to be regulated, morality is inherently controversial. People disagree about what morality prescribes, and uncertainty exists concerning the limits of permissi-

ble conduct and the nature and scope of one's moral obligations to others. In contrast, for these positivists at least, law is apparently concrete and uncontroversial. Moreover, when a dispute arises over whether or not something is law, there exists a decision procedure that, in the bulk of cases, settles the issue. Law is knowable and ascertainable; so that, while a person may not know the range of his moral obligations, he is aware of (or can find out) what the law expects of him. Commitment to the traditional legal values associated with the rule of law requires that law consist in knowable, largely uncontroversial fact; and it is this feature of law that positivism draws attention to and that underlies it.

One can reach the same characterization of law as consisting in uncontroversial, hard facts by ascribing to legal positivism the epistemological and semantic constraints of logical positivism on legal facts. For the logical positivists, moral judgments were meaningless, because they could not be verified by a reliable and essentially uncontroversial test. In order for statements of law to be meaningful, they must be verifiable by such a test (the epistemic conception of the rule of recognition). To be meaninful, therefore, law cannot be essentially controversial.

Once positivism is characterized as the view of law as consisting in hard facts, Dworkin's ascription of certain basic tenets to it is plausible, and his objections to them are compelling. First, law for positivism consists in rules rather than principles, because the legality of a rule depends on its formal characteristics—the manner and form of its enactment—whereas the legality of a moral principle will depend on its content. The legality of rules, therefore, will be essentially uncontroversial; the legal normativity of principles will be essentially controversial. Second, adjudication takes place in both hard and simple cases. Paradigm or simple cases are uncontroversial. The answer to them as a matter of law is clear, and the judge is obligated to provide it. Cases falling within the penumbra of a general rule, however, are uncertain. There is no uncontroversial answer as a matter of law to them, and judges must go beyond the law to exercise their discretion in order to resolve them. Controversy implies the absence of legal duty, and to the extent to which legal rules have controversial instances, positivism is committed to a theory of discretion in the resolution of disputes involving them. Third, positivism must be committed to a rule of recognition in both the epistemic and the semantic senses, for the rule of recognition not only sets out the conditions of legality, it provides the mechanism by which one settles disputes about what, on a particular matter, the law is. The rule of recognition for the positivist is the principle by which particular propositions of law are verified. Relatedly, the conditions of legality set forth in the rule of recognition must be ones of pedigree or form; otherwise the norm will fail to provide a reliable principle for verifying and adjudicating competing claims about the law. Finally, law and morality are distinct (the separability thesis) because law consists in hard facts, while morality does not.

Unfortunately for positivism, if the distinction between law and morality is motivated by commitment to law as uncontroversial, hard facts, it must be abandoned because, as Dworkin rightly argues, law is controversial, and even where controversial may involve matters of obligation and right rather than discretion. . . .

I want to offer an alternative version of positivism that, like the law-as-hard-facts conception, is a form of positive positivism. The form of positive positivism I want to characterize and defend has, as its point, not that law is largely uncontroversial—it need not be—but that law is ultimately conventional: that the authority of law is a matter of its acceptance by officials.

4. Positive Positivism: Law as Social Convention

It is well known that one can meet the objections to positivism Dworkin advances in MOR-I by constructing a rule of recognition (in the semantic sense) that permits moral principles as well as rules to be binding legal standards.[6] Briefly, the argument is this: Even if some moral principles are legally binding, not every moral principle is a legal one. Therefore, a test must exist for distinguishing moral principles that are legally binding from those that are not. The characteristic of legally binding moral principles that distinguishes them from nonbinding moral principles can be captured in a clause in the relevant rule of recognition. In other words, a rule is a legal rule if it possesses characteristic C; and a moral principle is a legal principle if it possesses characteristic C_1. The rule of recognition then states that a norm is a legal one if and only if it possesses either C or C_1. Once this rule of recognition is formulated, everything Dworkin ascribes to positivism, other than the model

of rules, survives. The (semantic) rule of recognition survives, since whether a norm is a legal one does not depend on whether it is a rule or a principle but on whether it satisfies the conditions of legality set forth in a rule of recognition. The separability thesis survives just so long as not every conceivable legal system has in its rule of recognition a C_1 clause—that is, a clause that sets out conditions of legality for some moral principles—or if it has such a clause, there exists at least one conceivable legal system in which no principle satisfies that clause. Finally, one argument for judicial discretion—the one that relies not on controversy but on the exhaustibility of legal standards—survives. That is, only a determinate number of standards possess either C or C_1, so that a case may arise in which no legal standard under the rule of recognition is suitable or adequate to its resolution. In such cases, judges must appeal to nonlegal standards to resolve disputes.[7]

Given Dworkin's view of positivism as law consisting in hard facts, he might simply object to this line of defense by noting that the "rule of recognition" formed by the conjunction of the conditions of legality for both principles and rules could not be a rule of recognition in the positivist sense, because its reference to morality would make it inherently controversial. Put another way, a controversial rule of recognition could not be a rule of recognition in the epistemic sense; it could not provide a reliable verification principle. For that reason, it could not be a rule of recognition in the positivist sense. Interestingly, that is not quite the argument Dworkin advances. To be sure, he argues that a rule of recognition of this sort could not constitute a rule of recognition in the positivist sense. Moreover, he argues that such a rule would be inherently controversial. But the argument does not end with the allegation that such a rule would be controversial. The controversial character of the rule is important for Dworkin, not because it is incompatible with law as hard fact or because a controversial rule cannot be a reliable verification principle, but because a controversial rule of recognition cannot be a social rule. A controversial rule of recognition cannot be a conventional one, or one whose authority depends on its acceptance.

At the outset of the essay I distinguished between two kinds of constraints that might be imposed on the rule of recognition: those having to do with substantive conditions of legality and those having to do with the authority of the rule of recognition itself. The difference between Dworkin's arguments against positivism in MOR-I and Model of Rules II (MOR-II) is that, in the former essay, the version of positivism he objects to is constrained in the first way—legality must be determined by a noncontentful (or pedigree) test—whereas the version of positivism he objects to in MOR-II is constrained in the second way—the rule of recognition's authority must be a matter of convention.

Against the law-as-convention version of positivism, Dworkin actually advances four related arguments, none of which, I want to argue, is ultimately convincing. These are what I shall refer to as (1) the social rule argument; (2) the pedigree argument; (3) the controversy argument; and (4) the moral argument.[8]

4.1. The Social Rule Argument

Legal obligations are imposed by valid legal norms. A rule or principle is a valid one provided it satisfies the conditions of legality set forth in the rule of recognition. The question Dworkin raises in MOR-II concerns the nature of duties under the rule of recognition itself. Does the rule of recognition impose duties on judges because they accept it or because the rule is defensible within a more comprehensive moral theory of law? For Dworkin this is the question of whether the rule of recognition is a social or a normative rule.

Dworkin's first argument in MOR-II against law-as-convention positivism is that the social rule theory provides an inadequate general theory of duty. The argument is this: According to the social rule theory, an individual has an obligation to act in a particular way only if (1) there is a general practice of acting in that way and (2) the rule that is constructed or built up from the practice is accepted from an internal point of view. To accept a rule from an internal point of view is to use it normatively as providing reasons both for acting in accordance with it and for criticizing departures from it. But as Dworkin rightly notes, there may be duties even where no social practice exists, or where a contrary practice prevails. This is just another way of saying that not every duty is one of conventional morality.

If the positivist's thesis is that the social rule theory provides an adequate account of the source of all noninstitutional duties or of the meaning of all claims about such duties, it is surely mistaken. Not all duties imposed by rules are imposed by conventional rules. Fortunately, the law-as-convention version of positivism makes no such claim. The question is not whether the social rule theory is adequate to account for duties generally; it is whether the theory accounts for the duty of judges under a rule of recognition. An inadequate general theory of obligation may be an adequate theory of judicial duty. Were one to take the social rule argument seriously, it would amount to the odd claim that the rule of recognition could not be a social rule and, therefore, that obligations under it could not be ones of conventional morality, simply because not every duty-imposing rule is a social rule.

4.2. The Pedigree Argument

The first serious argument Dworkin makes against the social rule theory of judicial obligation relies, in part, on the argument in MOR-I. In meeting the objection to MOR-I, I constructed a rule of recognition that set out distinct conditions of legality for both rules (C) and moral principles C_1). Let us abbreviate this rule as "C and C_1." Dworkin's claim is that such a rule cannot be a social rule.

The argument is this: The truth conditions in "C and C_1" make reference to moral principles as well as to legal rules. Unlike legal rules, moral principles cannot be identified by their pedigree. Because determining which of a community's moral principles are legal ones requires reliance upon the content of principles, controversy over legality will naturally arise. But if there is substantial controversy, then there cannot be convergence of behavior sufficient to specify a social rule. The social rule theory requires convergence of behavior, that is, a social practice. A nonpedigree standard implies controversy; controversy implies the absence of a social practice; the absence of the requisite social practice means that the rule cannot be a social rule. A rule of recognition that made reference to morality—the kind of rule of recognition we constructed to overcome Dworkin's objections in MOR-I—could not be a social rule and, therefore, could not be a rule of recognition in the positivist sense.

The argument moves too quickly. Not every reference that a rule of recognition might make to morality would be inherently controversial. It does not follow from the fact that "C and C_1" refers to moral principles that this rule cannot determine legality in virtue of some noncontentful characteristic of moral principles. For example, C_1 could be an "entrenchment" requirement of the sort Rolf Sartorius has proposed, so that whether a moral principle is a legal principle will depend on whether it is mentioned in preambles to legislation and in other authoritative documents: the more mentions, the more weight the principle receives.[9] Or C_1 could state that a moral principle is a legal principle only if it is widely shared by members of the community. In short, the legality of a moral principle could be determined by some of its noncontentful characteristics. In such cases, to determine which moral principles are legally binding would be no more troublesome or controversial than to determine which rules are legal ones.

Though not every reference to morality will render a rule of recognition controversial, some ways of identifying which of a community's moral principles are law will. Suppose C_1 makes moral truth a condition of legality, so that a moral principle could not be part of a community's law unless it were true. Whereas its entrenchment is not a controversial characteristic of a moral principle, its truth is. Any rule of recognition that made moral truth a condition of legality would be controversial. A controversial rule of recognition results in divergence of behavior sufficient to undermine its claim to being a social rule. If a rule of recognition is not a social rule, it cannot be a rule of recognition in the positivist sense.

Not every possible rule of recognition, therefore, would be a social rule. For example, the rule "the law is whatever is morally right" could never be a rule of recognition in the positivist sense. Because positivism of the sort I want to defend holds that law is everywhere conventional—that (in the language of this discussion) the rule of recognition in every community is a social rule—it must be mistaken.

4.3. The Controversy Argument

Dworkin's view is that the rule of recognition in any jurisdiction is either a social rule or a normative rule; it imposes a duty, in other words, either because it is accepted or because it is true. Law-as-convention positivism is the view that, in every community, the rule of recognition is a social rule. At this level, negative positivism is the view that, in at least one conceivable community, the rule of recognition is a social rule. Natural law theory would then be the view that, in every conceivable legal system, the rule of recognition is a normative rule. Dworkin's claim is that the rule of recognition is a normative rule, and therein lies the justification for placing him within the natural law tradition.

The argument of the previous section is compatible with some rules of recognition being norma-tive rules and others being social rules. For example, a rule of recognition that made no reference to morality or, if it did, referred only to noncontentful features of moral principles, might, for all that the previous argument shows, still be a social rule. If it were, Dworkin's arguments, based on the controversial nature of rules of recognition that refer to morality, would be inadequate to establish the normative theory of law.

What Dworkin needs is an argument that no rule of recognition can be a social rule: that regardless of the conditions of legality it sets forth, no rule of recognition can account for certain features of law unless it is a normative rule. Dworkin has such an argument and it appears to be this: Regardless of the specific conditions of legality it sets forth, every rule of recognition will give rise to controversy at some point. For example, a rule that made no reference to morality could still give rise to controversy concerning either the weight to be given to precedent or the question of whether—and if so, to what extent—the present legislature could bind a future one. Though the rule itself would not be controversial, particular instances of it would be. Were the rule of recognition a social rule, it could not impose duties on judges in such controversial applications. In those controversial cases, the social rule interpretation of the rule of recognition could not account for the rule's imposing an obligation on judges. That is because, in the social rule theory, obligations derive from convergent practice; and in both the controversial and the as yet unresolved cases there exists no convergent practice or opinion from which an obligation might derive.

The rule of recognition is either a social rule or a normative rule. If it imposes obligations in controversial cases, it cannot be a social rule. Therefore, if the rule of recognition imposes a duty upon judges in controversial cases, it must be a normative rule. Because the rule of recognition in every community is a normative rule, the obligations of judges under it are ones of critical rather than conventional morality; and the ultimate authority of law is a matter of morality, not convention.

The argument from controversy presupposes that judges are bound by duty, even in controversial cases, under the rule of recognition. Positivism, it appears, is committed to judicial discretion in such cases and is, therefore, unable to explain either the source or nature of the duty. Because the social rule theory of judicial obligation is unable to explain the fact of judicial obligation in controversial cases, it must be false and, therefore, its alternative, the normative rule theory, must be true.

One response a positivist might make to Dworkin's argument is to deny that in such cases judges are bound by duty, in which case the failure of the social rule theory to account for judicial duty would not be troublesome. Dworkin quickly dismisses the plausibility of this response with the offhand remark that such a view likens law to a game in which the participants agree in advance that there are no right answers and no duties where sufficient controversy or doubt exists regarding the requirements of a rule. The analogy to a game is supposed to embarrass positivism, but it need not. Anyone even superficially familiar with Hart's work knows that the bulk of examples he draws upon to illustrate his claims about rules, law and the nature of adjudication are drawn from games like baseball and chess. So the positivist might welcome, rather than eschew, the analogy to games.

Whether it is advanced to support or to criticize positivism, the alleged analogy to games is unsatisfying. The more interesting tack is to suppose along with Dworkin that judges may be obligated by a rule of recognition, even in its controversial applications, and then ask whether, in spite of Dworkin's arguments to the contrary, the social rule theory can explain this feature of law.

4.4. The Moral Argument

That Dworkin takes judicial obligations in cases involving controversial applications of the rule of recognition to be ones of critical morality rather than conventional practice is illustrated by the moral argument. Unlike the previous arguments I have outlined, the moral argument is direct and affirmative in the sense that, instead of trying to establish the inadequacies of the social rule theory, its purpose is to provide direct support for the normative interpretation of the rule of recognition. The argument is simply this: In resolving hard or controversial cases that arise under the rule of recognition, judges do not typically cite the practice or opinions of other judges. Because these cases are controversial, there exists no convergent practice among judges to cite. Instead, in order to resolve these disputes, judges typically appeal to principles of political morality. For example, in determining how much weight to give precedent, judges may apply alternative conceptions of fairness. If, as the social rule theory claims, the source of a judge's duty depends on the rule or principle he cites

as its basis, the sources of judicial obligation in these controversial cases are the principles of political morality judges cite as essential to the resolution of the dispute. The duty of judges in controversial cases can only be explained if the rule of recognition is a normative one whose authority depends on its moral merits; whose normativity, in other words, depends on moral argument of precisely the sort judges appear to engage in.

4.5. Summary

Dworkin has three distinct, powerful arguments against law-as-convention positivism. Each argument has a slightly different character and force. The point of the pedigree argument is that a rule of recognition that makes reference to the content of moral principles as a condition of their legality will spur controversy and, because it will, it cannot be a social rule, or, therefore, a rule of recognition in the positivist sense. The argument is weak in the sense that, even if sound, it would be inadequate to establish the normative account of the rule of recognition. Only controversial rules of recognition fail to be social rules; for all the argument shows, uncontroversial rules of recognition may be social rules.

The more general argument from controversy appears to fill the gap left by the pedigree argument. Here the argument is not that every rule of recognition will be systematically controversial. Instead, the argument relies on the plain fact that even basically uncontroversial rules of recognition will have controversial instances. The social rule theory cannot account for judicial obligation in the face of controversy. If the rule of recognition imposes an obligation on judges in controversial cases, as Dworkin presumes it does, the obligation can be accounted for only if the rule is a normative one whose capacity to impose a duty does not depend on widespread convergence of conduct or opinion. The point of the argument can be put in weaker or stronger terms. One can say simply that obligations in controversial cases exist and positivism cannot account for them; or one can put the point in terms of natural law theory as the claim that the duties that exist are ones of critical morality rather than conventional practice.

The point of the moral argument is that, in resolving hard cases, judges appear to rely on principles of political morality rather than on convergent social practice. Judges apparently believe that they are bound to resolve these controversies and, more important, that their duty to resolve them in one way rather than another depends on the principles of morality to which they appeal.

5. Convention and Controversy

Each of the objections to the social rule theory can be met.[10] Consider the pedigree argument first; that is, the claim that a rule of recognition which refers to morality—which has a C_1 clause satisfied by some norm—will be controversial and, therefore, cannot be a social rule of recognition. Suppose the clause in the rule of recognition states, "The law is whatever is morally correct." The controversy among judges does not arise over the content of the rule of recognition itself. It arises over which norms satisfy the standards set forth in it. The divergence in behavior among officials as exemplified in their identifying difference standards as legal ones does not establish their failure to accept the same rule of recognition. On the contrary, judges accept the same truth conditions for propositions of law; that is, that law consists in moral truth. They disagree about which propositions satisfy those conditions. While there may be no agreement whatsoever regarding which standards are legal ones—since there is no agreed-upon standard for determining the truth of a moral principle—there is complete agreement among judges concerning the standard of legality. That judges reach different conclusions regarding the law of a community does not mean that they are employing different standards of legality. Since disagreement concerning which principles satisfy the rule of recognition presupposes that judges accept the same rule of recognition, the sort of controversy envisaged by the pedigree argument is compatible with the conventionalist account of the authority of the rule of recognition.

Notice, however, that were we to understand the rule of recognition epistemically, as providing a reliable test for identifying law, rather than as specifying truth conditions for statements of law, the sort of controversy generated by a rule of recognition like the rule "the law is whatever is morally correct" would be problematic, since the proposed rule of recognition would be incapable of providing a reliable test for identifying legal norms. This just draws our attention once again both to the importance of distinguishing between the epistemic and semantic interpretations of the rule of recognition, and to the necessity of insisting upon the semantic interpretation of it.

Even on the semantic interpretation, the phrase "controversy in the rule of recognition" is ambiguous. Controversy may arise, as it did in the previous case, over which norms satisfy the conditions of legality set forth in the rule of recognition; or it can arise over the conditions of legality set out in the rule of recognition. Cases of the first sort are the ones Dworkin envisions arising from a rule of recognition that includes a clause specifying legality conditions for moral principles. These cases are not problematic, because controversy presupposes agreement about and acceptance of the rule of recognition. In contrast, the claim that every rule of recognition will be controversial in some of its details is precisely the claim that, in some cases, controversy will arise over the content or proper formulation of the rule of recognition itself. The question that these cases pose is not whether judges agree about which norms satisfy the same rule of recognition; rather, it is whether judges can be said to be applying the same rule. Since the social rule theory requires of the rule of recognition that its formulation be specified by convergence of behavior or belief, the controversy concerning the proper formulation of the rule means that the rule cannot be a social rule and, therefore, that it cannot be a rule of recognition in the positivist sense.

One way of interpreting Dworkin's claim is that, wherever controversy exists in the proper formulation of a rule, the rule cannot be a conventional or social rule. This is counterintuitive, since all rules—those of conventional as well as critical morality—are vague at points and, therefore, their application in some context will be controversial. If we take Dworkin to be making the argument that the existence of controversy is straightforwardly incompatible with the idea of a social rule, then no rule could be a social rule. Certainly, in spite of the controversial nature of all rules governing behavior, we are able to distinguish (at least in broad terms) the conventional rules from those whose authority depends on their truth.

A more sympathetic and plausible reading of Dworkin is that he does not mean to contest the existence of social rules. Instead his claim is that social rules cannot account for duties beyond the range of convergent practice. Social rules cannot explain duties in controversial cases. With respect to the rule of recognition, the social rule theory cannot account for the obligation of judges to give the correct formulation of the rule of recognition in its controversial instances. On the assumption that judges have such an obligation, the social rule theory fails. Only a normative interpretation of the rule of recognition can explain the duty in cases of divergent opinions or conduct, since the duty, according to the normative theory, does not derive from convergent practice but from sound moral argument.

Schematically, Dworkin's argument is as follows:

(1) Every rule of recognition will be controversial with respect to its scope and, therefore, with respect to the nature and scope of the obligations it imposes.

(2) Nevertheless, in resolving disputes involving controversial aspects of the rule, judges are under an obligation, as they are in the uncontroversial cases, to give the right answer.

(3) The social rule theory which requires convergence of behavior as a condition of an obligation cannot account for the obligation of judges in (2).

(4) Therefore, positivism cannot account for judicial obligation in (2).

(5) Therefore, only a normative theory of law in which the duty of judges depends on moral argument rather than convergent practice can account for judicial duty in (2).

As I suggested earlier, a positivist might respond by denying the truth of (2), that is, by denying that judges are obligated in controversial cases in which behavior and opinion diverge. Hart, for one, denies (2), and he appears to do so because he accepts (3). That he denies (2) is made evident by his characterizing these kinds of cases as involving "uncertainty in the rule of recognition" in which "all that succeeds is success." If a positivist were to deny (2) to meet Dworkin's objections on the ground that he (the positivist) accepts (3), it would be fair to accuse him of begging the question. He would be denying the existence of judicial obligation simply because his theory cannot account for it. Moreover, from a strategic point of view, it would be better to leave open the question whether such duties exist, rather than to preclude the very possibility of their existence as a consequence of the theory; otherwise, any argument that made the existence of such duties conceivable would have the effect of completely undermining the theory. Notice, however, that Dworkin is led to an analogous position, since his argument for the normative theory of law—i.e., (5)—requires that judges are under obligations in every conceivable case—i.e., (2). The social rule theory logically precludes judicial obligation in such

cases; the normative theory requires it. Both theories of law will fail, just in case the existence of judicial duty in controversial cases involving the rule of recognition is a contingent feature of law. In other words, if it turns out that in some legal systems judges have an obligation to provide a particular formulation of the rule of recognition when controversy arises over its proper formulation, whereas in other legal systems no such duty exists and judges are free to exercise discretion—at least until one or another formulation takes hold—both the theory that logically precludes judicial duties in all controversial cases and the one that logically entails such duties will fail.

Denying the existence of the duties to which Dworkin draws attention is a strategy that will not serve the positivist well. One alternative would be to admit the existence of the duty in some cases, but to give up the social rule theory according to which the nature and scope of a duty are completely specified by convergent practice in favor of some other theory concerning the way in which conventional or social rules give rise to duties. There is a promising line of argument I am not prepared to discuss here. However, it seems to me that the discussion of conventions in David Lewis's brilliant book *Convention*[11] might provide the theoretical foundations for an alternative to the standard social rule theory. Briefly, the idea is that the duties imposed by social rules or conventions are the results of expectations that arise from efforts to coordinate behavior. Vested, warranted expectations may extend beyond the area of convergent practice, in which case the obligations to which a social rule gives rise might cover controversial, as well as uncontroversial, cases.[12]

Another alternative strategy, the one I have been trying to develop, follows the social rule theory in restricting the duty imposed by a conventional rule to the area of convergent practice. In this view, if controversy arises in the rule of recognition itself, it does not follow that the judges are free to exercise discretion in providing a formulation of the rule. What counts is not whether controversy exists, but whether there exists a practice among judges of resolving the controversy in a particular way. And to answer the question of whether such a practice exists, we do not look to the rule of recognition—whose conditions of legality are presumably in dispute—but to the social rule constituted by the behavior of judges in applying the rule of recognition. Whether a duty exists will depend, in part, on whether the judges have developed an accepted social practice of resolving these controversies in a particular way.

Suppose that, in applying the rule of recognition, judges have developed a practice of resolving controversial instances of it. Suppose further that in some jurisdictions, for example, the United States and England, judges, by and large, resolve such disputes, as Dworkin believes they do, by providing arguments of principle; so that in determining, for example, whether and to what extent the Supreme Court can review the constitutionality of federal legislation, judges argue from principles of political morality, for example the separation of powers and so on. According to Dworkin, we should have a controversy in the rule of recognition itself that judges would be required to resolve in the appropriate way; and the obligation of judges would derive from principles of morality that constitute the best argument. This is the essence of what I referred to as the "moral argument," and it shows that the rule of recognition is a normative, not a social, rule.

For the traditional positivist, we should have a case in which no obligation existed, where all that succeeded was success: a case in which the judges' recourse to the principles of political morality necessarily involved an exercise of discretion.

Both of these positions are mistaken. If, as Dworkin supposes, judges as a general rule look to moral principles in resolving controversial features of the rule of recognition, then there exists a practice among them of resolving controversial aspects of the rule of recognition in that way; that is, as the moral argument suggests judges in the United States and England do. If this is, in fact, the practice of judges in constitutional democracies like ours—as it must be if Dworkin's arguments are to be taken seriously—and if the practice is critically accepted by judges, then there is a legal duty even in controversial cases: a duty that does not derive from the principles judges cite (as in Dworkin) but from their acceptance of the practice of resolving these disputes by offering substantive moral arguments. All that Dworkin's arguments really show is that judges have adopted critically the practice that the best moral argument wins, which explains both their appeal to substantive moral principles and, contrary to the traditional positivist, their duty to make the appeal.

What, in Dworkin's view, is evidence for the normative theory of the rule of recognition—that is, general and widespread appeal to moral principle to resolve controversies in it—is, in my view, evidence of the existence of a social practice among judges of resolving such disputes in a particular way; a practice that specifies part of the social rule regarding judicial behavior. The appeal of substantive moral argument is, then, perfectly compatible with the conventionalist account of law.

To argue that the appeal to moral argument is compatible with the conventionalist account is not to establish that account, since the appeal to moral argument as a vehicle of dispute resolution is also consistent with the normative theory of law. One could argue that, at most, my argument shows only that Dworkin's arguments, which rely on both the controversial nature of law and the appeal to moral principle to resolve controversy, are inadequate to undermine positivism. We need some further reason to choose between the normative and conventional theories of law.

For the normative theory of law to be correct, judges must be under a legal obligation to resolve controversies arising in every conceivable rule of recognition by reliance on substantive moral argument. That is because Dworkin's version of the normative theory entails the existence of judicial duty in all cases, and because the resolution of the dispute must involve moral argument. After all, if the rule of recognition is, as Dworkin claims, a normative rule, then its authority rests on sound moral argument, and the resolution of disputes concerning its scope must call for moral argument. Were judges to rely on anything else, the authority of the rule of recognition would not be a matter of its moral merits; or if they appeal to nothing at all, then in such jurisdictions we would have reason to believe that judges are under no particular obligation to resolve a controversy in the rule of recognition.

The real acid test seems to be not whether positivism of the sort I am developing can account for judicial obligations in the kinds of cases we are discussing, but whether these obligations constitute a necessary feature of law which, in every jurisdiction, is imposed by moral principle. As long as the existence of such duties is a contingent feature of law, as is the duty to resolve disputes by appealing to moral argument, the normative theory of law is a less plausible account than is the conventionalist theory. Indeed, it seems straightforwardly false, since we can imagine immature legal systems (which are legal systems nonetheless) in which no practice for resolving disputes in the rule of recognition has yet developed—where all that succeeds is success. Or we could imagine the development of considerably less attractive practices for resolving such disputes, for example, the flip of a coin: heads, defendant wins; tails, plaintiff does. In the first sort of legal system, it would seem odd to say judges were legally bound to resolve such disputes (though they might always be morally bound to do so), since no practice had as yet developed. Eventually, such a practice is likely to develop, and the range of judicial discretion will narrow as the practice becomes widespread and critically accepted. As the second example shows, the practice that finally develops need not conform to judicial practice in the United States and England. Though judicial discretion narrows as the range of judicial obligation expands, it may do so in a way that is considerably less attractive than the moral argument envisions; in a way that is, in fact, less attractive than a system in which all that succeeds is success.

Unlike traditional positivism, which has trouble explaining judicial behavior in mature legal systems, and the normative theory of law, which has difficulty explaining developing and immature legal systems (for reasons that the first precludes obligations in controversial cases, while the second requires them), law-as-convention positivism understands such duties to be a contingent feature of law that can be explained as arising from the critical acceptance of a practice of dispute resolution, rather than from the principles of morality which judges under one kind of practice might cite.

6. Conclusion

Dworkin makes three correct observations about the controversial nature of some legal standards:

1. A legal system can (and does in the United States and Britain) recognize certain standards as part of the law even though they are "essentially controversial" in the sense that there may be disagreements among judges as to which these are, and there is no decision procedure which, even in principle, can demonstrate what they are, and so settle disagreements.

2. Among such essential controversial legal standards are moral principles owing their status as

law to their being "true" moral principles, though their "truth" cannot be demonstrated by any agreed-upon test.

3. The availability of such controversial principles fills the "gaps" left by ordinary sources of law, which may be partially undetermined, vague or conflicting, so that, at least with respect to the resolution of disputes involving standards subordinate to the rule of recognition, a judge never has to exercise lawmaking power or "discretion" to fill the gaps or remove the indeterminacy if such moral principles are a part of the law.

In this essay, I have drawn distinctions among three versions of positivism and have discussed their relationship to Dworkin's claims: (1) "negative positivism," the view that the legal system need not recognize as law "controversial" moral standards; (2) "positive, hard-facts positivism," the view that controversial standards cannot be regarded as law and, hence, rejects Dworkin's three points; and (3) "positive, social rule positivism," which insists only on the conventional status of the rule of recognition but accepts Dworkin's three points.

Since the inclusion of controversial moral principles is not a necessary feature of the concept of law, Dworkin's arguments to the effect that such principles figure in judicial practice in the United States and England are inadequate to undermine the very weak claim of negative positivism. On the other hand, if Dworkin is right—and I am inclined to think that he is—in thinking that controversial moral principles sometimes figure in legal argument, then any form of positivism that is committed to the essential noncontroversial nature of law is mistaken. Finally, what I have tried to do is to develop a form of positivism which accepts the controversial nature of some legal reasoning, while denying that this is incompatible with the essential, affirmative claim of the theory that law is everywhere conventional in nature. If I am correct, there is a form of positivism which can do justice to Dworkin's insights while rendering his objections harmless.[13]

---

1. Dworkin's claim that positivism is committed to a pedigree standard of legality is too narrow. What he means to argue, I believe, is that positivism is committed to some form of "noncontentful" criterion of legality, of which a pedigree standard would be one. For ease of exposition, I shall use "pedigree

test" broadly to mean any sort of noncontentful criterion of legality.
2. See below, secs. 2 and 5.
3. The phrase "truth as a moral principle and a condition of legality" does seem a bit awkward. However, any other phrase, such

as "morality as a condition of legality" or "moral content as a condition of legality," would be ambiguous, since it would be unclear whether the separability thesis was a claim about the relationship between law and critical morality or between law and conventional morality. My understanding of the separability thesis is as a denial of a constitutive relationship between law and critical morality. Other interpretations of the separability thesis are discussed in the text immediately following this note.

4. This seems to be the form of positivism David Lyons advances to meet Dworkin's objections to positivism. Cf. David Lyons, "Review: Principles, Positivism, and Legal Theory," Yale Law Journal 87 (1977): 415.

5. But see Rolf Sartorius, "Social Policy and Judicial Legislation," American Philosophical Quarterly 8 (1971): 151, and Jules Coleman, "Review: Taking Rights Seriously," California Law Review 66 (1978): 885.

6. See above, note 5.

7. Often overlooked is the fact that there are two distinct arguments for discretion: One relies on the controversial nature of penumbral cases involving general terms; the other relies on the finiteness of legal standards. The first argument is actually rooted in a theory of language; the second, which would survive a rejection of that theory, relies on gaps in the law. See Coleman, above, note 5.

8. Dworkin does not explicitly distinguish among these various arguments, nor does he label any of them. The labels and distinctions are mine.

9. Sartorius, "Social Policy and Judicial Legislation." Dworkin himself discusses, but wrongly rejects, this possibility. See "Model of Rules I," in Ronald Dworkin, Taking Rights Seriously (1977), p. 977. See also C. L. Ten's useful discussion "The Soundest Theory of Law," Mind 88 (1979): 522.

10. There are two ways we might understand the notion of a social rule. Under one interpretation, not every rule of recognition would be a social rule; under the other, each would be. As both Hart and Dworkin use the term, a social rule is a practice, and the nature of the practice determines the scope of the rule and the extent of the duties it imposes. The rule that men must doff their hats upon entering church is a social rule in this sense. Not every rule of recognition, however, is a social rule in this sense, for two reasons. First, at least in some jurisdictions, the content of the rule may be specified prior to the existence of an appropriate practice. For example, the formulation of the Constitution of the United States did not require the existence of the relevant judicial practice; it preceded the practice. No doubt ambiguities and other uncertainties in the rule are resolved through judicial practice; nevertheless, the general form and nature of the rule had been specified without regard to practice. Second, whereas Dworkin's contrast between social rule and normative rule theories of law turns on the manner in which legal rules give rise to duties, the rule of recognition is not itself a duty-imposing rule. We might construct a broader notion of a social rule. In this sense a rule will be a social rule if its existence or authority depends, in part, on the existence of a social practice. Here the requirement is not that the rule's proper formulation be specified by practice. Instead, the claim is that the authority of the rule depends on the existence of a practice. The rule itself may be specifiable, at least in general terms and at some points in time, without regard to the practice. However, in the absence of the practice, the rule is empty in that it is incapable of providing justifications for action. In short, its normativity depends on the practice, though its content need not be specified by it. Every rule of recognition for the positivist is a social rule in this sense.

11. David Lewis, Convention: A Philosophical Study (1969).

12. Gerald Postema has been trying to develop an alternative to the social rule theory that relies heavily on Lewis's theory of conventions. See "Coordination and Convention at the Foundations of Law," Journal of Legal Studies 11 (1982): 165.

13. I have refrained from discussing the argument against positivism that Dworkin advances in his brilliant essay "Hard Cases," because in that essay Dworkin reveals himself to be much more of a conventionalist than he would have us believe. The main purpose of that essay is to provide a theory of adjudication that makes plain the sense in which right answers and judicial obligations exist in controversial cases. If Dworkin makes his case for right answers, positivism—at least versions of it that deny judicial duty in the face of controversy—must be mistaken. Moreover, Dworkin attempts to show that the theory of adjudication which provides right answers necessarily makes morality part of the concept of law. Some comments regarding at least this latter claim are in order. Dworkin's general theory of adjudication may be explicated as follows. A case, A, comes before an appellate judge. The judge must decide whether to give a decision in favor of the defendant (decision D) or in favor of the plaintiff, P. In making his decision, the judge notes that there exists a large body of settled law, S, that is suitably purged of its "mistakes." (Dworkin has a theory of the way in which judges identify mistaken decisions.) Once S has been purged of mistakes, it can be systematized. The judge is required then to construct a theory of law that best explains and justifies S by subsuming S under a set of general principles that constitute the best explanation of S. These principles constitute the soundest theory of the existing law (STL). Dworkin employs the standard philosophic notion of explanation, so that if STL explains S, then S follows logically or theoretically from STL. Once STL is constructed, the judge must ask whether either D or P follows from it. If either statement follows logically from STL, the case presents no problem for the positivist. In the event that neither D nor P follows logically from STL, the case is one that, for the positivists at least, calls for discretion, since both conclusions are equally inadequately warranted by the existing law. Dworkin's theory of adjudication here departs from positivism. For while neither D nor P is entailed by STL, either D or P, but not both, "coheres" of "fits" best with it. While neither a decision in favor of the plaintiff nor one in favor of the defendant is a logical consequence of the soundest theory of law, one, but not the other, is a coherence consequence of it. Whichever is the coherence consequence is the "right" answer, the one the judge is obligated to provide. More important, in determining the right answer the judge is required to invoke consideration of morality, since the soundest theory of law not only explains the settled law but justifies it as well. While I have other systematic objections to the argument for right answers, I doubt that the theory of adjudication Dworkin outlines accurately describes judicial practice everywhere, or that it is a necessary feature of legal practice. More important for our present purposes, the claim that determining right answers necessarily involves a moral theory of law which is incompatible with the conventionalist account of law is simply mistaken. On the contrary, Dworkin's argument is thoroughly conventionalist in nature. First, Dworkin must be committed to some standard version of a rule of recognition, since he is committed to a judge's being able to identify the existing body of settled law. Like the positivists he criticizes, Dworkin is, therefore, committed to an epistemic rule of recognition—at least for determining settled law. In Dworkin's view, the judge must construct a theory of law that explains the settled law once it is discovered. The theory of law consists in a set of principles which explain and justify S. The argument for the claim that the soundest theory of law is a moral theory rests either on the requirement that the principles justify the law or on the claim that the principles which constitute the theory are moral principles. In neither case can the argument be sustained. Dworkin's argument for the justification requirement relies on a deeper principle of political responsibility; the judge must be able to give reasons in support of his decisions by showing a consistency between this and previous, similar cases. The notion of justification, however, is ambiguous. There are both weaker and stronger notions of justification. On the other hand, there is the notion of justifica-

tion that is part of critical morality according to which if a principle or decision is justified it is morally defensible. In this sense, bad law can never be morally justified. But Dworkin (rightly) believes that bad law can be law nonetheless, so he cannot mean that the best theory of law justifies the existing law in the sense that it shows the law to be morally defensible. It is clear, then, that the principle of political responsibility requires the weaker notion of justification. This notion is institu-

tional in nature and is akin to the requirement of consistency or formal justice. This notion of justification does not establish the link between law and critical morality necessary to undermine positivism. The argument that the best theory of law is a moral theory because it consists in a set of moral principles fails primarily because the principles which constitute the best theory do not do so because they are true, but because they best systematize the existing law.

Law from the Perspective of the Judge

THE DILEMMAS OF JUDGES WHO MUST INTERPRET "IMMORAL LAWS"*

Joel Feinberg

Filling in the Gaps in Human Law with Precepts of the Natural Law

Perhaps the most distinctive tenet of natural law theory is that morality—or some sector of morality, notably justice—is not simply a useful criterion for evaluating any given system of human law, and not simply a desirable feature to import into law. In natural law theory, morality is an essential part of law as it is. Some reference to morality (that is, to critical, objective, natural morality, not simply to the conventional morality that happens to prevail in one place or another) must be made as part of the very analysis of what human law is as well as what substantive rules it contains. According to natural law theorists, this connection is a necessary one, derived from conceptual analysis, or definition, of the terms involved. It is not, therefore, a merely contingent connection that could vanish in time as human institutions change.

Legal positivists have been especially puzzled by this claim. What are the ways, they ask, in which human law could be thought to connect with a moral law that is only discovered by human beings, not invented or created by them? One natural law reply is that judges must appeal to natural justice in those "hard cases," as they are called, where the law seems somehow incomplete or indeterminate, yet judgment is required anyway. There are at least three types of hard case. First, the case before the court may be one in which a statute's wording is vague and the court must decide, by eliminating the linguistic indeterminacy, whether a defendant is properly convicted of violating it. Suppose a person is charged with violating a local ordinance against "reckless" or "drunk driving," because while drunk he was discovered riding a horse along the side of a public road. Suppose the facts are not contested. He was drunk; he was on horseback; he was moving along a public road. What is at issue is whether horseback riding is a form of driving. Suppose that because of vagueness the legal issue cannot be settled on linguistic grounds alone. Suppose further that conscientious efforts by the judge to determine the intentions of the original legislators one hundred years earlier are totally frustrated. It is commonly said that, in circumstances like this, where there is a gap in the positive law, the judge is free to legislate on her own and decide the culpability of the horseman on grounds of public policy, including

---

*Written specifically for this book. Previously published in earlier editions.

effects on the economic interests of local businesses. At this point, a somewhat cautious natural law theorist might agree, though his misgivings might lead him to add that, if any principle of natural justice is applicable to the issues in the gap of the positive law, they take instant priority over considerations of any other kind. In fact, insofar as justice does apply in the gap, it is no real gap at all, because natural justice brings with itself a kind of automatic legal relevance. This is especially true when the judge's reasonings "in the gap" lead to results that conflict with principles of fairness that are only implicit in the written part of the law or that can be presumed to apply in the gap simply because it goes without saying that at least some minimal reasonableness is an essential element of law. Minimal reasonableness is, after all, part of the very concept of law, whether put explicitly in the language of a statute or not.

In other words, a vaguely written statute might leave out any mention of fairness or unfairness, in which case, natural justice, though unstated, must be assumed to cover the omission. Or the statute might, in a way, be overwritten, making explicit judgments of fairness that are incorrect, since they conflict with the models of fairness that are a part of natural law. One principle of justice thought to derive from natural law, for example, maintains that justice consists in the exclusion of arbitrary inequalities in the allocation of the benefits or burdens of citizenship. As Aristotle put it, relevantly similar cases are to be treated in similar ways and relevantly dissimilar cases, in dissimilar ways and in direct proportion to the degree of dissimilarity between them.[1] Interpreting relevance can be a difficult matter, but some of the irrelevant dissimilarities, at least, can be easily spotted. In deciding which of two persons, A or B, is to be taxed more heavily, conscripted into military service, awarded the starring role in a stage play,[2] or appointed to an appellate court, skin color, as such, is self-evidently irrelevant. So any rule for settling such matters that treats skin color as relevant, has not excluded the arbitrary. There may or may not exist some cases in which gender *is* relevant. But that there exist *any* such cases at all is controversial and a reason for reserving special scrutiny (as our constitutional tradition puts it) for claims that the dissimilarities between men and women are *ever* relevant. Perhaps women's relative muscular weakness renders them less suitable for heavy physical labor than men, or more vulnerable to harm, say, in military combat. Or perhaps their greater biological fitness for the care of infants gives them a priority for work in maternity wards, etc. The point is that some such *reason* must be offered, defended, and then examined with very careful scrutiny if discriminatory treatment based on gender is to pass the test of natural justice. This test is presumed to be implicit in all substantive legal rules, but should be especially visible where there is an interstice (gap) in the written law.

Natural law theorists are especially persuasive when they point to examples of a kind of unreasonableness that undermines fairness in a perfectly transparent fashion. In these cases the unreasonable claims are in a statute's language when that language is interpreted with almost childish literalness; natural justice, on the other hand, lingers in the interstices, unspoken.

A specimen example is *People v. Johnson,*[3] a New York case from 1967.[4]

> The defendant was charged with the violation of a statute designed to regulate the resale of theatre tickets, in that she did sell two tickets to an opera for $40 each, which tickets were originally priced at $20 each. The court found the defendant not guilty. It appeared that the defendant had purchased the tickets for $20 each in the hope of making them the key to a reunion with her estranged husband. When her husband refused to accompany her, she decided not to attend the opera, and placed an ad in a local newspaper inviting offers to purchase the tickets. In response to the ad a city police inspector telephoned the defendant. He and a policewoman went to the defendant's apartment, agreed upon a price of $40 a ticket, and after the exchange was made the officers disclosed their identity and placed the defendant under arrest, charged with the resale of tickets of admission. . . . The court could not believe that it was the legislative intent to embrace a case such as the one at bar within the ambit of the statute. Rather, the court said, the statute was designed to apply to those engaged in the business of reselling tickets, and the court observed that "business" has been described as a word of large import, rather than a mere isolated transaction. . . . The court found that the prosecution's contention that any sale, even to a relative or friend, of a ticket . . . with or without profit, constituted a violation of the law, was unacceptable, and a reductio ad absurdum [of the prosecution's case].

There was not even an apparent gap in this case. The conflict with justice was located entirely in what was said in the statute and its interpretation by the prosecution. Here the prosecution provided its own interpretation of the imprecise words in the statute in such a way that the words applying to the case at bar were utterly unreasonable and unfair. No statute could be that arbitrary and still be valid law! So, if this statute is valid law, it must be interpreted in such a way that it does not conflict with the minimal rationality and fairness that natural law contributes to all valid human law.

The judge in *People v. Johnson* never mentions natural justice or natural law, but it is not far off the mark to take his case for acquittal to be an appeal to natural justice. Its main argument is not a survey of relevant precedents nor does it depend on the exact language or plain meaning of a statute. There is no insistence on the fact that explicit exceptions do not appear in the wording of the statute. Rather, the judge relies on the conviction that neither valid law nor legislative intent could be as crazy as this statute is when it is not understood to contain tacit exceptions. And when the exceptions are made explicit by sensible judicial interpretation, the statute is seen to be reasonable.

I trust that it is not too misleading to characterize an argument as an appeal to "natural justice" if it appeals to a fairness or reasonableness that is based upon considerations other than or in addition to "the letter of the law." Some will appeal to standard rational principles of justice, like the Aristotelian exclusion of arbitrary inequalities or the principle of fair opportunity. Tacit appeals to natural justice then can be used to support an interpretation of a legal judgment or rule, on the one hand, or a declaration of its validity or invalidity, on the other. Typically, such appeals are used, as in *People v. Johnson,* both to support an interpretation and in an intertwined fashion, a judgment of validity or invalidity. The interpretation of this statute must be so and so because, otherwise, the statute would be laughably unreasonable and cryably unfair, hence invalid, even though we didn't think of it as invalid in the beginning. That is one way the argument might go. Alternatively, it might concede that the statute is properly interpreted as such and such and then judge it invalid because it leads to extreme unfairness, as properly interpreted, and valid law cannot be that unjust.

How severely unfair must a statute be if it is properly to be declared invalid on the ground of conflict with natural justice? The difficulty of this ques-

tion is perhaps the chief impediment in the way of accepting the natural law doctrine as a theory of legal validity. Cicero, Augustine, and Aquinas all espoused the doctrine (or at least gave lip service to it) that *lex iniusta non est lex* (an unjust law is no law at all). When we think of cases like *People v. Johnson*—or, better, those actual or hypothetical cases like *People v. Johnson* except that interpretations like the prosecution's in that case are explicitly endorsed in the statute itself—we can be very easily tempted by the *"non est lex"* position. But it is a sobering thought that many or most statutes accepted as valid by the courts, partly because of the legitimacy of their origins (the procedures by which they were enacted) are at least to some degree unfair to someone or other. Some are extremely unfair to whole classes of people. Sales taxes, for example, since they are regressive, hurt the poor more than the wealthy. As a result, they are unfair, but even the thousands of citizens who share that opinion recognize, nevertheless, that the statutes imposing the taxes are valid laws creating moral obligations to comply. It is almost impossible to imagine the chaos that would result if everyone honestly believed that unjust laws are not laws at all, but only acts of force obliging compliance without morally obligating anyone to comply.

In addition to statutes whose key words (like "drive") are vague, there are at least two other types of situation that can seem to present judges with gaps, or interstices, in the law. A second type of hard case results from another class of words used in the formulation of legal rules and principles, those that express what have come to be known as essentially contested concepts. In an example of Ronald Dworkin's,[5] a statute may render void all "sacrilegious" contracts, requiring a judge to decide in a particular case whether a contract signed on a Sunday is truly sacrilegious. Similarly, a court may have to decide whether a lower judge's sentencing of a convicted criminal is truly "cruel"; or whether a given price is "just compensation"; or whether some behavior was "due," "reasonable," or "appropriate" in the circumstances. According to some theories at least, the judge is on her own in these cases too; she must apply her own moral standards—that is, what she honestly believes are the objectively correct moral standards—to the case at issue. Insofar as the law requires the judge to speak first as a moralist and only then as a jurist, these are hard cases too.

Finally there are cases that are hard because they are "cases of first impression" with no binding precedent nor even a close analogy to any prior cases in the judge's jurisdiction. The lack of precedent may be because the facts are novel or it may be because, though the facts are familiar, the bringing of a suit under those facts is unprecedented. In the former category are recent suits for the custody of frozen embryos or for the removal of feeding tubes from a patient in a persistent vegetative state. In the second category, to select just one example, was the first tort suit for emotional damage to a relative of the direct victim of a negligently caused accident.

In both types of hard case described in the preceding two paragraphs, the judge appears to be required not only to legislate, but to legislate in a special way, not by appealing to general policy considerations as a genuine legislature might do, or to a guess about "legislative intentions," or a dictionary's description of the common usage of words like *drive, death* (in the feeding tubes case), or *damage.* Rather, the judge is called upon to decide the case—if it is to be decided at all—by affirming and defending a substantive moral judgment and thus engaging in a type of reasoning for which the written law provides very little guidance. Is it *fair* to make a negligent motorist pay for a purely psychological kind of suffering, with no physical basis, of the direct victim's aunt who learns in a telephone call of injury to her nephew? Is it fair, to a husband filing for divorce from his wife, for the wife to preserve, over his protest, the embryo that they had earlier agreed to create by the fertilization in vitro of her ovum by his sperm, for implantation in her womb? Which is the more important interest here: the wife's interest at the age of forty in bearing a child of her own (this may be her last chance) or her ex-husband's desire not to have a child of his raised by a biological mother he despises? Is a contract signed on the sabbath truly sacrilegious? All of these questions are issues some judge had once to decide, with clear guidance neither from statute nor precedent, but only by the application of some commonly acknowledged or rationally certified principle of natural justice to an unusual-fact situation. Critics of "judicial activism"[6] often say that this construal of the situation suffers the fatal flaw of permitting the judge to apply *her own* values or appeal to *her own* moral convictions as if it would be better if she appealed to someone else's moral principles that she does not personally share. Of course the principles she uses must be "her own"—that is, principles that she genuinely believes in. Otherwise, her opinion in the case would lack conviction and she would lack sincerity and integrity. Those principles, however, are

relevant and proper not because they are hers. Rather, they are hers because she thinks they are cogent for quite independent reasons, because the reasoning that leads her to them is sound, and because the principle of natural justice that she invokes is correct. There can be no certainty about that, of course, but practical certainty is hard to come by even in those complex legal decisions that confront no gap, involve no purely moral reasoning, and require no leap across the chasm to natural justice.

Natural Law as a Handful of Partly Uninterpreted Abstract Principles

If any of the propositions of the natural law are in some sense a part of the human law too, it must be the more abstract ones. The natural law itself should be thought of as more like a constitution than a municipal code and not at all like the complete set of particularized rules both procedural and substantive—that is, statutes, judgments, and judicial precedents. Some book collections of rules require whole buildings for their storage. The natural law may be a collection of principles, precepts, and very general rules; if so, it is a collection of only the most general of them, before they are actually applied to fact situations. The result of their application will be particularized rules about safety precautions in boiler factories; hours in which the drivers of ice cream trucks are permitted to ring bells; the maximal percentage of alcohol permitted in the blood of car drivers, but perhaps not horse and mule drivers; distinctions between grades of burglary; etc. (I deliberately make this list as miscellaneous as possible. I don't think that Aquinas, for example, conceived of the natural law as even mentioning alcohol, ice cream, gasoline combustion vehicles, boiler factories, and so on. It is more likely, I think, that the natural law resembles the Ten Commandments, or perhaps a small, very small, list of maxims of justice, all put in the abstract, like Aristotle's formulae for distinguishing between genuine equality of treatment and invidious discrimination. The United States Constitution, with its Bill of Rights and its Fourteenth Amendment, come to think of it, might make a better model than even the Ten Commandments and the conclusions of Aristotle's theory of distributive justice. In short, if we wrote down the "natural law," it might appear as a list of ten or twelve moral judgments of a very abstract kind and the whole printed document might be no more than two or three pages long. Perhaps there could be a single ultimate principle, or two or three. Indeed, John Rawls sums everything up in two principles of justice; his utilitarian opponents, in one.[7] Blackstone wrote that we should live honestly, should hurt nobody, and should render to everybody his due, "to which three general precepts Justinian has reduced the whole doctrine of law."[8]) Less abstract but more thorough philosophers might formulate the requirements of equal justice; several more principles of liberty; and still a few others, spelling out the principles of autonomy (what is now misleadingly called "privacy"[9]). Absolute orders of priority among the principles, to guide judges to decisions in cases where principles seem to conflict, would probably be impossible. No mechanical decision procedure in these cases could substitute for moral sensibility, analogical reasoning, and Solom- onic wisdom.[10] A statement of the full content of natural law would not only contain the principles that protect citizens from their governments, but also the principles that protect them from each other. Those principles might include the most general—responsibility, justification, and excuse—as well as the first principles of tort and contract liability, child custodianship, and property rights. Perhaps our full statement of the natural law at this point would come to seven or eight printed pages, a statement longer than the Ten Commandments but approximately the same length as the Constitution with its amendments. In fact, a system of human law that consisted of no more than that brief statement of natural law would be very much like one that could lead judges to leap to the constitutional level immediately in every case, a system that could cut the rest of the law adrift.

We can think of the abstract natural law precepts, in this model, as related in one or both of two ways to the more particular judgments and rules of the human law with which they exist. Natural law functions both as a progenitor of human law rules or a standard of legitimacy by which the complex and particularized rules are judged valid or not. Typically, I should think, the general (natural) and particular (positive) rules are not allowed to conflict because the natural rules have themselves been used to produce the positive ones, by application to ever more complex factual circumstances and ever more refined restatements of the generating rules themselves as they spin off exceptive clauses and the like. If a generating rule seems to conflict with some of its offspring, it is understandable that, other things

being equal, the more concrete derived judgments should be the ones that are invalidated, since they are inconsistent with the rational precepts that were to have produced them in the first place.

Consequently, a town ordinance that permits blacks to sit only in the back row of a public bus is flatly inconsistent with a precept of natural law requiring that law not be used to enforce arbitrary inequalities. In that case the ordinance, in contradicting a principle of justice, is itself shown to be unjust and, therefore (the difficult step), legally invalid. As Cicero and Augustine would have said, it is as if there were no law (governing the distribution of bus seats by race) at all. It is instead just a blunt and forcible way of putting blacks in their place, as guns or clubs might do. The American Supreme Court came to the same result (*non est lex*) *not explicitly via natural law,* but in virtue of the supreme authority of the *U.S. Constitution,* whose Fourteenth Amendment is itself subject to a kind of natural law interpretation, especially when it invites its judicial interpreters to apply moral standards of what is fitting, appropriate, due, reasonable, unreasonable, cruel, excessive, impartial, equal, private, and so on. Where can the judge turn to find answers to subtle moral questions if not to the objective moral judgments discovered by reason rather than merely invented to serve one's pleasure? That zone, the argument concludes, is the realm of natural law.

Some natural law theorists, of whom Blackstone is perhaps the most typical example, give more than a routine respectful nod to positive law. They believe that positive law rightfully prevails *except* where it contains "flat absurdity or injustice."[11] Only when it is extremely unfair and downright irrational is an otherwise legitimate positive law invalidated by its content. This seems to be simply another way of saying that positive law is to prevail except where it contains a gap but that, within the gap and until it is closed by the enactment of new positive law, natural law is to prevail. If the natural law in the gap conflicts with the positive law that surrounds the gap, then positive law wins out. In these respects, this interstitial theory of natural law is the very opposite of the "higher law" version of the natural law theory associated with Ghandi and Martin Luther King, Jr.

From examples like this we can see that positivists often differ only in degree and emphasis from other positivists, just as natural law partisans often differ only in such ways from other natural law advocates. Each group of philosophers contains people who respect both established law and its duties of fidelity and obedience, on the one hand, and precepts of justice with their duties of reasonable fairness, on the other. Given the conflicting claims to superior authority of these positive and natural rules, it is not surprising that some nominal positivists bend over backward to accommodate natural justice,[12] and some natural law theorists in their writings make at least a respectful nod to such positivist precepts as that expressed by *stare decisis*.[13]

Even pure positivists who insist that law is one thing and morality another, and never shall the one concept be reduced to the other, are likely, as we have seen, to interpret what their rivals call natural law as a set of objective criteria for evaluating a given statute or a given set of established positive rules as good or bad, just or unjust, efficient or cumbersome. They agree with their natural law friends that positive law *ought* to be just and that the criteria of justice are themselves objective truths accessible to reason, denying only that these standards of evaluation are themselves actually part of the law. The positivist writers, on the other hand, who are most respectful of natural law are those described above who would let enacted or judicially established law prevail except where there are gaps in the positive law itself. These gaps are a consequence of the open texture of language, the unavoidability of essentially contested concepts in the wording of statutes and constitutions, and the legal vacuums produced by unprecedented factual circumstances. Such vacuums are often the consequence of new technology or sometimes simply a reflection of the fact that every precedent in the law is a link in a chain of cases that goes back to an original precedent that was itself decided in the absence of still earlier relevant precedent. Some otherwise positivist judges would insist that courts always decide these cases of first impression on moral grounds, by appealing directly to natural justice, for example. Anti-slavery judges in the nineteenth century, torn apart by the conflict between their anti-slavery consciences and their sworn duty as judges to uphold the established law, tried hard to reinterpret some laws regarded by their colleagues as established. These judges tried to show that the laws were not really established, because gaps existed in them. In some of these instances it was difficult to know whether to classify the judge as a positivist or a natural law theorist, since he tried so hard to find gaps in the positive law into which he could cram as much natural law as possible.

Most of the theories about how morality or natural law is related to positive or human law are, in one of the ways discussed, compromises between two distinct and often conflicting kinds of value. At one extreme, we have the higher law version of natural law theory, which pays little respect to positive law as such. (The fact that segregation statutes in the South were properly enacted by legitimate rule-making bodies had very little weight with them.) At the other extreme, pure positivism, even when sympathetic to the goal of suffusing more justice into the law, had no sympathy for the view that *lex iniusta non est lex*, that unjust requirements are already excluded from law by definition. Apart from these groups, the other theories can be understood as efforts somehow to have it both ways, to be a natural law theorist who respects the moral importance of established law or a positivist with a very tender sense of justice, particularly pertaining to the operations of his or her country's legal system. These matters may seem at first to be merely problems for scholars and philosophers trying to achieve consistency, but when we turn to the moral obligation of obedience to law, we soon discover that they mask conflicts of practical commitment, sometimes with matters of life or death riding on their outcome.

Fuller, Radbruch, and Hart: The German Experience with Nazism

Perhaps the most influential of the non-Thomist natural law theories in the twentieth century was that of Lon Fuller. Fuller insisted on the essential connection between law and morality, but his secularized version of legal naturalism had no theological grounding. Moreover, morality provides criteria, in Fuller's view, for the existence of a *legal system,* not criteria for the validity of a single rule or statute. It is possible then, according to Fuller, for an unjust law to be a valid law. But if the whole network of rules and rule-making powers, or a substantial subsection thereof, is antithetical to morality, then it is no longer a functioning legal system; it is, at best, another method of social control based on arbitrary power.

The morality that Fuller held essential to the existence of a legal system is wholly procedural and does not apply directly to the substantive content of regulations and statutes. Fuller denied that there is some higher law, external to established law, to which the latter must correspond if it is to exist. The morality that is essential to law Fuller calls "the internal morality of law" or "the morality that makes law possible." In his book *The Morality of Law* he sketches the principles of this internal morality:[14]

1. The rules must be general and not mere ad hoc commands.
2. There can be no secret (unpromulgated) rules.
3. There can be no retroactive rules.
4. The rules must be understandable by those to whom they apply.
5. The rules must not be either self-contradictory or contradictory as a group.
6. The rules must not demand actions that are beyond their subjects' powers to perform.
7. The rules must not be constantly changing.
8. There must be some minimal correspondence between what the rules say and how they are administered or interpreted by the courts.

A total failure in respect to any one of these principles, or a partial failure in respect to most or all of them, implies not simply that there is a bad legal system, but that there is not a legal system at all.

One consequence of Fuller's conception is that the existence of a legal system is always a matter of degree, since the degree of conformity to the internal morality of law can itself be a matter of degree. Some critics of Fuller found degrees of existence to be an odd notion. Other critics, including even some who could make sense of it, objected to Fuller's use of the word "morality" for the principles of order that make a legal system, whether just or not, workable. "Why not call them the conditions for effective lawmaking, or the maxims of legal craftsmanship?" they asked. A traditional legal naturalist might say of some particular positive law of the Nazi era, "This is so evil, it cannot be a law." In most of these cases, Fuller claims, one could usually have said instead: "This thing is a product of a system so oblivious to the (inner) morality of law that it is not entitled to be called a law."

In their famous debate in *The Harvard Law Review* in 1958 and 1959, Fuller and H. L. A. Hart differed over the legal consequences in the postwar period of actions performed under the laws (pseudo-laws?) of the Nazi regime. Fuller staunchly defended, and Hart respectfully criticized, the position of Gustav Radbruch. Radbruch, once a leading German legal positivist, had converted to a traditional natural law theory in his efforts to deal with the claims of German citizens in response to moral outrages against them in the Nazi era by acts that were considered perfectly legal at the time committed. Despite their philosophical differences over the relations between law and morality, Radbruch, Hart, and Fuller came to similar practical conclusions. German citizens had been under no overriding moral obligation to obey the Nazi statutes, they all concluded. Fuller held this view because the statutes were the product of a system that could not claim to be a legal system; Radbruch, because the individual statutes were too evil to be legally valid; and Hart, because the statutes, though legally valid, were too morally evil to be obeyed, since there are moral obligations that can, in given cases, outweigh the moral obligation to obey valid law.

These differences were so subtle that some commentators suspected that they were theoretically insignificant. Lloyd L. Weinreb, for example, asked "Can it possibly make so much difference whether we say, 'This enactment is too immoral to obligate us; therefore it is not law' or 'This law is too immoral to obligate us; therefore it ought not to be obeyed?'"[15] It is easy to sympathize with Weinreb's complaint, but in what space remains, I shall try to clarify the controversy and reformulate the obedience problem in a way that recaptures its importance and its poignancy. Most but by no means all writers believe that there is a moral obligation to obey the valid laws of one's community, especially in a country that is genuinely democratic and by and large just.[16] In the past I have had some difficulty accepting the arguments usually made in support of this belief, but I must admit that it has almost a common-sense status for the great majority of people who hold it, so I am more than willing to assume it here for the sake of argument. To affirm it, after all, is very much like saying that there is a moral obligation to keep one's promises or to tell the truth. Notoriously, life is capable of creating circumstances in which these "moral obligations" conflict so that, whatever one does, one will be violating at least one of them. So, for example, there may be circumstances such that, if I tell the truth, I will be breaking a promise and, if I keep my promise, I will be telling a lie. Instead of concluding that whatever we do in those circumstances will be wrong, philosophers have reinterpreted the moral principles, imposing the duties as conditional. We have a general moral obligation to tell the truth, for example, except when we are under another moral obligation that is even more stringent in the circumstances, and there may indeed be such a conflicting obligation. Moral obligations, then, do differ in degrees of stringency, or weight, and vary in such a way that it is impossible in the abstract to formulate a hierarchy of weightiness on the moral scales, a hierarchy that will hold whatever the circumstances are like. In some circumstances the duty to tell the truth takes priority; in others, the duty to keep a promise. It all depends on the circumstances.

According to H. L. A. Hart, we do have a moral obligation to obey any valid law, even an unjust or evil one. But we also have a moral obligation to oppose injustice and, when a valid law reaches a certain degree of evil, the obligation to obey is outweighed by an even more stringent moral obligation to resist. Insofar as the statute in question is a valid one, we are tugged one way; insofar as it is immoral, it tugs in the other—sometimes it tugs even harder. The moral obligation to obey the law is an example, therefore, of what some writers call a prima facie obligation (abbreviated henceforth as PFO).

Not in every case is a PFO a decisive moral reason, but it is always a relevant supporting reason and one that would be conclusive if no other relevant reason of greater strength applied to the situation. Hart's account is "candid," he says, because it allows us to say both of these things: that the validity of an applicable rule is always a reason, and a powerful one, for obeying it (or if one is a judge, for applying it), but that it is not necessarily a decisive reason when it comes into conflict with moral PFOs of other kinds. This account, Hart maintains, explains exactly and truly what we are doing when we conscientiously disobey the law. We are acting illegally and we know it. Fidelity to enacted law is morally required of us, but it is not the whole of what is morally required of us. Some things, at some times, may be even more important morally, and it is disingenuous to label these things as law too. That would be to disguise even from ourselves what we are really doing—namely, deliberately disobeying the law for the sake of something we deem more important.

Duty Versus Conscience: The American Experience with Slavery

Some of the moral duties generally believed to be created by laws are private duties—for example, the negative duties not to harm others or to be rude or tactless to them, and the positive duties to be sociable and cooperative. Some of the private duties can be interpreted as the duties of a *citizen:* to stay informed, to vote, to pay one's bills and taxes. Still others are the duties of a *neighbor:* to maintain the exterior appearances of one's property and to be prepared to help one's neighbors in emergencies and, at any time, to do minor favors, like taking in a neighbor's mail when she is on vacation. Examples of these kinds might tempt us to the view that all duties are in a sense public—that is, derived from one's occupancy of an office in some institution. The temptation is reinforced by our ability, usually, to add the words *as an office holder* to our description of our own duties. I have duties not only as a citizen and as a neighbor, but also as a father and as a husband, and some of my duties are as a teacher or policeman (or whatever my job happens to be). A family is a relatively private sort of institution—compared, say, to a corporation or a jury—but it is some sort of institution. And there are still other duties that are more private still, deriving from no institutional office at all, public or private, but rather from my status as a human being among other mostly unrelated human beings. Our duties to strangers encountered in lonely places (our duties not to beat and rob them, for example) are duties we have simply as human beings, not as institutional office holders of any kind—not private, like the family, not more public, like the employer-corporation.

On the other hand, many of our more important and determinate duties are near the public end of the spectrum. A so-called public official is a person with a very specific set of duties derived from his or her job. These public duties are added to those moral duties that the official shares with everyone. Some public officials, like tenured judges, hold their offices for extended periods of time. Others occupy temporary offices created for specific tasks. A good example of the latter would be the office of juror in a public trial in a criminal court. To understand what it is to be a judge or a juror is just to know what the duties are that define the job. Those duties then descend on a person when he or she is actually sworn in as a judge or juror. What creates the special duties of the job is often an oath in which the designate swears to discharge the job-defining duties to the best of personal ability.

The juror solemnly promises to obey the judge's instructions, chief among which is to base one's verdict strictly on the evidence and find the defendant guilty only if the presented evidence establishes guilt beyond a reasonable doubt. It is also the juror's duty to vote for the defendant's acquittal if and only if the evidence leaves a reasonable doubt of guilt. From a solemn promise, sworn in a public oath, derives the juror's clear duty not to acquit unless the evidence does leave the required residue of doubt. And yet the court, in a number of ways, seems almost to encourage juries to cheat! The jury members, for example, have both a *moral duty* to honor their oath and (let us imagine) to convict the accused thereby, and a *legal power* to acquit without answering to anyone. Jury deliberations are secret, they are not subject to review after the trial; jurors may not be subjected to any penalty for bad judgment or for dereliction of official duty; and acquittal verdicts may not be appealed or overturned because of the constitutional protection against double jeopardy. It is evident that there is no way to prevent a jury from acquitting a clearly guilty defendant when conviction would offend their consciences— when, for example, the jurors must pass judgment on a clearly guilty eight-year-old child charged with stealing a turnip during the early Victorian period, when such a petty theft was a capital crime. In such cases the jury knows that it can set the child free by "voting its conscience" instead of doing its duty. And yet juries are instructed that they have, individually and collectively, an unqualified duty to follow the judge's instructions and put their consciences aside as they decide on guilt or innocence according to the evidence alone. Each juror takes a solemn oath to do just that. So it appears that the law, in a perfectly explicit way, confers a power on juries to do what they have an equally explicit duty not to do.

As things now stand, conscientious jurors in morally difficult cases are in an unenviable position. From the purely legal standpoint, their position is not so difficult. Their duty is to decide according to the evidence only. If the evidence leaves no reasonable doubt of guilt, their duty is to convict. But human beings are more than the sum of the duties of their stations, and the morally right way to act may violate any given one of their official duties or even the sum total of their duties on balance. What morality requires of a person, in morally difficult circumstances, is not something to be mechanically determined by an examination of the person's office or role-centered duties. An individual must on rare occasions have the courage to rise above all that and obey the dictates of conscience. One's conscience may be wholly convincing, considered only on its own terms. But its conflict with duty will nevertheless make the occasion for decision morally complex and difficult. It is no laughing matter, morally speaking, deliberately to violate one's own privately acknowledged duties, and our public institutions would be gravely endangered if their officials as a matter of routine were prepared to do that. The circumstances must be extreme, and the emphasis on duty strong and unremitting, if an official is even to consider such a drastic course. A

juror has no moral right to violate the solemn oath on the ground that there would probably be some unfairness in punishing the defendant, even though he or she is plainly guilty, or because the juror disapproves of the statute the defendant is charged with breaking. Rather, the jurors must place a substantial surcharge[17] on departures from their official obligations. Conviction must seem more than unfair; it must seem unconscionable, a gross injustice given the defendant's undeniable moral right to do what he or she did. A single juror who makes these moral judgments can nullify the judge's instructions quite surreptitiously, so that no one will ever know what has happened. Sometimes, in morally desperate circumstances, that is what a juror should do, since secret nullification does less damage to a just institution (jury trials as currently instituted) than open and clear nullification would do. But departures from duty—any duty—should never be taken lightly.

The Moral Duties of Judges

When we discuss disobedience of ordinary citizens, either to the validly enacted statutes of their communities or to the rules defining their own official roles, if any, in their community's legal system, the quarrels between positivists and natural law theorists are likely to seem arid and picky. What difference does it make, we might ask in our impatience, whether this extremely unjust statute is too wicked really to be a statute at all (despite its impeccable pedigree), as the natural law theorist might maintain, or that it is a legal statute all right, but one that is too wicked to obey, as the positivist would have it? The positivist would admit that, insofar as it is a valid statute, he or she has a moral obligation to obey it, but argue that that prima facie obligation (PFO) has little weight when placed on the scales against stronger PFOs that will outweigh it in these circumstances. In any event, the positivist and the natural law theorist will be allies against any wicked dictatorship that tries to disguise its unjust commands by representing them as valid law (as they may or may not be). Neither will have any respect for the egregiously unjust content of the law, or pseudo-law, that they disobey. So what practical difference can there be between them, and between the legal philosophies they espouse?

The conscientious judge's situation is quite different, especially when he or she is a judge in the nation's highest appellate court. This judge will have a conscience that could on occasion be in conflict with the duties of office, duties the judge has solemnly sworn to discharge. But the judge does not have legal power of the same degree of effectiveness as that of the ordinary citizen or the juror. Paradoxically, the higher we climb in the court system, the less effective power to breach official duties do we find. I suspect that is because the duties themselves, at that level, are regarded with awe and thought to be of maximal or supreme stringency. After all, the Supreme Court justice has solemnly, and with great publicity, sworn to uphold the highest source of law in the land, the Constitution itself. No justice can take *that* duty lightly. Moreover, the Supreme Court judge is not protected by the same degree of secrecy as the mere juror. Nor can he or she so easily escape sanctions afterward. The Supreme Court justice is subject to impeachment, and subject to great social pressure to give an accounting of each judicial decision and mode of argument. Such a judge is not truly free to be candid and confess that he or she knowingly violated a most sacred promise to the public and did so in order to satisfy personal conscience. Very likely the critics will respond that a willingness to break so important a promise betrays not so much a sensitive conscience as a conscience insensitive to the moral bindingness of voluntary commitments.

It is puzzling to know how to exercise our terminological options in this situation. Most of us, I think, would be made uncomfortable by talk of a conflict between duty and conscience. After all, our ordinary role- or job-connected duties also have a voice in the chorus that is conscience. Moreover, a person could say without being incoherent that conscience forbids him or her from being derelict in (other) duties, or that he or she has a duty to obey conscience. And yet there *is* an intuitive distinction between, say, my duty as a teacher and all or most of my other duties combined. The collective voice of the other duties may have the timbre and tone that we attribute to conscience.

The best historical example of an intractable struggle within the forum of a judge's mind between the duties of public office and the duties of private conscience is that which tormented large sections of the American judiciary in the decades preceding the Civil War. A number of distinguished judges of profound and genuine abolitionist convictions, men who hated slavery with an intense moral passion, struggled to reconcile their consciences with what looked like their plain constitutional duty: the duty to order the return of escaped slaves to their southern masters. On one side of these intrapersonal conflicts was a role-duty as stringent and weighty on the moral scales as role-duties ever are, partly because it derived from the most basic source of law in our legal system, the Constitution itself, and partly because it was so undeniably explicit, precise, and unambiguous. On the other side was a moral consensus against human slavery. This consensus dated back to the early Christians, Stoic philosophers, and even Roman jurists and included the leading political philosophers of the seventeenth and eighteenth centuries—Locke, Puffendorf, Montesquieu—and the ideological fathers of the French and American Revolutions. Every schoolchild could recite passages from the Declaration of Independence; the Constitutional Preamble; and the speeches of Patrick Henry, Madison, and Jefferson (ironically, all from the southern slave-holding state of Virginia). These works affirmed the natural rights of *all* people, whatever the positive laws of their governments might say or leave unsaid, to the contrary. Moreover, these rights were said to be noncontroversial because their existence was *self-evident.* Taken together, all this authority constituted as powerful a display of intellectual reinforcement for a consensus of conscience that anyone could ever hope for, even though much of its support under pressure turned out to be mere lip service and political rhetoric.

By 1850, most of the American judiciary joined most of the educated public in thinking of the Constitution, in critical part, as a compromise over slavery.[18] The compromise consisted of the agreement of the slave-holding states to join the union, provided that the new nation's Constitution recognized and promised to preserve the legal legitimacy of slavery in those states that wanted to keep the practice. Those who were impressed by this interpretation could point to five provisions in the original Articles that were evidence for it, chief of which was "the bloody clause," as Wendell Phillips called it.[19] This clause was the original fugitive slave provision, the price paid by the free states, according to the Great Compromise theory, for having the benefits of an enlarged union from the beginning of national independence. The fugitive slave clause in the original federal Constitution (superseded after the Civil War by the Thirteenth Amendment) declared that

> No person held to service or labor in one
> state, under the law thereof, escaping into
> another, shall, in consequence of any law or
> regulation therein, be discharged from such

service or labor, but shall be delivered up on claim of the party to whom such service or labor may be due.

Thus, if Massachusetts enacted a statute requiring that fugitive slaves be fully liberated upon crossing their borders and permitted to stay on, as free persons in permanent residence there, the statute would be clearly unconstitutional; it would be void ab initio in virtue of this clause. Slave owners from the escaped slave's state could then dispatch slave hunters to Massachusetts to capture the escapee; certify with the local authorities that the hunter was reclaiming his employer's property; and return the wretched slave, in shackles, to servitude. Periodically, the slave would be intercepted by local citizens and rescued, at least for a time. Often these conflicts got into the courts, as would-be rescuers and their aiders and abettors appealed convictions for interfering with property, or the slave owners petitioned for return of their property. Almost invariably the slavers triumphed in court, in virtue of that inescapable barrier to justice and humanity, the bloody clause. It cannot have been a pleasant experience for the judges, particularly those of abolitionist conviction and natural law philosophy. In his penetrating history of the legal struggles against slavery in the first half of the nineteenth century, Robert Cover distinguishes five possible responses of a judge caught in the grip of a duty-versus-conscience struggle.[20] (Actually he mentions only four choices, but a fifth is clearly implicit in his discussion.)

1. He may apply the law against his conscience.
2. He may apply conscience and be faithless to the law.
3. He may resign.
4. Or he may cheat, [and] state that the law is not what he believes it to be, and thus preserve an appearance (to others) of the conformity to law and morality.

Finally, there is a fifth possibility. The judge may adopt an ameliorist solution. He "may introduce his own sense of what 'ought to be' interstitially, where no hard law yet exists."[21]

All five of these choices were actually made and/or advocated by otherwise abolitionist judges. Most of them stopped resisting the clear language of the bloody clause. There it was in plain English, a clear constitutional recognition of slavery. Clearly, a given judge's duty as a judge was to obey the explicit dictates of a Constitution that could no longer

be respected and morally embraced. It was of course a literal bloody shame that thousands of human beings were oppressed and, at best, treated as animals. But it must be remembered that such results are not the personal responsibility of the judge but, rather, commands of the impersonal voice of the law. The judge's job is to discover the law and then be its voice, totally uninfluenced by his personal opinions, even by his moral convictions. He can say "Not I, directly or indirectly . . . but the law, which is given to me and is my master, says thus."[22]

At first that kind of political eloquence functioned primarily as a line of defense for the judge. As such, it was an argument from humility, more a self-minimizing kind of apology than a full-blooded justification. But the fuller justification, usually forthcoming, was simply to opt for legal positivism, except perhaps in respect to those gaps in the positive law, where one can hope to introduce natural law interstitially in virtue of "a sort of bend-over-backward principle . . . an obligation to achieve a profreedom [anti-slavery] result unless there is a very specific, concrete positive law that prevents it."[23] Perhaps it was possible at the time of the Constitutional Convention to deny that the fugitive slave clause was specific or concrete. But the fugitive slave clause was a kind of invitation to Congress and to state legislatures to provide their own detailed implementation language. The Fugitive Slave Acts of 1793 and 1850 enjoined very specific procedures to be used in capturing and returning fugitive slaves— none of which were at all advantageous to the fugitive. Northern abolitionists loudly accused Congress of interfering with (more irony) states' rights, in particular the Constitutional rights of the states to establish their own rules providing more due process for the prisoner and his rescuers both (including a jury trial guaranteed elsewhere in the Constitution). By 1850 very few interstices were left in those statutes that further restricted the rights of the escaped slave. By then the bend-over-backward principle was rarely used and, in fact, often explicitly rejected. Ameliorist natural law theories intended only for that diminishing interstitial area of the positive law tended to be absorbed by the "legal duty" option and the legal positivism that was its foundation.

The second option was for the judge to abandon the very law he was sworn to apply and to apply instead the dictates of his own conscience. It is difficult to understand, of course, how such reasonings could be explained by the judge in presenting his conclusions to the public. Could he write an opinion affirming his conscientious conviction that slavery is monumental injustice and cruelty, rejected almost everywhere as contrary to the laws of nature (morality) and therefore impossible for a right-thinking person to promote? Could he continue by pointing out that his clear legal duty would require that he contribute to the strengthening of slavery and that, therefore, he had decided to reject his legal duty (his duty as a judge) and vote instead for the position recommended by his conscience? It would be acceptable to the public if he affirmed those premises but drew a different conclusion from them—namely, that he must resign his appointment as a judge immediately and not take part at all in the legal proceedings that are already under way. That is the third option, resignation, a choice that was very popular with abolitionist judges. But that is altogether different from saying "I know my duty but I am not going to do it. I will do what is contrary to my duty instead." I can imagine that universal condemnation and impeachment would await the judge at the end of that line. And his colleagues would hector him repeatedly about what the legal system would be like if every judge felt free to renounce his duty whenever it conflicted with one of his own moral beliefs.

The resignation option was chosen by Wendell Phillips, who not only resigned his own judgeship, but wrote a book advocating resignation by public officials and the organizing of a political party encouraging withdrawal and noncooperation. In his book[24] Phillips quotes from the letter of resignation of one Francis Jackson, who wrote that

> "The oath to support the Constitution of the United States is a solemn promise to do that which is a violation of the natural rights of man, and a sin in the sight of God. . . . I withdraw all profession of allegiance to it [The Constitution] and all my voluntary efforts to sustain it." . . . More and more, it appeared the question ought not to be put, "How should a judge of integrity decide these cases?" but rather "How can a man of integrity judge these cases [at all]?"

The making of dramatic resignations conjures up pictures of heroic resistance, but in some instances there is a suspicion that *self-indulgence* might be the better term. If a judge's resignation is motivated entirely by his desire to preserve his own moral purity, so that his hands will not be soiled with the blood of others, then he makes a poor hero, though his conduct on his own behalf might have required considerable courage. But wouldn't a more fruitful use of his courage and a craftier use of the power of his office, if any, be more commendable? What help does he give the suffering slaves by concentrating his efforts on his own integrity? I suspect that efforts to preserve integrity in situations like these will inevitably be self-defeating, because true integrity requires more effective resistance and less narcissistic self-concern. "It is a waste to refuse to use accessible power for a good purpose. . . ."[25]

Few did, and few would now, embrace the fourth choice, requiring the conscientious but frustrated judge to cheat. That can hardly be the kind of advice that one would expect to find in a law manual, a text, or casebook. The advice to violate legal norms in order to avoid morally unacceptable results cannot itself be a legal norm; an enumeration of the duties of a judge can hardly include the duty to cheat when there is no other way to produce a just result. Still, we should note that the moral situation of an abolitionist judge at a hearing concerning the fate of an escaped slave is basically no different from that of a juror in a trial of an eight-year-old child for the capital offense of stealing a turnip from a neighbor's fields. The main relevant differences are that the juror's cheating is secret and may never be known; the judge's opportunities are not as great. Moreover, the judge speaks officially on behalf of the nation's legal system; the juror speaks only to a question of fact. The juror's "cheating" consists simply in lying about those facts in order to prevent suffering and injustice. Both the juror and the judge must pay a price for the nullification they achieve by their untruthfulness. But we are all threatened more by the judge, who because of greater visibility and greater impact generally, has a greater potential for harming the system if the scheme goes awry. In both cases great emphasis must be put on the importance of legal duty, and its strict bindingness, if we are to ensure that misrepresentation happen only rarely, in the most extreme cases, and not as a general rule.

The chief opponent of the resignation school, Lysander Spooner, was also the chief spokesman for the cheating alternative. He did not convince many judges, so far as we know, but one cannot but smile at his ingenuity.[26]

> Spooner was willing to treat the problem *arguendo* as one of a judge who had sworn to uphold an unjust constitution (even though he, Spooner, believed that the U.S. Constitution is properly interpreted as a just nonslavery

instrument). Spooner acknowledged that the dominant position seemed to be that such a judge should resign. But he thought that the proper analogy was one of a man given a weapon on condition that he kill an innocent and helpless victim. In such a situation, Spooner argued, it is proper to make the promise, keep the weapon, and use it to defend rather than attack the victim. To give up the sword, to resign the judicial office, is "only a specimen of the honor that is said to prevail among thieves."

In both cases, that of the judge torn between morality (conscience) and law (duty) and that of the party who accepts his neighbor's weapon, the cheating consists of breaking a promise to uphold the law even when it conflicts with morality or, in Spooner's example, to kill the innocent third party. The receiver of his friend's weapon could certainly not ever justify *keeping* his promise to his neighbor to kill the third party. Suppose, nevertheless, that he does keep his promise and shoots the third party dead with the weapon given him for that purpose by his neighbor. "I hated having to kill him," he might say, "but if I had saved him instead, that would have been to break my promise, and I couldn't do *that!*" The abiding message of this analogy is that duties to keep one's promises don't *always and necessarily* take precedence over the prima facie duties with which they may conflict.

In Closing: A Friendly Philosophical Dialogue

Do we need a conception of natural law to do justice to the claims that morality makes on legislators and judges? William James once wrote that "Every difference must make a difference."[27] That is to say that, if two theories are distinct in meaning, it must be because there is at least some conceivable difference it would make to our experience if one, but not the other, were true. Alternatively, if some single theory has a sense to it, that sense must be the difference we can imagine for our experience if the theory happened to be true. Whether that pragmatic theory of meaning is correct is a technical question well beyond the scope of this paper. But its full adequacy aside, the theory can provide useful assistance to our understanding of a philosophical proposition. It advises us simply to look for the difference it

would make in our lives if the proposition were true and creates a presumption at least that, if its truth would make no practical difference, then there is really no theoretical difference either, between its being true and its being false.

More precisely, our questions are these: "Does morality have to pretend to be literally a part of law in order for it to perform its function as protector of human interests and ground of political obligations?" "Does it really matter to any of our practical purposes and values whether we think of morality as inside, or outside, or both inside and outside our legal codes?" We saw earlier that we expect jural laws of a variety of kinds to impose moral obligations on the citizens who are subject to them. The criminal code, for example, imposes obligations of obedience on everybody, whereas the rules defining public offices—either relatively permanent, like the office of judge, or relatively temporary, like the office of juror—impose moral obligations only on their occupants. In addition, the making of promises and the swearing of oaths are legal mechanisms for generating official duties. In the same way, ordinary promises between citizens generate ordinary moral obligations between them, whether enforceable by the state or not. Likewise, social roles, both when filled voluntarily (like that of husband or wife) and even when filled involuntarily (like that of daughter or son), are recognized generators of moral obligation. Our classification approaches completeness when we add mention of informal social roles (like that of neighbor) and private institutional roles, offices, or jobs (like that defined by the duties of a janitor or the duties of a chief executive officer in a private corporation). All of these duties are or can be moral duties—both those generated by private rules and procedures, informal or institutional, and those derived from legal rules, both those that apply to all citizens alike and those that impose the moral obligations of public officials and are peculiar to them.

Earlier I discussed the moral obligations normally imposed by a legal system, at least in a democratic, more or less just country, on all citizens. Sometimes particular statutes in such a system are extremely unjust or even irrational ("crazy," as we say), and questions arise whether our normal obligation to obey *any* valid law is weakened or even dissolved in this case. For a judge presiding over a trial of a citizen for violating such a "law," the problem to be dealt with is one of judicial *duty*. Does the normal duty as a judge, to apply the law as it is written, get weakened or suspended in the case at bar because of the immoral content of the governing statute? For the defendant, a private citizen occupying no judicial office, the problem is, or was, one of private conscience. The statute the defendant deliberately violated was so utterly wicked, she didn't think it could possibly have any obligatory force. Moreover, she could not act as the law seemed to enjoin her to act, without a severe crisis of conscience.

Suppose, for example, that the statute defines a capital offense—perhaps not an act so utterly trivial as stealing a turnip, but close. It forbids any derogatory oral statement about the country's political leader, on pain of death, and requires the persons overhearing such a statement to inform the police. If they fail to do so, they are subject to life imprisonment at hard labor. Moreover, the conscience-stricken citizen has learned that the law was not debated in her country's parliament but only given a unanimous rubber-stamp approval ordered secretly by the country's leader. The parliamentary approval was intended to place an ex post facto veneer of legality over the punishment of a dissident, which had occurred a few days earlier. The legal system is now obviously breaking down and has reached the point where Lon Fuller is prepared to pronounce it nearly dead.

The positivistic H. L. A. Hart concluded about this only partly fictitious case that the law deliberately broken by the conscientious citizen was indeed a valid statute in the legal system (if that system still existed), having been duly enacted by an elected legislature in accordance with the procedure prescribed by the country's unamended ancient constitution. Nevertheless, he found it so extremely wicked that his conscience too would forbid him from obeying it. As a legal philosopher, he would admit that the offending law was valid; as a moral philosopher, he would deny that he was under a moral obligation, all things considered, to obey it, since the moral obligation of obedience normally generated by a valid law was not produced in this case.

On the other side, Lon Fuller, in the position of the conscientious citizen, would also have disobeyed, but he would have denied that he had broken a valid law in any operative legal system. When the content of a rule is that wicked, cruel, and unjust and the methods of generating it so corrupt, then it is no legal rule at all, but only a pretender to legal status. And since it was not a valid legal rule and/or the legal system of which it might have been a part hardly exists any more, of course it does not generate a duty derived from the general capacity of valid law to generate moral obligations of obedience. Ergo, Fuller would conclude, he was under no obligation to obey.

And so Hart and Fuller, for all their philosophical quarreling, would be allies in the political arena and perhaps cell mates in the same prison. Is there really any actual difference between their philosophies, then? Do we have an answer to Lloyd Weinreb, who wonders what possible difference it makes whether we describe the moral situation in Nazi Germany as Fuller did (no legal system, no obligation of obedience) or as Hart did (a valid law but too evil to obey)?

I think we can say that, if there is an important theoretical difference between these two positions, it is not because of any important practical difference they yield. The ruthless dictator, after all, would have them both butchered. As we have seen, Hart did claim a small advantage for his position in what he called the merit of candor. As he reconstructs the practical reasoning of two dissidents, one a legal positivist and the other a natural law theorist, the positivist would tally up the score in such a way that disobedience would have a huge balance over obedience but not a complete shutout. The score might be 9 to 1 (these numbers, of course, are not to be taken seriously), but that one point would register on any sensitive conscience, since it is the minimal force that comes from the recognition of a valid law. For the positivist there is a conflict of prima facie obligations: the PFO of obedience to valid law (here represented as weakly as possible) versus the PFOs (all of them here at maximal strength) to oppose injustice, to prevent suffering, to speak truth, and more. It is a one-sided conflict, Hart would say, but a conflict for all that, and to characterize it in that fashion is to exercise the virtue of candor. Fuller, on the other side, would tally the score as 10 to 0 against obedience. For him there was no conflict at all, since all the relevant PFOs spoke with one voice, and there was no valid law involved that might bring the moral duty of fidelity to law into play.

I conclude, then, that the famous differences between the positivist and the natural law theorist on the question of the private citizen's moral obligation to obey the law do not amount to much. But I am reluctant to draw the further inference, without some caution, that the difference between legal positivism and natural law theory, as *general* accounts of the relation between law and morality, don't come to much. I don't wish to be hasty and skeptical about that, not after studying the way those called positivists and those called natural law theorists divided over the vital political issue of fugitive slave laws that, in the end, split the country and exploded into a bloody conflagration.

There is at least one possibly significant way in which the Hart-Fuller problem, inspired by the historical record of the Nazi government of Germany and the fugitive slave issue of the shaky American union between the Revolution and Civil War, can be shown to make a difference. In our example from Fuller and Hart, we are concerned with the moral obligations people had *as private citizens* to obey the law. In the example from the Civil War period, we are dealing with the moral obligations that one class of public officials (appellate judges) had to interpret and apply laws that others had written. Let us explore, then, how the *judge's* moral obligations might be importantly different depending on whether he is a positivist or a natural law theorist.

This time let us consider how a fictitious Supreme Court judge, who happens to be a theorist of natural law (NL), might have debated that matter with a time-traveling judge from the twentieth century, who happens to be a legal positivist (LP).

LP: Surely it is as clear as it ever is in law that the Fugitive Slave Acts are valid law, whatever reservations we have about their content. The question of legal validity in America is settled by reference to the Constitution, and that document, our ultimate "rule of recognition," goes out of its way, in Article IV, to recognize the legitimacy of human slavery, and it very explicitly requires that escaped slaves "shall be delivered up" on claim of their masters.

NL: We both know that the reason why this statement was included in the Constitution is that it was part of the original bargain that induced the slave states to join the Union in the first place. But, in any complete and accurate consideration of a judge's moral obligations when an appeal of the fugitive or his rescuer comes before him, that can hardly be the end of the matter. You and your colleagues have within your collective power the fate not just of this one wretched human being—sick, undernourished, and devastated psychologically, and subject to who knows how many fierce beatings upon return—but also, in virtue of precedents, thousands more who will follow.

LP: I sincerely and deeply regret that my actions may have those terrible results. You know that I hate the institution of human chattel slavery

just as much as you do, and I have opposed it just as long, and just as strenuously, as you have. But I don't see how I have any choice in the matter. I didn't make that loathsome law nor do I have the power to change it. My job is simply to apply the law as it is, indeed, as others have written it. I may have political convictions *as a private citizen* about the moral merits or demerits of the laws I am to apply, but my duty *as a judge* is to determine what the law is, not what it ought to be. In short, I am here to make strictly legal judgments. Moral judgments are for others, and I am sworn to put them aside.

NL: But I insist that you cannot separate law and morality in that facile and complacent fashion. Certain minimal conditions of reasonableness and fairness must be presumed to be a part, usually an unwritten implicit part, of any valid law. Cicero said that and so did Augustine, Aquinas, and the leading writers of our own revolutionary period. And surely our own Constitution is full of testimony to the natural rights of man and the moral foundation of all legitimate government. The fugitive slave clause flies in the teeth of all that. Its presence in the Constitution renders that document incoherent and contradictory. There cannot be an ultimate source of positive law, as our Constitution claims to be, whose parts are mutually contradictory. When all but one part of the document affirms human rights to freedom, equality, autonomy, and the means to happiness, and one specific part explicitly denies those rights, then clearly the only reasonable way to restore coherence is to invalidate that one clashing part.

LP: Good heavens, look at what you are saying! You say that the fugitive slave clause conflicts with morality, human rights, and justice. But even if that were so, it would not follow that it is not valid law! Are you suggesting that a part of the Constitution itself could be unconstitutional? Look who is talking about inconsistency and contradiction!

NL: No, it makes no sense to say that the Constitution, or one of its parts, could be unconstitutional. But the Constitution could suffer a kind of disability analogous to unconstitutionality. It could conflict sharply with a basic principle of morality—a principle of justice, or equality, or humaneness, or autonomy.

LP: I agree that there are certain abstract principles of morality that, despite their appearance as vacuous and imprecise—or perhaps because of it—are objective truths endorsed by a large and confident consensus. Justice, for example, excludes arbitrary inequalities. We can all agree on that precept, provided it is kept abstract. There will be more disagreements when we try to decide whether a given inequality is arbitrary or when a dissimilarity—say, in skin color—is relevant as a ground for dissimilar or unequal treatment. I concede further that there is some reason to be optimistic about the possibility of strong consensus even about those more determinate derivative moral judgments. But my main point is that my duty as a judge, to which I was solemnly sworn, is to interpret and apply only what is internal to the law. We both have the highest respect for morality, even perhaps as much as for law. But morality is something outside of law, and I am only to consider what is inside law, so to speak.

NL: Well that seems to be the nub of the disagreement between us. I am strongly inclined to say that the basic principles of justice, for example, have a home within every actual legal system, or a kind of implicit presence in the interstices of every legal statute, in effect putting a limit on how far that statute can drift away from justice without losing the character of legality. The Fugitive Slave Acts, I should say, are about as far from conformity with that internal justice requirement as it is possible to get. You need not fear violating your judicial duty by declaring them, because of their extreme immorality, null and void as law.

LP: Would that it were that simple! What can it mean for a moral principle to be "part" of a legal rule? Or for morality to be "implicit in the interstices" of law? This smacks of obscurantism. Normally, law and morality are understood as contrasting. Law is law and morality is morality. You would convert a generic distinction into one between a genus and one of its own species. Instead of morality having a character different enough from law's to disqualify it as something properly called law, you juggle the terms about so that morality suddenly becomes a species of law rather than a contrasting genus. And not only is morality itself a kind of law, even a part of a system of positive law, it now becomes a *higher* kind of law, or a test of what else can be or not be law. Why don't we simply say, with Bishop Butler,[28] that "a thing is what it is and not another thing" and add that a system of law that fails to measure up to the standards of morality is a pretty lousy system of law?

NL: But still law?

LP: Yes, still law.

NL: Would you then have decided cases in 1850 in such a way that certain northern states would be prevented from declaring a fugitive slave to be a free citizen and welcoming him or her to permanent residence?

LP: I couldn't say now. Your question is too hypothetical.

NL: But can you think of *any* circumstances in which your legal philosophy would permit you to decide a case in accordance with the abstract principles of justice instead of the plain meaning of the terms in which the governing rule is stated?

LP: Maybe my legal philosophy is not where we should turn. Try my moral philosophy instead. I might have no doubt at all what my duty as a judge requires of me. But as a full human being, not just a judge, I may be so appalled morally at what my legal duty requires that my conscience will tell me not to do my judicial duty.

NL: Give me an example other than the fugitive slave example.

LP: Well, this is a bit fanciful, but suppose that back in the days before women had the franchise (back in your time) somebody introduced a bill, in the usual way, on the floor of a state legislature. Imagine that a quorum of legislators were in attendance, in accordance with the state's constitutional requirement for valid lawmaking, and they astonish the world by passing the bill into law. The bill legalizes rape in that state. I would not hesitate to judge that a valid law had just been created, but I would be prepared, as the morally sensitive human being I am, to throttle personally any young scoundrel I would see who was attempting a legal rape. I wouldn't care that his behavior was legal. I would beat the hell out of him anyway.

NL: But judge, you are now talking about your duties, liberties, and liabilities as an ordinary private citizen. What I want to know is whether you would discharge your judicial duty (as you see it) to uphold this law the first time the question of its constitutionality arises or whether, in the same spirit as that manifested in your attack on the scoundrel in the other example, you would vote to invalidate the statute because of its conflict with justice and morality?

LP: Well, maybe I would declare it invalid for the reason you mention, but if I did that I might want to conceal what my real reason was. I don't want the world to think that I would shrink from my duty for the wrong kind of reason. There would probably be something in the state constitution I could cite as conflicting with the statute, thus entailing its unconstitutionality. Its injustice and immorality needn't be mentioned.

NL: If you *were* to refer to the statute's injustice or inhumanity, would you be going outside of the law for your justification?

LP: Yes, I would. I think the conceptual distinction between law and morality is too useful to undermine as you keep trying to do. But as I said before, I might nevertheless choose to go outside the law in violation of my legal duty, because when I take into account all the prima facie obligations (PFOs) that I am subject to as a human being, my judicial duty (which is also one of my moral duties) may be outbalanced by the other PFOs that have a bearing in those circumstances on my decision.

NL: Your reasoning, then, is precisely parallel to that of H. L. A. Hart in his discussion of the moral duties of ordinary citizens when confronted with extremely unjust laws that they know, in addition, to be the work of thoroughly corrupt legislatures. In both examples, we are dealing with the problem of determining our resultant bottom-line duties as human beings when there is conflict among the various PFOs to which we are subject, including the very special and stringent PFOs of a public official generated in part by the solemn promises of office. Does the fact that the deliberating individual in the second example is a *judge,* with an additional kind of duty to throw on the deliberative scales, make no difference then? Or is there no real difference between the positions of the natural law theorist and the legal positivist in respect to their judgments about the duties of judges?

LP: I would say that there is some difference but perhaps not as much as I thought before this discussion. What confuses or troubles me most is the abundance of distinctions among types of duty that this discussion generates. Assume that we

are discussing purely moral philosophy and our question is of quite the same kind as if we asked whether in some hypothetical case a person should do his or her moral duty (PFO) to tell the truth and thereby violate in those unusual circumstances the duty (PFO) to keep a promise. In that event, we may be talking about moral duties that do not come from the definition of some role, station, or office. The conflicting PFOs are PFOs to which the person is subject simply as a human being. In deciding, he will have to weigh, so to speak, these PFOs against one another and then be moved in the direction of the weightier one. One PFO may outweigh (or "outscore," to use our earlier sports metaphor) the other by an overwhelming amount (a score of 10 to 1 or 9 to 1, as in the earlier example) or the score may be close—perhaps 5 to 4 or 4 to 5, as in the fugitive slave dilemma.

Perhaps, in the majority of cases where the decision to be made has this form, at least one of the contending PFOs will derive from the definition of a social role or a job assignment or office occupied by the decision maker, but even then the role or office duty will be just one among the several that have relevance to the decision. Some PFOs will derive from very general and ill-defined roles we all have, for example, the role of citizen. In the Nazi example debated by Fuller and Hart, these two eminent legal philosophers agreed that the PFOs they had *as citizens* to obey the law were outweighed by far by other PFOs they had, perhaps also as citizens, to oppose social injustice. The bottom-line duty,[29] as you called it, is by definition the PFO that carries the day. Adjusting this terminology to fit our moral priorities is a very difficult and even dangerous thing. It is dangerous because it may lead us to overlook the way our terminology can commit us to positions that we do not hold, positions whose truth or falsity, before argument, should be open questions. Thus we can think of the duty that "carries the day" as being identical by definition with a duty we have as human beings, not merely as role players or job or office holders. But that begs the question in favor of a controversial substantive position— namely, that when role and office duties clash with more general nonrole and nonoffice duties, the latter must *always* win out. A person's duty as a judge, for example, can never be as weighty as a clashing duty that he or she has quite apart from any role, relation, or job, or any promise already made. More confusion can result if we think of the winning duty as the one we will *call* our duty as human beings. Then, if on argumentative or intuitive grounds, we find that a competing PFO, which we have as role or office occupants, seems weightier, we will have to call *that* duty the duty we have as human beings. This result undermines our original distinction.

We also have available, as a way of referring to the bottom-line duty, the term *conscientious duty*. That is a term commonly reserved, I suspect, for the bottom-line winner, because it seems odd that a lesser PFO could outweigh a PFO of conscience. After all, it is conscience that "sits on the throne." But if in fact a role duty *can* outweigh a stringent nonrole duty in certain circumstances, and that is at least a genuine possibility, then, I suppose, we should have to say "Ignore your conscience and do your role duty instead." But that sounds so cynical, even if inadvertently so, that we should probably avoid that usage. But suppose we define *conscientious duty* as the duty that is the weightiest of the competing duties before us. Then, when the duty that seems intuitively to win out is a role duty, we would have to call *it* the voice of conscience, and the distinction between conscientious duties and role duties is undermined. It would be better in advance of argument not to identify the bottom-line duty (the one that carries the day), by definition, with any other category.

[Pausing for breath] Wow, these things are complicated! Am I still on the right track?

NL: Yes, I think so. You have already made enough distinctions to cover the Hart-Fuller case. There the personal moral decision of the citizen was to overrule the individual's PFO to obey the valid laws of the community, and do instead the PFO (also as a citizen? more likely, simply as a human being) to oppose injustice, particularly political injustice. Now what further distinction must we make, I wonder, to apply to the PFOs of the *judge* in our two examples? Consider (1) the historical example of the fugitive slave cases and (2) your strange example of the legalization of rape.

LP: In the judicial cases, we simply have the possibility of new PFOs that are present only when the moral deliberator is a judge. The judge must deliberate on two levels. The first is entirely legal. He or she must look inside the law for rules, statutes, precedents, and the other appro-

priate legal data that might enable a judicial decision. But the judge is not a mere computer. First of all, before a judge is ever a judge, he or she is a human being made of flesh and blood, not merely of computer chips, and subject to many more PFOs than simply that of the job of judge. Normally his or her PFOs as judge are extremely stringent and the opposing PFOs on the scale are greatly outweighed, so that deliberation is quick and easy. But normally the judge doesn't have to put the evil of human slavery or of rape on the scales at all. But in this case the comparative "weight measurement" is extremely close. After hours of weighing and reweighing, the judge sees that the more stringent PFO is not the duty as a judge but instead the duty as a human being.

NL: Now we are precisely at the point where a difference will appear, if it is to appear at all. What should the human being–judge do at this point, and how can he do it? His counterpart in the private citizen example at this point omits legal duty—the legal duty, say, to inform on a neighbor or a spouse. The private citizen leaves town without an exit permit. He or she writes a farewell letter that condemns the country's political leader, then sends a copy to a newspaper for publication as a letter to the editor. The citizen fires shots at policemen when they are trying to arrest a known dissident; joins the underground resistance; and renounces once and for all, as in a declaration of war, the PFO to obey the laws of the government. The judge could well be a natural law theorist (like me or Lon Fuller) who denies that the citizen is breaking a law at all through all these rebellious activities, since there are no laws to break. That makes it extremely easy. But a colleague of this judge could just as well be a legal positivist like you or H. L. A. Hart, in disagreement with the judge over whether the citizen is breaking a law but morally bound to behavior no different from that of the other judge. So far, their philosophical differences make no difference to their conduct.

When the human being–judge decides that his PFOs to resist injustice, which he has as a human being, outweigh the PFO that derives from the definition of his job, even when the latter is reinforced by his PFO to keep his promises and honor his oaths, what does he do? Here the parallel with the case of the private citizen begins to break down. The judge can overrule the actions of a lower court in judging the appeal before him, even though the opposite course appeared clearly to be the legally correct one. But the judge cannot do that secretly, so that nobody notices it, and then sneak out of town like a common criminal. He must stand up in a public forum and declare his conclusion and the legal reasons supporting it. In effect, he will be either presenting arguments that support a conclusion other than the one he declares to be correct or (equivalently) arguing, not really for the course that it is his duty as judge to certify, but rather for the course that it is his moral duty as citizen perhaps, but more likely *as* human being, to do. After that, he can avoid the hubbub by resigning his judgeship, but that would probably be a self-defeating thing to do, since he would be replaced by a more reliably "dutiful" judge, who in time would find a way to undo whatever he had achieved.

Now if the judge were a legal positivist, he would find it impossible to give a straightforward legal argument for the conclusion his conscience would have him declare. He would have to admit that a judge can only refer to matters internal to the law in arguing for a legal conclusion and that, by his lights, questions about justice and injustice are external to the law and therefore may not be considered. That leaves him only the option of giving all the arguments that support his bottom-line duty as a human being and violating his duty as a judge. If he is candid, then, he must in effect tell the world that he did not reach the judgment that it was his duty as a judge to reach, but rather the judgment imposed on him by his conscience. That would be almost as shocking as a confession of a crime. Your fellow legal positivists would lead the chase, denouncing as usurpation any judge's claim that he has discretion to appeal to wider considerations to settle a question of law. In the period before the American Civil War, Great Britain's Lord Camden was often quoted: "The discretion of a judge is the law of tyrants. . . . [At] its best it is often-times caprice—[at] its worst, it is every vice, folly, and passion to which human nature is liable." I think that, if the positivists knew more people like *you,* they would be less unwilling to confer on a judge the discretion to appeal to natural justice in arguments. But as this quotation shows, it was not that most of them disparaged justice. It was

rather that most of them distrusted *people,* especially people in positions of power, like judges.

LP: Perhaps the only legitimate course for the judge in hard cases of the sort we have been considering, in effect, is to *cheat,* paradoxical though that would be. If I were a judge in one of the fugitive slave appeals, I could try to present as plausible an argument as I could find for invalidating the bloody clause without once mentioning such external factors as its natural injustice, arbitrariness, inhumanity, and so on. I could say that the recognition of slavery was at odds with the whole drift of the Constitution and the other foundational documents of our government. I could show the banner of states rights (a huge irony in 1860) and deny the power of the federal government to prevent individual (northern) states from holding fugitives until their lot could be determined by the state's own rules of due process, including the trial by jury guaranteed by the federal Constitution. I could try all those gambits, but it would be a heroic, uphill, losing fight. After all, good friend, the damned bloody clause in Article IV came right out and said that fugitive slaves must be "delivered up" as soon as an authenticated representative of their owner made claim to them. There is simply no way around that, even for so wily a lawyer as me.

Anyway, even if my cleverness enabled me to make some sort of standard argument for the morally preferable outcome, albeit a hopelessly unpersuasive one, that would simply help to gum up the law and create tricky precedents of the kind that any self-respecting positivist would abhor. So the position of the morally conscientious legal positivist judge in these examples is an unenviable one. Would the morally conscientious judge who is an advocate of natural law theory be in any better a position?

NL: Well, I for one, would be much better off. In my theory, when I appeal to natural justice, I am appealing to something internal to the law. I do not have to concede, as you would, that contrary to my oath I am going outside the law for considerations that will support my legal conclusions. And in response to those who will accuse me of substituting merely my own opinions about morality and justice, subjective and ungrounded as they are thought to be, for the straightforward and objective dictates of the law, I can cite a dazzling array of authorities—from Cicero, Aquinas, and Blackstone, down to Jefferson, and in our own time Lincoln—for the proposition that the principles of justice are objective and rooted securely in the nature of things, independent of anyone's mere opinion. It would be hard to pin the label *moral crackpot* on me or my mere opinions, so long as I am in *that* company.

LP: There is a subtle point, I think, about a source of discomfort that would apply as well to the natural law theorist as to the positivist in their roles as judges. There is something essentially *public* about the judge's reasons for acting. The judge's reasons, even those that he might give for what is essentially an act of judicial nullification, become a part of the official record, where they remain forever in a position to influence the future course of the law. The judge is an official spokesman for the state; there is something impersonal about that arrangement that makes it peculiarly jolting for a judge to introduce predominately autobiographical materials into his reasonings about the validity of laws, for example. And that is just what is done by the judge, whether he be a positivist or a natural law partisan, when he states and defends a position about his own duties, not as a judge, but as a human being.

In this respect the judge's dilemmas that we have been considering differ from both the moral dilemmas of the ordinary citizen as citizen or as human being, on the one hand, and that of other officials, like jurors, on the other. The juror, for example, makes nothing public but her verdict. She is not required to give her reasons even for that. Her defiant act of jury nullification, if any, is done in secret, and its reasons and supporting argument become part of no record. Moreover, the juror, in theory, decides only about the facts. She is in no position, therefore, to influence the future course of law. And in no sense does she speak for the state.

I must admit at this point that the only place where one's stand on the positivism–natural law controversy seems to have practical effects is the situation in which the philosophers are also judges and they have good reason to find their personal, moral duties as human beings even more stringent than their sworn duties as judges when those duties are weighed on the scales of conscience, all things considered. The main practical difference made in these circumstances by one's philosophical stance seems to be to the disadvantage of my allies, the legal positivists. Their position, as we said, is more uncomfortable than that of their natural law counterparts. Comfort, to be sure, is much to be preferred to discomfort. But isn't there a limit to the relevance of such a consideration when we come to evaluate theories as true or false? Is there not even a limit to the relevance of discomfort to a determination of whether the two theories really have *differences* in their morally important consequences?

I am glad that we had this chat, even though we are a long way from resolution of the problems that engage us. I must confess that you have made natural law theory a good deal more plausible than I ever believed it was. But I can hardly accept it at this stage of our discussions, for I must first be led to understand one of the tenets that is both obscure and central to natural law theory: namely, the notion that moral principles are a part of, or identical with, or essentially connected to, legal rules or are themselves legal rules of a special implicit kind; or that as "higher law" they are part and parcel of every legal system, capable of invalidating any other legal rules whose content conflicts with their own; or that they fill the interstices of all legal systems, and similar claims. If you could explain how morality got into the law in the first place or what it can mean to say that its necessary presence within every legal system is conceptually entailed by the very idea of law, I would be more friendly to your view. The consequences of natural law theory in courts of law have often been benign, but until these notions are clarified, I am unwilling to accept the theory as true.

NL: I too enjoyed our philosophic exchange, but we must get together again soon to continue our discussion right where you left it. In the meantime, permit me also a moment of politeness. You have succeeded in puzzling me about my own theory, and if only to that extent, leading me to have more respect for legal positivism. But if I too am a bit uncertain what it means to assert that deep and fundamental moral principles are implicitly a part of every legal system, simply as a definitional truth like "All true laws are promulgated" or "Secret laws are not true laws," I am much less puzzled about what it means to *advocate* or *recommend* that some moral precepts be acknowledged as part of *our* legal system, not because of some alleged conceptual truth that ties *all* legal systems to certain moral precepts necessarily, but rather because such a measure would promote both justice and efficiency, and that is reason enough. You ask how morality got into the law. Part of the answer to that question, especially in respect to the minimal requirements of fairness and reasonableness, is that *we put it there.* If it seems not to be there at all in our legal system, then our legislators ought to put it there.

LP: But I'm not sure that our suspicious legislators would be very enthusiastic about that suggestion! They are happy to give lip service to such glittering ideas as justice and morality, but when it comes to practical action, they would probably let us down.

NL: We would have a better chance if we emphasized that it is only a bare minimal morality that we would put into law. We ask only that they agree that there is (or should be) a limit to how crazy, mean, cruel, or senseless a law (or legal interpretation) can be. To my mind, the natural law theory, which assures us that morality is already in law, is most persuasive when it is the relatively noncontroversial minimal morality we are talking about. Then I can say something that strikes your ear as obscure and rhapsodical— that morality is just naturally there growing like flowers on a bed of law—and say this while confident that I can get even good legal positivists like yourself to join our efforts to *make* this true, even if it is not already true by nature.

LP: What, then, do you propose, you compromised former natural law theorist?

NL: It's very simple. I would have moral principles (at first very abstract and not very controversial ones) made quite explicit, perhaps in an asterisked endnote at the bottom of the page on which every bill of legislation and every enacted statute is printed, just as the words "We are an equal opportunity employer," or words to that effect, now appear on the official sta-

tionery of many universities. At first, the explicit statement should be quite minimal, ruling out only extremely unjust and irrational rules, judgments, verdicts, and sentences. Once it is understood that there *is* such a super-rule or higher law, in our system, the way is open for courts to find some laws to be invalid for no other reason than their conflict with (those) principles of justice. It would have to be heavily emphasized, of course, that simple unfairness and commonplace unreasonableness are not enough, that only transparently flawed legislation could be invalidated in this fashion: flagrant, gross, and outrageous injustice, and utterly crazy pointless unreasonableness. Anyone who has made even a casual perusal of casebooks knows, however, that such flagrant flaws are frequently found in the arguments of prosecutors, judges, and others. And to the objection that this procedure would give too much power to judges, who in turn would use their new discretion in capricious ways, I would reply by pointing to the other places in the law where judges are invited to apply their own standards to determine what is substantial, reasonable, excessive, cruel, fitting, appropriate, due, and other such predicates. A legal system in the modern world could hardly get along without such open-textured and essentially contested terms and the discretion they bring with them. My proposal would only empower courts to filter out the most extreme unreasonableness and unfairness from our laws, without giving discretion to judges to enter into the deeper questions of justice on their own, without controls. And legal philosophers need no longer be puzzled about what it means to say that moral precepts are a part of our legal system (if not all other legal systems). They need only look at the printed message at the bottom of the page.

---

1. Aristotle, *Nicomachean Ethics*, 1131 a 32–3 (paraphrased).
2. Some purists might insist that Shakespeare's *Othello* requires that Desdemona be white and Othello black and that a black actress and a white actor in those roles would distract an audience into missing a good deal of the dramatic clash that Shakespeare was trying to exploit. A more reasonable view now, however, is that audiences can be expected not to be distracted by so very irrelevant a thing as skin color and therefore can be relied upon to provide their own appropriate projection of historic setting. One must admit, however, that a switch in gender might overtax an audience's imaginative resources.
3. *People v. Johnson* (1967) 52 *Misc 2d* 1087, 278 *NYS* 2d 80.
4. The quotation is from Lynn C. Cobb, "Annotation, Validity of State or Local Regulation Dealing with Resale of Tickets to Theatrical or Sporting Events," American Law Reports, 3d, *Cases and Annotations*, vol. 81 (1977), p. 672.4.

5. Ronald Dworkin, "Hard Cases" in *Taking Rights Seriously* (Cambridge, Mass.: Harvard University Press, 1971).

6. For a critique of judicial activism, see Robert H. Bork, *The Tempting of America* (New York: Free Press, 1990).

7. Compare John Rawls, *A Theory of Justice* (Cambridge, Mass.: Harvard University Press, 1971), pp. 54–117, and J. S. Mill, *Utilitarianism* (1861), chap. 1.

8. Sir William Blackstone, *Commentaries on the Laws of England*, vol. 1 (Chicago: University of Chicago Press, 1979), p. 40.

9. See Joel Feinberg, *Harm to Self* (New York: Oxford University Press, 1986), pp. 87–94, on the differences between privacy, in the ordinary sense, and autonomy, or self-determination.

10. That occasions for "Solomonic wisdom" still exist is shown by recent well-publicized cases in the United States of hospital-switched babies later suing for "divorce" from their biological parents.

11. Blackstone, *op. cit.* (see note 8), 1:70.

12. See Robert M. Cover, *Justice Accused: Antislavery and the Judicial Process* (New Haven, Conn.: Yale University Press, 1975), p. 62: "The court can assert a sort of bend-over-backward principle by which there is an obligation to achieve a profreedom (antislavery) result unless there is a very specific, concrete positive law that prevents it."

13. R. Dworkin, "The Model of Rules" in *Taking Rights Seriously* (Cambridge, Mass.: Harvard University Press, 1977). In his interesting discussion of the distinction between legal rules and legal principles, Dworkin treats *stare decisis* as an example of a conservative principle.

14. Lon L. Fuller, *The Morality of Law* (New Haven, Conn.: Yale University Press, 1964), pp. 33–38.

15. Lloyd L. Weinreb, *Natural Law and Justice* (Cambridge, Mass.: Harvard University Press, 1987), p. 4.

16. Exceptions to this consensus include Rolf Sartorius, *Individual Conduct and Social Norms* (Belmont, Calif.: Wadsworth, 1975); A. John Simmons, *Moral Principles and Political Obligations* (Princeton: Princeton University Press, 1979); M.B.E. Smith, "Is There a Prima Facie Obligation to Obey the Law?" *Yale Law Journal* 82 (1973).

17. Mortimer and Sanford Kadish, *Discretion to Disobey* (Palo Alto, California: Stanford University Press, 1973), pp. 27–28.

18. Cover, *op. cit.* (see note 12), pp. 151 ff.

19. Cover, *Ibid.*, p. 171.

20. *Ibid.*, p. 6.

21. *Loc. cit.*

22. Francis Lieber, *Political Ethics*, 2nd ed. (Philadelphia: Lippincott, 1875), I: 344, as quoted by Cover, *op. cit.*, p. 147.

23. Cover, see note 12.

24. Wendell Phillips, *The Constitution: A Pro-Slavery Compact*, quoted by Cover, *op. cit.*, pp. 153, 178.

25. Cover, *op. cit.*, p. 158.

26. Lysander Spooner, *The Unconstitutionality of Slavery*, quoted by Cover, *loc. cit.*

27. William James, "What Pragmatism Means" in *Essays in Pragmatism* (New York: Hafner Publishing, 1948), p. 144.

28. Joseph Butler, Bishop of Durham, 1662–1752. I do not know the exact source.

29. There are at least six phrases we can use to give definition to the PFO that wins out in the competition, in some specific set of circumstances, with other PFOs that are less weighty in those circumstances. We can refer to (1) a resultant (as opposed to a component) duty; (2) a bottom-line duty; (3) an "all things considered" duty; (4) (the term used by W. P. Ross) the duty sans phrase, or the duty without the qualifying phrase *prima facie;* (5) the duty that trumps; or (6) the duty that carries the day.

THE MODEL OF RULES*

Ronald M. Dworkin

Embarrassing Questions

Lawyers lean heavily on the connected concepts of legal right and legal obligation. We say that someone has a legal right or duty, and we take that statement as a sound basis for making claims and demands, and for criticizing the acts of public officials. But our understanding of these concepts is remarkably fragile, and we fall into trouble when we try to say what legal rights and obligations are. We say glibly that whether someone has a legal obligation is determined by applying "the law" to the particular facts of this case, but this is not a helpful answer, because we have the same difficulties with the concept of law.

We are used to summing up our troubles in the classic questions of jurisprudence: What is "the law"? When two sides disagree, as often happens, about a proposition "of law," what are they disagreeing about, and how shall we decide which side is right? Why do we call what "the law" says a matter of legal "obligation"? Is "obligation" here just a term of art, meaning only "what the law says"? Or does legal obligation have something to do with moral obligation? Can we say that we have, in principle at least, the same reasons for meeting our legal obligations that we have for meeting our moral obligations?

These are not puzzles for the cupboard, to be taken down on rainy days for fun. They are sources of continuing embarrassment, and they nag at our attention. They embarrass us in dealing with particular problems that we must solve, one way or another. Suppose a novel right-of-privacy case comes to court, and there is no statute or precedent either granting or denying the particular right of anonymity claimed by the plaintiff. What role in the court's decision should be played by the fact that most people in the community think that private individuals are "morally" entitled to that particular privacy? Suppose

the Supreme Court orders some prisoner freed because the police used procedures that the Court now says are constitutionally forbidden, although the Court's earlier decisions upheld these procedures. Must the Court, to be consistent, free all other prisoners previously convicted through these same procedures?[1] Conceptual puzzles about "the law" and "legal obligation" become acute when a court is confronted with a problem like this.

These eruptions signal a chronic disease. Day in and day out we send people to jail, or take money away from them, or make them do things they do not want to do, under coercion of force, and we justify all of this by speaking of such persons as having broken the law or having failed to meet their legal obligations, or having interfered with other people's legal rights. Even in clear cases (a bank robber or a willful breach of contract), when we are confident that someone had a legal obligation and broke it, we are not able to give a satisfactory account of what that means, or why that entitles the state to punish or coerce him. We may feel confident that what we are doing is proper, but until we can identify the principles we are following we cannot be sure that they are sufficient, or whether we are applying them consistently. In less clear cases, when the issue of whether an obligation has been broken is for some reason controversial, the pitch of these nagging questions rises, and our responsibility to find answers deepens.

Certain lawyers (we may call them "nominalists") urge that we solve these problems by ignoring them. In their view the concepts of "legal obligation" and "the law" are myths, invented and sustained by lawyers for a dismal mix of conscious and subconscious motives. The puzzles we find in these concepts are merely symptoms that they are myths. They are unsolvable because unreal, and our concern with them is just one feature of our enslavement. We would do better to flush away the puzzles

---

*From 35 *University of Chicago Law Review* 14 (1967). Reprinted by permission of the author and the publisher.

and the concepts altogether, and pursue our important social objectives without this excess baggage.

This is a tempting suggestion, but it has fatal drawbacks. Before we can decide that our concepts of law and of legal obligation are myths, we must decide what they are. We must be able to state, at least roughly, what it is we all believe that is wrong. But the nerve of our problem is that we have great difficulty in doing just that. Indeed, when we ask what law is and what legal obligations are, we are asking for a theory of how we use these concepts and of the conceptual commitments our use entails. We cannot conclude, before we have such a general theory, that our practices are stupid or superstitious.

Of course, the nominalists think they know how the rest of us use these concepts. They think that when we speak of "the law," we mean a set of timeless rules stocked in some conceptual warehouse awaiting discovery by judges, and that when we speak of legal obligation we mean the invisible chains these mysterious rules somehow drape around us. The theory that there are such rules and chains they call "mechanical jurisprudence," and they are right in ridiculing its practitioners. Their difficulty, however, lies in finding practitioners to ridicule. So far they have had little luck in caging and exhibiting mechanical jurisprudence (all specimens captured—even Blackstone and Joseph Beale—have had to be released after careful reading of their texts).

In any event, it is clear that most lawyers have nothing like this in mind when they speak of the law and of legal obligation. A superficial examination of our practices is enough to show this, for we speak of laws changing and evolving, and of legal obligation sometimes being problematical. In these and other ways we show that we are not addicted to mechanical jurisprudence.

Nevertheless, we do use the concepts of law and legal obligation, and we do suppose that society's warrant to punish and coerce is written in that currency. It may be that when the details of this practice are laid bare, the concepts we do use will be shown to be as silly and as thick with illusion as those the nominalists invented. If so, then we shall have to find other ways to describe what we do, and either provide other justifications or change our practices. But until we have discovered this and made these adjustments, we cannot accept the nominalists' premature invitation to turn our backs on the problems our present concepts provide.

Of course the suggestion that we stop talking about "the law" and "legal obligation" is mostly bluff.

These concepts are too deeply cemented into the structure of our political practices—they cannot be given up like cigarettes or hats. Some of the nominalists have half-admitted this and said that the myths they condemn should be thought of as Platonic myths and retained to seduce the masses into order. This is perhaps not so cynical a suggestion as it seems; perhaps it is a covert hedging of a dubious bet.

If we boil away the bluff, the nominalist attack reduces to an attack on mechanical jurisprudence. Through the lines of the attack, and in spite of the heroic calls for the death of law, the nominalists themselves have offered an analysis of how the terms "law" and "legal obligation" should be used which is not very different from that of more classical philosophers. Nominalists present their analysis as a model of how legal institutions (particularly courts) "really operate." But their model differs mainly in emphasis from the theory first made popular by the nineteenth century philosopher John Austin, and now accepted in one form or another by most working and academic lawyers who hold views on jurisprudence. I shall call this theory, with some historical looseness, "positivism." I want to examine the soundness of positivism, particularly in the powerful form that Professor H. L. A. Hart of Oxford has given to it. I choose to focus on his position, not only because of its clarity and elegance, but because here, as almost everywhere else in legal philosophy, constructive thought must start with a consideration of his views.

Positivism

Positivism has a few central and organizing propositions as its skeleton, and though not every philosopher who is called a positivist would subscribe to these in the way I present them, they do define the general position I want to examine. These key tenets may be stated as follows:

(a) The law of a community is a set of special rules used by the community directly or indirectly for the purpose of determining which behavior will be punished or coerced by the public power. These special rules can be identified and distinguished by specific criteria, by tests having to do not with their content but with their *pedigree* or the manner in which they were adopted or developed. These tests of pedigree can be used to distinguish valid legal rules from spurious legal rules (rules which lawyers and litigants wrongly argue are rules of law) and also from other sorts of social rules (generally lumped together as "moral rules") that the community follows but does not enforce through public power.

(b) The set of these valid legal rules is exhaustive of "the law," so that if someone's case is not clearly covered by such a rule (because there is none that seems appropriate, or those that seem appropriate are vague, or for some other reason) then that case cannot be decided by "applying the law." It must be decided by some official, like a judge, "exercising his discretion," which means reaching beyond the law for some other sort of standard to guide him in manufacturing a fresh legal rule or supplementing an old one.

(c) To say that someone has a "legal obligation" is to say that his case falls under a valid legal rule that requires him to do or to forbear from doing something. (To say he has a legal right, or has a legal power of some sort, or a legal privilege or immunity, is to assert, in a shorthand way, that others have actual or hypothetical legal obligations to act or not to act in certain ways touching him.) In the absence of such a valid legal rule there is no legal obligation; it follows that when the judge decides an issue by exercising his discretion, he is not enforcing a legal obligation as to that issue.

This is only the skeleton of positivism. The flesh is arranged differently by different positivists, and some even tinker with the bones. Different versions differ chiefly in their description of the fundamental test of pedigree a rule must meet to count as a rule of law.

Austin, for example, framed his version of the fundamental test as a series of interlocking definitions and distinctions.[2] He defined having an obligation as lying under a rule, a rule as a general command, and a command as an expression of desire that others behave in a particular way, backed by the power and will to enforce that expression in the event of disobedience. He distinguished classes of rules (legal, moral or religious) according to which person or group is the author of the general command the rule represents. In each political community, he thought, one will find a sovereign—a person or a determinate group whom the rest obey habitually, but who is not in the habit of obeying anyone else. The legal rules of a community are the general commands its sovereign has deployed. Austin's definition of legal obligation followed from this definition of law. One has a legal obligation, he thought, if one is among the addressees of some general order of the sovereign, and is in danger of suffering a sanction unless he obeys that order.

Of course, the sovereign cannot provide for all contingencies through any scheme of orders, and some of his orders will inevitably be vague or have furry edges. Therefore (according to Austin) the sovereign grants those who enforce the law (judges) discretion to make fresh orders when novel or troublesome cases are presented. The judges then make new rules or adapt old rules, and the sovereign either overturns their creations, or tacitly confirms them by failing to do so.

Austin's model is quite beautiful in its simplicity. It asserts the first tenet of positivism, that the law is a set of rules specially selected to govern public order, and offers a simple factual test—what has the sovereign commanded?—as the sole criterion for identifying those special rules. In time, however, those who studied and tried to apply Austin's model found it too simple. Many objections were raised, among which were two that seemed fundamental. First, Austin's key assumption that in each community a determinate group or institution can be found, which is in ultimate control of all other groups, seemed not to hold in a complex society. Political control in a modern nation is pluralistic and shifting, a matter of more or less, of compromise and cooperation and alliance, so that it is often impossible to say that any person or group has that dramatic control necessary to qualify as an Austinian sovereign. One wants to say, in the United States for example, that the "people" are sovereign. But this means almost nothing, and in itself provides no test for determining what the "people" have commanded, or distinguishing their legal from their social or moral commands.

Second, critics began to realize that Austin's analysis fails entirely to account for, even to recognize, certain striking facts about the attitudes we take toward "the law." We make an important distinction between law and even the general orders of a gangster. We feel that the law's strictures—and its sanctions—are different in that they are obligatory in a way that the outlaw's commands are not. Austin's analysis has no place for any such distinction, because it defines an obligation as subjection to the threat of force, and so founds the authority of law entirely on the sovereign's ability and will to harm those who disobey. Perhaps the distinction we make is illusory—perhaps our feelings of some special authority attaching to the law is based on religious hangover or another sort of mass self-deception. But Austin does not demonstrate this, and we are entitled to insist that an analysis of our concept of law either acknowledge and explain our attitudes, or show why they are mistaken.

H. L. A. Hart's version of positivism is more complex than Austin's, in two ways. First, he recognizes, as Austin did not, the rules are of different logical kinds (Hart distinguishes two kinds, which he calls "primary" and "secondary" rules). Second, he rejects Austin's theory that a rule is a kind of command, and substitutes a more elaborate general analysis of what rules are. We must pause over each of these points, and then note how they merge in Hart's concept of law.

Hart's distinction between primary and secondary rules is of great importance.[3] Primary rules are those that grant rights or impose obligations upon members of the community. The rules of the criminal law that forbid us to rob, murder or drive too fast are good examples of primary rules. Secondary rules are those that stipulate how, and by whom, such primary rules may be formed, recognized, modified or extinguished. The rules that stipulate how Congress is composed, and how it enacts legislation, are examples of secondary rules. Rules about forming contracts and executing wills are also secondary rules because they stipulate how very particular rules governing particular legal obligations (that is, the terms of a contract or the provisions of a will) come into existence and are changed.

His general analysis of rules is also of great importance.[4] Austin had said that every rule is a general command, and that a person is obligated under a rule if he is liable to be hurt should he disobey it. Hart points out that this obliterates the distinction between being *obliged* to do something and being *obligated* to do it. If one is bound by a rule he is obligated, not merely obliged, to do what it provides, and therefore being bound by a rule must be different from being subject to an injury if one disobeys an order. A rule differs from an order, among other ways, by being *normative,* by setting a standard of behavior that has a call on its subject beyond the threat that may enforce it. A rule can never be binding just because some person with physical power wants it to be so. He must have *authority* to issue the rule or it is no rule, and such authority can only come from another rule which is already binding on those to whom he speaks. That is the difference between a valid law and the orders of a gunman.

So Hart offers a general theory of rules that does not make their authority depend upon the physical power of their authors. If we examine the way different rules come into being, he tells us, and attend to the distinction between primary and secondary rules, we see that there are two possible sources of a rule's authority.[5]

(a) A rule may become binding upon a group of people because that group through its practices *accepts* the rule as a standard for its conduct. It is not enough that the group simply conforms to a pattern of behavior: even though most Englishmen may go to the movies on Saturday evening, they have not accepted a rule requiring that they do so. A practice constitutes the acceptance of a rule only when those who follow the practice regard the rule as binding, and recognize the rule as a reason or justification for their own behavior and as a reason for criticizing the behavior of others who do not obey it.

(b) A rule may also become binding in quite a different way, namely by being enacted in conformity with some *secondary* rule that stipulates that rules so enacted shall be binding. If the constitution of a club stipulates, for example, that by-laws may be adopted by a majority of the members, then particular by-laws so voted are binding upon all the members, not because of any practice of acceptance of these particular by-laws, but because the constitution says so. We use the concept of *validity* in this connection: rules binding because they have been created in a manner stipulated by some secondary rule are called "valid" rules. Thus we can record Hart's fundamental distinction this way: a rule may be binding (a) because it is accepted or (b) because it is valid.

Hart's concept of law is a construction of these various distinctions.[6] Primitive communities have only primary rules, and these are binding entirely because of practices of acceptance. Such communities cannot be said to have "law," because there is no way to distinguish a set of legal rules from amongst other social rules, as the first tenet of positivism requires. But when a particular community has developed a fundamental secondary rule that stipulates how legal rules are to be identified, the idea of a distinct set of legal rules, and thus of law, is born.

Hart calls such a fundamental secondary rule a "rule of recognition." The rule of recognition of a given community may be relatively simple ("What the king enacts is law") or it may be very complex (the United States Constitution, with all its difficulties of interpretation, may be considered a single rule of recognition). The demonstration that a particular rule is valid may therefore require tracing a complicated chain of validity back from that particular rule ultimately to the fundamental rule.

Thus a parking ordinance of the city of New Haven is valid because it is adopted by a city council, pursuant to the procedures and within the competence specified by the municipal law adopted by the state of Connecticut, in conformity with the procedures and within the competence specified by the constitution of the state of Connecticut, which was in turn adopted consistently with the requirements of the United States Constitution.

Of course, a rule of recognition cannot itself be valid, because by hypothesis it is ultimate, and so cannot meet tests stipulated by a more fundamental rule. The rule of recognition is the sole rule in a legal system whose binding force depends upon its acceptance. If we wish to know what rule of recognition a particular community has adopted or follows, we must observe how its citizens, and particularly its officials, behave. We must observe what ultimate arguments they accept as showing the validity of a particular rule, and what ultimate arguments they use to criticize other officials or institutions. We can apply no mechanical test, but there is no danger of our confusing the rule of recognition of a community with its rules of morality. The rule of recognition is identified by the fact that its province is the operation of the governmental apparatus of legislatures, courts, agencies, policemen, and the rest.

In this way Hart rescues the fundamentals of positivism from Austin's mistakes. Hart agrees with Austin that valid rules of law may be created through the acts of officials and public institutions. But Austin thought that the authority of these institutions lay only in their monopoly of power. Hart finds their authority in the background of constitutional standards against which they act, constitutional standards that have been accepted, in the form of a fundamental rule of recognition, by the community which they govern. This background legitimates the decisions of government and gives them the cast and call of obligation that the naked commands of Austin's sovereign lacked. Hart's theory differs from Austin's also, in recognizing that different communities use different ultimate tests of law, and that some allow other means of creating law than the deliberate act of a legislative institution. Hart mentions "long customary practice" and "the relation [of a rule] to judicial decisions" as other criteria that are often used, though generally along with and subordinate to the test of legislation.

So Hart's version of positivism is more complex than Austin's, and his test for valid rules of law is more sophisticated. In one respect, however, the two models are very similar. Hart, like Austin, recognizes that legal rules have fuzzy edges (he speaks of them as having "open texture") and, again like Austin, he accounts for troublesome cases by saying that judges have had to exercise discretion to decide these cases by fresh legislation.[7] (I shall later try to show why one who thinks of law as a special set of rules is almost inevitably drawn to account for difficult cases in terms of someone's exercise of discretion.)

Rules, Principles, and Policies

I want to make a general attack on positivism, and I shall use H. L. A. Hart's version as a target, when a particular target is needed. My strategy will be organized around the fact that when lawyers reason or dispute about legal rights and obligations, particularly in those hard cases when our problems with these concepts seem most acute, they make use of standards that do not function as rules, but operate differently as principles, policies, and other sorts of standards. Positivism, I shall argue, is a model of and for a system of rules, and its central notion of a single fundamental test for law forces us to miss the important roles of these standards that are not rules.

I just spoke of "principles, policies, and other sorts of standards." Most often I shall use the term "principle" generically, to refer to the whole set of these standards other than rules; occasionally, however, I shall be more precise, and distinguish between principles and policies. Although nothing in the present argument will turn on the distinction, I should state how I draw it. I call a "policy" that kind of standard that sets out a goal to be reached, generally an improvement in some economic, political, or social feature of the community (though some goals are negative, in that they stipulate that some present feature is to be protected from adverse change). I call a "principle" a standard that is to be observed, not because it will advance or secure an economic, political, or social situation deemed desirable, but because it is a requirement of justice or fairness or some other dimension of morality. Thus the standard that automobile accidents are to be decreased is a policy, and the standard that no man may profit by his own wrong a principle. The distinction can be collapsed by construing a principle as stating a social goal (that is, the goal of a society in which no man profits by his own wrong), or by construing a policy as stating a principle (that is, the principle that the goal the policy embraces is a worthy one) or by adopting the utilitarian thesis that principles of justice are disguised statements of goals (securing the greatest happiness of the greatest number). In some contexts the distinction has uses which are lost if it is thus collapsed.[8]

My immediate purpose, however, is to distinguish principles in the generic sense from rules, and I shall start by collecting some examples of the former. The examples I offer are chosen haphazardly; almost any case in a law school casebook would provide examples that would serve as well. In 1889 a New York court, in the famous case of *Riggs v. Palmer*,[9] had to decide whether an heir named in the will of his grandfather could inherit under that will, even though he had murdered his grandfather to do so. The court began its reasoning with this admission: "It is quite true that statutes regulating the making, proof and effect of wills, and the devolution of property, if literally construed, and if their force and effect can in no way and under no circumstances be controlled or modified, give this property to the murderer."[10] But the court continued to note that "all laws as well as all contracts may be controlled in their operation and effect by general, fundamental maxims of the common law. No one shall be permitted to profit by his own fraud, or to take advantage of his own wrong, or to found any claim upon his own iniquity, or to acquire property by his own crime."[11] The murderer did not receive his inheritance.

In 1960, a New Jersey court was faced, in *Henningsen v. Bloomfield Motors, Inc.*,[12] with the important question of whether (or how much) an auto- mobile manufacturer may limit his liability in case the automobile is defective. Henningsen had bought a car, and signed a contract which said that the manufacturer's liability for defects was limited to "making good" defective parts—"this warranty being expressly in lieu of all other warranties, obligations or liabilities." Henningsen argued that, at least in the circumstances of his case, the manufacturer ought not to be protected by this limitation, and ought to be liable for the medical and other expenses of persons injured in a crash. He was not able to point to any statute, or to any established rule of law, that prevented the manufacturer from standing on the contract. The court nevertheless agreed with Henningsen. At various points in the court's argument the following appeals to standards are made: (a) "[W]e must keep in mind the general principle that, in the absence of fraud, one who does not choose to read a contract before signing it cannot later relieve himself of its burdens."[13] (b) "In applying that

principle, the basic tenet of freedom of competent parties to contract is a factor of importance."[14] (c) "Freedom of contract is not such an immutable doctrine as to admit of no qualification in the area in which we are concerned."[15] (d) "In a society such as ours where the automobile is a common and necessary adjunct of daily life, and where its use is so fraught with danger to the driver, passengers and the public, the manufacturer is under a special obligation in connection with the construction, promotion and sale of his cars. Consequently, the courts must examine purchase agreements closely to see if consumer and public interests are treated fairly."[16] (e) " '[I]s there any principle which is more familiar or more firmly embedded in the history of Anglo-American law than the basic doctrine that the courts will not permit themselves to be used as instruments of inequity and injustice?' "[17] (f) " 'More specifically, the courts generally refuse to lend themselves to the enforcement of a "bargain" in which one party has unjustly taken advantage of the economic necessities of another. . . .' "[18]

The standards set out in these quotations are not the sort we think of as legal rules. They seem very different from propositions like "The maximum legal speed on the turnpike is sixty miles an hour" or "A will is invalid unless signed by three witnesses." They are different because they are legal principles rather than legal rules.

The difference between legal principles and legal rules is a logical distinction. Both sets of standards point to particular decisions about legal obligation in particular circumstances, but they differ in the character of the direction they give. Rules are applicable in an all-or-nothing fashion. If the facts a rule stipulates are given, then either the rule is valid, in which case the answer it supplies must be accepted, or it is not, in which case it contributes nothing to the decision.

This all-or-nothing is seen most plainly if we look at the way rules operate, not in law, but in some enterprise they dominate—a game, for example. In baseball a rule provides that if the batter has had three strikes, he is out. An official cannot consistently acknowledge that this is an accurate statement of a baseball rule, and decide that a batter who has had three strikes is not out. Of course, a rule may have exceptions (the batter who has taken three strikes is not out if the catcher drops the third strike). However, an accurate statement of the rule would take this exception into account, and any that did not would be incomplete. If the list of exceptions is very large, it would be too clumsy to repeat them each time the rule is cited; there is, however, no reason in theory why they could not all be added on, and the more that are, the more accurate is the statement of the rule.

If we take baseball rules as a model, we find that rules of law, like the rule that a will is invalid unless signed by three witnesses, fit the model well. If the requirement of three witnesses is a valid legal rule, then it cannot be that a will has been signed by only two witnesses and is valid. The rule might have exceptions, but if it does then it is inaccurate and incomplete to state the rule so simply, without enumerating the exceptions. In theory, at least, the exceptions could all be listed, and the more of them that are, the more complete is the statement of the rule.

But this is not the way the sample principles in the quotations operate. Even those which look most like rules do not set out legal consequences that follow automatically when the conditions provided are met. We say that our law respects the principle that no man may profit from his own wrong, but we do not mean that the law never permits a man to profit from wrongs he commits. In fact, people often profit, perfectly legally, from their legal wrongs. The most notorious case is adverse possession—if I trespass on your land long enough, some day I will gain a right to cross your land whenever I please. There are many less dramatic examples. If a man leaves one job, breaking a contract, to take a much higher paying job, he may have to pay damages to his first employer, but he is usually entitled to keep his new salary. If a man jumps bail and crosses state lines to make a brilliant investment in another state, he may be sent back to jail, but he will keep his profits.

We do not treat these—and countless other counter-instances that can easily be imagined—as showing that the principle about profiting from one's wrongs is not a principle of our legal system, or that it is incomplete and needs qualifying exceptions. We do not treat counter-instances as exceptions (at least not exceptions in the way in which a catcher's dropping the third strike is an exception) because we could not hope to capture these counter-instances simply by a more extended statement of the principle. They are not, even in theory, subject to enumeration, because we would have to include not only these cases (like adverse possession) in which some institution has already provided that profit can be gained through a wrong, but also those numberless imaginary cases in which we know in advance that

the principle would not hold. Listing some of these might sharpen our sense of the principle's weight (I shall mention that dimension in a moment), but it would not make for a more accurate or complete statement of the principle.

A principle like "No man may profit from his own wrong" does not even purport to set out conditions that make its application necessary. Rather, it states a reason that argues in one direction, but does not necessitate a particular decision. If a man has or is about to receive something, as a direct result of something illegal he did to get it, then that is a reason which the law will take into account in deciding whether he should keep it. There may be other principles or policies arguing in the other direction—a policy of securing title, for example, or a principle limiting punishment to what the legislature has stipulated. If so, our principle may not prevail, but that does not mean that it is not a principle of our legal system, because in the next case, when these contravening considerations are absent or less weighty, the principle may be decisive. All that is meant, when we say that a particular principle is a principle of our law, is that the principle is one which officials must take into account, if it is relevant, as a consideration inclining in one direction or another.

The logical distinction between rules and principles appears more clearly when we consider principles that do not even look like rules. Consider the proposition, set out under "(d)" in the excerpts from the *Henningsen* opinion, that "the manufacturer is under a special obligation in connection with the construction, promotion and sale of his cars." This does not even purport to define the specific duties such a special obligation entails, or to tell us what rights automobile consumers acquire as a result. It merely states—and this is an essential link in the *Henningsen* argument—that automobile manufacturers must be held to higher standards than other manufacturers, and are less entitled to rely on the competing principle of freedom of contract. It does not mean that they may never rely on that principle, or that courts may rewrite automobile purchase contracts at will; it means only that if a particular clause seems unfair or burdensome, courts have less reason to enforce the clause than if it were for the purchase of neckties. The "special obligation" counts in favor, but does not in itself necessitate, a decision refusing to enforce the terms of an automobile purchase contract.

This first difference between rules and principles entails another. Principles have a dimension that rules do not—the dimension of weight or importance. When principles intersect (the policy of protecting automobile consumers intersecting with principles of freedom of contract, for example), one who must resolve the conflict has to take into account the relative weight of each. This cannot be, of course, an exact measurement, and the judgment that a particular principle or policy is more important than another will often be a controversial one. Nevertheless, it is an integral part of the concept of a principle that it has this dimension, that it makes sense to ask how important or how weighty it is.

Rules do not have this dimension. We can speak of rules as being *functionally* important or unimportant (the baseball rule that three strikes are out is more important than the rule that runners may advance on a balk, because the game would be much more changed with the first rule altered than the second). In this sense, one legal rule may be more important than another because it has a greater or more important role in regulating behavior. But we cannot say that one rule is more important than another within the system of rules, so that when two rules conflict one supersedes the other by virtue of its greater weight. If two rules conflict, one of them cannot be a valid rule. The decision as to which is valid, and which must be abandoned or recast, must be made by appealing to considerations beyond the rules themselves. A legal system might regulate such conflicts by other rules, which prefer the rule enacted by the higher authority, or the rule enacted later, or the more specific rule, or something of that sort. A legal system may also prefer the rule supported by the more important principles. (Our own legal system uses both of these techniques.)

It is not always clear from the form of a standard whether it is a rule or a principle. "A will is invalid unless signed by three witnesses" is not very different in form from "A man may not profit from his own wrong," but one who knows something of American laws knows that he must take the first as stating a rule and the second as stating a principle. In many cases the distinction is difficult to make—it may not have been settled how the standard should operate, and this issue may itself be a focus of controversy. The First Amendment to the United States Constitution contains the provision that Congress shall not abridge freedom of speech. Is this a rule, so that if a particular law does abridge freedom of speech, it follows that it is unconstitutional? Those who claim that the first amendment is "an absolute" say that it must

be taken in this way, that is, as a rule. Or does it merely state a principle, so that when an abridgement of speech is discovered, it is unconstitutional unless the context presents some other policy or principle which in the circumstances is weighty enough to permit the abridgement? That is the position of those who argue for what is called the "clear and present danger" test or some other form of "balancing."

Sometimes a rule and a principle can play much the same role, and the difference between them is almost a matter of form alone. The first section of the Sherman Act states that every contract in restraint of trade shall be void. The Supreme Court had to make the decision whether this provision should be treated as a rule in its own terms (striking down every contract "which restrains trade," which almost any contract does) or as a principle, providing a reason for striking down a contract in the absence of effective contrary policies. The Court construed the provision as a rule, but treated that rule as containing the word "unreasonable," and as prohibiting only "unreasonable" restraints of trade.[19] This allowed the provision to function logically as a rule (whenever a court finds that the restraint is "unreasonable" it is bound to hold the contract invalid) and substantially as a principle (a court must take into account a variety of other principles and policies in determining whether a particular restraint in particular economic circumstances is "unreasonable").

Words like "reasonable," "negligent," "unjust," and "significant" often perform just this function. Each of these terms makes the application of the rule which contains it depend to some extent upon principles or policies lying beyond the rule, and in this way makes that rule itself more like a principle. But they do not quite turn the rule into a principle, because even the least confining of these terms restricts the *kind* of other principles and policies on which the rule depends. If we are bound by a rule that says that "unreasonable" contracts are void, or that grossly "unfair" contracts will not be enforced, much more judgment is required than if the quoted terms were omitted. But suppose a case in which some consideration of policy or principle suggests that a contract should be enforced even though its restraint is not reasonable, or even though it is grossly unfair. Enforcing these contracts would be forbidden by our rules, and thus permitted only if these rules were abandoned or modified. If we were dealing, however, not with a rule but with a policy against enforcing unreasonable contracts, or a principle that unfair contracts ought not to be enforced, the contracts could be enforced without alteration of the law.

Principles and the Concept of Law

Once we identify legal principles as separate sorts of standards, different from legal rules, we are suddenly aware of them all around us. Law teachers teach them, lawbooks cite them, legal historians celebrate them. But they seem most energetically at work, carrying most weight, in difficult lawsuits like *Riggs* and *Henningsen*. In cases like these principles play an essential part in arguments supporting judgments about particular legal rights and obligations. After the case is decided, we may say that the case stands for a particular rule (that is, the rule that one who murders is not eligible to take under the will of his victim). But the rule does not exist before the case is decided; the court cites principles as its justification for adopting and applying a new rule. In *Riggs*, the court cited the principle that no man may profit from his own wrong as a background standard against which to read the statute of wills and in this way justified a new interpretation of that statute. In *Henningsen*, the court cited a variety of intersecting principles and policies as authority for a new rule respecting manufacturer's liability for automobile defects.

An analysis of the concept of legal obligation must therefore account for the important role of principles in reaching particular decisions of law. There are two very different tacks we might take.

(a) We might treat legal principles the way we treat legal rules and say that some principles are binding as law and must be taken into account by judges and lawyers who make decisions of legal obligation. If we took this tack, we should say that in the United States, at least, the "law" includes principles as well as rules.

(b) We might, on the other hand, deny that principles can be binding the way some rules are. We would say, instead, that in cases like *Riggs* or *Henningsen* the judge reaches beyond the rules that he is bound to apply (reaches, that is, beyond the "law") for extralegal principles he is free to follow if he wishes.

One might think that there is not much difference between these two lines of attack, that it is only a verbal question of how one wants to use the word "law." But that is a mistake, because the choice between these two accounts has the greatest conse-

quences for an analysis of legal obligation. It is a choice between two *concepts* of a legal principle, a choice we can clarify by comparing it to a choice we might make between two concepts of a legal rule. We sometimes say of someone that he "makes it a rule" to do something, when we mean that he has chosen to follow a certain practice. We might say that someone has made it a rule, for example, to run a mile before breakfast because he wants to be healthy and believes in a regimen. We do not mean, when we say this, that he is *bound* by the rule that he must run a mile before breakfast, or even that he regards it as binding upon him. Accepting a rule as binding is something different from making it a rule to do something. If we use Hart's example again, there is a difference between saying that Englishmen make it a rule to see a movie once a week, and saying that the English have a rule that one must see a movie once a week. The second implies that if an Englishman does not follow the rule, he is subject to criticism or censure, but the first does not. The first does not exclude the possibility of a sort of criticism—we can say that one who does not see movies is neglecting his education—but we do not suggest that he is doing something wrong *just* in not following the rule.[20]

If we think of the judges of a community as a group, we could describe the rules of law they follow in these two different ways. We could say, for instance, that in a certain state the judges make it a rule not to enforce wills unless there are three witnesses. This would not imply that the rare judge who enforces such a will is doing anything wrong just for that reason. On the other hand we can say that in that state a rule of law requires judges not to enforce such wills; this does imply that a judge who enforces them is doing something wrong. Hart, Austin and other positivists, of course, would insist on this latter account of legal rules; they would not at all be satisfied with the "make it a rule" account. It is not a verbal question of which account is right. It is a question of which describes the social situation more accurately. Other important issues turn on which description we accept. If judges simply "make it a rule" not to enforce certain contracts, for example, then we cannot say, before the decision, that anyone is "entitled" to that result, and that proposition cannot enter into any justification we might offer for the decision.

The two lines of attack on principles parallel these two accounts of rules. The first tack treats principles as binding upon judges, so that they are wrong not to apply the principles when they are pertinent. The second tack treats principles as summaries of what most judges "make it a principle" to do when forced to go beyond the standards that bind them. The choice between these approaches will affect, perhaps even determine, the answer we can give to the question whether the judge in a hard case like *Riggs* or *Henningsen* is attempting to enforce preexisting legal rights and obligations. If we take the first tack, we are still free to argue that because such judges are applying binding legal standards they are enforcing legal rights and obligations. But if we take the second, we are out of court on that issue, and we must acknowledge that the murderer's family in *Riggs* and the manufacturer in *Henningsen* were deprived of their property by an act of judicial discretion applied *ex post facto*. This may not shock many readers—the notion of judicial discretion has percolated through the legal community—but it does illustrate one of the most nettlesome of the puzzles that drive philosophers to worry about legal obligation. If taking property away in cases like these cannot be justified by appealing to an established obligation, yet another justification must be found, and nothing satisfactory has yet been supplied.

In my skeleton diagram of positivism, previously set out, I listed the doctrine of judicial discretion as the second tenet. Positivists hold that when a case is not covered by a clear rule, a judge must exercise his discretion to decide that case by what amounts to a fresh piece of legislation. There may be an important connection between this doctrine and the question of which of the two approaches to legal principles we must take. We shall therefore want to ask whether the doctrine is correct, and whether it implies the second approach, as it seems on its face to do. En route to these issues, however, we shall have to polish our understanding of the concept of discretion. I shall try to show how certain confusions about that concept, and in particular a failure to discriminate different senses in which it is used, account for the popularity of the doctrine of discretion. I shall argue that in the sense in which the doctrine does have a bearing on our treatment of principles, it is entirely unsupported by the arguments the positivists use to defend it.

Discretion

The concept of discretion was lifted by the positivists from ordinary language, and to understand it we must put it back *in habitat* for a moment. What does it mean, in ordinary life, to say that someone "has dis-

cretion"? The first thing to notice is that the concept is out of place in all but very special contexts. For example, you would not say that I either do or do not have discretion to choose a house for my family. It is not true that I have "no discretion" in making that choice, and yet it would be almost equally misleading to say that I do have discretion. The concept of discretion is at home in only one sort of context: when someone is in general charged with making decisions subject to standards set by a particular authority. It makes sense to speak of the discretion of a sergeant who is subject to orders of superiors, or the discretion of a sports official or contest judge who is governed by a rule book or the terms of the contest. Discretion, like the hole in a doughnut, does not exist except as an area left open by a surrounding belt of restriction. It is therefore a relative concept. It always makes sense to ask, "Discretion under which standards?" or "Discretion as to which authority?" Generally the context will make the answer to this plain, but in some cases the official may have discretion from one standpoint though not from another.

Like almost all terms, the precise meaning of "discretion" is affected by features of the context. The term is always colored by the background of understood information against which it is used. Although the shadings are many, it will be helpful for us to recognize some gross distinctions.

Sometimes we use "discretion" in a weak sense, simply to say that for some reason the standards an official must apply cannot be applied mechanically but demand the use of judgment. We use this weak sense when the context does not already make that clear, when the background our audience assumes does not contain that piece of information. Thus we might say, "The sergeant's orders left him a great deal of discretion." To those who do not know what the sergeant's orders were or who do not know something that made those orders vague or hard to carry out. It would make perfect sense to add, by way of amplification, that the lieutenant had ordered the sergeant to take his five most experienced men on patrol but that it was hard to determine which were the most experienced.

Sometimes we use the term in a different weak sense, to say only that some official has final authority to make a decision and cannot be reviewed and reversed by any other official. We speak this way when the official is part of a hierarchy of officials structured so that some have higher authority but in which the patterns of authority are different for different classes of decision. Thus we might say that in baseball certain decisions, like the decision whether the ball or the runner reached second base first, are left to the discretion of the second base umpire, if we mean that on this issue the head umpire has no power to substitute his own judgment if he disagrees.

I call both of these senses weak to distinguish them from a stronger sense. We use "discretion" sometimes not merely to say that an official must use judgment in applying the standards set for him by authority, or that no one will review that exercise of judgment, but to say that on some issue he is simply not bound by standards set by the authority in question. In this sense we say that a sergeant has discretion who has been told to pick any five men for patrol he chooses or that a judge in a dog show has discretion to judge airedales before boxers if the rules do not stipulate an order of events. We use this sense not to comment on the vagueness or difficulty of the standards, or on who has the final word in applying them, but on their range and the decisions they purport to control. If the sergeant is told to take the five most experienced men, he does not have discretion in this strong sense because that order purports to govern his decision. The boxing referee who must decide which fighter has been the more aggressive does not have discretion, in the strong sense, for the same reason.[21]

If anyone said that the sergeant or the referee had discretion in these cases, we should have to understand him, if the context permitted, as using the term in one of the weak senses. Suppose, for example, the lieutenant ordered the sergeant to select the five men he deemed most experienced, and then added that the sergeant had discretion to choose them. Or the rules provided that the referee should award the round to the more aggressive fighter, with discretion in selecting him. We should have to understand these statements in the second weak sense, as speaking to the question of review of the decision. The first weak sense—that the decisions take judgment—would be otiose, and the third, strong sense is excluded by the statements themselves.

We must avoid one tempting confusion. The strong sense of discretion is not tantamount to license, and does not exclude criticism. Almost any situation in which a person acts (including those in which there is no question of decision under special authority, and so no question of discretion) makes relevant certain standards of rationality, fairness and effectiveness. We criticize each other's acts in terms of these standards, and there is no reason not to do so when the acts are within the center rather than beyond the

perimeter of the doughnut of special authority. So we can say that the sergeant who was given discretion (in the strong sense) to pick a patrol did so stupidly or maliciously or carelessly, or that the judge who had discretion in the order of viewing dogs made a mistake because he took boxers first although there were only three airedales and many more boxers. An official's discretion means not that he is free to decide without recourse to standards of sense and fairness, but only that his decision is not controlled by a standard furnished by the particular authority we have in mind when we raise the question of discretion. Of course this latter sort of freedom is important; that is why we have the strong sense of discretion. Someone who has discretion in this third sense can be criticized, but not for being disobedient, as in the case of the soldier. He can be said to have made a mistake, but not to have deprived a participant of a decision to which he was entitled, as in the case of a sports official or contest judge.

We may now return, with these observations in hand, to the positivists' doctrine of judicial discretion. That doctrine argues that if a case is not controlled by an established rule, the judge must decide it by exercising discretion. We want to examine this doctrine and to test its bearing on our treatment of principles; but first we must ask in which sense of discretion we are to understand it.

Some nominalists argue that judges always have discretion, even when a clear rule is in point, because judges are ultimately the final arbiters of the law. This doctrine of discretion uses the second weak sense of that term, because it makes the point that no higher authority reviews the decisions of the highest court. It therefore has no bearing on the issue of how we account for principles, any more than it bears on how we account for rules.

The positivists do not mean their doctrine this way, because they say that a judge has no discretion when a clear and established rule is available. If we attend to the positivists' arguments for the doctrine, we may suspect that they use discretion in the first weak sense to mean only that judges must sometimes exercise judgment in applying legal standards. Their arguments call attention to the fact that some rules of law are vague (Professor Hart, for example, says that all rules of law have "open texture"), and that some cases arise (like *Henningsen*) in which no established rule seems to be suitable. They emphasize that judges must sometimes agonize over points of law, and that two equally trained and intelligent judges will often disagree.

These points are easily made; they are commonplace to anyone who has any familiarity with law. Indeed, that is the difficulty with assuming that positivists mean to use "discretion" in this weak sense. The proposition that, when no clear rule is available discretion in the sense of judgment must be used, is a tautology. It has no bearing, moreover, on the problem of how to account for legal principles. It is perfectly consistent to say that the judge in *Riggs*, for example, had to use judgment, and that he was bound to follow the principle that no man may profit from his own wrong. The positivists speak as if their doctrine of judicial discretion is an insight rather than a tautology, and as if it does have a bearing on the treatment of principles. Hart, for example, says that when the judge's discretion is in play, we can no longer speak of his being bound by standards, but must speak rather of what standards he "characteristically uses."[22] Hart thinks that when judges have discretion, the principles they cite must be treated on our second approach, as what courts "make it a principle" to do.

It therefore seems that positivists, at least sometimes, take their doctrine in the third, strong sense of discretion. In that sense it does bear on the treatment of principles; indeed, in that sense it is nothing less than a restatement of our second approach. It is the same thing to say that when a judge runs out of rules he has discretion, in the sense that he is not bound by any standards from the authority of law, as to say that the legal standards judges cite other than rules are not binding on them.

So we must examine the doctrine of judicial discretion in the strong sense. (I shall henceforth use the term "discretion" in that sense.) Do the principles judges cite in cases like *Riggs* or *Henningsen* control their decisions, as the sergeant's orders to take the most experienced men or the referee's duty to choose the more aggressive fighter control the decisions of these officials? What arguments could a positivist supply to show that they do not?

(1) A positivist might argue that principles cannot be binding or obligatory. That would be a mistake. It is always a question, of course, whether any particular principle is *in fact* binding upon some legal official. But there is nothing in the logical character of a principle that renders it incapable of binding him. Suppose that the judge in *Henningsen* had failed to take any account of the principle that automobile manufacturers have a special obligation to their consumers, or the principle that the courts seek to protect those whose bargaining position is weak,

but had simply decided for the defendant by citing the principle of freedom of contract without more. His critics would not have been content to point out that he had not taken account of considerations that other judges have been attending to for some time. Most would have said that it was his duty to take the measure of these principles and that the plaintiff was entitled to have him do so. We mean no more, when we say that a rule is binding upon a judge, than that he must follow it if it applies, and that if he does not he will on that account have made a mistake.

It will not do to say that in a case like *Henningsen* the court is only "morally" obligated to take particular principles into account, or that it is "institutionally" obligated, or obligated as a matter of judicial "craft," or something of that sort. The question will still remain why this type of obligation (whatever we call it) is different from the obligation that rules impose upon judges, and why it entitles us to say that principles and policies are not part of the law but are merely extralegal standards "courts characteristically use."

(2) A positivist might argue that even though some principles are binding, in the sense that the judge must take them into account, they cannot determine a particular result. This is a harder argument to assess because it is not clear what it means for a standard to "determine" a result. Perhaps it means that the standard *dictates* the result whenever it applies so that nothing else counts. If so, then it is certainly true that individual principles do not determine results, but that is only another way of saying that principles are not rules. Only rules dictate results, come what may. When a contrary result has been reached, the rule has been abandoned or changed. Principles do not work that way; they incline a decision one way, though not conclusively, and they survive intact when they do not prevail. This seems no reason for concluding that judges who must reckon with principles have discretion because a set of principles can dictate a result. If a judge believes that principles he is bound to recognize point in one direction and that principles pointing in the other direction, if any, are not of equal weight, then he must decide accordingly, just as he must follow what he believes to be a binding rule. He may, of course, be wrong in his assessment of the principles, but he may also be wrong in his judgment that the rule is binding. The sergeant and the referee, we might add, are often in the same boat. No one factor dictates which soldiers are the most experienced or which fighter the more aggressive. These officials must make judgments of the relative

weights of these various factors; they do not on that account have discretion.

(3) A positivist might argue that principles cannot count as law because their authority, and even more so their weight, are congenitally *controversial*. It is true that generally we cannot *demonstrate* the authority or weight of a particular principle as we can sometimes demonstrate the validity of a rule by locating it in an act of Congress or in the opinion of an authoritative court. Instead, we make a case for a principle, and for its weight, by appealing to an amalgam of practice and other principles in which the implications of legislative and judicial history figure along with appeals to community practices and understandings. There is no litmus paper for testing the soundness of such a case—it is a matter of judgment, and reasonable men may disagree. But again this does not distinguish the judge from other officials who do not have discretion. The sergeant has no litmus paper for experience, the referee none for aggressiveness. Neither of these has discretion, because he is bound to reach an understanding, controversial or not, of what his orders or the rules require, and to act on that understanding. That is the judge's duty as well.

Of course, if the positivists are right in another of the doctrines—the theory that in each legal system there is an ultimate test for binding law like Professor Hart's rule of recognition—it follows that principles are not binding law. But the incompatibility of principles with the positivists' theory can hardly be taken as an argument that principles must be treated any particular way. That begs the question; we are interested in the status of principles because we want to evaluate the positivists' model. The positivist cannot defend his theory of a rule of recognition by fiat; if principles are not amenable to a test he must show some other reason why they cannot count as law. Since principles seem to play a role in arguments about legal obligation (witness, again *Riggs* and *Henningsen*), a model that provides for that role has some initial advantage over one that excludes it, and the latter cannot properly be inveighed in its own support.

These are the most obvious of the arguments a positivist might use for the doctrine of discretion in the strong sense, and for the second approach to principles. I shall mention one strong counterargument against that doctrine and in favor of the first approach. Unless at least some principles are acknowledged to be binding upon judges, requiring them as a set to reach particular decisions, then no rules, or very few rules, can be said to be binding upon them either.

In most American jurisdictions, and now in England also, the higher courts not infrequently reject established rules. Common law rules—those developed by earlier court decisions—are sometimes overruled directly, and sometimes radically altered by further development. Statutory rules are subjected to interpretation and reinterpretation, sometimes even when the result is not to carry out what is called the "legislative intent."[23] If courts had discretion to change established rules, then these rules would of course not be binding upon them, and so would not be law on the positivists' model. The positivist must therefore argue that there are standards, themselves binding upon judges, that determine when a judge may overrule or alter an established rule, and when he may not.

When, then, is a judge permitted to change an existing rule of law? Principles figure in the answer in two ways. First, it is necessary, though not sufficient, that the judge find that the change would advance some policy or serve some principle, which policy or principle thus justifies the change. In *Riggs* the change (a new interpretation of the statute of wills) was justified by the principle that no man should profit from his own wrong; in *Henningsen* certain rules about automobile manufacturers' liability were altered on the basis of the principles and policies I quoted from the opinion of the court.

But not any principle will do to justify a change, or no rule would ever be safe. There must be some principles that count and others that do not, and there must be some principles that count for more than others. It could not depend on the judge's own preferences amongst a sea of respectable extralegal standards, any one in principle eligible, because if that were the case we could not say that any rules were binding. We could always imagine a judge whose preferences amongst extralegal standards were such as would justify a shift or radical reinterpretation of even the most entrenched rule.

Second, any judge who proposes to change existing doctrine must take account of some important standards that argue against departures from established doctrine, and these standards are also for the most part principles. They include the doctrine of "legislative supremacy," a set of principles and policies that require the courts to pay a qualified deference to the acts of the legislature. They also include the doctrine of precedent, another set of principles and policies reflecting the equities and efficiencies of consistency. The doctrines of legislative supremacy and precedent incline toward the *status quo*, each within its sphere, but they do not command it. Judges are not free, however, to pick and choose amongst the principles and policies that make up these doctrines—if they were, again, no rule could be said to be binding.

Consider, therefore, what someone implies who says that a particular rule is binding. He may imply that the rule is affirmatively supported by principles the court is not free to disregard, and which are collectively more weighty than other principles that argue for a change. If not, he implies that any change would be condemned by a combination of conservative principles of legislative supremacy and precedent that the court is not free to ignore. Very often, he will imply both, for the conservative principles, being principles and not rules, are usually not powerful enough to save a common law rule or an aging statute that is entirely unsupported by substantive principles the court is bound to respect. Either of these implications, of course, treats a body of principles and policies as law in the sense that rules are; it treats them as standards binding upon the officials of a community, controlling their decisions of legal right and obligation.

We are left with this issue. If the positivists' theory of judicial discretion is either trivial because it uses "discretion" in a weak sense, or unsupported because the various arguments we can supply in its defense fall short, why have so many careful and intelligent lawyers embraced it? We can have no confidence in our treatment of that theory unless we can deal with that question. It is not enough to note (although perhaps it contributes to the explanation) that "discretion" has different senses that may be confused. We do not confuse these senses when we are not thinking about law.

Part of the explanation, at least, lies in a lawyer's natural tendency to associate laws and rules, and to think of "the law" as a collection or system of rules. Roscoe Pound, who diagnosed this tendency long ago, thought that English-speaking lawyers were tricked into it by the fact that English uses the same word, changing only the article, for "a law" and "the law."[24] (Other languages, on the contrary, use two words: "loi" and "droit," for example, and "Gesetz" and "Recht.") This may have had its effect, with the English-speaking positivists, because the expression "a law" certainly does suggest a rule. But the principal reason for associating law with rules runs deeper, and lies, I think, in the fact that legal education has for a long time consisted of teaching and examining those established rules that form the cutting edge of law.

In any event, if a lawyer thinks of law as a system of rules, and yet recognizes, as he must, that judges change old rules and introduce new ones, he will come naturally to the theory of judicial discretion in the strong sense. In those other systems of rules with which he has experience (like games), the rules are the only special authority that govern official decisions, so that if an umpire could change a rule, he would have discretion as to the subject matter of that rule. Any principles umpires might mention when changing the rules would represent only their "characteristic" preferences. Positivists treat law like baseball revised in this way.

There is another, more subtle consequence of this initial assumption that law is a system of rules. When the positivists do attend to principles and policies, they treat them as rules *manqué*. They assume that if they are standards of law they must be rules, and so they read them as standards that are trying to be rules. When a positivist hears someone argue that legal principles are part of the law, he understands this to be an argument for what he calls the "higher law" theory, that these principles are the rules of a law above the law.[25] He refutes this theory by pointing out that these "rules" are sometimes followed and sometimes not, that for every "rule" like "no man shall profit from his own wrong" there is another competing "rule" like "the law favors security of title," and that there is no way to test the validity of "rules" like these. He concludes that these principles and policies are not valid rules of a law above the law, which is true, because they are not rules at all. He also concludes that they are extralegal standards which each judge selects according to his own rights in the exercise of his discretion, which is false. It is as if a zoologist had proved that fish are not mammals, and then concluded that they are really only plants.

The Rule of Recognition

This discussion was provoked by our two competing accounts of legal principles. We have been exploring the second account, which the positivists seem to adopt through their doctrine of judicial discretion, and we have discovered grave difficulties. It is time to return to the fork in the road. What if we adopt the first approach? What would the consequences of this be for the skeletal structure of positivism? Of course we should have to drop the second tenet, the doctrine of judicial discretion (or, in the alternative, to make plain that the doctrine is to be read merely to say that judges must often exercise judgment). Would we also have to abandon or modify the first tenet, the proposition that law is distinguished by tests of the sort that can be set out in a master rule like Professor Hart's rule of recognition? If principles of the *Riggs* and *Henningsen* sort are to count as law, and we are nevertheless to preserve the notion of a master rule for law, then we must be able to deploy some test that all (and only) the principles that do count as law meet. Let us begin with the test Hart suggests for identifying valid *rules* of law, to see whether these can be made to work for principles as well.

Most rules of law, according to Hart, are valid because some competent institution enacted them. Some were created by a legislature, in the form of statutory enactments. Others were created by judges who formulated them to decide particular cases, and thus established them as precedents for the future. But this test of pedigree will not work for the *Riggs* and *Henningsen* principles. The origin of these as legal principles lies not in a particular decision of some legislature or court, but in a sense of appropriateness developed in the profession and the public over time. Their continued power depends upon this sense of appropriateness being sustained. If it no longer seemed unfair to allow people to profit by their wrongs, or fair to place special burdens upon oligopolies that manufacture potentially dangerous machines, these principles would no longer play much of a role in new cases, even if they had never been overruled or repealed. (Indeed, it hardly makes sense to speak of principles like these as being "overruled" or "repealed." When they decline they are eroded, not torpedoed.)

True, if we were challenged to back up our claim that some principle is a principle of law, we would mention any prior cases in which that principle was cited, or figured in the argument. We would also mention any statute that seemed to exemplify that principle (even better if the principle was cited in the preamble of the statute, or in the committee reports or other legislative documents that accompanied it). Unless we could find some such institutional support, we would probably fail to make out our case, and the more support we found, the more weight we could claim for the principle.

Yet we could not devise any formula for testing how much and what kind of institutional support is necessary to make a principle a legal principle, still less to fix its weight at a particular order of magnitude. We argue for a particular principle by grappling with a whole set of shifting, developing and interacting standards (themselves principles rather than rules) about institutional responsibility, statutory interpretation, the persuasive force of various sorts of precedent, the relation of all these to contemporary moral practices, and hosts of other such standards. We could not bolt all of these together into a single "rule," even a complex one, and if we could the result would bear little relation to Hart's picture of a rule of recognition, which is the picture of a fairly stable master rule specifying "some feature or features possession of which by a suggested rule is taken as a conclusive affirmative indicating that it is a rule. . . . "26

Moreover, the techniques we apply in arguing for another principle do not stand (as Hart's rule of recognition is designed to) on an entirely different level from the principles they support. Hart's sharp distinction between acceptance and validity does not hold. If we are arguing for the principle that a man should not profit from his own wrong, we could cite the acts of courts and legislatures that exemplify it, but this speaks as much to the principle's acceptance as its validity. (It seems odd to speak of a principle as being valid at all, perhaps because validity is an all-or-nothing concept, appropriate for rules, but inconsistent with a principle's dimension of weight.) If we are asked (as we might well be) to defend the particular doctrine of precedent, or the particular technique of statutory interpretation, that we used in this argument, we should certainly cite the practice of others in using that doctrine or technique. But we should also cite other general principles that we believe support that practice, and this introduces a note of validity into the chord of acceptance. We might argue, for example, that the use we make of earlier cases and statutes is supported by a particular analysis of the point of practice of legislation or the doctrine of precedent, or by the principles of democratic theory, or by a particular position on the proper division of authority between national and local institutions, or something else of that sort. Nor is this path of support a one-way street leading to some ultimate principle resting on acceptance alone. Our principles of legislation, precedent, democracy, or federalism might be challenged too; and if they were we should argue for them, not only in terms of practice, but in terms of each other and in terms of the implications of trends of judicial and legislative decisions, even though this last would involve appealing to those same doctrines of interpretation we justified through the principles we are now trying to support. At this level of abstraction, in other words, principles rather hang together than link together.

So even though principles draw support from the official acts of legal institutions, they do not have a simple or direct enough connection with these acts to frame that connection in terms of criteria specified by some ultimate master rule of recognition. Is there any other route by which principles might be brought under such a rule?

Hart does say that a master rule might designate as law not only rules enacted by particular legal institutions, but rules established by custom as well. He has in mind a problem that bothered other positivists, including Austin. Many of our most ancient legal rules were never explicitly created by a legislature or a court. When they made their first appearance in legal opinions and texts, they were treated as already being part of the law because they represented the customary practice of the community, or some specialized part of it, like the business community. (The examples ordinarily given are rules of mercantile practice, like the rules governing what rights arise under a standard form of commercial paper.[27]) Since Austin thought that all law was the command of a determinate sovereign, he held that these customary practices were not law until the courts (as agents of the sovereign) recognized them, and that the courts were indulging in a fiction in pretending otherwise. But that seemed arbitrary. If everyone thought custom might in itself be law, the fact that Austin's theory said otherwise was not persuasive.

Hart reversed Austin on this point. The master rule, he says, might stipulate that some custom counts as law even before the courts recognize it. But he does not face the difficulty this raises for this general theory, because he does not attempt to set out the criteria a master rule might use for this purpose. It cannot use, as its only criterion, the provision that the community regard the practice as *morally* binding, for this would not distinguish legal customary rules from moral customary rules, and of course not all of the community's long-standing customary moral obligations are enforced as law. If, on the other hand, the test is whether the community regards the customary practice as *legally* binding, the whole point of the master rule is undercut, at least for this class of legal rules. The master rule, says Hart, marks the transformation from a primitive society to one with law, because it provides a test for determining social rules of law other than by measuring their acceptance. But if the master rule says merely that whatever other rules the community accepts as legally binding are legally binding, then it provides no such test at all, beyond the test we should use were there no master rule. The master rule becomes (for these cases) a nonrule of recognition; we might as well say that every primitive society has a secondary rule of recognition, namely the rule that whatever is accepted as binding is binding. Hart himself, in discussing international law, ridicules the idea that such a rule could be a rule of recognition, by describing the proposed rule as "an empty repetition of the mere fact that the society concerned . . . observes certain standards of conduct as obligatory rules."[28]

Hart's treatment of custom amounts, indeed, to a confession that there are at least some rules of law that are not binding because they are valid under standards laid down by a master rule but are binding—like the master rule—because they are accepted as binding by the community. This chips at the neat pyramidal architecture we admired in Hart's theory: we can no longer say that only the master rule is binding because of its acceptance, all other rules being valid under its terms.

This is perhaps only a chip, because the customary rules Hart has in mind are no longer a very significant part of the law. But it does suggest that Hart would be reluctant to widen the damage by bringing under the head of "custom" all those crucial principles and policies we have been discussing. If he were to call these part of the law and yet admit that the only test of their force lies in the degree to which they are accepted as law by the community or some part thereof, he would very sharply reduce that area of the law over which his master rule held any dominion. It is not just that all the principles and policies would escape its sway, though that would be bad enough. Once these principles and policies are accepted as law, and thus as standards judges must follow in determining legal obligations, it would follow that *rules* like those announced for the first time in *Riggs* and *Henningsen* owe their force at least in part to the authority of principles and policies, and so not entirely to the master rule of recognition.

So we cannot adapt Hart's version of positivism by modifying his rule of recognition to embrace principles. No tests of pedigree, relating principles to acts of legislation, can be formulated, nor can his concept of customary law, itself an exception to the first tenet of positivism, be made to serve without abandoning that tenet altogether. One more possibility must be considered, however. If no rule of recognition can provide a test for identifying principles, why not say that principles are ultimate, and form the rule of recognition of our law? The answer to the general question "What is valid law in an American jurisdiction?" would then require us to state all the principles (as well as ultimate constitutional rules) in force in that jurisdiction at the time, together with appropriate assignments of weight. A positivist might then regard the complete set of these standards as the rule of recognition of the jurisdiction. This solution has the attraction of paradox, but of course it is an unconditional surrender. If we simply designate our rule of recognition by the phrase "the complete set of principles in force," we achieve only the tautology that law is law. If, instead, we tried actually to list all the principles in force we would fail. They are controversial, their weight is all important, they are numberless, and they shift and change so fast that the start of our list would be obsolete before we reached the middle. Even if we succeeded, we would not have a key for law because there would be nothing left for our key to unlock.

I conclude that if we treat principles as law we must reject the positivists' first tenet, that the law of a community is distinguished from other social standards by some test in the form of a master rule. We have already decided that we must then abandon the second tenet—the doctrine of judicial discretion—or clarify it into triviality. What of the third tenet, the positivists' theory of legal obligation?

This theory holds that a legal obligation exists when (and only when) an established rule of law imposes such an obligation. It follows from this that in a hard case—when no such established rule can be found—there is no legal obligation until the judge creates a new rule for the future. The judge may apply that new rule to the parties in the case, but this is *ex post facto* legislation, not the enforcement of an existing obligation.

The positivists' doctrine of discretion (in the strong sense) required this view of legal obligation, because if a judge has discretion there can be no legal right or obligation—no entitlement—that he must enforce. Once we abandon that doctrine, however, and treat principles as law, we raise the possibility that a legal obligation might be imposed by a constellation of principles as well as by an established rule. We might want to say that a legal obligation exists whenever the case supporting such an obligation, in terms of binding legal principles of different sorts, is stronger than the case against it.

Of course, many questions would have to be answered before we could accept that view of legal obligation. If there is no rule of recognition, no test for law in that sense, how do we decide which principles are to count, and how much, in making such a case? How do we decide whether one case is better than another? If legal obligation rests on an undemonstrable judgment of that sort, how can it provide a justification for a judicial decision that one party had a legal obligation? Does this view of obligation square with the way lawyers, judges and laymen speak, and is it consistent with our attitudes about moral obligation? Does this analysis help us to deal with the classical jurisprudential puzzles about the nature of law?

These questions must be faced, but even the questions promise more than positivism provides. Positivism, on its own thesis, stops short of just those puzzling, hard cases that send us to look for theories of law. When we reach these cases, the positivist remits us to a doctrine of discretion that leads nowhere and tells nothing. His picture of law as a system of rules has exercised a tenacious hold on our imagination, perhaps through its very simplicity. If we shake ourselves loose from this model of rules, we may be able to build a model truer to the complexity and sophistication of our own practices.

---

1. See *Linkletter v. Walker,* 381 U.S. 618 (1965).
2. J. Austin, The Province of Jurisprudence Determined (1832).
3. See H. L. A. Hart, The Concept of Law 89–96 (1961).
4. *Id.* at 79–88.
5. *Id.* at 97–107.
6. *Id. passim,* particularly ch. VI.
7. *Id.,* ch. VII.
8. See Dworkin, *Wasserstrom: The Judicial Decision,* 75 Ethics 47 (1964), reprinted as *Does Law Have a Function?,* 74 *Yale L. J.* 640 (1965).
9. 115 N.Y. 506, 22 *N.E.* at 188 (1889).
10. *Id.* at 509, 22 *N.E.* at 189.
11. *Id.* at 511, 22 *N.E.* at 190.
12. 32 *N.J.* 358, 161 *A.2d* 69 (1960).
13. *Id.* at 386, 161 *A.2d* at 84.
14. *Id.*
15. *Id.* at 388, 161 *A.2d* at 86.
16. *Id.* at 387, 161 *A.2d* at 85.
17. *Id.* at 389, 161 *A.2d* at 86 quoting Frankfurter, J., in *United States v. Bethlehem Steel,* 315 U.S. 289, 326 (1942).
18. *Id.*
19. *Standard Oil v. United States,* 221 U.S. 1, 60 (1911); *United States v. American Tobacco Co.,* 221 U.S. 106, 180 (1911).

20. The distinction is in substance the same as that made by Rawls, *Two Concepts of Rules*, 64 *Philosophical Rev.* 3 (1955).

21. I have not spoken of that jurisprudential favorite, "limited" discretion, because that concept presents no special difficulties if we remember the relativity of discretion. Suppose the sergeant is told to choose from "amongst" experienced men, or to "take experience into account." We might say either that he has (limited) discretion in picking his patrol, or (full) discretion to either pick amongst experienced men or decide what else to take into account.

22. H. L. A. Hart, The Concept of Law 144 (1961).

23. See Wellington & Albert, *Statutory Interpretation and the Political Process: A Comment on Sinclair v. Atkinson*, 72 *Yale L. J.* 1547 (1963).

24. R. Pound, An Introduction to the Philosophy of Law 56 (rev. ed. 1954).

25. See, e.g., Dickinson, *The Law Behind Law* (pts. 1 & 2), 29 Colum. L. Rev. 112, 254 (1929).

26. H. L. A. Hart, The Concept of Law 92 (1961).

27. See Note, *Custom and Trade Usage: Its Application to Commercial Dealings and the Common Law,* 55 Colum. L. Rev. 1192 (1955), and materials cited therein at 1193 n.1. As that note makes plain, the actual practices of courts in recognizing trade customs follow the pattern of applying a set of general principles and policies rather than a test that could be captured as part of a rule of recognition.

28. H. L. A. Hart, The Concept of Law 230 (1961).

*RIGGS V. PALMER**

Court of Appeals of New York, 1889

Rights of Legatees— Murder of Testator

The law of New York relating to the probate of wills and the distributions of estates will not be construed so as to secure the benefit of a will to a legatee who has killed the testator in order to prevent a revocation of the will. GRAY and DANFORTH, J J., dissenting.

Appeal from supreme court, general term, third department.

Leslie W. Russell, for appellants. *W. M. Hawkins,* for respondents.

EARL, J. on the 13th day of August 1880, Francis B. Palmer made his last will and testament, in which he gave small legacies to his two daughters, Mrs. Riggs and Mrs. Preston, the plaintiffs in this action, and the remainder of his estate to his grandson, the defendant Elmer E. Palmer, subject to the support of Susan Palmer, his mother, with a gift over to the two daughters, subject to the support of Mrs. Palmer in case Elmer should survive him and die under age, unmarried, and without any issue. The testator, at the date of his will, owned a farm, and considerable personal property. He was a widower,

and thereafter, in March, 1882, he was married to Mrs. Bresee, with whom, before his marriage, he entered into an antenuptial contract, in which it was agreed that in lieu of dower and all other claims upon his estate in case she survived him she should have her support upon his farm during her life, and such support was expressly charged upon the farm. At the date of the will, and subsequently to the death of the testator, Elmer lived with him as a member of his family, and at his death was 16 years old. He knew of the provisions made in his favor in the will, and, that he might prevent his grandfather from revoking such provisions, which he had manifested some intention to do, and to obtain the speedy enjoyment and immediate possession of his property, he willfully murdered him by poisoning him. He now claims the property, and the sole question for our determination is, can he have it?

The defendants say that the testator is dead; that his will was made in due form, and has been admitted to probate; and that therefore it must have effect according to the letter of the law. It is quite true that statutes regulating the making, proof, and effect of wills and the devolution of property, if literally construed, and if their force and effect can in no way and under no circumstances be controlled or modified, give this property to the murderer. The purpose of those statutes was to enable testators to dispose of their estates to the objects of their bounty at death, and to carry into effect their final wishes legally expressed; and in considering and giving effect to them this purpose must be kept in view. It was the intention of the law-makers that the donees in a will should have the property given to them. But it never could have been their intention that a donee who murdered the testator to make the will operative should have any benefit under it. If such a case had been present to their minds, and it had been supposed necessary to make some provision of law to meet it, it cannot be doubted that they would have provided for it. It is a familiar canon of construction that a thing which is within the intention of the makers of a statute is as much within the statute as if it were within the letter; and a thing which is within the letter of the statute is not within the statute unless it be within the intention of the makers. The writers of laws do not always express their intention perfectly, but either exceed it or fall short of it, so that judges are to collect it from probable or rational conjectures only, and this is called "rational interpretation;" and Rutherford, in his Institutes, (page 420) says: "Where we make use of rational interpretation, sometimes we restrain the meaning of the writer so as to take in less, and sometimes we extend or enlarge his meaning so as to take in more, than his words express." Such a construction ought to be put upon a statute as will best answer the intention which the makers had in view. . . . Many cases are mentioned where it was held that matters embraced in the general words of statutes nevertheless were not within the statutes, because it could not have been the intention of the law-makers that they should be included. They were taken out of the statutes by an equitable construction; and it is said in Bacon: "By an equitable construction a case not within the letter of a statute is sometimes holden to be within the meaning, because it is within the mischief for which a remedy is provided. The reason for such construction is that the law-makers could not set down every case in express terms. In order to form a right judgment whether a case be within the equity of a statute, it is a good way to suppose the law-maker present, and that you have asked him this question: Did you intend to comprehend this case? Then you must give yourself such answer as you imagine he, being an upright and reasonable man, would have given. If this be that he did mean to comprehend it, you may

safely hold the case to be within the equity of the statute; for while you do no more than he would have done, you do not act contrary to the statute, but in conformity thereto." (9 Bac. Abr. 248.) In some cases the letter of a legislative act is restrained by an equitable construction; in others, it is enlarged; in others, the construction is contrary to the letter. . . . If the law-makers could, as to this case, be consulted, would they say that they intended by their general language that the property of a testator or of an ancestor should pass to one who had taken his life for the express purpose of getting his property? In 1 Bl. Comm. 91, the learned author, speaking of the construction of statutes, says: "If there arise out of them collaterally any absurd consequences manifestly contradictory to common reason, they are with regard to those collateral consequences void. Where some collateral matter arises out of the general words, and happens to be unreasonable, there the judges are in decency to conclude that this consequence was not foreseen by the parliament, and therefore they are at liberty to expound the statute by equity, and only *quo ad hoc* disregard it;" and he gives as an illustration, if an act of parliament gives a man power to try all causes that arise within his manor of Dale, yet, if a cause should arise in which he himself is party, the act is construed not to extend to that, because it is unreasonable that any man should determine his own quarrel. There was a statute in Bologna that whoever drew blood in the streets should be severely punished, and yet it was held not to apply to the case of a barber who opened a vein in the street. It is commanded in the decalogue that no work shall be done upon the Sabbath, and yet giving the command a rational interpretation founded upon its design the Infallible Judge held that it did not prohibit works of necessity, charity, or benevolence on that day.

What could be more unreasonable than to suppose that it was the legislative intention in the general laws passed for the orderly peaceable, and just devolution of property that they should have operation in favor of one who murdered his ancestor that he might speedily come into the possession of his estate? Such an intention is inconceivable. We need not, therefore, be much troubled by the general language contained in the laws. Besides, all laws, as well as all contracts, may be controlled in their operation and effect by general, fundamental maxims of the common law. No one shall be permitted to profit by his own fraud, or to take advantage of his own wrong, or to found any claim upon his own iniquity, or to acquire property by his own crime. These maxims are dictated by public policy, have their foundation in universal law administered in all civilized countries, and have nowhere been superseded by statutes. They were applied in the decision of the case of *Insurance Co. v. Armstrong,* 117 U. S. 599, 6 Sup. Ct. Rep. 877. There it was held that the person who procured a policy upon the life of another, payable at his death, and then murdered the assured to make the policy payable, could not recover thereon. Mr. Justice FIELD, writing the opinion, said: "Independently of any proof of the motives of Hunter in obtaining the policy, and even assuming that they were just and proper, he forfeited all rights under it when, to secure its immediate payment, he murdered the assured. It would be a reproach to the jurisprudence of the country if one could recover insurance money payable on the death of a party whose life he had feloniously taken. As well might he recover insurance money upon a building that he had willfully fired." These maxims, without any statute giving them force or operation, frequently control the effect and nullify the language of wills. A will procured by fraud and deception, like any other instrument, may be decreed void, and set aside; and so a particular portion of a will may be excluded from probate, or held inoperative, if induced by the fraud or undue influence of the person in whose favor it is. . . . So a will may contain provisions which are immoral, irreligious, or against public policy, and they will be held void.

Here there was no certainty that this murderer would survive the testator, or that the testator would not change his will, and there was no certainty that he would get this property if nature was allowed to take its course. He therefore murdered the testator expressly to vest himself with an estate. Under such circumstances, what law, human or divine, will allow him to take the estate and enjoy the fruits of his crime? The will spoke and became operative at the death of the testator. He caused that death, and thus by his crime made it speak and have operation. Shall it speak and operate in his favor? If he had met the testator, and taken his property by force, he would have had no title to it. Shall he acquire title by murdering him? If he had gone to the testator's house, and by force compelled him, or by fraud or undue influence had induced him, to will him his property, the law would not allow him to hold it. But can he give effect and operation to a will by murder, and yet take the property? To answer these questions in the affirmative it seems to me would be a reproach to the jurisprudence of our state, and an

offense against public policy. Under the civil law, evolved from the general principles of natural law and justice by many generations of jurisconsults, philosophers, and statesmen, one cannot take property by inheritance or will from an ancestor or benefactor whom he has murdered. . . . In the Civil Code of Lower Canada the provisions on the subject in the Code Napoleon have been substantially copied. But, so far as I can find, in no country where the common law prevails has it been deemed important to enact a law to provide for such a case. Our revisers and law-makers were familiar with the civil law, and they did not deem it important to incorporate into our statutes its provisions upon this subject. This is not a *casus omissus.* It was evidently supposed that the maxims of the common law were sufficient to regulate such a case, and that a specific enactment for that purpose was not needed. For the same reasons the defendant Palmer cannot take any of this property as heir. Just before the murder he was not an heir, and it was not certain that he ever would be. He might have died before his grandfather, or might have been disinherited by him. He made himself an heir by the murder, and he seeks to take property as the fruit of his crime. What has before been said to him as legatee applies to him with equal force as an heir. He cannot vest himself with title by crime. My view of this case does not inflict upon Elmer any greater or other punishment for his crime than the law specifies. It takes from him no property, but simply holds that he shall not acquire property by his crime, and thus be rewarded for its commission.

Our attention is called to *Owens v. Owens,* 100 N. C. 240, 6 S. E. Rep. 794, as a case quite like this. There a wife had been convicted of being an accessory before the fact to the murder of her husband, and it was held that she was nevertheless entitled to dower. I am unwilling to assent to the doctrine of that case. The statutes provide dower for a wife who has the misfortune to survive her husband, and thus lose his support and protection. It is clear beyond their purpose to make provision for a wife who by her own crime makes herself a widow, and willfully and intentionally deprives herself of the support and protection of her husband. As she might have died before him, and thus never have been his widow, she cannot by her crime vest herself with an estate. The principle which lies at the bottom of the maxim *volenti non fit injuria* should be applied to such a case, and a widow should not, for the purpose of acquiring, as such, property rights, be permitted to allege a widowhood which she has wickedly and intentionally created.

The facts found entitled the plaintiffs to the relief they sought. The error of the referee was in his conclusion of law. Instead of granting a new trial, therefore, I think the proper judgment upon the facts found should be ordered here. The facts have been passed upon twice with the same result,—first upon the trial of Palmer for murder, and then by the referee in this action. We are therefore of opinion that the ends of justice do not require that they should again come in question. The judgment of the general term and that entered upon the report of the referee should therefore be reversed, and judgment should be entered as follows: That Elmer E. Palmer and the administrator be enjoined from using any of the personalty or real estate left by the testator for Elmer's benefit; that the devise and bequest in the will to Elmer be declared ineffective to pass the title to him; that by reason of the crime of murder committed upon the grandfather he is deprived of any interest in the estate left by him; that the plaintiffs are the true owners of the real and personal estate left by the testator, subject to the charge in favor of Elmer's mother and the widow of the testator, under the antenuptial agreement, and that the plaintiffs have costs in all the courts against Elmer. All concur, except GRAY, J., who reads dissenting opinion, and DANFORTH, J., concurs.

GRAY, J., (*dissenting*). This appeal represents an extraordinary state of facts, and the case, in respect to them, I believe, is without precedent in this state. The respondent, a lad of 16 years of age, being aware of the provisions in his grandfather's will, which constituted him the residuary legatee of the testator's estate, caused his death by poison, in 1882. For this crime he was tried, and was convicted of murder in the second degree, and at the time of the commencement of this action he was serving out his sentence in the state reformatory. This action was brought by two of the children of the testator for the purpose of having those provisions of the will in the respondent's favor canceled and annulled. The appellants' argument for a reversal of the judgment, which dismissed their complaint, is that the respondent unlawfully prevented a revocation of the existing will, or a new will from being made, by his crime; and that he terminated the enjoyment by the testator of his property, and effected his own succession to it, by the same crime. They say that to permit the respondent to take the property willed to him would be to permit him to take advantage of his own wrong. To sustain their position the appellants' counsel has submitted an able and elaborate brief, and, if I believed that the decision of the question could be effected by considerations of an equitable nature, I should not hesitate to assent to views which commend themselves to the conscience. But the matter does not lie within the domain of conscience. We are bound by the rigid rules of law, which have been established by the legislature, and within the limits of which the determination of this question is confined. The question we are dealing with is whether a testamentary disposition can be altered, or a will revoked, after the testator's death, through an appeal to the courts, when the legislature has by its enactments prescribed exactly when and how wills may be made, altered, and revoked, and apparently, as it seems to me, when they have been fully complied with, has left no room for the exercise of an equitable jurisdiction by courts over such matters. Modern jurisprudence, in recognizing the right of the individual, under more or less restrictions, to dispose of his property after his death, subjects it to legislative control, both as to extent and as to mode of exercise. Complete freedom of testamentary disposition of one's property has not been and is not the universal rule, as we see from the provisions of the Napoleonic Code, from the systems of jurisprudence in countries which are modeled upon the Roman law, and from the statutes of many of our states. To the statutory restraints which are imposed upon the disposition of one's property by will are added strict and systematic statutory rules for the execution, alteration, and revocation of the will, which must be, at least substantially, if not exactly, followed to insure validity and performance. The reason for the establishment of such rules, we may naturally assume, consists in the purpose to create those safeguards about these grave and important acts which experience has demonstrated to be the wisest and surest. That freedom which is permitted to be exercised in the testamentary disposition of one's estate by the laws of the state is subject to its being exercised in conformity with the regulations of the statutes. The capacity and the power of the individual to dispose of his property after death, and the mode by which that power can be exercised, are matters of which the legislature has assumed the entire control, and has undertaken to regulate with comprehensive particularity.

The appellants' argument is not helped by reference to those rules of the civil law, or to those laws of other governments, by which the heir, or legatee, is excluded from benefit under the testament if he has been convicted of killing, or attempting to kill, the testator. In the absence of such legislation here, the courts are not empowered to institute such a system of remedial justice. The deprivation of the heir of his testamentary succession by the Roman law, when guilty of such a crime, plainly was intended to be in the nature of a punishment imposed upon him. The succession, in such a case of guilt, escheated to the exchequer. . . . I concede that rules of law which annul testamentary provisions made for the benefit of those who have become unworthy of them may be based on principles of equity and of natural justice. It is quite reasonable to suppose that a testator would revoke or alter his will, where his mind has been so angered and changed as to make him unwilling to have his will executed as it stood. But these principles only suggest sufficient reasons for the enactment of laws to meet such cases.

The statutes of this state have prescribed various ways in which a will may be altered or revoked; but the very provision defining the modes of alterations and revocation implies a prohibition of alteration or revocation in any other way. The words of the section of the statute are: "No will in writing, except in the cases hereinafter mentioned, nor any part thereof, shall be revoked or altered otherwise," etc. Where, therefore, none of the cases mentioned are met by the facts, and the revocation is not in the way described in the section, the will of the testator is unalterable. I think that a valid will must continue as a will always, unless revoked in the manner provided by the statutes. Mere intention to revoke a will does not have the effect of revocation. The intention to revoke is necessary to constitute the effective revocation of a will, but it must be demonstrated by one of the acts contemplated by the statute. As WOODWORTH, J., said in *Dan v. Brown,* 4 Cow. 490; "Revocation is an act of the mind, which must be demonstrated by some outward and visible sign of revocation." The same learned judge said in that case: "The rule is that if the testator lets the will stand until he dies, it is his will; if he does not suffer it to do so, it is not his will.". . . The finding of fact of the referee that presumably the testator would have altered his will had he known of his grandson's murderous intent cannot affect the question. We may concede it to the fullest extent; but still the cardinal objection is undisposed of,—that the making and the revocation of a will are purely matters of statutory regulation, by which the court is bound in the determination of questions relating to these acts. Two cases,—in this state and in Kentucky,—at an early day, seem to me to be much in point. *Gains v. Gains,* 2 A. K. Marsh. 190, was decided by the Kentucky court of appeals in 1820. It was there urged that the testator intended to have destroyed his will, and that he was forcibly prevented from doing so by the defendant in error or devisee; and it was insisted that the will, though not expressly, was thereby virtually, revoked. The court held, as the act concerning wills prescribed that manner in which a will might be revoked, that, as none of the acts evidencing revocation were done, the intention could not be substituted for the act. In that case the will was snatched away, and forcibly retained. In 1854, Surrogate BRADFORD, whose opinions are entitled to the highest consideration, decided the case of *Leaycraft v. Simmons,* 3 Bradf. Sur. 35. In that case the testator, a man of 89 years of age, desired to make a codicil to his will, in order to enlarge the provisions for his daughter. His son, having custody of the instrument, and the one to be prejudiced by the change, refused to produce the will at the testator's request, for the purpose of alteration. The learned surrogate refers to the provisions of the civil law for such and other cases of unworthy conduct in the heir or legatee, and says: "Our statute has undertaken to prescribe the mode in which wills can be revoked [citing the statutory provision]. This is the law by which I am governed in passing upon questions touching the revocation of wills. The whole of this subject is now regulated by statute; and a mere intention to revoke, however well authenticated, or however defeated, is not sufficient." And he held that the will must be admitted to probate. I may refer also to a case in the Pennsylvania courts. In that state the statute prescribed the mode for repealing or altering a will, and in *Clingan v. Micheltree,* 31 Pa. St. 25, the supreme court of the state held, where a will was kept from destruction by the fraud and misrepresentation of the devisee, that to declare it canceled as against the fraudulent party would be to enlarge the statute. I cannot find any support for the argument that the respondent's succession to the property should be avoided because of his criminal act, when the laws are silent. Public policy does not demand it; for the demands of public policy are satisfied by the proper execution of the laws and the punishment of the crime. There has been no convention between the testator and his legatee; nor is there any such contractual element, in such a disposition of property by a testator, as to impose or imply conditions in the legatee. The appellants' argument practically amounts to this: that, as the legatee has been guilty of a crime, by the commission of which he is placed in a position to sooner receive the benefits of the testamentary provision, his rights to the property should be forfeited, and he should be divested of his estate. To allow their argument to prevail would involve the diversion by the court of the testator's estate into the hands of persons whom, possibly enough, for all we know, the testator might not have chosen or desired as its recipients. Practically the court is asked to make another will for the testator. The laws do not warrant this judicial action, and mere presumption would not be strong enough to sustain it. But, more than this, to concede the appellants' views would involve the imposition of an additional punishment or penalty upon the respondent. What power or warrant have the courts to add to the respondent's penalties by depriving him of property? The law has punished him for his crime, and we may not say that it was an insufficient punishment. In the trial and punishment of the respondent the law has vindicated itself for the outrage which he committed, and further judicial utterance upon the subject of punishment or deprivation of rights is barred. We may not, in the language of the court in *People v. Thornton,* 25 Hun. 456, "enhance the pains, penalties, and forfeitures provided by law for the punishment of crime." The judgment should be affirmed, with costs.

DANFORTH, J., concurs.

INTEGRITY IN LAW*

Ronald Dworkin

The McLoughlin Case

. . . Mrs. McLoughlin's husband and four children were injured in an automobile accident in England at about 4 P.M. on October 19, 1973. She heard about the accident at home from a neighbor at about 6 P.M. and went immediately to the hospital, where she learned that her daughter was dead and saw the serious condition of her husband and other children. She suffered nervous shock and later sued the defendant driver, whose negligence had caused the accident, as well as other parties who were in different ways involved, for compensation for her emotional injuries. Her lawyer pointed to several earlier decisions of English courts awarding compensation to people who had suffered emotional injury on seeing serious injury to a close relative. But in all these cases the plaintiff had either been at the scene of the accident or had arrived within minutes. In a 1972 case, for example, a wife recovered—won compensation—for emotional injury; she had come upon the body of her husband immediately after his fatal accident. In 1967 a man who was not related to any of the victims of a train crash worked for hours trying to rescue victims and suffered nervous shock from the experience. He was allowed to recover. Mrs. McLoughlin's lawyer relied on these cases as precedents, decisions which had made it part of the law that people in her position are entitled to compensation. . . .

The judge before whom Mrs. McLoughlin first brought her suit, the trial judge, decided that the precedents her lawyer cited, about others who had recovered compensation for emotional injury suffered when they saw accident victims, were distinguishable because in all those cases the shock had occurred at the scene of the accident while she was shocked some two hours later and in a different place. Of course not every difference in the facts of two cases makes the earlier one distinguishable: no

---

*From *Law's Empire* (Cambridge, MA: Harvard University Press, 1986) 24–29, 225–75. Endnotes have been edited and renumbered.

one could think it mattered if Mrs. McLoughlin was younger than the plaintiffs in the earlier cases.

The trial judge thought that suffering injury away from the scene was an important difference because it meant that Mrs. McLoughlin's injury was not "foreseeable" in the way that the injury to the other plaintiffs had been. Judges in both Britain and America follow the common law principle that people who act carelessly are liable only for reasonably foreseeable injuries to others, injuries a reasonable person would anticipate if he reflected on the matter. The trial judge was bound by the doctrine of precedent to recognize that emotional injury to close relatives at the scene of an accident is reasonably foreseeable, but he said that injury to a mother who saw the results of the accident later is not. So he thought he could distinguish the putative precedents in that way and decided against Mrs. McLoughlin's claim.

She appealed his decision to the next highest court in the British hierarchy, the Court of Appeal. That court affirmed the trial judge's decision—it refused her appeal and let his decision stand—but not on the argument he had used. The Court of Appeal said it *was* reasonably foreseeable that a mother would rush to the hospital to see her injured family and that she would suffer emotional shock from seeing them in the condition Mrs. McLoughlin found. That court distinguished the precedents not on that ground but for the very different reason that what it called "policy" justified a distinction. The precedents had established liability for emotional injury in certain restricted circumstances, but the Court of Appeal said that recognizing a larger area of liability, embracing injuries to relatives not at the scene, would have a variety of adverse consequences for the community as a whole. It would encourage many more lawsuits for emotional injuries, and this would exacerbate the problem of congestion in the courts. It would open new opportunities for fraudulent claims by people who had not really suffered serious emotional damage but could find doctors to testify that they had. It would increase the cost of liability insurance, making it more expensive to drive and perhaps preventing some poor people from driving at all. The claims of those who had suffered genuine emotional injury away from the scene would be harder to prove, and the uncertainties of litigation might complicate their condition and delay their recovery.

Mrs. McLoughlin appealed the decision once more, to the House of Lords, which reversed the Court of Appeal and ordered a new trial. The decision was unanimous, but their lordships disagreed about what they called the true state of the law. Several of them said that policy reasons, of the sort described by the Court of Appeal, might in some circumstances be sufficient to distinguish a line of precedents and so justify a judge's refusal to extend the principle of those cases to a larger area of liability. But they did not think these policy reasons were of sufficient plausibility or merit in Mrs. McLoughlin's case. They did not believe that the risk of a "flood" of litigation was sufficiently grave, and they said the courts should be able to distinguish genuine from fraudulent claims even among those whose putative injury was suffered several hours after the accident. They did not undertake to say when good policy arguments might be available to limit recovery for emotional injury; they left it an open question, for example, whether Mrs. McLoughlin's sister in Australia (if she had one) could recover for the shock she might have in reading about the accident weeks or months later in a letter.

Two of their lordships took a very different view of the law. They said it would be wrong for courts to deny recovery to an otherwise meritorious plaintiff for the *kinds* of reasons the Court of Appeal had mentioned and which the other law lords had said might be sufficient in some circumstances. The precedents should be regarded as distinguishable, they said, only if the moral *principles* assumed in the earlier cases for some reason did not apply to the plaintiff in the same way. And once it is conceded that the damage to a mother in the hospital hours after an accident is reasonably foreseeable to a careless driver, then no difference in moral principle can be found between the two cases. Congestion in the courts or a rise in the price of automobile liability insurance, they said, however inconvenient these might be to the community as a whole, cannot justify refusing to enforce individual rights and duties that have been recognized and enforced before. They said these were the wrong sorts of arguments to make to judges as arguments of law, however cogent they might be if addressed to legislators as arguments for a change in the law. (Lord Scarman's opinion was particularly clear and strong on this point.) The argument among their lordships revealed an important difference of opinion about the proper role of considerations of policy in deciding what result parties to a lawsuit are entitled to have. . . .

A Large View

. . . Law as integrity denies that statements of law are either the backward-looking factual reports of conventionalism or the forward-looking instrumental programs of legal pragmatism. It insists that legal claims are interpretive judgments and therefore combine backward- and forward-looking elements; they interpret contemporary legal practice seen as an unfolding political narrative. So law as integrity rejects as unhelpful the ancient question whether judges find or invent law; we understand legal reasoning, it suggests, only by seeing the sense in which they do both and neither.

Integrity and Interpretation

The adjudicative principle of integrity instructs judges to identify legal rights and duties, so far as possible, on the assumption that they were all created by a single author—the community personified—expressing a coherent conception of justice and fairness. We form our third conception of law, our third view of what rights and duties flow from past political decisions, by restating this instruction as a thesis about the grounds of law. According to law as integrity, propositions of law are true if they figure in or follow from the principles of justice, fairness, and procedural due process that provide the best constructive interpretation of the community's legal practice. Deciding whether the law grants Mrs. McLoughlin compensation for her injury, for example, means deciding whether legal practice is seen in a better light if we assume the community has accepted the principle that people in her position are entitled to compensation. . . .

Integrity and History

History matters in law as integrity: very much but only in a certain way. Integrity does not require consistency in principle over all historical stages of a community's law; it does not require that judges try to understand the law they enforce as continuous in principle with the abandoned law of a previous century or even a previous generation. It commands a horizontal rather than vertical consistency of principle across the range of the legal standards the community now enforces. It insists that the law—the rights and duties that flow from past collective decisions and for that reason license or require coer-

cion—contains not only the narrow explicit content of these decisions but also, more broadly, the scheme of principles necessary to justify them. History matters because that scheme of principle must justify the standing as well as the content of these past decisions. Our justification for treating the Endangered Species Act as law, unless and until it is repealed, crucially includes the fact that Congress enacted it, and any justification we supply for treating that fact as crucial must itself accommodate the way we treat other events in our political past.

Law as integrity, then, begins in the present and pursues the past only so far as and in the way its contemporary focus dictates. It does not aim to recapture, even for present law, the ideals or practical purposes of the politicians who first created it. It aims rather to justify what they did (sometimes including, as we shall see, what they said) in an overall story worth telling now, a story with a complex claim: that present practice can be organized by and justified in principles sufficiently attractive to provide an honorable future. Law as integrity deplores the mechanism of the older "law is law" view as well as the cynicism of the newer "realism." It sees both views as rooted in the same false dichotomy of finding and inventing law. When a judge declares that a particular principle is instinct in law, he reports not a simple-minded claim about the motives of past statesmen, a claim a wise cynic can easily refute, but an interpretive proposal: that the principle both fits and justifies some complex part of legal practice, that it provides an attractive way to see, in the structure of that practice, the consistency of principle integrity requires. Law's optimism is in that way conceptual; claims of law are endemically constructive, just in virtue of the kind of claims they are. This optimism may be misplaced: legal practice may in the end yield to nothing but a deeply skeptical interpretation. But that is not inevitable just because a community's history is one of great change and conflict. An imaginative interpretation can be constructed on morally complicated, even ambiguous terrain.

The Chain of Law

The Chain Novel

. . . [C]reative interpretation takes its formal structure from the idea of intention, not (at least not necessarily) because it aims to discover the purposes of any particular historical person or group but because it aims to impose purpose over the text or data or tradition being interpreted. Since all creative interpretation shares this feature, and therefore has a normative aspect or component, we profit from comparing law with other forms or occasions of interpretation. We can usefully compare the judge deciding what the law is on some issue not only with the citizens of courtesy deciding what that tradition requires, but with the literary critic teasing out the various dimensions of value in a complex play or poem.

Judges, however, are authors as well as critics. A judge deciding *McLoughlin* or *Brown* adds to the tradition he interprets; future judges confront a new tradition that includes what he has done. Of course literary criticism contributes to the traditions of art in which authors work; the character and importance of that contribution are themselves issues in critical theory. But the contribution of judges is more direct, and the distinction between author and interpreter more a matter of different aspects of the same process. We can find an even more fruitful comparison between literature and law, therefore, by constructing an artificial genre of literature that we might call the chain novel.

In this enterprise a group of novelists writes a novel *seriatim;* each novelist in the chain interprets the chapters he has been given in order to write a new chapter, which is then added to what the next novelist receives, and so on. Each has the job of writing his chapter so as to make the novel being constructed the best it can be, and the complexity of this task models the complexity of deciding a hard case under law as integrity. The imaginary literary enterprise is fantastic but not unrecognizable. Some novels have actually been written in this way, though mainly for a debunking purpose, and certain parlor games for rainy weekends in English country houses have something of the same structure. Television soap operas span decades with the same characters and some minimal continuity of personality and plot, though they are written by different teams of authors even in different weeks. In our example, however, the novelists are expected to take their responsibilities of continuity more seriously; they aim jointly to create, so far as they can, a single unified novel that is the best it can be.[1]

Each novelist aims to make a single novel of the material he has been given, what he adds to it, and (so far as he can control this) what his successors will want or be able to add. He must try to make this the best novel it can be construed as the

work of a single author rather than, as is the fact, the product of many different hands. That calls for an overall judgment on his part, or a series of overall judgments as he writes and rewrites. He must take up some view about the novel in progress, some working theory about its characters, plot, genre, theme, and point, in order to decide what counts as continuing it and not as beginning anew. If he is a good critic, his view of these matters will be complicated and multifaceted, because the value of a decent novel cannot be captured from a single perspective. He will aim to find layers and currents of meaning rather than a single, exhaustive theme. We can, however, in our now familiar way give some structure to any interpretation he adopts, by distinguishing two dimensions on which it must be tested. The first is what we have been calling the dimension of fit. He cannot adopt any interpretation, however complex, if he believes that no single author who set out to write a novel with the various readings of character, plot, theme, and point that interpretation describes could have written substantially the text he has been given. That does not mean his interpretation must fit every bit of the text. It is not disqualified simply because he claims that some lines or tropes are accidental, or even that some events of plot are mistakes because they work against the literary ambitions the interpretation states. But the interpretation he takes up must nevertheless flow throughout the text; it must have general explanatory power, and it is flawed if it leaves unexplained some major structural aspect of the text, a subplot treated as having great dramatic importance or a dominant and repeated metaphor. If no interpretation can be found that is not flawed in that way, then the chain novelist will not be able fully to meet his assignment; he will have to settle for an interpretation that captures most of the text, conceding that it is not wholly successful. Perhaps even that partial success is unavailable; perhaps every interpretation he considers is inconsistent with the bulk of the material supplied to him. In that case he must abandon the enterprise, for the consequence of taking the interpretive attitude toward the text in question is then a piece of internal skepticism: that nothing can count as continuing the novel rather than beginning anew.

He may find, not that no single interpretation fits the bulk of the text, but that more than one does. The second dimension of interpretation then requires him to judge which of these eligible readings makes the work in progress best, all things considered. At this point his more substantive aesthetic judgments, about the importance or insight or realism or beauty of different ideas the novel might be taken to express, come into play. But the formal and structural considerations that dominate on the first dimension figure on the second as well, for even when neither of two interpretations is disqualified out of hand as explaining too little, one may show the text in a better light because it fits more of the text or provides a more interesting integration of style and content. So the distinction between the two dimensions is less crucial or profound than it might seem. It is a useful analytical device that helps us give structure to any interpreter's working theory or style. He will form a sense of when an interpretation fits so poorly that it is unnecessary to consider its substantive appeal, because he knows that this cannot outweigh its embarrassments of fit in deciding whether it makes the novel better, everything taken into account, than its rivals. This sense will define the first dimension for him. But he need not reduce his intuitive sense to any precise formula; he would rarely need to decide whether some interpretation barely survives or barely fails, because a bare survivor, no matter how ambitious or interesting it claimed the text to be, would almost certainly fail in the overall comparison with other interpretations whose fit was evident.

We can now appreciate the range of different kinds of judgments that are blended in this overall comparison. Judgments about textual coherence and integrity, reflecting different formal literary values, are interwoven with more substantive aesthetic judgments that themselves assume different literary aims. Yet these various kinds of judgments, of each general kind, remain distinct enough to check one another in an overall assessment, and it is that possibility of contest, particularly between textual and substantive judgments, that distinguishes a chain novelist's assignment from more independent creative writing. Nor can we draw any flat distinction between the stage at which a chain novelist interprets the text he has been given and the stage at which he adds his own chapter, guided by the interpretation he has settled on. When he begins to write he might discover in what he has written a different, perhaps radically different, interpretation. Or he might find it impossible to write in the tone or theme he first took up, and that will lead him to reconsider other interpretations he first rejected. In either case he returns to the text to reconsider the lines it makes eligible.

Scrooge

We can expand this abstract description of the chain novelist's judgment through an example. Suppose you are a novelist well down the chain. Suppose Dickens never wrote *A Christmas Carol,* and the text you are furnished, though written by several people, happens to be the first part of that short novel. You consider these two interpretations of the central character: Scrooge is inherently and irredeemably evil, an embodiment of the untarnished wickedness of human nature freed from the disguises of convention he rejects; or Scrooge is inherently good but progressively corrupted by the false values and perverse demands of high capitalist society. Obviously it will make an enormous difference to the way you continue the story which of these interpretations you adopt. If you have been given almost all of *A Christmas Carol* with only the very end to be written— Scrooge has already had his dreams, repented, and sent his turkey—it is too late for you to make him irredeemably wicked, assuming you think, as most interpreters would, that the text will not bear that interpretation without too much strain. I do not mean that no interpreter could possibly think Scrooge inherently evil after his supposed redemption. Someone might take that putative redemption to be a final act of hypocrisy, though only at the cost of taking much else in the text not at face value. This would be a poor interpretation, not because no one could think it a good one, but because it is in fact, on all the criteria so far described, a poor one.

But now suppose you have been given only the first few sections of *A Christmas Carol.* You find that neither of the two interpretations you are considering is decisively ruled out by anything in the text so far; perhaps one would better explain some minor incidents of plot that must be left unconnected on the other, but each interpretation can be seen generally to flow through the abbreviated text as a whole. A competent novelist who set out to write a novel along either of the lines suggested could well have written what you find on the pages. In that case you have a further decision to make. Your assignment is to make of the text the best it can be, and you will therefore choose the interpretation you believe makes the work more significant or otherwise better. That decision will probably (though not inevitably) depend on whether you think that real people somewhat like Scrooge are born bad or are corrupted by capitalism. But it will depend on much else as well, because your aesthetic convictions are not so simple as to make only this aspect of a novel relevant to its overall success. Suppose you think that one interpretation integrates not only plot but image and setting as well; the social interpretation accounts, for example, for the sharp contrast between the individualistic fittings and partitions of Scrooge's countinghouse and the communitarian formlessness of Bob Cratchit's household. Now your aesthetic judgment—about which reading makes the continuing novel better as a novel—is itself more complex because it must identify and trade off different dimensions of value in a novel. Suppose you believe that the original sin reading is much the more accurate depiction of human nature, but that the sociorealist reading provides a deeper and more interesting formal structure for the novel. You must then ask yourself which interpretation makes the work of art better on the whole. You may never have reflected on that sort of question before—perhaps the tradition of criticim in which you have been trained takes it for granted that one or the other of these dimensions is the more important—but that is no reason why you may not do so now. Once you make up your mind you will believe that the correct interpretation of Scrooge's character is the interpretation that makes the novel better on the whole, so judged.

This contrived example is complex enough to provoke the following apparently important question. Is your judgment about the best way to interpret and continue the sections you have been given of *A Christmas Carol* a free or a constrained judgment? Are you free to give effect to your own assumptions and attitudes about what novels should be like? Or are you bound to ignore these because you are enslaved by a text you cannot alter? The answer is plain enough: neither of these two crude descriptions—of total creative freedom or mechanical textual constraint—captures your situation, because each must in some way be qualified by the other. You will sense creative freedom when you compare your task with some relatively more mechanical one, like direct translation of a text into a foreign language. But you will sense constraint when you compare it with some relatively less guided one, like beginning a new novel of your own.

It is important not only to notice this contrast between elements of artistic freedom and textual constraint but also not to misunderstand its character. It is *not* a contrast between those aspects of in-

terpretation that are dependent on and those that are independent of the interpreter's aesthetic convictions. And it is not a contrast between those aspects that may be and those that cannot be controversial. For the constraints that you sense as limits to your freedom to read *A Christmas Carol* so as to make Scrooge irredeemably evil are as much matters of judgment and conviction, about which different chain novelists might disagree, as the convictions and attitudes you call on in deciding whether the novel would have been better if he had been irredeemably evil. If the latter convictions are "subjective" (I use the language of external skepticism, reluctantly, because some readers will find it helpful here) then so are the former. Both major types of convictions any interpreter has—about which readings fit the text better or worse and about which of two readings makes the novel substantively better—are internal to his overall scheme of beliefs and attitudes; neither type is independent of that scheme in some way that the other is not. . . .

Our chain-novel example has so far been distorted by the unrealistic assumption that the text you were furnished miraculously had the unity of something written by a single author. Even if each of the previous novelists in the chain took his responsibilities very seriously indeed, the text you were given would show the marks of its history, and you would have to tailor your style of interpretation to that circumstance. You might not find any interpretation that flows through the text, that fits everything the material you have been given treats as important. You must lower your sights (as conscientious writers who join the team of an interminable soap opera might do) by trying to construct an interpretation that fits the bulk of what you take to be artistically most fundamental in the text. More than one interpretation may survive this more relaxed test. To choose among these, you must turn to your background aesthetic convictions, including those you will regard as formal. Possibly no interpretation will survive even the relaxed test. That is the skeptical possibility I mentioned earlier: you will then end by abandoning the project, rejecting your assignment as impossible. But you cannot know in advance that you will reach that skeptical result. You must try first. The chain-novel fantasy will be useful in the later argument in various ways, but that is the most important lesson it teaches. The wise-sounding judgment that no one interpretation could be best must be earned and defended like any other interpretive claim.

A Misleading Objection

A chain novelist, then, has many difficult decisions to make, and different chain novelists can be expected to make these differently. But his decisions do not include, nor are they properly summarized as, the decision whether and how far he should depart from the novel-in-progress he has been furnished. For he has nothing he *can* depart from or cleave to until he has constructed a novel-in-process from the text, and the various decisions we have canvassed are all decisions he must make just to do this. Suppose you have decided that a sociorealist interpretation of the opening sections of *A Christmas Carol* makes that text, on balance, the best novel-so-far it can be, and so you continue the novel as an exploration of the uniformly degrading master-servant relation under capitalism rather than as a study of original sin. Now suppose someone accuses you of rewriting the "real" novel to produce a different one that you like better. If he means that the "real" novel can be discovered in some way other than by a process of interpretation of the sort you conducted, then he has misunderstood not only the chain-novel enterprise but the nature of literature and criticism. Of course, he may mean only that he disagrees with the particular interpretive and aesthetic convictions on which you relied. In that case your disagreement is not that he thinks you should respect the text, while you think you are free to ignore it. Your disagreement is more interesting: you disagree about what respecting this text means.

Law: The Question of Emotional Damages

Law as integrity asks a judge deciding a common-law case like *McLoughlin* to think of himself as an author in the chain of common law. He knows that other judges have decided cases that, although not exactly like his case, deal with related problems; he must think of their decisions as part of a long story he must interpret and then continue, according to his own judgment of how to make the developing story as good as it can be. (Of course the best story for him means best from the standpoint of political morality, not aesthetics.) We can make a rough distinction once again between two main dimensions of this interpretive judgment. The judge's decision— his postinterpretive conclusions—must be drawn from an interpretation that both fits and justifies

what has gone before, so far as that is possible. But in law as in literature the interplay between fit and justification is complex. Just as interpretation within a chain novel is for each interpreter a delicate balance among different types of literary and artistic attitudes, so in law it is a delicate balance among political convictions of different sorts; in law as in literature these must be sufficiently related yet disjoint to allow an overall judgment that trades off an interpretation's success on one type of standard against its failure on another. I must try to exhibit that complex structure of legal interpretation, and I shall use for that purpose an imaginary judge of superhuman intellectual power and patience who accepts law as integrity.

Call him Hercules.[2] In this and the next several chapters we follow his career by noticing the types of judgments he must make and tensions he must resolve in deciding a variety of cases. But I offer this caution in advance. We must not suppose that his answers to the various questions he encounters *define* law as integrity as a general conception of law. They are the answers I now think best. But law as integrity consists in an approach, in questions rather than answers, and other lawyers and judges who accept it would give different answers from his to the questions it asks. You might think other answers would be better. (So might I, after further thought.) You might, for example, reject Hercules' views about how far people's legal rights depend on the reasons past judges offered for their decisions enforcing these rights, or you might not share his respect for what I shall call "local priority" in common-law decisions. If you reject these discrete views because you think them poor constructive interpretations of legal practice, however, you have not rejected law as integrity but rather have joined its enterprise.

Six Interpretations

Hercules must decide *McLoughlin*. Both sides in that case cited precedents; each argued that a decision in its favor would count as going on as before, as continuing the story begun by the judges who decided those precedent cases. Hercules must form his own view about that issue. Just as a chain novelist must find, if he can, some coherent view of character and theme such that a hypothetical single author with that view could have written at least the bulk of the novel so far, Hercules must find, if he can, some coherent theory about legal rights to compensation for emotional injury such that a single political official with that theory could have reached most of the results the precedents report.

He is a careful judge, a judge of method. He begins by setting out various candidates for the best interpretation of the precedent cases even before he reads them. Suppose he makes the following short list:

(1) No one has a moral right to compensation except for physical injury.

(2) People have a moral right to compensation for emotional injury suffered at the scene of an accident against anyone whose carelessness caused the accident but have no right to compensation for emotional injury suffered later.

(3) People should recover compensation for emotional injury when a practice of requiring compensation in their circumstances would diminish the overall costs of accidents or otherwise make the community richer in the long run.

(4) People have a moral right to compensation for any injury, emotional or physical, that is the direct consequence of careless conduct, no matter how unlikely or unforeseeable it is that that conduct would result in that injury.

(5) People have a moral right to compensation for emotional or physical injury that is the consequence of careless conduct, but only if that injury was reasonably foreseeable by the person who acted carelessly.

(6) People have a moral right to compensation for reasonably foreseeable injury but not in circumstances when recognizing such a right would impose massive and destructive financial burdens on people who have been careless out of proportion to their moral fault.

These are all relatively concrete statements about rights and, allowing for a complexity in (3) we explore just below, they contradict one another. No more than one can figure in a single interpretation of the emotional injury cases. (I postpone the more complex case in which Hercules constructs an interpretation from competitive rather than contradictory principles, that is, from principles that can live together in an overall moral or political theory though they sometimes pull in different directions.)[3] Even so, this is only a partial list of the contradictory interpretations someone might wish to consider; Hercules chooses it as his initial short list because he knows that the principles captured in these interpretations have actually been discussed in the legal literature. It will obviously make a great difference

which of these principles he believes provides the best interpretation of the precedents and so the nerve of his postinterpretive judgment. If he settles on (1) or (2), he must decide for Mr. O'Brian; if on (4), for Mrs. McLoughlin. Each of the others requires further thought, but the line of reasoning each suggests is different. (3) invites an economic calculation. Would it reduce the cost of accidents to extend liability to emotional injury away from the scene? Or is there some reason to think that the most efficient line is drawn just between emotional injuries at and those away from the scene? (5) requires a judgment about foreseeability of injury, which seems to be very different, and (6) a judgment both about foreseeability and the cumulative risk of financial responsibility if certain injuries away from the scene are included.

Hercules begins testing each interpretation on his short list by asking whether a single political official could have given the verdicts of the precedent cases if that official were consciously and coherently enforcing the principles that form the interpretation. He will therefore dismiss interpretation (1) at once. No one who believed that people never have rights to compensation for emotional injury could have reached the results of those past decisions cited in *McLoughlin* that allowed compensation. Hercules will also dismiss interpretation (2), though for a different reason. Unlike (1), (2) fits the past decisions; someone who accepted (2) as a standard would have reached these decisions, because they all allowed recovery for emotional injury at the scene and none allowed recovery for injury away from it. But (2) fails as an interpretation of the required kind because it does not state a principle of justice at all. It draws a line that it leaves arbitrary and unconnected to any more general moral or political consideration.

What about (3)? It might fit the past decisions, but only in the following way. Hercules might discover through economic analysis that someone who accepted the economic theory expressed by (3) and who wished to reduce the community's accident costs would have made just those decisions. But it is far from obvious that (3) states any principle of justice or fairness. . . .

Law as integrity asks judges to assume, so far as this is possible, that the law is structured by a coherent set of principles about justice and fairness and procedural due process, and it asks them to enforce these in the fresh cases that come before them, so that each person's situation is fair and just according to the same standards. That style of adjudication respects the ambition integrity assumes, the ambition to be a community of principle. But . . . integrity does not recommend what would be perverse, that we should all be governed by the same goals and strategies of policy on every occasion. It does not insist that a legislature that enacts one set of rules about compensation today, in order to make the community richer on the whole, is in any way committed to serve that same goal of policy tomorrow. For it might then have other goals to seek, not necessarily in place of wealth but beside it, and integrity does not frown on this diversity. Our account of interpretation, and our consequent elimination of interpretation (3) read as a naked appeal to policy, reflects a discrimination already latent in the ideal of integrity itself.

We reach the same conclusion in the context of *McLoughlin* through a different route, by further reflection on what we have learned about interpretation. An interpretation aims to show what is interpreted in the best light possible, and an interpretation of any part of our law must therefore attend not only to the substance of the decisions made by earlier officials but also to how—by which officials in which circumstances—these decisions were made. A legislature does not need reasons of principle to justify the rules it enacts about driving, including rules about compensation for accidents, even though these rules will create rights and duties for the future that will then be enforced by coercive threat. A legislature may justify its decision to create new rights for the future by showing how these will contribute, as a matter of sound policy, to the overall good of the community as a whole. There are limits to this kind of justification. . . . The general good may not be used to justify the death penalty for careless driving. But the legislature need not show that citizens already have a moral right to compensation for injury under particular circumstances in order to justify a statute awarding damages in those circumstances.

Law as integrity assumes, however, that judges are in a very different position from legislators. It does not fit the character of a community of principle that a judge should have authority to hold people liable in damages for acting in a way he concedes they had no legal duty not to act. So when judges construct rules of liability not recognized before, they are not free in the way I just said legislators are. Judges must make their common-law decisions on grounds of principle, not policy: they must deploy arguments why the parties actually had the "novel" legal rights and duties they enforce at

the time the parties acted or at some other pertinent time in the past.[4] A legal pragmatist would reject that claim. But Hercules rejects pragmatism. He follows law as integrity and therefore wants an interpretation of what judges did in the earlier emotional damage cases that shows them acting in the way he approves, not in the way he thinks judges must decline to act. It does not follow that he must dismiss interpretation (3) read . . . as supposing that past judges acted to protect a general legal right to compensation when this would make the community richer. For if people actually have such a right, others have a corresponding duty, and judges do not act unjustly in ordering the police to enforce it. The argument disqualifies interpretation (3) only when this is read to deny any such general duty and to rest on grounds of policy alone.

Expanding the Range

Interpretations (4), (5), and (6) do, however, seem to pass these initial tests. The principles of each fit the past emotional injury decisions, at least on first glance, if only because none of these precedents presented facts that would discriminate among them. Hercules must now ask, as the next stage of his investigation, whether any one of the three must be ruled out because it is incompatible with the bulk of legal practice more generally. He must test each interpretation against other past judicial decisions, beyond those involving emotional injury, that might be thought to engage them. Suppose he discovers, for example, that past decisions provide compensation for physical injury caused by careless driving only if the injury was reasonably foreseeable. That would rule out interpretation (4) unless he can find some principled distinction between physical and emotional injury that explains why the conditions for compensation should be more restrictive for the former than the latter, which seems extremely unlikely.

Law as integrity, then, requires a judge to test his interpretation of any part of the great network of political structures and decisions of his community by asking whether it could form part of a coherent theory justifying the network as a whole. No actual judge could compose anything approaching a full interpretation of all of his community's law at once. That is why we are imagining a Herculean judge of superhuman talents and endless time. But an actual judge can imitate Hercules in a limited way. He can allow the scope of his interpretation to fan out from the cases immediately in point to cases in the same

general area or department of law, and then still farther, so far as this seems promising. In practice even
this limited process will be largely unconscious: an
experienced judge will have a sufficient sense of the
terrain surrounding his immediate problem to know
instinctively which interpretation of a small set of
cases would survive if the range it must fit were expanded. But sometimes the expansion will be deliberate and controversial. Lawyers celebrate dozens of
decisions of that character, including several on
which the modern law of negligence was built.[5]
Scholarship offers other important examples.[6]

Suppose a modest expansion of Hercules'
range of inquiry does show that plaintiffs are denied
compensation if their physical injury was not reasonably foreseeable at the time the careless defendant acted, thus ruling out interpretation (4). But this
does not eliminate either (5) or (6). He must expand
his survey further. He must look also to cases involving economic rather than physical or emotional injury, where damages are potentially very great: for
example, he must look to cases in which professional advisers like surveyors or accountants are
sued for losses others suffer through their negligence. Interpretation (5) suggests that such liability
might be unlimited in amount, no matter how ruinous in total, provided that the damage is foreseeable, and (6) suggests, on the contrary, that liability
is limited just because of the frightening sums it
might otherwise reach. If one interpretation is uniformly contradicted by cases of that sort and finds
no support in any other area of doctrine Hercules
might later inspect, and the other is confirmed by
the expansion, he will regard the former as ineligible, and the latter alone will have survived. But suppose he finds, when he expands his study in this
way, a mixed pattern. Past decisions permit extended liability for members of some professions but
not for those of others, and this mixed pattern holds
for other areas of doctrine that Hercules, in the exercise of his imaginative skill, finds pertinent.

The contradiction he has discovered, though
genuine, is not in itself so deep or pervasive as to
justify a skeptical interpretation of legal practice as a
whole, for the problem of unlimited damages, while
important, is not so fundamental that contradiction
within it destroys the integrity of the larger system.
So Hercules turns to the second main dimension, but
here, as in the chain-novel example, questions of fit
surface again, because an interpretation is *pro tanto*
more satisfactory if it shows less damage to integrity
than its rival. He will therefore consider whether in-

terpretation (5) fits the expanded legal record better
than (6). But this cannot be a merely mechanical decision; he cannot simply count the number of past
decisions that must be conceded to be "mistakes" on
each interpretation. For these numbers may reflect
only accidents like the number of cases that happen
to have come to court and not been settled before
verdict. He must take into account not only the
numbers of decisions counting for each interpretation, but whether the decisions expressing one principle seem more important or fundamental or
wideranging than the decisions expressing the other.
Suppose interpretation (6) fits only those past judicial decisions involving charges of negligence
against one particular profession—say, lawyers—
and interpretation (5) justifies all other cases, involving all other professions, and also fits other kinds of
economic damage cases as well. Interpretation (5)
then fits the legal record better on the whole, even
if the number of cases involving lawyers is for some
reason numerically greater, unless the argument
shifts again, as it well might, when the field of study
expands even more.

Now suppose a different possibility: that
though liability has in many and varied cases actually been limited to an amount less than interpretation (5) would allow, the opinions attached to these
cases made no mention of the principle of interpretation (6), which has in fact never before been recognized in official judicial rhetoric. Does that show
that interpretation (5) fits the legal record much better, or that interpretation (6) is ineligible after all?
Judges in fact divide about this issue of fit. Some
would not seriously consider interpretation (6) if no
past judicial opinion or legislative statement had
ever explicitly mentioned its principle. Others reject
this constraint and accept that the best interpretation of some line of cases may lie in a principle that
has never been recognized explicitly but that nevertheless offers a brilliant account of the actual decisions, showing them in a better light than ever before.[7] Hercules will confront this issue as a special
question of political morality. The political history
of the community is *pro tanto* a better history, he
thinks, if it shows judges making plain to their public, through their opinions, the path that later judges
guided by integrity will follow and if it shows judges
making decisions that give voice as well as effect to
convictions about morality that are widespread
through the community. Judicial opinions formally
announced in law reports, moreover, are themselves
acts of the community personified that, particularly

if recent, must be taken into the embrace of integrity. These are among his reasons for somewhat preferring an interpretation that is not too novel, not too far divorced from what past judges and other officials said as well as did. But he must set these reasons against his more substantive political convictions about the relative moral value of the two interpretations, and if he believes that interpretation (6) is much superior from that perspective, he will think he makes the legal record better overall by selecting it even at the cost of the more procedural values. Fitting what judges did is more important than fitting what they said.

Now suppose an even more unpatterned record. Hercules finds that unlimited liability has been enforced against a number of professions but has not been enforced against a roughly equal number of others, that no principle can explain the distinction, that judicial rhetoric is as split as the actual decisions, and that this split extends into other kinds of actions for economic damage. He might expand his field of survey still further, and the picture might change if he does. But let us suppose he is satisfied that it will not. He will then decide that the question of fit can play no more useful role in his deliberations even on the second dimension. He must now emphasize the more plainly substantive aspects of that dimension: he must decide which interpretation shows the legal record to be the best it can be from the standpoint of substantive political morality. He will compose and compare two stories. The first supposes that the community personified has adopted and is enforcing the principle of foreseeability as its test of moral responsibility for damage caused by negligence, that the various decisions it has reached are intended to give effect to that principle, though it has often lapsed and reached decisions that foreseeability would condemn. The second supposes, instead, that the community has adopted and is enforcing the principle of foreseeability limited by some overall ceiling on liability, though it has often lapsed from that principle. Which story shows the community in a better light, all things considered, from the standpoint of political morality?

Hercules' answer will depend on his convictions about the two constituent virtues of political morality we have considered: justice and fairness. It will depend, that is, not only on his beliefs about which of these principles is superior as a matter of abstract justice but also about which should be followed, as a matter of political fairness, in a community whose members have the moral convictions his fellow citizens have. In some cases the two kinds of

judgment—the judgment of justice and that of fairness—will come together. If Hercules and the public at large share the view that people are entitled to be compensated fully whenever they are injured by others' carelessness, without regard to how harsh this requirement might turn out to be, then he will think that interpretation (5) is plainly the better of the two in play. But the two judgments will sometimes pull in different directions. He may think that interpretation (6) is better on grounds of abstract justice, but know that this is a radical view not shared by any substantial portion of the public and unknown in the political and moral rhetoric of the times. He might then decide that the story in which the state insists on the view he thinks right, but against the wishes of the people as a whole, is a poorer story, on balance. He would be preferring fairness to justice in these circumstances, and that preference would reflect a higher-order level of his own political convictions, namely his convictions about how a decent government committed to both fairness and justice should adjudicate between the two in this sort of case.

Judges will have different ideas of fairness, about the role each citizen's opinion should ideally play in the state's decision about which principles of justice to enforce through its central police power. They will have different higher-level opinions about the best resolution of conflicts between these two political ideals. No judge is likely to hold the simplistic theory that fairness is automatically to be preferred to justice or vice versa. Most judges will think that the balance between the opinions of the community and the demands of abstract justice must be struck differently in different kinds of cases. Perhaps in ordinary commercial or private law cases, like *McLoughlin,* an interpretation supported in popular morality will be deemed superior to one that is not, provided it is not thought very much inferior as a matter of abstract justice. But many judges will think the interpretive force of popular morality very much weaker in constitutional cases like *Brown,* because they will think the point of the Constitution is in part to protect individuals from what the majority thinks right.

Local Priority

I must call special attention to a feature of Hercules' practice that has not yet clearly emerged. His judgments of fit expand out from the immediate case before him in a series of concentric circles. He asks which interpretations on his initial list fit past emotional injury cases, then which ones fit cases of accidental damage to the person more generally, then which fit damage to economic interests, and so on into areas each further and further from the original *McLoughlin* issue. This procedure gives a kind of local priority to what we might call "departments" of law. If Hercules finds that neither of two principles is flatly contradicted by the accidental damage cases of his jurisdiction, he expands his study into, say, contract cases to see which of these principles, if either, fits contract decisions better. But in Hercules' view, if one principle does *not* fit accident law at all—if it is contradicted by almost every decision in the area that might have confirmed it—this counts dramatically against it as an eligible interpretation of that body of law, even if it fits other areas of the law superbly. He will not treat this doctrine of local priority as absolute, however; he will be ready to override it, as we shall soon see, in some circumstances.

The compartmentalization of law into separate departments is a prominent feature of legal practice. Law schools divide courses and their libraries divide treatises to distinguish emotional from economic or physical injury, intentional from unintentional torts, tort from crime, contract from other parts of common law, private from public law, and constitutional law from other parts of public law. Legal and judicial arguments respect these traditional divisions. Judicial opinions normally begin by assigning the case in hand to some department of law, and the precedents and statutes considered are usually drawn exclusively from that department. Often the initial classification is both controversial and crucial.

Compartmentalization suits both conventionalism and pragmatism, though for different reasons. Departments of law are based on tradition, which seems to support conventionalism, and they provide a strategy a pragmatist can manipulate in telling his noble lies: he can explain that his new doctrine need not be consistent in principle with past decisions because the latter, properly understood, belong to a different department. Law as integrity has a more complex attitude toward departments of law. Its general spirit condemns them, because the adjudicative principle of integrity asks judges to make the law coherent as a whole, so far as they can, and this might be better done by ignoring academic boundaries and reforming some departments of law radically to make them more consistent in principle with others. But law as integrity is interpretive, and compartmentalization is a feature of legal practice no competent interpretation can ignore.

Hercules responds to these competing impulses by seeking a constructive interpretation of compartmentalization. He tries to find an explanation of the practice of dividing law into departments that shows that practice in its best light. The boundaries between departments usually match popular opinion; many people think that intentional harm is more blameworthy than careless harm, that the state needs a very different kind of justification to declare someone guilty of a crime than it needs to require him to pay compensation for damage he has caused, that promises and other forms of explicit agreement or consent are a special kind of reason for state coercion, and so forth. Dividing departments of law to match that sort of opinion promotes predictability and guards against sudden official reinterpretations that uproot large areas of law, and it does this in a way that promotes a deeper aim of law as integrity. If legal compartments make sense to people at large, they encourage the protestant attitude integrity favors, because they allow ordinary people as well as hard-pressed judges to interpret law within practical boundaries that seem natural and intuitive.

Hercules accepts that account of the point of compartmentalization, and he shapes his doctrine of local priority accordingly. He allows the doctrine most force when the boundaries between traditional departments of law track widely held moral principles distinguishing types of fault or responsibility, and the substance of each department reflects those moral principles. The distinction between criminal and civil law meets that test. Suppose Hercules thinks, contrary to most people's opinion, that being made to pay compensation is just as bad as being made to pay a fine, and therefore that the distinction between criminal and civil law is unsound in principle. He will nevertheless defer to local priority. He will not claim that criminal and civil law should be treated as one department; he will not argue that a criminal defendant's guilt need only be established as probable rather than beyond a reasonable doubt because the probable standard fits the combined department as well as any other.

But Hercules will not be so ready to defer to local priority when his test is not met, when traditional boundaries between departments have become mechanical and arbitrary, either because popular morality has shifted or because the substance of the departments no longer reflects popular opinion.[8] Compartments of law do sometimes grow arbitrary and isolated from popular conviction in that way, particularly when the central rules of the departments were developed in different periods. Suppose the legal tradition of a community has for many decades separated nuisance law, which concerns the discomfort of interference that activities on one person's land cause to neighbors, from negligence law, which concerns the physical or economic or emotional injuries someone's carelessness inflicts on others. Suppose that the judges who decided the crucial nuisance cases disdained any economic test for nuisance; they said that an activity counts as a nuisance, and must therefore be stopped, when it is not a "natural" or traditional use of the land, so that someone who starts a factory on land traditionally used for farming is guilty of nuisance even though the factory is an economically more efficient use. But suppose that in recent years judges have begun to make economic cost crucial for negligence. They say that someone's failure to take precautions against injuring others is negligent, so that he is liable for the resulting injury if the precaution was "reasonable" in the circumstances, and that the economic cost of the precaution counts in deciding whether it was in fact reasonable.

The distinction between negligence and nuisance law no longer meets Hercules' test, if it ever did. It makes some sense to distinguish nuisance from negligence if we assume that nuisance is intentional while negligence is unintentional; then the distinction tracks the popular principle that it is worse to injure someone knowingly than unknowingly. But the developments in negligence law I just described are not consistent with that view of the distinction, because failing to guard against an accident is not necessarily unintentional in the required sense. So Hercules would be ready to ignore the traditional boundary between these two departments of law. If he thought that the "natural use" test was silly, and the economic cost test much more just, he would argue that the negligence and nuisance precedents should be seen as one body of law, and that the economic cost test is a superior interpretation of that unified body. His argument would probably be made easier by other legal events that already had occurred. The intellectual climate that produced the later negligence decisions would have begun to erode the assumption of the earlier nuisance cases, that novel enterprises that annoy people are necessarily legal wrongs. Perhaps the legislature would have adopted special statutes rearranging liability for some new forms of inconvenience, like airport noise, that the "natural" theory has decided or would decide in what seems the wrong way, for example. Or perhaps judges would have decided airport cases by straining the historical meaning of "natural" to reach decisions that seemed sensible given developing technology. Hercules would cite these changes as supporting his interpretive argument consolidating nuisance and negligence. If he persuades the profession to his view, nuisance and negligence will no longer be distinct departments of law but joint tenants of a new province which will shortly attract a new name attached to new law school courses and new treatises. This prcess is in fact under way in Anglo-American law, as is, though less securely, a new unification of private law that blurs even the long-established and once much firmer boundary between contract and tort. . . .

Some Familiar Objections

Hercules Is Playing Politics

Hercules has completed his labors in *McLoughlin*. He declares that the best interpretation of the emotional damage cases, all things considered, is (5): the law allows compensation for all emotional injury directly caused by careless driving and foreseeable by a reasonably thoughtful motorist. But he concedes that in reaching that conclusion he has relied on his own opinion that this principle is better—fairer and more just—than any other that is eligible on what he takes to be the right criteria of fit. He also concedes that this opinion is controversial: it is not shared by all of his fellow judges, some of whom therefore think that some other interpretation, for example (6), is superior. What complaints are his arguments likely to attract? The first in the list I propose to consider accuses Hercules of ignoring the actual law of emotional injury and substituting his own views about what the law should be.

How shall we understand this objection? We might take it in two very different ways. It might mean that Hercules was wrong to seek to justify his interpretation by appealing to justice and fairness because it does not even survive the proper threshold test of fit. We cannot assume, without reviewing the cases Hercules consulted, that this argument is mistaken. Perhaps this time Hercules nodded; perhaps if he had expanded the range of his study of precedents further he would have discovered that only one interpretation did survive, and this discovery would then have settled the law, for him, without engaging his opinions about the justice of requiring compensation for accidents. But it is hardly plausible that even the strictest threshold test of fit will always permit only one interpretation, so the objection, understood this way, would not be a general objection to Hercules' methods of adjudication but only a complaint that he had misapplied his own methods in the particular case at hand.

We should therefore consider the second, more interesting reading of the objection: this claims that a judge must never rely on his personal convictions about fairness or justice the way Hercules did in this instance. Suppose the critic says, "The correct interpretation of a line of past decisions can always be discovered by morally neutral means, because the correct interpretation is just a matter of discovering what principles the judges who made these decisions intended to lay down, and that is just a matter of historical fact." Hercules will point out that this critic needs a political reason for his dictum that interpretations must match the intentions of past judges. That is an extreme form of the position we have already considered, that an interpretation is better if it fits what past judges said as well as did, and even that weaker claim depends on the special arguments of political morality I described. The critic supposes that these special reasons are not only strong but commanding; that they are so powerful that a judge always does wrong even to consider an interpretation that does not meet the standard they set, no matter how well that interpretation ties together, explains, and justifies past decisions.

So Hercules' critic, if his argument is to have any power, is not relying on politically neutral interpretive convictions after all. He, too, has engaged his own background convictions of political morality. He thinks the political values that support his interpretive style are of such fundamental importance as to eliminate any competing commands of justice altogether. That may be a plausible position, but it is hardly uncontroversial and is in no sense neutral. His difference with Hercules is not, as he first suggested, about whether political morality is relevant in deciding what the law is, but about which principles of morality are sound and therefore decisive of that issue. So the first, crude objection, that Hercules has substituted his own political convictions for the politically neutral correct interpretation of the past law, is an album of confusions.

Hercules Is a Fraud

The second objection is more sophisticated. Now the critic says, "It is absurd to suppose that there is any single correct interpretation of the emotional injury cases. Since we have discovered two interpretations of these cases, neither of which can be preferred to the other on 'neutral' grounds of fit, no judge would be forced by the adjudicative principle of integrity to accept either. Hercules has chosen one on frankly political grounds; his choice reflects only his own political morality. He has no choice in the circumstances but to legislate in that way. Nevertheless it is fraudulent for him to claim that he has discovered, through his political choice, what the *law* is. He is only offering his own opinion about what it should be."

This objection will seem powerful to many readers, and we must take care not to weaken it by making it seem to claim more than it does. It does not try to reinstate the idea of conventionalism, that when convention runs out a judge is free to improve the law according to the right legislative standards; still less the idea of pragmatism that he is always free to do this, checked only by considerations of strategy. It acknowledges that judges must choose between interpretations that survive the test of fit. It insists only that there can be no best interpretation when more than one survives that test. It is an objection, as I have framed it, from within the general idea of law as integrity; it tries to protect that idea from corruption by fraud.

Is the objection sound? Why is it fraudulent, or even confusing, for Hercules to offer his judgment as a judgment of law? Once again, two somewhat different answers—two ways of elaborating the objection—are available, and we cannot do credit to the objection unless we distinguish them and consider each. The first elaboration is this: "Hercules' claim is fraudulent because it suggests that there can be a right answer to the question whether interpretation (5) or (6) is fairer or more just; since political morality is subjective there cannot be a single right answer to that question, but only answers." . . . The second elaboration does not rely on skepticism: "Hercules is a fraud even if morality is objective and even if he is right that the principle of foreseeability he settled on is objectively fairer and more just. He is a fraud because he pretends he has discovered what the law is, but he has only discovered what it should be." That is the form of the objection I shall consider here.

We ask of a conception of law that it provide an account of the grounds of law—the circumstances under which claims about what the law is should be accepted as true or sound—that shows why law licenses coercion. Law as integrity replies that the grounds of law lie in integrity, in the best constructive interpretation of past legal decisions, and that law is therefore sensitive to justice in the way Hercules recognizes. So there is no way Hercules *can* report his conclusion about Mrs. McLoughlin's case except to say that the law, as he understands it, is in her favor. If he said what the critic recommends, that she has no legal right to win but has a moral right that he proposes to honor, he would be *misstating* his view of the matter. He would think that a true account of some situations—if he found the law too immoral to enforce, for example—but not of this one. A critic might disagree with Hercules at many levels. He might reject law as integrity in favor of conventionalism or pragmatism or some other conception of law. Or he might accept it but reach different conclusions from Hercules because he holds different ideas about the necessary requirements of fit, or different convictions about fairness or justice or the relation between them. But he can regard Hercules' use of "law" as fraudulent (or grammatically wrong) only if he suffers from the semantic sting, only if he assumes that claims of law are somehow out of order when they are not drawn directly from some set of factual criteria for law every competent lawyer accepts.

One aspect of the present objection, however, might be thought immune from my arguments against the rest. Even if we agree that Hercules' conclusions about Mrs. McLoughlin are properly presented as conclusions of law, it might seem extravagant to claim that these conclusions in any way follow from integrity understood as a distinct political ideal. Would it not be more accurate to say that integrity is at work in Hercules' calculations just up to the point at which he has rejected all interpre-tations that fail the threshold test of fit, but that integrity plays no part in selecting among those that survive that test? Should we not say that his conception of law is really two conceptions: law as integrity supplemented, when integrity gives out, by some version of natural law theory? This is not a very important objection; it only suggests a different way of reporting the conclusions it no longer challenges. Nevertheless the observation that prompts it is too crude. For it is a mistake to think that the idea of integrity is irrelevant to Hercules' decision once that decision is no longer a matter of his convictions about fit but draws on his sense of fairness or justice as well.

The spirit of integrity, which we located in fraternity, would be outraged if Hercules were to make his decision in any way other than by choosing the interpretation that he believes best from the standpoint of political morality as a whole. We accept integrity as a political ideal because we want to treat our political community as one of principle, and the citizens of a community of principle aim not simply at common principles, as if uniformity were all they wanted, but the best common principles politics can find. Integrity is distinct from justice and fairness, but it is bound to them in that way: integrity makes no sense except among people who want fairness and justice as well. So Hercules' final choice of the interpretation he believes sounder on the whole—fairer and more just in the right relation—flows from his initial commitment to integrity. He makes that choice at the moment and in the way integrity both permits and requires, and it is therefore deeply misleading to say that he has abandoned the ideal at just that point. . . .

———————————

1. Perhaps this is an impossible assignment; perhaps the project is doomed to produce not just an impossibly bad novel but no novel at all, because the best theory of art requires a single creator or, if more than one, that each must have some control over the whole. (But what about legends and jokes? What about the Old Testament, or, on some theories, the *Iliad?*) I need not push that question further, because I am interested only in the fact that the assignment makes sense, that each of the novelists in the chain can have some grasp of what he is asked to do, whatever misgivings he might have about the value or character of what will then be produced.
2. Hercules played an important part in Ronald Dworkin, *Taking Rights Seriously* (Cambridge, Mass.: Harvard University Press, 1978, chap. 4.
3. See the discussion of critical legal studies later in this article.
4. See *Taking Rights Seriously,* chap. 4.
5. See *Thomas v. Winchester,* 6 N.Y. 397, and *MacPherson v. Buick Motor Co.,* 217 N.Y. 382, 111 N.E. 1050.
6. C. Haar and D. Fessler, *The Wrong Side of the Tracks* (New York, 1986), is a recent example of integrity working on a large canvas.
7. See, for example, Benjamin Cardozo's decision in *Hynes v. New York Central R.R. Co.,* 231 N.Y. 229.
8. The disagreement between Lords Diplock and Edmund Davies, on the one hand, and Viscount Dilhourne on the other, in the notorious blasphemy case *R. v. Lemon* [1979] I All ER 898, illustrates the importance of not ignoring this connection between changes in popular morality and the boundaries of local priority. The former insisted that the law of blasphemy be interpreted to reflect developments in other parts of criminal law; the latter that blasphemy, for some unexplained reason, be counted an isolated domain of its own.

THE THIRD THEORY OF LAW*

J. L. Mackie

I have resisted the temptation to entitle this paper "Taking Rights Seriously and Playing Fast and Loose with the Law." But it will become plain, as I go on, why I was tempted.

Professor Dworkin's theory of law is now well known, especially since the publication of his book, *Taking Rights Seriously.*[1] But it may be as well to review it, and show how some of his main theses fit together.

I call it the third theory of law because it contrasts both with legal positivism and with the doctrine of natural law, and is in some ways intermediate between the two. The natural law doctrine is well summarized by Blackstone: "This law of nature being coeval with mankind and dictated by God himself is of course superior in obligation to any other. It is binding over the whole globe, in all countries and at all times. No human laws are of any validity if contrary to this, and such of them as are valid derive their force and all their authority, mediately or immediately, from this original."[2] This entails that a judge, relying on his rational knowledge of natural law, may overrule even what appears to be the settled law of the land—unambiguous and regularly enacted statutes or clearly relevant and unopposed precedents—and declare that the apparently settled law is not the law. Against this, I think that Professor Dworkin would concede that all law is made somehow by human beings, and that the (detailed) question, What is the law? makes sense only if construed as asking, What is at a certain time the law of England, or of France, or of the United States, or of South Dakota? The validity of a law is wholly relative to the legal system to which it belongs. Consequently the finding out of what is the law is an empirical task, not a matter of *a priori* reasoning. But, this being conceded, Professor Dworkin stresses a series of contrasts between his view and legal pos-

itivism, even such a cautious form of positivism as Professor Hart's.

First, he holds that the law consists not only of rules but also of principles, the distinction between these being logical: "Rules are applicable in an all-or-nothing fashion," whereas principles have the extra dimension of weight (*TRS*, pp. 22–28).

Secondly, he rejects the positivist notion of a single ultimate or fundamental test for law, such as Professor Hart's "rule of recognition." In its place he puts the sort of reasoning that he ascribes, in "Hard Cases," to his imaginary judge, Hercules. Some parts of the law in a certain jurisdiction are settled and relatively uncontroversial, in the constitution or statutes or precedents. Hercules uses these as data, seeking the theory, in terms of further rights and principles, which best explains and justifies this settled law. Having developed this theory, he then applies it to the hard case (*TRS*, pp. 105–23).

Thirdly, and as a result of this method, Professor Dworkin holds that in any sufficiently rich legal system (notably in that of England no less than in that of the United States) the question, What is the law on this issue? always has a right answer, discoverable in principle, and it is the duty of the judge to try to discover it. One of the parties will always have a right to a decision in his favor. "Judicial decisions enforce existing political rights." There is a theoretical possibility of a tie, a dead heat, between competing sets of principles when all relevant considerations have been taken into account, but this is so unlikely that it may in practice be ignored. (See *TRS*, pp. 81, 279–90, esp. 286–87.)

Consequently, and fourthly, though judges in hard or controversial cases have discretion in the weak sense that they are called upon to exercise judgment—they are not supplied with any cut and dried decision procedure—they never have discretion in

the strong sense which would exclude a duty to decide the case one way rather than the other (*TRS,* pp.
31–35, 68–71).

Fifthly, though it is really only another way of
making the same point, Professor Dworkin holds
that even in a hard case one does not reach a stage
where the law has run out before it has yielded a
decision, and the judge has to make some new law
to deal with a new problem. Judges never need to
act, even surreptitiously, as legislators, though he
has allowed that they may in fact do so as they
sometimes do when they make a mistake or when
they prospectively overrule a clear precedent.[3]

A sixth point is a further consequence of this.
If judges were in effect legislating, it would be appropriate for them to do so in the light of considerations of policy—in particular, of utility or the general
welfare of the community or the known will of the
majority of the people. But if they are not legislating
but still discovering an already existing law, they
must confine themselves to considerations of principle; if they let policy outweigh principle, they will
be sacrificing someone's rights in order to benefit or
satisfy others, and this is unjust. There is, however,
an exception to this point. It holds uniformly in civil
cases, Professor Dworkin says, but only asymmetrically in criminal cases. The accused may have a right
to be acquitted, but the prosecution never has a right
to a conviction. So a court may sometimes justly acquit, for reasons of policy, someone who is in fact
guilty (*TRS,* pp. 82–100).

Seventhly, Professor Dworkin rejects the traditional positivist separation of law from morality. However, this is a tricky issue. The legal positivism he has
explicitly taken as his main target is that of Professor
Hart, and Professor Hart recognizes many ways in
which law and morality are closely linked. For example, he says, "In some systems, as in the United States,
the ultimate criteria of legal validity explicitly incorporate principles of justice or substantive moral values . . ." ". . . statutes may be a mere legal shell and
demand by their express terms to be filled out with
the aid of moral principles; the range of enforceable
contracts may be limited by reference to conceptions
of morality and fairness . . ." and "Judicial decision,
especially on matters of high constitutional import,
often involves a choice between moral values. . . ."
But one point on which Professor Hart stands firm is
that we can sometimes say, "This is law but too iniquitous to obey or apply," rather than, "Because this is
iniquitous it is not law." He argues (against supporters of natural law) that it is both more clearheaded

and morally better to allow that something can be
valid law and yet evil.[4] It is not clear to me whether
Professor Dworkin would deny this. But he makes
the following important point. The task which he assigns to Hercules in "Hard Cases" is to find the theory
that best explains and justifies the settled law, and to
use this theory to decide otherwise unsettled issues.
He construes the phrase "best explains and justifies"
as including a moral dimension; Hercules has to find
the morally best justification of the constitution,
statutes, practices, and so on which are not in dispute.
In doing this, Hercules must himself make substantive moral judgments, and not merely take account of
conventional morality, of widely accepted social rules
(*TRS,* pp. 123–28; cf. pp. 206–22).

This third theory of law combines descriptive
with prescriptive elements. On the one hand, Professor Dworkin is claiming that it gives the best theoretical understanding of legal procedures and legal
reasoning actually at work in such systems as those of
England and the United States. But on the other, he
wants it to be more explicitly accepted and more consciously followed. He wants it to become a truer description than it yet is, whereas some views that might
count as interpretations of the positivist model—
for example, the "strict constructionist" view favored
by ex-President Nixon—would, he thinks, have deplorable results (*TRS,* pp. 131–49).

It follows that discussion of this theory must
also be on more than one level. We are concerned
with both its truth as a description and its merit as a
recommendation. Let us consider it first as a description. Professor Dworkin argues that courts do, in fact,
appeal to principles as distinct from rules and that
no coherent description of their procedures can be
given by a theory which recognizes only rules as
constituting the law. This must, I think, be conceded.
But he further maintains that the way in which judges
reason in hard cases is some approximation to that
which he ascribes to his "superhuman judge," Hercules; and such a view is much more controversial.
Along with other aspects of his descriptive theory it
needs to be checked empirically and in detail. But
some general preliminary comments can be made.

First, there is a distinction—and there may be
a divergence—between what judges say they are
doing, what they think they are doing, and the most
accurate objective description of what they actually
are doing. They may say and even believe that they
are discovering and applying an already existing
law, they may be following procedures which assume this as their aim, and yet they may in fact be

making new law. Such a divergence is not even improbable, because even where new law is being made, it will seem fairer if this fact is concealed and the decision is believed to enforce only presently existing rights; and because the making of new law will usually mean only that existing rules or principles are extended somewhat beyond their previous field of application.

Secondly, even though legal reasoning in hard cases involves appeals to principles and rights and is affected by "the gravitational force of precedents," it does not follow that it does or must or even should work in terms of a complete theory of the underlying law for the jurisdiction in question. The superhuman Hercules is, as his name indicates, a mythical figure, and human judges will always operate in a more limited way. However, the practical force of Professor Dworkin's account is that it allows and encourages judges to bring to bear upon a controversial case general considerations and notions about rights which are supported by elements in the settled law that are remote from the case in hand. We may or may not want this; but I would stress that this holistic treatment of the law is in no way required by the admission that legal reasoning appeals to principles as well as to rules. That admission allows such remote control, but does not require it.

Thirdly, though legal reasoning in hard cases refers to rights, this does not entail that it can take no account of interests. Admittedly, to take rights seriously is to see them as having some resistance to interests; in particular, it is to recognize that the rights of an individual will often justify a decision in his favor which is against the interests of the community as a whole. However, Professor Dworkin himself does not regard all rights as absolute, but admits that they may sometimes be overruled by community interest. And when rights conflict with one another, interests may help to determine which right is the stronger in the particular circumstances.

There is no doubt that judges sometimes argue in this way, as in *Miller v. Jackson and Another,* heard in the British Court of Appeal—reported in *The Times,* 7 April 1977. The plaintiff lived in a house built in 1972 near a village cricket ground which had been used for over seventy years. He sought an injunction to prevent the club members from playing cricket unless they took adequate steps to prevent stray balls from hitting his house and garden. There is a conflict of rights here: *prima facie* the club has a right to go on playing cricket and the plaintiff has a right to enjoy his home and garden in

safety. The court refused, by two to one, to grant the injunction. The judges on the majority side spoke of the public interest and also stressed that the injunction sought was a discretionary remedy. Lord Denning said that the public interest lay in protecting the environment by preserving playing fields in the face of mounting development and enabling our youth to enjoy the benefits of outdoor games, in contrast to the private interest, which lay in securing the privacy of a home and garden without intrusion or interference. Lord Justice Cumming-Bruce said that in considering whether to exercise a judicial discretion to grant an injunction the court was under a duty to consider the interests of the public. That is, they seemed to think that while each party had a *prima facie* right, when these rights came into conflict the importance of the public interest made the cricket club's right the stronger. Professor Dworkin may deplore such reasoning, but he can hardly deny that it occurs, nor can he argue that it should not occur merely because in a hard case there are appeals to principles and rights.

Fourthly, it would be a mere fallacy (which I want to guard against, but do not accuse Professor Dworkin of committing) to argue from the premise that hard cases should be reasoned (partly) in terms of rights—including *prima facie,* non-absolute rights—to the conclusion that in such a case one party must have a (final or resultant) right to a decision in his favor.

Fifthly, there is a weakness in the argument that an exactly equal balance between the considerations on either side is so unlikely that it is almost certain that one party will have an antecedent right to win (*TRS,* pp. 286–87). This argument assumes too simple a metric for the strength of considerations, that such strengths are always commensurable on a linear scale, so that the strength of the case for one side must be either greater than that of the case for the other side, or less, or else they must be equal in the sense of being so finely balanced that even the slightest additional force on either side would make it the stronger. But in fact considerations may be imperfectly commensurable, so that neither of the opposing cases is stronger than the other, and yet they are not finely balanced. Consider the analogous question about three brothers: Is Peter more like James than he is like John? There may be an objectively right and determinable answer to this question, but again there may not. It may be that the only correct reply is that Peter is more like James in some ways and more like John in others, and that there is no objective reason for putting more weight on the former points of resemblance than on the latter or vice versa. While we might say that Peter's likeness to James is equal to his likeness to John (because neither is determinately the greater), this does not mean that any slight additional resemblance to either would decide the issue; hence, it does not mean that this equality expresses an improbably exact balance.

Sixthly, we must note an implication of Professor Dworkin's inclusion of a moral dimension in the reasoning he assigns to Hercules. Hercules' judgment about what the law is on some specific issue depends on what he finds to be the best explanatory and justificatory theory of the settled law. So what the law is, on Professor Dworkin's view, may crucially depend on what is morally best—what is best, not what is conventionally regarded as best in that society. Now I would argue, though I cannot do so here, that moral judgments of this kind have an irreducibly subjective element.[5] If so, then Professor Dworkin's theory automatically injects a corresponding subjectivity into statements about what the law is. Of course, Professor Dworkin is right in arguing that the moral judgments people make—and this may also be true for those that Hercules can be presumed to make—are not, in general, reports of socially established rules or even such reports conjoined with the speaker's acceptance or endorsement of those rules (*TRS,* pp. 45–58). Moral judgments typically include what I call a claim to objectivity and to the objectivity precisely of their prescriptive authority. But these claims, I maintain, are always false. Prescriptive moral judgments are really subjective, though those who make them commonly think that they are objectively valid and mean them to be objectively valid. Suppose Hercules and another judge in the same jurisdiction, both following Professor Dworkin's methods, reach different conclusions about what the law on some issue is because each has reasoned coherently in the light of his own moral views. Though each of them will sincerely and consistently believe that the law already is as he determines it, I maintain that they will both be wrong. The grounds on which they rely fail to determine an objective preexisting law. Whichever judge's opinion wins the day in the final court of appeal will become the law and will then be the law. The judges who finally decide the case will have been legislating, though they will sincerely, consistently, and rationally believe that they have not. By making a choice determined by their subjective moral judgments for which they honestly but mis-

takenly claim objective validity, they will have been making law on an issue on which there was previously no determinate law, on which they had no antecedent duty to decide one way rather than the other, and on which neither party had a right to a decision in his favor.

These six general points cast doubt on some parts of Professor Dworkin's descriptive theory, but they should be tested along with the theory, against actual examples of hard cases. I now want to leave the question of description and consider the merits of the third theory as a recommendation. I can do this best by going straight to a concrete example, taken from the legal history of the United States. Professor Dworkin, in a review of Robert M. Cover's book *Justice Accused,* applies his theory to cases which arose before the American Civil War under the Fugitive Slave Acts.[6]

He finds it puzzling that such judges as Joseph Story and Lemuel Shaw, though themselves strongly opposed to slavery, enforced these acts, sending alleged runaway slaves back from states in which slavery was not permitted to states where it still existed and from which they were alleged to have escaped. But why is there a puzzle? Were these judges not, as they themselves said, simply doing their legal duty of enforcing what was then the law of the land, despite the fact that it conflicted with their own moral views? Professor Dworkin argues that it is not so simple. The relevant law was not settled: these cases were controversial. Though the judges in question explicitly denied this, in their deeper thinking they admitted it. But then, being legal positivists, they concluded that they had to legislate, to make new law by their findings. But why, then, did they not make the law in accordance with their moral convictions and their sense of justice? Because, says Professor Dworkin, following Cover, they saw themselves as subordinate legislators only, bound to make the law in harmony with the discoverable intentions of the superior legislators in Congress and, earlier, in the Constitutional Convention. These legislators had, in their several enactments, created and maintained a compromise between the slave states and the nonslave states; therefore, sending an alleged slave back to the state from which he had come was the natural fulfillment of that compromise.

According to Professor Dworkin, the reasoning of these judges was a "failure of jurisprudence." If they had been adherents, not of positivism, but of the third theory, they could have found in the general structure of the American Constitution "a conception of individual freedom antagonistic to slavery, a conception of procedural justice that condemned the procedures established by the Fugitive Slave Acts, and a conception of federalism inconsistent with the idea that the State of Massachusetts had no power to supervise the capture of men and women within its territory." These principles were "more central to the law than were the particular and transitory policies of the slavery compromise."

It is not in dispute that if these judges had been adherents of the natural law doctrine—as evidently they were not—they might have refused to enforce the Fugitive Slave Acts. Then the judges would have held that even if the Acts were settled law in the sense of being unambiguous and regularly enacted statutes, they were not genuine law because they violated principles of justice and natural right which were prior to any man-made system of law. The problem is whether the third theory would have yielded the same result.

First, was the law really not settled? Professor Dworkin says that the (federal) Fugitive Slave Acts "left open many questions of procedure, particularly about the power of the free states themselves to impose restrictions on the process in the interests of the alleged slave." And Massachusetts had enacted such restrictions. However, the judges held that these restrictions were overruled by the federal laws, and this seems to follow from a straightforward interpretation of Article VI of the United States Constitution: "This Constitution, and the laws of the United States which shall be made in pursuance thereof, . . . shall be the supreme law of the land; and the judges in every State shall be bound thereby, anything in the constitution or laws of any State notwithstanding." Professor Dworkin refers also to "narrowly legalistic and verbal arguments" on behalf of the alleged slaves, but arguments of that description, too easily produced, will not show that the law was not, for all that, settled. The only ground on which he can claim, in a way that is even initially plausible, that the law was not settled, is that the procedures laid down in these acts "offended ordinary notions of due process." The federal official who returned the alleged slave to his purported master was "a mere commissioner who received a higher fee if the alleged slave was sent back than if he was not, there was no question of a jury trial, and the defendant was not allowed to contest whether he was in fact a slave, that issue being left to be decided in the slave state after his return."

But it is far from clear that these provisions offend against due process. They would be defended on the ground that these proceedings were only preliminary: the legal issue about the fugitive's status was still to be decided in the state from which he had come, and that, surely, was where witnesses to his identity and status would be available. He was not being deprived of liberty without due process of law; the due process would take place in, say, Virginia. This argument could be rebutted only by casting doubt on the legal respectability of the Virginia courts, and whatever private doubts the Massachusetts judges may have had about this, it was an essential part of the federal compromise that they should not be guided by such doubts in their legal decisions. Article IV, Section 1, of the Constitution says that "full faith and credit shall be given in each State to the public acts, records, and judicial proceedings of any other State." The Virginia slaveowner could have argued that if he were not allowed to get his slave back without bringing a large number of witnesses five hundred miles so as to have his claim heard before a Massachusetts jury which was likely to be hostile to the very institution of slavery on which his claim was based, he would be, in effect, being deprived of his property, namely the slave, without due process of law. Article IV, Section 2, of the Constitution is quite explicit: "No person held to service or labor in one State, under the laws thereof, escaping into another, shall, in consequence of any law or regulation therein, be discharged from such service or labor, but shall be delivered up on claim of the party to whom such service or labor may be due."

That, in the face of all this, Professor Dworkin can hold that the law was not settled brings out an important characteristic of his theory, highly relevant to the assessment of its merits as a recommendation: the third theory often takes as unsettled issues which on a legal positivist view belong clearly to the realm of settled law.

But suppose that the law was not settled, and that a judge at the time had tried to decide these cases by Professor Dworkin's method. What conclusion would he have reached? Hercules, being a product of Professor Dworkin's imagination, would no doubt have argued as Professor Dworkin does. But let us invent another mythical judge, say Rhadamanthus.[7] He might have argued as follows:

What principles that are relevant to this case are implicit in the settled law? The fundamental fact is the Union itself, which arose out of an alliance, against Britain, of thirteen separate and very different colonies. It was recognized from the start that these colonies, and the states which they have become, have diverse institutions and ways of life. The Union exists and can survive only through compromises on issues where these differing institutions and ways of life come into conflict. One salient principle, then, enshrined as clearly as anything could be in the federal Constitution and in various statutes, is that the rights which individuals have by virtue of the institutions of the states in which they live are to be protected throughout the Union. A Virginian slave-owner's property in his slaves is one of these rights; the clear intention of Article IV, Section 2, of the Constitution and of the Fugitive Slave Acts is to protect this right. Therefore, whatever merely technical defects may be found in them the law of the land, as determined by the third theory of law which I hold, is that the alleged slave should be returned from Massachusetts to Virginia, where it can be properly decided, by the evidence of many witnesses, whether he is in fact the slave of the man who claims him.

The contrary view, that the Constitution presupposes a conception of freedom antagonistic to slavery, cannot be upheld. Jefferson, who actually wrote the Declaration of Independence, and who later was mainly responsible for the amendments which most strongly assert individual rights, was himself a slave-owner. The individual freedom which the Constitution presupposes was never intended to apply to slaves. Nor will the requirements of procedural justice, which can indeed be seen as principles enshrined in the settled law, support a finding in favor of the alleged slave. On the presumption that slave-owners have legally valid property rights in their slaves, procedural justice will best be secured by sending the alleged slave back. The conception of federalism does no doubt give the state of Massachusetts the power to supervise the capture of men and women in its territory, but this power must be exercised in ways that respect the institutions of Virginia and the rights of citizens of Virginia, especially as these are further protected by federal law.

Even if Joseph Story and Lemuel Shaw had shared Professor Dworkin's theory of jurisprudence,

they might still have followed Rhadamanthus rather than Hercules and, without for a moment abandoning their reliance on principles on their concern for rights, might have reached just those decisions they did reach by a more positivistic route. This brings out a second characteristic of the third theory, highly relevant to the assessment of its merits as a recommendation: the rights thesis, like the natural law doctrine that it in some ways resembles, is a two-edged weapon. It is particularly risky for an opponent of slavery and of racial discrimination to appeal to states' rights within a federal system. The special importance which Professor Dworkin, in his essays on applied jurisprudence (*TRS*, pp. 206–58), gives to the right to equality is not a necessary consequence of the rights thesis as such.

A third important characteristic of Professor Dworkin's theory is that its adoption would tend to make the law not only less certain but also less determinate than it would be on the rival positivist view. Of course, it is never completely determinate. Reasonable judges may well disagree on hard cases, whatever theory of jurisprudence they hold. But the third theory introduces a further source of indeterminacy. It is well known that the inference from a precedent to a general rule supposed to be implicit in it is not watertight; but a much larger degree of freedom is introduced if the judge has to frame hypotheses, not merely about rules which apply directly to cases, but also about far more general and abstract principles of justice and their implications. Professor Dworkin would deny this. He would say that it is legal positivism that would make the law in hard cases indeterminate, since it envisages situations in which the law as a whole, not merely the settled law, has run out. Judges are then called upon to legislate, bringing in consideration of policy as well as morality, and it tells judges that they thus have discretion in the strong sense. His theory, on the other hand, holds that there is on every issue a determinate and, in principle, discoverable, though perhaps not settled or certain, law.

This is why I am tempted to speak of professor Dworkin playing fast and loose with the law.[8] The alleged determinacy of the law in hard cases is a myth, and the practical effect of the acceptance of this myth would be to give, in three ways, a larger scope for what is in reality judicial legislation. First, it would shift the boundary between the settled and the unsettled law, it would make what on another view would be easy cases into hard ones. Secondly, this approach would encourage a holistic treatment of the law, letting very general principles and remote parts of the law bear upon each specific issue. Thirdly, it would encourage judges, in this holistic treatment, to rely upon their necessarily subjective views about a supposedly objective morality.

The third theory of law is thus a plea for a more speculative and enterprising handling by judges of their traditional materials and data. Like the natural law doctrine, this theory allows the consciences and the speculations of judges to intervene more significantly between what the legislative and executive branches try to do—or, for whatever reason, leave undone—and the law as it actually operates. We know well that people's prejudices, training, and social position—the movements in which they are caught up and the ideologies linked with these—strongly influence their consciences and their speculations. Whether we consider this a merit or a demerit depends upon our judgment of the judges, and particularly upon comparative judgments we make between them, the legislators, and the holders of executive office. Which of these three, with their characteristic methods and the influences to which they are exposed or from which they are sheltered, are the more to be trusted with the opportunity for partly independent decision in the making and remaking of the law? Should we give up some certainty and determinacy about what the law is, and some freedom for legislators to decide what it shall be, in order to give greater weight to what judges will see as people's rights or just claims? I do not know what answer to give, but I want it to be clear that this is the choice.

---

1. Ronald Dworkin, *Taking Rights Seriously* (London, 1977).
2. Commentaries, quoted by Julius Stone, *The Providence and Function of Law* (Sydney, 1946), p. 227.
3. *TRS*, pp. 82–84. Professor Dworkin gave this clarification in reply to a question from Professor Sir Rupert Cross at a seminar on Hard Cases in Oxford, 12 May 1976.
4. H. L. A. Hart, *The Concept of Law* (Oxford, 1961), pp. 181–207, esp. 199–200 and 205–207.
5. I have argued for this view in Chapter 1 of my *Ethics: Inventing Right and Wrong* (Harmondsworth, 1977).
6. *The Times Literary Supplement*, 5 December 1975.
7. Cf. Plato, *The Apology of Socrates* 40^c–41^a: "Would it be such a bad journey if one arrived in Hades, having got rid of the self-styled judges here, and found the true judges who are said to have jurisdiction there, Minos and Rhadamanthus and Aeacus and Triptolemus and such other demigods as were just during their lives?"
8. Cf. *Oxford English Dictionary*: "Fast and loose: A cheating game played with a stick and a belt or string, so arranged that a spectator would think he could make the latter fast by placing a stick through its intricate folds, whereas the operator could detach it at once."

THE PATH OF THE LAW*

O. W. Holmes, Jr.

When we study law we are not studying a mystery but a well known profession. We are studying what we shall want in order to appear before judges, or to advise people in such a way as to keep them out of court. The reasons why it is a profession, why people will pay lawyers to argue for them or to advise them is that in societies like ours the command of the public force is intrusted to the judges in certain cases, and the whole power of the state will be put forth, if necessary, to carry out their judgments and decrees. People want to know under what circumstances and how far they will run the risk of coming against what is so much stronger than themselves, and hence it becomes a business to find out when this danger is to be feared. The object of our study, then, is prediction, the prediction of the incidence of the public force through the instrumentality of the courts.

The means of the study are a body of reports, of treatises, and of statutes, in this country and in England, extending back for six hundred years, and now increasing annually by hundreds. In these sibylline leaves are gathered the scattered prophecies of the past upon the cases in which the axe will fall. These are what properly have been called the oracles of the law. Far the most important and pretty nearly the whole meaning of every new effort of legal thought is to make these prophecies more precise, and to generalize them into a thoroughly connected system. The process is one, from a lawyer's statement of a case, eliminating as it does all the dramatic elements with which his client's story has clothed it, and retaining only the facts of legal import, up to the final analyses and abstract universals of theoretic jurisprudence. The reason why a lawyer does not mention that his client wore a white hat when he made a contract, while Mrs. Quickly would be sure to dwell upon it along with the parcel gilt goblet and the sea-coal fire, is that he foresees that the public force will act in the same way whatever his client had upon his head. It is to make the pro-

phecies easier to be remembered and to be understood that the teachings of the decisions of the past are put into general propositions and gathered into text-books, or that statutes are passed in a general form. The primary rights and duties with which jurisprudence busies itself again are nothing but prophecies. One of the many evil effects of the confusion between legal and moral ideas, about which I shall have something to say in a moment, is that theory is apt to get the cart before the horse, and to consider the right or the duty as something existing apart from and independent of the consequences of its breach, to which certain sanctions are added afterward. But, as I shall try to show, a legal duty so called is nothing but a prediction that if a man does or omits certain things he will be made to suffer in this or that way by judgment of the court;—and so of a legal right.

The number of our predictions when generalized and reduced to a system is not unmanageably large. They present themselves as a finite body of dogma which may be mastered within a reasonable time. It is a great mistake to be frightened by the ever increasing number of reports. The reports of a given jurisdiction in the course of a generation take up pretty much the whole body of the law, and restate it from the present point of view. We could reconstruct the corpus from them if all that went before were burned. The use of the earlier reports is mainly historical, a use about which I shall have something to say before I have finished.

I wish, if I can, to lay down some first principles for the study of this body of dogma or systematized prediction which we call the law, for men who want to use it as the instrument of their business to enable them to prophesy in their turn, and, as bearing upon the study, I wish to point out an ideal which as yet our law has not attained.

The first thing for a business-like understanding of the matter is to understand its limits, and

*Oliver Wendell Holmes, "The Path of the Law," *Harvard Law Review,* vol. 10 (1897), pp. 457–68.

therefore I think it desirable at once to point out and dispel a confusion between morality and law, which sometimes rises to the height of conscious theory, and more often and indeed constantly is making trouble in detail without reaching the point of consciousness. You can see very plainly that a bad man has as much reason as a good one for wishing to avoid an encounter with the public force, and therefore you can see the practical importance of the distinction between morality and law. A man who cares nothing for an ethical rule which is believed and practised by his neighbors is likely nevertheless to care a good deal to avoid being made to pay money, and will want to keep out of jail if he can.

I take it for granted that no hearer of mine will misinterpret what I have to say as the language of cynicism. The law is the witness and external deposit of our moral life. Its history is the history of the moral development of the race. The practice of it, in spite of popular jests, tends to make good citizens and good men. When I emphasize the difference between law and morals I do so with reference to a single end, that of learning and understanding the law. For that purpose you must definitely master its specific marks, and it is for that that I ask you for the moment to imagine yourselves indifferent to other and greater things.

I do not say that there is not a wider point of view from which the distinction between law and morals becomes of secondary or no importance, as all mathematical distinctions vanish in presence of the infinite. But I do say that that distinction is of the first importance for the object which we are here to consider,—a right study and mastery of the law as a business with well understood limits, a body of dogma enclosed within definite lines. I have just shown the practical reason for saying so. If you want to know the law and nothing else, you must look at it as a bad man, who cares only for the material consequences which such knowledge enables him to predict, not as a good one, who finds his reasons for conduct, whether inside the law or outside of it, in the vaguer sanctions of conscience. The theoretical importance of the distinction is no less, if you would reason on your subject aright. The law is full of phraseology drawn from morals, and by the mere force of language continually invites us to pass from one domain to the other without perceiving it, as we are sure to do unless we have the boundary constantly before our minds. The law talks about rights, and duties, and malice, and intent, and negligence, and so forth, and nothing is easier, or, I may say, more common in legal

reasoning, than to take these words in their moral sense, at some stage of the argument, and so to drop into fallacy. For instance, when we speak of the rights of man in a moral sense, we mean to mark the limits of interference with individual freedom which we think are prescribed by conscience, or by our ideal, however reached. Yet it is certain that many laws have been enforced in the past, and it is likely that some are enforced now, which are condemned by the most enlightened opinion of the time, or which at all events pass the limit of interference as many consciences would draw it. Manifestly, therefore, nothing but confusion of thought can result from assuming that the rights of man in a moral sense are equally rights in the sense of the Constitution and the law. No doubt simple and extreme cases can be put of imaginable laws which the statute-making power would not dare to enact, even in the absence of written constitutional prohibitions, because the community would rise in rebellion and fight; and this gives some plausibility to the proposition that the law, if not a part of morality, is limited by it. But this limit of power is not coextensive with any system of morals. For the most part it falls far within the lines of any such system, and in some cases may extend beyond them, for reasons drawn from the habits of a particular people at a particular time. I once heard the late Professor Agassiz say that a German population would rise if you added two cents to the price of a glass of beer. A statute in such a case would be empty words, not because it was wrong, but because it could not be enforced. No one will deny that wrong statutes can be and are enforced, and we should not all agree as to which were the wrong ones.

The confusion with which I am dealing besets confessedly legal conceptions. Take the fundamental question, What constitutes the law? You will find some text writers telling you that it is something different from what is decided by the courts of Massachusetts or England, that it is a system of reason, that it is a deduction from principles of ethics or admitted axioms or what not, which may or may not coincide with the decisions. But if we take the view of our friend the bad man we shall find that he does not care two straws for the axioms or deductions, but that he does want to know what the Massachusetts or English courts are likely to do in fact. I am much of his mind. The prophecies of what the courts will do in fact, and nothing more pretentious, are what I mean by the law.

Take again a notion which as popularly understood is the widest conception which the law contains;—the notion of legal duty, to which already I have referred. We fill the word with all the content which we draw from morals. But what does it mean to a bad man? Mainly, and in the first place, a prophecy that if he does certain things he will be subjected to disagreeable consequences by way of imprisonment or compulsory payment of money. But from his point of view, what is the difference between being fined and being taxed a certain sum for doing a certain thing? That his point of view is the test of legal principles is shown by the many discussions which have arisen in the courts on the very question whether a given statutory liability is a penalty or a tax. On the answer to this question depends the decision whether conduct is legally wrong or right, and also whether a man is under compulsion or free. Leaving the criminal law on one side, what is the difference between the liability under the mill acts or statutes authorizing a taking by eminent domain and the liability for what we call a wrongful conversion of property where restoration is out of the question? In both cases the party taking another man's property has to pay its fair value as assessed by a jury, and no more. What significance is there in calling one taking right and another wrong from the point of view of the law? It does not matter, so far as the given consequence, the compulsory payment, is concerned, whether the act to which it is attached is described in terms of praise or in terms of blame, or whether the law purports to prohibit it or allow it. If it matters at all, still speaking from the bad man's point of view, it must be because in one case and not in the other some further disadvantages, or at least some further consequences, are attached to the act by the law. The only other disadvantages thus attached to it which I ever have been able to think of are to be found in two somewhat insignificant legal doctrines, both of which might be abolished without much disturbance. One is, that a contract to do a prohibited act is unlawful, and the other, that, if one of two or more joint wrongdoers has to pay all the damages, he cannot recover contribution from his fellows. And that I believe is all. You see how the vague circumference of the notion of duty shrinks and at the same time grows more precise when we wash it with cynical acid and expel everything except the object of our study, the operations of the law.

Nowhere is the confusion between legal and moral ideas more manifest than in the law of contract. Among other things, here again the so called primary rights and duties are invested with a mystic significance beyond what can be assigned and explained. The duty to keep a contract at common law means a prediction that you must pay damages if you do not keep it,—and nothing else. If you commit a tort, you are liable to pay a compensatory sum. If you commit a contract, you are liable to pay a compensatory sum unless the promised event comes to pass, and that is all the difference. But such a mode of looking at the matter stinks in the nostrils of those who think it advantageous to get as much ethics into the law as they can. It was good enough for Lord Coke, however, and here, as in many other cases, I am content to abide with him. In *Bromage v. Genning*,[1] a prohibition was sought in the King's Beach against a suit in the marches of Wales for the specific performance of a covenant to grant a lease, and Coke said that it would subvert the intention of the covenantor, since he intends it to be at his election either to lose the damages or to make the lease. Sergeant Harris for the plaintiff confessed that he moved the matter against his conscience, and a prohibition was granted. This goes further than we should go now, but it shows what I venture to say has been the common law point of view from the beginning, although Mr. Harriman, in his very able little book upon Contracts has been misled, as I humbly think, to a different conclusion.

I have spoken only of the common law, because there are some cases in which a logical justification can be found for speaking of civil liabilities as imposing duties in an intelligible sense. These are the relatively few in which equity will grant an injunction, and will enforce it by putting the defendant in prison or otherwise punishing him unless he complies with the order of the court. But I hardly think it advisable to shape general theory from the exception, and I think it would be better to cease troubling ourselves about primary rights and sanctions altogether, than to describe our prophecies concerning the liabilities commonly imposed by the law in those inappropriate terms.

I mentioned, as other examples of the use by the law of words drawn from morals, malice, intent, and negligence. It is enough to take malice as it is used in the law of civil liability for wrongs,—what we lawyers call the law of torts,—to show you that it means something different in law from what it means in morals, and also to show how the difference has been obscured by giving to principles which have little or nothing to do with each other the same name. Three hundred years ago a parson preached a sermon and told a story out of Fox's Book of Martyrs of a man who had assisted at the torture of one of the saints, and afterward died, suffering compensatory inward torment. It happened that Fox was wrong. The man was alive and chanced to hear the sermon, and thereupon he sued the parson. Chief Justice Wray instructed the jury that the defendant was not liable, because the story was told innocently, without malice. He took malice in the moral sense, as importing a malevolent motive. But nowadays no one doubts that a man may be liable, without any malevolent motive at all, for false statements manifestly calculated to inflict temporal damage. In stating the case in pleading, we still should call the defendant's conduct malicious; but, in my opinion at least, the word means nothing about motives, or even about the defendant's attitude toward the future, but only signifies that the tendency of his conduct under the known circumstances was very plainly to cause the plaintiff temporal harm.[2]

In the law of contract the use of moral phraseology has led to equal confusion, as I have shown in part already, but only in part. Morals deal with the actual internal state of the individual's mind, what he actually intends. From the time of the Romans down to now, this mode of dealing has affected the language of the law as to contract, and the language used has reacted upon the thought. We talk about a contract as a meeting of the minds of the parties, and thence it is inferred in various cases that there is no contract because their minds have not met; that is, because they have intended different things or because one party has not known of the assent of the other. Yet nothing is more certain than that parties may be bound by a contract to things which neither of them intended, and when one does not know of the other's assent. Suppose a contract is executed in due form and in writing to deliver a lecture, mentioning no time. One of the parties thinks that the promise will be construed to mean at once, within a week. The other thinks that it means when he is ready. The court says that it means within a reasonable time. The parties are bound by the contract as it is interpreted by the court, yet neither of them meant what the court declares that they have said. In my opinion no one will understand the true theory of contract or be able even to discuss some fundamental questions intelligently until he has understood that all contracts are formal, that the making of a contract depends not on the agreement of two minds in one intention, but on the agreement of two sets of external signs,—not on the parties' having *meant* the same thing but on their having *said* the same thing. Furthermore, as the signs may be addressed to one

sense or another,—to sight or to hearing,—on the nature of the sign will depend the moment when the contract is made. If the sign is tangible, for instance, a letter, the contract is made when the letter of acceptance is delivered. If it is necessary that the minds of the parties meet, there will be no contract until the acceptance can be read,—none, for example, if the acceptance be snatched from the hand of the offerer by a third person.

This is not the time to work out a theory in detail, or to answer many obvious doubts and questions which are suggested by these general views. I know of none which are not easy to answer, but what I am trying to do now is only by a series of hints to throw some light on the narrow path of legal doctrine, and upon two pitfalls which, as it seems to me, lie perilously near to it. Of the first of these I have said enough. I hope that my illustrations have shown the danger, both to speculation and to practice, of confounding morality with law, and the trap which legal language lays for us on that side of our way. For my own part, I often doubt whether it would not be a gain if every word of moral significance could be banished from the law altogether, and other words adopted which should convey legal ideas uncolored by anything outside the law. We should lose the fossil records of a good deal of history and the majesty got from ethical associations, but by ridding ourselves of an unnecessary confusion we should gain very much in the clearness of our thought.

So much for the limits of the law. The next thing which I wish to consider is what are the forces which determine its content and its growth. You may assume, with Hobbes and Bentham and Austin, that all law emanates from the sovereign, even when the first human beings to enunciate it are the judges, or you may think that law is the voice of the Zeitgeist, or what you like. It is all one to my present purpose. Even if every decision required the sanction of an emperor with despotic power and a whimsical turn of mind, we should be interested nonetheless, still with a view to prediction, in discovering some order, some rational explanation, and some principle of growth for the rules which he laid down. In every system there are such explanations and principles to be found. It is with regard to them that a second fallacy comes in, which I think it important to expose.

The fallacy to which I refer is the notion that the only force at work in the development of the law is logic. In the broadest sense, indeed, that notion would be true. The postulate on which we think about the universe is that there is a fixed quantitative

relation between every phenomenon and its antecedents and consequents. If there is such a thing
as a phenomenon without these fixed quantitative
relations, it is a miracle. It is outside the law of cause
and effect, and as such transcends our power of
thought, or at least is something to or from which we
cannot reason. The condition of our thinking about
the universe is that it is capable of being thought
about rationally, or, in other words, that every part
of it is effect and cause in the same sense in which
those parts are with which we are most familiar. So
in the broadest sense it is true that the law is a logical development, like everything else. The danger of
which I speak is not the admission that the principles governing other phenomena also govern the
law, but the notion that a given system, ours, for instance, can be worked out like mathematics from
some general axioms of conduct. This is the natural
error of the schools, but it is not confined to them. I
once heard a very eminent judge say that he never
let a decision go until he was absolutely sure that it
was right. So judicial dissent often is blamed, as if it
meant simply that one side or the other were not
doing their sums right, and, if they would take more
trouble, agreement inevitably would come.

This mode of thinking is entirely natural. The
training of lawyers is a training in logic. The
processes of analogy, discrimination, and deduction
are those in which they are most at home. The language of judicial decision is mainly the language of
logic. And the logical method and form flatter that
longing for certainty and for repose which is in every
human mind. But certainly generally is illusion, and
repose is not the destiny of man. Behind the logical
form lies a judgment as to the relative worth and importance of competing legislative grounds, often an
inarticulate and unconscious judgment, it is true, and
yet the very root and nerve of the whole proceeding. You can give any conclusion a logical form. You
always can imply a condition in a contract. But why
do you imply it? It is because of some belief as to
the practice of the community or of a class, or because of some opinion as to policy, or, in short, because of some attitude of yours upon a matter not
capable of exact quantitative measurement, and
therefore not capable of founding exact logical conclusions. Such matters really are battle grounds
where the means do not exist for determinations that
shall be good for all time, and where the decision
can do no more than embody the preference of a
given body in a given time and place. We do not realize how large a part of our law is open to recon-

sideration upon a slight change in the habit of the
public mind. No concrete proposition is self-evident,
no matter how ready we may be to accept it, not
even Mr. Herbert Spencer's, Every man has a right
to do what he wills, provided he interferes not with
a like right on the part of his neighbors.

Why is a false and injurious statement privileged, if it is made honestly in giving information
about a servant? It is because it has been thought
more important that information should be given
freely, than that a man should be protected from what
under other circumstances would be an actionable
wrong. Why is a man at liberty to set up a business
which he knows will ruin his neighbor? It is because
the public good is supposed to be best subserved by
free competition. Obviously such judgments of relative importance may vary in different times and
places. Why does a judge instruct a jury that an employer is not liable to an employee for an injury received in the course of his employment unless he is
negligent, and why do the jury generally find for the
plaintiff if the case is allowed to go to them? It is because the traditional policy of our law is to confine liability to cases where a prudent man might have
foreseen the injury, or at least the danger, while the
inclination of a very large part of the community is to
make certain classes of persons insure the safety of
those with whom they deal. Since the last words were
written, I have seen the requirement of such insurance put forth as part of the programme of one of the
best known labor organizations. There is a concealed,
half conscious battle on the question of legislative
policy, and if any one thinks that it can be settled
deductively, or once for all, I only can say that I think
he is theoretically wrong, and that I am certain that
his conclusion will not be accepted in practice
semper ubique et ab omnibus.

Indeed, I think that even now our theory upon
this matter is open to reconsideration, although I am
not prepared to say how I should decide if a reconsideration were proposed. Our law of torts comes
from the old days of isolated, ungeneralized wrongs,
assaults, slanders, and the like, where the damages
might be taken to lie where they fell by legal judgment. But the torts with which our courts are kept
busy today are mainly the incidents of certain well
known businesses. They are injuries to person or
property by railroads, factories, and the like. The liability for them is estimated, and sooner or later goes
into the price paid by the public. The public really
pays the damages, and the question of liability, if
pressed far enough, is really the question how far it

is desirable that the public should insure the safety of those whose work it uses. It might be said that in such cases the chance of a jury finding for the defendant is merely a chance, once in a while rather arbitrarily interrupting the regular course of recovery, most likely in the case of an unusually conscientious plaintiff, and therefore better done away with. On the other hand, the economic value even of a life to the community can be estimated, and no recovery, it may be said, ought to go beyond that amount. It is conceivable that some day in certain cases we may find ourselves imitating, on a higher plane, the tariff for life and limb which we see in the Leges Barbarorum.

I think that the judges themselves have failed adequately to recognize their duty of weighing considerations of social advantage. The duty is inevitable, and the result of the often proclaimed judicial aversion to deal with such considerations is simply to leave the very ground and foundation of judgments inarticulate, and often unconscious, as I have said. When socialism first began to be talked about, the comfortable classes of the community were a good deal frightened. I suspect that this fear has influenced judicial action both here and in England, yet it is certain that it is not a conscious factor in the decisions to which I refer. I think that something similar has led people who no longer hope to control the legislatures to look to the courts as expounders of the Constitutions, and that in some courts new principles have been discovered outside the bodies of those instruments, which may be generalized into acceptance of the economic doctrines which prevailed about fifty years ago, and a wholesale prohibition of what a tribunal of lawyers does not think about right. I cannot but believe that if the training of lawyers led them habitually to consider more definitely and explicitly the social advantage on which the rule they lay down must be justified, they sometimes would hesitate where now they are confident, and see that really they were taking sides upon debatable and often burning questions.

---

1. I Roll. Rep. 368.

2. See *Hanson v. Globe Newspaper Co.,* 159 *Mass.* 293, 302.

LEGAL REALISM*

Jerome Frank

We have talked much of the law. But what is "the law"? A complete definition would be impossible and even a working definition would exhaust the patience of the reader. But it may not be amiss to inquire what, in a rough sense, the law means to the average man of our times when he consults his lawyer.

The Jones family owned the Blue & Gray Taxi Company, a corporation incorporated in Kentucky. That company made a contract with the A. & B. Railroad Company, also a Kentucky corporation, by which it was agreed that the Blue & Gray Taxi Company was to have the exclusive privilege of soliciting taxicab business on and adjacent to the railroad company's depot.

A rival taxicab company, owned by the Williams family, the Purple Taxi Company, began to ignore this contract; it solicited business and parked its taxicabs in places assigned by the railroad company to the Blue & Gray Company and sought in other ways to deprive the Blue & Gray Company of the benefits conferred on it by the agreement with the railroad.

The Jones family were angered; their profits derived from the Blue & Gray stock, which they owned, were threatened. They consulted their lawyer, a Louisville practitioner, and this, we may conjecture, is about what he told them: "I'm afraid your contract is not legally valid. I've examined several decisions of the highest court of Kentucky and they pretty clearly indicate that you can't get away with that kind of an agreement in this state. The Kentucky court holds such a contract to be bad as creating an unlawful monopoly. But I'll think the matter over. You come back tomorrow and I'll try meanwhile to find some way out."

So, the next day, the Joneses returned. And this time their lawyer said he thought he had discovered how to get the contract sustained: "You see, it's this way. In most courts, except those of Kentucky and of a few other states, an agreement like this is perfectly good. But, unfortunately, as things now stand, you'll have to go into the Kentucky courts.

"If we can manage to get our case tried in the federal court, there's a fair chance that we'll get a different result, because I think the federal court will follow the majority rule and not the Kentucky rule. I'm not sure of that, but it's worth trying.

"So this is what we'll do. We'll form a new Blue & Gray Company in Tennessee. And your Kentucky Blue & Gray Company will transfer all its assets to the new Tennessee Blue & Gray Company. Then we'll have the railroad company execute a new contract with the new Tennessee Blue & Gray Company, and at the same time cancel the old contract and, soon after, dissolve the old Kentucky Blue & Gray Company."

"But," interrupted one of the Joneses, "what good will all that monkey-business do?"

The lawyer smiled broadly. "Just this," he replied with pride in his cleverness: "The A. & B. Railroad Company is organized in Kentucky. So is the Purple Taxi which we want to get at. The federal court will treat these companies as if they were citizens of Kentucky. Now, a corporation which is a citizen of Kentucky can't bring this kind of suit in the federal court against other corporations which are also citizens of Kentucky. But if your company becomes a Tennessee corporation, it will be considered as if it were a citizen of Tennessee. Then your new Tennessee company can sue the other two in the federal court, because the suit will be held to be one between citizens of different states. And that kind of suit, based on what we lawyers call 'diversity of citizenship,' can be brought in the federal

*Jerome Frank, "Legal Realism," from *Law and the Modern Mind* (New York: Doubleday and Co. Anchor edition, 1963), 46–52. Originally published by Brentanos, Inc. in 1930. Copyright © 1930, 1933, 1949 by Coward McCann, Inc. Copyright reviewed in 1958 by Florence K. Frank. Copyright © 1930 by Brentanos, Inc. Reprinted by arrangement with Barbara Kiastern and Peter Smith Publisher, Inc.

court by a corporation which organized in Tennessee against corporations which are citizens of another state, Kentucky. And the federal court, as I said, ought to sustain your contract."

"That sounds pretty slick," said one of the Joneses admiringly. "Are you sure it will work?"

"No," answered the lawyer. "You can't ever be absolutely sure about such a plan. I can't find any case completely holding our way on all these facts. But I'm satisfied that's the law and that that's the way the federal court ought to decide. I won't guarantee success. But I recommend trying out my suggestion." His advise was followed. Shortly after the new Tennessee Blue & Gray Company was organized and had entered into the new contract, suit was brought by the Joneses' new Blue & Gray Corporation of Tennessee in the Federal District Court against the competing Purple Company and the railroad company. In this suit, the Blue & Gray Taxi Company of Tennessee asked the court to prevent interference with the carrying out of its railroad contract.

As the Joneses' lawyer had hoped, the federal court held, against the protest of the Purple Company's lawyer, first, that such a suit could be brought in the federal court and, second, that the contract was valid. Accordingly the court enjoined the Purple Company from interfering with the depot business of the Joneses' Blue & Gray Company. The Joneses were elated, for now their profits seemed once more assured.

But not for long. The other side appealed the case to the Federal Circuit Court of Appeals. And the Joneses' lawyer was somewhat worried that that court might reverse the lower federal court. But it didn't, and the Joneses again were happy.

Still the Purple Company persisted. It took the case to the Supreme Court of the United States. That Court consists of nine judges. And the Joneses' lawyer couldn't be certain just how those judges would line up on all the questions involved. "Some new men on the bench, and you never can tell about Holmes and Brandeis. They're very erratic," was his comment.

When the United States Supreme Court gave its decision, it was found that six of the nine judges agreed with counsel for the Joneses. Three justices (Homes, Brandeis, and Stone) were of the contrary opinion. But the majority governs in the United States Supreme Court, and the Joneses' prosperity was at last firmly established.

Now, what was "the law" for the Joneses, who owned the Blue & Gray Company, and the Williamscs, who owned the Purple Company? The an-

swer will depend on the date of the question. If asked before the new Tennessee Company acquired this contract, it might have been said that it was almost surely "the law" that the Joneses would lose; for any suit involving the validity of that contract could then have been brought only in the Kentucky state court and the prior decisions of that court seemed adverse to such an agreement.

After the suggestion of the Joneses' lawyer was carried out and the new Tennessee corporation owned the contract, "the law" was more doubtful. Many lawyers would have agreed with the Joneses' lawyer that there was a good chance that the Jones family would be victorious if suit were brought in the federal courts. But probably an equal number would have disagreed: they would have said that the formation of the new Tennessee company was a trick used to get out of the Kentucky courts and into the federal court, a trick of which the federal court would not approve. Or that, regardless of that question, the federal court would follow the well-settled Kentucky rule as to the invalidity of such contracts as creating unlawful monopolies (especially because the use of Kentucky real estate was involved) and that therefore the federal court would decide against the Joneses. "The law," at any time before the decision of the United States Supreme Court, was indeed unsettled. (That is, it was unsettled whether the Williamses had the energy, patience, and money to push an appeal. If not, then the decision of the lower federal court was the actual settled law for the Jones and Williams families.) No one could know what the court would decide. Would it follow the Kentucky cases? If so, the law was that no "rights" were conferred by the contract. Would it refuse to follow the Kentucky cases? If so, rights were conferred by the contract. To speak of settled law governing that controversy, or of the fixed legal rights of those parties, as antedating the decision of the Supreme Court, is mere verbiage. If two more judges on that bench had agreed with Justices Holmes, Brandeis, and Stone, the law and the rights of the parties would have been of a directly opposite kind.

After the decision, "the law" was fixed. There were no other courts to which an appeal could be directed. The judgment of the United States Supreme Court could not be disturbed and the legal "rights" of the Joneses and the Williamses were everlastingly established.

We may now venture a rough definition of law from the point of view of the average man: For any particular lay person, the law, with respect to any particular set of facts, is a decision of a court with respect to those facts so far as that decision affects that particular person. Until a court has passed on those facts no law on that subject is yet in existence. Prior to such a decision, the only law available is the opinion of lawyers as to the law relating to that person and to those facts. Such opinion is not actually law but only a guess as to what a court will decide. (The United States Supreme Court has wittily been called the "court of ultimate conjecture.")

Law, then, as to any given situation is either (*a*) actual law, that is, a specific past decision, as to that situation, or (*b*) probable law, that is, a guess as to a specific future decision.

Usually when a client consults his lawyer about "the law," his purpose is to ascertain not what the courts have actually decided in the past but what the courts will probably decide in the future. He asks,

"Have I a right, as a stockholder of the American Taffy Company of Indiana, to look at the corporate books?" Or, "Do I have to pay an inheritance tax to the State of New York on bonds left me by my deceased wife, if our residence was in Ohio, but the bonds, at the time of her death, were in a safety-deposit box in New York?" Or, "Is there a right of 'peaceful' picketing in a strike in the State of California?" Or, "If Jones sells me his Chicago shoe business and agrees not to compete for ten years, will the agreement be binding?" The answers (although they may run "There is such a right," "The law is that the property is not taxable," "Such picketing is unlawful," "The agreement is not legally binding") are in fact prophecies or predictions of judicial action. It is from this point of view that the practice of law has been aptly termed an art of prediction. . . .

Interpretive Construction in the Substantive Criminal Law*

Mark Kelman

Legal argument has a standard, and putatively rational, form: It states overarching purposes to the legal system, and from those purposes it deduces answers to specific doctrinal dilemmas. This article examines the standard doctrinal arguments routinely made by judges and commentators on the substantive criminal law.[1] I do not wish to challenge any results these commentators may reach, except insofar as it is important to challenge some universally held beliefs in order to counter claims that there are easy criminal law cases. Instead, I want to challenge the

falsely complacent sense that the arguments, while grounded in politically controversial purposes, are deduced or derived in a rational and coherent fashion once the purposes are settled.[2] I will be contending, in essence, that legal argument has two phases, interpretive construction and rational rhetoricism, and that the former, a vital step which undercuts the rationality of the latter, goes virtually unexamined.

By interpretive construction, I refer to processes by which concrete situations are reduced to substantive legal controversies: It refers both to the

---

*The author wishes to thank Paul Brest, Tom Heller, John Kaplan, Duncan Kennedy, Bob Rabin, and especially Tom Grey for their helpful comments on an earlier draft, as well as Don Creach for his research assistance. Errors remain mine. This research was supported by the Stanford Legal Research Fund, made possible by a bequest from the Estate of Ira S. Lillick and by gifts from Roderick E. and Carla A. Hills and other friends of the Stanford Law School. Mark Kelman is Associate Professor of Law, Stanford University. A. B. 1972, J. D. 1976, Harvard University. From 33 *Stanford Law Review* 591 (April 1981). Endnotes have been edited and renumbered.

way we construe a factual situation and to the way we frame the possible rules to handle the situation. What then follows logically, if not chronologically, is rational rhetoricism—the process of presenting the legal conclusions that result when interpretive constructs are applied to the "facts." This rhetorical process is the "stuff" of admirable legal analysis: distinguishing and analyzing cases, applying familiar policies to unobvious fact patterns, and emphasizing the degree to which we can rely on the least controversial underlying values. These rhetorical techniques are so intellectually complex that there is a powerful tendency to elevate falsely the importance of intellect in actual legal decisionmaking, to fail to see the interpretive construction that makes the wise posturing possible. I will look behind (or unpack) this rhetoric to the selection of "relevant" categories and "relevant" facts. At the same time, I will try to understand the appeal of the well-argued case, an appeal clearly felt by so many of my colleagues and students.

Part I of this article briefly summarizes the various interpretive constructs that pervade substantive criminal law. These constructs are sometimes unconscious techniques of sorting out legal material and are sometimes consciously held political or philosophical beliefs, although even the consciously held beliefs function so that the users seem unaware of them. Parts II and III discuss the process by which conscious and unconscious constructs settle doctrinal issues. I will try to illustrate how each of these interpretive constructs "operates," how a legal-sounding argument can be made only *after* a situation is characterized nonrationally, so that the advocate seems able to deduce a single result on principle. For example, I will show that issues of the voluntariness of a defendant's conduct can be resolved only *after* we have agreed, for reasons outside of our rational discourse, to include within the relevant time frame some obviously voluntary act that contributes to the ultimate harm. I will try to demonstrate the unresolved and unresolvable inconsistency in using such interpretive constructs in standard discourse; for instance, we neither frame time the same way in all criminal law settings nor do we ever explain why we use one time frame or another. Finally, I will suggest what role interpretive construction plays—why the interpreter does what he does, although I offer my accounts of why "analysts" do what they do with more trepidation than I have when I offer my account of what they are doing.

Though it may appear to some that I have nonrandomly selected the cases in which these in-terpretive constructs are involved, this charge strikes me as unwarranted. First, though the group of "hard" cases I have selected may seem unrepresentative, I have simply selected nearly *all* of the issues that I cover teaching a traditional substantive criminal law course, using a good casebook[3] that certainly was not edited with my concerns in mind. Second, and more importantly, I have attempted in Part IV to extend the discussion of interpretive constructs to the sorts of "easy" cases that legal commentators never bother to discuss, cases with few apparent puzzling aspects. If the interpretations I discuss are at work in these "easy" cases, they are at stake in *every* case.

I. A General Summary of Interpretive Constructs

Legal argument can be made only *after* a fact pattern is characterized by interpretive constructs. Once these constructs operate, a single legal result seems inevitable, a result seemingly deduced on general principle. These constructs appear both in conscious and unconscious forms in standard legal discourse. Before examining in detail how interpretive constructs reify substantive "textbook" law, it will be useful to examine them more precisely.

A. Four Unconscious Interpretive Constructs

Unconscious interpretive constructs shape the way we view disruptive incidents, but they are never identified or discussed by judges or commentators. There are basically four forms of unconscious constructs, two dealing with "time-framing" and two dealing with problems of categorization. I discuss unconscious constructs before conscious ones because the former are often used to avoid issues inherent in the latter, issues that the legal analysts are most prone to be aware are controversial, perhaps insoluble, and highly politicized.

1. Broad and Narrow Time Frames We put people on trial. People exist over time; they have long, involved personal histories. We prosecute particular acts—untoward incidents—that these people commit. But even these incidents have a history: Things occur before or after incidents that seem relevant to our judgment of what the perpetrator did. Sometimes we incorporate facts about the defendant's personal history.[4] Other times, we incorporate facts about events preceding[5] or post-dating[6] the criminal incident. But an interpreter can readily focus solely on the isolated criminal incident, as if all we can learn of value in assessing culpability can be seen with that narrower time focus.

Most often, though not invariably, the arational choice between narrow and broad time frames keeps us from having to deal with more explicit political questions arising from one conscious interpretive construct—the conflict between intentionalism and determinism. Often, conduct is deemed involuntary (or determined) rather than freely willed (or intentional) because we do not consider the defendant's earlier decisions that may have put him in the position of apparent choicelessness. Conversely, conduct that could be viewed as freely willed or voluntary if we looked only at the precise moment of the criminal incident is sometimes deemed involuntary because we open up the time frame to look at prior events that seem to compel or determine the defendant's conduct at the time of the incident. The use of "time-framing" as interpretive *method* blocks the perception that intentionalist or determinist issues could be substantively at stake. If one has somehow convinced oneself that the incident, narrow time-framed focus is the appropriate *technique* for interpreting criminal law material, there is simply no background data one can use, either to provide the grist for a determinist account or to locate a prior sphere of choice in a seemingly constricted world. The interpretive "choice" between narrow and broad time frames affects not only controversial, doctrinally tricky legal cases, but also "easy" cases, because narrow time-framing fends off, at the methodological level, the possibility of doing determinist analyses.

2. Disjoined and Unified Accounts   A second unconscious interpretive construct relating to time involves the tension between disjoined and unified accounts of incidents. Many legally significant situations seem to require a somewhat broad time frame, at least in the sense that we feel we must look beyond a single moment in time and account, in some fashion, for some clearly relevant earlier moment. The earlier "moment" may be the time at which a defendant made some judgment about the situation she was in, some judgment that at least contributed to the ultimate decision to act criminally. For instance, the defendant negligently believes she must use deadly force to defend herself and then she intentionally kills someone, having formed that belief. Alterna-

tively, the earlier moment may simply be the moment at which the defendant initiated the chain of events that culminated in criminal results. For instance, the defendant may shoot at X, but the bullet will miss X and then kill Y, an unforeseeably present bystander.

Once we agree to look at these earlier moments, we must decide whether to disjoin or unify the earlier moment with the later moment. We can treat all the relevant facts as constituting a single incident, or we can disjoin the events into two separate incidents.

Once this arational interpretive decision is made, the question of criminal culpability is forever biased. Is a negligent decision to kill followed by an intentional killing a negligent or intentional act? Is the person who misses X and shoots Y someone who commits two crimes—attempted murder of X plus, say, reckless homicide of Y—or one crime—an intentional murder of a person? Sometimes, unifying two arguably separate incidents allows us to avoid making a hard-to-justify assertion that the arguably second incident or decision was determined by the first. Often, other interests are at stake in separating or joining a series of incidents.

3. Broad and Narrow Views of Intent   A third unconscious construct involves broad and narrow views of intent. Each time someone acts, we can say with fair confidence that, in the absence of some claim of accident, he intended to do precisely the acts that he has done. But we have difficulty categorizing those acts, because an individual set of acts may, in the observer's eyes, be an instance of a number of different categories of acts. For example, when the defendant intends to undertake certain deeds constituting a particular crime, it feels both misleading in significant ways, and perfectly proper in others, to assert that the defendant intended the particular crime. On one hand, it is odd to think of actors as viewing the world in criminal law categories when they act. On the other hand, it is equally odd to think of actors as focusing in their consciousness only on the most precise physical motions they undertake. Thus, when we talk of the requisite intent to commit assault *with intent* to commit murder, it is peculiar to think *either* that the defendant must have mentally focused his conduct on the broadly interpreted *crime* of murder (with all its complications, *e.g.,* that he must intend to act with malice, premeditation, nonprovocation, nonjustification, etc.), or that it is sufficient that he simply focused on the physical *motions* which would predicate the crime (*e.g.,* pulling the trigger on the gun, which we may deem murder if, in fact, he acted with what we call malice, nonprovocation, etc.).

Similarly, a defendant may perform suspicious acts not in themselves criminal or abandon a particular criminal attempt. We wonder whether the defendant, in the first case, can accurately be thought of as intending only the precise acts he committed or whether, in some broader sense, he *intended* some apter deeds which we would deem criminal acts. Likewise, in the second case, we wonder whether the defendant abandoned only the one criminal incident or abandoned the criminal category of which that incident is but an instance.

4. Bread and Narrow Views of the Defendant   A fourth unconscious construct is that the interpreter may view defendants in broad or narrow terms. Each defendant is a unique individual, with a unique set of perceptions and capabilities. Every crime is committed in a unique setting. At the same time, every defendant has general human traits, and is thus a representative of the broader category of human beings. Similarly, the setting in which a crime is committed is an instance of those settings in which the crime is generally committed, and the features of the more general situation could be ascribed to the particular situation. By varying our interpretive focus, by particularizing at times and categorizing at others, substantive criminal law reaches all manner of results. Shifts in these perspectives underlie efforts to make doctrinal categories appear more cogent than they actually are.

B. Conscious Interpretive Constructs

Just as unconscious constructs shape the way we view disruptive incidents, conscious constructs settle doctrinal issues while obscuring the nondeductive nature of legal discourse. I discuss two forms of conscious construction: the choice between intentionalistic and deterministic accounts of human conduct, and the choice between stating legal commands in the form of precise rules or vague ad hoc standards. While judges and commentators seem to be aware of these constructs, they discuss them only as *general* philosophical themes in the criminal law.

But I will argue that any consciously stated "grand" choices elevating intentionalism or rules, determinism or standards, as *the* solution to legal dilemmas is inevitably partial. The "victory" of one framework or the other is a temporary one that can never be made with assurance or comfort. Each as-

sertion manifests no more than a momentary expression of feelings that remain contradictory and unresolved. Most significantly, arguments based on these explicitly political issues feel less "legal" than arguments grounded in traditional doctrinal categories. Perhaps more important for this article, I will also argue that the *un-self-conscious* assertion of the inexorability of applying one or the other poles in these controversies to a particular setting settles many doctrinal issues, though the problematic nature of chosen doctrine would become more apparent if the use of interpretive constructs surfaced. In this sense, these interpretive constructs function just like the four unconscious constructs. Though they are conscious political positions when employed at a general level, they may function as unreasoned presuppositions that solve cases while obscuring the dissonant, fundamentally nondeductive nature of legal discourse.

1. Intentionalism and Determinism   Intentionalism is the principle that human conduct results from free choice.[7] An intentionalist interpretation of an incident gives moral weight to autonomous choice and expresses the indeterminacy of future actions.[8] Determinism, on the other hand, implies that subsequent behavior is causally connected to prior events. A determinist interpretation considers behavior by looking backward, and it expresses no moral respect or condemnation of these predetermined acts.[9]

Most basic issues of the criminal law are issues of the applicability of an intentionalist model.[10] Notions of blameworthiness and deterrence[11] are both based on the assumption that criminal actors make intentional choices. Of course, criminal jurisprudence *acknowledges* the plausibility of a determinist discourse, but it *acts* as if the intentionalist discourse is ultimately complete, coherent, and convincing.[12] It is quite apparent, however, that standard criminal law doctrine often interprets facts in deterministic modes. For example, duress, insanity, and provocation are determinist excuses for otherwise criminal conduct.

2. Rules versus Standards   An overarching conflict within our legal system pertains to the form that legal pronouncements should take.[13] Our legal system bounces fitfully between "clearly defined, highly administrable, general rules"[14] and "equitable standards producing ad hoc decisions with relatively little precedential value."[15]

Rules seem, on the positive side, capable of uniform and nonprejudicial application. They define spheres of autonomy and privacy and spheres of duty by giving clear notice to citizens of the legal consequences of their conduct. The void-for-vagueness and strict construction doctrines both resonate in the rule-respecting liberal tradition. On the negative side, rules will inevitably be both over- and underinclusive according to the purposes reasonably attributable to the law.[16] This not only leads to random injustice when particular culpable parties are acquitted[17] and nonculpable parties are convicted,[18] but it enables people to calculate privately optimal levels of undesirable behavior that are within the precise confines of the law.[19]

Standards alleviate the problems of nonpurposive applications of legal commands to particular cases. On the other hand, they may be difficult to administer or may be enforced in a biased, unequal, and uncertain fashion. The use of standards in the criminal law is rampant. Whether we are talking about requirements of "malice" in homicide law, looking at regulatory statutes that are openly vague in proscribing *unreasonable* restraints of trade,[20] or considering the use of discretion in prosecution and sentencing, it is difficult to deny that avoiding vagueness is more important as ideology than in practice. In any argument within our culture, *both* of these modes of framing legal commands are simultaneously appealing and unappealing; neither has killer force.[21] Because neither position can dominate the other, legal arguments about the desirable form of legal commands are not just oscillating, unsettled, and unbalanced, but the choice of one resolution or the other ultimately feels like a product of whim—a reflection of one's most recent overreaction to the follies of the previously adopted form.

II. Unconscious Interpretive Constructs

Having examined the interpretive constructs in general, I shall now apply the four unconscious constructs to doctrinally "hard" cases in the substantive criminal law. This part illustrates how each construct is used and how certain results are apparently mandated only after an unwarranted interpretation is made. I shall also try in this section to account for the appearance of particular constructs in particular fact situations. Though I am generally skeptical of accounts of construction, it is most often my belief that interpretive construction appears to enable the legal analyst to avoid dealing with fundamental political problems.

A. Broad and Narrow Time Frames

1. Narrow Time-Framing   Generally speaking, narrow time frames buttress the traditionally asserted intentionalism of the criminal justice system. In a number of doctrinal areas, though, conduct is deemed to be involuntary or otherwise outside the responsibility of the defendant even though, if we interpret the relevant legal material as including earlier decisions (that is, if we broaden the time frame), we can interpret the *course* of conduct that culminates in criminal harm as chosen.

Status versus conduct distinction. The tensions of time-framing are evident in the status versus conduct distinction. In *United States v. Moore,*[22] Judge Wright, in dissent, argued that a statute proscribing narcotics possession should not apply to drug addicts, because possession merely manifests their status of being addicted. He contended that drug addicts cannot be deterred from or blamed for possessing narcotics *because* their addiction rendered them choiceless.[23] Since punishment is inappropriate unless its deterrence or retributory aims are met, it is inapt here.

Fully addicted people truly may not be deterrable by the prospect of punishment at the *moment* when they decide to possess or use drugs. In Judge Wright's narrow view of the relevant legal material, the defendant may be nondeterrable because his then-pressing desire makes him oblivious to the costs imposed by state punishment. But once we broaden the time frame, we can see that even the particular use by the addict in *Moore* would have been less likely if addicts were punished. Assuming, as one must in applying deterrence theories, that actors calculate rationally and try to avoid pain, we know that if a person can be punished at *any* future time he uses drugs, not just in the pre-addiction period, he will be less prone to start using drugs. But, of course, if the person who ultimately came to trial had not made the initial uses, he would not have become an addict or made the particular use we are concerned with.[24]

Precisely the same objection can be made to Judge Wright's argument that the status of addiction cannot be deemed blameworthy. Even if we should not blame people for *being* sick, we may well blame them for *becoming* sick. The addict may seem blameless in the narrow time frame, but in a broader time frame he may well be blameworthy. Certainly, it is not at all uncommon or bizarre for a parent to blame (and punish) a child who goes out of the house in a storm without adequate raingear for *getting* a cold, even though the same parent would not punish the child for the "status" of *being* ill. Venereal disease is another clear case: That VD is generally considered a disease hardly precludes us from blaming its victims, because they *contracted* it through *earlier* voluntary acts.[25]

Judge Wright dismissed, in conclusory fashion, the possibility of using a broader time frame in assessing retributive demands.[26] Presumably, Judge Wright used a very *narrow* time frame here to reach the determinist result he would like to reach by using the very *broadest* one: I surmise that the judge actually believes that the initial "voluntary" drug uses are themselves determined by social and environmental pressures that predate those early uses. Despairing of the possibility of applying a very wide time focus and a more general determinism, he avoided this political confrontation by constructing the legal "material" in terms of the traditional *incident* focus, a focus which the majority implicitly rejected in the following conclusory terms:

> The gist of appellant's argument is that "the common law has long held that the capacity to control behavior is a prerequisite for criminal responsibility."
>
> It is inescapable that the logic of appellant's argument, if valid, would carry over to all other illegal acts of any type whose purpose was to obtain narcotics.[27]

If we take it as given that we *must* punish the people we are now punishing—and a lot of those people are stealing to obtain narcotics—then we must avoid Judge Wright's incident-based determinism. But this is simply a functionalist complacency, the belief that things are right because they are done: a world view hardly more or less acceptable than any other political assertion (*e.g.,* things can be presumed to be wrong, if done, because the world we see is pretty crummy), and hardly the outcome of piercing legal analysis.

The voluntary act requirement. Unconscious shifting between broad and narrow time frames also arises in applying the criminal law's voluntary act requirement. In *Martin v. State,*[28] police officers arrested the defendant at his home and took him onto a public highway, where the defendant used loud and profane language. He was convicted under a statute prohibiting public exhibition of a drunken condition. The appellate court reversed, holding that the defen-

dant was involuntarily and forcibly carried to the public place by the arresting officers. The court concluded, uncontroversially, that an involuntary act cannot give rise to liability.[29] But in *People v. Decina,*[30] the court sustained the defendant's conviction for negligent homicide, though at the time his car struck the victims, he was unconscious as a result of an epileptic fit, not voluntarily operating the vehicle. The court held that the defendant was culpable because he had made a conscious decision to drive, knowing that an epileptic attack was possible.[31]

The hidden interpretive time-framing construct becomes visible when one tries to square *Martin* with *Decina.* In *Decina,* the court opened up the time frame, declaring that if the defendant commits a voluntary act at time one which poses a risk of causing an involuntary harm later—drives the car knowing he is a blackout-prone epileptic—then the second act—crashing while unconscious—will be deemed voluntary. But the defendant in *Martin,* as well, may have done *something* voluntarily (before the police came) that posed a risk that he would get arrested and carried into public in his drunken state. While it is plausible that Martin was arrested on an old warrant[32] and could not foresee that he would wind up in public on this occasion, it is quite possible that the defendant was arrested for activity he was engaging in at home: for instance, beating his wife.[33] Why did the court not consider saying that the voluntary act at time one (wife beating) both posed a risk of and caused a harmful involuntary act at time two (public drunkenness) and assessing the voluntariness of the alleged criminal act with reference to the wider time-framed scenario? It cannot be that the involuntary, harmful act at time two was unforeseeable.[34] The probability of an epileptic blackout is almost certainly far lower than the probability of ending up in public after engaging in behavior likely to draw police attention. Arguments that we are less concerned with people "thinking ahead" to avoid public drunkenness than unconscious driving seem inadequate as well; the penalties for public drunkenness are presumably set lower to reflect the relative lack of gravity of the offense. Ultimately, the *Martin* finding of voluntariness "works" not because it is "right," but because all the hard points disappear in the initial interpretive construction of the potentially relevant fats.[35]

Hostility to strict liability. Commentators who attack the use of strict liability in criminal law invariably use narrow time-framing. They imply that the defendant deemed guilty of an offense which allows no mental state excuses as to some element of the crime is treated unjustly because he could somehow not avoid criminality. Look, for instance, at H. L. A. Hart's comments on criminal responsibility:

> The reason why, according to modern ideas, strict liability is odious, and appears as a sacrifice of a valued principle . . . is that those whom we punish should have had, when they acted, the normal capacities . . . for doing what the law requires and abstaining from what it forbids. . . . [T]he moral protest is that it is morally wrong to punish because "he could not have helped it" or "he could not have done otherwise" or "he had no real choice."[36]

But this implication is not valid. Often, the actor could readily avoid liability—so that all metaphors of "unobeyable laws," or "helpless victims" are inappropriate—if we simply broaden the time frame. Chief Justice Burger did precisely this in *United States v. Park*.[37] *Park* sustained a conviction of a responsible corporate official for shipping adulterated food, though the official had not been "aware of wrongdoing." The Chief Justice argued that corporate officials voluntarily assume a duty to ensure that violations will not occur when they take on managerial responsibility. . . .[38]

2. Broad Time-Framing Much criminal law doctrine departs from the traditional incident focus and opens up the time frame. Broad time frame construction is most often used when deterministic discourse supplants the usual intentionalism. The substantive doctrines of duress, subjective entrapment, provocation, and insanity are examples of such uses of broad time-framing.[39] These doctrines describe how certain blameworthy acts are in fact blameless because rooted in or determined by factors that preceded the criminal incident. The question, of course, is why the broad time frame is selected in these cases, while it continues to be excluded as methodologically inappropriate in most other cases for no apparent reason.

Broad time-framing unrelated to determinism and intentionalism also occurs in other areas of the substantive criminal law. The time frame can be opened up to account for events both prior and subsequent to the criminal incident.

Abandonment. The basic decision to allow *any* abandonment defense follows a wide time-framed interpretive construction.[40] The defendant has already committed some act which, if interrupted by external forces, would constitute an offense, an attempt of some other substantive crime. Yet we judge the act innocent because of the defendant's *subsequent* failure to consummate the harm. Although many reasons for this widened time frame have been offered, none overcomes the fundamentally nonrational, interpretive aspect of the initial broadening of focus. Some deterrence-oriented theorists suggest that an abandonment defense provides incentives to avoid the consummation of harm.[41] But there are surely a number of "completed" crimes whose harm can be as effectively "undone" as can the abandoned attempt: An embezzler, for instance, may return money to victims unaware of their loss[42] and "undo" as much harm as the person who desists from an assault with intent to commit rape because the victim talks him out of continuing.[43]

Retributively oriented commentators note that abandonment makes us reassess our vision of the defendant's blameworthiness or deviance.[44] Of course, if we admitted evidence of post-criminal conduct (whether remorse, restitution, condonation, or reform) into *every* trial, we would frequently change our views of the defendant's blameworthiness. Once more, the act of interpretation, the open time frame, *allows* the policy conclusion.

Broad time-framing is used in the abandonment area because the general rule-oriented nature of the criminal law has already stumbled in the less rule-like attempt area. Attempt law is generally problematic in our legal culture because it is inexorably less rule-like than the law of consummated harms; the actus reus of "attempting" refers not so much to particular proscribed acts[45] as to unavoidably noncategorizable acts which, in the particular case, seem to give evidence of the particular defendant's subjective disposition to act criminally. To commit rape is to force carnal knowledge of a woman; to attempt rape is to do sufficient acts to indicate that one *would* force carnal knowledge. Whether the requisite "sufficient" acts include the precise acts of undressing, fondling, cornering, isolating from public view, using force, and/or simply implying that force will be used is inevitably a case-by-case determination. I suspect that the use of a forward-looking broad time frame in considering the blameworthiness of an attempter is the predictable outcome of the breakdown of the rule-like form. The system demands all available information about defendant's blameworthiness, taken from as wide a period as possible, as soon as it departs from the rule-like form.

The attachment to overtly political Rule of Law ideals *precludes* a general broadening of time focus in the traditional consummated harm case; the idea is that blameworthiness must be conclusively presumed from the performance of one of the proscribed acts in one of the narrow time-framed blameworthy fashions. Once we allow ourselves to recognize the breakdowns in our inevitably imprecise conclusive presumptions, we see the strains of legalism. To recognize that we were probably thinking about the unremorseful, nonrestitutionary thief when we set out general penalties for larceny is to remind ourselves of the limit of the universalistic model. But we can avoid overtly political defenses of obviously inapt conclusive presumptions by implying that, as a matter of *method,* our factual inquiry simply does not go forward once a criminal act is complete.

The undefended, but deviant, broad time frame appears in constructing an abandonment defense because of the inevitable breakdown of pure legalist form in the attempt area. Since we *cannot* infer blame from a single act, because no such act is present in attempting, we move, at the very least, to more partial Rule of Law strictures: We try to infer a disposition to perform one of the still automatically blameworthy acts. But this does not imply, as Fletcher seems to believe,[46] the *logical* necessity of allowing an abandonment defense: Once one performs acts indicating a firm intention to commit blameworthy criminal acts, there is no rational reason not to treat the performance of these acts as conclusively presumed proof of criminal intent. Of course, such a conclusive presumption would be inaccurate, as all conclusive presumptions are; the abandoning defendant demonstrates that our presumption that defendants who have "attempted" are firmly resolved to commit crimes is sometimes wrong. But the remorseful consummated criminal would equally well demonstrate that conclusive presumptions about the need to incapacitate, reform, or blame a person because he has committed some crime can be inapt. The abandonment defense, then, appears not because a forward-looking broad time frame is logically better suited to attempt law, but because the always available policy attacks on rules (and conclusive presumptions) are allowed sway only in an area where the rule-form is already weakened by the imprecision of the definition of the act upon which criminal liability is predicated. . . .

B. Disjoined and Unified Accounts of "Incidents"

A second unconscious interpretive construct is the choice between "disjoined" and "unified" accounts of relevant legal facts. Substantive criminal law unknowingly, or at least without rational argument, shifts between viewing a series of significant events as a single incident or as separate incidents.

1. Imperfect Self-Defense Imperfect self-defense doctrine is one example of the arational choice between disjoined and unified accounts of incidents. In these cases, the defendant genuinely believes that the ultimate victim is attacking him with deadly force that cannot be warded off unless he counters with deadly force, but a reasonable person in the defendant's position would not believe this.[47] Holding this negligent but genuine belief, the defendant intentionally kills the victim. Is the homicide intentional or negligent? On the one hand, we might view the killing incident as temporally disjoined; a negligent perception of the need to kill is *followed* by an intentional killing. Under this view, the defendant is more blameworthy than the traditional negligent killer (*e.g.,* the bad driver,[48] the person who plays with guns[49]), because he has focused on the issue of whether to take human life and has gone ahead and done it. On the other hand, if the perception of the need to kill and the conduct are unified as a single incident, we will not see the killing as worse than the traditional negligent killing. The Model Penal Code,[50] reflecting a partial judicial and legislative trend,[51] considers such defendants guilty only of negligent homicide. The Code does not recognize, if only to deny its importance, the distinction between deliberately taking human life under unreasonable perceptions and taking life without being subjectively aware of the risk of death.

In contrast, in *United States v. Calley,*[52] the defendant deliberately shot Vietnamese villagers after unreasonably believing that he was lawfully ordered to do so. The court held that Calley committed intentional murder, even if he believed he was acting under orders, because: "The acts of a subordinate done in compliance with an unlawful order given him by his superior are [not] excused . . . [if] the superior's order is one which a man of ordinary sense and understanding would, under the circumstances, know to be unlawful. . . ."[53] The court, without comment or apparent awareness, disjoined a potentially unified incident, classifying negligent perception *followed by* the legally relevant intentional killing as separate incidents, each incident to be judged on its own merits.

One might believe that the intentional killing should be separate from the perception in this particular case because the Calley "incident" occurred over a longer period than does the typical imperfect self-defense incident. Calley did have a longer time to consider his perceptions *before* he killed intentionally. But that reasoning is hard to fathom: As long as Calley *still* believed at the time he killed that he was acting legally, he is like the imperfect self-defender. Both could say: "At the moment I pulled the trigger, intentionally killing the victim, I believed that I was legally authorized to kill. Although my belief was unreasonable, it was not based on a misunderstanding of legal duties. I simply misapplied these legal norms to the particulars of this case."

We must recognize that disjoined time-framing has made a hard case seem easy. The unstated, unjustified, disjoined perspective of *Calley* suppresses the sense that the actor did not kill in the manner the worst intentional killers do—with a subjective sense of wrongfulness. On the other hand, the Model Penal Code's unified perspective similarly suppresses the recognition that negligent self-defenders cause death differently than do ordinary negligent killers in that they at least sense the presence of death.

The Model Penal Code's perspective is, I would guess, intended to preserve the "rule-like" nature of the Code's mens rea categories.[54] The disjoined perspective would require a finding that the defendant is somewhat "worse" than the typical negligent killer, though perhaps still "better" than the typical purposeful one. Yet the Code's intermediate categories do not aptly portray the defendant, for he certainly does not kill "recklessly" or with "knowledge." This implies that "blameworthiness" is not aptly summarized by the Code's categories, an implication quite unsettling to the politically significant notion that the blameworthy mental state, a necessary condition to conviction, a core element of the definition of each offense, can be precisely described in a rule-like form.[55] Moreover, the disjoined perspective raises, if only metaphorically, the highly unsettling determinist position that it is not enough to know that the defendant acted intentionally without inquiring into the *roots* of his intention. If we treat the negligent self-defender as a partly excused intentional killer, one partly exculpated because the roots

of his intentional decision to kill are clearly less than culpable, we are led to wonder why we should not *always* inquire into the temporally separated background of the vicious will. Perhaps we should always ask how culpable the defendant was in *becoming* an intentional criminal. Interpretive construction suppresses this disturbing question: We unify when we want to account for but deny that we are looking at the background of an intentional act; we disjoin and focus on the "second" incident when we want to obliterate the past altogether. . . .

C. Broad and Narrow Views of Intent

A third unconscious construct is the unstated choice between broad and narrow views of the actor's intent. A narrow view assumes that the actor intends only the precise physical act he performs. A broad view assumes that the precise act is an instance of some broader category of acts the actor intends.

1. Impossible Attempts   The shifting between broad and narrow views that unconsciously occurs in the criminal law is evident in the doctrine of impossible attempts. The typical attempt case has a decidedly temporal dimension; the defendant fails to cause harm because his criminal conduct is incomplete, interrupted, or thwarted. In impossible attempts, the defendant completes the physical acts, yet no criminally cognizable harm occurs.

Courts and commentators must deal with four categories of impossibility: pure legal impossibility, traditional legal impossibility, legal/factual impossibility, and factual impossibility. In pure legal impossibility the defendant aims to violate a criminal proscription, but no criminal statute actually proscribes his conduct, nor does any statute proscribe an apter version of his intention.[56] Similarly, in traditional legal impossibility, the defendant's *acts* do not violate a criminal proscription. However, an existing criminal prohibition does narrowly describe the defendant's *aim*.[57] In the third category, legal/factual impossibility, the defendant again fails to consummate the harm. This time, however, it is because of a fairly particularized mistake about the *legal attributes* of the situation he faces.[58] The mistake preventing harm is not a pure legal mistake—believing it is illegal to receive stolen goods when it is in fact legal—nor a traditional legal mistake—believing that goods attained through fraud are stolen when the jurisdiction does not describe fraudulently obtained goods as stolen for purposes of the stolen goods receipt statute. Rather the mistake concerns the *legal status* of the particular goods—attempting to receive stolen goods that have been "recovered" by the police. Finally, in factual impossibility the defendant fails to cause harm because he mistakenly perceives the probability of effectiveness of his conduct. His mistake concerns some nonlegal fact. The classic case involves defendants convicted of attempted larceny when they stick their hands into empty pockets.[59]

I believe that the lines drawn among, and the arguments separating, these four categories are generally based on submerged interpretive shifts between broad and narrow views of the defendant's intent. When we view the defendant as intending only precise physical acts, we acquit the defendant because these precise acts do not constitute a crime. On the other hand, when we view the defendant as intending a broader category of acts, an apter version of the acts he did, we inculpate the defendant for attempting a crime. These interpretive shifts can be seen if we analyze the doctrinal positions of the major commentators in two paradigm cases—*Wilson v. State*[60] and *People v. Jaffe*.[61] In *Wilson,* defendant was acquitted of a forgery because he changed numbers rather than letters on a check—a case of traditional legal impossibility, since the change in numbers was not a material alteration of the check and the crime of forgery requires material alterations. In *Jaffe,* the defendant was acquitted of a charge of attempting to receive stolen goods because the stolen goods he thought he was to receive had been recovered by the police, and hence were no longer stolen—a case of legal/factual impossibility.

Lafave and Scott, reflecting both the Model Penal Code[62] and traditional commentators,[63] make nonrational interpretive switches in distinguishing traditional legal impossibility from legal/factual impossibility. They argue:

> In Wilson the defendant may have thought he was committing a crime, but if he did it was not because he intended to do something that the criminal law prohibited but rather because he was ignorant of the material alteration requirement of the crime of forgery. In Jaffe, on the other hand, what the defendant intended to do was a crime and if the facts had been as the defendant believed them to be he would have been guilty of the completed crime.[64]

Lafave and Scott simply interpret, without rationale, Wilson's intent narrowly and Jaffe's intent broadly. They view Wilson as intending the most precise deed imaginable—altering the numbers on the check—rather than as intending a broader category of acts—intending to receive money from a bank by aptly altering an instrument. They view Jaffe as intending a broader category of acts—receiving stolen property—rather than intending a precise act—receiving the particular goods that were actually delivered to him. Viewed narrowly, Jaffe "thought he was committing a crime" but was not because the criminal law does not prohibit receiving unstolen goods. Similarly, viewed broadly, Wilson intended to violate the law of forgery; had he *correctly* altered the instrument (so as to make a bank pay him money), he would have been guilty of the completed crime.[65]

Fletcher, desiring to inculpate *only* factually impossible attempters, sets out a more refined and elegant test than do the earlier commentators. In essence, Fletcher argues as follows: The general category of "attempting" must be objectively defined so as to satisfy constraints proscribing vague statutes. What does it mean, in ordinary language, to attempt or try to do a certain something? To attempt something means that it is part of the rational motivation of the actor that all conditions defining that certain something be present. How do we know if someone attempts [to fix a faucet on Saturday] when he fixes it on Sunday, believing it to be Saturday? We know that he attempts the bracketed act only if a rational person's motivation changes when he is informed of the counterfactual nature of all the assumptions contained in the brackets. For example, someone who fixes a faucet while mistakenly believing that the capital of California is Sausalito would not be affected if he were to find out that Sacramento is the capital;[66] thus, he does not attempt to [fix a faucet if the capital is Sausalito].

Fletcher's account of "attempting" is interesting,[67] but its application to the cases hinges on how broadly or narrowly the crime which is arguably attempted is defined.[68] Fletcher says the empty-pocket pickpocket is guilty of attempted larceny because larceny is defined as [taking money from a full pocket], and the rational pickpocket would not stick his hand in the pocket if he knew the pocket were empty. The counterfactual assumption contained in the bracketed definition of the crime affects his rational motivation. But Fletcher says that Jaffe is not guilty of attempting [to receive stolen property] because he is indifferent to whether the property is stolen. If anything, Jaffe would be more willing to receive unstolen property.[69] Similarly, Fletcher says that Wilson does not attempt to [forge a check] because he is indifferent to whether the money is received by way of forgery.[70]

Fletcher engages in the simplest kind of nonrational interpretive construction here. To inculpate, he defines the attempted crime in terms of the precise physical acts consummating the harm. To exculpate, he defines the attempted crime in broad, categorical terms, focusing on the legal attributes of the situation. Thus, he does not ask the categorical question of whether the would-be pickpocket is attempting to [steal money from a pocket]. Of course, the pickpocket is indifferent to whether the money received is stolen. Nor does Fletcher define the crime of forgery as [getting money from a bank by apt means] and ask whether Wilson has attempted *that* particular criminal act. If he did, Wilson would be guilty under Fletcher's rational motivation test: Had Wilson known his alterations were ineffective to get money, he would not have made them.

The writing in this field uniformly supports exculpating defendants in traditional legal impossibility cases. Thus, a narrow interpretation of intention must be used. It probably arises from an unstated desire to preserve the rule form of the criminal law in a rather trivial case. All the posturing done to ensure that no one is convicted of attempting a crime when his acts do not precisely correspond to the definition of the consummated crime is charmingly ludicrous. We tolerate far greater vagueness in everything from the definition of murder to sentencing and probation policy. If anyone asserted, as a straightforward political matter, that these cases were an important bulwark against governmental arbitrariness and citizen insecurity, I suspect that the statement would be written in an ironic trope. Once more, I sense that "the lady doth protest too much." We suppress our real queasiness about the breakdown of legalism by rallying around its banner with staggeringly inappropriate gusto in unimportant circumstances. . . .

2. Aiding and Abetting   [Another] example of shifts between broad and narrow intent occurs in doctrine relating to aiding and abetting the sale of a proscribed good. In *People v. Gordon,*[71] the defendant referred an undercover agent to a seller of marijuana and was charged with the accessorial crime of facilitation.[72] Because neither purchase nor possession of marijuana by the agent is a felony, the defendant could not be convicted for aiding the undercover agent. Moreover, the appeals court acquitted the defendant of facilitating the seller's felonious sale because the seller could not possibly have intended to commit the crime of selling marijuana to the agent at the time of the referral.[73]

The interpretive problem here is apparent: The court assumes that when the statute says that the facilitation must aid a party who "intends to commit a crime," a *categorical* intent—to sell marijuana generally, rather than to commit a number of specific crimes—is irrelevant. The court implies that even a drug dealer constantly in the business of making sales *never* intends to commit a crime until the moment of commission, because he never intends to sell to *the* person he ultimately sells to. But why stop with the identity? Does a drug dealer ever intend a crime unless he knows beforehand exactly when and where he will sell, or what the buyer will be wearing? While the result seems somewhat silly here, the narrow interpretive construct the court uses is neither uncommon nor attackable in anything but result-oriented terms. . . .[74]

D. Broad and Narrow Views of the Defendant

A fourth unconscious interpretive construct involves shifts between broad and narrow views of the defendant. The defendant can be viewed as a person with specific traits or as an instance of some broader class of people.

1. Concurrence Doctrine   The shift between broad and narrow views of the defendant occurs in concurrence doctrine, which requires a union between actus reus and mens rea. Doctrinally, blameworthiness in the criminal law is not supposed to be a hovering wickedness; it is supposed to attach to particular harmful acts. Thus, in *Regina v. Cunningham,* the court held that a defendant who negligently broke a gas line while trying to steal coins from the gas meter had to have purposely, knowingly, or recklessly poisoned the victim to be convicted.[75] The court refused to transfer the requisite mental state from the defendant's attempt to steal coins to the poisoning. Except for felony-murder, we (purportedly) do not transfer or impute the mens rea of one crime to another one; on the contrary, the actus reus and mens rea must concur. Yet, as I shall demonstrate, concurrence doctrine can readily be (and has readily been) interpreted away by altering the focus on the defendant and his circumstances.

Assume that larceny and poisoning are the two different crimes in *Cunningham,* and that poisoning can be committed purposely, recklessly, or negligently.[76] The breadth of focus on the defendant's behavior can be manipulated in two ways. Assume we want the defendant convicted of negligent poisoning, believing that breaking a gas meter posed an unreasonable, unjustified risk of poisoning that a reasonable man would not have suffered. The Model Penal Code definition of negligence requires that the risk taken must be one that would be avoided by a reasonable person "*in the actor's* situation." The interpretive question is whether to view defendant as a member of a narrowly defined class—the class of gas meter thieves—or a broader class of persons—those dealing with gas meters in general or those people dealing with poisonous substances in general. If we focus on the defendant's most particularized situation, that of a thief, we see that he may have been as careful as any thief—for thieves rush around carelessly—while if his situation is that of the typical meterman, he may have been unreasonably careless. If the narrow view is appropriate, a seemingly perverse result occurs: Thieves are less likely to be inculpated for negligent poisoning than are gas line repairmen because, if we focus narrowly on their particular situation, they can be expected to take fewer precautions.

Before dismissing the narrow focus, one should note that through a second manipulation of interpretive focus, the defendant can more readily be convicted through use of this focus. Model Penal Code definitions of both recklessness and negligence require the creation of substantial *and* unjustifiable risk. Risks created by repairmen are generally justified by the social value of the repairs. But the same risk may be unjustifiably high if one is talking about the more focused, narrower version of defendant's activity—*stealing. Nearly any risk* of poisoning is unjustifiably high if one weighs the risks against the benefits of stealing, a presumptively socially valueless activity.

Ultimately, of course, a narrow focus on the defendant's activity undercuts concurrence doctrine. Nearly any defendant can be convicted of a higher crime which can be committed negligently as well as recklessly, and many defendants can be convicted where the higher crime must be committed at least recklessly, once one assesses the justifiability of the actor's risk-taking in the criminal context he actually acted in. A conviction-prone interpreter can apply a methodologically nondefensible broad focus in assessing what constitutes reasonable precaution and an equally indefensible narrow focus on the nature of the risk, and thereby interpret away the concurrence doctrine.[77]

2. Provocation   The role of broad and narrow views of the defendant is explicit in provocation doctrine. In many jurisdictions, an intentional homicide is punished less severely if the defendant was reasonably provoked; the grade of the crime may be reduced to manslaughter.[78] The problem, as courts[79] and commentators[80] recognize, is that there exists no convincing interpretation of reasonable provocation. The *ordinary* man would *never* be provoked to take another life by jibes, assaults, or even the bad fortune of discovering adultery in progress.[81] So when we say that a defendant was reasonably provoked to kill, we *cannot* mean that the defendant's conduct was typical of people in similar situations.[82] Nor does the narrowest view of reasonableness acceptably define provocation: Someone just like the defendant, with all his fears, foibles, and disabilities, would *obviously* be provoked to kill under the same pressures he faced, because that someone just *did*.

Courts include or exclude certain traits of the defendant in the profile of the typical individual to whom the defendant's conduct is to be compared. For instance, a court may say that it is irrelevant that a particular defendant is generally impotent in assessing whether a prostitute's taunts on the subject are reasonable provoking;[83] commentators respond that the defendant's reaction ought to be compared to the reasonable impotent man's.[84] Presumably, everyone tries to exclude from his vision of the typical man to whom the defendant is to be compared all the narrow-focused traits the defendant has that the criminal law is designed to alter—hotheadedness, hypersensitivity, proclivity toward violence—but this line ultimately collapses. Of course the criminal code is not trying to deter or to blame impotence itself. But if the impotent as a group pose a menace because impotence is associated with hypersensitivity, if they are prone to violence when confronted by situations that routinely confront people, it is not clear why we would want to exculpate them. Ultimately, the real battle here is between our asserted determinist (excusing) notions of impotence and our intentionalist (inculpatory) models of hotheadedness. Unconscious interpretive construction avoids this more openly political battle: As we take a broader, more categorical view of the typical provoked defendant, fewer and fewer defendants appear to have acted reasonably.

3. The Omission/Commission Problem   Broad and narrow views of intent, along with disjoined and unified accounts of incidents, are unconsciously employed in trying to solve the omission/commission problems in the criminal law. Since the criminal law requires that the defendant perform some voluntary act, a common issue is whether the defendant has committed some act or simply failed to act. Unless the defendant has a duty to act,[85] an omission is not culpable. Of course, the line between omissions and commissions is blurry. There is considerable circularity in claiming that a defendant can be culpable only if he has committed an act, when we often describe an event in active conduct terms rather than passively if we have already (somehow) determined that the party is culpable. For instance, a parent who *does not feed* a child may readily be said to *starve* the child—to commit an act—while a stranger would be said to *fail to feed*—a passive nonact.[86]

Consider the following case. Defendant, a skid row grocer, routinely sells wood alcohol to chronic alcoholics, knowing that they drink it with only moderate ill effects. One day, he switches the brand of wood alcohol at his store to a brand with higher alcohol contents; he is perhaps knowing, perhaps reckless, perhaps negligent as to the fact that they will die if they drink it. The bottles, though, contain warning labels which the chronic alcoholics could, at least in theory, read.

If we view this as an omissions case, a case in which the defendant "failed to warn," it is probable that defendant will not have the actus reus for homicide, since there is no "duty to warn." The legal deduction from the interpreted facts is orderly and rather clear-cut. On the other hand, if we conceive of this as a *poisoning* case, then we are more likely to inculpate the defendant.

Of course, nearly *every* poisoning case can be interpreted in an omissions mode (depending on both the time-framing characterization and the breadth of focus). At some point in time after a victim is likely to ingest a poisonous substance, the defendant merely "fails to warn" the victim. Failing to warn is *temporally* most proximate to the death. Generally, though, we treat the *earlier* placing of the poison as the more morally relevant act. The grocer, however, is not traditionally held culpable for this earlier act, because it seems to resemble a "routine" commercial act, placing an item out for sale. But we now see the unwarranted interpretive construction. If we focus broadly on the grocer's act—as an instance of the broad category of routine commercial activities by grocers—it seems unexceptionable. Coupling this broad view of the defendant's conduct with a time-dissociated or -disjoined view of the poisoning incident, we have a routine sale followed by a morally but not legally culpable failure to warn. If, on the other hand, we focus more narrowly on *this* grocer's acts in *these* particular circumstances—making more toxic wood alcohol available to an unusual group of customers who are likely to ingest the wood alcohol—and then interpret that sale plus the subsequent failure to warn as comprising the typical mode of a single unified poisoning incident (secretly making poison available for ingestion), the defendant appears more culpable.[87]

The interpretive construction is more entrenched in the commonly debated omissions case of the easily saved drowning child.[88] Whether the would-be defendant who stands nearby is characterized as "failing to rescue" or as "drowning" the child is again interpretive. The active verb-form ("drowning") is a more plausible description of the scene if we think of the defendant in his precise circumstances—near the child, viewing the child—than if we think of him simply as an *instance* of all of mankind unrelated to the child. When opponents of liability in the drowning case speak of the inability to fully discharge a duty to save,[89] they are unconsciously seeing the defendant in his broadest terms—as a member of the broad class of mankind responsible for seeking out whatever drowning victims they can find—rather than as the particular person at the scene of the drowning.

Similarly, applying the ordinary or categorical mental state to the particular defendant may cause confusion. In typical "omissions" cases, the defendant does not deliberately seek the proscribed result; we are unlikely to use active commission verbs unless our standard case is one of purpose. If, for instance, someone who stands by while a child drowns has said to a parent, "I'll watch your kid swim while you're away" *in order* to ensure that the kid dies, we would be prone to call this an intentional killing, not an intentional failure to save. Presumably, mens rea requirements can account for a particular defendant's culpability; it is unnecessary to find the absence of an actus reus[90] because most "similarly situated" persons would lack the mens rea requisite for conviction.

Drowning incidents, like poisoning incidents, are arguably divisible: In the standard active case, we focus on the act of putting the victim in peril, of shoving him in the water, and let the failure to rescue, the more temporally immediate cause of death, fade from the picture. The categorical focus suppresses the relevance of failing to rescue.

The political debate over omissions duties is sufficiently familiar that I need only mention the underlying significance of the interpretive battle. At the level of criminal justice system results, members of the dominant classes are not particularly threatened by inevitably circumscribed charges of failing to discharge positive duties, though these charges would likely be more randomly distributed across class than most charges. At the ideological level, though, the sense of blamelessness and self-righteousness one can feel in the face of the correctable suffering of others is buttressed forcefully by drawing a rigid distinction between acts and nonacts. Once more, the association between blame and *disruption,* critical to conservative dominance, is solidified: One cannot be a criminal actor when one simply lets things go on as they are, regardless of the consequences.

4. An Analogue: Causation   Just as unconscious shifts in viewing the defendant affect substantive results, so do shifts between broad and narrow views of causation. Here is a standard causation problem: The defendant hits the victim on the head and the victim ultimately dies. Homicide requires not just the actus reus and mens rea, but a harm; the blameworthy blow must cause the death. Assume that this particular victim does not die on the spot but on the trip to the hospital in an ambulance.

The defendant is not culpable unless he is both a "but-for" cause and a culpable "proximate" cause of the death.[91] Clearly, the defendant is the but-for cause of death, since the victim would not have been in the ambulance but for the blow. But is the defendant the proximate cause? Ignoring the circularity of traditional *definitions* of proximate cause,[92] the interpretive problem is that everything looks accidental when looked at too particularly. Moreover, there is no defensible scheme for aggregating "similar" events. For instance, assume that there is a 50% chance, ex ante, that the victim will die if hit. This 50% chance is, of course, a sum of many different possibilities. For our purposes, a few possible categories will be sufficient: There is a 49% chance of dying on the spot or after responsible ambulance and hospital care, a 0.8% chance of dying as a result of hospital negligence, a 0.1% chance of dying as a result of malicious care in the hospital or ambulance, and a 0.1% chance of the ambulance having a fatal crash.

Of course, from the broadest perspective *none* of these deaths is *accidental,* in that hitting foreseeably leads to death. But is the broadest category appropriate? What if the victim dies in an ambulance crash, and ambulances crash no more often than do other vehicles? Presumably, at least if we break off that mode of death as a relevant category, the defendant will not be culpable.[93] But do we subcategorize further? Assume that ambulances are more dangerous than normal vehicles because they speed and run lights. What if the defendant is killed in an ambulance crash that is not of the sort that makes ambulances more dangerous than other vehicles— for example, what if the ambulance is rear-ended while peacefully stopped in the hospital driveway, not sideswiped as it dashes through an intersection?

Legal systems devise a number of aggregating and disaggregating presumptions. For instance, when someone dies after a blow to the head, it is insignificant which vein burst or where the clot was. Each of these *forms* of death will be aggregated so that they are deemed predictable and nonaccidental. On the other hand, the condition of the victim, though it may dramatically affect the chances of death and is thus causally related, is never treated as relevant in deciding whether a particular death is accidental. A victim in bad shape will be implicitly disaggregated, precipitated out from the class of victims in general, so that the death appears nonaccidental.[94]

But conventional aggregating devices are incomplete—I have no idea how our legal culture would deal with the ambulance accident cases—and arbitrary. It is not simply that the typical proximate cause standard is circular.[95] The more serious concern is that even less subjectively stated standards for "improbable" or "accidental" are meaningless in the absence of nondefensible interpretations of the breadth of focus of the "category" of the event whose probability is to be ascertained.

III. Conscious Interpretive Constructs

Conscious interpretive constructs, like the unconscious ones, operate to avoid fundamental political problems. This part applies the two conscious constructs to the substantive criminal law.

A. Intentionalism and Determinism

Anglo-American courts and commentators assert that our criminal justice system is based on the supposition of "free will" or intentionalistic conduct.[96] Of course, though, in a number of areas we allow determinist excusing conceptions of the defendant to be considered. This residual determinism negates the simplest claims justifying the generally asserted intentionalism, *i.e.,* that a determinist discourse is somehow technically infeasible or methodologically inapplicable to legal contexts. The standard methodological objections to a more general determinism are twofold: first, a simple skepticism about the *necessity* of any effect following from any cause, and second, a distrust of our capacity to account for the roots of particular decisions that explain the *precise* conduct that the actor ultimately engaged in. Yet, these objections apply as well to the uses of determinism that we do tolerate. . . .

1. Apparent Determinism: Insanity and Diminished Capacity The insanity "defense" is best understood as the portion of the trial that determines whether to incarcerate the defendant in a prison or a mental institution.[97] But for a variety of both practical[98] and "theoretical"[99] reasons, it is seen as a genuine defense. Certainly, diminished capacity constitutes a partially exculpatory defense.[100]

Along with the defense of infancy, the insanity defense is determinism's most obvious domain in the criminal law. Without speculating on the cultural history of this particular determinism, I wish to note two things. First, the hegemonic power of medical models and "hard science" in our culture made insanity as a disease appear more concrete, more thing-like than other explained forms of deviance.[101] Second, and more interesting, I share Katz's sense that the criminal justice system must distinguish between two classes of defendants who might, in a nonlegal context, seem equally "crazy." The legal system will dismiss as insane those defendants who, while acting in a fashion we deem "medically explicable," *reinforce* our abstract social practices. Other defendants, equally "explicable" in their actions, may be disorientingly deviant, may implicitly *attack* our abstract social practices, and these defendants will not be dismissed, but actively suppressed, corrected and put away.[102]

Compare the following hypotheticals. Defendant A (a classically legally insane person) says, "I killed the victim because I thought he was a snake, about to attack me." This delusion is nondisorienting at the abstract level; the defendant's implicit rule structure is socially acceptable. (Once we perceive objects as snakes, we too shoot them.) Defendant B (a disorienting deviant) says, "I killed the victim be-

cause he is an exploitative pig who deserves to die." While in the culture's ordinary discourse, desert *is rooted in* the law—people deserve punishment if they violate the law, people deserve to own property the law says they are entitled to—disorienting deviants root the law in their own concept of desert. For the society in general, law is the universal, applied in particular cases to determine desert. The disorienting deviant is disorienting precisely because his own sense of desert is the universal; law is just a particular application.

A more general, medically based determinism does not enable us to screen out and condemn disorienting deviants. Concerning the insanity defense, it is important to realize that we only occasionally decide to listen to the doctors' accounts of personality. If we were to admit the possibility of a more general determinism, doctors might well be glad to describe the psychic roots of all harm-causing behavior. We could not make any good arguments, in terms of the explanatory capabilities of psychiatrists, to restrict the occasions on which we would listen to their descriptions to those occasions on which a defendant's atypical thought and moral structure is nondisorienting. But rather than make difficult explicit political arguments that we must condemn the disorienting deviant, whether he is psychologically explicable or not, we fall back on the pseudo-methodological claim that we are simply applying the usual rule that determinist discourse is unavailable.[103]

B. Rules versus Standards

Conscious interpretive construction exists in the choice between rules and standards. At the philosophical level, the liberal state's commitment to a rule-like criminal law is pervasive and grandiose. Jerome Hall's comments are typical: "The principle of legality is in some ways the most fundamental of all the principles. . . . The essence of this principle of legality is limitation on penalization by the State's officials, effected by the prescription and application of specific rules."[104] Yet, in practice, limiting a legal system to mechanical application of rigidly defined rules is both practically unthinkable and substantively objectionable. We must explore the strong antirule tendency in a supposedly rule-worshipping legal culture.

1. Preparation versus Attempt Courts and commentators alike have offered a variety of tests to distinguish between nonpunishable "mere preparation" and culpable "attempts" to commit crimes. The basic tension in defining this actus reus of attempting seems relatively straightforward. We punish attempts (despite the general absence of harm)[105] for two reasons: first, because the actor has manifested the same blameworthy disposition as any other criminal, the lack of harm is a fortuity outside his control;[106] second, because we wish to deter people from taking steps that ordinarily result in harm, and it may add significantly to deterrence to punish people even when they fail in their aim.[107] Of course, the failure to consummate the harm makes us doubt whether the actor had the malicious resolve of the typical effective offender. If the defendant is apprehended when we are still especially uncertain about the resoluteness of the criminal plan, we call the action "preparation."

My claim is that the tests *labeling* or *defining* attempts can easily be aligned along a continuum of rule-like to standard-like. That is, tests may be framed in terms that are mechanically applicable and categorical or in terms that are ad hoc. All these tests will seem unsatisfactory in precisely the way that *no* rule form or standard form of doctrine can *ever* be satisfactory.

Under the most rule-like test, an actor has not attempted a crime until he has taken the last possible step within his control to consummate the harm.[108] This test can be applied uniformly, without regard to the defendant's personal qualities. Moreover, it leaves maximum room for people to engage in not-yet-harmful conduct without state intrusion. Unfortunately, the test is obviously underinclusive—a defendant would be acquitted of attempting murder in a slow poisoning case until the last dose of a fatal series of doses was given; some significant crimes would be impossible to attempt—*e.g.,* rape and theft, where there is always some other act to be taken before the crime is complete. Moreover, a regime in which this test is employed will discourage the police from taking preventative action to stop crimes if they are afraid to "blow" convictions. Furthermore, this test enables people to plan their harmful conduct in a roundabout fashion so as to eliminate a major purpose of attempt law—it enables them to assure that they will either cause harm or go unpunished.[109] Finally, a rule-like attempt definition puts pressure on the broader legal regime to establish other rule-like preparatory crimes (*e.g.,* curfew violations, loitering) to permit early police intervention. Thus, to gain the *procedural* freedom inherent in the rule form—freedom from the arbitrariness of random state enforcement—the society may end up restricting *substantive* freedom. If the police cannot stop nighttime strollers who seem suspicious—because suspiciousness is too vague a standard—and if citizens deeply fear nighttime breakins, one solution is to ban *all* nighttime strolling. This would be a highly intrusive limit on substantive autonomy within a formally free and rule-like system.[110]

The second test is relatively rule-like: An action constitutes an attempt only if it is unequivocally directed towards the consummation of a crime.[111] Since this test focuses on how the act appears, without regard to the actor, the test is less likely to be prejudicially enforced against "criminal types." Of course, whether one can recognize when an act is unequivocally directed at harm without regard to one's belief about what the actor is likely to do next, a belief based on suppositions about the actor, not the act, is highly problematic. But if the test is taken seriously in its most rule-like sense, it is plausible that *no* conduct will be deemed unequivocally oriented towards the consummation of harm.[112] For instance, attempted rape would be impossible, since no acts prior to intercourse are unequivocally inconsistent with a design to molest rather than rape. But if the test is read as proscribing "acts unequivocally directed at harm under the circumstances for that person" it dissolves into the Model Penal Code test,[113] with all the problems of a standard-like test.

The third test is moderately rule-like and moderately standard-like, with the faults or virtues of both. An act constitutes an attempt when it reveals a physical or dangerous proximity to the consummated harm[114] or if it would have resulted in the harm but for an unforeseen interruption.[115] If we read "proximity" as relating to how close we believe *that* actor was to causing harm, the test is as standard-like as the Model Penal Code test. If we read it in physical terms, it is as rule-like as the "last possible step" test. In applying the "unforeseen interruption" test the question is whether we are allowed to consider our belief about the particular defendant's propensity to desist. If we are, the test is like the Model Penal Code's. If we simply consider the natural physical circumstances of acts that are irretrievably done when judging whether harm would have occurred but for unusual circumstances, the test reverts once more to the "last possible step" test.

Under the Model Penal Code test, an act constitutes an attempt if it is strongly corroborative of the actor's criminal intention.[116] This test allows no roundabout schemes that are immune from attempt law. The police need not wait to intervene until danger rises in order to preserve a potential conviction.[117] People fortuitously interrupted before they have taken all the necessary steps to consummate the harm are not freed. On the other hand, when the fact-finder suspects the defendant is a "criminal sort" or is simply prejudiced against the defendant, acts consistent with both criminal and noncriminal plans are likely to be deemed corroborative of a criminal plan.[118] No one has clear notice about what is and is not permitted when the ultimate legal standard varies so much with the fact-finder's opinion.

Ultimately, I sense that no one is comfortable with any of these tests. An "argument" for one simply suppresses the terror of the rules/standards dilemma that faces any actor within our culture.[119] The position ultimately settled on is simply a temporary assertion. . . .

2. Vagueness Doctrine   One plausible account of the invalidation of vague statutes is that the Constitution (or, in Britain, a more general principle of criminal law)[120] *mandates* a rule-like criminal code. Certainly, courts invalidating statutes as unconstitutionally vague make the usual pleas for clearly administrable rules. In *Papachristou v. City of Jacksonville,*[121] for instance, Justice Douglas wrote that an ordinance is void for vagueness if it:

> "fails to give a person of ordinary intelligence fair notice that his contemplated conduct is forbidden" . . . and . . . [if] it encourages arbitrary and erratic arrests and convictions. . . .
>
> It furnishes a convenient tool for "harsh and discriminatory enforcement by local prosecuting officials, against particular groups deemed to merit their displeasure."[122]

The problem with viewing the vagueness doctrine as "settling" the rule/standard tension is that the void-for-vagueness strictures are rarely used, though so many statutes are undeniably fuzzy. Thus, we must account for the judiciary's occasional invalidation of ambiguous laws. A coherent account focuses on the interaction of a series of "standards" and "policies" disparaging or supporting vagueness that are themselves exceedingly vague, rather than on some hypothetical "quantum" of vagueness. Thus, ironically, the "rule system" is upheld only occasionally, and in a very un-rule-like fashion.

A detailed account of the vagueness doctrine is unnecessary given Professor Amsterdam's seminal work.[123] It is enough to say that the outcome of any case is unpredictable without at least considering three factors: facts and values, core conduct, and nearby conduct.

The first factor asks whether the court believes the statute *could* have been written more precisely. Statutes may refer to facts, to values-as-facts, or to values. For example, a statute refers to values if it says, "Don't be obscene"; it refers to values-as-facts if it says, "Don't say things that the average citizen of Pensacola would consider obscene"; and it refers to facts if it says, "Don't say any of the following 'dirty words.'" Generally, within this culture, values are considered individual and widely dispersed.[124] Thus, *any* statute making reference to values will *inevitably* seem vague: There can be no precise understanding of the content of any "value" since that content is not communally shared. All else being equal, courts are generally more tolerant of vagueness where value references are inevitable than where the legislature *could* define facts more precisely.[125]

The second factor asks whether the court believes that the core conduct described by the statute— conduct clearly fitting *within* its murky boundaries—is substantively innocent. In *Papachristou,* for instance, the Jacksonville ordinance outlawed "neglecting all business and habitually spending . . . time . . . where alcoholic beverages are sold or served."[126] This is not a particularly vague description of the illicit activity *unless* one assumes, as did Justice Douglas, that it cannot *possibly* be intended to apply to "members of golf clubs and city clubs."[127] Vagueness doctrine—a procedure-oriented constitutional jurisprudence—is in this manner used to strike down substantively objectionable statutes.[128]

Thus, there is a second layer of irony in dealing with vagueness doctrine. It is designed to invalidate generalized statutes like "Don't do bad things" because what is "bad" is unknown and unknowable in a culture premised on the subjectivity of value. Yet a major criterion for invalidating a statute is that the conduct it proscribes is substantively approved, not "bad." The judge must thus know what is least knowable.

The third factor makes this worry even more apparent. Vagueness doctrine is *predominantly* used when the conduct that is *ambiguously* covered by the statute, conduct that the court fears will be deterred because citizens are unsure whether or not it falls within the ambit of the statute, is either affirmatively constitutionally protected[129] or at least desirable.[130] When this "nearby" conduct is unprotected or affirmatively undesirable in the judge's eyes, courts are less likely to overturn.[131] Naturally, the court's interpretation of the breadth of conduct that may be deterred is quite flexible. For instance, does a facially vague statute outlawing vexatious phone-calling[132] chill protected "speech" or less protected "telephoning to strangers"? From the rules/standards vantage point, the critical observation is that the "rule-like" form of law is not preserved in rule-like fashion: Substantive standards are used to define the occasions on which rules are required.

IV. The Easy Case

Parts II and III delineated the conscious and unconscious use of interpretative construction in the traditional "hard" cases of substantive criminal law. It would be possible to claim that interpretive construction is at work only in the tricky but rare gray area cases which implicate the sort of elevated doctrine that occupies academic commentators and appellate courts. The criminal justice system predominantly processes much *simpler* facts: The harm is consummated, the precise act is "intended," the act and intent concur, and there are no legally cognizable mistakes. Paradigmatic "easy cases" are ones in which a defendant wishes to kill a nonprovoking victim and, without the slightest thought that he is defending himself, kills the victim, or a thief takes property he knows belongs to another.

This part shows that even to inculpate these defendants with any sense of consistency, one must perform all the critical interpretive steps illustrated in parts II and III. My purpose is to show that interpretive constructs are at work in *every* case.

A. Conscious Interpretation

Both the basic intentionalist assertion and the purported devotion to the rule form apply to the "easy case." The significance of rejecting a determinist discourse is made most obvious by the panic that retributionists feel when confronting a more full-blown determinism. They worry about the criminal law being "swallowed up." It is quite plausible that we could still incarcerate in order to incapacitate those persons whose unacceptable conduct was perfectly understood. However, losing the illusion that we are treating criminals justly, rather than simply conveniently, would alter both our beliefs about the cruelty of our punishment practices and our more ordinary beliefs about merit. If we came to conceive of the typical criminal act as just one more horror in a lifelong parade of never-ending horrors, we might still decide to conquer and subdue the criminal, but we would not self-righteously condemn him.

The concern over rule-bound precision in drafting a criminal code is most readily seen in the "easy case" in the context of debates over punishment policy.[133] Devotion to rule-form is harder to see, though more politically significant, in understanding a key ideological basis for excluding nondisruptive harms (*e.g.,* unnecessary deaths caused by routine commercial dealings) from the criminal code. It is difficult to imagine rule-like forms proscribing *unreasonably* dangerous conduct, particularly conduct not taken on single discrete occasions by single actors to whom the harm can easily be attributed. These may be seen as "easy" cases of noncriminality solely *because* of an unshakably strong procedural norm against vagueness.

B. Unconscious Interpretation

More interesting, though, is the way the more obscured, un-self-conscious interpretive constructs serve to buttress conventional blaming practices. This section applies the four unconscious constructs to the easy cases.

1. Broad and Narrow Time Frames   Choosing a time frame is critical for a number of reasons. Most critically, the interpreter's ability to convince himself of the legitimacy, or better, the necessity of a narrow focus eliminates the more obvious political tensions inherent in the choice of an intentionalist account. Narrow time-framing simply excludes all the potentially explanatory background data.[134] For instance, a criminologist's familiar category for homicide—that the crime is fundamentally victim-precipitated[135]— disappears in ordinary criminal law discourse, except in those rare provocation cases where the victim enrages the perpetrator just before the killing, rather than over some longer time period. The distinction between those who are partially exculpated because they were enraged once (provoked), and those who are inculpated though they were tortured for years before reacting makes no sense as a matter of retribution[136] and only superficial sense in terms of deterrence.[137] Ultimately, I suspect, the distinction is grounded in a nearly primeval fear of the collapse of the easy case: If long-term interactions are appropriate subjects of judicial scrutiny, then there is indeed no certainty in blaming.

2. Disjoined and Unified Accounts Disjoined time-framing eases blaming practices where an exculpatory, broad time-framed determinism presses on the would-be condemnor. The quasi-methodological notion is that the ultimate criminal act, even if comprehensively grounded in prior experience, must be separated from its backdrop. While we sometimes unify an overt criminal decision with its backdrop,[138] our more usual technique is to say, in essence, that the criminal moment stands separate, as a matter of technique, from even obviously relevant background.

But while narrow or disjoined time-framing is connected with the artificial and problematic restriction of "excused" behavior, its more politically central role may be in its suppression of the recognition of something akin to the "justification" of behavior. Take our easy-case thief. It is true that he alters the current holdings of property, but the legitimacy of these holdings is politically contingent and problematic. It does not matter, for our purposes, whether these present property holdings can be satisfactorily justified in the eyes of some relevant group or other. The justification of the distribution of goods that preceded the "theft" is decidedly *not* an issue in any particular criminal trial. The incidental focus that supports this limitation of issues—a focus that blurs the "crime" by freezing or taking for granted the background conditions in which the "crime" is committed—serves important ideological purposes. First, it normalizes, sanitizes, and decriminalizes the property holdings of dominating groups, which are unlikely to be traceable to single, easily identified *disruptive* incidents. The dominant rarely appear "criminal" when the implicit theory of criminality is *disruption,* when the only sort of crime we comfortably discuss is temporally limited. Second, the incidental focus decontextualizes, delegitimatizes, and thereby criminalizes the activities of the dispossessed. Instead of viewing, say, theft and episodic violence as part of a dynamic struggle for control over resources, as one group's more or less self-conscious "strategy" to counter another long-term strategy of control over "privately held" means of production and concomitant definitions of job roles and productivity,[139] and control over the state and its resources,[140] a narrow time-framed focus views each act of theft as occurring outside of history.

Note the implicit disjunctive, nonunified interpretation of time: Criminal trials implicitly assume that property systems are *followed by* theft rather than that real property systems are continually being created by a social struggle that includes everything from alternately encouraging and discouraging the flow of illegal aliens[141] to "stealing." The political beliefs flowing from the unified perspective are naturally by no means unambiguous. On the other hand, if one becomes fully smugly functionalist and views *everything* as part of some single, unified grand scheme, punishing labeled thieves is just another aspect of the ultimate "system" of property. On the other hand, the unified perspective may be counter-complacent as well: If "taking" is just another technique for getting distributive shares straight, "antitaking" (punishment for theft) seems like a simple act of force, a victory for one group in a dynamic struggle rather than a restoration of some prepolitical equilibrium.

Just as the ordinarily asserted narrow time frame inculpates the "easy case" defendant by denying him both determinist excuses and contextual justifications, so an asserted broad and unified time frame precludes labeling as criminal those who sell unsafe products or those who insist on the performance of unsafe work. Rather than viewing the introduction of an unsafe product onto the market as a reckless act which later causes harm, exculpating interpretations focus on the act as *part* of a longer-term process of market interaction. In this long-term process, the victim's (buyer's) participation is deemed crucial; the focus is precisely opposite that of the typical criminal law analysis in which the victim's participation (precipitation) is irrelevant. The marketing of dangerous products is interpreted simply as a *part* of a *generally* justified system of producing and exchanging goods. The sale of a particular dangerous product is not viewed as a disruptive departure from a more narrowly normatively justified system in which *safe* goods are produced and marketed. Instead, it is seen as one part of a properly equilibrated system of distribution where goods, not harms, are delivered. The otherwise criminal act gains legitimacy because it need not justify *itself;* one need show only that production is worthwhile, not that this production serves any of the purposes that generally make production worthwhile. Contrast that account with the typical criminal law account of the thief: Theft is deemed to represent a departure from a normatively justified general system of property rights rather than as a part of the establishment of a normatively justified system. Each instance of theft must be justified on its own; it is not enough to claim that the distributive scheme that would exist in a world without thieves would be normatively less desirable on the whole than the system that has emerged in a world with thieves. . . . .

3. Broad and Narrow Views of the Defendant   The interpretive decision characterizing defendants either in terms of capacities generally available to people or in terms of their own capacities is germane to the stability of the "easy case" because of its connection with the intentionalism/determinism rule. If one looks back at our first discussion of provocation, the relationship of subcategorization to "easy case" blame is readily apparent. Serious crimes inevitably require meaningful capacity to conform as a prerequisite to liability. Capacity, though, can be assessed either in terms of general human capabilities which the defendant, as a human, is improperly syllogistically presumed to possess[142] *or* narrowly, negating the possibility of capacity.[143] There must be some *implicit,* undefended comparison of the defendant to some person who has avoided crime before anyone can be inculpated. The killer who kills for money—arguably the easiest case of premeditated, malicious murder—might be impossibly complex, were it not for an odd category trick. What could it mean to say that someone who kills for money understands the sanctity of life, such that we would say he "comprehend[ed] his duty to govern his actions in accord[ance] with the duty imposed by law,"[144] or to "maturely and meaningfully reflect upon the gravity of his contemplated act"?[145] Presumably, we get around these problems by categorizing the hired killer as just another commercial actor, able, like any buyer or seller of goods, to accept or reject offers after determining whether they are in his interest.

V. Conclusion

I can interpret my own task of deconstructing rhetoric in three distinct, though not wholly incompatible, fashions. First, I can view the piece as a rather traditional legal realist's plea for the "politicization" of legal discourse. One might view my arguments as having the following structure: The courts and commentators purport to solve the particular doctrinal dilemma, but their "solutions" use an unsupportable "interpretation" or "characterization" to make the case appear manageable. Had they been doing "good" legal analysis, they would instead "balance" the substantive policy concerns at stake to

reach a well-reasoned result.

I have very limited sympathy for this account. First of all, this account fails to come to grips with a central and undeniable fact: Perfectly competent and intelligent commentators continue to mask so-called policy with a powerful residual conceptualism. The commentators I have cited are hardly Langdellians, the courts hardly premodern. I am dealing almost exclusively with the masters of realist thinking. Second, and quite related, I sense that the policy-balancing act that the traditional realist advocates *never* takes very full hold, both because it renders all legal outcomes highly ad hoc and because it makes legal discourse seem less distinct from nonlegal argument. Third, by failing to deconstruct the mechanisms needed to maintain the persistence of conceptualist solutions, traditional realists are unable to see that the culture's *blindness* to its constructs is critical. Thought takes on a natural, apolitical, noncontingent quality unless it is subject to ordered deconstruction.

A second plausible account of my work is that I am attempting to account for the existence of interpretive construction, and that identifying the forms that characterization takes is just one important step towards understanding the process of interpretation at a broader level. At various points I have accounted for the appearance of a particular interpretive construct as manifesting a simple class conflict between those protecting the position that the legal system routinely allows them from sudden, incidental disruption, and those disfavored by the routine distortion of benefits that the legal system generates. Naturally, those disfavored by the ordinary legal distributions of economic power are most prone to use means generally considered criminal.

Interpretive construction could play very distinct roles in this class conflict. It is possible that each construction might correspond to the political program of a social class. I would call this view "construction determinism": a belief that the interpretive technique an analyst uses is itself a product of the social class he politically supports. Alternatively, each legal *result* could correspond to the political program of a social group, and interpretive construction may serve simply to *cover up* the result-oriented, overtly political nature of resolving disputes. I would call this view "result determinism": a belief that the "bottom line" of any case results from class conflict, and the interpretive technique is just a ruse to hide a primitive assertion of power to promote one's selfish interests behind a mask of legal deductions. Finally, it may be that maintaining the appearance (or illusion) of legal argument is a significant political program of any dominant social class, so that making formal arguments which do not refer to the unexplainable interpretations that actually ground the arguments may sometimes be more vital than maintaining either the construction or particular results. I would call this "legal form determinism": a belief that the preservation of the faith in an orderly, nonarbitrary distribution of political and economic benefits is more central to dominant classes than either the result of any particular case or the preservation of the dominance of any one construction.

Throughout the essay, I have proffered all these sorts of explanations. I argued, for instance, in Part IV, that the most basic task of a dominant group is to identify criminality with disruption, with incidents that break the ordinary flow of distribution of burdens and benefits. My claim was that certain characterizations or constructions are most compatible with that end. In Part II, I frequently gave "result-oriented" explanations, made claims that an advocate of a certain position constructs the legal material simply to reach a desired result, and that the result is based on some *real* interest in winning a certain class of cases, either because they are significant to maintaining economic or political control or because they help solidify a certain ideological story that is helpful to maintaining domination. Finally, even in those cases when it seemed as if no one could possibly care about construction form or results in a particular setting, there is always the fallback claim that a legal system ought not to have gaps; it ought to look as if *every* case can be resolved by some similar "scientific" method.

A third account of my enterprise is that the interpretive constructs I note are not politically meaningful at all, but simply inexplicably unpatterned mediators of experience, the inevitably nonrational filters we need to be able to perceive or talk at all. If that were the case, my role would be largely aesthetic: I speak on behalf of those who no longer like to listen to people making arguments that mask a hidden structure of "nonarguments" with insistent, false rigor. In the preface to their property casebook, Professors Casner and Leach wrote that, "In order to move the student along the road of becoming a lawyer, he must be subjected to close analytical testing that rejects generalities or approximations. We think this must come at the beginning of his law study to get him to recognize and abhor superficiality."[146] I don't know whether to laugh or cry. When the unwarranted conceptualist garbage is cleared

away, dominant legal thought is nothing *but* some more or less plausible common-wisdom banalities, superficialities, and generalities, little more on close analysis than a tiresome, repetitive assertion of complacency that "we do pretty well, all considered, when you think of all the tough concerns we've got to balance." Legal thought *does* have its rigorous moments, but these are largely grounded in weak and shifting sands. There is some substance, but we tend to run for cover when it appears.

In the criminal law, two substantive concerns recur. Intentional action and rule-like form are purportedly necessary to construct our ordinary jurisprudence. But no one truly believes in absolute intentionalism or in rules, though the departures from the polar positions are vague and weakly defended. We must avoid the issues in order to talk like lawyers, partly because we have so little to say about them that is not deeply contradictory and ambivalent. What is worse for the lawyer rhetoritician is that when we assert a bottom line, we are rarely very convincing. We rarely do more than restate some utterly nonlegal functionalist preference, some pompous version of Pollyanna's principles, or some equally nonlegal anger or contempt for a system in which the comfortable beneficiaries of a rule structure cash in on their strengths and self-righteously condemn those marginalized by the most central social and collective decisions—the decisions about how rights, duties, and privileges are created and enforced. Rather than face our inability to speak, we hide the uses of standards and determinist discourses, or proclaim, loudly if not clearly, that when we are *obviously* using them, we are in an "exceptional" circumstance.

Most often, we avoid the issues altogether by constructing the legal material in terms of apparently well-established conceptualist dogma, looking to concepts that, at some broad level, are doubtless policy-"justified" (somewhere or other). As best I can tell, we do these interpretive constructions utterly un-self-consciously. I have never seen or heard anyone declare that they are framing time broadly or narrowly, unifying or disjoining an incident, broadly or narrowly categorizing a defendant's actual or required intent or a defendant's being or circumstances, let alone explain why they are doing it. It is illuminating and disquieting to see that we are nonrationally constructing the legal world over and over again; it is a privilege to discern some structure to this madness, a privilege one gets when a system feels unjust and unnatural. The outsider sees patterns that the insider, committed to keeping the enterprise afloat, never sees; structuring the practices of others is a funny and fun form of dismissal.

One real conclusion, one possible bottom line, is that I've constructed a very elaborate, schematized, and conceptual piece of winking dismissal: Here's what they say, this is how far they have gotten. You know what? There's not much to it.

---

1. This article does not review the traditional rationales of punishment—deterrence, retribution, detention, or rehabilitation. For general discussions of these traditional rationales, see, *e.g.*, J. Hall, *General Principles of Criminal Law*, 296–324 (2d ed. 1960); H. L. A. Hart, *Punishment and Responsibility* (1968); W. LaFave & A. Scott, *Handbook on Criminal Law* § 5 (1972); H. Packer, *The Limits of the Criminal Sanction* 9–70 (1968); *The Philosophy of Punishment* (H. Acton ed. 1969).

   For an analysis of a wide range of doctrine seen through the eyes of a deterrence-oriented theorist, see G. Williams, *Criminal Law: The General Part* (2d ed. 1961); for a retributionist's view, see G. Fletcher, *Rethinking Criminal Law* (1978).

   Nor does this article speculate on the origins of particular proscriptions of any criminal code. *See, e.g.*, L. Freidman, *A History of American Law* 256–58, 508–12 (1973); E. Thompson, *Whigs and Hunters* (1975).

2. For discussions of the complacency-inducing, conservatizing impact of the perceived separatedness of legal and political discourse, see Heller, *Is the Charitable Exemption from Property Taxation an Easy Case? General Concerns About Legal Economics and Jurisprudence*, in *Essays on the Law and Economics of Local Governments* 183, 201–7 (D. Rubinfeld ed. 1979); Kennedy, *The Structure of Blackstone's Commentaries*, 28 *Buffalo L. Rev.* 209, 214–19, 346–50 (1979); Kennedy, *Form and Substance in Private Law Adjudication*, 89 *Harv. L. Rev.* 1685, 1760–66 (1976).

3. S. Kadish & M. Paulsen, *Criminal Law and Its Processes* (3d ed. 1975).

4. For example, we incorporate facts about a defendant's personal history in raising the insanity defense.

5. *E.g.*, in raising the defense of duress.

6. *E.g.*, in raising the defense of abandonment.

7. Intentionalism gives "an account of experience which looks forward from the moment of human choice." Heller, *supra* note 2, at 237.

8. An intentionalist expresses "the indeterminancy of future action, the potential for a free exercise of intentional action implicit in indeterminate behavior. Necessarily, an existential phenomenology must take seriously the concepts of intentionality and responsibility and an ethical theory which gives moral weight to individual, autonomous choice." *Id.*

   For a fuller account of responsibility-demanding existentialist phenomenology, see H. Fingarette, *The Self in Transformation: Psychoanalysis, Philosophy and the Life of the Spirit* 162–69 (1963).

9. In a determinist discourse, the interpreter "reconsider[s] our behavior by looking backward across a series of acts . . . [rearranging] these acts by positing relations or theories which demonstrate their connectedness. This connectedness however implies their necessary succession, the determination of the later events once the sequence is grasped. . . . What is predetermined merits no moral respect or condemnation." Heller, *supra* note 2, at 237.

10. The standard text writers all must at some point refute the relevance of determinism to the criminal law. *See, e.g.*, G. Fletcher, *supra* note 1, §§ 6.4.3, 10.3.1; J. Hall, *supra* note 1, at 455–60; H. L. A. Hart, *supra* note 1, at 28–31, 179–85; H. Packer, *supra* note 1, at 74–75; G. Williams, *supra* note 1, § 173, at 547–49.

11. Environmental and genetic factors determine people's relative tastes for criminal activity, but they generally do not render peo-
ple utterly insensitive to punishment. Thus, a determinist who feels uncomfortable blaming someone prone to criminality might still find it worthwhile to punish in order to lower the amount of crime. Full-blown deterrence theorists generally suppose a great deal of rationality in the decision to pursue criminal ventures. *E.g.* Ehrlich, *Participation in Illegitimate Activities: A Theoretical and Empirical Investigation*, 81 J. Pol. Econ. 521 (1973). Determinists are more skeptical about whether many criminals act so rationally, since an indifference to consequences may be one of the prominent determined effects of deprivation. As a result, the price effects of higher punishment may be dimmed. *See, e.g.*, Gardiner, *The Purposes of Criminal Punishment*, 21 Mod. L. Rev. 117, 122–23 (1958); California Assembly Committee on Criminal Procedure, Progress Report: Deterrent Effects of Criminal Sanctions 7 (1968).

12. *See, e.g., State v. Sikora*, 44 N.J. 453, 470, 210 A.2d 193, 202 (1965) ("Criminal blameworthiness cannot be judged on a basis that negates free will and excuses the offense, wholly or partially, on opinion evidence that the offender . . . was predetermined to act the way he did at that time."); *id.* at 475–76, 210 A.2d at 205 (Weintraub, C. J., concurring) ("[The psychiatrist] traces a man's every deed to some cause truly beyond the actor's own making. . . . Now this is interesting, and I will not quarrel with any of it. But the question is whether it has anything to do with the crime of murder. I think it does not."); H. Packer, *supra* note 1, at 74–75.

13. A fuller account of this conflict, assessing it as central to our legal culture, is given in Kennedy, *Form and Substance in Private Law Adjudication*, 89 *Harv. L. Rev.* 1685 (1976).

14. *Id.* at 1685.

15. *Id.*

16. Take a simple example: a statutory rape law designed to protect innocent girls from the sexual pressures of the sophisticated. In its rule form, the age of consent is given as, say, 16. Some girls under 16 will be perfectly sophisticated, however, and some over 16 will not be.

17. *See, e.g., Lewis v. Commonwealth*, 184 Va. 69, 34 S.E. 2d 309 (1945) (defendant not guilty of disorderly conduct on a bus when disorderly conduct statute referred only to cars, trains, and cabooses); *Rex v. Bazeley*, 168 Eng. Rep. 517 (1799) (when embezzlement was not contemplated by traditional legal category of larceny, bank teller who appropriated a note found not guilty because it was in his possession when he appropriated it).

18. *See, e.g., Regina v. Dudley & Stephens*, [1884] 14 Q.B. 273, 288 (lifeboat passengers who killed a sick boy to survive found guilty of murder, because "compassion for the criminal . . . [must not] change or weaken in any manner the legal definition of the crime").

19. This problem is better recognized in private law than in criminal law. It is perhaps the dominant problem in tax law, where the courts affirm the rights of taxpayers to minimize tax liabilities as long as they follow the rules, *e.g., Gregory v. Helvering*, 293 U.S. 465 (1935), but recharacterize transactions when taxpayers' characterizations fall outside of what "the statute intended." *Knetsch v. United States*, 364 U.S. 361, 365 (1960) (quoting *Gregory v. Helvering*, 293 U.S. at 469).

20. *See, e.g.*, 15 U.S.C. § 45(a) (1976 & Supp. III 1979).

21. Much of the technique of Socratic first-year law teaching involves the teacher driving the student towards a rule position and countering with a parade of horrible cases in which actors

within the culture abuse the precisely framed rules, or driving the student towards advocacy of a vague, purposive standard and countering with a parade of horrors about the "nonlegal," flat-based, bigoted system the student has created.

22. 486 *F. 2d* 1139 (D.C. Cir. 1973).

23. Judge Wright stated, "[R]ecognition of a defense of 'addiction' for crimes such as possession of narcotics is consistent not only with our historic common law notions of criminal responsibility and moral accountability, but also with the traditional goals of penology—retribution, deterrence, isolation and rehabilitation.

    "... [T]he retributive theory of criminal justice looks solely to the past.... Revenge, if it is ever to be legitimate, must be premised on moral blameworthiness, and what segment of our society would feel its need for retribution satisfied when it wreaks vengeance upon those who are diseased because of their disease? ...

    "The most widely employed argument in favor of punishing addicts for crimes such as possession of narcotics is that such punishment or threat of punishment has a substantial deterrent effect.... [But d]eterrence presupposes rationality.... In the case of the narcotic addict, however, the normal sense of reason, which is so essential to effective functioning of deterrence, is overcome by the psychological and physiological compulsions of the disease. As a result, it is widely agreed that the threat of even harsh prison sentences cannot deter the addict from using and possessing the drug." *Id.* at 1242–44.

24. Thus, to use obviously artificial numbers, assume the person on day one prevalues all future drug uses at 100 and prevalues punishment for use at (–200). However, there is only a 1 in 4 chance of being caught using before he is addicted. He may then use the drugs, since the expected value of use (100) exceeds the negative expected value of punishment ($\frac{1}{4} \times (-200)$ or (–50)). Use may lead to the pressing desire of addiction, so at the time of the particular use for which he is arrested, drug use may have reached a value of, say, 50,000, so that, in Wright's terms, he is nondeterrable.

    If a potential drug user knows he will be punished even if addicted, he may never use drugs at all. Thus, even postaddiction drug use is less likely if we broaden the time frame to include the defendant's earlier decisions to use drugs.

25. In his concurring opinion in *Robinson v. California*, 370 U.S. 660, 676–78 (1962), Justice Douglas argued that it is unconstitutionally cruel and unusual to punish a person for being an addict, since addiction is an illness. But why are we morally duty-bound to treat, rather than to condemn, sick people, if we believe that having an illness is not an inevitably disconnected incident, but may be part of an historical process to which the ill person voluntarily contributed?

    Besides the time-framing issue, his argument is ambiguous in two other ways: First, what does it mean to say that addiction is an illness? If, for instance, an illness is something doctors can treat, would addiction count? Second, even if addiction is an illness and illnesses must be treated, how do we know that punishment is not a form of treatment or that traditional "treatment" is not, at least when unwanted, punishment? *See In re* De La O, 59 Cal. 2d 128, 378 P.2d 793, 28 Cal. Rptr. 489 (1963) (upholding mandatory civil commitment program for addicts because it was not deemed punishment under *Robinson*).

26. Judge Wright noted that "there may have been a time in the past before the addict lost control when he made a conscious decision to use drugs. But imposition of punishment on this basis would violate the long-standing rule that '[t]he law looks to the immediate, and not to the remote cause; to the actual state of the party, and not to the causes, which remotely produced it.'" 486 F.2d at 1243 (quoting *United States v. Drew,* 25 F. Cas. 913, 914 (C.C.D. Mass. 1828) (No. 14,993)).

27. 486 *F. 2d* at 1145.

28. 31 *Ala. App.* 334, 17 So. 2d 427 (1944).

29. *Id.* at 335, 17 *So.* 2d at 427.

30. 2 *N.Y.* 2d 133, 138 *N.E.* 2d 799, 157 *N.Y.S.* 2d 558 (1956).

31. *Id.* at 139–40, 138 *N.E.* 2d at 803–4, 157 *N.Y.S.* 2d at 565.

32. In a truly intentionalist discourse, the hypothetical fact that Martin did not foresee arrest on the particular occasion that he was drunk (*e.g.*, when he was arrested on a past warrant) would still not preclude a finding of voluntariness, at least if the arrest was valid. (An invalid arrest, as in *Finch v. State,* 101 *Ga. App.* 73, 112 *S.E.* 2d 824 (1960), would make the public appearance that follows seem involuntary in a broad time frame as well.) One of the risks one (voluntarily) takes when one performs acts for which one ultimately may be arrested is that one will someday be forced to go places with the police, when *they* want to go and not when the individual wants to. This sort of broad voluntary reading of human intention typifies traditional assumption of risk doctrine, in which a worker is deemed to contract away his rights to a safe workplace when he makes a deal that includes, but makes no explicit reference to, the abnormal risks of the workplace.

33. Courts do not examine whether the defendant's voluntary acts brought the police to his home just prior to the arrest. Instead, they unconsciously use a narrow time frame in assessing voluntariness. Cases where the defendant clearly took such recent acts, *e.g., Marshall v. State,* 70 *Ga. App.* 106, 27 *S.E.* 2d 702 (1943) (defendant arrested after a reported disturbance at a soda plant); *People v. Lane,* 8 *Misc.* 2d 325, 32 *N.Y.S.* 2d 61 (1942) (defendant taken from a friend's apartment by police after he began fighting with the friend's guest); *People v. Brown,* 64 *Misc.* 677, 120 *N.Y.S.* 859 (1909) (defendant hauled away from a private house because he had been "licking his horse"), read just like the cases where the root of the public appearance is unsure or unclear, *e.g., Martin v. State,* 31 *Ala. App.* 334, 17 *So.* 2d 427 (1944); *Gunn v. State,* 37 *Ga. App.* 333, 140 *S.E.* 524 (1927); *Reddick v. State,* 35 *Ga. App.* 256, 132 *S.E.* 645 (1926).

    Two recent California cases do broaden the time frame in looking at the voluntariness of a public appearance. *People v. Perez,* 64 *Cal. App.* 3d 297, 134 *Cal. Rptr.* 338 (2d Dist. 1976); *People v. Olson,* 18 *Cal. App.* 3d 592, 96 *Cal. Rptr.* 132 (2d Dist. 1971) (both deciding questions of suppressing evidence obtained after arrest, rather than validity of drunk-in-public conviction).

34. First, one must note that the court made no foreseeability arguments; the interpretive characterization of the situation precluded the need for such an argument. Second, in courts using narrow time frames, a defendant who is involuntarily brought into public, even when he could clearly foresee that involuntary appearance would occur, will be acquitted of a drunk-in-public charge. *See, e.g., Moody v. State,* 131 *Ga. App.* 355, 206 *S.E.* 2d 79 (1974) (defendant brought by deputy sheriff into public in response to subpoena; court did not see that although presence in public may not have been voluntary over the short run, it was clearly foreseeable).

35. The case ultimately may be better understood as involving issues traditionally raised either as entrapment, *see* notes 135–36 *infra* and accompanying text (*i.e.,* the police may simply be too entwined in this particular violation to sustain a conviction), or justification, *see* notes 192–93 *infra* and accompanying text (*i.e.,* we actually *want* Martin to violate the drunk-in-public law in these particular circumstances, because, on balance, we like obedience to police much more than we dislike public drunkenness). The interpretive construction may obviate the need to apply inevitably vague entrapment and justification doctrines; thus, it expands the core of the criminal law covered by rules rather than ad hoc standards.

36. H. L. A. Hart, *supra* note 1, at 152.

    See J. Feinberg, *Doing and Deserving* 111–12 (1970) ("[S]trict liability to *imprisonment* ... 'has been held by many to be incompatible with the basic requirements of our Anglo-American, and indeed, any civilized jurisprudence.' ... [T]he reason why strict liability to imprisonment (punishment) is so much more repugnant to our sense of justice than is strict liability to fine (penalty) is simply that imprisonment in modern times has taken on the symbolism of public reprobation.... We are familiar with the practice of penalizing persons for 'offenses' *they could not help*. It happens every day in football games, business firms, traffic courts, and the like. But there is something very odd and offensive in *punishing* people for admittedly faultless conduct. . . .") (second emphasis added) (footnotes omitted).

All the major commentators, with the partial exception of Wasserstrom, *Strict Liability in the Criminal Law,* 12 *Stan. L. Rev.* 731 (1960), share this hostility to strict liability. *See, e.g.,* G. Fletcher, *supra* note 1, § 9.3, at 717–36; J. Hall, *supra* note 1, at 342–59; H. Packer, *supra* note 1, at 121–31; G. Williams, *supra* note 1, § 89; Wechsler, *The Challenge of a Model Penal Code,* 65 *Harv. L. Rev.* 1097, 1108–9 (1952). The Model Penal Code predicates criminality only on negligence, recklessness, purpose, or knowledge. Model Penal Code § 2.05 (Tent. Draft No. 4, 1955) provides that any strict liability "crime" can be no worse than a "violation," with no nonmonetary penalties.

37. 421 *U.S.* 658 (1975).

38. Chief Justice Burger wrote: "Thus *Dotterweich* and the cases which have followed reveal that in providing sanctions which reach and touch the individuals who execute the corporate mission—and this is by no means necessarily confined to a single corporate agent or employee—the Act imposes not only a positive duty to seek out and remedy violations when they occur but also, and primarily, a duty to implement measures that will insure that violations will not occur. The requirements of foresight and vigilance imposed on responsible corporate agents are beyond question demanding, and perhaps onerous, *but they are no more stringent than the public has a right to expect of those who voluntarily assume positions of authority* in business enterprises whose services and products affect the health and well-being of the public that supports them. . . .

"The Act does not, as we observed in *Dotterweich,* make criminal liability turn on 'awareness of some wrongdoing' or 'conscious fraud.' The duty imposed by Congress on responsible corporate agents is, we emphasize, one that requires the highest standard of foresight and vigilance, but the Act, in its criminal aspect, *does not require that which is objectively impossible." Id.* at 672–73 (emphasis added).

39. *See infra.* Part III.

40. *See, e.g.,* Model Penal Code § 5.01(4) (Tent. Draft No. 10, 1960), exculpating an actor who completely and voluntarily renounces an unconsummated criminal plan, even though he had already done enough so that were he interrupted by external forces, he would be guilty of attempt. *Cf. People v. Staples,* 6 *Cal. App. 3d* 61, 85 *Cal. Rptr.* 589 (2d Dist. 1970) (denying that voluntary abandonment is a good defense).

41. *See, e.g.,* W. LaFave & A. Scott, *supra* note 1, § 60, at 450; G. Williams, *supra* note 1, § 199, at 620–21.

42. G. Fletcher, *supra* note 1, § 3.3.8, at 186.

43. *See Le Barron v. State,* 32 *Wis. 2d* 294, 145 *N.W. 2d* 79 (1966).

44. G. Fletcher, *supra* note 1, § 3.3.8, at 187–88.

45. *See* the discussion of distinguishing preparation from attempt, notes 167–80 *infra* and accompanying text. H. Packer, *supra* note 1, at 100 states: "[A]ll of us frequently make moves in the direction of criminal activity, thereby satisfying this essential element of the attempt concept. It is, therefore, instructive to note the doctrinal mechanisms whose function it is, baldly put, to keep from making criminals of us all." The difficulties of squaring this vague doctrine with legalism are discussed in *id.* at 101; G. Fletcher, *supra* note 1, § 3.3.4, at 157–59.

46. Fletcher argues not precisely that the abandonment undermines our sense that the defendant is a blameworthy harm-causer, but that it undermines the far more specific criminal intent that he feels is required to carry out a crime. G. Fletcher, *supra* note 1, § 3.3.8, at 189. This more complex vision, though, is ultimately circular: It is based solely on Fletcher's notion that consummated harms are more than simply indicators of blameworthiness or need for reformation, incapacitation, etc., *cf.* Model Penal Code § 1.02(1) (Proposed Official Draft 1962) ("The general purposes of the provisions governing the definition of offenses are: . . . (b) to subject to public control persons whose conduct *indicates* that they are disposed to commit crimes.") (emphasis added),

while attempts, uniquely, are simply indicators. But the validity of the vision of attempts as indicators of blameworthiness and completed harms as inexorably blameworthy, without regard to the rest of the defendant's revealed attitude about harming, is precisely the question here; it cannot be used to provide the answer to the question of whether the open time frame used in the abandonment defense is uniquely appropriate.

47. I will not discuss whether a reasonable belief in the necessity of self-defense is a belief the ordinary man would have in the circumstances *or* a belief generated by a reasonable process, given the physical and/or emotional perceptions the defendant actually has. The problem is analogous to the problem of interpreting "reasonable provocation."

48. *See, e.g., Jones v. Commonwealth,* 213 *Ky,* 356, 281 *S.W.* 164 (1926).

49. *See, e.g., State v. Tucker,* 865 *S.C.* 211, 68 *S.E.* 523 (1910).

50. Model Penal Code § 2.02(10) (Proposed Official Draft 1962).

51. *See, e.g., Allison v. State,* 74 *Ark.* 444, 86 *S.W.* 409 (1905); *State v. Thomas,* 184 *N.C.* 757, 114 *S.E.* 834 (1972); *Commonwealth v. Colandro,* 231 *Pa.* 343, 80 *A.* 571 (1911); *Ill. Ann. Stat.* ch. 38, § 9-2 (Smith-Hurd 1979); *Wis. Stat. Ann.* § 940.05 (West Supp. 1980).

52. 46 *C.M.R.* 1131, *aff'd,* 22 *C.M.A.* 534 (1973).

53. *Id.* at 1183.

54. *See* Model Penal Code § 2.02 (Proposed Official Draft 1962) (describing levels of blameworthiness).

55. *See* H. Packer, *supra* note 1, at 107: "If one is engaged in drafting a criminal code, *which must prescribe precisely what has to be proven to convict of crime and precisely what distinctions separate one crime from another* when the same external facts are present (as, for example, in differentiating murder from manslaughter), there can be no doubt that the positive approach [which "attempts to identify particular states of mind"] is much the superior. . . . It is no accident that the positive approach is adopted in the masterly legislative construct underlying the American Law Institute's Model Penal Code." (emphasis added) (quoted material in brackets is from *id.* at 105).

56. For instance, defendant possesses liquor, believing he is breaking the law, though in fact Prohibition has been repealed. All commentators exculpate defendant.

57. A classic example is *Wilson v. State,* 85 *Miss.* 687, 38 *So.* 46 (1905). The trial court convicted defendant of attempting to commit forgery when he changed the *numbers* on a check. Defendant was unaware that changing the numbers, rather than the letters, is not a forgery. The appeals court, subsequently supported by all the commentators, reversed.

Professor John Kaplan suggested to me that "enlightened" commentators do not share this judgment of *Wilson.* This is an area where I am unsure who I am allowed to attack without being accused of picking on small-fry. The *Wilson* result is supported by the major writers, and I have been unable to find it explicitly attacked. G. Fletcher, *supra* note 1, § 3.3.7, at 178; J. Hall, *supra* note 1, at 595–98; G. Williams, *supra* note 1, § 205; Enker, *Impossibility in Criminal Attempts—Legality and the Legal Process,* 53 *Minn. L. Rev.* 665 (1969); Hughes, *One Further Footnote on Attempting the Impossible,* 42 *N.Y.U.L. Rev.* 1005 (1967).

58. The classic case is *People v. Jaffe,* 185 *N.Y.* 497, 78 *N.E.* 169 (1906). Defendant attempted to receive what he thought were stolen goods. Actually, police had recovered the goods. The court exculpated defendant. Some commentators agree, *see* G. Fletcher, *supra* note 1, § 3.3.7, at 182; Enker, *supra* note 75, at 694, but some do not, *see* J. Hall, *supra* note 1, at 598; Deusner, *The Doctrine of Impossibility in the Law of Criminal Attempts,* 4 *Crim. L. Bull.* 398 (1968); Hughes, *supra* note 75, at 1009; Sayre, *Criminal Attempts,* 41 *Harv. L. Rev.* 821, 853–54 (1928).

59. *See, e.g., People v. Fiegelman,* 33 *Cal. App. 2d* 100, 91 *P. 2d* 156 (4th Dist. 1939); *People v. Moran,* 123 *N.Y.* 254, 25 *N.E. 2d* 412 (1890). *Cf. Mullen v. State,* 45 *Ala.* 43 (1871) (defendant shot at victim with defective weapon, incapable of causing harm); *State v. Morretti,* 52 *N.J.* 182, 244 *A. 2d* 499 (1968) (defendant tried to perform illegal abortion on woman who was not in fact pregnant).

60. 85 *Miss.* 687, 38 *So.* 46 (1905). *See* note 57 *supra.*
61. 185 *N.Y.* 497, 78 *N.E.* 169 (1906). *See* note 58 *supra.*
62. Model Penal Code § 5.01(a) (Proposed Official Draft 1962).
63. *See, e.g.,* J. Hall, *supra* note 1, at 594–99.
64. W. LaFave & A. Scott, *supra* note 1, § 60, at 443.
65. The nonrational choice between broad and narrow interpretations of intention recurs no matter how one states the policy issue. One might claim that Wilson is harmless because if he keeps changing numbers on checks, he'll never take anyone's money, whereas if the pickpocket keeps sticking his hands in pockets, someday he'll steal. Such a claim involves an unwarranted interpretation of Wilson as someone mentally fixed on changing numbers rather than on getting money. One could just as plausibly say, "If you keep sticking hands in *empty* pockets, you'll never steal anything." The claim that a defendant doing the "same" thing will not cause harm follows from an unwarranted narrow view of what the "same" thing is. Narrowly viewed, Wilson repeats precisely the same acts. Yet we imagine the pickpockets as doing more apt versions of some broader category of acts.

    One might argue that Wilson should not be convicted because had he obtained money from the bank by altering numbers, that money would have been a gift from the bank rather than the proceeds of forgery, whereas the pickpocket's getting money from a pocket is a theft. Once more, the interpretation of the facts is indefensibly inconsistent. Had the pickpocket received money through the *precise* means he used—for instance, after he stuck his hands in an *empty* pocket, had the would-be victim said, "You must be desperate. Here's a twenty for your trouble"—then *that* receipt would not have been the proceeds of theft. And had Wilson received money by altering the instrument effectively, he would have been guilty of forgery. In *any* impossibility case, the *precise* means used do not result in harm. Otherwise, we would not be talking about attempts.
66. G. Fletcher, *supra* note 1, § 3.3.4, at 160–66.
67. Although it is not my main complaint with Fletcher's test, I should note that the test leads to some peculiar results. Take, for instance, the case of *United States v. Thomas,* 13 C.M.A. 278, 32 C.M.R. 278 (1962), in which the defendant had sexual intercourse with a dead woman. Has he attempted rape? Under Fletcher's theory, the defendant is *less* likely to be convicted of attempted rape if he is indifferent to whether the victim is alive.
68. It is noteworthy that Fletcher makes the categorization errors he makes, since he seems aware that LaFave and Scott have ignored the categorization issues I have described. G. Fletcher, *supra* note 1, § 3.3.7, at 178–79.
69. *Id.* § 3.3.4, at 161–62. It is interesting that Fletcher's argument is wrong on its own terms. If one views the receiver of goods as wondering whether the goods are stolen or recovered, this legal attribute question will matter a great deal to the person's "rational motivation." Only a rather self-destructive fence agrees to receive goods he knew were recovered; the hovering presence of the police deters most.
70. *Id.* § 2.2.1, at 82.
71. 32 *N.Y. 2d* 62, 295 *N.E. 2d* 777, 343 *N.Y.S. 2d* 103 (1973).
72. *See N.Y. Penal Law* § 115.00 (McKinney 1975), which provides that a person is guilty of criminal facilitation when "believing it probable that he is rendering aid to a person who intends to commit a crime, he engages in conduct which provides such person with means or opportunity for the commission thereof and which in fact aids such person to commit a felony."
73. 32 *N.Y. 2d* at 66, 295 *N.E. 2d* at 780, 343 *N.Y.S. 2d* at 106.
74. A result of conviction could have been reached by applying an equally arational broad view of intent, as is done in cases of transferred intent.

    When a defendant intentionally shoots at X, but hits and kills Y, courts traditionally hold her guilty of intentional homicide, saying the intent transfers from one victim to another. *See, e.g., Mayweather v. State,* 29 *Ariz.* 460, 242 *P.* 864 (1926). The defendant might claim that while she may be guilty of attempting to kill X, the killing of Y was at worst negligent. That claim gets lost in the interpretive shuffle when the court says that the defendant intended to kill a person, and then it defines *that* intent, rather than the narrow intent to kill X, as the relevant, requisite intent for murder. Similarly, the *Gordon* court could have found that the defendant displayed the intent to sell drugs and defined *that* as the requisite intent.

    It may be fair to presume that people *generally* set out to kill particular people rather than to kill, while people set out to sell drugs rather than to sell them to particular people. But this is a probabilistic generalization rather than a necessary truth. Some killers *are* more interested in killing than in killing particular enemies; many drug dealers really do select the people to whom they sell.
75. [1957] 2 *Q.B.* 396, 401.
76. Model Penal Code § 2.02 (Proposed Official Draft 1962) states:

    "(1) . . . a person is not guilty of an offense unless he acted purposely, knowingly, recklessly, or negligently, as the law may require, with respect to each material element of the offense.

    "(2) *Kinds of Culpability Defined.*

    "(a) *Purposely.*

    "A person acts purposely . . .

    "(1) if . . . it is his conscious object to engage in conduct of that nature or to cause such a result . . .

    "(b) *Knowingly* . . .

    "(c) *Recklessly.*

    "A person acts recklessly with respect to a material element of an offense when he consciously disregards a substantial and unjustifiable risk that the material element exists or will result from his conduct. The risk must be of such a nature and degree that considering the nature and purpose of the actor's conduct and the circumstances known to him, its disregard involves a gross deviation from the standard of conduct that a law-abiding person would observe in the actor's situation.

    "(d) *Negligently.*

    "A person acts negligently with respect to a material element of an offense when he should be aware of a substantial and unjustifiable risk that the material element exists or will result from his conduct. The risk must be of such a nature and degree that the actor's failure to perceive it, considering the nature and purpose of his conduct and the circumstances known to him, involves a gross deviation from the standard of care that a reasonable person would observe in the actor's situation."
77. To illustrate further, assume that there are two different classes of fire offenses, malicious damage (burning fields) and the more serious offense of arson (burning structures). The black letter concurrence rule would state that if a person intentionally burns a field, "unaware" of the possibility that a structure will be burned, he cannot be convicted of arson. But it is quite clear to me that if we take two persons—one having a marshmallow roast with his Boy Scout troop and the other deliberately burning a field—who pose equally small risks of burning a building and are each aware of this risk, the malicious damager's risk-taking activity will be interpreted narrowly (and thus be deemed unjustifiably risky or reckless) to overcome the supposed strictures of concurrence doctrine.

    Since the interpretations will be made by fact-finders (prosecutors deciding which crimes to charge, juries instructed by judges who read them abstractions about "substantial and unjustifiable risks"), it is not likely that appellate court decisions will show the extent of the breakdown of formal concurrence doctrine. Nevertheless, one can find appellate cases where the breakdown is rather overt, *see, e.g., Caywood v. Commonwealth,* 13 *Ky. Op.* 576 (1885) (defendant may be guilty of poisoning though unaware of the poisonous character of the drug given to excite the animal passions of a girl as part of what was undoubtedly another crime—seduction). *Accord, State v. Schaub,* 231 *Minn.* 512, 44 *N.W. 2d* 61 (1950) (defendant tried to commit suicide by gas; when landlord later flicked light switch, spark ignited gas; building blew up, killing landlord's wife; no issue of mental state vis à vis death considered in discussing conviction for second degree manslaughter); *People v.*

Vizzini, 78 Misc. 2d 1040, 359 *N.Y.S. 2d* 143 (1974) (firefighter union leaders who deliberately falsified a strike vote charged with reckless endangerment for calling a walkout; court sustained conviction though the proof of mental state on reckless endangerment, as opposed to coercion charge inherent in distorting strike vote, seems rather threadbare).

78. *See, e.g.*, Model Penal Code § 210.3(1)(b) (Proposed Official Draft 1962): "Criminal homicide constitutes manslaughter when . . . a homicide which would otherwise be murder is committed under the influence of extreme mental or emotional disturbance for which there is reasonable explanation or excuse. The reasonableness of such explanation or excuse shall be determined from the viewpoint of a person in the actor's situation under the circumstances as he believes them to be." *Accord, Del. Code Ann.* tit. 11, §§ 632, 641 (1979); *Minn. Stat. Ann.* § 609.20 (West 1964); *N.Y. Penal Law* § 125.25(1)(a) (McKinney 1975); *Utah Code Ann.* § 76-5-205 (1978).

79. *See, e.g., Bedder v. Director of Public Prosecutions*, [1954] 1 *W.L.R.* 1119 (H.L.) (impotent defendant insulted by prostitute's taunts is not reasonably provoked if his reaction is typical only of impotent men).

80. *See, e.g.*, G. Fletcher, *supra* note 1, § 4.2.1, at 247.

81. *See* Williams, *Provocation and the Reasonable Man*, 1954 *Crim. L. Rev.* 740, 751–52.

82. We *might* mean that the typical person would be *more likely* to kill. *See, e.g.*, G. Fletcher, *supra* note 1, 4.2.1, at 248; Wechsler & Michael, *A Rationale of the Law of Homicide II*, 37 *Colum. L. Rev.* 1261, 1281–82 (1937) ("While it is true, it is also beside the point, that most men do not kill on even the gravest provocation; the point is that the more strongly they would be moved to kill . . . the less does [the actor's] succumbing serve to differentiate his character from theirs"). But this formula still evades the categorization problem: When assessing the *situation* the average person "faces," are elements of the particular person's character part of a *quasi-external situation* or not?

83. See *Bedder v. Director of Public Prosecutions*, [1954] 1 W.L.R. 1119 H.L.). *But cf. Regina v. Raney*, 29 Crim. App. 14 (1942) (provocation inherent in knocking out the crutch of a one-legged man judged by the reaction of one-legged men to the incident).

84. *See, e.g.*, G. Fletcher, *supra* note 1, § 4.2.1, at 248–49.

85. *See Jones v. United States*, 308 F. 2d 307 (D.C. Cir. 1962) ("There are at least four situations in which the failure to act may constitute breach of a legal duty. One can be held criminally liable: first, where a statute imposes a duty to care for another; second, where one stands in a certain status relationship to another; third, where one has assumed a contractual duty to care for another; and fourth, where one has voluntarily assumed the care of another and so secluded the helpless person as to prevent others from rendering aid") (footnotes omitted).

86. G. Fletcher, *supra* note 1, § 8.2.3, at 601–2 recognizes this point. Fletcher uses the active verb form to determine the proper legal results, though the general verb form may simply reflect probabilistic assumptions about how events usually happen. For example, if *generally* speaking, strangers *allow to drown* rather than *drown*, we may use the passive verb form as a matter of supposition even when blame is more reasonable in the particular case.

87. Fletcher may acknowledge this, *id.* at 602, but I sense he views these cases as more extraordinary than I am suggesting.

88. *See, e.g.*, J. Hall, *supra* note 1, at 210; Dawson, *Negotiorum Gestio: The Altruistic Intermeddler*, 74 *Harv. L. Rev.* 1073, 1101–8 (1961).

89. *See, e.g.*, Kleinig, *Good Samaritanism*, 5 *Phil. & Pub. Aff.* 381 (1976); Trammel, *Tooley's Moral Symmetry Principle*, 5 *Phil. & Pub. Aff.* 305 (1976). For a response somewhat parallel to the one presented here, see Broot, *Dischargeability, Optionality, and the Duty to Save Lives*, 8 *Phil. & Pub. Aff.* 194 (1979).

90. Fletcher actually does argue that whether a particular defendant has actively killed ought to be answered on the basis of our suppositions about whether most people who do the physical deeds that the defendant did are killers. The *typical*

failure to render aid does not constitute a primary form of harm. This explains, I believe, the *intuitive oddity* of "intending" a particular result by failure to intervene. I agree with Fletcher wholeheartedly, but I draw from his observation the conclusion that intuitions and common verbal practices, grounded as they are in generalizations that fit particular circumstances poorly, are a most untrustworthy basis for stable, ultimately legitimated argument. Making people recognize that they are simply falling back on a probabilistic—but not especially applicable—supposition is a standard way of unsettling their sense of making reflective "rational decisions" of the sort that rationalist legal systems are supposed to make.

91. "With crimes so defined as to require not merely conduct but also a specified result of conduct, the defendant's conduct must be the 'legal' or 'proximate' cause. . . . [I]t must be determined that the defendant's conduct was the cause in fact of the result [and] . . . that any variation between the result intended . . . or hazarded . . . and the result actually achieved is not so extraordinary that it would be unfair to hold the defendant responsible for the actual result." W. LaFave & A. Scott, *supra* note 1, § 35, at 246. *See also* their discussion of doctrinal issues and cases in causation, *id.* § 33, at 246–51.

92. The Model Penal Code states that a defendant is deemed to cause a result that is "not too remote or accidental in its occurrence to have a [just] bearing on the actor's liability." Model Penal Code § 2.03(2)(b) (Proposed Official Draft 1962) (brackets in original).

93. In the analogous area of torts, "coincidence" cases do not give rise to liability. *See, e.g., Berry v. Borough of Sugar Notch*, 191 *Pa.* 345, 43 *A.* 240 (1899) (no liability when streetcar, traveling at excessive speed along route, gets hit by falling tree; negligent conduct must increase the probability of the harm that occurred, in order to cause it). *See also* Shavell, *An Analysis of Causation and the Scope of Liability in the Law of Torts*, 9 *J. Legal Studies* 463 (1980).

94. Was it predictable that "a person" would die if tapped? Was it predictable that a hemophiliac would die if tapped? Do we judge probability by referring to the broader group of human beings of whom hemophiliacs are instances, or narrow the focus? If we interpret broadly, we are prone to say, "Hemophilia caused the death"; if the latter, "the defendant caused it."

95. The logic says a defendant must cause a harm to be justly punished, and a defendant causes a harm when it is not so accidental as to make it unjust to punish him.

96. *See, e.g.*, Heller, *supra* note 2, at 237.

97. *See, e.g., id.* § 10.4.4, at 835.

98. A defendant "acquitted" by reason of insanity is held involuntarily in a facility. But the party may not be civilly committed or held in a treatment facility once he is "cured," regardless of whether he has been detained as long as he would have been had he been convicted and incarcerated in a prison. *See, e.g., Bolton v. Harris*, 395 *F.* 2d 642 (D.C. Cir. 1968).

99. *See, e.g.*, H. Packer, *supra* note 1, at 132 ("Let us . . . assume . . . that . . . a verdict [of not guilty by reason of insanity] . . . operates to deprive the person of liberty through confinement in an institution . . . in most respects very like a prison. . . . We must [still] put up with the bother of the insanity defense because to exclude it is to deprive the criminal law of its chief paradigm of free will.")

100. *See, e.g., People v. Conley*, 64 *Cal. 2d* 310, 411 *P. 2d* 911, 49 *Cal. Rptr.* 815 (1966) (diminished capacity, an inability to comprehend one's duty to govern one's actions under duty imposed by law, negates possibility of finding malice requisite to conviction for either first or second degree murder).

101. *See, e.g.*, J. Hall, *supra* note 1, at 449–54, 466–72 (criticizing the extension of psychiatric defenses because psychiatrists are inadequately scientific). "The problem of mental disease and criminal responsibility has, therefore, the appearance of utter simplicity. It is merely a matter of finding out which harm doers had a serious mental disease at the legally relevant time, and the experts in that kind of disease are psychiatrists. . . . It

happens, however, that a very large number, perhaps half, of the practicing psychiatrists in this country are not doctors of medicine . . ." *Id.* at 449.

102. A. Katz, *Studies in Boundary Theory* (unpublished ms. draft on file with *Stanford Law Review*) at 44–46.

103. The prototypical defendant excused for duress is likewise exculpated because his deviant acts are nondisorienting. The acts represent the kind of response that some (dominant) "we" would make to the pressures of some "they." The general determinist's duress plea is unacceptable because it disorientingly switches "we's" with "they's": "We" (who profess at least some sort of control over the social world) become a "they"— a source of horror—while "they"—the supposed source of horror—simply have typical, unexceptionable reactions to our unwarranted intrusions on their "real" characters.

104. J. Hall, *supra* note 1, at 25, 28.

105. Some attempts cause an apprehension of harm when the would-be victim is aware that the attempt is being made, or they cause anxiety when the victim learns the attempt was made. *See, e.g., id.* at 218.

106. *See, e.g.,* Schulhofer, *Harm and Punishment: A Critique of Emphasis on the Results of Conduct in the Criminal Law, 122 U. Pa. L. Rev.* 1497, 1519–21 (1974); Model Penal Code, § 5.01, Comment (Tent. Draft No. 10, 1960).

107. There may be people who would be willing to endure criminal punishment if they had the satisfaction of causing the harm they desired. Such persons would not be effectively deterred unless attempts were criminalized. *See* H. L. A. Hart, *supra* note 1, at 129.

108. *Rex v. Eagleton,* 169 *Eng. Rep.* 766 (1855). The case test was definitively rejected in *Rex v. White,* [1910] 2 *K.B.* 124 (in a case of slow poisoning, the last dose of poison needed to kill need not be administered to constitute the offense of attempted murder).

109. Fletcher recognizes the advantages and disadvantages of the tests. G. Fletcher, *supra* note 1, §§ 3.3.1, 3.3.2.

110. *Cf.* Katz & Teitelbaum, *PINS Jurisdiction, The Vagueness Doctrine, and The Rule of Law,* 53 *Ind. L.J.* 1 (1978) (noting that a command from the judge to the teen in need of supervision that is rule-like and consistent with procedural norms of freedom, like "obey *all* parental commands," restricts substantive autonomy more than a command that is a good deal vaguer and therefore less consistent with procedural norms of freedom, like "obey all *reasonable* commands").

111. *The King v. Barker,* [1924] *N.Z.L.R.* 865 (Ct. App.). Fletcher is fond of this test. G. Fletcher, *supra* note 1, § 3.3.2, at 142–45.

112. *See* G. Williams, *supra* note 1, § 202, at 630 (noting that a man approaching a haystack with a lighted match may simply intend to light his pipe).

113. *See* notes 116–18 *infra* and accompanying text.

114. *See, e.g., Hyde v. United States,* 225 *U.S.* 347, 387 (1912).

115. *Commonwealth v. Peaslee,* 177 *Mass.* 267, 59 *N.E.* 55 (1901) (opinion by Holmes, C.J.).

116. Model Penal Code § 5.01 (Proposed Official Draft 1962).

117. G. Williams, *supra* note 1, § 203, at 632, particularly emphasizes this point.

118. *E.g.,* activity described as "casing the joint" may be preparation for a larceny or a manifestation of curiosity about the way a neighborhood looks.

119. Reading the works in this field, *e.g.,* G. Fletcher, *supra* note 1, §§ 3.3.1, 3.3.2; J. Hall, *supra* note 1, at 576–86; G. Williams, *supra* note 1, §§ 201–3; Wechsler, Jones & Korn, *The Treatment of Inchoate Crimes in the Model Penal Code of the American Law Institute: Attempt, Solicitation, and Conspiracy,* 61 *Colum. L. Rev.* 571, 585–611 (1961), one senses that the problem is truly exasperating for each commentator, but that each sees the need to assert a solution. *But see* H. Packer, *supra* note 1, at 100–2 (viewing all the tests as nonsensical, though viewing the effort to avoid punishing preparation as a significant antipreventive detention effort).

120. *See* G. Williams, *supra* note 1, § 185, at 578.

121. 405 *U.S.* 156 (1972).

122. *Id.* at 162, 170 (quoting, respectively, *United States v. Harriss,* 347 *U.S.* 612, 617 (1953) and *Thornhill v. Alabama,* 310 *U.S.* 88, 97–98 (1940).

123. Note, *The Void-for-Vagueness Doctrine in the Supreme Court,* 109 *U. Pa. L. Rev.* 67 (1960).

124. For a discussion of the liberal culture's premise of the subjectivity of values, see R. Unger, *Knowledge and Politics* 51–55, 76–81, 88–104 (1975).

125. *Compare, e.g., Keeler v. Superior Court,* 2 *Cal. 3d* 619, 470 *P. 2d* 617, 87 *Cal. Rptr.* 481 (1970) (homicide statute not extended to apply to killing of fetus; statute could readily be drawn to encompass fetuses) *with Johnson v. Phoenix City Court,* 24 *Ariz. App.* 63, 535 *P. 2d* 1067 (1975) (upholding laws against lewd and immoral behavior, presumably because varieties of lewdness would be difficult to specify). Of course, a number of "vague" statutes must be limited to ensure that conduct protected by the first amendment is not proscribed. *See, e.g., Coates v. City of Cincinnati,* 402 *U.S.* 611 (1971) (ordinance prohibiting three or more persons from assembling on sidewalk and annoying passers-by); *In re Bushman,* 1 *Cal. 3d* 767, 463 *P. 2d* 727, 83 *Cal. Rptr.* 375 (1970) (statute prohibiting disturbance of peace; defendant claimed to be engaging in "symbolic speech").

126. 405 *U.S.* at 156 n. 1.

127. *Id.* at 164.

128. *See* Tribe, *The Puzzling Persistence of Process-Based Constitutional Theories,* 89 *Yale L.J.* 1063 (1980). Tribe discusses the use of ostensibly procedural norms to reach substantive results. In part, of course, one of the traditional "procedural" concerns in vagueness doctrine—that potential defendants know the criminal law—is implicated whenever "generally innocent" conduct is proscribed. Since few citizens read the statutes to learn the law, a statute proscribing conduct few would imagine illegal is likely to be unknown. Still, the substantive aspects of the decision seem powerful; it is unlikely that public announcements would cure the defects Douglas was getting at in *Papachristou.*

129. *See, e.g., Interstate Circuit, Inc. v. City of Dallas,* 390 *U.S.* 676 (1968); *NAACP v. Button,* 371 *U.S.* 415 (1963); *Winters v. New York,* 333 *U.S.* 507 (1948) (each discussing a possible chilling effect on exercise of the first amendment right to freedom of speech).

130. *See, e.g., Papachristou v. City of Jacksonville,* 405 *U.S.* 156, 164 (1972) (extolling virtues of strolling and loafing, activities arguably covered by vagrancy statute).

131. *See, e.g., Rose v. Locke,* 423 *U.S.* 48 (1975) (upholding a statute proscribing "crimes against nature," even as applied to cunnilingus).

132. *See, e.g.,* Cal. Penal Code § 653m (West Supp. 1981): "Every person who with intent to annoy telephones another and addresses to or about such other person any *obscene* language . . . [is punishable]" (emphasis added).

133. For example, there have been many attacks on the broad discretion involved in parole practice. *See, e.g.,* N. Morris, *The Future of Imprisonment* 35–36 (1974); Bronstein, *Rules for Playing God, Civ. Lib. Rev.,* Summer 1974, at 116, 120; Loewenstein, *Bringing the Rule of Law to Parole,* 8 *Clearinghouse Rev.* 769, 775 (1975). *Contra,* Breitel, *Controls in Criminal Law Enforcement,* 27 *U. Chi. L. Rev.* 427 (1960).

The trend toward more rule-like forms in sentencing and parole provisions reflects the hostility toward discretion. *See, e.g.,* McGee, *California's New Determinate Sentencing Act, Fed. Probation,* Mar. 1978, at 3, 8–9; Taylor, *In Search of Equity: The Oregon Parole Matrix, Fed. Probation,* Mar. 1979, at 52, 56. *See generally* Citizens' Inquiry on Parole & Criminal Justice, Inc., *Report on New York Parole: A Summary,* 11 *Crim. L. Bull.* 273 (1975) (urging nondiscretionary release provisions); O'Leary, *Parole Theory and Outcomes Reexamined,* 11 *Crim. L. Bull.* 304 (1975) (rebuttal).

134. For instance, it excludes the sort of pseudo-scientific analysis of behavior in Delgado, *Ascription of Criminal States of Mind: Toward a Defense Theory for the Coercively Persuaded ("Brainwashed") Defendant*, 63 *Minn. L. Rev.* 1 (1978).

135. *See, e.g.*, M. Wolfgang, *Patterns in Criminal Homicide* 245–65 (1958); Gobert, *Victim Precipitation*, 77 *Colum. L. Rev.* 511, 530–34 (1977).

136. In ordinary discourse, a party who kills after he has been repeatedly provoked would almost certainly be deemed less culpable than one who boils over and kills the first time he is so provoked. Somehow, in legal discourse, the fact that the long-term provoked defendant has managed to squelch his violent reactions in the past makes him more culpable when he finally gives in. The legal discourse makes sense only if we assume that a person should leave rather than slowly build up an uncontrollable rage—an assumption that depends on the exaggerated assertions that the person is aware of his rage and that there are no other reasons that compel him to stay in spite of that rage.

137. Deterrence theory, I take it, assumes that the short-run provoked party is blind to the criminal law signals; the longer-run provoked party ought to have time to consider the jailer and leave if he fears he is being worked into a frenzy. Again, this strikes me as a phenomenologically unsound reading of many cases of long-run provocation: People may get upset and then find themselves, for a moment that need last no longer than that which the traditionally provoked party faces, in an unforeseeable oblivious-to-punishment rage.

138. For instance, we can ground the decision to kill in the perception of the need to defend oneself and judge the defendant's blameworthiness as to the whole scene.

139. *See, e.g.*, Stone, *The Origins of Job Structure in the Steel Industry*, *Rev. Radical Pol. Econ.*, Summer 1974, at 113 (arguing that the extensive division of labor in the steel industry is not technically mandated, but serves to immunize steel bosses from effective in-plant opposition).

140. *See, e.g.*, P. Baran & P. Sweezy, *Monopoly Capital* (1966).

141. *See* S. Castles & G. Kosack, *Immigrant Workers and Class Structure in Western Europe* (1973) (discussing impact of "guest workers" in dampening labor's hopes for larger share of national income).

142. *E.g.*, "Humans have the capacity to conform to law. Defendant is a human. Therefore, defendant has the capacity to conform to the law."

143. *E.g.*, "Defendant is only truly like himself. That person did not resist criminality. Therefore, we have no real reason to believe that someone truly like the defendant can resist criminality."

144. *People v. Conley*, 64 *Cal. 2d* 310, 322, 411 *P. 2d* 911, 918, 49 *Cal. Rptr.* 815, 822 (1966) (defining malice).

145. *People v. Wolff*, 61 *Cal. 2d* 795, 821, 394 *P. 2d* 959, 975, 40 *Cal. Rptr.* 271, 287 (1964) (defining premeditation).

146. A. Casner & W. Leach, *Cases and Text on Property* vii (2d ed. 1969).

The Moral Obligation to Obey the Law

CRITO*

Plato

SOCRATES: Here already, Crito? Surely it is still early?

CRITO: Indeed it is.

SOCRATES: About what time?

CRITO: Just before dawn.

SOCRATES: I wonder that the warder paid any attention to you.

CRITO: He is used to me now, Socrates, because I come here so often. Besides, he is under some small obligation to me.

SOCRATES: Have you only just come, or have you been here for long?

CRITO: Fairly long.

SOCRATES: Then why didn't you wake me at once, instead of sitting by my bed so quietly?

CRITO: I wouldn't dream of such a thing, Socrates. I only wish I were not so sleepless and depressed myself. I have been wondering at you, because I saw how comfortably you were sleeping, and I deliberately didn't wake you because I wanted you to go on being as comfortable as you could. I have often felt before in the course of my life how fortunate you are in your disposition, but I feel it more than ever now in your pres-ent misfortune when I see how easily and placidly you put up with it.

SOCRATES: Well, really, Crito, it would be hardly suitable for a man of my age to resent having to die.

CRITO: Other people just as old as you are get involved in these misfortunes, Socrates, but their age doesn't keep them from resenting it when they find themselves in your position.

SOCRATES: Quite true. But tell me, why have you come so early?

CRITO: Because I bring bad news, Socrates—not so bad from your point of view, I suppose, but it will be very hard to bear for me and your other friends, and I think that I shall find it hardest of all.

SOCRATES: Why, what is this news? Has the boat come in from Delos—the boat which ends my reprieve when it arrives?

CRITO: It hasn't actually come in yet, but I expect that it will be here today, judging from the report of some people who have just arrived from Sunium and left it there. It's quite clear from their account

*Hugh Tredennick, trans. From Edith Hamilton and Huntington Cairnes, eds., *The Collected Dialogues of Plato* (Princeton: Princeton University Press, 1961).

that it will be here today, and so by tomorrow, Socrates, you will have to . . . to end your life.

SOCRATES: Well, Crito, I hope that it may be for the best. If the gods will it so, so be it. All the same, I don't think it will arrive today.

CRITO: What makes you think that?

SOCRATES: I will try to explain. I think I am right in saying that I have to die on the day after the boat arrives?

CRITO: That's what the authorities say, at any rate.

SOCRATES: Then I don't think it will arrive on this day that is just beginning, but on the day after. I am going by a dream that I had in the night, only a little while ago. It looks as though you were right not to wake me up.

CRITO: Why, what was the dream about?

SOCRATES: I thought I saw a gloriously beautiful woman dressed in white robes, who came up to me and addressed me in these words: Socrates, 'To the pleasant land of Phthia on the third day thou shalt come.'[1]

CRITO: Your dream makes no sense, Socrates.

SOCRATES: To my mind, Crito, it is perfectly clear.

CRITO: Too clear, apparently. But look here, Socrates, it is still not too late to take my advice and escape. Your death means a double calamity for me. I shall not only lose a friend whom I can never possibly replace, but besides a great many people who don't know you and me very well will be sure to think that I let you down, because I could have saved you if I had been willing to spend the money. And what could be more contemptible than to get a name for thinking more of money than of your friends? Most people will never believe that it was you who refused to leave this place although we tried our hardest to persuade you.

SOCRATES: But my dear Crito, why should we pay so much attention to what 'most people' think? The really reasonable people, who have more claim to be considered, will believe that the facts are exactly as they are.

CRITO: You can see for yourself, Socrates, that one has to think of popular opinion as well. Your present position is quite enough to show that the capacity of ordinary people for causing trouble is not confined to petty annoyances, but has hardly any limits if you once get a bad name with them.

SOCRATES: I only wish that ordinary people *had* an unlimited capacity for doing harm; then they might have an unlimited power for doing good, which would be a splendid thing, if it were so. Actually they have neither. They cannot make a man wise or stupid; they simply act at random.

CRITO: Have it that way if you like, but tell me this, Socrates. I hope that you aren't worrying about the possible effects on me and the rest of your friends, and thinking that if you escape we shall have trouble with informers for having helped you to get away, and have to forfeit all our property or pay an enormous fine, or even incur some further punishment? If any idea like that is troubling you, you can dismiss it altogether. We are quite entitled to run that risk in saving you, and even worse, if necessary. Take my advice, and be reasonable.

SOCRATES: All that you say is very much in my mind, Crito, and a great deal more besides.

CRITO: Very well, then, don't let it distress you. I know some people who are willing to rescue you from here and get you out of the country for quite a moderate sum. And then surely you realize how cheap these informers are to buy off; we shan't need much money to settle them, and I think you've got enough of my money for yourself already. And then even supposing that in your anxiety for my safety you feel that you oughtn't to spend my money, there are these foreign gentlemen staying in Athens who are quite willing to spend theirs. One of them, Simmias of Thebes, has actually brought the money with him for this very purpose, and Cebes and a number of others are quite ready to do the same. So, as I say, you mustn't let any fears on these grounds make you slacken your efforts to escape, and you mustn't feel any misgivings about what you said at your trial—that you wouldn't know what to do with yourself if you left this country. Wherever you go, there are plenty of places where you will find a welcome, and if you choose to go to Thessaly, I have friends there who will make much of you and give you complete protection, so that no one in Thessaly can interfere with you.

Besides, Socrates, I don't even feel that it is right for you to try to do what you are doing, throwing away your life when you might save it. You are doing your best to treat yourself in exactly the same way as your enemies would, or rather did, when they wanted to ruin you. What is more, it seems to me that you are letting your sons down too. You have it in your power to finish their bringing-up and education, and instead of that you are proposing to go off and desert them, and so far as you are concerned they will have to take their chance. And what sort of chance are they likely to get? The sort of thing that usually happens to orphans when they lose their parents. Either one ought not to have children at all, or one ought to see their upbringing and education through to the end. It strikes me that you are taking the line of least resistance, whereas you ought to make the choice of a good man and a brave one, considering that you profess to have made goodness your object all through life. Really, I am ashamed, both on your account and on ours, your friends'. It will look as though we had played something like a coward's part all through this affair of yours. First there was the way you came into court when it was quite unnecessary—that was the first act. Then there was the conduct of the defense—that was the second. And finally, to complete the farce, we get this situation, which makes it appear that we have let you slip out of our hands through some lack of courage and enterprise on our part, because we didn't save you, and you didn't save yourself, when

it would have been quite possible and practicable, if we had been any use at all.

There, Socrates, if you aren't careful, besides the suffering there will be all this disgrace for you and us to bear. Come, make up your mind. Really it's too late for that now; you ought to have it made up already. There is no alternative; the whole thing must be carried through during this coming night. If we lose any more time, it can't be done; it will be too late. I appeal to you, Socrates, on every ground; take my advice and please don't be unreasonable!

SOCRATES: My dear Crito, I appreciate your warm feelings very much—that is, assuming that they have some justification. If not, the stronger they are, the harder they will be to deal with. Very well, then, we must consider whether we ought to follow your advice or not. You know that this is not a new idea of mine; it has always been my nature never to accept advice from any of my friends unless reflection shows that it is the best course that reason offers. I cannot abandon the principles which I used to hold in the past simply because this accident has happened to me; they seem to me to be much as they were, and I respect and regard the same principles now as before. So unless we can find better principles on this occasion, you can be quite sure that I shall not agree with you—not even if the power of the people conjures up fresh hordes of bogies to terrify our childish minds, by subjecting us to chains and executions and confiscations of our property.

Well, then, how can we consider the question most reasonably? Suppose that we begin by reverting to this view which you hold about people's opinions. Was it always right to argue that some opinions should be taken seriously but not others? Or was it always wrong? Perhaps it was right before the question of my death arose, but now we can see clearly that it was a mistaken persistence in a point of view which was really irresponsible nonsense. I should like very much to inquire into this problem, Crito, with your help, and to see whether the argument will appear in any different light to me now that I am in this position, or whether it will remain the same, and whether we shall dismiss it or accept it.

Serious thinkers, I believe, have always held some such view as the one which I mentioned just now, that some of the opinions which people entertain should be respected, and others should not. Now I ask you, Crito, don't you think that this is a sound principle? You are safe from the prospect of dying tomorrow, in all human probability, and you are not likely to have your judgment upset by this impending calamity. Consider, then, don't you think that this is a sound enough principle, that one should not regard all the opinions that people hold, but only some and not others? What do you say? Isn't that a fair statement?

CRITO: Yes, it is.

SOCRATES: In other words, one should regard the good ones and not the bad?

CRITO: Yes.

SOCRATES: The opinions of the wise being good, and the opinions of the foolish bad?

CRITO: Naturally.

SOCRATES: To pass on, then, what do you think of the sort of illustration that I used to employ? When a man is in training, and taking it seriously, does he pay attention to all praise and criticism and opinion indiscriminately, or only when it comes from the one qualified person, the actual doctor or trainer?

CRITO: Only when it comes from the one qualified person.

SOCRATES: Then he should be afraid of the criticism and welcome the praise of the one qualified person, but not those of the general public.

CRITO: Obviously.

SOCRATES: So he ought to regulate his actions and exercises and eating and drinking by the judgment of his instructor, who has expert knowledge, rather than by the opinions of the rest of the public.

CRITO: Yes, that is so.

SOCRATES: Very well. Now if he disobeys the one man and disregards his opinion and commendations, and pays attention to the advice of the many who have no expert knowledge, surely he will suffer some bad effect?

CRITO: Certainly.

SOCRATES: And what is this bad effect? Where is it produced? I mean, in what part of the disobedient person?

CRITO: His body, obviously; that is what suffers.

SOCRATES: Very good. Well now, tell me, Crito— we don't want to go through all the examples one by one—does this apply as a general rule, and above all to the sort of actions which we are trying to decide about, just and unjust, honorable and dishonorable, good and bad? Ought we to be guided and intimidated by the opinion of the many or by that of the one—assuming that there is someone with expert knowledge? Is it true that we ought to respect and fear this person more than all the rest put together, and that if we do not follow his guidance we shall spoil and mutilate that part of us which, as we used to say, is improved by right conduct and destroyed by wrong? Or is this all nonsense?

CRITO: No, I think it is true, Socrates.

SOCRATES: Then consider the next step. There is a part of us which is improved by healthy actions and ruined by unhealthy ones. If we spoil it by taking the advice of non-experts, will life be worth living when this part is once ruined? The part I mean is the body. Do you accept this?

CRITO: Yes.

SOCRATES: Well, is life worth living with a body which is worn out and ruined in health?

CRITO: Certainly not.

SOCRATES: What about the part of us which is mutilated by wrong actions and benefited by right ones? Is life worth living with this part ruined? Or do we believe that this part of us, whatever it may be, in which right and wrong operate, is of less importance than the body?

CRITO: Certainly not.

SOCRATES: It is really more precious?

CRITO: Much more.

SOCRATES: In that case, my dear fellow, what we ought to consider is not so much what people in general will say about us but how we stand with the expert in right and wrong, the one authority, who represents the actual truth. So in the first place your proposition is not correct when you say that we should consider popular opinion in questions of what is right and honorable and good, or the opposite. Of course one might object, All the same, the people have the power to put us to death.

CRITO: No doubt about that! Quite true, Socrates. It is a possible objection.

SOCRATES: But so far as I can see, my dear fellow, the argument which we have just been through is quite unaffected by it. At the same time I should like you to consider whether we are still satisfied on this point, that the really important thing is not to live; but to live well.

CRITO: Why, yes.

SOCRATES: And that to live well means the same thing as to live honorably or rightly?

CRITO: Yes.

SOCRATES: Then in the light of this agreement we must consider whether or not it is right for me to try to get away without an official discharge. If it turns out to be right, we must make the attempt; if not, we must let it drop. As for the considerations you raise about expense and reputation and bringing up children, I am afraid, Crito, that they represent the reflections of the ordinary public, who put people to death, and would bring them back to life if they could, with equal indifference to reason. Our real duty, I fancy, since the argument leads that way, is to consider one question only, the one which we raised just now. Shall we be acting rightly in paying money and showing gratitude to these people who are going to rescue me, and in escaping or arranging the escape ourselves, or shall we really be acting wrongly in doing all this? If it becomes clear that such conduct is wrong, I cannot help thinking that the question whether we are sure to die, or to suffer any other ill effect for that matter, if we stand our ground and take no

action, ought not to weigh with us at all in comparison with the risk of doing what is wrong.

CRITO: I agree with what you say, Socrates, but I wish you would consider what we ought to *do*.

SOCRATES: Let us look at it together, my dear fellow; and if you can challenge any of my arguments, do so and I will listen to you; but if you can't, be a good fellow and stop telling me over and over again that I ought to leave this place without official permission. I am very anxious to obtain your approval before I adopt the course which I have in mind. I don't want to act against your convictions. Now give your attention to the starting point of this inquiry—I hope that you will be satisfied with my way of stating it—and try to answer my questions to the best of your judgment.

CRITO: Well, I will try.

SOCRATES: Do we say that one must never willingly do wrong, or does it depend upon circumstances? Is it true, as we have often agreed before, that there is no sense in which wrongdoing is good or honorable? Or have we jettisoned all our former convictions in these last few days? Can you and I at our age, Crito, have spent all these years in serious discussions without realizing that we were no better than a pair of children? Surely the truth is just what we have always said. Whatever the popular view is, and whether the alternative is pleasanter than the present one or even harder to bear, the fact remains that to do wrong is in every sense bad and dishonorable for the person who does it. Is that our view, or not?

CRITO: Yes, it is.

SOCRATES: Then in no circumstances must one do wrong.

CRITO: No.

SOCRATES: In that case one must not even do wrong when one is wronged, which most people regard as the natural course.

CRITO: Apparently not.

SOCRATES: Tell me another thing, Crito. Ought one to do injuries or not?

CRITO: Surely not, Socrates.

SOCRATES: And tell me, is it right to do an injury in retaliation, as most people believe, or not?

CRITO: No, never.

SOCRATES: Because, I suppose, there is no difference between injuring people and wronging them.

CRITO: Exactly.

SOCRATES: So one ought not to return a wrong or an injury to any person, whatever the provocation is. Now be careful, Crito, that in making these single admissions you do not end by admitting something contrary to your real beliefs. I know that there are and always will be few people who think like this, and consequently between those who do think so and those who do not there can be no agreement on principle; they must always feel contempt when they observe one another's decisions. I want even you to consider very carefully whether you share my views and agree with me, and whether we can proceed with our discussion from the established hypothesis that it is never right to do a wrong or return a wrong or defend oneself against injury by retaliation, or whether you dissociate yourself from any share in this view as a basis for discussion. I have held it for a long time, and still hold it, but if you have formed any other opinion, say so and tell me what it is. If, on the other hand, you stand by what we have said, listen to my next point.

CRITO: Yes, I stand by it and agree with you. Go on.

SOCRATES: Well, here is my next point, or rather question. Ought one to fulfill all one's agreements, provided that they are right, or break them?

CRITO: One ought to fulfill them.

SOCRATES: Then consider the logical consequence. If we leave this place without first persuading the state to let us go, are we or are we not doing an injury, and doing it in a quarter where it is least justifiable? Are we or are we not abiding by our just agreements?

CRITO: I can't answer your question, Socrates. I am not clear in my mind.

SOCRATES: Look at it in this way. Suppose that while we were preparing to run away from here—or however one should describe it—the laws and constitution of Athens were to come and confront us and ask this question, Now, Socrates, what are you proposing to do? Can you deny that by this act which you are contemplating you intend, so far as you have the power, to destroy us, the laws, and the whole state as well? Do you imagine that a city can continue to exist and not be turned upside down, if the legal judgments which are pronounced in it have no force but are nullified and destroyed by private persons?

How shall we answer this question, Crito, and others of the same kind? There is much that could be said, especially by a professional advocate, to protest against the invalidation of this law which enacts that judgments once pronounced shall be binding. Shall we say, Yes, I do intend to destroy the laws, because the state wronged me by passing a faulty judgment at my trial? Is this to be our answer, or what?

CRITO: What you have just said, by all means, Socrates.

SOCRATES: Then what supposing the laws say, Was there provision for this in the agreement between you and us, Socrates? Or did you undertake to abide by whatever judgments the state pronounced?

If we expressed surprise at such language, they would probably say, Never mind our language, Socrates, but answer our questions; after all, you are accustomed to the method of question and answer. Come now, what charge do you bring against us and the state, that you are trying to destroy us? Did we not give you life in the first place? Was it not through us that your father married your mother and begot you? Tell us, have you any complaint against those of us laws that deal with marriage?

No, none, I should say.

Well, have you any against the laws which deal with children's upbringing and education, such as you had yourself? Are you not grateful to those of us laws which were instituted for this end, for requiring your father to give you a cultural and physical education?

Yes, I should say.

Very good. Then since you have been born and brought up and educated, can you deny, in the first place, that you were our child and servant, both you and your ancestors? And if this is so, do you imagine that what is right for us is equally right for you, and that whatever we try to do to you, you are justified in retaliating? You did not have equality of rights with your father, or your employer—supposing that you had had one—to enable you to retaliate. You were not allowed to answer back when you were scolded or to hit back when you were beaten, or to do a great many other things of the same kind. Do you expect to have such license against your country and its laws that if we try to put you to death in the belief that it is right to do so, you on your part will try your hardest to destroy your country and us its laws in return? And will you, the true devotee of goodness, claim that you are justified in doing so? Are you so wise as to have forgotten that compared with your mother and father and all the rest of your ancestors your country is something far more precious, more venerable, more sacred, and held in greater honor both among gods and among all reasonable men? Do you not realize that you are even more bound to respect and placate the anger of your country than your father's anger? That if you cannot persuade your country you must do whatever it orders, and patiently submit to any punishment that it imposes, whether it be flogging or imprisonment? And if it leads you out to war, to be wounded or killed, you must comply, and it is right that you should do so. You must not give way or retreat or abandon your position. Both in war and in the law courts and everywhere else you must do whatever your city and your country command, or else persuade them in accordance with universal justice, but violence is a sin even against your parents, and it is a far greater sin against your country.

What shall we say to this, Crito—that what the laws say is true, or not?

CRITO: Yes, I think so.

SOCRATES: Consider, then, Socrates, the laws would probably continue, whether it is also true for us to say that what you are now trying to do to us is not right. Although we have brought you into the world and reared you and educated you, and given you and all your fellow citizens a share in all the good things at our disposal, nevertheless by the very fact of granting our permission we openly proclaim this principle, that any Athenian, on attaining to manhood and seeing for himself the political organization of the state and us its laws, is permitted, if he is not satisfied with us, to take his property and go away wherever he likes. If any of you chooses to go to one of our colonies, supposing that he should not be satisfied with us and the state, or to emigrate to any other country, not one of us laws hinders or prevents him from going away wherever he likes, without any loss of property. On the other hand, if any one of you stands his ground when he can see how we administer justice and the rest of our public organization, we hold that by so doing he has in fact undertaken to do anything that we tell him. And we maintain that anyone who disobeys is guilty of doing wrong on three separate counts: first because we are his parents, and secondly because we are his guardians, and thirdly because, after promising obedience, he is neither obeying us nor persuading us to change our decision if we are at fault in any way. And although all our orders are in the form of proposals, not of savage commands, and we give him the choice of either persuading us or doing what we say, he is actually doing neither. These are the charges, Socrates, to which we say that you will be liable if you do what you are contemplating, and you will not be the least culpable of your fellow countrymen, but one of the most guilty.

If I asked why, they would no doubt pounce upon me with perfect justice and point out that there are very few people in Athens who have entered into this agreement with them as explicitly as I have. They would say, Socrates, we have substantial evidence that you are satisfied with us and with the state. You would not have been so exceptionally reluctant to cross the borders of your country if you had not been exceptionally attached to it. You have never left the city to attend a festival or for any other purpose, except on some military expedition. You have never traveled abroad as other people do, and you have never felt the impulse to acquaint yourself with another country or constitution. You have been content with us and with our city. You have definitely chosen us, and undertaken to observe us in all your activities as a citizen, and as the crowning proof that you are satisfied with our city, you have begotten children in it. Furthermore, even at the time of your trial you could have proposed the penalty of banishment, if you had chosen to do so—that is, you could have done then with the sanction of the state what you are now trying to do without it. But whereas at that time you made a noble show of indifference if you had to die, and in fact preferred death, as you said, to banishment, now you show no respect for your earlier professions, and no regard for us, the laws, whom you are trying to destroy. You are behaving like the lowest type of menial, trying to run away in spite of the contracts and undertakings by which you agreed to live as a member of our state. Now first answer this question. Are we or are we not speaking the truth when we say that you have undertaken, in deed if not in word, to live your life as a citizen in obedience to us?

What are we to say to that, Crito? Are we not bound to admit it?

CRITO: We cannot help it, Socrates.

SOCRATES: It is a fact, then, they would say, that you are breaking covenants and undertakings made with us, although you made them under no compulsion or misunderstanding, and were not compelled to decide in a limited time. You had seventy years in which you could have left the country, if you were not satisfied with us or felt that the agreements were unfair. You did not choose Sparta or Crete—your favorite models of good government—or any other Greek or foreign state. You could not have absented yourself from the city less if you had been lame or blind or decrepit in some other way. It is quite obvious that you stand by yourself above all other Athenians in your affection for this city and for us its laws. Who would care for a city without laws? And now, after all this, are you not going to stand by your agreement? Yes, you are, Socrates, if you will take our advice, and then you will at least escape being laughed at for leaving the city.

We invite you to consider what good you will do to yourself or your friends if you commit this breach of faith and stain your conscience. It is fairly obvious that the risk of being banished and either losing their citizenship or having their property confiscated will extend to your friends as well. As for yourself, if you go to one of the neighboring states, such as Thebes or Megara, which are both well governed, you will enter them as an enemy to their constitution, and all good patriots will eye you with suspicion as a destroyer of law and order. Incidentally you will confirm the opinion of the jurors who tried you that they gave a correct verdict; a destroyer of laws might very well be supposed to have a destructive influence upon young and foolish human beings. Do you intend, then, to avoid well-governed states and the higher forms of human society? And if you do, will life be worth living? Or will you approach these people and have the impudence to converse with them? What arguments will you use, Socrates? The same which you used here, that goodness and integrity, institutions and laws, are the most precious possessions of mankind? Do you not think that Socrates and everything about him will appear in a disreputable light? You certainly ought to think so.

But perhaps you will retire from this part of the world and go to Crito's friends in Thessaly? That is the home of indiscipline and laxity, and no doubt they would enjoy hearing the amusing story of how you managed to run away from prison by arraying yourself in some costume or putting on a shepherd's smock or some other conventional run-away's disguise, and altering your personal appearance. And will no one comment on the fact that an old man of your age, probably with only a short time left to live, should dare to cling so greedily to life, at the price of violating the most stringent laws? Perhaps not, if you avoid irritating anyone. Otherwise, Socrates, you will hear a good many humiliating comments. So you will live as the toady and slave of all the populace, literally 'roistering in Thessaly,' as though you had left this country for Thessaly to attend a banquet there. And where will your discussions about goodness and uprightness be then, we should like to know? But of course you want to live for your children's sake, so that you may be able to bring them up and educate them. Indeed! By first taking them off to Thessaly and making foreigners of them, so that they may have that additional enjoyment? Or if that is not your intention, supposing that they are brought up here with you still alive, will they be better cared for and educated without you, because of course your friends will look after them? Will they look after your children if you go away to Thessaly, and not if you go away to the next world? Surely if those who profess to be your friends are worth anything, you must believe that they would care for them.

No, Socrates, be advised by us your guardians, and do not think more of your children or of your life or of anything else than you think of what is right, so that when you enter the next world you may have all this to plead in your defense before the authorities there. It seems clear that if you do this thing, neither you nor any of your friends will be the better for it or be more upright or have a cleaner conscience here in this world, nor will it be better for you when you reach the next. As it is, you will leave this place, when you do, as the victim of a wrong done not by us, the laws, but by your fellow men. But if you leave in that dishonorable way, returning wrong for wrong and evil for evil, breaking your agreements and covenants with us, and injuring those whom you least ought to injure—yourself, your friends, your country, and us—then you will have to face our anger in your lifetime, and in that place beyond when the laws of the other world know that you have tried, so far as you could, to destroy even us their brothers, they will not receive you with a kindly welcome. Do not take Crito's advice, but follow ours.

That, my dear friend Crito, I do assure you, is what I seem to hear them saying, just as a mystic seems to hear the strains of music, and the sound of their arguments rings so loudly in my head that I cannot hear the other side. I warn you that, as my opinion stands at present, it will be useless to urge a different view. However, if you think that you will do any good by it, say what you like.

CRITO: No, Socrates, I have nothing to say.

SOCRATES: Then give it up, Crito, and let us follow this course, since God points out the way.

---

1. *Iliad* 9.363.

LETTER FROM BIRMINGHAM JAIL*

Martin Luther King, Jr.

April 16, 1963

My Dear Fellow Clergymen:

While confined here in the Birmingham city jail, I came across your recent statement calling my present activities "unwise and untimely." Seldom do I pause to answer criticism of my work and ideas. If I sought to answer all the criticisms that cross my desk, my secretaries would have little time for anything other than such correspondence in the course of the day, and I would have no time for constructive work. But since I feel that you are men of genuine good will and that your criticisms are sincerely set forth, I want to try to answer your statement in what I hope will be patient and reasonable terms.

I think I should indicate why I am here in Birmingham, since you have been influenced by the view which argues against "outsiders coming in." I have the honor of serving as president of the Southern Christian Leadership Conference, an organization operating in every southern state, with headquarters in Atlanta, Georgia. We have some eighty-five affiliated organizations across the South, and one of them is the Alabama Christian Movement for Human Rights. Frequently we share staff, educational and financial resources with our affiliates. Several months ago the affiliate here in Birmingham asked us to be on call to engage in a nonviolent direct-action program if such were deemed necessary. We readily consented, and when the hour came we lived up to our promise. So I, along with several members of my staff, am here because I was invited here. I am here because I have organizational ties here.

But more basically, I am in Birmingham because injustice is here. Just as the prophets of the eighth century B.C. left their villages and carried their "thus saith the Lord" far beyond the boundaries of their home towns, and just as the Apostle Paul left his village of Tarsus and carried the gospel of Jesus Christ to the far corners of the Greco-Roman world, so am I compelled to carry the gospel of freedom beyond my own home town. Like Paul, I must constantly respond to the Macedonian call for aid.

Moreover, I am cognizant of the interrelatedness of all communities and states. I cannot sit idly by in Atlanta and not be concerned about what happens in Birmingham. Injustice anywhere is a threat to justice everywhere. We are caught in an inescapable network of mutuality, tied in a single garment of destiny. Whatever affects one directly, affects all indirectly. Never again can we afford to live with the narrow, provincial "outside agitator" idea. Anyone who lives inside the United States can never be considered an outsider anywhere within its bounds.

You deplore the demonstrations taking place in Birmingham. But your statement, I am sorry to say, fails to express a similar concern for the conditions that brought about the demonstrations. I am sure that none of you would want to rest content with the superficial kind of social analysis that deals merely with effects and does not grapple with underlying causes. It is unfortunate that demonstrations are taking place in Birmingham, but it is even more unfortunate that the city's white power structure left the Negro community with no alternative.

In any nonviolent campaign there are four basic steps: collection of the facts to determine whether injustices exist; negotiation; self-purification; and direct action. We have gone through all these steps in Birmingham. There can be no gainsaying the fact that racial injustice engulfs this community. Birmingham is probably the most thoroughly segregated city in the United States. Its ugly record of brutality is widely known. Negroes have experienced grossly unjust treatment in the courts. There have been more unsolved bombings of Negro homes and churches in Birmingham than in any other city in the nation.

---

*Reprinted by arrangement with the heirs to the estate of Martin Luther King, Jr., c/o Joan Daves Agency as agent for the proprietor.

These are the hard, brutal facts of the case. On the basis of these conditions, Negro leaders sought to negotiate with the city fathers. But the latter consistently refused to engage in good-faith negotiation.

Then, last September, came the opportunity to talk with leaders of Birmingham's economic community. In the course of the negotiations, certain promises were made by the merchants—for example, to remove the stores' humiliating racial signs. On the basis of these promises, the Reverend Fred Shuttlesworth and the leaders of the Alabama Christian Movement for Human Rights agreed to a moratorium on all demonstrations. As the weeks and months went by, we realized that we were the victims of a broken promise. A few signs, briefly removed, returned; the others remained.

As in so many past experiences, our hopes had been blasted, and the shadow of deep disappointment settled upon us. We had no alternative except to prepare for direct action, whereby we would present our very bodies as a means of laying our case before the conscience of the local and the national community. Mindful of the difficulties involved, we decided to undertake a process of self-purification. We began a series of workshops on nonviolence, and we repeatedly asked ourselves: "Are you able to accept blows without retaliating?" "Are you able to endure the ordeal of jail?" We decided to schedule our direct-action program for the Easter season, realizing that except for Christmas, this is the main shopping period of the year. Knowing that a strong economic-withdrawal program would be the by-product of direct action, we felt that this would be the best time to bring pressure to bear on the merchants for the needed change.

Then it occurred to us that Birmingham's mayoral election was coming up in March, and we speedily decided to postpone action until after election day. When we discovered that the Commissioner of Public Safety, Eugene "Bull" Connor, had piled up enough votes to be in the run-off, we decided again to postpone action until the day after the run-off so that the demonstrations could not be used to cloud the issues. Like many others, we waited to see Mr. Connor defeated, and to this end we endured postponement after postponement. Having aided in this community need, we felt that our direct-action program could be delayed no longer.

You may well ask: "Why direct action? Why sit-ins, marches and so forth? Isn't negotiation a better path?" You are quite right in calling for negotiation. Indeed, this is the very purpose of direct action.

Nonviolent direct action seeks to create such a crisis and foster such a tension that a community which has constantly refused to negotiate is forced to confront the issue. It seeks so to dramatize the issue that it can no longer be ignored. My citing the creation of tension as part of the work of the nonviolent-resister may sound rather shocking. But I must confess that I am not afraid of the word "tension." I have earnestly opposed violent tension, but there is a type of constructive, nonviolent tension which is necessary for growth. Just as Socrates felt that it was necessary to create a tension in the mind so that individuals could rise from the bondage of myths and half-truths to the unfettered realm of creative analysis and objective appraisal, so must we see the need for nonviolent gadflies to create the kind of tension in society that will help men rise from the dark depths of prejudice and racism to the majestic heights of understanding and brotherhood.

The purpose of our direct-action program is to create a situation so crisis-packed that it will inevitably open the door to negotiation. I therefore concur with you in your call for negotiation. Too long has our beloved Southland been bogged down in a tragic effort to live in monologue rather than dialogue.

One of the basic points in your statement is that the action that I and my associates have taken in Birmingham is untimely. Some have asked: "Why didn't you give the new city administration time to act?" The only answer that I can give to this query is that the new Birmingham administration must be prodded about as much as the outgoing one, before it will act. We are sadly mistaken if we feel that the election of Albert Boutwell as mayor will bring the millennium to Birmingham. While Mr. Boutwell is a much more gentle person than Mr. Connor, they are both segregationists, dedicated to maintenance of the status quo. I have hope that Mr. Boutwell will be reasonable enough to see the futility of massive resistance to desegregation. But he will not see this without pressure from devotees of civil rights. My friends, I must say to you that we have not made a single gain in civil rights without determined legal and nonviolent pressure. Lamentably, it is an historical fact that privileged groups seldom give up their privileges voluntarily. Individuals may see the moral light and voluntarily give up their unjust posture; but, as Reinhold Niebuhr has reminded us, groups tend to be more immoral than individuals.

We know through painful experience that freedom is never voluntarily given by the oppressor; it must be demanded by the oppressed. Frankly, I have yet to engage in a direct-action campaign that was "well timed" in the view of those who have not suffered unduly from the disease of segregation. For years now I have heard the word "Wait!" It rings in the ear of every Negro with piercing familiarity. This "Wait" has almost always meant "Never." We must come to see, with one of our distinguished jurists, that "justice too long delayed is justice denied."

We have waited for more than 340 years for our constitutional and God-given rights. The nations of Asia and Africa are moving with jetlike speed toward gaining political independence, but we still creep at horse-and-buggy pace toward gaining a cup of coffee at a lunch counter. Perhaps it is easy for those who have never felt the stinging darts of segregation to say, "Wait." But when you have seen vicious mobs lynch your mothers and fathers at will and drown your sisters and brothers at whim; when you have seen hate-filled policemen curse, kick and even kill your black brothers and sisters; when you see the vast majority of your twenty million Negro brothers smothering in an airtight cage of poverty in the midst of an affluent society; when you suddenly find your tongue twisted and your speech stammering as you seek to explain to your six-year-old daughter why she can't go to the public amusement park that has just been advertised on television, and see tears welling up in her eyes when she is told that Funtown is closed to colored children, and see ominous clouds of inferiority beginning to form in her little mental sky, and see her beginning to distort her personality by developing an unconscious bitterness toward white people; when you have to concoct an answer for a five-year-old son who is asking: "Daddy, why do white people treat colored people so mean?"; when you take a cross-country drive and find it necessary to sleep night after night in the uncomfortable corners of your automobile because no motel will accept you; when you are humiliated day in and day out by nagging signs reading "white" and "colored"; when your first name becomes "nigger," your middle name becomes "boy" (however old you are) and your last name becomes "John," and your wife and mother are never given the respected title "Mrs."; when you are harried by day and haunted by night by the fact that you are a Negro, living constantly at tiptoe stance, never quite knowing what to expect next, and are plagued with inner fears and outer resentments; when you are forever fighting a degenerating sense of "nobodiness"—then you will understand why we find it difficult to wait. There comes a time when the cup of endurance runs over,

and men are no longer willing to be plunged into the abyss of despair. I hope, sirs, you can understand our legitimate and unavoidable impatience.

You express a great deal of anxiety over our willingness to break laws. This is certainly a legitimate concern. Since we so diligently urge people to obey the Supreme Court's decision of 1954 outlawing segregation in the public schools, at first glance it may seem rather paradoxical for us consciously to break laws. One may well ask: "How can you advocate breaking some laws and obeying others?" The answer lies in the fact that there are two types of laws: just and unjust. I would be the first to advocate obeying just laws. One has not only a legal but a moral responsibility to obey just laws. Conversely, one has a moral responsibility to disobey unjust laws. I would agree with St. Augustine that "an unjust law is no law at all."

Now, what is the difference between the two? How does one determine whether a law is just or unjust? A just law is a man-made code that squares with the moral law or the law of God. An unjust law is a code that is out of harmony with the moral law. To put it in the terms of St. Thomas Aquinas: An unjust law is a human law that is not rooted in eternal and natural law. Any law that uplifts human personality is just. Any law that degrades human personality is unjust. All segregation statutes are unjust because segregation distorts the soul and damages the personality. It gives the segregator a false sense of superiority and the segregated a false sense of inferiority. Segregation, to use the terminology of the Jewish philosopher Martin Buber, substitutes an "I-it" relationship for an "I-thou" relationship and ends up relegating persons to the status of things. Hence segregation is not only politically, economically and sociologically unsound, it is morally wrong and sinful. Paul Tillich has said that sin is separation. Is not segregation an existential expression of man's tragic separation, his awful estrangement, his terrible sinfulness? Thus it is that I can urge men to obey the 1954 decision of the Supreme Court, for it is morally right; and I can urge them to disobey segregation ordinances, for they are morally wrong.

Let us consider a more concrete example of just and unjust laws. An unjust law is a code that a numerical or power majority group compels a minority group to obey but does not make binding on itself. This is *difference* made legal. By the same token, a just law is a code that a majority compels a minority to follow and that it is willing to follow itself. This is *sameness* made legal.

Let me give another explanation. A law is unjust if it is inflicted on a minority that, as a result of being denied the right to vote, had no part in enacting or devising the law. Who can say that the legislature of Alabama which set up that state's segregation laws was democratically elected? Throughout Alabama all sorts of devious methods are used to prevent Negroes from becoming registered voters, and there are some counties in which, even though Negroes constitute a majority of the population, not a single Negro is registered. Can any law enacted under such circumstances be considered democratically structured?

Sometimes a law is just on its face and unjust in its application. For instance, I have been arrested on a charge of parading without a permit. Now, there is nothing wrong in having an ordinance which requires a permit for a parade. But such an ordinance becomes unjust when it is used to maintain segregation and to deny citizens the First-Amendment privilege of peaceful assembly and protest.

I hope you are able to see the distinction I am trying to point out. In no sense do I advocate evading or defying the law, as would the rabid segregationist. That would lead to anarchy. One who breaks an unjust law must do so openly, lovingly, and with a willingness to accept the penalty. I submit that an individual who breaks a law that conscience tells him is unjust, and who willingly accepts the penalty of imprisonment in order to arouse the conscience of the community over its injustice, is in reality expressing the highest respect for law.

Of course, there is nothing new about this kind of civil disobedience. It was evidenced sublimely in the refusal of Shadrach, Meshach and Abednego to obey the laws of Nebuchadnezzar, on the ground that a higher moral law was at stake. It was practiced superbly by the early Christians, who were willing to face hungry lions and the excruciating pain of chopping blocks rather than submit to certain unjust laws of the Roman Empire. To a degree, academic freedom is a reality today because Socrates practiced civil disobedience. In our own nation, the Boston Tea Party represented a massive act of civil disobedience.

We should never forget that everything Adolf Hitler did in Germany was "legal" and everything the Hungarian freedom fighters did in Hungary was "illegal." It was "illegal" to aid and comfort a Jew in Hitler's Germany. Even so, I am sure that, had I lived in Germany at the time, I would have aided and comforted my Jewish brothers. If today I lived in a Communist country where certain principles dear to the Christian faith are suppressed, I would openly advocate disobeying that country's antireligious laws.

I must make two honest confessions to you, my Christian and Jewish brothers. First, I must confess that over the past few years I have been gravely disappointed with the white moderate. I have almost reached the regrettable conclusion that the Negro's great stumbling block in his stride toward freedom is not the White Citizen's Counciler or the Ku Klux Klanner, but the white moderate, who is more devoted to "order" than to justice; who prefers a negative peace which is the absence of tension to a positive peace which is the presence of justice; who constantly says: "I agree with you in the goal you seek, but I cannot agree with your methods of direct action"; who paternalistically believes he can set the timetable for another man's freedom; who lives by a mythical concept of time and who constantly advises the Negro to wait for a "more convenient season." Shallow understanding from people of good will is more frustrating than absolute misunderstanding from people of ill will. Lukewarm acceptance is much more bewildering than outright rejection.

I had hoped that the white moderate would understand that law and order exist for the purpose of establishing justice and that when they fail in this purpose they become the dangerously structured dams that block the flow of social progress. I had hoped that the white moderate would understand that the present tension in the South is a necessary phase of the transition from an obnoxious negative peace, in which the Negro passively accepted his unjust plight, to a substantive and positive peace, in which all men will respect the dignity and worth of human personality. Actually, we who engage in nonviolent direct action are not the creators of tension. We merely bring to the surface the hidden tension that is already alive. We bring it out in the open, where it can be seen and dealt with. Like a boil that can never be cured so long as it is covered up but must be opened with all its ugliness to the natural medicines of air and light, injustice must be exposed, with all the tension its exposure creates, to the light of human conscience and the air of national opinion before it can be cured.

In your statement you assert that our actions, even though peaceful, must be condemned because they precipitate violence. But is this a logical assertion? Isn't this like condemning a robbed man because his possession of money precipitated the evil act of robbery? Isn't this like condemning Socrates because his unswerving commitment to truth and his philosophical inquiries precipitated the act by the misguided populace in which they made him drink hemlock? Isn't this like condemning Jesus because his unique God-consciousness and never-ceasing devotion to God's will precipitated the evil act of crucifixion? We must come to see that, as the federal courts have consistently affirmed, it is wrong to urge an individual to cease his efforts to gain his basic constitutional rights because the quest may precipitate violence. Society must protect the robbed and punish the robber.

I had also hoped that the white moderate would reject the myth concerning time in relation to the struggle for freedom. I have just received a letter from a white brother in Texas. He writes: "All Christians know that the colored people will receive equal rights eventually, but it is possible that you are in too great a religious hurry. It has taken Christianity almost two thousand years to accomplish what it has. The teachings of Christ take time to come to earth." Such an attitude stems from a tragic misconception of time, from the strangely irrational notion that there is something in the very flow of time that will inevitably cure all ills. Actually, time itself is neutral; it can be used either destructively or constructively. More and more I feel that the people of ill will have used time much more effectively than have the people of good will. We will have to repent in this generation not merely for the hateful words and actions of the bad people but for the appalling silence of the good people. Human progress never rolls in on wheels of inevitability; it comes through the tireless efforts of men willing to be co-workers with God, and without this hard work, time itself becomes an ally of the forces of social stagnation. We must use time creatively, in the knowledge that the time is always ripe to do right. Now is the time to make real the promise of democracy and transform our pending national elegy into a creative psalm of brotherhood. Now is the time to lift our national policy from the quicksand of racial injustice to the solid rock of human dignity.

You speak of our activity in Birmingham as extreme. At first I was rather disappointed that fellow clergymen would see my nonviolent efforts as those of an extremist. I began thinking about the fact that I stand in the middle of two opposing forces in the Negro community. One is a force of complacency, made up in part of Negroes who, as a result of long years of oppression, are so drained of self-respect and a sense of "somebodiness" that they have adjusted to segregation; and in part of a few middle-class Negroes who, because of a degree of academic and economic security and because in some ways they profit by seg-regation, have become insensitive to the problems of the masses. The other force is one of bitterness and hatred, and it comes perilously close to advocating violence. It is expressed in the various black nationalist groups that are springing up across the nation, the largest and best-known being Elijah Muhammad's Muslim movement. Nourished by the Negro's frustration over the continued existence of racial discrimination, this movement is made up of people who have lost faith in America, who have absolutely repudiated Christianity, and who have concluded that the white man is an incorrigible "devil."

I have tried to stand between these two forces, saying that we need emulate neither the "do-nothingism" of the complacent nor the hatred and despair of the black nationalist. For there is the more excellent way of love and nonviolent protest. I am grateful to God that, through the influence of the Negro church, the way of nonviolence became an integral part of our struggle.

If this philosophy had not emerged, by now many streets of the South would, I am convinced, be flowing with blood. And I am further convinced that if our white brothers dismiss as "rabble-rousers" and "outside agitators" those of us who employ nonviolent direct action, and if they refuse to support our nonviolent efforts, millions of Negroes will, out of frustration and despair, seek solace and security in black-nationalist ideologies—a development that would inevitably lead to a frightening racial nightmare.

Oppressed people cannot remain oppressed forever. The yearning for freedom eventually manifests itself, and that is what has happened to the American Negro. Something within has reminded him of his birthright of freedom, and something without has reminded him that it can be gained. Consciously or unconsciously, he has been caught up by the *Zeitgeist,* and with his black brothers of Africa and his brown and yellow brothers of Asia, South America and the Caribbean, the United States Negro is moving with a sense of great urgency toward the promised land of racial justice. If one recognizes this vital urge that has engulfed the Negro community, one should readily understand why public demonstrations are taking place. The Negro has many pent-up resentments and latent frustrations, and he must release them. So let him march; let him make prayer pilgrimages to the city hall; let him go on freedom rides—and try to understand why he must do so. If his repressed emotions are not released in nonviolent ways, they will seek expression through violence; this is not a threat but a fact of history. So I have not said to my people: "Get rid of your discontent." Rather, I have tried to say that this normal and healthy discontent can be channeled into the creative outlet of nonviolent direct action. And now this approach is being termed extremist.

But though I was initially disappointed at being categorized as an extremist, as I continued to think about the matter I gradually gained a measure of satisfaction from the label. Was not Jesus an extremist for love: "Love your enemies, bless them that curse you, do good to them that hate you, and pray for them which despitefully use you, and persecute you." Was not Amos an extremist for justice: "Let justice roll down like waters and righteousness like an everflowing stream." Was not Paul an extremist for the Christian gospel: "I bear in my body the marks of the Lord Jesus." Was not Martin Luther an extremist: "Here I stand; I cannot do otherwise, so help me God." And John Bunyan: "I will stay in jail to the end of my days before I make a butchery of my conscience." And Abraham Lincoln: "This nation cannot survive half slave and half free." And Thomas Jefferson: "We hold these truths to be self-evident, that all men are created equal. . . ." So the question is not whether we will be extremists, but what kind of extremists we will be. Will we be extremists for hate or for love? Will we be extremists for the preservation of injustice or for the extension of justice? In that dramatic scene on Calvary's hill three men were crucified. We must never forget that all three were crucified for the same crime—the crime of extremism. Two were extremists for immorality, and thus fell below their environment. The other, Jesus Christ, was an extremist for love, truth and goodness, and thereby rose above his environment. Perhaps the South, the nation and the world are in dire need of creative extremists.

I had hoped that the white moderate would see this need. Perhaps I was too optimistic; perhaps I expected too much. I suppose I should have realized that few members of the oppressor race can understand the deep groans and passionate yearnings of the oppressed race, and still fewer have the vision to see that injustice must be rooted out by strong, persistent and determined action. I am thankful, however, that some of our white brothers in the South have grasped the meaning of this social revolution and committed themselves to it. They are still all too few in quantity, but they are big in quality. Some—such as Ralph McGill, Lillian Smith, Harry Golden, James McBride Dabbs, Ann Braden and Sarah Patton Boyle—have written about our struggle in eloquent and prophetic terms. Others have

marched with us down nameless streets of the South. They have languished in filthy, roach-infested jails, suffering the abuse and brutality of policemen who view them as "dirty nigger-lovers." Unlike so many of their moderate brothers and sisters, they have recognized the urgency of the moment and sensed the need for powerful "action" antidotes to combat the disease of segregation.

Let me take note of my other major disappointment. I have been so greatly disappointed with the white church and its leadership. Of course, there are some notable exceptions. I am not unmindful of the fact that each of you has taken some significant stands on this issue. I commend you, Reverend Stallings, for your Christian stand on this past Sunday, in welcoming Negroes to your worship service on a nonsegregated basis. I commend the Catholic leaders of this state for integrating Spring Hill College several years ago.

But despite these notable exceptions, I must honestly reiterate that I have been disappointed with the church. I do not say this as one of those negative critics who can always find something wrong with the church. I say this as a minister of the gospel, who loves the church; who was nurtured in its bosom; who has been sustained by its spiritual blessings and who will remain true to it as long as the cord of life shall lengthen.

When I was suddenly catapulted into the leadership of the bus protest in Montgomery, Alabama, a few years ago, I felt we would be supported by the white church. I felt that the white ministers, priests and rabbis of the South would be among our strongest allies. Instead, some have been outright opponents, refusing to understand the freedom movement and misrepresenting its leaders; all too many others have been more cautious than courageous and have remained silent behind the anesthetizing security of stained-glass windows.

In spite of my shattered dreams, I came to Birmingham with the hope that the white religious leadership of this community would see the justice of our cause and, with deep moral concern, would serve as the channel through which our just grievances could reach the power structure. I had hoped that each of you would understand. But again I have been disappointed.

I have heard numerous southern religious leaders admonish their worshippers to comply with a desegregation decision because it is the law, but I have longed to hear white ministers declare: "Follow this decree because integration is morally right and because the Negro is your brother." In the midst of blatant injustices inflicted upon the Negro, I have watched white churchmen stand on the sidelines and mouth pious irrelevancies and sanctimonious trivialities. In the midst of a mighty struggle to rid our nation of racial and economic injustice, I have heard many ministers say: "Those are social issues, with which the gospel has no real concern." And I have watched many churches commit themselves to a completely otherworldly religion which makes a strange, unBiblical distinction between body and soul, between the sacred and the secular.

I have traveled the length and breadth of Alabama, Mississippi and all the other southern states. On sweltering summer days and crisp autumn mornings I have looked at the South's beautiful churches with their lofty spires pointing heavenward. I have beheld the impressive outlines of her massive religious education buildings. Over and over I have found myself asking: "What kind of people worship here? Who is their God? Where were their voices when the lips of Governor Barnett dripped with words of interposition and nullification? Where were they when Governor Wallace gave a clarion call for defiance and hatred? Where were their voices of support when bruised and weary Negro men and women decided to rise from the dark dungeons of complacency to the bright hills of creative protest?"

Yes, these questions are still in my mind. In deep disappointment I have wept over the laxity of the church. But be assured that my tears have been tears of love. There can be no deep disappointment where there is not deep love. Yes, I love the church. How could I do otherwise? I am in the rather unique position of being the son, the grandson and the great-grandson of preachers. Yes, I see the church as the body of Christ. But, oh! How we have blemished and scarred that body through social neglect and through fear of being nonconformists.

There was a time when the church was very powerful—in the time when the early Christians rejoiced at being deemed worthy to suffer for what they believed. In those days the church was not merely a thermometer that recorded the ideas and principles of popular opinion; it was a thermostat that transformed the mores of society. Whenever the early Christians entered a town, the people in power became disturbed and immediately sought to convict the Christians for being "disturbers of the peace" and "outside agitators." But the Christians pressed on, in the conviction that they were "a colony of heaven," called to obey God rather than man. Small in number, they were big in commitment. They were too God-intoxicated to be "astronomically intimidated." By their effort and example they brought an end to such ancient evils as infanticide and gladiatorial contests.

Things are different now. So often the contemporary church is a weak, ineffectual voice with an uncertain sound. So often it is an archdefender of the status quo. Far from being disturbed by the presence of the church, the power structure of the average community is consoled by the church's silent—and often even vocal—sanction of things as they are.

But the judgment of God is upon the church as never before. If today's church does not recapture the sacrificial spirit of the early church, it will lose its authenticity, forfeit the loyalty of millions, and be dismissed as an irrelevant social club with no meaning for the twentieth century. Every day I meet young people whose disappointment with the church has turned into outright disgust.

Perhaps I have once again been too optimistic. Is organized religion too inextricably bound to the status quo to save our nation and the world? Perhaps I must turn my faith to the inner spiritual church, the church within the church, as the true *ekklesia* and the hope of the world. But again I am thankful to God that some noble souls from the ranks of organized religion have broken loose from the paralyzing chains of conformity and joined us as active partners in the struggle for freedom. They have left their secure congregations and walked the streets of Albany, Georgia, with us. They have gone down the highways of the South on tortuous rides for freedom. Yes, they have gone to jail with us. Some have been dismissed from their churches, have lost the support of their bishops and fellow ministers. But they have acted in the faith that right defeated is stronger than evil triumphant. Their witness has been the spiritual salt that has preserved the true meaning of the gospel in these troubled times. They have carved a tunnel of hope through the dark mountain of disappointment.

I hope the church as a whole will meet the challenge of this decisive hour. But even if the church does not come to the aid of justice, I have no despair about the future. I have no fear about the outcome of our struggle in Birmingham, even if our motives are at present misunderstood. We will reach the goal of freedom in Birmingham and all over the nation, because the goal of America is freedom. Abused and scorned though we may be, our destiny is tied up with America's destiny. Before the pilgrims landed at Plymouth, we were here. Before the pen of Jefferson etched the majestic words of the Declaration of

Independence across the pages of history, we were here. For more than two centuries our forebears labored in this country without wages; they made cotton king; they built the homes of their masters while suffering gross injustice and shameful humiliation—and yet out of a bottomless vitality they continued to thrive and develop. If the inexpressible cruelties of slavery could not stop us, the opposition we now face will surely fail. We will win our freedom because the sacred heritage of our nation and the eternal will of God are embodied in our echoing demands.

Before closing I feel impelled to mention one other point in your statement that has troubled me profoundly. You warmly commended the Birmingham police force for keeping "order" and "preventing violence." I doubt you would have so warmly commended the police force if you had seen its dogs sinking their teeth into unarmed, nonviolent Negroes. I doubt that you would so quickly commend the policemen if you were to observe their ugly and inhumane treatment of Negroes here in the city jail; if you were to watch them push and curse old Negro women and young Negro girls; if you were to see them slap and kick old Negro men and young boys; if you were to observe them, as they did on two occasions, refuse to give us food because we wanted to sing our grace together. I cannot join you in your praise of the Birmingham police department.

It is true that the police have exercised a degree of discipline in handling the demonstrators. In this sense they have conducted themselves rather "nonviolently" in public. But for what purpose? To preserve the evil system of segregation. Over the past few years I have consistently preached that nonviolence demands that the means we use must be as pure as the ends we seek. I have tried to make clear that it is wrong to use immoral means to attain moral ends. But now I must affirm that it is just as wrong, or perhaps even more so, to use moral means to preserve immoral ends. Perhaps Mr. Connor and his policemen have been rather nonviolent in public, as was Chief Pritchett in Albany, Georgia, but they have used the moral means of nonviolence to maintain the immoral end of racial injustice. As T. S. Eliot has said: "The last temptation is the greatest treason: To do the right deed for the wrong reason."

I wish you had commended the Negro sit-inners and demonstrators of Birmingham for their sublime courage, their willingness to suffer and their amazing discipline in the midst of great provocation. One day the South will recognize its real heroes. They

will be the James Merediths, with the noble sense of purpose that enables them to face jeering and hostile mobs, and with the agonizing loneliness that characterizes the life of the pioneer. They will be old, oppressed, battered Negro women, symbolized in a seventy-two-year-old woman in Montgomery, Alabama, who rose up with a sense of dignity and with her people decided not to ride segregated buses, and who responded with ungrammatical profundity to one who inquired about her weariness: "My feets is tired, but my soul is at rest." They will be the young high school and college students, the young ministers of the gospel and a host of their elders, courageously and nonviolently sitting in at lunch counters and willingly going to jail for conscience' sake. One day the South will know that when these disinherited children of God sat down at lunch counters, they were in reality standing up for what is best in the American dream and for the most sacred values in our Judaeo-Christian heritage, thereby bringing our nation back to those great wells of democracy which were dug deep by the founding fathers in their formulation of the Constitution and the Declaration of Independence.

Never before have I written so long a letter. I'm afraid it is much too long to take your precious time. I can assure you that it would have been much shorter if I had been writing from a comfortable desk, but what else can one do when he is alone in a narrow jail cell, other than write long letters, think long thoughts and pray long prayers?

If I have said anything in this letter that overstates the truth and indicates an unreasonable impatience, I beg you to forgive me. If I have said anything that understates the truth and indicates my having a patience that allows me to settle for anything less than brotherhood, I beg God to forgive me.

I hope this letter finds you strong in the faith. I also hope that circumstances will soon make it possible for me to meet each of you, not as an integrationist or a civil-rights leader but as a fellow clergyman and a Christian brother. Let us all hope that the dark clouds of racial prejudice will soon pass away and the deep fog of misunderstanding will be lifted from our fear-drenched communities, and in some not too distant tomorrow the radiant stars of love and brotherhood will shine over our great nation with all their scintillating beauty.

Yours for the cause of Peace and Brotherhood,
Martin Luther King, Jr.

DIFFERENCE MADE LEGAL: THE COURT AND DR. KING*

David Luban

> No set of legal institutions or prescriptions exists apart from the narratives that locate it and give it meaning. For every constitution there is an epic, for each decalogue a scripture. Once understood in the context of the narratives that give it meaning, law becomes not merely a system of rules to be observed, but a world in which we live.
>
> —*Robert Cover*[1]

> No fact that is a cause is for that very reason historical. It becomes historical posthumously, as it were, through events that may be separated from it by thousands of years. A historian who takes this as his point of departure stops telling the sequence of events like the beads of a rosary. Instead, he grasps the constellation which his own era has formed with a definite earlier one. Thus he establishes a conception of the present as the "time of the now" which is shot through with chips of Messianic time.
>
> —*Walter Benjamin*[2]

Legal argument is a struggle for the privilege of recounting the past. To the victor goes the right to infuse a constitutional clause, or a statute, or a series of prior decisions with the meaning that it will henceforth bear by recounting its circumstances of origin and assigning its place in history. I shall call such a historical placement of legal materials a *political narrative*. A string of precedents, a legislative history, an examination of framers' intent are all political narratives. To the victor goes also the right to recite what I shall call the *local narrative* constituting "the facts of the case at hand," and, following on these two rights, the additional right to pronounce the correspondence or mirroring of each narrative in the other that renders further argument unnecessary.

By "correspondence" and "mirroring" I mean that legal argument aims to show that *these facts* precisely exemplify the political problem that *this body of law* was intended to solve and, conversely, that the history of this body of law precisely prefigures the problem that led to the present litigation. To legitimize legal argument it is essential that the political and local narratives mirror each other precisely. For if an advocate or a judge were to admit that the legislative history or the precedents in a case were ambiguous, or that the facts before the court failed to square with past political narratives in important respects, the argument would lose its aura of authority and invite a self-proliferating skepticism rather than conviction. It is to avoid this deflationary loss of aura that political and local narratives must dovetail in an improbable mutual correspondence that legitimizes both the favored conclusion and the political narrative that embeds it. . . .

When you control the power of recounting history, you have therefore won a legal argument, for a legal argument is nothing but the confluence of a political narrative culminating in a proposition of law (which, as Cover suggests in my epigraph, attains meaning only when it is embedded in such a narrative) and a local narrative of events surrounding the lives of the litigants. Forcing these two

*For their help in trying to bring earlier drafts of this article under some semblance of control, I would like to thank David Bogen, Paul Kahn, Judith Lichtenberg, Richard Pildes, Peter Quint, Sara Vance, Robert Wachbroit, Steven Winter, and Gordon Young. From 87 *Michigan Law Review* 2152 (1989). Endnotes have been edited and renumbered.

narratives into correspondence imparts whatever power of conviction legal argumentation possesses.

This accounts for an experience that most lawyers have had, namely reading a majority appellate opinion and at first blush finding it thoroughly convincing, its arguments flowing inevitably from the precedents and the facts; then reading a dissenting opinion and finding it equally compelling. When we closely compare the two, we find that the authors have recounted a carefully edited selection of the facts of the case—what I have called a local narrative—together with a precedential or constitutional or legislative history (a political narrative) contrived to exhibit an (illusory?) correspondence with the local narrative. As Benjamin puts it in the passage I have taken as my second epigraph, the author of a legal argument "grasps the constellation which his own era has formed with a definite earlier one," and out of that constellation radiates the authority and conviction of the argument. . . .[3]

Holmes was therefore wrong: The life of the law is neither logic nor experience, but narrative and the only partially civilized struggle for the power it conveys. To put the point in slightly different terms, legal argument is at bottom neither analytic nor empirical, but rather historical. The life of the law is not a vision of the future but a vision of the past; its passions are unleashed, to use Benjamin's words, "by the image of enslaved ancestors rather than that of liberated grandchildren. . . ."[4]

My aim in this essay is to contrast two legal retellings of the same event: a set of demonstrations sponsored by the Southern Christian Leadership Conference in Birmingham, Alabama, in 1963 that led to the arrest and incarceration of Martin Luther King, Jr. One is the Supreme Court majority opinion in *Walker v. City of Birmingham,* sustaining King's conviction;[5] the other, King's own defense of his actions in his *Letter from Birmingham Jail.*[6] I wish to show how the self-same event entails radically different legal consequences when it appears in different narratives, one the Supreme Court's official voice, the other the excluded voice of one of the defendants whose condemnation the Supreme Court affirmed. In each, I shall be focusing on aspects usually thought of as literary or "rhetorical": the structure of narrative, the voice, the range of allusion, the questions that the authors intended to invoke and—equally importantly—those they hoped or had to forestall. If "rhetorical" is meant to indicate conviction through narrative rather than logical procedures, I accept the label; if "rhetorical" is meant to contrast with legiti-

mate argumentation, I reject it. For I have been claiming so far that legal argument gains legitimacy just to the extent that it is able to ground the authority of its own narratives. The criticisms I shall offer of both the Court's opinion and King's *Letter* are criticisms of narrative vision as much as logical coherence. . . .

I. Project Confrontation

In January 1963, the Southern Christian Leadership Conference (SCLC) held a retreat in Georgia to discuss strategy for a concerted attack on segregation in Birmingham, Alabama.[7] Project C—for "confrontation"—would consist of demonstrations and boycotts of Birmingham's downtown businesses during the normally busy Easter shopping season.

Birmingham itself had recently begun to display some sentiment for change in its segregationist ways. A group of whites headed by the Chamber of Commerce president campaigned to alter Birmingham's municipal government by abolishing the offices of the three segregationist commissioners (including the notoriously racist Commissioner of Public Safety, Theophilus Eugene "Bull" Connor) who then ran the city. The voters agreed to move to a mayoral system, and in a special election Connor was defeated by a more moderate segregationist named Albert Boutwell. Connor went to court to demand that he be allowed to finish his term of office as Commissioner of Public Safety,[8] and while this matter was pending Birmingham was governed by what was in effect two city governments, each passing its own laws and conducting city business after its own fashion; municipal checks were signed by both Connor and Boutwell. Some Birmingham whites hoped that SCLC would cancel the Easter demonstrations in order to give the new government a chance to show what it could do; but the SCLC leadership—which had previously cancelled demonstrations to allow the run-off election between Connor and Boutwell to proceed without the pressure of demonstrations—went ahead with Project C.

A Birmingham city ordinance required the demonstrators to obtain a parade permit from the city commission. On April 3, Mrs. Lola Hendricks, representing the demonstrators, approached Connor to request a permit; Connor replied "No, you will not get a permit in Birmingham, Alabama to picket. I will picket you over to the City Jail." On April 5— one week before Good Friday—Connor replied to a second, telegraphic, request for a parade permit with another refusal. The demonstrators proceeded with their protests.

Project C included plans for the Reverend Martin Luther King, Jr., to place himself in a position to be arrested on Good Friday, April 12. Late Wednesday evening, April 10, Connor obtained an *ex parte* injunction from Alabama Circuit Court Judge W. A. Jenkins, Jr., forbidding civil rights leaders, including all the leaders of Project C, from taking part in or encouraging demonstrations. The injunction was served at 1 A.M. on Thursday, and the SCLC leadership debated how to respond to it. King feared that complying with the injunction would deflate the protest, as had happened the previous summer in Albany, Georgia. He went ahead with the planned demonstration the following day, and was arrested; a second demonstration took place on Easter Sunday, April 14. Subsequently Judge Jenkins found several of the demonstrators guilty of criminal contempt and sentenced each of them (including King) to five days in jail and a $50 fine.[9] It is this conviction that the *Walker* Court upheld.

This ends the sequence of events recounted in *Walker* and King's *Letter*. But the larger chronicle of the Birmingham campaign did not end with King's arrest. Subsequently the demonstrators embarked on a strategy of marches by school children, leading to literally thousands of arrests. As the demonstrations continued, Bull Connor upped the level of official response, ordering that fire hoses and police dogs be turned on the demonstrators. Television news horrified its audiences with the spectacle of children bowled over by hoses that hit with enough force to rip the bark off trees. White moderates and the SCLC leadership undertook negotiations that led to a settlement announced on May 10. On May 11, the Ku Klux Klan staged a rally; after the meeting, the motel at which King had been staying and the home of his brother were bombed. Crowds of angry blacks rioted, and eventually President Kennedy sent in federal troops.[10] A month later, Alabama Governor George Wallace personally blocked the entrance of a University of Alabama building to prevent the entrance of two black students whose admission had been ordered by a federal court. Evidently this was the last straw. That same day, President Kennedy spoke on national television to announce that he was seeking comprehensive civil rights legislation that eventually became the Civil Rights Act of 1964. The summer ended with the March on Washington at which King delivered his "I have a dream" oration;

in a sense, the civil rights act and the march were the culminating events of Project C.

But let us return to King's original April arrest. While King was in jail, eight white clergyman—significantly, they were liberals who had publicly opposed Governor George Wallace's "Segregation Forever!" speech[11] took out a full-page advertisement in the *Birmingham News* denouncing the demonstrators' actions. King responded from his cell, writing in the newspaper's margins until he was able to obtain paper; after he was permitted visitors, King's manuscript was typed by his friends and returned to him in jail for revisions. His *Letter from Birmingham Jail* attracted little attention at first.[12] It was eventually printed by the American Friends Service Committee and reprinted in numerous periodicals; it is perhaps the most famous document to emerge from the civil rights movement.[13]

At their contempt hearing, the civil rights leaders averred that the parade permit ordinance and Judge Jenkins' *ex parte* injunction were unconstitutional; the judge, however, refused to consider the issue, since the demonstrators had never attempted to get the injunction dissolved. Eventually the United States Supreme Court agreed that the ordinance on which the injunction rested was unconstitutional.[14] Nevertheless, the Court in *Walker* declined to overturn the demonstrators' convictions for criminal contempt, holding that even a constitutionally questionable court order must be obeyed—the so-called "*Mine Workers* rule" derived from *United States v. United Mine Workers*.[15]

Point and counterpoint: King's *Letter* has become one of the great classics in the literature of civil disobedience, both for its philosophy and for the soul-stirring magnificence of its language. No one has called Potter Stewart's *Walker* opinion a classic (in what might be called the literature of civil obedience), but its status as a Supreme Court precedent makes it the functional equivalent of a "classic."[16] Both *Walker* and the *Letter* address an ancient question, a question that more than any other defines the very subject of legal philosophy: that, of course, is the question of whether we lie under an obligation to obey unjust legal directives, including directives ordering our punishment for disobeying other unjust directives. All political philosophy, from Plato's *Apology* and *Crito* on, is driven by this question; all our political hopes and aspirations are contained in the descriptive and argumentative materials we use to answer it. It is those materials that form our topic.[17]

II. The *Walker* Decision

A. *The Narrative of Authority*

How does one describe a legally significant event? There is, I hazard, no such thing as an absolutely neutral description of the facts—"writing degree zero"[18]—and one's choice of focus, of beginning and end, and of voice may already contain the answers to crucial questions.

The Court's *Walker* opinion adopts the voice and viewpoint of governmental authority and recites a simple story of authority vindicated. As we shall see, authority is the protagonist, the subject of the narrative, and the narrative itself is simple and straightforward. Authority takes prudent (if possibly excessive) precautions to protect the community against danger. Well-meaning but shortsighted demonstrators recklessly bypass those precautions. All of authority's worst fears are subsequently confirmed. Then the demonstrators attempt to avoid legal accountability for their actions. Needless to say—and after such a narrative, it is indeed needless to say—the Court declines to assist them in this enterprise.

Stewart's opinion begins (without introduction) with unnamed "city officials" going to court to obtain their injunction; in this narrative, therefore, an official act is the initiating event, and city officials are its protagonists. Stewart provides no background or context for the demonstrations or the demonstrators' motives; nor does he provide any clue to the segregationist history and predilections of Birmingham or of Bull Connor; nor does he allude to the fact that the lame duck commissioners were in their last three days of office after having been voted out in what amounted to a referendum on their racial policies. He merely quotes the allegations by "officials of Birmingham" that the demonstrations were "'calculated to provoke breaches of the peace,' 'threaten[ed] the safety, peace and tranquility of the City,' and placed 'an undue burden and strain upon the manpower of the Police Department.'"[19]

He then devotes three paragraphs to insinuations that as events subsequently unfolded these official fears were fully confirmed. In the first of these paragraphs, he quotes an angry complaint by one of the petitioners that in past demonstrations state courts had favored local law enforcement, and "if the police couldn't handle it, the mob would,"[20] thus suggesting that even the demonstrators understood the potential dangers of such confrontations.[21] The next paragraph notes that on Good Friday "a large crowd gathered," the onlookers "'clapping, and hollering, and [w]hooping.'" Members of this crowd "spilled" out into the street.[22]

Stewart's third descriptive paragraph portrays the Easter Sunday demonstration in the following terms: "Some 300 or 400 people from among the onlookers followed in a crowd that occupied the entire width of the street and overflowed onto the sidewalks. Violence occurred. Members of the crowd threw rocks that injured a newspaperman and damaged a police motorcycle."[23] The reference to a crowd overflowing onto the sidewalks, like the earlier reference to a crowd spilling out into the street, is intended to buttress the Court's subsequent argument validating "the strong interest of state and local governments in regulating the use of their streets and other public places" since "the free passage of traffic and the prevention of public disorder and violence become important objects of legitimate state concern."[24]

The three paragraphs also introduce a second theme: the willfulness of the demonstrators. The demonstrators distributed a statement "declaring their intention to disobey the injunction";[25] they "announced that '[i]njunction or no injunction we are going to march tomorrow'";[26] "calls for volunteers to 'walk' and go to jail were made."[27] And the angry complaint that state courts favored anti-demonstration local law enforcement suggests that the demonstrators had little respect for state courts.

Thus, the Court's exposition of facts has consisted so far of a theme—the city officials' justifiable concerns about the forthcoming demonstrations—a second theme—the demonstrators' defiant intentions—and a tragic climax, the vindication of authority as its fears were born out in the event by whooping and hollering crowds spilling into the street and by violence. The Court immediately lays this sonata-form exposition next to the rule of law that an "injunction duly issuing out of a court of general jurisdiction with equity powers upon pleadings properly invoking its action, and served upon persons made parties therein and within the jurisdiction, must be obeyed by them however erroneous the action of the court may be. . . ."[28]

Only then does the Court frame its legal issue:

We are asked to say that the Constitution compelled Alabama to allow the petitioners to violate this injunction, to organize and engage in these mass street parades and demonstrations, without any previous effort on their

part to have the injunction dissolved or modified, or any attempt to secure a parade permit
in accordance with its terms.[29]

Framed this way, the legal question is of course
self-answering; but it also provokes from the Court a
further description of the facts of the case that is worthy of note. According to the Court, the petitioners
had not made "any attempt to secure a parade permit
in accordance with [the injunction's] terms"; they "did
not apply for a permit either to the commission itself
or to any commissioner after the injunction issued."[30]
Now in fact, Mrs. Lola Hendricks, a member of the
petitioners' organization, had attempted to obtain a
parade permit *before* the injunction issued, and had
been threatened with jail by Bull Connor (who also
turned down a second request). Inasmuch as it was
Connor and the other commissioners who obtained
the injunction, it is plain enough that they were not
about to issue the parade permit the next day, and so
the Court is clearly insisting on a formality for formality's sake alone. The Court mentions the Hendricks
incident, but stresses that Mrs. Hendricks was "*not a
petitioner in this case*."[31] This was literally true, but
the Court is being a bit cute at this point by ignoring
the fact that she represented the petitioners' organization and sought the permit on the organization's behalf. This fact evidently has no relevance, and so it
disappears from the narrative—it is of a piece with
the remarkable absence of civil rights organizations
and the civil rights movement from Stewart's dramatis
personae. The very existence of political collectivities
other than governmental authority is missing from the
Court's narrative vocabulary—only government and
individuals (sometimes acting alone, sometimes
whooping it up in unstructured mobs) form a part of
Walker's ontology.

In any event, Connor "had . . . made clear that
he was without power to grant the permit alone,
since the issuance of such permits was the responsibility of the entire city commission."[32] Now Chief
Justice Warren alluded in his dissenting opinion to
claims made by the petitioners that "parade permits
had uniformly been issued for all other groups by
the city clerk on the request of the traffic bureau of
the police department, which was under Commissioner Connor's direction. The requirement that the
approval of the full Commission be obtained was applied only to this one group."[33] Nevertheless, Connor "had made clear" his incapacity to act; note the
success-verb construction, which carries with it the
twin implications that what Connor said was true,

and that—because he had made it clear—the
demonstrators were on notice of its truth.

The Court then turns to its legal arguments.
First, it insists that although the Birmingham statute
and the *ex parte* injunction both raise "substantial
constitutional issues," neither "was transparently invalid or had only a frivolous pretense to validity."[34]
This is because "the free passage of traffic and the
prevention of public disorder and violence become
important objects of legitimate state concern,"[35] and
(as we have seen) problems of traffic and disorder actually arose during the Birmingham demonstrations.

Because the statute and injunction were not
transparently invalid, the Court argues, the demonstrators should have proceeded immediately to court
to test them.

> There was an interim of two days between
> the issuance of the injunction and the Good
> Friday march. The petitioners give absolutely
> no explanation of why they did not make
> some application to the state court during that
> period. . . . It cannot be presumed that the
> Alabama courts would have ignored the peti-
> tioners' constitutional claims.[36]

For, and this is both the Court's ultimate argument and final paragraph,

> in the fair administration of justice no man
> can be judge in his own case, however ex-
> alted his station, however righteous his mo-
> tives, and irrespective of his race, color,
> politics, or religion. This Court cannot hold
> that the petitioners were constitutionally free
> to ignore all the procedures of the law and
> carry their battle to the streets. One may sym-
> pathize with the petitioners' impatient com-
> mitment to their cause. But respect for judicial
> process is a small price to pay for the civiliz-
> ing hand of law, which alone can give abid-
> ing meaning to constitutional freedom.[37]

Here the Court echoes Felix Frankfurter's concurring
opinion in *United Mine Workers:*

> Only when a court is so obviously traveling
> outside its orbit as to be merely usurping
> judicial forms and facilities, may an order
> issued by a court be disobeyed and treated
> as though it were a letter to a newspaper.
> Short of an indisputable want of authority
> on the part of a court, the very existence of
> a court presupposes its power to entertain a

controversy, if only to decide, after deliberation, that it has no power over the particular
controversy. Whether a defendant may be
brought to the bar of justice is not for the
defendant himself to decide. . . .

There can be no free society without
law administered through an independent
judiciary. If one man can be allowed to determine for himself what is law, every man can.
That means first chaos, then tyranny.[38]

There was a certain irony in Frankfurter's statement,
an irony that moves us from the local history of the
Birmingham events recounted in *Walker* to the political history encapsulated in the *Mine Workers* rule.
Howat,[39] the Court's principal precedent in *Walker,*
was a labor injunction case (as was *United Mine
Workers* itself), and it is clear from *Walker's* reliance
on *Howat* that the Court's political history assimilates
Judge Jenkins' injunction against the Birmingham
march to past uses of injunctions in labor disputes.

The labor injunction was a tool of union busting in the late nineteenth and early twentieth centuries. The parallels with Project C are clear: labor
unions, like the civil rights demonstrators, sought to
launch coordinated demonstrations and actions
against their employers. Like Bull Connor, the employers would turn to sympathetic judges in order
to enjoin these demonstrations and thereby to
defuse the movement. The classic study of the labor
injunction, launching a devastating attack on it, was
co-authored by none other than Frankfurter.[40]
Though the *Walker* majority fails to mention the fact,
Chief Justice Warren's dissenting opinion alludes to
the unsavory political history encoded in *Howat* and
United Mine Workers (and cites Frankfurter's
book).[41] It is a political history of judicial power
pressed or manipulated into service by entrenched
interests in order to stifle social change. And indeed,
it is a political history to which *Walker* subsequently
contributed: in the year following the decision, at
least fifty-four injunctions were employed by university administrators against the student movement,
and—in another ironic historical twist—*Walker* was
used to buttress labor injunctions in sectors not covered by the federal anti-injunction laws that Frankfurter had been instrumental in creating.[42] *Walker's*
political narrative conceals and extends a secret history of judicial authority ("secret," of course, because
the Court elects to leave unmentioned the history of
the use of injunctions registered in *Howat*)[43] It is
that history that we must now explore.

B. The Republic of Laws
and "Transparent Invalidity"

The rhetorical structure of the Court's opinion suggests that it is making something like the following
argument:

(1) The city officials' concerns about traffic and row-
diness were born out in fact, and so, *a fortiori,*
they were reasonable concerns.
(2) Because their concerns were reasonable, the injunction (and the statute upon which it was
based), though arguably unconstitutional, was
not *transparently* unconstitutional (the court
was not, in Frankfurter's words, "*obviously* traveling outside its orbit").
(3) Had the injunction been transparently unconstitutional, the demonstrators would perhaps have
been within their rights to disobey.
(4) However, on the assumption that its unconstitutionality was debatable, the only legitimate
course for the demonstrators to follow was to
test it in court.
(5) The rule of law instructing them to this effect
was clear, and they were on notice of it.
(6) Since the demonstrators did not attempt to test
the injunction's constitutionality in court, they
can be punished for disobeying it.

Even the various dissenters appear to accept
the validity of this argument, disagreeing not with its
jurisprudence but with steps (2) or (5). Thus, Chief
Justice Warren believes that the statute "is patently
unconstitutional on its face,"[44] Justice Douglas
agrees that it is "unconstitutional on its face or
patently unconstitutional as applied,"[45] and Justice
Brennan, though he insists that his opinion does not
deal with the merits of the constitutional claim, accepts the contention "that the ordinance and injunction are in fact facially unconstitutional."[46] Similarly,
the various dissenters contest the applicability of
Howat, though to different extents. Warren believes
that it was weakened by subsequent decisions,[47]
Douglas stresses that its rule makes an exception
when "'the question of jurisdiction' is 'frivolous and
not substantial'"[48] hence, when the ordinance is
"unconstitutional on its face or patently unconstitutional as applied"; and Brennan accepts *Howat* as a
"premise," arguing that the interest it underwrites
can be outweighed.[49]

Clearly, however, the heart of the Court's treatise on civil obedience lies in the jurisprudential
premise of its argument, with which even the dis-

senters appear to agree. I repeat it for emphasis: (3) *Had the injunction been transparently unconstitutional, the demonstrators would perhaps have been within their rights to disobey. (4) However, on the assumption that its unconstitutionality was debatable, the only legitimate course for the demonstrators to follow was to test its constitutionality in court.*

Now the Court never actually *says* that if the injunction's unconstitutionality had been transparent the demonstrators would have been free to disobey it; as we shall see the Court's rhetorical stance did not permit it to say such a thing. But Stewart devotes almost a third of his opinion to demonstrating that the statute and injunction were not "transparently invalid," none of which would be relevant unless transparent invalidity might affect the outcome of the case.

This is a point worth emphasizing, because it points to a remarkable incoherence in the opinion (as well as Frankfurter's *Mine Workers* concurrence). Remember that the Court's decisive argument rests on the familiar maxim that no one can be a judge in his own case. The statute and injunction may have been unconstitutional, but that is for a court to decide, not for the demonstrators to judge on their own.

If this argument holds at all, it holds regardless of whether the statute and injunction were "transparently invalid." For even then, if it is left to the demonstrators to determine transparent invalidity, they are acting as judges in their own case. Since the Court will not permit anyone to be judge in his own case, the Court had no need to insist that the statute and injunction were not transparently invalid; it had no need to recite a set of facts designed to underscore that the statute and injunction were not transparently invalid. In fact, it had no need for most of its opinion.

The opinion is a remarkable instance of protesting too much. The Court's fervent desire to prove a point (that the statute and injunction were not transparently invalid), even though the Court's argument renders that point irrelevant, points to an abiding and deeply buried anxiety—a kind of Banquo's ghost—that the Court dared not acknowledge but that it could not help addressing.

The anxiety arises from the political narratives that give meaning to American constitutionalism. The very notion of the rule of law and not of men, which goes back as far as Plato,[50] implies a limit to what authority can do, and thus contains within it the concept of *ultra vires* action. Moreover, the theory of popular sovereignty says that when governmental authority runs out the actual exercise of sovereignty devolves back to the people.[51] Finally,

the idea that law must be public, and publicly comprehensible, implies that there must be some point at which ordinary citizens can know that an action is *ultra vires* and thus that the power to disobey has devolved upon them. That is the point of transparent unconstitutionality to which the Court refers. The concept of transparent unconstitutionality, and the right to disobey transparently unconstitutional injunctions, is thus a linchpin of the legitimacy of American government: take it away and you must abandon the rule of law, or popular sovereignty, or the publicity of law.

The Court cannot quite bring itself to acknowledge this point, however, for a very good reason: an open acknowledgment that we are entitled to disobey transparently unconstitutional injunctions would invite us to judge constitutionality for ourselves, thereby undermining the authority of the courts. Clearly it is this possibility that the *Walker* Court is most concerned to foreclose. The political narratives underlying the authority of American courts vest ultimate power—including the ultimate power of understanding the law—not in the courts but in the citizenry, and insists that courts' authority is bounded. In *Walker,* however, the Court confronted the question of who is to determine the bounds of judicial authority. . . .

[T]he court's political narrative yokes the Constitution to the history of the labor injunction—of union busting. Its fundamental effect is to convert the notion of a transparently unconstitutional injunction into a kind of half-chimerical ideal. It is not quite mythical, for we can imagine that even the Court would find transparently unconstitutional an injunction saying "It is hereby ordered that the Constitution of the United States of America is suspended."[52] But in *Walker* the Court comes close to saying that anything less extreme—anything that authority takes the slightest care to disguise, thereby presenting a litigiable issue—is not *transparently* unconstitutional.

After all, in *Walker* we are confronted with an injunction that could hardly have been more irregular: it was issued *ex parte,* with less than a day available for appeal, at the behest of commissioners who had lost their mandate.[53] It would irreparably damage the demonstrators—a standard legal reason for not granting an injunction—by causing their moment to pass,[54] and it was based on an extraordinarily broadly worded statute granting the commissioners virtually unfettered power of prior restraint, inasmuch as mere "convenience" was included as a ground for denying parade permits.[55]

Nevertheless, the Court insists (what the dissenters deny) that this injunction is not transparently invalid.

The message could hardly be made more plain: provided that authority exerts the slightest effort to trick out its injunction in the trappings of legality, the injunction is not transparently unconstitutional and the citizen's power to defy it with impunity evaporates. *Walker* virtually issues instructions to judges and other officials about how to insulate an injunction from the possibility of being legitimately disobeyed. On the assumption that judges and other officials will follow these instructions in the future, the Court thus simultaneously presupposes and denies the jurisprudential premise of constitutionalism—that a citizen may disobey a transparently invalid injunction. . . .

C. The Naked Assertion of Judicial Authority

I have spoken only of the transparent invalidity of Judge Jenkins' injunction, not of the underlying statute, though the Court and dissenters discuss both. That is because the *Walker* opinion really concerns only the former, and indeed a key legal issue revolves around its asymmetrical treatment of injunctions and statutes, hence of judges and legislatures.

As Chief Justice Warren emphasizes in his dissent, one cannot be punished for violating an unconstitutional statute, and indeed it may be impossible to gain standing to test the statute in court unless one disobeys it.[56] Yet the *Walker* decision holds that the demonstrators can be punished for contempt when they violate an unconstitutional injunction. Evidently the authority of courts matters in a way that the authority of legislatures does not. Why?

The answer cannot be because of any constitutional superiority of the judicial process over the legislative process. For the issue in *Walker* is whether the petitioners can test an *unconstitutional* court order by disobeying it; the unconstitutionality of the order is one of the givens of the problem, and the difference in the processes by which an unconstitutional order issues therefore drops out of consideration. Unconstitutionality is unconstitutionality. The Court treats court orders as different in *kind* from legislative enactments, whereas the judicial and legislative processes differ only in degree (of accuracy, responsiveness, law-abidingness, whatever).

Indeed, what is most apparent in *Walker* is the Court's anxiety to uphold judicial authority as such,

as though it were civilization's final, frail barrier against a lurking catastrophe.[57] Hence the Court's final sentence: "But respect for judicial process is a small price to pay for the civilizing hand of law, which alone can give abiding meaning to constitutional freedom."[58] If I am right, the Supreme Court wanted to preclude the very possibility of testing the validity of injunctions by disobeying them because it viewed injunctions as utterly different in kind from statutes, as final barriers against civil anarchy. Frankfurter says this explicitly in the passage we quoted above: "the very existence of a court"—hence, its existence as such, regardless of its legitimacy—"presupposes its power to entertain a controversy. . . . There can be no free society without law administered through an independent judiciary. If one man can be allowed to determine for himself what is law, every man can. That means first chaos, then tyranny."[59] A restraining order is a last ditch attempt to stop something from happening, to pull the plug on an impending event, and the Court apparently believed that there must be some device that enables the authorities to pull the plug on an impending event.

This, I am convinced, is the heart of the *Walker* decision. The Court saw itself confronting a challenge to the judiciary's ultimate authority, the authority to stop events from getting out of hand; the Court was willing to go to almost any length in order to uphold that authority. As we have seen, ample grounds existed for the Court to find for the petitioners in a decision narrowly tailored to the facts: the *ex parte* hearing, its timing, the fact that Bull Connor had been voted out of office, his treatment of Mrs. Hendricks, his history of racism (known to the Court from prior cases)[60] not to mention the well-known commitment of the SCLC to nonviolence. Each could have provided a convenient hook for a favorable decision.[61] The fact that the Court did not rest content with allowing even a narrow exception to the inviolability of court orders shows that it feared even the slightest diminution of judicial ability to stop events.

This is particularly striking in view of the Supreme Court's general support for the civil rights movement and civil rights demonstrations in the years preceding *Walker*.[62] In hindsight, *Walker* (together with the *Adderley* decision handed down seven months before[63]) in fact marks a turning point in the Court's attitude, away from the civil rights movement and in the direction of greater emphasis on civil order. In his dissenting opinion, Justice Brennan lets us know why: "We cannot permit fears of 'riots' and 'civil disobedience' generated by slogans like 'Black Power' to divert our attention from what is here at stake. . . ."[64] *Walker* was decided in 1966, when the nonviolent civil rights movement was metamorphosing into greater militance and the country had witnessed riots in Watts and Harlem spread elsewhere; by 1966, the slogan "Burn, baby, burn!" had raised the fear of self-fueling riots. The Court saw itself confronting a very real possibility of losing its grip.[65]

This perhaps makes the Court's response more comprehensible; it does nothing to render it justifiable. The entire question of the legitimacy of judicial authority remains begged, and begged to its depths. Authority "needs" to be able to stop social protest from getting out of hand. It "needs" to be able to freeze the status quo in emergency situations, even by unconstitutional means. Why is that? To be sure, violence is an intrinsically terrible thing; but the Supreme Court of the United States did not base the "need" to stop matters from getting out of hand on grounds of pacifism, for the United States government is in no respect pacifist.[66] The status quo is itself always maintained by violence, and never more so than in the case of Jim Crow.[67] The ultimate question remains: Why should courts be able legitimately to reserve the power to preserve an unjust status quo of which they are a part, even for a single second, by means that exceed their authority?[68] (This, too, after all, is an example of being a judge in one's own case.)

To freeze the status quo inevitably does more than delay social protest. It destroys it. Social protest is always a miraculous phenomenon; it is irrational for an individual to participate in collective action for social change even when the collective action is itself rational; whether or not the action occurs will never turn on the participation of a single individual, so for each individual it makes more sense to leave the risks and labor to others than to participate.[69] Since this is true for all individuals, social protest is almost always stillborn, suffocated by cords of inertia, mistrust, and self-interest. Moreover, because members of victimized groups typically live in environments with little economic security, it may be more rational for them to emphasize the short run over the long, and thus consent to a substantial level of oppression that nevertheless offers a livelihood, rather than choosing the risky path of seeking structural change.[70]

Social protest can occur only when individuals are stirred in their souls, stirred to act in a way that is not individually rational. For years, or decades, even centuries, the routine of oppression proceeds uninterrupted. Then, inexplicably, at certain privileged moments the curtain lifts and political action flames into existence. At a rally in Manila, or a shipyard strike in Gdansk, or a public funeral in Beijing, or a segregated bus in Montgomery, something unpredictable happens to interrupt the timid calculations of individual rationality. In Benjamin's words,

> Where thinking suddenly stops in a configuration pregnant with tensions, it gives that configuration a shock, by which it crystallizes into a monad. . . . In this structure [the historical materialist] recognizes the sign of a Messianic cessation of happening. . . . He takes cognizance of it in order to blast a specific era out of the homogeneous course of history. . . .[71]

But if that moment—"shot through," as Benjamin says, "with chips of Messianic time"[72] passes, if the momentum of social protest is interrupted, the miracle will no longer occur. The protestors lose their faith, or they must return to their families and jobs, or the media go home, or the instant of dialectical sympathy between the protestors and the larger community, which would draw the larger community into the movement, evaporates. Wyatt Walker recollected: "One option we eliminated was going to court to try to get the injunction dissolved. We knew this would tie us up in court at least ten days to two weeks, and even then we might not get it dissolved. We would have a lengthy lawsuit to appeal but no Birmingham campaign. All of our planning and organizing, a year's effort, would have been in vain, and that was exactly what the city was trying to accomplish by going to court."[73] Bull Connor and Judge Jenkins understood that for a protest movement delay means death. Authority *always* understands that for a protest movement, delay means death. The Supreme Court of the United States understood it. In the *Walker* decision, the Court imposed, so far as it was able, a death sentence on social protest. By what right did the Court cast its vote for existent injustice over social change? Why is a court's claim to authority greater than that of the civil rights movement?

One answer, of course, is that judges are democratically elected or chosen by democratically elected representatives. But this is scarcely a decisive argument, for two reasons: first, in many cases (and notably the case of blacks in the South of 1963) the protest movement has had no part in the democratic process (and the process is itself stacked against oppressed people); and second, the question turns on *unconstitutional* injunctions issued by democratically elected judges.

Ultimately, the *Walker* Court reserved for the judiciary the authority to stifle social protest by any means, constitutional or not. Its assertion of authority is naked, unsupported by anything other than the assertion itself. . . .

III. King's *Letter*

Addressing the NAACP in Atlanta nine months before the Birmingham march, King reminded his law-oriented audience that "legislation and court orders can only declare rights. They can never thoroughly deliver them. Only when the people themselves begin to act are rights on paper given life blood."[74] So apt is this response to the final sentences of Stewart's *Walker* opinion that it is almost as though King had peered into the future to read it. Where the Court sought its panacea in "the civilizing hand of law" rather than "the petitioners' impatient commitment to their cause,"[75] King found legal rights only where "the people themselves begin to act." In the same Atlanta speech King sounded some of the motifs that would later appear in his *Letter,* and indeed employed several of the similes and comparisons that we shall later examine; in part, the Atlanta speech amounts to a prototype of the *Letter*. It shows how deeply King was thinking about the basic tension between juridical institutions and community as the true source of legal authority.

King's *Letter* is a prophetic call to community; so much is obvious from the moment that he enunciates his basic thought: "We are caught in an inescapable network of mutuality, tied in a single garment of destiny."[76] And by its invocation of community—an entity or category so strikingly absent in the *Walker* opinion—King's is a voicing of the Birmingham events that is supplementary or dual to the *Walker* Court's. . . . But King, like the Court, is unsure whether to issue his call in religious or secular terms. The *Letter* in fact has it both ways; therein lies its power but also its deficiency. I shall explain this by looking closely at King's political narratives, his identifications of the actions of himself and his fellow demonstrators with episodes of a larger, more universal history—or, more precisely, with several such histories, some of which are religious in character, some secular. First, to help orient the reader, I briefly summarize the *Letter*.

After an initial greeting to his "fellow clergymen,"[77] King addresses the various accusations that the eight clergymen had leveled in their newspaper advertisement. To the charge that he and his fellow organizers are outside agitators, King asserts the "interrelatedness of all communities and states," and likens himself to St. Paul answering the Macedonian call.[78] To the charge that the demonstrations are "unwise and untimely," King responds by reviewing Birmingham's history of racism and of broken promises to the civil rights movement and outlines the careful steps taken by the campaign to prepare itself for nonviolence.[79] To the charge that the demonstrators have substituted confrontation for negotiation, King responds that it is naive to believe that negotiation will ever take place unless the demonstrators have forced it by creating a "tension" in the community.[80] To the charge that the demonstrators are forcing the issue before giving the Boutwell administration time to do what it can in race relations, King suggests that Boutwell, like Connor, is a segregationist, differing from the latter only in that Connor is more crude. In the most moving and urgent paragraph of the *Letter,* he meditates bitterly on the evils of segregation to illustrate one of his main themes: that "it is easy for those who have never felt the stinging darts of segregation to say, 'Wait,'"[81] but wholly unreasonable to expect long-suffering blacks to remain patient in their suffering.

Next, King addresses a charge that is close to the issue in *Walker*. How can King ask whites to comply with *Brown v. Board of Education* if he is himself prepared to disobey a court order that he doesn't like? In response, King sketches an argument based on a series of distinctions from the natural law tradition: One is obligated to obey just law, but to disobey unjust law. Just law is law that uplifts human personality, whereas unjust law is law that degrades it. Segregation laws, by giving whites a false sense of superiority and blacks a false sense of inferiority, degrade human personality, whereas an integrationist decree such as *Brown* uplifts it and is consequently just. Alternatively, just law is law that applies evenhandedly to minorities and majorities—it is "sameness made legal"—whereas unjust law is law that does not—it is "difference made legal"; by this criterion as well, segregation laws and *Brown* differ fundamentally. Finally, a just law, such as an ordinance requiring marchers to obtain a parade permit, can be enforced selectively (as in Judge Jenkins's injunction), in which case it too is difference made legal and hence unjust. *Ergo, Brown's* decree must be obeyed and segregation laws (including Judge Jenkins's injunction) must be disobeyed.[82]

After answering the white clergymen's accusations, King launches his own. He expresses dismay at white "moderates," who are "more devoted to 'order' than to justice," who agree with the movement's goals but characterize all of its methods as too extreme, and who believe fallaciously that the passage of time will in and of itself end segregation without demonstrators forcing matters.[83] In response, he condemns "the strangely irrational notion that there is something in the very flow of time that will inevitably cure all ills";[84] he then reminds his readers that it is not his nonviolent movement but black nationalist groups such as the Muslims who stand at the extreme of the race issue.[85] King then reflects that on second thought he should willingly accept the "extremist" label, for it puts him in very good company. Since it will concern us later, I reproduce this vital paragraph here for convenience:

> But though I was initially disappointed at being categorized as an extremist, as I continued to think about the matter I gradually gained a measure of satisfaction from the label. Was not Jesus an extremist for love: "Love your enemies, bless them that curse you, do good to them that hate you, and pray for them which despitefully use you, and persecute you." Was not Amos an extremist for justice: "Let justice roll down like waters and righteousness like an ever-flowing stream." Was not Paul an extremist for the Christian gospel: "I bear in my body the marks of the Lord Jesus." Was not Martin Luther an extremist: "Here I stand; I cannot do otherwise, so help me God." And John Bunyan: "I will stay in jail to the end of my days before I make a butchery of my conscience." And Abraham Lincoln: "This nation cannot survive half slave and half free." And Thomas Jefferson: "We hold these truths to be self-evident, that all men are created equal. . . ."[86]

For future reference, let us refer to this as the "extremism passage." We shall return to it several times.

In the concluding pages of the *Letter*, King excoriates the white churches for their failure to embrace the cause of civil rights as a fundamental moral matter.[87] In a prophetic mode, King castigates the churches for urging compliance with civil rights laws merely as a matter of prudence rather than welcoming blacks as brothers and sisters;[88] he thunders that

the churches themselves will face a day of reckoning for their moral failings.[89] Finally, King criticizes the clergymen for congratulating the Birmingham police for "preventing violence"; King bitterly points out that this ignores the police dogs and the violence employed by the police out of sight of the cameras, not to mention that their public restraint was merely a tactic in the service of segregation.[90] In the end, however, King offers a conciliatory closing salutation: "I hope this letter finds you strong in the faith. I also hope that circumstances will soon make it possible for me to meet each of you, not as an integrationist or a civil rights leader but as a fellow clergyman and a Christian brother."[91]

This, however, is a bare summary. The true meaning of the *Letter* lies more in the detailed narratives King offers than in the larger structure of his argument. I shall be focusing on King's identifications of himself and his fellow demonstrators with a variegated but carefully chosen collection of other historical actors. In what I have labeled the "extremism passage,"[92] and elsewhere in the *Letter*, King identifies with biblical characters (Paul, Amos, Jesus, Shadrach, Meshach, and Abednego); with Christian dissidents (unnamed Christian martyrs, Luther, Bunyan); with theological thinkers (Augustine, Aquinas, Buber, Tillich); with American . egalitarians (Jefferson, Lincoln); and with the patron saint of civil disobedience (Socrates). Together, these self-identifications generate a dense and, as we shall see, multiply ambiguous political narrative.

A. *King's Local Narrative*

My primary focus will be on King's political narratives, his efforts to make legal sense of a larger history of which the Birmingham campaign forms just one episode, rather than his local narrative of the Birmingham events. This is because King's local narrative—his description of the Birmingham campaign—tries not to be self-contained, but rather points explicitly outside itself toward the larger political narrative. The local narrative is, to borrow a term from the philosophy of science, "theory laden" to a remarkable extent. King organizes his account of the Birmingham campaign around a theory of direct action rather than a chronological sequence of events. "In any nonviolent campaign there are four basic steps: collection of the facts to determine whether injustices exist; negotiation; self-purification; and direct action. We have gone through all these steps in Birmingham."[93] Having propounded this schema, King proceeds in ordered sequence to describe Birmingham's racist predilections ("to determine whether injustices exist"), the events leading up to the demonstrations, including prior attempts at negotiation ("negotiation"), and the planning of the demonstrations, including workshops in nonviolence ("self-purification"). The local narrative he develops in this way is richer and more inclusive than that of the *Walker* Court; instead of a reductionist recounting of the event as an encounter between authority and individuals, King's narrative vocabulary also includes the civil rights organization and the Birmingham white community itself.

What is noteworthy about King's local narrative, however—apart from the striking set of categories he uses to organize it—is that he says virtually nothing about the demonstrations themselves, the fourth step of his schematism ("direct action"). Or rather, he says virtually nothing about the march, the crowds, the arrest, or the injunction.[94] Instead, he recounts the events by describing what he takes to be the political and spiritual import of direct action:

> Nonviolent direct action seeks to create such a crisis and foster such a tension that a community which has constantly refused to negotiate is forced to confront the issue. It seeks so to dramatize the issue that it can no longer be ignored. . . . Just as Socrates felt that it was necessary to create a tension in the mind so that individuals could rise from the bondage of myths and half-truths to the unfettered realm of creative analysis and objective appraisal, so must we see the need for nonviolent gadflies to create the kind of tension in society that will help men rise from the dark depths of prejudice and racism to the majestic heights of understanding and brotherhood.
>
> The purpose of our direct-action program is to create a situation so crisis-packed that it will inevitably open the door to negotiation.[95]

King, I believe, purposely refuses to recount the events without subsuming them within an account of their purpose.[96] In his narrative vocabulary, a march or a sit-in simply resists flat-footedly behavioral narration. A sit-in attempts to dramatize an issue, and thus to refer beyond itself. And so to describe it in behavioral terms without building that dramatic function into the description would be as misleading as a description of Othello choking Desdemona that omits the fact that the action is occurring in a play. To take another example—one that is highly perti-

nent to King's spiritualized understanding of a direct action campaign—a religious revelation may well resist flatfootedly behavioral narration. ("St. So-and-So knelt in prayer. Two hours later she stood up. That's all, folks!") The physical events that transpired on April 12, 1963 are, in King's narrative apparatus, shadow-events or bare husks whose recitation—here we must think of Stewart's local narrative in *Walker*—misleads and misses the truth of what occurred: a local narrative of crisis and creative tension. . . .[97]

B. King's Biblical Allusions

The literary prototype of King's *Letter* is immediately apparent: the letter is modeled after the epistles of Paul.[98] King confirms this when he writes, "[J]ust as the Apostle Paul left his little village of Tarsus and carried the gospel of Jesus Christ to the far corners of the Greco-Roman world, so am I compelled to carry the gospel of freedom beyond my own home town. Like Paul, I must constantly respond to the Macedonian call for aid."[99] The reference is to the Book of Acts. "And a vision appeared to Paul in the night: a man of Macedonia was standing beseeching him and saying, Come over to Macedonia, and help us."[100] As we shall see, it is highly significant that King likens himself to Paul of the Book of Acts, for this Book is the portion of the Bible closest in its utopian and communitarian ecstasy to King's own basic thought, "We are caught in an inescapable network of mutuality, tied in a single garment of destiny. Whatever affects one directly, affects all indirectly."[101]

None of King's biblical guises—Paul, Amos, Jesus, or even Shadrach, Meshach, and Abednego—are accidental. But Paul's is the most evident, since his guise shapes the literary form of the *Letter*. Why does King assume the guise of Paul? The answer should be clear when we recollect his audience: eight white clergymen. For King, the fact that they were white and the fact that they were clergy combined irresistibly to suggest a parallel with Paul's evangelism, his efforts to weld the people of many nations into a City of God. Paul's epistles are directed to small, insular Christian communities amid larger unbelieving nations. The *Letter* is nothing short of a reminder to brethren in Christ that, black or white, they are, indeed, brethren in Christ, therefore bound together by a bond that knows no distinction of skin color.[102]

The *Letter* is more particular than that, however, as we realize when we turn to the Biblical passages to which King refers. These are: the Book of

Acts, the Book of Amos, Paul's Epistle to the Galatians, the Sermon on the Mount, and the Book of Daniel. I take these up in turn.[103]

In structure, recall, King's *Letter* proceeds from a justification of the Project C demonstrations and of nonviolent civil disobedience more generally to an Old Testament denunciation of contemporary iniquity, particularly the iniquity of pusillanimous white "moderates" and the Southern churches. King moves along a course from communitarian creed to prophetic menace: "But the judgment of God is upon the church as never before."[104] All this is on the surface; but it is also in the depths, contained in the biblical allusions that King deploys, knowing that the clergy who read it would embed it in the biblical narratives it invokes.

Thus, the prophetic stance of King's *Letter* is exhibited clearly in the contrast between the early Christians described in the most explicitly communitarian—even communistic—passages of Acts, the Book to which King points us in his evocation of Paul's call from the Macedonians, and the corrupted Israelites whose religious offerings God angrily rejects in the denunciations of Amos to which King later alludes. Thus the Book of Acts: "And all who believed were together and had all things in common; and they sold their possessions and goods and distributed them to all, as any had need."[105] "Now the company of those who believed were of one heart and soul, and no one said that any of the things which he possessed was his own, but they had everything in common."[106] "There was not a needy person among them, for as many as were possessors of lands or houses sold them, and brought the proceeds of what was sold and laid it at the apostles' feet; and distribution was made to each as any had need."[107] It is noteworthy, and scarcely coincidental, that Marx remembered these passages when, in his most utopian writing, he attributed to the future communist society the principle "from each according to his ability, to each according to his needs!"[108] For these passages from Acts have inspired utopian communists for over a thousand years.[109] Moreover, they inspired the Social Gospel theologian Walter Rauschenbusch to draw parallels between the Bible and Marxism, in a book that impressed King deeply in his seminary days.[110]

This is the City of God as it should be. Compare this with King's reference to the Book of Amos, one of the Bible's most vituperative denunciations of the actual community's unrighteousness. The line he quotes from Amos is this: "Let justice roll down

like waters and righteousness like an ever-flowing stream."[111] Amos' line appears in the context of a ghastly denunciation of a corrupted Israel:

> Therefore because you trample upon the poor and take from him exactions of wheat, you have built houses of hewn stone, but you shall not dwell in them; you have planted pleasant vineyards, but you shall not drink their wine. For I know how many are your transgressions, and how great are your sins— you who afflict the righteous, who take a bribe, and turn aside the needy in the gate.[112]

The applicability of these charges to the segregated South need scarcely be remarked ("turning aside the needy in the gate" may well stand as a literal description of Bull Connor's action in arresting King and his fellow demonstrators as they marched to downtown Birmingham). And because of these sins, religious observances will avail the unrighteous not at all:

> I hate, I despise your feasts, and I take no delight in your solemn assemblies. Even though you offer me your burnt offerings and cereal offerings, I will not accept them, and the peace offerings of your fatted beasts I will not look upon. Take away from me the noise of your songs; to the melody of your harps I will not listen. *But let justice roll down like waters, and righteousness like an ever-flowing stream.*[113]

The line King quotes thus appears in a passage that would convey a stern, even terrifying reminder to the clergymen to whom King's letter is addressed.

As I noted earlier, King likens himself (for the second time in the *Letter*) to Paul immediately following his reference to Amos in the extremism passage. This reference too directs us to a biblical passage fraught with significance, for it bears with startling directness on King's confrontation with the courts. The line King quotes, "I bear in my body the marks of the Lord Jesus,"[114] appears at the end of the Epistle to the Galatians, the most fervid of all New Testament declarations that love and community stand above the law. Paul could not be more blunt: "Christ redeemed us from the curse of the law. . . ."[115] And again: "Now before faith came, we were confined under the law, kept under restraint until faith should be revealed. So that the law was our custodian until Christ came, that we might be justified by faith. But now that faith has come, we are no longer under a custodian. . . ."[116] Paul evokes the mystical, hence translegal, character of egalitarian community in language that resonates with King's aspirations for the redeemed American polity: "There is neither Jew nor Greek, there is neither slave nor free, there is neither male nor female; for you are all one in Christ Jesus."[117] (Compare this with the finale of the "I have a dream" speech: "all of God's children—black men and white men, Jews and Gentiles, Protestants and Catholics—will be able to join hands. . . .") "For the whole law is fulfilled in one word, 'You shall love your neighbor as yourself.'"[118] Community and brotherhood in faith trump fidelity to established law. Indeed, the Book of Acts, which we have seen forms one of King's referential reservoirs, itself contains an explicit statement of the same antinomian principle: "We must obey God rather than men."[119]

This carries us quite naturally to King's reference to Jesus. The "Love your enemies" verse that King quotes in the extremism passage appears, of course, in the Sermon on the Mount.[120] Significantly, it is the continuation of this verse: "You have heard that it was said, 'You shall love your neighbor and hate your enemy.' But I say to you, *Love your enemies and pray for those who persecute you.*"[121] Christ's allusion here is to *Leviticus* 19:18, "You shall not take vengeance or bear any grudge against the sons of your own people, but you shall love your neighbor as yourself: I am the Lord." He interprets the Levitican injunction to love your neighbor as a negative pregnant: an implicit restriction of the injunction to those who are like oneself; the Sermon on the Mount radicalizes the message of love by extending it to those unlike oneself. Small wonder that King would invoke this biblical passage, since extending the injunction of love from one's own people to all people is precisely the universalist and cosmopolitan theme of King's *Letter.*[122]

A more important point is this. We recall that in the Epistle to the Galatians, to which King alludes shortly after his reference to Jesus, Paul takes this passage from the Sermon on the Mount to reject the Mosaic law. ("Christ redeemed us from the curse of the law. . . . For the whole law is fulfilled in one word, 'You shall love your neighbor as yourself.'"[123]) Yet this is not how Christ himself characterized the Sermon's import. On the contrary, Christ cautions, "Think not that I have come to abolish the law and the prophets; I have come not to abolish them but to fulfil them. For truly, I say to you, till heaven and earth pass away, not an iota, not a dot, will pass from the law until all is accomplished."[124]

Now it is possible to reconcile Paul's and Christ's characterizations of what Christ has done to the law when he proclaims "Love your neighbor as yourself." Christ has proclaimed, "I am not come to abolish [the law] but to fulfill," and Paul satisfies the letter of this warning when he writes, "For the whole law is fulfilled in one word, You shall love your neighbor as yourself." Yet that is surely not what Christ preached in the Sermon, where "You shall love your neighbor as yourself" appears as but one of a dozen or more revaluations of the Mosaic law, occupying no privileged position. Paul's is an idiosyncratic reinterpretation of Christ's own word, transforming the Sermon on the Mount into an antinomian religion of love.

There is, however, another way to reconcile the attitudes toward law expressed in these two biblical passages (if not their religious substance). Paul understands the Sermon on the Mount to be Christ's radicalization, or purposive revaluation, of the Mosaic law—a radicalization that amounts to its rejection. Christ demands the fulfillment of the law's underlying purpose, which indeed annihilates it as (mis)interpreted by the "scribes and Pharisees."[125] On this reading, Paul's antinomian dicta merely make explicit what was indeed implicit in the Sermon: that in the fulfillment of the law's spirit lies the destruction of its received juristic interpretation. And King, by juxtaposing the Sermon with Paul's epistle to the Galatians, invites his readers to interpret the sermon in just this way: as an authoritative unofficial reading of the law that in effect overthrows the official reading. As we shall see, King's own analysis of legality in the *Letter* takes just such a tack.

Notwithstanding this interpretive finesse, there is no denying that Paul's "Christ has redeemed us from the curse of the law" and the Sermon on the Mount's "Do not think that I have come to abolish the Law" are quite different in tenor and import—the latter assuming the mantle of legality, the former proclaiming what Kierkegaard would have deemed a "teleological suspension of the legal."[126] It will be part of my argument that King's *Letter* itself vacillates between these two stances, with important consequences.

The fact that King evidently saw no inconsistency between the Sermon on the Mount and the epistle to the Galatians is important, for Paul's equation of the law's end with the law's fulfillment readily transposes into a justification of King's civil rights activity: if there is any obvious legal theme to the *Letter* it is that the end of the segregationist legal order is the fulfillment, the purposive revaluation, of the constitutional promise of equal protection. (I return to this point below.) King's is an authoritative unofficial reading of the Constitution that overthrows Southern officials' readings. . . .

Let me summarize my reading of King's biblical allusions. The key points are these.

(1) King underscores his own communitarianism by invoking the God-intoxicated, overtly communistic, egalitarian Christian community of the Book of Acts.

(2) King places the cosmopolitan and universalist message of the civil rights movement side-by-side with cosmopolitan and universalist passages of the Bible such as "There is neither Jew nor Greek, there is neither slave nor free, there is neither male nor female; for you are all one in Christ Jesus"[127] and the Sermon on the Mount.

(3) King echoes his denunciation of the existing church by alluding to Amos' denunciations of Israel for empty, impious observances of a law that has become merely formal.

(4) Crucially, King singles out passages in which the formal legality of Israel is either fulfilled— *aufgehoben,* to utilize Hegel's word once again—by the Christian law of love or, in the important alternative, annihilated by it.[128] That is, King points ambiguously in the incompatible directions of a higher law of love or a divine antinomianism. And thus the earlier themes of communitarianism, cosmopolitanism, and denunciation waffle dangerously between natural law legalism—a theme that is capable of purely secular development—and mystical anarchism, a doctrine of love grounded in the revelation of divinity. Insofar as King identifies himself more closely with Paul than with Jesus, he seems to tilt a bit more toward the latter alternative.

(5) This is in no way to deny that King speaks often and reverently of the law: the natural law and legalist strain in the *Letter* is totally authentic. Yet legalism, too, becomes a communitarian and universalist tool in King's hands. For it is clear that King advocates what Levinson calls the "protestant" mode of legal interpretation, in which the individual, or at any rate the nonhierarchical community, retains ultimate interpretive authority. As we have seen, the *Walker* Court has built its entire argument around the necessity of the catholic approach, in which the

Court/Church—the *curia*—is the sole repository of interpretive authority. Levinson's eloquent argument for the coincidence of religious and constitutional hermeneutics is nowhere more telling than in the contrast between *Walker* and King's *Letter.* The contrast is simply Catholicism and Protestantism revisited. Indeed, in King's *Letter* "protestant" interpretation of the Constitution quite simply coincides with Protestantism itself, King's own religious commitment. This makes two of King's other self-identifications in the extremism passage fall immediately into place: "Was not Martin Luther an extremist: 'Here I stand; I cannot do otherwise, so help me God.' And John Bunyan: 'I will stay in jail to the end of my days before I make a butchery of my conscience.'"[129] Luther's "stand," of course, inaugurated the Protestant reformation, and Bunyan was jailed for his Puritan preaching.[130]

(6) Finally, it is clear that King's chain of religious self-identifications, his transposition of the Birmingham events into a biblical key, offers a political narrative that refigures and reconstitutes the legal meaning of those events. In the sense explicated in my opening discussion, King's "biblicizing" of the Birmingham campaign in the *Letter* is legal argumentation in the full and unqualified sense.

C. King's Natural Law Theory

The ambivalence I have described between King's natural law legalism and what I have called his mystical anarchism pervades the argumentative or conceptual portion of the *Letter* just as it does the chain of biblical self-identifications. King's argument arises, recall, as an attempt to explain why he is willing to disobey a court order while continuing to urge white obedience to the Supreme Court's desegregation orders: "[T]here are two types of law: just and unjust. . . . One has not only a legal but a moral responsibility to obey just laws. Conversely, one has a moral responsibility to disobey unjust laws. I would agree with St. Augustine that 'an unjust law is no law at all.'"[131] King then offers what I take to be two separate accounts of the distinction between just and unjust laws. The first is a theological and mystical account:

> A just law is a manmade code that squares with the moral law or the law of God. An unjust law is a code that is out of harmony with the moral law. To put it in the terms of St. Thomas Aquinas: An unjust law is a

human law that is not rooted in eternal law and natural law. Any law that uplifts human personality is just. Any law that degrades human personality is unjust. All segregation statutes are unjust because segregation distorts the soul and damages the personality. It gives the segregator a false sense of superiority and the segregated a false sense of inferiority. Segregation, to use the terminology of the Jewish philosopher Martin Buber, substitutes an "I-it" relationship for an "I-thou" relationship and ends up relegating persons to the status of things. Hence segregation is not only politically, economically and sociologically unsound, it is morally wrong and sinful. Paul Tillich has said that sin is separation. Is not segregation an existential expression of man's tragic separation, his awful estrangement, his terrible sinfulness? Thus it is that I can urge men to obey the 1954 decision of the Supreme Court, for it is morally right; and I can urge them to disobey segregation ordinances, for they are morally wrong.[132]

The second is a secular and essentially liberal argument based on considerations of fairness:

> An unjust law is a code that a numerical or power[ful] majority group compels a minority group to obey but does not make binding on itself. This is *difference* made legal. By the same token, a just law is a code that a majority compels a minority to follow and that it is willing to follow itself. This is *sameness* made legal.
>
> Let me give another explanation. A law is unjust if it is inflicted on a minority that, as a result of being denied the right to vote, had no part in enacting or devising the law. . . . Can any law enacted under such circumstances be considered democratically structured?
>
> Sometimes a law is just on its face and unjust in its application. For instance, I have been arrested on a charge of parading without a permit. Now, there is nothing wrong in having an ordinance which requires a permit for a parade. But such an ordinance becomes unjust when it is used to maintain segregation and to deny citizens the First Amendment privilege of peaceful assembly and protest.[133]

I take it that the difference between these two descriptions of natural law theory is readily apparent

even on the surface. The first implicitly presumes that "eternal law and natural law" are fulfilled by the end of separation between human beings, the effacement of boundary and even of the very possibility of boundary signified by Buber's "basic word I-thou." For Buber, indeed, it understates matters even to say that "I-thou" entails a fusion of I and thou, for the very thought of two distinct entities that fuse belongs itself to the sphere of I-it. Here King's thought is close to Paul's insistence in Galatians that divine law achieves its fulfillment in the single injunction to love, and that "you are all one in Christ Jesus." This is communitarianism as mystical union.

By contrast, the second characterization of natural law as "sameness made legal" emphasizes values of process, participation, and democratic equality. In my view it is best understood as a version of the fair play argument of Hart and Rawls, according to which we are obligated to obey the law only insofar as the law is a cooperative enterprise requiring and receiving widespread compliance to achieve its beneficial aims.[134] Insofar as the law is unfair ("difference made legal"), it cannot be understood as such a generally beneficial cooperative scheme, and thus it loses its obligatory character.

To lay my cards on the table, I believe that this argument is exactly right.[135] But make no mistake: it is an argument wholly secular in character. It rests on a premise of human political equality that presumes no theological revelation of human unity in Christ (or out of Christ, for that matter). This premise arises from a nonbiblical political narrative of the American Constitution; indeed, we shall see that King himself provides such a narrative in the extremism passage when he likens himself to Jefferson and Lincoln.

The fair play argument, moreover, is grounded in the characteristically liberal political relationship of *mutual respect,* not in the mystical and loving communitarianism implicit in King's invocation of Buber and Tillich.[136] Obviously, the two arguments parallel each other in important respects: both ground legal obligation in equality, both attack the monstrous premise of white superiority underlying racial segregation, and both vindicate disobedience to segregation-preserving laws as well as obedience to the Court's *Brown* decision. But the difference between love and respect as defining relationships for the egalitarian community decisively distinguishes the two arguments. The purpose of any community-defining relationship is to establish social trust, but love and respect do so in quite different ways.[137] For the primary concern of love is to abolish the distance between people, while that of respect is to maintain it. . . .

In short, the two versions of King's natural law argument in the *Letter* correspond to the ambiguity between viewing the Christian narrative as a perfection of the law and as the mystical *Aufhebung* of it implicit in King's earlier juxtaposition of the Sermon on the Mount with Galatians.

D. *King's American Allusions*

This ambiguity emerges as well in the difference between King's biblical and secular political narratives. Just as King's biblical allusions in the extremism passage point—ambiguously, to be sure—in the direction of antinomian mysticism, his secular allusions point toward liberal natural law egalitarianism. The secular argument, recall, derives egalitarianism from the notion of fairness incipient in natural law. This entails a particular political narrative of American constitutionalism, one that tells the story of constitutional progress as the drive toward emancipation and equality.

Thus we find, immediately after King likens himself to Jesus, Amos, Paul, Luther, and Bunyan in the extremism passage, the invocation of Lincoln and Jefferson: "Was not Martin Luther an extremist. . . . And John Bunyan. . . . And Abraham Lincoln: 'This nation cannot survive half slave and half free.' And Thomas Jefferson: 'We hold these truths to be self-evident, that all men are created equal. . . .' "[138]

Jefferson and Lincoln are well-coupled. After all, it was Lincoln who, in the Gettysburg Address, claimed that the true meaning of America lay in Jefferson's Declaration of Independence rather than in the Constitution: he characterized America as "a new nation . . . dedicated to the proposition that all men are created equal." Dulled by long familiarity, we are inclined to read this sentence without giving it a second thought (or even a first thought), without realizing that it is a powerfully heretical—because deconstitutionalized—interpretation of the meaning of American history.[139] King's political narrative draws a straight line from Jefferson and Lincoln through the civil war Amendments that finally constitutionalized this interpretation to the civil rights movement, and indicates that egalitarianism is the imminent truth of America.

He also, if I read him aright, alludes in the most powerful passage of the *Letter* to another link in this political narrative, the Court's opinion in *Brown v. Board of Education*. King bitterly meditates on his experience as a black parent,

> when you suddenly find your tongue twisted and your speech stammering as you seek to explain to your six-year-old daughter why she can't go to the public amusement park that has just been advertised on television, and see tears welling up in her eyes when she is told that Funtown is closed to colored children, and see ominous clouds of inferiority beginning to form in her little mental sky, and see her beginning to distort her personality by developing an unconscious bitterness toward white people. . . .[140]

Surely King is here alluding to Kenneth Clark's experiments on self-perceptions of inferiority among black children, which formed the sociological linchpin of the *Brown* opinion. Rhetorically, the allusion is strikingly well-suited to the white clergymen to whom the *Letter* was addressed; just as his biblical allusions attempted to preach Christian community to the clergymen, the allusion to *Brown* attempts to remind white Americans of their unkept promise of equality. As part of a political narrative, *Brown* is another point on the line from Jefferson through Lincoln and the fourteenth amendment to the civil rights movement—a narrative line that aims to recall the promise of egalitarian constitutionalism incipient in *Brown* as a continuation of Lincoln's and Jefferson's political vision.

To summarize my reading so far, I have been tracing two versions of communitarianism in King's *Letter*: a religious and antinomian communitarianism based on love, and a liberal natural law egalitarianism aiming at communities based on respect. King's biblical narratives, particularly his self-identification with Paul, point ambiguously toward the former, whereas his American political narrative clearly points in the latter direction.

E. *King's Socratic Allusion*

King's *Letter* incorporates one final self-identification. At two points King likens his own actions in Birmingham and those of his fellow demonstrators to Socrates, who "felt that it was necessary to create a tension in the mind so that individuals could rise from the bondage of myths and half-truths to the unfettered realm of creative analysis and objective appraisal."[141] King goes on to analogize the Birmingham demonstrators to "nonviolent gadflies," Socrates' self-description in the *Apology*.[142] Later he alludes again to the condemnation of Socrates: "Isn't [condemning the Birmingham demonstrators for provoking violence] like condemning Socrates because his unswerving commitment to truth and his philosophical inquiries precipitated the act by the misguided populace in which they made him drink hemlock?"[143] Though I shall later have occasion to doubt the appropriateness of the Socratic analogy, there is indeed an uncanny parallel between the moral and legal problem posed by King's arrest and a perplexing dilemma posed in Plato's *Apology* and *Crito*.

The dilemma is easily seen. In the *Apology* Socrates boasts that he has always been unwilling to comply with unjust official orders, including court orders. Thus, when the Thirty Tyrants had ordered him to arrest Leon the Salaminian unjustly, so as "to implicate as many in their crimes as they could," Socrates merely went home; he tells his jurors that he would have died for his disobedience had the government not fallen soon after.[144] And earlier in his defense Socrates provokes his jurors by telling them that if they were to order him, on pain of death, to abandon his philosophical activities, he would reply: "Men of Athens, I respect and love you, but I shall obey the god rather than you, and while I live and am able to continue, I shall never give up philosophy."[145]

The *Apology* is thus the protean text of conscientious disobedience, and King's appropriation of the figure of Socrates seems completely clear. In the *Crito,* however, the convicted Socrates refuses to flee his impending execution, offering a series of arguments that he is obligated to obey the laws, including his own unjust death sentence. These arguments, based on consent or the "social contract," on gratitude, on the citizen's tutelage under government, and on the dire consequences were everyone to disobey, have shaped all subsequent philosophical discussions of the subject.[146] The facial contradiction with the *Apology* could scarcely be more striking, and it has puzzled generations of commentators. If it is wrong to disobey even unjust laws and court orders, why did Socrates disobey the Thirty Tyrants? How could he boast that he would continue to practice philosophy in the face of a court order to desist? On the other hand, if it is right to disobey an unjust edict, why should Socrates have complied with his death sentence?

Recently, Richard Kraut has offered a remarkable interpretation of the *Crito* aiming to show that, far from an encomium to absolute obedience and submission, it is actually a powerful argument on behalf of civil disobedience that is fully consistent with

the *Apology*.[147] Kraut focuses on Socrates' careful phrasing of his arguments for obedience in the *Crito*. Rather than concluding categorically that one must obey the laws, Socrates three times phrases the injunction in the alternative: one must *either* persuade the state as to the nature of justice *or else* obey.[148] Now this may suggest that Socrates is offering the unhelpful thought that the citizen may try to get a law changed or repealed, but if he fails he must obey. Since in practice one will seldom be able to get a law repealed, this suggestion amounts to precisely the encomium to absolute obedience.

Kraut responds that the forum Socrates had in mind for persuasion is not the legislature but the court.[149] And persuasion is not an attempt to get the law changed *before* obeying it, but an attempt to argue against a criminal conviction *after* disobeying it. That is, Socrates' position amounts to permitting one to disobey an unjust law provided one is subsequently willing to offer a defense in court, and accept the punishment if the jury rejects that defense.

Kraut's reading of the *Crito* makes a lot of the text fall into place, and ingeniously resolves the facial contradiction between the *Apology* and the *Crito*.[150] However, there is one situation that Kraut's reading fails to resolve. What if a court, unpersuaded by the disobedient citizen, does not punish him for disobedience but merely reiterates the order to obey? That, after all, is the hypothetical situation Socrates himself raises in which at the conclusion of his trial the jury orders him to abandon philosophy. He tells the jurors that he will disobey; but since he has failed to persuade, must he not obey?

The problem is this. Kraut seems to assume that disobedience will precede persuasion: you are hailed into court because you have disobeyed. Then you attempt to persuade, and if you fail you take your punishment. But when the court responds not with punishment but with another order, persuasion has failed *before* the choice between obedience and disobedience to the new order must be made. Now, surely, Socrates' persuade-or-obey conclusion leaves you no option but obedience; for it is plainly no answer to suggest disobeying the new court order, being hailed into court again, attempting once again to persuade, failing, receiving another court order, disobeying, and so on ad infinitum. That is simply a ruse for making an end run around the "obey" horn of the dilemma. No: if Socrates fails at persuasion and is subsequently ordered to abandon philosophy, Kraut's version of the persuade-or-obey doctrine requires obedience. Yet Socrates has told us he will disobey. And so the contradiction has not, after all, been resolved.

The basic dilemma between conscience and obligation reappears, that is, when a citizen is faced with an unjust court order (rather than an unjust punishment). It is this problem, in almost precisely this form, that the Birmingham events raise. One political narrative, then—the narrative of conscientious disobedience, from Socrates on—stands ready to offer placement to the argument between the *Walker* Court and King.

I do not mean to suggest that when he alluded to Socrates in the *Letter* King had anything in mind as specific as the textual inconsistency between the *Apology* and the *Crito,* to say nothing of classicists' arguments about it. Significantly, however, King invoked both dialogues in his Atlanta NAACP address, which (I noted earlier) amounts to a preliminary version of portions of the *Letter:* "Come if you will to Plato's *Dialogues.* Open the *Crito* or the *Apology.* See Socrates practicing civil disobedience."[151] In the *Letter,* King clearly *did* have the *Apology* itself in mind and the dilemma between conscience and obedience is the explicit subject matter of the *Letter*'s argumentative portion. And we have seen King's own resolution of the dilemma. He offers an argument for the moral obligation to obey the law that is distinct from the standard arguments of the *Crito;* all of those arguments attempt to explain the obligation to obey the law as an obligation to the state, whereas the fair-play argument offered by King explains it as an obligation to one's fellow citizens. It is a communitarian, rather than a statist, argument for obedience to just laws. And it yields the conclusion that this obligation exists only when the law in question reflects "sameness made legal" rather than "difference made legal"—only, that is, when the law is fair. Thus, King maintains the tradition of the *Apology* by abandoning the statism implicit in the *Crito.*

Where does the Socratic narrative of civil disobedience fit into the tension between mystical anarchism and natural law legalism I have been stressing? At first Socrates seems to belong in the second camp: natural law is closely tied to the rationalist ethical vision that appears in numerous Socratic dialogues, particularly the *Euthyphro* (and, ambiguously, the *Phaedo,* where the rationalism assumes distinctly mystical overtones). Moreover, Plato has long been identified as a principal source for the natural law tradition.

Nevertheless, it is noteworthy that neither in the *Apology* nor elsewhere does Socrates claim to be responding to a "higher law." Rather, he repeatedly says that he is responding to a divine call. Socrates tells us that the god at Delphi originally launched his philosophical career,[152] and he reveals to the Athenians that he is guided in all his endeavors by a divine voice, his famous *daimon,* that warns him whenever he is about to do anything wrong.[153] Socrates' *daimon* is instantly recognizable as what later ages would call "the voice of conscience"; and it is important to realize that Socrates identifies conscience, and therefore conscientious disobedience, with fidelity to a supernatural being. Viewed as the prototypical conscientious disobedient, as King clearly views him, Socrates is much more the religious saint than the natural law adherent. And so King's Socratic self-identification falls more plausibly on the side of his mystical anarchism than on the side of his natural law legalism.

IV. The Tension Between Religion and Politics

So far my examination has stayed reasonably close to the actual language and range of allusion within *Walker* and King's *Letter.* In this section, I wish to venture further afield and explore the consequences this examination carries for social change as well as legal argument. I shall be borrowing again from Benjamin's *Theses,* but also from a remarkably interesting essay on civil disobedience written by Hannah Arendt during the height of the Black Power, student, and anti-war movements, an essay that trenchantly addresses some of the issues I have raised.[154]

A. Arendt on the Self-Misunderstanding of Civil Disobedience

It should be clear from our foregoing examination that King's *Letter* contains a narrative complexity and richness wholly absent from the *Walker* opinion.[155] It also, I fear, contains a fundamental self-*mis*understanding with serious consequences. King's Socratic allusion may serve us as a point of entry to the discussion of this self-misunderstanding.

In her extraordinary essay on civil disobedience, Hannah Arendt points out the falseness of identifying politically motivated civil disobedience with the figure of Socrates (and of Thoreau as well).[156] As we have seen, Socrates opposes his conscience, which we might think of as an organ attuned to the supernatural, to the demands of the state. Conscientious civil disobedients are essentially solitary figures in communion with divinity; they are essentially unpolitical. Thus, the tension between King's mystical anarchism and his natural law legalism points to a tension between conscience and politics in his thought that effaces the political character of the movement by comprehending it through supernatural political narratives. Arendt writes:

> Here, as elsewhere, conscience is unpolitical. It is not primarily interested in the world where the wrong is committed or in the consequences that the wrong will have for the future course of the world. It does not say, with Jefferson, "I tremble *for my country* when I reflect that God is just; that His justice cannot sleep forever," because it trembles for the individual self and its integrity.[157]

The point, once made, is obvious: there is an important sense in which Socrates, like Paul and Amos and Shadrach and Luther and Bunyan, does not belong in the same political narrative as the Southern Christian Leadership Conference. The defining relationship of Socrates' public stance, like the figures in the biblical narratives, was a relationship with a divine voice.[158] This relationship, to be sure, manifested itself in a politically significant action, but in the case of Socrates that was happenstance. This is in no way to deny the obvious, namely that religiously inspired people can be canny politicians and publicists. Paul and Luther were. But, unless we take Paul and Luther to be lying at the core of their being, their political acumen accrued to them (to speak scholastically) *per accidens;* it was their God-consciousness that defined their public stance *per essens.* And so the theological narratives contained in King's *Letter* may actually suppress or displace an explicitly political self-understanding of political action by substituting relationships with the divinity for political relationships. . . .[159]

Lest these suggestions create a misunderstanding, let me emphasize that I have chosen to analyze King's *Letter* not because of its narrative weaknesses, but because of its overwhelming strength. More importantly, I have been concerned throughout this essay to stress that the *non*biblical strand of the *Letter* promotes a remarkably attractive—let me go so far as to say "true"—political and legal theory. It is my view that King has pointed the way to a truly liberal communitarianism (a political possibility that philosophers have often neglected or denied[160]); that his fair-play

version of natural law resolves the Platonic problem of political obligation; and that his narrative of American political history from Jefferson to Lincoln to *Brown* to Project C displays the fourteenth amendment to our Constitution in what may well be the best light it can truthfully sustain.[161] These are virtues for which we may well be moved to abandon the antinomianism of the epistle to the Galatians and the political narrative of supernaturally-inspired conscientious disobedience from Socrates through Bunyan. . . .

V. Conclusion: On Our Weak Messianic Power

My discussion of King's *Letter* has attempted to separate out two strains of his thinking, one essentially religious and one essentially secular. I have urged the priority of the secular side, both as a more credible form of communitarian political association and as a more authentic basis for political action.

At the same time, however, I have suggested that political authority and political action are best understood in terms that are thoroughly theological. Benjamin's *Theses,* upon which I have relied so extensively in this essay, speaks recurrently about the messianic nature of political upheaval. To speak of the Messiah is to speak of a miraculous intervention into human affairs inaugurating an epoch that has broken decisively with what has hitherto constituted our history. Benjamin thus implies that political action amounts to just such a miraculous intervention.

Benjamin evokes a specifically Jewish tradition of messianism.[162] On this view the Messiah occupies a uniquely past-oriented and backward-looking position: the Messiah's purpose is not only, indeed not even primarily, to create a better future, but rather to redeem the past and make meaningful the sufferings of the Jewish people. Benjamin speaks in the final thesis about a rabbinic tradition that prohibits Jews from investigating the future,[163] and earlier he had emphasized that the spirit of sacrifice is "nourished by the image of enslaved ancestors rather than that of liberated grandchildren."[164] Political action is messianic not only because it blasts the present moment out of the continuum of history, but because its aim is first and foremost to redeem the past.

This is not meant figuratively; rather, Benjamin—like King—suggests that political action transforms the structure of history, interrupting the calendrical sequence ("homogeneous, empty time") and stitching together past and present, so that the present redeems the past by reenacting it—literally, by *becoming* it.

What can this mean? The notion of discrete moments in the calendrical sequence fusing is, of course, a highly mystical one, and, we may fear, it is for that very reason a nonsensical one. Indeed, the claim that discrete—numerically distinct—moments are numerically identical is simply a self-contradiction. What Benjamin had in mind, I believe, was not the numerical identity of past and present, but rather bringing the past back to life through celebration and commemoration, particularly where these include not just retelling the past but reenacting it. "The initial day of a calendar serves as a historical time-lapse camera. And, basically, it is the same day that keeps recurring in the guise of holidays, which are days of remembrance. Thus the calendars do not measure time as clocks do. . . ."[165] Here Benjamin may have had in mind not only the theological notion of holidays—holy days—as interruptions of clock-time devoted to remembrance, but also the thought that Nietzsche once described as the "high point of the meditation": "That *everything recurs* is the closest *approximation of a world of becoming to a world of being*."[166] A series of reenactments is the closest mortal approximation to immortality; we resurrect and redeem enslaved ancestors by refighting their battles for freedom.

Here it is useful to draw an analogy to improvisatory musical pieces, such as jazz compositions, which are realized differently in each performance. No archetype exists, and we understand precisely what it means to say that the piece is brought to life, and indeed lives, only in its realizations, even though the realizations differ widely from one another. In the same category as jazz compositions we may place many folk-arts: dances that have never been notated but are simply handed down from dancer to dancer, epic poems in preliterate societies, folk songs, and—most to the point—folk tales and stories. Such stories exist only in the retelling, and their retelling, like all acts of collective memory, revives the past by commemorating it. The very etymology of the word "commemorate"—literally, commemorate, "to remember together"—suggests the combining of two epochs in one memory, and the collective character of that memory.

Benjamin's idea amounts to the assertion that political action should be seen as a device of collective memory in precisely this sense.[167] In Benjamin's words: "There is a secret agreement between past generations and the present one. Our coming was expected on earth. Like every generation that preceded us, we have been endowed with a *weak* Messianic power, a power to which the past has a claim."[168] It is a "weak" Messianic power, of course, because no generation is truly the Messiah promised by religion; we will not end history, and believing that we can is a millenarian delusion.[169] Our power to act is messianic nonetheless because our victorious struggle for the privilege of recounting the past makes sense of past suffering. The successful outcome of the Birmingham campaign makes sense of the deaths incurred by the campaign, and, to a certain ("weak") extent, the sufferings endured by 400 years of black experience in America.

I am laboring this point because I believe it is central not only for a theory of political action but also for a theory of legal argument. It is, indeed, the view of legal argument that I sketched at the outset of this essay: legal argument succeeds when it demonstrates that a local narrative has reenacted an episode of a political narrative, and thus that the two have become stitched together, paired in affinity. Legal argument understood as persuasion, hence as political action, works in a medium of historical time that is backward-looking and redemptive in structure.

This account contrasts starkly with another influential view of legal argument: on this view, which Ronald Dworkin has called "pragmatism," legal argument is entirely forward-looking, seeking only to create a better future and remaining generally oblivious to the past.[170] On this view . . . a legal argument consists largely of an attempt to predict and assess the likely future consequences of a judicial decision; it seeks to show that a certain outcome would yield the best consequences overall.

My quarrel is not with the notion that we should aim to achieve the best consequences overall, but rather with the notion that the best consequences are to be sought by peering into the future—in Frankfurter's words, attempting "[t]o pierce the curtain of the future, to give shape and visage to mysteries still in the womb of time."[171] Partly, this is because I have little faith in our predictive powers; more fundamentally, however, I am arguing that the consequences we seek are in large measure to be sought in the past—as Benjamin says, "our image of happiness is indissolubly bound up with the image of redemption."[172] We achieve happiness in the thought that we have resurrected the memory of our dead ancestors, rescued their history from the defamations of their enemies, and therefore given ourselves a past that makes us comprehensible.[173] That is the true function of legal narrative.

Perhaps the most self-conscious example of an exclusively forward-looking view of the sort I am criticizing is found not in legal pragmatism, but in Marx. At the beginning of his greatest historical work, *The Eighteenth Brumaire of Louis Bonaparte*, Marx writes, "Hegel remarks somewhere that all great, world-historical facts and personages occur, as it were, twice. He has forgotten to add: the first time as tragedy, the second as farce."[174] Marx understands full well that revolutionary action is typically backward-looking, seeking to explain itself by assimilation to a political narrative of the past; but unlike Benjamin (and me), he finds the attempt to be farcical, grotesque superstition:

> The tradition of all the dead generations weighs like a nightmare on the brain of the living. And just when they seem engaged in revolutionizing themselves and things, in creating something entirely new, precisely in such epochs of revolutionary crisis they anxiously conjure up the spirits of the past to their service and borrow from them names, battle slogans and costumes in order to present the new scene of world history in this time-honoured disguise and this borrowed language. Thus Luther donned the mask of the Apostle Paul, the Revolution of 1789 to 1814 draped itself alternately as the Roman Republic and the Roman Empire, and the Revolution of 1848 knew nothing better to do than to parody, in turn, 1789, and the revolutionary tradition of 1793 to 1795.
>
> . . . Similarly, at another stage of development, . . . Cromwell and the English people had borrowed speech, passions and illusions from the Old Testament for their bourgeois revolution. When the real aim had been achieved, when the bourgeois transformation of English society had been accomplished, Locke supplanted Habakkuk.[175]

After heaping his considerable scorn on backward-looking, ghost-ridden and superstitious revolutionaries, Marx arrives at this passionate exhortation:

> The social revolution of the nineteenth century cannot draw its poetry from the past, but only from the future. It cannot begin with itself before it has stripped off all superstition

in regard to the past. Earlier revolutions required world-historical recollections in order to drug themselves concerning their own content. In order to arrive at its own content, the revolution of the nineteenth century must let the dead bury their dead.[176]

It has been my argument that these brave and passionate words amount to a profound misunderstanding of our possibilities of action. Marx aims to eliminate superstition and theology, to disenchant us; similarly, legal pragmatists aim at a disenchanted view of legal argument. In my view, it cannot be done; let me turn for the last time to Walter Benjamin, who offered the following parable in criticism of the scientific and disenchanted vision offered by orthodox Marxism:

> The story is told of an automaton constructed in such a way that it could play a winning game of chess, answering each move of an opponent with a countermove. A puppet in Turkish attire and with a hookah in its mouth sat before a chessboard placed on a large table. A system of mirrors created the illusion that this table was transparent from all sides. Actually, a little hunchback who was an expert chess player sat inside and guided the puppet's hand by means of strings. One can image a philosophical counterpart to this device. The puppet called "historical materialism" is to win all the time. It can easily be a match for anyone if it enlists the services of theology, which today, as we know, is wizened and has to keep out of sight.[177]

This parable returns us to King, but also to *Walker*. In Benjamin's ingenious jest we may find not only a critique of Marx, who was forced to smuggle in his theology in the form of a necessitarian theory of historical change, but a moral applicable to the *Walker* Court as well. Instead of calling Benjamin's puppet "historical materialism," call it "the civilizing hand of law," which must win all the time if the judicial suppression of social protest is to be justified. I have argued that the Court buttresses its preposterous deification of law's efficacy by a theological reliance on authority, and this may serve as the hunchback crouching beneath the table. The mirrors that disguise the hunchback are the unmentioned premises of constitutionalism and popular sovereignty, which the Court seems to evoke when it speaks of "constitutional freedom," but which in reality serve only to deflect our attention from the authoritarian hand that drives the opinion.

Martin Luther King, on the other hand, found no need to hide theology under the table. In King's case the critical portion of my argument has been different: it is that the real theology required by King is not a biblical or even Socratic doctrine of conscience, but rather an understanding of the essentially redemptive character of political action itself. And just as the real political narrative underwriting the Supreme Court's authority ought to be the suppressed "protestant" narrative of constitutionalism under popular sovereignty, the real political narrative that embeds and fulfills the Birmingham campaign ought to be the narrative of constitutional egalitarianism and natural law legalism in Jefferson, Lincoln, and *Brown*. The two halves of my argument converge: *our* history—the history of black and white Americans, of protesters and the Supreme Court, that would allow us to speak of any history as a common possession—is a narrative of communitarian liberalism that redeems our past oppressions and iniquities. It is the narrative of social protest and moments of "creative tension" that remind us of unkept promises and of the moral emergency in which we live.

---

1. Cover, *The Supreme Court, 1982 Term—Foreword:* Nomos *and Narrative,* 97 *Harv. L. Rev.* 4, 4–5 (1983).
2. W. Benjamin, *Theses on the Philosophy of History,* in *Illuminations* 255, 265 (H. Arendt ed. 1968). The phrase "time of the now" translates *"Jetztzeit,"* and refers (Benjamin's editor tells us) to the mystical "standing now," the moment in which (to quote *Henry IV* Part 1, Act v, sc. 4, ll. 82–83) "time, that takes survey of all the world, must have a stop." *Cf.* W. Benjamin, *supra,* at 263 n.*.
3. W. Benjamin, *supra* note 2, at 265.
4. *Id.* at 263.
5. 388 *U.S.* 307 (1967) (criminal contempt conviction of King and other demonstrators for violating injunction not invalidated by likely unconstitutionality of injunction).
6. M. L. King, *Letter from Birmingham Jail,* in *Why We Can't Wait* 77 (1963) [hereinafter King, *Letter*]. Since much of my essay consists of a close reading of the *Walker* opinion and King's *Letter,* a reader may be well advised to read through them first; neither is especially lengthy. Indeed, since much of my argument at the beginning and end of the present essay is drawn from W. Benjamin, *supra* note 2, I shall have the temerity to suggest reading these as well (they amount to only 11 pages).
7. My account of these events is drawn from T. Branch, *supra* note 24, at 688–747; D. Garrow, *supra* note 20, at 225–67; M. L. King, *supra* note 13; J. Williams, *Eyes on the Prize: America's Civil Rights Years 1954–65,* at 181–89 (1987); and especially A. Westin & B. Mahoney, *The Trial of Martin Luther King* (1974), as well as from the *Walker* opinion.
8. *See Connor v. State,* 153 *So. 2d* 787 (Ala. 1963); *see also Reid v. City of Birmingham,* 150 *So. 2d* 735 (Ala. 1963).
9. For an account of the trial, see A. Westin & B. Mahoney, *supra* note 7, at 95–126, 141–42.
10. T. Branch, *supra* note 24, at 756–802.
11. *Id.* at 738.
12. *Id.* at 744.
13. For a detailed account of the letter's composition, see *id.* at 737–45.
14. *Shuttlesworth v. City of Birmingham,* 394 *U.S.* 147 (1969).
15. 330 *U.S.* 258 (1947).
16. Roughly: a classic is a piece you can't ignore when you write in the canon.
17. There is, to be sure, this difference between the questions raised by *Walker* and King's *Letter: Walker* is concerned with the obligation to obey unconstitutional directives (whether or not they are just), whereas King is concerned with the obligation to obey unjust directives (whether or not they are constitutional). Yet clearly the inquiries are close to each other in spirit, and there may be significant substantive overlap as well: an unconstitutional directive is at least *prima facie* unjust since it amounts to an illegitimate exercise of authority, and an unjust directive may run afoul of the constitutional principles of due process and equal protection.
18. Writing degree zero: "a colourless writing. . . . The new neutral writing takes its place in the midst of all those ejaculations and judgments, without becoming involved in any of them; it consists precisely in their absence. . . . it deliberately foregoes any elegance or ornament. . . ." R. Barthes, *Writing Degree Zero and Elements of Semiology* 76–78 (A. Lavers & C. Smith trans. 1967).
19. *Walker v. City of Birmingham,* 388 *U.S.* 307, 309 (1967).
20. 388 *U.S.* at 310.
21. As they surely did: less than two years before, the Freedom Riders were brutally beaten when their bus arrived at the Birmingham terminal, after the Birmingham police had agreed to give the Ku Klux Klan fifteen uninterrupted minutes to assault the riders. T. Branch, *supra* note 24, at 420. Such circumstances raise in a graphic way, however, the question of why the demonstrations should be halted rather than monitored and protected. King raises this question explicitly:

     In your statement you assert that our actions, even though peaceful, must be condemned because they precipitate violence. But is this a logical assertion? Isn't this like condemning a robbed man because his possession of money precipitated the evil act of robbery? Isn't this like condemning Socrates because his unswerving commitment to truth and his philosophical inquiries precipitated the act by the misguided populace in which they made him drink hemlock? Isn't this like condemning Jesus because his unique God-consciousness and never-ceasing devotion to God's will precipitated the evil act of crucifixion?

     King, *Letter, supra* note 13, at 85.
22. 388 *U.S.* at 310–11.
23. 388 *U.S.* at 311. Note the construction "Violence occurred." By making "violence" the subject of the sentence Stewart obviates the necessity of attributing the violence, though in the next sentence he explains that "members of the crowd," not the demonstrators, threw rocks. As Justice Brennan's dissenting opinion points out, there were only three rock-throwers, and the rock-throwing occurred after (in anger at?) the arrest of King, Shuttlesworth, and Walker. 388 *U.S.* at 341 (Brennan, J., dissenting).
24. 388 *U.S.* at 315–16. As we shall see, the very fact that the Court found it necessary to make this argument points to a fundamental problem with the Court's opinion.
25. 388 *U.S.* at 310.
26. 388 *U.S.* at 310.
27. 388 *U.S.* at 311.

28. 388 *U.S.* at 314 (quoting *Howat v. Kansas,* 258 *U.S.* 181, 189–90 [1922]). Note the rhythmic concatenation of formulaic legalisms piled one on top of the other. Rhetorically, this serves the function of infusing the conclusion with a sense of syllogistic inevitability. (What are all those carefully catalogued legalisms doing there unless they are minor premises of a deductive application of some rule of law presumably known by the Court? Therefore the conclusion must be right.)

29. 388 *U.S.* at 315.

30. 388 *U.S.* at 315, 318.

31. 388 *U.S.* at 317, n.9 (emphasis in original).

32. 388 *U.S.* at 317–18.

33. 388 *U.S.* at 326 (Warren, C. J., dissenting); *see also* A. Westin & B. Mahoney, *supra* note 25, at 105–6, 121 (detailing the petitioners' arguments presented at trial).

34. 388 *U.S.* at 315, 316.

35. 388 *U.S.* at 316.

36. 388 *U.S.* at 318–19. In fact, the petitioners did not have two days since the injunction was not served until the day before the scheduled demonstration. (Though they knew all day Wednesday that Connor was preparing to obtain an injunction. T. Branch, *supra* note 24, at 727.) Norman Amaker, one of the movement's lawyers, recollects "that there was never any serious discussion of counseling the leaders to go into court to seek relief prior to the Good Friday march. Going into court would have required foregoing the weekend marches. . . ." A. Westin & B. Mahoney, *supra* note 25, at 80.

37. 388 *U.S.* at 320–21 (footnote omitted).

38. *United States v. United Mineworkers,* 330 *U.S.* 258, 309–10, 312 (1947) (Frankfurter, J., concurring).

39. *Howat v. Kansas,* 258 *U.S.* 181 (1922).

40. F. Frankfurter & N. Greene, *The Labor Injunction* (1930). Later, the injunction device would be pressed into service by opponents of the Progressive movement in order to prevent the enforcement of Progressive legislation. *See* O. Fiss, *The Civil Rights Injunction* 1–4 (1978).

41. *Walker,* 388 *U.S.* at 330–31 (Warren, C. J., dissenting).

42. A. Westin & B. Mahoney, *supra* note 25, at 277–78. The statistic on university injunctions is from Note, *Equity on the Campus: The Limits of Injunctive Regulation of University Protest,* 80 *Yale L.J.* 987, 987 (1971).

43. Another political narrative the *Walker* Court buries by exercising its victor's prerogative of assigning the meaning it chooses to past events lies in its use of previous Court opinions. The Court describes the *Howat* rule, 258 *U.S.* at 189–90, *quoted supra* text accompanying note 46, as "consistent with the rule of law followed by the federal courts," and cites a string of cases in support of this claim. *Walker,* 388 *U.S.* at 314 & n.5. But in fact two of the cases cited—*Ex parte* Rowland, 104 *U.S.* 604 (1881), and *In re* Ayers, 123 *U.S.* 443 (1887)—stand for precisely the opposite proposition. *Howat* requires obedience to invalid orders on pain of contempt, whereas *Rowland* and *Ayers,* like the related cases *In re* Sawyer, 124 *U.S.* 200 (1888), and *Ex parte* Fisk, 113 *U.S.* 713 (1885), hold that disobedience of an invalid court order cannot be punished as contempt. (For clear statements of this holding, see *Fisk,* 113 *U.S.* at 718, and *Rowland,* 104 *U.S.* at 612.)

44. *Walker,* 388 *U.S.* at 328 (Warren, C. J., dissenting).

45. 388 *U.S.* at 338 (Douglas, J., dissenting).

46. 388 *U.S.* at 342 (Brennan, J., dissenting).

47. 388 *U.S.* at 332 & n.9 (Warren, C. J., dissenting) (citing *In re* Green, 369 *U.S.* 689 (1962)).

48. 388 *U.S.* at 337 (Douglas, J., dissenting) (quoting *United States v. United Mine Workers,* 330 *U.S.* 258, 293 (1947)).

49. 388 *U.S.* at 343–44 (Brennan, J., dissenting).

50. Plato, *Laws* *715d. *But cf.* Plato, *Statesman* *294a–97b, for his doubts about the efficacy of the rule of law.

51. Thus also the ninth and tenth amendments to the Constitution.

52. Nor is this a wholly fictitious scenario: *Cooper v. Aaron,* 358 *U.S.* 1 (1958), an opinion that every Justice signed individually for emphasis, was provoked by Arkansas Governor Orville Faubus' declaration that the Supreme Court's *Brown* decision was not binding.

53. In other cases the Court recognized the validity of the first two of these reasons: in *Carroll v. President & Commissioners of Princess Anne,* 393 *U.S.* 175 (1968), the Court backed off from *Walker* by insisting that injunctions restraining the exercise of first amendment rights cannot be issued *ex parte* unless it is impossible to notify the opposing parties in time to allow them to be heard; and in *Freedman v. Maryland,* 380 *U.S.* 51 (1965), the Court had recognized that a speedy hearing and appeal are constitutionally required in a different first amendment context, namely censorship proceedings against a movie.

54. For three reasons: first, demonstrators gathered from around the country cannot tarry indefinitely in Birmingham while waiting for the courts to rule on the injunction's validity; second, the religious symbolism of holding the demonstrations on Good Friday and Easter Sunday was important, and those days come but once a year; third, the demonstrations were intended to target downtown businesses during the extra-busy Easter shopping season, and that season is relatively short. *See* A. Westin & B. Mahoney, *supra* note 7, at 76. Moreover, the Court itself later recognized that when complying with a court order would do irreparable damage because it would subsequently be impossible to "unring the bell," one could defy the order without facing conviction for contempt if the order was invalid. *Maness v. Meyers,* 419 *U.S.* 449, 460 (1975).

55. Indeed, in *Shuttlesworth v. City of Birmingham,* 394 *U.S.* 147 (1969), the Court found this ordinance to be unconstitutional. Oddly enough, this opinion too was authored by Justice Stewart, who noted that the ordinance conferred on the City Commission "virtually unbridled and absolute power to prohibit any 'parade,' 'procession,' or 'demonstration' on the city's streets or public ways," so that it "fell squarely within the ambit of the many decisions of this Court over the last 30 years, holding that a law subjecting the exercise of First Amendment freedoms to the prior restraint of a license, without narrow, objective, and definite standards to guide the licensing authority, is unconstitutional." Strikingly, Stewart cited numerous decisions that "have made clear that a person faced with such an unconstitutional licensing law may ignore it and engage with impunity in the exercise of the right of free expression for which the law purports to require a license." *Shuttlesworth,* 394 *U.S.* at 150–51 (footnotes omitted).

56. *Walker v. City of Birmingham,* 388 *U.S.* 307, 327 (1967) (Warren, C. J., dissenting).

57. Similar concerns emerge in cases about judicial tort immunity. The most notable is *Stump v. Sparkman,* 435 *U.S.* 349 (1978), in which the Court found that a trial judge who had ordered a teenager sterilized at the *ex parte* request of the teenager's mother was immune from tort liability. Indeed, it is only in the most bizarre of circumstances that judicial immunity dissolves. *See, e.g., Zarcone v. Perry,* 572 *F. 2d* 52 (2d Cir. 1978) (upholding punitive damages against a traffic judge who had ordered a street vendor brought into his courtroom in manacles because he had sold the judge a bad cup of coffee).

58. *Walker,* 388 *U.S.* at 321.

59. *United States v. United Mine Workers,* 330 *U.S.* 258, 310, 312 (1947).

60. In his dissent, Chief Justice Warren cites five cases and two governmental reports that take official notice of "[t]he attitude of the city administration in general and of its Public Safety Commissioner in particular. . . ." *Walker,* 388 *U.S.* at 325 n.1 (Warren, C. J., dissenting).

61. Westin and Mahoney argue that the Court should have found in favor of King in an opinion narrowly tailored to the exceptional facts. A. Westin & B. Mahoney, *supra* note 7, at 286–89.

62. *See, e.g., Cox v. Louisiana,* 379 *U.S.* 559 (1965) (protecting demonstrators from state suppression); *Fields v. South Carolina,* 375 *U.S.* 44 (1963) (same); *Edwards v. South Carolina,* 372 *U.S.* 229 (1963) (same).

63. *Adderley v. Florida,* 385 *U.S.* 39 (1966) was the first Supreme Court case in the 1960s upholding the convictions of nonviolent demonstrators. A. Westin & B. Mahoney, *supra* note 7, at 205.

64. *Walker,* 388 *U.S.* at 349 (Brennan, J., dissenting).

65. This is a major theme in A. Westin & B. Mahoney, *supra* note 7.

66. An important case prefiguring *Walker* that runs contrary to my general line of argument here is *United States v. Shipp,* 203 *U.S.* 563 (1906). In that case, the Supreme Court issued an order preventing the execution of Johnson, a black man convicted of raping a white woman, pending appeal. A lynch-mob gathered at the jail and Shipp, the sheriff guarding the prisoner, joined forces with the mob to carry out the lynching. Shipp was convicted of contempt of court. He argued that the Supreme Court had no jurisdiction for its order, and therefore that he could not be punished for contemning it. The Court rejected this argument in a discussion that links the necessity of preventing violence with the question-begging assertion of the Court's "catholic" authority to determine the limits of its own authority: "Until its judgment declining jurisdiction should be announced, it [*i.e.,* the Supreme Court] had authority from the necessity of the case to make orders to preserve the existing conditions and the subject of the petition. . . ." *Shipp,* 203 *U.S.* at 573.

Shipp appears to illustrate the necessity of some social mechanism to "pull the plug" on events that threaten to get out of hand, leading to incidents as appalling as the lynching of Johnson. But why should it be judicial authority? Why not the sheriff? In *Shipp,* of course, the answer is that the sheriff was part of the mob. But must it therefore be a judge? We can imagine judges who also fail to do their job for the same reasons as the sheriff; we could imagine the Supreme Court, or any other authority, failing to do its job for racist reasons. The argument from the need for a social mechanism to freeze events in their tracks to the vindication of judicial authority is thus a complete *non sequitur.* To see this clearly, consider a case cognate to *Shipp:* Johnson is unjustly convicted, and the unjust conviction is upheld by the Supreme Court. Now events are threatening to get out of hand: Johnson is about to be executed. What is needed, clearly, is some social mechanism to "pull the plug" on these events. Since all the authorities are united in their determination to execute Johnson unjustly, the task falls to a mob of Johnson's supporters, who rescue him dramatically from jail. Here the need for a social mechanism to freeze events in their tracks, in order to stop unjust violence, vindicates mob rebellion against judicial authority, just as in *Shipp* it vindicates judicial authority itself.

67. The history of violence employed to maintain Jim Crow goes all the way back to the dissolution of Reconstruction. *See, e.g., United States v. Cruikshank,* 92 *U.S.* 542 (1875) (denying federal authority to punish private individuals for forcibly breaking up a black political meeting and thereby hindering the exercise by blacks of the right to vote). For an eloquent reminder that law rests on violence, see Cover, *Violence and the Word,* 95 *Yale L.J.* 1601 (1986).

68. In his *Letter,* King writes: "I have almost reached the regrettable conclusion that the Negro's great stumbling block in his stride toward freedom is not the White Citizen's Counciler or Ku Klux Klanner, but the white moderate, who is more devoted to 'order' than to justice. . . ." King, *Letter, supra* note 6, at 87. The debate over whether the highest legal value is order or justice is an old one; I have sketched arguments about this issue in ancient Greek literature, and argued that the pursuit of order at the expense of justice is faulty. *See* Luban, *Some Greek Trials: Order and Justice in Homer, Hesiod, Aeschylus, and Plato,* 54 *Tenn. L. Rev.* 279 (1987).

69. This argument was explored initially in M. Olson, *The Logic of Collective Action: Public Goods and the Theory of Groups* (rev. ed. 1971). *See also* R. Hardin, *Collective Action* (1982). This argument is applied to the analysis of revolutionary social change in Buchanan, *Revolutionary Motivation and Rationality,* 9 *Phil. & Pub. Affs.* 59 (1979). *But see* G. Kavka, *Hobbesian Moral and Political Theory* 266–79 (1986), for an argument that revolution-

ary participation can be rational. On the relationship between collective action problems and the legal system, see D. Luban, *Lawyers and Justice: An Ethical Study* 364–91 (1988).

70. *See* J. Cohen & J. Rogers, *Rules of the Game: American Politics and the Central America Movement* (1986) (a succinct statement of the obstacles facing social protest movements in America); J. Cohen & J. Rogers, *On Democracy: Toward a Transformation of American Society* 47–87 (1983); Przeworski, *Proletariat into a Class: The Process of Class Formation from Karl Kautsky's* The Class Struggle *to Recent Controversies,* 7 *Pol. & Socy.* 343 (1977); Przeworski, *Material Bases of Consent: Economics and Politics in a Hegemonic System,* 1 *Pol. Power & Soc. Theory* 21 (1980); Przeworski, *Social Democracy as a Historical Phenomenon, New Left Rev.,* July–Aug. 1980, at 27; Przeworski & Wallerstein, *The Structure of Class Conflict in Democratic Capitalist Societies,* 76 *Am. Pol. Sci. Rev.* 215 (1982).

71. W. Benjamin, *supra* note 2, at 264–65.

72. *Id.* at 265.

73. *Quoted in* A. Westin & B. Mahoney, *supra* note 7, at 76.

74. *Quoted in* T. Branch, *Parting the Waters: America in the King Years* (1988).

75. *Walker v. City of Birmingham,* 388 *U.S.* 307, 321 (1967).

76. King, *Letter, supra* note 6, at 79.

77. *Id.* at 77.

78. *Id.* at 78.

79. *Id.* at 79–81.

80. *Id.* at 81–82.

81. *Id.* at 82–83.

82. *Id.* at 84–86.

83. *Id.* at 87–93.

84. *Id.* at 89.

85. *Id.* at 90–92.

86. *Id.* at 92.

87. *Id.* at 93–98.

88. *Id.* at 94.

89. *Id.* at 96.

90. *Id.* at 98–99.

91. *Id.* at 100.

92. *Supra* note 86 and accompanying text.

93. King, *Letter, supra* note 6, at 79.

94. He does, however, describe these events in his 1964 memoir of the Birmingham campaign. M. L. King, *New Day in Birmingham,* in *Why We Can't Wait* 55–75 (1964).

95. King, *Letter, supra* note 13, at 81–82.

96. This, of course, is a strategy that runs the risk of self-deception or even whitewash, of substituting an idealized picture of what one hoped to do for an accurate rendition of what one in fact did. In my view, however, the Birmingham campaign actually lived up to the description that King offers in the *Letter,* so no self-deception or whitewash actually occurs.

97. This is not to deny that sometimes it is appropriate to insist on the behavioral narration. The terrorist group insists that it merely dramatized the plight of its people (by setting off a car-bomb in a crowded street); we rightly insist that what it did was set off a car-bomb in a crowded street. The administration claims that it is signaling support for democratic institutions in Central America; we rightly insist that it is aiding and abetting right-wing murders and tortures. When the dramatic act is *malum in se,* when it consists of support for violence or violation of human rights, that fact swamps the expressive character of the act and becomes the only appropriate description. In the case of the Birmingham campaign, however, this is not the circumstance, and it would be as misleading to describe the demonstration as an unauthorized parade as it would to describe it as a pleasant stroll down the street.

98. Consider, for example, King's closing salutation: "I hope this letter finds you strong in the faith. I also hope that circumstances will soon make it possible for me to meet each of you, not as an integrationist or a civil-rights leader but as a fellow clergyman and a Christian brother." King, *Letter, supra* note 6, at 100. The contemporary references apart, the language

resonates with Paul's various salutations (perhaps especially with *Ephesians,* when Paul like King was a prisoner).

99. King, *Letter, supra* note 13, at 78.

100. *Acts* 16:9. (I use the Revised Standard Version of the Bible except where noted.)

101. King, *Letter, supra* note 6, at 79.

102. King's rhetoric, however, did not sway Episcopal Bishop C. C. Jones Carpenter, the instigator of the clerical attack on King that provoked the *Letter.*

> Bishop Carpenter sat down in his study with a copy of King's mammoth reply. He read the letter through to the end, then turned to his bishop coadjutor, George Murray, with a sigh of resignation. "This is what you get when you try to do something," he said. "You get it from both sides. George, you just have to live with that." Carpenter felt abused and misunderstood for his efforts to act as a progressive force in race relations. The clash of emotion turned him, like his great-grandfather, into a more strident Confederate.

T. Branch, *supra* note 24, at 745.

103. In an order chosen for ease of exposition, though it is not King's own order.

104. King, *Letter, supra* note 6, at 96.

105. *Acts* 2:44–45.

106. *Acts* 4:32.

107. *Acts* 4:34–35.

108. K. Marx, *Critique of the Gotha Programme* 10 (C. Dutt ed. 1938).

109. *See* N. Cohn, *The Pursuit of the Millennium* 194, 197 (rev. ed. 1970).

110. *See* T. Branch, *supra* note 24, at 73.

111. King, *Letter, supra* note 6, at 92.

112. *Amos* 5:11–12.

113. *Amos* 5:21–24 (emphasis added). The line was evidently dear to King, for he repeated it in the "I have a dream" speech in the March on Washington a few months later; moreover, King had used it in the first political speech in his career, the address to the mass meeting called after the arrest of Rosa Parks for refusing to move to the back of the bus in Montgomery that propelled him to leadership of the Montgomery bus boycott.

114. King, *Letter, supra* note 6, at 92 (quoting *Galatians* 6:17).

115. *Galatians* 3:13.

116. *Galatians* 3:23–25.

117. *Galatians* 3:28.

118. *Galatians* 5:14. *See Leviticus* 19:18, which places "You shall love your neighbor as yourself" as but one of the Mosaic commandments—though Hillel would later enunciate the Golden Rule as the entire teaching of the Torah.

> Robert Cover has offered a complex argument that Paul, in *Galatians* 4:22–31, invokes a hidden subversive theme, closely tied to the problem of legal legitimacy that we have been examining, that animated the entire Old Testament. Cover, *supra* note 1, at 19–25. One of the most important Mosaic laws concerned the right of the firstborn to a double portion of the father's inheritance. *Deuteronomy* 21:15–17. As Cover points out, this law is violated in the stories of Cain and Abel, of Ishmael and Isaac, of Jacob and Esau, of Joseph and his brothers, of Solomon's rise to the Davidic throne, of Moses' dominance over Aaron, of the Prophet Samuel's birth and assumption of the place of Eli, and of David's succession to the throne of Saul—each of which involves a catapulting of a younger son over the elders. Cover argues that the meaning of this tension between the law of succession and these key biblical narratives is "first, that the rule of succession can be overturned; second, that it takes a conviction of divine destiny to overturn it; and third, that divine destiny is likely to manifest itself precisely in overturning this specific rule." Cover, *supra* note 1, at 22. It is to one of these stories, that of Hagar and Ishmael, that Paul points in the passage in Galatians, which Cover characterizes as a "revolutionary allegorical extension of the typology." *Id.* at 24. It is not my argument that King himself drew these connections; but it *is* my argu-

ment that King meant consciously to invoke a biblical text that glorifies the violation of legal precepts in the name of divine destiny.

119. *Acts* 5:29. Cover refers to this principle as "a religious rule of recognition," functionally equivalent and therefore directly contradictory to the supremacy clause of article VI, section 2 of the Constitution. Cover, *supra* note 1, at 30.

120. *Matthew* 5:44.

121. *Matthew* 5:43–44 (emphasis added).

122. It is worth pointing out that the traditional Jewish understanding of *Leviticus* 19:18 is *not* "Love your neighbor and hate your enemy," but rather is fully as universalist and cosmopolitan as Christ's own message. *See* J. Hertz, *The Pentateuch and Haftorahs* 501 nn. 563–64 (2d ed. 1981); *see also* A. Cohen, Everyman's Talmud 212–16 (1949). This is one of the theological points that divides Jews from Christians.

123. *Galatians* 3:13, 5:14.

124. *Matthew* 5:17–18.

125. *Matthew* 5:20.

126. Kierkegaard actually spoke of the teleological suspension of the ethical, not the legal. S. Kierkegaard, *Fear and Trembling* 64–77 (Lowrie trans. 1954). He used the term to describe Abraham's murderous attempt to sacrifice Isaac, which could be justified teleologically by reference to the miraculous commandment of God, though viewed from the sphere of the ethical it could never be regarded as anything but a transgression.

127. *Galatians* 3:28.

128. In this respect, the New Testament allusions are fully consistent with Amos' denunciation of Israel's empty formalities and the King James Bible's version of *Daniel* 3:25 as a prefiguration of the New Testament. In all of them, Christians are likely to identify the *Aufhebung* of formal legality by love with the *Aufhebung* of the Old Testament by the New.

129. King, *Letter, supra* note 6, at 92. Note that this is the continuation of the extremism passage we have been examining.

130. However, Luther's own stance toward secular authority is considerably more quiescent than King's. *See* Luther, *Temporal Authority: To What Extent It Should Be Obeyed,* in *Luther: Selected Political Writings* 51 (J. M. Porter ed. 1974). Moreover, I find it disturbing that King should liken himself to a tormented, dismal, and half-mad fanatic such as Bunyan. I write this footnote on February 16, 1989, as the newspapers report that an Iranian cleric has offered a one million dollar reward to any faithful Moslem who assassinates Salman Rushdie for his "blasphemous" novel Satanic Verses. Bunyan had more in common with this vicious cleric than with either King or Luther (though Luther himself burned the works of Pope Leo). For a delightfully opinionated but illuminating discussion, see Macaulay's article on Bunyan. 4 *Encyclopaedia Britannica* 389 (14th ed. 1937). For a more sympathetic account, see C. Hill, *A Soldier and a Poor Man: John Bunyan and His Church* 1628–1688 (1989).

131. King, *Letter, supra* note 6, at 84.

132. *Id.* at 85.

133. *Id.* at 85–86.

134. Rawls, *Legal Obligation and the Duty of Fair Play,* in *Law and Philosophy* 3, 9–10 (S. Hook ed. 1964); Hart, *Are There Any Natural Rights?,* 64 *Phil. Rev.* 175, 185 (1955).

135. *See* D. Luban, *supra* note 69, at 32–49 (wherein I elaborate a solidarity-based theory of legal obligation understood as fair play, derived from King's *Letter*).

136. On the distinction between respect and love, see Luban, *The Quality of Justice,* 66 *Denver L. Rev.* 381, 413–16 (1989).

137. On trust as a defining relationship in moral and political theory, see N. Luhmann, *Trust: A Mechanism for the Reduction of Social Complexity,* in *Trust and Power* 1 (1979); Baier, *Trust and Antitrust,* 96 *Ethics* 231 (1986); Baier, *What Do Women Want in a Moral Theory?,* 19 *Nous* 53 (1985); Luban, *Legal Modernism,* 84 *Mich. L. Rev.* 1656, 1688–89 (1986).

138. King, *Letter, supra* note 6, at 92.

139. *See* G. Wills, *Inventing America: Jefferson's Declaration of Independence* xiv–xxiv (1978).

140. King, *Letter, supra* note 6, at 81.
141. King, *Letter, supra* note 6, at 81; *see also id.* at 87. As we have seen, the imagery of removing fetters binding us to myths and half-truths comes from Plato's *Republic.*
142. *See* Plato, *Apology* *30e.
143. King, *Letter, supra* note 6, at 88–89.
144. Plato, *supra* note 185, at *32c–e.
145. *Id.* at *39d.
146. They are, however, unsound, and their unsoundness has been remarked often in the history of philosophy. *See* Luban, *supra* note 69, at 36–37.
147. R. Kraut, *Socrates and the State* 54–90 (1984). *But see id.* at 75–76 (concerning the difference between Socratic conscientious disobedience and civil disobedience for expressive and political purposes).
148. Plato, *Crito, supra* note 142, at *51c–52d.
149. *See* R. Kraut, *supra* note 147, at 55–56.
150. A very different, perhaps even more persuasive, resolution of the contradiction has been offered by Ernest Weinrib. Weinrib suggests that Socrates never believed his arguments for obedience to the law in the first place. This is strikingly signalled by the fact that Socrates does not offer the arguments in his own voice, but rather puts them in the "mouth" of the personified laws. It is signalled equally strikingly when, at the conclusion of the dialogue, Socrates likens the arguments to Corybantic flute-playing, a technique for curing madness by inducing a musical frenzy in its sufferer. This is surely a strange characterization of serious arguments. Weinrib, *Obedience to the Law in Plato's* Crito, 27 *Am. J. Juris.* 85 (1982). While Weinrib's may well be the right reading of the *Crito,* I do not consider it here, since after all even if the textual problem is resolved in this way, the dilemma of obedience and disobedience is not.
151. *Quoted* in T. Branch, at 599.
152. Plato, *supra* note 142, at *20c–21e.
153. *Id.* at 115, 139, 141.
154. H. Arendt, *Civil Disobedience,* in *Crises of the Republic* 51–102 (1972).
155. Not to mention that the argument concerning obedience to the law is better.
156. Arendt, *supra* note 160, at 58–68.
157. *Id.* at 60–61 (footnote omitted) (quoting T. Jefferson, *Notes on the State of Virginia,* Query XVIII (1781–85)).
158. This is not to deny that King, too, was guided by a divine voice. Consider his recollections in M. L. King, *Stride Toward Freedom: The Montgomery Story* 134–35 (1958):

> It seemed as though I could hear the quiet assurance of an inner voice saying: "Martin Luther, stand up for righteousness. Stand up for justice. Stand up for truth. And lo I will be with you, even until the end of the world." . . . I heard the voice of Jesus saying still to fight on. He promised never to leave me, never to leave me alone. No never alone. No never alone. He promised never to leave me, never to leave me alone.

I mean to be saying only that King's revelation does not constitute the public meaning of his actions nor those of the civil rights movement more generally.
159. The Situationist theorist Guy Debord writes perceptively: "Modern revolutionary expectations are not irrational continuations of the religious passion of millenarianism, as Norman Cohn thought he had demonstrated in *The Pursuit of the Millennium.* On the contrary, millenarianism, revolutionary class struggle speaking the language of religion for the last time, is already a modern revolutionary tendency which as yet lacks *the consciousness that it is historical.* The millenarians had to lose because they could not recognize the revolution as their own operation." The Society of the Spectacle sec. 138 (unauthorized ed. 1970). It is ironic that Debord, writing only five years after the Birmingham campaign, evidently believed that revolution spoke the language of religion for the last time in the sixteenth century.
160. *See, e.g.,* A. MacIntyre, *After Virtue* (1981); M. Sandel, *Liberalism and the Limits of Justice* (1982); R. Unger, *Knowledge and Politics* (1975).
161. I believe, moreover, that King's liberal communitarianism harmonizes with the three premises of American constitutionalism I identified in my discussion of *Walker,* namely the rule of law, popular sovereignty, and the publicity of law—precisely the premises that the Court found it necessary to finesse.
162. Benjamin wrote the *Theses* as a response to his friend Gershom Scholem's masterpiece, G. Scholem, *Major Trends in Jewish Mysticism* (1941). On the personal meaning of the *Theses,* and especially the famous "angel of history" thesis (Thesis 9), see Scholem, *Walter Benjamin and His Angel,* in *On Jews and Judaism in Crisis* 198–236 (W. Dannhauser ed. 1976). The *Theses* were provoked by Scholem's discussions of the seventeenth-century Sabbatian movement, a millenarian popular movement that convulsed all of Judaism and that bears great similarity to chiliastic movements in Christendom, including the Anabaptists. *See* G. Scholem, *Sabbatai Sevi: The Mystical Messiah* 93–102 (1973). Yet Jewish mysticism could also be connected with liberalism, as was the case with Spinoza, who befriended English radicals as well as Dutch republicans, and defended liberalism against messianism after his excommunication by rabbis who would in a few years openly embrace Sabbatai Sevi. *See* L. Feuer, *Spinoza and the Rise of Liberalism* 29–30, 47–57 (1958).
163. W. Benjamin, *supra* note 2, at 266.
164. *Id.* at 262.
165. *Id.* at 261.
166. F. Nietzsche, *The Will to Power* 330 sec. 617 (W. Kornhauser ed., R. Hollingdale & W. Kaufmann trans. 1967).
167. I have discussed the relationship between narrative, poetry, political action, and collective memory in Luban, *Explaining Dark Times: Hannah Arendt's Theory of Theory,* 50 *Soc. Res.* 215 (1983). It is hardly surprising that Arendt's views, which I discuss in that essay, are close to Benjamin's: Arendt closely studied Benjamin's *Theses,* and in fact was responsible for their survival. Benjamin entrusted the manuscript of the *Theses* to Arendt, who smuggled it out of occupied France and brought it to New York; Benjamin himself committed suicide when he was turned back at the Spanish border as he attempted to flee the Nazis. *See* E. Young-Bruehl, *Hannah Arendt: For Love of the World* 160–63 (1982).
168. W. Benjamin, *supra* note 2, at 256.
169. *See* Luban, *supra* note 137, at 1684–85, 1694.
170. R. Dworkin, *Law's Empire* 95, 151–75 (1986) (Pragmatism is the view "that judges do and should make whatever decisions seem to them best for the community's future, not counting any form of consistency with the past as valuable for its own sake."). Utilitarian theories of adjudication are obvious examples of pragmatism. For an example of a rule-utilitarian theory, see R. Wasserstrom, *The Judicial Decision* (1961).
171. F. Frankfurter, *The Judicial Process and the Supreme Court,* in *Of Law and Men* 39 (P. Elman ed. 1956).
172. W. Benjamin, *supra* note 2, at 256.
173. In this sense, the sharp distinction I have drawn between forward-looking and backward-looking understandings of action and argument blurs: the redemption of the past *is* one of the consequences we hope for in the future, and, as Cover, *supra* note 1, insists, narratives of the past will include our ancestors' prophecies of their and our futures. Thus, the backward-looking gaze will see the future reflected in the mirror of ancestral prophecies, just as the forward-looking gaze will find future happiness indissolubly bound up with the redemption of past wrongs and sufferings. The difference in emphasis and valuation the two understandings place on the past nevertheless remains decisive. (My thanks to Paul Kahn for stressing to me the extent to which past and future are caught up with each other.)
174. K. Marx, *The Eighteenth Brumaire of Louis Bonaparte* 13 (C. Dutt ed. 1957) (3d German ed. 1883).
175. *Id.* at 13–14 (footnote omitted).
176. *Id.* at 16.
177. W. Benjamin, *supra* note 2, at 255.

PART TWO

Liberty

Under what conditions, and for what reasons, can the presumption in favor of political liberty be overridden? This is not merely an abstract question addressed to philosophers, but an unavoidable practical question to be faced by every democratic legislator. In effect, it is a question of the limits beyond which restrictive lawmaking is morally illegitimate.

The Case for Self-Determination

John Stuart Mill, the first essayist presented in this part, gives the classic liberal answer to the question. Restriction of the liberty of one citizen, he argues, can be justified only to prevent harm to others. We can refer to Mill's position as the "harm to others principle," or, more succinctly, the harm principle. Several things should be noted about this principle at the outset. First, by *harm,* Mill means not only direct personal injury such as broken bones or the loss of money but also more diffuse social harms such as air pollution or the impairment of public institutions. Second, the principle does not propose a sufficient condition for the restriction of liberty, because some harms to others are too slight to outbalance the very real harm or danger involved in the restriction of liberty. Thus, in close cases, legislators must balance the value of the interests to be restricted by proposed coercive legislation *and* the collateral costs of enforcing any coercive law, on the one hand, against the value of the interests to be protected by the proposed legislation, on the other. It is only when the probable harms prevented by the statute are greater than those that it will cause that the legislation is justified. Finally, the harm principle should be interpreted as a claim about *reasons*. Only one kind of consideration is ever morally relevant to the justification of coercion, namely, that it is necessary to prevent harm to others. It is never a relevant reason that the conduct to be restricted is merely offensive (as opposed to harmful) or even that it is intrinsically immoral, nor is it relevant that coercion is necessary to prevent a person from harming himself or herself (as opposed to others).

Challenges to Self-Determination: Legal Paternalism

No one would disagree that prevention of harm to others is always a relevant reason for coercion, but many disagree with Mill's contention that it is the *only* relevant consideration. Thus, no one will seriously suggest that laws against battery, larceny, and homicide are unjustified, but many maintain that the state is also justified, at least in some circumstances, in prohibiting (1) actions that hurt or endanger the actor (the principle of legal paternalism), (2) "immoralities" even when they harm no one but their perpetrators (the principle of legal moralism), and (3) conduct that is offensive though not harmful to others (the offense principle).[1] These rival doctrines cannot easily be proved or refuted in the abstract. Rather, they are best judged by how faithfully they reflect, and how systematically they organize, our considered judgments in particular cases; for such principles, after all, purport to be explicit renderings of the axioms to which we are committed by the most confident judgments we make in everyday discourse about problems of liberty. The main areas of controversy in which such problems arise are those concerning unorthodox expressions of opinion, "morals offenses" in the criminal law (especially when committed in private by solitary individuals or among consenting adults), pornography and obscenity (when offered or displayed to the public or to nonconsenting individuals), activities that are harmful or dangerous to those who voluntarily engage in them (voluntary suicide and euthanasia), otherwise harmless invasions of the privacy of others, and conscientious acts of civil disobedience. The cautious theorist will begin with Mill's harm principle as an account of at least one set of reasons that are always relevant in such controversies and then apply it to the various problem areas to determine the extent, if any, to which it must be supplemented to provide solutions that are both plausible and consistent. In particular, we must decide, in each area, whether we need have recourse to the offense principle, legal moralism, or legal paternalism.

Under most of the problem area headings, there is still another kind of controversy to be settled, namely, whether even the unsupplemented harm principle can justify too *much* coercion, and whether, therefore, doing justice to our considered judgments requires also a doctrine of *natural rights,* which limits the applicability of the harm principle (or any of the other liberty-limiting principles that might apply at all). Perhaps this kind of question arises most prominently in the area of free expression of opinion. There is no doubt that expressions of opinion, in speech or writing, do often cause vast amounts of harm. Politicians sometimes advocate policies that would lead to disastrous consequences if adopted, and scientists sometimes defend theories that are false and detrimental to scientific progress. If we apply the harm principle in a straightforward, unqualified way—by prohibiting all particular expressions that seem, on the best evidence, likely to cause more harm than good—we might very well justify widespread invasions of what we should naturally take to be a moral right of free speech. To avoid this embarrassing consequence, the partisan of the harm principle will have to propose subtle refinements and mediating norms for the application of this principle, weighing such matters as the balancing of rival interests and social costs and the measurements of probabilities, dangers, and risks.

In a broader analysis of paternalism, Gerald Dworkin considers, in a comprehensive and systematic way, the question of whether paternalistic statutes (defined roughly as those interfering with a person's liberty "for his own good") are ever justi-

fied. He treats Mill's absolutistic position with respect but points out how widespread paternalistic restrictions are and how drastic their total elimination would be. Laws requiring hunters to wear red caps, and motorcyclists to wear helmets, or those requiring medical prescriptions for certain therapeutic drugs, for example, seem innocuous to most of us. Even more so are laws that actually protect children and incompetents from their own folly and those which persons regard as "social insurance" against their own future decisions that might be not only dangerous but also irreversible. Dworkin then attempts to find criteria that can be used to separate unjustified paternalistic restrictions from those he thinks any rational person would welcome.

Constitutional Privacy

The idea of privacy made a major new entry into American constitutional law through the celebrated case of *Griswold v. Connecticut,* decided by the United States Supreme Court in 1965. (See also the contribution of Robert Bork to Part Two of this book.) The opinions in that case raise a variety of genuinely philosophical issues and might have been included with equal relevance in any of the first three sections in Part One. The decision overturned a Connecticut statute making the use of contraceptives by any person a criminal offense. That statute was unconstitutional, Mr. Justice Douglas wrote, because it violated a right of marital privacy "older than the Bill of Rights" but included in the "penumbra" of the First, Fourth, Fifth, Eighth, Ninth, and Fourteenth Amendments. A penumbra of a right is a set of further rights not specifically guaranteed in so many words but properly inferable from the primary right either as necessary means for its fulfillment or as implied by it in certain factual circumstances not necessarily foreseen by those who formulated it. Thus, the right to read whatever one wishes is in the penumbra of the right of free expression if only because the latter, which is mentioned in the Constitution, would have little point if it existed without the former, which is not mentioned in the Constitution.

Similarly, the Constitution does not specifically spell out a right of marital privacy. The dissenters on the Court (Justices Stewart and Black) were suspicious of the technique of finding anything a judge thinks just and reasonable in the penumbra of a specific guarantee. Justice Goldberg in his concurring opinion had rested his case for a constitutional right of marital privacy on the Ninth Amendment's reference to fundamental rights "retained by the people," and Justices Harlan and White in their concurring opinions (not reprinted here) derived the unconstitutionality of the anticontraception statute from its capriciousness, irrationality, and offensiveness to a "sense of fairness and justice." A careful reader of Part One of this book will recognize here the overtones of the natural law tradition, whereas in justice Black's dissenting opinion, a skeptical stricture on the catchwords of natural justice, there is the powerful echo of the tradition of legal positivism.

The doctrine of privacy applied by the majority opinions in *Griswold* affirms that there is a domain in which the individual's own choice must reign supreme. *Eisenstadt v. Baird* (1972) extended the right of marital privacy to individuals, married or single, allowing them to use contraceptives if they so choose and freeing them of governmental intrusion in an area that is their business alone. In *Loving v. Virginia* (1967), privacy was made the basis of a person's right freely to decide to marry a person of another race. In *Stanley v. Georgia* (1969), a right to view pornographic films or tapes in one's own home was also said to be implied by the fundamental right to privacy, and in 1973 in *Roe v. Wade,* a right to choose an abortion was similarly derived. Throughout this period, there was both controversy and confusion. The latter was caused, according to some critics, by a misnaming of the constitutional right in question. The relevant right, for these critics, is one of *autonomy* (self-government) in some fundamental areas of life, not *privacy,* which is quite another thing.

The most controversial of the "privacy" decisions has been the famous abortion case of 1973, *Roe v. Wade,* which extended the right of privacy to a woman's autonomous choice of whether to terminate her pregnancy during the first two trimesters. Here a woman's autonomy had to be balanced against the state's growing interest in the potentiality of human life, which can become dominant in the third trimester. Abortion is unique among other privacy issues in requiring courts and critics to consider not only moral principles and constitutional precedents, but also conceptual or metaphysical questions such as "What is a person?" In the *Casey* case (1992) the court settled twenty years of intense controversy by explicitly upholding *Roe v. Wade.* In so doing, however, it kindled new quarrels by permitting more grounds for state regulation of abortions—even to the point of placing a substantial obstacle in the path of a

woman seeking an abortion during the first two trimesters. Thus, another constitutional criterion was born: the "undue burden standard," which permits legislatures to regulate up to a point but not beyond. Beyond that point, according to the standard, the burden placed on a woman bent on exercising her constitutional privacy right becomes an undue burden.

By 1986, the year in which *Bowers v. Hardwick* was decided, the positivist position was that of the court's new majority. The new majority challenged the new minority to find, in the explicit language of the Constitution itself, a right to practice sodomy—or at least to find a general constitutional principle, with impeccable credentials from which that specific right follows logically. This Supreme Court case probably presents the clearest confrontation yet between legal moralists, who would restrict "immoral" behavior even when discreet and harmless and the intellectual descendants of Mill, who find legitimate only those restrictions of liberty that protect people from harms or risks of harm to which they have not voluntarily consented.

Freedom of Expression and Its Limits

In the first essay in this section, Joel Feinberg considers further how the harm principle must be qualified if it is to guarantee free expression of opinion in a morally satisfactory way. He examines first the relatively noncontroversial limits on free speech imposed by Anglo-American law: civil liability for defamatory utterances and for nondefamatory statements that reveal information that is properly private, criminal liability for irresponsible statements that cause panics or riots, laws against incitements to crime, and (more controversially) sedition. They are considered in part because each raises its own questions of interest for the philosophy of law and in part because each provides a challenge for the harm principle to provide a rationale for sensible restrictions on liberty that will not at the same time justify restrictions on free speech unacceptable to Mill and other liberals. Feinberg then attempts to provide a philosophical rationale for justice Holmes's "clear and present danger" test, and concludes with comments on the inevitable balancing of interests so central to the harm principle approach to problems of liberty.

One kind of case that has caused some difficulty for liberal advocates of free speech is the public use of "obscene" language—even when that language is used to express political opinion. This sort of problem for the free-speech advocate was dramatically illustrated in the United States Supreme Court case of *Cohen v. California* in 1971. Cohen was convicted by a Los Angeles municipal Court for lingering in the corridors of a public building wearing a jacket emblazoned with the words "Fuck the Draft." In his appeal to the Supreme Court of California and later to the United States Supreme Court, Cohen claimed that his right to free speech, guaranteed by the First and Fourteenth Amendments, had been violated. The California authorities argued that they had properly applied against him a valid statute forbidding "willfully . . . offensive conduct." Now there are two ways in which a written or spoken statement can be offensive: It can express an opinion that some auditors might find offensive, or it can express an opinion in language that is itself offensive, independent of the substantive message it conveys. Neither the United States Constitution nor the libertarian principles of free expression of opinion espoused by Mill and Feinberg would permit legal interference with free speech in order to prevent the expression of an "offensive" opinion. However, restrictions on obscene, scurrilous, and incitive words, quite apart from their role in the expression of unpopular opinion, might well be justified by the offense principle, and indeed by the Constitution itself insofar as it tacitly employs the offense principle to mark out a class of exceptions to the free speech guarantee. Justice Harlan, however, rejected this approach to the case. He argued that the free expression of opinion, protected by the Constitution, extends not merely to the proposition declared by a statement but also to the speaker's (or writer's) emotions or the intensity of his or her attitudes—in the case at hand, "the depths of his feelings against the Vietnam War and the draft." Harlan's distinction points to an important function of what are ordinarily called obscene words: Unseemly epithets can shock and jolt and, in virtue of their very character as socially unacceptable, give expression to intense feelings more accurately than any other words in the language.

In *Village of Skokie v. National Socialist Party of America,* the Supreme Court of Illinois carried out the mandate of a previous United States Supreme Court decision. The decision allowed a march by the American Nazi Party through a predominantly Jewish suburb of Chicago. The focal issue was whether the use of swastikas by the marchers was protected by the First Amendment's protection of free speech.

The Court regarded the swastika as a form of protected symbolic expression that cannot be banned because of the offense it may cause or even because of the violence it may provoke. The Court held that the "fighting words" exception to First Amendment protection did not apply here. In addition, the Court maintained that the fact that those who would be upset by the sight of swastikas could avoid it without great inconvenience distinguished this case from other cases involving intrusion into the home or a captive audience. (On the other side it was argued that severe psychic hurt can be produced without actual physical confrontation.) Following *Cohen, Skokie* naturally invites comparison of the nature and degree of the offense in the two cases: on the one hand, hearing or seeing the obscene word *fuck* in a public place, and, on the other, witnessing the proud and threatening display of the symbol of the political party under whose sponsorship unspeakably brutal and genocidal slaughterings took place.

In *Texas v. Johnson* a third type of offensiveness is described for comparison with the other two: that which follows the witnessing of a wanton (one is almost tempted to say sacrilegious) destruction of a politically sacred symbol. For the philosopher as well as the judge, the three types of offensiveness and the cases to which they give rise require consistency of treatment. In turn this requirement for consistency may require that apparently similar cases nevertheless be distinguished in some morally relevant way or that dissimilar results, despite their various differences, be reconciled—that is, shown to be similar in some crucially relevant respect.

In recent years another class of odious expressions has led to fresh legislative efforts to delimit free speech. Public humiliation of groups—such as racial and ethnic minorities, political dissenters, and homosexuals—and sexual harassment, usually of women, has become a political issue. Extremely insulting signs or utterances referring to these and other groups occurred in such circumstances as to be clearly within the law—both the criminal law and the civil law of nuisance and defamation. These uses of language came to be called hate speech, and legislatures in a number of states tried to draft statutes stating the conditions under which it is prohibited. To the consternation of most students and faculty members, a large number of cases of alleged hate speech occurred on university campuses, where free speech and free inquiry have always been especially treasured. No sooner were new rules formulated than hard cases for their application stimulated new controversy. Thomas

Grey, professor of law at Stanford University, was one of the earliest to draft rules governing student conduct in this area. His lucid article highlights the pitfalls threatening all new codes. In particular, his account of the conflict between civil rights and civil liberties explains how traditional liberal values can lead not only to disagreements among liberals on specific issues but also to conflicts within the minds or hearts of particular liberal individuals who may, as a result, be too confused to take a stand. In regard to resolving dilemmas of this kind. Grey's article shows the value of careful philosophical methods.

Principles of Constitutional Interpretation

"Congress shall make no law . . . abridging the freedom of speech, or of the press." Those are the words, and the only words, contained in the U.S. Constitution—all in the First Amendment—to guide courts in deciding so-called free-speech cases. Fourteen words by the grammarian's measure, but only four that actually breed the notorious perplexity that free speech cases engender: namely, the words "abridging," "freedom," "speech," and "press." Never in the history of political institutions have so many scholars poured so many words into the interpretation of so few. The original words are few, without question, but the value attached to those words by political figures and

legal scholars has been almost beyond measure. Their constant reinterpretation has been a labor of love.

The more philosophical a judge or scholarly commentator is, the more likely he or she is to pause frequently to ask just what the rules are in the game of interpretation. What makes an authoritative interpretation of a short and cryptic constitutional passage? Does the interpreter find all the clues inside the text itself? Or are there principles of justice outside the text to which he or she can legitimately refer in order to make better sense of the few clues provided by text itself? Is evidence of the founding fathers' intentions ever relevant? Is it ever not relevant? Is anything apart from such evidence ever relevant?

Disagreement about the answers to these questions has created the leading current controversy over the limits of law, or the boundaries of liberty. It is perhaps accurate (though too simple) to say that the chief focus of these controversies is the status of the so-called right of privacy, as spelled out in *Griswold v. Connecticut* and several dozen other Supreme Court cases that followed in Griswold's wake.[2] The problem is that the Constitution nowhere explicitly confers a right of that name on all citizens, so the Court must explain where a basic right can come from if not from the Constitution. Alternatively, if the right is in the Constitution, but only tacitly expressed or sketchily suggested, that needs explanation too. For either of these purposes, a full and detailed legal philosophy is required.

---

1. Some liberal writers who would normally follow Mill do not go quite so far as Mill does on the issue of offensiveness. These writers would allow that offense to others can be an acceptable reason for prohibitory statutes usually, but a good or decisive reason only rarely, when a complex of other conditions are satisfied. See Joel Feinberg, *Offense to Others* (New York: Oxford University Press, 1986), chapter 1. Feinberg and the authors of the Model Penal Code are among those who would restrict penal statutes to harmful and (in some cases) offensive behavior.

2. In *Griswold,* Justice Douglas's passionate tribute to the institution of marriage made it seem as though a main part of the point

of *Griswold* was to protect marriage and restrict the right to use contraceptives to married couples. But seven years later, in *Eisenstadt v. Baird,* 405 U.S. 438 (1972), the Supreme Court clearly indicated that the right of privacy recognized in *Griswold* could not be limited to married couples: "If the right of privacy means anything, it is the right of the individual, married or single, to be free from unwarranted governmental intrusion into matters so fundamentally affecting a person as the decision whether to bear or beget a child."

The Case for Self-Determination

ON LIBERTY*

John Stuart Mill

The object of this Essay is to assert one very simple principle, as entitled to govern absolutely the dealings of society with the individual in the way of compulsion and control, whether the means used be physical force in the form of legal penalties, or the moral coercion of public opinion. That principle is, that the sole end for which mankind are warranted, individually or collectively, in interfering with the liberty of action of any of their number, is self-protection. That the only purpose for which power can be rightfully exercised over any member of a civilized community, against his will, is to prevent harm to others. His own good, either physical or moral, is not a sufficient warrant. He cannot rightfully be compelled to do or forbear because it will be better for him to do so, because it will make him happier, because, in the opinions of others, to do so would be wise, or even right. These are good reasons for remonstrating with him, or reasoning with him, or persuading him, or entreating him, but not for compelling him, or visiting him with any evil, in case he do otherwise. To justify that, the conduct from which it is desired to deter him must be calculated to produce evil to some one else. The only part of the conduct of any one, for which he is amenable to society, is that which concerns others. In the part which merely concerns himself, his independence is, of right, absolute. Over himself, over his own body and mind, the individual is sovereign.

It is, perhaps, hardly necessary to say that this doctrine is meant to apply only to human beings in the maturity of their faculties. We are not speaking of children, or of young persons below the age which the law may fix as that of manhood or womanhood. Those who are still in a state to require being taken care of by others, must be protected against their own actions as well as against external injury. For the same reason, we may leave out of consideration those backward states of society in which the race itself may be considered as in its nonage. The early difficulties in the way of spontaneous progress are so great, that there is seldom any choice of means for overcoming them; and a ruler full of the spirit of improvement is warranted in the use of any expedients that will attain an end, perhaps otherwise unattainable. Despotism is a legitimate mode of government in dealing with barbarians, provided the end be their improvement, and the means justified by actually effecting that end. Liberty, as a principle, has no application to any state of things anterior to the time when mankind have become capable of being improved by free and equal discussion. Until then, there is nothing for them but implicit obedience to an Akbar or a Charlemagne, if they are so fortunate as to find one. But as soon as mankind have attained the capacity of being guided to their own improvement by conviction or persuasion (a period long since reached in

---

*From *On Liberty*, excerpts from Chapters I and II, and all of Chapter IV. First published in 1859.

all nations with whom we need here concern ourselves), compulsion, either in the direct form or in that of pains and penalties for non-compliance, is no longer admissible as a means to their own good, and justifiable only for the security of others.

It is proper to state that I forego any advantage which could be derived to my argument from the idea of abstract right, as a thing independent of utility. I regard utility as the ultimate appeal on all ethical questions; but it must be utility in the largest sense, grounded on the permanent interests of man as a progressive being. Those interests, I contend, authorize the subjection of individual spontaneity to external control, only in respect to those actions of each, which concern the interest of other people. If any one does an act hurtful to others, there is a *prima facie* case for punishing him, by law, or, where legal penalties are not safely applicable, by general disapprobation. There are also many positive acts for the benefit of others, which he may rightfully be compelled to perform; such as, to give evidence in a court of justice; to bear his fair share in the common defence, or in any other joint work necessary to the interest of the society of which he enjoys the protection; and to perform certain acts of individual beneficence, such as saving a fellow creature's life, or interposing to protect the defenceless against ill-usage, things which whenever it is obviously a man's duty to do, he may rightfully be made responsible to society for not doing. A person may cause evil to others not only by his actions but by his inaction, and in either case he is justly accountable to them for the injury. The latter case, it is true, requires a much more cautious exercise of compulsion than the former. To make any one answerable for doing evil to others, is the rule; to make him answerable for not preventing evil, is, comparatively speaking, the exception. Yet there are many cases clear enough and grave enough to justify that exception. In all things which regard the external relations of the individual, he is *de jure* amenable to those whose interests are concerned, and if need be, to society as their protector. There are often good reasons for not holding him to the responsibility; but these reasons must arise from the special expediencies of the case: either because it is a kind of case in which he is on the whole likely to act better, when left to his own discretion, than when controlled in any way in which society have it in their power to control him; or because the attempt to exercise control would produce other evils, greater than those which it would prevent. When such reasons as these

preclude the enforcement of responsibility, the conscience of the agent himself should step into the vacant judgment-seat, and protect those interests of others which have no external protection; judging himself all the more rigidly, because the case does not admit of his being made accountable to the judgment of his fellow-creatures.

But there is a sphere of action in which society, as distinguished from the individual, has, if any, only an indirect interest; comprehending all that portion of a person's life and conduct which affects only himself, or, if it also affects others, only with their free, voluntary, and undeceived consent and participation. When I say only himself, I mean directly, and in the first instance: for whatever affects himself, may affect others *through* himself; and the objection which may be grounded on this contingency, will receive consideration in the sequel. This, then, is the appropriate region of human liberty. It comprises, first, the inward domain of consciousness; demanding liberty of conscience, in the most comprehensive sense; liberty of thought and feeling; absolute freedom of opinion and sentiment on all subjects, practical or speculative, scientific, moral, or theological. The liberty of expressing and publishing opinions may seem to fall under a different principle, since it belongs to that part of the conduct of an individual which concerns other people; but, being almost of as much importance as the liberty of thought itself, and resting in great part on the same reasons, is practically inseparable from it. Secondly, the principle requires liberty of tastes and pursuits; of framing the plan of our life to suit our own character; of doing as we like, subject to such consequences as may follow; without impediment from our fellow-creatures, so long as what we do does not harm them, even though they should think our conduct foolish, perverse, or wrong. Thirdly, from this liberty of each individual, follows the liberty, within the same limits, of combination among individuals; freedom to unite, for any purpose not involving harm to others: the persons combining being supposed to be of full age, and not forced or deceived.

No society on which these liberties are not, on the whole, respected, is free, whatever may be its form of government; and none is completely free in which they do not exist absolute and unqualified. The only freedom which deserves the name, is that of pursuing our own good in our own way, so long as we do not attempt to deprive others of theirs, or impede their efforts to obtain it. Each is the proper guardian of his own health, whether bodily, or mental and spiritual. Mankind are greater gainers by suffering each other to live as seems good to themselves, than by compelling each to live as seems good to the rest. . . .

We have now recognized the necessity to the mental well-being of mankind (on which all their other well-being depends) of freedom of opinion, and freedom of the expression of opinion, on four distinct grounds; which we will now briefly recapitulate.

First, if any opinion is compelled to silence that opinion may, for aught we can certainly know, be true. To deny this is to assume our own infallibility.

Secondly, though the silenced opinion be an error, it may, and very commonly does, contain a portion of truth; and since the general or prevailing opinion on any subject is rarely or never the whole truth, it is only by the collision of adverse opinions that the remainder of the truth has any chance of being supplied.

Thirdly, even if the received opinion be not only true, but the whole truth; unless it is suffered to be, and actually is vigorously and earnestly contested, it will, by most of those who receive it, be held in the manner of a prejudice, with little comprehension or feeling of its rational grounds. And not only this, but, fourthly, the meaning of the doctrine itself will be in danger of being lost, or enfeebled, and deprived of its vital effect on the character and conduct: the dogma becoming a mere formal profession, inefficacious for good, but cumbering the ground, and preventing the growth of any real and heartfelt conviction from reason or personal experience. . . .

Of the Limits to the Authority of Society over the Individual

What, then, is the rightful limit to the sovereignty of the individual over himself? Where does the authority of society begin? How much of human life should be assigned to individuality, and how much to society?

Each will receive its proper share, if each has that which more particularly concerns it. To individuality should belong the part of life in which it is chiefly the individual that is interested; to society, the part which chiefly interests society.

Though society is not founded on a contract, and though no good purpose is answered by inventing a contract in order to deduce social obligations

from it, every one who receives the protection of society owes a return for the benefit, and the fact of living in society renders it indispensable that each should be bound to observe a certain line of conduct towards the rest. This conduct consists, first, in not injuring the interests of one another; or rather certain interests, which, either by express legal provision or by tacit understanding, ought to be considered as rights; and secondly, in each person's bearing his share (to be fixed on some equitable principle) of the labors and sacrifices incurred for defending the society or its members from injury and molestation. These conditions society is justified in enforcing, at all costs to those who endeavor to withhold fulfillment. Nor is this all that society may do. The acts of an individual may be hurtful to others, or wanting in due consideration for their welfare, without going the length of violating any of their constituted rights. The offender may then be justly punished by opinion, though not by law. As soon as any part of a person's conduct affects prejudicially the interests of others, society has jurisdiction over it, and the question whether the general welfare will or will not be promoted by interfering with it, becomes open to discussion. But there is no room for entertaining any such question when a person's conduct affects the interests of no persons besides himself, or needs not affect them unless they like (all the persons concerned being of full age, and the ordinary amount of understanding). In all such cases there should be perfect freedom, legal and social, to do the action and stand the consequences.

It would be a great misunderstanding of this doctrine, to suppose that it is one of selfish indifference, which pretends that human beings have no business with each other's conduct in life, and that they should not concern themselves about the well-doing or well-being of one another, unless their own interest is involved. Instead of any diminution, there is need of a great increase of disinterested exertion to promote the good of others. But disinterested benevolence can find other instruments to persuade people to their good, than whips and scourges, either of the literal or the metaphorical sort. I am the last person to undervalue the self-regarding virtues; they are only second in importance, if even second, to the social. It is equally the business of education to cultivate both. But even education works by conviction and persuasion as well as by compulsion, and it is by the former only that, when the period of education is past, the self-regarding virtues should be inculcated. Human beings owe to each other help to distinguish the better from the worse, and encouragement to choose the former and avoid the latter. They should be forever stimulating each other to increased exercise of their higher faculties, and increased direction of their feelings and aims towards wise instead of foolish, elevating instead of degrading, objects and contemplations. But neither one person, nor any number of persons, is warranted in saying to another human creature of ripe years, that he shall not do with his life for his own benefit what he chooses to do with it. He is the person most interested in his own well-being: the interest which any other person, except in cases of strong personal attachment, can have in it, is trifling, compared with that which he himself has; the interest which society has in him individually (except as to his conduct to others) is fractional, and altogether indirect: while, with respect to his own feelings and circumstances, the most ordinary man or woman has means of knowledge immeasurably surpassing those that can be possessed by anyone else. The interference of society to overrule his judgment and purposes in what only regards himself, must be grounded on general presumptions; which may be altogether wrong, and even if right, are as likely as not to be misapplied to individual cases, by persons no better acquainted with the circumstances of such cases than those are who look at them merely from without. In this department, therefore, of human affairs, individuality has its proper field of action. In the conduct of human beings towards one another, it is necessary that general rules should for the most part be observed, in order that people may know what they have to expect; but in each person's own concerns, his individual spontaneity is entitled to free exercise. Considerations to aid his judgment, exhortations to strengthen his will, may be offered to him, even obtruded on him, by others; but he, himself, is the final judge. All errors which he is likely to commit against advice and warning, are far outweighed by the evil of allowing others to constrain him to what they deem his good.

I do not mean that the feelings with which a person is regarded by others, ought not to be in any way affected by his self-regarding qualities or deficiencies. This is neither possible nor desirable. If he is eminent in any of the qualities which conduce to his own good, he is, so far, a proper object of admiration. He is so much the nearer to the ideal perfection of human nature. If he is grossly deficient in those qualities, a sentiment the opposite of admiration will follow. There is a degree of folly, and a de-

gree of what may be called (though the phrase is not unobjectionable) lowness or depravation of taste, which, though it cannot justify doing harm to the person who manifests it, renders him necessarily and properly a subject of distaste, or, in extreme cases, even of contempt: a person would not have the opposite qualities in due strength without entertaining these feelings. Though doing no wrong to anyone, a person may so act as to compel us to judge him, and feel to him, as a fool, or as a being of an inferior order: and since this judgment and feeling are a fact which he would prefer to avoid, it is doing him a service to warn him of it beforehand, as of any other disagreeable consequence to which he exposes himself. It would be well, indeed, if this good office were much more freely rendered than the common notions of politeness at present permit, and if one person could honestly point out to another that he thinks him in fault, without being considered unmannerly or presuming. We have a right, also, in various ways, to act upon our unfavorable opinion of any one, not to the oppression of his individuality, but in the exercise of ours. We are not bound, for example, to seek his society; we have a right to avoid it (though not to parade the avoidance), for we have a right to choose the society most acceptable to us. We have a right, and it may be our duty to caution others against him, if we think his example or conversation likely to have a pernicious effect on those with whom he associates. We may give others a preference over him in optional good offices, except those which tend to his improvement. In these various modes a person may suffer very severe penalties at the hands of others, for faults which directly concern only himself; but he suffers these penalties only in so far as they are the natural, and, as it were, the spontaneous consequences of the faults themselves, not because they are purposely inflicted on him for the sake of punishment. A person who shows rashness, obstinacy, self-conceit—who cannot live within moderate means—who cannot restrain himself from hurtful indulgences—who pursues animal pleasures at the expense of those of feelings and intellect—must expect to be lowered in the opinion of others, and to have a less share of their favorable sentiments, but of this he has no right to complain, unless he has merited their favor by special excellence in his social relations and has thus established a title to their good offices, which is not affected by his demerits towards himself.

What I contend for is, that the inconveniences which are strictly inseparable from the unfavorable judgment of others, are the only ones to which a person should ever be subjected for that portion of his conduct and character which concerns his own good, but which does not affect the interests of others in their relations with him. Acts injurious to others require a totally different treatment. Encroachment on their rights; infliction on them of any loss or damage not justified by his own rights; falsehood or duplicity in dealing with them; unfair or ungenerous use of advantages over them; even selfish abstinence from defending them against injury—these are fit objects of moral reprobation, and, in grave cases, of moral retribution and punishment. And not only these acts, but the dispositions which lead to them, are properly immoral, and fit subjects of disapprobation which may rise to abhorrence. Cruelty of disposition; malice and ill-nature; that most anti-social and odious of all passions, envy; dissimulation and insincerity; irascibility on insufficient cause, and resentment disproportioned to the provocation; the love of domineering over others; the desire to engross more than one's share of advantages (the πλεονεξία of the Greeks); the pride which derives gratification from the abasement of others; the egotism which thinks self and its concerns more important than every-thing else, and decides all doubtful questions in his own favor—these are moral vices, and constitute a bad and odious moral character: unlike the self-regarding faults previously mentioned, which are not properly immoralities, and to whatever pitch they may be carried, do not constitute wickedness. They may be proofs of any amount of folly, or want of personal dignity and self-respect; but they are only a subject of moral reprobation when they involve a breach of duty to others, for whose sake the individual is bound to have care for himself. What are called duties to ourselves are not socially obligatory, unless circumstances render them at the same time duties to others. The term duty to oneself, when it means anything more than prudence, means self-respect or self-development; and for none of these is any one accountable to his fellow-creatures, because for none of them is it for the good of mankind that he be held accountable to them.

The distinction between the loss of consideration which a person may rightly incur by defect of prudence or of personal dignity, and the reprobation which is due to him for an offence against the rights of others, is not a merely nominal distinction. It makes a vast difference both in our feelings and in our conduct towards him, whether he displeases us in things in which we think we have a right to control him, or in things in which we know that we have not. If he displeases us, we may express our distaste, and we may stand aloof from a person as well as from a thing that displeases us; but we shall not therefore feel called on to make his life uncomfortable. We shall reflect that he already bears, or will bear, the whole penalty of his error; if he spoils his life by mismanagement, we shall not, for that reason, desire to spoil it still further: instead of wishing to punish him, we shall rather endeavor to alleviate his punishment, by showing him how he may avoid or cure the evils his conduct tends to bring upon him. He may be to us an object of pity, perhaps of dislike, but not of anger or resentment; we shall not treat him like an enemy of society: the worst we shall think ourselves justified in doing is leaving him to himself, if we do not interfere benevolently by showing interest or concern for him. It is far otherwise if he has infringed the rules necessary for the protection of his fellow-creatures, individually or collectively. The evil consequences of his acts do not then fall on himself, but on others; and society, as the protector of all its members, must retaliate on him; must inflict pain on him for the express purpose of punishment, and must take care that it be sufficiently severe. In the one case, he is an offender at our bar, and we are called on not only to sit in judgment on him, but, in one shape or another, to execute our own sentence: in the other case, it is not our part to inflict any suffering on him, except what may incidentally follow from our using the same liberty in the regulation of our own affairs, which we allow to him in his.

The distinction here pointed out between the part of a person's life which concerns only himself, and that which concerns others, many persons will refuse to admit. How (it may be asked) can any part of the conduct of a member of society be a matter of indifference to the other members? No person is an entirely isolated being; it is impossible for a person to do anything seriously or permanently hurtful to himself, without mischief reaching at least to his near connections, and often far beyond them. If he injures his property, he does harm to those who directly or indirectly derived support from it, and usually diminishes, by a greater or less amount, the general resources of the community. If he deteriorates his bodily or mental faculties, he not only brings evil upon all who depended on him for any portion of their happiness, but disqualifies himself for rendering the services which he owes to his fellow-creatures generally; perhaps becomes a burden on their affection or benevolence; and if such conduct were very frequent, hardly any offence that is committed would detract more from the general sum of good. Finally, if by his vices or follies a person does no direct harm to others, he is nevertheless (it may be said) injurious by his example; and ought to be compelled to control himself, for the sake of those whom the sight or knowledge of his conduct might corrupt or mislead.

And even (it will be added) if the consequences of misconduct could be confined to the vicious or thoughtless individual, ought society to abandon to their own guidance those who are manifestly unfit for it? If protection against themselves is confessedly due to children and persons under age, is not society equally bound to afford it to persons of mature years who are equally incapable of self-government? If gambling, or drunkenness, or incontinence, or idleness, or uncleanliness, are as injurious to happiness, and as great a hindrance to improvement, as many or most of the acts prohibited by law, why (it may be asked) should not law, so far as is consistent with practicability and social convenience, endeavor to repress these also? And as a supplement to the unavoidable imperfections of law, ought not opinion at least to organize a powerful police against these vices, and visit rigidly with social penalties those who are known to practise them? There is no question here (it may be said) about restricting individuality, or impeding the trial of new and original experiments in living. The only things it is sought to prevent are things which have been tried and condemned from the beginning of the world until now; things which experience has shown not to be useful or suitable to any person's individuality. There must be some length of time and amount of experience, after which a moral or prudential truth may be regarded as established: and it is merely desired to prevent generation after generation from falling over the same precipice which has been fatal to their predecessors.

I fully admit that the mischief which a person does to himself, may seriously affect, both through their sympathies and their interests, those nearly connected with him, and in a minor degree, society at large. When, by conduct of this sort, a person is led to violate a distinct and assignable obligation to any other person or persons, the case is taken out of the self-regarding class, and becomes amenable to moral disapprobation in the proper sense of the term. If, for example, a man, through intemperance or extravagance, becomes unable to pay his debts,

or, having undertaken the moral responsibility of a family, becomes from the same cause incapable of supporting or educating them, he is deservedly reprobated, and might be justly punished; but it is for the breach of duty to his family or creditors, not for the extravagance. If the resources which ought to have been devoted to them, had been diverted from them for the most prudent investment, the moral culpability would have been the same. George Barnwell murdered his uncle to get money for his mistress, but if he had done it to set himself up in business, he would equally have been hanged. Again, in the frequent case of a man who causes grief to his family by addiction to bad habits, he deserves reproach for his unkindness or ingratitude; but so he may for cultivating habits not in themselves vicious, if they are painful to those with whom he passes his life, or who from personal ties are dependent on him for their comfort. Whoever fails in the consideration generally due to the interests and feelings of others, not being compelled by some more imperative duty, or justified by allowable self-preference, is a subject of moral disapprobation for that failure, but not for the cause of it, nor for the errors, merely personal to himself, which may have remotely led to it. In like manner; when a person disables himself, by conduct purely self-regarding, from the performance of some definite duty incumbent on him to the public, he is guilty of a social offence. No person ought to be punished simply for being drunk; but a soldier or a policeman should be punished for being drunk on duty. Whenever, in short, there is a definite damage, or a definite risk of damage, either to an individual or to the public, the case is taken out of the province of liberty, and placed in that of morality or law.

But with regard to the merely contingent, or, as it may be called, constructive injury which a person causes to society, by conduct which neither violates any specific duty to the public, nor occasions perceptible hurt to any assignable individual except himself; the inconvenience is one which society can afford to bear, for the sake of the greater good of human freedom. If grown persons are to be punished for not taking proper care of themselves, I would rather it were for their own sake, than under pretence of preventing them from impairing their capacity of rendering to society benefits which society does not pretend it has a right to exact. But I cannot consent to argue the point as if society had no means of bringing its weaker members up to its ordinary standard of rational conduct, except waiting till they do something irrational, and then punishing them, legally or morally, for it. Society has had absolute power over them during all the early portion of their existence: it has had the whole period of childhood and nonage in which to try whether it could make them capable of rational conduct in life. The existing generation is master both of the training and the entire circumstances of the generation to come; it cannot indeed make them perfectly wise and good, because it is itself so lamentably deficient in goodness and wisdom; and its best efforts are not always, in individual cases, its most successful ones; but it is perfectly well able to make the rising generation, as a whole, as good as, and a little better than, itself. If society lets any considerable number of its members grow up mere children, incapable of being acted on by rational consideration of distant motives, society has itself to blame for the consequences. Armed not only with all the powers of education, but with the ascendency which the authority of a received opinion always exercises over the minds who are least fitted to judge for themselves; and aided by the *natural* penalties which cannot be prevented from falling on those who incur the distaste or the contempt of those who know them; let not society pretend that it needs, besides all this, the power to issue commands and enforce obedience in the personal concerns of individuals, in which, on all principles of justice and policy, the decision ought to rest with those who are to abide the consequences. Nor is there anything which tends more to discredit and frustrate the better means of influencing conduct, than a resort to the worse. If there be among those whom it is attempted to coerce into prudence or temperance, any of the material of which vigorous and independent characters are made, they will infallibly rebel against the yoke. No such person will ever feel that others have a right to control him in his concerns, such as they have to prevent him from injuring them in theirs; and it easily comes to be considered a mark of spirit and courage to fly in the face of such usurped authority, and do with ostentation the exact opposite of what it enjoins; as in the fashion of grossness which succeeded, in the time of Charles II, to the fanatical moral intolerance of the Puritans. With respect to what is said of the necessity of protecting society from the bad example set to others by the vicious or the self-indulgent; it is true that bad example may have a pernicious effect, especially the example of doing wrong to others with impunity to the wrongdoer. But we are now speaking of conduct which, while it does no wrong

to others, is supposed to do great harm to the agent himself: and I do not see how those who believe this, can think otherwise than that the example, on the whole, must be more salutary than hurtful, since, if it displays the misconduct, it displays also the painful or degrading consequences which, if the conduct is justly censured, must be supposed to be in all or most cases attendant on it.

But the strongest of all the arguments against the interference of the public with purely personal conduct, is that when it does interfere, the odds are that it interferes wrongly, and in the wrong place. On questions of social morality, of duty to others, the opinion of the public, that is, of an overruling majority, though often wrong, is likely to be still oftener right; because on such questions they are only required to judge of their own interests; of the manner in which some mode of conduct, if allowed to be practised, would affect themselves. But the opinion of a similar majority, imposed as a law on the minority, on questions of self-regarding conduct, is quite as likely to be wrong as right; for in these cases public opinion means, at the best, some people's opinion of what is good or bad for other people; while very often it does not even mean that; the public, with the most perfect indifference, passing over the pleasure or convenience of those whose conduct they censure, and considering only their own preference. There are many who consider as an injury to themselves any conduct which they have a distaste for, and resent it as an outrage to their feelings; as a religious bigot, when charged with disregarding the religious feelings of others, has been known to retort that they disregard his feelings, by persisting in their abominable worship or creed. But there is no parity between the feeling of a person for his own opinion, and the feeling of another who is offended at his holding it; no more than between the desire of a thief to take a purse, and the desire of the right owner to keep it. And a person's taste is as much his own peculiar concern as his opinion or his purse. It is easy for any one to imagine an ideal public, which leaves the freedom and choice of individuals in all uncertain matters undisturbed, and only requires them to abstain from modes of conduct which universal experience has condemned. But where has there been seen a public which set any such limit to its censorship? or when does the public trouble itself about universal experience? In its interferences with personal conduct it is seldom thinking of anything but the enormity of acting or feeling differently from itself; and this standard of judgment, thinly disguised, is held up to mankind as the dictate of religion and philosophy, by nine tenths of all moralists and speculative writers. These teach that things are right because they are right; because we feel them to be so. They tell us to search in our own minds and hearts for laws of conduct binding on ourselves and on all others. What can the poor public do but apply these instructions, and make their own personal feelings of good and evil, if they are tolerably unanimous in them, obligatory on all the world?

The evil here pointed out is not one which exists only in theory; and it may perhaps be expected that I should specify the instances in which the public of this age and country improperly invests its own preferences with the character of moral laws. I am not writing an essay on the aberrations of existing moral feeling. That is too weighty a subject to be discussed parenthetically, and by way of illustration. Yet examples are necessary, to show that the principle I maintain is of serious and practical moment, and that I am not endeavoring to erect a barrier against imaginary evils. And it is not difficult to show, by abundant instances, that to extend the bounds of what may be called moral police, until it encroaches on the most unquestionably legitimate liberty of the individual, is one of the most universal of all human propensities.

As a first instance, consider the antipathies which men cherish on no better grounds than that persons whose religious opinions are different from theirs, do not practise their religious observances, especially their religious abstinences. To cite a rather trivial example, nothing in the creed or practice of Christians does more to envenom the hatred of Mahomedans against them, than the fact of their eating pork. There are few acts which Christians and Europeans regard with more unaffected disgust, than Mussulmans regard this particular mode of satisfying hunger. It is, in the first place, an offence against their religion; but this circumstance by no means explains either the degree or the kind of their repugnance; for wine also is forbidden by their religion, and to partake of it is by all Mussulmans accounted wrong, but not disgusting. Their aversion to the flesh of the "unclean beast" is, on the contrary, of that peculiar character, resembling an instinctive antipathy, which the idea of uncleanness, when once it thoroughly sinks into the feelings, seems always to excite even in those whose personal habits are anything but scrupulously cleanly, and of which the sentiment of religious impurity, so intense in the

Hindoos, is a remarkable example. Suppose now that in a people, of whom the majority were Mussulmans, that majority should insist upon not permitting pork to be eaten within the limits of the country. This would be nothing new in Mahomedan countries.[1] Would it be a legitimate exercise of the moral authority of public opinion? and if not, why not? The practice is really revolting to such a public. They also sincerely think that it is forbidden and abhorred by the Deity. Neither could the prohibition be censured as religious persecution. It might be religious in its origin, but it would not be persecution for religion, since nobody's religion makes it a duty to eat pork. The only tenable ground of condemnation would be, that with the personal tastes and self-regarding concerns of individuals the public has no business to interfere.

To come somewhat nearer home: the majority of Spaniards consider it a gross impiety, offensive in the highest degree to the Supreme Being, to worship him in any other manner than the Roman Catholic; and no other public worship is lawful on Spanish soil. The people of all Southern Europe look upon a married clergy as not only irreligious, but unchaste, indecent, gross, disgusting. What do Protestants think of these perfectly sincere feelings, and of the attempt to enforce them against non-Catholics? Yet, if mankind are justified in interfering with each other's liberty in things which do not concern the interests of others, on what principle is it possible consistently to exclude these cases? or who can blame people for desiring to suppress what they regard as a scandal in the sight of God and man? No stronger case can be shown for prohibiting anything which is regarded as a personal immorality, than is made out for suppressing these practices in the eyes of those who regard them as impieties; and unless we are willing to adopt the logic of persecutors, and to say that we may persecute others because we are right, and that they must not persecute us because they are wrong, we must beware of admitting a principle of which we should resent as a gross injustice the application to ourselves.

The preceding instances may be objected to, although unreasonably, as drawn from contingencies impossible among us: opinion, in this country, not being likely to enforce abstinence from meats, or to interfere with people for worshipping, and for either marrying or not marrying, according to their creed or inclination. The next example, however, shall be taken from an interference with liberty which we have by no means passed all danger of.

Wherever the puritans have been sufficiently powerful, as in New England, and in Great Britain at the time of the Commonwealth, they have endeavored, with considerable success, to put down all public, and nearly all private, amusements: especially music, dancing, public games, or other assemblages for purposes of diversion, and the theatre. There are still in this country large bodies of persons by whose notions of morality and religion these recreations are condemned; and those persons belonging chiefly to the middle class, who are the ascendant power in the present social and political condition of the kingdom, it is by no means impossible that persons of these sentiments may at some time or other command a majority in Parliament. How will the remaining portion of the community like to have the amusements that shall be permitted to them regulated by the religious and moral sentiments of the stricter Calvinists and Methodists? Would they not, with considerable peremptoriness, desire these intrusively pious members of society to mind their own business? This is precisely what should be said to every government and every public, who have the pretension that no person shall enjoy any pleasure which they think wrong. But if the principle of the pretension be admitted, no one can reasonably object to its being acted on in the sense of the majority, or other preponderating power in the country; and all persons must be ready to conform to the idea of a Christian commonwealth, as understood by the early settlers in New England, if a religious profession similar to theirs should ever succeed in regaining its lost ground, as religions supposed to be declining have so often been known to do.

To imagine other contingency, perhaps more likely to be realized than the one last mentioned. There is confessedly a strong tendency in the modern world towards a democratic constitution of society, accompanied or not by popular political institutions. It is affirmed that in the country where this tendency is most completely realized—where both society and the government are most democratic—the United States—the feeling of the majority, to whom any appearance of a more showy or costly style of living than they can hope to rival is disagreeable, operates as a tolerably effectual sumptuary law, and that in many parts of the Union it is really difficult for a person possessing a very large income, to find any mode of spending it, which will not incur popular disapprobation. Though such statements as these are doubtless much exaggerated as a representation of existing facts, the state of

things they describe is not only a conceivable and possible, but a probable result of democratic feeling, combined with the notion that the public has a right to a veto on the manner in which individuals shall spend their incomes. We have only further to suppose a considerable diffusion of Socialist opinions, and it may become infamous in the eyes of the majority to possess more property than some very small amount, or any income not earned by manual labor. Opinions similar in principle to these, already prevail widely among the artisan class, and weigh oppressively on those who are amenable to the opinion chiefly of that class, namely, its own members. It is known that the bad workmen who form the majority of the operatives in many branches of industry, are decidedly of opinion that bad workmen ought to receive the same wages as good, and that no one ought to be allowed, through piecework or otherwise, to earn by superior skill or industry more than others can without it. And they employ a moral police, which occasionally becomes a physical one, to deter skilful workmen from receiving, and employers from giving, a larger remuneration for a more useful service. If the public have any jurisdiction over private concerns, I cannot see that these people are in fault, or that any individual's particular public can be blamed for asserting the same authority over his individual conduct, which the general public asserts over people in general.

But, without dwelling upon suppositious cases, there are, in our own day, gross usurpations upon the liberty of private life actually practised, and still greater ones threatened with some expectation of success, and opinions proposed which assert an unlimited right in the public not only to prohibit by law everything which it thinks wrong, but in order to get at what it thinks wrong, to prohibit any number of things which it admits to be innocent.

Under the name of preventing intemperance, the people of one English colony, and of nearly half the United States, have been interdicted by law from making any use whatever of fermented drinks, except for medical purposes: for prohibition of their sale is in fact, as it is intended to be, prohibition of their use. And though the impracticability of executing the law has caused its repeal in several of the States which had adopted it, including the one from which it derives its name, an attempt has notwithstanding been commenced, and is prosecuted with considerable zeal by many of the professed philanthropists, to agitate for a similar law in this country. The association, or "Alliance" as it terms itself, which has been formed for this purpose, has acquired some notoriety through the publicity given to a correspondence between its Secretary and one of the very few English public men who hold that a politician's opinions ought to be founded on principles. Lord Stanley's share in this correspondence is calculated to strengthen the hopes already built on him, by those who know how rare such qualities as are manifested in some of his public appearances, unhappily are among those who figure in political life. The organ of the Alliance, who would "deeply deplore the recognition of any principle which could be wrested to justify bigotry and persecution," undertakes to point out the "broad and impassable barrier" which divides such principles from those of the association. "All matters relating to thought, opinion, conscience, appear to me," he says, "to be without the sphere of legislation; all pertaining to social act, habit, relation, subject only to a discretionary power vested in the State itself, and not in the individual, to be within it." No mention is made of a third class, different from either of these, viz., acts and habits which are not social, but individual; although it is to this class, surely, that the act of drinking fermented liquors belongs. Selling fermented liquors, however, is trading, and trading is a social act. But the infringement complained of is not on the liberty of the seller, but on that of the buyer and consumer; since the State might just as well forbid him to drink wine, as purposely make it impossible for him to obtain it. The Secretary, however, says, "I claim, as a citizen, a right to legislate whenever my social rights are invaded by the social act of another." And now for the definition of these "social rights." "If anything invades my social rights, certainly the traffic in strong drink does. It destroys my primary right of security, by constantly creating and stimulating social disorder. It invades my right of equality, by deriving a profit from the creation of a misery, I am taxed to support. It impedes my right to free moral and intellectual development, by surrounding my path with dangers, and by weakening and demoralizing society, from which I have a right to claim mutual aid and intercourse." A theory of "social rights," the like of which probably never before found its way into distinct language—being nothing short of this—that it is the absolute social right of every individual, that every other individual shall act in every respect exactly as he ought; that whosoever fails thereof in the smallest particular, violates my social right, and entitles me to demand from the legislature the removal of the grievance. So monstrous a principle is far more dangerous than any

single interference with liberty; there is no violation of liberty which it would not justify; it acknowledges no right to any freedom whatever, except perhaps to that of holding opinions in secret, without ever disclosing them: for the moment an opinion which I consider noxious, passes any one's lips, it invades all the "social rights" attributed to me by the Alliance. The doctrine ascribes to all mankind a vested interest in each other's moral, intellectual, and even physical perfection, to be defined by each claimant according to his own standard.

Another important example of illegitimate interference with the rightful liberty of the individual, not simply threatened, but long since carried into triumphant effect, is Sabbatarian legislation. Without doubt, abstinence on one day in the week, so far as the exigencies of life permit, from the usual daily occupation, though in no respect religiously binding on any except Jews, it is a highly beneficial custom. And inasmuch as this custom cannot be observed without a general consent to that effect among the industrious classes, therefore, in so far as some persons by working may impose the same necessity on others, it may be allowable and right that the law should guarantee to each, the observance by others of the custom, by suspending the greater operations of industry on a particular day. But this justification, grounded on the direct interest which others have in each individual's observance of the practice, does not apply to the self-chosen occupations in which a person may think fit to employ his leisure; nor does it hold good, in the smallest degree, for legal restrictions on amusements. It is true that the amusement of some is the day's work of others; but the pleasure, not to say the useful recreation, of many, is worth the labor of a few, provided the occupation is freely chosen, and can be freely resigned. The operatives are perfectly right in thinking that if all worked on Sunday seven days' work would have to be given for six days' wages: but so long as the great mass of employments are suspended, the small number who for the enjoyment of others must still work, obtain a proportional increase of earnings; and they are not obliged to follow those occupations, if they prefer leisure to emolument. If a further remedy is sought, it might be found in the establishment by custom of a holiday on some other day of the week for those particular classes of persons. The only ground, therefore, on which restrictions on Sunday amusements can be defended, must be that they are religiously wrong; a motive of legislation which never can be too earnestly protested again. "Deorum injuriae Diis curae." It remains to be proved that society or any of its officers holds a commission from on high to avenge any supposed offence to Omnipotence, which is not also a wrong to our fellow-creatures. The notion that it is one man's duty that another should be religious, was the foundation of all the religious persecutions ever perpetrated, and if admitted, would fully justify them. Though the feeling which breaks out in the repeated attempts to stop railway travelling on Sunday, in the resistance to the opening of Museums, and the like, has not the cruelty of the old persecutors, the state of mind indicated by it is fundamentally the same. It is a determination not to tolerate others in doing what is permitted by their religion, because it is not permitted by the persecutor's religion. It is a belief that God not only abominates the act of the misbeliever, but will not hold us guiltless if we leave him unmolested.

I cannot refrain from adding to these examples of the little account commonly made of human liberty, the language of downright persecution which breaks out from the press of this country, whenever it feels called on to notice the remarkable phenomenon of Mormonism. Much might be said on the unexpected and instructive fact, that an alleged new revelation, and a religion founded on it, the product of palpable imposture, not even supported by the *prestige* of extraordinary qualities in its founder, is believed by hundreds of thousands, and has been made the foundation of a society, in the age of newspapers, railways, and the electric telegraph. What here concerns us is, that this religion, like other and better religions, has its martyrs; that its prophet and founder was, for his teaching, put to death by a mob; that others of its adherents lost their lives by the same lawless violence; that they were forcibly expelled, in a body, from the country in which they first grew up; while, now that they have been chased into a solitary recess in the midst of a desert, many of this country openly declare that it would be right (only that it is not convenient) to send an expedition against them, and compel them by force to conform to the opinion of other people. The article of the Mormonite doctrine which is the chief provocative to the antipathy which thus breaks through the ordinary restraints of religious tolerance, is its sanction of polygamy; which, though permitted to Mahomedans, and Hindoos, and Chinese, seems to excite unquenchable animosity when practised by persons who speak English, and profess to be a kind of Christians. No one has a deeper disapprobation than I have of the Mormon institution;

both for other reasons, and because, far from being in any way countenanced by the principle of liberty, it is a direct infraction of that principle, being a mere riveting of the chains of one half of the community, and an emancipation of the other from reciprocity of obligation towards them. Still, it must be remembered that this relation is as much voluntary on the part of the women concerned in it, and who may be deemed the sufferers by it, as is the case with any other form of the marriage institution; and however surprising this fact may appear, it has its explanation in the common ideas and customs of the world, which teaching women to think marriage the one thing needful, make it intelligible that many a woman should prefer being one of several wives, to not being a wife at all. Other countries are not asked to recognize such unions, or release any portion of their inhabitants from their own laws on the score of Mormonite opinions. But when the dissentients have conceded to the hostile sentiments of others, far more than could justly be demanded; when they have left the countries to which their doctrines were unacceptable, and established themselves in a remote corner of the earth, which they have been the first to render habitable to human beings; it is difficult to see on what principles but those of tyranny they can be prevented from living there under what laws they please, provided they commit no aggression on other nations, and allow perfect freedom of departure to those who are dissatisfied with their ways. A recent writer, in some respects of considerable merit, proposes (to use his own words) not a crusade, but a *civilizade,* against this polygamous community, to put an end to what seems to him a retrograde step in civilization. It also appears so to me, but I am not aware that any community has a right to force another to be civilized. So long as the sufferers by the bad law do not invoke assistance from other communities, I cannot admit that persons entirely unconnected with them ought to step in and require that a condition of things with which all who are directly interested appear to be satisfied, should be put an end to because it is a scandal to persons some thousands of miles distant, who have no part or concern in it. Let them send missionaries, if they please, to preach against it; and let them, by any fair means (of which silencing the teachers is not one), oppose the progress of similar doctrines among their own people. If civilization has got the better of barbarism when barbarism had the world to itself, it is too much to profess to be afraid lest barbarism, after having been fairly got under, should revive and conquer civilization. A civilization that can thus succumb to its vanquished enemy must first have become so degenerate, that neither its appointed priests and teachers, nor anybody else, has the capacity, or will take the trouble, to stand up for it. If this be so, the sooner such a civilization receives notice to quit, the better. It can only go on from bad to worse, until destroyed and regenerated (like the Western Empire) by energetic barbarians.

---

1. The case of the Bombay Parsees is a curious instance in point. When this industrious and enterprising tribe, the descendants of the Persian fire-worshippers, flying from their native country before the Caliphs, arrived in Western India, they were admitted to toleration by the Hindoo sovereigns, on condition of not eating beef. When those regions afterwards fell under the dominion of Mahomedan conquerors, the Parsees obtained from them a continuance of indulgence, on condition of refraining from pork. What was at first obedience to authority became a second nature, and the Parsees to this day abstain both from beef and pork. Though not required by their religion, the double abstinence has had time to grow into a custom of their tribe; and custom, in the East, is a religion.

Challenges to Self-Determination

PATERNALISM*

Gerald Dworkin

Neither one person, nor any number of persons, is warranted in saying to another human creature of ripe years, that he shall not do with his life for his own benefit what he chooses to do with it.

—Mill

I do not want to go along with a volunteer basis. I think a fellow should be compelled to become better and not let him use his discretion whether he wants to get smarter, more healthy or more honest.

—General Hershey

I take as my starting point the "one very simple principle" proclaimed by Mill *On Liberty* . . .

That principle is, that the sole end for which mankind are warranted, individually or collectively, in interfering with the liberty of action of any of their number, is self-protection. That the only purpose for which power can be rightfully exercised over any member of a civilized community, against his will, is to prevent harm to others. He cannot rightfully be compelled to do or forbear because it will be better for him to do so, because it will make him happier, because, in the opinion of others, to do so would be wise, or even right.

This principle is neither "one" nor "very simple." It is at least two principles; one asserting that self-protection or the prevention of harm to others is sometimes a sufficient warrant and the other claiming that the individual's own good is *never* a sufficient warrant for the exercise of compulsion either by the society as a whole or by its individual members. I assume that no one, with the possible exception of extreme pacifists or anarchists, questions the correctness of the first half of the principle. This essay is an examination of the negative claim embodied in Mill's principle—the objection to paternalistic interferences with a man's liberty.

I

By paternalism I shall understand roughly the interference with a person's liberty of action justified by reasons referring exclusively to the welfare, good, happiness, needs, interests or values of the person being coerced. One is always well-advised to illustrate one's definitions by examples but it is not easy to find "pure" examples of paternalistic interferences. For almost any piece of legislation is justified by several different kinds of reasons and even if historically a piece of legislation can be shown to have been introduced for purely paternalistic motives, it may be that advocates of the legislation with an antipaternalistic outlook can find sufficient reasons justifying the legislation without appealing to the

*From *Morality and the Law*, edited by Richard A. Wasserstrom. Copyright © 1971 by Wadsworth Publishing Company, Inc., Belmont, California 94002. Reprinted by permission of the publisher and the author.

reasons which were originally adduced to support it. Thus, for example, it may be that the original legislation requiring motorcyclists to wear safety helmets was introduced for purely paternalistic reasons. But the Rhode Island Supreme Court recently upheld such legislation on the grounds that it was "not persuaded that the legislature is powerless to prohibit individuals from pursuing a course of conduct which could conceivably result in their becoming public charges," thus clearly introducing reasons of a quite different kind. Now I regard this decision as being based on reasoning of a very dubious nature but it illustrates the kind of problem one has in finding examples. The following is a list of the kinds of interferences I have in mind as being paternalistic.

II

1. Laws requiring motorcyclists to wear safety helmets when operating their machines.
2. Laws forbidding persons from swimming at a public beach when lifeguards are not on duty.
3. Laws making suicide a criminal offense.
4. Laws making it illegal for women and children to work at certain types of jobs.
5. Laws regulating certain kinds of sexual conduct, for example, homosexuality among consenting adults in private.
6. Laws regulating the use of certain drugs which may have harmful consequences to the user but do not lead to antisocial conduct.
7. Laws requiring a license to engage in certain professions with those not receiving a license subject to fine or jail sentence if they do engage in the practice.
8. Laws compelling people to spend a specified fraction of their income on the purchase of retirement annuities (Social Security).
9. Laws forbidding various forms of gambling (often justified on the grounds that the poor are more likely to throw away their money on such activities than the rich who can afford to).
10. Laws regulating the maximum rates of interest for loans.
11. Laws against duelling.

In addition to laws which attach criminal or civil penalties to certain kinds of action there are laws, rules, regulations, decrees which make it either difficult or impossible for people to carry out their plans and which are also justified on paternalistic grounds. Examples of this are:

1. Laws regulating the types of contracts which will be upheld as valid by the courts, for example (an example of Mill's to which I shall return), no man may make a valid contract for perpetual involuntary servitude.
2. Not allowing assumption of risk as a defense to an action based on the violation of a safety statute.
3. Not allowing as a defense to a charge of murder or assault the consent of the victim.
4. Requiring members of certain religious sects to have compulsory blood transfusions. This is made possible by not allowing the patient to have recourse to civil suits for assault and battery and by means of injunctions.
5. Civil commitment procedures when these are specifically justified on the basis of preventing the person being committed from harming himself. The D. C. Hospitalization of the Mentally Ill Act provides for involuntary hospitalization of a person who "is mentally ill, and because of that illness, is likely to injure himself or others if allowed to remain at liberty." The term injure in this context applies to unintentional as well as intentional injuries.

All of my examples are of existing restrictions on the liberty of individuals. Obviously one can think of interferences which have not yet been imposed. Thus one might ban the sale of cigarettes, or require that people wear safety belts in automobiles (as opposed to merely having them installed), enforcing this by not allowing a motorist to sue for injuries even when caused by other drivers if the motorist was not wearing a seat belt at the time of the accident.

I shall not be concerned with activities which though defended on paternalistic grounds are not interferences with the liberty of persons, for example, the giving of subsidies in kind rather than in cash on the grounds that the recipients would not spend the money on the goods which they really need, or not including a $1,000 deductible provision in a basic protection automobile insurance plan on the ground that the people who would elect it could least afford it. Nor shall I be concerned with measures such as "truth-in-advertising" acts and Pure Food and Drug legislation which are often attacked as paternalistic but which should not be considered so. In these cases all that is provided—it is true by the use of compulsion—is information which it is presumed that rational persons are interested in having in order to make wise decisions. There is no interference with the liberty of the consumer unless one wants to stretch a point beyond good sense and say that his liberty to apply for a loan without knowing the true rate of interest is diminished. It is true that sometimes there is sentiment for going further than providing information, for example when laws against usurious interest are passed preventing those who might wish to contract loans at high rates of interest from doing so, and these measures may correctly be considered paternalistic.

III

Bearing these examples in mind, let me return to a characterization of paternalism. I said earlier that I meant by the term, roughly, interference with a person's liberty for his own good. But, as some of the examples show, the class of persons whose good is involved is not always identical with the class of persons whose freedom is restricted. Thus, in the case of professional licensing it is the practitioner who is directly interfered with but it is the would-be patient whose interests are presumably being served. Not allowing the consent of the victim to be a defense to certain types of crime primarily affects the would-be aggressor but it is the interests of the willing victim that we are trying to protect. Sometimes a person may fall into both classes as would be the case if we banned the manufacture and sale of cigarettes and a given manufacturer happened to be a smoker as well.

Thus we may first divide paternalistic interferences into "pure" and "impure" cases. In "pure" paternalism the class of persons whose freedom is restricted is identical with the class of persons whose benefit is intended to be promoted by such restrictions. Examples: the making of suicide a crime, requiring passengers in automobiles to wear seat belts, requiring a Christian Scientist to receive a blood transfusion. In the case of "impure" paternalism in trying to protect the welfare of a class of persons we find that the only way to do so will involve restricting the freedom of other persons besides those who are benefitted. Now it might be thought that there are no cases of "impure" paternalism since any such case could always be justified on nonpaternalistic grounds, that is, in terms of preventing harm to others. Thus

we might ban cigarette manufacturers from continuing to manufacture their product on the grounds that we are preventing them from causing illness to others in the same way that we prevent other manufacturers from releasing pollutants into the atmosphere, thereby causing danger to the members of the community. The difference is, however, that in the former but not the latter case the harm is of such a nature that it could be avoided by those individuals affected if they so chose. The incurring of the harm requires, so to speak, the active cooperation of the victim. It would be mistaken theoretically and hypocritical in practice to assert that our interference in such cases is just like our interference in standard cases of protecting others from harm. At the very least someone interfered with in this way can reply that no one is complaining about his activities. It may be that impure paternalism requires arguments or reasons of a stronger kind in order to be justified, since there are persons who are losing a portion of their liberty and they do not even have the solace of having it be done "in their own interest." Of course in some sense, if paternalistic justifications are ever correct, then we are protecting others, we are preventing some from injuring others, but it is important to see the differences between this and the standard case.

Paternalism then will always involve limitations on the liberty of some individuals in their own interest but it may also extend to interferences with the liberty of parties whose interests are not in question.

IV

Finally, by way of some more preliminary analysis, I want to distinguish paternalistic interference with liberty from a related type with which it is often confused. Consider, for example, legislation which forbids employees to work more than, say, forty hours per week. It is sometimes argued that such legislation is paternalistic for if employees desired such a restriction on their hours of work they could agree among themselves to impose it voluntarily. But because they do not the society imposes its own conception of their best interests upon them by the use of coercion. Hence this is paternalism.

Now it may be that some legislation of this nature is, in fact, paternalistically motivated. I am not denying that. All I want to point out is that there is another possible way of justifying such measures which is not paternalistic in nature. It is not paternalistic because, as Mill puts it in a similar context, such measures are "required not to overrule the judgment of individuals respecting their own interest, but to give effect to that judgment: they being unable to give effect to it except by concert, which concert again cannot be effectual unless it receives validity and sanction from the law" (Principles of Political Economy).

The line of reasoning here is a familiar one first found in Hobbes and developed with great sophistication by contemporary economists in the last decade or so. There are restrictions which are in the interests of a class of persons taken collectively but are such that the immediate interest of each individual is furthered by his violating the rule when others adhere to it. In such cases the individuals involved may need the use of compulsion to give effect to their collective judgment of their own interest by guaranteeing each individual compliance by the others. In these cases compulsion is not used to achieve some benefit which is not recognized to be a benefit by those concerned, but rather because it is the only feasible means of achieving some benefit which *is* recognized as such by all concerned. This way of viewing matters provides us with another characterization of paternalism in general. Paternalism might be thought of as the use of coercion to achieve a good which is not recognized as such by those persons for whom the good is intended. Again while this formulation captures the heart of the matter—it is surely what Mill is objecting to in *On Liberty*—the matter is not always quite like that. For example, when we force motorcyclists to wear helmets we are trying to promote a good—the protection of the person from injury—which is surely recognized by most of the individuals concerned. It is not that a cyclist doesn't value his bodily integrity; rather, as a supporter of such legislation would put it, he either places, perhaps irrationally, another value or good (freedom from wearing a helmet) above that of physical well-being or, perhaps, while recognizing the danger in the abstract, he either does not fully appreciate it or he underestimates the likelihood of its occurring. But now we are approaching the question of possible justifications of paternalistic measures and the rest of this essay will be devoted to that question.

V

I shall begin for dialectical purposes by discussing Mill's objections to paternalism and then go on to discuss more positive proposals.

An initial feature that strikes one is the absolute nature of Mill's prohibitions against paternalism. It is so unlike the carefully qualified admonitions of Mill and his fellow utilitarians on other moral issues. He speaks of self-protection as the *sole* end warranting coercion, of the individual's own goals as *never* being a sufficient warrant. Contrast this with his discussion of the prohibition against lying in *Utilitarianism*:

> Yet that even this rule, sacred as it is, admits of possible exception, is acknowledged by all moralists, the chief of which is where the withholding of some fact . . . would save an individual . . . from great and unmerited evil.

The same tentativeness is present when he deals with justice:

> It is confessedly unjust to break faith with any one: to violate an engagement, either express or implied, or disappoint expectations raised by our own conduct, at least if we have raised these expectations knowingly and voluntarily. Like all the other obligations of justice already spoken of, this one is not regarded as absolute, but as capable of being overruled by a stronger obligation of justice on the other side.

This anomaly calls for some explanation. The structure of Mill's argument is as follows:

1. Since restraint is an evil the burden of proof is on those who propose such restraint.
2. Since the conduct which is being considered is purely self-regarding, the normal appeal to the protection of the interests of others is not available.
3. Therefore we have to consider whether reasons involving reference to the individual's own good, happiness, welfare, or interests are sufficient to overcome the burden of justification.
4. We either cannot advance the interests of the individual by compulsion, or the attempt to do so involves evils which outweigh the good done.
5. Hence the promotion of the individual's own interests does not provide a sufficient warrant for the use of compulsion.

Clearly the operative premise here is (4), and it is bolstered by claims about the status of the individual as judge and appraiser of his welfare, interests, needs, et cetera:

With respect to his own feelings and circumstances, the most ordinary man or woman has means of knowledge immeasurably surpassing those that can be possessed by any one else.

He is the man most interested in his own well-being: the interest which any other person, except in cases of strong personal attachment, can have in it is trifling, compared to that which he himself has.

These claims are used to support the following generalizations concerning the utility of compulsion for paternalistic purposes.

The interferences of society to overrule his judgment and purposes in what only regards himself must be grounded on general presumptions; which may be altogether wrong, and even if right, are as likely as not to be misapplied to individual cases.

But the strongest of all the arguments against the interference of the public with purely personal conduct is that when it does interfere, the odds are that it interferes wrongly and in the wrong place.

All errors which the individual is likely to commit against advice and warning are far outweighed by the evil of allowing others to constrain him to what they deem his good.

Performing the utilitarian calculations by balancing the advantages and disadvantages, we find that: "Mankind are greater gainers by suffering each other to live as seems good to themselves, than by compelling each other to live as seems good to the rest." Ergo, (4).

This classical case of a utilitarian argument with all the premises spelled out is not the only line of reasoning present in Mill's discussion. There are asides, and more than asides, which look quite different and I shall deal with them later. But this is clearly the main channel of Mill's thought and it is one which has been subjected to vigorous attack from the moment it appeared—most often by fellow utilitarians. The link that they have usually seized on is, as Fitzjames Stephen put it in *Liberty, Equality, Fraternity*, the absence of proof that the "mass of adults are so well acquainted with their own interests and so much disposed to pursue them that no compulsion or restraint put upon them by any others for the purpose of promoting their interest can

really promote them." Even so sympathetic a critic as H. L. A. Hart is forced to the conclusion that:

> In Chapter 5 of his essay [On Liberty] Mill carried his protests against paternalism to lengths that may now appear to us as fantastic. . . . No doubt if we no longer sympathise with his criticism this is due, in part, to a general decline in the belief that individuals know their own interest best.
>
> Mill endows the average individual with "too much of the psychology of a middle-aged man whose desires are relatively fixed, not liable to be artificially stimulated by external influences; who knows what he wants and what gives him satisfaction or happiness; and who pursues these things when he can."

Now it is interesting to note that Mill himself was aware of some of the limitations on the doctrine that the individual is the best judge of his own interests. In his discussion of government intervention in general (even where the intervention does not interfere with liberty but provides alternative institutions to those of the market) after making claims which are parallel to those just discussed, for example, "People understand their own business and their own interests better, and care for them more, than the government does, or can be expected to do," he goes on to an intelligent discussion of the "very large and conspicuous exceptions" to the maxim that:

> Most persons take a juster and more intelligent view of their own interest, and of the means of promoting it than can either be prescribed to them by a general enactment of the legislature, or pointed out in the particular case by a public functionary.

Thus there are things

> of which the utility does not consist in ministering to inclinations, nor in serving the daily uses of life, and the want of which is least felt where the need is greatest. This is peculiarly true of those things which are chiefly useful as tending to raise the character of human beings. The uncultivated cannot be competent judges of cultivation. Those who most need to be made wiser and better, usually desire it least, and, if they desire it, would be incapable of finding the way to it by their own lights.

. . . A second exception to the doctrine that individuals are the best judges of their own interest, is when an individual attempts to decide irrevocably now what will be best for his interest at some future and distant time. The presumption in favor of individual judgment is only legitimate, where the judgment is grounded on actual, and especially on present, personal experience; not where it is formed antecedently to experience, and not suffered to be reversed even after experience has condemned it.

The upshot of these exceptions is that Mill does not declare that there should never be government interference with the economy but rather that

. . . in every instance, the burden of making out a strong case should be thrown not on those who resist but those who recommend government interference. Letting alone, in short, should be the general practice: every departure from it, unless required by some great good, is a certain evil.

In short, we get a presumption, not an absolute prohibition. The question is why doesn't the argument against paternalism go the same way?

I suggest that the answer lies in seeing that in addition to a purely utilitarian argument Mill uses another as well. As a utilitarian, Mill has to show, in Fitzjames Stephen's words, that: "Self-protection apart, no good object can be attained by any compulsion which is not in itself a greater evil than the absence of the object which the compulsion obtains." To show this is impossible, one reason being that it isn't true. Preventing a man from selling himself into slavery (a paternalistic measure which Mill himself accepts as legitimate), or from taking heroin, or from driving a car without wearing seat belts may constitute a lesser evil than allowing him to do any of these things. A consistent utilitarian can only argue against paternalism on the grounds that it (as a matter of fact) does not maximize the good. It is always a contingent question that may be returned by the evidence. But there is also a noncontingent argument which runs through *On Liberty*. When Mill states that "there is a part of the life of every person who has come to years of discretion, within which the individuality of that person ought to reign uncontrolled either by any other person or by the public collectively," he is saying something about what it means to be a person, an autonomous agent. It is

because coercing a person for his own good denies this status as an independent entity that Mill objects to it so strongly and in such absolute terms. To be able to choose is a good that is independent of the wisdom of what is chosen. A man's "mode of laying out his existence is the best, not because it is the best in itself, but because it is his own mode." It is the privilege and proper condition of a human being, arrived at the maturity of his faculties, to use and interpret experience in his own way.

As further evidence of this line of reasoning in Mill, consider the one exception to his prohibition against paternalism.

In this and most civilised countries, for example, an engagement by which a person should sell himself, or allow himself to be sold, as a slave, would be null and void; neither enforced by law nor by opinion. The ground for thus limiting his power of voluntarily disposing of his own lot in life, is apparent, and is very clearly seen in this extreme case. The reason for not interfering, unless for the sake of others, with a person's voluntary acts, is consideration for his liberty. His voluntary choice is evidence that what he so chooses is desirable, or at least endurable, to him, and his good is on the whole best provided for by allowing him to take his own means of pursuing it. But by selling himself for a slave, he abdicates his liberty; he foregoes any future use of it beyond that single act. He therefore defeats, in his own case, the very purpose which is the justification of allowing him to dispose of himself. He is no longer free; but is thenceforth in a position which has no longer the presumption in its favour, that would be afforded by his voluntarily remaining in it. The principle of freedom cannot require that he should be free not to be free. It is not freedom to be allowed to alienate his freedom.

Now leaving aside the fudging on the meaning of freedom in the last line, it is clear that part of this argument is incorrect. While it is true that *future* choices of the slave are not reasons for thinking that what he chooses then is desirable for him, what is at issue is limiting his immediate choice; and since this choice is made freely, the individual may be correct in thinking that his interests are best provided for by entering such a contract. But the main consideration for not allowing such a contract is the need to preserve the liberty of the person to make future choices. This gives us a principle—a very narrow one—by which to justify some paternalistic interferences. Paternalism is justified only to preserve a wider range of freedom for the individual in question. How far this principle could be extended, whether it can justify all the cases in which we are inclined upon reflection to think paternalistic measures justified, remains to be discussed. What I have tried to show so far is that there are two strains of argument in Mill—one a straight-forward utilitarian mode of reasoning and one which relies not on the goods which free choice leads to but on the absolute value of the choice itself. The first cannot establish any absolute prohibition but at most a presumption and indeed a fairly weak one given some fairly plausible assumptions about human psychology; the second, while a stronger line of argument, seems to me to allow on its own grounds a wider range of paternalism than might be suspected. I turn now to a consideration of these matters.

VI

We might begin looking for principles governing the acceptable use of paternalistic power in cases where it is generally agreed that it is legitimate. Even Mill intends his principles to be applicable only to mature individuals, not those in what he calls "non-age." What is it that justifies us in interfering with children? The fact that they lack some of the emotional and cognitive capacities required in order to make fully rational decisions. It is an empirical question to just what extent children have an adequate conception of their own present and future interests but there is not much doubt that there are many deficiencies. For example, it is very difficult for a child to defer gratification for any considerable period of time. Given these deficiencies and given the very real and permanent dangers that may befall the child, it becomes not only permissible but even a duty of the parent to restrict the child's freedom in various ways. There is however an important moral limitation on the exercise of such parental power which is provided by the notion of the child eventually coming to see the correctness of his parent's interventions. Parental paternalism may be thought of as a wager by the parent on the child's subsequent recognition of the wisdom of the restrictions. There is an emphasis on what could be called future-oriented consent—on what the child will come to welcome, rather than on what he does welcome.

The essence of this idea has been incorporated by idealist philosophers into various types of "real-will" theory as applied to fully adult persons. Extensions of paternalism are argued for by claiming that in various respects, chronologically mature individuals share the same deficiencies in knowledge, capacity to think rationally, and the ability to carry out decisions that children possess. Hence in interfering with such people we are in effect doing what they would do if they were fully rational. Hence we are not really opposing their will, hence we are not really interfering with their freedom. The dangers of this move have been sufficiently exposed by Berlin in his *Two Concepts of Liberty*. I see no gain in theoretical clarity nor in practical advantage in trying to pass over the real nature of the interferences with liberty that we impose on others. Still the basic notion of consent is important and seems to me the only acceptable way of trying to delimit an area of justified paternalism.

Let me start by considering a case where the consent is not hypothetical in nature. Under certain conditions it is rational for an individual to agree that others should force him to act in ways which, at the time of action, the individual may not see as desirable. If, for example, a man knows that he is subject to breaking his resolves when temptation is present, he may ask a friend to refuse to entertain his requests at some later stage.

A classical example is given in the *Odyssey* when Odysseus commands his men to tie him to the mast and refuse all future orders to be set free, because he knows the power of the Sirens to enchant men with their songs. Here we are on relatively sound ground in later refusing Odysseus' request to be set free. He may even claim to have changed his mind but, since it is *just* such changes that he wished to guard against, we are entitled to ignore them.

A process analogous to this may take place on a social rather than individual basis. An electorate may mandate its representatives to pass legislation which when it comes time to "pay the price" may be unpalatable. I may believe that a tax increase is necessary to halt inflation though I may resent the lower pay check each month. However in both this case and that of Odysseus, the measure to be enforced is specifically requested by the party involved and at some point in time there is genuine consent and agreement on the part of those persons whose liberty is infringed. Such is not the case for the paternalistic measures we have been speaking about. What must be involved here is not consent to specific measures but rather consent to a system of government, run by elected representatives, with an understanding that they may act to safeguard our interests in certain limited ways.

I suggest that since we are all aware of our irrational propensities, deficiencies in cognitive and emotional capacities, and avoidable and unavoidable ignorance, it is rational and prudent for us to in effect take out "social insurance policies." We may argue for and against proposed paternalistic measures in terms of what fully rational individuals would accept as forms of protection. Now clearly, since the initial agreement is not about specific measures we are dealing with a more-or-less blank check and therefore there have to be carefully defined limits. What I am looking for are certain kinds of conditions which make it plausible to suppose that rational men could reach agreement to limit their liberty even when other men's interest are not affected.

Of course as in any kind of agreement schema there are great difficulties in deciding what rational individuals would or would not accept. Particularly in sensitive areas of personal liberty, there is always a danger of the dispute over agreement and rationality being a disguised version of evaluative and normative disagreement.

Let me suggest types of situations in which it seems plausible to suppose that fully rational individuals would agree to having paternalistic restrictions imposed upon them. It is reasonable to suppose that there are "goods" such as health which any person would want to have in order to pursue his own good—no matter how that good is conceived. This is an argument used in connection with compulsory education for children but it seems to me that it can be extended to other goods which have this character. Then one could agree that the attainment of such goods should be promoted even when not recognized to be such, at the moment, by the individuals concerned.

An immediate difficulty arises from the fact that men are always faced with competing goods and that there may be reasons why even a value such as health—or indeed life—may be overridden by competing values. Thus the problem with the Christian Scientist and blood transfusions. It may be more important for him to reject "impure substances" than to go on living. The difficult problem that must be faced is whether one can give sense to the notion of a person irrationally attaching weights to competing values.

Consider a person who knows the statistical data on the probability of being injured when not wearing seat belts in an automobile and knows the types of gravity of the various injuries. He also insists that the inconvenience attached to fastening the belt every time he gets in and out of the car outweighs for him the possible risks to himself. I am inclined in this case to think that such a weighing is irrational. Given his life plans, which we are assuming are those of the average person, his interests and commitments already undertaken, I think it is safe to predict that we can find inconsistencies in his calculations at some point. I am assuming that this is not a man who for some conscious or unconscious reasons is trying to injure himself nor is he a man who just likes to "live dangerously." I am assuming that he is like us in all the relevant respects but just puts an enormously high negative value on inconvenience—one which does not seem comprehensible or reasonable.

It is always possible, of course, to assimilate this person to creatures like myself. I, also, neglect to fasten my seat belt and I concede such behavior is not rational but not because I weigh the inconvenience differently from those who fasten the belts. It is just that having made (roughly) the same calculation as everybody else, I ignore it in my actions. [Note: a much better case of weakness of the will than those usually given in ethics tests.] A plausible explanation for this deplorable habit is that although I know in some intellectual sense what the probabilities and risks are I do not fully appreciate them in an emotionally genuine manner.

We have two distinct types of situation in which a man acts in a nonrational fashion. In one case he attaches incorrect weights to some of his values; in the other he neglects to act in accordance with his actual preferences and desires. Clearly there is a stronger and more persuasive argument for paternalism in the latter situation. Here we are really not—by assumption—imposing a good on another person. But why may we not extend our interference to what we might call evaluative delusions? After all, in the case of cognitive delusions we are prepared, often, to act against the expressed will of the person involved. If a man believes that when he jumps out the window he will float upwards—Robert Nozick's example—would not we detain him, forcibly if necessary? The reply will be that this man doesn't wish to be injured and if we could convince him that he is mistaken as to the consequences of his action, he would not wish to perform the action. But part of what is involved in claiming that the man who doesn't fasten his seatbelts is attaching an incorrect weight to the inconvenience of fastening them is that if he were to be involved in an accident and severely injured he would look back and admit that the inconvenience wasn't as bad as all that. So there is a sense in which, if I could convince him of the consequences of his action, he also would not wish to continue his present course of action. Now the notion of consequences being used here is covering a lot of ground. In one case it's being used to indicate what will or can happen as a result of a course of action and in the other it's making a prediction about the future evaluation of the consequences—in the first sense—of a course of action. And whatever the difference between facts and values—whether it be hard and fast or soft and slow—we are genuinely more reluctant to consent to interferences where evaluative differences are the issue. Let me now consider another factor which comes into play in some of these situations which may make an important difference in our willingness to consent to paternalistic restrictions.

Some of the decisions we make are of such a character that they produce changes which are in one or another way irreversible. Situations are created in which it is difficult or impossible to return to anything like the initial stage at which the decision was made. In particular, some of these changes will make it impossible to continue to make reasoned choices in the future. I am thinking specifically of decisions which involve taking drugs that are physically or psychologically addictive and those which are destructive of one's mental and physical capacities.

I suggest we think of the imposition of paternalistic interferences in situations of this kind as being a kind of insurance policy which we take out against making decisions which are far-reaching, potentially dangerous and irreversible. Each of these factors is important. Clearly there are many decisions we make that are relatively irreversible. In deciding to learn to play chess, I could predict in view of my general interest in games that some portion of my free time was going to be preempted and that it would not be easy to give up the game once I acquired a certain competence. But my whole life style was not going to be jeopardized in an extreme manner. Further it might be argued that even with addictive drugs such as heroin one's normal life plans would not be seriously interfered with if an inexpensive and adequate supply were readily available. So this type of argument might have a much narrower scope than appears to be the case at first.

A second class of cases concerns decisions which are made under extreme psychological and sociological pressures. I am not thinking here of the making of the decision as being something one is pressured into—for example, a good reason for making duelling illegal is that unless this is done many people might have to manifest their courage and integrity in ways in which they would rather not do so—but rather of decisions, such as that to commit suicide, which are usually made at a point where the individual is not thinking clearly and calmly about the nature of his decision. In addition, of course, this comes under the previous heading of all-too-irrevocable decisions. Now there are practical steps which a society could take if it wanted to decrease the possibility of suicide—for example not paying social security benefits to the survivors or, as religious institutions do, not allowing persons to be buried with the same status as natural deaths. I think we may count these as interferences with the liberty of persons to attempt suicide and the question is whether they are justifiable.

Using my argument schema the question is whether rational individuals would consent to such limitations. I see no reason for them to consent to an absolute prohibition but I do think it is reasonable for them to agree to some kind of enforced waiting period. Since we are all aware of the possibility of temporary states, such as great fear or depression, that are inimical to the making of well-informed and rational decisions, it would be prudent for all of us if there were some kind of institutional arrangement whereby we were restrained from making a decision which is so irreversible. What this would be like in practice is difficult to envisage and it may be that if no practical arrangements were feasible we would have to conclude that there should be no restriction at all on this kind of action. But we might have a "cooling off" period, in much the same way that we now require couples who file for divorce to go through a waiting period. Or, more far-fetched, we might imagine a Suicide Board composed of a psychologist and another member picked up by applicant. The Board would be required to meet and talk with the person proposing to take his life, though its approval would not be required.

A third class of decisions—these classes are not supposed to be disjoint—involves dangers which are either not sufficiently understood or appreciated correctly by the persons involved. Let me illustrate, using the example of cigarette smoking, a number of possible cases.

1. A man may not know the facts—for example, smoking between one and two packs a day

shortens life expectancy 6.2 years, the costs and pain of the illness caused by smoking, et cetera.

2. A man may know the facts, wish to stop smoking, but not have the requisite willpower.

3. A man may know the facts but not have them play the correct role in his calculation because, say, he discounts the danger psychologically since it is remote in time and/or inflates the attractiveness of other consequences of his decision which he regards as beneficial.

In case 1 what is called for is education, the posting of warnings, et cetera. In case 2 there is no theoretical problem. We are not imposing a good on someone who rejects it. We are simply using coercion to enable people to carry out their own goals. (Note: There obviously is a difficulty in that only a subclass of the individuals affected wish to be prevented from doing what they are doing.) In case 3 there is a sense in which we are imposing a good on someone in that given his current appraisal of the facts he doesn't wish to be restricted. But in another sense we are not imposing a good since what is being claimed—and what must be shown or at least argued for—is that an accurate accounting on his part would lead him to reject his current course of action. Now we all know that such cases exist, that we are prone to disregarding dangers that are only possibilities, that immediate pleasures are often magnified and distorted.

If in addition the dangers are severe and far-reaching, we could agree to allow the state a certain degree of power to intervene in such situations. The difficulty is in specifying in advance, even vaguely, the class of cases in which intervention will be legitimate. A related difficulty is that of drawing a line so that it is not the case that all ultra-hazardous activities are ruled out, for example, mountain-climbing, bull-fighting, sports-car racing, et cetera. There are some risks—even very great ones—which a person is entitled to take with his life.

A good deal depends on the nature of the deprivation—for example, does it prevent the person from engaging in the activity completely or merely limit his participation—and how important to the nature of the activity is the absence of restriction when this is weighed against the role that the activity plays in the life of the person. In the case of automobile seat belts, for example, the restriction is trivial in nature, interferes not at all with the use or enjoyment of the activity, and does, I am assuming, considerably reduce a high risk of serious injury. Whereas,

for example, making mountain-climbing illegal completely prevents a person from engaging in an activity which may play an important role in his life and his conception of the person he is.

In general, the easiest cases to handle are those which can be argued about in the terms which Mill thought to be so important—a concern not just for the happiness or welfare, in some broad sense, of the individual but rather a concern for the autonomy and freedom of the person. I suggest that we would be most likely to consent to paternalism in those instances in which it preserves and enhances for the individual his ability to rationally consider and carry out his own decisions.

I have suggested in this essay a number of types of situations in which it seems plausible that rational men would agree to granting the legislative powers of a society the right to impose restrictions on what Mill calls "self-regarding" conduct. However, rational men knowing something about the resources of ignorance, ill-will and stupidity available to the lawmakers of a society—a good case in point is the history of drug legislation in the United States—will be concerned to limit such intervention to a minimum. I suggest in closing two principles designed to achieve this end.

In all cases of paternalistic legislation there must be a heavy and clear burden of proof placed on the authorities to demonstrate the exact nature of the harmful effects (or beneficial consequences) to be avoided (or achieved) and the probability of their occurrence. The burden of proof here is twofold— what lawyers distinguish as the burden of going forward and the burden of persuasion. That the authorities have the burden of going forward means that it is up to them to raise the question and bring forward evidence of the evils to be avoided. Unlike the case of new drugs, where the manufacturer must produce some evidence that the drug has been tested and found not harmful, no citizen has to show with respect to self-regarding conduct that it is not harmful or promotes his best interest. In addition the nature and cogency of the evidence for the harmfulness of the course of action must be set at a high level. To paraphrase a formulation of the burden of proof for criminal proceedings—better two men ruin themselves than one man be unjustly deprived of liberty.

Finally I suggest a principle of the least restrictive alternative. If there is an alternative way of accomplishing the desired end without restricting liberty although it may involve great expense, inconvenience, et cetera, the society must adopt it.

Constitutional Privacy

GRISWOLD V. CONNECTICUT*

United States Supreme Court, 1965

MR. JUSTICE DOUGLAS delivered the opinion of the Court.

Appellant Griswold is Executive Director of the Planned Parenthood League of Connecticut. Appellant Buxton is a licensed physician and a professor at the Yale Medical School who served as Medical Director for the League at its Center in New Haven—a center open and operating from November 1 to November 10, 1961, when appellants were arrested.

They gave information, instruction, and medical advice to *married persons* as to the means of preventing conception. They examined the wife and prescribed the best contraceptive device or material for her use. Fees were usually charged, although some couples were serviced free.

The statutes whose constitutionality is involved in this appeal are §§ 53-32 and 54-196 of the General Statutes of Connecticut (1958 rev.). The former provides:

Any person who uses any drug, medicinal article or instrument for the purpose of preventing conception shall be fined not less than fifty dollars or imprisoned not less than sixty days nor more than one year or be both fined and imprisoned.

Section 54-196 provides:

Any person who assists, abets, counsels, causes, hires or commands another to commit any offense may be prosecuted and punished as if he were the principal offender.

The appellants were found guilty as accessories and fined $100 each, against the claim that the accessory statute as so applied violated the Fourteenth Amendment. The Appellate Division of the Circuit Court affirmed. The Supreme Court of Errors affirmed that judgment.

We think that appellants have standing to raise the constitutional rights of the married people with whom they had a professional relationship. . . . Certainly the accessory should have standing to assert that the offense which he is charged with assisting is not, or cannot constitutionally be, a crime. . . .

Coming to the merits, we are met with a wide range of questions that implicate the Due Process Clause of the Fourteenth Amendment. Overtones of some arguments suggest that *Lochner v. New York,* 198 U.S. 45, should be our guide. But we decline that invitation. We do not sit as a super-legislature to determine the wisdom, need, and propriety of laws that touch economic problems, business affairs, or social conditions. This law, however, operates directly on an intimate relation of husband and wife and their physician's role in one aspect of that relation.

The association of people is not mentioned in the Constitution nor in the Bill of Rights. The right to educate a child in a school of the parents' choice—whether public or private or parochial—

*381 *U.S.* 479 (1965). Excerpts only. Footnotes renumbered. Citations omitted.

is also not mentioned. Nor is the right to study any particular subject or any foreign language. Yet the First Amendment has been construed to include certain of those rights.

By *Pierce v. Society of Sisters,* the right to educate one's children as one chooses is made applicable to the States by the force of the First and Fourteenth Amendments. By *Meyer v. Nebraska,* the same dignity is given the right to study the German language in a private school. In other words, the State may not, consistently with the spirit of the First Amendment, contract the spectrum of available knowledge. The right of freedom of speech and press includes not only the right to utter or to print, but the right to distribute, the right to receive, the right to read and freedom of inquiry, freedom of thought, and freedom to teach—indeed the freedom of the entire university community. Without those peripheral rights the specific rights would be less secure. . . .

In *NAACP v. Alabama,* 357 *U.S.* 449, 462, we protected the "freedom to associate and privacy in one's associations," noting that freedom of association was a peripheral First Amendment right. Disclosure of membership lists of a constitutionally valid association, we held, was invalid "as entailing the likelihood of a substantial restraint upon the exercise by petitioner's members of their right to freedom of association." *Ibid.* In other words, the First Amendment has a penumbra where privacy is protected from governmental intrusion. In like context, we have protected forms of "association" that are not political in the customary sense but pertain to the social, legal, and economic benefit of the members. In *Schware v. Board of Bar Examiners,* 353 *U.S.* 232, we held it not permissible to bar a lawyer from practice, because he had once been a member of the Communist Party. The man's "association with that Party" was not shown to be "anything more than a political faith in a political party" and was not action of a kind proving bad moral character.

Those cases involved more than the "right of assembly"—a right that extends to all irrespective of their race or ideology. The right of "association," like the right of belief, is more than the right to attend a meeting; it includes the right to express one's attitudes or philosophies by membership in a group or by affiliation with it or by other lawful means. Association in that context is a form of expression of opinion; and while it is not expressly included in the First Amendment its existence is necessary in making the express guarantees fully meaningful.

The foregoing cases suggest that specific guarantees in the Bill of Rights have penumbras, formed by emanations from those guarantees that help give them life and substance. Various guarantees create zones of privacy. The right of association contained in the penumbra of the First Amendment is one, as we have seen. The Third Amendment in its prohibition against the quartering of soldiers "in any house" in time of peace without the consent of the owner is another facet of that privacy. The Fourth Amendment explicitly affirms the "right of the people to be secure in their persons, houses, papers, and effects, against unreasonable searches and seizures." The Fifth Amendment in its Self-Incrimination Clause enables the citizen to create a zone of privacy which government may not force him to surrender to his detriment. The Ninth Amendment provides: "The enumeration in the Constitution, of certain rights, shall not be construed to deny or disparage others retained by the people."

The Fourth and Fifth Amendments were described in *Boyd v. United States,* 116 *U.S.* 616, 630, as protection against all governmental invasions "of the sanctity of a man's home and the privacies of life." We recently referred in *Mapp v. Ohio,* 367 *U.S.* 643, 656, to the Fourth Amendment as creating a "right to privacy, no less important than any other right carefully and particularly reserved to the people." These cases bear witness that the right of privacy which presses for recognition here is a legitimate one.

The present case, then, concerns a relationship lying within the zone of privacy created by several fundamental constitutional guarantees. And it concerns a law which, in forbidding the *use* of contraceptives rather than regulating their manufacture or sale, seeks to achieve its goals by means having a maximum destructive impact upon that relationship. Such a law cannot stand in light of the familiar principle, so often applied by this Court, that a "governmental purpose to control or prevent activities constitutionally subject to state regulation may not be achieved by means which sweep unnecessarily broadly and thereby invade the area of protected freedoms." *NAACP v. Alabama,* 377 *U.S.* 288, 307. Would we allow the police to search the sacred precincts of marital bedrooms for telltale signs of the use of contraceptives? The very idea is repulsive to the notions of privacy surrounding the marriage relationship.

We deal with a right of privacy older than the Bill of Rights—older than our political parties, older

than our school system. Marriage is a coming together for better or for worse, hopefully enduring,
and intimate to the degree of being sacred. It is an
association that promotes a way of life, not causes;
a harmony in living, not political faiths; a bilateral
loyalty, not commercial or social projects. Yet it is
an association for as noble a purpose as any involved in our prior decisions.
Reversed.

MR. JUSTICE GOLDBERG, whom THE CHIEF JUS-
TICE and MR. JUSTICE BRENNAN join, concurring. . . .
My Brother Stewart dissents on the ground that he
"can find no . . . general right of privacy in the Bill
of Rights, in any other part of the Constitution, or in
any case ever before decided by this Court." He
would require a more explicit guarantee than the
one which the Court derives from several constitutional amendments. This Court, however, has never
held that the Bill of Rights or the Fourteenth Amendment protects only those rights that the Constitution
specifically mentions by name. . . .

My Brother Stewart, while characterizing the
Connecticut birth control law as "an uncommonly silly
law," would nevertheless let it stand on the ground
that it is not for the courts to "'substitute their social
and economic beliefs for the judgment of legislative
bodies, who are elected to pass laws.'" Elsewhere, I
have stated that "[w]hile I quite agree with Mr. Justice
Brandeis that . . . 'a . . . State may . . . serve as a laboratory; and try novel social and economic experiments,' I do not believe that this includes the power
to experiment with the fundamental liberties of citizens. . . ." The vice of the dissenters' views is that it
would permit such experimentation by the States in
the area of the fundamental personal rights of its citizens. I cannot agree that the Constitution grants such
either to the States or to the Federal Government.

The logic of the dissents would sanction federal or state legislation that seems to me even more
plainly unconstitutional than the statute before us.
Surely the Government, absent a showing of a compelling subordinating state interest, could not decree
that all husbands and wives must be sterilized after
two children have been born to them. Yet by their
reasoning such an invasion of marital privacy would
not be subject to constitutional challenge because,
while it might be "silly," no provision of the Constitution specifically prevents the Government from
curtailing the marital right to bear children and raise
a family. While it may shock some of my Brethren

that the Court today holds that the Constitution protects the right of marital privacy in my view it is far
more shocking to believe that the personal liberty
guaranteed by the Constitution does not include protection against such totalitarian limitation of family
size, which is at complete variance with our constitutional concepts. Yet, if upon a showing of a slender basis of rationality, a law outlawing voluntary
birth control by married persons is valid, then, by
the same reasoning a law requiring compulsory birth
control also would seem to be valid. In my view,
however, both types of law would unjustifiably intrude upon rights of marital privacy which are constitutionally protected.

In a long series of cases this Court has held
that where fundamental personal liberties are involved, they may not be abridged by the States simply on a showing that a regulatory statute has some
rational relationship to the effectuation of a proper
state purpose. "Where there is a significant encroachment upon personal liberty, the State may
prevail only upon showing a subordinating interest
which is compelling," *Bates v. Little Rock,* 361 *U.S.*
516, 524. The law must be shown "necessary, and
not merely rationally related, to the accomplishment
of a permissible state policy." *McLaughlin v. Florida,*
379 *U.S.* 184, 196.

Although the Connecticut birth-control law obviously encroaches upon a fundamental personal liberty, the State does not show that the law serves any
"subordinating [state] interest which is compelling" or
that it is "necessary . . . to the accomplishment of a
permissible state policy." The State, at most, argues
that there is some rational relation between this
statute and what is admittedly a legitimate subject of
state concern—the discouraging of extra-marital relations. It says that preventing the use of birth-control
devices by married persons helps prevent the indulgence by some in such extra-marital relations. The rationality of this justification is dubious, particularly in
light of the admitted widespread availability to all persons in the State of Connecticut, unmarried as well as
married, of birth-control devices for the prevention of
disease, as distinguished from the prevention of conception. But, in any event, it is clear that the state interest in safeguarding marital fidelity can be served
by a more discriminately tailored statute, which does
not, like the present one, sweep unnecessarily
broadly, reaching far beyond the evil sought to
be dealt with and intruding upon the privacy of all
married couples. Here, as elsewhere, "[p]recision of

regulation must be the touchstone in an area so closely touching our most precious freedoms." *NAACP v. Button,* 371 *U.S.* 415, 438. The State of Connecticut does have statutes, the constitutionality of which is beyond doubt, which prohibit adultery and fornication. These statutes demonstrate that means for achieving the same basic purpose of protecting marital fidelity are available to Connecticut without the need to "invade the area of protected freedoms." *NAACP v. Alabama, supra,* at 307.

Finally, it should be said of the Court's holding today that it in no way interferes with a State's proper regulation of sexual promiscuity or misconduct. As my Brother Harlan so well stated in his dissenting opinion in *Poe v. Ullman,*

> Adultery, homosexuality and the like are sexual intimacies which the State forbids . . . but the intimacy of husband and wife is necessarily an essential and accepted feature of the institution of marriage, an institution which the State not only must allow, but which always and in every age it has fostered and protected. It is one thing when the State exerts its power either to forbid extra-marital sexuality . . . or to say who may marry, but it is quite another when, having acknowledged a marriage and the intimacies inherent in it, it undertakes to regulate by means of the criminal law the details of that intimacy.

In sum, I believe that the right of privacy in the marital relation is fundamental and basic—a personal right "retained by the people" within the meaning of the Ninth Amendment. Connecticut cannot constitutionally abridge this fundamental right, which is protected by the Fourteenth Amendment from infringement by the States. I agree with the Court that petitioners' convictions must therefore be reversed. . . .

Mr. Justice BLACK, with whom Mr. Justice STEWART joins, dissenting.

I agree with my Brother Stewart's dissenting opinion. And like him I do not to any extent whatever base my view that this Connecticut law is constitutional on a belief that the law is wise or that its policy is a good one. In order that there may be no room at all to doubt why I vote as I do, I feel constrained to add that the law is every bit as offensive to me as it is to my Brethren of the majority and my Brothers Harlan, White and Goldberg who, reciting reasons why it is offensive to them, hold it unconstitutional. There is no single one of the graphic and eloquent strictures

and criticisms fired at the policy of this Connecticut law either by the Court's opinion or by those of my concurring Brethren to which I cannot subscribe—except their conclusion that the evil qualities they see in the law make it unconstitutional. . . .

The Court talks about a constitutional "right of privacy" as though there is some constitutional provision or provisions forbidding any law ever to be passed which might abridge the "privacy" of individuals. But there is not. There are, of course, guarantees in certain specific constitutional provisions which are designed in part to protect privacy at certain times and places with respect to certain activities. Such, for example, is the Fourth Amendment's guarantee against "unreasonable searches and seizures." But I think it belittles that Amendment to talk about it as though it protects nothing but "privacy." To treat it that way is to give it a niggardly interpretation, not the kind of liberal reading I think any Bill of Rights provision should be given. The average man would very likely not have his feelings soothed any more by having his property seized openly than by having it seized privately and by stealth. He simply wants his property left alone. And a person can be just as much, if not more, irritated, annoyed and injured by an unceremonious public arrest by a policeman as he is by a seizure in the privacy of his office or home.

One of the most effective ways of diluting or expanding a constitutionally guaranteed right is to substitute for the crucial word or words of a constitutional guarantee another word or words, more or less flexible and more or less restricted in meaning. This fact is well illustrated by the use of the term "right of privacy" as a comprehensive substitute for the Fourth Amendment's guarantee against "unreasonable searches and seizures." "Privacy" is a broad, abstract and ambiguous concept which can easily be shrunken in meaning but which can also, on the other hand, easily be interpreted as a constitutional ban against many things other than searches and seizures. I have expressed the view many times that First Amendment freedoms, for example, have suffered from a failure of the courts to stick to the simple language of the First Amendment in construing it, instead of invoking multitudes of words substituted for those the Framers used. For these reasons I get nowhere in this case by talk about a constitutional "right of privacy" as an emanation from one or more constitutional provisions. I like my privacy as well as the next one, but I am nevertheless compelled to admit that government has a right to invade it unless prohibited by some specific constitutional provision. For these reasons I cannot agree with the Court's judgment and the reasons it gives for holding this Connecticut law unconstitutional. . . .

The due process argument which my Brothers Harlan and White adopt here is based, as their opinions indicate, on the premise that this Court is vested with power to invalidate all state laws that it considers to be arbitrary, capricious, unreasonable, or oppressive, or on this Court's belief that a particular state law under scrutiny has no "rational or justifying" purpose, or is offensive to a "sense of fairness and justice." If these formulas based on "natural justice," or others which mean the same thing,[1] are to prevail, they require judges to determine what is or is not constitutional on the basis of their own appraisal of what laws are unwise or unnecessary. The power to make such decisions is of course that of a legislative body. Surely it has to be admitted that no provision of the Constitution specifically gives such blanket power to courts to exercise such a supervisory veto over the wisdom and value of legislative policies and to hold unconstitutional those laws which they believe unwise or dangerous. I readily admit that no legislative body, state or national, should pass laws that can justly be given any of the invidious labels invoked as constitutional excuses to strike down state laws. But perhaps it is not too much to say that no legislative body ever does pass laws without believing that they will accomplish a sane, rational, wise and justifiable purpose. While I completely subscribe to the holding of *Marbury v. Madison,* and subsequent cases, that our Court has constitutional power to strike down statutes, state or federal, that violate commands of the Federal Constitution, I do not believe that we are granted power by the Due Process Clause or any other constitutional provision or provisions to measure constitutionality by our belief that legislation is arbitrary, capricious or unreasonable, or accomplishes no justifiable purpose, or is offensive to our own notions of "civilized standards of conduct."[2] Such an appraisal of the wisdom of legislation is an attribute of the power to make laws, not of the power to interpret them. The use by federal courts of such a formula or doctrine or whatnot to veto federal or state laws simply takes away from Congress and States the power to make laws based on their own judgment of fairness and wisdom and transfers that power to this Court for ultimate determination—a power which was specifically denied to federal courts by the convention that framed the Constitution. . . .

My Brother Goldberg has adopted the recent discovery[3] that the Ninth Amendment as well as the Due Process Clause can be used by this Court as authority to strike down all state legislation which this Court thinks violates "fundamental principles of liberty and justice," or is contrary to the "traditions and [collective] conscience of our people." He also states, without proof satisfactory to me, that in making decisions on this basis judges will not consider "their personal and private notions." One may ask how they can avoid considering them. Our Court certainly has no machinery with which to take a Gallup Poll.[4] And the scientific miracles of this age have not yet produced a gadget which the Court can use to determine what traditions are rooted in the "[collective] conscience of our people." Moreover, one would certainly have to look far beyond the language of the Ninth Amendment[5] to find that the Framers vested in this Court any such awesome veto powers over lawmaking, either by the States or by the Congress. Nor does anything in the history of the Amendment offer any support for such a shocking doctrine. The whole history of the adoption of the Constitution and Bill of Rights points the other way, and the very material quoted by my Brother Goldberg shows that the Ninth Amendment was intended to protect against the idea that "by enumerating particular exceptions to the grant of power" to the Federal Government, "those rights which were not singled out, were intended to be assigned into the hands of the General Government [the United States], and were consequently insecure."[6] That Amendment was passed, not to broaden the powers of this Court or any other department of "the General Government," but, as every student of history knows, to assure the people that the Constitution in all its provisions was intended to limit the Federal Government to the powers granted expressly or by necessary implication. If any broad, unlimited power to hold laws unconstitutional because they offend what this Court conceives to be the "[collective] conscience of our people" is vested in this Court by the Ninth Amendment, the Fourteenth Amendment, or any other provision of the Constitution, it was not given by the Framers, but rather has been bestowed on the Court by the Court. This fact is perhaps responsible for the peculiar phenomenon that for a period of a century and a half no serious suggestion was ever made that the Ninth Amendment, enacted to protect state powers against federal invasion, could be used as a weapon of federal power to prevent state legislatures from passing laws they consider appropriate to govern local affairs. Use of any such broad, unbounded judicial authority would make of this Court's members a day-to-day constitutional convention.

1. A collection of the catchwords and catch phrases invoked by judges who would strike down under the Fourteenth Amendment laws which offend their notions of natural justice would fill many pages. Thus it has been said that this Court can forbid state action which "shocks the conscience," *Rochin v. California*, 342 *U.S.* 165, 172, sufficiently to "shock itself into the protective arms of the Constitution," *Irvine v. California*, 347 *U.S.* 128, 138 (concurring opinion). It has been urged that States may not run counter to the "decencies of civilized conduct," *Rochin, supra,* at 173, or "some principle of justice so rooted in the traditions, and conscience of our people as to be ranked as fundamental," *Snyder v. Massachusetts,* 291 *U.S.* 97, 105, or to "those canons of decency and fairness which express the notions of justice of English-speaking peoples," *Malinski v. New York,* 324 *U.S.* 401, 417 (concurring opinion), or to "the community's sense of fair play and decency," *Rochin, supra,* at 173. It has been said that we must decide whether a state law is "fair, reasonable and appropriate," or is rather "an unreasonable, unnecessary and arbitrary interference with the right of the individual to his personal liberty or to enter into . . . contracts," *Lochner v. New York,* 198 *U.S.* 45, 56. States, under this philosophy, cannot act in conflict with "deeply rooted feelings of the community," *Haley v. Ohio,* 332 *U.S.* 596, 604 (separate opinion), or with "fundamental notions of fairness and justice," *id.,* 607. See also, e.g., *Wolf v. Colorado,* 338 *U.S.* 25, 27 ("rights . . . basic to our free society"); *Hebert v. Louisiana,* 272 *U.S.* 312, 316 ("fundamental principles of liberty and justice"); *Adkins v. Children's Hospital,* 261 *U.S.* 525, 561 ("arbitrary restraint of . . . liberties"); *Betts v. Brady,* 316 *U.S.* 455, 462 ("denial of fundamental fairness, shocking to the universal sense of justice"); *Poe v. Ullman,* 367 *U.S.* 497, 539 (dissenting opinion) ("intolerable and unjustifiable"). Perhaps the clearest, frankest and briefest explanation of how this due process approach works is the statement in another case handed down today that this Court is to invoke the Due Process Clause to strike down state procedures or laws which it can "not tolerate." *Linkletter v. Walker, post,* p. 618, at 631.

2. See Hand, The Bill of Rights (1958) 70: "[J]udges are seldom content merely to annul the particular solution before them; they do not, indeed they may not, say that taking all things into consideration, the legislators' solution is too strong for the judicial stomach. On the contrary they wrap up their veto in a protective veil of adjectives such as 'arbitrary,' 'artificial,' 'normal,' 'reasonable,' 'inherent,' 'fundamental,' or 'essential,' whose office usually, though quite innocently, is to disguise what they are doing and impute to it a derivation far more impressive than their personal preferences, which are all that in fact lie behind the decision." [Citations omitted—Eds.].

3. See Patterson, The Forgotten Ninth Amendment (1955). Mr. Patterson urges that the Ninth Amendment be used to protect unspecified "natural and inalienable rights." P. 4. The Introduction by Roscoe Pound states that "there is a marked revival of natural law ideas throughout the world. Interest in the Ninth Amendment is a symptom of that revival." P. iii.

4. Of course one cannot be oblivious to the fact that Mr. Gallup has already published the results of a poll which he says show that 46% of the people in this country believe schools should teach about birth control. Washington Post, May 21, 1965, p. 2, col. 1. I can hardly believe, however, that Brother Goldberg would view 46% of the persons polled as so overwhelming a proportion that this Court may now rely on it to declare that the Connecticut law infringes "fundamental" rights, and overrule the long-standing view of the people of Connecticut expressed through their elected representatives.

5. U.S. Const., Amend. IX, provides: "The enumeration in the Constitution, of certain rights, shall not be construed to deny or disparage others retained by the people."

6. Annuals of Congress 439.

ROE V. WADE *

United States Supreme Court, 1973

In decisions handed down on January 22, 1973, the U.S. Supreme Court declared unconstitutional the Texas and Georgia abortion laws. The Texas case, *Roe v. Wade,* concerned a statute which restricted legal abortions to those deemed necessary to save the woman's life. The Georgia case, *Doe v. Bolton,* dealt with a state law permitting abortions only when required by the woman's health, or to prevent birth of a deformed child, or when pregnancy resulted from rape. The court's invalidation of these laws implied that similarly restrictive laws in most other states are also unconstitutional.

Majority Opinion by Justice Harry A. Blackmun (Concurred in by Six Others)

. . . A recent review of the common law precedents argues . . . that even post-quickening abortion was never established as a common law crime. This is of some importance because while most American courts ruled, in holding or dictum, that abortion of an unquickened fetus was not criminal under their received common law, others followed Coke in stating that abortion of a quick fetus was a "misprison," a term they translated to mean "misdemeanor." That their reliance on Coke on this aspect of the law was uncritical and, apparently in all the reported cases, dictum (due probably to the paucity of common law prosecutions for post-quickening abortion), makes it now appear doubtful that abortion was ever firmly established as a common law crime even with respect to the destruction of a quick fetus. . . .

It is thus apparent that at common law, at the time of the adoption of our Constitution, and throughout the major portion of the 19th century, abortion was viewed with less disfavor than under most American statutes currently in effect. Phrasing it another way, a woman enjoyed a substantially broader right to terminate a pregnancy than she does in most States today. At least with respect to the early stage of pregnancy, and very possibly without such a limitation, the opportunity to make this choice was present in this country well into the 19th century. Even later, the law continued for some time to treat less punitively an abortion procured in early pregnancy. . .

Three reasons have been advanced to explain historically the enactment of criminal abortion laws in the 19th century and to justify their continued existence.

It has been argued occasionally that these laws were the product of a Victorian social concern to discourage illicit sexual conduct. Texas, however, does not advance this justification in the present case, and it appears that no court or commentator has taken the argument seriously. . . .

A second reason is concerned with abortion as a medical procedure. When most criminal abortion laws were first enacted, the procedure was a hazardous one for the woman. This was particularly true prior to the development of antisepsis. Antiseptic techniques, of course, were based on discoveries by Lister, Pasteur, and others first announced in 1867, but were not generally accepted and employed until about the turn of the century. Abortion mortality was high. Even after 1900, and perhaps until as late as the development of antibiotics in the 1940's, standard modern techniques such as dilation and curettage were not nearly so safe as they are today. Thus it has been argued that a State's real concern in enacting a criminal abortion law was to protect the pregnant woman, that is, to restrain her from submitting to a procedure that placed her life in serious jeopardy.

Modern medical techniques have altered this situation. Appellants and various *amici* refer to medical data indicating that abortion in early pregnancy,

---

that is, prior to the end of first trimester, although not without its risk, is now relatively safe. Mortality rates for women undergoing early abortions, where the procedure is legal, appear to be as low as or lower than the rates for normal childbirth. Consequently, any interest of the State in protecting the woman from an inherently hazardous procedure, except when it would be equally dangerous for her to forgo it, has largely disappeared. Of course, important state interests in the area of health and medical standards do remain. The State has a legitimate interest in seeing to it that abortion, like any other medical procedure, is performed under circumstances that insure maximum safety for the patient. This interest obviously extends at least to the performing physician and his staff, to the facilities involved, to the availability of after-care, and to adequate provision for any complication or emergency that might arise. The prevalence of high mortality rates at illegal "abortion mills" strengthens, rather than weakens, the State's interest in regulating the conditions under which abortions are performed. Moreover, the risk to the woman increases as her pregnancy continues. Thus the State retains a definite interest in protecting the woman's own health and safety when an abortion is performed at a late stage of pregnancy.

The third reason is the State's interest—some phrase it in terms of duty—in protecting prenatal life. Some of the argument for this justification rests on the theory that a new human life is present from the moment of conception. . . .

Parties challenging state abortion laws have sharply disputed in some courts the contention that a purpose of these laws, when enacted, was to protect prenatal life. Pointing to the absence of legislative history to support the contention, they claim that most state laws were designed solely to protect the woman. Because medical advances have lessened this concern, at least with respect to abortion in early pregnancy, they argue that with respect to such abortions the laws can no longer be justified by any state interest. There is some scholarly support for this view of original purpose. The few state courts called upon to interpret their laws in the late 19th and early 20th centuries did focus on the State's interest in protecting the woman's health rather than in preserving embryo and fetus. . . .

The Constitution does not explicitly mention any right of privacy. In a line of decisions, however, going back perhaps as far as *Union Pacific R. Co. v. Botsford,* 141 *U.S.* 250, 251 (1891), the Court has recognized that a right of personal privacy, or a guaran-

tee of certain areas or zones of privacy, does exist under the Constitution. In varying contexts the Court or individual Justices have indeed found at least the roots of that right in the First Amendment, . . . in the Fourth and Fifth Amendments . . . in the penumbras of the Bill of Rights . . . in the Ninth Amendment . . . or in the concept of liberty guaranteed by the first section of the Fourteenth Amendment. . . . These decisions make it clear that only personal rights that can be deemed "fundamental" or "implicit in the concept of ordered liberty," . . . are included in this guarantee of personal privacy. They also make it clear that the right has some extension to activities relating to marriage, . . . procreation, . . . contraception, . . . family relationships, . . . and child rearing and education. . . .

This right of privacy, whether it be founded in the Fourteenth Amendment's concept of personal liberty and restrictions upon state action, as we feel it is, or, as the District Court determined, in the Ninth Amendment's reservation of rights to the people, is broad enough to encompass a woman's decision whether or not to terminate her pregnancy. . . .

. . . Appellants and some *amici* argue that the woman's right is absolute and that she is entitled to terminate her pregnancy at whatever time, in whatever way, and for whatever reason she alone chooses. With this we do not agree. Appellants' arguments that Texas either has no valid interest at all in regulating the abortion decision, or no interest strong enough to support any limitation upon the woman's sole determination, is unpersuasive. The Court's decisions recognizing a right of privacy also acknowledge that some state regulation in areas protected by that right is appropriate. As noted above, a state may properly assert important interests in safe-guarding health, in maintaining medical standards, and in protecting potential life. At some point in pregnancy, these respective interests become sufficiently compelling to sustain regulation of the factors that govern the abortion decision. The privacy right involved, therefore, cannot be said to be absolute. . . .

We therefore conclude that the right of personal privacy includes the abortion decision, but that this right is not unqualified and must be considered against important state interests in regulation.

We note that those federal and state courts that have recently considered abortion law challenges have reached the same conclusion. . . .

Although the results are divided, most of these courts have agreed that the right of privacy, however based, is broad enough to cover the abortion decision; that the right, nonetheless, is not absolute and is subject to some limitations; and that at some point the state interests as to protection of health, medical standards, and prenatal life, become dominant. We agree with this approach.

The appellee and certain *amici* argue that the fetus is a "person" within the language and meaning of the Fourteenth Amendment. In support of this they outline at length and in detail the well-known facts of fetal development. If this suggestion of personhood is established, the appellant's case, of course, collapses, for the fetus' right to life is then guaranteed specifically by the Amendment. The appellant conceded as much on reargument. On the other hand, the appellee conceded on reargument that no case could be cited that holds that a fetus is a person within the meaning of the Fourteenth Amendment.

All this, together with our observation, *supra,* that throughout the major portion of the 19th century prevailing legal abortion practices were far freer than they are today, persuades us that the word "person," as used in the Fourteenth Amendment, does not include the unborn. . . . Indeed, our decision in *United States v. Vuitch,* 402 *U.S.* 62 (1971), inferentially is to the same effect, for we would not have indulged in statutory interpretation favorable to abortion in specified circumstances if the necessary consequence was the termination of life entitled to Fourteenth Amendment protection.

. . . As we have intimated above, it is reasonable and appropriate for a State to decide that at some point in time another interest, that of health of the mother or that of potential human life, becomes significantly involved. The woman's privacy is no longer sole and any right of privacy she possesses must be measured accordingly.

. . . We need not resolve the difficult question of when life begins. When those trained in the respective disciplines of medicine, philosophy, and theology are unable to arrive at any consensus, the judiciary, at this point in the development of man's knowledge, is not in a position to speculate as to the answer.

It should be sufficient to note briefly the wide divergence of thinking on this most sensitive and difficult question. There has always been strong support for the view that life does not begin until live birth. This was the belief of the Stoics. It appears to be the predominant, though not the unanimous, attitude of the Jewish faith. It may be taken to represent also the position of a large segment of the Protestant community, insofar as that can be ascertained; organized groups that have taken a formal position on the abortion issue have generally regarded abortion as a matter for the conscience of the individual and her family. As we have noted, the common law found greater significance in quickening. Physicians and their scientific colleagues have regarded that event with less interest and have tended to focus either upon conception or upon live birth or upon the interim point at which the fetus becomes "viable," that is, potentially able to live outside the mother's womb, albeit with artificial aid. Viability is usually placed at about seven months (28 weeks) but may occur earlier, even at 24 weeks. . . .

In areas other than criminal abortion the law has been reluctant to endorse any theory that life, as we recognize it, begins before live birth or to accord legal rights to the unborn except in narrowly defined situations and except when the rights are contingent upon live birth. . . . In short, the unborn have never been recognized in the law as persons in the whole sense.

In view of all this, we do not agree that, by adopting one theory of life, Texas may override the rights of the pregnant woman that are at stake. We repeat, however, that the State does have an important and legitimate interest in preserving and protecting the health of the pregnant woman, whether she be a resident of the State or a nonresident who seeks medical consultation and treatment there, and that it has still *another* important and legitimate interest in protecting the potentiality of human life. These interests are separate and distinct. Each grows in substantiality as the woman approaches term and, at a point during pregnancy, each becomes "compelling."

With respect to the State's important and legitimate interest in the health of the mother, the "compelling" point, in the light of present medical knowledge, is at approximately the end of the first trimester. This is so because of the now established medical fact . . . that until the end of the first trimester mortality in abortion is less than mortality in normal childbirth. It follows that, from and after this point, a State may regulate the abortion procedure to the extent that the regulation reasonably relates to the preservation and protection of maternal health. Examples of permissible state regulation in this area are requirements as to the qualifications of the person who is to perform the abortion; as to the licensure of that person; as to the facility in which the procedure is to be performed, that is, whether it must be a hospital or may be a clinic or some other place of less-than-hospital status; as to the licensing of the facility; and the like.

This means, on the other hand, that, for the period of pregnancy prior to this "compelling" point, the attending physician, in consultation with his patient, is free to determine, without regulation by the State, that in his medical judgment the patient's pregnancy should be terminated. If that decision is reached, the judgment may be effectuated by an abortion free of interference by the State.

With respect to the State's important and legitimate interest in potential life, the "compelling" point is at viability. . . . State regulation protective of fetal life after viability thus has both logical and biological justifications. If the State is interested in protecting fetal life after viability, it may go so far as to proscribe abortion during that period except when it is necessary to preserve the life or health of the mother. . . .

To summarize and repeat:

1. A state criminal abortion statute of the current Texas type, that excepts from criminality only a *life saving* procedure on behalf of the mother, without regard to pregnancy stage and without recognition of the other interests involved, is violative of the Due Process Clause of the Fourteenth Amendment.
    (a) For the stage prior to approximately the end of the first trimester, the abortion decision and its effectuation must be left to the medical judgment of the pregnant woman's attending physician.
    (b) For the stage subsequent to approximately the end of the first trimester, the State, in promoting its interest in the health of the mother, may, if it chooses, regulate the abortion procedure in ways that are reasonably related to maternal health.
    (c) For the stage subsequent to viability the State, in promoting its interest in the potentiality of human life, may, if it chooses, regulate, and even proscribe, abortion except where it is necessary, in appropriate medical judgment, for the preservation of the life or health of the mother.
2. The State may define the term "physician," as it has been employed in the preceding numbered paragraphs of this Part XI of this opinion, to mean only a physician currently licensed by the State, and may proscribe any abortion by a person who is not a physician as so defined.

. . . The decision leaves the State free to place increasing restrictions on abortion as the period of pregnancy lengthens, so long as those restrictions are tailored to the recognized state interests. The decision vindicates the right of the physician to administer medical treatment according to his professional judgment up to the points where important state interests provide compelling justifications for intervention. Up to those points the abortion decision in all its aspects is inherently, and primarily, a medical decision, and basic responsibility for it must rest with the physician. If an individual practitioner abuses the privilege of exercising proper medical judgment, the usual remedies, judicial and intraprofessional, are available. . . .

Dissent by Justice Byron R. White (Concurred in by Justice William H. Rehnquist)

At the heart of the controversy in these cases are those recurring pregnancies that pose no danger whatsoever to the life or health of the mother but are nevertheless unwanted for any one or more of a variety of reasons—convenience, family planning, economics, dislike of children, the embarrassment of illegitimacy, etc. The common claim before us is that for any one of such reasons, or for no reason at all, and without asserting or claiming any threat to life or health, any woman is entitled to an abortion at her request if she is able to find a medical advisor willing to undertake the procedure.

The Court for the most part sustains this position: During the period prior to the time the fetus becomes viable, the Constitution of the United States values the convenience, whim or caprice of the putative mother more than the life or potential life of the fetus; the Constitution, therefore, guarantees the right to an abortion as against any state law or policy seeking to protect the fetus from an abortion not prompted by more compelling reasons of the mother.

With all due respect, I dissent. I find nothing in the language or history of the Constitution to support the Court's judgment. . . . As an exercise of raw judicial power, the Court perhaps has authority to do what it does today; but in my view its judgment is an improvident and extravagant exercise of the power of judicial review which the Constitution extends to this Court.

The Court apparently values the convenience of the pregnant mother more than the continued existence and development of the life or potential life which she carries. . . .

It is my view, therefore, that the Texas statute is not constitutionally infirm because it denies abortions to those who seek to serve only their convenience rather than to protect their life or health. . . .

PLANNED PARENTHOOD OF S.E. PENNSYLVANIA V. CASEY *

United States Supreme Court, 1992

JUSTICE O'CONNOR, JUSTICE KENNEDY, AND JUSTICE SOUTER announced the judgment of the Court:

At issue in these cases are five provisions of the Pennsylvania Abortion Control Act of 1982 as amended in 1988 and 1989. The Act requires that a woman seeking an abortion give her informed consent prior to the abortion procedure, and specifies that she be provided with certain information at least 24 hours before the abortion is performed. For a minor to obtain an abortion, the Act requires the informed consent of one of her parents, but provides for a judicial bypass option if the minor does not wish to or cannot obtain a parent's consent. Another provision of the Act requires that, unless certain exceptions apply, a married woman seeking an abortion must sign a statement indicating that she has notified her husband of her intended abortion. The Act exempts compliance with these three requirements in the event of a "medical emergency," which is defined in § 3203 of the Act. In addition to the above provisions regulating the performance of abortions, the Act imposes certain reporting requirements on facilities that provide abortion services. . . .

After considering the fundamental constitutional questions resolved by *Roe*, principles of institutional integrity, and the rule of stare decisis, we are led to conclude this: the essential holding of *Roe v. Wade* should be retained and once again reaffirmed.

It must be stated at the outset and with clarity that *Roe*'s essential holding, the holding we reaffirm, has three parts. First is a recognition of the right of the woman to choose to have an abortion before viability and to obtain it without undue interference from the State. Before viability, the State's interests are not strong enough to support a prohibition of abortion or the imposition of a substantial obstacle to the woman's effective right to elect the procedure. Second is a confirmation of the State's power to restrict abortions after fetal viability, if the law contains exceptions for pregnancies which endanger a woman's life or health. And third is the principle that the State has legitimate interests from the outset of the pregnancy in protecting the health of the woman and the life of the fetus that may become a child. These principles do not contradict one another; and we adhere to each. . . .

The Court's duty in the present case is clear. In 1973, it confronted the already divisive issue of governmental power to limit personal choice to undergo abortion, for which it provided a new resolution based on the due process guaranteed by the Fourteenth Amendment. Whether or not a new social consensus is developing on that issue, its divisiveness is no less today than in 1973, and pressure to overrule the decision, like pressure to retain it, has grown only more intense. A decision to overrule *Roe*'s essential holding under the existing circumstances would address error, if error there was, at the cost of both profound and unnecessary damage to the Court's legitimacy, and to the Nation's commitment to the rule of law. It is therefore imperative to adhere to the essence of *Roe*'s original decision, and we do so today. . . .

From what we have said so far it follows that it is a constitutional liberty of the woman to have some freedom to terminate her pregnancy. We conclude that the basic decision in *Roe* was based on a constitutional analysis which we cannot now repudiate. The woman's liberty is not so unlimited, however, that from the outset the State cannot show its concern for the life of the unborn, and at a later point in fetal development the State's interest in life

*112 *S. Ct.* 2791 (1992).

has sufficient force so that the right of the woman to terminate the pregnancy can be restricted.

That brings us, of course, to the point where much criticism has been directed at *Roe,* a criticism that always inheres when the Court draws a specific rule from what in the Constitution is but a general standard. We conclude, however, that the urgent claims of the woman to retain the ultimate control over her destiny and her body, claims implicit in the meaning of liberty, require us to perform that function. Liberty must not be extinguished for want of a line that is clear. And it falls to us to give some real substance to the woman's liberty to determine whether to carry her pregnancy to full term.

We conclude the line should be drawn at viability, so that before that time the woman has a right to choose to terminate her pregnancy. We adhere to this principle for two reasons. First, as we have said, is the doctrine of stare decisis. Any judicial act of linedrawing may seem somewhat arbitrary, but *Roe* was a reasoned statement, elaborated with great care. We have twice reaffirmed it in the face of great opposition. Although we must overrule those parts of *Thornburgh* and *Akron I* which, in our view, are inconsistent with *Roe*'s statement that the State has a legitimate interest in promoting the life or potential life of the unborn, the central premise of those cases represents an unbroken commitment by this Court to the essential holding of *Roe.* It is that premise which we reaffirm today.

The second reason is that the concept of viability, as we noted in *Roe,* is the time at which there is a realistic possibility of maintaining and nourishing a life outside the womb, so that the independent existence of the second life can in reason and all fairness be the object of state protection that now overrides the rights of the woman. Consistent with other constitutional norms, legislatures may draw lines which appear arbitrary without the necessity of offering a justification. But courts may not. We must justify the lines we draw. And there is no line other than viability which is more workable. To be sure, as we have said, there may be some medical developments that affect the precise point of viability, but this is an imprecision within tolerable limits given that the medical community and all those who must apply its discoveries will continue to explore the matter. The viability line also has, as a practical matter, an element of fairness. In some broad sense it might be said that a woman who fails to act before viability has consented to the State's intervention on behalf of the developing child.

The woman's right to terminate her pregnancy before viability is the most central principle of *Roe v. Wade*. It is a rule of law and a component of liberty we cannot renounce. . . .

Yet it must be remembered that *Roe v. Wade* speaks with clarity in establishing not only the woman's liberty but also the State's "important and legitimate interest in potential life." That portion of the decision in *Roe* has been given too little acknowledgement and implementation by the Court in its subsequent cases. Those cases decided that any regulation touching upon the abortion decision must survive strict scrutiny, to be sustained only if drawn in narrow terms to further a compelling state interest. Not all of the cases decided under that formulation can be reconciled with the holding in *Roe* itself that the State has legitimate interests in the health of the woman and in protecting the potential life within her. In resolving this tension, we choose to rely upon *Roe,* as against the later cases.

Roe established a trimester framework to govern abortion regulations. Under this elaborate but rigid construct, almost no regulation at all is permitted during the first trimester of pregnancy; regulations designed to protect the woman's health, but not to further the State's interest in potential life, are permitted during the second trimester; and during the third trimester, when the fetus is viable, prohibitions are permitted provided the life or health of the mother is not at stake. Most of our cases since *Roe* have involved the application of rules derived from the trimester framework.

The trimester framework no doubt was erected to ensure that the woman's right to choose not become so subordinate to the State's interest in promoting fetal life that her choice exists in theory but not in fact. We do not agree, however, that the trimester approach is necessary to accomplish this objective. A framework of this rigidity was unnecessary and in its later interpretation sometimes contradicted the State's permissible exercise of its powers.

Though the woman has a right to choose to terminate or continue her pregnancy before viability, it does not at all follow that the State is prohibited from taking steps to ensure that this choice is thoughtful and informed. Even in the earliest stages of pregnancy, the State may enact rules and regulations designed to encourage her to know that there are philosophical and social arguments of great weight that can be brought to bear in favor of continuing the pregnancy to full term and that there are procedures and institutions to allow adoption of unwanted children as well as a certain degree of state assistance if the mother chooses to raise the child herself. "'[T]he Constitution does not forbid a State or city, pursuant to democratic processes, from expressing a preference for normal childbirth.'" *Webster v. Reproductive Health Services*. . . .

We reject the trimester framework, which we do not consider to be part of the essential holding of *Roe*. Measures aimed at ensuring that a woman's choice contemplates the consequences for the fetus do not necessarily interfere with the right recognized in *Roe*, although those measures have been found to be inconsistent with the rigid trimester framework announced in that case. A logical reading of the central holding in *Roe* itself, and a necessary reconciliation of the liberty of the woman and the interest of the State in promoting prenatal life, require, in our view, that we abandon the trimester framework as a rigid prohibition on all previability regulation aimed at the protection of fetal life. The trimester framework suffers from these basic flaws: in its formulation it misconceives the nature of the pregnant woman's interest; and in practice it undervalues the State's interest in potential life, as recognized in *Roe*.

As our jurisprudence relating to all liberties save perhaps abortion has recognized, not every law which makes a right more difficult to exercise is, ipso facto, an infringement of that right. An example clarifies the point. We have held that not every ballot access limitation amounts to an infringement of the right to vote. Rather, the States are granted substantial flexibility in establishing the framework within which voters choose the candidates for whom they wish to vote.

The abortion right is similar. Numerous forms of state regulation might have the incidental effect of increasing the cost or decreasing the availability of medical care, whether for abortion or any other medical procedure. The fact that a law which serves a valid purpose, one not designed to strike at the right itself, has the incidental effect of making it more difficult or more expensive to procure an abortion cannot be enough to invalidate it. Only where state regulation imposes an undue burden on a woman's ability to make this decision does the power of the State reach into the heart of the liberty protected by the Due Process Clause.

These considerations of the nature of the abortion right illustrate that it is an overstatement to

describe it as a right to decide whether to have an abortion "without interference from the State," *Planned Parenthood of Central Mo. v. Danforth*. All abortion regulations interfere to some degree with a woman's ability to decide whether to terminate her pregnancy. It is, as a consequence, not surprising that despite the protestations contained in the original *Roe* opinion to the effect that the Court was not recognizing an absolute right, the Court's experience applying the trimester framework has led to the striking down of some abortion regulations which in no real sense deprived women of the ultimate decision. Those decisions went too far because the right recognized by *Roe* is a right "to be free from unwarranted governmental intrusion into matters so fundamentally affecting a person as the decision whether to bear or beget a child." *Eisenstadt v. Baird*. Not all governmental intrusion is of necessity unwarranted; and that brings us to the other basic flaw in the trimester framework: even in *Roe*'s terms, in practice it undervalues the State's interest in the potential life within the woman. *Roe v. Wade* was express in its recognition of the State's "important and legitimate interest[s] in preserving and protecting the health of the pregnant woman [and] in protecting the potentiality of human life." The trimester framework, however, does not fulfill *Roe*'s own promise that the State has an interest in protecting fetal life or potential life. *Roe* began the contradiction by using the trimester framework to forbid any regulation of abortion designed to advance that interest before viability. Before viability, *Roe* and subsequent cases treat all governmental attempts to influence a woman's decision on behalf of the potential life within her as unwarranted. This treatment is, in our judgment, incompatible with the recognition that there is a substantial state interest in potential life throughout pregnancy.

The very notion that the State has a substantial interest in potential life leads to the conclusion that not all regulations must be deemed unwarranted. Not all burdens on the right to decide whether to terminate a pregnancy will be undue. In our view, the undue burden standard is the appropriate means of reconciling the State's interest with the woman's constitutionally protected liberty.

A finding of an undue burden is a shorthand for the conclusion that a state regulation has the purpose or effect of placing a substantial obstacle in the path of a woman seeking an abortion of a nonviable fetus. A statute with this purpose is invalid because the means chosen by the State to further the interest in potential life must be calculated to inform the woman's free choice, not hinder it. And a statute which, while furthering the interest in potential life or some other valid state interest, has the effect of placing a substantial obstacle in the path of a woman's choice cannot be considered a permissible means of serving its legitimate ends. To the extent that the opinions of the Court or of individual Justices use the undue burden standard in a manner that is inconsistent with this analysis, we set out what in our view should be the controlling standard. In our considered judgment, an undue burden is an unconstitutional burden. . . .

Some guiding principles should emerge. What is at stake is the woman's right to make the ultimate decision, not a right to be insulated from all others in doing so. Regulations which do no more than create a structural mechanism by which the State, or the parent or guardian of a minor, may express profound respect for the life of the unborn are permitted, if they are not a substantial obstacle to the woman's exercise of the right to choose. Unless it has that effect on her right of choice, a state measure designed to persuade her to choose childbirth over abortion will be upheld if reasonably related to that goal. Regulations designed to foster the health of a woman seeking an abortion are valid if they do not constitute an undue burden.

Even when jurists reason from shared premises, some disagreement is inevitable. That is to be expected in the application of any legal standard which must accommodate life's complexity. We do not expect it to be otherwise with respect to the undue burden standard. We give this summary:

(a) To protect the central right recognized by *Roe v. Wade* while at the same time accommodating the State's profound interest in potential life, we will employ the undue burden analysis as explained in this opinion. An undue burden exists, and therefore a provision of law is invalid, if its purpose or effect is to place a substantial obstacle in the path of a woman seeking an abortion before the fetus attains viability.

(b) We reject the rigid trimester framework of *Roe v. Wade.* To promote the State's profound interest in potential life, throughout pregnancy the State may take measures to ensure that the woman's choice is informed, and measures designed to advance this interest will not be invalidated as long as their purpose is to persuade the woman to choose childbirth over abortion. These measures must not be an undue burden on the right.

(c) As with any medical procedure, the State may enact regulations to further the health or safety of a woman seeking an abortion. Unnecessary health regulations that have the purpose or effect of presenting a substantial obstacle to a woman seeking an abortion impose an undue burden on the right.

(d) Our adoption of the undue burden analysis does not disturb the central holding of *Roe v. Wade,* and we reaffirm that holding. Regardless of whether exceptions are made for particular circumstances, a State may not prohibit any woman from making the ultimate decision to terminate her pregnancy before viability.

(e) We also reaffirm *Roe's* holding that "subsequent to viability, the State in promoting its interest in the potentiality of human life may, if it chooses, regulate, and even proscribe, abortion except where it is necessary, in appropriate medical judgment, for the preservation of the life or health of the mother." *Roe v. Wade,* 410 *U.S.,* at 164-165, 93 *S.Ct.,* at 732.

These principles control our assessment of the Pennsylvania statute. . . .

The Court of Appeals applied what it believed to be the undue burden standard and upheld each of the provisions except for the husband notification requirement. We agree generally with this conclusion. . .

BOWERS V. HARDWICK*

United States Supreme Court, 1986

JUSTICE WHITE delivered the opinion of the Court.

In August 1982, respondent was charged with violating the Georgia statute criminalizing sodomy[1] by committing that act with another adult male in the bedroom of respondent's home. After a preliminary hearing, the District Attorney decided not to present the matter to the grand jury unless further evidence developed.

Respondent then brought suit in the Federal District Court, challenging the constitutionality of the statute insofar as it criminalized consensual sodomy.[2] He asserted that he was a practicing homosexual, that the Georgia sodomy statute, as administered by the defendants, placed him in imminent danger of arrest, and that the statute for several reasons violates the Federal Constitution. The District Court granted the defendants' motion to dismiss for failure to state a claim, relying on *Doe v. Commonwealth's Attorney for the City of Richmond,* 403 F.Supp. 1199 (ED Va. 1975), which this Court summarily affirmed, 425 U.S. 901, 96 S.Ct. 1489, 47 L.Ed.2d 751 (1976).

A divided panel of the Court of Appeals for the Eleventh Circuit reversed. . . . The court first held that, because *Doe* was distinguishable and in any event had been undermined by later decisions, our summary affirmance in that case did not require affirmance of the District Court. Relying on our decisions in *Griswold v. Connecticut, . . . Eisenstadt v. Baird, . . . Stanley v. Georgia, . . .* and *Roe v. Wade, . . .* the court went on to hold that the Georgia statute violated respondent's fundamental rights because his homosexual activity is a private and intimate association that is beyond the reach of state regulation by reason of the Ninth Amendment and the Due Process Clause of the Fourteenth Amendment. The case was remanded for trial, at which, to prevail, the State would have to prove that the statute is supported by a compelling interest and is the most narrowly drawn means of achieving that end.

Because other Courts of Appeals have arrived at judgments contrary to that of the Eleventh Circuit in this case, we granted the State's petition for certiorari questioning the holding that its sodomy statute violates the fundamental rights of homosexuals. We agree with the State that the Court of Appeals erred, and hence reverse its judgment.

This case does not require a judgment on whether laws against sodomy between consenting adults in general, or between homosexuals in particular, are wise or desirable. It raises no question about the right or propriety of state legislative decisions to repeal their laws that criminalize homosexual sodomy, or of state court decisions invalidating those laws on state constitutional grounds. The issue presented is whether the Federal Constitution confers a fundamental right upon homosexuals to engage in sodomy and hence invalidates the laws of the many States that still make such conduct illegal and have done so for a very long time. The case also calls for some judgment about the limits of the Court's role in carrying out its constitutional mandate.

We first register our disagreement with the Court of Appeals and with respondent that the Court's prior cases have construed the Constitution to confer a right of privacy that extends to homosexual sodomy and for all intents and purposes have decided this case. The reach of this line of cases was sketched in *Carey v. Population Services International, . . . Pierce v. Society of Sisters, . . .* and *Meyer v. Nebraska, . . .* were described as dealing with child rearing and education; *Prince v. Massachusetts, . . .* with family relationships; *Skinner v. Oklahoma ex xel. Williamson, . . .* with procreation; *Loving v. Virginia, . . .* with marriage; *Griswold v. Connecticut, supra,* and *Eisenstadt v. Baird, supra,* with contraception; and *Roe v. Wade, . . .* with abortion. The latter three cases were interpreted as construing the Due Process Clause of the Fourteenth Amendment

*487 *U.S.* 186 (1986). Endnotes edited and renumbered.

to confer a fundamental individual right to decide whether or not to beget or bear a child. . . .

Accepting the decisions in these cases and the above description of them, we think it evident that none of the rights announced in those cases bears any resemblance to the claimed constitutional right of homosexuals to engage in acts of sodomy that is asserted in this case. No connection between family, marriage, or procreation on the one hand and homosexual activity on the other has been demonstrated, either by the Court of Appeals or by respondent. Moreover, any claim that these cases nevertheless stand for the proposition that any kind of private sexual conduct between consenting adults is constitutionally insulated from state proscription is unsupportable. Indeed, the Court's opinion in *Carey* twice asserted that the privacy right, which the *Griswold* line of cases found to be one of the protections provided by the Due Process Clause, did not reach so far. . . .

Precedent aside, however, respondent would have us announce, as the Court of Appeals did, a fundamental right to engage in homosexual sodomy. This we are quite unwilling to do. It is true that despite the language of the Due Process Clauses of the Fifth and Fourteenth Amendments, which appears to focus only on the processes by which life, liberty, or property is taken, the cases are legion in which those Clauses have been interpreted to have substantive content, subsuming rights that to a great extent are immune from federal or state regulation or proscription. Among such cases are those recognizing rights that have little or no textual support in the constitutional language. *Meyer, Prince,* and *Pierce* fall in this category, as do the privacy cases from *Griswold* to *Carey.*

Striving to assure itself and the public that announcing rights not readily identifiable in the Constitution's text involves much more than the imposition of the Justices' own choice of values on the States and the Federal government, the Court has sought to identify the nature of the rights qualifying for heightened judicial protection. In *Palko v. Connecticut,* . . . it was said that this category includes those fundamental liberties that are "implicit in the concept of ordered liberty," such that "neither liberty nor justice would exist if [they] were sacrificed." A different description of fundamental liberties appeared in *Moore v. East Cleveland,* . . . (opinion of POWELL, J.), where they are characterized as those liberties that are "deeply rooted in this Nation's history and tradition." . . .

It is obvious to us that neither of these formulations would extend a fundamental right to homosexuals to engage in acts of consensual sodomy. Proscriptions against that conduct have ancient roots. See generally, Survey on the Constitutional Right to Privacy in the Context of Homosexual Activity, 40 *U.Miami L.Rev.* 521, 525 (1986). Sodomy was a criminal offense at common law and was forbidden by the laws of the original thirteen States when they ratified the Bill of Rights. In 1868, when the Fourteenth Amendment was ratified, all but 5 of the 37 States in the Union had criminal sodomy laws. In fact, until 1961, all 50 States outlawed sodomy, and today, 24 States and the District of Columbia continue to provide criminal penalties for sodomy performed in private and between consenting adults. Survey, *U.Miami L.Rev., supra,* at 524, n. 9. Against this background, to claim that a right to engage in such conduct is "deeply rooted in this Nation's history and tradition" or "implicit in the concept of ordered liberty" is, at best, facetious.

Nor are we inclined to take a more expansive view of our authority to discover new fundamental rights imbedded in the Due Process Clause. The Court is most vulnerable and comes nearest to illegitimacy when it deals with judge-made constitutional law having little or no cognizable roots in the language or design of the Constitution. That this is so was painfully demonstrated by the face-off between the Executive and the Court in the 1930s, which resulted in the repudiation of much of the substantive gloss that the Court had placed on the Due Process Clause of the Fifth and Fourteenth Amendments. There should be, therefore, great resistance to expand the substantive reach of those Clauses, particularly if it requires redefining the category of rights deemed to be fundamental. Otherwise, the Judiciary necessarily takes to itself further authority to govern the country without express constitutional authority. The claimed right pressed on us today falls far short of overcoming this resistance.

Respondent, however, asserts that the result should be different where the homosexual conduct occurs in the privacy of the home. He relies on *Stanley v. Georgia,* . . . where the Court held that the First Amendment prevents conviction for possessing and reading obscene material in the privacy of his home: "If the First Amendment means anything, it means that a State has no business telling a man, sitting alone in his house, what books he may read or what films he may watch." . . .

Stanley did protect conduct that would not have been protected outside the home, and it partially prevented the enforcement of state obscenity laws; but the decision was firmly grounded in the First Amendment. The right pressed upon us here has no similar support in the text of the Constitution, and it does not qualify for recognition under the prevailing principles for construing the Fourteenth Amendment. Its limits are also difficult to discern. Plainly enough, otherwise illegal conduct is not always immunized whenever it occurs in the home. Victimless crimes, such as the possession and use of illegal drugs do not escape the law where they are committed at home. *Stanley* itself recognized that its holding offered no protection for the possession in the home of drugs, firearms, or stolen goods. *Id.,* at 568, n. 11, 89 *S.Ct.,* at 1249, n. 11. And if respondent's submission is limited to the voluntary sexual conduct between consenting adults, it would be difficult, except by fiat, to limit the claimed right to homosexual conduct while leaving exposed to prosecution adultery, incest, and other sexual crimes even though they are committed in the home. We are unwilling to start down that road.

Even if the conduct at issue here is not a fundamental right, respondent asserts that there must be a rational basis for the law and that there is none in this case other than the presumed belief of a majority of the electorate in Georgia that homosexual sodomy is immoral and unacceptable. This is said to be an inadequate rationale to support the law. The law, however, is constantly based on notions of morality, and if all laws representing essentially moral choices are to be invalidated under the Due Process Clause, the courts will be very busy indeed. Even respondent makes no such claim, but insists that majority sentiments about the morality of homosexuality should be declared inadequate. We do not agree, and are unpersuaded that the sodomy laws of some 25 States should be invalidated on this basis.

Accordingly, the judgment of the Court of Appeals is

Reversed.

CHIEF JUSTICE BURGER, concurring.

I join the Court's opinion, but I write separately to underscore my view that in constitutional terms there is no such thing as a fundamental right to commit homosexual sodomy.

As the Court notes, *ante* at—, the proscriptions against sodomy have very "ancient roots." Decisions of individuals relating to homosexual conduct have been subject to state intervention throughout the history of Western Civilization. Condemnation of those practices is firmly rooted in Judaeo-Christian moral and ethical standards. Homosexual sodomy was a capital crime under Roman law. See *Code Theod.* 9.7.6; *Code Just.* 9.9.31. See also D. Bailey, *Homosexuality in the Western Christian Tradition* 70–81 (1975). During the English Reformation when powers of the ecclesiastical courts were transferred to the King's Courts, the first English statute criminalizing sodomy was passed. 25 Hen. VIII, c. 6. Blackstone described "the infamous crime against nature" as an offense of "deeper malignity" than rape, an heinous act "the very mention of which is a disgrace to human nature," and "a crime not fit to be named." Blackstone's Commentaries 215. The common law of England, including its prohibition of sodomy, became the received law of Georgia and the other Colonies. In 1816 the Georgia Legislature passed the statute at issue here, and that statute has been continuously in force in one form or another since that time. To hold that the act of homosexual sodomy is somehow protected as a fundamental right would be to cast aside millennia of moral teaching.

This is essentially not a question of personal "preferences" but rather of the legislative authority of the State. I find nothing in the Constitution depriving a State of the power to enact the statute challenged here.

JUSTICE POWELL, concurring.

I join the opinion of the Court. I agree with the Court that there is no fundamental right—*i.e.,* no substantive right under the Due Process Clause—such as that claimed by respondent, and found to exist by the Court of Appeals. This is not to suggest, however, that respondent may not be protected by the Eighth Amendment of the Constitution. The Georgia statute at issue in this case, Ga.Code Ann. § 16-6-2, authorizes a court to imprison a person for up to 20 years for a single private, consensual act of sodomy. In my view, a prison sentence for such conduct—certainly a sentence of long duration—would create a serious Eighth Amendment issue. Under the Georgia statute a single act of sodomy, even in the private setting of a home, is a felony comparable in terms of the possible sentence imposed to serious felonies such as aggravated battery, § 16-5-24, first degree arson, § 16-7-60 and robbery, § 16-8-40.[3]

In this case, however, respondent has not been tried, much less convicted and sentenced.

Moreover, respondent has not raised the Eighth Amendment issue below. For these reasons this constitutional argument is not before us.

JUSTICE BLACKMUN, with whom JUSTICE BRENNAN, JUSTICE MARSHALL, and JUSTICE STEVENS join, dissenting.

This case is no more about "a fundamental right to engage in homosexual sodomy," as the Court purports to declare, . . . than *Stanley v. Georgia*, . . . was about a fundamental right to watch obscene movies, or *Katz v. United States*, . . . was about a fundamental right to place interstate bets from a telephone booth. Rather, this case is about "the most comprehensive of rights and the right most valued by civilized men," namely, "the right to be let alone." *Olmstead v. United States*, 277 *U.S.* 438, 478, 48 *S.Ct.* 564, 572, 72 *L.Ed.* 944 (1928) (BRANDEIS, J., dissenting).

The statute at issue, *Ga.Code Ann.* § 16-6-2, denies individuals the right to decide for themselves whether to engage in particular forms of private, consensual sexual activity. The Court concludes that § 16-6-2 is valid essentially because "the laws of . . . many States . . . still make such conduct illegal and have done so for a very long time." . . . But the fact that the moral judgments expressed by statutes like § 16-6-2 may be "natural and familiar . . . ought not to conclude our judgment upon the question whether statutes embodying them conflict with the Constitution of the United States." *Roe v. Wade*, . . . quoting *Lochner v. New York*, . . . (HOLMES, J., dissenting). Like Justice Holmes, I believe that "[i]t is revolting to have no better reason for a rule of law than that so it was laid down in the time of Henry IV. It is still more revolting if the grounds upon which it was laid down have vanished long since, and the rule simply persists from blind imitation of the past." Holmes, The Path of the Law, 10 Harv.L.Rev. 457, 469 (1897). I believe we must analyze respondent's claim in the light of the values that underlie the constitutional right to privacy. If that right means anything, it means that, before Georgia can prosecute its citizens for making choices about the most intimate aspects of their lives, it must do more than assert that the choice they have made is an "'abominable crime not fit to be named among Christians,'" . . .

I.

In its haste to reverse the Court of Appeals and hold that the Constitution does not confe[r] a fundamental right upon homosexuals to engage in sodomy," *ante,*

at 2843, the Court relegates the actual statute being challenged to a footnote and ignores the procedural posture of the case before it. A fair reading of the statute and of the complaint clearly reveals that the majority has distorted the question this case presents.

First, the Court's almost obsessive focus on homosexual activity is particularly hard to justify in light of the broad language Georgia has used. Unlike the Court, the Georgia Legislature has not proceeded on the assumption that homosexuals are so different from other citizens that their lives may be controlled in a way that would not be tolerated if it limited the choices of those other citizens. . . . Rather, Georgia has provided that "[a] person commits the offense of sodomy when he performs or submits to any sexual act involving the sex organs of one person and the mouth or anus of another." *Ga.Code Ann.* § 16-6-2(a). The sex or status of the persons who engage in the act is irrelevant as a matter of state law. In fact, to the extent I can discern a legislative purpose for Georgia's 1968 enactment of § 16-6-2, that purpose seems to have been to broaden the coverage of the law to reach heterosexual as well as homosexual activity.[4] I therefore see no basis for the Court's decision to treat this case as an "as applied" challenge to § 16-6-2, . . . or for Georgia's attempt, both in its brief and at oral argument, to defend § 16-6-2 solely on the grounds that it prohibits homosexual activity. Michael Hardwick's standing may rest in significant part on Georgia's apparent willingness to enforce against homosexuals a law it seems not to have any desire to enforce against heterosexuals. . . . But his claim that § 16-6-2 involves an unconstitutional intrusion into his privacy and his right of intimate association does not depend in any way on his sexual orientation.

Second, I disagree with the Court's refusal to consider whether § 16-6-2 runs afoul of the Eighth or Ninth Amendments or the Equal Protection Clause of the Fourteenth Amendment. . . . Respondent's complaint expressly invoked the Ninth Amendment, see App. 6, and he relied heavily before this Court on *Griswold v. Connecticut*, . . . which identifies that Amendment as one of the specific constitutional provisions giving "life and substance" to our understanding of privacy. . . . More importantly, the procedural posture of the case requires that we affirm the Court of Appeals' judgment if there is *any* ground on which respondent may be entitled to relief. This case is before us on petitioner's motion to dismiss for failure to state a claim. . . . It is a well-settled principle of law that "a complaint should not be dismissed merely because a plaintiff's allegations do not support the particular legal theory he advances, for the court is under a duty to examine the complaint to determine if the allegations provide for relief on any possible theory." . . . Thus, even if respondent did not advance claims based on the Eighth or Ninth Amendments, or on the Equal Protection Clause, his complaint should not be dismissed if any of those provisions could entitle him to relief. I need not reach either the Eighth Amendment or the Equal Protection Clause issues because I believe that Hardwick has stated a cognizable claim that § 16-6-2 interferes with constitutionally protected interests in privacy and freedom of intimate association. But neither the Eighth Amendment nor the Equal Protection Clause is so clearly irrelevant that a claim resting on either provision should be peremptorily dismissed.[5] The Court's cramped reading of the issue before it makes for a short opinion, but it does little to make for a persuasive one.

II

"Our cases long have recognized that the Constitution embodies a promise that a certain private sphere of individual liberty will be kept largely beyond the reach of government." *Thornburgh v. American Coll. of Obst. & Gyn.,* . . . In construing the right to privacy, the Court has proceeded along two somewhat distinct, albeit complementary, lines. First, it has recognized a privacy interest with reference to certain *decisions* that are properly for the individual to make. . . . Second, it has recognized a privacy interest with reference to certain *places* without regard for the particular activities in which the individuals who occupy them are engaged. . . . The case before us implicates both the decisional and the spatial aspects of the right to privacy.

A

The Court concludes today that none of our prior cases dealing with various decisions that individuals are entitled to make free of governmental interference "bears any resemblance to the claimed constitutional right of homosexuals to engage in acts of sodomy that is asserted in this case." . . . While it is true that these cases may be characterized by their connection to protection of the family, . . . the Court's conclusion that they extend no further than this boundary ignores the warning in *Moore v. East*

Cleveland, . . . against "clos[ing] our eyes to the basic reasons why certain rights associated with the family have been accorded shelter under the Fourteenth Amendment's Due Process Clause." We protect those rights not because they contribute, in some direct and material way, to the general public welfare, but because they form so central a part of an individual's life. "[T]he concept of privacy embodies the 'moral fact that a person belongs to himself and not others nor to society as a whole.'" . . . And so we protect the decision whether to marry precisely because marriage "is an association that promotes a way of life, not causes; a harmony in living, not political faiths; a bilateral loyalty, not commercial or social projects." *Griswold v. Connecticut.* . . . We protect the decision whether to have a child because parenthood alters so dramatically an individual's self-definition, not because of demographic considerations or the Bible's command to be fruitful and multiply. Cf. *Thornburgh v. American Coll. of Obst. & Gyn., supra,*—U.S., at—,n. 6. 106 S.Ct., at 2188, n. 6 (STEVENS, J., concurring). And we protect the family because it contributes so powerfully to the happiness of individuals, not because of a preference for stereotypical households. . . . The Court recognized in *Roberts* . . . that the "ability independently to define one's identity that is central to any concept of liberty" cannot truly be exercised in a vacuum; we all depend on the "emotional enrichment of close ties with others." . . .

Only the most willful blindness could obscure the fact that sexual intimacy is "a sensitive, key relationship of human existence, central to family life, community welfare, and the development of human personality," . . . The fact that individuals define themselves in a significant way through their intimate sexual relationships with others suggests, in a Nation as diverse as ours, that there may be many "right" ways of conducting those relationships, and that much of the richness of a relationship will come from the freedom an individual has to *choose* the form and nature of these intensely personal bonds. See Karst, The Freedom of Intimate Association, 89 Yale L.J. 624, 637 (1980). . . .

In a variety of circumstances we have recognized that a necessary corollary of giving individuals freedom to choose how to conduct their lives is acceptance of the fact that different individuals will make different choices. For example, in holding that the clearly important state interest in public education should give way to a competing claim by the Amish to the effect that extended formal schooling threatened their way of life, the Court declared: "There can be no assumption that today's majority is 'right' and the Amish and others like them are 'wrong.' A way of life that is odd or even erratic but interferes with no rights or interests of others is not to be condemned because it is different." *Wisconsin v. Yoder. . . .* The Court claims that its decision today merely refuses to recognize a fundamental right to engage in homosexual sodomy; what the Court really has refused to recognize is the fundamental interest all individuals have in controlling the nature of their intimate associations with others.

B

The behavior for which Hardwick faces prosecution occurred in his own home, a place to which the Fourth Amendment attaches special significance. The Court's treatment of this aspect of the case is symptomatic of its overall refusal to consider the broad principles that have informed our treatment of privacy in specific cases. Just as the right to privacy is more than the mere aggregation of a number of entitlements to engage in specific behavior, so too, protecting the physical integrity of the home is more than merely a means of protecting specific activities that often take place there. Even when our understanding of the contours of the right to privacy depends on "reference to a 'place,'" . . . "the essence of a Fourth Amendment violation is 'not the breaking of [a person's] doors, and the rummaging of his drawers,' but rather is 'the invasion of his indefeasible right of personal security, personal liberty and private property.'" . . .

The Court's interpretation of the pivotal case of *Stanley v. Georgia, . . .* is entirely unconvincing. *Stanley* held that Georgia's undoubted power to punish the public distribution of constitutionally unprotected, obscene material did not permit the State to punish the private possession of such material. According to the majority here, *Stanley* relied entirely on the First Amendment, and thus, it is claimed, sheds no light on cases not involving printed materials. . . . But that is not what *Stanley* said. Rather, the *Stanley* Court anchored its holding in the Fourth Amendment's special protection for the individual in his home:

"The makers of our Constitution undertook to secure conditions favorable to the pursuit of happiness. They recognized the significance of man's spiritual nature, of his feelings and of his intellect. They knew that only a part of the pain, pleasure and satisfactions of life are to be found in material things. They sought to protect Americans in their beliefs, their thoughts, their emotions and their sensations."

These are the rights that appellant is asserting in the case before us. He is asserting the right to read or observe what he pleases—the right to satisfy his intellectual and emotional needs in the privacy of his own home. . . ."

The central place that *Stanley* gives Justice Brandeis' dissent in *Olmstead,* a case raising *no* First Amendment claim, shows that *Stanley* rested as much on the Court's understanding of the Fourth Amendment as it did on the First. Indeed, in *Paris Adult Theatre I v. Slaton, . . .* suggested that reliance on the Fourth Amendment not only supported the Court's outcome in *Stanley* but actually was *necessary* to it: "If obscene material unprotected by the First Amendment in itself carried with it a 'penumbra' of constitutionally protected privacy, this Court would not have found it necessary to decide *Stanley* on the narrow basis of the 'privacy of the home,' which was hardly more than a reaffirmation that 'a man's home is his castle.'" . . . "The right of the people to be secure in their . . . houses," expressly guaranteed by the Fourth Amendment, is perhaps the most "textual" of the various constitutional provisions that inform our understanding of the right to privacy, and thus I cannot agree with the Court's statement that "[t]he right pressed upon us here has no . . . support in the text of the Constitution," . . . Indeed, the right of an individual to conduct intimate relationships in the intimacy of his or her own home seems to me to be the heart of the Constitution's protection of privacy.

III

The Court's failure to comprehend the magnitude of the liberty interests at stake in this case leads it to slight the question whether petitioner, on behalf of the State, has justified Georgia's infringement on these interests. I believe that neither of the two general justifications for § 16-6-2 that petitioner has advanced warrants dismissing respondent's challenge for failure to state a claim.

First, petitioner asserts that the acts made criminal by the statute may have serious adverse consequences for "the general public health and welfare," such as spreading communicable diseases or fostering other criminal activity. . . . Inasmuch as this case was dismissed by the District Court on the pleadings, it is not surprising that the record before us is barren of any evidence to support petitioner's claim.[6] In light of the state of the record, I see no justification for the Court's attempt to equate the private, consensual sexual activity at issue here with the "possession in the home of drugs, firearms, or stolen goods," . . . to which *Stanley* refused to extend its protection. . . . None of the behavior so mentioned in *Stanley* can properly be viewed as "[v]ictimless," . . . drugs and weapons are inherently dangerous, . . . and for property to be "stolen," someone must have been wrongfully deprived of it. Nothing in the record before the Court provides any justification for finding the activity forbidden by § 16-6-2 to be physically dangerous, either to the persons engaged in it or to others.

The core of petitioner's defense of § 16-6-2, however, is that respondent and others who engage in the conduct prohibited by § 16-6-2 interfere with Georgia's exercise of the "'right of the Nation and of the States to maintain a decent society,'" . . . Essentially, petitioner argues, and the Court agrees, that the fact that the acts described in § 16-6-2 "for hundreds of years, if not thousands, have been uniformly condemned as immoral" is a sufficient reason to permit a State to ban them today. . . .

I cannot agree that either the length of time a majority has held its convictions or the passions with which it defends them can withdraw legislation from this Court's scrutiny. . . . As Justice Jackson wrote so eloquently for the Court in *West Virginia Board of Education v. Barnette,* . . . "we apply the limitations of the Constitution with no fear that freedom to be intellectually and spiritually diverse or even contrary will disintegrate the social organization. . . . [F]reedom to differ is not limited to things that do not matter much. That would be a mere shadow of freedom. The test of its substance is the right to differ as to things that touch the heart of the existing order." See also Karst, 89 Yale L.J., at 627. It is precisely because the issue raised by this case touches the heart of what makes individuals what they are that we should be especially sensitive to the rights of those whose choices upset the majority.

The assertion that "traditional Judaeo-Christian values proscribe" the conduct involved, Brief for Petitioner 20, cannot provide an adequate justification for § 16-6-2. That certain, but by no means all, religious groups condemn the behavior at issue gives the State no license to impose their judgments on the entire citizenry. The legitimacy of secular legisla-

tion depends instead on whether the State can advance some justification for its law beyond its conformity to religious doctrine. . . . Thus, far from buttressing his case, petitioner's invocation of Leviticus, Romans, St. Thomas Aquinas, and sodomy's heretical status during the Middle Ages undermines his suggestion that § 16-6-2 represents a legitimate use of secular coercive power.[7] A State can no more punish private behavior because of religious intolerance than it can punish such behavior because of racial animus. "The Constitution cannot control such prejudices, but neither can it tolerate them. Private biases may be outside the reach of the law, but the law cannot, directly or indirectly give them effect." . . . No matter how uncomfortable a certain group may make the majority of this Court, we have held that "[m]ere public intolerance or animosity cannot constitutionally justify the deprivation of a person's physical liberty." . . .

Nor can § 16-6-2 be justified as a "morally neutral" exercise of Georgia's power to "protect the public environment," . . . Certainly, some private behavior can affect the fabric of society as a whole. Reasonable people may differ about whether particular sexual acts are moral or immoral, but "we have ample evidence for believing that people will not abandon morality, will not think any better of murder, cruelty and dishonesty, merely because some private sexual practice which they abominate is not punished by the law." H. L. A. Hart, Immorality and Treason, reprinted in The Law as Literature 220, 225 (L. Blom-Cooper ed. 1961). Petitioner and the Court fail to see the difference between laws that protect public sensibilities and those that enforce private morality. Statutes banning public sexual activity are entirely consistent with protecting the individual's liberty interest in decisions concerning sexual relations: the same recognition that those decisions are intensely private which justifies protecting them from governmental interference can justify protecting individuals from unwilling exposure to the sexual activities of others. But the mere fact that intimate behavior may be punished when it takes place in public cannot dictate how States can regulate intimate behavior that occurs in intimate places. See *Paris Adult Theatre I,* . . . ("marital intercourse on a street corner or a theater stage" can be forbidden despite the constitutional protection identified in *Griswold v. Connecticut.* . . .

This case involves no real interference with the rights of others, for the mere knowledge that other individuals do not adhere to one's value system cannot be a legally cognizable interest, . . . let alone an interest that can justify invading the houses, hearts, and minds of citizens who choose to live their lives differently.

IV

It took but three years for the Court to see the error in its analysis in *Minersville School District v. Gobitis* . . . and to recognize that the threat to national cohesion posed by a refusal to salute the flag was vastly outweighed by the threat to those same values posed by compelling such a salute. . . . I can only hope that here, too, the Court soon will reconsider its analysis and conclude that depriving individuals of the right to choose for themselves how to conduct their intimate relationships poses a far greater threat to the values most deeply rooted in our Nation's history than tolerance of nonconformity could ever do. Because I think the Court today betrays those values, I dissent.

JUSTICE STEVENS, with whom JUSTICE BRENNAN and JUSTICE MARSHALL join, dissenting.

Like the statute that is challenged in this case,[8] the rationale of the Court's opinion applies equally to the prohibited conduct regardless of whether the parties who engage in it are married or unmarried, or are of the same or different sexes. Sodomy was condemned as an odious and sinful type of behavior during the formative period of the common law. That condemnation was equally damning for heterosexual and homosexual sodomy. Moreover, it provided no special exemption for married couples.[9] The license to cohabit and to produce legitimate offspring simply did not include any permission to engage in sexual conduct that was considered a "crime against nature."

The history of the Georgia statute before us clearly reveals this traditional prohibition of heterosexual, as well as homosexual, sodomy.[10] Indeed, at one point in the 20th century, Georgia's law was construed to permit certain sexual conduct between homosexual women even though such conduct was prohibited between heterosexuals. The history of the statutes cited by the majority as proof for the proposition that sodomy is not constitutionally protected, . . . similarly reveals a prohibition on heterosexual, as well as homosexual, sodomy.

Because the Georgia statute expresses the traditional view that sodomy is an immoral kind of conduct regardless of the identity of the persons who engage in it, I believe that a proper analysis of its constitutionality requires consideration of two questions: First, may a State totally prohibit the described conduct by means of a neutral law applying without exception to all persons subject to its jurisdiction? If not, may the State save the statute by announcing that it will only enforce the law against homosexuals? The two questions merit separate discussion.

I

Our prior cases make two propositions abundantly clear. First, the fact that the governing majority in a State has traditionally viewed a particular practice as immoral is not a sufficient reason for upholding a law prohibiting the practice; neither history nor tradition could save a law prohibiting miscegenation from constitutional attack. Second, individual decisions by married persons, concerning the intimacies of their physical relationship, even when not intended to produce offspring, are a form of "liberty" protected by the Due Process Clause of the Fourteenth Amendment. *Griswold v. Connecticut*. . . . Moreover, this protection extends to intimate choices by unmarried as well as married persons. . . .

In consideration of claims of this kind, the Court has emphasized the individual interest in privacy, but its decisions have actually been animated by an even more fundamental concern. As I wrote some years ago:

> These cases do not deal with the individual's
> interest in protection from unwarranted public
> attention, comment, or exploitation. They
> deal, rather, with the individual's right to make
> certain unusually important decisions that will
> affect his own, or his family's, destiny. The
> Court has referred to such decisions as impli-
> cating "basic values," as being "fundamental,"
> and as being dignified by history and tradi-
> tion. The character of the Court's language in
> these cases brings to mind the origins of the
> American heritage of freedom—the abiding
> interest in individual liberty that makes certain
> state intrusions on the citizen's right to decide
> how he will live his own life intolerable.
> Guided by history, our tradition of respect for
> the dignity of individual choice in matters of
> conscience and the restraints implicit in the

federal system, federal judges have accepted the responsibility for recognition and protection of these rights in appropriate cases. . . .

Society has every right to encourage its individual members to follow particular traditions in expressing affection for one another and in gratifying their personal desires. It, of course, may prohibit an individual from imposing his will on another to satisfy his own selfish interests. It also may prevent an individual from interfering with, or violating, a legally sanctioned and protected relationship, such as marriage. And it may explain the relative advantages and disadvantages of different forms of intimate expression. But when individual married couples are isolated from observation by others, the way in which they voluntarily choose to conduct their intimate relations is a matter for them—not the State—to decide. The essential "liberty" that animated the development of the law in cases like *Griswold, Eisenstadt,* and *Carey* surely embraces the right to engage in nonreproductive, sexual conduct that others may consider offensive or immoral.

Paradoxical as it may seem, our prior cases thus establish that a State may not prohibit sodomy within "the sacred precincts of marital bedrooms," *Griswold,* . . . or, indeed, between unmarried heterosexual adults. *Eisenstadt.* . . . In all events, it is perfectly clear that the State of Georgia may not totally prohibit the conduct proscribed by § 16-6-2 of the Georgia Criminal Code.

II

If the Georgia statute cannot be enforced as it is written—if the conduct it seeks to prohibit is a protected form of liberty for the vast majority of Georgia's citizens—the State must assume the burden of justifying a selective application of its law. Either the persons to whom Georgia seeks to apply its statute do not have the same interest in "liberty" that others have, or there must be a reason why the State may be permitted to apply a generally applicable law to certain persons that it does not apply to others.

The first possibility is plainly unacceptable. Although the meaning of the principle that "all men are created equal" is not always clear, it surely must mean that every free citizen has the same interest in "liberty" that the members of the majority share. From the standpoint of the individual, the homosexual and the heterosexual have the same interest in

deciding how he will live his own life, and, more narrowly, how he will conduct himself in his personal and voluntary associations with his companions. State intrusion into the private conduct of either is equally burdensome. The second possibility is similarly unacceptable. A policy of selective application must be supported by a neutral and legitimate interest— something more substantial than a habitual dislike for, or ignorance about, the disfavored group. Neither the State nor the Court has identified any such interest in this case. The Court has posited as a justification for the Georgia statute "the presumed belief of a majority of the electorate in Georgia that homosexual sodomy is immoral and unacceptable." . . . But the Georgia electorate has expressed no such belief—instead, its representatives enacted a law that presumably reflects the belief that *all sodomy* is immoral and unacceptable. Unless the Court is prepared to conclude that such a law is constitutional, it may not rely on the work product of the Georgia Legislature to support its holding. For the Georgia statute does not single out homosexuals as a separate class meriting special disfavored treatment.

Nor, indeed, does the Georgia prosecutor even believe that all homosexuals who violate this statute should be punished. This conclusion is evident from the fact that the respondent in this very case has formally acknowledged in his complaint and in court that he has engaged, and intends to continue to engage, in the prohibited conduct, yet the State has elected not to process criminal charges against him. As JUSTICE POWELL points out, moreover, Georgia's prohibition on private, consensual sodomy has not been enforced for decades. The record of nonenforcement, in this case and in the last several decades, belies the Attorney General's representations about the importance of the State's selective application of its generally applicable law.

Both the Georgia statute and the Georgia prosecutor thus completely fail to provide the Court with any support for the conclusion that homosexual sodomy, *simpliciter,* is considered unacceptable conduct in that State, and that the burden of justifying a selective application of the generally applicable law has been met.

III

The Court orders the dismissal of respondent's complaint even though the State's statute prohibits all sodomy; even though that prohibition is concededly unconstitutional with respect to heterosexuals; and even though the State's *post hoc* explanations for selective application are belied by the State's own actions. At the very least, I think it clear at this early stage of the litigation that respondent has alleged a constitutional claim sufficient to withstand a motion to dismiss.

I respectfully dissent.

---

1. *Ga.Code Ann.* § 16-6-2 (1984) provides, in pertinent part, as follows:

   "(a) A person commits the offense of sodomy when he performs or submits to any sexual act involving the sex organs of one person and the mouth or anus of another. . . .

   "(b) A person convicted of the offense of sodomy shall be punished by imprisonment for not less than one nor more than 20 years. . . ."

2. John and Mary Doe were also plaintiffs in the action. They alleged that they wished to engage in sexual activity proscribed by § 16-6-2 in the privacy of their home, App. 3, and that they had been "chilled and deterred" from engaging in such activity by both the existence of the statute and Hardwick's arrest. *Id.*, at 5. The District Court held, however, that because they had neither sustained, nor were in immediate danger of sustaining, any direct injury from the enforcement of the statute, they did not have proper standing to maintain the action. *Id.*, at 18. The Court of Appeals affirmed the District Court's judgment dismissing the Does' claim for lack of standing. 760 *F.2d* 1202, 1206–1207 (1985), and the Does do not challenge that holding in this Court.

   The only claim properly before the Court, therefore, is Hardwick's challenge to the Georgia statute as applied to consensual homosexual sodomy. We express no opinion on the constitutionality of the Georgia statute as applied to other acts of sodomy.

3. It was conceded at oral argument that, prior to the complaint against respondent Hardwick, there had been no reported decision involving prosecution for private homosexual sodomy under this statute for several decades. See *Thompson v. Aldredge*, 187 *Ga.* 467, 200 *S.E.* 799 (1939). Moreover, the State has declined to present the criminal charge against Hardwick to a grand jury, and this is a suit for declaratory judgment brought by respondents challenging the validity of the statute. The history of nonenforcement suggests the moribund character today of laws criminalizing this type of private, consensual conduct. Some 26 states have repealed similar statutes. But the constitutional validity of the Georgia statute was put in issue by respondents, and for the reasons stated by the Court, I cannot say that conduct condemned for hundreds of years has now become a fundamental right.

4. Until 1968, Georgia defined sodomy as "the carnal knowledge and connection against the order of nature, by man with man, or in the same unnatural manner with woman." *Ga. Crim.Code* § 26-5901 (1933). In *Thompson v. Aldredge*, 187 *Ga.* 467, 200 S.E. 799 (1939), the Georgia Supreme Court held that § 26-5901 did not prohibit lesbian activity. And in *Riley v. Garrett*, 219 *Ga.* 345, 133 *S.E.2d* 367 (1963), the Georgia Supreme Court held that § 26-5901 did not prohibit heterosexual cunnilingus. Georgia passed the act-specific statute currently in force "perhaps in response to the restrictive court decisions such as Riley." Note, The Crimes Against Nature, 16 *J.Pub.L.* 159, 167, n. 47 (1967).

5. In *Robinson v. California*, 370 *U.S.* 660, 82 *S.Ct.* 1417, 8 *L.Ed.2d* 758 (1962), the Court held that the Eighth Amendment barred convicting a defendant due to his "status" as a narcotics addict, since that condition was "apparently an illness which may be contracted innocently or involuntarily." *Id.*, at 667, 82 S.Ct., at 1420. In *Powell v. Texas*, 392 *U.S.* 514, 88 *S.Ct.* 2145, 20 *L.Ed.2d* 1254 (1968), where the Court refused to extend Robinson to punishment of public drunkenness by a chronic alcoholic, one of the factors relied on by Justice MARSHALL, in writing the plurality opinion, was that Texas had not "attempted to regulate appellant's behavior in the privacy of his own home." *Id.*, at 532, 88 S.Ct., at 2154. Justice WHITE wrote separately:

   "Analysis of this difficult case is not advanced by preoccupation with the label 'condition.' In *Robinson* the Court dealt with 'a statute which makes the "status" of narcotic addiction a criminal offense. . . .' 370 *U.S.*, at 666 [82 *S.Ct.*, at 1420]. By precluding criminal conviction for such a 'status' the Court was dealing with a condition brought about by acts remote in time from the application of the criminal sanctions contemplated, a condition which was relatively permanent in duration, and a condition of great magnitude and significance in terms of human behavior and values. . . . If it were necessary to distinguish between 'acts' and 'conditions' for purposes of the Eighth Amendment, I would adhere to the concept of 'condition' implicit in the opinion in *Robinson*. . . . The proper subject of inquiry is whether volitional acts brought about the 'condition' and whether those acts are sufficiently proximate to the 'condition' for it to be permissible to impose penal sanctions on the 'condition.'" *Id.*, 392 *U.S.*, at 550–551, n. 2, 88 *S.Ct.*, at 2163, n. 2.

   Despite historical views of homosexuality, it is no longer viewed by mental health professionals as a "disease" or disorder. See Brief for American Psychological Association and American Public Health Association as *Amici Curiae* 8–11. But, obviously, neither is it simply a matter of deliberate personal election. Homosexual orientation may well form part of the very fiber of an individual's personality. Consequently, under Justice WHITE's analysis in *Powell,* the Eighth Amendment may pose a constitutional barrier to sending an individual to prison for acting on that attraction regardless of the circumstances. An individual's ability to make constitutionally protected "decisions concerning sexual relations," *Carey v. Population Services International*, 431 *U.S.* 678, 711, 97 *S.Ct.* 2010, 2029, 52 *L.Ed.2d* 675 (1977) (POWELL, J., concurring in part and concurring in the judgment), is rendered empty indeed if he or she is given no real choice but a life without any physical intimacy.

   With respect to the Equal Protection Clause's applicability to § 16-6-2, I note that Georgia's exclusive stress before this Court on its interest in prosecuting homosexual activity despite the gender-neutral terms of the statute may raise serious questions of discriminatory enforcement, questions that cannot be disposed of before this Court on a motion to dismiss. See *Yick Wo v. Hopkins*, 118 *U.S.* 356, 373–374, 6 *S.Ct.* 1064, 1072–1073, 30 *L.Ed.* 220 (1886). The legislature having decided that the sex of the participants is irrelevant to the legality of the acts, I do not see why the State can defend § 16-6-2 on the ground that individuals singled out for prosecution are of the same sex as their partners. Thus, under the circumstances of this case, a claim under the Equal Protection Clause may well be available without having to reach the more controversial question whether homosexuals are a suspect class. See, *e.g., Rowland v. Mad River Local School District*,— U.S.—,—, 105 *S.Ct.* 1373,—, 84 *L.Ed.2d* 392 (1985) (BRENNAN, J., dissenting from denial of certiorari); Note, The Constitutional Status of Sexual Orientation: Homosexuality as a Suspect Classification, 98 *Harv. L.Rev.* 1285 (1985).

6. Even if a court faced with a challenge to § 16-6-2 were to apply simple rational-basis scrutiny to the statute, Georgia would be

required to show an actual connection between the forbidden acts and the ill effects it seeks to prevent. The connection between the acts prohibited by § 16-6-2 and the harms identified by petitioner in his brief before this Court is a subject of hot dispute, hardly amenable to dismissal under Federal Rule of Civil Procedure 12(b)(6).

7. The theological nature of the origin of Anglo-American anti-sodomy statutes is patent. It was not until 1533 that sodomy was made a secular offense in England. 25 Hen. VIII, cap. 6. Until that time, the offense was, in Sir James Stephen's words, "merely ecclesiastical." 2 J. Stephen, A History of the Criminal Law of England 430 (1883). Pollock and Maitland similarly observed that "[t]he crime against nature . . . was so closely connected with heresy that the vulgar had but one name for both." 2 F. Pollock & F. Maitland, The History of English Law 554 (1895). The transfer of jurisdiction over prosecutions for sodomy to the secular courts seems primarily due to the alteration of ecclesiastical jurisdiction attendant on England's break with the Roman Catholic Church, rather than to any new understanding of the sovereign's interest in preventing or punishing the behavior involved. Cf. E. Coke, The Third Part of the Institutes of the Laws of England, ch. 10 (4th ed. 1797).

8. See *Ga. Code Ann.* § 16-6-2(a) (1984) ("A person commits the offense of sodomy when he performs or submits to any sexual act involving the sex organs of one person and the mouth or anus of another").

9. See J. May, The Law of Crimes § 203 (2d ed. 1893) ("Sodomy, otherwise called buggery, bestiality, and the crime against nature, is the unnatural copulation of two persons with each other, or of a human being with a beast. . . . It may be committed by a man with a man, by a man with a beast, or by a woman with a beast, or by a man with a woman—his wife, in which case, if she consents, she is an accomplice").

10. The predecessor of the current Georgia statute provided, "Sodomy is the carnal knowledge and connection against the order of nature, by man with man, or in the same unnatural manner with woman." *Ga.Code,* Tit. 1, Pt. 4, § 4251 (1861). This prohibition of heterosexual sodomy was not purely hortatory. See, eg., *Comer v. State, 21 Ga.App.* 306, 94 *S.E.* 314 (1917) (affirming prosecution for consensual heterosexual sodomy).

Freedom of Expression and Its Limits

LIMITS TO THE FREE EXPRESSION OF OPINION*

Joel Feinberg

The purpose of this essay is to determine how the liberal principles that support free expression of opinion generally also define the limits to what the law can permit to be said. The liberal principle in question, put vaguely, is that state coercion is justified only to prevent personal or public harm. That more harm than good can be expected to come from suppression of dissenting opinions in politics and religion has been amply documented by experience and argument, but concentration on this important truth, despite its salutary practical effects, is likely to mislead us into thinking that the liberal "harm principle" is simple in its meaning and easy in its application. For that reason, this essay will only summarize (in Part I) the impressive case for total freedom of expression of opinions of certain kinds in normal contexts, and concentrate instead (in Part II) on the types of expressions *excluded* by the harm principle: defamation and "malicious truth," invasions of privacy, and expressions that cause others to do harm (those that cause panics, provoke retaliatory violence, or incite others to crime or insurrection). Part III will examine the traditional crime of "sedition," and conclude that it is not properly among the categories of expressions excluded by the harm principle. Among the other lessons that will emerge from these exercises, I hope, is that the

harm principle is a largely empty formula in urgent need of supplementation by tests for determining the relative importance of conflicting interests and by measures of the degree to which interests are endangered by free expressions.

I The Case for Freedom

The classic case for free expression of opinion was made by John Stuart Mill.[1] Mill's purpose in his famous chapter "Of the Liberty of Thought and Discussion" was to consider, as a beginning, just one class of actions and how his "harm principle" applied to them. The actions in question were instances of expressing orally or in print opinions about matters of fact, and about historical, scientific, theological, philosophical, political, and moral questions. Mill's conclusion was that suppressing such expressions is always more harmful than the expressions themselves would be and therefore is never justified. But don't expressions of opinion *ever* harm others? Of course they do, and it would be silly to ascribe to Mill the absurd contrary view. Expressions of opinion harm others when they are: defamatory (libelous or slanderous), seditious, incitive to violence, mali-

---

*This article first appeared in the first edition of this anthology, 1975.

cious publications of damaging or embarrassing truths, or invasions of privacy. In fact, in classifying an expression under one of these headings, we are *ipso facto* declaring that it is harmful. Mill is not radical about this. Putting these obviously harmful expressions to one side (he is best understood as asking) is there any [further] ground for suppressing mere "opinions"? To *this* question Mill's answer is radical and absolutist: If an expression cannot be subsumed under one of these standard headings for harmfulness, then it can never be sufficiently injurious to be justifiably suppressed. Apart from direct harm to assignable persons, no other ground is ever a sufficient reason for overriding the presumption in favor of liberty. One may *never* properly suppress an expression on the grounds, for example, that it is immoral, shocking to sensibilities, annoying, heretical, unorthodox, or "dangerous," and especially not on the ground simply that it is false.

Expressions of opinion thus occupy a very privileged position, in Mill's view. That is because their suppression, he contends, is not only a private injury to the coerced party but also and inevitably a very serious harm to the public in general. The argument has two distinct branches. The first has us consider the possibility that the suppressed opinion is wholly or partially true. On this assumption, of course, repression will have the harmful social consequence of loss of truth.

The crucial contention in this wing of the argument, however, is much stronger than that. Mill contends that there is *always* a chance, for all we can know, that the suppressed opinion is at least partially true, so that the act of repression itself necessarily involves some risk. Moreover, the risk is always an unreasonable one, never worth taking, since the risk of its alternative—permitting free expression generally—to our interest in acquiring knowledge and avoiding error, is negligible. By letting every opinion, no matter how "certainly true," be challenged, we minimize the risk of permanent commitment to falsehood. In the process, of course, we allow some falsehoods to be expressed, but since the truth is not denied its champions either, there is very little risk that the tolerated falsehood will become permanently enthroned. The balance of favorable risks then is clearly on the side of absolute freedom of expression.

This argument is especially convincing in the world of science, where no hypothesis bears its evidence on its face, and old errors are continually exposed by new and easily duplicable evidence and by more careful and refined experimental techniques. Even totalitarian regimes have learned that it is in their own interest to permit physicists and plant geneticists to go their theoretical ways unencumbered by ideological restrictions. Sometimes, to be sure, the truth of a scientific theory is so apparent that it is well worth acting on even though it strains governmental priorities to do so and requires large investment of funds; but this very confidence, Mill argued, is justified only when every interested party has had an opportunity to refute the theory. In respect at least to scientific theories, the more open to attack an opinion is, the more confident we can eventually be of its truth. That "no one has disproved it yet" is a convincing reason for accepting a theory only when everyone has been free to try.

To deny that it is possible for a given opinion to be true, Mill maintained, is to assume one's own infallibility. This is no doubt an overstatement, but what does seem clear is that to deny that a given proposition can possibly be true is to assume one's own infallibility with respect to though of course not one's infallibility generally. To say that one cannot possibly be wrong in holding a given belief is to say that one knows that one's knowledge of its truth is authentic. We claim to know infallibly when we claim to know that we know. It is also clear, I think, that we are sometimes justified in making such claims. I know that I know that 2 + 3 = 5, that I am seated at my desk writing, and that New York is in the United States. In the face of challenges from the relentless epistemological skeptic, I may have to admit that I don't know *how* I know these things, but it doesn't follow from that that I don't know them. It seems then that there is no risk, after all, in suppressing some opinions, namely, the denials of such truisms.

Yet what could ever be the point of forbidding persons from denying that 2 + 3 = 5 or that New York is in the United States? There is surely no danger that general confidence in these true propositions would be undermined. There is no risk of loss of truth, I suppose, in suppressing their denials, but also no risk in allowing them free circulation. Conceding that we can know truisms infallibly, therefore, can hardly commit us to approve of the suppression of their denials, at least so long as we adhere, with Mill, exclusively to the harm principle. More importantly, there are serious risks involved in granting any mere man or group of men the power to draw the line between those opinions that are known infallibly to be true and those not so known, in order to ban expression of the former. Surely, if there is one thing that is *not* infallibly known, it is how to draw *that* line.

In any case, when we leave tautologies and truisms behind and consider only those larger questions of substance, doctrines about which have in fact been banned by rulers in the past as certainly false (for example, the shape of the earth, the cause of disease, the wisdom of certain wars or economic policies, and the morality of certain kinds of conduct) our own fallibility is amply documented by history. The sad fact is that at every previous stage of history including the recent past there have been questions of the highest importance about which nearly *everyone,* including the wisest and most powerful, has been dead wrong. The more important the doctrines, then, the greater the risk we run in forbidding expressions of disagreement.

Mill's account, in this first wing of his argument, of the public interest in the discovery and effective dissemination of truth has many important practical implications. Mill himself thought that we should seek out our ideological enemies and offer them public forums in which to present and defend their views, or failing that, hire "devil's advocates" to defend unpopular positions in schools and in popular debates. Mill's reasons for these proposals also provide the grounding for the so-called "adversary theory of politics." The argument is (in the words of Zechariah Chafee): "Truth can be sifted out from falsehood only if the government is vigorously and constantly crossexamined. . . . Legal proceedings prove that an opponent makes the best cross-examiner."[2] This states the rationale of the two-party system exactly. The role of the out-party is like that of the prosecutor in a criminal trial, or plaintiff in a civil action. It is a vitally important role too. Numerous historical instances suggest that we are in grave danger when both parties agree. Witness, for example, the Vietnam debacle, which was the outcome of a twenty-year "bipartisan foreign policy." Foreign policy decisions are as difficult as they are important; hence the need for constant reexamination, probing for difficulties and soft spots, bringing to light new and relevant facts, and subjecting to doubt hitherto unquestioned first premises. Without these aids, we tend to drift quite complacently into dead ends and quagmires.[3]

The second branch of the argument has us assume that the unorthodox opinion we are tempted to suppress really is false anyway. Even in this case, Mill insists, we will all be the losers, in the end, for banning it. When people are not forced by the stimulus of dissent to rethink the grounds of their convictions, then their beliefs tend to wither and decay. The rationales of the tenets are forgotten, their vital direction and value lost, their very meaning altered, until at last they are held in the manner of dead dogmas rather than living truths.

No part of Mill's argument in *On Liberty* is more impressive than his case for totally free expression of opinion. It is especially ingenious in that it rests entirely on social advantages and foregoes all help that might come from appeals to "the inalienable right to say what one pleases whether it's good for society or not." But that very utilitarian ingenuity may be its Achilles heel; for if liberty of expression is justified only because it is socially useful, then some might think that it is justified only *when* it is socially useful. The possibility of special circumstances in which repression is still *more* useful is real enough to disturb allies of Mill who love liberty fully as much as he and would seek therefore a still more solid foundation for it. But even if the case for absolute liberty of opinion must rest ultimately on some theory of natural rights, Mill has given that case powerful utilitarian reinforcement.

II Limits to Freedom

Despite the impressive case for complete liberty of expression, there are obvious instances where permitting a person to speak his mind freely will cause more harm than good all around. These instances have been lumped together in various distinct legal categories whose names have come to stand for torts or crimes and to suggest, by a powerful linguistic convention, unpermitted wrongdoing. Thus, there can be no more right to defame or to incite to riot than there can be a right way, in Aristotle's example,[4] to commit adultery. Underlying these linguistic conventions, however, are a settled residue of interest weightings as well as actual and hypothetical applications of the harm principle, often filled in or mediated in various ways by principles of other kinds. The various categories of excluded expressions are worth examining not only for the light they throw on the harm principle, but also for the conceptual and normative problems each raises on its own for political theory.

1. Defamation and "Malicious Truth"

Defamatory statements are those that damage a person's reputation by their expression to third parties in a manner that "tends to diminish the esteem in which the plaintiff is held, or to excite adverse feelings or opinions against him."[5] The primary mode of discouraging defamers in countries adhering to the common law has been the threat of civil liability to a court-enforced order to pay cash to the injured party in compensation for the harm done his reputation. In cases of especially malicious defamation, the defendant may be ordered to pay a stiff fine ("punitive damages") to the plaintiff as well. Only in the most egregious cases (and rarely even then) has criminal liability been imposed for defamation, but nevertheless the threat of civil suit as sufficient to entitle us to say that our law does not leave citizens (generally) free to defame one another. Here then is one clear limit to our freedom of expression.

Not all expressions that harm another's reputation, of course, are legally forbidden. Even when damaging defamation has been proved by the plaintiff, the defendant may yet escape liability by establishing one of two kinds of defense. He may argue that his utterance or publication was "privileged," or simply that it is *true*. The former defense is established by showing either that the defendant, in virtue of his public office or his special relation to the plaintiff, has been granted an absolute immunity from liability for defamation (for example, he spoke in a judicial or legislative proceeding, or he had the prior consent of the plaintiff), or that he had a prior immunity contingent on the reasonableness of his conduct. Examples of this category of privilege are the immunity of a person protecting himself or another by a warning that someone is of poor character, or of a drama, literary, or political critic making "fair comment" of an extremely unfavorable kind about a performance, a book, or a policy. These immunities are still other examples of public policies that protect an interest (in this case, the interest in reputation) just to the point where the protection interferes with interests deemed more important—either to the public in general or to other private individuals. These policies imply that a person's reputation is a precious thing that deserves legal protection just as his life, health, and property do, but on the other hand, a certain amount of rough handling of reputations is to be expected in courtrooms, in the heated spontaneous debates of legislative chambers, in reviews of works presented to the public for critical comment, and in the rough-and-tumble competition among eminent persons for power or public acclaim. To withhold immunities in these special contexts would be to allow nervous in-

hibitions to keep hard truths out of law courts to the detriment of justice, or out of legislatures to the detriment of the laws themselves; or to make critics overly cautious, to the detriment of those who rely on their judgments; or to make political commentators overly deferential to power and authority, to the detriment of reform.

There is, however, no public interest in keeping those who are not in these special contexts uninhibited when they speak or write about others. Indeed, we should all be nervous when we make unfavorable comments, perhaps not on the ground that feelings and reputations will simply be damaged (there may be both justice and social gain in such damage), but at least on the ground that the unfavorable comment may be *false*. In a way, the rationale for the defamation action at law is the opposite of Mill's case for the free expression of opinion. The great public interest in possessing the truth in science, philosophy, politics, and so on, is best served by keeping everyone uninhibited in the expression of his views; but there are areas where there is a greater interest in avoiding falsehood than in acquiring truth, and here we are best served by keeping people very nervous indeed when they are tempted to speak their minds.

Once the plaintiff has proved that the defendant has published a defamatory statement about him, the defendant may avoid liability in another way, namely, by showing that the statement in question is *true*. "Out of a tender regard for reputations," writes Professor Prosser, "the law presumes in the first instance that all defamation is false, and the defendant has the burden of pleading and proving its truth."[6] In the large majority of American jurisdictions, truth is a "complete defense" which will relieve the defendant of liability even when he published his defamation merely out of spite, in the absence of any reasonable social purpose. One wonders why this should be. Is the public interest in "the truth" so great that it should always override a private person's interest in his own reputation? An affirmative answer, I should think, would require considerable argument.

Most of the historical rationales for the truth defense worked out in the courts and in legal treatises will not stand scrutiny. They all founder, I think, on the following kind of case. A New York girl supports her drug addiction by working as a prostitute in a seedy environment of crime and corruption. After a brief jail sentence, she decides to reform, and travels to the Far West to begin her life anew. She marries a respectable young man, becomes a leader in civic and church affairs, and raises a large and happy family. Then twenty years after her arrival in town, her neurotically jealous neighbor learns of her past, and publishes a lurid but accurate account of it for the eyes of the whole community. As a consequence, her "friends" and associates snub her; she is asked to resign her post as church leader; gossipmongers prattle ceaselessly about her; and obscene inscriptions appear on her property and in her mail. She dare not sue her neighbor for defamation since the defamatory report is wholly true. She has been wronged, but she has no legal remedy.

Applied to this case the leading rationales for the truth defense are altogether unconvincing. One argument claims that the true gravamen of the wrong in defamation is the deception practiced on the public in misrepresenting the truth, so that where there is no misrepresentation there is no injury—as if the injury to the reformed sinner is of no account. A variant of this argument holds the reformed sinner to be deserving of exposure on the ground that he (or she) in covering up his past deceives the public, thereby compounding the earlier delinquency. If this sort of "deception" is morally blameworthy, then so is every form of 'covering up the truth,' from cosmetics to window blinds! Others have argued that a delinquent plaintiff should not be allowed any standing in court because of his established bad character. A related contention is that "a person is in no position to complain of a reputation which is consistent with his actual character and behavior."[7] Both of these rationales apply well enough to the unrepentant sinner, but work nothing but injustice and suffering on the reformed person, on the plaintiff defamed in some way that does not reflect upon his character, or on the person whose "immoralities" have been wholly private and scrupulously kept from the public eye. It does not follow from the fact that a person's reputation is consistent with the truth that it is "deserved."

The most plausible kind of argument for the truth defense is that it serves some kind of overriding public interest. Some have argued that fear of eventual exposure can serve as effectively as the threat of punishment to *deter* wrongdoing. This argument justifies a kind of endless social penalty and is therefore more cruel than a system of criminal law, which usually permits a wrongdoer to wipe his slate clean. Others have claimed that exposure of character flaws and past sins protects the community by warning it of dangerous or untrustworthy persons.

That argument is well put (but without endorsement) by Harper and James when they refer to ". . . the social desirability as a general matter, of leaving individuals free to warn the public of antisocial members of the community, provided only that the person furnishing the information take the risk of its being false."[8] (Blackstone went so far as to assert that the defendant who can show the truth of his defamatory remarks has rendered a public service in exposing the plaintiff and deserves the public's gratitude[9]). This line of argument is convincing enough when restricted to public-spirited defamers and socially dangerous plaintiffs; but it lacks all plausibility when applied to the malicious and useless exposure of past misdeeds, or to nonmoral failings and "moral" flaws of a wholly private and well-concealed kind.

How precious a thing, after all, is this thing denoted by the glittering abstract noun, the "Truth"? The truth in general is a great and noble cause, a kind of public treasury more important than any particular person's feelings; but the truth about a particular person may be of no great value at all except to that person. When the personal interest in reputation outweighs the dilute public interest in truth (and there is no doubt that this is sometimes the case) then it must be protected even at some cost to our general knowledge of the truth. The truth, like any other commodity, is not so valuable that it is a bargain at *any* cost. A growing number of American states have now modified the truth defense so that it applies only when the defamatory statement has been published with good motives, or is necessary for some reasonable public purpose, or (in some cases) both. The change is welcome.

In summary, the harm principle would permit all harmless statements about others whether true or false (harmless statements by definition are not defamatory), but it would impose liability for all defamatory false statements and all seriously defamatory true statements except those that serve (or seem likely to serve) some beneficial social purpose.

2. Invasions of Privacy

Still other expressions are neither defamatory nor false, and yet they can unjustly wound the persons they describe all the same. These do not invade the interest in a good reputation so much as a special kind of interest in peace of mind, sometimes called a sense of dignity, sometimes the enjoyment of solitude, but most commonly termed the interest in personal privacy. As the legal "right to privacy" is now understood, it embraces a miscellany of things, protecting the right-holder not only from "physical intrusions upon his solitude" and "publicity given to his name or likeness or to private information about him" without his permission, but also from being placed "in a false light [but without defamation] in the public eye" and from the "commercial appropriation of elements of his personality."[10] (Some of these are really invasions of one's property rights through unpermitted commercial exploitation of one's name, image, personality, and so on. For that reason it has been urged that the invaded right in these cases be called "the right to publicity.") What concerns us here are statements conveying true and nondefamatory information about the plaintiff, of a very intimate and properly private kind, gathered and published without his consent, often to his shame and mortification. Business advantage and journalistic profit have become ever stronger motives for such statements, and the invention of tiny, very sensitive snooping devices has made the data easier than ever to come by.

Since the "invasion of privacy" tort has been recognized, plaintiffs have recovered damages from defendants who have shadowed them, looked into their windows, investigated their bank accounts, and tapped their telephone wires. In many of these cases, the court's judgment protected the plaintiff's interest in "being let alone," but in other cases the interest protected was not merely this, or not this at all, but rather the interest in *not being known about*. If there is a right not to be known about in some respects by anyone, then *a fortiori* there is a right not to be known about, in those respects by nearly everyone. Privacy law has also protected the interests of those who don't want details of their lives called to the public's attention and made the subject of public wonder, amusement, discussion, analysis, or debate. Hence some plaintiffs have recovered from defendants who have published embarrassing details of their illness or physical deformity; their personal letters or unpublished notes, or inventories of their possessions; their photographs in a "good looks" popularity contest, or in a "before and after" advertisement for baldness or obesity cures, or on the labels of tomato cans; and from defendants who have published descriptions of the plaintiffs' sexual relations, hygienic habits, and other very personal matters. No life, of course, can be kept wholly private, or immune from public inspection even in some of its most personal aspects. "No one enjoys being stared at," Harper and James remind us, yet if a person "goes out on the street he [can have] no legal objection to people looking at him."[11] On the other hand, life would be hardly tolerable if there were no secrets we could keep (away from "the street"), no preserve of dignity, no guaranteed solitude.

There would probably be very little controversy over the existence of a right to privacy were it not the case that the interest in being let alone is frequently in conflict with other interests that seem at least equally deserving of protection. Even where the right is recognized by law, it is qualified by the recognition of very large classes of privileged expressions. First of all, like most other torts and crimes, the charge of invasion of privacy is completely defeated by proof that the plaintiff gave his consent to the defendant's conduct. Secondly, and more interestingly, the right of privacy can conflict with the constitutionally guaranteed freedom of the press, which, according to Prosser, "justifies the publication of news and all other matters of legitimate public interest and concern."[12] For a court to adjudicate between a paper's right to publish and an individual's right to privacy then, it must employ some standard for determining what is of legitimate public concern or, what amounts to the same thing, which news about a person is "fit to print." Such legal standards are always in the making, never finished, but the standard of "legitimate interest" has begun to take on a definite shape. American courts have decided, first of all, that "the person who intentionally puts himself in the public eye . . . has no right to complain of any publicity which reasonably bears on his activity."[13] The rationale for this judgment invokes the maxim that a person is not wronged by that to which he consents, or by that the risk of which he has freely assumed. The person who steps into the public spotlight ought to know what he is letting himself in for; hence the law presumes that he *does* know, and therefore that he is asking for it. Much the same kind of presumption lies behind the "fair comment" defense in defamation cases: The person who voluntarily publishes his own work is presumed to be inviting criticism and is therefore not entitled to complain when the criticism is adverse or harsh, providing only that it is relevant and not personally abusive. One can put oneself voluntarily into the public eye by running for or occupying public office; by becoming an actor, musician, entertainer, poet, or novelist; by inventing an interesting device or making a geographical or scientific discovery; or even by becoming wealthy. Once a person has become a public figure, he has sacrificed much of his right of privacy to the public's legitimate curiosity.

Of course, one never forfeits *all* rights of privacy; even the public figure has a right to the privacy of his very most intimate affairs. (This may, however, be very small consolation to him.)

One cannot always escape the privilege of the press to invade one's privacy simply by avoiding public roles and offices, for the public spotlight can catch up with anyone. "Reluctant public characters" are nonetheless public and therefore, according to the courts, as legitimate objects of public curiosity as the voluntary public figures. Those unfortunates who attract attention unwillingly by becoming involved, even as victims, in accidents, or by being accused of crimes, or even as innocent bystanders to interesting events, have become "news," and therefore subject to the public's right to know. They maintain this unhappy status "until they have reverted to the lawful and unexciting life led by the great bulk of the community," but until then, "they are subject to the privileges which publishers have to satisfy the curiosity of the public as to their leaders, heroes, villains, and victims."[14] Again, the privilege to publish is not unlimited so that "the courts must somehow draw the distinction between conduct which outrages the common decencies and goes beyond what the public mores will tolerate, and that which the plaintiff must be expected in the circumstances to endure."[15]

When interests of quite different kinds head toward collisions, how can one determine which has the right of way? This problem, which lies behind the most puzzling questions about the grounds for liberty and coercion, tends to be concealed by broadly stated principles. The conflict between the personal interest in privacy and the public curiosity is one of the best illustrations of the problem, but it is hardly unique. In defamation cases, as we have seen, there is often a conflict between the public interest in truth and the plaintiff's interest in his own good name. In nuisance law, there is a conflict between the plaintiff's interest in the peaceful enjoyment of his land and the defendant's interest in keeping a hogpen, or a howling dog, or a small boiler factory. In suburban neighborhoods, the residents' interest in quiet often conflicts with motorcyclists' interest in cheap and speedy transportation. In buses and trains, one passenger's interest in privacy[16] can conflict with another's interest in listening to rock and roll music on a portable radio, or for that matter, with the interests of two nearby passengers in making unavoidably audible, but avoidably inane, conversation. The principle of "the more freedom the better" doesn't tell us whose freedom must give way in these competitive situations.

The invasion of privacy cases are among the very clearest examples of the inevitable clash of interests in populous modern communities. They are, moreover, examples that show that solving the problem is not just a matter of minimizing harm all around. Harm is the invasion of an interest, and invasions do differ in degree, but when interests of radically different kinds are invaded to the same degree, where is the greater harm? Perhaps we should say that some interests are more important than others in the sense that harm to them is likely to lead to greater damage to the whole economy of personal (or as the case may be, community) interests than harm to the lesser interest, just as harm to one's heart or brain will do more damage to one's bodily health than an "equal degree" of harm to less vital organs. Determining which interests are more "vital" in an analogous sense would be no easy task, but even if we could settle this matter, there would remain serious difficulties. In the first place, interests pile up and reinforce one another. My interest in peace and quiet may be more vital in my system than the motorcyclist's interests in speed, excitement, and economy are in his, but there is also the interest of the cyclist's employer in having workers efficiently transported to his factory, and the economic interest of the community in general (including me) in the flourishing of the factory owner's business; the interest of the motorcycle manufacturers in their own profits; the interest of the police and others (perhaps including me) in providing a relatively harmless outlet for adolescent exuberance, and in not having a difficult rule to enforce. There may be nowhere near so great a buildup of reinforcing interests, personal and public, in the quietude of my neighborhood.

There is still another kind of consideration that complicates the delicate task of interest-balancing. Interests differ not only in the extent to which they are thwarted, in their importance or "vitality," and the degree to which they are backed up by other interests, but also in their inherent moral quality. Some interests, simply by reason of their very natures, we might think better worth protecting than others. The interest in knowing the intimate details of Brigitte Bardot's married sex life (the subject of a sensational lawsuit in France) is a morally repugnant peeping tom's interest. The sadist's interest in having others suffer pain is a morbid interest. The interest in divulging a celebrity's private conversations is a busybody's interest. It is probably not conducive to the public good to encourage development of the character flaws from which these interests spring, but even if there were social advantage in the individual vices, there would be a case against protecting their spawned interests, based upon their inherent unworthiness. The interests in understanding, diagnosing, and simply being apprised of newsworthy events might well outbalance a given individual's reluctance to be known about, but photographs and descriptions with no plausible appeal except to the morbid and sensational can have very little weight in the scales.

3. Causing Panic

Defamatory statements, "malicious truths," and statements that wrongfully invade privacy do harm to the persons they are about by conveying information or falsehood to third parties. Their publication tends to instill certain beliefs in others, and the very existence of those beliefs constitutes a harm to the person spoken or written about. Other classes of injurious expressions do harm in a rather different way, namely, by causing those who listen to them (or more rarely, those who read them) to act in violent or otherwise harmful ways. In these cases, the expressions need not be about any specifiable persons, or if they are about persons, those individuals are not necessarily the victims of the subsequent harm. When spoken words cause panic, breach the peace, or incite to crime or revolt, a variety of important interests, personal and social, will be seriously harmed. Such expressions, therefore, are typically proscribed by the criminal, and not merely the civil, law.

"The most stringent protection of free speech," wrote Holmes in his most celebrated opinion, "would not protect a man in falsely shouting fire in a theatre and causing a panic."[17] In some circumstances a person can cause even more harm by *truthfully* shouting "Fire!" in a crowded theater, for the flames and smoke might reinforce the tendency of his words to cause panic, and the fire itself might block exits, leading the hysterical crowds to push and trample. But we do not, and cannot fairly, hold the excited alarm sounder criminally responsible for his warning when it was in fact true and shouted with good intentions. We can hardly demand on pain of punishment that persons pick their words carefully in emergencies, when emotions naturally run high and there is no time for judicious deliberation. A person's warning shout in such circumstances is hardly to be treated as a full-fledged voluntary act at all. Perhaps it can be condemned as negligent, but given the

mitigating circumstances, such negligence hardly amounts to the gross and wanton kind that can be a basis of criminal liability. The law, then, can only punish harmful words of this class when they are spoken or written with the intention of causing the harm that in fact ensues, or when they are spoken or written in conscious disregard of a high and unreasonable risk that the harm will ensue. The practical joker in a crowded auditorium who whispers to his comrade, "Watch me start a panic," and then shouts "Fire!" could be convicted for using words intentionally to cause a panic. The prankster who is willing to risk a general panic just for the fun of alarming one particular person in the audience could fairly be convicted for the grossly reckless use of dangerous words. Indeed, his recklessness is akin to that of the motorist who drives at an excessive speed just to frighten a timorous passenger.

Suppose, however, that the theater is virtually empty, and as the lights come on at the end of the film, our perverse or dim-witted jokester shouts "Fire! Fire!" just for the sake of confusing the three or four other patrons and alarming the ushers. The ushers quickly see through the ruse and suffer only a few moments of anxiety, and the patrons walk quickly to the exits and depart. No harm to speak of has been done; nor could any have reasonably been anticipated. This example shows how very important are the surrounding circumstances of an utterance to the question of its permissibility. Given the presumptive case for liberty in general, and especially the powerful social interest in leaving persons free to use *words* as they see fit, there can be a countervailing case for suppression on the grounds of the words' dangerous tendency only when the danger in fact is great and the tendency immediate. These matters are determined not only by the particular words used, but by the objective character of the surrounding circumstances—what lawyers call "the time, place, and manner" of utterance.

The question of legal permissibility should not be confused with that of moral blameworthiness or even with civil liability. The practical joker, even in relatively harmless circumstances, is no moral paragon. But then neither are the liar, the vulgarian, the rude man, and the scandalmonger, most of whose faults are not fit subjects for penal legislation. We cannot make every instance of mendacity, rudeness, and malicious gossip criminal, but we can protect people from the serious injury that comes from fraud, battery, or defamation. Similarly, practical jokers should be blamed but not punished, unless their tricks reach the threshold of serious danger to others. On the other hand, almost all lies, bad tales, jokes, and tricks create some risk, and there is no injustice in making the perpetrator compensate (as opposed to being punished) even his unlikely victim. Thus, if a patron in the nearly empty theater described above sprains an ankle in hurrying towards an exit, there is no injustice in requiring the jokester to pay the medical expenses.

It is established in our law that when words did not in fact cause harm the speaker may nevertheless be punished for having uttered them only if there was high danger when they were spoken that serious harm would result. This condition of course could be satisfied even though the harm in fact was averted: Not everything probable becomes actual. Similarly, for a person rightly to be punished even for harm in fact caused by his words, the harm in its resultant magnitude must have been an objectively probable consequence of the spoken words in the circumstances; otherwise the speaker will be punished for an unforeseeable fluke. In either case, then, the clear and present danger that serious harm will follow a speaker's words is necessary if he is rightly to be punished.

As we have seen, punishment for the harm caused by words is proper only if the speaker caused the harm either *intentionally* or *recklessly*. Both of these "mental conditions" of guilt require the satisfaction of the clear and present danger formula, or something like it. Consider recklessness first. For there to be recklessness there must really be a substantial risk consciously and unreasonably run. A speaker is not being reckless if he utters words that have only a remote and speculative tendency to cause panics or riots.

Intentional harm-causing by words raises more complications. Suppose an evil-minded person wishes to cause a panic and believes what is false and wholly unsupported by any real evidence, namely, that his words will have that effect. Imagine that he attends a meeting of the Policemen's Benevolent Association and, at what he takes to be the strategic moment, he stands up and shrieks, "There's a mouse under my chair!" Perhaps these words would cause a panic at a meeting of Girl Scouts but it merely produces a round of contemptuous laughter here. Wanting a panic and sincerely believing that one is causing a panic by one's words, then, are not sufficient. Suppose however we complicate the story so that by some wholly unforeseeable fluke the spoken words do precipitate a panic. The story is

hard to invent at this point, but let us imagine that one patrolman laughs so hard that he tips over his chair causing another to drop his pipe, starting a fire, igniting live bullets, et cetera. Now, in addition to evil desire, and conscious belief in causal efficacy, we have a third important element: The words actually do initiate a causal process resulting in the desired panic. But these conditions still are not sufficient to permit us to say that the speaker *intentionally caused* a panic. Without the antecedent objective probability that a panic would follow these words in these circumstances, we have only a bizarre but tragic coincidence.

We would say much the same thing of a superstitious lady who "attempts" to start a riot by magic means. In an inconspicuous corner of a darkened theater, she sticks pins into a doll and mutters under her breath a magic incantation designed to produce a panic. Of course this doesn't work in the way intended, but a nearsighted and neurotic passerby observes her, takes the doll to be a real baby, and screams. The hoped-for panic then really follows. The evil lady cannot be found guilty of intentionally causing a panic, even though she intended to cause one and really did cause (or at least initiate a causal process that resulted in) one. She can be condemned for having very evil motives. But if people are sufficiently ignorant and impotent, the law, applying the harm principle, allows them to be as evil as they wish.

4. Provoking Retaliatory Violence

Suppose a person utters words which have as their unhappy effects violence directed *at him* by his angry audience, counterviolence by his friends and protectors, and escalation into a riotous breach of the peace. This is still another way of causing harm by words. Should the speaker be punished? In almost every conceivable case, the answer should be No. There is a sense, of course, in which the speaker did not start the physical violence. He used only words, and while words can sting and infuriate, they are not instruments of violence in the same sense that fists, knives, guns, and clubs are. If the law suppresses public speech, either by withholding permits in advance or punishing afterwards, simply on the ground that the expressed views are so unpopular that some auditors can be expected to start fighting, then the law punishes some for the criminal proclivities of others. "A man does not become a criminal because someone else assaults him . . . ," writes

Zechariah Chafee. Moreover, he continues, on any such theory, "a small number of intolerant men . . . can prevent *any kind* of meeting. . . . A gathering which expressed the sentiment of a majority of law-abiding citizens would become illegal because a small gang of hoodlums threatened to invade the hall."[18] When violent response to speech threatens, the obvious remedy is not suppression, but rather increased police protection.

So much seems evident, but there may be some exceptions. Some words uttered in public places in the presence of many unwilling auditors may be so abusive or otherwise offensive as to be "reasonably considered a direct provocation to violence."[19] The captive auditor, after all, is not looking for trouble as he walks the public streets intent on his private errands. If he is forced to listen, as he walks past a street meeting, to speakers denouncing and ridiculing his religion, and forced to notice a banner with a large and abusive caricature of the Pope,[20] his blood might reasonably be expected to boil. Antireligious and anticlerical opinions, of course, no matter how unpopular, are entitled to the full protection of the law. Even abusive, virulent, and mocking expressions of such views are entitled to full protection if uttered to private gatherings, in private or privately reserved places. Such expressions become provocative only when made in public places to captive auditors.

What makes an expression "provocative?" Surely, if words are to be suppressed on the ground that they are provocative of violence, they must be more than merely "provoking," else all unpopular opinions will be suppressed, to the great public loss. As far as I know, the concept of provocation has received thorough legal elaboration only in the law of homicide, where provocation reduces a charge of murder to that of manslaughter, thus functioning as a kind of mitigating consideration rather than as a justification or complete excuse. In the common law, for there to be sufficient provocation to mitigate: (1) The behavior of the victim must have been so aggravating that it would have produced "such excitement and passion as would obscure the reason of an ordinary man and induce him . . . to strike the blow."[21] (2) There must not have elapsed so much time between the provocation and the violence that a reasonable man's blood would have cooled. (3) But for the victim's provocation the violence would not have occurred. In short, provocation mitigates only when it in fact produces a reason-numbing rage in the attacker and is such that it could be expected to pro-

duce such a rage in any normal person in his circumstances. Nazi emblems might be expected to have this effect on a former inmate of a Nazi death camp, but the Democratic party line cannot be sufficiently provocative to excuse a violent Republican, and similarly the other way round. Indeed, in the law of homicide, *no mere words alone,* no matter how abusive or scurrilous, can be adequate provocation to justify or totally excuse killing as a response.

There would seem to be equally good reason not to consider mere words either as justifying or totally excusing nonlethal acts of violence. The "reasonable person" in a democracy must be presumed to have enough self-control to refrain from violent responses to odious words and doctrines. If he is followed, insulted, taunted, and challenged, he can get injunctive relief, or bring charges against his tormentor as a nuisance; if there is no time for this and he is backed to the wall he may be justified in using "reasonable force" in self-defense; or if he is followed to his own home, he can use the police to remove the nuisance. But if he is not personally harrassed in these ways, he can turn on his heels and leave the provocation behind, and this is what the law, perhaps, should require of him.

Only when public speech satisfies stringent tests qualifying it as "direct provocation to violence," (if that is possible at all) will the harm principle justify its suppression. But there are many possible modes of suppression, and some are far more restrictive of liberty than others. Orders to cease and desist on pain of arrest are most economical, for they permit the speaker to continue to air his views in a nonprovocative way or else retire with his audience to a less public place. Lawful removal of the provocation (as a public nuisance) may be more satisfactory than permitting violent response to it, and is infinitely preferable to punishing the speaker. Nowhere in the law where provocation is considered as a defense do the rules deem the proven provoker (the victim) a criminal himself! At best his conduct mitigates the crime of his attacker, who is the only criminal.

One final point. While it is conceivable that some public *speech* can satisfy the common law test for provocation by being so aggravating that even a reasonable person could be expected to lose control of his reason when exposed to it, this can never be true of books. One can always escape the provocation of the printed word simply by declining to read it, and where escape from provocation is that easy, no "reasonable person" will succumb to it.

5. Incitement to Crime or Insurrection

In the criminal law, anyone who "counsels, commands, or encourages another to commit a crime" is himself guilty of the resultant crime as an "accessory before the fact." Counseling, commanding, and encouraging, however, must consist in more than merely uttering certain words in the presence of others. Surely there must also be serious (as opposed to playful) intent and some possibility at least of the words having their desired effect. It is not possible that these conditions can be satisfied if I tell my secretary that she should overthrow the United States government, or if a speaker tells an audience of bank presidents that they should practice embezzlement whenever they can. These situations are analogous to the efforts to start a panic by magical means or to panic policemen with words about mice.

The problem of interpreting the meaning of a rule making the counseling of crime itself a crime is similar, I should think, to that raised by a statute forbidding the planting of a certain kind of plant. One does not violate such a statute if he scatters the appropriate kind of seeds on asphalt pavement or in barren desert, even with evil intent. (Again, if you are stupid enough, the law—insofar as it derives from the harm principle—can allow you to be as evil as you wish.) To violate the statute, either one would have to dig a little hole in the appropriate sort of soil, deposit the appropriate seeds, cultivate, fertilize, allow for sufficient water, protect against winds, worms, and dogs; *or* one would have to find suitable conditions ready-made, where the soil is already receptive and merely dropping the seeds will create a substantial likelihood that plants will grow and thrive. By analogy, even words of advice, if they are to count as incitements to crime, must fall on reasonably receptive ears. The harm principle provides a ready rationale for this requirement. If we permit coercive repression of nondangerous words we will confer such abundant powers on the repressive organs of the state that they are certain to be abused. Moreover, we will so inhibit persons in their employment of language as to discourage both spontaneity and serious moral discussion, thus doing a great deal of harm and virtually no good at all. (The only "gain," if it is that, to be expected from looser standards of interpretation would be that nondangerous persons with evil motives could be scooped up in the state's tighter nets and punished.)

Counseling others to crime is not the only use of speech that can be described as incitement. We must also come to terms with instigating, egging on, and inflaming others to violence. Even Mill conceded that the opinion that "corn dealers are starvers of the poor," which deserves protection when published in the press, may nevertheless "justly incur punishment when delivered orally to an excited mob assembled before the house of a corn dealer. . . ."[22] The metaphor of planting seeds in receptive soil is perhaps less apt for this situation than the commonly employed "spark and tinder" analogy. Words which merely express legitimate though unpopular opinion in one context become "incendiary" when addressed to an already inflammable mob. As Chafee put it: "Smoking is all right, but not in a powder magazine."[23] Of course the man who carries a cigar into a powder magazine may not know that the cigar he is carrying is lighted, or he may not know that he has entered a powder magazine. He may plead his lack of intention afterward (if he is still alive) as a defense. Similarly, the man who speaks his opinion to what he takes to be a calm audience, or an excited audience with *different* axes all ground fine, may plead his ignorance in good faith as a defense. But "the law" (as judges are fond of saying) "presumes that a man intends the natural and probable consequences of his actions," so that a defendant who denies that he intended to cause a riot may have the burden of proving his innocent intention to the jury.

In summary, there are two points to emphasize in connection with the punishment of inflammatory incitements. First, the audience must really be tinder, that is to say not merely sullen, but angry to the point of frenzy, and so predisposed to violence. A left-wing radical should be permitted to deliver a revolutionary tirade before the ladies of the D.A.R., even if his final words are "to the barricades!", for that would be to light a match not in a powder magazine but in a Turkish steam bath. Second, no one should be punished for inciting others to violence unless he used words intentionally, or at least recklessly, with respect to that consequence. Otherwise at best a speaker will be punished for his mere negligence, and at worst he will be punished though perfectly innocent.

There is one further problem raised by the concept of incitement as a crime. It might well be asked how one person—the inciter—can be held criminally responsible for the free and deliberate actions of another person—the one who is incited by his words. This problem is common to both kinds of incitement, counseling and inflaming or egging on, but it seems especially puzzling in the case of advising and persuading; for the deliberate, thoughtful, unforced, and undeceived acceptance of the advice of another person is without question itself a voluntary act. Yet there may well be cases which are such that had not the advice been given, the crime would never have been perpetrated, so that the advisor can truly be said to have "got" the advisee to do something he might otherwise never have done. In this case, the initiative was the advisor's, and his advice was the crucial causal factor that led to the criminal act, so that it would be no abuse of usage to call it "the cause." And yet, for all of that, no one *forced* the advisee to act; he could have rejected the advice, but he didn't.

If there is the appearance of paradox in this account, or in the very idea of one person's causing another to act voluntarily, it is no doubt the result of an unduly restrictive conception of what a cause is. There are, of course, a great many ways of causing another person to behave in a given way by the use of words. If we sneak up behind him and shout "boo!" we may startle him so that he jumps and shrieks. In this case our word functioned as a cause not in virtue of its meaning or the mediation of the other person's understanding, but simply as a noise, and the person's startled reaction to this physical stimulus was as involuntary as an eye-twitch or a knee-jerk. Some philosophers would restrict the notion of causing behavior to cases of this kind, but there is no good reason for such a restriction, and a strong case can be built against it based both on its capacity to breed paradox and on common sense and usage. I can "get" an acquaintance to say "Good morning" by putting myself directly in his line of vision, smiling, and saying "Good morning" to him. If I do these things and he predictably responds in the way I intended, I can surely say that my behavior was the cause, in those circumstances, of his behavior; for my conduct is not only a circumstance but for which his action would not have occurred, it is also a circumstance which, when added to those already present, made the difference between his speaking and remaining silent. Yet I did not force him to speak; I did not deceive him; I did not trick him. Rather I exploited those of his known policies and dispositions that made him antecedently "receptive" to my words. To deny that I caused him to act voluntarily, in short, is either to confuse causation with compulsion (a venerable philosophical mistake) or to regard one person's initiative as incompatible with another person's responsibility.[24]

In any case, where one person causes another to act voluntarily either by giving him advice or information or by otherwise capitalizing on his carefully studied dispositions and policies, there is no reason why *both* persons should not be held responsible for the act if it should be criminal. It is just as if the law made it criminal to contribute to a human explosion either by being human dynamite or by being a human spark: either by being predisposed by one's character to crime or by one's passions to violence, or else by providing the words or materials which could fully be anticipated to incite the violent or criminal conduct of others. It is surely no reasonable defense of the spark to say that but for the dynamite there would have been no explosion. Nor is it any more reasonable to defend the dynamite by arguing that but for the spark it should have remained forever quiescent.

There is probably even less reason for excluding from responsibility the speaker haranguing an inflammable mob on the grounds that the individuals in the throng are free adults capable of refraining from violence in the circumstances. A mob might well be understood as a kind of fictitious collective person whose passions are much more easily manipulated and whose actions more easily maneuvered than those of individual persons. If one looks at it this way, the caused behavior of an inflamed mob may be a good deal less than fully voluntary, even though the component individuals in it, being free adults, are all acting voluntarily on their own responsibility.

III Sedition

Causing panic, provoking violence, and inciting to crime or insurrection are all made punishable by what Chafee calls "the normal criminal law of words."[25] The relevant common law categories are riot, breach of the peace, solicitation, and incitement. All these crimes, as we have seen, require either intentionally harmful or reckless conduct, and all of them require, in addition—and for reasons partly derived from and explicable by the harm principle—that there be some objective likelihood that the relevant sort of harm will be produced by the words uttered in the circumstances. In addition to these traditional common law crimes, many governments have considered it necessary to create statutes making *sedition* a crime. It will be useful to consider the question of sedition against the background of the normal criminal law of words, for this will lead us quickly to two conclusions. The first is that sedition laws are wholly unnecessary to avert the harm they are ostensibly aimed at. The second is that if we must nevertheless put up with sedition laws, they must be applied by the courts in accordance with the same standards of objective likelihood and immediate danger that govern the application of the laws against provoking and inciting violence. Otherwise sedition statutes are likely to do far more social harm than good. Such laws when properly interpreted by enforcers and courts are at best legal redundancies. At worst they are corrosive of the values normally protected by freedom of expression.

The word "sedition," which in its oldest, prelegal sense meant simply divisiveness and strife, has never been the name of a crime in the English common law. Rather the adjective "seditious" forms part of the name of the common law crimes of "seditious words," "seditious libel," and "seditious conspiracy." Apparently the common ingredient in these offenses was so-called "seditious intent." The legal definition of "seditious intent" has changed over the centuries. In the beginning any spoken or written words which in fact had a tendency, however remote, to cause dissension or to weaken the grip of governmental authorities, and were spoken or published intentionally (with or without the further purpose of weakening the government or causing dissension) were held to manifest the requisite intent. In the fifteenth and sixteenth centuries, for example, publicly to call the king a fool, even in jest, was to risk capital punishment. There was to be less danger somewhat later for authors of *printed* words; for all books and printed papers had to be submitted in advance to the censorship (a practice denounced in Milton's eloquent *Areopagitica*), so that authors of politically dangerous words risked not punishment but only prior restraint. There is little evidence, however, that many of them felt more free as a consequence of this development.

The abandonment of the censorship in 1695 was widely hailed as a triumph for freedom of the press, but it was soon replaced by an equally repressive and far more cruel series of criminal trials for "seditious libel." Juries were permitted to decide only narrow factual questions, whereas the matter of "seditious intent" was left up to very conservative judges who knew well where their own personal interests lay. Moreover, truth was not permitted as a defense[26]—a legal restriction which in effect destroyed all right of adverse political criticism. Zechariah Chafee[27] has argued convincingly that the First Amendment to the United States Constitution was proposed and adopted by men who were con-

sciously reacting against the common law of seditious libel, and in particular against the applications of that law in the English trials of the time. "Reform" (of sorts) came in England through Fox's Libel Act of 1792, which allowed juries to decide the question of seditious intent and permitted the truth defense if the opinions were published with good motives. (The ill-advised and short-lived American Sedition Act of 1798 was modeled after this act.) In the hysterical reaction to the French Revolution and the Napoleonic Wars, however, juries proved to be even more savage than judges, and hundreds were punished even for the mildest political unorthodoxy.

Throughout most of the nineteenth century, the prevailing definition of seditious intent in English law derived from a statute passed during the repressive heyday of the Fox Act sedition trials. Men were punished for publishing any words with:

> the intention of (1) exciting disaffection, hatred, or contempt against the sovereign, or the government and constitution of the kingdom, or either house of parliament, or the administration of justice, or (2) exciting his majesty's subjects to attempt, otherwise than by lawful means, the alteration of any matter in church or state by law established, or (3) to promote feelings of ill will and hostility between different classes.[28]

In short, the three possible modes of seditious libel were defamation of the institutions or officers of the government, incitement to unlawful acts, and a use of language that tends toward the breach of the peace "between classes." The normal criminal law of words sufficiently covers the last two modes; and the civil law of defamation would apply to the first. The criminal law, as we have seen, employs a clear and present danger test for incitement and breach of peace, and does so for good reasons derived from the harm principle and the analysis of "intentional causing." For other good reasons, also derived from the harm principle, the law of defamation privileges fair comment on public officials, and gives no protection at all to institutions. So there would seem to be no further need, at least none demonstrated by the harm principle, for a criminal law of sedition.[29]

Still, many have thought that the harm principle requires sedition laws, and some still do. The issue boils down to the question of whether the normal law of words with its strict standard of immediate danger is too lax to prevent serious harms, and whether, therefore, it needs supplementing by sedition laws employing the looser standards of "bad tendency" and "presumptive intent." By the standard of bad tendency, words can be punished for their dangerous propensity "long before there is any probability that they will break out into unlawful acts";[30] and by the test of presumptive intent, it is necessary only that the defendant intended to publish his words, not that he intended further harm by them. It is clear that most authors of sedition statutes have meant them to be interpreted by the courts in accordance with the tests of bad tendency and presumptive intent (although the United States Supreme Court has in recent decades declared that such interpretations are contrary to the First Amendment of the Constitution). Part of the rationale for the older tests was that if words make a definite contribution to a situation which is on its way to being dangerous, it is folly not to punish them well before that situation reaches the threshold of actual harm. There may seem to be no harm in piling up twigs as such, but if this is done with the purpose (or even the likely outcome) of starting a fire eventually, why not stop it now before it is too late? Those who favor this argument have often employed the harm principle also to defend laws against institutional defamation. The reason why it should be unlawful to bring the Constitution or the courts (or even the *flag*) into disrepute by one's words, they argue, is not simply that such words are offensive, but rather that they tend to undermine respect and loyalty and thereby contribute to more serious harm in the long run.

The focus of the disagreement over sedition laws is the status of *advocacy*. The normal law of words quite clearly outlaws counseling, urging, or demanding (under certain conditions) that others resort to crime or engage in riots, assassinations, or insurrections. But what if a person uses language not directly to counsel or call for violence but rather (where this is different) to *advocate* it? In the wake of the Russian Revolution, many working class parties in America and Europe adopted some variant of an ideology which declared that the propertied classes derived their wealth from the systematic exploitation of the poor; capitalists controlled the major media of news and opinion as well as parliaments and legislators; the grievances of the workers therefore could not be remedied through normal political channels but required instead direct pressure through such means as general strikes, boycotts, and mass demonstrations; and that the working class would inevitably be triumphant in its struggle, expropriate the exploiters, and itself run industry.

Spokesmen for this ideology were known for their flamboyant rhetoric, which invariably contained such terms as "arise," "struggle," "victory," and "revolution." Such persons were commonly charged with violations of the Federal Espionage Act during and after World War I, of state sedition laws during the 1920s, and, after World War II, of the Smith Act. Often the key charge in the indictment was "teaching or advocating" riot, assassination, or the violent overthrow of the government.

Trials of Marxists for advocacy of revolution tended to be extremely difficult and problematic partly because it was never clear whether revolution in any usual sense was something taught and approved by them, and partly because it was unclear whether the form of reference to revolution in the Marxist ideology amounted to "advocacy" of it. Marxists disagreed among themselves over the first point. Many thought that forms of group pressure well short of open violence would be sufficient to overturn the capitalists; others thought that "eventually" (when is that?), when conditions were at last ripe, a brief violent seizure of power might be necessary. Does this, in any case, amount to the advocacy of revolution? If it is criminal advocacy to teach that there are conceivable circumstances under which revolution would be justified, then almost everyone, including this author, "advocates" revolution. Suppose one holds further that the "conceivable justifying conditions" may one day become actual, or that it is even probable that they will be actual at some indeterminate future time. Is this to count as criminal advocacy?

Not according to Justice Holmes in his famous opinion in *U.S. v. Schenk.* Schenk and others had encouraged draft resistance in 1917 by mailing circulars denouncing conscription as unconstitutional and urging in very emotional prose that draft-eligible men "assert their rights." The lower court found this to be advocacy of unlawful conduct, a violation, in particular, of the Espionage Act of 1917. The Supreme Court upheld the conviction but nevertheless laid down in the words of O. W. Holmes the test which was to be applied, in a more generous spirit, in later cases: "The question in every case is whether the words . . . are used in such circumstances and are of such a nature as to create a clear and present danger that they will bring about the substantive evils that Congress has a right to prevent." Since Congress has the right to raise armies, any efforts to interfere by words or action with the exercise of that right are punishable. But the clear and present danger standard brings advocacy under the same kind of test as that used for incitement in the normal law of words. One can "advocate" draft resistance over one's breakfast table to one's daughter (though perhaps not to one's son), but not to a sullen group waiting to be sworn in at the induction center.

There is, on the other hand, never any real danger in this country in permitting the open advocacy of *revolution,* except, perhaps, as Chafee puts it, "in extraordinary times of great tension." He continues:

> The chances of success are so infinitesimal that the probability of any serious attempt following the utterances seems too slight to make them punishable. . . . This is especially true if the speaker urges revolution at some future day, so that no immediate check is needed to save the country.[31]

Advocacy of assassination, on the other hand, is less easily tolerated. In the first place, the soil is always more receptive to that seed. It is not that potential assassins are more numerous than potential revolutionaries, although at most times that is true. Potential assassins include among their number persons who are contorted beyond reason by hate, mentally unstable persons, and unpredictable crackpots. Further, a successful assassination requires only one good shot. Since it is more likely to be tried and easier to achieve, its danger is always more "clear and present." There will be many circumstances, therefore, in which Holmes's test would permit advocacy of revolution but punish advocacy of assassination. Still in most contexts of utterance it would punish neither. It should no doubt be criminal for a prominent politician to advocate assassination of the president in a talk over national television, or in a letter to the *New York Times,*[32] but when a patron of a neighborhood tavern heatedly announces to his fellow drinkers that "the bum ought to be shot," the president's life will not be significantly endangered. There are times and places where it doesn't matter in the slightest how carelessly one chooses one's words, and others where one's choice of words can be a matter of life and death.

I shall, in conclusion, sketch a rationale for the clear and present danger test, as a kind of mediating standard for the application of the harm principle in the area of political expression. The natural challenge to the use of that test has been adumbrated above. It is true, one might concede, that the teaching of Communist ideology here and now will not create a clear and present danger of violent revolu-

tion. Every one knows that, including the Communists. Every trip, however, begins with some first steps, and that includes trips to forbidden destinations. The beginning steps are meant to increase numbers, add strength, and pick up momentum at later stages. To switch the metaphor to one used previously, the Communists are not just casting seeds on barren ground; their words are also meant to cultivate the ground and irrigate it. If the law prohibits planting a certain kind of shrub and we see people storing the forbidden seeds, garden tools, and fertilizer, and actually digging trenches for irrigation pipes, why wait until they are ready to plant the seed before stopping them? Even at these early stages of preparation, they are clearly attempting to achieve what is forbidden. So the argument goes.

The metaphor employed by the argument, however, is not very favorable to its cause. There is a world of difference between making plans and preparations for a future crime and actually launching an attempt, and this distinction has long been recognized by the ordinary criminal law. Mere preparations without actual steps in the direction of perpetration are not sufficient for the crime of attempt (though if preparation involves talking with collaborators, it may constitute the crime of conspiracy). Not even preliminary "steps" are sufficient; for "the act must reach far enough toward the accomplishment of the desired result to amount to the commencement of the consummation."[33] So the first faltering steps of a surpassingly difficult fifty-year trip toward an illegal goal can hardly qualify as an "attempt" in either the legal or the everyday sense.

If the journey is a collective enterprise, the participants could be charged with *conspiracy* without any violation of usage. The question is whether it would be sound public policy to suppress dissenting voices in this manner so long before they reach the threshold of public danger. The argument to the contrary has been given very clear statement in our time by Zechariah Chafee. Consider what interests are involved when the state employs some coercive technique to prevent a private individual or group from expressing an opinion on some issue of public policy, or from teaching or advocating some political ideology. Chafee would have us put these various interests in the balance to determine their relative weights. In the one pan of the scale, there are the private interests of the suppressed individual or group in having their opinions heard and shared, and in winning support and eventual acceptance for them. These interests will be effectively squelched by state suppression. In the other pan is the public interest in peace and order, and the preservation of democratic institutions. These interests may be endangered to some degree by the advocacy of radical ideologies. Now if these are the only interests involved, there is no question that the public interest (which after all includes all or most private interests) sits heavier in the pan. There is, however, another public interest involved of very considerable weight. That is the public interest in the discovery and dissemination of all information that can have any bearing on public policy, and of all opinions about what public policy should be. The dangers that come from neglecting *that* interest are enormous at all times. (See Part I above.) And the more dangerous the times—the more serious the questions before the country's decision makers (and *especially* when these are questions of war and peace)—the more important it is to keep open all the possible avenues to truth and wisdom.

Only the interest in national safety can outweigh the public interest in open discussion, but *it sits in the scale only to the degree that it is actually imperiled*. From the point of view of the public interest alone, with no consideration whatever of individual rights, it would be folly to sacrifice the social benefits of free speech for the bare possibility that the public safety may be somewhat affected. The greater the certainty and imminence of danger, however, the more the interest in public safety moves on to the scale, until at the point of clear and present danger it is heavy enough to tip the scales its way.

The scales analogy, of course, is only an elaborate metaphor for the sorts of deliberations that must go on among enforcers and interpreters of the law when distinct public interests come into conflict. These clashes of interest are most likely to occur in times of excitement and stress when interest "balancing" calls for a clear eye, a sensitive scale, and a steady hand. At such times the clear and present danger rule is a difficult one to apply, but other guides to decision have invariably gone wrong, while the clear and present danger test has hardly ever been seriously tried. Perhaps that helps account, to some degree, for the sorry human record of cruelty, injustice, and war.

---

1. In Chapter Two of *On Liberty,* not reprinted in this volume.
2. Zechariah Chafee, Jr., *Free Speech in the United States* (1941), p. 33.
3. This point applies especially to discussions of moral, social, political, legal, and economic questions, as well as matters of governmental policy, domestic and foreign. "Cross-examination" in science and philosophy is perhaps less important.
4. Aristotle, *Nicomachean Ethics,* Bk. II, Chap. 6, 1107a. "When a man commits adultery, there is no point in asking whether it was with the right woman or at the right time or in the right way, for to do anything like that is simply wrong."
5. William L. Prosser, *Handbook of the Law of Torts,* 2nd ed. (St. Paul: West Publishing Co., 1955), p. 584.
6. *Ibid.,* p. 631.
7. Fowler V. Harper and Fleming James, Jr., *The Law of Torts* (Boston: Little, Brown and Co., 1956), Vol. I, p. 416. The authors do not endorse this view.
8. *Ibid.*
9. William Blackstone, *Commentaries on the Laws of England,* Vol. III, 1765 Reprint (Boston: Beacon Press, 1962), p. 125.
10. Prosser, *op. cit.,* p. 644.
11. Harper and James, *op. cit.,* p. 680.
12. Prosser, *op. cit.,* p. 642.
13. *Loc. cit.*
14. American Law Institute, *Restatement of the Law of Torts* (St. Paul, 1934) § 867, comment c.
15. Prosser, *op. cit.,* p. 644.
16. "There are two aspects of the interest in seclusion. First, the interest in preventing others from seeing and hearing what one does and says. Second, the interest in avoiding seeing and hearing what other people do and say. . . . It may be as distasteful to suffer the intrusions of a garrulous and unwelcome guest as to discover an eavesdropper or peeper." Harper and James, *op. cit.,* p. 681. (Emphasis added.)
17. *Schenck v. United States,* 249 U.S. 47 (1919).
18. Chafee, *op. cit.,* pp. 152, 161, 426. cf. *Terminiello v. Chicago* 337 U.S. 1, (1949).
19. Chafee, *op. cit.,* p. 426.
20. *Ibid.,* p. 161.
21. *Toler v. State,* 152 Tenn. 1, 13, 260 S.W. 134 (1923).
22. Mill, *op. cit.,* pp. 67–8.
23. Chafee, *op. cit.,* p. 397.
24. For a more detailed exposition of this view see my "Causing Voluntary Actions" in *Doing and Deserving* (Princeton, N.J.: Princeton University Press, 1970), p. 152.
25. Chafee, *op. cit.,* p. 149.
26. In the words of the great common law judge, William Murray, First Earl of Mansfield, "The Greater the Truth, the Greater the Libel," hence Robert Burns's playful lines in his poem, "The Reproof":
    "Dost not know that old Mansfield
    Who writes like the Bible,
    Says the more 'tis a truth, sir,
    The more 'tis a libel?"
27. Chafee, *op. cit.,* pp. 18–22.
28. *Ibid.,* p. 506.
29. Such things, however, as patriotic sensibilities are capable of being highly offended by certain kinds of language. The rationale of sedition laws, therefore, may very well derive from the "offense-principle," which warrants prohibition of offensive behavior even when it is (otherwise) harmless.
30. Chafee, *op. cit.,* p. 24.
31. *Ibid.,* p. 175.
32. In which case the newspaper too would be criminally responsible for publishing the letter.
33. *Lee v. Commonwealth,* 144 Va. 594, 599, 131 S.E. 212, 214 (1926) as quoted in Rollin M. Perkins, *Criminal Law* (Brooklyn Foundation Press, 1957), p. 482.

COHEN V. CALIFORNIA*

United States Supreme Court, 1971

Opinion of the Court

MR. JUSTICE HARLAN delivered the opinion of the Court.

This case may seem at first blush too inconsequential to find its way into our books, but the issue it presents is of no small constitutional significance.

Appellant Paul Robert Cohen was convicted in the Los Angeles Municipal Court of violating that part of California Penal Code § 415 which prohibits "maliciously and willfully disturb[ing] the peace or quiet of any neighborhood or person . . . by . . . offensive conduct. . . ."[1] He was given 30 days' imprisonment. The facts upon which his conviction rests are detailed in the opinion of the Court of Appeal of California, Second Appellate District, as follows:

"On April 26, 1968, the defendant was observed in the Los Angeles County Courthouse in the corridor outside of division 20 of the municipal court wearing a jacket bearing the words 'Fuck the Draft' which were plainly visible. There were women and children present in the corridor. The defendant was arrested. The defendant testified that he wore the jacket knowing that the words were on the jacket as a means of informing the public of the depth of his feelings against the Vietnam War and the draft.

"The defendant did not engage in, nor threaten to engage in, nor did anyone as the result of his conduct in fact commit or threaten to commit any act of violence. The defendant did not make any loud or unusual noise, nor was there any evidence that he uttered any sound prior to his arrest."

In affirming the conviction the Court of Appeal held that "offensive conduct" means "behavior which has a tendency to provoke *others* to acts of violence or to in turn disturb the peace," and that the State had proved this element because, on the facts of this case, "[i]t was certainly reasonably foreseeable that such conduct might cause others to rise up to commit a violent act against the person of the defendant or attempt to forceably remove his jacket." The California Supreme Court declined review by a divided vote. We brought the case here, postponing the consideration of the question of our jurisdiction over this appeal to a hearing of the case on the merits. We now reverse.

I

In order to lay hands on the precise issue which this case involves, it is useful first to canvass various matters which this record does *not* present.

The conviction quite clearly rests upon the asserted offensiveness of the *words* Cohen used to convey his message to the public. The only "conduct" which the State sought to punish is the fact of communication. Thus, we deal here with a conviction resting solely upon "speech," not upon any separately identifiable conduct which allegedly was intended by Cohen to be perceived by others as expressive of particular views but which, on its face, does not necessarily convey any message and hence arguably could be regulated without effectively repressing Cohen's ability to express himself. Further, the State certainly lacks power to punish Cohen for the underlying content of the message the inscription conveyed. At least so long as there is no showing of an intent to incite disobedience to or disruption of the draft, Cohen could not, consistently with the First and Fourteenth Amendments, be punished for asserting the evident position on the inutility or immorality of the draft his jacket reflected.

Appellant's conviction, then, rests squarely upon his exercise of the "freedom of speech" protected from arbitrary governmental interference by

*408 *U.S.* 15 (1971). Some footnotes omitted. Citation omitted.

the Constitution and can be justified, if at all, only as a valid regulation of the manner in which he exercised that freedom, not as a permissible prohibition on the substantive message it conveys. This does not end the inquiry, of course, for the First and Fourteenth Amendments have never been thought to give absolute protection to every individual to speak whenever or wherever he pleases, or to use any form of address in any circumstances that he chooses. In this vein, too, however, we think it important to note that several issues typically associated with such problems are not presented here.

In the first place, Cohen was tried under a statute applicable throughout the entire State. Any attempt to support this conviction on the ground that the statute seeks to preserve an appropriately decorous atmosphere in the courthouse where Cohen was arrested must fail in the absence of any language in the statute that would have put appellant on notice that certain kinds of otherwise permissible speech or conduct would nevertheless, under California law, not be tolerated in certain places. No fair reading of the phrase "offensive conduct" can be said sufficiently to inform the ordinary person that distinctions between certain locations are thereby created.[2]

In the second place, as it comes to us, this case cannot be said to fall within those relatively few categories of instances where prior decisions have established the power of government to deal more comprehensively with certain forms of individual expression simply upon a showing that such a form was employed. This is not, for example, an obscenity case. Whatever else may be necessary to give rise to the States' broader power to prohibit obscene expression, such expression must be, in some significant way, erotic. It cannot plausibly be maintained that this vulgar allusion to the Selective Service System would conjure up such psychic stimulation in anyone likely to be confronted with Cohen's crudely defaced jacket.

This Court has also held that the States are free to ban the simple use, without a demonstration of additional justifying circumstances, of so-called "fighting words," those personally abusive epithets which, when addressed to the ordinary citizen, are, as a matter of common knowledge, inherently likely to provoke violent reaction. While the four-letter word displayed by Cohen in relation to the draft is not uncommonly employed in a personally provocative fashion, in this instance it was clearly not "directed to the person of the hearer." No individual actually or likely to be present could reasonably have regarded the words on appellant's jacket as a direct personal insult. Nor do we have here an instance of the exercise of the State's police power to prevent a speaker from intentionally provoking a given group to hostile reaction. There is, as noted above, no showing that anyone who saw Cohen was in fact violently aroused or that appellant intended such a result.

Finally, in arguments before this Court much has been made of the claim that Cohen's distasteful mode of expression was thrust upon unwilling or unsuspecting viewers, and that the State might therefore legitimately act as it did in order to protect the sensitive from otherwise unavoidable exposure to appellant's crude form of protest. Of course, the mere presumed presence of unwitting listeners or viewers does not serve automatically to justify curtailing all speech capable of giving offense. While this Court has recognized that government may properly act in many situations to prohibit intrusion into the privacy of the home of unwelcome views and ideas which cannot be totally banned from the public dialogue, we have at the same time consistently stressed that "we are often 'captives' outside the sanctuary of the home and subject to objectionable speech." The ability of government, consonant with the Constitution, to shut off discourse solely to protect others from hearing it is, in other words, dependent upon a showing that substantial privacy interests are being invaded in an essentially intolerable manner. Any broader view of this authority would effectively empower a majority to silence dissidents simply as a matter of personal predilections.

In this regard, persons confronted with Cohen's jacket were in a quite different posture than, say, those subjected to the raucous emissions of sound trucks blaring outside their residences. Those in the Los Angeles courthouse could effectively avoid further bombardment of their sensibilities simply by averting their eyes. And, while it may be that one has a more substantial claim to a recognizable privacy interest when walking through a courthouse corridor than, for example, strolling through Central Park, surely it is nothing like the interest in being free from unwanted expression in the confines of one's own home. Given the subtlety and complexity of the factors involved, if Cohen's "speech" was otherwise entitled to constitutional protection, we do not think the fact that some unwilling "listeners" in a public building may have been briefly exposed to it can serve to justify this breach of the peace conviction where, as here, there was no evidence that persons powerless to avoid appellant's conduct did in fact object to it, and where that portion of the statute upon which Cohen's conviction rests evinces no concern, either on its face or as construed by the California courts, with the special plight of the captive auditor, but, instead, indiscriminately sweeps within its prohibitions all "offensive conduct" that disturbs "any neighborhood or person."

II

Against this background, the issue flushed by this case stands out in bold relief. It is whether California can excise, as "offensive conduct," one particular scurrilous epithet from the public discourse, either upon the theory of the court below that its use is inherently likely to cause violent reaction or upon a more general assertion that the States, acting as guardians of public morality, may properly remove this offensive word from the public vocabulary.

The rationale of the California court is plainly untenable. At most it reflects an "undifferentiated fear or apprehension of disturbance [which] is not enough to overcome the right to freedom of expression." We have been shown no evidence that substantial numbers of citizens are standing ready to strike out physically at whomever may assault their sensibilities with execrations like that uttered by Cohen. There may be some persons about with such lawless and violent proclivities, but that is an insufficient base upon which to erect, consistently with constitutional values, a governmental power to force persons who wish to ventilate their dissident views into avoiding particular forms of expression. The argument amounts to little more than the self-defeating proposition that to avoid physical censorship of one who has not sought to provoke such a response by a hypothetical coterie of the violent and lawless, the States may more appropriately effectuate that censorship themselves.

Admittedly, it is not so obvious that the First and Fourteenth Amendments must be taken to disable the States from punishing public utterance of this unseemly expletive in order to maintain what they regard as a suitable level of discourse within the body politic. We think, however, that examination and reflection will reveal the shortcomings of a contrary viewpoint.

At the outset, we cannot overemphasize that, in our judgment, most situations where the State has a justifiable interest in regulating speech will fall within one or more of the various established exceptions, discussed above but not applicable here, to the usual rule that governmental bodies may not prescribe the form or content of individual expression. Equally important to our conclusion is the constitutional backdrop against which our decision must be made. The constitutional right of free expression is powerful medicine in a society as diverse and populous as ours. It is designed and intended to remove governmental restraints from the arena of public discussion, putting the decision as to what views shall be voiced largely into the hands of each of us, in the hope that use of such freedom will ultimately produce a more capable citizenry and more perfect polity and in the belief that no other approach would comport with the premise of individual dignity and choice upon which our political system rests.

To many, the immediate consequence of this freedom may often appear to be only verbal tumult, discord, and even offensive utterance. These are, however, within established limits, in truth necessary side effects of the broader enduring values which the process of open debate permits us to achieve. That the air may at times seem filled with verbal cacophony is, in this sense not a sign of weakness but of strength. We cannot lose sight of the fact that, in what otherwise might seem a trifling and annoying instance of individual distasteful abuse of a privilege, these fundamental societal values are truly implicated. That is why "[w]holly neutral futilities . . . come under the protection of free speech as fully as do Keats' poems or Donne's sermons," *Winters v. New York,* (1948) (Frankfurter, J., dissenting), and why "so long as the means are peaceful, the communication need not meet standards of acceptability," *Organization for a Better Austin v. Keefe,* (1971).

Against this perception of the constitutional policies involved, we discern certain more particularized considerations that peculiarly call for reversal of this conviction. First, the principle contended for by the State seems inherently boundless. How is one to distinguish this from any other offensive word? Surely the State has no right to cleanse public debate to the point where it is grammatically palatable to the most squeamish among us. Yet no readily ascertainable general principle exists for stopping short of that result were we to affirm the judgment below. For, while the particular four-letter word being litigated here is perhaps more distasteful than most others of its genre, it is nevertheless often true that one man's vulgarity is another's lyric. Indeed, we think it is largely because governmental officials cannot make principled distinctions in this area that the Constitution leaves matters of taste and style so largely to the individual.

Additionally, we cannot overlook the fact, because it is well illustrated by the episode involved here, that much linguistic expression serves a dual communicative function: it conveys not only ideas capable of relatively precise, detached explication, but otherwise inexpressible emotions as well. In fact, words are often chosen as much for their emotive as their cognitive force. We cannot sanction the view that the Constitution, while solicitous of the cognitive content of individual speech, has little or no regard for that emotive function which, practically speaking, may often be the more important element of the overall message sought to be communicated. Indeed, as Mr. Justice Frankfurter has said, "[o]ne of the prerogatives of American citizenship is the right to criticize public men and measures—and that means not only informed and responsible criticism but the freedom to speak foolishly and without moderation." *Baumgartner v. United States,* (1944).

Finally, and in the same vein, we cannot indulge the facile assumption that one can forbid particular words without also running a substantial risk of suppressing ideas in the process. Indeed, governments might soon seize upon the censorship of particular words as a convenient guise for banning the expression of unpopular views. We have been able, as noted above, to discern little social benefit that might result from running the risk of opening the door to such grave results.

It is, in sum, our judgment that, absent a more particularized and compelling reason for its actions, the State may not, consistently with the First and Fourteenth Amendments, make the simple public display here involved of this single four-letter expletive a criminal offense. Because that is the only arguably sustainable rationale for the conviction here at issue, the judgment below must be reversed.

Separate Opinion

Mr. Justice Blackmun, with whom THE CHIEF JUSTICE and Mr. Justice Black join.

I dissent, and I do so for two reasons:

1. Cohen's absurd and immature antic, in my view, was mainly conduct and little speech. The California Court of Appeal appears so to have described it, and I cannot characterize it otherwise. Further, the case appears to me to be well within the sphere of *Chaplinsky v. New Hampshire,* where Mr. Justice Murphy, a known champion of First Amendment freedoms, wrote for a unanimous bench. As a consequence, this Court's agonizing First Amendment values seems misplaced and unnecessary.

2. I am not at all certain that the California Court of Appeal's construction of § 415 is now the authoritative California construction. . . .

---

1. The statute provides in full:

   "Every person who maliciously and willfully disturbs the peace or quiet of any neighborhood or person, by loud or unusual noise, or by tumultuous or offensive conduct, or threatening, traducing, quarreling, challenging to fight, or fighting, or who, on the public streets of any unincorporated town, or upon the public highways in such unincorporated town, run any horse race, either for a wager or for amusement, or fire any gun or pistol in such unincorporated town, or use any vulgar language within the presence or hearing of women or children, in a loud and boisterous manner, is guilty of a misdemeanor, and upon conviction by any Court of competent jurisdiction shall be punished by fine not exceeding two hundred dollars, or by imprisonment in the County Jail for not more than ninety days, or by both fine and imprisonment, or either, at the discretion of the Court."

2. It is illuminating to note what transpired when Cohen entered a courtroom in the building. He removed his jacket and stood with it folded over his arm. Meanwhile, a policeman sent the presiding judge a note suggesting that Cohen be held in contempt of court. The judge declined to do so and Cohen was arrested by the officer only after he emerged from the courtroom.

VILLAGE OF SKOKIE V. NATIONAL SOCIALIST PARTY OF AMERICA*

Supreme Court of Illinois, 1978

PER CURIAM:

Plaintiff, the village of Skokie, filed a complaint in the circuit court of Cook County seeking to enjoin defendants, the National Socialist Party of America (the American Nazi Party) and 10 individuals as "officers and members" of the party, from engaging in certain activities while conducting a demonstration within the village. The circuit court issued an order enjoining certain conduct during the planned demonstration. The appellate court modified the injunction order, and, as modified, defendants are enjoined from "[i]ntentionally displaying the swastika on or off their persons, in the course of a demonstration, march, or parade." . . . We allowed defendants' petition for leave to appeal. . . .

The pleadings and the facts adduced at the hearing are fully set forth in the appellate court opinion, and only those matters necessary to the discussion of the issues will be repeated here. The facts are not disputed.

It is alleged in plaintiff's complaint that the "uniform of the National Socialist Party of America consists of the storm trooper uniform of the German Nazi Party embellished with the Nazi swastika"; that the plaintiff village has a population of about 70,000 persons of which approximately 40,500 persons are of "Jewish religion or Jewish ancestry" and of this latter number 5,000 to 7,000 are survivors of German concentration camps; that the defendant organization is "dedicated to the incitation of racial and religious hatred directed principally against individuals of Jewish faith or ancestry and non-Caucasians"; and that its members "have patterned their conduct, their uniform, their slogan and their tactics along the pattern of the German Nazi Party."

Defendants moved to dismiss the complaint. In an affidavit attached to defendants' motion to dismiss, defendant Frank Collin, who testified that he was "party leader," stated that on or about March 20, 1977, he sent officials of the plaintiff village a letter stating that the party members and supporters would hold a peaceable, public assembly in the village on May 1, 1977, to protest the Skokie Park District's requirement that the party procure $350,000 of insurance prior to the party's use of the Skokie public parks for public assemblies. The demonstration was to begin at 3 P.M., last 20 to 30 minutes, and consist of 30 to 50 demonstrators marching in single file, back and forth, in front of the village hall. The marchers were to wear uniforms which include a swastika emblem or armband. They were to carry a party banner containing a swastika emblem and signs containing such statements as "White Free Speech," "Free Speech for the White Man," and "Free Speech for White America." The demonstrators would not distribute handbills, make any derogatory statements directed to any ethnic or religious group, or obstruct traffic. They would cooperate with any reasonable police instructions or requests.

At the hearing on plaintiff's motion for an "emergency injunction" a resident of Skokie testified that he was a survivor of the Nazi holocaust. He further testified that the Jewish community in and around Skokie feels the purpose of the march in the "heart of the Jewish population" is to remind the two million survivors "that we are not through with you" and to show "that the Nazi threat is not over, it can happen again." Another resident of Skokie testified that as the result of defendants' announced intention to march in Skokie, 15 to 18 Jewish organizations,

---

*373 *N.E.* 2d 21 (Ill. 1978). Citation details deleted throughout.

within the village and surrounding area, were called and a counterdemonstration of an estimated 12,000 to 15,000 people was scheduled for the same day. There was opinion evidence that defendants' planned demonstration in Skokie would result in violence.

The circuit court entered an order enjoining defendants from "marching, walking or parading in the uniform of the National Socialist Party of America; marching, walking or parading or otherwise displaying the swastika on or off their person; distributing pamphlets or displaying any materials which incite or promote hatred against persons of Jewish faith or ancestry or hatred against persons of any faith or ancestry, race or religion" within the village of Skokie. The appellate court, as earlier noted, modified the order so that defendants were enjoined only from intentional display of the swastika during the Skokie demonstration.

The appellate court opinion adequately discussed and properly decided those issues arising from the portions of the injunction order which enjoined defendants from marching, walking, or parading, from distributing pamphlets or displaying materials, and from wearing the uniform of the National Socialist Party of America. The only issue remaining before this court is whether the circuit court order enjoining defendants from displaying the swastika violates the First Amendment rights of those defendants.

In defining the constitutional rights of the parties who come before this court, we are, of course, bound by the pronouncements of the United States Supreme Court in its interpretation of the United States Constitution. The decisions of that court, particularly *Cohen v. California* . . . in our opinion compel us to permit the demonstration as proposed, including display of the swastika.

"It is firmly settled that under our Constitution the public expression of ideas may not be prohibited merely because the ideas are themselves offensive to some of their hearers" . . . and it is entirely clear that the wearing of distinctive clothing can be symbolic expression of a thought or philosophy. The symbolic expression of thought falls within the free speech clause of the First Amendment . . . and the plaintiff village has the heavy burden of justifying the imposition of a prior restraint upon defendants' right of freedom of speech. . . . The village of Skokie seeks to meet this burden by application of the "fighting words" doctrine first enunciated in *Chaplinsky v. New Hampshire* (1942), . . . That doctrine was designed to permit punishment of extremely

hostile personal communication likely to cause immediate physical response, "no words being 'forbidden except such as have a direct tendency to cause acts of violence by the persons to whom, individually, the remark is addressed.'" . . . In *Cohen* the Supreme Court restated the description of fighting words as "those personally abusive epithets which, when addressed to the ordinary citizen, are, as a matter of common knowledge, inherently likely to provoke violent reaction." . . . Plaintiff urges, and the appellate court has held, that the exhibition of the Nazi symbol, the swastika, addresses to ordinary citizens a message which is tantamount to fighting words. Plaintiff further asks this court to extend *Chaplinsky,* which upheld a statute punishing the use of such words, and hold that the fighting-words doctrine permits a prior restraint on defendants' symbolic speech. In our judgment we are precluded from doing so.

In *Cohen,* defendant's conviction stemmed from wearing a jacket bearing the words "Fuck the Draft" in a Los Angeles County courthouse corridor. The Supreme Court for reasons we believe applicable here refused to find that the jacket inscription constituted fighting words. That court stated:

> The constitutional right of free expression is powerful medicine in a society as diverse and populous as ours. It is designed and intended to remove governmental restraints from the arena of public discussion, putting the decision as to what views shall be voiced largely into the hands of each of us, in the hope that use of such freedom will ultimately produce a more capable citizenry and more perfect polity and in the belief that no other approach would comport with the premise of individual dignity and choice upon which our political system rests. . . .

> To many, the immediate consequence of this freedom may often appear to be only verbal tumult, discord, and even offensive utterance. These are, however, within established limits, in truth necessary side effects of the broader enduring values which the process of open debate permits us to achieve. That the air may at times seem filled with verbal cacophony is, in this sense not a sign of weakness but of strength. We cannot lose sight of the fact that, in what otherwise might seem a trifling and annoying instance

of individual distasteful abuse of a privilege, these fundamental societal values are truly implicated . . . "so long as the means are peaceful, the communication need not meet standards of acceptability.". . .

Against this perception of the constitutional policies involved, we discern certain more particularized considerations that peculiarly call for reversal of this conviction. First, the principle contended for by the State seems inherently boundless. How is one to distinguish this from any other offensive word [emblem]? Surely the State has no right to cleanse public debate to the point where it is grammatically palatable to the most squeamish among us. Yet no readily ascertainable general principle exists for stopping short of that result were we to affirm the judgment below. For, while the particular four-letter word [emblem] being litigated here is perhaps more distasteful than most others of its genre, it is nevertheless often true that one man's vulgarity is another's lyric. Indeed, we think it is largely because governmental officials cannot make principled distinctions in this area that the Constitution leaves matters of taste and style so largely to the individual. . . .

Finally, and in the same vein, we cannot indulge the facile assumption that one can forbid particular words without also running a substantial risk of suppressing ideas in the process. Indeed, governments might soon seize upon the censorship of particular words [emblems] as a convenient guise for banning the expression of unpopular views. We have been able, as noted above, to discern little social benefit that might result from running the risk of opening the door to such grave results. . . .

The display of the swastika, as offensive to the principles of a free nation as the memories it recalls may be, is symbolic political speech intended to convey to the public the beliefs of those who display it. It does not, in our opinion, fall within the definition of "fighting words," and that doctrine cannot be used here to overcome the heavy presumption against the constitutional validity of a prior restraint.

Nor can we find that the swastika, while not representing fighting words, is nevertheless so offensive and peace threatening to the public that its display can be enjoined. We do not doubt that the sight of this symbol is abhorrent to the Jewish citizens of Skokie, and that the survivors of the Nazi persecutions, tormented by their recollections, may have strong feelings regarding its display. Yet it is entirely clear that this factor does not justify enjoining defendants' speech. The *Cohen* court spoke to this subject:

> Finally, in arguments before this Court much has been made of the claim that Cohen's distasteful mode of expression was thrust upon unwilling or unsuspecting viewers, and that the State might therefore legitimately act as it did in order to protect the sensitive from otherwise unavoidable exposure to appellant's crude form of protest. Of course, the mere presumed presence of unwitting listeners or viewers does not serve automatically to justify curtailing all speech capable of giving offense. . . . While this Court has recognized that government may properly act in many situations to prohibit intrusion into the privacy of the home of unwelcome views and ideas which cannot be totally banned from the public dialogue, e.g., *Rowan v. Post Office Dept.*, 397 *U.S.* 728, 90 *S.Ct.* 1484, 25 *L.Ed.2d* 736 (1970), we have at the same time consistently stressed that "we are often 'captives' outside the sanctuary of the home and subject to objectionable speech." *Id.*, at 738, 90 *S.Ct.* at 1491. The ability of government, consonant with the Constitution, to shut off discourse solely to protect others from hearing it is, in other words, dependent upon a showing that substantial privacy interests are being invaded in an essentially intolerable manner. Any broader view of this authority would effectively empower a majority to silence dissidents simply as a matter of personal predilections. . . .

Similarly, the Court of Appeals for the Seventh Circuit, in reversing the denial of defendant Collin's application for a permit to speak in Chicago's Marquette Park, noted that courts have consistently refused to ban speech because of the possibility of unlawful conduct by those opposed to the speaker's philosophy.

> Starting with *Terminiello v. City of Chicago*, . . . and continuing to *Gregory v. City of Chicago*,

. . . it has become patent that a hostile audience is not a basis for restraining otherwise legal First Amendment activity. As with many of the cases cited herein, if the actual behavior is not sufficient to sustain a conviction under a statute, then certainly the anticipation of such events cannot sustain the burden necessary to justify a prior restraint. . . .

Rockwell v. Morris . . . also involved an American Nazi leader, George Lincoln Rockwell, who challenged a bar to his use of a New York City park to hold a public demonstration where anti-Semitic speeches would be made. Although approximately 2 1/2 million Jewish New Yorkers were hostile to Rockwell's message, the court ordered that a permit to speak be granted, stating:

> A community need not wait to be subverted by street riots and storm troopers; but, also, it cannot, by its policemen or commissioners, suppress a speaker, in prior restraint, on the basis of news reports, hysteria, or inference that what he did yesterday, he will do today. Thus, too, if the speaker incites others to immediate unlawful action he may be punished —in a proper case, stopped when disorder actually impends; but this is not to be confused with unlawful action from others who seek unlawfully to suppress or punish the speaker.
>
> So, the unpopularity of views, their shocking quality, their obnoxiousness, and even their alarming impact is not enough. Otherwise, the preacher of any strange doctrine could be stopped; the anti-racist himself could be suppressed, if he undertakes to speak in "restricted" areas; and one who asks that public schools be open indiscriminately to all ethnic groups could be lawfully suppressed, if only he choose to speak where persuasion is needed most. . . .

In summary, as we read the controlling Supreme Court opinions, use of the swastika is a symbolic form of free speech entitled to First Amendment protections. Its display on uniforms or banners by those engaged in peaceful demonstrations cannot be totally precluded solely because that display may provoke a violent reaction by those who view it. Particularly is this true where, as here, there has been advance notice by the demonstrators

of their plans so that they have become, as the complaint alleges, "common knowledge" and those to whom sight of the swastika banner or uniforms would be offense are forewarned and need not view them. A speaker who gives prior notice of his message has not compelled a confrontation with those who voluntarily listen.

As to those who happen to be in a position to be involuntarily confronted with the swastika, the following observations from *Erznoznik v. City of Jacksonville* . . . are appropriate:

> The plain, if at all times disquieting, truth is that in our pluralistic society, constantly proliferating new and ingenious forms of expression, "we are inescapably captive audiences for many purposes." . . . Much that we encounter offends our esthetic, if not our political and moral, sensibilities. Nevertheless, the Constitution does not permit government to decide which types of otherwise protected speech are sufficiently offensive to require protection for the unwilling listener or viewer. Rather, absent the narrow circumstances described above [home intrusion or captive audience], the burden normally falls upon the viewer to 'avoid further bombardment of [his] sensibilities simply by averting [his] eyes. . . .

Thus by placing the burden upon the viewer to avoid further bombardment, the Supreme Court has permitted speakers to justify the initial intrusion into the citizen's sensibilities.

We accordingly, albeit reluctantly, conclude that the display of the swastika cannot be enjoined under the fighting-words exception to free speech, nor can anticipation of a hostile audience justify the prior restraint. Furthermore, *Cohen* and *Erznoznik* direct the citizens of Skokie that it is their burden to avoid the offensive symbol if they can do so without unreasonable inconvenience. Accordingly, we are constrained to reverse that part of the appellate court judgment enjoining the display of the swastika. That judgment is in all other respects affirmed.

Affirmed in part and reversed in part.

CLARK, Justice, dissenting.

TEXAS V. JOHNSON *

United States Supreme Court, 1989

Justice BRENNAN delivered the opinion of the Court.

After publicly burning an American flag as a means of political protest, Gregory Lee Johnson was convicted of desecrating a flag in violation of Texas law. This case presents the question whether his conviction is consistent with the First Amendment. We hold that it is not.

I

While the Republican National Convention was taking place in Dallas in 1984, respondent Johnson participated in a political demonstration dubbed the "Republican War Chest Tour." As explained in literature distributed by the demonstrators and in speeches made by them, the purpose of this event was to protest the policies of the Reagan administration and of certain Dallas-based corporations. The demonstrators marched through the Dallas streets, chanting political slogans and stopping at several corporate locations to stage "die-ins" intended to dramatize the consequences of nuclear war. On several occasions they spray-painted the walls of buildings and overturned potted plants, but Johnson himself took no part in such activities. He did, however, accept an American flag handed to him by a fellow protestor who had taken it from a flag pole outside one of the targeted buildings.

The demonstration ended in front of Dallas City Hall, where Johnson unfurled the American flag, doused it with kerosene, and set it on fire. While the flag burned, the protestors chanted, "America, the red, white, and blue, we spit on you." After the demonstrators dispersed, a witness to the flag-burning collected the flag's remains and buried them in his backyard. No one was physically injured or threatened with injury, though several witnesses testified that they had been seriously offended by the flag-burning.

Of the approximately 100 demonstrators, Johnson alone was charged with a crime. The only criminal offense with which he was charged was the desecration of a venerated object in violation of Tex. Penal Code Ann. § 42.09 (a)(3) (1989).[1] After a trial, he was convicted, sentenced to one year in prison, and fined $2,000. The Court of Appeals for the Fifth District of Texas at Dallas affirmed Johnson's conviction, . . . but the Texas Court of Criminal Appeals reversed, . . . holding that the State could not, consistent with the First Amendment, punish Johnson for burning the flag in these circumstances.

The Court of Criminal Appeals began by recognizing that Johnson's conduct was symbolic speech protected by the First Amendment: "Given the context of an organized demonstration, speeches, slogans, and the distribution of literature, anyone who observed appellant's act would have understood the message that appellant intended to convey. The act for which appellant was convicted was clearly 'speech' contemplated by the First Amendment." *Id.,* at 95. To justify Johnson's conviction for engaging in symbolic speech, the State asserted two interests: preserving the flag as a symbol of national unity and preventing breaches of the peace. The Court of Criminal Appeals held that neither interest supported his conviction.

Acknowledging that this Court had not yet decided whether the Government may criminally sanction flag desecration in order to preserve the flag's symbolic value, the Texas court nevertheless concluded that our decision in *West Virginia Board of Education v. Barnette,* . . . (1943), suggested that furthering this interest by curtailing speech was impermissible. "Recognizing that the right to differ is the centerpiece of our First Amendment freedoms," the court explained, "a government cannot mandate by

---

*109 *S. Ct.* 2533 (1989). Only an excerpt has been included here from the dissenting opinion.

fiat a feeling of unity in its citizens. Therefore, that very same government cannot carve out a symbol of unity and prescribe a set of approved messages to be associated with that symbol when it cannot mandate the status or feeling the symbol purports to represent." . . . Noting that the State had not shown that the flag was in "grave and immediate danger," *Barnette, supra,* . . . of being stripped of its symbolic value, the Texas court also decided that the flag's special status was not endangered by Johnson's conduct. . . .

As to the State's goal of preventing breaches of the peace, the court concluded that the flag-desecration statute was not drawn narrowly enough to encompass only those flag-burnings that were likely to result in a serious disturbance of the peace. And in fact, the court emphasized, the flag-burning in this particular case did not threaten such a reaction. "'Serious offense' occurred," the court admitted, "but there was no breach of peace nor does the record reflect that the situation was potentially explosive. One cannot equate 'serious offense' with incitement to breach the peace." . . . The court also stressed that another Texas statute, Tex. Penal Code Ann. § 42.01 (1989), prohibited breaches of the peace. Citing *Boos v. Barry,* . . . the court decided that § 42.01 demonstrated Texas' ability to prevent disturbances of the peace without punishing this flag desecration.

Because it reversed Johnson's conviction on the ground that § 42.09 was unconstitutional as applied to him, the state court did not address Johnson's argument that the statute was, on its face, unconstitutionally vague and overbroad. We granted certiorari, . . . and now affirm.

II

Johnson was convicted of flag desecration for burning the flag rather than for uttering insulting words.[2] This fact somewhat complicates our consideration of his conviction under the First Amendment. We must first determine whether Johnson's burning of the flag constituted expressive conduct, permitting him to invoke the First Amendment in challenging his conviction. . . . If his conduct was expressive, we next decide whether the State's regulation is related to the suppression of free expression. . . . If the State's regulation is not related to expression, then the less stringent standard we announced in *United States v. O'Brien* for regulations of noncommunicative conduct controls. . . . If it is, then we are out-

side of *O'Brien*'s test, and we must ask whether this interest justifies Johnson's conviction under a more demanding standard.[3] . . . A third possibility is that the State's asserted interest is simply not implicated on these facts, and in that event the interest drops out of the picture.

The First Amendment literally forbids the abridgement only of "speech," but we have long recognized that its protection does not end at the spoken or written word. While we have rejected "the view that an apparently limitless variety of conduct can be labeled 'speech' whenever the person engaging in the conduct intends thereby to express an idea," . . . we have acknowledged that conduct may be "sufficiently imbued with elements of communication to fall within the scope of the First and Fourteenth Amendments."

In deciding whether particular conduct possesses sufficient communicative elements to bring the First Amendment into play, we have asked whether "[a]n intent to convey a particularized message was present, and [whether] the likelihood was great that the message would be understood by those who viewed it." . . . Hence, we have recognized the expressive nature of students' wearing of black armbands to protest American military involvement in Vietnam, . . . of a sit-in by blacks in a "whites only" area to protest segregation, . . . of the wearing of American military uniforms in a dramatic presentation criticizing American involvement in Vietnam, . . . and of picketing about a wide variety of causes. . . .

Especially pertinent to this case are our decisions recognizing the communicative nature of conduct relating to flags. Attaching a peace sign to the flag, . . . saluting the flag, . . . and displaying a red flag, . . . we have held, all may find shelter under the First Amendment. See also *Smith v. Goguen* . . . (treating flag "contemptuously" by wearing pants with small flag sewn into their seat is expressive conduct). That we have had little difficulty identifying an expressive element in conduct relating to flags should not be surprising. The very purpose of a national flag is to serve as a symbol of our country; it is, one might say, "the one visible manifestation of two hundred years of nationhood."

Thus, we have observed:

[T]he flag salute is a form of utterance. Symbolism is a primitive but effective way of communicating ideas. The use of an emblem or flag to symbolize some system, idea, institution, or personality, is a short cut from mind to mind. Causes and nations, political parties, lodges and ecclesiastical groups seek to knit the loyalty of their followings to a flag or banner, a color or design.

. . . Pregnant with expressive content, the flag as readily signifies this Nation as does the combination of letters found in "America."

We have not automatically concluded, however, that any action taken with respect to our flag is expressive. Instead, in characterizing such action for First Amendment purposes, we have considered the context in which it occurred. In *Spence,* for example, we emphasized that Spence's taping of a peace sign to his flag was "roughly simultaneous with and concededly triggered by the Cambodian incursion and the Kent State tragedy." . . . The State of Washington had conceded, in fact, that Spence's conduct was a form of communication, and we stated that "the State's concession is inevitable on this record."

The State of Texas conceded for purposes of its oral argument in this case that Johnson's conduct was expressive conduct, . . . and this concession seems to us as prudent as was Washington's in *Spence.* Johnson burned an American flag as part—indeed, as the culmination—of a political demonstration that coincided with the convening of the Republican Party and its renomination of Ronald Reagan for President. The expressive, overtly political nature of this conduct was both intentional and overwhelmingly apparent. At his trial, Johnson explained his reasons for burning the flag as follows: "The American Flag was burned as Ronald Reagan was being renominated as President. And a more powerful statement of symbolic speech, whether you agree with it or not, couldn't have been made at that time. It's quite a just position [juxtaposition]. We had new patriotism and no patriotism." . . . In these circumstances, Johnson's burning of the flag was conduct "sufficiently imbued with elements of communication, . . . to implicate the First Amendment.

III

The Government generally has a freer hand in restricting expressive conduct than it has in restricting the written or spoken word. . . . It may not, however, proscribe particular conduct *because* it has expressive elements. "[W]hat might be termed the more generalized guarantee of freedom of expression makes the communicative nature of conduct an inadequate *basis* for singling out that conduct for pro-

scription. A law *directed at* the communicative nature of conduct must, like a law directed at speech itself, be justified by the substantial showing of need that the First Amendment requires." . . . It is, in short, not simply the verbal or nonverbal nature of the expression, but the governmental interest at stake, that helps to determine whether a restriction on that expression is valid.

Thus, although we have recognized that where "'speech' and 'nonspeech' elements are combined in the same course of conduct, a sufficiently important governmental interest in regulating the nonspeech element can justify incidental limitations on First Amendment freedoms," . . . we have limited the applicability of *O'Brien*'s relatively lenient standard to those cases in which "the governmental interest is unrelated to the suppression of free expression." . . . In stating, moreover, that *O'Brien*'s test "in the last analysis is little, if any, different from the standard applied to time, place, or manner restrictions," . . . we have highlighted the requirement that the governmental interest in question be unconnected to expression in order to come under *O'Brien*'s less demanding rule.

In order to decide whether *O'Brien*'s test applies here, therefore, we must decide whether Texas has asserted an interest in support of Johnson's conviction that is unrelated to the suppression of expression. If we find that an interest asserted by the State is simply not implicated on the facts before us, we need not ask whether *O'Brien*'s test applies. . . . The State offers two separate interests to justify this conviction: preventing breaches of the peace, and preserving the flag as a symbol of nationhood and national unity. We hold that the first interest is not implicated on this record and that the second is related to the suppression of expression.

A

Texas claims that its interest in preventing breaches of the peace justifies Johnson's conviction for flag desecration.[4] However, no disturbance of the peace actually occurred or threatened to occur because of Johnson's burning of the flag. Although the State stresses the disruptive behavior of the protestors during their march toward City Hall, . . . it admits that "no actual breach of the peace occurred at the time of the flagburning or in response to the flagburning." . . . The State's emphasis on the protestors' disorderly actions prior to arriving at City Hall is not only somewhat surprising given that no charges were brought on the basis of this conduct, but it also fails to show that a disturbance of the peace was a likely reaction to Johnson's conduct. The only evidence offered by the State at trial to show the reaction to Johnson's actions was the testimony of several persons who had been seriously offended by the flag-burning.

The State's position, therefore, amounts to a claim that an audience that takes serious offense at particular expression is necessarily likely to disturb the peace and that the expression may be prohibited on this basis.[5] Our precedents do not countenance such a presumption. On the contrary, they recognize that a principal "function of free speech under our system of government is to invite dispute. It may indeed best serve its high purpose when it induces a condition of unrest, creates dissatisfaction with conditions as they are, or even stirs people to anger." . . . It would be odd indeed to conclude *both* that "if it is the speaker's opinion that gives offense, that consequence is a reason for according it constitutional protection," . . . *and* that the Government may ban the expression of certain disagreeable ideas on the unsupported presumption that their very disagreeableness will provoke violence.

Thus, we have not permitted the Government to assume that every expression of a provocative idea will incite a riot, but have instead required careful consideration of the actual circumstances surrounding such expression, asking whether the expression "is directed to inciting or producing imminent lawless action and is likely to incite or produce such action." *Brandenburg v. Ohio,* . . . (reviewing circumstances surrounding rally and speeches by Ku Klux Klan). To accept Texas' arguments that it need only demonstrate "the potential for a breach of the peace, . . . and that every flag-burning necessarily possesses that potential, would be to eviscerate our holding in *Brandenburg.* This we decline to do.

Nor does Johnson's expressive conduct fall within that small class of "fighting words" that are "likely to provoke the average person to retaliation, and thereby cause a breach of the peace." . . . No reasonable onlooker would have regarded Johnson's generalized expression of dissatisfaction with the policies of the Federal Government as a direct personal insult or an invitation to exchange fisticuffs. . . .

We thus conclude that the State's interest in maintaining order is not implicated on these facts. The State need not worry that our holding will disable it from preserving the peace. We do not sug-

gest that the First Amendment forbids a State to prevent "imminent lawless action." . . . And, in fact, Texas already has a statute specifically prohibiting breaches of the peace, Tex. Penal Code Ann. § 42.01 (1989), which tends to confirm that Texas need not punish this flag desecration in order to keep the peace. . . .

B

The State also asserts an interest in preserving the flag as a symbol of nationhood and national unity. In *Spence,* we acknowledged that the Government's interest in preserving the flag's special symbolic value "is directly related to expression in the context of activity" such as affixing a peace symbol to a flag. . . . We are equally persuaded that this interest is related to expression in the case of Johnson's burning of the flag. The State, apparently, is concerned that such conduct will lead people to believe either that the flag does not stand for nationhood and national unity, but instead reflects other, less positive concepts, or that the concepts reflected in the flag do not in fact exist, that is, we do not enjoy unity as a Nation. These concerns blossom only when a person's treatment of the flag communicates some message, and thus are related "to the suppression of free expression" within the meaning of *O'Brien.* We are thus outside of *O'Brien*'s test altogether.

IV

It remains to consider whether the State's interest in preserving the flag as a symbol of nationhood and national unity justifies Johnson's conviction.

As in *Spence,* "[w]e are confronted with a case of prosecution for the expression of an idea through activity," and "[a]ccordingly, we must examine with particular care the interests advanced by [petitioner] to support its prosecution." 418 U.S., at 411. Johnson was not, we add, prosecuted for the expression of just any idea; he was prosecuted for his expression of dissatisfaction with the policies of this country, expression situated at the core of our First Amendment values. . . .

Moreover, Johnson was prosecuted because he knew that his politically charged expression would cause "serious offense." If he had burned the flag as a means of disposing of it because it was dirty or torn, he would not have been convicted of flag desecration under this Texas law: federal law designates burning as the preferred means of disposing of a flag "when it is in such condition that it is no longer a fitting emblem for display," . . . and Texas has no quarrel with this means of disposal. . . . The Texas law is thus not aimed at protecting the physical integrity of the flag in all circumstances, but is designed instead to protect it only against impairments that would cause serious offense to others.[6] Texas concedes as much: "Section 42.09(b) reaches only those severe acts of physical abuse of the flag carried out in a way likely to be offensive. The statute mandates intentional or knowing abuse, that is, the kind of mistreatment that is not innocent, but rather is intentionally designed to seriously offend other individuals." . . .

Whether Johnson's treatment of the flag violated Texas law thus depended on the likely communicative impact of his expressive conduct.[7] Our decision in *Boos v. Barry* . . . tells us that this restriction on Johnson's expression is content-based. In *Boos,* we considered the constitutionality of a law prohibiting "the display of any sign within 50 feet of a foreign embassy if that sign tends to bring that foreign government into 'public odium' or 'public disrepute.'" . . . Rejecting the argument that the law was content-neutral because it was justified by "our international law obligation to shield diplomats from speech that offends their dignity," . . . we held that a "[t]he emotive impact of speech on its audience is not a 'secondary effect'" unrelated to the content of the expression itself. . . .

According to the principles announced in *Boos,* Johnson's political expression was restricted because of the content of the message he conveyed. We must therefore subject the State's asserted interest in preserving the special symbolic character of the flag to "the most exacting scrutiny."[8] . . .

Texas argues that its interest in preserving the flag as a symbol of nationhood and national unity survives this close analysis. Quoting extensively from the writings of this Court chronicling the flag's historic and symbolic role in our society, the State emphasizes the "'special place'" reserved for the flag in our Nation. . . . The State's argument is not that it has an interest simply in maintaining the flag as a symbol of *something,* no matter what it symbolizes; indeed, if that were the State's position, it would be difficult to see how that interest is endangered by highly symbolic conduct such as Johnson's. Rather, the State's claim is that it has an interest in preserving the flag as a symbol of *nationhood* and *national unity,* a symbol with a determinate range of mean-

ings. . . . According to Texas, if one physically treats the flag in a way that would tend to cast doubt on either the idea that nationhood and national unity are the flag's referents or that national unity actually exists, the message conveyed thereby is a harmful one and therefore may be prohibited.[9]

If there is a bedrock principle underlying the First Amendment, it is that the Government may not prohibit the expression of an idea simply because society finds the idea itself offensive or disagreeable. . . .

We have not recognized an exception to this principle even where our flag has been involved. In *Street v. New York,* . . . we held that a State may not criminally punish a person for uttering words critical of the flag. Rejecting the argument that the conviction could be sustained on the ground that Street had "failed to show the respect for our national symbol which may properly be demanded of every citizen," we concluded that "the constitutionally guaranteed 'freedom to be intellectually . . . diverse or even contrary,' and the 'right to differ as to things that touch the heart of the existing order,' encompass the freedom to express publicly one's opinions about our flag, including those opinions which are defiant or contemptuous." . . . Nor may the Government, we have held, compel conduct that would evince respect for the flag. "To sustain the compulsory flag salute we are required to say that a Bill of Rights which guards the individual's right to speak his own mind, left it open to public authorities to compel him to utter what is not in his mind." . . .

In holding in *Barnette* that the Constitution did not leave this course open to the Government, Justice Jackson described one of our society's defining principles in words deserving of their frequent repetition: "If there is any fixed star in our constitutional constellation, it is that no official, high or petty, can prescribe what shall be orthodox in politics, nationalism, religion, or other matters of opinion or force citizens to confess by word or act their faith therein." . . . In *Spence,* we held that the same interest asserted by Texas here was insufficient to support a criminal conviction under a flag-misuse statute for the taping of a peace sign to an American flag. "Given the protected character of [Spence's] expression and in light of the fact that no interest the State may have in preserving the physical integrity of a privately owned flag was significantly impaired on these facts," we held, "the conviction must be invalidated." . . . See also *Goguen,* . . . (to convict a person who had sewn a flag onto the seat of his pants for "contemptuous" treatment of the flag would be "[t]o convict not to protect the physical integrity or to protect against acts interfering with the proper use of the flag, but to punish for communicating ideas unacceptable to the controlling majority in the legislature").

In short, nothing in our precedents suggests that a State may foster its own view of the flag by prohibiting expressive conduct relating to it.[10] To bring its argument outside our precedents, Texas attempts to convince us that even if its interest in preserving the flag's symbolic role does not allow it to prohibit words or some expressive conduct critical of the flag, it does permit it to forbid the outright destruction of the flag. The State's argument cannot depend here on the distinction between written or spoken words and nonverbal conduct. That distinction, we have shown, is of no moment where the nonverbal conduct is expressive, as it is here, and where the regulation of that conduct is related to expression, as it is here. . . . In addition, both *Barnette* and *Spence* involved expressive conduct, not only verbal communication, and both found that conduct protected.

Texas' focus on the precise nature of Johnson's expression, moreover, misses the point of our prior decisions: their enduring lesson, that the Government may not prohibit expression simply because it disagrees with its message, is not dependent on the particular mode in which one chooses to express an idea.[11] If we were to hold that a State may forbid flag-burning wherever it is likely to endanger the flag's symbolic role, but allow it wherever burning a flag promotes that role—as where, for example, a person ceremoniously burns a dirty flag—we would be saying that when it comes to impairing the flag's physical integrity, the flag itself may be used as a symbol—as a substitute for the written or spoken word or a "short cut from mind to mind"—only in one direction. We would be permitting a State to "prescribe what shall be orthodox" by saying that one may burn the flag to convey one's attitude toward it and its referents only if one does not endanger the flag's representation of nationhood and national unity.

We never before have held that the Government may ensure that a symbol be used to express only one view of that symbol or its referents. Indeed, in *Schacht v. United States,* we invalidated a federal statute permitting an actor portraying a member of one of our armed forces to "'wear the uniform of that armed force if the portrayal does not tend to discredit that armed force.'" . . . This proviso, we held, "which leaves Americans free to praise the war in Vietnam but can send persons like Schacht to prison

for opposing it, cannot survive in a country which has the First Amendment." . . .

We perceive no basis on which to hold that the principle underlying our decision in *Schacht* does not apply to this case. To conclude that the Government may permit designated symbols to be used to communicate only a limited set of messages would be to enter territory having no discernible or defensible boundaries. Could the Government, on this theory, prohibit the burning of state flags? Of copies of the Presidential seal? Of the Constitution? In evaluating these choices under the First Amendment, how would we decide which symbols were sufficiently special to warrant this unique status? To do so, we would be forced to consult our own political preferences, and impose them on the citizenry, in the very way that the First Amendment forbids us to do. . . .

There is, moreover, no indication—either in the text of the Constitution or in our cases interpreting it—that a separate juridical category exists for the American flag alone. Indeed, we would not be surprised to learn that the persons who framed our Constitution and wrote the Amendment that we now construe were not known for their reverence for the Union Jack. The First Amendment does not guarantee that other concepts virtually sacred to our Nation as a whole—such as the principle that discrimination on the basis of race is odious and destructive—will go unquestioned in the marketplace of ideas. . . . We decline, therefore, to create for the flag an exception to the joust of principles protected by the First Amendment.

It is not the State's ends, but its means, to which we object. It cannot be gainsaid that there is a special place reserved for the flag in this Nation, and thus we do not doubt that the Government has a legitimate interest in making efforts to "preserv[e] the national flag as an unalloyed symbol of our country." . . . We reject the suggestion, urged at oral argument by counsel for Johnson, that the Government lacks "any state interest whatsoever" in regulating the manner in which the flag may be displayed. . . . Congress has, for example, enacted precatory regulations describing the proper treatment of the flag, see 36 U.S.C. §§ 173–177, and we cast no doubt on the legitimacy of its interest in making such recommendations. To say that the Government has an interest in encouraging proper treatment of the flag, however, is not to say that it may criminally punish a person for burning a flag as a means of political protest. "National unity as an end which officials may foster by persuasion and example is not in question. The problem is whether under our Constitution compulsion as here employed is a permissible means for its achievement." . . .

We are fortified in today's conclusion by our conviction that forbidding criminal punishment for conduct such as Johnson's will not endanger the special role played by our flag or the feelings it inspires. To paraphrase Justice Holmes, we submit that nobody can suppose that this one gesture of an unknown man will change our Nation's attitude towards its flag. . . . Indeed, Texas' argument that the burning of an American flag "'is an act having a high likelihood to cause a breach of the peace,'" . . . and its statute's implicit assumption that physical mistreatment of the flag will lead to "serious offense," tend to confirm that the flag's special role is not in danger; if it were, no one would riot or take offense because a flag had been burned.

We are tempted to say, in fact, that the flag's deservedly cherished place in our community will be strengthened, not weakened, by our holding today. Our decision is a reaffirmation of the principles of freedom and inclusiveness that the flag best reflects, and of the conviction that our toleration of criticism such as Johnson's is a sign and source of our strength. Indeed, one of the proudest images of our flag, the one immortalized in our own national anthem, is of the bombardment it survived at Fort McHenry. It is the Nation's resilience, not its rigidity, that Texas sees reflected in the flag—and it is that resilience that we reassert today.

The way to preserve the flag's special role is not to punish those who feel differently about these matters. It is to persuade them that they are wrong. "To courageous, self-reliant men, with confidence in the power of free and fearless reasoning applied through the processes of popular government, no danger flowing from speech can be deemed clear and present, unless the incidence of the evil apprehended is so imminent that it may befall before there is opportunity for full discussion. If there be time to expose through discussion the falsehood and fallacies, to avert the evil by the processes of education, the remedy to be applied is more speech, not enforced silence." . . . And, precisely because it is our flag that is involved, one's response to the flag-burner may exploit the uniquely persuasive power of the flag itself. We can imagine no more appropriate response to burning a flag than waving one's own, no better way to counter a flag-burner's message than by saluting the flag that burns, no surer means of preserving the dignity even of the flag that

burned than by—as one witness here did—according its remains a respectful burial. We do not consecrate the flag by punishing its desecration, for in doing so we dilute the freedom that this cherished emblem represents.

V

Johnson was convicted for engaging in expressive conduct. The State's interest in preventing breaches of the peace does not support his conviction because Johnson's conduct did not threaten to disturb the peace. Nor does the State's interest in preserving the flag as a symbol of nationhood and national unity justify his criminal conviction for engaging in political expression. The judgment of the Texas Court of Criminal Appeals is therefore
Affirmed.

CHIEF JUSTICE REHNQUIST, with whom JUSTICE WHITE and JUSTICE O'CONNOR join, dissenting.

In holding this Texas statute unconstitutional, the Court ignores Justice Holmes' familiar aphorism that "a page of history is worth a volume of logic." . . . For more than 200 years, the American flag has occupied a unique position as the symbol of our Nation, a uniqueness that justifies a governmental prohibition against flag burning in the way respondent Johnson did here. . . .

The Court concludes its opinion with a regrettably patronizing civics lecture, presumably addressed to the Members of both Houses of Congress, the members of the 48 state legislatures that enacted prohibitions against flag burning, and the troops fighting under that flag in Vietnam who objected to its being burned: "The way to preserve the flag's special role is not to punish those who feel differently about these matters. It is to persuade them that they are wrong." . . . The Court's role as the final expositor of the Constitution is well established, but its role as a platonic guardian admonishing those responsible to public opinion as if they were truant school children has no similar place in our system of government. The cry of "no taxation without representation" animated those who revolted against the English Crown to found our Nation—the idea that those who submitted to government should have some say as to what kind of laws would be passed. Surely one of the high purposes of a democratic society is to legislate against conduct that is regarded as evil and profoundly offensive to the majority of people—whether it be murder, embezzlement, pollution, or flag burning.

Our Constitution wisely places limits on powers of legislative majorities to act, but the declaration of such limits by this Court "is, at all times, a question of much delicacy, which ought seldom, if ever, to be decided in the affirmative, in a doubtful case." *Fletcher v. Peck,* 6 Cranch 87, 128 (1810) (Marshall, C. J.). Uncritical extension of constitutional protection to the burning of the flag risks the frustration of the very purpose for which organized governments are instituted. The Court decides that the American flag is just another symbol, about which not only must opinions pro and con be tolerated, but for which the most minimal public respect may not be enjoined. The government may conscript men into the Armed Forces where they must fight and perhaps die for the flag, but the government may not prohibit the public burning of the banner under which they fight. I would uphold the Texas statute as applied in this case.[12]

---

1. Tex. Penal Code Ann. § 42.09 (1989) provides in full: "§ 42.09. Desecration of Venerated Object

(a) A person commits an offense if he intentionally or knowingly desecrates:

(1) a public monument;

(2) a place of worship or burial; or

(3) a state or national flag.

(b) For purposes of this section, 'desecrate' means deface, damage, or otherwise physically mistreat in a way that the actor knows will seriously offend one or more persons likely to observe or discover his action.

(c) An offense under this section is a Class A misdemeanor."

2. Because the prosecutor's closing argument observed that Johnson had led the protestors in chants denouncing the flag while it burned, Johnson suggests that he may have been convicted for uttering critical words rather than for burning the flag. Brief for Respondent 33–34. He relies on *Street v. New York,* 394 *U.S.* 576, 578 (1969), in which we reversed a conviction obtained under a New York statute that prohibited publicly defying or casting contempt on the flag "either by words or act" because we were persuaded that the defendant may have been convicted for his words alone. Unlike the law we faced in *Street,* however, the Texas flag-desecration statute does not on its face permit conviction for remarks critical of the flag, as Johnson himself admits. See Brief for Respondent 34. Nor was the jury in this case told that it could convict Johnson of flag desecration if it found only that he had uttered words critical of the flag and its referents.

Johnson emphasizes, though, that the jury was instructed—according to Texas' law of parties—that "'a person is criminally responsible for an offense committed by the conduct of another if acting with intent to promote or assist the commission of the offense, he solicits, encourages, directs, aids, or attempts to aid the other person to commit the offense.'" Brief for Respondent 2, n. 2, quoting 1 Record 49. The State offered this instruction because Johnson's defense was that he was not the person who had burned the flag. Johnson did not object to this instruction at trial, and although he challenged it on direct appeal, he did so only on the ground that there was insufficient evidence to support it. 706 *S. W.* 2d 120, 124 (Tex. App. 1986). It is only in this Court that Johnson has argued that the law-of-parties instruction might have led the jury to convict him for his words alone. Even if we were to find that this argument is properly raised here, however, we would conclude that it has no merit in these circumstances. The instruction would not have permitted a conviction merely for the pejorative nature of Johnson's words, and those words themselves did not encourage the burning of the flag as the instruction seems to require. Given the additional fact that "the bulk of the State's argument was premised on Johnson's culpability as a sole actor," *ibid.,* we find it too unlikely that the jury convicted Johnson on the basis of this alternative theory to consider reversing his conviction on this ground.

3. Although Johnson has raised a facial challenge to Texas' flag-desecration statute, we choose to resolve this case on the basis of his claim that the statute as applied to him violates the First Amendment. Section 42.09 regulates only physical conduct with respect to the flag, not the written or spoken word, and although one violates the statute only if one "knows" that one's physical treatment of the flag "will seriously offend one or more persons likely to observe or discover his action," *Tex. Penal Code Ann.* § 42.09(b) (1989), this fact does not necessarily mean that the statute applies only to expressive conduct protected by the First Amendment. Cf. *Smith v. Goguen,* 415 *U.S.* 566, 588 (1974) (WHITE, J., concurring in judgment) (statute prohibiting "contemptuous" treatment of flag encompasses only expressive conduct). A tired person might, for example, drag a flag through the mud, knowing that this conduct is likely to offend others, and yet have no thought of expressing any idea; neither the language nor the Texas courts' interpretations of the statute precludes the possibility that such a person would be prosecuted for flag desecration. Because the prosecution of a person who had not engaged in expressive conduct would pose a different case, and because we are capable of disposing of this case on narrower grounds, we address only Johnson's claim that § 42.09 as applied to political expression like his violates the First Amendment.

4. Relying on our decision in *Boos v. Barry,* 485 *U.S.* 312 (1988), Johnson argues that this state interest is related to the suppression of free expression within the meaning of *United States v. O'Brien,* 391 *U.S.* 367 (1968). He reasons that the violent reaction to flag-burnings feared by Texas would be the result of the message conveyed by them, and that this fact connects the State's interest to the suppression of expression. Brief for Respondent 12, n. 11. This view has found some favor in the lower courts. See *Monroe v. State Court of Fulton County,* 739 *F. 2d* 568, 574–575 (CA11 1984). Johnson's theory may overread *Boos* insofar as it suggests that a desire to prevent a violent audience reaction is "related to expression" in the same way that a desire to prevent an audience from being offended is "related to expression." Because we find that the State's interest in preventing breaches of the peace is not implicated on these facts, however, we need not venture further into this area.

5. There is, of course, a tension between this argument and the State's claim that one need not actually cause serious offense in order to violate § 42.09. See Brief for Petitioner 44.

6. Cf. *Smith v. Goguen,* 415 *U.S.,* at 590–591 (BLACKMUN, J., dissenting) (emphasizing that lower court appeared to have construed state statute so as to protect physical integrity of the flag in all circumstances); *id.,* at 597–598 (REHNQUIST, J., dissenting) (same).

7. Texas suggests that Johnson's conviction did not depend on the onlookers' reaction to the flag-burning because § 42.09 is violated only when a person physically mistreats the flag in a way that he "knows will seriously offend one or more persons likely to observe or discover his action." Tex. Penal Code Ann. §

42.09(b) *(1969)* (emphasis added). "The 'serious offense' language of the statute," Texas argues, "refers to an individual's intent and to the manner in which the conduct is effectuated, not to the reaction of the crowd." Brief for Petitioner 44. If the statute were aimed only at the actor's intent and not at the communicative impact of his actions, however, there would be little reason for the law to be triggered only when an audience is "likely" to be present. At Johnson's trial, indeed, the State itself seems not to have seen the distinction between knowledge and actual communicative impact that it now stresses; it proved the element of knowledge by offering the testimony of persons who had in fact been seriously offended by Johnson's conduct. *Id.,* at 6–7. In any event, we find the distinction between Texas' statute and one dependent on actual audience reaction too precious to be of constitutional significance. Both kinds of statutes clearly are aimed at protecting onlookers from being offended by the ideas expressed by the prohibited activity.

8. Our inquiry is, of course, bounded by the particular facts of this case and by the statute under which Johnson was convicted. There was no evidence that Johnson himself stole the flag he burned, Tr. of Oral Arg. 17, nor did the prosecution or the arguments urged in support of it depend on the theory that the flag was stolen. *Ibid.* Thus, our analysis does not rely on the way in which the flag was acquired, and nothing in our opinion should be taken to suggest that one is free to steal a flag so long as one later uses it to communicate an idea. We also emphasize that Johnson was prose-cuted only for flag desecration—not for trespass, disorderly conduct, or arson.

9. Texas claims that "Texas is not endorsing, protecting, avowing or prohibiting any particular philosophy." Brief for Petitioner 29. If Texas means to suggest that its asserted interest does not prefer Democrats over Socialists, or Republicans over Democrats, for example, then it is beside the point, for Johnson does not rely on such an argument. He argues instead that the State's desire to maintain the flag as a symbol of nationhood and national unity assumes that there is only one proper view of the flag. Thus, if Texas means to argue that its interest does not prefer any viewpoint over another, it is mistaken; surely one's attitude towards the flag and its referents is a viewpoint.

10. Our decision in *Halter v. Nebraska,* 205 *U.S.* 34 (1907), addressing the validity of a state law prohibiting certain commercial uses of the flag, is not to the contrary. That case was decided "nearly 20 years before the Court concluded that the First Amendment applies to the States by virtue of the Fourteenth Amendment." *Spence v. Washington,* 418 *U.S.* 405, 413, n. 7 (1974). More important, as we continually emphasized in *Halter* itself, that case involved purely commercial rather than political speech. 205 *U.S.,* at 38, 41, 42, 45.

Nor does *San Francisco Arts & Athletics v. Olympic Committee,* 483 *U.S.* 522, 524 (1987), addressing the validity of Congress' decision to "authoriz[e] the United States Olympic Committee to prohibit certain commercial and promotional uses of the word 'Olympic,'" relied upon by the dissent, post, at 9, even begin to tell us whether the Government may criminally punish physical conduct towards the flag engaged in as a means of political protest.

11. The dissent appears to believe that Johnson's conduct may be prohibited and, indeed, criminally sanctioned, because "his act . . . conveyed nothing that could not have been conveyed and was not conveyed just as forcefully in a dozen different ways." *Post,* at 10. Not only does this assertion sit uneasily next to the dissent's quite correct reminder that the flag occupies a unique position in our society—which demonstrates that messages conveyed without use of the flag are not "just as forcefu[l]" as those conveyed with it—but it also ignores the fact that, in *Spence,* supra, we "rejected summarily" this very claim. See 418 *U.S.,* at 411, n. 4.

12. In holding that the Texas statute as applied to Johnson violates the First Amendment, the Court does not consider Johnson's claims that the statute is unconstitutionally vague or overbroad. Brief for Respondent 24–30. I think those claims are without merit. In *New York State Club Assn. v. City of New York,* 487 *U.S.*—,—(1988), we stated that a facial challenge is only proper under the First Amendment when a statute can never be applied in a permissible manner or when, even if it may be validly applied to a particular defendant, it is so broad as to reach the protected speech of third parties. While Tex. Penal Code Ann. § 42.09 (1989) "may not satisfy those intent on finding fault at any cost, [it is] set out in terms that the ordinary person exercising ordinary common sense can sufficiently understand and comply with." *CSC v. Letter Carriers,* 413 *U.S.* 548, 579 (1973). By defining "desecrate" as "deface," "damage" or otherwise "physically mistreat" in a manner that the actor knows will "seriously offend" others, § 42.09 only prohibits flagrant acts of physical abuse and destruction of the flag of the sort at issue here—soaking a flag with lighter fluid and igniting it in public—and not any of the examples of improper flag etiquette cited in Respondent's brief.

CIVIL RIGHTS VERSUS CIVIL LIBERTIES:
The Case of Discriminatory Verbal Harassment*

Thomas C. Grey

The expression of a change of aspect is the expression of a *new* perception and at the same time of the perception's being unchanged.
—Wittgenstein, *Philosophical Investigations*[1]

American liberals believe that both civil liberties and civil rights are harmonious aspects of a basic commitment to human rights. But recently these two clusters of values have seemed increasingly to conflict—as, for example, with the feminist claim that the legal toleration of pornography, long a goal sought by civil libertarians, actually violates civil rights as a form of sex discrimination.

Here I propose an interpretation of the conflict of civil rights and civil liberties in its latest manifestation: the controversy over how to treat discriminatory verbal harassment on American campuses. I was involved with the controversy in a practical way at Stanford, where I helped draft a harassment regulation that was recently adopted by the university.

Like the pornography issue, the harassment problem illustrates the element of paradox in the conflict of civil-liberties and civil-rights perspectives or mentalities. This problem does not simply trigger familiar disagreements between liberals of a classical or libertarian orientation as against those of a welfare state or social democratic one—though it does sometimes do that. In my experience, the issue also has the power to appear to a single person in different shapes and suggest different solutions as it oscillates between being framed in civil-liberties and in civil-rights terms. At the same time, however, it remains recognizably

the same problem. It is thus a very practical and political example of the kind of tension noted by Wittgenstein in the aphorism that heads this essay—a puzzle of interpretive framing, of "seeing-as."

One of my aims in this essay is to bring the reader to share the sense of paradox that, for me, pervades the experience of trying to categorize and resolve the harassment issue. At the outset, let me sketch what I take to be the two main structural features of the clash between the civil-liberties and the civil-rights perspectives that this problem exemplifies.

First, the two approaches take contrasting views of intangible or psychic injury. The civil-liberties mentality, centrally concerned with protecting freedom of expression against censorship, tends to limit the kinds of harms that can justify abridgment of that freedom to traditionally recognized infringements of tangible interests in property and bodily security. In particular, claims that government can interfere with speech to protect sensibilities, emotional tranquility, or self-esteem—in general, *feelings*—are strongly disfavored. It is a "bedrock principle" of civil liberties that censorship is not justified to prevent even what is "deeply offensive to many."[2] The civil-libertarian counsel to fellow citizens is the traditional parental advice to the child wounded by insult or rejection: "Sticks and stones may break my bones, but words will never hurt me"—not hurt *enough,* that is, to justify the known costs of censorship.

By contrast, the civil-rights approach, with its roots in anti-discrimination law and social policy, is centrally concerned with injuries of stigma and

*[Thomas C. Grey expresses] thanks for excellent research assistance . . . to William Boyle, Jay Fowler, and John Tweedy. And [he is] also grateful for the editorial suggestions of Barbara Babcock, Barbara Fried, Mark Kelman, Richard Posner, Robert Rabin, Carol Rose, James Weinstein, Steven Shiffrin, and Steven Winter; of those who attended [the] faculty workshop at Boalt Hall, University of California, Berkeley; and of Ellen Paul and the other editors of *Social Philosophy & Policy*. Finally, special thanks, for inspiration, to Charles Lawrence III. From Grey, Thomas, "Civil Rights and Civil Liberties: The Case of Discriminatory Verbal Harassment," in *Social Philosophy and Policy* (1991). Reprinted by permission of Blackwell Publishers.

humiliation to those who are the victims of discrimination—conduct generating "feelings of inferiority"
that damage "hearts and minds," in the language of
the most famous American civil rights case.[3] The
point is not so much to protect a sphere of autonomy
or personal security from *intrusion* as to protect potentially marginal members of the community from
exclusion—from relegation, that is, to the status of
second-class citizens.

The second contrast is a related one: it comes
in the treatment of the public-private distinction. The
active state is traditionally conceived as the sole or
dominant threat to civil liberties. Civil libertarians do
not spend much of their time or energy seeking
ways to positively empower dissenters, deviants, and
nonconformists against the pressures brought on
them by unorganized public opinion, or by private
employers or landlords. The catalogue of civil liberties is certainly what Judge Richard Posner has called
the Constitution: "a charter of negative rather than
positive liberties."[4]

"But [to continue with the same quotation
from Judge Posner] where the liberty asserted is the
right to equal treatment irrespective of race or sex,
the analysis is more complex."[5] Under the civil-rights
perspective, defense of basic human rights is by no
means simply a matter of limiting state power. Government may deny equal protection by omission as
well as by action—for example, by refusing law enforcement protection to minorities. The tendency of
the civil-rights mentality is to favor the prohibition
of all invidious treatment that has the effect of "implying inferiority in civil society" to individuals on
the basis of their membership in identifiable social
groups.[6] This "anti-discrimination principle" goes
beyond cleansing government action of bias; it also
attacks discrimination on the suspect bases of race,
sex, and so on, in the other major institutions of civil
society. Thus the identification of a new form of invidious discrimination today typically brings with it
pressure for legislation against private as well as official discrimination of that kind in housing, employment, and education.[7]

When the conflict of civil-liberties and civil-
rights perspectives is described in terms of the structural features just sketched, it resonates with a
number of the binary oppositions of social philosophy: liberty against equality; liberty against democracy; individualism against collectivism; the methods
of economics and rational choice theory against those
of sociology and cultural anthropology. Though I
hope what I have to say here may intrigue those in-

terested in the practical implications of the standard
theoretical dichotomies, I do not analyze the harassment issue in these terms.

This is partly to avoid one of the temptations
of classic social philosophy, the urge to make it as
nearly as possible like geometry or physics. One
seeks, using this paradigm, to formulate contending
theoretical positions as models, stated as broadly
and at the same time as rigorously as possible.
Adopting this approach, one then sees an actual
controversy that brings these oppositions into play
as simply a manifestation of underlying theoretical
contradictions. The practical issue serves the purpose of forcing choice between the theories, just as
crucial experiments are supposed to force choice between rival scientific hypotheses. On the harassment
issue, the structural conflict between civil-liberties
and civil-rights approaches then naturally appears as
the vivid illustration of a contradiction between, for
example, opposed libertarian and egalitarian theories of liberalism. Intellectual rigor and respect for
consistency would then require forthright resolution
of the contradiction, most readily achieved by rejecting one of the conflicting alternatives.

This seems to me the wrong way to deal with
the harassment problem; indeed, it generally seems
the wrong way to deal with most theoretical disagreements as they bear on social, political, and legal
questions. Rarely can important theories in these
areas be plausibly formulated as models or axiom-
systems precise enough to give rise to "contradictions." Much more often the actual working theories
are perspectives, approaches, or mentalities constituted of more or less vague (but never completely
open-ended) clusters of goals, ideals, guidelines, and
presumptions. When theories this imprecise clash,
no principle of logic requires rejection of either one.

Methods of social philosophy that seek to formulate theories with maximum precision do so with
an eye to determinacy—they seek theories that can
actually *compel* results where they apply. Theories
that conflict over a practical issue then compel conflicting results; when a contradiction arises, one theory must be chosen to the exclusion of the other. Yet
in problematic practical situations, each of the conflicting theories (perspectives, approaches, mentalities) may have something valuable and even
essential to contribute to a resolution. In such situations, oversharpened theories tend to produce incomplete and one-sided outcomes, whereas a
pragmatist tolerance of theoretical ambiguity and imprecision can conduce to better results.

Such a situation is, it seems to me, presented by the issue of discriminatory harassment. This problem exemplifies something liberal pragmatists should accept as normal—a conflict between plural, sometimes incommensurable, structured clusters of values and principles, here the familiar ones surrounding the terms "civil liberties" and "civil rights." Where these conflicting approaches overlap, as they inevitably will, liberal democrats can identify a range of mediating solutions that respect the claims of both conflicting approaches. I offer the Stanford provision on discriminatory verbal harassment as an example of such a solution. But first I should more fully describe the practical issue and the opposed civil-rights and civil-liberties approaches to it.

I

There has recently been an upsurge in the number and intensity of reported incidents of racist, homophobic, and sexist abuse in American universities.[8] An extreme example was the incident reported at the University of Wisconsin in which white students followed a black woman student across campus shouting "We've never tried a nigger."[9] Perhaps less unequivocal in its implications was this exchange at Stanford: after a dormitory argument in which a black student had claimed that Ludwig van Beethoven was a mulatto and other students had objected to placing such stress on racial origins, two white students defaced a picture of the composer into a blackface caricature and posted it near the black student's room.[10] The question is: what disciplinary action (if any) is appropriate in such cases? A pure civil-rights approach treats the conduct in question as discriminatory harassment. Then principles of equal treatment not only entitle but *require* universities to punish the behavior, at least if it becomes sufficiently widespread to create a pervasively hostile environment. The analogy is to employers' obligations to deal with racial or sexual harassment by fellow employees in the workplace. When black or female employees must endure a barrage of race-or sex-based insults from co-workers, an employer who ignores the situation may be guilty of unlawful (and if a public employer, unconstitutional) race or sex discrimination.[11] Again I quote Judge Posner, certainly no civil-rights extremist:

> By taking no steps to prevent sexual harassment, the city created a worse working envi-

ronment for women than for men. . . . That is discrimination. . . . It is as if the city decided to provide restrooms for male but not female employees, and when pressed for a reason said it simply didn't care whether its female employees were comfortable or not.[12]

In the case in question, the sexual harassment included some physical contact and coercive sexual proposals by supervisors, as well as sexist obscenities and epithets from fellow workers. In discriminatory harassment cases, however, courts have not sharply differentiated between action and verbal abuse in evaluating claims by black or female employees. Typically, action and speech are blended together in a course of conduct that gives rise to liability for the employer when it creates an intolerably "hostile environment" for women or racial minority employees. In some cases, which the courts have not singled out for special treatment on this ground, harassment is found from speech alone—typically a stream of racist or sexist jokes, pictures, and epithets. To avoid liability, the employer must take reasonable steps to keep verbal as well as physical or otherwise coercive abuse below the level of a "sustained pattern of harassment."[13] The decisive question is not whether the harassment constitutes speech or action, but whether it is widespread and serious enough to go beyond what the courts judge must be tolerated as part of life's ordinary rough and tumble.

A civil rights approach to the verbal abuse problem on campus simply applies the doctrine of hostile environment discrimination to the university. Most educators, like most employers, are required by law (as they should feel required by fairness) to provide equal opportunity to women and students of color. Campus harassment can make the educational environment hostile, just as workplace harassment makes the employment environment so. Many campuses have already recognized this with respect to sexual harassment and have adopted disciplinary restrictions accordingly. There is no good reason why racial or anti-homosexual harassment should not be treated in the same way. As a legal matter, an unremedied "sustained pattern of harassment" might make the university itself guilty of unlawful discrimination.[14] Prudent and sensitive administrators will prohibit acts of harassment before the point at which the conduct cumulates into a sustained pattern and thus creates a legally actionable hostile environment.

An analysis like this can easily lead to a prohibition defined purely in terms of civil rights. Thus the University of Michigan, faced with an upsurge in racial harassment, enacted a prohibition against any "behavior, verbal or physical" that "stigmatizes or victimizes" an individual on the basis of race, sex, or other characteristics protected under the university's nondiscrimination policy and that has the "reasonably foreseeable effect of interfering with an individual's academic efforts," or "[c]reates an intimidating, hostile or demeaning environment for educational pursuits." This is a prohibition drafted to track the form of injury dealt with by the civil-rights approach—conduct contributing to a hostile environment that denies equal educational opportunity.[15]

And yet, in the first major case involving the regulation of campus verbal harassment, a federal district court struck this provision down on First Amendment grounds.[16] Civil libertarians applauded the opinion; they qualified their applause at the result only because the case seemed so easy that it did not establish a particularly powerful precedent for other cases of regulation of campus harassment. And an easy case it was—as soon as it was considered from the angle of a civil-liberties, rather than a civil-rights, approach.

Viewed through a First Amendment lens, the Michigan regulation—now seen as a "hate speech" or "group defamation" rule rather than a harassment prohibition—was a dramatically overbroad incursion into core areas of protected speech. Consider just one example of the kind of speech prohibited by the regulation, taken from the guidelines the university distributed to student to explain the new policy:

> A male student makes remarks in class like "Women just aren't as good in this field as men," thus creating a hostile learning atmosphere for female classmates.[17]

From this one can readily extrapolate to other statements (made in class or in a dorm hallway debate) that would violate the standard: arguing on the basis of IQ data that blacks are less intelligent than whites; that homosexuality is "unnatural," or is a disease; that women are naturally less creative than men.[18] The expression of these opinions is certainly experienced as "stigmatizing" and "demeaning" by many, probably most, students belonging to the groups thus insulted; when cumulated to create a climate of opinion, comments like these might well foreseeably "interfere with the academic efforts" of the students whose basic humanity or equal mental capacity they deny.

Because the Michigan regulation has been so universally condemned, it is important to understand how campus authorities might have drafted and enforced it the way they did. They evidently viewed the problem of verbal harassment from one perspective only: the perspective of civil rights. Viewed solely through the lens provided by anti-discrimination law and policy, the kind of statements to which the regulation was applied might well appear as more polite but no less demeaning versions of the kind of racist, sexist, or homophobic insults routinely prohibited under anti-harassment codes in the employment area.

Indeed, the very "politeness" of these statements might rationally be thought to make them *more* disabling to the educational performance of those exposed to them than are the relatively rare incidents involving gutter epithets. At most universities, the victims of the crudest insults can partly discount them because they clearly transgress the dominant mores. By contrast, the more academically respectable forms of denigration of blacks, women, and gays can be supported by evidence and argument, the forms of discourse with maximum credibility in the university. And the damage such statements do is probably enhanced when the stereotypes they reinforce deny the ability of groups of students to study and learn whose members already feel marginal on many campuses. The discourse of "statistics show . . ." and "environmental factors cannot fully explain . . ." may much more effectively create a hostile educational environment than "[Epithet] go home!"

But as soon as a civil-liberties perspective is brought to bear, the kind of speech reached by the Michigan regulation is readily seen as close to the core of the First Amendment. The record in the federal court challenge to the regulation, with a large number of complaints processed, and many resolved informally to require apology (and, in some cases, what looks suspiciously like University of Beijing-style "re-education")[19] in response to speech expressing views on issues of public and campus concern, did indeed present an easy case. If questions that go to the core of human rights and social policy issues cannot be freely debated on campuses, what issues can?

The regulation established a general, content-based regime of censorship of politically and socially controversial speech, with speech concerning issues of race, gender, and sexual orientation subject to special restriction. Worse, within that content-defined field of regulation, the censorship regime imposed a viewpoint-specific orthodoxy: students were allowed to state radical or liberal, but not conservative or reactionary, views on controverted issues. They could say that the mental abilities of blacks were equal to or greater than those of whites, but not lesser; that homosexuality was a culturally formed category of sexual preference or a natural inclination, but not a disease or a sin; that women's genetic endowments made them equal or superior to men in socially valued activities, but not inferior.[20]

Viewed from the civil-liberties perspective, regulations such as these are highly suspect because they are aimed squarely at the content of speech rather than at its incidental injurious consequences. Under current First Amendment doctrine, no restriction focused on the communicative impact of speech is permissible unless it is necessary to prevent serious and imminent harm; the harm in question cannot be simply offense, however strong and justified, at what is said. Finally, any restriction within these narrow confines must be "viewpoint neutral."

The underlying idea is that there must be no ideological censorship—no official regime of screening utterances for the political, moral, or social acceptability of the message they deliver.[21] "The First Amendment recognizes no such thing as a 'false' idea."[22] The idea behind this slogan need not be a paralyzed relativism. It can be a historically-founded liberal suspicion that officials are peculiarly unlikely to accurately distinguish falsity from truth under a regime of censorship, as expressed in Justice Jackson's classic *Barnette* opinion:

> If there is any star fixed in our constitutional constellation, it is that no official, high or petty, can prescribe what shall be orthodox in politics, nationalism, religion, or other matters of opinion . . .[23]

Or it can be a republican faith in the citizenry's ability to respond to bad speech with better speech, as in Justice Brandeis's equally classic *Whitney* opinion:

> Fear or serious injury alone cannot justify suppression of free speech. . . . Those who won our independence by revolution were not cowards. . . . If there be time to expose through discussion the falsehood and fallacies, to avert the evil by the processes of education, the remedy to be applied is more speech, not enforced silence.[24]

The civil-liberties analytical framework tends to confine regulation of campus verbal harassment to prohibiting conduct verging on assault, including perhaps tortious "intentional infliction of emotional distress" and certain face-to-face insults that are especially likely to provoke immediate violence—so-called "fighting words." Further, the civil-liberties framework requires that any speech regulations must be evenhanded; universities may not single out ideologically defined classes of provocations or verbal assaults for prohibition. This, let it be said, is the moderate civil-libertarian position. Civil-liberties purists find even the "emotional distress" and "fighting words" theories insufficiently content-neutral and so oppose *any* disciplinary measures against verbal harassment whatever—even in the extreme Wisconsin example I mentioned above.[25]

For some, of course, the civil-rights and civil-liberties approaches are not "perspectives" on this problem; rather, one or the other of these approaches simply states the reality of the situation. Thus on the civil-rights side, many students at Stanford were sincerely shocked when free speech concerns led university authorities not to prosecute the Beethoven poster episode at Stanford that I described above. A number of them described this as an instance of taking something that was clearly one thing—a racist atrocity, which if left unpunished established an officially condoned practice of discrimination—and "turning it into" a civil-liberties issue. Later in the year, when members of a left-activist student coalition seized (forcibly, but without causing personal injury or property damage) the office of the president of the university, they cited the Beethoven incident as one of their main grievances; when they were charged (and ultimately found guilty) under the university disciplinary code for the takeover, they said it was an irony that their "peaceful protest" had been punished while this clear incident of racist persecution had been treated as protected free speech.

On the other side, many civil libertarians simply do not see the problem as involving issues of civil rights or discrimination at all. It is *not* a clash of equal protection and free speech, they insist, but a pure civil liberties issue, in which fragile free speech values are threatened by powerful political pressure groups on liberal campuses. For these civil libertarians, protecting discriminatory verbal harassment is no different from protecting flag-burning; it represents the principled defense of reason against the perennial collective emotional impulse to censor, rather than answer, the speech of unpopular and often unpleasant dissenters.[26]

My own view is that there are plenty of good reasons, and plenty of worthy passions, on both sides of the issue. And they seem to me really to be *sides*—mutually incommensurable perspectives—rather than the poles of a well-defined continuum along which negotiators may approach each other in search of a solution that measurably splits the difference between them.[27] The epigraph to this essay occurs in the course of Wittgenstein's famous discussion of the ambiguous "duck-rabbit" drawing, which can appear as either a duck or a rabbit, depending on how you look at it.[28] You can learn facility at shifting between seeing the figure as a duck and seeing it as a rabbit, but at any moment it appears only in one aspect or the other. The campus harassment issue has something of the same quality.

II

Let me now describe the proposal I originally drafted, which was recently adopted as a disciplinary rule covering discriminatory verbal harassment at Stanford.[29] The provision is an attempt to accommodate competing values, to mediate the incommensurable conflict of civil-liberties and civil-rights approaches on this issue. I am not confident that it is better than other mediating solutions, though I can give a reason for the choice of each of its elements. But I do believe that some such accommodating solution, as against a "principled" choice implementing one approach to the exclusion of the other, is needed.[30]

The first section of the provision restates Stanford's policy on free expression, including an insistence that students must learn to "tolerate even expression of opinions which they find abhorrent." Counterposed is a second section restating the university's existing policy against discrimination "in the administration of its educational policies" on the basis of "sex, race, color, handicap, religion, sexual orientation, or national and ethnic origin," and adding that harassment on the basis of these characteristics can, when cumulated, constitute hostile environment discrimination under the policy. The third section notes that the free expression and anti-discrimination policies conflict on the issue of verbal harassment; it provides that "protected free expression ends and prohibited discriminatory harassment begins" at the point where expression of opinion becomes "personal vilification"

of a student on the basis of one of the characteristics stated in the anti-discrimination policy.

The operative part of the provision comes in the fourth and last section, which defines "personal vilification" as speech or other symbolic expression that (a) is intended to insult or stigmatize individuals on the basis of one of the designated characteristics; (b) is "addressed directly" to those insulted or stigmatized; and (c) makes use of "insulting or 'fighting' words," defined (quoting from *Chaplinsky v. New Hampshire*[31]) as words (or non-verbal symbols) that "by their very utterance inflict injury or tend to incite to an immediate breach of the peace."

Finally, the proposal adds a narrowing proviso designed to adapt the *Chaplinsky* insulting-or-fighting words concept to civil-rights enforcement. In the context of discriminatory harassment, punishable words (or symbols) are defined as those "commonly understood to convey direct and visceral hatred or contempt for human beings on the basis of" the characteristics specified in the anti-discrimination policy—a phrase meant to capture the sense of the common expression "racial epithets" and to extend it to other prohibited forms of discrimination.

To summarize, the rule would punish speech directed to individuals: speech meant to insult them on the basis of a protected characteristic that also makes use of one of the gutter epithets of bigotry. It thus adopts one element of what I have called the "moderate civil libertarian" view of harassment regulation; it prohibits only expression that falls roughly within the categories of fighting words or intentional infliction of emotional distress doctrines. The provision therefore only prohibits a very narrow category of expression, immunizing even the vilest hate speech addressed generally to a campus audience as well as many serious face-to-face discriminatory verbal assaults. Many students of color and other civil-rights advocates at Stanford have opposed it, for these reasons, as too weak an anti-discrimination measure.

At the same time, narrow as it is, the proposal retains enough of the civil-rights approach to trouble most civil libertarians. It seems to violate the second central civil-liberties tenet: not only can speech be regulated only to the minimum extent necessary to prevent immediate and otherwise unremediable harm; further, any speech regulation must be *neutral*—generally neutral as to content, certainly neutral as to viewpoint. The provision's apparent violation of the neutrality constraint results directly from its being framed as civil-rights protection or anti-discrimination measure.

To bring out the neutrality problem, I need to describe more fully the legal underpinnings of the proposal. It does not precisely track either of the most common bases for narrow discriminatory harassment regulations: the "fighting words" or "intentional infliction of emotional distress" rationales, which have been adopted at other universities in the wake of the Michigan case.[32] Rather, it draws on the relevant common elements in those two theories, adapting them to the context of a civil-rights–based campus harassment regulation.

In the *Chaplinsky* case, a unanimous Supreme Court excluded from First Amendment protection "insulting or 'fighting' words," those which "by their very utterance inflict injury" *or* that "tend to incite an immediate breach of the peace." Subsequent cases have focused on the "breach of the peace" half of the category, and the Court has made clear that its reach is narrow indeed; it has never affirmed a conviction under the doctrine since *Chaplinsky* itself in 1942.[33] During those years, the Court has also developed the "heckler's veto" doctrine as a counterweight to its "fighting words" proviso, putting the burden on law enforcement to protect speakers against threatened violence, rather than avoiding the violence by silencing the speaker.[34]

The heckler's veto analysis brings out the weakness in the "fighting words" doctrine as it was traditionally formulated. The concept seems to ask purely factual and predictive questions. Can imminent violence be expected from an audience? Are available law enforcement resources insufficient to protect the speaker? As many civil libertarians have argued, however, it seems inconsistent with free speech values to punish a speaker simply because the heckler's veto is made effective—because, that is, a sufficient number of thugs have plausibly threatened violence and available police protection is inadequate. A serious civil-libertarian presumption in favor of free speech seems to require some evaluation of what the speaker has said—are they really "*fighting* words"?—before silencing the speaker in the face of a hostile audience can be said to be a proper response.

The same requirement of normative evaluation of the speech must also apply, it seems, in the case of intentional infliction of emotional distress. And here, indeed, the evaluative element is explicitly built into the standard common law elements of the tort. The victim must foreseeably suffer severe emotional distress from what the defendant does or says, but this is not sufficient. In addition, the defendant's conduct must be, as Section 46 or the Torts

Restatement puts it, in unmistakably evaluative terms, "beyond all possible bounds of decency" and "regarded as atrocious and utterly intolerable in a civilized community"—in short, "outrageous."[35]

I suggest that we interpret the *Chaplinsky* category of "insulting or 'fighting' words" as designating utterances that at least meet the standard set by Restatement Section 46. For free speech purposes, though, the Section 46 standard is *too* purely evaluative—too vague.[36] But if the vagueness problem can be met (by delineating a category of utterances that *are* "outrageous" and are given further and more objective definition), then it would be reasonable—under *Chaplinsky*—to treat those utterances as subject to prohibition because they are likely *either* to provoke violence or to cause severe emotional distress.

The Stanford provision thus interprets *Chaplinsky*'s dual formulation to suggest a category of speech, objectively "insulting" in character, that attacks the very identity of its victim in such a way as to stimulate the familiar "fight or flight reaction." Among certain classes of hearers, particularly young males socialized to be physically aggressive, the typical reaction to a vile personal insult may be "fight." For others—many men; perhaps most children, most older people, most women; invalids—the typical reaction to this kind of verbal assault is some combination of extreme fear, numbness, and impotent rage: reactions calculated to produce the sort of "severe emotional distress" to which the Restatement of Torts makes reference. We should read *Chaplinsky,* in my view, to have identified two distinct kinds of reactions (fight or flight) to the same category of intolerable speech when it speaks, respectively, of utterances that "tend to incite an immediate breach of the peace" and those that "by their very utterance inflict injury."

The Stanford provision identifies discriminatory "personal vilification" as a class of utterances of which any instance is particularly likely to produce one or the other of the kinds of injury covered by the "fighting words" and "emotional distress" analysis. These are, in Richard Delgado's phrase, "words that wound"—utterances directed to members of groups specially subject to discrimination, intended to insult or stigmatize them, and making use of the small class of commonly recognized words or symbols that have no other function but to convey hatred and contempt for these groups.[37]

Professor Delgado offers as the test for liability under his proposal the requirement that the words directed to the victim be such as "a reasonable person would recognize as a racial insult." In a campus context, where claims of insult and ideological debate are often intertwined, this phrasing raises special, and I think avoidable, civil-liberties problems. Some ideas might be taken as racial or ethnic insults by virtue of their content alone: for example, claims that the Holocaust never happened, or that blacks are genetically inferior to whites. To avoid banning ideas as such on the basis of propositional content, on campus or elsewhere, the Stanford regulation prohibits only verbal abuse including actual racial epithets, or their equivalents for other forms of discrimination.[38] These are the all-too-familiar words that carry with them so inseparable a message of hatred and contempt that apologies are in order for the affront involved in even quoting them: "nigger," "kike," "faggot," "cunt," and the like.[39]

Racial and other discriminatory hatred and contempt can be effectively expressed without using these words, of course, but (partly in the interests of avoiding vagueness and its chilling effect) such cases are not included under the regulation. A white student can tell a black student, face-to-face, "you people are inferior and should not be here," but not be guilty of harassment. In addition, even gutter epithets are immunized when uttered to the campus or public at large, in order to give the widest possible leeway for speech in the public forum; the Klan or the neo-Nazis may demonstrate and display their symbols and shout their words of hatred with impunity. This very much narrows the reach of the proposal and exposes it to the charge, mentioned before, that it is mere tokenism. But at the same time, it helps meet traditional and legitimate civil-liberties concerns about public political expression, and about vagueness and its accompanying chilling effect.[40]

The Stanford provision has also been drafted with an eye on another concern—one rooted in the civil-rights perspective, and often noted as well in civil-libertarian objections to "hate speech" or "group defamation" regulations.[41] The concern is illustrated by one of the cases that occurred under the Michigan regulation. A black woman law student, in the course of a heated argument, called a classmate "white trash." She was charged with a violation of the harassment rule; she ultimately agreed to write a formal letter of apology to the classmate in settlement of the charge.

Under the Stanford provision, calling a white student "white trash" would not constitute harassment. In its commonly understood meaning, the term is (like "redneck") derogatory to the poor whites of

the rural South by virtue of their class, not their race.[42] If the student addressed came from that social background, and if class bias were a form of discrimination covered by the proposal (as it is not), there might be a disciplinary case. But as a white person, she is not a victim of discriminatory *racial* harassment; the term "white trash" is clearly not "commonly understood" to convey hatred or contempt for whites on the basis of their race as such—a requirement for liability under the provision. This is not to deny that the black woman student intended to express race-based hatred or contempt, or that she may have effectively conveyed a racial insult, just as a white student does who tells a black student that "you people are inferior and shouldn't be here." In neither case, though, is the regulation violated, because in neither case is there use of one of the required "commonly understood" assaultive epithets or symbols of discriminatory contempt.

The point of the "white trash" case can be generalized, and in a way that is most troubling to civil-libertarian defenders of viewpoint neutrality. As best I can see, there are *no* epithets in this society at this time that are "commonly understood" to convey hatred and contempt for whites *as such*. The same can be said, I believe, of males as such, and heterosexuals as such.[43] If this is indeed a sociolinguistic fact, it is of course one not fixed in stone; on the other hand, it is no accident. The denigrating epithets covered by the Stanford provision are able to inflict the serious and distinctive injuries characteristic of legally prohibited invidious discrimination because they strike at groups subjected to long-standing and deep-rooted prejudices widely held and disseminated throughout our culture. American children grow up with the negative stereotypes of blacks, women, and homosexuals in their bones and in their souls. This is tragically true, too, of children who are black, female, or later identify themselves as homosexual.

The denigrating epithets draw their capacity to impose the characteristic civil-rights injury to "hearts and minds" from the fact that they turn the whole socially and historically inculcated weight of these prejudices upon their victim. Each hatemonger who invokes one of these terms summons a vicious chorus in his support. It is because, given our cultural history, no such *general* prejudices strike against the dominant groups that there exist no comparable terms of universally understood hatred and contempt applicable to whites, males, and heterosexuals as such.[44]

III

The Stanford provision, then, while neutral on its face, will foreseeably be asymmetric in its application. This aspect of the provision allows its interpretation to reflect a state of affairs central to civil-rights analysis—the continued existence of asymmetric social relations of group domination and subjugation in the United States. Contrary to the democratic ideal, American society (like other societies) is still characterized by a hierarchy of relatively stable ascriptive status groups. To rephrase the point from the jargon of sociology to the rhetoric of movement politics, there still exist "oppressor" and "oppressed" (or, to lower the political pitch, "privileged" and "subordinated") groups, identified as such by characteristics such as race, gender, class, and sexual preference. Indeed, the civil-rights project can best be understood as at once premised on the existence of these groups' asymmetric power relations and aimed at the ultimate elimination of the asymmetries. (To describe it thus is not to decide in advance the debatable question of affirmative action—the question of whether symmetric or asymmetric policies are best suited to attain the goal.)

Given its narrow coverage, the Stanford provision obviously does not embody a particularly radical or utopian civil-rights approach. Its categories and its thrust largely reflect a civil-liberties perspective on the racial harassment problem. The exclusive remedy it contemplates for all but a tiny fraction of discriminatory speech is the one civil libertarians favor: more speech. But the features it adopts from a civil-rights approach still jar most civil libertarians; indeed, they jar me when I look at the problem through a civil-liberties lens. First, the provision lacks content-neutrality; it regulates only speech bearing on matters of race, gender, sexual orientation, and the like while neglecting other speech that might similarly provoke violence or cause similarly severe emotional distress. Second, and even more troubling, the rule bears asymmetrically on its restricted subject matter in a way that, to some, will seem inconsistent with viewpoint-neutrality.

That is, it may seem biased against the disfavored ideologies of racism, sexism, and homophobia, openly favoring "politically correct" egalitarians against their adversaries in the campus marketplace of opinion. It arguably takes from the bigots emotively powerful rhetorical weapons—the traditional hate epithets—without imposing comparable restrictions on the other side. It is as if terms like "commie" and "pinko" were barred from political debate, while "imperialist lackey" and "capitalist running dog" were allowed. This seems to violate official neutrality: the principle of "no orthodoxy in matters of opinion," "no such thing as a false idea."

This civil-libertarian objection helps bring out the deep structure of the conflict between the two approaches. From the civil rights perspective, there *are* false ideas and ideologies, among which white supremacy and related forms of bigotry are the paradigm examples. The insult and stigma involved in the imposition of supremacist ideologies on those whom they oppress and exclude from full citizenship attacks what John Rawls has called the most fundamental of those "primary goods" that government is established to allow individuals to pursue—those that form the basis of self-respect.[45] The protection of the basis of the individual's capacity for self-respect against violation by socially authoritative humiliation is as much at the heart of equal protection as is official viewpoint-neutrality in regulating the marketplace of ideas that is at the heart of free expression.

The analysis of the civil-rights approach in terms of preventing exclusion by the social imposition of caste-based stigma supplies the standard rationale for the central doctrine of modern anti-discrimination law: the rejection of the "separate but equal" version of Jim Crow.[46] The doctrinal problem was this: A state supplies equal (but separate) facilities to whites and blacks—schools, public parks, beaches, buses, amenities in public buildings, etc. How does this equality-preserving separation of the races violate the Constitution's prohibition of racially *unequal* treatment? The *Brown* line of cases answers that the inequality inheres in the subordinating character of the *message* delivered by the separation—the material state action, separate but equal segregation, viewed in isolation from its communicative impact, fully preserves equality. *Plessy* had said that if black people felt insulted by the separation, that was only their interpretation; *Brown* finally (and realistically) accepted that the insulting interpretation was the only plausible one.[47]

But the *Plessy* formula is a quite appropriate response to a complaint of discriminatory segregation in some social contents. Separation sometimes stigmatizes no one. The maintenance of separate men's and women's restrooms in public buildings, for example, does not by itself constitute invidious sex discrimination. But in the context of this society and its history, the Jim Crow variety of racial segregation imposed inequality because it rested on the assumption, and hence delivered the message, that whites were a superior caste to be protected from the polluting contact of their black inferiors. The insulting message, the wound inflicted by the authoritative endorsement of the "false idea" of white supremacy and black unworthiness, was what made Jim Crow unconstitutional.[48]

Essentially the same wound is the injury inflicted on minority, female, and gay students or employees when endemic verbal abuse renders educational or work environment discriminatorily "hostile" within the terms of discrimination law. In this sense, the focus on symbolic injury to the "hearts and minds" of black children in the desegregation cases supplies the basic authority for campus verbal harassment regulation; *Brown,* as Charles Lawrence strikingly argues, "may be read as regulating the content of racist speech."[49]

The civil-libertarian, dedicated to a principle of liberal official neutrality in the marketplace of ideas, sees this as a perverse misstatement of *Brown.* It ignores two crucial distinctions, the argument runs: speech vs. action, and public vs. private.[50] First, the civil-libertarian insists that the *practice* of white (or male, or heterosexual) supremacy must be kept distinct from its *preaching;* while the former violates the anti-discrimination principle, the latter is protected by the principle of free expression. Questions of the boundary between speech and action may present difficulty, but the structure is clear.

The point is quite general: the Constitution certainly requires the *practice* of republican government, due process, and non-establishment of religion, as well as non-discrimination. But equally central is the principle of free expression, which includes the freedom to *preach* dictatorship, summary justice, theocracy—or even universal censorship. And so, the argument continues, the same principle guarantees freedom to advocate racist and other inegalitarian doctrines—as, indeed, many First Amendment decisions firmly establish.[51]

Second, the argument continues, the invocation of *Brown* to support the suppression of racist speech ignores the public-private distinction, which is essential to the maintenance not only of free speech but also of such other civil liberties as freedom of religion. If *Brown* does perhaps strike at certain "speech" (more precisely, at the communicative element in certain actions), it is only at *official* speech, which has never been thought protected by a principle of free expression. What the First Amendment protects is the right of *private* individuals to deliver those same messages.

While the equal protection clause might, for example, prohibit a legislature from placing a white supremacist slogan on a state's seal, flag, public buildings, and the like, the First Amendment just as firmly protects the freedom of private individuals to put that slogan into free competition against more egalitarian ones in the marketplace of ideas. Not only the flag, but also a copy of the *Brown* decision, or a picture of Martin Luther King, can be defaced in public with impunity under the First Amendment—though of course, as the civil-libertarian usually adds, government officials should denounce such racist outrages, just as university authorities should denounce racist speech on campus while resolutely protecting it against coercive interference.

When we turn to look at the world through the civil-rights lens, though, we find much less clarity in the public-private distinction.[52] The civil-rights approach seeks to cleanse not only the state but civil society generally of racist and other bigoted practices. The formal constitutional expression of the public-private distinction, the state action doctrine, tends to break down in the area of discrimination law. Nothing approaching a clear line separates (prohibited) official encouragement or support of private discrimination on the one hand from (permissible) neutral toleration on the other. Judge Posner's words quoted earlier from the hostile environment discrimination case help make the point: states often deny the equal protection of the laws not by acting, but by omitting to act against private discriminatory action within such areas of responsibility as a government workplace. The point becomes more forceful as, with the growth of the modern welfare and regulatory state, government's sphere of activity broadens, and increased supervision of areas of private conduct brings with it more responsibility for that conduct.[53]

Further, when we look beyond formal constitutional doctrine, we find that our actual civil-rights practices place little weight on the public-private distinction. The social condemnation of a form of discrimination as invidious brings it within the anti-discrimination principle. This principle typically leads both to judicial prohibition of the official forms of prejudice and legislative prohibition where it appears "privately" in employment, housing, education, and public accommodations. By contrast, our civil-liberties practices exhibit no parallel tendency toward legislative protection of Nazis, Klansmen, and flag-burners against private discrimination. "Tolerance," a civil-rights word, and "toleration," a civil-liberties word, name quite different values.

And as I have already stressed, the civil-rights approach likewise does not sharply distinguish between speech and action. "Sticks and stones may break my bones, but words will never hurt me"—which expresses in homely form the First Amendment's Brandeisian ideal of self-reliant civic courage[54]—does not apply within a framework of analysis in which the central injury to be avoided is stigma and humiliation—injury to a socially constructed (and hence socially destructible) personality. Words and symbols are among the chief weapons for inflicting this form of injury. The point becomes clear when one reads the facts of some of the hostile environment discrimination cases; anyone will agree with Judge Posner that the victims in these cases have suffered discrimination in "terms and conditions of employment" as surely as if they had been made to do extra work for the same pay on account of their race or sex.[55]

These same hostile environment discrimination cases likewise provide some of the best examples of civil rights analysis that blur the "speech-action" as well as the "public-private" distinction. When a private employer is held liable under Title VII for not taking reasonable steps to prevent racist or sexist verbal assaults by employees on their fellow workers, the government is in effect imposing (as sovereign, not employer) a contentand viewpoint-specific regime of censorship on the speech of private employees. The American Civil Liberties Union has seen the point; it opposes liability for employers or schools who fail to prevent verbal sexual harassment that "has no other effect on its recipient than to create an unpleasant working [learning] environment."[56] But I have found that many good civil-libertarians see these hostile environment cases (at least in the employment context) through the civil-rights lens; they thus agree with current law in accepting that an employer should be obligated to police the workplace to some extent against even purely verbal abuse when it becomes so pervasive and differentially "unpleasant" on grounds of race or sex to affect employees' terms and conditions of employment.

IV

I have tried to suggest how the civil-liberties and civil-rights approaches overlap and clash on the issue of discriminatory harassment; apparently, no higher principle of comparable force and vitality can resolve their conflict.[57] Do these two approaches simply represent, respectively, rightand left-wing political tendencies within American liberalism? It is possible to tell the story that way: civil-liberties (and its marketplace of ideas) then represents a dying classical liberalism, while civil-rights (and its society of equal groups) represents a post-liberal social democracy struggling to be born. Or (to flip the political poles of the historical plot-line) civil liberties now represents the true liberal future at this moment of the end of history, while the asymmetric civil-rights project will be rejected along with other misguided attempts to inject communitarian ideals into the legal governance of free societies.

Both of these sketches operate on the "contradiction" hypothesis; they postulate, on the basis of the structural conflict between the civil-rights and civil-liberties approaches, that one should give way in the name of principled consistency. Following this analysis, one could press (from the right) toward a more formal and neutral "civil-liberties" style of anti-discrimination law or (from the left) toward a more substantive and result-oriented "civil-rights" version of free speech law.

The former move would incline toward an ideal of formal neutrality in civil-rights law, one that stressed not the abolition of caste or status-subordination by the elimination from law of "suspect classifications"—distinctions based upon individuals' immutable characteristics. The latter move would give a larger role in First Amendment law to correction of market imperfections in the marketplace of ideas, pursuing policies such as realistically equal access to media, opening debate to the participation of those previously silenced by social subordination, and so on. As this essay perhaps suggests, I am more inclined to go in the latter direction than in the former, but I am not inclined to go very far[58]—nothing like far enough to bring civil-liberties law into full consistency with the public-private and speech-action treatments characteristic of current civil-rights law.

What, then, is the alternative to seeing this incommensurable conflict as contradiction? My answer is already implicit in the body of the essay; it can be roughly captured by the slogan that the civil-rights approach embodies a *project,* which is to be carried on within a *framework* constituted by the civil-liberties approach. Civil rights has statable social goals, however utopian: the abolition of racism, sexism, and other forms of bigotry. It postulates disease-like social conditions and collective enemies; it then sets us the task of struggling against these and, ideally, eliminating them. The civil-rights mentality represents our collective self-commitment to a definite, though limited and negative, judgment about the nature of the good society, or at least the good society for us— it is one without castes (whether of race, or sex, or sexual orientation, or . . .). Civil-rights law is then conceived mainly as an *instrument* toward that end.

Note that this instrumental account of civil-rights doctrine characterizes even those who are unhappy with affirmative action and who tend to support a symmetric version of anti-discrimination law. First, in my experience, few adherents of this view support a wholehearted symmetry in practice. Second, the reason for this shows up in their arguments; they oppose affirmative action as counterproductive, as a poor strategy in the effort to attain what all concede to be the long-run goal: a caste-free society. To use race as a principle for distributing burdens and benefits, they argue, is to legitimize it as a ground for social action; this reinforces the tendency to revert to less benign uses in moments of social panic or pressure. These neutralists on civil rights are thus, at bottom, instrumentalists too; they share the same conception of the overriding goal, only disagreeing on the best means by which to pursue it.[59]

The civil-liberties approach, whether in its rightor left-wing versions, postulates no goal for society in the same sense. What would society look like if the "aims" of the First Amendment were achieved? It would be a society where people could in general say what they have to say, but this merely restates First Amendment doctrine in summary form without articulating a social goal at which it aims. Attempts to state positive goals for the First Amendment typically produce vague and eclectic wish-lists that are of little help in shaping free speech doctrine. A similar point could be made, I believe, of the free exercise clause and some aspects of the right of privacy. We cannot say anything very definite about how society would look if these civil-libertarian rights were fully realized.

We might fairly say that these provisions aim at an open society, but that is to say only that they aim at a society that might look like anything at all. Their very goallessness is in a sense the point of these provisions. They capture our skeptical sense that we do not, in general, know where we are going; we have no dominant *overall* collective project, and we want to keep it that way. The First Amendment, along with the other "civil liberties,"[60] is there to maintain possibilities, to keep the future open to the presently unpredictable workings of the human imagination. Its effective enforcement requires a strong dose of skepticism—not (a self-contradictory) "absolute relativism," but a skeptical *attitude* toward collectively-imposed substantive moral judgments. (This skepticism is not inconsistent with a fair degree of romanticism about the possible achievements of the unchecked human imagination.[61]) By contrast, the civil-rights approach, on its more limited subject (the intolerability of a system of group subordination or caste), is not skeptical at all— no more skeptical than were the abolitionists. (Of course, a degree of skepticism about the possibility of authoritatively ranking human beings, hence of identifying "natural aristocrats," also lends support to this limited egalitarian absolutism.)

In this contrast between the dominant skepticism of the civil libertarian and the dominant confidence of the civil-rights advocate lies the best answer to the objection that a narrow prohibition of discriminatory harassment violates "viewpoint-neutrality" by discriminating in favor of the Left against the Right on issues relevant to civil-rights concerns. The answer is that if the prohibition has been framed narrowly enough, it does preserve practical neutrality—that is, it does *not* differentially deprive any significant element in American political life of its rhetorical capital. I would argue that this is the case with the Stanford provision. The Right has no special stake in the free face-to-face use of epithets that perform no other function except to portray whole classes of Americans as subhuman and unworthy of full citizenship.

V

In conclusion, I must return to answer an objection to the Stanford provision that I have heard from critics of both the civil-rights and civil-liberties persuasions. This has to do with the charge that the regulation is drafted so narrowly as to make it "merely symbolic," a point that evidently engages one of the key differences between the two approaches. I readily agree that the provision prohibits very little of the behavior that creates the significantly discriminatory hostile environment that faces students of color and others on many campuses. So why bother with it? The point is made with special force by civil libertarians, who think the proposal exacts a high cost in principle through its incursions into the indivisible fabric of the First Amendment.

But egalitarians, on their side, can also object on principle to the provision as a form of tokenism.

I also concede that the main good the provision can do is through its educative or symbolic effect—though I would add that the harms its opponents see in it are likewise largely symbolic as well. The question then arises: why can we not get the same educative effect through official statements, declarations of concern, and the like, issued with appropriate vehemence by university authorities whenever serious incidents of racist verbal abuse occur? Let me suggest a partial answer by modifying a hypothetical situation I posed earlier.

Suppose a state legislature declared a "white supremacy day," perhaps invoking the descriptive and predictive terms of Justice Harlan's dissent in *Plessy v. Ferguson* as an ideal. ("The white race deems itself to be the dominant race in this country. And so it is. . . . So, I doubt not, it will continue for all time, if it remains true to its great heritage. . . ."[62]) That would be a terrible thing, but would it be unconstitutional? I think it would be—but I also admit there is at least some doubt as to the answer. On the other hand, there is no doubt at all that state imposition of racial segregation in public facilities, even if they maintain perfect material equality, are unconstitutional. Yet by hypothesis the injury, the stigma of official racial insult, is the same in both cases—or, if anything, more explicit and obvious in the case of "white supremacy day." Why is segregation more obviously unconstitutional?

One answer: because the government delivers the insult with more force (and hence compounds the injury) when the action expressing the insult *does* something, even if the thing done is (apart from the insult) not itself discriminatory. We think of government as primarily an instrument for the maintenance of law and order and the provision of material public goods.[63] Its ideological centrality in our lives derives mainly from its role as the primary repository of legitimated power in society. It provides such a "bully pulpit" largely *because* it already has so firm a grip on our attention through its coercive powers of taxation and law enforcement.

For this reason, government speaks most clearly when its message is delivered through the exercise of one of those powers, such as the provision of schools, parks, and the like. We think of joint resolutions designating state flowers and mayoral proclamations of schoolteacher week as quite apart from the serious business of government. The adoption of a racist resolution or motto, then, though unconstitutional, would not be as obviously so as would, say, resegregating the seats in the courthouse. When the government acts—when it does something—it puts its money where its mouth is.

Similarly, when a university administration backs its anti-racist pronouncements with action, it puts *its* money where its mouth is. The action, if it is to serve this purpose, must be independently justifiable—independently, that is, of the symbolic purpose. Authorities make the most effective statement when they are honestly concerned to do something *beyond* making a statement. And the action of punishing persons who violate the Stanford harassment regulation *is* justifiable independent of the statement it makes. It provides a remedy for an action that causes real pain and harm to real individuals while doing no good, and it may serve to deter such actions in the future.

Notice that the idea of the "main business of government" advanced here is derived from the classical liberal conception of the state, which in turn lies at the heart of the civil-liberties approach. In that conception, government exists to prevent private force and fraud and to supply tangible public goods by taxing and spending. And that is basically *all* it is there for; its other functions are either suspect or "merely symbolic." Yet throughout this essay I have contrasted that conception of government to one implicit in the civil-rights approach, which undermines traditional public-private distinctions as well as denying the automatic association of "merely" with "symbolic" or "intangible" when discussing of the kind of effects law and government should be centrally concerned with.

And yet, at the end, I revert to slogans involving a distinction between real state action and mere gesture! The point is that neither the civil-liberties nor the civil-rights approach will go away; sometimes, as here, one of them even feeds on the other. With that suggestion of the sometimes paradoxical interweaving of these perspectives, incommensurably co-existing at the heart of modern liberalism, let me call a halt to this very limited examination of their mutual relations.

Appendix: The Stanford Discriminatory Harassment Provision

Preamble

The Fundamental Standard requires that students act with "such respect for . . . the rights of others as is demanded of good citizens." Some incidents in recent years on campus have revealed doubt and disagreement about what this requirement means for students in the sensitive area where the right of free expression can conflict with the right to be free of invidious discrimination. The Student Conduct Legislative Council offers this interpretation to provide students and administrators with some guidance in this area.

Fundamental Standard Interpretation: Free Expression and Discriminatory Harassment

1. Stanford is committed to the principles of free inquiry and free expression. Students have the right to hold and vigorously defend and promote their opinions, thus entering them into the life of the University, there to flourish or wither according to their merits. Respect for this right requires that students tolerate even expression of opinions which they find abhorrent. Intimidation of students by other students in their exercise of this right, by violence or threat of violence, is therefore considered to be a violation of the Fundamental Standard.

2. Stanford is also committed to principles of equal opportunity and non-discrimination. Each student has the right of equal access to a Stanford education, without discrimination on the basis of sex, race, color, handicap, religion, sexual orientation, or national and ethnic origin. Harassment of students on the basis of any of these characteristics con-

tributes to a hostile environment that makes access to education for those subjected to it less than equal. Such discriminatory harassment is therefore considered to be a violation of the Fundamental Standard.

3. This interpretation of the Fundamental Standard is intended to clarify the point at which protected free expression ends and prohibited discriminatory harassment begins. Prohibited harassment includes discriminatory intimidation by threats of violence, and also includes personal vilification of students on the basis of their sex, race, color, handicap, religion, sexual orientation, or national and ethnic origin.

4. Speech or other expression constitutes harassment by personal vilification if it:

a) is intended to insult or stigmatize an individual or a small number of individuals on the basis of their sex, race, color, handicap, religion, sexual orientation, or national and ethnic origin; and

b) is addressed directly to the individual or individuals whom it insults or stigmatizes; and

c) makes use of insulting or "fighting" words or non-verbal symbols.

In the context of discriminatory harassment, insulting or "fighting" words or non-verbal symbols are those "which by their very utterance inflict injury or tend to incite to an immediate breach of the peace," and which are commonly understood to convey direct and visceral hatred or contempt for human beings on the basis of their sex, race, color, handicap, religion, sexual orientation, or national and ethnic origin.

---

1. Ludwig Wittgenstein, Philosophical Investigations 196e (New York: Macmillan, 1958).
2. United States v. Eichman, 110 S. Ct. 2404, 2410 (1990).
3. Brown v. Board of Education, 347 U.S. 483, 494 (1954).
4. Bohen v. City of East Chicago, 799 F.2d 1180, 1189–90 (7th Cir., 1986) (concurring opinion).
5. Ibid.
6. Strauder v. West Virginia, 100 U.S. (10 Otto) 303, 308 (1880).
7. See Paul Brest, "Foreword: In Defense of the Antidiscrimination Principle," Harvard Law Review, vol. 90 (1976), p. 1.
8. I will often make the oversimplifying assumption that all these forms of discrimination can and should be treated the same. Each form of insult has its own unique features and problems, however, and may ultimately generate its own distinct body oflegal doctrine, as does each form of discrimination recognized as "invidious" under equal protection law and civil rights statutes. I will, moreover, put discrimination against gays and lesbians in with the rest, though it has not yet been recognized as invidious under federal constitutional law. A number of state and local civil rights laws, and the anti-discrimination policies of many public

and private institutions (including Stanford) do prohibit sexual-preference discrimination, as in my view all should.
9. Time, May 23, 1989, p. 89.
10. I was faculty co-chair of the campus judicial council at Stanford when this incident occurred; no disciplinary charges were ultimately brought. Thereafter I worked on the drafting of a disciplinary standard to deal with racial harassment, which was adopted by the campus legislative body and became effective in June of 1990. The Beethoven incident is treated eloquently, strictly from a civil-rights perspective, in Patricia Williams, "The Obliging Shell: An Informal Essay on Formal Equal Opportunity," Michigan Law Review, vol. 87 (1989), pp. 2128, 2133–37.
11. The applicable legal provisions are (for most private employers) Title VII of the Civil Rights Act of 1964, which prohibits employers from discriminating against employees on the basis of race or sex in the "terms or conditions of employment," and (for public employers) the Fourteenth Amendment's requirement that no state may "deny to any person the equal protection of the laws," which has been construed to prohibit race and sex discrimination in public employment.

12. *Bohen v. East Chicago,* p. 1191. Judge Posner alternatively analyzed the employer's inaction as analogous to a selective withdrawal of protection, as if a government denied police protection to blacks, or failed to punish rapes alone among violent crimes.

13. In sex discrimination cases under Title VII, the courts distinguish between "quid pro quo" harassment (efforts to extract sexual favors in return for job retention or promotion) and "hostile environment" harassment of the kind described in the text. Racial harassment takes only the latter form. The Supreme Court recognized hostile environment sexual harassment as a Title VII violation in *Meritor Savings Bank v. Vinson,* 477 *U.S.* 57 (1986). On hostile environment discrimination, see *Rogers v. EEOC,* 454 *F. 2d* 234, 238 (5th Cir. 1971) ("sustained pattern of harassment"); *Bundy v. Jackson,* 641 *F. 2d* 934 (D. C. Cir. 1981), and *Henson v. City of Dundee,* 682 *F. 2d* 897 (11th Cir. 1982) (sexual harassment cases involving mixed quid pro quo and pure verbal harassment incidents); *Erebia v. Chrysler Plastics,* 722 *F. 2d* 1250 (6th Cir. 1985); *EEOC v. Murphy Motor Freight Lines,* 488 *F. Supp.* 381 (D. Minn. 1980) (employer failure to take action against racist insults of black employee by fellow workers held unlawful discrimination).

14. As with public employers, the Fourteenth Amendment prohibits public universities from discriminating on the basis of race or sex in providing educational services. Private universities receiving federal grants are subject to similar prohibitions under Title IX of the Civil Rights Act of 1964. In some states, statutes also prohibit discriminatory practices by private universities. Finally, most private universities in the United States have committed themselves to non-discrimination policies, which may give rise to contractual liability when a student can show discrimination that would be unlawful for a public university.

15. Indeed it was evidently drafted on the model of the Equal Employment Opportunity Commission guidelines, which define sexual harassment to include "verbal or physical conduct of a sexual nature" that "has the purpose or effect of unreasonably interfering with an individual's work performance or creating an intimidating, hostile, or offensive working environment." 29 CFR § 1604.11(a).

16. *Doe v. University of Michigan,* 721 *F. Supp.* 852 (E. D. Mich. 1989). See 856 for the text of the regulations.

17. *Doe v. Michigan,* p. 858. The Guide went on to warn students that "YOU are a harasser when . . . you comment in a derogatory way about a . . . group's . . . cultural origins, or religious beliefs"—a very sweeping restriction on the discussion of history and current events. Might not screening *The Last Temptation of Christ* or selling *The Satanic Verses* count as "derogatory comment" on a "group's religious beliefs"?

18. Under the University of Michigan regulation, a social work student was in fact prosecuted for expressing the view that homosexuality was a disease, for which he hoped to develop a counseling plan in a research class; *Doe v. Michigan,* p. 865. The other two statements propound views that I trust my readers will admit are widely held, or at least entertained, if relatively rarely expressed, on American campuses.

19. For example, a student who had recited a homophobic limerick in class plea-bargained the dropping of a charge against him under the Michigan regulations in return for a classroom apology, a letter of apology to the campus paper, and attendance at a "gay rap session;" *Doe v. University of Michigan,* p. 865. It has become a commonplace among civil-libertarian opponents of verbal harassment regulation to stress the utility of "education" (rather than disciplinary rules) as a remedy for campus discrimination, generally without much serious attention to the question of what such "education" may entail. In my own view, the worst of both worlds is achieved when multicultural sensitivity training (valuable as it can be when done well) is imposed as a penal sanction for harassment. I would sharply separate punishment of harassment (which should be confined to cases of intentional wrongdoing) from orientation efforts aimed at acquainting students and others with the diverse cultural backgrounds, expectations, and sensitivities they are likely to meet in the contemporary university.

20. The plaintiff in the Michigan case was a psychology graduate student working on the biological basis of differences in personality traits and mental abilities. He alleged, quite plausibly, that certain theories in his field could be perceived as sexist or racist, so that their discussion might be sanctionable under the policy. *Doe v. Michigan,* p. 858.

21. An excellent and often-cited doctrinal analysis, distinguishing the key terms of art's "communicative impact," "content," and "viewpoint," is Geoffrey Stone, "Content Regulation and the First Amendment," *William and Mary Law Review,* vol. 25 (1983), p. 189.

22. *Hustler Magazine v. Falwell,* 108 *S. Ct.* 876, 879 (1988); compare *Gertz v. Robert Welch,* 418 *U.S.* 323, 339 (1974).

23. *West Virginia State Board of Education v. Barnette,* 319 *U.S.* 624, 643 (1943). Compare *Texas v. Johnson,* 109 *S. Ct.* 2533, 2544: "If there is a bedrock principle underlying the First Amendment, it is that the government may not prohibit the expression of an idea because society finds the idea itself offensive or disagreeable."

24. *Whitney v. California,* 274 U. S. 357, 377 (1927).

25. The moderate view is especially well articulated, by a present General Counsel of the ACLU, in Nadine Strossen, "Regulating Campus Speech: A Modest Proposal," *Duke Law Journal,* p. 483. Strossen, like other moderates, is more skeptical of the "fighting words" than of the "emotional distress" rationale. The purist view is inferrable from Franklyn Haiman, *Speech and Law in a Free Society* (Chicago: University of Chicago, 1981). Haiman altogether rejects the "insulting or fighting words" doctrine, (pp. 132–35, 256–59); he would confine sanctions for verbal infliction of emotional distress to cases of injury through intentional factual misrepresentation (pp. 148–56).

26. It has been my personal experience in debating this issue with colleagues and students that few causes attract more powerful emotional adherence than does First Amendment absolutism. I make the point not to disparage this aspect of their commitment, but because civil libertarians frequently pose the verbal harassment issue (typically with analogy to the flag-burning issue) as a clash between "reason" on their side and "emotion" on the other. On the other side, not a few civil-rights egalitarians take up the same binary opposition between "reason" and "passion" and turn it around to accuse free speech defenders of the moral defect of cerebral and unfeeling elitism.

27. Incommensurable conflicts are, roughly, those we have to resolve in the absence of a satisfactory determining norm (substantive rule, agreed procedure, or common metric). They are not contradictions and need not be resolved "irrationally." A good discussion of value-incommensurability in the context of individual action can be found in Joseph Raz, *The Morality of Freedom,* 321–66 (Oxford: Clarendon Press, 1986).

28. Wittgenstein, *Philosophical Investigations,* p. 194.

29. The text of the Stanford regulation is given in the Appendix.

30. One example of an alternative mediating solution was the situation at Stanford before adoption of the harassment provision. The University's president and general counsel had said publicly that face-to-face use of racial epithets could be considered to violate the long-standing "Fundamental Standard" which required of students conduct manifesting such "respect for the rights of others as is expected of good citizens." Though that solution gave too little guidance to satisfy civil-liberties concerns in my view, it was in the same ballpark as the one later adopted. Other examples of mediating solutions include the regulation adopted at the University of California and the one proposed at the University of Texas. See note 32 below.

31. 315 *U.S.* 568, 572 (1942).

32. The University of California has adopted a prohibition on student harassment by "fighting words," defined as "those personally abusive epithets which, when directly addressed to any ordinary person are, in the context used and as a matter of common knowledge, inherently likely to provoke a violent reaction

whether or not they actually do so." These "include, but are not limited to" terms abusive in terms of race, sex, or the other categories of discrimination law. Harassment occurs when fighting words are used to "create a hostile and intimidating environment" which the utterer should know will interfere with the victim's education.

A committee at the University of Texas has proposed a regulation of "racial harassment" tracking the Restatement of Torts definition of intentional infliction of emotional distress, with the addition of the element of intent to "harass, intimidate, or humiliate . . . on account of race, color or national origin." Establishing a violation requires an actual showing of "severe emotional distress" on the part of the victim.

33. See *Cohen v. California*, 403 *U.S.* 15 (1971); *Gooding v. Wilson*, 405 *U.S.* 518 (1972).

34. Compare *Gregory v. Chicago*, 394 *U.S.* 111 (1969) with *Feiner v. New York*, 340 *U.S.* 315 (1951).

35. *Restatement of Torts*, 2d, sec. 46, comment (d).

36. "'Outrageousness' in the area of political and social discourse has an inherent subjectiveness about it which would allow a jury to impose liability on the basis of the jurors' tastes or views, or perhaps on the basis of their dislike of a particular expression." *Hustler Magazine v. Falwell*, 108 *S. Ct.* 876, 882. The Court's decision, however, does not foreclose granting tort damages under the "outrageousness" test for infliction of emotional distress through speech alone in a private or face-to-face context, rather than in a published and nationally distributed lampoon of an important public figure, such as was involved in Falwell.

37. Richard Delgado, "Words that Wound: A Tort Action for Racial Insults, Epithets, and Name-calling," *Harvard Civil Rights–Civil Liberties Law Review*, vol. 17 (1982), pp. 133–81. Professor Delgado has assembled on pp. 136–49 an impressive body of evidence and argument that supports the identification of racial verbal abuse as inflicting a distinctive and identifiable form of injury, and so qualifying as a distinctive wrong. His proposal is limited to racial insults.

38. Because I believe to this extent in the "no false ideas" strand of American First Amendment law, I reject group defamation and hate-speech prohibitions of the kind called for by the International Convention on the Elimination of All Forms of Racial Discrimination: "States Parties . . . shall declare as an offence publishable by law all dissemination of ideas based on racial superiority or hatred. . . ." Mari Matsuda ably argues the contrary view, urging modification of First Amendment law to permit the extension of a limited version of the international standard to this country in "Public Response to Racist Speech: Considering the Victim's Story," *Michigan Law Review*, vol. 87 (1989), p. 2320. As Professor Matsuda's article documents, many Western countries have such laws. The Canadian hate-speech statute is currently under review by the Supreme Court of Canada for its consistency with the free expression guarantee of the recently adopted Canadian Charter of Rights and Freedoms.

39. It would be possible, in the interests of maximum clarity, to attempt a comprehensive list of the "discriminatory fighting words" and equivalent visual symbols (swastikas, burning crosses, etc.). I think this would be a mistake; new examples of such words and symbols are constantly being invented by the creativity of the collective bigoted mind. Even without a definitive list, however, the Stanford regulation gives clearer notice of what will count as an offense than any other similar proposal I know. I should add that as I understand the provision, derogatory epithets aimed at (white) national origin groups ("dago," "Polack," etc.) would come within its terms to the extent they were determined to be still "commonly understood" to "convey direct and visceral hatred or contempt" on the basis of national origin.

40. The narrow confinement of the harassment regulation to the use of the gutter epithets also emphasizes that it is meant as an anti-discrimination provision, not a "civility rule." As a teacher,

I would not let students address each other in class using personally derogatory terms of any kind, and would exclude students who persisted in doing so. That is a civility rule, similar to those applied in most American parliamentary bodies. Such rules are not, in my opinion, appropriate for campus-wide enforcement. The campus should be thought of as primarily a general public forum, and secondarily as a workplace (the work of education). I would add that values of residential privacy may justify more stringent regulation of offensive speech in student dormitories than in classrooms or in public campus areas, but this is a complex issue which I cannot treat adequately here.

41. This is the concern raised by Justice Black in his dissent from the Supreme Court's decision sustaining conviction of a white racist pamphleteer under a group libel statute: "If there be any minority groups who hail this holding as their victory, they might consider the possible relevance of this ancient remark: 'Another such victory and I am undone.'" *Beauharnais v. Illinois*, 343 U.S. 250, 275 (1952).

42. Indeed in its usual sense, the term is implicitly racist toward people of color—with its implication of surprise that a white person would be "trash."

43. I realize that others might disagree with this, citing terms such as "honky," "gringo," "breeder," etc. But I myself do not know which of these terms are current and seriously-used epithets of hatred or contempt—evidence that they are not "commonly understood" as such. On the other side, no sentient black, Latino, or gay American has any doubt about the current standard insulting epithets for their groups.

44. A similar analysis applies to the unjustified use of the term "white racist," which many of my white students have invoked as the equivalent, applied to them, of the standard racial epithets as applied to the students of color. Leaving to one side whether unjustified use of a term like this inflicts the same level of injury, it does not in any event come within the class of injuries that concern civil-rights law and policy. The term "white racist" does not denigrate whites as such, any more than "black separatist racist" denigrates blacks as such. In addition, strong civil-liberties considerations distinguish the cases. Terms of political abuse like "white racist" (or "Stalinist," "Nazi," "terrorist") are sometimes accurately and appropriately applied to individuals in robust debate; exactly when they properly apply, however, is politically controversial. In contrast, the Stanford provision rests on the premise that the racial (and other) discriminatory gutter epithets it deals with are never appropriately directed at individuals; enforcement of the provision, therefore, does not involve the politically charged task of discriminating between justified and unjustified uses.

45. John Rawls, *A Theory of Justice* (Cambridge: Harvard, 1971), pp. 178–79, 440–46, 543–47.

46. *Brown v. Board of Education*, 347 *U.S.* 483 (1954); see also *Mayor of Baltimore v. Dawson*, 350 *U.S.* 877 (1955) (beaches); *Gayle v. Browder*, 352 *U.S.* 903 (1956) (buses); *Holmes v. City of Atlanta*, 350 *U.S.* 879 (1955) (golf courses); *Johnson v. Virginia*, 373 *U.S.* 61 (1963) (courthouses).

47. *Plessy v. Ferguson*, 163 *U.S.* 537, 551 (1896), rejecting the claim that "the enforced separation of the two races stamps the colored race with a badge of inferiority" on the ground that "[i]f this be so, it is not by reason of anything found in the act, but solely because the colored race chooses to put that construction upon it." *Compare Brown v. Board of Education*, 347 *U.S.* 483, 494 (1954).

48. Edmond Cahn early on offered this rationale as the proper interpretation of *Brown*:

As is observed in the ancient Babylonian Talmud, to shame and degrade a fellow-creature is to commit a kind of psychic mayhem upon him. Like an assailant's knife, humiliation slashes his self-respect and human dignity. He grows pale, the blood rushes from his face just as thought it had been shed. That is why we are accustomed to say he feels "wounded." . . .

So one speaks in terms of the most familiar and universally accepted standards of right and wrong when one remarks (1)

that racial segregation under government auspices inevitably inflicts humiliation, and (2) that official humiliation of innocent, law-abiding citizens is psychologically injurious and morally evil. . . .
"Jurisprudence," *New York University Law Review,* vol. 30 (1955), pp. 148–59.

49. Charles Lawrence III, "If He Hollers Let Him Go: Regulating Racist Speech on Campus," *Duke Law Journal,* vol. 1990, pp. 901, 909. My treatment of *Brown* has been much influenced by this excellent article.

50. Nadine Strossen contests the *Brown* analogy in these terms in her article cited above.

51. *Collin v. Smith,* 578 *F. 2d* 1197 (7th Cir. 1978), cert. denied 436 *U.S.* 953 (1978); *Brandenburg v. Ohio,* 395 *U.S.* 444 (1969); *Terminiello v. Chicago,* 337 *U.S.* 1 (1949). The Court has reiterated the point in significant dicta in the flag-burning cases. "The First Amendment does not guarantee that other concepts virtually sacred to our Nation as a whole—such as the principle that discrimination on the basis of race is odious and destructive—will go unchallenged in the marketplace of ideas." *Texas v. Johnson,* 109 *S. Ct.* 2533, 2544 (1989). "We are aware that desecration of the flag is deeply offensive to many. But the same might be said, for example, of virulent ethnic and religious epithets [citing Terminiello]. . . ." *United States v. Eichman,* 110 *S. Ct.* 2404, 2410 (1990).

52. The reliance of traditional civil-liberties law on a public-private distinction much stronger than we recognize elsewhere is the theme of Frank Michelman, "Conceptions of Democracy in American Constitutional Argument: The Case of Pornography Regulation," *Tennessee Law Review,* vol. 56 (1989), p. 291.

53. Thus in *Shelley v. Kraemer,* 334 *U.S.* 1 (1948), extensive legal supervision of the kinds of enforceable covenants running with the land rendered enforcement of a racially restrictive private covenant discriminatory state action; in *Terry v. Adams,* 345 *U.S.* 461 (1953), extensive state regulation of elections rendered the exclusionary practices of the formally private Texas Jaybird Democratic Club (in effect the white Democratic Party) discriminatory state action; in *Burton v. Wilmington Parking Authority,* 365 *U.S.* 715 (1961), public ownership and operation of a parking garage constitutionally entangled the state in the racial exclusion practiced by a privately-owned restaurant leasing space in the building.

54. See the language from Justice Brandeis's opinion in *Whitney v. California,* quoted in text accompanying note 24 above.

55. Thus in *Bohen v. East Chicago,* the plaintiff, a female fire department dispatcher, had to deal with a supervisor who was constantly "speaking to her entirely of sexual matters and describing his preferred sexual positions, Bohen's participation, and his expectations for her behavior." Further, she was "a continual target for obscene comments by firefighters and other male employees and was forced to listen to their filthy talk and descriptions of their sexual fantasies of which she was the object." A fire captain told her that "a forcible rape in some nearby flora would improve her disposition." 799 *F. 2d,* pp. 1182–83.
In *EEOC v. Murphy Motor Freight Lines,* 488 *F. Supp.* 381 (D. Minn. 1980), Ray Wells, a black dockman, was subjected regu-

larly to racial slurs on chalkboards attached to loading carts: "Ray Wells is a nigger," "The only good nigger is a dead nigger," "Niggers are a living example that Indians screwed buffalo." When Wells started eating in another room, his white co-workers wrote "niggers only" above the door. Management did nothing in response to complaints. See pp. 384–85.

56. *Policy Guide of the ACLU* (rev. ed. 1989), at 142, 400. The ACLU position requires distinguishing between (protected) verbal abuse that merely renders the environment "unpleasant" and that which crosses the line to inflicting actionable emotional distress—hardly a bright line. My thanks to Nadine Strossen for providing me the text of these ACLU provisions.

57. Which is not to say that verbal formulae may not be offered to supply formal or aesthetic resolution to liberal theory and hence present it as a closed system. John Rawls attempts such a closure with his lexical ordering of liberty over equal opportunity in *A Theory of Justice;* the difficulty is to defend the substance of this firm hierarchy. Joseph Raz supplies an attractive overarching account of "autonomy" as the supreme liberal value, resolving liberty-equality conflicts, in *The Morality of Freedom.* I myself prefer the frank pluralism of Isaiah Berlin in "Two Concepts of Liberty," *Four Essays on Liberty,* pp. 167–72 (London: Oxford, 1969).

58. Thus I sympathize with Owen Fiss's suggestions for moving First Amendment doctrine in a more realistically democratic direction in his "Free Speech and Social Structure," *Iowa Law Review,* vol. 71 (1986), p. 1405. On the other hand, I stop short of endorsing civil-rights-based bans on potentially broad content-defined categories of speech: racist speech, as endorsed by Mari Matsuda, "Public Response"; or sexist pornography, as in the trafficking provisions of the Indianapolis anti-pornography ordinance invalidated in *American Booksellers Assn'n v. Hudnut,* 771 *F. 2d* 323 (7th Cir. 1985).

59. Thus in the most "neutralist" of recent Supreme Court civil-rights decisions, *City of Richmond v. J. A. Croson,* 109 *S. Ct.* 706, 721 (1989), invalidating a municipal minority business set-aside program, the Court majority stated the grounds for treating even benign racial classifications as suspect in terms instrumental to an anti-caste goal: "Classifications based on race carry a danger of stigmatic harm. . . . They may in fact promote notions of racial inferiority and lead to a politics of racial hostility."

60. The First Amendment is also tied (as the free exercise and privacy rights are not) to the preservation of a functioning democratic system of government; however, there could conceivably be a working free speech guarantee, justified along the lines I suggest, even in a liberal but undemocratic state.

61. This romantic side of the civil-liberties mentality is very attractively presented in Steven Shiffrin, *The First Amendment, Democracy, and Romance* (Cambridge: Harvard University Press, 1990).

62. 163 *U.S.* 537, 559 (1896). Actual current controversies that raise this issue (though less starkly) include the continued official use by southern states of the Confederate flag.

63. This isn't true of government in all societies; see Clifford Geertz, *Negara: The Theater State in Nineteenth Century Bali* (Princeton: Princeton University Press, 1980).

Principles of Constitutional Interpretation

THE RIGHT OF PRIVACY:
The Construction of a Constitutional Time Bomb*

Robert H. Bork

The 1965 decision in *Griswold v. Connecticut*[1] was insignificant in itself but momentous for the future of constitutional law. Connecticut had an ancient statute making it criminal to use contraceptives. The state also had a general accessory statute allowing the punishment of any person who aided another in committing an offense. On its face, the statute criminalizing the use of contraceptives made no distinction between married couples and others. But the statute also had never been enforced against anyone who used contraceptives, married or not. There was, of course, no prospect that it ever would be enforced. If any Connecticut official had been mad enough to attempt enforcement, the law would at once have been removed from the books and the official from his office. Indeed, some Yale law professors had gotten the statute all the way to the Supreme Court a few years previously, and the Court had refused to decide it precisely because there was no showing that the law was ever enforced. The professors had some difficulty arranging a test case but finally managed to have two doctors who gave birth control information fined $100 apiece as accessories.

Such enforcement in the area as there was consisted of the occasional application of the accessory statute against birth control clinics, usually clinics that advertised. The situation was similar to the enforcement of many antigambling laws. They may cover all forms of gambling on their faces, but they are in fact enforced only against commercial gambling. An official who began arresting the priest at the church bingo party or friends having their monthly poker game at home would have made a most unwise career decision and would be quite unlikely to get a conviction. There are a number of statutes like these in various state codes, such as the statutes flatly prohibiting sodomy and other "unnatural practices," which apply on their faces to all couples, married or unmarried, heterosexual or homosexual. The statutes are never enforced, but legislators, who would be aghast at any enforcement effort, nevertheless often refuse to repeal them.

There is a problem with laws like these. They are kept in the codebooks as precatory statements, affirmations of moral principle. It is quite arguable that this is an improper use of law, most particularly of criminal law, that statutes should not be on the

---

books if no one intends to enforce them. It has been suggested that if anyone tried to enforce a law that had moldered in disuse for many years, the statute should be declared void by reason of desuetude or that the defendant should go free because the law had not provided fair warning.

But these were not the issues in *Griswold*. Indeed, getting off on such grounds was the last thing the defendants and their lawyers wanted. Since the lawyers had a difficult time getting the state even to fine two doctors as accessories, it seems obvious that the case was not arranged out of any fear of prosecution, and certainly not the prosecution of married couples. *Griswold* is more plausibly viewed as an attempt to enlist the Court on one side of one issue in a cultural struggle. Though the statute was originally enacted when the old Yankee culture dominated Connecticut politics, it was now quite popular with the Catholic hierarchy and with many lay Catholics whose religious values it paralleled. The case against the law was worked up by members of the Yale law school faculty and was supported by the Planned Parenthood Federation of America, Inc., the Catholic Council on Civil Liberties, and the American Civil Liberties Union. A ruling of unconstitutionality may have been sought as a statement that opposition to contraception is benighted and, therefore, a statement about whose cultural values are dominant. Be that as it may, the upshot was a new constitutional doctrine perfectly suited, and later used, to enlist the Court on the side of moral relativism in sexual matters.

Justice Douglas's majority opinion dealt with the case as if Connecticut had devoted itself to sexual fascism. "Would we allow the police to search the sacred precincts of marital bedrooms for telltale signs of the use of contraceptives? The very idea is repulsive to the notions of privacy surrounding the marriage relationship."[2] That was both true and entirely irrelevant to the case before the Court. Courts usually judge statutes by the way in which they are actually enforced, not by imagining horrible events that have never happened, never will happen, and could be stopped by courts if they ever seemed about to happen. Just as in *Skinner* he had treated a proposal to sterilize three-time felons as raising the specter of racial genocide, Douglas raised the stakes to the sky here by treating Connecticut as though it was threatening the institution of marriage. "We deal with a right of privacy older than the Bill of Rights—older than our political parties, older than our school system." The thought was incoherent. What the right of privacy's age in comparison with that of our political parties and school sys-

tem had to do with anything was unclear, and where the "right" came from if not from the Bill of Rights it is impossible to understand. No court had ever invalidated a statute on the basis of the right Douglas described. That makes it all the more perplexing that Douglas in fact purported to derive the right of privacy not from some pre-existing right or law of nature, but from the Bill of Rights. It is important to understand Justice Douglas's argument both because the method, though without merit, continually recurs in constitutional adjudication and because the "right of privacy" has become a loose canon in the law. Douglas began by pointing out that "specific guarantees in the Bill of Rights have penumbras, formed by emanations from those guarantees that help give them life and substance." There is nothing exceptional about that thought, other than the language of penumbras and emanations. Courts often give protection to a constitutional freedom by creating a buffer zone, by prohibiting a government from doing something not in itself forbidden but likely to lead to an invasion of a right specified in the Constitution. Douglas cited *NAACP v. Alabama*,[3] in which the Supreme Court held that the state could not force the disclosure of the organization's membership lists since that would have a deterrent effect upon the members' First Amendment rights of political and legal action. That may well have been part of the purpose of the statute. But for this anticipated effect upon guaranteed freedoms, there would be no constitutional objection to the required disclosure of membership. The right not to disclose had no life of its own independent of the rights specified in the first amendment.

Douglas named the buffer zone or "penumbra" of the First Amendment a protection of "privacy," although, in *NAACP v. Alabama*, of course, confidentiality of membership was required not for the sake of individual privacy but to protect the public activities of politics and litigation. Douglas then asserted that other amendments create "zones of privacy." These were the first, third (soldiers not to be quartered in private homes), fourth (ban on unreasonable searches and seizures), and fifth (freedom from self-incrimination). There was no particularly good reason to use the word "privacy" for the freedoms cited, except for the fact that the opinion was building toward those "sacred precincts of marital bedrooms." The phrase "areas of freedom" would have been more accurate since the provisions cited protect both private and public behavior.

None of the amendments cited, and none of their buffer or penumbral zones, covered the case before the Court. The Connecticut statute was not invalid under any provision of the Bill of Rights, no matter how extended. Since the statute in question did not threaten any guaranteed freedom, it did not fall within any "emanation." *Griswold v. Connecticut* was, therefore, not like *NAACP v. Alabama*. Justice Douglas bypassed that seemingly insuperable difficulty by simply asserting that the various separate "zones of privacy" created by each separate provision of the Bill of Rights somehow created a general but wholly undefined "right of privacy" that is independent of and lies outside any right or "zone of privacy" to be found in the Constitution. Douglas did not explain how it was that the Framers created five or six specific rights that could, with considerable stretching, be called "privacy," and, though the Framers chose not to create more, the Court could nevertheless invent a general right of privacy that the Framers had, inexplicably, left out. It really does not matter to the decision what the Bill of Rights covers or does not cover.

Douglas closed the *Griswold* opinion with a burst of passionate oratory. "Marriage is a coming together for better or for worse, hopefully enduring, and intimate to the degree of being sacred. It is an association that promotes a way of life, not causes; a harmony in living, not political faiths; a bilateral loyalty, not commercial or social projects. Yet it is an association for as noble a purpose as any involved in our prior decisions."[4] It is almost a matter for regret that Connecticut had not threatened the institution of marriage, or even attempted to prevent anyone from using contraceptives, since that left some admirable sentiments, expressed with rhetorical fervor, dangling irrelevantly in midair. But the protection of marriage was not the point of *Griswold*. The creation of a new device for judicial power to remake the Constitution was the point.

The *Griswold* opinion, of course, began by denying that any such power was being assumed. "[W]e are met with a wide range of questions that implicate the Due Process Clause of the 14th Amendment. Overtones of some arguments suggest that [*Lochner v. New York*] should be our guide. But we decline that invitation. . . . We do not sit as a super-legislature to determine the wisdom, need, and propriety of laws that touch economic problems, business affairs, or social conditions."[5] *Griswold,* as an assumption of judicial power unrelated to the Constitution is, however, indistinguishable from *Lochner*. And the nature of that power, its lack of rationale or structure, ensured that it could not be confined.

The Court majority said there was now a right of privacy but did not even intimate an answer to the question, "Privacy to do what?" People often take addictive drugs in private, some men physically abuse their wives and children in private, executives conspire to fix prices in private, Mafiosi confer with their button men in private. If these sound bizarre, one professor at a prominent law school has suggested that the right of privacy may create a right to engage in prostitution. Moreover, as we shall see, the Court has extended the right of privacy to activities that can in no sense be said to be done in private. The truth is that "privacy" will turn out to protect those activities that enough Justices to form a majority think ought to be protected and not activities with which they have little sympathy.

If one called the zones of the separate rights of the Bill of Rights zones of "freedom," which would be more accurate, then, should one care to follow Douglas's logic, the zones would add up to a general right of freedom independent of any provision of the Constitution. A general right of freedom—a constitutional right to be free of regulation by law—is a manifest impossibility. Such a right would posit a state of nature, and its law would be that of the jungle. If the Court had created a general "right of freedom," we would know at once, therefore, that the new right would necessarily be applied selectively, and, if we were given no explanation of the scope of the new right, we would know that the "right" was nothing more than a warrant judges had created for themselves to do whatever they wished. That . . . is precisely what happened with the new, general, undefined, and unexplained "right of privacy."

Justice Black's dissent stated: "I like my privacy as well as the next one, but I am nevertheless compelled to admit that government has a right to invade it unless prohibited by some specific constitutional provision."[6] He found none. "The Court talks about a constitutional 'right of privacy' as though there is some constitutional provision or provisions forbidding any law ever to be passed which might abridge the 'privacy' of individuals. But there is not." He pointed out that there are "certain specific constitutional provisions which are designed in part to protect privacy at certain times and places with respect to certain activities." But there was no general right of the sort Douglas had created. Justice Stewart's dissent referred to the statute as "an uncommonly silly law" but noted that its asininity was not before the Court.[7] He could "find no such general right of privacy in the Bill of Rights, in any other part of the

Constitution, or in any case ever before decided by this Court." He also observed that the "Court does not say how far the new constitutional right of pri-

vacy announced today extends." That was twenty-four years ago, and the Court still has not told us.

---

1. 381 *U.S.* 479 (1965).
2. *Id.* at 485–86.
3. 357 *U.S.* 449 (1958).
4. 381 *U.S.* at 486.

5. *Id.* at 481–82.
6. 381 *U.S.* at 507, 508, 510 (Black, J. dissenting).
7. 381 *U.S.* at 527, 530m.7 (Stewart, J., dissenting).

DISCOVERING FUNDAMENTAL VALUES*

John Hart Ely

[I]t remains to ask the hardest questions. Which values . . . qualify as sufficiently important or fundamental or whathaveyou to be vindicated by the Court against other values affirmed by legislative acts? And how is the Court to evolve and apply them?

—Alexander Bickel

No answer is what the wrong question begets. . . .

—Alexander Bickel

Since interpretivism[1]—at least a clause-bound version of interpretivism—is hoist by its own petard, we should look again, and more closely, at its traditional competitor. The prevailing academic line has held for some time that the Supreme Court should give content to the Constitution's open-ended provisions by identifying and enforcing upon the political branches those values that are, by one formula or another, truly important or fundamental. Indeed we are told this is inevitable: "there is simply no way for courts to review legislation in terms of the Constitution without repeatedly making difficult substantive choices among competing values, and indeed among inevitably controverted political, social, and moral

conceptions." "[C]onstitutional law must now be understood as the means by which effect is given to those ideas that from time to time are held to be fundamental. . . ." The Court is "an institution charged with the evolution and application of society's fundamental principles," and its "constitutional function," accordingly, is "to define values and proclaim principles."

The Judge's Own Values

The ultimate test of the Justices' work, I suggest, must be goodness. . . .

—J. Skelly Wright

The view that the judge, in enforcing the Constitution, should use his or her *own values* to measure the judgment of the political branches is a methodology that is seldom endorsed in so many words. As we proceed through the various methodologies that are, however, I think we shall sense in many cases that although the judge or commentator in question may be talking in terms of some "objective," nonpersonal method of identification, what he is really likely to

---

be "discovering," whether or not he is fully aware of it, are his own values. It is thus important at the outset to understand just why a "judge's own values" approach is unacceptable: that understanding will illumine the unacceptability of the entire enterprise.

How might one arrive at such a view? Much of the explanation seems to involve what might be called the fallacy of transformed realism. About forty years ago people "discovered" that judges were human and therefore were likely in a variety of legal contexts consciously or unconsciously to slip their personal values into their legal reasonings. From that earth-shattering insight it has seemed to some an easy inference that that is what judges *ought* to be doing. Two observations are in order, both obvious. The first is that such a "realist" theory of adjudication is not a theory of adjudication at all, in that it does not tell us *which* values should be imposed. The second is that the theory's "inference" does not even remotely follow: that people have always been tempted to steal does not mean that stealing is what they should be doing. This is all plain as a pikestaff, which means something else has to be going on. People who tend to this extreme realist view must consciously or unconsciously be envisioning a Court staffed by justices who think as they do. That assumption takes care of both the problems I've mentioned. It tells you what values are to be imposed (the commentator's own) and also explains (at least to the satisfaction of the commentator) why such a Court would be desirable. But it's a heroic assumption, and the argument that seems to score most heavily against such a "realist" outlook is one that is genuinely realistic—that there is absolutely no assurance that the Supreme Court's life-tenured members (or the other federal judges) will be persons who share your values.

But let that pass and grant the realists their strange assumption. There remains the immense and obvious problem of reconciling the attitude under discussion with the basic democratic theory of our government. At this point a distinction is drawn. In America it would not be an acceptable position that appointed judges should run the country, and that is not the position of the commentators under discussion. Saying the judges should run the country is different, however, and many have argued that it is significantly different, from saying the judges should use their own values to give content to the Constitution's open texture. Consistency with democratic theory will supposedly be found in the idea that the judiciary isn't really in a position to make much of a difference to the way the country is run. This assumption has impressive historical roots, running back to Hamilton's *Federalist* 78:

> Whoever attentively considers the different departments of power must perceive, that, in a government in which they are separated from each other, the judiciary, from the nature of its functions, will always be the least dangerous to the political rights of the Constitution; because it will be least in a capacity to annoy or injure them. . . . The judiciary . . . has no influence over either the sword or the purse; no direction either of the strength or of the wealth of the society; and can take no active resolution whatever. It may truly be said to have neither FORCE nor WILL, but merely judgment; and must ultimately depend upon the aid of the executive arm even for the efficacy of its judgments.

This must have made a good bit of sense at the outset of our nation: in the absence of precedent, the lack of independent enforcement machinery and the various constitutional checks on the judiciary must have seemed sufficient to ensure that it would play a quite insignificant role. What are harder to justify are the "realist" literature's *contemporary* iterations of Hamilton's assurances, most unrealistically untouched by two hundred years of experience. The Court may be purseless and swordless, but its ability importantly to influence the way the nation functions has proved great, and seems to be growing all the time. It may be true that the Court cannot *permanently* thwart the will of a solid majority, but it can certainly delay its implementation for decades—workmen's compensation, child labor, and unionization are among the more obvious examples—and to the people affected, that's likely to be forever.

The formal checks on the Court have surely not proved to be of much consequence. Congress's control over the budget of the federal courts—note, though, that it cannot constitutionally reduce judicial salaries—has proved an instrument too blunt to be of any real control potential. The country needs functioning and competent federal courts, and everybody knows it does. Despite the two-thirds requirement, impeachment *might* have developed into an effective mode of controlling decision. However, in part precisely because of our allegiance to the idea of an independent judiciary, it didn't, and today it is understood to be a weapon reserved for the grossest of cases. (It is no easier to impeach a justice than a President, as Richard Nixon learned, from both sides.) Congress's theoretical power to withdraw the Court's jurisdiction over certain classes of cases is so fraught with constitutional doubt that although talked about from time to time, it has not been invoked for over one hundred years. Altering the size of, or "packing," the Court was quite popular in the nineteenth century, but only once, during the Grant Administration, is it even arguable that it had its desired effect. And that is the last time it's been done. Franklin Roosevelt tried it, and although he failed, the prevailing mythology for a time was that his effort had pressured the Court into mending its ways. More recently discovered Court records have indicated, however, that the Court's "switch" was independent of (in fact prior to) the announcement of his plan. The message is mixed, but what now seems important about the episode is that an immensely popular President riding an immensely popular cause had his lance badly blunted by his assault on judicial independence.

There is also the possibility of constitutional amendment, but even when this course works it takes time—during which the Court's roadblock stays in place—and in any event it seldom works. Our recent experience with the Equal Rights Amendment, endorsed by both major parties and hardly advancing a radical proposition, corroborates the difficulty of amending the Constitution. In all our history only four decisions of the Supreme Court have been reversed by constitutional amendment. It is also true that often, though by no means always, the cooperation of political officials is required to enforce Supreme Court decisions. But they generally go along, however grudgingly: it is, after all, their perceived legal duty to do so. (One inclined to regard failure to obey as a viable means of controlling the Court would do well to reflect on the fact that the President of the United States—one hardly renowned for his reverence to the rule of law—did surrender those fatal tapes.) What's left is the fact that the President appoints and the Senate confirms the new members of the Court, and certainly there is something there. But it generally takes several successive presidential terms, and the concurrence of several successive Senates, to replace a majority of the justices. It has also proved hard to predict how someone in another line of work will function as a justice and one sometimes wonders whether the appointee who turns out differently from the way the President who appointed him expected is not the rule rather then the exception. (Truman and Eisen-

hower are both reported to have regarded Supreme Court appointments—Clark and Warren, respectively—as the worst mistakes they had made as President.) Nor is it the least bit unusual for a justice to sit for decades during which the issues are likely to have shifted markedly from those the President had in mind when the appointment was made.

So it can't be the actual invocation of the formal checks the realists mean to rely on in assuring us that the Court is no threat to influence importantly the governance of the country. The point tends to be made more mysteriously, generally in the language of "destruction." Thus we are told that the Court's "essentially anti-democratic character keeps it constantly in jeopardy of destruction": it knows "that frequent judicial intervention in the political process would generate such widespread political reaction that the Court would be destroyed in its wake." Readers who are even passingly familiar with the literature on judicial review of the 1960s and 1970s will recognize the theme: it is incanted as an article of faith and forms the foundation for much conservative "realism." But what is it supposed to mean? What sort of "destruction" is it that lurks around the activist corner? We're never exactly told, but to be coherent the idea has to be that although the formal checks appear to the naive observer to have atrophied, the Court knows better, and understands that if it gets too rambunctious—if it too regularly exercises what the public will understand are properly political functions—those checks will be invoked.

This isn't the way it works, and the justices know it isn't. Throughout its history the Court has been told it had better stick to its knitting or risk destruction, yet somehow "[t]he possibility of judicial emasculation by way of popular reaction against constitutional review by the courts has not in fact materialized in more than a century and a half of American experience." The warnings probably reached their peak during the Warren years; they were not notably heeded; yet nothing resembling destruction materialized. In fact the Court's power continued to grow, and probably has never been greater than it has been over the past two decades. For public persons know that one of the surest ways to acquire power is to assert it. "[J]udicial activism feeds on itself," Professors Karst and Horowitz have written. "The public has come to expect the Court to intervene against gross abuses. And so the Court must intervene." *Must* intervene"? I'd argue not, at least not as the formula is stated here. But "can get away with intervening"? For sure.

It's because everybody down deep knows this that few come right out and argue for the judge's own values as a source of constitutional judgment. Instead the search purports to be objective and value-neutral; the reference is to something "out there" waiting to be discovered, whether it be natural law or some supposed value consensus of historical America, today's America, or the America that is yet to be.

Natural Law

"Well, what may seem like the truth to you," said the seventeen-year-old bus driver and part-time philosopher, "may not, of course, seem like the truth to the other fella, you know."
"THEN THE OTHER FELLOW IS WRONG, IDIOT!"
—Philip Roth, *The Great American Novel*

At the time the original Constitution was ratified, and during the period leading up to the Fourteenth Amendment as well, a number of people espoused the existence of a system of natural law principles. "This law of nature being coeval with mankind and dictated by God himself is of course superior in obligation to any other. It is binding over the whole globe, in all countries and at all times. No human laws are of any validity if contrary to this. . . ." Some sort of natural law theory (which need not necessarily be deistic) thus seems an obvious candidate in the search for a source of values to give content to the Constitution's open-ended provisions.

The historical record here is not so uncomplicated as it is sometimes made to appear. As noted above, some of our nation's founders did not find the concept intelligible in any context, and even those who did "were seldom, if ever, guilty of confusing law with natural right." It therefore seems no oversight that the Constitution at no point adverts to the concept. Of course the Declaration of Independence had spoken in such terms. Part of the explanation for the difference is undoubtedly that intellectual fashions had changed somewhat over that eventful decade and a half. But surely that can't be all there was to it—ideas do not come and go so fast—and a more important factor seems to have been the critical difference in function between the two documents. The Declaration of Independence was, to put it bluntly, a brief (with certain features of an indictment). People writing briefs are likely, and often well advised, to throw in arguments of every hue. People writing briefs for revolution are obviously unlikely to have apparent positive law on their side, and are therefore well advised to rely on natural law.[2] This the argument for our Revolution did, combining natural law concepts with references to positive law, both English and colonial, to the genuine "will of the people," to the "rights of Englishmen"—in short, with references to anything that seemed to help. "It was the quarrel with Britain that forced Americans to reach upward and bring natural law down from the skies, to be converted into a political theory for use as a weapon in constitutional argument; in that capacity it was directed against British policies and was never intended as a method of analyzing the rights and wrongs of colonial life." The Constitution was not a brief, but a frame of government. A broadly accepted natural law philosophy surely could have found a place within it, presumably in the Bill of Rights. But such philosophies were not that broadly accepted. Since the earlier impetus that had moved the Declaration, the need to "make a case," was no longer present, these controversial doctrines were omitted, at least in anything resembling explicit form, from the later document.

Natural law was also part of the rhetoric of antislavery, but again it was just one arrow in the quiver. As suited their purposes, the abolitionists, like the revolutionaries before them, argued both positive law, now in the form of existing constitutional provisions, and natural law. And for them too, the latter reference was virtually unavoidable, since it took a purity of spirit that transcended judgment not to recognize that the original Constitution, candidly considered, not only did not outlaw slavery, but deliberately protected it. "When it was the fashion to speak and write of 'natural' law very few stopped to consider the exact significance of that commonplace of theological, economic, literary, and scientific, as well as political, thought. Particularly is this true of the use of theories of natural law in the heat of controversies. At such times it is the winning of a cause, not the discussion of problems of ontology, which occupies men's minds." *Justice Accused,* Robert Cover's fine recent book on antislavery and the judicial process, corroborates the conclusion that for early American lawyers, references to natural law and natural rights functioned as little more than signals for one's sense that the law was not as one felt it should be. This is not to say that "natural law" was entirely without perceived legal significance. It was thought to be invocable interstitially, when no aspect of positive law provided an applicable rule for the case at hand. But it was subordinate to applicable statutes and well-settled precedent as well as to constitutional provisions, and not generally perceived as a source of values on whose basis positive law could be constitutionally upset.

We shouldn't make too much of this historical record, though. If there is such a thing as natural law, and if it can be discovered, it would be folly, no matter what our ancestors did or didn't think, to ignore it as a source of constitutional values. It's not nice to fool Mother Nature, and even Congress and the President shouldn't be allowed to do so. The idea is a discredited one in our society, however, and for good reason. "[A]ll theories of natural law have a singular vagueness which is both an advantage and disadvantage in the application of the theories." The advantage, one gathers, is that you can invoke natural law to support anything you want. The disadvantage is that everybody understands that. Thus natural law has been summoned in support of all manner of causes in this country—some worthy, others nefarious—and often on both sides of the same issue. Perhaps the most explicit invocation of natural law in a Supreme Court opinion appears in Justice Bradley's 1872 opinion in *Bradwell v. Illinois,* denying Ms. Bradwell's application to become a lawyer:

> [T]he civil law, as well as nature herself, has always recognized a wide difference in the respective spheres and destinies of man and woman. . . . The constitution of the family organization, which is founded in the divine ordinance, as well as in the nature of things, indicates the domestic sphere as that which properly belongs to the domain and functions of womanhood. . . . The paramount destiny and mission of woman are to fulfill the noble and benign offices of wife and mother. This is the law of the Creator.

But in fact the list of causes natural law has supported is almost infinite.

> [N]atural law has had as its content whatever the individual in question desired to advocate. This has varied from a defence of theocracy to a defence of the complete separation of church and state, from revolutionary rights in 1776 to liberty of contract in recent judicial opinions, from the advocacy of universal adult suffrage to a defence of rigid limitations upon the voting power, from philosophical anarchy in 1849 with Thoreau to strict pater-

nalism five years later with Fitzhugh, from the advocacy of the inalienable right of secession to the assertion of the natural law of national supremacy, from the right of majority rule to the rights of vested interests.

It was, indeed, invoked on both sides of the slavery question. Calhoun cited natural law to "prove" the inferiority of blacks, and the Kentucky Constitution of 1850 and the Kansas Constitution of 1857 declared the right to own slaves "before and higher than any constitutional sanction." Small wonder, then, that abolitionists like Wendell Phillips came to realize that "[b]ecause 'nature' no longer spoke with a single voice, only the judge's conscience ultimately determined the source of right."

It has thus become increasingly evident that the only propositions with a prayer of passing themselves off as "natural law" are those so uselessly vague that no one will notice—something along the "No one should needlessly inflict suffering" line. "[A]ll the many attempts to build a moral and political doctrine upon the conception of a universal human nature have failed. They are repeatedly trapped in a dilemma. Either the allegedly universal ends are too few and abstract to give content to the idea of the good, or they are too numerous and concrete to be truly universal. One has to choose between triviality and implausibility." The concept has consequently all but disappeared in American discourse. The influence of religion has declined, but that isn't the real point: even persons who count themselves religious are unlikely to hold that the Almighty speaks with a sufficiently unambiguous ethical voice to help with today's difficult issues of public policy. Perhaps physical laws will be found "out there," though even that faith is fraying, but in any event moral laws will not. In 1931 Benjamin Wright wrote, in *American Interpretations of Natural Law:* "Since the Civil War the concept has been of importance only in the field of constitutional law. Here certain of the traditional individual rights doctrines have been taken over and woven into the fabric of due process of law and liberty of contract. In systematic theory it has served almost solely as an object of criticism." One thing has changed since 1931: constitutional lawyers have gotten the message, and the concept is no longer respectable in that context either.

This is not to say that the arguments against "moral absolutism" have not been overstated. It is no fairer to cite the dissenting "morality" of Adolf Hitler to prove the nonexistence of moral truth than it would be to invoke the views of the Flat Earth Society to prove there is not a correct position on the shape of the world. There *are* ethical positions so hopelessly at odds with assumptions most of us hold that we would be justified in labeling them (if not with absolute precision) "irrational." But the set of such propositions will turn out to be the mirror image of the set of propositions sufficiently vague and uncontroversial to pass themselves as "natural law": an example here would be the proposition that the infliction of needless suffering is morally acceptable. The existence of such a set of plainly unentertainable ethical propositions will obviously be no more relevant to constitutional disputes than will their plainly undeniable counterparts. Constitutional litigation will involve an action that has been approved by the legislative branch of the government involved or someone ultimately accountable thereto, whose action in addition has seemed sufficiently acceptable to a government lawyers' office to result in governmental defense in court. Such actions will involve a *choice* of evils (or goods). They may involve the infliction of suffering for reasons whose sufficiency on balance is open to argument; they will not involve the infliction of suffering that can fairly be labeled needless.

Another point that is sometimes made in this context is that what appear on the surface to be ethical disputes will often turn out on analysis to be disagreements over what the facts are. This position can be overstated. Some disputes—cruelty to animals and abortion are two—are over the appropriate breadth of the moral universe and not over any factual claim. More often, an apparent ethical dispute will preeminently involve a balancing or comparison of two or more quite well understood costs—abortion again, once fetuses are admitted to the universe of moral concern, is an example—and this is a paradigmatically ethical dispute. It is undoubtedly true, however, that at least some apparent moral disagreements do hide different factual assumptions. What follows for the constitutional context, though? That courts should resolve the disputes, by finding the actual facts and applying to them what all, presumably, would then agree—let's pass *that* problem—was the appropriate moral principle? That can't be right. In the first place, it isn't clear why judges should be the ones to find the facts in such situations. Broad questions of public policy are likely to involve what are called, uncoincidentally, "legislative facts," or broad factual generalizations, as opposed to specific "adjudicative facts." The conventional wisdom here, that courts are markedly worse than legislatures at determining leg-

islative facts, surely can stand significant qualification—but at the same time there isn't any reason to suppose they are better at it. More fundamentally, these are likely to be situations in which the facts are inherently intractable, not susceptible to resolution in any way that would satisfy all observers. The ancient, and recently reheated, controversy over whether the death penalty actually deters homicides is a good example. It shows us what is genuinely likely to be at stake in public policy controversies, namely questions of *how public institutions should behave under conditions of empirical uncertainty*. That factual uncertainty is an element of a problem does not mean the problem is not a profoundly moral one, or that it is one courts have any superior claim to being able or entitled to solve.

When I was a lad studying philosophy in the late 1950s, epistemology and logic were all the rage, and moral and political philosophy were sneered at by knowledgeables: after all, one couldn't really *reason* about ethical issues, could one? That day, happily, has passed: people *do* reason about such issues and some of them number among our most renowned contemporary philosophers. But the kind of reasoning that is involved in the arguments of contemporary moral philosophers proceeds from ethical principles or conclusions it is felt the reader is likely already to accept to other conclusions or principles he or she might not previously have perceived as related in the way the writer suggests. Surely this is reasoning, for reasoning in other areas consists in nothing more. But note the critical appeal at the outset to acceptance of the initial proposition or conclusion: the inference proceeds, as it must, from one "ought" to another. We have learned once again that we *can* reason about moral issues, but reasoning about ethical issues is not the same as discovering absolute ethical truth. So we're where we were: our society does not, rightly does not, accept the notion of a discoverable and objectively valid set of moral principles, at least not a set that could plausibly serve to overturn the decisions of our elected representatives.

Neutral Principles

In 1959 Herbert Wechsler delivered a widely heralded lecture, which became a widely heralded article, entitled "Toward Neutral Principles of Constitutional Law." He argued that the Supreme Court, rather than functioning as a "naked power organ" simply announcing its conclusions ad hoc, should proceed on the basis of principles that transcend the case at bar and treat like cases alike. Having announced such a principle in one case, the Court should then proceed unflinchingly to apply it to all others it controls. Consciousness of this obligation to the future will obviously help shape the principle the Court will formulate, and thus the result it will reach, in the first case. (What he said, in short, is that the Court should act in a principled fashion.)

Even this suggestion has had its detractors. There are those who will wax quite eloquent on the byzantine beauty of what is sometimes called the common law method, one of reaching what instinctively seem the right results in a series of cases, and only later (if at all?) enunciating the principle that explains the pattern—a sort of connect-the-dots exercise. This quarrel is of no concern to us here, though obviously I wouldn't have written this book if I weren't with Wechsler on *that* point. What is relevant here is that as embellished by the subsequent literature, Wechsler's suggestion was given another dimension, one it is not entirely clear he intended. "Neutral principles" became not simply an appropriate *requirement* for judicial behavior but also, in the minds of much of the profession, a *source* of constitutional judgment—a sufficient as well as necessary condition of legitimate constitutional decision-making. The articulation of a neutral principle, the idea seems sometimes to run, is itself sufficient guarantee that the Court is behaving appropriately.

We needn't spend long on this suggestion. Its unambiguous endorsement has been rare, and its fallacy has been pointed out by others. An insistence on "neutral principles" does not by itself tell us anything useful about the appropriate content of those principles or how the Court should derive the values they embody. The requirement means initially—this much is easy in theory, though we all know people who don't abide by it—that a principle, once promulgated, is to be applied to all cases it controls and not just when one is in the mood. But that can't be enough: the principle that "Freedom of speech is guaranteed to Republicans" would not satisfy us as "neutral," no matter how unblinkingly it was applied. Thus some degree of generality must also be required to make a principle count as "neutral" in Wechsler's sense. Even in the unlikely event that we could agree on what degree of generality should be required, however, we still would not have arrived at a formula that would guarantee the *appropriateness* of the principle. The principle that "Legislatures can do whatever they want"—even if (especially if) un-

blinkingly applied—would obviously be unacceptable, but hardly because of inadequate generality.

"Neutral principles" has often served as a code term for judicial conservatism, probably because Wechsler himself originally used the concept in criticizing *Brown v. Board of Education* as wrongly decided. But it needn't have been so: there are neutral principles of every hue. (How about "No racial segregation, ever"?) In fact the Warren Court probably came as close to the ideal as any of its predecessors: the problem for the commentators may actually have been too much generality, not too little. But however that may be, requirements of generality of principle and neutrality of application do not provide a source of substantive content.

Reason

> If a society were to design an institution which had the job of finding the society's set of moral principles and determining how they bear in concrete situations, that institution would be sharply different from one charged with proposing policies. . . . It would provide an environment conducive to rumination, reflection, and analysis. "Reason, not Power" would be the motto over its door.
>
> —Harry Wellington

The constitutional literature that has dominated the past thirty years has often insisted that judges, in seeking constitutional value judgments, should employ, in Alexander Bickel's words, "the method of reason familiar to the discourse of moral philosophy." "Judges have, or should have, the leisure, the training, and the insulation to follow the ways of the scholar in pursuing the ends of government." This view, like the others we are considering, seldom appears in unadulterated form. (Indeed, much of the point is that these various value sources, in their understandable confusion, fall all over one another.) It is, however, one of the more important presences.

Technically, of course, reason alone can't tell you anything: it can only connect premises to conclusions. To mean anything, the reference has to be somewhat richer, to implicate the invocation of premises along with the ways in which one reasons from them. The basic idea thus seems to be that moral philosophy is what constitutional law is properly about, that there exists a correct way of doing such philosophy, and that judges are better than others at identifying and engaging in it. Now I know lawyers are a cocky lot: the fact that our profession brings us into contact with many disciplines often generates the delusion that we have mastered them all. But surely the claim here cannot be that lawyers and judges are the best imaginable people to tell good moral philosophy from bad: members of the clergy, novelists, maybe historians, to say nothing of professional moral philosophers, all seem more sensible candidates for this job. I suppose that this isn't the relevant comparison, though, and that all that has to be demonstrated is that of the institutions existing in our government, courts are those best equipped to make moral judgments, in particular that they are better suited to the task than legislatures.

Since judges tend generally to be drawn from roughly the same ranks as legislators, the heart of the argument here is that moral judgments are sounder if made dispassionately, and that because of their comparative insulation judges are more likely so to make them. "[T]he environment in which legislators function makes difficult a bias-free perspective. It is often hard for law-makers to resist pressure from their constituents who react to particular events (a brutal murder, for instance) with a passion that conflicts with common morality." One might begin by questioning the alleged incompatibility between popular input on moral questions and "correct" moral judgment. In fact there are reasons for supposing that our moral sensors function *best* under the pressure of experience. Most of us did not fully wake up to the immorality of our most recent war until we were shown pictures of Vietnamese children being scalded by American napalm. Professor Bickel makes this point in what must have seemed to him an unrelated section of his book:

> There was an unforgettable scene . . . in one CBS newscast from New Orleans, of a white mother fairly foaming at the mouth with the effort to rivet her distracted little boy's attention and teach him how to hate. And repeatedly, the ugly, spitting curse, NIGGER! The effect, achieved on an unprecedented number of people with unprecedented speed, must have been something like what used to happen to individuals (the young Lincoln among them) at the sight of an actual slave auction, or like the slower influence on northern opinion of the fighting in "Bleeding Kansas" in 1854–55.

It is thus no surprise that the case that our "insulated" judiciary has done a better job of speaking for our better moral selves turns out to be historically shaky. "Can we really be sure that it was Marshall or Taney rather than Clay or Webster who did the better job of articulating values? Which of the Civil War Justices excelled Lincoln in voicing the hopes and goals of the republic? . . . Which Justice in the 1920's gave better tongue than Norris or LaFollette to the American dream?"

A more fundamental error underlies the view under consideration, however—an outsider's error, akin to the assumption nonlawyers frequently make that there is something called "the law" whose shape good lawyers will describe identically. (Whatever one's profession, I assume this phenomenon is recognizable.) The error here is one of assuming that something exists called "the method of moral philosophy" whose contours sensitive experts will agree on, that "there are only two kinds of reasoning—one is sound and the other is unsound." That is not the way things are. Some moral philosophers think utilitarianism is the answer; others feel just as strongly it is not. Some regard enforced economic redistribution as a moral imperative; others find it morally censurable. What may be the two most renowned recent works of moral and political philosophy, John Rawls's *A Theory of Justice* and Robert Nozick's *Anarchy, State and Utopia,* reach very different conclusions. There simply does not exist *a* method of moral philosophy.

Ronald Dworkin also succumbs to this error. Writing in 1972 he said:

> Constitutional law can make no genuine advance until it isolates the problem of rights against the state and makes that problem part of its own agenda. That argues for a fusion of constitutional law and moral theory, a connection that, incredibly, has yet to take place. It is perfectly understandable that lawyers dread contamination with moral philosophy, and particularly with those philosophers who talk about rights, because the spooky overtones of that concept threaten the graveyard of reason. But better philosophy is now available than the lawyers may remember. Professor Rawls of Harvard, for example, has published an abstract and complex book about justice which no constitutional lawyer will be able to ignore.

The invitation to judges seems clear: seek constitutional values in—that is, overrule political officials on the basis of—the writings of good contemporary moral philosophers, in particular the writings of Rawls. Rawls's book *is* fine. But how are judges to react to Dworkin's invitation when almost all the commentators on Rawls's work have expressed reservations about his conclusions? The Constitution may follow the flag, but is it really supposed to keep up with the *New York Review of Books?*

One might be tempted to suppose that there will be no systematic bias in the judges' rendition of "correct moral reasoning" aside from whatever derives from the philosophical axioms from which they begin. ("We like Rawls, you like Nozick. We win, 6–3. Statute invalidated.") That would certainly be bad enough, but the actual situation is likely to be somewhat worse. Experience suggests that in fact there will be a systematic bias in judicial choice of fundamental values, unsurprisingly in favor of the values of the upper-middle, professional class from which most lawyers and judges, and for that matter most moral philosophers, are drawn. People understandably think that what is important to them is what is important, and people like us are no exception.[3] Thus the list of values the Court and the commentators have tended to enshrine as fundamental is a list with which readers of this book will have little trouble identifying: expression, association, education, academic freedom, the privacy of the home, personal autonomy, even the right not to be locked in a stereotypically female sex role and supported by one's husband. But watch most fundamental-rights theorists start edging toward the door when someone mentions jobs, food, or housing: those are important, sure, but they aren't *fundamental.*

Thus the values judges are likely to single out as fundamental, to the extent that the selections do not simply reflect the political and ethical predispositions of the individuals concerned, are likely to have the smell of the lamp about them. They will be—and it would be unreasonable to expect otherwise if the task is so defined—the values of what Henry Hart without irony used to call "first-rate lawyers." The objection to "reason" as a source of fundamental values is therefore best stated in the alternative: either it is an empty source, in the same way "neutral principles" turned out to be an empty source, or, if not empty, it is so flagrantly elitist and undemocratic that it should be dismissed forthwith.[4] Our society did not make the constitutional decision

to move to near-universal suffrage only to turn around and have superimposed on popular decisions the values of first-rate lawyers. As Robert Dahl has observed, "After nearly twenty-five centuries, almost the only people who seem to be convinced of the advantages of being ruled by philosopher-kings are . . . a few philosophers."

Tradition

> Running men out of town on a rail is at least as much an American tradition as declaring unalienable rights.
>
> —Garry Wills

Tradition is an obvious place to seek fundamental values, but one whose problems are also obvious. The first is that people have come to understand that "tradition" can be invoked in support of almost any cause. There is obvious room to maneuver, along continua of both space and time, on the subject of which tradition to invoke. Whose traditions count? America's only? Why not the entire world's? (For some reason Justice Frankfurter liked to refer to the "traditions of the English-speaking people.") And what is the relevant time frame? All of history? Ante-constitutional only? Prior to the ratification of the provision whose construction is in issue? Why not, and indeed this seems the more usual reference, extending to the present day? (Once you're there, however, you're verging into a somewhat distinct approach.) And who is to say that the "tradition" must have been one endorsed by a majority? Is Henry David Thoreau an invocable part of American tradition? John Brown? John Calhoun? Jesus Christ? It's hard to see why not. Top all this off with the tremendous uncertainties in ascertaining anything very concrete about the intellectual or moral climates of ages passed, and you're in a position to prove almost anything to those who are predisposed to have it proved or, more candidly, to admit that tradition doesn't really generate an answer, at least not an answer sufficiently unequivocal to justify overturning the contrary judgment of a legislative body.[5]

The indications in *Regents of the University of California v. Bakke* that racial preferences for historically disadvantaged minorities are to be treated as (at least somewhat) constitutionally suspect were quite explicitly rooted in an appeal to tradition. "This perception of racial and ethnic distinctions is rooted in our Nation's constitutional and demographic history." And indeed Justice Powell was able to assemble a collection of historical statements to the effect that a person's legal status should not be affected by his race. Those statements, however, were made in the context of discussing whether whites should be permitted to advantage themselves at the expense of racial minorities: to quote them in the affirmative action context without taking account of that critical fact is to succumb to the understandable temptation to vary the relevant tradition's level of abstraction to make it come out right.

Even with respect to the use of racial discrimination to *dis*favor minorities, our country has two conflicting traditions: the egalitarian one to which most official documents have paid lip service over the past century, and the quite different and malevolent one that in fact has characterized much official and unofficial practice over the same period (and certainly before). Presumably no reader would wish to endorse the latter tradition, but I'd be interested to hear the argument that can make it go away. Assume that by some magic it will, however, and assume therefore a unitary American tradition against the use of racial classification to disadvantage minorities: even that contrivance will not, unless we cheat, generate a unitary tradition on the different question of whether racial minorities can be favored. In recent years there have been numerous official programs that give breaks of one sort or another to persons because of their minority race. It is true that in some earlier periods such programs did not exist, but that may have been because those concerned with improving the lot of minorities had their hands full attempting, generally unsuccessfully, to combat widespread official discrimination *against* minorities. In fact the only prior period during which affirmative action for racial minorities seems even to have been a realistic possibility was Reconstruction. Some did object, apparently in part on principle—the name of Andrew Johnson is one that comes to mind here—but it surely seems more relevant that the Reconstruction Congress, the same Congress that gave us the amendment under which Bakke brought his challenge, passed over Johnson's veto such explicit preferences for blacks as those contained in the Freedmen's Bureau Act of 1866. In the heat of debate one might attempt to identify Reconstruction as the relevant period from which to draw those traditions that should define our construction of the Fourteenth Amendment, and surely that seems no more disreputable than other appeals to tradition we have seen. The more honest conclu-

sion, however, is that one must look elsewhere to decide what racial and other groups are to be permitted constitutionally to do to and for each other. There does not exist an unambiguous American tradition on the question of whether racial majorities can act to aid minorities, and one can make it seem there is only by quoting out of context.

It is never satisfactory to rest one's whole objection to a constitutional theory on grounds of indeterminacy, if only because the implications of *any* nontrivial theory will be open to debate. There are, however, serious theoretical problems with tradition as a source of constitutional values. Its overtly backward-looking character highlights its undemocratic nature: it is hard to square with the theory of our government the proposition that yesterday's majority, assuming it was a majority, should control today's. Of course part of the point of the Constitution is to check today's majority. This observation simply compounds the problems with making tradition a source of constitutional values, however, since the provisions for which we are seeking a source of values were phrased in open-ended terms to admit the possibility of growth. (If one wanted to freeze a tradition, the sensible course would be to write it down.) Moreover, "[i]f the Constitution protects only interests which comport with traditional values, the persons most likely to be penalized for their way of life will be those least likely to receive judicial protection," and that flips the point of the provisions exactly upside down. Reliance on tradition therefore seems consistent with neither the basic theory of popular control nor the spirit of the majority-checking provisions to which we are seeking to give content. For these reasons the reference is invariably a passing one, buttressing what turns out to be the most common reference-in-chief, the genuine consensus of contemporary American thought.

Consensus

Few of us would march our sons and daughters off to war to preserve the citizen's right to see "Specified Sexual Activities" exhibited in the theaters of our choice.
—United States Supreme Court (1976)

The idea that society's "widely shared values" should give content to the Constitution's open-ended provisions—that "constitutional law must now be understood as expressing contemporary norms" turns out to be at the core of most "fundamental values" positions. Just as those who talk about tradition usually wind up with something like "today's values viewed in the light of tradition," something like contemporary value consensus almost inevitably ends up giving content to the inherently contentless notions of "reason" and "principle." The reference has received its clearest recent articulation by Harry Wellington, who put it in terms of "conventional" or "common" morality: "The Court's task is to ascertain the weight of the principle in conventional morality and to convert the moral principle into a legal one by connecting it with the body of constitutional law."

In theory this approach solves two problems we have seen with earlier ones. In theory it is not incomplete. Consensus or conventional morality is postulated as something "out there" that can be discovered. And in theory it is not undemocratic. Quite to the contrary, it is billed by Wellington as a "reference to the people." F. A. Hayek elaborates: "Only a demagogue can represent as 'anti-democratic' the limitations which long-term decisions and the general principles held by the people impose upon the power of temporary majorities."

I guess this makes me a demagogue, but I think both claims—that judicial references to popular consensus are not incomplete and that they are not undemocratic—are wrong. As to the first, there is a growing literature that argues that in fact there is no consensus to be discovered (and to the extent that one may seem to exist, that is likely to reflect only the domination of some groups by others). It is sometimes said that the American consensus disintegrated in the 1960s. That would be rebuttal enough, but in fact it may be only the recognition that is recent:

> The lack of common interest between master and slave is obvious. So is the relationship between the military during World War II and the Japanese-Americans who were herded into internment camps in an order whose constitutionality was upheld by the Supreme Court. Latter-day disputes concerning the legitimate role of race in governmental decision-making, whether for purposes of segregation or affirmative action, or the legitimacy of the state's allowing the cessation of the possibility of life, by abortion or euthanasia, also present differences of the greatest magnitude regarding conceptions of justice.

Even if we assume, however—though it's virtually self-contradictory to do so—that there *is* a consensus lurking out there that contradicts the judgment of our elected representatives, there would still remain the point, sufficient in itself, that that consensus is not reliably discoverable, at least not by courts. As Louis Jaffe once inquired:

> How does one isolate and discover a consensus on a question so abstruse as the existence of a fundamental right? The public may value a right and yet not believe it to be fundamental. The public may hold that the rights of parents are fundamental and yet have no view whether they include sending a child to a private school. There may be a profound ambiguity in the public conscience; it may profess to entertain a traditional ideal but be reluctant to act upon it. In such a situation might we not say that the judge will be free to follow either the traditional ideal or the existing practice, depending on the reaction of his own conscience? And in many cases will it not be true that there has been no general thinking on the issue?

Thus when one gets down to cases, one finds much the same mix we found when the reference was to "natural law"—a mix of the uselessly general and the controversially specific. Roberto Unger's observation about references to tradition seems equally applicable here: "To make the doctrine plausible in the absence of divinely revealed moral truth, its proponents rely on references to moral opinions shared by men of many different ages and societies. The more concrete the allusions to this allegedly timeless moral agreement, the less convincing they become. Therefore, to make their case the proponents of objective value must restrict themselves to a few abstract ideals whose vagueness allows almost any interpretation." Express skepticism about the existence of moral consensus to someone who claims it means something, and you're likely to be given some jejune maxim like "No one should profit from his own wrong." Ask for an actual case where a constitutional court could legitimately overrule a legislative judgment on the basis of a moral consensus, and things get a little strange. In *Breithaupt v. Abram,* decided in 1957, the Supreme Court held that the drawing of twenty cubic centimeters of blood from the unconscious body of the obviously unconsenting petitioner, and the subsequent use of that blood to convict him of drunk driving, did not deny him due process. In doing so it rather explicitly employed a consensus methodology: "[D]ue process is not measured by the yardstick of personal reactions . . . but by that whole community sense of 'decency and fairness' that has been woven by common experience into the fabric of acceptable conduct. It is on this bedrock that this Court has established the concept of due process." Bedrock indeed: what the Court fails to note, for all its talk of community sense, is that three of the nine justices dissented. The doubtful attribution of consensus is not, I should hasten to add, a technique reserved for "conservative" causes. In their separate concurring opinions in *Furman v. Georgia* (1972), Justices Brennan and Marshall argued quite directly that the death penalty was unconstitutional because it was out of accord with contemporary community values. The risk in such a claim is obvious, and in this case it was tragically realized. Following *Furman* there was a virtual stampede of state reenactments of the death penalty, and the clarity of that community reaction surely had much to do with the Court's turnaround on the issue. The commentators' readings of society's values are as questionable as those of the justices. Professor Bickel wrote: "I would assert that the rightness of the Court's decision in the *School Segregation Cases* can be demonstrated [in terms of an appeal to societal values]. I would deny, however, that any similar demonstration can be or was mounted . . . to show that a statute setting maximum hours or minimum wages violates fundamental presuppositions of our society." One can surely understand the goal that is evident here—to find a way of approving *Brown* while disapproving *Lochner*. And I think that combination can responsibly be defended, but not in these terms. I suppose it's possible, though in fact it seems unlikely, that by 1954 the values of most of the country—assuming, despite our federal system, that opinion nationwide is what should count here—had moved to the point of condemning "separate but equal" schooling. And obviously, given the existence of the legislation whose constitutionality was in issue, there were in some quarters serious reservations about laissez-faire capitalism around the time of *Lochner*. Bickel's *comparative* judgment, however, seems indefensible: racism of the sort that supported separate schools was into the 1950s (and remains today) a strong strain in American life, and laissez-faire capitalism was a philosophy that was very widely entertained around the turn of the century. Dean Wellington, developing the implications of his "conventional morality" approach, pronounces, if more hesitantly, the same dubious verdict as Bickel on *Lochner*'s roots in popular opinion. His ability to

distinguish propositions that conventional morality supports from those it does not is displayed even more impressively, however, in the area of abortion:

> I take some comfort in the fact that the American Law Institute's Model Penal Code also would permit abortion for rape, to save the life of the mother, or if "the child would be born with grave physical or mental defect." The work of the Institute is a check of sorts. Its conclusions are some evidence of society's moral position on these questions. It is, indeed, better evidence than state legislation, for the Institute, while not free of politics, is not nearly as subject to the pressures of special interest groups as is a legislature.
>
> The Institute, however, would permit abortion in additional situations, most importantly where there was "a substantial risk that continuance of the pregnancy would gravely impair the physical or mental health of the mother." I would like to be able to find support for that position in conventional morality, for it surely coincides with my personal preference. But the Institute's position is here the best evidence there is and that does not seem enough. I do not understand how, by noticing commonly held attitudes, one can conclude that a healthy fetus is less important than a sick mother.

It's quite a slalom, but I doubt that there's room on it for anyone besides Wellington.

Examples could be multiplied, but it should by now be clear that by viewing society's values through one's own spectacles—resolving apparent inconsistencies in popular thinking in the "appropriate" direction by favoring the "emergent over the recessive," the "general over the particular," or whatever[6]—one can convince oneself that some invocable consensus supports almost any position a civilized person might want to see supported. As elsewhere, though, it is hard to claim that this alone adds up to a dispositive argument: there does not exist a nontrivial constitutional theory that will not involve judgment calls. In fact I think this one is worse than most in that regard, but in any event the comparative judgment is devastating: as between courts and legislatures, it is clear that the latter are better situated to reflect consensus. Sophisticated commentary never tires of reminding us that legislatures are only imperfectly democratic. Beyond the fact that the appropriate answer is to make them more democratic, however, the point is one that may on analysis backfire. The existing anti-majoritarian influences in Congress and the state legislatures, capable though they may be of *blocking* legislation, are not well situated to get legislation passed in the face of majority opposition. That makes all the more untenable the suggestion under consideration, that courts should invalidate legislation in the name of a supposed contrary consensus. Beyond that, however, we may grant until we're blue in the face that legislatures aren't wholly democratic, but that isn't going to make courts more democratic than legislatures.

An appeal to consensus, or to consensus tempered by the judge's own values, may make some sense in a "common law" context, where the court is either filling in the gaps left by the legislature—"legislating interstitially," in Cardozo's phrase—or, perhaps, responding to a broad legislative delegation of decision-making authority. Since they are "standing in" for the legislature, courts presumably should try to behave as (good) legislatures behave, and that may involve combining their best estimate of popular opinion with their own best judgment. All too often commentators accustomed to working in fields other than constitutional law, fields where appeals to this sort of filtered consensus may make sense, seek to transfer their analytical techniques to the constitutional area without dropping a stitch. After all, the inference seems to run, law is law, isn't it, and if it made sense there it should make sense here. The problem is that the constitutional context is worlds away: the legislature has spoken, and the question is whether the court is to overrule it in a way that can be undone only by the cumbersome process of constitutional amendment. That is precisely what constitutional courts must do—quite often, I shall argue. But to do so on the theory that the legislature does not truly speak for the people's values, but the Court does, is ludicrous.

The notion that the genuine values of the people can most reliably be discerned by a nondemocratic elite is sometimes referred to in the literature as "the Führer principle," and indeed it was Adolf Hitler who said "My pride is that I know no statesman in the world who with greater right than I can say that he is the representative of his people." We know, however, that this is not an attitude limited to right-wing elites. "The Soviet definition" of democracy, as H. B. Mayo has written, also involves the "ancient error" of assuming that "the wishes of the people can be ascertained more accurately by some mysterious methods of intuition open to an elite rather than by allowing people to discuss and vote and decide freely." Apparently moderates are not immune either.

The final problem, the most fundamental of all, comes into perspective when you step back a couple of paces and think about why we're engaging in this entire exercise. There are two possible reasons one might look to consensus to give content to the Constitution's open-ended provisions. One *might* say one was seeking to protect the rights of the majority by ensuring that legislation truly reflect popular values. If that were the purpose, however, the legislative process would plainly be better suited to it than the judicial. This leaves the other possible reason for the reference, to protect the rights of individuals and minority groups against the actions of the majority. That, of course, is what we've been about in this chapter. No one suggests that we look to "natural law" or "tradition" to ensure that the majority's will is in fact being worked; such references are instead calculated to protect minorities from the unchecked exercise of the majority's will. Now think again about consensus as a possible source, and the message will come clear: it makes no sense to employ the value judgments of the majority. The consensus approach therefore derives what apparent strength it has from a muddle: its methodology, which people slide into accepting because of its similarity to what courts may do properly in common law contexts, has nothing to do with the tasks they can legitimately set themselves in the area of constitutional adjudication.

Predicting Progress

In his 1969 Holmes Lectures, subsequently published as *The Supreme Court and the Idea of Progress,* the thinking of Alexander Bickel apparently took a new tack. The Warren Court, he claimed, had tried to prefigure the future, to shape its constitutional principles in accord with its best estimate of what tomorrow's observers would be prepared to credit as progress. In this, he argued, it had failed: already the Warren Court's "bets on the future" were coming up political losers. Bickel was somewhat elusive about whether he himself was prepared to accredit "tomorrow's values" as a source of constitutional judgment: his formal claim was that that had been the criterion of the Warren Court and that by its own criterion that Court had to be judged a failure. Though the point is arguable, I believe there was a good deal of prescription folded into Bickel's description. In any event others, before and after, have endorsed the method, even if Bickel did not mean to.

The problems with this approach are the familiar ones, in more aggravated form. First—assuming for the moment that we really are talking about a predictive task—there is no reason to suppose that judges are well qualified to foresee the future development of popular opinion. Professor Bickel, whose historical sensitivity surely exceeded that of most lawyers and judges, fell on his face—or so at least it seems as of 1980—explaining a decade ago how the Warren Court's great desegregation and reapportionment decisions had (already!) become irrelevant. That only proves he was human—we've all mistaken ripples for waves. But that's exactly the point: prediction is a risky enterprise for anyone, and there is no warrant for an appointed judge's supposing he is so much better at it than the legislature that he is going to declare their efforts unconstitutional on the basis of his predictions.

In addition, the reference is antidemocratic on its face. Controlling today's generation by the values of its grandchildren is no more acceptable than controlling it by the values of its grandparents: a "liberal accelerator" is neither less nor more consistent with democratic theory than a "conservative brake." Superimposed on this problem is one I noted in connection with a contemporary consensus approach: the imposition of allegedly majoritarian values is a mindless way of going about protecting minorities, and stipulating that the majority is to be a future majority does not suddenly make sense of it. But even assuming that by some miracle of logic we could convince ourselves that the sensible way to protect today's minorities from today's majority is to impose on today's majority the values of tomorrow's majority, it would remain a myth that "the values of tomorrow's majority" are data that prescient courts can discover in a value-neutral way. For today's judicial decision (no matter what its source of judgment) will inevitably have an important influence on the values of tomorrow's majority. The "prophecies" of people in power have an inevitably self-fulfilling character, even when what is being "prophesied" is popular opinion. This may or may not be a bad thing, but it does mean that the Court cannot be heard to plead value-neutrality on the theory that it is "taking its values from the future" rather than imposing its values *on* it: the fact that things turned out as the Supreme Court predicted may prove only that the Supreme Court is the Supreme Court. Thus by predicting the

future the justices will unavoidably help shape it, and by shaping the future they will unavoidably, indeed this is the point of the methodology, shape the present. Assuming it works, that amounts to the imposition of the justices' own values. That's just what the fundamental value theorists promised they wouldn't do to us; the fact that it's done with mirrors shouldn't count as a defense. . . .

There are a couple of reasons why Alexander Bickel has been such a central character in this chapter. He was probably the most creative constitutional theorist of the past twenty years. And he ran the gamut of fundamental-value methodologies. His career[7] is thus a microcosm, and it testifies to the inevitable futility of trying to answer the wrong question: "Which values, among adequately neutral and general ones, qualify as sufficiently important or fundamental or whathaveyou to be vindicated by the Court against other values affirmed by legislative acts?" It wouldn't do, he acknowledged, for the justices simply to impose their own values: he recognized, as others have pretended not to, that given the enormous influence of the judiciary such a course would be fundamentally inconsistent with the first principles of our democracy. Nor did he suppose for a moment that there was some timeless set of objectively valid natural law principles out there to be discovered by judges or anyone else. And so he began his quest. He was one of the first to see that incanting "neutral principles" doesn't begin to tell you what those principles should be, and though he talked a lot about "reason" it was clear he understood that some other ingredient was needed. Tradition was too backward-looking, at least for a Robert Kennedy liberal, which is what Bickel was as late as 1968. Consensus—now that was promising, that could solve the countermajoritarian difficulty. But slowly he came to realize, though he never gave up on the idea altogether, that there probably wasn't any consensus respecting the sorts of issues that came before the Court, and that even if there had been, the Court was one of the last bodies we should trust to find it. Thus "the idea of progress." Bickel's posthumously published book, *The Morality of Consent,* suggests that he soon saw this too for what it was, a thinly veiled imposition of personal judicial values on the present and future. What, then, to fill the breach? Unfortunately, a pastiche of themes remembered, with particular stress this time on one that hadn't much attracted the young Alex Bickel: tradition. His good friend Robert Bork explained at Bickel's Memorial Service that this

Burkean ending meant that Bickel had finally "resolved the tension" between his political liberalism and his judicial conservatism. "To read his *New Republic* piece on Edmund Burke is to see that his political philosophy had come into alignment with his legal philosophy." I remember choking as Bork said this, not because I disagreed that Bickel's politics had moved somewhat toward the end—I can't account for *The Morality of Consent* without that assumption either—but rather because of Bork's suggestion that there had been a contradiction to be resolved. For one perfectly well *can* be a genuine political liberal and at the same time believe, out of a respect for the democratic process, that the Court

should keep its hands off the legislature's value judgments. I've calmed down, though, and now I can see how *someone who started with Bickel's premise,* that the proper role of the Court is the definition and imposition of values, might well after a lifetime of searching conclude that since nothing else works—since there isn't any impersonal value source out there waiting to be tapped—one might just as well "do the right thing" by imposing one's own values. It's a conclusion of desperation, but in this case an inevitable desperation. No answer is what the wrong question begets.

---

1. The author earlier defined interpretivism as the view that "judges should confine themselves to enforcing norms that are stated or clearly implicit in the written Constitution."—Ed.
2. This is not a new insight. "If the written law tells against our case, clearly we must appeal to the universal law, and insist on its greater equity and justice." Aristotle, "Rhetoric" 1375a, in *The Basic Works of Aristotle* 1374 (R. McKeon ed. 1941).
3. "And so we arrive at the result, that the pleasure of the intelligent part of the soul is the pleasantest of the three, and that he of us in whom this is the ruling principle has the pleasantest life.

   "Unquestionably, he said, the wise man speaks with authority when he approves of his own life." Plato, *The Republic,* Book IX, in 2 *The Dialogues of Plato* 455 (4th ed. B. Jowett 1953).
4. The danger that upper-middle-class judges and commentators will find upper-middle-class values fundamental is obviously present irrespective of methodology. I think it's exacerbated when "reason" is the supposed value source, however, partly because the values we have mentioned are the values of the "reasoning class," and partly because "reason," being inherently an empty source, may lend itself unusually well to being filled in by the values of one's own kind.
5. A related technique is to discredit a practice by associating it with a disreputable tradition. See, e.g., *Shaughnessy v. United States* ex rel. Mezei, 345 *U.S.* 206, 217–18 (1953) (Black, J., dissenting). The techniques of association and dissociation can obviously be used in tandem. See, e.g., *Poe v. Ullman,* 367 *U.S.* 497, 542 (1961) (Harlan, J., dissenting) (emphasis added): "The balance of which I speak is the balance struck by this country, having regard to what history teaches are the traditions from which it developed as well as the traditions from which it broke." This technique is virtually omnipotent, since there is no litmus that

   can separate prior practices that are properly regarded as part of our tradition from those the framers "must have been rebelling against" (though any commentator is likely almost automatically to assume that those of which he or she disapproves belong in the latter category).
6. Such techniques are evident in the work of consensus theorists generally, and are sometimes made explicit. Ronald Dworkin argues that community values must be refined by the judge in a way that removes prejudice, emotional reaction, rationalization, and "parroting," and in addition should be tested for sincerity and consistency. R. Dworkin, *Taking Rights Seriously* 126, 240–58 (1977). See also, e.g., Wellington, "Common Law Rules and Constitutional Double Standards: Some Notes on Adjudication," 83 *Yale L. J.* 221, 251 (1973) (courts "must be reasonably confident that they draw on conventional morality and screen out contemporary bias, passion, and prejudice, or indeed, that they distinguish cultivated taste from moral obligation"); Perry, "Substantive Due Process Revisited: Reflections on (and beyond) Recent Cases," 71 *Nw. U. L. Rev.* 417, 442 (1976) (distinction should be drawn between "the commands to which conventional moral culture subscribes and the commands to which it not only subscribes but believes should have the force of law"). Some such collection of "laundering" devices is plainly needed, lest one be forced to the conclusion that the law the legislature passed is likely to reflect the way contemporary community values bear on the issues in question. Cf. Note, "Legislative Purpose, Rationality, and Equal Protection," 82 *Yale L.J.* 123, 127–32, 135–37 (1972).
7. "Tragically foreshortened" is too trite for Alex, who was never trite, in intellectual or personal style.

CONSTITUTIONAL INTERPRETATION AND ORIGINAL MEANING*

David Lyons

I. Constitutional Originalism

By "originalism" I mean the familiar approach to constitutional adjudication that accords binding authority to the text of the Constitution or the intentions of its adopters. At least since Marbury, in which Chief Justice Marshall emphasized the significance of our Constitution's being a written document, originalism in one form or another has been a major theme in the American constitutional tradition.[1]

Indeed, originalism can seem to be the only plausible approach to judicial review. One might reason as follows: "A court cannot decide whether an official decision conforms to the Constitution without applying its rules. The Constitution was written down to fix its content, and its rules remain unchanged until it is amended. Courts have not been authorized to change the rules. So courts deciding cases under the Constitution should follow the rules there laid down. By what right would courts decide constitutional cases on any other grounds?"

That challenge is conveyed by writings on judicial review that are regarded as originalist. But it is misleading. Most of the positions that are condemned by contemporary originalists accept the authority of the Constitution.[2] Although originalists present the issue as fidelity to the Constitution, it primarily concerns, I shall argue, how the Constitution is to be interpreted.

A distinctively originalist mode of interpretation assumes that the doctrinal content of the Constitution was completely determined when it was adopted and that constitutional doctrines can be identified by a value-free factual study of the text or of "original in-

tent." It is part of my purpose to show that this type of theory is not only less plausible than its severest critics have suggested,[3] but that significant alternatives to it are available (sections II and III).

An approach to judicial review includes not only a theory of interpretation, which tells us how to understand the Constitution, but also a theory of adjudication, which tells us how to apply the Constitution so interpreted—how it should be used in constitutional cases. Originalist theory is not usually analyzed in this way, but we shall find that the distinction is needed when considering contemporary originalism.

One would expect a distinctively originalist approach to adjudication to hold that constitutional cases should be decided on the basis of doctrines in the "original" Constitution (that is, the Constitution interpreted in an originalist way), and on no other basis whatsoever. I shall show that contemporary theorists who present themselves as strict originalists accept rules for judicial review that cannot be found in or otherwise attributed to the "original" Constitution (sections IV–VI).

A third point I wish to make is that doctrines drawn from general philosophy—ideas about meaning and morals, for example—play a significant role in contemporary originalist theorizing. This point is important because these philosophical notions are dubious and controversial. It must be emphasized, however, that some of the same philosophical ideas have wide currency in legal theory generally.

Although originalism has relatively few defenders, its most prominent champions are highly placed within the federal government. These include Robert H. Bork,[4] Judge on the United States Court of Appeals for the District of Columbia Circuit, Edwin Meese III,[5]

---

*From Lyons, David. "Constitutional Interpretation and Original Meaning," in *Social Philosophy and Policy* (1987). Reprinted by permission of Blackwell Publishers.

Attorney General of the United States, and William H. Rehnquist,[6] Associate Justice of the United States Supreme Court. It is important for us to recognize the quality of the constitutional theories that are embraced by these responsible officials. This paper is, then, a critique of constitutional originalism. We need a better theory. Although I shall not offer one here, I shall suggest some requirements for an adequate theory of constitutional adjudication.

II. Original Intent

Paul Brest's definition of "originalism" mentions two variants—"textualism" and "intentionalism."[7] The difference between them is significant. This section deals with constitutional intentionalism, especially its need for justification and the difficulties of finding any.

An originalist mode of interpretation holds that the doctrinal content of the Constitution was fixed when (or by the time that) the Constitution was adopted,[8] and that constitutional doctrines can be identified by a value-free factual inquiry. An intentionalist version of originalism holds that we must understand the Constitution in terms of the "intentions" of its framers, adopters, or ratifiers,[9] such as the specific applications that they had in mind, those they would have been prepared to accept, or their larger purposes.[10]

Champions of "original intent" seem to regard that approach to constitutional interpretation as so obviously correct that it requires no justification; for none seems to be offered. So it will be useful to begin by noting some aspects of intentionalism that imply its need for justification.

Reference to "original intent" is inherently ambiguous. The following questions indicate some (but not all) of that ambiguity. Whose intentions count? The intentions of, for example, one who drafts a text or one who votes for it? Which intentions count? To establish as authoritative some particular text, or some text understood in a certain way, or to serve some identifiable larger purposes? Reference to original intent is problematic in other ways too. While two or more individuals can share an intention, it is by no means clear how (or whether it is always possible) to aggregate the relevant attitudes of the members of a group so as to determine their collective intentions.[11] The answer that one gives to such questions should affect originalist interpretation, so the selection of any particular criterion of original

intent as the basis for interpreting the Constitution requires specific justification. In the absence of a satisfactory rationale, we should regard any particular criterion of original intent as theoretically arbitrary. Sad to say, original intent theorists generally ignore these fundamental problems, despite their having systematically been surveyed in law reviews for at least two decades.[12]

But the differences among the various versions of originalist intentionalism do not chiefly concern us now. The point I would like to emphasize is that *any* intentionalist approach requires substantial justification. Intentionalism is a special theory of constitutional interpretation, not a platitude.

Early in our constitutional career, the Supreme Court refused to apply the Bill of Rights to the several states, holding that the first ten amendments restricted only the federal government, although their language does not explicitly limit most of those amendments in that way.[13] In so deciding, the Court made some reference to the intentions of "the framers." Although the Court's grounds for its decision went far beyond original intent, its reference to framers' intent might suggest that the Court followed that criterion of constitutional meaning instead of the apparent meaning of the authoritative text. If that were so, the Court would have followed a special theory of constitutional interpretation, and one that requires substantial justification.

In general, we recognize that we do not always mean what we say or write; *we* may mean something different from the meaning *of the language* that we use. This is reflected in our reading of legal instruments such as wills and contracts. It has also been observed, by advocates as well as critics of intentionalism, that the surest guide to authors' intent is the authoritative constitutional text itself. This is possible only because the text is understood to carry a meaning that stands on its own—that is independent of its authors' intentions.[14]

It follows that intentionalism is a special theory of constitutional interpretation, not a platitude. Either it derives from a failure to appreciate the distinction between the meaning of a text and what its authors meant to convey; or else it presupposes some reason for holding that the meaning of the constitutional text, unlike that of texts generally, is a matter of authors' intent. So intentionalism is either confused or else requires substantial justification.

What might justify intentionalist constitutional interpretation? Originalists might appeal to (1) the idea (not limited to law) that interpretation should generally be governed by authors' intentions; (2) a specifically legal canon of construction; or (3) some theory of political morality that implies that we are under an obligation to respect the intentions of the framers, adopters, or ratifiers.

(1) *Intentionalism as a general approach to interpretation.* The notion that textual interpretation seeks generally to determine authors' intentions is plausible when our primary concern is what some individual had in mind, as in the case of personal communications, studies of literary figures and, in law, wills and contracts. The question is whether our proper concern when interpreting an authoritative public text such as a constitution is to determine what its authors had in mind. The suggestion seems to me implausible.

I do not wish to deny that, just as a poem can be a political statement, law can be read as literature. But law's distinctive functions are significantly different from those of literature and personal communications. Law tells us what we must or must not do, threatening punishment for disobedience. It places the coercive power of the state behind some individuals' decisions. It quite literally regulates death and taxes, war and peace, debts and compensation, imprisonment, conscription and confiscation, and innumerable other matters of direct, vital interest to individuals, communities, and often all humanity. That is the explicit, normal business of the law, including the U.S. Constitution.

An important feature of law's normal business is that it requires justification. The same applies, of course, to judicial decisions, including those that turn upon legal interpretation. They require justification, too. The justification of judicial decisions, like the justification of the normal business of the law generally, cannot be understood in narrowly legalistic terms. Adequate justification concerns not merely whether something is required or allowed by law but, also, whether what the law does is what I have elsewhere called "defensible."[15] All of this suggests that the need for justification may properly regulate matters of legal and specifically constitutional interpretation and, thus, that these matters turn on political morality.

(2) *Intentionalism as a theory of legal interpretation.* Could intentionalism be based on a general canon of construction for legal instruments? The possibility is suggested by the fact that statutory construction is said to seek out "legislative intent." But there are several difficulties here. Insofar as constitutional intentionalism relies upon a canon of construction that derives from precedent or common law, there

will be some difficulty incorporating such a theory of interpretation into originalism, as I shall explain later.

Another problem is this. Conventions regulate the identification of "legislative intent," such as the authority given to official reports from legislative committees. Such conventions have only problematic application to the U.S. Constitution. The existence of such conventions suggests something else that seems important, namely, that the search for "legislative intent" is not a purely factual inquiry about a consensus that obtained at a particular historical moment. This is suggested also by the fact that statutory construction characteristically seeks to interpret legislation in as favorable a light as possible; for example, as a reasonable and legislatively legitimate means to a reasonable and legislatively legitimate means to be a reasonable and legislatively legitimate end. Such a normative bias can be explained by the fact that statutory construction seeks to provide, if possible, a grounding for judicial decisions that are justified. If what counts as "legislative intent" is in fact shaped by normative considerations, it could not serve as a model for "original intent," for those who endorse the latter as the criterion of constitutional meaning regard it as a plain matter of historical fact, accessible to a value-free inquiry.

Originalists assume that the Constitution is a morally adequate basis for judicial decisions (as well as for our political arrangements generally). The normative bias within interpretation to which I refer requires that we interpret the Constitution in such a way that it is, if possible, capable of performing that function.

If statutory construction is no help to constitutional intentionalism, what about the interpretation of other legal instruments, such as wills and contracts? The first point made about "legislative intent" applies here, too: insofar as constitutional intentionalism relies upon a canon of construction that derives from precedent or common law, there will be some difficulty incorporating such a theory of interpretation into originalism.

It might nonetheless be thought that an intentionalist interpretation of contracts[16] could serve as a model for constitutional intentionalism. That is because political rhetoric often refers to the Constitution as the upshot of a "social contract." Now, the idea of a "social contract" is invoked to argue for obedience to law, however objectionable on other grounds it might be, so long as it does not violate constitutional restrictions. This means that a "social contract" basis for intentionalism is dependent on a theory of political morality. To accept intentionalism on this basis, we must establish the legitimacy of a "social contract" argument and its valid application to this case.

(3) *Intentionalism as a theorem of political morality*. Our discussion suggests that we should seek a rationale for constitutional intentionalism in the political morality of constitutional creation and application, that is, in principles that explain why the Constitution is worthy of respect and morally binding. Two ideas are provided by political rhetoric. One, already noted, refers to a "social contract." Another, asserted within as well as outside the Constitution, holds that it comes from "the people."

The latter idea is promising because contemporary originalists, like most constitutional theorists, emphasize the predominantly "democratic" character of our constitutional arrangements. Representative government nicely complements popular sovereignty. Political rhetoric suggests that "the people" knowingly and freely agreed to respect government so long as it conforms to the Constitution, and that "the people" are accordingly bound by that agreement. But this does not yet yield the constitutional theory of original intent, which requires that the Constitution be understood in terms of the "intentions" of a special subclass of "the people," namely, the framers, adopters, or ratifiers, as opposed to (say) the understanding that one might have of the Constitution based on text meaning.

The present line of reasoning requires us to suppose, then, (a) that "the people" *contracted to accept the intentions of the authors,* by reference to which the Constitution must therefore be understood, and (b) that *this* makes the Constitution binding on us now. The theory seems fatally flawed.

(a) In the first place, only a small minority of the people of that time and place were permitted to participate in the original adoption process. We lack precise figures, but it should suffice for present purposes to observe that the process excluded not only many adult white males (and, of course, children) but also women, chattel slaves, and Native Americans. It could not have included more than a small fraction of the total population, and willing contractors would have amounted to a smaller fraction still.

In the second place, it is doubtful whether any such contractors would have been morally competent to create obligations to respect political arrangements that continued chattel slavery, second-class citizenship for women, and the subjugation of Native Americans. At the very least, those subject to such arrangements could not be bound by a constitution simply because it was agreeable to others.

(b) In the third place, it is unclear how contracts made by members of earlier generations can bind succeeding generations. This is not to suggest that law can bind only those who have given their consent. But the mere fact that some people some time in the past have accepted a political arrangement cannot by itself automatically bind others. More is required than that to show that later generations are bound.

But the rhetoric of popular sovereignty is nonetheless illuminating. It suggests a commitment to popular government, however narrowly that was at first conceived.[17] Furthermore, the Constitution is a piece of public, not private law. Our proper concern in interpreting it is not to implement the understanding of parties to a limited, private agreement or the personal wishes of a testator, but to establish the basis for political arrangements and justified judicial decisions that legitimately concern the community as a whole. Whatever else is needed for a theory of constitutional adjudication, the legitimate interest of the entire population strongly suggests that the primary criterion of constitutional meaning should be popular understanding, the basic index of which must be text meaning.

Consider the alternative. Interpretation in terms of the intentions of constitutional framers or ratifiers would seem to assume a conception of law like that of the classical legal positivists Bentham and Austin, according to which an exclusive subgroup of the population makes law for others to follow.[18] That is objectionable because of our interest in justification. Interpretation based on anything like that conception of the law will present formidable obstacles to justifying the Constitution, justifying compliance with morally deficient laws so long as they conform to the Constitution, and justifying judicial decisions that those laws require.

The upshot is that constitutional intentionalism is profoundly problematic. There is no obvious linguistic or moral basis for interpreting the Constitution by reference to the intentions of an exclusive political group, as opposed to the meaning of the text. When these considerations are combined with other substantial objections to intentionalism, the theory seems unpromising indeed.

III. Alternatives to Intentionalism

In this section, I argue that intentionalism does not win out by default, despite its deficiencies.

According to Brest's typology, the originalist alternative to intentionalism is textualism, which comes in two varieties. "A strict textualist purports to construe words and phrases very narrowly and precisely."[19] Brest appears to argue that this is untenable both as textual interpretation and as originalism: "An originalist would hold that, because interpretation is designed to capture the original understanding, the text must be understood in the contexts of the society that adopted it."[20] This means that textualism must be "moderate" to be plausible. "A moderate textualist takes account of the open-textured quality of language and reads the language of provisions in their social and linguistic contexts."[21]

In other words, Brest judges the only legitimate originalist alternative to intentionalism[22] to be a reading of constitutional language as "open textured."[23] Unfortunately, Brest does not explain what he takes this to mean. But his reference to the spurious precision of "strict" textualism suggests that we might understand "moderate textualism" by reference to Hart's use of "open-textured" when he introduced that technical term into legal theory.[24]

Following the received wisdom of the time, Hart held that all terms in "natural" languages (which include the language of the law) are "open-textured." An "open-textured" word has a core of determinate meaning, encompassing fact situations to which it uncontroversially applies, and a "penumbra" encompassing fact situations to which the term neither clearly applies nor clearly does not apply. The idea of "open texture" assumes that the meaning of a word is indeterminate whenever there are reasons both for and against applying the word. This aspect of the theory of "open texture" provides a theoretical rationale for a view that is widely accepted by legal theorists, namely, that legal language has indeterminate meaning insofar as its proper application is unclear.

On this understanding, to characterize constitutional language as "open textured" is to imply that the doctrines given by that language are incompletely formed. Provisions that many theorists seem to believe fit this description to an extreme degree include the so-called "vague clauses" guaranteeing "free speech," "due process," "just compensation," "equal protection," and the like. On the "open texture" model, these provisions are seen as having tiny cores of clear (and therefore determinate) meaning and relatively wide unclear (and therefore indeterminate) penumbras.

This is a politically significant idea. For it implies that, insofar as the judicial process of "interpret-ing" the Constitution makes its proper application clearer, the process really *changes* the Constitution by making its meaning more determinate. The clearer doctrines resulting from such "interpretations" could not then be attributed to the "original" Constitution. That is the view of constitutional language that Brest seems to regard as the ("moderate") originalist alternative to "strict" textualism.

Given this conception of the alternatives, we can better understand why originalists regard as most significant the dividing line between "strict" and "moderate" originalism. That is because moderate originalism appears to collapse into nonoriginalism.

Originalism regards the authority of the "original" Constitution as axiomatic, whereas nonoriginalism holds that adherence to the Constitution requires justification and that principles of political morality that are capable of providing such justification might also justify deviation from it.[25] To clarify this difference, we can distinguish two categories of doctrines that might be used in constitutional cases. Those that can and those that cannot truly be attributed to the Constitution may be called "constitutional" and "extraconstitutional," respectively. Nonoriginalism is prepared to consider using extra-constitutional doctrines in constitutional cases, whereas a distinctively originalist theory of adjudication would presumably reject any such use of them.

"Moderate" originalism regards unclear constitutional language as "open-textured," or inherently somewhat vague. It also accepts the judicial practice of deciding cases under unclear aspects of the Constitution. But it seems to regard the constitutional "interpretations" that are used as creating, and the resulting decisions as applying, doctrines that are extra-constitutional—judicial amendments to the "original" Constitution. On this view, "moderate" originalism's approach to deciding cases under unclear aspects of the Constitution *is equivalent to nonoriginalism.* Such decisions would be condemned by a "strict" originalist who holds that, as courts have no authority to amend the Constitution, they should refrain from doing so.[26]

It must be emphasized that the line of reasoning sketched in the last few paragraphs assumes that "moderate" textualism regards the Constitution as indeterminate insofar as its proper application is unclear. But we need not assume this; we need not accept the dubious assumption that the meaning of a text is indeterminate whenever it is unclear, or whenever interpretation of it would be controversial, so that the discovery of text meaning is impossible precisely when it is needed.

Instead of discussing these issues in the abstract, it will be useful to consider an approach which agrees that such language in the "original" Constitution does *not* provide *complete* doctrines of just compensation, free speech, and the like. This approach nevertheless provides grounds for attributing the doctrines resulting from sound interpretations to the Constitution. This will provide us with all that we require for present purposes, namely, an alternative to "strict" intentionalism that might justifiably assign meaning to the Constitution and enable courts to decide cases on constitutional grounds.

It has been suggested[27] that the so-called "vague clauses" incorporate "contested concepts." It is the nature of such a concept to admit of competing "conceptions" and thus routinely to *require* interpretation. Contested concepts do not have built-in criteria of application; they are more abstract than that. As a result, different people can use the same (contested) concept while accepting and employing different standards for its application. It would seem, for example, that general normative concepts, such as "right" and "wrong," "good" and "bad," "right" and "obligation," as well as more specific normative concepts, such as particular virtues and vices, are "contested" in this way. When people agree about the "facts" but disagree in their evaluations, their disagreement concerns the principles that determine the proper application of those concepts to particular cases.

The notion of a "contested concept" is explicitly used, for example, in Rawls's theory of social justice, the relevant part of which can be explained as follows. Imagine that you and I disagree about the substantive requirements of social justice. We then differ as to how the concept of justice applies; we differ, that is, about the principles of justice. This is possible if the concept of justice admits of different interpretations, or competing conceptions. That seems to be the case.

Rawls maintains that the mere concept of justice determines no detailed, substantive criteria of justice, only the skeletal requirement that there be no "arbitrary distinctions" between persons but, rather, "a proper balance between competing claims."[28] The task of a theory of justice is to show (not merely to claim) the superiority of one conception (one principle or set of principles) over competing conceptions as an interpretation of this requirement. The possibility of a uniquely correct interpretation of a provision incorporating the contested concept of justice, then, depends on the superior justifiability of a particular conception of justice.

Now consider a constitutional example. Past judicial interpretations aside,[29] a court applying the just compensation clause would not necessarily decide a case as the original authors would have done, nor would it automatically follow a more popular consensus of the time (even if either were possible). Instead, a court would understand the Constitution to mean precisely what it says and thus to require *just compensation*. A court would need to defend a particular conception of just compensation (that is, it would need to defend principles of justice appropriate to compensation) against the most plausible alternatives. It would then apply that conception to decide the case at bar.

Someone might be skeptical about the possibility of justifying such an interpretation. Someone might believe it is impossible to provide a rational defense of, say, principles of just compensation and might therefore claim that a court adopting this approach would inevitably impose its own arbitrary conception of just compensation instead of the conception embraced by the authors of the Constitution or by a broader "original" consensus. (It should be emphasized that, on this view, an "original" conception of just compensation is completely arbitrary and indefensible.) Someone might hold, in other words, that all such principles are inherently arbitrary, so that courts cannot possibly do what is required to implement this approach to the interpretation of "vague" constitutional language.[30] I shall not offer a general critique of such skepticism,[31] but I shall suggest below why it is reasonable to believe that there can be a best conception among competing conceptions of some contested concepts. I shall later show how philosophical skepticism about values is, in this context, incoherent.[32]

Contested concepts do not seem confined to morality and law. Their properties are at any rate similar to those of concepts referring to natural substances or phenomena, such as water and heat. On a plausible understanding of the development of science, for example, the caloric and kinetic theories of heat are (or at one time were) competing conceptions of the concept heat. This is suggested by the fact that "heat" refers to a physical phenomenon that is but partially and imperfectly identified by any prescientific verbal definition of the word, and that something very much like the idea of a contested concept is required to explain how there can be two theories of heat, that is, two different conceptions of the single concept heat.

If, as most people would agree, "heat" refers to a determinate physical phenomenon, there can be, in principle, a best theory of heat. This implies that there can be a best conception of a contested concept, at least in some cases. This suggests, in turn, that contested concepts in the Constitution might have best interpretations.

The kinetic theory of heat has displaced the caloric conception and is currently our best conception of heat. As this example implies, we may be justified in using *our* best conception even if it is not in fact *the* best. Similarly, just as our best conception of heat is liable to change, so we may expect change from time to time in our best conception of, say, just compensation. This involves no moral relativism.

Now if the idea that the Constitution includes contested concepts is correct, then to apply the Constitution in terms of their best interpretation is, in effect, to apply doctrines whose application is called for by the original Constitution. But, just as interpretation of the concept heat requires more than mere reflection, any interpretation of this type inevitably draws upon resources that are neither implicit in the text nor purely linguistic. It makes essential use of political argument, though at a relatively general or abstract level. So this alternative approach implies that a sound interpretation—one faithful to the meaning of the text—can include substantive doctrines that are not derivable from the text (even supplemented by its original social and linguistic context) but that are identifiable only by reasoning about political principles in the context of the federal system.

It is important to emphasize that this approach to constitutional interpretation, where applicable, requires that an interpreter go outside the "four corners" of the text, its strict linguistic implications, and the relatively specific intentions of its authors,[33] for interpretations and arguments supporting them. But, as this is done because it is understood to be required by the very nature of contested concepts found within the Constitution, both the strategy of argument and its results can claim fidelity to the Constitution. For this reason, the interpretive approach just sketched might reasonably be regarded as "originalist."

As usually understood, however, "originalism" assumes that constitutional doctrines must be identified by a value-free factual study of the text or of original intent and that doctrines that are not implicit in the "original" text or "understanding" cannot truly be attributed to the Constitution. It accordingly rejects without a hearing the possibility of attributing to the Constitution interpretations of those contested concepts that are in the Constitution. That possibility gives reason to withhold assent from the more familiar originalist theories.

IV. Originalist Adjudication

The Fourteenth Amendment says that no state "shall deny to any person within its jurisdiction the equal protection of the laws." The meaning of this provision is unclear. If (as some suggest) the provision does not have any determinate meaning, how should courts deal with cases under it? The Constitution does not tell us what we should then do.

As I have suggested, a comprehensive theory of judicial review can be understood as having two parts. A theory of interpretation purports to determine constitutional meaning. If well grounded, such a theory should be welcome when the text is unclear. Furthermore, anyone who holds the text to be misleading needs a good theory to justify such a claim.

But theories about judicial review go beyond straightforward interpretation; they include theories of adjudication, which purport to determine how the Constitution should be applied.[34] Such a theory is required if cases are decided when the meaning of the Constitution is undetermined, or to justify departure from the Constitution's implications.

To illustrate the latter possibility, consider Thayer's famous deferential doctrine.[35] Thayer argued that federal legislation should never be nullified by federal courts unless it cannot reasonably be doubted that the legislation violates the Constitution. He held that this judicial policy was needed to promote respect for federal law and to protect the courts from legislative interference.[36] Thayer did not assume that the Constitution has no determinate meaning when there is reasonable disagreement about its meaning. On the contrary, he insisted that the judiciary should not apply its best interpretation of the Constitution but should defer whenever it is possible to regard the legislature's actions as constitutional.

> [W]hen the ultimate question is . . .
> whether certain acts of another department,
> officer, or individual are legal or permissible,
> . . . *the ultimate question is not what is the
> true meaning of the constitution, but whether
> legislation is sustainable or not.*[37]

Thayer recommends, in effect, that the courts should sometimes refrain from enforcing the Constitution, even when they have a good, justifiable, and perhaps sound idea of what it means. That amounts to a special theory of adjudication (and, incidentally, one that seems decidedly extra-constitutional).

The distinctively originalist approach to adjudicating constitutional cases would seem to hold that they should be decided exclusively by doctrines that can be found in the "original" Constitution, that is, interpreted in an originalist way. There is a problem here. It is by no means clear that originalist theory can be found within the "original" Constitution. If originalism itself includes extra-constitutional doctrines, then insofar as a court applied and was guided by this theory of adjudication, it would decide cases in a nonoriginalist way!

It may accordingly seem reasonable to revise the originalist theory of adjudication so that originalism does not prohibit its own application. It would be modified to say that a doctrine may be applied within judicial review if, but only if, the doctrine either is attributable to the Constitution (in the sense required by an appropriate originalist theory of interpretation) or else is a doctrine of originalism itself.

That problem seemed easily solved. But it may suggest how difficult it is to embrace originalism unqualifiedly. Take another example. Raoul Berger's attack upon judicial decisions that fail to respect "framers' intent" leads him to suggest that courts should repudiate all decisions that cannot be grounded upon the Constitution so construed, regardless of "undesirable consequences."[38] But Berger hastily retreats from this proposal, saying:

> It would, however, be utterly unrealistic and probably impossible to undo the past in the face of the expectations that the segregation decisions, for example, have aroused in our black citizenry—expectations confirmed by every decent instinct. That is more than the courts should undertake and more, I believe, than the American people would desire.[39]

Berger's retreat appears unprincipled. At best, he invokes an undefined and undefended extra-constitutional principle of constitutional adjudication, which clashes with his originalist pretensions.

Henry Monaghan appears sensitive to Berger's problem. He too says that the school desegregation decisions should not be undone. Unlike Berger, however, Monaghan suggests a judicial principle that would permit leaving those decisions undisturbed, even though he questions their constitutional warrant. His solution is to advocate a doctrine of judicial precedent.[40]

The question now is whether a doctrine of judicial precedent can be attributed to the "original" Constitution. Monaghan appears not to think so. But he believes that such a doctrine can be justified because it serves "the long-run values of stability and predictability for ordering our most fundamental affairs."[41]

Monaghan does not seem to appreciate the awkwardness of his position. In offering a justification for a doctrine of precedent based on its desirable consequences, he commits himself to holding that judicial review may be regulated by *any* principles whose use would serve the same "long-run values." That would permit the use in judicial review of an indeterminate class of useful extra-constitutional principles.[42]

One might, alternatively, suggest that a doctrine of precedent was in fact provided by the "original" Constitution. For the Constitution was grafted upon a system whose common law heritage includes, of course, a doctrine requiring courts to respect judicial precedent.[43] The trouble with this way of reasoning, from an originalist perspective, is that it would render the Constitution much less limited doctrinally than originalists tend to view it. It would imply that the Constitution contains a multitude of common law principles.

Monaghan's predicament suggests the instability of originalism. If an originalist believes that there is justification for respecting a judicial principle that is no more controversial than precedent, he not only runs the risk of agreeing that constitutional cases may properly be decided by doctrines that cannot be attributed to the Constitution; he may become committed to accepting a relatively indeterminate theory of judicial review, incorporating all the principles of constitutional adjudication that can be justified by the criteria that are needed to justify a doctrine of precedent.

This point is generalizable. Contemporary originalists are often preoccupied with "restraining" the federal judiciary in constitutional cases and tend to embrace theories of adjudication that are designed in part to limit judicial nullification of decisions made by elected officials. The relevant judicial principles require justification. If such principles cannot be found in the "original" Constitution, they require justification by reference to some principles of political morality. The considerations that are adduced or required to justify such doctrines are capable of justifying an indefinite class of other doctrines that are relevant to constitutional adjudication. To endorse an extra-constitutional principle is to commit oneself to endorsing any other principle that is justifiable on the same grounds that justify the one endorsed. Such an approach to constitutional adjudication is hardly consistent with the spirit of originalism.

V. Democratic Sensibilities

Constitutional theorizing nowadays puts an emphasis upon "democracy" that we have so far neglected. It arises in contexts like the following. Intentionalists believe that our knowledge of constitutional meaning extends only so far as our knowledge of original intent. What remains unclear can be assigned no determinate meaning. If it is assumed that the "interpretation" and application of unclear aspects of the Constitution involves extra-constitutional doctrines, it would be natural for originalists to prefer that courts refrain from deciding such cases.

One who wishes to justify such a policy of "judicial restraint" might suggest that the defendant should win whenever law is unclear and therefore indeterminate, because then the burden of proof cannot effectively be shouldered by a plaintiff or appellant.[44] This reasoning seems warranted by the notion that courts should decide cases by reference to existing law. Not requiring extra-constitutional doctrines, it seems compatible with originalism.

But extensive use of the burden-of-proof rule would be problematic in our system. Suppose, for example, that district courts in different circuits, believing they had adequate constitutional grounds for doing so, decided similar cases, but did so differently. Suppose, further, that their decisions involved aspects of the Constitution that their respective circuit courts regarded as indeterminate because unclear. If the circuit courts invoked the burden-of-proof rule, the result would in effect establish conflicting constitutional doctrines in different circuits. The federal courts would seem to require some extra-constitutional doctrine to extricate us from that predicament.

The alternative basis for a policy of "judicial restraint" is an argument from "democracy," which concludes that nonelected judges should not nullify decisions made by "electorally accountable" officials. The reasoning may be understood as follows. Insofar as political arrangements are subject to popular control through elections, they are regarded by many constitutional theorists as respecting democratic values. In addition, our system involves a division of political power under which popularly elected legislatures are authorized to make law and the judiciary is conventionally understood as authorized to interpret and apply, but not to make law.

One who assumes that unclear law is indeterminate will also believe that judges must "legislate" whenever they decide "hard cases." This practice is tolerable, or even desirable, when kept to a minimum, judges are elected and, most importantly, elected legislatures are able, if they wish, to modify the results by means of subsequent legislation. This would normally be the case except when courts must rule on limits to the legislature's authority.

From that perspective, judicial review by the federal courts of decisions made by elected officials is most problematic. In the first place, federal judges are not elected, but are appointed with indefinite tenure. Popular control is more limited over the federal judiciary than over elected officials (or, more generally, over those who are considered "electorally accountable"—those who, for example, are appointed but serve at the pleasure of elected officials). In the second place, such review concerns the constitutionality of nonjudicial decisions. Decisions made by electorally accountable officials are liable to be nullified by nonelected federal judges, and electorally accountable officials will be unable to override those judicial decisions. It is accordingly held by many constitutional theorists that such judicial review severely strains democratic principles.

These same democratic sensibilities are most seriously offended when judicial review is thought to be combined with "judicial legislation." Therefore, when constitutional cases turn upon the testing of nonjudicial decisions against unclear constitutional provisions, legal theorists tend to suppose that any substantive decision involves judicial revision of the Constitution itself. On the basis of such reasoning, contemporary originalists sometimes hold that decisions made by officials who are answerable to the electorate should not be nullified by nonelected judges unless it is clear that those decisions violate the Constitution.[45]

Some constitutional theorists are thought to lack such scruples. They are accused of claiming that courts may take it upon themselves to change the supreme law of the land. An example of such thinking is discussed by Justice Rehnquist, who quotes from a brief filed in federal court on behalf of state prisoners as follows:

We are asking a great deal of the Court because other branches of government have abdicated their responsibility. . . . Prisoners are like other "discrete and insular" minorities for whom the Court must spread its protective umbrella because no other branch of government will do so. . . . This Court, as the voice and conscience of contemporary society, as the measure of the modern conception of human dignity, must declare that the [named prison] and all it represents offends the Constitution of the United States and will not be tolerated.[46]

Rehnquist understands this to imply that "nonelected members of the federal judiciary may address themselves to a social problem simply because other branches of government have failed or refused to do so."[47] Federal judges would then have "a roving commission to second-guess Congress, state legislatures, and state and federal administrative officers concerning what is best for the country."[48] Rehnquist accordingly describes such a view as "a formula for an end run around popular government, genuinely corrosive of the fundamental values of our democratic society."[49]

Rehnquist's rhetoric is fired by "democratic" flames, so let us look more closely at this argument from democracy. It challenges the legitimacy of judicial review. If we were to formulate the argument rigorously, its conclusion would amount to the following proposition:

Judicial review of a non-judicial decision violates democratic principles to the extent that the reviewing judiciary is less directly accountable to a popular electorate than is the non-judicial decision maker.

To reach this conclusion, a premise like the following is needed:

Democratic principles imply that the more directly accountable an official decision maker is to a popular electorate, the greater the priority that should be given her official decisions.

This claim is dubious. It assumes that democratic standards apply directly to the several branches of a political structure, although the several branches are supposed to complement each other so as to yield a structure that is democratic overall. On the contrary, just as various amendments to the Constitution can

be understood as promoting the system's respect for democratic values, rather than compromising that commitment, judicial review may be instrumental in securing that respect.

The sort of premise that seems to be needed by the standard argument against judicial review invokes "democracy" in a problematic way. It seems to invoke a theory of the Constitution. But no attempt is made to explain what relation such a view must have to the Constitution if the former is to qualify as a theory of the latter, no less how a particular theory might be defended. This is especially important because it is uncertain whether any view can both qualify as a theory of the Constitution, to be used in constitutional interpretation, and be reconciled with "strict" originalism.

More generally, the premise of the standard argument from democracy fails to reflect any appreciation of the values that might explain the importance of accountability to a popular electorate. It is implausible to suppose that "electoral accountability" is a fundamental value. That it is not is suggested, for example, by the qualifications that one would reasonably place on electoral accountability before it could serve in such a role; for example, that elections be free and fair. This strongly suggests that electoral accountability derives its importance from some more fundamental value, such as the right to participate in shaping the rules that may be enforced against oneself or, perhaps, political equality. These values and their relation to electoral accountability require clarification. Until we understand the basic values at stake, we can hardly determine the relation between judicial review and a commitment to democracy. And yet the literature on judicial review is silent on such matters.

Now, a federal judge might find it awkward to endorse the argument from democracy. For it suggests that the constitutional system is "democratic" in such a way as to make judicial review illegitimate. One who endorses such an argument might find it difficult to function honestly in the federal judiciary, where judicial review is firmly established.

It turns out, however, that the argument from democracy is used not to block judicial review but, rather, to establish a presumption against it. It is thought to counsel "restraint." This is illustrated by Rehnquist's response to the argument from democracy. He does not reject judicial review. He endorses it on the ground that the constitutional arrangements including judicial review are given by "the people."[50] Unfortunately, Rehnquist's version of this claim is no more plausible than the one we considered in section II. A specious argument receives a glib reply.

It should be observed, finally, that Rehnquist charges those he criticizes as favoring "the substitution of some other set of values for those which may be derived from the language and intent of the framers."[51] As this formulation suggests, his argument really turns on how the Constitution is to be understood. The quoted brief claimed, after all, that courts have a special responsibility to protect "discrete and insular minorities." This is a proposition with which some constitutional scholars agree.[52] They hold this responsibility to be based on the Constitution, not created by judicial fiat. Rehnquist disagrees with this interpretation and treats its proponents as if they recommend infidelity to the Constitution.

VI. The Wages of Skepticism

An initially more promising argument regarding judicial review is presented by Professor (now Judge) Bork, who begins by rejecting the crude argument from democracy and by describing our constitutional system as "Madisonian":

> A Madisonian system is not completely democratic, if by "democratic" we mean completely majoritarian. It assumes that in wide areas of life majorities are entitled to rule for no better reason than they are majorities. We need not pause here to examine the philosophical underpinnings of that assumption since it is a "given" in our society. . . .[53]

Bork refrains from reflecting on the values that are at stake. This may be deliberate, for reasons that will emerge presently. But it is unfortunate because Bork, too, appears to offer us a theory of the Constitution.

Bork claims that "the Madisonian model" has two "premises." One is "majoritarian," the other "counter-majoritarian."

> The model . . . assumes there are some areas of life a majority should not control. There are some things a majority should not do to us no matter how democratically it decides to do them.[54]

To reconcile these "premises," we charge the Supreme Court to "define both majority and minority freedom through the interpretation of the Constitution."[55] Thus Bork accepts the legitimacy of judicial review. But, he says,

> the Court's power is legitimate only if it has, and can demonstrate in reasoned opinions that it has, a valid theory, derived from the Constitution, of the respective spheres of majority and minority freedom. If it does not have such a theory but merely imposes its own value choices, or worse if it pretends to have a theory but actually follows its own predilections, the Court violates the postulates of the Madisonian model that alone justifies its power.[56]

This passage suggests Bork's concern that the Court not impose its own "value choices."

He explains that concern in the course of an argument that appears more promising than Rehnquist's because it deals with the issues at a more fundamental level. Bork's argument may be summarized as follows:

1. Judicial decisions *should be* "principled."
2. Judicial decisions either *make* or *implement* "value choices."
3. Judicial decisions that *implement* "value choices" *can* be "principled."
4. There is *no* "principled" way to *make* a "value choice."
5. Judicial decisions *should implement,* rather than make, "value choices."
6. Law-creation, such as legislation or the framing of a constitution, involves *making* "value choices."
7. "Courts [reviewing legislation] must accept any value choice the legislature makes unless it clearly runs contrary to a choice made in the framing of the Constitution."[57]

This argument is originalist in spirit, if not entirely in content. An originalist theory of interpretation is suggested by the notion that certain "value choices" were made by the framers and are now available to be implemented by the courts. This corresponds to the idea that Constitutional doctrines are fixed when the document is framed. An originalist theory of adjudication is suggested too, as Bork comes near to claiming that only those doctrines embodying the "framers' value choices" should be applied by the Court.

Note that the last step in the argument appears to presuppose a nonoriginalist principle:

Whenever the Constitution is unclear, the Court should defer to the legislature.

What basis could there be for such a doctrine of "restraint"? Bork has no grounds for suggesting, for example, that the practice of judicial review should be confined because it suffers under a cloud of illegitimacy. For, as we have seen, he has rejected the dubious argument from democracy, endorsed the practice of judicial review, and assigned it an indispensable constitutional function.

Here is one possible explanation of that last step in Bork's reasoning. As we have observed, many legal theorists embrace assumptions about meaning which lead them to believe that law is indeterminate when it is unclear. As we shall presently see, Bork explicitly endorses an even more radical type of philosophical skepticism—about value judgments generally. It would therefore not be out of keeping for Bork to indulge in the semantical skepticism that leaps from "unclear" to "indeterminate." This would lead him to reason that, when (a) the Constitution does not *clearly* contain a doctrine that is violated by a piece of legislation, then (b) the Constitution contains *no* such doctrine, (c) the legislation does not violate the Constitution, and (d) the legislation should accordingly be accepted by the Court.[58]

But the most serious difficulty with Bork's reasoning derives from his value skepticism. To see this, we might begin by asking what is meant by a "value choice." This expression is so commonplace in constitutional theory that we may need to remind ourselves that it is an artifact of theory. Compare the expression with "value judgment." "Value choice" omits any reference to judgment, and so encourages the suggestion of arbitrariness and discourages any contrary suggestion of rational defensibility. The difference fits nicely into Bork's strategy of argument, which explicitly invokes a general philosophical doctrine of skepticism about the rational defensibility of value judgments.

As we have seen, Bork defines the central problem of "Madisonian democracy" as the need to strike a balance between "majority and minority freedom."[59] It is precisely in this context that he says, for example:

> Every clash between a minority claiming freedom and a majority claiming power to regulate involves a choice between gratifications of the two groups. When the Constitution has not spoken, the Court will be able to find no

scale, other than its own value preferences, upon which to weigh the respective claims to pleasure.[60]

Bork has two examples. One is Griswold, which he views as a judicial choice between two "claims to pleasure" and their respective "gratifications." Another is "a hypothetical suit by an electric company and one of its customers to void a smoke pollution ordinance as unconstitutional. The cases are identical."[61]

To make Bork's position perfectly clear, we should consider a different example. Prior to the Fourteenth Amendment, Bork would presumably respond to a suit seeking invalidation of a law banning Jews and Catholics from certain occupations, as follows:

> There is no way of deciding these matters other than by reference to some system of moral or ethical values that has no objective or intrinsic validity of its own and about which men can and do differ. Where the Constitution does not embody the moral or ethical choice, the judge has no basis other than his own values upon which to set aside the community judgment embodied in the statute.[62]

My point is not that a refusal to invalidate the statute would have been unfaithful to the law, for the contrary interpretation is, unfortunately, plausible. My point is that Bork's express reason for a judicial policy of "restraint" is that all opposing positions, including the rejection of bigotry, are rationally indefensible, so that, lacking constitutional warrant, a judicial decision favoring one would be "unprincipled" *just because* any "preference" for one side or the other *could not be* "principled." Value "choices" are required to adjudicate between any two opposing views, because moral and political positions are in Bork's view equivalent to preferences. The judicial vindication of a morally motivated claim is likewise equivalent, in his eyes, to favoring one person's gratification over another's. But:

> There is no principled way to decide that one man's gratifications are more deserving of respect than another's or that one form of gratification is more worthy than another.[63]

Such "value choices" might be made by judges or derived from the Constitution. If made by judges, Bork maintains, the judicial decisions in which they are embodied are "unprincipled," because value judgments are in general "unprincipled."

> Where constitutional materials do not clearly specify the value to be preferred, there is no principled way to prefer any claimed human value to any other.[64]

But if the "value choices" are derived from the Constitution, then the judicial decisions implementing them are "principled."

It is important to emphasize that in these passages Bork is *not* simply asserting the standard originalist claim that judges reviewing legislation should not impose their own values, but should apply doctrines derived from the Constitution. For that is what he is trying to prove. He is arguing, in effect, that *when the Constitution is unclear and interpretation of it may seem to require moral reasoning,* judges should defer to the legislature. His philosophical skepticism is deployed to show that judges should make no value judgments when deciding constitutional cases.

That is relevant to an earlier argument of this paper. The alternative to "strict" originalism that was sketched in section III requires that courts applying "vague clauses" of the Constitution interpret "contested concepts," which requires reasoning about moral or political principles. Bork's view that judges should not make "value choices" seems to mean that courts should not engage in any such reasoning. Bork reasons: judicial review should be neutral, principled, and nonarbitrary; it is impossible to make value judgments that are neutral, principled, or nonarbitrary; so judges should not incorporate value judgments into their constitutional decisions.

Bork's value skepticism is assumed and applied without justification.[65] Needless to say, value skepticism cannot be found within the Constitution. Indeed, the two are clearly incompatible. Thus Bork invokes an *anti*-constitutional doctrine to significant effect.

It is worth noting that Bork's skepticism renders his overall position incoherent. Consider his claim that judges *should* decide constitutional cases in a certain way—that (as he seems to argue) they are *under an obligation* to do so. Bork writes as if he is providing a rational defense for that sort of conclusion about the responsible, legitimate use of judicial power. He appears to believe that his reasoning excludes contrary conceptions of judicial obligation. In his terminology, however, to embrace such a doctrine is to make a "value choice," which according to his value skepticism is irremediably

"unprincipled," or rationally indefensible.

The result is a dilemma for Bork. If it is possible to provide good reasons (as Bork purports to do) for his conception of the legitimate (justified, responsible) exercise of judicial power—reasons designed to show that his conception is superior to contrary conceptions—then "value choices" can be principled. On the one hand, the success of any argument for the attribution of an obligation to judges would refute his value skepticism and undermine his argument that value judgments have no legitimate place in constitutional adjudication. On the other hand, his wholesale value skepticism excludes the possibility that any conception of the legitimate exercise of judicial power might be rationally defensible; so his skepticism undermines his own argument for and resulting judgment about responsible adjudication.

Consider now Bork's notion that judges must rely upon the value judgments that are embedded in the Constitution if their decisions are to be "principled." Bork assumes that decisions involving the exercise of judicial review can be "principled" insofar as they are grounded upon constitutional doctrines. This apparently means that the decisions can be justified relative to, or conditional upon, those doctrines.

But conditional justification is only as good as its condition. Recall that one piece of Bork's argument goes as follows:

> Law-creation, such as legislation or the framing of a constitution, involves making "value choices."

Another piece says:

> There is no principled way to make a "value choice."

Put together, these pieces yield the conclusion that the "value choices" embodied in the Constitution and the corresponding doctrines are themselves "unprincipled" or, in other words, unjustifiable. But if the doctrines on which the justification of judicial decisions depends are themselves unjustifiable, then the same applies to those decisions.

This means that Bork is faced with another dilemma. On the one hand, if "value choices" are unjustifiable, then so are the "value choices" reflected in the Constitution, and the same applies to all that relies on them for justification. On the other hand, if some value judgments can be justified (such as the idea that the Constitution merits respect), then Bork's general value skepticism is unsound, and his main argument collapses.

Bork might seem to avoid this particular incoherence when he remarks that his value skepticism "is not applicable to legislation. Legislation requires value choice and cannot be principled in the sense under discussion."[66] Bork might seem to suggest that there is another sense of "principled" in which the "value choices" embodied in legislation (and thus the legislation itself) can be "principled." Bork might mean, for example, that, rationally defensible or not, legislation by popularly elected officials is *permissible* under both democratic principles and our constitutional system. He might also wish to infer from this that those subject to such laws are under an obligation to respect them.

But this interpretation would not enable Bork to avoid the dilemma. Either he accepts the idea that democratic standards *justify* political arrangements that satisfy them, or he rejects it, presumably because of his value skepticism. If he rejects the idea, then there is no apparent sense within Bork's skeptical system in which legislation or indeed our constitutional system can be justifiable; there is no apparent sense in which the Constitution can *truly* be said to merit respect, in which judges can *truly* be said to be under an obligation to respect it. If Bork believes that any of these value judgments can *truly* be justified,

then he must forsake his objection based on value skepticism to the exercise of moral judgment within judicial review.

VII. Conclusion

Originalism seems to derive its initial plausibility from a simplified conception of how written constitutions work. Interpretation in terms of original intent promises a stable, uncontroversial version of the Constitution. But intentionalism faces overwhelming difficulties and appears to lack compensating justification, either in political or linguistic terms. Seeing no promising alternatives, opponents of strict originalism have accepted the need for extra-constitutional doctrines in constitutional adjudication. Originalists appear to reject such heterodoxy, but they unselfconsciously embrace a variety of extra-constitutional doctrines. Their theorizing about the Constitution tends toward the superficially descriptive and has yet to face the substantive value commitments implicit even in ritualistic appeals to democracy. Just as the Constitution cannot be value-free, so our understanding of it must be informed by reflection on the principles it serves.

---

1. Brest, *The Misconceived Quest for the Original Understanding,* 60 *B.U. L. Rev.* 204 (1980).
2. At the same time, it seems that most if not all theorists hold that constitutional cases may sometimes be decided by rules that cannot be attributed to the Constitution. We shall touch on "nonoriginalism" in section III.
3. See, e.g., John Ely, Democracy and Distrust, ch. 2 (1980); Brest, *The Misconceived Quest;* Dworkin, *The Forum of Principle,* 56 *N.Y.U. L. Rev.* 469–500 (1981); and Schauer, *An Essay on Constitutional Language,* 29 *UCLA L. Rev.* 797 (1982). MacCallum, *Legislative Intent,* 75 *Yale L.J.* 754 (1966) applies here too.
4. Bork, *Neutral Principles and Some First Amendment Problems,* 47 *Indiana L.J.* 1 (1971).
5. Meese, *Construing the Constitution,* 19 *U.C. Davis L. Rev.* 22 (1985).
6. Rehnquist, *The Notion of a Living Constitution,* 54 *Texas L. Rev.* 693 (1976).
7. Brest also draws a distinction between "strict" and "moderate" originalism, which I take up below.
8. On this view, the meaning of an amendment would presumably be fixed when (or by the time) it was ratified, and its incorporation into the Constitution would presumably modify (and in that sense fix anew) the doctrinal content of the Constitution as a whole.
9. I shall occasionally use "author" to refer to such an exclusive subclass of the population.
10. This covers both species of intentionalism in Brest's typology. "Strict intentionalism requires the interpreter to determine how the adopters would have applied a provision to a given situation, and to apply it accordingly." (Brest, *The Misconceived Quest,* p. 222) This permits "intentions" to include general principles, as most original intent theorists appear to accept. "A moderate intentionalist applies a provision consistent with the adopters' intent at a relatively high level of generality, consistent with what is sometimes called 'the purpose of the provision'" (*ibid.,* p. 223) The words I have emphasized suggest the view that "intentions" are relatively concrete or specific whereas "purposes" are relatively abstract or general, so that an appeal to original intent, strictly speaking, should be limited to the former. Brest does not defend this view, which does not square with his definition of "strict intentionalism" and is not required by the concept of intent. On the relevance of abstract intentions, see Dworkin, *The Forum of Principle.*
11. The most plausible criterion in such cases—which are, of course, most directly relevant here—would refer to the meaning of a text that has been adopted as authoritative. But that criterion would subordinate intentionalism to textualism and would make authors' intent a derivative rather than a basic determinant of meaning. I am here considering intentionalism as a basic general theory of constitutional interpretation. I am not considering, for example, the idea that considerations of original intent may for one reason or another properly play a secondary, subordinate, or supplementary role in constitutional interpretation.
12. See Ely, *Democracy and Distrust;* Brest, *The Misconceived Quest;* Dworkin, *The Forum of Principle;* Schauer, *An Essay on Constitutional Language;* and MacCallum, *Legislative Intent.*

13. *Barron v. The Mayor and City Council of Baltimore*, 7 *Pet.* 243, 8 *L. Ed.* 672 (1833).

14. This point does not presuppose a general theory of text meaning. The argument of section III would seem to imply, however, that the meaning of a text is not determined solely by linguistic conventions.

15. See my *Derivability, Defensibility, and the Justification of Judicial Decisions*, 68 *The Monist* 325 (1985).

16. Insofar as such interpretation is, in fact, intentionalist. It seems relevant that contractual interpretation is not purely a matter of actual intent, but is also regulated by legal norms.

17. The idea of popular sovereignty was reflected in constitutional rhetoric from early on. It became increasingly reflected in the constitutional system as time passed, as major changes occurred in the Republic, including of course major constitutional amendments.

18. This aspect of that theory is discussed by H. L. A. Hart, The Concept of Law 41–43 (1961).

19. Brest, *The Misconceived Quest*, p. 204.

20. *ibid.*, p. 208.

21. *ibid.*, p. 223.

22. Actually, Brest seems to believe that moderate textualism amounts to the only plausible originalist alternative to "strict" intentionalism, as he says that "moderate textualism and intentionalism closely resemble each other in methodology and results." *ibid.*

23. *ibid.*, pp. 205, 223.

24. Hart, The Concept of Law, pp. 121–132.

25. Compare Brest, *The Misconceived Quest*, p. 225. For a work that might be considered "nonoriginalist," see M.J. Perry, The Constitution, The Courts, and Human Rights (1982).

26. We shall consider the originalist approach to this issue in section V.

27. R. Dworkin, Taking Rights Seriously 132–137 (1977). This suggestion is independent of other aspects of Dworkin's legal theory.

28. J. Rawls, A Theory Of Justice 5, 10 (1971).

29. If a court works under a doctrine of precedent, then the criterion of a justifiable interpretation cannot simply be fidelity to the "original" Constitution. In that case, past judicial interpretations can presumably affect the content of a justifiable interpretation, even when those past interpretations were mistaken. I ignore that complication here.

30. We should distinguish such philosophical skepticism about values from concern about the difficulty a court might have trying to identify the best conception of a contested political concept (even when the alternatives are severely limited in number) and from an appreciation of the fact that any attempt to identify the best conception is likely to be controversial. We may also assume that reasonable judges can differ in their interpretations. It should be emphasized, however, that approaches to judicial review that seek to avoid controversial interpretations of the Constitution cannot be assumed to be justifiable by reference to the "original" Constitution. That is precisely one of the points at issue here.

31. I address some aspects of this issue in Ethics and the Rule of Law, ch. 1 (1984).

32. Section VI.

33. Interpretation by reference to "original intent" also, of course, draws upon information outside the "four corners" of the text.

34. A theory of adjudication would seem to presuppose an independently determined interpretation of the Constitution, to fix whatever is (or is not) to be applied.

35. Thayer, *The Origin and Scope of the American Doctrine of Constitutional Law*, 7 *Harv. L. Rev.* 129 (1893).

36. These are Thayer's chief arguments for judicial deference. Although he nods in the direction of democratic sentiments, he expresses little respect for the virtue, sense, or competence of legislators, but he fears their collective power.

37. Thayer, *The Origin*, p. 150 (emphasis in the original).

38. R. Berger, Government By Judiciary 412 (1977).

39. *ibid.*, pp. 412–413.

40. Monaghan, *Our Perfect Constitution*, 56 *N.Y.U. L. Rev.* 387–391 (1981); and *Taking Supreme Court Decisions Seriously*, 39 *Maryland L. Rev.* 1–12 (1979).

We are presumably concerned here with precedents on the same court level, as distinct from precedents that are binding due to the hierarchical structure of a layered court system.

41. Monaghan, *Our Perfect Constitution*, p. 389; compare *Taking Supreme Court Decisions Seriously*, p. 7.

Lawyers seem to favor consequentialist arguments for precedent over the notion that precedent is grounded upon the fairness of treating like cases alike. For a discussion of this alternative, see Lyons, *Formal Justice and Judicial Precedent*, 38 *Vanderbilt L. Rev.* 495 (1985).

42. Perhaps Monaghan would like to limit the use of consequentialist argument in some unexplained way. It will be difficult to show, however, that such limitations are not ad hoc. Indeed, Monaghan's consequentialist strategy of argument threatens to get completely out of hand. For his argument commits him to approving all principles whose use would serve any values that are as desirable as "stability and predictability." It may also be noted that insofar as originalist doctrine, such as strict intentionalism, appeals to past judicial practice, its originalist credentials must be as problematic as those of a doctrine of precedent.

43. Monaghan distinguishes the doctrine of precedent that is needed for constitutional cases from "common law analogies" because of differences in details, and he may infer from these differences that the constitutional doctrine could not be based on common law traditions; *Taking Supreme Court Decisions Seriously*, p. 12. But that reasoning is dubious.

44. See, e.g., Van Alstyne, *Interpreting This Constitution: The Unhelpful Contributions of Special Theories of Judicial Review*, 35 *U. Fla. L. Rev.* 229 (1983).

45. This assumes, of course, that judicial review can be justified despite the argument from democracy. We shall return to that point presently.

46. Rehnquist, *The Notion of a Living Constitution*, 54 *Texas L. Rev.* 695 (1976).

47. ibid.

48. *ibid.*, p. 698.

49. *ibid.*, p. 706.

50. *ibid.*, p. 696.

51. *ibid.*, p. 695.

52. See, e.g., Ely, Democracy and Distrust.

53. Bork, *Neutral Principles*, pp. 2–3.

54. *ibid.*, p. 3.

55. *ibid.*

56. *ibid.*

57. *ibid.*, pp. 10–11.

58. This assumes the use of a burden-of-proof rule discussed in section V.

59. Bork, *Neutral Principles*, p. 3.

60. *ibid.*, p. 9.

61. *ibid.*

62. *ibid.*, p. 10.

63. *ibid.*, Bork's note explains: "The impossibility is related to that of making interpersonal comparisons of utilities." He apparently assumes that if there is any morally defensible criterion for making decisions (including those adjudicating interpersonal conflicts of interest), it is that they should maximize (in Bork's terms) "gratifications." The alleged impossibility to which he refers would make that criterion impossible to satisfy. Normative welfare economics avoids the problem by giving up the maximizing requirement and replacing it with a conception of economic efficiency, such as Pareto's, that requires no interpersonal comparisons of utility. Bork's note suggests that he is unaware of or refuses to consider either economic or deontological alternatives to classical utilitarianism.

64. *ibid.*, p. 8.

65. But see note 63.

66. Bork, *Neutral Principles*, p. 8.

PART THREE

Justice

The framework for discussing questions about justice comes to us rather directly from the ancient Greeks. Even when they disagreed strongly among themselves about the justice of particular political policies, the leading Greek philosophers were agreed that there is some basic connection between the ideas of justice and *equality*. But only the extreme radicals, those who called themselves "democrats," thought that in all the contexts of justice, benefits and burdens must be allocated with perfect equality. Aristotle maintained that distributive justice, for example, does not consist in absolute equality (that is, perfectly equal shares for all those among whom something is to be distributed) but rather in a proportionate equality, which is to say an equality of ratios. What justice requires, he insisted, is that equal cases be treated alike (equally), and that unequal cases be treated unalike (unequally), in direct proportion to the relevant differences (inequalities) between them, so that between any two persons the ratio between their shares ($S_1 : S_2$) should equal the ratio between their qualifying characteristics ($C_1 : C_2$).

Aristotle conceded that people disagree over which characteristics of persons should be taken into account in assessing their qualifications, but all parties to these disagreements (except those who insisted upon absolute equality) employed tacitly the notion of proportionate equality. However merit is conceived, for example, those for whom it would be the sole criterion in awarding shares would give one person twice as large a share of some benefit as they would to any other person deemed only half as meritorious. The common object of these distributors, even when they disagree over what merit is, is to divide shares into a ratio (2 : 1) equal to the ratio of the merits of the two persons (2 : 1). Such distribu-

tions are sometimes necessarily impressionistic (how can one person's merit be seen to be exactly one half of another's?). But, when the criterion of merit is exactly definable, and the shares themselves can be measured in terms of money, the calculations can sometimes achieve a mathematical precision.

Since any two persons will be unequal in some respects and equal in others, Aristotle's theory of distributive justice is incomplete until he tells us which personal characteristics are *relevant* factors to be considered in the balancing of ratios. Various criteria of relevance have been proposed by writers of different schools. Some have held that A's share should be to B's share as A's ability is to B's ability, or as A's moral virtue is to B's, or as A's labor is to B's, and so on. All the above maxims could be said to specify different forms of merit, so that a meritarian theorist would be one who held that the only personal characteristics relevant to a just distribution of goods are such forms of personal merit. Aristotle was undoubtedly a meritarian in this broad sense. Meritarian social philosophers, then, can disagree among themselves over which forms of merit are relevant and over criteria for assessing a given form of merit. In addition, they might hold that some forms of merit are relevant to some types of distribution, and other merits to other types. A nonmeritarian theory would find exclusive relevance in personal characteristics (for example, needs) that are in no sense merits, and of course mixed theories are also possible. Even a "democratic" or "equalitarian" theory, one that is wholly nonmeritarian, might plausibly be said to employ tacitly Aristotle's analysis of distributive justice as proportionate equality while rejecting of course Aristotle's suggested criteria of relevance. Even a perfect equalitarian would presumably wish to endorse such maxims as: A's share should be to B's share as A's needs are to B's needs, or as A's "infinite human worth" is to B's "infinite human worth" (that is, the same). It seems likely, therefore, that all complete theories of social justice must contain maxims specifying relevant characteristics, and that all of them presuppose Aristotle's formal analysis of distributive justice as proportionate equality between shares and relevant characteristics.

The Machinery of Justice: Three Sample Procedural Problems

In the modern world the principles of justice often seem far removed from the procedures of a legal system in operation. Attempts to do justice generate further problems of justice, which philosophers of law can take up with equal relish.

The essay by John H. Langbein, "Torture and Plea Bargaining," describes the serious problems that surround the procedure for disposing of most criminal cases in America today. Criminal accusations are made the subject of negotiation rather than of adjudication so that as little time, effort, and money as possible need be spent in dealing with criminal charges. Reducing the charge itself or reducing the sentence to be demanded on a particular charge is offered in exchange for a guilty plea so that the burdensome business of a trial can be avoided. The accused is very rarely a free bargaining agent, and the result is frequently a coerced conviction. In other cases where there is serious crime, insupportable leniency mocks the very reason for a system of criminal justice. The system encourages the plea bargainer to believe that after getting caught, it is a matter mainly of getting a good deal or not. This works against the cultivation of a general law-abiding attitude in that part of the community most prone to crime. The overdeveloped adversarial system makes plea bargaining in some form necessary, in Langbein's view, and its evils can only be escaped by fundamental reforms that take the sort of approach to criminal justice that is seen in European countries.

Kent Greenawalt discusses another problem for justice that arises through operation of somewhat rusty "machinery of justice": the dilemma of jury nullification. This is a problem only in countries that use the jury system as a way of finding the facts to which the relevant rules as specified in the instructions of the judge are to be applied. In the Anglo-American jury system, jurors are aware both that they have a duty to obey the judge's instructions and that they have a legal power to disobey those instructions when their consciences direct them to do so in the interest of justice to a defendant. Professor Greenawalt's proposed guide to the perplexed juror dovetails nicely with earlier essays on civil disobedience in Part One, though in Part Three the disobedience in question is that of an office holder (juror) and not that of an ordinary citizen.

The final article in this subsection presents a procedural problem concerning the moral limits of certain methods of criminal law enforcement. For many years, and in many countries, police have set traps for criminals by providing them with apparent opportunities, not to mention temptations and inducements, to commit crimes. In the majority of these cases, where the victim was predisposed to commit the very crime he is "trapped" into committing, there is no problem for justice. But as Gerald Dworkin points out, it is sometimes morally disturbing to realize that, but for the police conduct, this particular prisoner would never have committed this crime, now or ever. The importance of the conditional language, "but for the police conduct the crime would never have been committed" shows how central a philosophical issue can be to a practical issue in the law.

Justice and Compensation

Aristotle's concept of corrective justice (distinguished in the *Nichomachean Ethics* from distributive justice) is what we think of as the basis of compensation to an injured party when the one who injures is required to pay damages. The present edition includes new materials on the civil law and avoids imparting the impression that criminal law is the whole of law. Of course, the criminal law breeds legitimate and important philosophical problems, but the civil law governing suits between private individuals is just as important and just as representative. Therefore we have added articles on the role of law in resolving private quarrels.

The principle that we ought to clean up our messes, or that we should not be allowed to displace the costs of our activities onto others, expresses an attractive conception of the demands of fairness. The problem is to determine how to think about what constitutes the cost of an activity. When the rancher's cows trample the farmer's corn, should we think about the corn crop damage as a cost of ranching or of farming? In "Mischief and Misfortune," Coleman and Ripstein reject the idea that we can identify an activity's costs with its causal upshots and argue instead that the concept of an activity's costs is normative, in the sense that it requires a theory of what individuals owe one another by way of care. Only after we determine what the rancher and the farmer owe each other, in the relevant sense, can we determine whether the damage is a cost of farming or ranching.

One of the more perplexing questions about corrective justice is whether or not an original pattern of holdings must be just in order for the claims of corrective justice to be invokable. On the face of it, the affirmative answer appears plausible. In that case, corrective justice could be seen as an aspect of distributive justice, requiring us to return to others what we have no right to and thus protecting a fair initial division. Against this view, Stephen R. Perry argues, in "Loss, Agency and Responsibility for Outcomes: Three Conceptions of Corrective Justice," that the central idea in corrective justice is responsibility for outcomes. A person who is responsible for an untoward outcome has a duty to repair it whether or not doing so will reinstate a just pattern of holdings. The claims in corrective justice derive from personal responsibility, not from distributive justice.

Justice and Contract

Among the generally accepted functions of contract law are to distinguish legally binding agreements from nonbinding ones, to determine the rights and duties created by ambiguous contracts, and to indicate the consequences of a breach. But may the law of contracts also justifiably be used as an instrument for achieving some desired social distribution of wealth? In "Contract Law and Distributive Justice," Anthony Kronman contends that redistribution is indeed among the proper aims of contract law. Kronman carves out his position in opposition both to libertarians—who oppose any form of enforced redistribution—and liberals, who tend to favor taxation as the sole redistributive mechanism. Kronman argues that both taxation and contract law are justifiable instruments of redistribution and that the choice between them should be made on the basis of which is least costly and intrusive in a given situation.

Seldom has the justice of a private contract occasioned so much public debate as the agreement between Mr. and Mrs. Whitehead, on the one hand, and Mr. and Mrs. Stern, on the other, in the celebrated case of Baby M, settled in 1986 by the New Jersey Supreme Court. A large complex of philosophical and moral issues were involved in this case, as in most surrogate mother cases. The Baby M case, unfortunately, tends to blur these issues because it involved so many extraneous and unhappy elements—a badly drawn agreement, a predictable mind change, kidnap, assault and battery, passion, anger, and noise. That is a shame, because even by 1986 there had been several hundred smooth and uneventful cases of women contracting, for an agreed-upon fee, to carry a baby that another woman was physically unable to bear to parturition. In the Baby M case Mr. Stern had fertilized Mrs. Whitehead's ovum by artificial insemination, so that Baby M was descended genetically from the male adopter and the "gestational mother" (the woman who carried the child through gestation), but in other cases the ovum of the adopting woman herself is fertilized by her own husband's sperm and the resulting embryo is transferred to the surrogate's womb. In that kind of case the surrogate mother is not the biological mother.

Moral and policy issues involved in any case of surrogacy include the following: How can an act or transaction that is uncontroversially permissible when done without monetary charge be contrary to public policy, at the least, when done for money? How does money acquire this mysterious capacity to corrupt? (Prostitution is another example of this kind; so are sales by a next of kin of her deceased kinsman's healthy bodily organs, and sales, as opposed to charitable donations, of blood to hospitals.) Should lopsided contracts that protect the interests of one party far more than the other be enforceable, even at great cost to the naive and trusting weaker party? Or should the law be paternalistic and protect people from their own folly? Is there an important distinction between a court ordering damages for breach of contract and a court ordering specific performance? Can a woman ever give informed consent to an agreement that might lead her to relinquish a baby that she has (unforeseeably) decided to keep? Can we reconcile surrogacy contracts with the outright ban on the sale of babies? The articles by Robin Fox and Bonnie Steinbock differ somewhat in emphasis and attitude: Fox is less impressed than Steinbock by the liberty to make contractual commitments. But both articles illustrate how philosophers who are both sensitive and sensible can hope to achieve agreement even on vexatious and emotional moral issues.

Justice, Affirmative Action, and Racial Quotas

Invidiously discriminatory treatment in the distribution of benefits (including opportunities) and burdens is the essential feature of what Aristotle called distributive injustice. In the United States grossly discriminatory rules and practices have only recently begun to crumble, and for the first time in centuries there is hope that the ideal of equal opportunity will one day be fulfilled. To expect the effects of racial and sexual discrimination to vanish overnight with the abrogation of ancient rules, however, would be exceedingly naive. Many reformers, in fact, have been urging that the elimination of discriminatory practices is not enough, and that a kind of reverse discrimination, especially in the allocation of educational and professional opportunities for such groups as blacks and women, is required by social justice. Programs of affirmative action (that is, of active recruitment of minorities even in some cases at the expense of apparently better qualified majority males) are full of moral dangers and raise many misgivings even among those of us who find racism utterly odious. Chief of these misgivings is the fear that injustice to one group is being sought by means that are unjust to another, and that that is not an effective way to promote the cause of justice generally. Others have feared the effects on the beneficiaries themselves, as they become targets of skeptical disrespect from those who infer that they have found success in the world only because of favoritism. That general suspicion especially hurts those many professionally successful blacks who more than hold their own in fair competition with whites.

Because of these and similar worries, defenders of affirmative action programs have felt obliged to argue that justice is on the side of affirmative action. Those arguments, even when winning plaudits from those already inclined to agree, have not won many converts from among the skeptics. By and large, the arguments for affirmative action have been of two kinds. Forward-looking arguments base their case on the long-term contributions of pump-priming efforts now to increased economic parity and political power for blacks in the future, greater respect for blacks as more and more of them achieve middle-class status without the aid of special advantages, and more social stability and freedom from disruptive violence. Among other such consequential benefits, one can mention the benefit to black children that comes from having black schoolteachers, doctors, and other professionals to deal with daily.

The second class of arguments for affirmative action are backward looking. They focus on the great wrongs committed against blacks in the past and the enormous debt whites have inherited. These debts, the arguments state, require whites to rectify those wrongs through a program of reparations in which affirmative action plays a central role. Some of the arguments in these two categories have genuine merit and have scored points. But none has been very convincing to the firefighters, police, medical students, and professors who believe that they have lost their jobs, or their job security, just because their employers had to fill quotas assigned to minorities.

The controversy over affirmative action became the subject of a ballot referendum in 1996 in California, when the electorate of that state approved Proposition 209, amending the state constitution. The new amendment, which became Article I, sec. 31 of the California Constitution, is included here. It prohibits state or local governments, districts, public universities, colleges, schools, and other government instrumentalities from discriminating against or giving preferential treatment to any individual or group in public employment, public education, or public contracting on the basis of race, sex, color, ethnicity, or national origin.

The other two selections in this section are sympathetic to affirmative action but dissatisfied with the way it has been defended in the past, partly because of its inadequate message to resentful displaced whites (Nagel's emphasis) and partly because unexamined possibilities for justification, quite apart from the future advantage and past-looking reparation categories, have been neglected (Hill's emphasis). Although Nagel's article was published twenty years ago (1973), it sounds like a fresh new voice, in harmony with that of Hill, in his more recent article (1991).

Inequality and Gender

The final subsection of Part Three focuses primarily, though not exclusively, on legal injustices to women. It is undeniable that our laws are mainly the work of men in courts and legislatures that have rarely included women. There is no logical necessity, of course, that mostly male legislatures and judges must be unfair to women, but nonetheless there is a grave danger that men will not be able to share the point of view of women, that they will assume without thought that a woman's outlook on the world is essentially the same as their own in all particulars. In that event they will lack empathy with, and therefore understanding of, women in their roles as litigants in courts of law. As Kim Lane Scheppele puts it, "Women have experiences of the world that are not the same as men's," and failure to see the world through women's eyes leads first to misunderstanding and then, naturally enough, to injustice.

That is not to say that traditional legal rules are without exception entirely unfair to the women to whom they apply. Some of the cases considered in this section are genuinely controversial. But it is plain that many traditional legal rules—for example, those in the law of rape—have been severely unjust to women. Even these "plain" cases, however, are such that deciding how to improve things is complex and difficult and not at all obvious. The problems illustrated in the section are rape, sincere but unreasonable mistake as to consent, the battered-woman defense to homicide, and the so-called battered woman's syndrome, which can paralyze the resolve of women in serious danger from their husbands.

The final two selections expand the focus of the section to include gender-related injustices generally. *Michael M. v. Superior Court of Sonoma County* can be interpreted as illustrating an injustice to males, or at least males like the defendant, Michael M. Perhaps it shows how gender injustice need not, in the very nature of things, victimize women only. The petitioner in this U.S. Supreme Court case claimed that the California statutory rape statute unlawfully discriminated on the basis of gender, since men alone were criminally liable under the statute. Among other matters, the primary issue was whether the ground for treating men and women under the age of eighteen differently was an arbitrary one or whether the different roles of men and women in sexual relations were highly relevant to a legitimate state purpose in treating them differently. Many of the reforms that have helped women's "liberation" in the last two decades have proceeded from arguments that certain differences between men and women are arbitrary ones, not relevant to any legitimate regulative concern. In this case Chief Justice Rehnquist found a way of arguing that a statute that can send a 17 1/2-year-old male to prison for an "unlawful" sexual encounter with a 16 1/2-year-old female, but can impose no criminal liability on the female, is not unconstitutional discrimination on the basis of gender.

In the final selection of this section, Leslie Green considers a philosophical question with far-reaching implications for the rights of homosexuals: on what basis can or should we value an individual's choice to live according to his or her sexual orientation? Charles Taylor has argued that the value of a choice is determined by the cultural horizon in which it is made; in his view, the simple fact of being chosen cannot confer value on any part of a person's life. Green's response appeals to the modern ideal of authenticity—being true to oneself, rather than letting one's life path be dictated by tradition or the pressures of social conventions. If we accept authenticity as a genuine ideal, Green argues, then we need look no further for a reason to value and respect an individual's choice to express his or her deepest inclinations about love.

The Machinery of Justice: Three Sample Procedural Problems

TORTURE AND PLEA BARGAINING*

John H. Langbein

The American system of plea bargaining is becoming a subject of immense academic and public attention. A dozen books have appeared in the last year or so describing plea bargaining as observed in one forum or another. The law reviews are full of writing about the details; a special issue of the *Law and Society Review* is now offering 20 more articles. The general theme of much of the current writing is that although, arguably, plea bargaining might be in need of various operational reforms, the basic institution is natural, inevitable, universal, and just.

In this essay I shall set forth some of the case against plea bargaining from a perspective that must appear bizarre, although I hope to show that it is illuminating. I am going to contrast the modern American system of plea bargaining with the medieval European law of torture. My thesis is that there are remarkable parallels in origin, in function, and even in specific points of doctrine, between the law of torture and the law of plea bargaining. I shall suggest that these parallels expose some important truths about how criminal justice systems respond when their trial procedures fall into deep disorder.

The Law of Torture

For about half a millennium, from the middle of the thirteenth century to the middle of the eighteenth, a system of judicial torture lay at the heart of Continental criminal procedure. In our own day the very word "torture" is, gladly enough, a debased term. It has come to mean anything unpleasant, and we hear people speak of a tortured interpretation of a poem, or the torture of a dull dinner party. In discussions of contemporary criminal procedure we hear the word applied to describe illegal police practices or crowded prison conditions. But torture as the medieval European lawyers understood it had nothing to do with official misconduct or with criminal sanctions. Rather, the application of torture was a routine and judicially supervised feature of European criminal procedure. Under certain circumstances the law permitted the criminal courts to employ physical coercion against suspected criminals in order to induce them to confess. The law went to great lengths to limit this technique of extorting confessions to cases in which it was thought that the

*John H. Langbein, "Torture and Plea Bargaining," *The Public Interest*, No. 58, Winter 1980, pp. 43–61. Reprinted by permission of *The Public Interest*.

accused was highly likely to be guilty, and to surround the use of torture with other procedural safeguards that I shall discuss shortly.

This astonishing body of law grew up on the Continent as an adjunct to the law of proof—what we would call the system of trial—in cases of serious crime (for which the sanction was either death or severe physical maiming). The medieval law of proof was designed in the thirteenth century to replace an earlier system of proof, the ordeals, which the Roman Church effectively destroyed in the year 1215. The ordeals purported to achieve absolute certainty in criminal adjudication through the happy expedient of having the judgments rendered by God, who could not err. The replacement system of the thirteenth century aspired to achieve the same level of safeguard—absolute certainty—for human adjudication.

Although human judges were to replace God in the judgment seat, they would be governed by a law of proof so objective that it would make that dramatic substitution unobjectionable—a law of proof that would *eliminate human discretion* from the determination of guilt or innocence. Accordingly, the Italian Glossators who designed the system developed and entrenched the rule that conviction had to be based upon the testimony of two unimpeachable eyewitnesses to the gravamen of the crime—evidence that was, in the famous phrase, "clear as the noonday sun." Without these two eyewitnesses, a criminal court could not convict an accused who contested the charges against him. Only if the accused *voluntarily* confessed the offense could the court convict him without the eyewitness testimony.

Another way to appreciate the purpose of these rules is to understand their corollary: Conviction could not be based upon circumstantial evidence, because circumstantial evidence depends for its efficacy upon the subjective persuasion of the trier who decides whether to draw the inference of guilt from the evidence of circumstance. Thus, for example, it would not have mattered in this system that the suspect was seen running away from the murdered man's house and that the bloody dagger and the stolen loot were found in his possession. If no eyewitness saw him actually plunge the weapon into the victim, the court could not convict him.

In the history of Western culture no legal system has ever made a more valiant effort to perfect its safeguards and thereby to exclude completely the possibility of mistaken conviction. But the Europeans learned in due course the inevitable lesson. They had set the level of safeguard too high. They

had constructed a system of proof that could as a practical matter be effective only in cases involving overt crime or repentant criminals. Because society cannot long tolerate a legal system that lacks the capacity to convict unrepentant persons who commit clandestine crimes, something had to be done to extend the system to those cases. The two-eyewitness rule was hard to compromise or evade, but the confession rule seemed to invite the subterfuge that in fact resulted. To go from accepting a voluntary confession to coercing a confession from someone against whom there was already strong suspicion was a step that began increasingly to be taken. The law of torture grew up to regulate this process of generating confessions.

The spirit of safeguard that had inspired the unworkable formal law of proof also permeated the subterfuge. The largest chapter of the European law of torture concerned the prerequisites for examination under torture. The European jurists devised what Anglo-American lawyers would today call a rule of probable cause, designed to assure that only persons highly likely to be guilty would be examined under torture. Thus, torture was permitted only when a so-called "half proof" had been established against the suspect. That meant either one eyewitness, or circumstantial evidence of sufficient gravity, according to a fairly elaborate tariff. In the example where a suspect was caught with the dagger and the loot, each of those indicia would be a quarter proof. Together they cumulated to a half proof, which was sufficient to permit the authorities to dispatch the suspect for a session in the local torture chamber.

In this way the prohibition against using circumstantial evidence was overcome. The law of torture found a place for circumstantial evidence, but a nominally subsidiary place. Circumstantial evidence was not consulted directly on the ultimate question, guilt or innocence, but on a question of interlocutory procedure—whether or not to examine the accused under torture. Even there the law attempted to limit judicial discretion by promulgating predetermined, ostensibly objective criteria for evaluating the indicia and assigning them numerical values (quarter proofs, half proofs, and the like). Vast legal treatises were compiled on this jurisprudence of torture to guide the examining magistrate in determining whether there was probable cause for torture.

In order to achieve a verbal or technical reconciliation with the requirement of the formal law of proof that the confession be voluntary, the medieval lawyers treated a confession extracted under torture as involuntary, hence ineffective, unless the accused repeated it free from torture at a hearing that was held a day or so later. Often enough the accused who had confessed under torture did recant when asked to confirm his confession. But seldom to avail: The examination under torture could thereupon be repeated. An accused who confessed under torture, recanted, and then found himself tortured anew, learned quickly enough that only a "voluntary" confession at the ratification hearing would save him from further agony in the torture chamber.

Fortunately, more substantial safeguards were devised to govern the actual application of torture. These were rules designed to enhance the reliability of the resulting confession. Torture was not supposed to be used to elicit an abject, unsubstantiated confession of guilt. Rather, torture was supposed to be employed in such a way that the accused would disclose the factual detail of the crime—information which, in the words of a celebrated German statute of the year 1532, "no innocent person can know." The examining magistrate was forbidden to engage in so-called suggestive questioning, in which the examiner supplied the accused with the detail he wanted to hear from him. Moreover, the information admitted under torture was supposed to be investigated and verified to the extent feasible. If the accused confessed to the slaying, he was supposed to be asked where he put the dagger. If he said he buried it under the old oak tree, the magistrate was supposed to send someone to dig it up.

Alas, these safeguards never proved adequate to overcome the basic flaw in the system. Because torture tests the capacity of the accused to endure pain, rather than his veracity, the innocent might (as one sixteenth-century commentator put it) yield to "the pain and torment and confess things that they never did." If the examining magistrate engaged in suggestive questioning, even accidentally, his lapse could not always be detected or prevented. If the accused knew something about the crime, but was still innocent of it, what he did know might be enough to give his confession verisimilitude. In some jurisdictions the requirement of verification was not enforced, or was enforced indifferently.

These shortcomings in the law of torture were identified even in the Middle Ages and were the subject of emphatic complaint in Renaissance and early modern times. The Europeans looked ever more admiringly at England, where the jury system—operating without the two-eyewitness rule—had never needed the law of torture. In the eighteenth century,

as the law of torture was finally about to be abolished along with the system of proof that had required it, Beccaria and Voltaire became famous as critics of judicial torture; but they were latecomers to a critical legal literature nearly as old as the law of torture itself. Judicial torture survived the centuries not because its defects had been concealed, but in spite of their having been long revealed. The two-eyewitness rule had left European criminal procedure without a tolerable alternative. Having entrenched this unattainable level of safeguard in their formal trial procedure, the Europeans found themselves obliged to evade it through a subterfuge that they knew was defective. The coerced confession had to replace proof of guilt.

The Law of Plea Bargaining

I am now going to cross the centuries and cross the Atlantic in order to speak of the rise of plea bargaining in twentieth-century America. The account of the European law of torture that I just presented (which is based upon my monograph *Torture and the Law of Proof,* 1977), should stir among American readers an unpleasant sensation of the familiar, for the parallels between our modern plea bargaining system and the ancient system of judicial torture are many and chilling.

Let us begin by recollecting the rudiments of the American system of plea bargaining in cases of serious crime. Plea bargaining occurs when the prosecutor induces an accused criminal to confess guilt and to waive his right to trial in exchange for a more lenient criminal sanction than would be imposed if the accused were adjudicated guilty following trial. The prosecutor offers leniency either directly, in the form of a charge reduction, or indirectly, through the connivance of the judge, in the form of a recommendation for reduced sentence that the judge will follow. In exchange for procuring this leniency for the accused, the prosecutor is relieved of the need to prove the accused's guilt, and the court is spared having to adjudicate it. The court condemns the accused on the basis of his confession, without independent adjudication.

Plea bargaining is, therefore, a nontrial procedure for convicting and condemning the accused criminal. If you turn to the American Constitution in search of authority for plea bargaining, you will look in vain. Instead, you will find—in no less hallowed a place than the Bill of Rights—an opposite guarantee, a guarantee of trial. The Sixth Amendment provides: "In *all* criminal prosecutions, the accused shall enjoy the right to . . . trial . . . by an impartial jury . . ." (emphasis added).

In our day, jury trial continues to occupy its central place both in the formal law and in the mythology of the law. The Constitution has not changed, the courts pretend to enforce the defendant's right to jury trial, and television transmits a steady flow of dramas in which a courtroom contest for the verdict of the jury leads inexorably to the disclosure of the true culprit. In truth, criminal jury trial has largely disappeared in America. The criminal justice system now disposes of virtually all cases of serious crime through plea bargaining. In the major cities between 95 and 99 percent of felony convictions are by plea. This nontrial procedure has become the ordinary dispositive procedure of American law.

Why has our formal system of proof been set out of force and this nontrial system substituted for the trial procedure envisaged by the Framers? Scholars are only beginning to investigate the history of plea bargaining, but enough is known to permit us to speak with some confidence about the broad outline. In the two centuries from the mid-eighteenth to the mid-twentieth, a vast transformation overcame the Anglo-American institution of criminal jury trial, rendering it absolutely unworkable as an ordinary dispositive procedure and requiring the development of an alternative procedure, which we now recognize to be the plea bargaining system.

In eighteenth-century England jury trial was still a *summary proceeding*. In the Old Bailey in the 1730s we know that the court routinely processed between 12 and 20 jury trials for felony in a single day. A single jury would be impaneled and would hear evidence in numerous unrelated cases before retiring to formulate verdicts in all. Lawyers were not employed in the conduct of ordinary criminal trials, either for the prosecution or the defense. The trial judge called the witnesses (whom the local justice of the peace had bound over to appear), and the proceeding transpired as a relatively unstructured altercation between the witnesses and the accused. Plea bargaining was unknown—indeed, judges actively discouraged pleas of guilty even from defendants who tendered them voluntarily and without hope of sentencing concessions. In the 1790s, when the Americans were constitutionalizing English jury trial, it was still rapid and efficient. The trial of Hardy for high treason in 1794 was the first that ever lasted

more than one day, and the court seriously considered whether it had any power to adjourn. By contrast, we may note that the trial of Patricia Hearst for bank robbery in 1976 lasted 40 days and that the average felony jury trial in Los Angeles in 1968 required 7.2 days of trial time. In the eighteenth century the most characteristic (and time-consuming) features of modern jury trial, namely adversary procedure and the exclusionary rules of the law of criminal evidence, were still primitive and uncharacteristic. The accused's right to representation by retained counsel was not generalized to all felonies until the end of the eighteenth century in America and the nineteenth century in England. Appellate review was very restricted into the twentieth century; counsel for indigent accused was not required until the middle of this century. The practices that so protract modern American jury trials—extended *voir dire* (pretrial probing of the views and backgrounds of individual jurors for juror challenges), exclusionary rules and other evidentiary barriers, motions designed to provoke and preserve issues for appeal, maneuvers and speeches of counsel, intricate and often incomprehensible instructions to the jury—all are late growths in the long history of common-law criminal procedure. No wonder, then, that plea bargaining appears to have been a late-nineteenth-century growth that was scarcely acknowledged to exist in the United States before the 1920s. (The English are only now facing up to the fact of their dependence on plea bargaining.)

Nobody should be surprised that jury trial has undergone great changes over the last two centuries. It desperately needed reform. The level of safeguard against mistaken conviction was in several respects below what civilized peoples now require. What we will not understand until there has been research directed to the question, is why the pressure for greater safeguards led in the Anglo-American procedure to the law of evidence and the lawyerization of the trial, reforms that ultimately destroyed the system in the sense that they made jury trial so complicated and time-consuming as to be unworkable as the routine dispositive procedure.

Similar pressures for safeguards were being felt on the Continent in the same period, but they led to reforms in nonadversarial procedure that preserved the institution of trial. In the middle of the nineteenth century, when Continental criminal procedure was being given its modern shape, the draftsmen of the European codes routinely studied Anglo-American procedure as a reform model. They found much to admire and to borrow, but they resisted the temptation to adversary domination. Their experience with the way that their medieval rules of evidence had led to the law of torture also left them unwilling to imitate the nascent Anglo-American law of evidence. And they were unanimous in rejecting the institution of the guilty plea. As early as the 1850s German writers were saying that it was wrong for a court to sentence an accused on mere confession, without satisfying itself of his guilt.

Parallels to the Law of Torture

Let me now turn to my main theme—the parallels in function and doctrine between the medieval European system of judicial torture and our plea bargaining system. The starting point, which will be obvious from what I have thus far said, is that each of these substitute procedural systems arose in response to the breakdown of the formal system of trial that it subverted. Both the medieval European law of proof and the modern Anglo-American law of jury trial set out to safeguard the accused by circumscribing the discretion of the trier in criminal adjudication. The medieval Europeans were trying to eliminate the discretion of the professional judge by requiring him to adhere to objective criteria of proof. The Anglo-American trial system has been caught up over the last two centuries in an effort to protect the accused against the dangers of the jury system, in which laymen ignorant of the law return a one- or two-word verdict that they do not explain or justify. Each system found itself unable to recant directly on the unrealistic level of safeguard to which it had committed itself, and each then concentrated on inducing the accused to tender a confession that would waive his right to the safeguards.

The European law of torture preserved the medieval law of proof undisturbed for those easy cases in which there were two eyewitnesses or voluntary confession. But in the more difficult cases (where, I might add, safeguard was more important), the law of torture worked an absolutely fundamental change within the system of proof: It largely *eliminated the adjudicative function*. Once probable cause had been determined, the accused was made to concede his guilt rather than his accusers to prove it.

In twentieth-century America we have duplicated the central experience of medieval European criminal procedure. We have moved from an adjudicatory to a concessionary system. We coerce the accused against whom we find probable cause to confess his guilt. To be sure, our means are much more polite; we use no rack, no thumbscrew, no Spanish boot to mash his legs. But like the Europeans of distant centuries who did employ those machines, we make it terribly costly for an accused to claim his right to the constitutional safeguard of trial. We threaten him with a materially increased sanction if he avails himself of his right and is thereafter convicted. This sentencing differential is what makes plea bargaining coercive. There is, of course, a difference between having your limbs crushed if you refuse to confess, or suffering some extra years of imprisonment if you refuse to confess, but the difference is of degree, not kind. Plea bargaining, like torture, is coercive. Like the medieval Europeans, the Americans are now operating a procedural system that engages in condemnation without adjudication. The maxim of the medieval Glossators, no longer applicable to European law, now aptly describes American law: *Confessio est regina probationum,* confession is the queen of proof.

Supporters of plea bargaining typically maintain that a "mere" sentencing differential is not sufficiently coercive to pressure an innocent accused to convict himself. That point can be tested in the abstract simply by imagining a differential so great—for example, death versus a 50-cent fine—that any rational defendant would waive even the strongest defenses. The question of whether significant numbers of innocent people do plead guilty is not, of course, susceptible to empirical testing. It has been established that many of those who plead guilty claim that they are innocent. More importantly, prosecutors widely admit to bargaining hardest when the case is weakest, which is why the leading article on the subject, by Albert Alschuler ("The Prosecutor's Role in Plea Bargaining," University of Chicago Law Review, 1968), concluded that "the greatest pressures to plead guilty are brought to bear on defendants who may be innocent." Alschuler recounted one such case:

> San Francisco defense attorney Benjamin M. Davis recently represented a man charged with kidnapping and forcible rape. The defendant was innocent, Davis says, and after investigating the case Davis was confident of an acquittal. The prosecutor, who seems to have shared the defense attorney's opinion on this point, offered to permit a guilty plea to simple battery. Conviction on this charge would not

have led to a greater sentence than 30 days' imprisonment, and there was every likelihood that the defendant would be granted probation. When Davis informed his client of this offer, he emphasized that conviction at trial seemed highly improbable. The defendant's reply was simple: "I can't take the chance."

I do not think that great numbers of Americans plead guilty to offenses committed by strangers. (The European law of torture was also not supposed to apply in the easy cases where the accused could forthrightly explain away the evidence that might otherwise have given cause to examine him under torture.) I do believe that plea bargaining is used to coerce the waiver of tenable defenses, as in attorney Davis's example, and in cases where the offense has a complicated conceptual basis, as in tax and other white-collar crimes. Like the medieval law of torture, the sentencing differential in plea bargaining elicits confessions of guilt that would not be freely tendered, and some of the confessions are false. Plea bargaining is therefore coercive in the same sense as torture, although surely not in the same degree.

I do not mean to say that excesses of the plea bargaining system affect only the innocent who is coerced to plead guilty or the convict whose sentence is made more severe because he insisted on his right to trial. In other circumstances plea bargaining has been practiced in ways that result in unjustified leniency. Many observers have been struck by the extent of the concessions that prosecutors have been prepared to make in serious criminal cases in order to avoid having to go to trial. One Alaskan prosecutor told Alschuler in 1976 that "prosecutors can get rid of everything if they just go low enough. The police complained that we were giving cases away, and they were right."

I have said that European law attempted to devise safeguards for the use of torture that proved illusory; these measures bear an eerie resemblance to the supposed safeguards of the American law of plea bargaining. Foremost among the illusory safeguards of both systems is the doctrinal preoccupation with characterizing the induced waivers as voluntary. The Europeans made the torture victim repeat his confession "voluntarily," but under the threat of being tortured anew if he recanted. The American counterpart is Rule 11(d) of the Federal Rules of Criminal Procedure, which forbids the court from accepting a guilty plea without first "addressing the defendant personally in open court, determining that the plea

is voluntary and not the result of force or threats or of promises *apart from a plea agreement*." Of course, the plea agreement is the *source* of the coercion and already embodies the involuntariness.

The architects of the European law of torture sought to enhance the reliability of a torture-induced confession with other safeguards designed to substantiate its factual basis. We have said that they required a probable-cause determination for investigation under torture and that they directed the court to take steps to verify the accuracy of the confession by investigating some of its detail. We have explained why these measures were inadequate to protect many innocent suspects from torture, confession, and condemnation. Probable cause is not the same as guilt, and verification, even if undertaken in good faith, could easily fail as a safeguard, either because the matters confessed were not susceptible of physical or testimonial corroboration, or because the accused might know enough about the crime to lend verisimilitude to his confession even though he was not in fact the culprit.

The American law of plea bargaining has pursued a similar chimera: the requirement of "adequate factual basis for the plea." Federal Rule 11(f) provides that "the court should not enter judgment upon [a guilty] plea without making such inquiry as shall satisfy it that there is a factual basis for the plea." As with the tortured confession, so with the negotiated plea: Any case that has resisted dismissal for want of probable cause at the preliminary hearing will rest upon enough inculpating evidence to cast suspicion upon the accused. The function of trial, which plea bargaining eliminates, is to require the court to adjudicate whether the facts proven support an inference of guilt beyond a reasonable doubt. Consider, however, the case of *North Carolina* v. *Alford,* decided in this decade, in which the U.S. Supreme Court found it permissible to condemn without trial a defendant who had told the sentencing court: "I pleaded guilty on second degree murder because they said there is too much evidence, but I ain't shot no man. . . . I just pleaded guilty because they said if I didn't they would gas me for it. . . . I'm not guilty but I plead guilty." I invite you to compare Alford's statement with the explanation of one Johannes Julius, seventeenth-century burgomaster of Bamberg, who wrote from his dungeon cell where he was awaiting execution, in order to tell his daughter why he had confessed to witchcraft "for which I must die. It is all falsehood and invention, so help me God. . . . They never cease to torture until one says something."

The tortured confession is, of course, markedly less reliable than the negotiated plea, because the degree of coercion is greater. An accused is more likely to bear false witness against himself in order to escape further hours on the rack than to avoid risking a longer prison term. But the resulting moral quandary is the same. Judge Levin of Michigan was speaking of the negotiated guilty plea, but he could as well have been describing the tortured confession when he said, "there is no way of knowing whether a particular guilty plea was given because the accused believed he was guilty, or because of the promised concession." Beccaria might as well have been speaking of the coercion of plea bargaining when he said of the violence of torture that it "confounds and obliterates those minute differences between things which enable us at times to know truth from falsehood." The doctrine of adequate factual basis for the plea is no better substitute for proof beyond reasonable doubt than was the analogous doctrine in the law of torture. The factual unreliability of the negotiated plea has further consequences, quite apart from the increased danger of condemning an innocent man. In the plea bargaining that takes the form of charge bargaining (as opposed to sentence bargaining), the culprit is convicted not for what he did, but for something less opprobrious. When people who have murdered are said to be convicted of wounding, or when those caught stealing are nominally convicted of attempt or possession, cynicism about the processes of criminal justice is inevitably reinforced. This willful mislabelling plays havoc with our crime statistics, which explains in part why Americans—uniquely among Western peoples—attach so much importance to arrest records rather than to records of conviction. I think that the unreliability of the plea, the mislabelling of the offense, and the underlying want of adjudication all combine to weaken the moral force of the criminal law, and to increase the public's unease about the administration of criminal justice. The case of James Earl Ray is perhaps the best example of public dissatisfaction over the intrinsic failure of the plea bargaining system to establish the facts about crime and guilt in the forum of a public trial. Of course, not every trial resolves the question of guilt or innocence to public satisfaction. The Sacco-Vanzetti and Rosenberg cases continue to be relitigated in the forum of popular opinion. But plea bargaining leaves the public with what I believe to be a more pronounced sense of unease about the justness of results, because it avoids the open ventilation and critical evaluation of evidence that characterize public trial. (Just this concern appears to have motivated the government in the plea-bargained bribery case of Vice President Agnew to take extraordinary steps to assure the disclosure of the substance of the prosecution case.) It is interesting to remember that in Europe in the age of Beccaria and Voltaire, the want of adjudication and the unreliability of the law of torture had bred a strangely similar cynicism towards the criminal justice system of that day.

The Moral Blunder

Because plea bargaining involves condemnation without adjudication, it undermines a moral postulate of the criminal justice system so basic and elementary that in past centuries Anglo-American writers seldom bothered to express it: Serious criminal sanctions should only be imposed when the trier has examined the relevant evidence and found the accused guilty beyond reasonable doubt.

Why have we been able to construct a nontrial procedure that is irreconcilable with this fundamental proposition? A major reason is that we have been beguiled by the similarities between civil and criminal litigation in our lawyer-dominated procedural system. "What's wrong with settling cases?" the argument runs. "Surely society is correct not to insist on full-scale adjudication of every private grievance. If the parties are satisfied with their deal, there is no social interest in adjudication. Likewise in criminal adjudication: If the prosecutor and the accused can reach agreement about the sanction, hasn't the matter been satisfactorily concluded?"

The answer is that because the social interest in criminal adjudication differs importantly from that in civil cases, the deeply embedded policy in favor of negotiated (nontrial) settlement of civil disputes is misapplied when transposed to the criminal setting. There is good reason for treating adjudication as the norm in the criminal law, but as a last and exceptional resort in private law. Kenneth Kipnis has provided a wry illustration of the distinction with an example drawn from neither. Kipnis asks us to imagine a system of "grade bargaining," in which the teacher would offer a student a favorable grade in exchange for a waiver of the student's right to have the teacher read his examination paper. The teacher would save time, thus conserve his resources, and the student would not accept the teacher's grade offer unless he calculated it to be in his interest by comparison with his expected results from conventional grading.

We see instantly what is wrong with grade bargaining. Because third parties rely upon grades in admissions and hiring decisions, the grade bargain would adversely affect the legitimate interests of these outsiders. And because the grade is meant to inform the student about the teacher's perception of the comparative quality of his performance, the grade bargain would disserve the larger interest of the student.

Quite analogous objections apply to plea bargaining. Criminal sanctions are imposed for public purposes: certainly in order to deter future crime, probably still with the object of reforming at least some offenders, and perhaps still in the interest of retribution. Sentences that satisfy the accused's wish to minimize the sanction and the prosecutor's need to reduce his trial caseload are arrived at with only passing attention to these social interests. In particular, the enormous sentence differential needed to sustain the plea bargaining system is repugnant to any tenable theory of sentencing. We can scarcely claim to be tailoring the sentence to the crime when one of the largest aggravating factors we consult is whether the accused had the temerity to ask for his right to trial. The truth is that when an accused is convicted following jury trial, we customarily punish him twice: once for the crime, and then more severely for what the Constitution calls "enjoy[ing] the right to . . . trial . . . by an impartial jury."

Twenty years ago in a celebrated article the late Henry Hart compared so-called "civil commitment" for mental or contagious disease with imprisonment for criminal conviction. Many a prison is more pleasant than a nearby asylum. Why, then, do we treat the decision to imprison as the more serious and surround it with safeguards that, at least in theory, are more substantial than those for the civil-commitment process? Notwithstanding the operational similarity between civil and criminal sanctions, said Hart, there is a profound difference in purpose. "The core of the difference is that the patient has not incurred the moral condemnation of his community, whereas the convict has." The very stigma of criminal conviction is the source of much of the deterrent and retributive power of the criminal sanction. I believe that this moral force of the criminal sanction is partially dependent on the sanction having been imposed after rational inquiry and decision on the facts. Adjudication alone legitimates the infliction of serious criminal sanctions, because it alone is adequate to separate the innocent from the guilty and to establish the basis for proportioning punishment to the degree of culpability. To assert (as a defender of plea bargaining must) the equivalency of waiver and of adjudication is to overlook the distinctive characteristic of the criminal law.

The Prosecutor

Our law of plea bargaining has not only recapitulated much of the doctrinal folly of the law of torture, complete with the pathetic safeguards of voluntariness and factual basis, but it has also repeated the main institutional blunder of the law of torture. Plea bargaining concentrates effective control of criminal procedure in the hands of a single officer. Our formal law of trial envisages a division of responsibility. We expect the prosecutor to make the charging decision, the judge and especially the jury to adjudicate, and the judge to set the sentence. Plea bargaining merges these accusatory, determinative, and sanctional phases of the procedure in the hands of the prosecutor. Students of the history of the law of torture are reminded that the great psychological fallacy of the European inquisitorial procedure of that time was that it concentrated in the investigating magistrate the powers of accusation, investigation, torture, and condemnation. The single inquisitor who wielded those powers needed to have what one recent historian has called "superhuman capabilities [in order to] . . . keep himself in his decisional function free from the predisposing influences of his own instigating and investigating activity."

The dominant version of American plea bargaining makes similar demands: It requires the prosecutor to usurp the determinative and sentencing functions, hence to make himself judge in his own cause. There are dangers in this concentration of prosecutorial power. One need not necessarily accept Jimmy Hoffa's view that Robert Kennedy was conducting a personal and political vendetta against him in order to appreciate the danger that he might have been. The power to prosecute as we know it carries within itself the power to persecute. The modern public prosecutor commands the vast resources of the state for gathering and generating accusing evidence. We allowed him this power in large part because the criminal trial interposed the safeguard of adjudication against the danger that he might bring those resources to bear against an innocent citizen—whether on account of honest error, arbitrariness, or worse. But the plea bargaining system has largely dissolved that safeguard. While on the subject of institutional factors, I have one last comparison to advance. The point has been made, most recently by the Attorney General of Alaska, that preparing and taking cases to trial is much harder work than plea bargaining—for police, prosecutors, judges, and defense counsel. In short, convenience—or worse, sloth—is a factor that sustains plea bargaining. We suppose that this factor had a little to do with torture as well. As someone in India remarked to Sir James Fitzjames Stephen in 1872 about the proclivity of the native policemen for torturing suspects, "It is far pleasanter to sit comfortably in the shade rubbing red pepper into a poor devil's eyes than to go about in the sun hunting up evidence." If we were to generalize about this point, we might say that concessionary criminal-procedural systems like the plea bargaining system and the system of judicial torture may develop their own bureaucracies and constituencies. Here as elsewhere the old adage may apply that if necessity is the mother of invention, laziness is the father.

The Jurisprudence of Concession

Having developed these parallels between torture and plea bargaining, I want to draw some conclusions about what I regard as the lessons of the exercise. The most important is this: A legal system will do almost anything, tolerate almost anything, before it will admit the need for reform in its system of proof and trial. The law of torture endured for half a millennium although its dangers and defects had been understood virtually from the outset; and plea bargaining lives on although its evils are quite familiar to us all. What makes such shoddy subterfuges so tenacious is that they shield their legal systems from having to face up to the fact of breakdown in the formal law of proof and trial.

Why is it so hard for a legal system to reform a decadent system of proof? I think that there are two main reasons, one in a sense practical, the other ideological. From the standpoint of the practical, nothing seems quite so embedded in a legal system as the procedures for proof and trial, because most of what a legal system does is to decide matters of proof—what we call "fact finding." (Was the traffic light green or red? Was this accused the man who fired the shot or robbed the bank?) Blackstone em-

phasized this point in speaking of civil litigation, and it is even more true of criminal litigation. He said: "Experience will abundantly shew, that above a hundred of our lawsuits arise from disputed facts, for one where the law is doubted of." Every institution of the legal system is geared to the system of proof; forthright reconstruction would disturb, at one level or another, virtually every vested interest.

The inertia, the resistance to change that is associated with such deep-seated interests, is inevitably reinforced by the powerful ideological component that underlies a system of proof and trial. Adjudication, especially criminal adjudication, involves a profound intrusion into the lives of affected citizens. Consequently, in any society the adjudicative power must be rested on a theoretical basis that makes it palatable to the populace. Because the theory of proof purports to govern and explain the application of the adjudicative power, it plays a central role in legitimating the entire legal system. The medieval European law of proof assured people that the legal system would achieve certainty. The Anglo-American jury system invoked the inscrutable wisdom of the folk to justify its results. Each of these theories was ultimately untenable—the European theory virtually from its inception, the Anglo-American theory after a centuries-long transformation of jury procedure. Yet the ideological importance of these theories prevented either legal system from recanting them. For example, I have elsewhere pointed out how in the nineteenth century the ideological attachment to the jury retarded experimentation with juryless trial—that is, what we now call bench trial—while the plea bargaining system of juryless nontrial procedure was taking shape out of public sight. Like the medieval European lawyers before us, we have been unable to admit that our theory of proof has resulted in a level of procedural complexity and safeguard that renders our trial procedure unworkable in all but exceptional cases. We have responded to the breakdown of our formal system of proof by taking steps to perpetuate the ideology of the failed system, steps that closely resemble those taken by the architects of the law of torture. *Like the medieval Europeans, we have preserved an unworkable trial procedure in form, we have devised a substitute nontrial procedure to subvert the formal procedure, and we have arranged to place defendants under fierce pressure to "choose" the substitute.*

That this script could have been played out in a pair of legal cultures so remote from each other in time and place invites some suggestions about the adaptive processes of criminal procedural systems. First, there are intrinsic limits to the level of complexity and safeguard that even a civilized people can tolerate. If those limits are exceeded and the repressive capacity of the criminal justice system is thereby endangered, the system will respond by developing subterfuges that overcome the formal law. But subterfuges are intrinsically overbroad, precisely because they are not framed in a careful, explicit, and principled manner directed to achieving a proper balance between repression and safeguard. The upshot is that the criminal justice system is saddled with a lower level of safeguard than it could and would have achieved if it had not pretended to retain the unworkable formal system.

The medieval Europeans insisted on two eyewitnesses and wound up with a law of torture that allowed condemnation with no witnesses at all. American plea bargaining, in like fashion, sacrifices just those values that the unworkable system of adversary jury trial is meant to serve: lay participation in criminal adjudication, the presumption of innocence, the prosecutorial burden of proof beyond reasonable doubt, the right to confront and cross-examine accusers, the privilege against self-incrimination. Especially in its handling of the privilege against self-incrimination does American criminal procedure reach the outer bounds of incoherence. We have exaggerated the privilege to senseless lengths in formal doctrine, while in the plea bargaining system— which is our routine procedure for processing cases of serious crime— we have eliminated practically every trace of the privilege.

Furthermore, the sacrifice of our fundamental values through plea bargaining is needless. In its sad plea bargaining opinions of the 1970s, the Supreme Court has effectively admitted that for reasons of expediency American criminal justice cannot honor its promise of routine adversary criminal trial, but the Court has simply assumed that the present nontrial plea bargaining procedure is the inevitable alternative. There is, however, a middle path between the impossible system of routine adversary jury trial and the disgraceful nontrial system of plea bargaining. That path is a streamlined nonadversarial trial procedure.

Routine Nonadversarial Trials

The contemporary nonadversarial criminal justice systems of countries like West Germany have long demonstrated that advanced industrial societies can institute efficient criminal procedures that nevertheless provide for lay participation and for full adjudication in every case of serious crime. I have described the German system in detail in my *Comparative Criminal Procedure: Germany* (1977), and I have made no secret of my admiration for the brilliant balance that it strikes between safeguard and procedural effectiveness. Not the least of its achievements is that in cases of serious crime it functions with no plea bargaining whatsoever. Confessions are still tendered in many cases (41 percent in one sample), but they are not and cannot be bargained for; nor does a confession excuse the trial court from hearing sufficient evidence for conviction on what amounts to a beyond-reasonable-doubt standard of proof. In a trial procedure shorn of all the excesses of adversary procedure and the law of evidence, the time difference between trial without confession and trial with confession is not all that great. Because an accused will be put to trial whether he confesses or not, he cannot inflict significant costs upon the prosecution by contesting an overwhelming case. Confessions are tendered at trial not because they are rewarded, but because there is no advantage to be wrung from the procedural system by withholding them.

Plea bargaining is all but incomprehensible to the Europeans, whose ordinary dispositive procedure is workable without such evasions. In the German press, the judicial procedure surrounding the criminal conviction and resignation of Vice President Agnew was viewed with the sort of wonder normally inspired by reports of the customs of primitive tribes. The *Badische Zeitung* reported as the story unfolded in October 1973: "The resignation occurred as part of a 'cowtrade,' as it can only in the United States be imagined."

I hope that over the coming decades we who still live under criminal justice systems that engage in condemnation without adjudication will face up to the failure of adversary criminal procedure. I believe that we will find in modern Continental criminal procedure an irresistible model for reform. For the moment, however, I am left to conclude with a paradox. Today in lands where the law of torture once governed, peoples who live in contentment with their criminal justice systems look out across the sea in disbelief to the spectacle of plea bargaining in America, while American tourists come by the thousands each year to gawk in disbelief at the decaying torture chambers of medieval castles.

JURY NULLIFICATION*

Kent Greenawalt

The jury's power to nullify is the most obvious. In civil cases, a jury can decide against the party that has presented the most persuasive evidence; unless the evidence in favor of the losing party is extremely strong, the jury's decision will survive an appeal. Its power in criminal cases is more absolute; if it acquits, the constitutional rule against double jeopardy precludes further proceedings against the defendant. I will concentrate here on the role of the jury in criminal cases. Much of what is said also applies to civil cases, though, of course, the claim of the opposing party to have his lawful expectations satisfied is a powerful argument against subverting the rules of civil liability to his disadvantage.

Lay jurors in common-law countries can nullify the criminal law by acquitting a defendant they believe is guilty of the crime charged. They can also nullify the written law in a more moderate fashion, by returning a verdict for a lesser offense when they believe the defendant is guilty of the more serious offense with which he has been charged. One juror alone (or a minority of jurors in jurisdictions that allow conviction with less than unanimity) can, if sufficiently strong-willed and persistent, block application of the law to an offender by refusing to vote for conviction.

The Legal Authority of Juries

Whether or not jurors have legal authority to engage in such refusals to apply the law is a complex question. Their dispensing power has been a fundamental element of the administration of the criminal law since the medieval period, and indeed, because of the capital sentence for most homicides and thefts, was once a more integral aspect of the law's administration than it is now.[1] In the sixteenth and seventeenth centuries, jurors were occasionally fined and imprisoned for refusals to convict,[2] now when they acquit, not only is their verdict unreviewable, they are immune from any punishment for failing to fulfill their temporary official duty. Nevertheless, jurors are instructed to apply the law as the judge gives it to them, and they take an oath that they will do so; and despite three narrowly interpreted state constitutional standards that grant jurors authority to determine the law,[3] the earlier dispute over whether jurors are the ultimate finders of law as well as fact has now been decisively resolved: jurors must take the law according to the judge's instructions. Defendant's counsel can neither argue that the jury should disregard those instructions nor present evidence in favor of the proposition that the defendant should be acquitted despite violating the law.

How is the legal duty of jurors to be understood? One view is that the power of acquittal establishes a right of acquittal. As Chancellor James Kent put it, "The law must . . . have intended, in granting this power to a jury, to grant them a lawful and rightful power, or it would have provided a remedy against the undue exercise of it."[4] Without more, however, this position is too simple. The law may confer unreviewable power for a variety of reasons. Judges of highest courts, for example, have essentially unreviewable authority to determine the law, because in a practical system of government such power must be placed somewhere. Yet certainly some interpretations of law could be so egregious, so far beyond permissible bounds, that we should say the judges who made them violated their legal duty and acted outside their authority. In cases in which substantial evidence is produced against the defendant, jurors have, as George Christie has pointed out, effective power to convict on less than the reasonable doubt standard.[5] That is to say, if the jurors consciously determine that the evidence does not meet that requisite, but the defendant is probably guilty and is certainly a dangerous character who should be locked up, they can convict, and no other organ of government will be able to go behind their verdict and undo their finding of guilt. We should, nevertheless, hesitate to say that the jurors have legal authority to convict on less than beyond a reasonable doubt. Power does not necessarily demonstrate right.

The contrary position—that the jury's legal duty is always simply to apply the law as the judge instructs it—also presents some difficulties, because the undoubted power to acquit rests on something more than the impracticality of review. One of the historic arguments for jury trial is that a community check against enforcement of arbitrary laws and unduly harsh penalties is desirable; and jury refusals to convict publishers charged with seditious libel and petty thieves facing mandatory death penalties are celebrated as civilizing the administration of justice. Before the American Revolution, John Adams conceived the jury as introducing a democratic element into the executive function by which "the subject is guarded in the execution of the laws."[6] When the Supreme Court held that the Fourteenth Amendment required states to afford jury trials in criminal cases, the possibility of jury nullification was considered one of the characteristics making jury trial fundamental to our system of justice.[7] Since judges may direct judgment for either party in a civil case or acquittal in a criminal case, a judge's inability to direct a finding of guilt in a criminal trial rests not on impracticality, but on special solicitude for the criminal defendant—a sense that he should not be convicted without a supportive judgment by members of the community. Even such an apparently innocuous technique as requiring the jury to make particular findings of fact as well as returning a general verdict has been said to undercut its "historic function . . . of tempering rules of law by common sense."[8] Thus, the jury's power on occasion to nullify the law is viewed as a positive feature of its operation, one that is self-consciously protected by ancillary doctrines.

Finding each of the two simple competing views to be unsatisfactory, Mortimer and Sanford Kadish, in their insightful book *Discretion to Disobey*,[9] conclude that juries are under a legal obligation to follow instructions and have a legal right to disobey the instructions if the reasons for doing so are strong enough. Jurors are exemplars of officials who occupy "recourse roles" and who are permitted to depart from the prescribed means for exercising their roles when they believe the ends for which their roles are created will not be served if they fail to digress. The obligation to follow the prescribed means is like a promissory obligation in ordinary life—one that must be given considerable weight but can be overridden by very strong contrary reasons.

This account of the juror's responsibility under our system may make us somewhat uncomfortable, because we are used to thinking that the law forbids, requires, or permits actions. But the Kadish view reflects sophistication about subtle variations in the messages that may be conveyed to actors in a social enterprise.

One need only reflect on parental injunctions to small children to grasp the point. When my three boys have wanted to do things I regarded as part of the birthright of every youth but in later life saw as fraught with potential danger, such as walking on high walls, shooting metal clips with slingshots, throwing sticks and small rocks at the enemy of the moment, hitting brothers in assorted parts of the anatomy, and climbing out of windows, I have discovered that, whether I am presented with a fait accompli or involve myself before the event, my responses are modulated according to my feelings of danger and acceptability. For the actions I regard as the worst, I may say something like "This is absolutely forbidden. You should never do that. If you do it again, you will be seriously punished." On other occasions I say things like "That's a bad idea. You really shouldn't do that," or "That is really stupid. You know you can hurt someone (yourself) that way," or "I am very disappointed in you for doing X" (hitting a brother in a part of the body not absolutely forbidden), or "You really shouldn't do that, but if you must, be very careful." The last comment comes close to a grudging permission, but what I am struggling somehow to do in many instances is to avoid conveying a genuine permission, something that may connote approval or acceptance, and yet to steer clear of absolute prohibition. I should not want to make too much of this analogy, especially since what underlies my variations is a wish not to dilute the prohibitions of the worst acts or overburden the boys with absolute "no's" and a hope that their own sense of responsibility will develop—reasons quite different from those that underlie the uncertain signals the legal system conveys about jury responsibilities. But if a small amount of self-study reveals such variations in parental attempts to guide children, we should hardly be surprised that something as complicated as a legal system may not offer straightforward directions about the performance of some important responsibilities.

If the Kadishes are right that the legal authority of jurors cannot be described in simple terms, it does not follow that their own theoretical account is the most satisfactory. The thrust of their suggestions has a rather paradoxical air—that the obligation to apply the law faithfully continues in force even in those situations when nullification is warranted by the powerful reasons in its favor. As Kurt Baier has pointed out,[10] the conflict between possible nullification and applying the law is not just an ordinary conflict of obligations one cannot practically fulfill at the same time.[11] Nullification is logically incompatible with applying the law; if nullification is required by the ends of justice, one cannot conceivably fulfill that end of one's role and the obligation to apply the law. Without challenging the Kadish account of what jurors may do, Baier tries to dispel the element of paradox by suggesting that jurors should be thought to be under an obligation to follow instructions unless compliance would seriously frustrate some of the ends of their role.[12] In that event, they would cease to be under the obligation to apply the law faithfully.

I do not believe that Baier's revision is philosophically more compelling than the original account of the Kadishes. Having suggested that the obligations of promise and fair play may run into conflicts with more compelling duties of justice, I have assumed that obligations may be outweighed rather than cease, even when performance of the obligation is not logically compatible with satisfying the duty of justice. Imagine that A previously helped B to capture B's escaped slave; B has promised to do the same for A if the need arises. B, who has by now freed all his own slaves, sees A's escaped slave on his property. His obligations of promise and fair play toward A compete with his natural duties toward the slave. Performance of one duty is logically incompatible with performance of the other. I should say the promissory or fair play obligation is outweighed by the natural duty rather than nonexistent. Similarly, a jury's obligation to apply the law could be outweighed by its duty to do what is morally just in an individual case.

In any event, whatever the strength of Baier's position as an account of how outsiders should view the jury's responsibilities, it fails to capture the perplexities facing jurors themselves, who are not instructed about any authority to disregard instructions. Because no one tells them under what conditions they may nullify the law, they are likely to feel themselves being pulled in two different directions, with the uneasy feeling that whatever they do will be wrong from some point of view. The Kadish paradox is much more faithful to their disquieting dilemma than is Baier's simpler resolution.

Criteria for Nullification

Because judges do not instruct juries about their power to nullify the law, the dearth of writing on how conscientious jurors should exercise that power is not surprising; but I want to consider what standard might be applied by a thoughtful juror who is considering acquittal, even though he recognizes that application of the judge's instructions to the facts would yield a guilty verdict. Few now believe that lay jurors should supplant the judge's instructions with their own interpretations of the law, and such authority would be hard to defend. The authority that is implicitly conceded to jurors is rather that they may disregard the law when its application would be highly unjust. As the Kadishes put it, the jurors must place a "significant surcharge" on denial of their obligation to apply the law. A juror should not acquit unless he is firmly convinced that a gross injustice would be done by conviction. He must believe more than that the actor's motives were good or that the law is a bad one. He must think that the actor was performing an act that was clearly justified or was exercising an undeniable moral right. Ordinarily, he would have to think either that the law on which the prosecution is based is itself highly unjust or that the particular circumstances of the case are so far outside what the legislature had in mind that the law's application in this case would be unconscionable. In rare cases, for example, when jurors are strongly persuaded that protesters had an overwhelming powerful reason to break a law, acquittal may be warranted even though jurors do not consider the law itself unjust or the situation to be outside the legislature's intentions.

Perhaps the jury needs less strong reasons when the form of nullification is to reduce the crime involved (say from murder to manslaughter) without justification in the law and facts. Because the defendant will still be convicted and receive a sentence, the jury's defiance of the law in this situation is not quite so great.

One final distinction needs to be drawn. Some cases will present a genuine issue of guilt on the basis of the evidence, and an outsider may not be able to tell whether the jury honestly disbelieved the prosecutor's version of the facts or believed it but nevertheless determined not to convict. Indeed, the jurors voting for acquittal may represent both positions, and the jurors wishing to nullify may deceive the other jurors about the grounds for their votes. In such cases, nullification may be surreptitious; no one will be sure it has taken place.[13] Such violations of the ordinary premises of the system still require strong justification, but since the practical damage will be less if others are not aware of what has occurred, such manipulation may occasionally be warranted even if an open and clear nullification would not be.

The law itself supplies the guiding criteria for jury nullification only to a limited degree. In some cases, jurors may reach behind the letter of the broken law to its ascertainable spirit, perceiving that the individual violator was simply not a person that the legislature really wanted to penalize. In other instances, jurors may be aware that a particular prohibition is out of line with other, more important provisions of the law. For the most part, however, a juror must call on his own, individual sense of justice to decide if a legally warranted conviction would be so intolerable that he should not vote for it. Thus, if jury nullification is an instance in which agents "undertake actions outside the role's prescribed means to achieve the role's ends,"[14] the "ends" are general ones of justice and fairness. The jurors themselves will fill in the content of those ends, not from any special conception of the criminal law as it then exists, but from a less focused appreciation of when condemnation and punishment is acceptable.

Possible Reform

Practical interest in the status of jury nullification increased greatly with the trials of those who refused military service in Vietnam or protested the war there. Change in the present understanding of jury role could take place in either direction. Jury nullification could be more clearly labeled an illegitimate exercise of power, perhaps stripped of some of the support it now enjoys from tangential rules of law, no longer forming the basis of any constitutional doctrines about right to jury trial or providing a subject of admiration for thoughtful commentators. Conversely, jury nullification could be formally recognized, with juries instructed about their power and, perhaps, with lawyers presenting evidence and argument about the appropriateness of deciding against the law in particular cases.

There can be no doubt that jury nullification played a critical humanizing role during stages of English history when the substantive criminal law and its penalties were extremely harsh.[15] The lay jury has also served as an important safeguard against outright oppression. One can certainly conceive of systems of criminal justice that can do without lay jurors and their nullifying powers; but these systems would lack a significant check on official abuse. In any event, the tradition of such power is too deeply rooted in our law to be abandoned.

For the law implicitly to recognize and approve a power it does not admit to those who must exercise it is anomalous. Jurors lacking instructions about authority to nullify can hardly be expected to have reasonably compatible notions of when the duty to apply the law is outweighed by other considerations; on that score defendants are at the mercy of the private notions of members of their particular juries.

Formidable objections to a shift exist, however. If jury nullification could be effectively discouraged, jury power to prevent injustice would be diminished. If jury nullification were formally approved, the proper authority of the written law might be undermined. As all recognize, juries may nullify for bad reasons as well as good, and no one has yet thought of a formula that would produce nullification only in deserving cases. The sensible assumption is that if juries were instructed about their power to nullify, this would increase the instances of nullification; some of these would be just refusals to apply the law, others victories for prejudice or overly generous sympathy.

George Christie has made the further observation that such instructions would tend to have the undesirable effect of relieving the moral responsibility that jurors feel for nullification and increasing their sense of moral responsibility for convictions, because jurors could no longer view themselves as simple agents of the law sworn to do as it directs.[16] If defense attorneys could present evidence and argument in favor of nullification, the dangers of appeal to prejudice would be greatly enhanced, and trials of many political protesters would be turned into unconstrained debates over controversial political issues.

Some language should be discoverable that would alert all jurors to the existence of the nullification power but would indicate in the strongest terms that it should be reserved for only the most exceptional cases. Jurors might be told the following, for example: "Your basic responsibility is to apply the law as given in the judge's instructions. You do have the legal authority to acquit a defendant who is guilty under the law, but that should be done only in an extreme case of a terrible injustice." The gains in openness and consistency should outweigh any harm from a slight increase in instances of nullification. Because a crucial value of the law is its capacity to focus and narrow issues, however, to make cases turn on something other than the political and social sympathies of juries, no evidence or argument on the possibility of nullification should be permitted.

Judge Nullification

Judges in criminal cases also have some power to nullify the substantive law. In jury trials, they can direct jurors to acquit when evidence clearly supports a finding of guilt: when a trial is before the bench, a judge can acquit though persuaded of legal guilt. Such determinations are unreviewable, and the possibility of any disciplinary action for isolated instances of nullification is remote.

Judicial power to nullify the substantive law has never been suggested as a desirable feature of trial before judges, and the nonreviewability of their decisions to acquit may be thought to derive more from implications of the defendant's right against double jeopardy than from any sense that the judge is an appropriate agent to second guess the legislature about what behavior should be criminal. Judges are permanent officers of the law sworn to uphold the law, not representatives of community sentiment. In a system with jurors and judges, judges are much less appropriate candidates than jurors to assess the moral acceptability of applications of the law.[17] Perhaps in serious cases,[18] judges have no authority like that of the jury to engage in justified departures from the rules of the substantive law. If judges do have any authority to nullify the criminal law, it is much more limited than the parallel authority of juries.

Nevertheless, it is conceivable that some convictions would be so abhorrent that judicial defiance of the law would be defensible, and this conclusion may be true even if such action is considered to be outside the law in every sense. Given the judge's greater understanding of the law, its values may more fully inform his or her evaluation of possible justifications for nullification than will be true for jurors. Both because of the nature of the office and because they usually find a way of mitigating the rigors of the law through their sentencing power, judges will need much more powerful reasons than juries to engage in outright nullification.

Judges also have the power, in their roles as fact-finders, in their supervision of jurors, and even in their construal of the law, to achieve nullification of the civil law. Except when they resolve factual disputes, what trial court judges do is subject to appeal, but the reality often is that a case is not worth appealing and the powers of trial judges are frequently much greater than a formal analysis of their relation to appellate courts indicates. Nullification of the civil law means denial of legal rights to a litigant who is claiming them; but especially in areas of law in which the power of litigants is unequal, such as landlord-tenant, judges may sometimes be disposed to mitigate the rigor of applicable legal standards.

---

1. See, generally, T. A. Green, Verdict According to Conscience (1985).
2. Id. at 209.
3. Ga. Const. Art. 1, 32–201; Ind. Constr. Art. 1, § 19; Mo. Const. Art XV, § 19.
4. See M. Kadish and S. Kadish, Discretion to Disobey 51 (1973).
5. Christie, Lawful Departures from Legal Rules: "Jury Nullification" and Legitimated Disobedience, 62 Calif. L. Rev. 1289 (1974).
6. See J. Adams, Works III, 481, quoted and discussed in B. Bailyn, The Ideological Origins of the American Revolution 74 (1967).
7. *Duncan v. Louisiana,* 391 U.S. 145, 153 (1968).
8. *United States v. Spock,* 416 F.2d 165, 181 (1st Cir. 1969).
9. See note 23, supra.
10. See Baier, Book Review, 124 *U. Pa. L. Rev.* 561, 576 (1975). M. B. E. Smith has criticized the Kadishes' assumption that one can speak of legal obligations independently of moral obligations. Smith, Concerning Lawful Illegality, 83 *Yale L. J.* 1534 (1974).
11. If A has promised to pay B his only $2000, he cannot both fulfill the promise and pay $2000 for C's badly needed operation, but no logical compatibility exists between the two actions.

12. Id. at 581.
13. The initial grand jury disposition of the Bernhard Goetz case illustrates the possible uncertainty. Outsiders cannot be sure whether grand jurors refused to indict for homicide because they genuinely believed Goetz had a good claim of self-defense or because they just did not want to see him convicted given the circumstances surrounding his shooting of four youths.
14. Kadish and Kadish, supra note 23 at 31.
15. See Green, note 20 supra.
16. Christie, note 24 supra at 1304.
17. An assessment based on established constitutional or legislative criteria is much more appropriate for a judge. Both the application of the necessity defense and the interpretation of constitutional standards can involve judges in such assessments.
18. With respect to some petty offenses, such as traffic violations, it may be thought that judges have an implicit authority to decline to hold technically guilty offenders criminally liable.

THE SERPENT BEGUILED ME AND I DID EAT:
Entrapment and the Creation of Crime*

Gerald Dworkin

This paper examines the legitimacy of pro-active law enforcement techniques, i.e. the use of deception to produce the performance of a criminal act in circumstances where it can be observed by law enforcement officials. It argues that law enforcement officials should only be allowed to create the intent to commit a crime in individuals who they have probable cause to suppose are already engaged or intending to engage in criminal activity of a similar nature.

In the past few years a number of criminal prosecutions have brought to public attention the issue of entrapment: Abscam, the DeLorean cocaine trial, Operation Greylord, various sting fencing operations. The investigative techniques used in, say, Abscam while highly elaborate, expensive and ingenious are only one example of the range of investigative techniques with which I shall be concerned in this essay. What these techniques have in common is the use of deception to produce the performance of a criminal act under circumstances in which it can be observed by law enforcement officials. I shall use the term "pro-active enforcement" to cover such techniques and the question I shall be discussing is under what circumstances, if any, is the use of such measures legitimate.

1

Let me begin by saying something more about the nature of pro-active law enforcement and also by giving a fairly extensive sample of the use of such techniques. The sample will not only make clearer the nature of such operations but also provide a range of cases for testing judgments about the acceptability of such techniques.

Traditionally, law enforcement in our society has left most of the burden of reporting criminal offenses to private citizens. It is left to individuals, usually victims, to come forward with a complaint of criminal action and to provide much of the evidence in identifying and prosecuting the criminal. Government's role has been limited to various patrol activities and to reaction to complaint. Hence, the traditional notion of reactive law enforcement.

Recently the existence of "invisible offenses" has posed challenges to reactive law enforcement. Invisible offenses include not only the so-called victimless crimes, i.e. those crimes in which there are no complaints because all parties to the transaction are willing (drugs, vice, gambling) but also a variety of cases in which the victims are not aware of any criminal act. The patrons of a hotel are not aware of code violations whose existence is protected by the bribery of a building inspector. The purchasers of General Electric products were not aware of the fact that the price of the products they bought was affected by a price-fixing agreement. The customers of a bank are not aware of the loss of funds due to the embezzlement of a teller. There is another class of offenses which produces knowing victims but where, for a variety of reasons, the victims are not prepared to complain—blackmail, extortion, sexual harassment. We know from crime surveys that many victims of robbery and theft do not report these crimes either because of fear of harassment or because they believe it to be a waste of time.

Faced with the failure of the traditional modes of notification and investigative aid, law enforcement

*From Dworkin, Gerald. "The Serpent Beguiled Me and I Did Eat: Entrapment and the Creation of Crime," in *Law and Philosophy* vol. 4 (1985), pp. 17–39. Copyright © 1985 by D. Reidel Publishing Co., Dordrecht, Holland. Reprinted by permission of Kluwer Academic Publishers.

officials have turned to modes of investigation in which the reporting, observation and testimony can be done by the officials themselves. Detection of crime and investigation of crime proceed simultaneously. This is the arena of pro-active law enforcement. Originally used mainly in drug and vice investigations such techniques are now being used increasingly for many other kinds of crime. I shall enumerate a list of such techniques.

Decoy Operations

The New York City Street Crime Unit is a unit of the New York City Police Department which specializes in the techniques of "decoying and blending." The decoy is a police officer who assumes the role of a potential victim. He (or she) may play the role of derelict, shopper, grandmother, drunk, "john," cab driver, potential rape victim. The decoy is placed in an area where experience indicates it is likely the decoy will become a victim. The back-up blends into the street area near the decoy. When the decoy indicates that a crime has been committed the back-up team moves in for the arrest. A similar idea using inanimate objects occurs when decoy letters are sent to trap postal thieves.

In most decoy cases the potential offender is not targeted. But the same techniques can be used against specific suspects. In one case a Manhattan dentist was targeted after three patients had co plained that they had been molested while under anaesthesia. An undercover policewoman posed as a patient, accepted anaesthesia, and was kept under surveillance by a hidden camera. The dentist was arrested and the video evidence led to a conviction.

Sting Operations

Undercover agents take over a warehouse and announce that they are in the market to purchase stolen goods. They purchase goods brought to them and, after some period of time, arrest the sellers of the stolen property. Similar operations have involved running a pornographic bookstore in order to arrest film wholesalers.

Manna from Heaven Operations

Police leave a piece of luggage unattended at the Port Authority bus terminal and arrest those who attempt to walk off with it. As an integrity test for policemen money is left in an apartment, the door is left open, and an "open-door" call is put through to the police.

Honey-Pot Operations

Undercover agents provide opportunities for various criminal acts without actively soliciting them. They may, for example, open a garbage business in the hopes of becoming targets for extortion, or operate a bar in the hopes of being solicited for bribes by city inspectors.

Solicitation Operations

The most common mode of drug enforcement involves government agents offering to buy drugs from dealers. Similar methods are used to enforce laws against counterfeit currency and illegal firearms. In one of the more creative uses of such techniques the police fencing detail in Portland, Oregon purchased color television sets at wholesale prices (under an LEAA grant) and then made the rounds of bars offering to sell the sets very cheaply, claiming they were stolen. As part of the same operation randomly chosen appliance stores were approached with the same offer.

In the recent Operation Greylord in Cook County, Illinois, undercover agents staged a crime and arrest so that they could solicit offers to drop the charges for a payment.

In the course of soliciting a crime the government may play an active role in a criminal operation. In one extreme case involving liquor regulations an agent contacted two defendants with whom he had been previously involved in the production of bootleg alcohol and pressured them to re-establish operations. He offered to provide a still, a still-site, equipment and an operator. He then provided two thousand pounds of sugar at wholesale. The operation lasted for three years during which the government agent was the only customer.

Although the Ninth Circuit reversed this conviction it did not do so on grounds of entrapment. It did argue, however, that "the same underlying objections which render entrapment objectionable to American criminal justice are operative."[1] To see both why the court did not find entrapment, and what the underlying objectives referred to consist in, we must now examine the nature of the entrapment defense. Although my concern is with the normative issues raised by pro-active law enforcement, the legal doctrine of entrapment has been the focus of much of the discussion of such issues, and many of the conceptual and normative distinctions are present in the legal discussion.

2

Entrapment is a defense to a criminal charge. The defendant asserts a claim that he ought not to be held legally liable for some criminal act. It is a defense which originally was a judicial creation although it has since been codified in a number of states including Illinois, New York and Alaska. It is also interesting to note that as a bar to criminal liability it is virtually exclusive to the criminal jurisprudence of the United States.

It is a very narrow defense in that it only applies when the entrapment is performed by a government agent. It is not available to those who are enticed into criminal acts by private citizens. The term government agents, however, includes all employees of government, and in certain circumstances private citizens working for a government agent will count as government agents.

Entrapment occurs when government agents procure the commission of a criminal act by someone who, except for the solicitation, persuasion, or enticement, would not have committed the crime. Both the conditions under which entrapment will be found and the theoretical foundations of the defense are matters of legal dispute. Originally, state and federal courts based the defense on estoppel and public policy. But in 1932 the Supreme Court replaced these with the legal fiction that Congress implicitly excludes entrapment whenever it enacts a criminal statute. The court held that if the police implant in the mind of an innocent person the disposition to commit an offense it is unfair to find such a person guilty. We see here the two elements which recur through the future development of the doctrine—the innocence or predisposition of the offender and the inducement to commit the offense.

Sorrells contains the two main views about the justification of the entrapment defense.[2] The majority focuses on entrapment as a defense in the standard sense of the term, i.e. as a factor affecting the culpability or innocence of the offender. If somebody is found innocent by virtue of entrapment then, on this view, it is similar to being found innocent by virtue of mistake of fact. The offender is not,

or not as, culpable. As an excuse, entrapment is focused on the conduct of the defendant and his relative blameworthiness.

The concurring view, on the other hand, focuses not on the culpability of the offender but on the integrity of the judicial process and the legitimacy of the methods used by the police. The defendant is excused, not because he is less culpable, but because the government has acted in an illegitimate fashion. The point of the defense is not to exculpate offenders but to monitor police behavior.

Parallel to these different views of the nature and function of the defence has been the development of two different standards for the applicability of the defense. What has come to be called the "subjective" test concentrates on the offender's state of mind. With whom did the intent to commit the crime originate? Was the defendant predisposed to commit the crime? Would this particular defendant have committed this particular crime in the absence of the government's conduct? On the view that the defense affects culpability, only those not predisposed to commit the offense will be excused. That is why the defendant in Greene, who had a prior history of violation of liquor regulations, could not invoke entrapment.

The "objective" test, sometimes called the "hypothetical person" test focuses on the conduct of the police, not the defendant. It asks whether the methods used would have led a hypothetical law-abiding citizen to commit the crime in question. As the California Supreme Court put it:

> [We] are not concerned with who first conceived or who willingly, reluctantly, acquiesced in a criminal project. What we do care about is how much and what manner of persuasion, pressure and cajoling are brought to bear by law enforcement officials to induce persons to commit crime. . . . The proper test of entrapment in California is the following: was the conduct of the law-enforcement agent likely to induce a normally law-abiding person to commit the offense.[3]

Note that on this view it does not matter whether or not this defendant was predisposed. If a hypothetical nonpredisposed person would have been likely to commit the crime because of the actions of the police this defendant is let off, not because he is innocent, but because the government conduct cannot be condoned.

The two views cannot be integrated into a single theory. For on the view which emphasizes the innocence of those induced to perform criminal acts it should be irrelevant whether or not the entrapping parties are government agents or private citizens. And on the view which emphasizes the conduct of government agents, it should be irrelevant whether or not the suspect was predisposed to commit the crime.

Because the dominant opinion in the Supreme Court has favored the subjective test of entrapment, and most defendants have a criminal record which makes it difficult to demonstrate lack of predisposition, the entrapment defense remains limited in scope, rarely used, and even less rarely successful.

The legal literature on entrapment consists almost exclusively in expositions of the Supreme Court's various views about the doctrine, and normative questions are usually confined to arguing the relative merits of subjective vs. objective tests.[4] The much larger and important issue of the legitimacy of government created crime is ignored. What values are threatened by the use of pro-active methods of law enforcement? Ought we to distinguish between public officials and private citizens as targets of such techniques? Ought criminals have a right to complain about efficient methods of investigating and detecting their crimes? If certain crimes, e.g. bribery, can only (or most efficiently) be detected by these methods then does a norm of equal enforcement of the law favor such techniques?

3

The central moral concern with pro-active law enforcement techniques is that they manufacture or create crime in order that offenders be prosecuted and punished. They do not discover criminal activity; they create it. I take it that there is some common understanding of these terms such that if this were an accurate and apt description of certain law enforcement methods there would be a decisive objection to their use.

Consider, for example, the scenario of *U.S. v. Ordner*.[5] Ordner, a commercial blaster and firearms manufacturer, with no previous history of lawbreaking, was approached by a government informer at a gun show. The informer, working with the government in the hope of reducing his sentence in a pending case, offered to introduce Ordner to a contractor who might have some blasting work for him. When

Ordner went to meet the contractor, he was instead confronted with an elaborate scheme concocted by agents of the Bureau of Alcohol, Tax and Firearms to resemble a meeting of an underworld gang. Ordner eventually provided the blueprint and directed the assembly of five hundred "penguns." This is clearly an instance of the creation of criminal activity by law enforcement agents. What are the elements that distinguish the creation or manufacture of crime from its investigation and detection?

If one looks back at the range of operations listed earlier one sees that there are various means by which agents contrive to have criminal acts performed in their presence (other than maintaining surveillance of the suspect or a potential crime scene). They can suggest the crime be committed, offer various incentives, use coercion, provide some of the means needed to commit the crime, participate in the commission of the crime, arrange the presence of a potential victim, arrange the presence of a valuable object in an unsecure context, offer to buy or sell contraband, appeal to sentiments of friendship.

On at least one view all of these might count as the creation of criminal activity. Suppose we defined the creation of criminal activity as occurring whenever the police acted in such a way that they caused criminal activity to occur. According to one idea of cause which has played an important role in tort law, one event is said to cause another if it is a necessary condition for its occurrence. This is referred to as "but for" causation. But for the presence of the event in question the other event would not have occurred. Now it is a feature of all pro-active techniques that but for the actions of law enforcement officials the crime for which the defendants are charged would, almost certainly, not have been committed.

Thus, if a policeman rides on a bus with a wallet in his back pocket, and his pocket is picked, but for the actions of the policeman his wallet would not have been stolen. If an officer, suspecting short weighting, makes a purchase of meat at a supermarket, weighs it and finds it short weighted, then this particular fraudulent sale would not have been committed if the government had not acted. Yet, in these cases, it does not seem that the culpability of defendants is reduced, or that the methods go beyond some idea of what is fair.

One way to see this is to note that in an ordinary mugging the presence of the victim is a but for cause of the crime. If this little old lady had not been walking her dog in the park, her mugging would not have occurred. But, surely, she did not create or manufacture crime. The contribution of the state has to go beyond simply providing a potential victim, as in decoy operations.

If, however, the decoy is made to look particularly vulnerable and the "reward" particularly attractive, then questions of temptation and the overcoming of the will raise issues of causation and responsibility. If the crime is made sufficiently "easier" or sufficiently attractive then, as social scientists who leave wallets lying about in phone booths find out, almost any of us is likely to commit a crime.

It is relevant here to note that the increased probability does not occur simply as a forseen consequence of governmental action. A case of this would be the decision to shift patrols to a high-crime area foreseeing that there would be an increase in crime in the section of town with reduced patrols. But in the cases we are considering the point of the action is to increase the likelihood that a crime will be committed in the presence of the police.

If somebody commits a crime, and would not have done so absent the efforts of the state to make the crime easier, has the state created crime? To help in thinking about this let us look at other parts of the law which have developed theory on similar matters. In tort law it is common to invoke the idea that if one neglects to take precautions against harm one is liable for the harm that comes about, even if the harm is brought about by others. Thus a house painter was held liable for the loss of goods stolen by a thief who entered when the painter failed to lock the front door. But the language of the courts in such cases is not that the negligent party causes the wrongdoer to do what he does, or that he causes the harm that results. Rather it is that one has a duty to guard against such harm. Providing others with the opportunity to do harm may ground liability but not because it causes the harm.

In the criminal law there is also a distinction drawn between providing an opportunity to commit a crime and inducing others to commit crime. With respect to criminal responsibility a person is only held to have caused another to act if he makes use of threats, lies or the exercise of authority to induce another to act.

With respect to civil liability for the acts of others the accepted view is that one individual must do something which is directly addressed to the other person such as uttering a threat, or making a false statement, or exploiting personal influence. It is only when the agent led to act is less than fully competent, as in the case of young children, that the mere providing of a temptation counts as causing another to act—as in the doctrine of "attractive nuisance."

Both on grounds of conformity with other legal doctrine and harmony with commonsense notions of causation it is reasonable not to count the mere provision of opportunity to commit a crime as the manufacture or creation of crime. It is only if the opportunity is made sufficiently attractive that creation of opportunities can be regarded as temptation. The danger of such techniques is that they may lead persons to commit crimes who have not engaged in similar activities before. The person who walks away with the "abandoned" suitcase in the Port Authority building may not have been disposed to steal anything at all. In such cases there is the danger that one may not merely shift the scene of criminal activity but create crime that otherwise would not have occurred.

The offer to buy drugs, sex or stolen goods from those already engaged in their sale, or letting it be known that one is available for a bribe, does more than merely make it easier to commit a crime. It invites the criminal to act. Again, this does not seem sufficient to categorize the activity as the creation of crime since although the particular sale might not have taken place had it not been for the offer to engage in the transaction, by hypothesis one is dealing with those already engaged in criminal activity. Leaving aside complications, such as the fact that sting fencing operations may encourage individuals to commit burglaries by providing a ready outlet at above-market prices, such offers are on the portion of the spectrum closer to shifting the scene of criminal activity.

An interesting comparison is between the offer to sell as opposed to buy contraband. This seems a more questionable practice but it is not apparent where the difference lies. It is a crime to buy as well as sell contraband. Both transactions rely on the willingness of an offender to engage in the transaction. While it is true that the danger to society is usually greater from the seller than the buyer this seems to be relevant to what crimes to aim at, not at which techniques are permissible. Moreover, it does not seem particularly outrageous to let it be known that one is willing to sell one's services as a contract murderer (for the purpose of apprehending a buyer of such services).

I believe this is explained by the contingent fact that the offer to sell is more likely to be made without knowledge that a particular individual is already embarked on a course of criminal conduct.

This is why the Oregon case of going into bars and offering to sell supposedly stolen televisions seems to be the creation of crime, while the offer to sell one's services as a contract murderer does not. In the former the state is, in effect, making a random test of the corruptability of the general public.

The next step up from merely providing an opportunity, or merely offering to engage in a criminal transaction, is to provide the necessary means for the commission of a crime. Consider for example the facts in the Twigg case.[6] Robert Kubica after being arrested on charges of illegally manufacturing speed, pled guilty and agreed to assist the Drug Enforcement Administration in prosecuting other offenders. At the request of DEA officials he contacted an acquaintance, Henry Neville, and proposed they set up a laboratory for manufacturing speed. Kubica assumed responsibility for acquiring the necessary equipment, raw materials and a production site. The DEA supplied all of these plus an ingredient essential to the manufacture which, while legal, was difficult to obtain. Twigg joined the operation at the invitation of Neville. Kubica alone had the technical knowledge and skills necessary to manufacture the drug and had complete charge of the laboratory. The Court reversed on the grounds that when Kubica contacted him, Neville

> was not engaged in any illicit drug activity. Using Kubica, and actively participating with him, the DEA agents deceptively implanted the criminal design in Neville's mind. . . . This egregious conduct on the part of government agents generated new crimes by the defendant merely for the sake of pressing criminal charges against him when, as far as the record reveals, he was lawfully and peacefully minding his own affairs. Fundamental fairness does not permit us to countenance such actions by law enforcement officials and prosecution for a crime so fomented will be barred.[7]

I should suppose fundamental fairness would raise some problems about this case even if the intent to commit the crime arose in Neville. Imagine that he approached Kubica saying he would like to manufacture some speed but, unfortunately, lacked the raw materials, the technical skills, the capital, and the equipment. Kubica then supplies them all and Neville is then arrested. What is the harm that the state seeks to avoid by such prosecutions?

Nevertheless the court is focusing on the right factor in the creation of crime—the origin of criminal intent. The essential question for determining

when crime has been created is what the role of government is in causing the offender to form the specific intent to commit the crime in question. The issue of predisposition, which runs through the entrapment commentary, is a red herring. We are not interested in the general willingness of an offender to commit crime but in whether he has formed the intent to engage in a specific crime if the opportunity presents itself. In so far as only an opportunity is offered, then if the offender is using it to realize a pre-existing purpose the origin of intent is in him. If the government, in Learned Hand's phrase, "solicits, proposes, initiates, broaches or suggests" the offense then the origin of the intent lodges with the state.

Real situations are, of course, complicated by overdetermination. Suppose, for example, I form the intent to commit a crime if and only if I am solicited to do so by someone else. Or suppose I form the intent to steal something, but cannot overcome a residual fear of being apprehended, and it is only your encouragement that enables me to carry out the original intent.

The fact that there are difficult questions about determining the origin of intent only shows that the question of whether crime has been manufactured is often hard to settle. And that is something we already knew. If the ambiguities and difficulties in determining the origin of intent match those in deciding whether crime has been created that is all one can demand in terms of a satisfactory analysis.

Given our understanding of the idea of the creation of crime in terms of origin of intent we can now pass to the normative issues. Is it legitimate, and if so under what conditions, for the government to create criminal activity?

4

To answer this question one must have some general view about the underlying purpose and rules of fairness which are embedded in the particular system of criminal law-enforcement we have adopted. The legitimacy of particular law-enforcement techniques is necessarily relative to a particular conception or model of criminal justice. At most an argument for condemning particular modes of enforcement will be of the form "If you accept a particular ideal of the purposes and fairness of attaching criminal sanctions to rules of conduct, then these methods will be inconsistent or not cohere with such an ideal."

I shall sketch the outlines of what I believe to be an ideal of the principles of distribution applied to criminal sanctions embedded in our current practice and jurisprudence.

1. Criminal sanctions constitute an interference with the liberty of the members of a society.
2. They are justified, at least in part, by their contribution to the adherence of citizens to justifiable standards of conduct.
3. Individuals ought to have a broad area of autonomy, i.e. self-determination, in the choice of behavior and the formation of goals and purposes.
4. There is a conflict between maximizing autonomy and promoting fundamental human goods such as security of possessions, personal integrity and opportunity. One way of mitigating this conflict is to allow individuals to choose whether or not to become subject to criminal sanctions by presenting them with reasons against certain conduct (sanctions) and letting them make the decision to comply or not. Individuals who are legitimately punished have self-selected themselves for such treatment.
5. The criminal law is not to be thought of as a price system, i.e. as it being indifferent whether a citizen obeys the law or violates it but pays the price of the sanction. The criminal law is meant to be obeyed. Certain behaviors are forbidden and others are required, and while the citizen is given a choice (in the sense that the behaviors are not made impossible) his will is constrained to make the correct choice.

These propositions have implications for very different aspects of the criminal justice system. They affect the substantive content of legal standards, e.g. standards which are very difficult or impossible to obey would be ruled out. They affect procedural issues, e.g. laws should be prospective in application. They affect the excusing conditions we ought to allow. And they affect the types of law-enforcement techniques we should regard as legitimate.

In light of the above propositions the normative issue may be phrased in the following manner: what methods of apprehending and detecting offenders are consistent with the view of a system of criminal sanctions as a choosing system and as the enforcement of law, i.e. authoritative rules backed by sanctions. I am claiming that it is not consistent with such a system that law enforcement officials attempt to see if they can cause a person to commit a crime by suggesting or encouraging in any way that a crime be committed.

It is not that such suggestions are improper only if they are such as to overwhelm the will. The use of coercion, excessive temptation, and fraud are obviously inconsistent with the view that we are only entitled to punish those offenders who willingly choose to commit crimes. I am arguing for the much stronger view that it is not proper to solicit, encourage, or suggest crime even if this is done by no stronger means than verbal suggestion. It is not that the offender can complain after the fact that his will was overborne. It is that we, any of us, can complain before the fact that it is not the purpose of officers of the law to encourage crime for the purpose of punishing it.

For the law is set up to forbid people to engage in certain kinds of behavior. In effect it is commanding "Do not do this." And it shows that it is commanding, as opposed to requesting or advising by saying that it will impose sanctions on those who refuse to conform. It will "humble the will" to use Fingarette's language.[8]

But for a law enforcement official to encourage, suggest, or invite crime is to, in effect, be saying "Do this." It is certainly unfair to the citizen to be invited to do that which the law forbids him to do. But it is more than unfair; it is conceptually incoherent. Of course this incoherence does not appear to the person being entrapped since he is not aware of the official capacity of his entrapper. And the incapacity is concealed from the official since he thinks of himself as trying to detect a criminal—the thought being that an honest citizen will simply refuse the invitation. From the standpoint of one trying to understand and evaluate the system, however, the conflict is clear.

It is important to note that we are not literally involved in a contradiction as we would be, for example, if the Statutes both commanded and forbade that a certain action be done. Nor is it a pragmatic contradiction, in the sense of being self-defeating. The person who says "P but I do not believe P" takes back with the latter part of his assertion what he implies with the former part. Nor is it self-defeating in the sense that it cannot be useful to engage in such behavior in order to increase overall compliance with the legal system. It is not as if one part of the criminal justice system (the police) are trying to undo what another part (the legislature) is trying to accomplish. ·

It is not always incoherent to invite someone to do the very act which one is trying to get them to avoid doing. Consider a parent trying to teach a child not to touch the stove. In the case of a particularly recalcitrant child the most effective technique might be to encourage the child to touch the stove in one's presence. The slight pain now will teach the child to avoid a greater pain later. But this is surely not the model being used by the police. They are interested either in deterring others or in punishing guilty people. The end being served is not that of the person being invited to commit the crime.

I suppose we can (barely) make sense of a system of rules forbidding certain behavior which is enforced by inviting people to commit the forbidden acts and then punishing them for doing so. But such a system violates elementary standards of coherence and fairness.

To encourage the commission of a crime in the absence of any reason to believe the individual is already engaged in a course of criminal conduct is to be a tester of virtue, not a detector of crime.

As a way of insuring against such testing of virtue I suggest that whenever the action of creating an intent to commit a criminal act would render a private citizen liable to criminal charges as accessory or co-conspirator, public officials should be allowed to perform such acts as would create such an intent only if they have probable cause to suppose that the individuals approached are already engaged or are intending to engage in activity of a similar nature. If they offer to buy contraband from specific individuals they should have probable cause to believe those individuals are already engaged in such transactions. If they offer to sell stolen goods to individuals, they ought to have probable cause to believe such individuals are already buying stolen goods. If they offer bribes to public officials, then they should have probable cause to suppose that the officials are already corrupt; not just corruptible.

To use an analogy we do not think it proper for police to engage in random searches of homes in order to detect possible criminal activity. Why then should we allow random solicitation or encouragement of criminal activity? I have heard it argued that on grounds of equitable law enforcement it is wrong to allow those who may have corrupt dispositions, but have been fortunate enough not to have been given the opportunity to exercise them, to escape punishment when their less fortunate counterparts are caught. After all if we had offered them a bribe they would have taken it. This counter-factual seems to me an interesting piece of data for God, but not for the FBI. Suggesting the commission of a crime, even to wicked people, is not a legitimate function of a system of law enforcement.[9]

Although my discussion has been much broader than the topic of Abscam I would like to apply the discussion to Abscam, partly because it has caused so much controversy and partly because it is a difficult case to form a judgment about. Abscam is not one case but many since there were a number of different public officials involved. But basically the actual solicitation of crime involved either offering money to secure residency for the "shiek" or the offer to finance a titanium mine in return for using political office to secure government contracts. It is the latter case (Senator Williams) that I wish to focus upon.

The charges against Williams and his attorney related to a titanium mine and processing plant. Williams' investment group consisting of himself, his attorney Feinberg, Katz, Errichetti (the mayor of Camden) and Sandy Williams sought financing to acquire the titanium enterprise. Through Errichetti the group contacted Melvin Weinberg, a convicted swindler who was working for the government, and an undercover agent, Anthony Amoroso. The latter pair posed as members of Abdul Enterprises, an investment firm pretending to represent wealthy Arabs. Criminal charges arose out of the promise requested by the undercover agent as a condition for the financing, that Williams would use his power and influence to obtain government contracts for purchasing the titanium to be produced.

My own reading of the trial transcripts and the due process hearings that followed the conviction of Williams convinces me that Senator Williams acted in a corrupt and morally indefensible manner. Quite independently of the outcome of the criminal charges the Senate Ethics Committee acted entirely correctly in recommending that Williams be expelled from the Senate—an outcome he avoided by resigning.

On the legal issue of entrapment the trial judge denied Williams's motions to dismiss the indictment on grounds of entrapment and the Supreme Court concurred. What this shows, in my view, is that the current legal doctrine of entrapment is too narrowly construed because I believe the best reading of the evidence shows that Williams's crime was created and manufactured by the state, that there was no probable cause for targeting Williams, and that, in accordance with my earlier argument, it was improper to procede with prosecution. I can, in this appendix, only briefly highlight what I believe to be the grounds supporting my reading of the evidence. I shall be ignoring various aspects of the investigation which raise due process questions of their own, such as the reliability of Weinberg, the chief government informant, the absence of control over Weinberg by government agents, the absence of written reports summarizing conversations that were not recorded. I will focus only on the entrapment issues.

Was there probable cause for targeting Williams? The U.S. Attorney who supervised the investigation stated that he "had no reason to question the integrity of Senator Harrison Williams." The Special Agent in Charge, John Good, testified the government was "starting with a clean slate." Nowhere is there evidence of a predicate to investigate. It is the absence of such a predicate, not the question of predisposition, which I regard as crucial to the legitimacy of soliciting or encouraging crime.

As to the question of where the suggestion for criminal activity arose one has to read the evidence and note when and how often the suggestion for illegal conduct arose with the informant or government agents. The titanium venture itself was a legitimate business venture. The criminal elements included using political influence to get government contracts, concealing one's interest in the mine, and so forth. Consider these conversations. MW is Melvin Weinberg, the government informant. SW is Sandy Williams, friend and business associate of Senator Williams. TD is an FBI agent. AF is Williams attorney and business associate. GK is a business associate of Williams.

MW: Allright, now what about, uh, let me ask you a question. There's a lot of government contracts that, ya know, on the chemicals.

SW: Right.

MW: Now, can Williams get us the bids on them.

SW: Well, I don't know about that. The main thing is with this Cyanamid thing . . .

MW: Yeah.

SW: They've got customers they've had for twenty, thirty, forty years. . . . And if we wanna increase our business, we'll have to, we'll have to go into like Sherman-Williams and people like that and try to get their business away from somebody else.

TD: Is he going to be able to steer any kind of contracts from the Committees that he's going to get involved with? I mean . . .

AF: Well, this I didn't know until now I have to ask him that.

GK: He's not a guy, he's not a doer, you know, quietly behind the scene, you know, he, uh, may move a little bit . . . but let me tell you this here

between you and me, he's in a very, very powerful position here, the committees that he heads, you understand?

MW: Yeah.

GK: But he doesn't use that power for any advantages.

MW: Oh, how can we make him use it?

In this exchange the associates of Williams did not raise the issue of government contracts, and in every case where the government did so, they acted in a neutral or discouraging fashion. With respect to concealing his interest in the mine notice how in this conversation between Feinberg, Weinberg and Da Vito, the suggestion of concealing the interest arises from the government.

MW: That's in the mine though. But on the other thing there he, in fact you may we may put the 20 percent in his name even. I don't think he can though.

TD: Well, if he puts . . .

AF: I don't know, we haven't decided yet. We're gonna both examine the law involving his side investments which he . . .

MW: I don't think he can.

AF: He can put it in his wife's name or someone else.

MW: They could chase that too fast.

TD: Yeah.

MW: Come on, you're an attorney, you know that.

AF: I know that.

TD: Any, anything that he puts . . .

AF: I'm not sure that he's forbidden.

MW: Sure he is if he's going to get us open doors. Come on, you know that's a conflict of interest. He'll be sitting with Nixon out in Clemente there.

Perhaps the most controversial aspect of the investigation involves the coaching session between Weinberg and Williams just prior to Williams's meeting with the "shiek." This is the backstage maneuvers before the on-camera performance. Here is Weinberg telling Williams what to say.

MW: Forget the mine. Don't even mention the mine. . . . [Tell him] how high you are in the Senate. . . . He's interested in you . . . Who you know in the Senate can do you favors. . . . Without you there is no deal. You are the deal. You put this together. You worked on this and you got the government contracts. Without me there is no government contracts. . . . Mention, you know, come on as strong as possible. . . . You gotta just play and blow your horn. The louder you blow and mention names, who you control. And that's it, it goes no further. It's all talk, all bullshit.

But with all this effort the meeting with the shiek proves inconclusive. In November 1979, the prosecutors held a meeting to review the evidence against Williams and came to the conclusion that further investigative efforts were required.

> Relative to the matter concerning US Senator Harrison Williams of New Jersey, the following was decided:
>
> 1. It will be necessary to recontact US Senator Williams to attempt to obtain an overt action on his part regarding the sponsorship of some type of legislation, i.e. tax cover for titanium mine and/or import quotas for titanium mine.
>
> 2. It was also suggested that attempts should be made to elicit from US Senator Williams whether or not he wanted his shares hidden, through discussions concerning reporting of personal taxes and official acts that he promised to provide.

The prosecutors subsequently decided to add the "asylum scenario" that had been used so successfully against other Congressmen. A meeting between Williams and the shiek was held in which the shiek offered Williams money to obtain permanent residency in the United States. Williams refused the money, although he did go on to link his assistance on the immigration matter to the financing of the titanium venture. Incidentally, this meeting which was video-taped and observed by the investigators was interrupted at one point by a phone call by an FBI agent who instructed the shiek as to what he should say to Williams. The agent later testified as to the purpose of the interruption: "It was clear from the way the conversation was going on that it wasn't quite as specific as we would have liked it to have been."

I suggest that what we had in this case was not an investigation of whether Senator Williams was breaking the law but an effort to see if he could be induced to do so. That he was apparently quite willing to be so induced is not at issue. The issue is whether it is legitimate to substitute for the question. "Is this individual, who we have reason to suspect of corrupt activity, acting in a corrupt manner?" the question "Can we corrupt this individual who we have no reason to believe is corrupt?"

I do not deny that political corruption is a very difficult crime to detect by normal investigative techniques. I also do not believe that it is impermissible to use deception and trickery in the attempt to uncover such corruption. But I do not believe that it is legitimate to solicit and encourage such corruption unless we have evidence that the targeted individuals are already engaged in such corruption.[10]

---

1. *Greene v. United States,* 454 F. 2nd 783 (9th Cir. 1971).
2. *Sorrells v. United States,* 287 U.S. 435 (1932).
3. *People v. Barraza,* 23 Cal. 3rd 675 (1979).
4. Some exceptions include Park, *The Entrapment Controversy,* 60 *Minn. L. Rev.* 163 (1976). Goldstein, *For Harold Laswell: Some Reflections on Human Dignity, Entrapment, Informed Consent and the Plea Bargain,* 84 *Yale L.J.* 683 (1975). *Causation and Intention in the Entrapment Defense,* 28 *UCLA Law J.* 859 (1981).
5. 554 F. 2d 24 (2d Circ.), 434 U.S. 824 (1977).
6. *U.S. v. Twigg,* 558 F. 2d 373 (3d Cir. 1978).
7. Id. at 381.
8. H. Fingarette, *Punishment and Suffering,* Proceedings and Addresses of the American Philosophical Society, v. 50, 1977 p. 510.
9. I have ignored in my argument any discussion of the practical consequences of law enforcement officials engaging in the creation of crime. My argument has been addressed to matters of principle rather than practice. I believe, however, that considerations of likely consequences strengthens the argument. The work of Gary Marx, a sociologist from MIT, is the best source for the dangers of undercover police work in general. Here are some of the problems that he worries about.
    (a) The lack of effective supervision of informers and police.
    (b) The possibility of damage to unwitting victims and third parties.
    (c) The possibility of police participating in real crimes to gain the confidence of the targeted suspects.
    (d) The use of selective targeting against political opponents.
    (e) The corrupting effect on police of pretending to be corrupt.
    (f) Excessive invasion of privacy.
    (g) Stimulation of criminal activity, e.g. through offering to purchase stolen goods.
10. A version of this paper was read at the Eastern Division Meetings of the American Philosophical Association. My commentators at the meeting were Gerald Postema and Patricia White. I am indebted to them, and in particular to Postema, for helpful suggestions and criticisms.

Justice and Compensation

MISCHIEF AND MISFORTUNE
Annual McGill Lecture in Jurisprudence and Public Policy[*]

Jules Coleman and Arthur Ripstein

Introduction: The Interdependence of Corrective and Distributive Justice

Questions of distributive justice may seem far removed from those of tort theory. Corrective justice concerns the rectification of losses owing to private wrongs. In contrast, distributive justice concerns the general allocation of resources, benefits, opportunities, and the like. The duty to repair under corrective justice is *agent specific*—only wrongdoers need make up the losses of others. The duties imposed by distributive justice are, in contrast, *agent general*—everyone has a duty to create and sustain just distributions. Aristotle, the first to distinguish the two forms of justice, argued that corrective and distributive justice represent distinct and mutually irreducible modes of moral reasoning.[1]

In spite of these analytic or conceptual distinctions, some advocates of economic analysis have tried to reduce both forms of justice to a common denominator, typically either overall utility or economic efficiency. But, one does not have to believe that corrective and distributive justice are reducible to some other moral ideal in order to see important connections between them. First, in order to sustain a just distribution, the effects of wrongful transfers must be annulled. In this way, the institutions of distributive justice require institutions of corrective justice. Second, a practice of corrective justice has the effect of sustaining the prevailing distribution of resources by annulling the effects of certain changes in it. Because corrective justice imposes a *moral* reason on agents to make good others' losses, in doing so it sustains the prevailing distribution. It follows that not every distribution will be sufficiently just to warrant protection by such a practice. Only some distributions can be sustainable by a practice of corrective justice; a requirement that unjust losses be rectified only makes sense provided holdings are not entirely unjust. Thus, corrective justice imposes constraints on the existing institutions of distribution. To the extent that tort law helps shape our conception of corrective justice, this means that it is impossible

*We are grateful to audiences at Chicago-Kent School of Law, McGill University, Faculty of Law, The University of Manitoba, U.C.L.A., The University of Southern California, the University of Toronto, Western New England School of Law, and Yale Law School. Many people have given us helpful written comments. We are especially grateful to Gregory Keating for convincing us we did not mean some of the things that we had said about strict liability in earlier versions. 41 McGill Law Journal 91 © McGill Law Journal 1995. Endnotes have been edited and renumbered.

to entirely separate tort law from the institutions and demands of both distributive and corrective justice.[2]

Corrective and distributive justice are connected in another way as well. However distributive shares are to be fixed, their value will depend, in part, on the tort regime that is in effect. Depending on which transfers are considered wrongful and which not, the particular bundles of goods that individuals hold may turn out to have very different values. Just as corrective justice sustains existing distributions, so the value of distributive shares depends on ways of correcting wrongs.

We hope to show a further connection between distributive and corrective justice. Life is full of unplanned and unanticipated events, and even its best, planned aspects build on the result of earlier chance. Chance has a downside, of course. Its name is misfortune. We want to suggest that both tort law and the institutions of distributive justice can be understood as responses to the question: who owns which of life's misfortunes? We can distinguish between liberal and non-liberal answers to this question, and between liberal and non-liberal institutions of tort law and distribution. Part of what it means to refer to institutions as "liberal" is that they aspire to express a conception of equality. In the case of both tort law and distributive institutions, that conception of equality aspires to allocate misfortune and its burdens *fairly*. What does fairness require in the allocation of misfortune?

If we focus on misfortune's costs, one plausible suggestion is represented by the principle that each of us should bear the costs of our own activities. In economic vocabulary, no one should be allowed to displace the costs of their activities. So put, the principle has the ring of a tautology; if someone else ends up bearing the costs of one's activity, they turn out not to be one's own costs after all. But the point is normative as well as conceptual: however we might fix which costs belong to whom, it is surely unfair that some should end up bearing costs imposed by others.

I. The Principle of Fairness

1. Let us refer to the claim that each person should bear the costs of her activities as the principle of fairness. That principle requires a conception of the costs of an activity. Any form of liberalism must answer the question of where misfortunes properly lie in a way

that satisfies the principle of fairness. Different forms of liberalism will provide different interpretations of the principle, and what it requires by the way of institutions of tort law and distributive justice. In part, different conceptions of what the principle requires result from the fact that competing interpretations of liberalism offer conflicting conceptions of an activity's costs. In fact, we will argue that the two poles of broadly liberal thought—libertarianism and egalitarianism—adopt the same general conception of an activity's costs. This conception identifies the costs of an activity with its causal upshots.

If we identify the cost of an activity with its causal upshots, it may seem that the principle of fairness would require that we annul any losses our activities cause. That in turn suggests a system of generalized strict liability in torts, which would make injurers liable for any and all injuries they cause. Each of us should bear the costs our conduct imposes on others; otherwise, we force others to bear costs which are properly ours—the costs resulting from the expression of our agency through our decisions and choices. Put differently, strict liability looks like it is simply the idea that one should internalize all the externalities of one's conduct. If strict liability is necessary to prevent individuals from displacing costs onto others, then fault liability would allow individuals to displace some of their costs, presumably by imposing those costs an injurer *faultlessly* causes his victims. Faultlessly caused costs are, thus, displaced from injurer to victim.

In the same way, and for much the same reasons, some defenders of a tort system based exclusively on strict liability have maintained that the same principle, where one should bear the costs of one's activities, also lends support to non-redistributive economic institutions. Individuals have no duty to share in the misfortune of others unless they are causally responsible for having brought it about. Unfortunate individuals who manage to shift the burdens of misfortune to others who did not bring them about would otherwise impose external costs on them, no less than injurers do. In the same way that causal responsibility is enough to justify imposing the costs of misfortune on an injurer in tort, so the absence of causal responsibility is enough to block imposing the burdens of misfortune on others more generally. Because redistributive policies aim to have individuals shoulder the costs of misfortunes they did not cause, such policies are morally impermissible. For the libertarian, the principle of fairness requires a system of strict liability and the absence of coercive redistribution; strict liability for accidents and leaving life's standing misfortunes where they fall.

2. The libertarian is not alone in attempting to claim the principle that people should bear the costs of their choices. Where the libertarian emphasizes personal responsibility for misfortune, the liberal egalitarian emphasizes a communal responsibility to remedy the misfortunes of birth and status. According to the liberal egalitarian, we should all be made to share in all of life's misfortunes except for those we make for ourselves by our own choices. Only the misfortunes our choices bring to us are ours to bear alone. Where the libertarian emphasizes the misfortunes we cause others through our choices, the egalitarian liberal emphasizes those we create for ourselves though our choices, preference, and tastes.

Libertarians like Richard Epstein oppose redistribution,[3] whereas such liberal egalitarians as Ronald Dworkin[4] and John Roemer[5] favor substantial redistribution. Yet both positions draw support from the same general principle of fairness. Even more importantly, in spite of very different views about what the principle requires, they share a conception of the costs of activities. In both cases, the underlying thought is that responsibility is fixed by such concepts as cause, agency, and especially, control. For the libertarian, the costs of my activities include those costs that my activities cause others; for the liberal egalitarian, the costs of my activities are the results of the choices I make regarding my fair share of resources. If I choose to cultivate a taste for philosophy, the costs of so doing are mine alone to bear. No one else has a responsibility to make good my loss.

3. How can libertarians and liberal egalitarians accept the same general principle of fairness, interpret it in light of the same general conception of an activity's costs yet support radically different views about what that principle requires in the way of political institutions? The difference between the libertarian and the liberal egalitarian depends on the fact that they adopt different default rules. The libertarian claims that in the absence of causal responsibility, the costs of misfortune should lie where they fall—on victims. The liberal egalitarian holds the opposite default rule: misfortunes that are nobody's causal responsibility are to be held in common. Like the libertarian and the liberal egalitarian, we accept the principle of fairness in the allocation of the costs of misfortune. We reject, however, their shared conception of an activity's costs. Any theory that allows individuals to fix the costs of their own activities involves a *subjective* measure of those costs. The costs of my activities are fixed entirely

by some fact about *me:* my control over them, my causal responsibility for them, my intentions, the risks I mean to take or impose. On any such account, those features would matter in the same way, regardless of the activity in which I was engaged. Any such conception of the costs of an activity not only fails to honour the principle that one should bear the costs of one's activities but has the rather perverse consequence of allowing individuals *to determine what those costs are.*

In contrast, we will argue that only an *objective* measure of costs can honour the liberal principle of fairness. In explicating this idea, we defend the view that any measure of the costs of an activity is normative and depends on an analytically prior account of what each of us owes one another. Only when we know what each of us owes the other can we determine who owns the costs of misfortunes that arise in the course of our interactions. Whether the loss you suffer when my business succeeds in taking clients away from you is yours or mine does not depend on whether my business activity is the cause of your loss; instead, it depends on whether I owe you a duty not to interfere with your business interests, whether constraints of fairness limit competition. It depends, in other words, on what we owe one another with respect to competitive business practices, and whether in competing with you I violate or comply with those obligations.

We will argue that the only way to honour the principle of fairness is by employing a normative conception of what we owe each other. To the extent that such an account is supposed to honour the principle of fairness, those duties must be specified objectively. We will argue that an objective measure of the costs of an activity needs more than activity-neutral concepts like choice, cause, and agency. Instead, any plausible account will depend on the value of the activities in which we are engaged and the ways in which those activities figure in our lives—how they matter to us and why. Having shown this, we will demonstrate why the search for an appropriate default rule for dealing with all misfortunes is misconceived.

A. An Objective Standard of Costs

4. At this point, we offer no general theory of the duties we owe one another. Indeed, we may not even agree with each other about the specifics of the theory that our argument claims to be necessary. We share, however, the view that the principle of fairness requires an objective measure of costs and an account,

therefore, of our responsibilities to one another. We also share a commitment to the central idea of this essay, namely, that there is a right way of thinking about how to formulate and construct the general theory of obligations, which is implicit in the idea of bearing the costs of one's choices. In tort law, it is represented by a particular conception of liability. That conception is more nearly explicit in the fault standard than in the strict liability rules that govern particular areas of tort liability but is at work in both. In each case, liberty and security interests, which everyone can be supposed to share, determine the occasions for liability. In institutions of distributive justice, it is represented by the strategy of what John Rawls calls "primary goods".[6] Rawls describes primary goods as all-purpose means—things that anyone can be presumed to want in pursuit of whatever conception of the good they might have. Both rely on an interpersonal measure of value, of what is important in an individual's life and why. These concerns are often controversial. But controversy is unavoidable.

Our motives for defending these ways of looking at both liability and distributive justice and for emphasizing the connection between the two are not narrowly analytical. One great attraction of the family of views we reject is that it seems to give expression to an ideal of *neutrality*. Each person is free to cultivate her various tastes (liberal egalitarian) or engage in whatever non-criminal activities she wishes (libertarian). The state maintains its neutrality with respect to those differing conceptions of the good and, in this way at least, purports to respect each individual's moral independence. All the state is called on to do is to protect fairness by ensuring that each person bear the costs of whichever activities he or she happens to choose.

Our view, in contrast, is that any measure of the costs of an activity presupposes substantive and contestable conceptions of what is necessary or important to living a life in a liberal political culture. As a result, it is impossible for liberalism, or any other regime insisting on fairness as its central virtue, to be neutral in this way. We cannot be neutral with respect to all subjective accounts of what the elements of a good or meaningful life are. If we are to provide a defensible distinction between the misfortunes that are mine to bear and those that fall on others or should be held in common, while honouring the principle of equality, then we must appeal to objective measures of the value of various activities and their importance in our lives—how they matter and why—not by retreat to the seemingly neutral high ground of the concepts of choice, control, or human agency.

If a standard is objective, it has to take a stand on which subjectively-felt harms count and, therefore, cannot be entirely neutral about what matters in life. Such non-neutrality does not require that it take a stand on every disputed question. Indeed, a plausible liberal view of what matters in life maintains that part of a valuable life is being able to make one's own decisions about certain important questions. More generally, a liberal commitment to toleration is honoured by describing those interests in general terms, so that they are protected however people decide to exercise them. In addition, of course, non-neutrality need not translate into a policy of actively promoting particular activities. By letting the importance of activities figure into determining the costs of choices, various goods can be recognized without being openly promoted.

The questions that we claim are required to allocate misfortune fairly are substantive questions that many would like to avoid. Many, doubtless, wish to avoid the further political issue of who gets to answer such questions. Indeed, one of the great attractions to many of libertarianism and the liberal egalitarianism of Dworkin and Roemer is that they seem to substitute personal choice and control for public judgement. But, difficult questions cannot be avoided if we want to allocate misfortunes while honouring the idea that people should bear the costs of their choices. The questions raised by that appealing, if elusive, idea are normative all the way down.

II. Misfortune

5. We will explore these issues in legal and political philosophy through the lens of misfortune. We do not offer an analysis or general unifying conception of misfortune but simply look at particular misfortunes. Some misfortunes are thought of as injustices, in need of some form of repair; others are thought of as "mere" misfortunes. A variety of political institutions and strategies deal with misfortunes, including regulation, tort liability, and criminal sanction. Some try to prevent misfortunes; others simply attempt to shift their costs from one person to another. By reflecting on our practices for dealing with misfortunes, we can see what ideals and commitments they express. Perhaps, we can also gain sufficient critical distance from those practices to determine whether they are reflectively acceptable.

While we can always ask whose bad luck any particular misfortune is, analytically, only three answers seem to be available: the misfortune either belongs to the person it befell, to some other particular person(s),[7] or to the community as a whole. Tort law, traditionally, concerns itself only with shifting losses from one person to another, while distributive justice typically looks to questions of which misfortunes are to be held in common. Thus, we might say that tort law is concerned primarily with the "event" misfortunes of human agency, whereas the institutions of distributive justice focus primarily on the "standing" misfortunes of birth and place.

A. Misfortune and the Hobbesian World of Perfect Agency

6. It may be helpful to begin by identifying two extreme positions one might adopt in dealing with misfortune. At one extreme lies a Hobbesian state of nature,[8] in which all misfortunes are simply allowed to lie where they fall. Fortune is allowed full sway at every level. Holmes recommends this as a default position, remarking that the cumbersome machinery of the law should only be used to move a loss from one person to another when there is a compelling reason to do so.[9]

In the Hobbesian state of nature, there is no state, law, or other cumbersome machinery. As a result, there is no agency to shift losses. Of course, people might displace various misfortunes from themselves onto others—displacing their hunger by taking someone else's food or injuring another while attending to their own wants. If they succeed in any such endeavours, the misfortunes now lie where they most recently fell. Even deliberate shifting can be thought of as the full reign of fortune, because whether someone is in a position to shift their losses to another is itself a matter of fortune—at least from the perspective of the new owner of the misfortune. They just happened to be in the wrong place at the wrong time.

Hobbes himself describes the state of nature as a sort of cautionary tale, an explanation of why there must be limits on the misfortunes people are allowed to cause each other. Nobody has seriously recommended, however, that the state of nature is a normative ideal. It purports to be a world of pure agency with no room for ideas of concern or respect for others, let alone for even the thinnest idea of community or of a common fate.

B. Misfortune and the World of Perfect Community

7. At the other extreme lies the ideal of a perfect community in which all misfortunes are held in common. Whatever goes wrong and for whatever reason, all share in the costs. Hence the effects on particular persons of fortune are cancelled entirely. Where the Hobbesian state of nature is a world of pure agency with no community, this world is one in which the search for perfect community abandons the idea of agency altogether.

Here too it is difficult to think of anyone who fully endorses such a view. Perhaps some readings of utilitarianism hold out an ideal of perfect community, insofar as they suppose that gains are to be maximized and losses minimized, quite apart from who they might happen to belong to.[10] The other candidates are probably some of those theories that are considered and rejected by Robert Nozick under the name "patterned" theories of justice. Nozick hopes to tar all egalitarian and redistributive schemes by criticizing patterned distributions, but no theory anyone else has put forward is fully patterned.[11] Again, no-fault compensation schemes spread misfortunes on a limited scale but typically wait for accidents to happen before compensating. They are limited to particular misfortunes and maintain a distinction between those misfortunes which suddenly interrupt life, and those accidents of birth that form the background of some peoples' lives. The Soviet jurist Evgeny Pashukanis comes closest to actually endorsing such a view when he suggests that the idea of individual responsibility is a relic of a deformed social system, which will give way to a system in which problems are solved and losses made good as they come up.[12]

C. Misfortune and the Principle of Fairness

8. Neither the world of perfect agency nor the world of perfect community would be much of a place to live. For present purposes, the important point is that they share a single failing; neither has room for the idea that people should bear the full costs of their choices. Hobbes describes the state of nature in a way that makes the lack of security its most salient and troubling feature. But life in such a state would not only be solitary, poor, nasty, brutish, and short. It would also be terribly unfair. If I injure you in the

Hobbesian state of nature, it is your problem not mine. Whether through malice or indifference, people could take advantage of the efforts of others and displace the costs of their activities onto them. The world of perfect community is unfair in similar ways. If I injure you or fritter away my share of resources, I don't lose my place at the common trough. Costs imposed by the lazy, the vicious, and the self-indulgent must be spread no less than those that fall on the disadvantaged, the needy, or the injured. . . .

III. Libertarianism: Causation as a Measure of Misfortune

9. In spite of its emphasis on agency, the problem with the Hobbesian state of nature lies in its inability to distinguish between misfortunes one person creates for another, and those that are merely bad luck. The state of nature elides the distinction between mischief and misfortune. If this is the problem, the solution should be apparent. Some line must be drawn between those misfortunes that lie where they fall, and those that properly belong to some other person. The most obvious place to look for that distinction, consistent with the emphasis on agency, is in a distinction between what a person does and what (merely) happens. That is, what is needed is a line between the sufferings that one person *causes* another, and those that are merely the result of *chance*. The former must be compensated, the latter left where they have fallen. The resulting position is a regime of generalized strict liability for accidents, which allows no further non-voluntary wealth transfers. Basically, this is the libertarian solution.

In this way, libertarianism is one step removed from the Hobbesian state of nature. It seeks to capture the essential importance of agency in a way that is consistent with the liberal picture of fairness, something the state of nature cannot do. In the libertarian picture, the Hobbesian position serves as a default rule. Misfortunes do not simply lie where they fall. Instead, they lie where they have fallen unless they result from the causal agency of some other individual—in which case they are shifted to that person. So understood, the libertarian approach might be thought of as more accurately and adequately representing the ideal of pure agency.

Libertarians tend to focus on the particular misfortunes that are the standard province of tort law—manglings by defective bottles, chainsaws, drugs, and forklifts. But, that focus is not (just) the result of a morbid fascination with manglings. It is of a piece with their opposition to redistribution. A night-watchman state charged solely with protecting property rights, and a regime of generalized strict liability in tort law come as a package.

The underlying view is this: what I do is mine, what is mine I own; what is not mine, I do not own. The costs my conduct imposes (that is, causes) are the result of what I do and thus mine; I own them. I have to take back the costs my conduct has imposed on you, not so much to rectify your loss but to give me what is mine. In contrast, if the costs that have befallen you are not the result of what I do, then they are not mine to bear. That does not automatically mean they are yours to bear, instead; they belong to whoever's conduct caused them. If the misfortune that befalls you is your doing, you own it. If it is no one's doing, it belongs to no one; it is the result of chance, not agency. At this juncture, the default rule comes in. If a loss is no one's property but just the result of chance, then it must lie where it has fallen. The default rule is itself justified by a further appeal to agency: if, by chance, misfortune befalls you, it is yours, not because you deserve it, but because nobody else does. Shifting a loss to someone who did not cause it violates their agency. So it is yours just because it happened to you, just as your own body is yours. Chance plays an important role in both directions: whether or not my activity injures you may well depend on factors outside anyone's control, as will all of those natural facts not attributable to any human agency. For the libertarian, this way of dividing agency and chance is essential to the idea that people should bear the costs of their activities. . . .

A. The Inadequacy of Causation as a Measure of Agency

10. If causation is a good starting point, it does not get us far; for causation is everywhere. Ronald Coase and Guido Calabresi independently invented law and economics when they realized that both injurer and victim cause any injury.[13] The point is, of course, older than that; in the seventeenth century, Pascal made essentially the same point: "I have often commented that the sole cause of man's unhappiness is that he does not know how to sit quietly in his room."[14] The injurer's role is obvious, for the reasons that libertarian advocates of generalized strict liability focus on. But, the victim's role is no less real. In all

but the most bizarre cases,[15] the accident could have been prevented had the victim stayed home, taken a different route, or whatever. Thus, any injury is always a joint product, which must somehow be divided between the parties. If causation is made the basis for shifting losses, two questions can be asked in every case of injury. First, was the defendant the cause of the injury? Second, was the plaintiff? The trouble is that the answer to both questions seems to always be "yes". If we understand the causal question in terms of what would have happened but for the act of the defendant (plaintiff), we are likely to get the same result for every accident: both the injurer and the plaintiff cause the injury. Thus, we seem to find everyone liable for everything.

A tempting response to the problem of too many causes is to draw a distinction between causes and conditions. Thus, the libertarian might hope to claim that the injurer's act is the cause of the injury, while the victim's is merely a condition. Both are necessary conditions, and so but-for causes. Only one is the cause, because only one seems to have made a crucial difference. In ordinary parlance, we have no difficulty distinguishing between a match as a cause of a fire and the presence of oxygen as a mere condition. In the same way, the libertarian might hope to keep strict liability general by assigning losses to those who cause them, rather than to the bystanders who are the mere conditions of them.

The distinction between causes and conditions can be of no real help to the defender of generalized strict liability. Any account of causation that will be adequate to account for the distinction between causes and mere conditions in scientific and common-sense explanations will, in virtue of that very adequacy, fail to solve the libertarian's problem with causation. The legal account of causation requires uniqueness, while ordinary causal explanations do not. Any account of causation in non-legal contexts needs to accommodate the fact that, in ordinary discourse, the distinction between causes and conditions is contextual and malleable. For example, in some circumstances we might say that a match was caused to ignite by being struck, taking the presence of oxygen to be merely a background condition. In other, less familiar, circumstances we might say that the presence of oxygen was the cause. Therefore, we can give different answers to causal questions about the same event depending on our interests. The malleability of the distinction reflects the deeper fact that the two causal explanations are not incompatible. The person who claims that striking caused the

match to ignite, and the one who claims it was the presence of oxygen do not disagree about causation. At most, they disagree about what is interesting about the situation both seek to make sense of, and neither would declare the other's purported explanation irrelevant—the very fact that enables Pascal and Coase to claim that causation is reciprocal.

Some accounts of causation have sought to narrow its scope by reserving the name "cause" for those conditions which are not normal or typical.[16] Putting aside the difficulties any such account has in making sense of such banal claims as "evaporation causes cooling" or "eating causes weight gain", it is of no use to the libertarian. What counts as unusual will often depend on the circumstances and the purposes of the inquiry. The unusual event may change depending on whether our interests in the causal inquiry are *explanatory, predictive,* or *engineering.* If we want to control or engineer the future, we might look to conditions that would be of less interest if we sought, instead, to understand the past in a detailed way. Until we know what we are doing, we cannot identify causes.

The libertarian had hoped to embrace a general regime of strict liability as an interpretation of the idea that people should bear the costs of their activities. But, any attempt to retrieve that idea by narrowing the range of causation faces a dilemma. If we concede that the explanatory interest we are pursuing in identifying causes is tied to our interest in assigning liability, we must first interpret the idea that people should bear the costs of their choices in order to know our explanatory purposes in establishing liability. Of course, if we need an interpretation of the principle in order to distinguish causes from conditions, causation cannot itself provide the basis for an interpretation. Thus, causation provides no leverage in distinguishing plaintiff from defendant, unless we already have some other way to distinguish them.[17] Alternatively, the libertarian might insist that liability be assigned on the basis of what would seem to be the most natural causal explanation quite apart from concerns about liability. This time, the problem is slightly different. If the libertarian appeals to some merely explanatory, predictive, or engineering interests, then all connection between agency and liability is lost. The problem is not that we cannot distinguish among causes; it is that we cannot do so in a way consistent with the idea of agency and the simple idea underlying libertarianism, namely, that there is a conceptual connection between what I do and the costs of my activities. Instead, agency must give way to predictability or, worse yet from the libertarian's point of view, (social) engineering.

B. The Inadequacy of Strict Liability Based on Causal Paradigms

11. Epstein, for one, is aware that there are problems in distinguishing various causes and suggests that we must narrow our notion of causation to include something less than all cases of "but-for" causation. Instead, Epstein insists, we can look to the clear paradigms of causation which the law recognizes. He focuses on force, fright, compulsion, and the setting of dangerous conditions as the paradigms of causal connection.[18] If it is true that not every causal connection can suffice to ground ownership or liability, the question is, why pick these as our paradigms? Why not use Bob Dylan's more comprehensive list? I might compete with you, beat you, cheat you, or mistreat you, simplify you, classify, deny, defy or crucify you, select you, dissect you, inspect you, or reject you.[19] All of these things I might do are ways in which I could, and often do, cause harm to you. Some of these are even plausible grounds of liability, others not. Without an account of the obviousness of Epstein's paradigms, we are in danger of losing sight of what makes them obvious.

Again, the point is not that causation's reach cannot be appropriately narrowed, but that attempts like Epstein's turn out to be unprincipled: there is no rationale for them that does not beg important questions. Although the law may have no choice but to work outward from paradigm cases, Epstein's paradigms seem an *ad hoc* collection designed to get his preferred result. Why are not other omissions, besides the setting of dangerous conditions, the paradigmatic cases of causes that create a basis for liability? Again, why not focus on other, equally paradigmatic actions: I might *embarrass* you into spilling your coffee, *goad* you into hitting someone else, or *humiliate* you. In each of these cases, we need far more detail in order to assess whether your injury would be compensable. With each of these examples, certain questions cry out for answers in establishing liability: Did you deserve humiliation? Are you too easily embarrassed or frightened? Should you have stood up in the face of my goading? The same applies to any number of the other examples of action that might be thought to be paradigmatic. We seem to need a conception of the boundaries between persons before we can determine ownership. But if we do, the appeal of strict liability as a way of drawing a line between what I do and what happens evaporates. For it is no longer the fact that I caused you harm that makes it mine but something else. It seems liability can only be assessed once we have answered questions about things other than causation.

Worse yet, Epstein's paradigms look suspiciously like they avoid the difficult questions by presupposing answers to them. We do not need to ask whether I frightened you carefully, or if you yielded to my force too readily. That is not because these idioms are particularly causal, but because it is so difficult to figure out what would count as exercising care in forcing someone to do something or frightening them. In the same way, any distinction between the setting of dangerous conditions and the mere setting of conditions, seems to turn on what those conditions are, rather than on any causal notions. The line between dangerous and safe conditions cannot depend on whether the defendant could have made them safer, on pain of falling back into Pascal's world. The defendant always could have done something, and the plaintiff virtually always could have avoided them; but without an account of dangerous conditions, the paradigm of force includes too much.[20] The line can only be drawn in terms of some idea of how dangerous conditions are allowed to get.

Our claim is not that there are no principled ways of drawing distinctions between but-for causes. Our point is that any principled distinctions are also normative. What counts as a cause will depend on what turns on the answer.

We are not the first to point to the pervasive problems of indeterminacy that plague Epstein's defense of strict liability. Indeed, no one has been as powerful and sustained a critic of it as has Stephen Perry.[21] One might wonder why its appeal persists despite what strike many as obvious problems. One answer is that the libertarian's root concern is with the idea of self-ownership. Since (it is supposed) we own ourselves, any harm that one person does another must be thought of on the model of a person (or piece of property) straying onto another person's property. If I trespass on your land, it does not matter whether or not I was being careful—I still need to leave. The libertarian wants to generalize this idea to cover all of tort law—I am liable if I harm you, regardless of how careful I was being. If I cross your boundaries, I am liable, regardless. Hence the appeal of strict liability; but this is also its fatal flaw. Even if we stick to metaphors of borders and boundary crossing, we need some account of where the boundaries between persons are to be drawn. Causation cannot do the job. It merely presupposes that the job has already been done.

One other way in which the reach of this interpretation of strict liability might be narrowed, while keeping it general, is by holding people responsible not for all they have caused but only for the *intended* consequences of their actions. This approach looks promising, since those who intend to frighten, force, compel, or set dangerous conditions plainly differ from those who are frightened, forced, compelled, or unwittingly walk into dangerous conditions. It also has a certain natural attractiveness, as evidenced by the way children often defend themselves against charges of carelessness by saying, "But I didn't mean to." It is difficult to think of anyone who has actually put this view forward, though one might expect it of someone who came to tort law after thinking about the criminal law.

The naturalness of such a suggestion aside, its application would be counterintuitive at best: if I intend to hit you on the head but instead hit you on the shoulder, surely I should not be entirely relieved of liability, or your injury treated no differently than it would be were you hit by a bolt of lightning.

The more serious problem with the suggestion is deeper: limiting liability to intended consequences undermines the idea that it is supposed to express, namely, that people should bear the costs of their choices. For it effectively says that each person gets to decide what will and will not count as a cost of her activity. I determine the intended consequences of my conduct: after all, they are the consequences I intend. I can be liable only for them. Therefore, I determine the costs of my activity, so long as I do not want to harm you. Rather than being justified on the grounds that it expresses the idea that one should bear the costs of one's activities, this suggestion is, instead, a way of determining what those costs are; and it is a normatively unattractive way at that. For the intuitive idea is surely that people should bear the costs that their activities *impose* on *others;* it is not the idea that they are free to determine what those costs are. There can be no measurement of such costs unless we have some independent criteria for measuring them.

IV. Fault as a Measure of Misfortune

12. How can the costs of activities be measured? The most plausible illustration of the answer can be found in the fault system. We offer the fault system

for purposes of illustration because its analytical structure is clear. However, our discussion of it is not meant to suggest that there is no room in a legal system for particular areas of strict liability. As we shall show, where strict liability is defensible, it is best understood as employing the same type of reasoning that the fault system exemplifies. In defensible areas of strict liability, the boundaries between what a person does and what merely happens are given by moral boundaries and protected interests.

Instead of supposing that the duty to repair is a matter of causal relations or crossing prior natural boundaries, the fault system recognizes that the boundary between persons can only be understood in terms of our duties to each other. Thus, its inquiries are normative, not scientific or even folk-scientific. It narrows the scope of liability for harms caused to others by imposing a requirement of reasonable care. So long as I am careful, I am not liable for harms that I cause you. Those misfortunes are yours, as though they had been caused by some natural event. If I am careless, then I am liable for whatever harms I cause you—those misfortunes are mine, costs of my activity which I must bear. The whole point of the fault system is that when I am careless I may own more than the intended consequences of my actions; hence, the duty to repair.

Drawing the boundary between us in terms of the fault standard solves the problem of determining what counts as the cost of my activity. The fault system acknowledges the importance of concepts like control, agency, and choice. But, those concepts only work in concert with substantive judgements about why various activities matter to us and about the ways in which they do. That is, the fault system requires a substantive political theory. Indeed, because there is no natural feature to mark such boundaries, the fault system cannot help but make judgements about the importance of various activities.

In a liberal regime, the fault system aims to treat parties as equals, protecting each equally from the other and granting each a like liberty. In order to protect both liberty and equality, it must suppose plaintiff and defendant to have both liberty interests in going about their affairs and security interests in avoiding losses due to the activities of others. In so supposing, it does not look to how strongly either plaintiff or defendant feels about either liberty or security. For to do so would reproduce the problems with limiting liability to the intended consequences of actions, making each person's security depend on the particular priorities of his or her injurer. Those difficulties would be doubled because each person's liberty would depend on the particular sensibilities of his or her potential victims. It also does not (because it cannot) recognize either a generic interest in either doing what you want, or in being secure against all injuries. Instead, the amount of risk you can faultlessly expose me to depends *on what you are doing* and on the *kind* of harm that might eventuate.

A. Boundary Crossing

13. The fault standard invokes the idea that you and I have duties to one another. We can, if we like, put this in the libertarian's vocabulary of boundary crossings as the claim that each has a duty to repair should they cross the other's boundaries. Two caveats are required. First, such a duty presupposes independently established boundaries, whereas the whole point of fault is to help fix those borders. The boundaries between us are normative, fixed not by space but by the scope of the duties we owe one another. Second, I might violate my duty and thereby "cross" my own boundary, within which I am free of liability for harms I might cause—for example, by failing to exercise reasonable care—yet fail, through the good fortune of us both, to cross your boundary, if my lack of care causes no harm to you. That is, there is a moral space between our boundaries where fortune lurks. Crossing my own boundary does not entail that I thereby cross yours.

Because my crossing your border requires not only that I fail to meet my duty to you, but that in doing so I harm you as well, invoking the importance of fault does not require giving up on agency or causation. On the contrary, the fault system lets us see why agency matters at all. Liability depends on the fact that I am an agent, capable of acting in keeping with my duties. Were I not an agent, I could neither discharge nor fail to discharge any duty to you. The fault standard also explains why causation matters. Causation turns my failure to discharge my duty to you into a crossing of your boundary. Without fault, causation does not signify a boundary crossing; without causation, crossing my boundary does not mean I have crossed yours.

Third, and most importantly, while the concept of fault is understood in terms of reasonable care, the concept of reasonable care is to be understood as taking into account not just the relevant liberty and security interests of the parties but the relative *value* of the activities in which they are engaged. The measure cannot just be their evaluation of those activities but must, in some sense, be the value those activities actually have. This last point requires further elaboration.

B. Establishing the Boundary Line: Balancing Liberty and Security Interests

14. To see the way the importance of various activities enters into the fault system, think of the fault standard as dividing the risks of injury between plaintiff and defendant.[22] When an accident occurs, the fault system assigns the misfortune to the defendant if negligent, otherwise to the plaintiff. If all of the risk were to lie with the defendant—strict liability, in other words—the defendant would always act at his peril. If all the risk were to lie with the plaintiff—holding the defendant liable only for intended consequences—the plaintiff's security would be hostage to the defendant's action. Since neither extreme treats liberty or security interests equally or fairly, neither alternative is acceptable as a way of giving expression to the liberal idea of fairness or equality. The fault system solves this problem by supposing that the dividing line must be somewhere in between. Establishing the line depends on the particular liberty interests and security interests that are at stake.

For example, the liberty to drive without brakes is not sufficiently important to allow others to be exposed to injury from a car that is unable to stop in a timely fashion. In contrast, the person with an eggshell skull's interest in being able to go out is too important to make them bear the full risk. Yet, other examples, empirically like the eggshell skull, get treated differently. A rule of contributory or comparative negligence limits the plaintiff's recovery if his or her activity made the injury more likely or more costly, despite the fact that there would have been no injury at all had the defendant exercised appropriate care. By ignoring Pascal's advice and going out, the eggshell skull makes the activities of negligent people more costly, just as the person who walks on railway tracks does. Yet the defendant is liable for the full extent of the eggshell's injuries but not the trackwalker's. Although each would be fine if nobody else was careless, they get treated very differently. In the trackwalker's case, a rule of contributory or comparative negligence is applied which limits the plaintiff's recovery if his or her activity made the injury more likely or more costly, despite the fact that there would have been no injury at all had the defendant exercised appropriate care. These are standard examples, so familiar that their presuppositions are hidden. They depend on substantive, though familiar, judgements about the importance of various liberty and security interests. They also provide models through which other activities get classified.

Does carrying out one's perceived religious duties get treated as the equivalent of having an eggshell skull or as the equivalent of walking on railroad tracks?[23] The only way to answer such a question is to defend a substantive, if controversial, conception of the role of religion in our society. A general rule of contributory negligence requires plaintiffs to mitigate damages. Yet if someone fails to mitigate on recognized religious grounds, the defendant may well be liable for the full amount.[24] This is a reflection of the idea that the reasonable person would give more weight to certain of her religious convictions than to saving a negligent defendant money. Yet if the plaintiff fails to mitigate for other reasons, however deeply felt, damages are reduced accordingly. In other words, it is not how deeply religious convictions are felt that matters, for that would not distinguish religious conviction from other beliefs as a defense against failure to mitigate. Rather, what matters about religious beliefs is connected with a view of the ways religion matters to people.[25] Not all sincerely felt religious beliefs can be accommodated within such a model; tort rules that seek to accommodate religion in this way cannot pretend to be neutral.

Again, rescuers are allowed to expose themselves to risks that would normally preclude recovery from their injurers. Although the special treatment accorded rescuers is sometimes described in terms of foreseeability,[26] a more honest way of looking at the special treatment accorded rescuers supposes their activity to be important enough to make them bear proportionately less risk.[27]

The claim here is not that these cases invariably strike the balance correctly. Rather, it is that implicit in the fault system is the need to come to an understanding of the substantive value of various activities, their importance to us in a liberal society, and the ways they matter to us individually and collectively. Of course, neither judges nor juries normally think of themselves as engaged in an inquiry into the importance of various activities. Instead, they ask what a reasonable person would do in such circumstances—a person who had enough foresight to see what was likely to happen and appropriate regard for the interests of others. But, the construct of the reasonable person incorporates answers to

questions about which things matter and how they matter—we might even say that the reasonable person embodies them. Judges sometimes also appeal to what is customary or conventional. This, too, reflects implicit judgements about the importance of various activities. Provided that background conditions are otherwise fair, they enable people to take the costs of their activities into account by making those costs visible. In circumstances in which almost everyone engages in the same activities, and all are equally likely to be both plaintiff and defendant, a customary-activity rule may be a reasonable proxy for a substantive examination of the interests that are at stake. That is simply because in such circumstances (if they ever existed), everyone is engaged in the same activities and so has the same liberty and security interests in relation to them.[28]

C. An Objective Measure of Fault

15. The same considerations that support this interpretation of the fault system and argue against the intended consequences thesis explain why the fault required for liability in torts must be *objective*. Because fault is supposed to measure the costs of activities fairly and across individuals, it cannot be understood subjectively in terms of good faith efforts at care. To do so would create, yet again, the problem that faced strict liability for the intended consequences of actions: it would make each injurer the determiner of his or her exposure to liability. Thus, what counted as the costs of an activity would vary wildly. As a result, the scope of each person's right to security would depend on the decisions of others. The idea that people should bear the costs of their activities would be replaced with the very different and less appealing idea that people should do the best they can—at whatever they choose to do.

We have defended the fault system as a way of establishing the boundary between those misfortunes that are the injurer's to bear, and those that are to remain the misfortune of the victim. Such a boundary is necessary if we are to understand and give content to the principle that one ought to bear the costs of one's activities. The fault system accomplishes this, moreover, only by determining the relative importance of various activities, the ways they matter in people's lives, and why.

We might put the connection between morally defined boundaries and the requirement of causation in Kantian terms: an agent can either follow the moral law or fail to do so. For the agent who follows the moral law, his agency—for which consequences of his or her actions he or she is responsible or owns—pretty much ends with the intended consequences of his or her action. The situation is very different for the person who acts contrary to the moral law. In so doing, he or she takes authority upon himself or herself that he or she does not rightly have, and opens himself or herself up to the causal upshots of his or her conduct in ways in which the person who follows the moral law does not. Consequences of his or her wrong are his or hers to own, whether intended, or even foreseen, or not, including some consequences that would not have occurred but for the conduct of others. The scope of bad luck expands as a result of violating the moral law.[29]

Simply substitute fault for the moral law. The person who is at fault opens himself or herself up to liability for unintended consequences of his conduct, including some that would not have occurred but for the conduct of others. The conduct of others may be a but-for cause of the harm, but the agent's fault distinguishes his or her conduct from that of others. Of course, if the plaintiff is also at fault, both have a similar claim to own the costs of misfortune. Fault, far from rendering causation and agency otiose, actually defines the scope of their relevance.

D. Limiting Liability

16. Still, fault need not open one up to unlimited consequences of one's conduct. So long as we understand the boundaries between persons in terms of the libertarian's spatial metaphors, it seems as though any boundary crossing must open up unlimited responsibility. The result is a sort of "outlaw" theory—having done wrong, one becomes liable without limit for an infinity of consequences. However, if we understand the boundaries between persons as existing in moral rather than geometric space, we see that the fault system can coherently hold someone liable only for the losses that are within the risk implicit in the violated standard of care. The standard of care divides particular risks between the parties, and if one fails to exercise appropriate care, then he or she is liable for any harms following from that particular risk. Because different degrees of care are called for in relation to different activities and different risks, violating a standard of care is not enough to establish liability for consequences that result from unforeseeable causal chains. To establish liability in such circumstances would be to let unlimited liability in through the back door.[30]

There are (at least) two different ways the fault system can be understood: we can distinguish between the activities one chooses and one's execution of them. The first, more standard interpretation of fault holds that fault marks a failure in execution: the failure to render reasonable care, given the activity one has chosen. On this view, the standard of care owed varies with the activities in which one is engaged. Each agent is presumed to have an absolute liberty with respect to the choice of activities.[31] An agent is free of fault provided that the care taken is deemed appropriate to the activity.[32]

We are explicating an importantly different view of the fault principle. On this view, it requires that, in acting, each person takes into account the costs his or her action may impose on others. Thus, the question is not whether I am being careful by the standards of what I am doing, but whether I am being appropriately careful in light of my neighbour's interests in security and mine in liberty. The importance of my particular activities enters into defining the appropriate degree of care, not by holding me to a standard appropriate to the activity but in fixing the degree of liberty appropriate to those engaged in that sort of activity.

Only this conception of fault can provide an objective measure of the costs of my activity that will enable us to honour the liberal principle of fairness that one should bear the costs of one's own activities. To hold me only to taking such precautions as are reasonable or cost-justified for those engaging in that activity would mark a move back to a subjective standard, and hold others' security hostage to my choice of activities. Rather than protecting each equally from the others, such a rule would surrender security to an unlimited liberty interest in choosing activities, however dangerous, provided one took precautions customary to those activities. Thus, it would be a minor variant on limiting liability to intended consequences. Because the standard of care protects both liberty and security and is supposed to respect equally our interests in both, we cannot avoid looking at the activities themselves. The same logic that requires that we look to degrees of care, at all, requires us to look to the values of those activities. Judgements of what conduct is at fault or unreasonable involve both.

E. A Nuanced Objective Standard

17. Talk about objective standards makes some people uneasy. The idea of objectivity may suggest

that such standards are somehow eternal and exist quite apart from questions about which interests people have and how important they are. Any such conception of objectivity might well be suspected of being little more than a smoke screen for interests that are already well-entrenched.[33] But we mean something considerably more modest.[34] Precisely because the fault standard turns on substantive views about the importance of various activities, its contours will always be open to debate. It is objective in a negative sense, inasmuch as it is not subjective, that is, the limits of liability are not fixed by the views, interests, or abilities of either of the parties to a tort action. Instead, it protects the interests in both liberty and security that everyone is assumed to have. On the basis of those interests, it asks whether a reasonable person is entitled to have a particular interest protected. The importance, and even existence, of particular interests is often controversial, and the common law has sometimes been indifferent to what now seem significant interests and concerned about insignificant ones. Clear examples of such indifference can be found in the absence, until recently, of any legal recognition of the interest that women have in being free of sexual harassment. The appropriate response to such indifference, however, is to move to a more nuanced objective standard, not a subjective one. New causes of action for sexual harassment have developed in just this way.[35] Rather than allowing the victim to be the sole judge of the costs of the harasser's activities, such torts sometimes import a "reasonable woman" standard, which aims to recognize both the (potential) harasser's interest in self-expression and the (potential) victim's interest in being free of behaviour she perceives as inappropriate. While such a standard may carry risks of stereotyping, when properly deployed it works in the same way as traditional objective tests are supposed to. The standard is objective in that it divides the risk between the parties, allowing both the possibility that the plaintiff is being too sensitive, and that the defendant is behaving inappropriately though in good faith. Exactly where the line is drawn depends on the importance of those two interests—a matter that is sure to be hotly contested. Recent feminist scholarship and advocacy have changed our views about the boundaries of both sensitivity and good faith in such circumstances. What they have changed, however incompletely, are views about the costs of various activities and who should bear them.[36]

F. Strict Liability as a Measure of Misfortune in Rights Violations

18. Having argued that we must look to the importance of various activities in order to set boundaries between persons capable of honouring the principle that we should bear the costs of our activities rather than displacing them, we return for a moment to consider a final effort to do without such an inquiry. The goal of such an argument, recall, is to justify shifting the costs of some misfortunes while avoiding anything like a moralized notion of fault and relying in its place on agency, control, and the like. The first two interpretations of generalized strict liability relied on narrowing the causal condition: the first by introducing a distinction between causal and background conditions, the second by introducing the notion of the intended consequences of one's conduct. We found both of these wanting: the first because, in narrowing the range of causes, it lost contact with the principle it was supposed to express, the second because it allowed individuals to determine what counts as the cost of their activities, thus, violating the principle it was supposed to express.

Our argument so far has been that we cannot determine the costs of activities by focusing on activity-neutral concepts like cause, control, and agency. Instead, the costs of one's activities depend on what one owes others, which, in turn, depends on the activities on which individuals are engaged: why they matter and in what ways. The concept of duties between parties is expressed by the fault principle. Once we have a fault principle, we have a concept of boundaries between parties and, thus, a role for causation and agency. The question is whether we need to introduce fault in order to create these boundaries. What is it about fault that allows it to do this job? Can the same task be accomplished in a way that is consistent with a general principle of strict liability?

Suppose we re-cast libertarianism as the view that the costs of misfortune lie on those they happen to befall unless they result from the *rights-invasive* conduct of another.[37] In such a view, it is not enough that the harm result from another's agency. The harm must also consist in the invasion of a right. Such a view draws a boundary between the misfortunes that are an injurer's bad luck to bear, and those that are to remain the victim's responsibility. Thus, it creates a basis for determining the costs of various activities. It does so, moreover, without introducing the concept of fault.

This modification does not introduce the concept of fault, but it does introduce all of the same substantive normative considerations that figure in determining one's obligations of care to others. Moreover, rights can serve as premises in arguments about who is liable to whom *only because who has what right is itself the conclusion of a prior argument of precisely the sort that we have been invoking*. Ascriptions of rights are the conclusions of arguments regarding the relative importance of various activities and the weight that the relative security and liberty interests ought to command. Thus, a libertarian who introduces the concept of a rights invasion introduces precisely the same sort of normative considerations that underwrite the fault standard; and in so doing, the libertarian risks losing touch with the connection between agency and ownership, which makes the principle intuitively plausible in the first place.

A regime of strict liability for rights violations faces another problem as well: strict liability for rights violations turns out to be little more than a requirement that harm be caused if a boundary has been crossed. Not only do boundaries need to be defined in ways that cannot avoid substantive moral judgements, but we also need to be careful about how we understand those boundaries. If we think of them in the libertarian's standard spatial terms and suppose that one is responsible for the full consequences of one's action once those boundaries are crossed, any rights violation seems to open the violator up to all of the consequences of his or her action. But as we have suggested, this is neither how tort law works, nor is it an appealing account of corrective justice. Boundaries need to be understood in terms of liberty interests and the risks to security interests. If they are, boundary crossing can be thought of as opening the wrongdoer up to the risks that were ignored in the boundary crossing, rather than as a sort of forfeiture of any ability to disown consequences of his or her actions.[38]

So far, our target has been a general theory of strict liability, which is a normative view about how the costs of misfortune are to be generally allocated. Our discussion has focused on the normative thesis, not on the strict liability rules that have found their way into a variety of areas of tort law. That focus reflects our concern with the fairness of any general principle for allocating the costs of misfortune. We began with the simple thought that fairness precludes individuals from displacing the costs of their activities onto others. We showed why such a principle cannot be coherently understood as the requirement that people bear all of the costs that they cause others. We have tried to defend two claims against this apparently plausible position. First, the concept of the costs of an activity cannot be understood in terms of causation alone. Instead, it requires an account of the duties between the parties. Second, any account of the duties of parties to each other invokes inquiries into the substantive value of various activities and the seriousness of various harms in order to assess the relevant liberty and security interests of the parties.

G. Fault as a Measure—Conclusion

19. We conclude this section by considering whether existing legal practices can be thought of as giving expression to this understanding of fault and the liberal principle of fairness on which it rests. Of course, in a system of decentralized courts in numerous jurisdictions, there may be no principled path through all of the rationales that have been offered in tort decisions. But, an apparently more serious problem is that the conventional view claims that a large class of cases are adjudicated under a principle of strict liability. What can we say about these cases? We cannot take this question up in any detail here, but our view is that important areas in which strict liability is employed as a rule for deciding cases turn on precisely the same sort of reasoning that we have illustrated in our discussion of the fault system.

Consider first *Rylands v. Fletcher*,[39] the case which has been taught to generations of torts students as the leading example of strict liability in the nineteenth century. In that case, the defendant's reservoir leaked into mine shafts under the plaintiff's property. The defendant was held liable despite the Court accepting that he had exercised considerable care in constructing the reservoir. The decision was cast in terms of a distinction between natural and non-natural uses and imposed strict liability for non-customary uses. Liability for mining or agriculture requires that the plaintiff establish the defendant's fault; liability for unusual activities requires a showing of causation only. Thus, the defendant can be liable even if he exercised reasonable or, even, exceptional care. Yet, the Court's reasoning turns out to be considerably more subtle. A landowner must answer for the "natural and anticipated consequences" of keeping something mischievous on his property.[40] For certain types of activities, no amount of care will do. This is not the same as claiming that the defendant's conduct is wrong in a way that would justify prohibiting him from engaging in it, nor even wrong in a way that justifies granting injunctive relief to the plaintiff. Rather, engaging in the conduct is permissible, but any way of engaging in it imposes risks, which the person engaging in it must bear. Thus, any costs resulting from the activity must lie with the defendant. The defendant's duty to the plaintiff is defined accordingly. The rationale is to be found in the relatively greater importance of the plaintiff's security interest than the defendant's liberty interest. No amount of care is sufficient because engaging in the activity itself poses too great a risk to others.

So understood, important areas of strict liability involve the same sort of judgements about the importance of various liberty and security interests as does the fault system as we have explained it. Imposing liability in such circumstances is thus an instance of the general strategy we have been advocating. If the standard of care is supposed to protect people equally from each other, it cannot leave one person free to choose any activity and then exercise care in relation to that activity. The choice of activities may itself expose others to undue risks. In certain circumstances, the normality or otherwise of the use is a reliable indicator for the riskiness of such activities. In circumstances in which almost everyone engages in the same activities, and all are equally likely to be both plaintiff and defendant, a customary activity rule may be a reasonable proxy for a substantive examination of the interests that are at stake. But that is because in such circumstances, everyone is engaged in the same activities and, so, has the same interests in relation to them.[41]

V. Liberal Egalitarianism: Choice as a Measure of Misfortune

20. So far, we have focused on variations of the libertarian view of event misfortunes. The libertarian is committed to the same view of standing misfortunes. As a result, that part of his view is subject to the same objections—demarcating the class of losses that do not result from agency is no less difficult than specifying whose agency is involved in other losses.[42] Rather than continuing to focus on the libertarian, however, we want to take up the liberal-egalitarian view of the standing misfortunes of birth and status. . . .

Where the libertarian would be happy with the state of nature but for its failure to distinguish between those who keep to themselves and those who harm others, the liberal egalitarian would be happy with the world of perfect community but for the fact that it treats hardworking ants and lazy grasshoppers alike. The remedy for the libertarian is to introduce a requirement of agency as a condition of liability. The remedy for the liberal egalitarian is to give everyone a fair share of resources, rectifying those misfortunes that nobody can help but allowing those who wish to husband their share of resources to their own advantage.

All brute luck is held in common, its effects are cancelled. Only option luck, the result of voluntary risk-taking, plays a role in Dworkin's scheme. Thus, the liberal egalitarian appeals to "a certain view of the distinction between a person and his circumstances and assigns his tastes and ambitions to his person, and his physical and mental powers to his circumstances."[43]

If the libertarian could be said to be committed to the ideal that individuals must bear the costs of their agency, the liberal egalitarian could be said to be committed to a strikingly similar interpretation of the idea that people should bear the costs of their choices. Where they differ is in their account of the conditions under which this requirement makes sense. For the liberal egalitarian, the principle that individuals should bear the costs of their choices—and the misfortunes of option luck—applies only if certain background conditions are met. These are represented by the idea of equality of resources: provided that people have fair shares of resources to begin with, it makes sense to ask that they bear the costs of their choices. If, however, initial holdings of resources are unfairly distributed, the idea of bearing the costs of choices is under-defined. People cannot be said to bear the costs of their choices, because the costs they end up bearing reflect initial holdings as much as the choices themselves. . . .

The liberal egalitarian's view reflects a particular interpretation of the idea that people should bear the costs of their choice, which makes the idea of a choice turn on whether or not something is within a person's control. The interpretation of fairness might be summed up as follows: how well or badly a person's life goes should not depend on things they cannot control. Thus, the exception to perfect community in cases of option luck gets some of its appeal from the twin ideas that people should not be made to bear the costs of things they cannot control, and that they should bear the costs of the tastes they choose to develop. The distinction Dworkin draws between expensive needs and expensive tastes rests on the idea that tastes are the sorts of things that people can control. Again, the idea of option luck is just the idea that someone could have contented themselves with their share of resources but, having decided to take a chance, must bear its cost. In addition, behind the idea of brute luck lies the idea that some things simply happen, beyond the reach of anyone's control.

22. Appealing as these intuitive ideas are, they turn out to be rather less clear when applied to specific cases. Just as philosophers love to find causation everywhere, so economists are fond of claiming that virtually any human action can be represented as a calculated gamble. Often, the probabilities are sufficiently high or low that ordinary people overlook the risks; but they are no less real for that. Every action has costs in terms of opportunities foregone, and so anything anyone does can be treated as exposing oneself to risk: if I invest in Beta and other people choose V.H.S., I took a risk and lost. Likewise, if I invest in tubes and the world chooses transistors, or I invest in LP's and the world chooses CDs. In each of these cases, there may be some temptation to suppose that I did not need to take the risk, so that, although the outcomes themselves were not within my control, my exposure to them was. But tamer choices also have the same implications: if I work hard on the family farm, the industrial age may overtake me. If I plant canola the same year everyone else does, the drop in prices may overtake me, or the weather may turn bad, hurting all of us. If I follow Pascal's advice and stay in my room, I may get bedsores.

Not every misfortune, however, should be treated as option luck to be borne by the person it befell simply because they implicitly took a calculated risk in leaving the house or getting out of bed in the morning. Part of the problem is that if we construe risk so expansively, we lose the connection with control that first made it appealing. But if instead we limit the idea of risk to those circumstances in which the person could in fact control the outcome, the results are still stranger. If you and I are both trying to build a better mousetrap, and I outsell you, society would have to indemnify you. Indeed, any risk that did not work out would have to be treated as brute luck, thus, leaving the category of option luck all but empty. Like causation in the libertarian's account, option luck seems to be everywhere and so provides no way of deciding to whom particular misfortunes belong.

The libertarian is one step in from the state of nature and the liberal egalitarian one in from the perfect community. Not surprisingly, their difficulties are parallel. Each wants to carve out an exception to an otherwise attractive extreme position. Each wants the exception to accommodate the idea that people should bear the costs of their actions, and each tries to carve out the exception by looking to such value-neutral features of action as causation, intention, and control. Any neutral feature of human action, however, will also be generic and, as a result, too pervasive to neatly demarcate an exception. . . .

VI. Primary Goods as a Measure of Misfortune

25. With his idea of primary goods, Rawls offers us . . . a strategy for deciding which risks matter and how. Rawls introduces primary goods as the basis for fair distributive shares. He offers them as things people can reasonably be expected to want as much as possible of, and thus, any inequalities in their distribution must be justified. Like the fault system, primary goods provide an objective standard for measuring costs. A public measure of important interests makes interpersonal judgements of fairness possible and lets us distinguish between those misfortunes that lie where they fall, and those that are to be thought of as belonging to everyone. Like the fault standard, in order to be up to the task, an index of primary goods cannot adapt itself to individual idiosyncrasies. Some people might have different values—thinking that being a good juggler is essential to any decent life— and object to the choice to pool risks other than those on their preferred list. After all, they are being asked to give up other things for benefits they do not actually want. The person who wants other goods, however, does not have a claim in justice against others. Nor does the person who is unhappy with his or her share, nor the person who finds that, say, liberty makes life more difficult. None of these people have a claim in justice because each effectively asks that their own view be allowed to fix what does and does not count as a cost of their activity to others. If we are to give sense to the idea of people bearing the costs of their activities, we need to decide which things count as a person's activities and which do not. Leaving it up to each person to decide which risks to bear and which others must bear undoes the idea of people bearing the costs of their activities to others, for each person both sets the costs of their activities to others and is subject to the choices of others. Treating people as equals requires a common currency.

Control cannot be used to determine what things count as the costs of an activity for the same reasons that tort liability cannot be limited to the intended or actually foreseen consequences of actions. The difficulty with limiting tort liability to intended or actually foreseen consequences is that it leaves the determination of the costs of various activities as a matter of idiosyncratic individual choices. These were not choices about which activities to engage in (which do rightly enter into determining the costs of various activities) but choices about what counted as those costs. The only way to measure costs fairly is to measure them objectively, to measure them in a way that makes it possible to say, "You should have been more careful," or "You should have taken the dangers to others into account."

At the same time, we do not want to say such things about everything that the person might have done in aid of another's security. Only the important ones; hence the fault system. In just the same way, if we limit the place of option luck to those things of which a person knew the risks or, in fact, controlled, we lose any measure of the costs of activities to others in favor of what the person took to be the costs of those activities. In consequence, we lose the ability to make a point essential to the idea of bearing the costs of one's choices: "You ought to have realized there was a risk involved," or "You should have realized that was going to turn out to be so expensive that it would get in the way of the rest of your life." But, of course, we do not want to say such things about everything that someone might have done something about. Hence we need a solution parallel to the fault system.

Once we see that what is really at issue is not control but the importance of the various aspects of a person's life, some supposed problems for liberals disappear. Libertarians are fond of taunting liberals with the charge that economic redistribution cannot be distinguished from such gruesome practices as redistributing body parts to those who need them.[44] So long as we suppose that we can get substantive politics out of action theory, the charge is worrisome; but once we recognize the inescapability of substantive judgements about the importance of various activities and security interests, the charge becomes less interesting. For we can plausibly suppose bodily integrity to matter enough that body parts cannot be redistributed simply because others find them useful.

We can also insist that property rights need not be thought of in the same way as is bodily integrity. The libertarian might stick to his guns, hoping to show that property is just as important as bodily integrity. But showing that would require a substantive argument about the importance of various activities, not conceptual legerdemain about agency and the like.

So we must reject the view that we can settle questions about the costs of activities by invoking concepts like control or choice, not because these concepts make no sense, but rather, because their content cannot be fixed independently of engaging in normative argument about the values of various activities to us and the ways in which they matter in people's lives. We need something like a public index of goods.

Some candidates are easy: a modicum of wealth, health and education at least. A particular person's lack of these is a misfortune that we all have a responsibility to rectify. This is not because such circumstances are necessarily beyond the person's control but, rather, because of the ways in which such goods are substantively important in people's lives. There is no liberal theory worthy of the name that is neutral on such matters. Liberalism must face up to questions about misfortune and bad luck that are political throughout. To answer these questions together is to be a liberal-political community. Such a community need not share all misfortunes but must share a vision of what is to count as the costs of various activities.[45]

If neutrality is not a genuine option, however, toleration still is. Fairness and toleration fit together if the interests protected by primary goods include liberty interests in deciding what to do about important matters and security interests in the wherewithal to pursue the choices one makes. But to protect this sort of toleration, other putative security interests, including some that many people may think important, may need to be ignored. Thus, any interest that some might claim in cultural survival[46] or a secure moral climate must be rejected. Here, too, any index of primary goods will be controversial. Some resolution to these questions is required, however, if the idea that people should not displace costs onto others is to be honoured. The liberal commitment to toleration is expressed in the same way by broadly-defined liberty and security interests in tort law.

Conclusion

26. The libertarian and the egalitarian differ in their default rule for misfortunes but not in their rule for the other cases. Both aspire to neutrality, so both think that the default position itself can be given a neutral definition. But it cannot; it establishes boundaries between persons, and must be negotiated in the same substantive way that any other boundary is. Once we see that it must be negotiated, however, we also see that there need be no single default rule either. Instead, we always face the question of whether a misfortune should lie where it falls, be shifted to some other particular person, or be held in common. Because the boundaries between persons reflect judgements about the importance of various activities and security interests, the question of where some particular cost lies—like the related question of what counts as taking a risk—must have a substantive answer. Looking for an appealing default position only makes sense if a neutral rule is available to define exceptions to it.

Both an objective standard in tort and primary goods for distributive justice require balancing very different things against each other; but it does not require that they share some other, underlying feature that makes them commensurate. Indeed, the point of fixing an objective standard is to provide a way of measuring the costs of activities across persons. Doing so does not depend on a prior commensurability but provides a public measure that makes it possible to measure costs across persons.[47] Money provides a helpful, if potentially misleading, example. Prices do not mean that the things people pay for are all enjoyed in the same way, or even that one person deciding her priorities can reduce them to a single scale. But it does make it possible to measure opportunity costs across persons, leaving each to decide what her priorities are, while constraining her to take account of the costs to others.[48]

We began by saying that questions about what counts as a primary good, or what counts as reasonable care, invite disagreement, even among otherwise reasonable people. In fact, we probably even disagree with each other about such questions. But if we want to make sense of the idea of people bearing the costs of their activities, we cannot avoid (or evade) them.

1. See Aristotle, *Ethics*, trans. J. A. K. Thomson (London: Penguin, 1984) at 176–79.
2. This much we take to have shown in our (separate) previous works (see: J. L. Coleman, *Risks and Wrongs* (Cambridge: Cambridge University Press, 1992); A. Ripstein, "Equality, Luck, and Responsibility" (1994) 23 *Phil. & Pub. Aff.* 3). The current project builds on our previous work, but it aims to make a much more radical point. The thesis of this paper is that in important and underappreciated ways the problems of distributive and tort law are the same.
3. See R. Epstein, "Luck" (1988) 6 *Soc. Phil. & Pol'y* 17.
4. See R. Dworkin, "What is Equality? Part 2: Equality of Resources" (1981) 10 *Phil. & Pub. Aff.* 283 [hereinafter "Equality of Resources"].
5. See J. E. Roemer, "A Pragmatic Theory of Responsibility for the Egalitarian Planner" (1993) 22 *Phil. & Pub. Aff.* 146. See also G. A. Cohen, "On the Currency of Egalitarian Justice" (1989) 99 *Ethics* 906.
6. J. Rawls, *A Theory of Justice* (Cambridge, Mass.: Belknap Press, 1971) at 90.
7. Losses may appropriately lie with some group smaller than the entire community. For analytical purposes (depending on the details) we can think of such situations either in terms of losses lying with several individuals or with some community appropriate to the loss.
8. See T. Hobbes, *Leviathan* (Oxford: Basil Blackwell, 1955) at 80.
9. See O. W. Holmes Jr., *The Common Law* (New York: Dover, 1991) at 96.
10. This is the feature of utilitarianism that leads Rawls to conclude that it "does not take seriously the distinction between persons" (Rawls, *supra* note 6 at 27).
11. See R. Nozick, *Anarchy, State, and Utopia* (New York: Basic Books, 1974) at 156. The position that Dworkin considers, and rejects, under the name "equality of Welfare" might count as fully patterned and as representing the idea that all misfortunes are held in common. Since welfare is equalized under such a scheme, misfortune, as well as everything else, is held in common (see R. Dworkin, "What is Equality? Part 1: Equality of Welfare" (1981) 10 *Phil. & Pub. Aff.* 185 [hereinafter "Equality of Welfare"]). See also T. Scanlon, "Nozick on Rights, Liberty, and Property" in J. Paul, ed., *Reading Nozick: Essays on Anarchy, State, and Utopia* (Towtowa, N.J.: Rowman & Littlefield, 1981) 107.
12. See E. B. Pashukanis, *Law and Marxism: A General Theory*, trans. B. Einhorn (London: Pluto Press, 1983) at 109–33.
13. See: R. H. Coase, "The Problem of Social Cost" (1960) 3 *J. L. & Econ.* 1; G. Calabresi, "Some Thoughts on Risk Distribution and the Law of Torts" (1961) 70 *Yale L. J.* 499.
14. B. Pascal, *Pensées*, trans. A. J. Krailsheimer (London: Penguin, 1976) at 67.
15. See *e.g. Tomaki Juda v. United States*, 6 *Cl. Ct.* 441 (1984) in which the plaintiff was forcibly removed from his home in bikini atoll to allow nuclear weapons testing and then returned when radiation levels were dangerously high. In that case, presumably nothing the plaintiff could have done would have prevented the injury.
16. See J. L. Mackie, *The Cement of the Universe: A Study of Causation* (Oxford: Clarendon Press, 1973).
17. More embarrassing still, if we tie liability to causation and causation to what is atypical, the boundaries of a person's activity turn out to depend largely on how many other people engage in it. When white students at the University of Georgia rioted to

protest integration, a number of them screamed insults at the lone black student in a dormitory: "[D]oes she realize she's causing all this trouble?" (C. Trillin, "An Education in Georgia" *The New Yorker* (16 July 1963) 30 at 67, quoted in J. Feinberg, "Action and Responsibility" in A. R. White, ed., *The Philosophy of Action* (London: Oxford University Press, 1968) 95 at 115–16). While many libertarians oppose anti-discrimination laws, presumably few would want to rest any judgements of liability on the claim that the black student caused the riot.

More generally, tying causation, and thus, liability to statistical infrequency not only does badly as an interpretation of the idea that people should bear the costs of their choices, it also betrays another idea that libertarians claim to embrace, namely, that of attaching priority to individual liberty to do novel and interesting things.

18. See *Strict Liability, supra* note 13 at 166–80.
19. See B. Dylan, "All I Really Want to Do" on *B. Dylan's Greatest Hits,* vol. 2 (New York: Columbia Records, 1970).
20. See S. R. Perry, "The Impossibility of General Strict Liability" (1988) 1 *Can. J. Law & Jur.* 147.
21. See Perry, *ibid.*
22. The risks being divided are always risks of particular injuries (see Part IV.D., below).
23. See: *Meistrich v. Casino Arena Attractions Inc.,* 155 A.2d 90, 31 N.J. 29 (1959); *Lange v. Hoyt,* 159 A. 575, 82 *A.L.R.* 486 (Conn. 1932).
24. See G. Calabresi, *Ideals, Beliefs, Attitudes, and the Law: Private Law Perspectives on a Public Law Problem* (Syracuse: Syracuse University Press, 1985).
25. Such an account would presumably offer some explanation of why religious beliefs are typically deeply felt. But, it is not the depth of the feeling that counts.
26. As Justice Cardozo put it: "Danger invites rescue" (*Wagner v. International Railway Co.,* 133 *N.E.* 437, 232 *N.Y.* 176 (Ct. App. 1923).
27. For example:
   When one risks his life, or places himself in a position of great danger, in an effort to save the life of another, or to protect another, who is exposed to a sudden peril, or in danger of great bodily harm, it is held that such exposure and risk is not negligent. The law has so high a regard for human life that it will not impute negligence to an effort to preserve it, unless made under circumstances as to constitute rashness in the judgment of prudent persons (*Peyton v. Texas & P. Railway Co.,* 6 *So.* 690 at 691, 41 *La.Ann.* 861 (1889)).
28. Both liberty and security interests are typically described broadly. For example, a defendant has an interest in walking, not in walking to some particular place. As we shall explain below, at text accompanying notes 56ff, broadly described interests are a hallmark of liberal views about toleration but should not be mistaken for neutrality.
29. See I. Kant, "On a Supposed Right to Lie from Altruistic Motives" in *Critique of Practical Reason,* trans. L. W. Beck (Chicago: University of Chicago Press, 1949) 346.
30. Even in those areas in which liability is strict—that is, no showing of fault is required—it does not thereby become unlimited (see *infra* note 41).
31. On a variant of this view, there is presumed to be something like an activity-neutral criterion of what degree of care would have been reasonable or due. So, in this view, we might say that fault is in the manner of execution, and the standard of care is independent of the activity chosen. This view represents a logical possibility, rather than a position anyone has seriously put forward.
32. This is the view of fault that underlies the Learned Hand formula, at least in its non-economic interpretations. The root idea is that the benefits to someone participating in an activity serve to fix the degree of care that should be attached to the security interests of others.
33. See *e.g.* C. A. MacKinnon, *Toward a Feminist Theory of the State* (Cambridge, Mass.: Harvard University Press, 1989). For a discussion of Professor MacKinnon's views, see especially S. Haslanger, "On Being Objective and Being Objectified" in L. M. Anthony & L. Witt, eds., *A Mind of One's Own: Feminist Essays on Reason and Objectivity* (Boulder, Colo.: Westview Press, 1993) 85.
34. We have both discussed objectivity in our previous work (see especially: A. Ripstein, "Questionable Objectivity" (1993) 27 *Nous* 355; J. Coleman & B. Leiter, "Determinacy, Objectivity, and Authority" (1993) 142 *Penn. L. Rev.* 549).
35. Although these are typically statutory rather than tort based, they turn on all of the same issues of reasonableness.
36. See *e.g.:* K. Abrams, "Gender Discrimination and the Transformation of Workplace Norms" (1989) 42 *Vand. L. Rev.* 1183 at 1197–1214; S. Estrich, "Sex At Work" (1991) 43 *Stan. L. Rev.* 813 at 842 (advocating reasonableness standards that recognize the seriousness of women's interests and the limited importance of men's interest in harassment). As Estrich points out, the danger is that the wrong objective standard will be applied (*ibid.* at 843). See also *Ellison v. Brady,* 924 F.2d 872 (9th Cir. 1991). Despite the court's claim that the standard is "not fault based" (*ibid.* at 879), its reasoning plainly is. Robert S. Adler and Ellen R. Peirce argue that a reasonable woman standard must be unfair because it may hold men liable even though they are trying their best (see R. S. Adler & E. R. Peirce, "The Legal, Ethical, and Social Implications of the 'Reasonable Woman' Standard in Sexual Harassment Cases" (1993) 61 *Fordham L. Rev.* 773 at 826). On our interpretation of objective standards, any standard that protects people equally from each other may make someone liable for harms they unwittingly cause. The alternative is to make one person's well-meaning indifference the measure of another's interests. Our account also avoids the alleged difficulties with reasonableness standards considered by N. S. Ehrenreich, "Pluralist Myths and Powerless Men: The Ideology of Reasonableness in Sexual Harassment Law" (1990) 99 *Yale L.J.* 1177.
37. Judith Jarvis Thomson seems to advocate a structurally similar view (though not as an interpretation of libertarianism) (see J. J. Thomson, *Realm of Rights* [Cambridge, Mass.: Harvard University Press, 1990]).
38. Of course, rights could be structured to incorporate these concerns. But if they are, any remaining connection with strict liability is lost. Without the dogmas, there is no strict liability left.
39. (1866), L.R. 1 Ex. 265, 4 H. & C. 263, aff'd (1868), L.R. 3 H.L. 330, 19 L.T. 220 (H.L.) [hereinafter cited to L.R. 1 Ex.].
40. *Ibid.* at 279–80.
41. Other strict liability areas can be understood in a similar way. For example, master-servant liability reflects the view that employing people to engage in risky activities is itself a risky activity so that no amount of care in selecting employees will do. Justice Cardozo says as much in *Leonbruno v. Champlain Silk Mills,* 128 *N.E.* 711, 229 *N.Y.* 470 (Ct. App. 1920) [hereinafter *Leonbruno* cited to *N.E.*]: "The claimant while engaged in the performance of his duties in the employer's factory was struck in an eye by an apple which one of his fellow-servants, a boy, was throwing in sport at another". The accident was one "arising out of and in the course of employment . . . since the claimant was injured, not merely while he was in a factory, but because he was in a factory, in touch with associations and conditions inseparable from factory life. The risks of such associations and conditions were risks of the employment" (*Leonbruno, ibid.* at 711). The basic assumption is that in keeping a group of employees working together at a dull job, you do so knowing that there will be horseplay that may injure someone. Thus, you are liable, as you would be if you brought together any other set of dangerous forces you can expect to be unable to control. The reason is simple: the security interest of those who may be injured is important enough and the employer's interest in saving expenses insignificant enough that the former outweighs the latter. This is not to say that anyone who employs others is really "at fault" for so doing but only that they must bear the costs of their risky activity.

The same factors can limit the reach of strict liability in areas in which it is otherwise important. In *Williams v. RCA Co.*, 376 *N.E. 2d* 37, 59 *Il.* 229 (Ct. App. 1978) [hereinafter *Williams*], a security guard was injured because his walkie-talkie failed when he was seeking assistance to apprehend an intruder. In *Klages v. General Ordnance Equipment Co.* 367 *A. 2d* 304, 240 *Pa. S.* 356 (1976), the failure of a can of mace was grounds for liability because it was brought into the stream of commerce as a crime-prevention device. The court in *Williams* held that the manufacturer was not liable for a risk for which its product was not designed. Once again, risks are allocated on the basis of various liberty and security interests. In this case, the court held that the defendant's interest in selling its product did not require it to indemnify all users against all possible risks, despite the general rule of strict liability.

42. That is, if agency is everywhere but-for causation is, then virtually all misfortunes will be compensable, while if agency's reach is narrower, we need some way of specifying how to narrow it.

43. "Equality of Resources", *supra* note 4 at 302.

44. This, no doubt, grows out of the idea that ownership begins with owning one's body; hence, any taking of property is no different from a taking of a body part (see *e.g.*: Nozick, *supra* note 11 at 206; J. Narveson, "On Dworkinian Equality" (1983) 1 *Soc. Phil. & Pol'y* 1). In defending Dworkin's views, Will Kymlicka concedes that liberals should be concerned by this accusation (see W. Kymlicka, *Contemporary Political Philosophy: An Introduction* (Oxford: Clarendon Press, 1990) at 154).

45. Maybe, partly because we seem to be talking about everything at once here, and partly because one of us (Coleman) talks about it in everything he writes in torts these days, a few words are in order about generalized no-fault compensation schemes, such as the New Zealand model (see: Royal Commission to Inquire into and Report Upon Workers' Compensation, *Compensation for Personal Injury in New Zealand* (Wellington, 1967); K. H. Marks, "A First in National No-Fault: The Accident Compensation Act 1972 of New Zealand" (1973) 47 *Austl. L.J.* 516. For a discussion of implicit subsidies for motorcyclists, and others engaging in risky activities, see G. T. Schwartz, "National Health Care Reform On Trial: A National Health Care Program: What Its Effect Would Be On American Tort Law and Malpractice Law" (1994) 79 *Cornell L. Rev.* 1339 at 1356). Anyone writing about corrective justice and fault (with the possible exception of libertarians, who, as we have seen, have no room for fault in their accounts) needs to explain why the eclipse of fault in favor of a system of generalized, social insurance is not a loss of something morally significant. The general strategy of objective standards requires a substantive, though thin, index of primary goods in determining what counts as the cost of various activities. Narrow social insurance schemes, such as healthcare programs, rest on the idea that the risks of certain misfortunes created by a host of everyday activities are to be held in common. (In the case of health care, these range from eating and exercise habits to methods of transportation and types of employment as well as sexual activities and the types of public places one frequents.) The rationale for treating health in this way is that it is a primary good, important to everyone's life plans whatever they may be. A generalized social insurance scheme seeks to go one step further, protecting against all harms occasioned by accidental interactions of two or more parties. As such, it treats losses occasioned by accidents in the same way many health-care schemes treat illness. So described, such a scheme may sound unattractive for any number of reasons, not the least of which being that the class of accidents protected against does not seem like a morally significant category. There may also be losses of other important goods in a society that make accident avoidance a central primary good, since any change in an index will have impacts elsewhere. But if such a good is deemed important enough, there is no sacrifice to the general way of looking at misfortune that we have put forward here.

46. See *e.g.* C. Taylor, *Multiculturalism and the Politics of Recognition: An Essay* (Princeton: Princeton University Press, 1992): "Political society is not neutral between those who value remaining true to the culture of our ancestors and those who might want to cut loose in the name of some individual goal of self-development" (*ibid.* at 58).

47. See *e.g.*: J. Raz, *The Morality of Freedom* (Oxford: Clarendon Press, 1986); A. Sen & B. Williams, *Utilitarianism and Beyond* (Cambridge: Cambridge University Press, 1982) at 17–18. Those who insist that incommensurability entails arbitrariness share a questionable view of rationality with those who insist that choice entails commensurability. Both suppose that the only way something can be rational is if it reflects the application of a *quasi*-mechanical procedure—utterly free of judgement or evaluation—to some set of independently describable facts. Like the advocate of strict liability, the person espousing such a view hopes to avoid difficult choices, either by defining them out of existence or by pretending they do not matter. Both err in supposing that the fact that our practices incorporate contestable viewpoints undermines the possibility of their legitimacy. The only thing it undermines is the possibility of a certain kind of justification for them. But the problem is with the model of what a justification must look like, not with the practices.

There is another, quite different worry about incommensurability that grows out of the fear that any weighing will be done by someone, incorporating reasons that others may not share. Worries about commensurability may get part of their edge from the fact that any such decision places costs on some people that, were those people free to dictate the terms of association, they might wish to place elsewhere. There may be no vocabulary of the importance of goods that is acceptable to all in advance—which is precisely why fairness requires a common measure of costs. Apples and oranges might get balanced differently by different balancers. People do disagree about the importance of various liberty and security interests, and those disagreements are often in good faith, not just struggles for relative advantage. If that is the worry, it is worth taking seriously; but its only possible solution lies in institutional mechanisms to protect important interests in setting such boundaries.

This political worry must not be confused with a different worry, according to which fairness requires judging people only by standards they accept in advance. That view, if it makes sense at all, collapses into the sort of subjectivism that makes the idea of people bearing the costs of their choices incoherent. Nor should it be confused with a different political worry, according to which any particular balance between various liberty and security interests must be unfair because it might have come out differently. Though initially plausible, such a worry makes no sense, for it amounts to the view that since institutions are always imperfect, justice is neither possible nor desirable.

48. If we think of negligent injuries as belonging to the wrongdoer, two initially puzzling features of current tort practices become readily understandable. First, monetary damages for nonpecuniary losses make sense. Money can seldom make an injured plaintiff entirely whole. However, if we suppose that an injury resulting from negligence belongs to the wrongdoer, monetary damages provide a way of placing the cost of the negligence on the wrongdoer's shoulders. The wrongdoer must forego other things to make up the injury, just as he or she would have to have done had the injury been only to him or herself. Of course, injurers are often insured and, so, do not end up bearing those costs directly. Here, too, the idea that the wrongdoer owns the injury is illuminating: just as I can insure against injuries to myself, so can I insure against other injuries that belong to me.

LOSS, AGENCY, AND RESPONSIBILITY FOR OUTCOMES:
Three Conceptions of Corrective Justice[*]

Stephen R. Perry

Introduction

It is often claimed that the principle of corrective justice is, or ought to be, the theoretical mainspring of tort law. But this claim cannot be properly evaluated unless we know what corrective justice is. The idea that it is centrally concerned with the payment of compensation for certain losses that one person's conduct has caused another is generally accepted. It is also accepted, at least by the writers on corrective justice I shall discuss in this paper, that an important element of corrective justice is a notion of wrongfulness. Beyond this limited common ground, however, there exists deep disagreement.

Over the past decade or so two very different conceptions of corrective justice have figured prominently in the legal literature. Each takes as its starting-point, and attempts to ground corrective justice in the normative significance of, a different aspect of the common ground just described. According to the first conception, which was until recently defended by Jules Coleman, the starting-point is the fact that someone has suffered a loss. The particular notion of wrongfulness the theory employs is predicated of loss, and it takes the elimination or annulment of so-called wrongful losses to be the point of corrective justice.[1] Following Coleman, this can be called the annulment conception of corrective justice. According to the second conception, the best-known advocate of which is Ernest Weinrib, the starting-point for understanding and justifying corrective justice is the injurer's conduct. More precisely, Weinrib begins with the fact that the injurer exercised her powers of agency. On this view, the

relevant notion of wrongfulness is predicated of conduct rather than loss: the victim has a right to be compensated by the injurer precisely because the injurer acted wrongfully towards him.[2] For reasons that will become apparent later, I shall call this the Kantian/Hegelian conception of corrective justice.

The annulment and Kantian/Hegelian theories of corrective justice both give rise to a number of different problems,[3] but I shall argue in the first and second sections of this article that their respective major deficiencies turn out to be complementary. In each case the central difficulty is an inability to transcend the theory's own starting-point so as to take appropriate account of the particular feature of harmful interactions that the other theory treats as *its* starting-point. Thus the annulment view cannot non-arbitrarily limit the losses that fall within its scope to those caused by human agency. The Kantian/Hegelian conception, by contrast, is unable to justify a remedy of compensation for loss, as opposed to a remedy of, say, punishing the injurer for his wrong-doing. The lesson to be learned, I shall suggest, is that an adequate account of corrective justice must attribute an independent normative significance to the victim's loss, on the one hand, and to the injurer's exercise of agency, on the other.

In the final section of the article I outline a third conception of corrective justice, which I call the comparative conception, that meets this test of adequacy. The comparative conception treats agency and loss as each being normatively significant in its own right, and there is accordingly a sense in which it combines the best aspects of the annulment and Kantian/Hegelian theories. It is not, however, a simple composite of the other two positions, since its starting-point is an understanding of agency very different from that of the Kantian/Hegelian conception. According to this understanding, persons have a certain kind of special responsibility for all the sufficiently proximate outcomes of their actions, even where their conduct in causing the outcome could not be said to have exhibited fault.

Such a notion of "outcome-responsibility" is required to ground an adequate conception of corrective justice because otherwise there would be no normative link between particular injurers and their victims; the normative significance of agency and loss would have to be taken into account in some way that did not depend on the injurer/victim relationship, such as by means of a general distributive scheme of some kind. But outcome-responsibility does not give rise by itself to an obligation to compensate. Rather it sets the stage for a comparative inquiry, the conclusion of which will sometimes be that the injurer does have an obligation of this kind. The primary (but not exclusive) focus of this inquiry is two-fold: the existence and extent of fault in the injurer's conduct, on the one hand, and the nature and seriousness of the setback to the victim's well-being, on the other. I should emphasize that it is not my purpose in this article to present either a complete defence of the comparative conception of corrective justice, or a detailed account of the manner in which it would resolve specific kinds of disputes.[4] Rather the purpose is simply to outline, in light of the deficiencies of the two theories that have held sway in recent years, what an adequate conception of corrective justice would look like.

The Annulment Conception

The chief proponent of the annulment conception of corrective justice has been, at least until recently, Jules Coleman.[5] This conception takes the point of corrective justice to be the elimination, rectification or annulment of wrongful gains and losses. Since we are at present concerned with reparation only, not restitution, we can ignore wrongful gains and concentrate on wrongful losses.[6] The proposition that wrongful losses should be rectified or annulled Coleman calls the *annulment thesis*. He characterizes as "wrongful" those losses that result from either wrongful conduct or the invasion of a right. Conduct is wrongful if it does not comply with relevant norms

of conduct. Wrongful conduct that causes harm might or might not involve the invasion of a right. If it does, the right is said to have been *violated*. But innocent or justifiable conduct can also give rise to a rights invasion, in which case the right is said to have been *infringed*. Coleman apparently regards infringement cases as coextensive with necessity cases, in which one person takes or destroys the property of another in order to save her own life. On Coleman's analysis, the conduct of the person in the necessitous state is justified, but even so it infringes the right of the property-owner. The loss the latter suffers is thus a wrongful loss, and it falls within the purview of corrective justice. One reason why Coleman thought that wrongfulness is properly predicated, so far as corrective justice is concerned, of the victim's loss rather than the injurer's conduct was his view that in cases such as these the victim has a claim to repair even though the injurer did not act wrongfully.

Wrongful losses are thus caused, according to Coleman, by conduct that either is wrongful or invades a right. In both cases the loss is the result of an exercise of human agency, and Coleman expressly insisted that a loss could only be subject to the principle of corrective justice if it possessed this feature.[7] The annulment conception of corrective justice says that wrongful losses should be eliminated or annulled. But the responsibility of annulment does not fall to specific persons, and in particular it does not fall to the injurer (or injurers) who caused the loss. The annulment conception does not, in other words, give rise to agent-relative reasons for action.[8] It requires, rather, that a certain state of affairs be brought about through a reallocation of material resources within the relevant community. There might be more than one way of achieving this state of affairs, and the responsibility for doing so is in some sense a general one. This general responsibility conceivably rests, at least initially, with all members of the community as individuals, in which case corrective justice gives rise, on the annulment view, to agent-neutral reasons for action. But a shared responsibility of this kind would presumably generate a collective action problem, and this would eventually lead to its being delegated to the state. It is also possible that the responsibility rests with the state from the outset, as a collective responsibility flowing from an appropriate theory of political morality. In either case it is the state that would ultimately be charged with deciding how wrongful losses are to be annulled. . . .

So far as the distinction between wrongful and other kinds of losses is concerned, Coleman suggested that a person who had suffered a wrongful loss would have a *right* or a claim in justice to recover it, whereas someone who had suffered an identical loss that was not wrongful in his sense would not; the community might have moral reasons to compensate the latter victim, but no obligation or reason of justice to do so.[9] As we have seen, however, the moral right of the former victim would ultimately be held, not against the person who had acted wrongfully or invaded her right, but against the state or community at large. Such a right would presumably be justified by the fact of loss rather than by the manner in which the loss came about, so there is no obvious reason why the victim who suffered a materially identical but non-wrongful loss should not have a similar right. Given the assumption that the responsibility for annulling losses rests with the state, the claim that there is a morally stronger case for rectifying wrongful losses than non-wrongful ones looks arbitrary.

The important point underlying the comments in the preceding paragraph is this. The most plausible reason why the state or the community at large should have an independent responsibility to annul losses—i.e., a responsibility that is assumed not to derive from some other, non-collective responsibility taken to be primary, such as that of an injurer—rests on the fact that a loss constitutes an interference with human well-being. The maintenance or promotion of human well-being is a matter of general moral concern, and hence of normative significance. It gives rise, in other words, to moral reasons for action that are in some sense pervasive or diffuse. On one interpretation of the annulment thesis presented above, these reasons apply, at least initially, to everyone—i.e., they are agent-neutral—although the responsibility in question would no doubt come to be delegated to the state. On the other interpretation, the relevant reasons belong *ab initio* to the state, regarded as a distinct moral entity of some kind. In neither case, however, is there any basis for distinguishing between the ways that an interference with well-being came about; it is the interference itself, and not its source, that is of moral significance in this context. There is thus no basis for the annulment thesis to attribute any normative significance to the fact that a loss is wrongful in Coleman's sense, and hence to the fact that it resulted from an exercise of human agency. The point of a general or collective responsibility to annul losses can only be to provide compensation for the setback to well-being that a loss represents. As has been persuasively argued by those critics of tort law who re-

gard it as nothing but a failed or defective compensation system, there is no justification for determining which losses are to be compensated by looking to whether they were the result of fault or, more generally, of human agency. . . .

The preceding discussion suggests that the most basic normative concept underlying the annulment thesis is not loss but rather need, which is one of the concepts that ultimately informs distributive justice at the political level. This is not to deny that the category of loss, or at least of sudden and drastic loss, may be deserving of special consideration within the theory of distributive justice, because of the impact that such losses can have on formed expectations and existing life-plans. Something like this is suggested by the instances of ad hoc compensation that states sometimes make available to the victims of mass disasters, the consequences of which cannot readily be insured against. But any special consideration accorded to losses must still be fitted within a more general framework of distributive justice, the purpose of which is to ensure that material resources capable of sustaining or contributing to well-being are fairly distributed.

Coleman now acknowledges that the annulment thesis is best understood in terms of distributive rather than corrective justice.[10] But even if the annulment thesis turns out not to perform as originally promised, there is still much to be said for the underlying idea that any principle of compensation for loss must be normatively grounded in a theory of human well-being. A conception of the normative significance of well-being is not sufficient to justify a principle of corrective justice, but it is, I shall argue, necessary. The annulment thesis goes wrong in assuming that a principle of compensation can only generate agent-neutral or political reasons for action. As we shall see, however, there can also be agent-relative reasons for compensating persons who have suffered losses, and it is reasons of this kind to which corrective justice properly conceived gives rise. The justification for that principle is more complex than the argument supporting the annulment thesis, but it must still take the independent normative significance of human well-being as one of its starting-points.

The Kantian/Hegelian Conception

The Kantian/Hegelian conception of corrective justice that Ernest Weinrib defends assumes from the outset that corrective justice must be understood in terms of agent-relative reasons for action rather than agent-neutral or political reasons. More particularly, it is assumed that corrective justice is a matter of obligations on the part of injurers to pay compensation and correlative rights on the part of their victims to be compensated. The obligations in question arise only for persons who have wrongfully injured others, and the corresponding rights are held only against those injurers. So far as formal structure is concerned, this view is much more in keeping than the annulment thesis with the traditional understanding of corrective justice. But a substantive argument must still be offered to show why agent-relative moral obligations of this kind exist. Weinrib's argument is embedded in a more general theory of legal formalism, but it is possible to isolate the elements that are intended to justify his conception of corrective justice in particular. The starting-point is a Kantian/Hegelian understanding of moral agency. Normativity, in the form of general norms governing the interaction of self-determining agents, is said to be inherent in the very concept of free will or agency. At one level, which we can call the primary level, these norms set limits on what self-determining agents can do in the pursuit of their own ends in circumstances where action to attain those ends might impinge on other agents. Weinrib maintains that these limits are determined by what he calls the universality of the free will, which he says is the basis of the normativity inherent in agency. These primary norms define what counts as wrongful conduct towards other persons. They generate obligations not to behave wrongfully towards others, and correlative rights on the part of all persons not to be wronged.

The primary norms just described resemble in some respects the side constraints discussed by Robert Nozick: they place certain restrictions on what a person can do in the pursuit of her own ends that flow from the rights of all self-determining agents not to be wronged.[11] But this is not the end of the matter so far as corrective justice is concerned, since it is common ground that the core of corrective justice is a right to repair on the part of at least some persons who have suffered a loss at the hands of someone else. For the Kantian/Hegelian conception, this is a matter of the appropriate remedy to be imposed for violations of the primary norms that lead to harm. Not surprisingly, Weinrib maintains that the remedy required is the payment of compensation by the injurer: "The obligation to compensate is the juridical reflex of an antecedent obligation not

to wrong."[12] His Kantian/Hegelian normative schema thus contains a secondary or remedial level of norms that set out obligations of repair and corresponding rights to be made whole. Weinrib describes these remedial rights and their correlative obligations as one aspect of an "intrinsic ordering" that "traces the progression from doing to suffering."[13] Speaking of negligence law in particular, he states that its "bipolar procedure", which he says matches the bipolarity of doing and suffering, "transforms the victim's right to be free from wrongful suffering at the actor's hand into a remedy whereby the actor undoes, so far as possible, the injurious consequences."[14] He also refers to compensation as a reversal of the progression of doing and suffering.

Weinrib discusses the nature of remedial rights and obligations of repair in the context of tort law, but it is clear that he thinks the institutional doctrines and procedures of tort simply reflect an antecedent normative structure that is determined by the nature of agency and not by social practices. Weinrib does not, however, actually argue that normativity is inherent in agency; he simply asserts it. This is unsatisfactory in light of the powerful critique of the Kantian rationalist project that has been offered by Bernard Williams, among others,[15] but I shall pass over that point. Let me assume that Weinrib can produce an argument of Kantian or Hegelian pedigree capable of justifying the primary norms that define wrongdoing. Establishing the validity of primary norms does not automatically establish that compensation is the appropriate remedy for violations of them that lead to harm. Without further argument the idea of reversing the progression of doing and suffering just begs the question, and the same is true of a claim that the victim's right is transformed into a remedy that undoes the injurious consequences. There is, at the very least, a conceptual gap here.

The existence of this gap can be made clearer by considering the way that Weinrib refers interchangeably to annulling wrongfulness and annulling wrongful loss.[16] Annulling wrongfulness is presumably accomplished by punishment. Annulling wrongful loss is a matter of providing compensation. Even if we assume that instances of wrongdoing that result in harm demand, as a conceptual and normative matter, *some* remedy, what reason is there for concluding that the appropriate remedy is ever anything other than punishment? It will not do to say that punishment is a public and not a private matter, for two reasons. First, it is not clear that punishment is *necessarily* a public matter. Second, the appropriateness of private remedies is one of the points at issue here. This is not just a quibbling demand for an airtight argument in support of a conclusion that perhaps strikes many people as intuitively obvious, and hence as not being in need of this kind of justification. There are two responses that can be made to a claim that Weinrib is being held to an unrealistically high standard of argumentation. First, since it is Weinrib himself who says that the validity of norms is a matter of conceptual entailment, it can hardly be inappropriate to point out that he has not met that standard with respect to the remedial norms of corrective justice. Second and more importantly, there is reason to think that the conceptual gap between primary and secondary norms cannot be bridged within Weinrib's Kantian/Hegelian schema.[17]

The second response requires elaboration. We should observe, to begin with, that the universality of the will from which the normativity inherent in agency is supposed to flow is derived from the capacity of the free will "to abstract from any particular object of choice."[18] Weinrib refers to the norms governing interaction that he says inhere in agency by the Hegelian term "abstract right." Abstract right demands respect for persons and personality. Personality is defined, following Hegel, as "the *capacity* for rights."[19] "Right" is defined again following Hegel, as "an existent of any sort embodying the free will."[20] Free will is embodied in one's own body and can, as a result of certain kinds of acts, also be embodied in a material thing, which then becomes property. Weinrib draws a sharp distinction between right and what he calls advantage. In abstracting from particular objects of choice abstract right also abstracts, he says, from "the particularity of advantage."[21] "Advantage" is a term he employs in a fairly loose way to refer to all notions of interest, welfare or well-being. Weinrib states that "[w]hereas rights are morally relevant because of their conceptual connection with free will, advantages have no independent normative significance; it takes further argument to give them moral force."[22] He contrasts a model of private law based on rights with one based on advantages. In the latter model, "advantages and disadvantages are the original elements of analysis."[23] The model of right, however, is underpinned by abstract right, in which "advantages are valued not for their own sake but only inasmuch as they represent embodiments of an abstractly free will."[24]

The reason the conceptual gap between primary norms prohibiting wrongdoing and secondary norms specifying a remedy of repair seems un-

bridgeable for the Kantian/Hegelian theory is this. The core of any conception of corrective justice is a right to receive compensation for loss suffered. But a loss is just an interference with the victim's well-being. In Weinrib's terminology, it is an interference with an advantage, or a disadvantaging. For Weinrib, however, advantages have no independent normative significance, and are not valued for their own sake. They have value only as embodiments of the free will. As he says at one point, "[i]n abstract right the significance of particular rights consists *solely* in their being actualizations of [the] capacity [for rights] and not in their contribution to the satisfaction of the right holders' interests."[25] And again: "Instead of being conceived as the particular benefits enjoyed by particular persons, the rights of private law are seen as expressions of the universal nature of the will's freedom."[26] It would thus seem that the normative significance abstract right confers on rights, and in particular on the rights persons have in their bodies and material property, has nothing to do with any material benefit to them or with satisfaction of their interests. In other words, it has nothing to do with what Weinrib calls advantage, or, in a more standard terminology, with persons' well-being. But compensation for loss is clearly a matter of undoing an interference with well-being. How can a theory that gives such short shrift to well-being even have logical room for a compensatory remedy, let alone produce a conceptual derivation of it?

Could Weinrib respond that the statements quoted in the two preceding paragraphs are somewhat infelicitously phrased, and that what he really meant to say was that abstract right simply supplies the justificatory ground for the normative significance of well-being as that notion is usually understood? Could he claim, in other words, that when he says advantages are not valued for their own sake, his point is that they have no value apart from abstract right and that it is precisely because of abstract right that they can be said to have value *as advantages*, i.e., as aspects of well-being? The answer to these questions must be no. There are two main points to be considered in this connection. First, there is no evident basis for extracting a conception of well-being from abstract right; certainly Weinrib presents no argument to show that this is possible. Moreover if he were to make such an argument he would no longer be in a position to draw a sharp distinction between right and advantage, and this would lead to a blurring or collapse of the corresponding models of private law. If a full-blooded conception of well-being were to gain a toe-hold in the model of right at the remedial stage, for the reason that abstract right justified a concern for well-being as such, how could it be contained there? The misfeasance requirement of private law that Weinrib defends so vigorously could well be undermined in such a transformed theory, for example.[27] If abstract right treated the well-being associated with, say, bodily integrity and health as important for its own sake, then it is far from clear that it would not require persons to promote those interests in others and not just refrain from actively interfering with them.

The second point to be considered is that the normative significance abstract right confers on advantages within Weinrib's Kantian/Hegelian schema is clear, and it has nothing to do with their being instruments or aspects of well-being. Advantages are valued because "they represent embodiments of an abstractly free will;"[28] the significance of the rights that are associated with particular advantages "consists solely in their being actualizations of [the] capacity [for rights] and not in their contribution to the satisfaction of the right holders' interests."[29] "Capacity for rights" and "moral personality" refer in Weinrib's Hegelian terminology to the same concept, so the normative significance of advantages is clearly just that they are bearers of moral personality. Nor does their importance in this respect have anything to do with well-being, as the preceding quotation shows. This cannot be dismissed as a matter of infelicitous phrasing, since the same point also emerges very clearly from an examination of the nature of wrongdoing in the Kantian/Hegelian schema.

In its most abstract formulation, the wrongdoing that is prohibited by norms at the primary level consists of showing disrespect for moral personality. Limiting our attention for the moment to the paradigm example of intentional wrongdoing, it is important to observe that intentionally showing disrespect for personality is *not* the same as intentionally harming the embodiments of personality, i.e., intentionally interfering with certain advantages or interests. This is true, moreover, even though one way to show disrespect for personality is to harm its embodiment, as this example of Weinrib's makes clear: "[M]y murdering someone would be inconsistent with his having the capacity for rights, since I would be treating him as a thing that was available to my purposes and, thus, not an embodiment of free will."[30] So far as abstract right is concerned, however, the harm must be the disrespect shown, not the interference with an advantage regarded as an aspect of well-being (in the example,

loss of life). The same point emerges in the context of property damage when Weinrib says that abstract right "does not guarantee any specific condition or value to what is owned," and that it "accounts for ownership in a way that makes the condition of particular owned things *irrelevant*."[31] Weinrib goes on to say that "[a]lthough your injuring something that is mine may reduce the satisfaction I derive from it, what was injured nevertheless remains mine."[32] The clear implication here is that the harm, so far as corrective justice is concerned, is neither the physical damage nor the setback to well-being that this might occasion. This again leaves the insult to personality that is manifested by an intentional act of damaging another's property as the only plausible candidate for harm in abstract right. Advantages can thus serve their assigned role as bearers of personality in Weinrib's normative schema without our having to assume that they have any moral significance qua aspects of well-being.

It was noted earlier that even though intentionally harming the embodiments of personality is one way of intentionally showing disrespect for personality, the two are not equivalent. This suggests that it is possible intentionally to show disrespect for personality, thereby causing harm in the corrective justice sense, without intentionally harming its embodiment. Consider, for example, the case of a murder attempt that fails. No embodiment of free will is harmed, but surely the would-be murderer has shown as much disrespect for the intended victim's moral personality as if the attempt had succeeded. Consider as well the following case. I place my coat upon a sleeping person because I do not want to put it on the dirty floor. Using someone as a coat-rack is clearly "treating him as a thing . . . available to my purposes and, thus, not as an embodiment of free will."[33] The action thus intentionally evinces disrespect for moral personality even though it did not cause, was not intended to cause, and could not be expected to cause personal injury, i.e., harm to the embodiment of personality. In both the attempted murder and coat-rack scenarios the insult to personality nonetheless constitutes harm in the sense of abstract right.

The preceding discussion makes clear that abstract right does not, need not, and cannot treat advantages as normatively significant because they are aspects of well-being; their importance within the Kantian/Hegelian schema is simply as bearers of moral personality. Any suggestion to the contrary is bound to turn on an equivocation between "advantage" understood as an embodiment of personality, and "advantage" understood as an aspect of well-being.

What, then, are we to say about the question of remedy within the Kantian/Hegelian schema? There are two points to bear in mind. The first is that a remedy of compensation cannot be appropriate, because it treats an interference with well-being as normatively significant in its own right in a way that abstract right forbids.[34] As Weinrib himself notes in connection with cases of property damage, the condition of particular owned things is irrelevant for abstract right. The second point is that for abstract right, wrongdoing is a show of disrespect for personality, and harm is the insult shown. In other words, the wrong and the harm are very closely connected, if not identical. This strongly suggests that the remedial stage will inevitably have to deal with, and attempt somehow to undo or rectify, the wrong and the harm together.[35] One possibility is that the wrongdoer should be made to see that she has an obligation to offer a sincere apology or show of contrition. Within the context of a legal system, however, the most fitting remedy is surely punishment. In the Kantian tradition punishment is conceived, after all, precisely in terms of the annulment or nullification of a wrong. Furthermore, this view of the appropriate juridical response to wrongdoing within the Kantian/Hegelian schema is consistent with the fact that the schema can, as I have argued elsewhere,[36] only encompass wrongdoing that is culpable or blameworthy; notwithstanding Weinrib's assertions to the contrary, there is no place within the schema for an objective standard of care.

The punishment thesis is implicitly supported by Weinrib's discussion of intentional wrongs, which he calls "takings." He states that takings are "wrongs that constitute general denials of the validity of right," and that liability in tort "juridically nullifies this denial."[37] But the denial of right consists in the disrespect intentionally shown to personality, not in any physical harm or appropriation that might result, so the appropriate form of nullification is one that addresses the disrespect. This again points towards punishment rather than liability to pay compensation as the proper juridical response. Moreover, as we saw in connection with the attempted murder example, harm in the sense of insult to personality occurs whether or not a would-be taker succeeds in causing physical damage or appropriating another's property. As Weinrib says, "the taker *attempts* to assert dominion over something that is already a physical or proprietary embodiment of another's personality."[38] There has clearly been a denial of right in Weinrib's sense even if the attempt

fails, however, so nullification is required. It obviously cannot take the form of liability to compensate, since by hypothesis there has been no interference with the intended victim's well-being. Punishment is, again, the only plausible alternative. Punishment would similarly seem to be called for in cases like the coat-rack hypothetical described earlier, in which the wrongdoer intentionally shows disrespect for personality but neither causes nor intends to cause harm to an embodiment of personality.

The Kantian/Hegelian conception of corrective justice is thus defective in that it cannot accommodate, let alone justify, the core characteristic of corrective justice, namely, a right to be compensated for loss. Even if we grant Weinrib his claim that normativity is inherent in agency, a gap in the theory soon comes to light: he gives us no reason to think that this conceptually-derived normativity requires that losses resulting from violations of primary norms should be compensated. In fact the difficulty is more serious still, since the gap appears unbridgeable: the normativity in question is underpinned by the Hegelian concept of abstract right, and abstract right categorically denies that human well-being as such has any normative significance. The Kantian/ Hegelian conception thus faces a difficulty that is the mirror-image of the one encountered by the annulment theory. Put somewhat crudely, the one cannot get from agency to loss, while the other cannot get from loss to agency. The Kantian/Hegelian theory is nonetheless correct to conceive of corrective justice in terms of agent-relative obligations of repair on the part of injurers and correlative rights to be compensated on the part of their victims, even if it cannot provide the necessary substantive justification for those rights and obligations. And it is correct to take the normative significance of agency as *one* starting-point in the justification of corrective justice, although it goes wrong in treating this as the only starting-point. As we shall see, it also misunderstands just what the normative significance of agency for corrective justice is.

The Comparative Conception

A Preliminary Difficulty

As was noted in the introduction, it is common ground that corrective justice is centrally concerned with the payment of compensation for certain losses that one person's conduct has caused another.

Traditionally it has also been accepted that the victim's right to repair is correlative of an obligation to compensate owed by the injurer and the injurer alone. The annulment thesis rejected correlativity and agent-relativity, and in consequence it collapsed into a theory of general distributive justice. It is of course possible that there simply is no independent principle of corrective justice,[39] but if there is, the obligations it yields must be both limited to injurers and correlative of victims' rights. What we are seeking, then, is a justification for corrective justice that incorporates these constraints.

The discussion in the preceding two sections suggests that the justification we are looking for cannot be based on the normative significance of either loss or agency alone. The annulment conception begins with the reasonable premise that an interference with the well-being of one person—a loss—can affect the reasons for action of others; but it cannot limit the scope of the resulting principle to losses caused by human agency, let alone insist, as in fact it does not try to do, that the relevant reasons apply to injurers alone. The Kantian/Hegelian conception begins with the equally reasonable premise that a wrongful exercise of agency calls for the agent to atone or make amends in some way; but it cannot show, and indeed is precluded by its assumptions about well-being from showing, that the appropriate forms of making amends include an obligation to pay compensation when wrongful conduct causes loss.

It might seem plausible to think that the justification we seek could be achieved just by combining these two premises (minus the Kantian/Hegelian theory's problematic assumptions about well-being). The idea would be something like this. Engaging in wrongful conduct has various normative consequences for the wrongdoer. The interference with individual well-being that loss represents is capable of affecting other persons' reasons for action. Where A's wrongdoing causes loss to B, at least one of the normative consequences for A is that he has an obligation—i.e., a particular type of reason for action—to compensate B for the loss. This is because it is morally preferable that, as between a wrongdoer and an innocent victim, the former rather than the latter should suffer the interference with well-being that either the original loss or the payment of compensation entails. This can be characterized as an argument of localized distributive justice. Similar arguments are common in tort cases,[40] and some theorists have employed them as well. To take one example, George Fletcher's proposed justification for correlative rights and obligations of repair relies on a general distributive principle of equal security and, implicitly, on a localized distributive principle at the level of remedy.[41]

The argument just sketched is on the right track, but it will not do as it stands. This is because the localized character of the argument, which limits its application to particular wrongdoers and their victims, cannot be justified. There is thus no basis for saying that a wrongdoer's obligation to pay is owed to the particular victim he harmed, or that a victim has a right to be compensated by the particular person who injured her. Without more, there is no reason not to extend the argument so as to make all wrongdoers who cause harm collectively responsible for all wrongful losses that were caused by any one of them, or indeed to make all wrongdoers, whether or not they actually caused anybody harm, collectively responsible for all wrongful losses and possibly for other social burdens as well, such as losses not caused by human agency. In fact one possible scheme of this sort, in which all faulty drivers would be collectively responsible for all losses caused by driving, has been proposed by Coleman.[42] Such schemes would be justified by a distributive principle that called for wrongfully-inflicted losses (and perhaps other social burdens) to be allocated among persons in accordance with the degree to which they had exhibited certain kinds of moral deficiency. This principle is a natural generalization of the localized distributive principle discussed in the preceding paragraph, which says that a loss is more appropriately borne by the wrongdoer who caused it than by the victim who suffered it. In the absence of some reason for creating a distributive scheme limited to these two parties, a generalization along these lines seems unavoidable.

The justification for correlative rights and obligations of repair that we seek thus requires that we establish responsibility, not just for wrongdoing, but for the particular loss caused. Consider the Kantian/Hegelian conception once again. It begins with the idea that certain normative consequences attach to a wrongful exercise of agency. But it does not permit normative significance to be attached to the *outcomes* of particular actions, let alone to outcomes that constitute losses. This is in fact a very Kantian theme. A conception of faulty conduct does turn out to be important for corrective justice, but something more (in addition to the idea that losses are normatively significant in their own right) is needed as well. I shall suggest that a more complex account of agency, in which the outcomes of actions play a role in the moral assessment of those actions and in the determination of subsequent reasons for action, supplies the missing element.

Agent-Regret, Outcome-Responsibility and Compensation

Bernard Williams has argued, persuasively and with much insight, that the assessment and justification of action is in some contexts "essentially retrospective,"[43] in the sense that it is concerned first and foremost with the outcome of action rather than with its motivation. He suggests that retrospective justification of this kind sometimes depends on the outcome of an action in a way that cannot be captured by rules for the antecedent guidance of conduct, and thus depends in part on luck. If the agent's action turns out badly, either for the agent herself or for someone else, she will ordinarily feel what Williams terms "agent-regret". This is regret directed not just at the outcome of the action but at the action itself viewed retrospectively, in light of the outcome.

Agent-regret is not, according to Williams, restricted to cases of voluntary agency. By this he means that the sentiment is appropriately felt not just with respect to actions giving rise to outcomes that are related to ends intentionally aimed at, but in other cases as well. Nor is it restricted to outcomes that primarily affect only the agent. In cases in which the outcome has adverse effects for someone else, agent-regret takes on a moral dimension. Williams' example is of a driver who accidentally and without fault runs over a child. The driver will, he says, experience agent-regret where a spectator would not, at least unless the spectator has the "agent's thought" that he himself might have prevented the injury. The fact that the driver has occasion to experience agent-regret is in part a matter of moral luck, since the occurrence of the accident is partly due to factors beyond his control. (The same would be true, although possibly to a lesser degree, even if the driver had been at fault.) In the case of actions that adversely affect others, agent-regret will normally take the form of a wish on the agent's part that he had not acted as he did, or at least that he had not had to act as he did.[44] Williams also notes that other persons besides the driver will view his situation as being different from that of the spectator, since "there is something special about the driver's relation to this happening, something which cannot merely be eliminated by the consideration that it was not his fault."[45]

A spectator who witnessed the running over of the child might regret the incident, in the sense of wishing that things had been otherwise, but he would not have a wish that *he* had acted otherwise. The agent-regret of the driver and the regret of the spectator differ not only in the content of the sentiment felt, but also in the way their respective sentiments are expressed: "The lorry-driver may act in some way which he hopes will constitute or at least symbolize some kind of recompense or restitution, and this will be an expression of agent-regret."[46] This is a crucially important point, because it suggests that agent-regret is not just a sentiment but a truly normative notion that can directly affect present reasons for action. We have moved from the retrospective evaluation of one's past actions to a conception of responsibility of some kind for the outcomes of those actions. And while Williams cannot be taken as saying that this is anything other than a subjective and voluntary assumption of responsibility by the individual agent, his observation that the agent is generally recognized to stand in a special relation to the harmful event suggests at least the possibility of a more objective and public conception of responsibility. Let me label such conceptions of responsibility, both subjective and objective, as "outcome-responsibility."[47] It is important to make clear that outcome-responsibility does not necessarily carry with it an obligation to compensate, or even a non-peremptory reason to do so. It is a more general normative notion that may, for example, simply give rise to reasons to obtain assistance, or to express one's regret to the person harmed. But while outcome-responsibility may not be a sufficient condition for recognizing an obligation of repair it is, I wish to suggest, a necessary condition: it is the *basis* of an obligation to compensate. . . .

What is the basis of agent-regret itself, and why does it ground a conception of responsibility for outcomes? Why should we think that even in cases of culpable harm there is responsibility for the particular outcome, as opposed to responsibility simply for behaving badly? And why should we think there is a conception of responsibility that extends beyond the judgment of voluntary, culpable action, meaning action undertaken with an intent to cause harm or with knowledge that harm is likely to result? There is, I believe, no answer to these questions that will straightforwardly *justify* outcome-responsibility, which is too fundamental a notion to be subject to justification, but some sense of why we regard these matters as we do can be gained by reflecting on the following considerations. As agents we act with the intention of producing an effect of some sort under a certain description, and our sense of agency is such that when we succeed we regard the effect, in an important and fundamental sense, as ours: by exercising our powers of voluntary agency we have made a difference in the world, and we identify with the result. In cases of harm-producing actions involving wrongful intent it is appropriate that we regard the action with agent-regret, which in such a case means wishing that we had acted otherwise so as not to have produced the harmful outcome. But we cannot change the past, so agent-regret properly takes on a normative aspect that may affect our present and future reasons for action vis-à-vis the outcome in question. It is transformed, in other words, into a conception of outcome-responsibility. Exactly how our reasons for action are affected is not at this point in issue; what matters is that they are affected.

Similar considerations apply to at least some unintended consequences.[48] As persons capable of self-reflective thought we are aware that we do not have complete control over either our own character and identities as agents, or the physical environment in which we act. Things may, for a variety of reasons, turn out differently from what we expect, in the sense either that the result is itself completely different or that it possesses unexpected qualities. But the fact that things turn out unexpectedly is not a sufficient reason to disassociate ourselves from the outcomes we produce. As in the case of intended outcomes, we are aware that our exercise of agency has made a difference in the world, and given our knowledge of the circumstances under which we necessarily act—i.e., our lack of complete control over our own natures and our environment—it may be that we should likewise identify with at least some outcomes that were unintended. If so, they too will be ours, and if they involve adverse effects for others we should similarly experience agent-regret and accept the possibility of its transformation into a normative conception of outcome-responsibility.

When should we identify with unintended consequences in this way? Although it will not be possible to justify the following answer here,[49] I wish to suggest that we ordinarily do and should so identify *at least* in circumstances which are of such a character that we would generally be capable, in situations of that kind, of acting so as to avoid the harm, even if we were not capable of so acting on

the particular occasion due to, in the usual case, a failure of foresight. Because of the close connection between avoidability and foreseeability, the resulting conception of responsibility is an essentially epistemic one: it coincides for the most part with the notion of reasonable foreseeability, which is the most important determinant of a duty of care in negligence law. This conception of outcome-responsibility is not equivalent to fault, however, since fault is concerned with conduct that would constitute *breach* of a duty of care. Outcome-responsibility thus understood is objective in two senses. First, it does not depend on the subjective capacities of the particular agent to have acted otherwise on the particular occasion—subjectivity in this sense is, if not actually meaningless, at least without philosophical or practical interest[50]—and second, it is appropriately attributed to agents even if they did not happen on the occasion in question to feel the sentiment of agent-regret. The concept of outcome-responsibility is rooted in the sense of agent-regret that persons normally feel with respect to certain of their actions that produced harmful but avoidable outcomes, but it is not simply to be identified with that sentiment.

If the points urged in the preceding paragraph are correct, the heart of outcome-responsibility is a notion of avoidability. Avoidability is not the same as fault, since there is no necessary connotation that the agent *should* have acted otherwise. But a person who experiences agent-regret will nonetheless wish that she had acted otherwise, or at least that she had not had to act as she did, so that the harm in question would not have occurred. But the past cannot be undone, and hence the normative focus shifts to the present and future. The agent's reasons for action are affected, but this does not necessarily carry with it an obligation to compensate; the agent may have reasons only to obtain assistance, express regret, or make what Williams calls symbolic recompense. The possibility is at least raised, however, that she should pay full compensation, which means attempting to undo the harmful outcome entirely, to the extent that this is possible to achieve. The loss represents an interference with the victim's well-being, and it is capable of being transferred, at least up to a point, by the payment of compensation. In the nature of things, the victim will have to bear the loss if no one else has a reason to shoulder it. The injurer, by virtue of her outcome-responsibility, potentially has just such a reason. This sets the stage for a comparative inquiry of the following kind: which of these two should most appropriately suffer the interference with well-being that *either* the original loss *or* the payment of compensation necessarily entails?

Given that a loss represents a setback to well-being, it is appropriate to ask the question just posed within the framework of an interest theory of rights. I employ Joseph Raz's version of the interest theory for this purpose. According to Raz, a person has a right if, *inter alia,* his interest or well-being is a sufficient reason to hold someone else to be under a duty or obligation.[51] (An interest I take to be an aspect of well-being.) On this view, rights are *grounds* of obligations in others. "Holding someone to be under an obligation" could mean either judging him to have an obligation or, in an institutional context, imposing an obligation on him.[52] In general, determining whether there is "sufficient reason" to hold someone to be under an obligation requires us to look at the nature and importance of the interest at stake, on the one hand, and the nature and importance of the conduct from which it would be protected if a right were recognized or imposed, on the other. This involves a moral balancing that cannot be reduced to a calculus or decision procedure of some kind. Nor is there any claim, as there is in Weinrib's theory, that the content of rights can be determined by conceptual argument alone.

Let me assume for the moment that we are dealing with an outcome-responsible injurer and a victim who has suffered a setback to a particularly important interest, such as his person or tangible property. One circumstance in which it clearly seems just that the comparative inquiry should favour the victim and recognize an obligation on the part of the injurer to pay compensation is the presence of culpable fault in the injurer's harmful act. I shall assume that there exists, independently of any principles of reparation, a primary moral obligation (together with the appropriate correlative right) not to intentionally or knowingly harm or attempt to harm the person or property of another, or to intentionally or knowingly subject either his person or property to a substantial degree of risk of harm (i.e., to treat his person or property recklessly), without justification for doing so.[53] A breach of this obligation involves culpable fault. A person who culpably injures another has not only done something he could have avoided doing (which makes him outcome-responsible); he has also done something he *should* have avoided doing. In these circumstances the moral equities seem clear. The injurer's outcome-responsibility takes the form of a secondary obliga-

tion to repair the loss. This obligation is correlative of, and grounded by, a secondary right on the victim's part that protects the interest affected.

Are there other circumstances in which the comparative inquiry should impose a similar obligation? Although I shall not go into the matter here, a strong argument can be made that the Razzian comparative inquiry justifies compensation for damage to the fundamental interests of person and property which results from conduct that fails to comply with an objective negligence standard.[54] In general, the comparative inquiry focuses primarily but not exclusively on two factors: first, on the nature of the injurer's conduct in causing the damage, and in particular on whether her conduct exhibited fault of some kind, and second, on the nature of the victim's detrimentally affected interest.[55] These two factors are not independent of one another. Thus harm to some interests gives rise to an obligation to compensate only if the harm-causing action fell within a certain range of conduct, whereas for other interests, the existence of such an obligation depends on whether the harm-causing action fell within a different range.[56]

For the purposes of corrective justice, wrongdoing can thus be said to be interest-sensitive. This is reflected in the law of torts, where some interests are protected against intentional harm but unprotected against negligence, while others that are protected against malicious harm may, under certain circumstances, be unprotected against either intentional or negligent interference.[57] Consider also the difference between the law of negligence and the law of nuisance: the former determines liability by reference to a certain level of permissible risk,[58] whereas the latter determines liability by reference to a certain level of permissible *harm*.[59] This means that the interest protected by nuisance, namely, the use and enjoyment of real property, can permissibly be harmed intentionally, at least up to a point, although if the motivation is malice the law may call the interfering action a nuisance anyway and impose legal liability.[60] Another point to be noted is that the comparative inquiry, and consequently tort law, may impose an obligation to compensate for certain kinds of justified conduct that would nonetheless be wrongful in the absence of a specific justifying factor. Necessity cases such as *Vincent v. Lake Erie Transportation Co.*[61] are of this type, for example. The defendant's action in intentionally damaging the plaintiff's property is justified by the need to counter some serious threat to the former's life or health. The action is nonetheless in a certain sense fault-like, since its intentional nature would make it wrongful were it not for the situation of necessity. This fault-like aspect is what tips the balance and justifies, on the comparative approach, the payment of compensation.[62]

It seems useful to add a comment on the resemblance the comparative inquiry bears to the argument of localized distributive justice discussed earlier.[63] There is clearly a similarity of approach here, but I think it would be misleading to characterize the comparative inquiry as an instance of a localized distributive argument.[64] As the above discussion makes clear, there is no single criterion of distribution, such as a particular conception of fault, that can be applied in a uniform way in all cases. Rather the inquiry is an open-ended one: it is possible to take many different factors into consideration, and there is no pre-established list of what these are. Moreover there is an asymmetry as regards the positions of those in the "distributive group." The victim is included because in the nature of things he will have to continue to bear the loss he has experienced if no one else has a reason to take it on. The injurer is included because she is outcome-responsible for the loss, and hence potentially has a reason to shoulder it herself. The comparative inquiry is simply a process of determining whether, all things considered, the injurer really does have such a reason, in the form of an obligation to pay compensation. There is really nothing to be gained by calling this inquiry a scheme of localized distributive justice.

The discussion of the preceding three paragraphs suggests that the comparative inquiry called for by the comparative conception of corrective justice is a fairly open-ended affair, which can take a number of different kinds of consideration into account. This suggests in turn that corrective justice is less a matter of fixed substantive principles than it is a framework for certain kinds of moral argument. It will not be possible to consider further the character and scope of such argument here, or to attempt to determine in greater detail what results the comparative inquiry demands in various specific types of case. These are matters that must be left for another occasion.

---

1. See, e.g., Coleman, "Tort Law and the Demands of Corrective Justice" (1992) 67 *Indiana L.J.* 349, 357; Coleman, "Property, Wrongfulness and the Duty to Compensate" (1987) 63 *Chi.-Kent L. Rev.* 451; Coleman, "Moral Theories of Torts: Their Scope and Limits: Part II" (1983) 2 *Law & Phil.* 5; Coleman, "Corrective Justice and Wrongful Gain" (1982) 11 *J. of Legal Stud.* 421.

2. See e.g., Weinrib, "Corrective Justice" (1992) 77 *Iowa L. Rev.* (forthcoming); Weinrib, "The Special Morality of Tort Law" (1989) 34 *McGill L.J.* 403; Weinrib, "Understanding Tort Law" (1989) 23 *Valparaiso L. Rev.* 485; Weinrib, "Right and Advantage in Private Law" (1989) 10 *Cardozo L. Rev.* 1283; Weinrib, "Causation and Wrongdoing" (1987) 63 *Chi.-Kent L. Rev.* 407.

3. I advance a general critique of the annulment conception in Perry, "Comment on Coleman: Corrective Justice" (1992) 67 *Indiana L. Rev.* 381, and of the Kantian/Hegelian conception in Perry, "The Moral Foundations of Tort Law" (1992) 77 *Iowa L. Rev.* (forthcoming). I criticize the more comprehensive theory of legal formalism in which Weinrib embeds the Kantian/Hegelian conception in Perry, "Professor Weinrib's Formalism: The Not-So-Empty Sepulchre" (1993) 16 *Harv. J. of L. & Pub. Policy* (forthcoming).

4. For a more detailed characterization and defence of the comparative conception of corrective justice, see the discussion of the "volitionist/distributive" argument in Perry, "The Moral Foundations of Tort Law" *supra*, note 3.

5. Coleman has recently acknowledged that the annulment conception of corrective justice must be modified. See Coleman, *Risks and Wrongs* (Cambridge: Cambridge University Press, 1992); Coleman, "The Mixed Conception of Corrective Justice" (1992) 77 *Iowa L. Rev.* (forthcoming). I discuss the new theory of corrective justice Coleman presents in these works in Perry, "The Mixed Conception of Corrective Justice" (1992) 15 *Harv. J. of L. & Pub. Policy* 917. I argue there that his new theory turns out, on analysis and reconstruction, to be similar in essential respects to the view to be argued for in this article.

6. The following discussion is based on Coleman, "Moral Theories of Torts: Part II" *supra*, note 1 at 16–25; Coleman, "Tort Law and the Demands of Corrective Justice" *supra*, note 1 at 369–70.

7. Coleman, "Tort Law and the Demands of Corrective Justice" *supra*, note 1 at 371–72.

8. On the distinction between agent-relative and agent-neutral reasons for action, see D. Parfit, *Reasons and Persons* (New York: Oxford University Press, 1984) at 143; T. Nagel, *The View from Nowhere* (New York: Oxford University Press, 1986) at 152–53.

9. Coleman, "Justice and the Argument for No-Fault" (1975) 3 *Soc. Theory & Prac.* 161, at 173. See also the discussion in Coleman, "Tort Law and the Demands of Corrective Justice" *supra*, note 1 at 371–72.

10. *Supra*, note 5.

11. R. Nozick, *Anarchy, State and Utopia* (New York: Basic Books, 1974) at 28–35.

12. "The Special Morality of Tort Law" *supra*, note 2 at 409.

13. Weinrib, "Understanding Tort Law" *supra*, note 2 at 524.

14. *Ibid.*

15. B. Williams, *Ethics and the Limits of Philosophy* (Cambridge: Harvard University Press, 1985) Ch. 4. See also P. Foot, *Virtues and Vices* (Berkeley: University of California Press, 1978) Chs. 11, 12.

16. See Weinrib, "Causation and Wrongdoing" *supra*, note 2 at 434–35.

17. Cf. Sager, "Righting Rights" (1989) 10 *Cardozo L. Rev.* 1311 at 1322, 1325–29.

18. Weinrib, "Right and Advantage" *supra*, note 2 at 1288.

19. *Ibid.* at 1290, quoting G. Hegel, *Philosophy of Right* (New York: Oxford University Press, 1967) para. 36 (emphasis Weinrib's).

20. Weinrib, "Right and Advantage" *supra*, note 2 at 1287, quoting G. Hegel, *supra*, note 19 para. 29.

21. Weinrib, "Right and Advantage" *supra*, note 2 at 1286.

22. *Ibid.* at 1297.

23. *Ibid.* at 1285.
24. *Ibid.* at 1286.
25. *Ibid.* at 1290 (emphasis added).
26. *Ibid.* at 1286.
27. "Personality denotes indifference to the particularity of an actor's interests. The requirement on every person to respect others as persons does not, therefore, import an obligation to assist in the satisfaction of anyone else's interests. Indeed it denies such an obligation." Weinrib, "Right and Advantage" *supra,* note 2 at 1291.
28. *Ibid.* at 1286.
29. *Ibid.* at 1290.
30. *Ibid.* at 1292.
31. *Ibid.* at 1302 (emphasis added).
32. *Ibid.*
33. *Ibid.* at 1292.
34. This oversimplifies somewhat. Abstract right presumably has room for a compensatory remedy that permits damages to be awarded for insult to personality only. This would resemble an award of aggravated damages in existing tort law.
35. If "wrongful loss" is understood as harm in the form of insult to personality, then Weinrib's practice of referring interchangeably to annulling wrongfulness and annulling wrongful loss begins to make sense. See *supra,* note 16.
36. Perry, "The Moral Foundations of Tort Law" *supra,* note 3.
37. Weinrib, "Right and Advantage" *supra,* note 2 at 1303. Elsewhere Weinrib has stated that "criminal law falls under corrective justice," adding that the presence of *mens rea* involves a rejection by the criminal of "the very idea of the formal equality of corrective justice." Weinrib, "Legal Formalism: On the Immanent Rationality of Law" (1988), 97 *Yale L.J.* 949, at 982–83 n. 73. Weinrib goes on to say that in such cases, "state prosecution and punishment undoes the general wrong." This shows that criminal punishment is a remedy that is at least *available* within the Kantian/Hegelian conception of corrective justice to "nullify" certain wrongs. My arguments that, first, Weinrib's understanding of corrective justice has no room for a compensatory remedy and, second, it permits the rectification of only culpable wrongs (i.e. wrongs that import *mens rea*), point to the conclusion that punishment is the *sole* remedy that the Kantian/Hegelian conception is justified in deploying.
38. Weinrib, "Right and Advantage" *supra,* note 2 at 1303.
39. See, e.g., Alexander, "Causation and Corrective Justice: Does Tort Law Make Sense?" (1987) 6 *Law & Phil.* 1.
40. See *Sindell v. Abbott Laboratories* (1980), 607 P. 2d 924 (Cal. S.C.) at 936: "The most persuasive reason for finding plaintiff states a cause of action is that . . . as between an innocent plaintiff and negligent defendants, the latter should bear the cost of the injury".
41. Fletcher, "Fairness and Utility in Tort Theory" (1972) 85 *Harv. L. Rev.* 537, at 550. I argue that Fletcher implicitly relies on a localized distributive principle in Perry, "The Moral Foundations of Tort Law" *supra,* note 3. At one stage Jules Coleman also advanced a localized distributive argument, but he did not assume that it would have pre-institutional moral force; it would only take hold within an existing institution like tort law. This version of the argument is compatible with the annulment conception of corrective justice, since it must view the (at least partially) independent justification for the tort system, rather than corrective justice itself, as the source of agent-relative, correlative obligations for injurers. It also avoids the criticism of localized distributive arguments presented in the text. It is problematic for other reasons, however, because it presupposes the soundness of the annulment conception.
42. Coleman, "On the Moral Argument for the Fault System" (1974) 71 *J. Phil.* 473, at 484–85. Cf. Coleman, "Moral Theories of Torts: Their Scope and Limits: Part I" (1982) 1 *Law & Phil.* 371, at 375–76. Coleman calls this scheme the "at-fault pool."
43. Williams, "Moral Luck," in his *Moral Luck* (New York: Cambridge University Press, 1981) 20, at 24. There is also a very useful and pertinent discussion of moral luck in Nagel, "Moral Luck," in his *Mortal Questions* (1979) 24.
44. Williams rightly notes that agent-regret and the wish to have acted otherwise cannot be entirely assimilated in cases involving projects voluntarily undertaken, but that is not an issue with which we need be concerned here. Williams does not give an example of a situation in which the agent wishes, not that he had not acted as he did, but that he had not had to act as he did, but an example would presumably be a necessity case, i.e., a case in which the agent damages or destroys property in order to save himself from serious injury or death.
45. Williams, "Moral Luck" *supra,* note 43, at 28.
46. *Ibid.*
47. I borrow this term from Tony Honoré, even though my characterization of the notion differs in some important respects from his. See Honoré, "Responsibility and Luck" (1988) 104 *L.Q.R.* 530. I analyze Honoré's conception of outcome-responsibility, and offer a reconstruction of it, in Perry, "The Moral Foundations of Tort Law" *supra,* note 3.
48. The discussion in this paragraph has been influenced by Bernard Williams' article "Voluntary Acts and Responsible Agents" (1990) 10 *Oxford J. of Legal Stud.* 1. See in particular Williams' remarks on p. 10.
49. I argue for the conclusions in this paragraph in Perry, "Risk, Avoidability and Tort Law" (unpublished manuscript).
50. Cf. Perry, *ibid.;* Honoré, "Can and Can't" (1964), 73 *Mind* 463; Honoré, "Responsibility and Luck" *supra,* note 50, at 549–52; D. Dennett, *Elbow Room: The Varieties of Free Will Worth Wanting* (Cambridge: M.I.T. Press, 1985), Ch. 6.
51. For the purposes of this paper, I do not distinguish between duties and obligations.
52. *Ibid.* at 171–72.
53. In theory this obligation could be justified by a Kantian/Hegelian conceptual argument of the sort Weinrib favours, at least so long as it did not deny the possibility of a reparative remedy by assuming away the normative significance of well-being. I do not think that such arguments are in fact possible, although that it is too large an issue to be considered here. See further Williams, *Ethics and the Limits of Philosophy, supra,* note 15, ch. 4.
54. See Perry, "The Moral Foundations of Tort Law" *supra,* note 3; Perry, "Risk, Avoidability and Tort Law" *supra,* note 49.
55. For purposes of this article I shall ignore an important complicating factor, which is that often, perhaps even usually, the injurer will not be the only person who is outcome-responsible for the harm in question; third parties or, more importantly, the victim, may be outcome-responsible as well. See further Perry, "The Moral Foundations of Tort Law" *supra,* note 3; Perry, "Risk, Avoidability and Tort Law" *supra,* note 49. In such cases it will be necessary for the comparative inquiry to take account of the conduct of the third party or victim as well as that of the "primary" injurer, and if such conduct is faulty a proportional splitting of the loss may be appropriate. This is, essentially, how modern regimes of contributory negligence and contribution among tortfeasors work.
56. See further Perry, "Comment on Coleman" *supra,* note 3 at 404–8.
57. It is by no means clear how the Kantian/Hegelian conception of corrective justice would account for this fact. The only interests that it conceives corrective justice as protecting are "embodiments of personality," and whatever interests possess this quality would seem to be protected against the same types of personality-insulting wrongful conduct (according to Weinrib, intentional harm and negligence). In fact, bodily integrity and tangible property are the only two protected interests in tort law that Weinrib discusses.
58. See *Bolton v. Stone,* [1951] A.C. 850, 867.
59. This is recognized in the law by the "live and let live" principle. *Bamford v. Turnley* (1862), 3 B. & S. 66, at 83–84, 122 *E.R.* 27, at 32 (Ex. Ch.), per Bramwell B. See also Epstein, "Nuisance Law: Corrective Justice and Its Utilitarian Constraints" (1979) 8 *J. of Legal Stud.* 49, at 82–87.
60. *Hollywood Silver Fox Farms v. Emmett,* [1936] 2 *K.B.* 408 (C.A.).

61. (1910), 109 *Minn.* 456, 124 *N.W.* 221.
62. See further the discussion of necessity cases in Perry, "The Mixed Conception of Corrective Justice" *supra,* note 5. It is, again, by no means clear how the Kantian/Hegelian theory would account for necessity cases. Either the injurer's act of intentionally damaging someone else's property constituted a show of disrespect for an embodiment of personality, in which case it was wrongful and therefore unjustifiable, or else it did not constitute a show of disrespect, in which case compensation is presumably not owed.
63. Text at notes 39–42.
64. I made this mistake in Perry, "The Moral Foundations of Tort Law" *supra,* note 3.

Justice and Contract

CONTRACT LAW AND DISTRIBUTIVE JUSTICE*

Anthony T. Kronman

Within broad limits, our legal system leaves individuals free to dispose of their property as they wish, either by giving it away or by transferring it in exchange for the property of others. The freedom individuals enjoy in this regard includes the power to make contracts, legally binding agreements that provide for the exchange of property on terms fixed by the parties. Among contract scholars, there is nearly universal agreement that the law of contracts, the tangled mass of legal rules that regulate the process of private exchange, has three legitimate functions: first, to specify which agreements are legally binding and which are not;[1] second, to define the rights and duties created by enforceable but otherwise ambiguous agreements;[2] and finally, to indicate the consequences of an unexcused breach.[3] Beyond this, however, it has sometimes been suggested that the law of contracts should also be used as an instrument of distributive justice and that those responsible for choosing or designing rules of contract law—courts and legislatures—should do so with an eye to their distributional effects in a self-conscious effort to achieve a fair division of wealth among the members of society.[4]

There are, in fact, many rules of contract law that are deliberately intended to promote a distributional end of some sort. Obvious examples include: usury laws limiting the interest that can be charged on loans;[5] implied, but nevertheless nondisclaimable, warranties of quality or habitability;[6] and minimum wage laws.[7] The object of each of these rules is to shift wealth from one group—lenders, sellers, landlords, employers—to another—borrowers, buyers, tenants, workers—presumably in accordance with some principle of distributive justice, by altering the terms on which individuals are allowed to contract. Can legal rules of this sort be defended? More generally, is it ever appropriate to use the law of contracts—understood in the broad sense in which I have been using the term—as an instrument of redistribution, or should the legal rules that govern the process of private exchange be fashioned without regard to their impact on the distribution of wealth in society?

Libertarians, who deny that the state is ever justified in forcibly redistributing wealth from one individual or group to another, answer this question in the negative.[8] Surprisingly, many liberals, who believe that at least some compulsory redistribution of wealth is morally acceptable, even required, give the same answer.[9] The libertarian's opposition to the use of contract law as a mechanism for redistribution derives from his general belief that the compulsory transfer of wealth is theft, regardless of how it is accomplished.[10] By contrast, liberals who oppose the use of contract law as a redistributive device do so because they believe that distributional objectives

*An earlier version of this Article was presented as part of the Wilson Day Program at the University of Rochester on October 10, 1979. I am grateful to Bruce Ackerman, Owen Fiss, Arthur Leff, and Jerry Mashaw for their helpful comments on a prior draft. Anthony Kronman is Professor of Law, Yale Law School. From 89 *Yale Law Journal* 472 (1980).

(whose basic legitimacy they accept) are always better achieved through the tax system than through the detailed regulation of individual transactions.[11]

Thus, despite their fundamentally different views regarding the moral legitimacy of forced redistribution, liberals and libertarians often find themselves defending a similar conception of contract law. While lawyers and philosophers in both camps approvingly describe the role that contract law plays in reducing the cost of the exchange process itself and emphasize the importance of protecting those engaged in the process against threats of physical violence and other unacceptable forms of coercion,[12] there also appears to be widespread agreement, on both sides, that the legal rules regulating voluntary exchanges between individuals should not be selected or designed with an eye to their distributional consequences. It is tempting to conclude that this conception of contract law, which I shall call the nondistributive conception, must be correct if those with such sharply divergent views on the most basic questions of distributive justice agree on its soundness.

In this Article, I argue that the non-distributive conception of contract law cannot be supported on either liberal or libertarian grounds, and defend the view that rules of contract law should be used to implement distributional goals whenever alternative ways of doing so are likely to be more costly or intrusive. The Article is divided into two parts. In the first part I examine the libertarian theory of contractual exchange and argue, against the standard libertarian view, that considerations of distributive justice not only *ought* to be taken into account in designing rules for exchange, but *must* be taken into account if the law of contracts is to have even minimum moral acceptability. My aim here is to show that the idea of voluntary agreement—an idea central to the libertarian theory of justice in exchange—cannot be understood except as a distributional concept, and to demonstrate that the notion of individual liberty, taken by itself, offers no guidance in determining which of the many forms of advantage-taking possible in exchange relations render an agreement involuntary and therefore unenforceable on libertarian grounds. Having established this general point, I propose a simple test, similar in form to Rawls's difference principle,[13] for deciding which kinds of advantage-taking should be permitted and which should not, and argue that this test is the one libertarians ought to accept as being most compatible with the moral premises of libertarianism itself.

In the second part of the Article, I challenge the standard liberal preference for taxation as a method of redistribution. The choice of a redistributive method involves moral issues as well as questions of expediency. In my view, however, a blanket preference for taxation is not justified by considerations of either sort. There is no reason to think that taxation is always the most neutral and least intrusive way of redistributing wealth, nor is there reason to think it is always the most efficient means of achieving a given distributive goal. Which method of redistribution has these desirable properties will depend, in any particular case, on circumstantial factors; neither method is inherently superior to the other. And while any redistributive scheme is bound to involve a conflict between distributive justice and individual liberty, the existence of this conflict, although it raises serious difficulties for liberal theory in general, does not provide a reason for adopting a non-distributive conception of contract law.

There are important, but different lessons to be learned from both the liberal and libertarian opposition to using the law of contracts for distributive purposes, and I shall attempt to clarify these in the course of my argument. However, while both views contribute to our understanding of the difficulties involved in treating the law of contracts as a mechanism for redistributing wealth, neither view justifies the claim, implicit in the writings of liberals and libertarians alike, that there is something *morally* wrong with using contract law in this way.[14]

I. Distributive Justice and the Libertarian Theory of Exchange

A. *Voluntary Exchange*

The libertarian theory of contract law is premised upon the belief that individuals have a moral right to make whatever voluntary agreements they wish for the exchange of their own property, so long as the rights of third parties are not violated as a result. For a libertarian, there are only two grounds on which an agreement to exchange property may be impeached: first, that it infringes the rights of someone not a party to the agreement itself, and second, that one of the individuals agreeing to the exchange was coerced into doing so, and thus did not give his agreement voluntarily. Imagine a judge charged with responsibility for enforcing contracts between the members of a particular community. So long as the judge acts in a way consistent with libertarian principles, he need ask himself only two questions whenever a contract dispute arises: Did the party now said to be in breach voluntarily agree to do what the other party wants him to do? Will performance of the agreement violate the rights of third parties? If the answers are "yes" and "no," respectively, the contract must be enforced, regardless of its consequences for the welfare of the individuals involved. If the judge refuses to enforce a particular contract merely because it has certain distributional consequences, or if he adopts a general rule invalidating an entire class of contracts for similar reasons, his actions are indefensible on libertarian grounds. Taking distributional effects into account in this way is inconsistent with the libertarian conception of individual freedom and violates the basic entitlement on which that conception rests.

The question of when an agreement violates the rights of third parties—as opposed to merely diminishing their welfare—is a difficult and interesting one, but I shall say nothing about it here.[15] I want, instead, to focus on the second libertarian requirement for the enforcement of agreements—the requirement of voluntariness. Putting aside its effect on third party rights, the only thing about an agreement that matters, from a libertarian point of view, is the process by which it is reached. This is sometimes expressed by saying that the libertarian conception of contractual exchange is backward-looking or historical,[16] concerned with how agreements are made but not with their distributive consequences. . . .

But when is an agreement voluntary? For a libertarian, committed to the notion that all voluntary agreements must be enforced, the widest view of voluntariness is almost surely unacceptable. Suppose that I sign a contract to sell my house for $5,000 after being physically threatened by the buyer. It is possible to characterize my agreement as voluntary in one sense: after considering the alternatives, I have concluded that my self-interest is best served by signing and have deliberately implemented a perfectly rational decision by doing precisely that. Described in this general way, my agreement to sell appears in the same light that it would if, for example, I had not been threatened but signed the contract because I thought $5,000 a good price for the house. Under this description, however, my act of signing will be involuntary only if it is not motivated by a decision of any sort at all on my part. Such would be the case, for example, if the purchaser forcibly grabbed my hand and guided it over the document himself, or

commanded me to sign the contract while I was in an hypnotic state.

There is, of course, nothing logically absurd about drawing the line between voluntary and involuntary agreements at this point, but I doubt most libertarians would wish to do so. Among other things, defining voluntariness in this way conflicts with deeply entrenched notions of moral responsibility. In assessing the voluntariness of an agreement, it is not enough merely to determine that the agreement was motivated by a deliberate decision of some sort; we also want to know something about the circumstances under which it was given. But if this is true, the problem of drawing a line between agreements that are voluntary and agreements that are not—a problem the libertarian must confront if the idea of voluntary exchange is to have any meaning at all—can be understood as the problem of specifying the conditions that must be present before we will consider an agreement to have been voluntarily concluded. Put differently, unless the libertarian is prepared to accept a very broad concept of voluntariness, which equates voluntary agreement with rational choice, he must specify the various circumstances under which even a deliberately given, rational agreement will be held to have been coerced.[17]

B. Advantage-Taking

Whenever a promisor complains that his agreement was coerced and therefore ought not to be enforced, he should be understood as claiming that the agreement was given under circumstances that rendered it involuntary. In making an argument of this sort, a promisor may point to many different circumstances or conditions: he may say, for example, that his agreement was involuntary because he lacked the mental and emotional capacities required to appreciate its consequences[18] or a promisor may claim that he was threatened or deceived by the other party,[19] or that his agreement was given at a time he was hard-pressed for cash and therefore had no choice but to accept the terms proposed by the promisee[20] or a promisor may assert that his agreement was involuntary because he, unlike the other party, was ignorant of certain facts which, if known at the time of contracting, would have led him to make a different agreement or no agreement at all;[21] or he may say that the other party had a monopoly of some scarce resource—the only water hole or the best cow or the strongest shoulders in town—a monopoly which enabled him to dictate terms of sale to the promisor, making their agreement what is sometimes called a "contract of adhesion."[22]

In some of these cases, the circumstances allegedly making the promisor's agreement involuntary is an incapacity of the promisor himself—his insanity, youth, ignorance or impecuniousness. In others, the involuntariness of the promisor's agreement is attributable to an act by the other party—a fraudulent deception or threat of physical harm. Finally, in some cases, it is the other party's monopolization of a scarce resource and the market power he enjoys as a result which (it is claimed) renders the promisor's agreement involuntary. In each case, however, the promisor is asserting that his agreement, although deliberately given, lacked voluntariness because of the circumstances under which it was made—circumstances that in one way or another restricted his range of alternatives to a point where the promisor's choice could be said to be free in name only.[23]

The problem, of course, is to determine when the circumstances under which an agreement is given deprive it of its voluntariness in this sense. In my view, this problem is equivalent to another—the problem of determining which of the many forms of advantage-taking possible in exchange relationships are compatible with the libertarian conception of individual freedom. The latter way of stating the problem may appear to raise new and distinct issues but in fact it does not. In each of the hypothetical cases considered above, the promisee enjoys an advantage of some sort which he has attempted to exploit for his own benefit. The advantage may consist in his superior information, intellect, or judgment, in the monopoly he enjoys with regard to a particular resource, or in his possession of a powerful instrument of violence or a gift for deception. In each of these cases, the fundamental question is whether the promisee should be permitted to exploit his advantage to the detriment of the other party, or whether permitting him to do so will deprive the other party of the freedom that is necessary, from a libertarian point of view, to make his promise truly voluntary and therefore binding.[24]

The term "advantage-taking" is often used in a pejorative fashion, to refer to conduct we find morally objectionable or think the law should disallow. I mean the term to be understood in a broader sense, however, as including even those methods of gain the law allows and morality accepts (or perhaps even approves). In this broad sense, there is advantage-taking in every contractual exchange. Indeed, in mutually advantageous exchanges, there is advantage-taking by both parties. Suppose I have a cow you want, and you have a horse I want, and we agree to exchange our animals. The fact that you want my cow gives me an advantage I can exploit by insisting that you give me your horse in return. Your ownership of the horse gives you a symmetrical advantage over me. Each of us exploits the advantage we possess and—in this transaction at least—are both made better off as a result. This might seem to make my broad conception of advantage-taking empty or trivial. There is, however, an important reason for using the term in the unconventionally broad way that I do. By using the term to refer to *all* types of advantage-taking—those we tolerate as well as those we do not—attention is focused more sharply on the need to explain why the illicit methods of gain for which we normally reserve the term are thought to be objectionable.

In order to give meaningful content to the idea of voluntary exchange, a libertarian theory of contract law must provide an explanation of precisely this sort. However, although some principle or rule is needed as a basis for deciding which forms of advantage-taking should be allowed and which should not be, it is unclear what this principle or rule might be. Suppose, for example, that my neighbor threatens to shoot me unless I agree to buy his house. If there is one thing which must be treated as a condition for voluntary exchange, it is the absence of direct physical compulsion of the sort involved in this first case. But suppose that instead of threatening me with physical harm, the seller merely lies to me about the house—he tells me, for example, that water pipes inaccessibly buried beneath the basement are copper when in fact he knows them to be made of iron, an inferior material. Ought such advantage-taking be allowed?[25] While it is possible to justify advantage-taking of this sort on the grounds that only physical coercion should be disallowed, there is no good reason for making *this* distinction the decisive one. Moreover, even if one fastens on the physical nature of the advantage-taking act, explicit misrepresentation can be characterized in a way that gives it a physical character as well, for example by saying that the misrepresentation is communicated by soundwaves which stimulate an auditory response in the listener which in turn provokes a neural change that causes him to sign the contract. This may be fanciful, but it suggests that with enough imagination any form of advantage-taking can be characterized as a physical intrusion,[26] and the question of when such a characterization is appropriate cannot be answered by simply repeating that it is the physical nature of the act which makes it objectionable.

At this point, many will be tempted to acknowledge explicit misrepresentation as an illegitimate form of advantage-taking, but insist that the line be drawn there—limiting the conditions necessary for voluntary exchange to two (absence of physical coercion and fraud). Suppose, however, that the seller makes no threats and tells no lies, but does say things that, although true, are meant to encourage me to draw a false conclusion about the condition of the house and to inspect the premises less carefully than I might otherwise. (The seller tells me, for example, that the house has been inspected by an exterminator from the Acme Termite Company every six months for the last ten years, which is true, but neglects to inform me that during his last visit the exterminator discovered a termite infestation which the seller has failed to cure.) By telling me only certain things about the house, and not others, the seller intends to throw me off the track and thereby take advantage of my ignorance and naiveté. The same is true if he tells me nothing at all, but simply fails to reveal a defect he knows I am unaware of—a case of pure nondisclosure.[27]

Should this last form of advantage-taking be allowed? At this point, undoubtedly, many will be inclined to say I have only myself to blame for drawing an incorrect inference from the seller's truthful representations and for failing to take precautionary measures such as having the house inspected by an expert. But why is this a good reason for holding me to my bargain here, but not in the previous cases as well? I can, for example, protect myself against the risk that I will be forced to sign a contract at gunpoint by hiring a bodyguard to accompany me wherever I go; and I can protect myself against the danger of explicit misrepresentation by requiring the other party to take a lie detector test or, more simply, by insisting that he warrant the house to be free of pests or any other possible defect that happens to concern me. Why isn't my failure to protect myself in these cases a good reason for enforcing the agreement I have made?

In attempting to sort out these various forms of advantage-taking, a number of distinctions suggest themselves—for example, the distinction between physical and non-physical advantage-taking, or between those forms of advantage-taking that can be prevented by the victim and those that cannot. None, however, provides a principled basis for de-termining which forms of advantage-taking ought to be allowed. Each can be interpreted in different ways, yielding different results, and the distinctions themselves provide no guidance in deciding which of the competing interpretations is the right one. An independent principle of some sort is required to determine the scope and relevance of these distinctions, and consequently it is that principle, whatever it might be, rather than the distinctions themselves that explains why we ought to allow some forms of advantage-taking but not others.

C. The Principle of Paretianism

While there are many principles that might conceivably perform this function, the libertarian may be inclined to think that only one is morally acceptable. This principle, which I shall call the liberty principle, states that advantage-taking by one party to an agreement should be allowed unless it infringes the rights or liberty of the other party. The liberty principle has an appealing directness and simplicity. It does not, however, provide a satisfactory test for discriminating between acceptable and unacceptable forms of advantage-taking in the exchange process, but rather begs the question it is meant to answer.

For the liberty principle to be of any help at all, we must already know when an individual is entitled to complain that his liberty has been violated and to know this, we must know what rights he has. For example, we cannot say whether the liberty principle is violated if one person takes advantage of another by concealing valuable information in the course of an exchange, unless we have already decided that it is part of the first person's liberty that he be allowed to exploit the information he possesses in this way and not a part of the other person's liberty that he be free from such exploitation. The liberty principle does not purport to tell us what rights people actually have but assumes that we possess such knowledge independently of the principle itself.

How can we acquire the independent knowledge of rights needed to give the liberty principle meaning? Someone might claim that we can acquire such knowledge simply by looking to see what rights people have either by nature or convention. But rights cannot be ascertained in this way. Every claim concerning rights is necessarily embedded in a controversial theory: the only way to justify the claim that a person has a certain right is to argue that he does, and this means deploying a contestable theory[28] that cannot itself be verified or disproven by simply looking to see what is the case. In order to apply the liberty principle, we must already have a theory of rights. Because it does not itself supply such a theory, the liberty principle, standing alone, provides no guidance in deciding which forms of advantage-taking ought to be allowed.

If a direct appeal to the liberty principle is unhelpful, the libertarian is confronted with the problem of finding an alternative basis for distinguishing between acceptable and unacceptable forms of advantage-taking in the exchange process. A number of different principles suggest themselves, but three seem to me especially significant and I shall limit myself to these.

First, a libertarian might adopt the view that some people are simply better than others—more intelligent, beautiful, or noble—and argue that being a better person gives an individual the right to exploit his inferiors in certain ways.[29] A full elaboration of this view, which rests upon what may be called the doctrine of natural superiority, would require the following: a specification of the respects in which people differ as to their worth; a defense of the claim that worthiness is a legitimate ground for the assignment of rights and duties; and an account of the types of exploitation that can be justified by an appeal to the superiority of the exploiting party.

Second, a libertarian might attempt to justify certain forms of advantage-taking by arguing that they increase the total amount of some desired good such as happiness. Classical utilitarianism is the most familiar example of such a view; for convenience, I shall refer to the view itself as utilitarianism.[30]

Finally, a libertarian might attempt to distinguish between different forms of transactional advantage-taking by invoking the interest of the disadvantaged party himself. In some cases, it is reasonable to think that a person who has been taken advantage of in a particular way will be better off in the long run if the kind of advantage-taking in question is allowed than he would be were it prohibited. Whenever this is true, a libertarian might argue the advantage-taking should be permitted and in all other cases forbidden. I shall call this third view paretianism because of its close connection with the idea of Pareto efficiency.[31]

Each of these three principles provides an intelligible criterion for discriminating between acceptable and unacceptable forms of advantage-taking in the exchange process. Each leads to different results. All three rely upon something other than the bare idea of individual liberty and are therefore immune

from the special criticisms to which the liberty principle is subject. Only the last of these three principles, however, is consistent with the basic ethical commitments of libertarianism; if a libertarian were required to choose among the three, the only one that he could choose without abandoning his most fundamental moral beliefs would be the third.[32]

In the first place, libertarianism is a strongly egalitarian theory. According to the libertarian, all individuals are equal in what, from a moral perspective, is the most important respect—in their basic right to freedom from the interference of others. This feature of libertarianism rules out the doctrine of natural superiority as a basis for discriminating between acceptable and unacceptable forms of advantage-taking. The doctrine of natural superiority not only leads to non-egalitarian results, as may libertarianism itself, but also rests upon a notion of differential worthiness wholly incompatible with the libertarian conception of individual equality. There is no way of incorporating the doctrine of natural superiority within the framework of a libertarian theory of rights.

In addition to being strongly egalitarian, libertarianism is also an individualistic theory in the sense that it assigns a unique value to the autonomy of the individual person. Any principle, such as utilitarianism, that purports to evaluate states of affairs solely on the basis of the total amount of some good they happen to contain is capable of taking the idea of autonomy into account only indirectly; utilitarianism can give weight to the independence of individuals only insofar as their independence contributes to something else which is taken to be good in itself.[33] Given the peculiar strength of his commitment to individual autonomy—to the idea that individuals have moral "boundaries" which must be respected even if more happiness or welfare could be produced by disregarding them[34]— the libertarian must also reject utilitarianism as a basis for distinguishing between acceptable and unacceptable forms of advantage-taking. This leaves only paretianism, which states that a particular form of advantage-taking should be allowed if it works to the longrun benefit of those disadvantaged by it, but not otherwise—a principle that is neither anti-individualistic, since it does not make the sum or total of any impersonal good the touchstone of evaluation, nor anti-egalitarian.[35]

An important ambiguity in the principle of paretianism may seem to cast doubt on this claim, however. Suppose that Jim sells Fred a watch and lies to him about its condition. Should Jim be permitted to exploit Fred by deliberately defrauding him? On the assumption that paretianism is a strongly individualistic principle, one might conclude that it requires us to answer this question by considering the longrun effect of Jim's deceit on Fred's individual welfare. There are good reasons, however, for not interpreting the principle in this way. To begin with, it would probably be impossible for courts to make such highly individualized assessments, except in rare cases, and in any event, an approach of this sort would create uncertainty and deprive legal rules of their predictability. Moreover, unlike a court, a legislature must evaluate the effects of proposed rules on classes of persons rather than on particular, identifiable individuals. For these reasons, a strictly individualistic interpretation of paretianism is likely to make the principle unworkable in all but a few cases.

How should the principle be interpreted, then? Although the matter is by no means free from difficulty, one reasonable approach is to interpret paretianism as requiring only that the welfare of *most people* who are taken advantage of in a particular way be increased by the kind of advantage-taking in question.[36] If one adopts this view, in order to resolve the dispute between Jim and Fred, it is only necessary to decide whether most victims of fraud will be better off in the longrun, all things considered, if conduct such as Jim's is legally tolerated.

This interpretation of the principle of paretianism makes the principle easier to apply. At the same time, however, it appears to diminish the difference between paretianism and utilitarianism by substituting the overall welfare of a group for the welfare of a particular individual. But despite this appearance of similarity,[37] there are two related respects in which these principles remain distinguishable from one another. In the first place, paretianism and utilitarianism may lead to different results where the group of persons harmed by a particular form of advantage-taking represents a permanently distinct subset of society as a whole, since in cases of this sort, it is always possible that total welfare will increase while the welfare of the disadvantaged group declines. Assume, for example, that most people with low IQs are disadvantaged in their transactions with brighter people. Whether this kind of advantage-taking should be allowed depends entirely, for the utilitarian, on the total amount of welfare that it yields. If one adopts the principle of paretianism, on the other hand, advantage-taking by those with superior intellectual endowments can be justified only if it increases the longrun welfare of those with low IQs.

This points to a second and more fundamental difference between the two principles. The principle of paretianism ultimately rests on the notion that one person should be permitted to make himself better off at another's expense only if it is to the benefit of both that he be allowed to do so. By contrast, utilitarianism—as I use the term—is premised on the belief that more welfare is always better than less, regardless of how it is distributed. For a utilitarian, an increase in the total quantum of welfare is ethically significant in its own right; from the standpoint of paretianism, an increase of this sort has no meaning by itself. To be sure, a utilitarian may be driven to adopt paretianism as the best available method for measuring increases in total welfare,[38] but the principle of paretianism can never have independent ethical significance for the true utilitarian. Likewise, someone committed to paretianism may conclude that a simple summing of utilities is the only practical way of implementing *his* favored principle, but nevertheless reject the utilitarian notion that greater total welfare is a moral good in its own right, regardless of how it happens to be distributed among individuals. Thus, even where utilitarianism and paretianism converge to the same practical result, they do so for different reasons, arriving at a common conclusion from fundamentally different starting points.

In comparing moral principles, it is important to consider the reasons they provide for acting in certain ways, as well as the actions they require and forbid.[39] Utilitarianism and paretianism offer strikingly different justifications for permitting certain forms of advantage-taking in the exchange process. Paretianism permits only those forms of advantage-taking that work to the benefit of all concerned, a requirement rooted in the conviction that every person has an equal right not to have his own welfare reduced for the sole purpose of increasing someone else's.[40] This constraint expresses, in a powerful way, respect for the integrity of individuals, and distinguishes paretianism from every ethical theory—including utilitarianism—that treats the maximization of some impersonal good as an end in itself. Since he is committed to the idea of individual integrity, the libertarian has good reason to prefer the principle of paretianism over utilitarianism and to adopt the former principle as a basis for discriminating between acceptable and unacceptable forms of advantage-taking in exchange transactions.

D. Paretianism Applied

I want now to indicate, in a more concrete way, how the principle of paretianism can be used to give meaningful content to the idea of voluntary exchange by helping us decide which kinds of advantage-taking should be permitted and which should not. Let me begin with a relatively easy case.[41] Suppose that A owns a piece of property that, unbeknownst to A, contains a rich mineral deposit of some sort. B, a trained geologist, inspects the property (from the air, let us assume), discovers the deposit, and without disclosing what he knows, offers to buy the land from A at a price well below its true value. A agrees, and then later attempts to rescind the contract on the ground that B's failure to reveal what he knew about the property amounted to fraud. The general question here is whether buyers who have deliberately acquired superior information should be permitted to exploit their advantage by making contracts without revealing what they know or believe to be true. Except in special cases,[42] the law does not require disclosure by well-informed buyers, at least where their information is the product of a deliberate search. This rule can be defended in the following way. If B has made a deliberate investment in acquiring the information that gives him an advantage in his transaction with A, imposing a duty of disclosure will prevent him from reaping the fruits of his investment and thereby discourage others from making similar investments in the future. But this means that a smaller amount of useful geological information will be produced. As a result, the efficient allocation of land, the allocation of individual parcels to their best use, will be impaired. It is plausible to argue that this will hurt those at an informational disadvantage in particular exchanges more than they would be helped by imposing a duty of full disclosure in sale transactions such as the one involved here. For example, although imposing a duty of this sort will enable A to back out of a disadvantageous transaction with B, it will also increase the price A has to pay for oil and aluminum because the incentive to make the investment necessary to determine which pieces of land contain these resources in the first place will have been weakened as a result. Thus, a legal rule permitting B to buy A's property without disclosing its true worth arguably works to A's own benefit, since it provides a stimulus for the production of efficiency-enhancing information. This is, in any event, the kind of argument required by the principle of paretianism.

Although paretianism justifies certain types of advantage-taking,[43] it clearly rules out others. Suppose, for example, that B forces A to sell his property by threatening A with physical harm. If B's behavior does not bar enforcement of the contract, A himself may on other occasions be able to benefit from such a rule by coercing others to make agreements against their will. In the longrun, however, it is unlikely that A will be better off if physical coercion is permitted in the exchange process; as long as the means of violence are distributed in a relatively even fashion, there is no reason to think that A's gains from such a rule will exceed his losses. More importantly, a rule of this sort would give people an incentive to shift scarce resources from productive uses—uses that increase everyone's level of material well-being—to nonproductive ones (the development of more powerful weapons and better bulletproof vests) that improve no one's position but merely maintain the status quo. A legal rule permitting physical coercion in the exchange process would therefore have exactly the opposite effect of a rule permitting well-informed buyers to exploit deliberately acquired information.

The same is true of fraud (the deliberate production of misinformation).[44] If B agrees to purchase A's automobile after A has lied to him about its mechanical condition, enforcing B's agreement despite A's fraud will hurt B and benefit A. The next time, however, A may be the victim and B the successful defrauder. Once again, there is no reason to think that most people will benefit from a rule permitting fraud; indeed, this is impossible, since total gains from such a rule will exactly equal total losses. Moreover, adopting a rule of this sort would give everyone an incentive to invest in the detection of fraudulent representations. Such investments yield information, but only of a nonproductive kind. It is to everyone's advantage that resources be devoted to other uses; a rule prohibiting fraud in exchange transactions encourages precisely that result.

Of course, the principle of paretianism does not always yield so clear an answer as these cases might suggest. Suppose, for example, that A is aware of an important defect in his own property—a termite infestation, say—and merely fails to inform B of the defect's presence. A is surely exploiting his superior information at B's expense; in this respect, A's conduct is indistinguishable from B's in the situation described earlier—when B offers to buy A's property without revealing what he knows about its true value. Moreover, A's information, like B's, is productive in nature, because it reveals a fact that must be taken into account if the allocation of scarce resources is to be as efficient as possible. Unlike *B*'s information, however, *A*'s knowledge regarding the termites may be the product of casual observations made while living in the house, rather than the result of a deliberate and costly search. If so, a rule requiring *A* to disclose what he knows about the termites will have no, or only a small, effect on the production of such information. Moreover, a rule of this sort will reduce *B*'s own inspection costs—which are likely to be higher than *A*'s, given *B*'s unfamiliarity with the property.[45] Assuming that most people will be buyers about as often as they are sellers, one may perhaps tentatively conclude that their gains from a legal rule requiring sellers to disclose substantial, nonvisible defects will exceed the occasional losses they suffer as a result.

It does not follow, of course, that most people will be made better off if sellers of all sorts are required to disclose defects of every kind. Beyond a certain point, a rule requiring disclosure may have significant and undesirable incentive effects, and in some cases, the buyer's own search costs are likely to be so low as to trivialize the benefits he receives from disclosure. Even in this difficult area, however, the principle of paretianism provides guidance by indicating the kind of argument that must be made in order to justify any particular disclosure rule, whether it be a broad or narrow one. . . .[46]

G. Advantage-taking and Differences in Wealth

At this point, most libertarians would probably respond by claiming that I have shown the libertarian theory of contract law to be a theory of distributive justice in only a limited or perhaps even trivial respect. While conceding that the notion of voluntary exchange cannot be given meaning without specifying how rights to transactional advantages *in the exchange process itself* are to be distributed, a libertarian might argue that this can be done without attaching any importance whatsoever to the distributional *consequences* of those exchanges in which there has been no impermissible advantage-taking. So long as there has been no advantage-taking of this sort, he might argue, agreements should be enforced regardless of their impact on the distribution of wealth in society. On this view, contractual limitations of the sort mentioned at the be-

ginning of the Article—restrictions on interest rates, minimum wage laws, and nondisclaimable warranties—would be wholly unjustified if one assumes their purpose is not to insure voluntariness in exchange transactions, but to alter the distribution of wealth that results from the free exchange of property itself. In this way, a libertarian might concede that a limited theory of distributive justice is needed to explicate the notion of voluntary exchange, yet still maintain that his view is meaningfully different from that of anyone who believes it appropriate to manipulate the private law of contracts in order to achieve a more desirable distribution of wealth in society.

This position can be interpreted in one of two different ways. First, the claim may be that differences in wealth created or maintained by contractual exchange need not be justified by invoking the same principle of distributive justice, whatever it might be, that we appeal to in justifying various forms of advantage-taking in exchange relationships. On this view, differences in wealth that result from the free exchange of property are not to be thought of as requiring any justification at all, unlike the assignment of rights to transactional advantages in the exchange process; while the latter poses a problem of distributive justice, the former does not. I shall call this interpretation of the position the strong interpretation.

A second, weaker interpretation is also possible. Someone defending the position in question can be understood as claiming either that disparities in wealth which result from the free exchange of property *are* justified, on the same basis that certain forms of transactional advantage-taking are, or that existing disparities in wealth are *not* justified but should be corrected in some other way than by manipulating the rules for private exchange. I call this second interpretation weak because it accepts what the first interpretation questions—the claim that differences in wealth resulting from free exchange stand as much in need of justification as the exploitation of differential advantages in the exchange process itself.

In my view, the first of these two interpretations must be rejected since it rests upon an essentially arbitrary distinction between different kinds of wealth and the advantages associated with them, and fails to recognize that disparities in wealth resulting from one transaction become an advantage in the next. If we ask whether an individual should be permitted to exploit his superior information or intelligence in transactions with others, the answer—at least the answer the law gives[47]—is "sometimes and under certain circumstances." In order to explain why the possessor of these valuable resources should be allowed to exploit them in some ways but not others, appeal must be made to a principle of distributive justice. The same ought to be true if we ask whether someone with a substantial bank account should be allowed to take advantage of his superior wealth in transacting with other, less wealthy individuals. In the first place, if we define a person's wealth as comprising the sum total of revenue-generating assets which the law permits him to exploit for his own benefit, his wealth will include things like information, intelligence and physical strength, as well as dollars in the bank. If we prohibit someone from exploiting potentially valuable information or skills (for example, the skill of deception) we thereby decrease his wealth just as surely as if we were to take some money from his bank account and burn it or transfer it into a common fund. Second, it is wrong to think of money—wealth in the narrow sense—as anything other than a transactional advantage, an advantage which gives its possessor a leg up in the exchange process. Money enables an individual to acquire other transactional advantages (for example, superior information), to withstand pressures that might otherwise force him to make agreements on less favorable terms, to outbid competitors, etc.; other things equal, the more money an individual has, the better he is likely to do in his transactions with other persons. In fact, money not only gives its possessor a transactional advantage: unlike intelligence or physical strength, it gives him nothing else. A sailor stranded alone on a desert island may benefit from his physical and mental abilities; unless he has someone to transact with, however, the money in his pocket does him no good at all.

For these reasons, no one should be allowed to exploit his financial resources in transactions with others to any greater extent than he should be allowed to exploit his superior intelligence, strength or information. It is true that each of these represents wealth of a different kind and gives its possessor a distinct advantage in transacting with others. But it is unclear why any importance should be attached to differences of this sort. If one kind of advantage-taking—that based on superior information, for example—must be justified by showing that it is consistent with a particular conception of distributive justice, other kinds of advantage-taking, including those attributable to inequalities of a financial sort, should be justified in the same way. It is simply arbitrary to assert that some forms of advantage-taking must be justified but others need not be.

It does not follow, of course, that the rich should be forbidden to exploit their financial power in transacting with the poor. Whether and to what extent they should will depend upon the principle of distributive justice one adopts and factual details relevant to the principle's application. There is, however, no *a priori* reason for regarding a rule of contract law that is intended to reduce inequalities of wealth (in the narrow sense) as any more objectionable than rules prohibiting fraud or requiring the disclosure of certain kinds of information, which also redistribute wealth (in the broad sense) from one group of individuals to another. Although there may be a sound reason for opposing a rule of contract law whose purpose is to shift resources from the rich to the poor,[48] the reason cannot be that the special financial advantages enjoyed by the rich fall outside the scope of the principle of distributive justice that controls the assignment of rights to other kinds of transactional advantages. Therefore, the only sensible interpretation of the libertarian's position is the second or weak interpretation: when a libertarian asserts that contract law should not be used to redistribute wealth from the rich to the poor, he must be claiming either that existing inequalities of wealth *are* justified (for example, on utilitarian or paretianist grounds) or that contract law is an unsuitable instrument for correcting those inequalities which are unjustifiable. Stating the libertarian position in this way, however, eliminates the most fundamental difference between liberal and libertarian theories of contract law.

II. Taxation and Contractual Regulation

A. Two Methods of Redistribution

A liberal theory of society, as I am using the term here, is one that approves forced redistributions of wealth, at least up to a point, as a means of achieving a fair division of material resources among the members of society. All theories of this sort are distinguishable from libertarianism, which regards compulsory transfers aimed at achieving distributive fairness as a kind of theft. For the purposes of this argument, a liberal theory of society may be defined as one that: 1) assumes there is some characteristic or attribute of individuals in virtue of which they may be said to deserve a share of society's wealth and purports to describe the pattern of holdings that would result if this principle of desert were the sole or at least the primary basis for the distribution of material resources; 2) treats this ideal pattern as an evaluative standard by which to assess the fairness of the distribution that actually obtains in any given society; and 3) assigns to the state the task of bringing the existing distribution of wealth into conformity with the ideal one.[49]

There are, of course, many different theories that fit this general description, some of which may be regarded as illiberal by the proponents of others. Disagreements of this sort reflect the fact that two persons who both accept the legitimacy of forced redistribution may nevertheless endorse different principles of desert and therefore disagree as to which pattern of holdings would be an ideally just one. Such disagreements are often quite sharp and I do not mean to minimize their philosophical importance. In what follows, however, I shall ignore these differences and continue to use the term "liberal theory" in the broad sense defined above. There is significant agreement, among the proponents of otherwise distinguishable conceptions of distributive justice, regarding the appropriate *method* of achieving a fair division of wealth in society and it is this point of agreement that I am especially interested in challenging here.[50]

It will be useful to begin by contrasting two different methods for redistributing wealth. One method is taxation. To illustrate how taxation works, assume that every individual in society is given his fair share of society's resources, and then left free to transact with others on whatever terms he wishes. The initial assignment of shares will necessarily conform to a pattern of some sort, the pattern itself depending upon one's theory of distributive justice. Over time, however, the overall pattern of individual holdings is bound to diverge from the original and ideal one. As both critics and defenders of liberalism have pointed out,[51] this divergence is the unintended consequence of numerous private transactions between different individuals, all attempting to advance their self-interest in legitimate ways. However, when the resulting array of individual holdings is inconsistent with the principle of desert underlying the original distribution of wealth, it must be modified by a corrective redistribution. If taxation is adopted as a method of redistribution, those who now have more than they deserve will be required to make an ap-

propriate payment to the state, and the funds collected in this fashion will be transferred to those whose holdings are unjustly small. In this way, the original pattern of holdings can be re-established, and distributive justice preserved.

A second method for achieving distributive justice involves a more direct regulation of the terms on which individuals are allowed to transact with one another. I shall call this method of redistribution contractual regulation. To illustrate, suppose once again that everyone is given his fair share of society's resources. This time, however, instead of leaving people free to transact as they please and imposing a periodic tax on their wealth, an attempt is made to preserve the fairness of the original distribution of resources by restricting the terms on which individuals are permitted to alter their holdings through voluntary exchange—by forbidding certain transactions and, perhaps, by requiring others. Minimum wage laws, for example, impose restrictions of this sort: such laws attempt to insure a fair distribution of wealth between workers and employers by specifying, in part, the terms on which workers may contract to sell their labor.

As between these two methods at redistribution—taxation and the direct contractual regulation of individual transactions—many liberal theorists appear to have a pronounced preference for the first. For example, both in his book and in subsequent articles, John Rawls insists on a distinction between what he terms the "basic structure" of society, on the one hand, and "rules applying directly to individuals and associations and to be followed by them in particular transactions" on the other.[52] According to Rawls, the principles of distributive justice must be considered in designing the institutions that comprise the basic structure of society, including, in particular, the tax and transfer system. The function of the basic structure, on Rawls's view, is to establish and maintain a framework of entitlements that satisfies the principles of distributive justice, within which individuals remain free to pursue their own ends through voluntary transactions with others, "secure in the knowledge," as he puts it, "that elsewhere in the social system the necessary corrections to preserve background justice are being made."[53] Rawls of course recognizes that there must be rules governing private transactions between individuals, but he argues that these transactional rules should be "framed to leave individuals . . . free to act effectively in pursuit of their ends and without excessive constraints."[54] In Rawls's theory, rules of this sort are assigned only a facilitative role: their proper function is to keep the exchange process running smoothly by eliminating coercion and reducing the transaction costs associated with the process itself.[55] It is Rawls's view that rules governing private exchange between individuals, unlike the tax laws, should not be manipulated to help achieve a fair distribution of wealth among the members of society. More strongly, it seems to be Rawls's view that the law of contracts *cannot* be used in this way without illegitimately infringing the right of individuals to pursue their own conception of the good, free from excessive governmental interference. At several points, Rawls speaks of a "division of labor" between "the basic structure [of society] and the rules applying directly to particular transactions,"[56] the implication being that the distinctive distributive function of one is no business of the other.

Rawls's preference for taxation as a method of preserving "background justice" and his reluctance to view the private law of contracts as an equally appropriate vehicle for redistributing wealth reflect an attitude shared by many liberal thinkers.[57] Is it possible to justify this preference for taxation and the non-distributive conception of contract law that it entails?

One argument that is sometimes made by liberal theorists in support of a non-distributive conception of contract law may be dismissed at the outset. Suppose we have settled on a principle for evaluating the fairness of different wealth distributions. The argument I have in mind states that it would be wrong to assess particular transactions and to resolve the disputes arising out of them by appealing directly to the distributional principle we have chosen.[58] There is no reason to think that judges or anyone else can correctly assess the distributional consequences of particular transactions; more importantly, if every transaction could be invalidated for its failure to conform to the principle in question, individual expectations would be frustrated and voluntary arrangements rendered insecure. Instead, the argument goes, transactional disputes should be decided by applying the relevant rules of law in a formalistic fashion, that is, without regard to the distributional consequences of the decision itself, and the redistribution of wealth should be left to the tax system instead.

This argument rests upon a confusion. Even if one agrees, for the reasons indicated, that in particular cases judges and others charged with responsibility for policing individual transactions should apply established legal rules regardless of their distributional consequences, it does not follow that distributional effects should also be ignored in the initial design of a system of transactional rules or in the choice of new rules to supplement or amend those that already exist. It is one thing to evaluate individual transactions from a distributive perspective; it is another to evaluate the rules governing transactions from the same point of view.[59] Naturally, if one adopts the latter approach, there may be individual cases in which the distributive purpose of a particular rule is frustrated rather than advanced by its application. But this is the inevitable consequence of having a system of adjudication based upon generally applicable norms rather than ad hoc determinations, and does not provide a reason for ignoring distributive considerations in the original choice or amendment of these transactional norms themselves. If we ought to design rules of contract law without regard to their distributive effect, it must be for some reason other than the one I have just stated.

B. Redistribution, Neutrality and Individual Freedom

Two further arguments, based on moral considerations, may be offered for preferring taxation to contractual regulation as a means of redistributing wealth, and it is these I now want to consider. First, it can be argued that unlike taxation, contractual regulation discriminates between different pursuits by prohibiting some forms of exchange but not others, and is therefore inconsistent with the view, central to most liberal theories, that the state should remain neutral between the aims and activities of its citizens, so far as possible. Second, it can also be argued that taxation leaves more room for individual freedom than does a system of regulation that attempts to insure distributive justice by manipulating the rules of private exchange.

These two claims lie at the heart of the liberal preference for taxation. What do they purport to establish? On the one hand, each claim can be understood as asserting that taxation and regulation have invariant characteristics which necessarily make any tax scheme more neutral and less intrusive than a system of regulatory control designed to achieve the same end. If this were true, one would always be justified in choosing taxation as a method for redistributing wealth. On the other hand, these same two claims can be understood, in a more modest fashion, as asserting only that circumstantial factors, which vary from one situation to the next, often make taxation the better of the two methods. If one adopts the latter view, any preference for taxation will be contingent on contextual considerations which may (and I think do) sometimes warrant the pursuit of distributional goals through a regulatory scheme instead. In my judgment, it is the latter view which is the correct one: there is nothing about taxation that necessarily gives it greater neutrality or makes it less restrictive of individual liberty than contractual regulation, although in some cases a tax scheme may be preferable for both reasons.

Consider, first, the question of neutrality: is taxation, by its nature, a more neutral method of redistribution than contractual regulation? Suppose that a fair distribution of wealth could most easily be achieved by regulating or even prohibiting a particular class of transactions not thought to be objectionable in their own right—for example, those involving the sale of a few basic goods such as food and shelter. Even if it were the least costly way of reaching our distributional goal, a regulatory regime of this sort might be rejected on the ground that it unfairly discriminates against one particular group of citizens—those who would benefit, financially or otherwise, if the transactions in question were left unregulated—by imposing the full burden of the distributive scheme on them alone. More generally, in evaluating alternative methods for redistributing wealth, it is always necessary to consider how broadly the burdens of redistribution are spread: if a particular method imposes these costs only on some of those who ought to bear them, this by itself counts against adopting the method in question.

This general consideration, however, applies to taxation and contractual regulation alike, and does not warrant a universal preference for the former method. Any workable scheme for redistributing wealth is bound to discriminate unfairly in favor of some individuals or activities. This is true even of the simplest income tax, which gives an unjustified advantage to those who have more than they deserve but are nevertheless able to accomplish their ends in ways that do not produce taxable income. A selective income tax (such as the one we actually have) that applies only to the income from certain types of transactions or a sales tax on specific items designed to finance a system of redistributive transfer payments are more obvious examples of discriminatory taxes. But just as taxes vary in their neutrality, so do contractual regulations: a law re-

quiring bakers to sell their bread at a fixed price spreads the burdens of redistribution less widely than a law requiring all employers to pay their workers a minimum wage. Neutrality is a property that each method of redistribution may possess to varying degrees, and therefore even though we should always prefer less discriminatory arrangements to more discriminatory ones, this does not mean that we ought in every case to choose taxation as the appropriate means for redistributing wealth. In any particular instance, whether taxation is the least discriminatory way of achieving a given distributional end will depend upon the circumstances and the types of taxation and contractual regulation that are being compared. The relative neutrality of these two methods cannot be ascertained in advance since it is not a function of anything inherent in their nature.

Now consider the second moral argument for preferring taxation to contractual regulation as a method of redistribution—that taxation is less restrictive of individual liberty. To begin with, this may be understood as a claim about the frequency of intervention required by these alternative methods of redistribution. While taxation requires only a periodic interference in the lives of individuals, the direct regulation of transactions appears to necessitate continuous state involvement in individual affairs. Since it is sensible to prefer less frequent intrusions to more frequent ones, this might seem a good reason for preferring taxation as a method of redistribution.

This argument is unconvincing, however. In the first place, some taxes (sales taxes, for example) *do* apply continuously, to every individual transaction, and we do not think them objectionable for this reason alone. The argument is plausible only if we think of every redistributive tax as being like a periodic tax on income. We are tempted to do this, of course, because the income tax (unlike most other taxes) has an explicit redistributive purpose. It would be a mistake, however, to think that non-income taxes cannot perform a similar redistributive function: a special sales tax on luxury items might be an example.

Second, even if a tax is only applied at periodic intervals, it represents a continuous interference in the lives of individuals in precisely the sense suggested above. Suppose, for example, that the state imposes a progressive income tax that must be paid annually and that treats all income in the same way, regardless of its source. Throughout the year, every income-generating transaction that an individual makes is subject to the tax in question; the tax casts a shadow, as it were, over the whole of his economic life. Just as a minimum wage law prevents workers and employers from making certain kinds of contracts, an annual income tax restricts the contractual freedom of those subject to it. The existence of such a tax makes it impossible for anyone to form a contract that does not have as one of its implied terms a requirement that both parties share their income from the contract with the state. In many transactions, this implied requirement is also likely to affect other aspects of the parties' relationship, limiting their choice of additional terms, and even dictating the very structure of the transaction.[60]

All of this makes it wrong, in my view, to maintain that a periodic tax on income is a less frequently intrusive method of redistribution than the direct regulation of individual transactions. At this point, it might be objected that an income tax is in any case less *deeply* intrusive even if the restrictions it imposes apply continuously. Taxation appears to be less intrusive because it only takes money from people, leaving them free to arrange their affairs in the way that best realizes other, non-pecuniary ends. Regulation, by contrast, limits the sorts of transactions individuals may arrange for themselves and thus seems more restrictive of personal liberty.[61] Thus, one might argue, while regulation forbids people from doing certain sorts of things, a tax scheme merely requires those subject to the tax to share with the state the fruits of their voluntary transactions with other individuals.

This apparent difference in the restrictiveness of these two methods of redistribution is illusory, however. In the first place, it is misleading to say that contractual regulation forbids people from doing things but a tax scheme does not. A tax on income, for example, forbids people to keep what they have earned in income-producing transactions without making an appropriate payment to the state. If an individual finds this prohibition too restrictive, he can always shift his resources, including his time and personal labor, to activities which do not produce income, or which produce income and other goods—such as leisure—in differing proportions. By the same token, if the law requires that a certain class of agreements be made on terms specified by the state, individuals making such agreements remain free to abandon them in favor of other, unregulated transactions. In either case, of course, those subject to the tax or regulatory limitation may remain free to avoid it only in a theoretical sense: in an exchange economy, most of us must earn income in order to survive, and an employer who wants to avoid the impact of a law fixing the minimum compensation he must pay his workers can do so only by going out of business. In my view, however, this underscores the similarity—not the difference—of taxation and contractual regulation as methods of redistribution, and casts doubt on the claim that one is more restrictive of individual liberty than the other. . . .

C. Efficiency and Administrative Cost

Of course, it might be the case that taxation is invariably a more efficient and administratively simpler way of redistributing wealth, and should therefore be preferred to contractual regulation on this ground alone. This claim may be understood in two different ways. First, someone making the claim may be asserting that contractual regulation, unlike taxation, is almost always counterproductive in the sense that it leaves its intended beneficiaries worse off than they would otherwise be. This is an argument frequently made, for example, with regard to minimum wage and rent control laws.[62] If a landlord can only charge his tenants some statutorily-fixed amount, the argument goes, he will have an incentive to reduce maintenance and take his property out of the rental market altogether, to the disadvantage of renters or at least poor renters. This may be true but it does not show the alleged superiority of taxation as a method of redistribution. If we impose a tax on rental income and do not restrict the terms on which landlords are allowed to rent, rents will rise accordingly, again to the disadvantage of the poor.[63]

Naturally, it is irrational to adopt any redistributive scheme if it leaves its intended beneficiaries worse off than they would otherwise be. This is a general requirement, however, that applies to redistributive arrangements of all sorts. In my view, it does not support a blanket preference for taxation. Even if contractual regulation often hurts those it is meant to help, there is no reason to think that taxation is not frequently counterproductive as well. This question is an empirical one which must be resolved on a case-by-case basis, in the light of detailed information about the circumstances likely to influence the effectiveness of each method of redistribution.

The claim that taxation is more efficient than contractual regulation can also be understood as a claim about their comparative administrative costs. Even if taxation is on the whole equally restrictive of individual freedom, and has equally undesirable incentive effects, one can argue that tax schemes are by their nature easier to administer and therefore less costly than regulatory arrangements designed to achieve the same end. But this argument, too, is unconvincing. Suppose, for example, that a particular racial group has in the past been discriminated against in both the housing and employment markets, as a result of which the group currently has an undeservedly small share of society's wealth. One way of improving the group's material circumstances is to impose restrictions on the exchange process in both markets by forbidding employers and those who sell or rent real property to discriminate on the basis of race. Alternatively, one might attempt to accomplish the same end without contractual regulation of any sort, through an appropriate set of taxes and subsidies. For example, employers who hire members of the group might be rewarded by a reduction in their taxes, and group members might themselves be given whatever additional funds they need to overcome the prejudice of landlords and sellers and bid scarce housing resources away from nonmembers.[64] In this case, however, reliance on the tax system as a means of redistributing wealth is likely to entail much higher costs of administration than its regulatory counterpart. It is plausible to think that at least up to a point, the group's material prospects can most easily be improved by imposing a few simple restrictions on the contractual rights of those whose past discrimination has created the present inequity.

More generally, contractual regulation always has at least *one* advantage over taxation from an administrative point of view. Under a redistributive tax scheme, wealth must first be collected by the state and then redistributed to the beneficiaries of the tax. Each of these two steps has administrative costs. By contrast, if a redistributive restriction on contractual freedom achieves its intended purpose, it causes a direct transfer of wealth from one group to another without any mediation by the state. Other things being equal, this means a reduction in administrative costs.

Of course, other things are *not* always equal. There are additional administrative costs associated with any redistributive scheme, including, in particular, the cost of enforcing it, and these costs will sometimes be sufficiently high under a regulatory arrangement to offset whatever administrative advantage such an arrangement might have.[65] It is unlikely that this will always be the case, however. Is there reason to think, for example, that a minimum wage law will be more expensive to enforce than a tax on income (designed to benefit the working poor) which relies on self-reporting by individuals subject to the tax? In either case, some of those burdened by the redistributive scheme will attempt to circumvent it by concealing the details of their transactions with others, and in both cases, preventive measures must be adopted which make concealment of this sort more difficult. There is, however, no *a priori* basis for believing that one scheme will be more costly to police than the other, at least if the provisions contained in both schemes are equally simple or complex. Considerations of administrative cost may justify efforts to simplify any redistributive method one adopts, but they do not warrant a blanket preference for taxation. Here, too, circumstantial factors will be decisive—dictating in some cases the choice of a tax system, in others the imposition of restrictions on exchange, and in many a mix of the two. Like predictions regarding incentive effects, considerations of administrative cost almost certainly favor the use of different redistributive methods in different situations.

Conclusion

If one believes it is morally acceptable for the state to forcibly redistribute wealth from one group to another, the only question that remains is how the redistribution should be accomplished. I have described two methods of redistributing wealth, taxation and the regulatory control of private transactions, and have argued that the choice between them ought to be made on the basis of contextual considerations that are likely to vary from one situation to the next.

Both methods may be more or less neutral in effect and both are costly to administer. Each necessarily imposes limitations on individual liberty and, on occasion, has incentive effects that make its adoption irrational. These are considerations we must always keep in view in choosing between the two methods, but they do not invariably dictate the same choice: instead, they are likely to suggest that sometimes one method, sometimes the other, most often, perhaps, a mix of the two, is the best way of achieving whatever distributional goal we have set for ourselves. I have attempted to show (admittedly, in a casual way) that a blanket preference for taxation is unwarranted, and that contractual regulation will on occasion be the least intrusive and most efficient way of redistributing wealth to those who have a legitimate claim to a larger share of society's resources. If I am right in thinking this is so, distributive considerations should be permitted to influence our choice of contract rules, as circumstances dictate, and should not be flatly excluded from the domain of private exchange for what are alleged to be principled reasons.

I would like to conclude by returning briefly to the problem of liberty and fairness. I have argued that distributive fairness can only be achieved, by taxation or contractual regulation, at some sacrifice in individual liberty. This claim reflects what I believe is the core of truth in Nozick's assertion[66] that the implementation of any patterned conception of justice is bound to require interference in people's lives. As I have suggested, however, the conflict between these values is not itself a reason for abandoning liberalism and embracing libertarianism, nor is it a reason for endorsing a non-distributive conception of contract law. But the conflict does present any liberal theory with a central and difficult challenge—the challenge of elaborating a reasoned basis for reconciling the claims of liberty and fairness, without abandoning either. The measure of success achieved by a liberal theory of society will depend, in large part, upon the extent to which it is able to avoid arbitrariness at just this point.

----

1. *See* 1 A. Corbin, *Contracts* 2 (1963); *cf.* U.C.C. § 1-201(11) (1972) ("'Contract' means the total legal obligation which results from the parties' agreement. . . .")

2. *See, e.g.,* G. Tullock, *The Logic of the Law* 47 (1971) (one function of contract law is to save parties inconvenience of drafting very long agreements by providing rules of interpretation); Farnsworth, *Disputes Over Omission in Contracts,* 68 *Colum. L. Rev.* 860, 860 n.2 (1968) (court, having determined a contract exists, cannot refuse to apply it even in case for which parties did not expressly provide); *cf.* U.C.C. §§ 2-310, 2-511(1) (1972) (prescribing certain conditions to be considered part of all contracts "unless otherwise agreed" by parties).

3. *See, e.g.,* O. Holmes, *The Common Law* 227 (M. Howe ed. 1963); Farnsworth, *Legal Remedies for Breach of Contract,* 70 *Colum. L. Rev.* 1145, 1147 (1970). In recent years, a number of writers have advocated an economic approach to the problem of defining the appropriate remedies for breach. *See, e.g.,* Barton, *The Economic Basis of Damages for Breach of Contract,* 1 *J. Legal Stud.* 277 (1972); Priest, *Breach and Remedy for the Tender of Nonconforming Goods Under the Uniform Commercial Code: An Economic Approach,* 91 *Harv. L. Rev.* 960 (1978).

4. *See, e.g.,* Ackerman, *Regulating Slum Housing Markets on Behalf of the Poor: Of Housing Codes, Housing Subsidies and Income Redistribution Policy,* 80 *Yale L.J.* 1093, 1098 (1973) (housing codes, if properly enforced, can play important role in "war on poverty"); Kennedy, *Form and Substance in Private Law Adjudication,* 89 *Harv. L. Rev.* 1685, 1778 (1976) (contract law an "ideal context" for judicial task of creating "altruistic order"); Michelman, *Norms and Normativity in the Economic Theory of Law,* 62 *Minn. L. Rev.* 1015, 1016–37 (1978) (housing-code regulation of rental contracts justifiable as redistributive measure even if not demonstrably "efficient" in economic sense).

5. *See, e.g.,* Conn. Gen. Stat. § 37-4 (1979); *N.Y. Banking Law* § 173-1 (McKinney 1971).

6. *Javins v. First Nat'l Realty Corp.,* 428 F.2d 1071, 1079–82 (D.C. Cir.), *cert. denied,* 400 U.S. 925 (1970) (housing lease includes implied warranty of habitability).

7. *See,* 29 U.S.C. § 206(a)(1) (1976).

8. *See* F. Hayek, *The Constitution of Liberty* 93–102, 133–61 (1961) (redistribution of wealth restricts liberty and inappropriately attempts to align compensation with moral worth); R. Nozick, *Anarchy, State and Utopia* 140–53, 167–74 (1974) (property rights, established by principles of acquisition and transfer, should be inviolate); Buchanan, *Political Equality and Private Property: The Distributional Paradox,* in *Markets and Morals* 69–84 (G. Dworkin, G. Bennett, & P. Brown eds. 1977) (individual freedom inconsistent with forced economic equality); Epstein, *Unconscionability: A Critical Reappraisal,* 18 *J. L. & Econ.* 293, 293–94 (1975) (contract law provides individuals with a "sphere of influence" in which they are not required to justify their activity to the state).

9. *See* C. Fried, *Right and Wrong* 143–50 (1978); J. Rawls, *A Theory of Justice* 87–88, 274–79 (1971); Grey, *Property and Need: The Welfare State and Theories of Distributive Justice,* 28 *Stan. L. Rev.* 877, 890 n.38 (1976); Rawls, *The Basic Structure as Subject,* in *Values and Morals* 47, 54–55 (A. Golman & J. Kim eds. 1978) [hereinafter cited as *Basic Structure*]; C. DeMuth, Regulatory Costs and the "Regulatory Budget" 9 (Dec. 1979) (Discussion Paper, Faculty Project on Regulation, John F. Kennedy School of Government, Harvard University). *But cf.* Dworkin, *Liberalism,* in *Public and Private Morality* 133 (S. Hampshire ed. 1978) (preference for redistribution by taxation rather than regulation not essential to liberalism).

10. *See, e.g.,* R. Nozick, *supra* note 8, at 172.

11. *See, e.g., Basic Structure, supra* note 9, at 55, 65.

12. *Compare id.* at 54–55 (fraud example) *with* R. Nozick, *supra* note 8, at 150 (same).

13. *See, e.g.,* Epstein, *supra* note 8, at 293–95; *Basic Structure, supra* note 9, at 65.

14. *See* J. Rawls, *supra* note 9, at 60, 83, 302–03 (difference principle states that inequalities should be "arranged so that they are both to the greatest benefit of the least advantaged . . . and attached to offices and positions open to all").

15. The distinction between actions that violate a person's rights and those that merely reduce his welfare is developed in R. Nozick, *supra* note 8, at 57–84.

16. *See id.* at 153–55.

17. *See generally* Nozick, *Coercion,* in *Philosophy, Science, and Method, Essays in Honor of Ernest Nagel* (1969).

18. *See, e.g., Faber v. Sweet Style Mfg. Corp.,* 242 N.Y.S.2d 763, 40 Misc. 2d 212 (1963) (plaintiff claimed to suffer from manic-depressive psychosis).

19. *See, e.g., Schupp v. Davey Tree Expert Co.,* 235 Mich. 268, 209 N.W. 85 (1926) (plaintiff signed contract after being assured he would not be bound by its terms).

20. *See, e.g., Hackley v. Headley,* 45 Mich. 569, 8 N.W. 511 (1881) (plaintiff, unable to afford to sue for amount due him under contract, accepted note for lesser amount and gave receipt for full balance due).

21. *See, e.g., Sherwood v. Walker,* 66 Mich. 568, 33 N.W. 919 (1887) (sale of cow rescinded where the animal, assumed by both parties to be barren, later proved otherwise): *Obde v. Schlemeyer,* 56 Wash. 2d 449, 353 P.2d 672 (1960) (seller of home under duty to disclose termite infestation). For a theoretical discussion of the scope of the seller's duty to disclose, see Kronman, *Mistake, Disclosing Information, and the Law of Contracts,* 7 *J. Legal Stud.* 1 (1978).

22. Contracts of adhesion are standardized contracts characteristically used by large firms in every transaction for products or services of a certain kind. The use of such contracts can have profound implications for ordinary notions of freedom of contract:

> The weaker party, in need of the goods or services, is frequently not in a position to shop around for better terms, either because the author of the contract has a monopoly (natural or artificial) or because all competitors use the same clauses. His contractual intention is but a subjection more or less voluntary to terms dictated by the stronger party, terms whose consequences are often understood only in a vague way, if at all.

Kessler, *Contracts of Adhesion—Some Thoughts About Freedom of Contract,* 43 Colum. L. Rev. 629, 632 (1943). For a more recent discussion of adhesion contracts, see Leff, *Unconscionability and the Code—the Emperor's New Clause,* 115 U. Pa. L. Rev. 485, 504–08 (1967).

23. *Cf.* Scanlon, *Nozick on Rights, Liberty, and Property,* 6 *Phil. & Pub. Affairs* 3, 17 (1976) (idea of consent implies that choice occurs against some background of alternatives).

24. *Cf. id.* at 19 (adequate conceptions of "consent" and "freedom" would not legitimate loss of control over one's life resulting from unequal bargaining power).

25. This kind of advantage-taking does not differ significantly from deception that does not involve a spoken lie. Suppose that my neighbor makes no threats and tells no lies but merely covers over evidence of an existing termite infestation so completely that even an expert will now be unable to discover their presence in the house. *See DeJoseph v. Zambelli,* 392 Pa. 24, 139 A.2d 644 (1958). If I agree to buy the house after having had it inspected by an exterminator, should I be released from my agreement when the termites later make themselves known? It is difficult to see what reason there could be for not disallowing this form of advantage-talking if explicit misrepresentation is forbidden, other than the fact here the deception is accomplished without a spoken lie. But this reason is hardly a good one since the seller has done things which are, in any meaningful sense, fully the equivalent of a deliberately uttered falsehood. So either it was a mistake to disallow one form of advantage-taking, or it is a mistake to permit the other: they ought to stand or fall together.

26. For an ingenious effort to assimilate verbal influence to physical action, see Epstein, *A Theory of Strict Liability,* 2 J. *Legal Stud.* 151, 172–74 (1973). According to Professor Epstein, defendants whose words frighten someone may thereby commit the tort of assault. If the frightened person suffers injury attributable to fright, or injures someone else in an attempt to flee, his reactions are not "volitional" on Professor Epstein's view, and should therefore be regarded as the physical acts of the defendant.

27. In many jurisdictions, a seller is now required by law to disclose the presence of termites in a dwelling, despite the buyer's failure to make inquiries. *See, e.g., Williams v. Benson,* 3 Mich. App. 9, 141 N.W.2d 650 (1966); *Cohen v. Blessing,* 259 S.C. 400, 192 S.E.2d 204 (1972); *Obde v. Schlemeyer,* 56 Wash. 2d 449, 353 P.2d 672 (1960).

28. My argument here is that individual liberty is an "essentially contested concept," as that term is defined by W. B. Gallie. *See* Gallie, *Essentially Contested Concepts,* 56 *Proc. Aristotelian Soc'y* 167, 167–68 (1956). According to Gallie's formulation, a concept should be considered "essentially contestable" when it is evaluative as well as descriptive and has such diverse criteria of applicability that analysis of ordinary usage yields no single, preferred definition. The question which is the "best" definition is thus open to argument. The libertarian's failure to provide such an argument for his definition of individual liberty is criticized in Scanlon, *supra* note 23, at 3. For useful discussions of the disputable meaning of abstract concepts, see R. Dworkin, *Taking Rights Seriously* 134–35 (1977) (distinguishing concepts from "conceptions" offered as elucidations of them); S. Hampshire, *Thought and Action* 230–31 (1959) (disputes about boundaries necessarily involve disputes about host of connected notions).

29. *See* F. Nietzsche, *The Will to Power* §§ 901–902, 926 (Vintage ed. 1968).

30. For an energetic defense and an equally spirited critique of utilitarianism, see J. Smart & B. Williams, *Utilitarianism: For and Against* (1973).

31. Principles similar to paretianism have been discussed in connection with a range of legal problems. *See, e.g.,* C. Fried, *An Anatomy of Values* 187–91 (1970) ("risk pool" concept in tort law); Epstein, *Nuisance Law: Corrective Justice and its Utilitarian Constraints,* 8 *J. Legal Stud.* 49, 77–78 (1979) (implicit in-kind compensation in nuisance law); Michelman, *Property, Utility, and Fairness: Comments on the Ethical Foundations of "Just Compensation" Law,* 80 *Harv. L. Rev.* 1165, 1194–96, 1222–24 (1967) (distribution of longrun benefits and losses in eminent domain law); Polinsky, *Probabilistic Compensation Criteria,* 86 *Q.J. Econ.* 407, 420–21 (1972) (paretian criterion defined in terms of longrun probabilities); Posner, *The Ethical and Political Basis of the Efficiency Norm in Common Law Adjudication* (forthcoming in 8 *Hofstra L. Rev.* (1980)) (*ex ante* compensation). For a discussion of the ethical implications of the Pareto principle, see Coleman, *Efficiency, Exchange and Auction: Philosophic Aspects of the Economic Approach to Law* (forthcoming in 68 *Calif. L. Rev.* (1980)).

32. Libertarians therefore face the following choice: show that the liberty principle does in fact yield a determinate solution to the problem of specifying which forms of advantage-taking are legitimate; acknowledge the vacuousness of the liberty principle but argue that some other principle, different from the three I have considered, is the best one; or, finally, accept paretianism as the appropriate standard by which to assess the legitimacy of the various kinds of advantage-taking possible in exchange transactions. Even from a libertarian point of view, the last alternative seems to me the most attractive of the three and in what follows I shall assume that this is in fact the choice most libertarians would make.

33. This is true even of utilitarian theories that treat individual autonomy as an intrinsic good to be maximized, perhaps along with other intrinsic goods. If autonomy is made a maximand in this sense, then any limitations can be placed on a person's freedom so long as they yield a greater total amount of freedom overall. But this is to deny that persons have autonomy in the sense in which I am using the term. Respect for the autonomy of persons means that individuals cannot be restricted in their freedom solely for the purpose of increasing the overall amount of some desired good, including freedom itself.

34. Libertarian theorists often express the concept of individual autonomy in terms of the related notion of personal "boundaries." *See* R. Nozick, *supra* note 8, at 57–87; Epstein, *supra* note 30, at 50–54. The notion of boundaries suggests that each moral agent possesses a natural right to be free from violations of his body, and, more problematically, a similar right to be free from imposition of constraints on choice that are incompatible with moral personhood. His commitment to the idea of personal boundaries requires the libertarian to reject any theory, such as utilitarianism, that permits the violation of boundaries whenever the sum of some impersonal good can be advanced by doing so.

35. The latter point is developed more fully in a later section. *See* pp. 491–93 *infra.*

36. The practical necessity of evaluating rules by reference to their effects on classes rather than on particular individuals has been recognized previously. *See* J. Rawls, *supra* note 9, at 98. Rawls keys his difference principle to the welfare of the least advantaged class rather than the least advantaged person, and argues that a theory intended to protect individuals can employ general classifications with complete internal consistency when such classifications afford fuller protection to individuals than any other "practicable" scheme. *See id.*

37. For a fuller discussion of the differences between paretianism and utilitarianism as ethical theories, see Kronman, *Wealth Maximization As a Normative Principle* (forthcoming in 9 *J. Legal Stud.* (1980)).

38. *See, e.g.,* Coleman, *supra* note 30; Posner, *supra* note 30.

39. *See* Kant's *Critique of Practical Reason and Other Works on the Theory of Ethics* 4–5 (6th ed. T. Abbott trans. 1909).

40. This conviction is an element of Rawls's theory as well. *See* J. Rawls, *supra* note 9, at 3–4, 22–27.

41. For a fuller discussion of this and similar cases, see Kronman, *supra* note 21 at 9–18.

42. An example of such a case is a situation in which there is a prior fiduciary relationship between the parties.

43. Arguments similar to the one in text can be made to justify taking advantage of superior acumen or intelligence. *See* J. Rawls, *supra* note 9, at 100–08.

44. *See* R. Posner, *Economic Analysis of Law* 80–84 (2d ed. 1977).

45. *See* Kronman, *supra* note 21 at 13–14.

46. Although the application of the principle of paretianism in difficult cases may require the resolution of factual questions that the professional economist is best equipped to answer, it would be a mistake to think that the principle states merely an economic test for assessing different forms of advantage-taking in exchange transactions. It would be more accurate to say that paretianism provides the morally inspired framework within which technical economic issues (for example, those regarding the incentive effects of a proposed disclosure rule) must be debated.

47. *Compare Pratt Land & Improvement Co. v. McClain,* 135 Ala. 452, 456, 33 So. 185, 187 (1902) ("a purchaser [of real estate] though having superior judgment of values, does not commit fraud merely by purchasing without disclosing his knowledge of value") *with Equitable Life Assurance Soc'y of United States v. McElroy,* 83 F. 631 (8th Cir. 1897) (insurance contract set aside due to nondisclosure of operation for appendicitis during period between signing of application and completion of contract).

48. *See* Schwartz, *A Reexamination of Nonsubstantive Unconscionability,* 63 *Va. L. Rev.* 1053, 1056–59 (1977).

49. This characterization of liberal theories follows the account of "patterned" conceptions of justice elaborated in R. Nozick, *supra* note 8, at 155–64.

50. The point of agreement is a preference for taxation as a method of redistributing wealth. This preference is shared by liberal theorists whose principles of distributive justice differ significantly in other respects. *Compare Basic Structure, supra* note 9, at 54–55 *with* J. Mill, *Principles of Political Economy* 795–822, 966–69 (W. Ashley ed. 1923).

51. *See e.g.,* R. Nozick, *supra* note 8, at 160–64; *Basic Structure, supra* note 9, at 64.

52. *Basic Structure, supra* note 9, at 55.

53. *Id.*

54. *Id.*

55. *Id.* at 54–55.

56. *See, e.g., id.* at 66.

57. *See, e.g.,* C. Fried, *supra* note 9, at 143–50; Grey, *supra* note 9, at 890 n.38.

58. *See* J. Rawls, *supra* note 9, at 87–88; *Basic Structure, supra* note 9, at 54, 65.

59. *Cf.* Rawls, *Two Concepts of Rules,* 64 *Phil. Rev.* 3 (1955) (reasons used to justify choice of system of social rules may not properly be invoked to justify departures from those rules once the system is established).

60. For example, tax considerations are paramount in the planning of corporate mergers, liquidations, and reorganizations.

61. Rawls implicitly endorses this view of regulation. *See Basic Structure, supra* note 9, at 65.

62. *See, e.g.,* R. Heilbroner, *The Economic Problem* 521 (3d ed. 1972) (minimum wage laws); R. Posner, *supra* note 45, at 356–59 (housing codes imposing minimum standards of habitability on slum dwellings); Komesar, *Return to Slumville: A Critique of the Ackerman Analysis of Housing Code Enforcement and the Poor,* 82 *Yale L.J.* 1175, 1180–93 (1973) (same); Stigler, *Director's Law of Public Income Redistribution,* 13 *J. L. & Econ.* 1, 2–3 (1970) (minimum wage laws).

63. Of course, if some other group is taxed in order to generate the funds with which to subsidize low-income tenants, the behavior of landlords may be relatively unaffected. By the same token, however, it may be possible to improve the welfare of low-income renters by imposing contractual restrictions other than rent control, for example, a minimum wage law. But either of these alternative arrangements may itself have undesirable incentive effects that work to the disadvantage of poor people generally and hence to the disadvantage of poor renters.

64. For a discussion of individuals' "taste for discrimination," see G. Becker, *The Economics of Discrimination* 16–17 (2d ed. 1971).

65. These include not only the direct costs of organizing, staffing, and maintaining a regulatory agency, but also the drain on the economy that results from the forced diversion of private sector resources away from their best economic uses. *See, e.g.,* Posner, *Taxation by Regulation,* 2 *Bell J. Econ. & Management Sci.* 22 (1971) (regulation should be considered branch of public finance); DeMuth, *supra* note 9, at 10–17 (discussing and criticizing proposal that federal agencies should be forced to estimate costs of policies before implementing them).

66. R. Nozick, *supra* note 8, at 163.

BABIES FOR SALE:
Reflections on the Baby M Case[*]

Robin Fox

Can you write a commercial contract for a baby? Can a man buy his own child? Who owns the frozen embryos of a dead woman; can they be willed to third parties? It has been five years since the controversial and emotional "Baby M" case was legally settled, but we have barely begun to understand its implications.

The public read the headlines and moved on. But given advances in the so-called "New Birth Technologies" we are faced with a bewildering future for the very definition of the family, if not of the individual. In a world awash with rhetoric about family values, there are lessons to be learned from a close examination of the case and the public reaction to it.

We are a civilization obsessed with the model of the individual contractor as the ultimate social unit. In some ways, as Sir Henry Maine forcefully reminded us, the shift from social relations based on Status — what sociologists would now call "ascribed status"— to those based on Contract is the major shift in Western society over the historic period. The model for relations of Status was of course kinship—the family. A king was the father of his nation; God was the father of his people; the Church was the mother of us all. In the world of Contract, however, all parties are equal and autonomous contractors bound by their agreements. Society itself is such a contractual arrangement. The islands of Status, like slavery, have gradually been swept away, especially in the United States. Here, as Lawrence Friedman so graphically describes it, King Contract triumphed in the nineteenth and twentieth centuries as the model for *all* agreements between those acting rationally in their own interests.

One area held out for Status: the family. Or did it? This is the issue the Baby M case raised. And while there was indeed a settlement of sorts, it was an uneasy one, and one that was not convincing to a large segment of the American public. For Mary Beth Whitehead had not just demanded to keep "her" baby; she had challenged the power of almighty Contract. She issued this challenge in the name of motherhood. But as we shall see, motherhood, for all its hype, is a slender reed in the contractual wind.

A Contract Forbidding Bonds

In March 1986 a baby girl was born to Mary Beth Whitehead, a housewife in Brick Township, New Jersey. It was her third child—she already had a girl (Tuesday) and a boy (Ryan); she called it Sara Elizabeth. Mr. Whitehead, however—at that point employed as a garbage collector—was not Sara's father. The baby had been conceived and born as a result of a contractual agreement between the Whiteheads and William and Elizabeth Stern, a biochemist and physician respectively, of Tenafly, New Jersey, whereby Mrs. Whitehead was artificially inseminated with Mr. Stern's sperm. The contract was drawn up on February 6, 1985 by a lawyer, Noel Keane, of The Infertility Center of New York, a private organization concerned with bringing together infertile couples and potential surrogate mothers. The Center's fee for this service was $7,500.

The motives of the parties seemed fairly clear at the time. Mrs. Stern was unable to bear children for medical reasons. Mr. Stern had lost all his family

*From Fox, Robin. "Babies for Sale," in *The Public Interest*, no. 111 ('93), pp. 14–40. Reprinted here by permission of National Affairs, Inc.

in the Nazi genocide and desperately wanted to have a child of his own blood as a kind of psycho-physical replacement for the lost kin. Mrs. White-head saw an advertisement for the clinic, and considering her family's marginal economic condi-tion and the relative ease and pleasure with which she had already twice given birth, felt capable of performing as a surrogate mother. She was to re-ceive $10,000 for her services and all expenses would be paid by the Sterns. The parties met, Bill and Betsy liked Mary Beth, and she felt well-disposed to them. Richard Whitehead at first was dubious but eventually agreed. The contract—or "Surrogate Parenting Agreement"—was accepted and signed.

Let us pause here to consider this all-important contract. Right up front it states, in Clause 2, that "the sole purpose of this Agreement is to enable William Stern and his infertile wife to have a child which is biologically related to William Stern." In the next clause it puts the whole issue on the line:

> MARY BETH WHITEHEAD, Surrogate, represents that she is capable of conceiving children. MARY BETH WHITEHEAD understands and agrees that in the best interests of the child, she will not form or attempt to form a parent-child relationship with any child or children she may conceive, carry to term and give birth to, pursuant to the provisions of this Agree-ment, and shall freely surrender custody to WILLIAM STERN, Natural Father, immediately upon birth of the child and terminate all parental rights to said child pursuant to this agreement.

So before any of the details—even before any mention of the artificial insemination—the contract insists that the natural mother of the child who must "conceive, carry to term and give birth to" it, should not "form a parent-child relationship" with it. Clearly this must refer to the post-birth situation since, we must immediately ask, how can the mother *not* form a relationship with the child to whom she has been so intimately attached for nine months? And if, as there is much evidence to show, the most funda-mental point of this parent-fetus bonding process occurs at birth itself, then short of bypassing the ac-tual birth process how can the mother voluntarily refuse to form such a bond?

The contract, however, not only assumes she can but makes this the most fundamental of its con-ditions. It is as if the designer (Keane) knew in ad-

vance that the most difficult part of such an agree-ment was not the numerous medical details, but the prohibition of a natural process: that it was this that was most likely to derail the proceedings and there-fore had to be gotten out of the way first.

The next provision obtains Richard White-head's agreement to the same conditions and to the artificial insemination, and "rebut[s] the presumption of paternity of any offspring conceived and born pursuant to aforementioned agreement." This is be-cause the law, in the absence of proof to the con-trary, does assume any children born to a wife to be the natural children of her husband. (This goes back to Roman law. *Pater est quem nuptiae demonstrant:* the legal father of a child is he who can show mar-riage to the mother.) The third provision of this clause enjoins Mrs. Whitehead to cooperate in med-ical examinations, carry the baby to term, and sur-render all parental rights.

The next clause concerns the payment of the fees and expenses, and includes agreement to pater-nity testing. If Stern is found not to be the father, then the deal is off, and the Whiteheads must reim-burse the Sterns for all expenses incurred.

Clause 5 asks the Whiteheads to "understand and assume all risks, including the risk of death, which are incidental to conception, pregnancy and childbirth, including, but not limited to, postpartum complications." Clause 6 demands "psychiatric eval-uations" of the Whiteheads, and permits a release of these to ICNY or the Sterns. The evaluation was in-deed made and the psychiatrist, Joan Einwohner, concluded thus:

> It is the examiner's impression that Ms. Whitehead is sincere in her plan to become a surrogate mother and that she has thought extensively about the plan. However, I do have some concern about her tendency to deny feelings and think it would be impor-tant to explore with her in somewhat more depth whether she will be able to relinquish the child in the end.

There was more to this effect. The explorations in more depth never took place, and this evaluation was never communicated to the Sterns by ICNY.

The issue of miscarriage was then addressed. If the miscarriage occurred before the fifth month—no compensation for the mother; if after the fifth month, she would receive $1,000 for her services. Physical examinations and the possibility of no preg-nancy were then dealt with. Then, in Clause 13, came the matter of abortion:

> MARY BETH WHITEHEAD, Surrogate, agrees that she will not abort the child once conceived except, if in the professional medical opinion of the inseminating physician, such action is necessary for the physical health of MARY BETH WHITEHEAD or the child has been determined by said physician to be physiologically abnormal. MARY BETH WHITEHEAD further agrees, upon the request of said physician to undergo amniocentesis or similar tests to detect genetic and congenital defects. In the event that said test reveals that the fetus is genetically or congenitally abnormal, MARY BETH WHITEHEAD, Surrogate, agrees to abort the fetus upon demand of WILLIAM STERN, Natural Father, in which case the fee paid to the Surrogate will be in accordance with paragraph 10. If MARY BETH WHITEHEAD refuses to abort the fetus upon demand of WILLIAM STERN, his obligations as stated in this agreement shall cease forthwith, except as to obligations of paternity imposed by statute.

Thus the contract was not for a child as such but for *a genetically and physiologically perfect child*. Anything less could lead to a demand for abortion, and if this was refused, then the "surrogate" was stuck with the defective infant, no fee, and no expenses. The "natural father" would be in the clear. The next clause does admit that some such defects cannot be detected in advance, and if these occur then Stern "assumes the legal responsibility" for any such child. This is remarkably vague compared with the harsh specificity of the conditions imposed on the mother. Does "legal responsibility" extend to permanent custody or refer only to acknowledgement of paternity and child support?

In Clause 15, the "surrogate" agrees not to "smoke cigarettes, drink alcoholic beverages, use illegal drugs or take non-prescription medications," etc. And in the final clause Richard Whitehead agrees to execute a "refusal of consent" form. In this, Richard expressly refuses his consent to the artificial insemination while agreeing to all the other clauses. This is necessary so that Richard cannot be "declared or considered to be the legal father of the child conceived thereby."

I have spelled out the conditions of the contract for several reasons. Without knowing precisely what was in the contract it would be hard to have any sensible discussion (although much passionate debate was undertaken by parties who had never read the contract and had no idea what the specific provisions were). Also, as we have seen, the contract was loaded in favor of the "natural father" from the start, as one might expect since he was paying the fees. With a stroke of the pen, and the payment of a hefty sum of money, he appeared to gain enormous control over "the surrogate": He could require insemination, amniocentesis, the regulation of maternal habits, prevention of the formation of parent-child bonds, risk of death, and even abortion (if the child were imperfect). Very few of those who insisted that "a contract was a contract" and that Mrs. Whitehead was bound to submit to its clauses, knew the clauses even existed in this form.

This was a contract, for a monetary consideration, concerning the conception, gestation, birth, and custody of a human being, in which a natural mother was asked to agree not to develop any maternal feelings, and to turn over her child unconditionally to the sperm donor who had paid for this privilege. But there it was. She had "freely entered into" the contract. She was of sound mind. She was not coerced by anything but financial need.

Bonds Negate the Contract

But when Sara was born on March 27, 1986, the arrangement fell apart. Mrs. Whitehead did not want to give up the baby. She was flooded with feelings of guilt over surrendering Sara as well as guilt over disappointing the Sterns. But it came to her with overpowering strength that she was selling her baby "like a slave." She couldn't do it. The bond was simply too strong. She was allowed to take the baby home, but the Sterns insisted on their rights and eventually, with grief and desperation, Mrs. Whitehead gave up the child. The Sterns immediately named it Melissa and started the adoption process. Mrs. Whitehead refused to go through with the adoption and would not accept the $10,000. She was in such a distraught state that on March 30 the Sterns agreed to let her have the child "for a few days." When she again refused to relinquish the baby, the Sterns, armed with a lawyer (Gary Skolof), adoption papers, and the agreement, successfully applied for a court order to claim Sara/Melissa.

Their claim was heard by Superior Court Judge Harvey Sorkow on May 5th. Mrs. Whitehead had been breast-feeding the baby for forty days at this point. She was not represented at the hearings and the judge never interviewed her. He depended solely on the testimony of the Sterns' lawyer. The judge apparently had no qualms about the legitimacy of the contract and issued an *ex parte* order giving the Sterns sole custody. The grounds were that Mary Beth Whitehead had shown "mental instability" in her refusal to honor the contract, and that she might flee with the baby.

A bizarre scenario followed, almost Kafkaesque in its details, many of which cannot be given here since it is not the drama that concerns us but the legal issues. In summary, on May 5th, immediately after obtaining the order, the Sterns alerted the local police in Brick Township and descended on the Whitehead home with their court order. They produced the order, which demanded the surrender of one "Melissa Elizabeth Stern." They were momentarily stalled when the Whiteheads claimed no such baby existed and showed a legal birth certificate for "Sara Elizabeth Whitehead." While the police puzzled over this discrepancy, the infant was passed through a back window to Mr. Whitehead, who indeed fled with her to Mary Beth's parents' home in Florida. Once the disappearing trick was discovered, Mrs. Whitehead was handcuffed and arrested by the police, who later released her since they could not find any actual basis for arrest. Once released she too fled to Florida to join her husband and the baby and she resumed breast-feeding.

They stayed successfully in hiding, making fifteen moves over the course of almost three months, during which time Mrs. Whitehead repeatedly called William Stern to try to persuade him to stop the hunt and let her keep the baby, promising joint custody if he agreed. He refused to agree, taped the conversations (including Mary Beth's threats of suicide) on the advice of his lawyer, and hired private detectives to find the Whiteheads. Judge Sorkow had frozen the Whiteheads' bank account, the bank was about to foreclose on their mortgage, and they were out of funds. A judge in Florida issued an order, based on Sorkow's *ex parte* order, for repossession of the child. Later, when faced with all the facts, he rescinded the order, but by then it was too late.

The Sterns waited until Mrs. Whitehead was in a hospital being treated for an infection, then sent in armed private detectives and local police to the Florida home. Mary Beth's mother was manhandled and thrown to the ground. The baby was pulled from her crib, taken back to the police station, and handed over to the Sterns, who took her back to

New Jersey. She had been breast-feeding for 123 days at this point, and the judge ordered her weaned by the police. The Whiteheads returned to New Jersey, but were not allowed to see her for more than five weeks, when the judge allowed twice-weekly visits of one hour in a supervised facility with guards present. Mrs. Whitehead was specifically prohibited from breastfeeding her baby; her children were not allowed to see their sister. The Whiteheads by this time had a lawyer—on a *pro bono* basis, since they had no money—and they sued for custody. Suits, countersuits, motions, and petitions followed, until at last the trial date, before the same judge whose order had set in motion this bizarre train of events, was set for January 5, 1987, in the New Jersey Superior Court, Family Division, in Hackensack.

When Is a Deal Not a Deal?

The story so far is bizarre enough, but the layman may be excused for wondering why the courts could not quickly and easily settle the issue. Yet the baby was conceived and born under circumstances for which no exact legal precedent existed. Nor was there any state or federal legislation which entirely covered the case. It was not unequivocally a simple custody matter, nor was it just an issue of legal adoption, nor was it a blatant case of "baby selling." States have laws covering these cases, but the surrogate mother case was, to say the least, murky. No statute or precedent seemed to cover it clearly. Hence the intense general, legal, and media interest in the "Baby M" trial as it had now become.

Whose baby was she? Did she belong to the mother who bore her, and hence the mother's legal husband, or did she belong to the genetic father who had a contract for her? Seventy percent of the public, according to polls by the *Bergen Record* and *Newsweek,* believed that "she signed a contract, she should hand over the baby." The minority (less than 20 percent) felt "a baby can't be taken from its natural mother, contract or no contract." The law had no immediate answer.

The response of the overwhelming public majority is interesting. The sanctity of contracts was elevated over the sanctity of motherhood. And indeed the law does by and large encourage contracts and holds the keeping of them to be a good thing. But the public was misled in thinking that if a contract or agreement is signed, then that is that: The conditions must be met. In fact, while any contract may be drawn up, the courts may or may not decide to honor it in the event of a breach of the contract by one party. They may very well decide that the contract was not legal in the first place, since there are some things about which we may not write contracts. But even if they decide it was legal, the issue then becomes: What kind of restitution will they order to the injured party? In the case in question, Mary Beth Whitehead (and her husband) might well have been in breach of the contract, but the question remained: Would the courts order "specific performance" of the contract—that is, the handing over of the child to the injured parties (the Sterns)—or would they decide that a monetary penalty (damages) and costs to the injured party would suffice?

Contrary to public opinion, courts have traditionally been reluctant to order specific performance. And this reluctance has been particularly strong in what are called "personal service" contracts—typically contracts of employment. They have been reluctant because to enforce such a contract is tantamount to enforcing servitude. If someone breaks a contract of employment, by leaving a job before the specified time for example, then a court will certainly award damages to the employer, but it will rarely insist that the term of service be completed, since this would interfere with what is seen as a basic constitutional right to freedom of movement. Employees are not serfs. Similarly with the contract of marriage: If one partner breaches this contract, then damages may be awarded to the other, but the court will never insist that the partner in breach of the contract be forced to continue in the marriage. People who hold the "a deal is a deal" principle rarely seem to invoke this when it comes to their own divorces.

New Jersey, following this general rule, is reluctant to enforce specific performance of personal service contracts. In fact the standard as applied in New Jersey is particularly exacting compared to other states. New Jersey further insists that specific performance should not be granted when it is either contrary to the public interest or would require the court to act inequitably. The New Jersey Supreme Court had ruled that specific performance should be denied if it violates basic principles of human dignity or would be "harsh and oppressive" to one of the parties. Thus with contracts to bear children and renounce parental rights, courts should be unwilling to enforce compliance when one or both parties are resistant.

But for the moment we are simply trying to establish that there is no simple "a deal is a deal" doctrine as far as the law is concerned, and that in this the law is a lot wiser than the public. But then, that is one reason we have the law in the first place: to protect us against our own worst instincts (or perhaps, more exactly, our own worst social and historical constructs). As far as specific performance is concerned, the law seems clear: If there exists a market where one can obtain an adequate substitute, then the contract should not be enforced. And "subjective harm" is not the issue. That you desperately wanted the specific item in question (sentimental value, perhaps) is not at issue. You can get an adequate substitute. This establishes that performance of a contract is by no means automatic, and one might well argue that a sperm-donor father has a "market" out there in which he can obtain an adequate substitute. The substitute will still be his child. As A. Corbin, an expert on contract law, has stated, the onus is on the party seeking specific performance to prove that "a substantial equivalent for all practical purposes" is not readily obtainable from others in exchange for a monetary payment.

It is again remarkable how many people, presented with this argument, respond that it is "repugnant" to discuss a child in this manner—as the subject of a monetary agreement. These are often the same people who saw nothing wrong with the contract in the first place and insisted passionately that it should be upheld!

Equally, we have to consider the issue of "informed consent." A valid contract is unenforceable if one of the parties was, for example, under duress, or if relevant information was withheld from any of the parties, or for any reason that renders one of the parties not in a position to give "informed consent" to the document. Thus if you have a gun to my head when I sign, or if I am legally insane, then even though my signature is on the contract the court will declare it void. In this case, even if we regard the contract as valid in establishing parental rights for Mr. Stern, can we hold it as valid in *extinguishing* the parental rights of Mary Beth Whitehead? Can a woman in fact ever give "informed consent" to a promise to relinquish the child of her body? When it comes to giving up a child for adoption, for example, every state except Wyoming holds that *consent to adoption prior to birth is invalid unless ratified after birth.*

The question, then, is open: Should a surrogate mother have fewer rights in this matter than the mother of a baby put up for adoption? There is here, it might be argued, a genetic father with rights in the child. This is not disputed. In the adoption case there is a genetic father also, but he is rarely ever consulted. The issue is, as we have said, whether an agreement is sufficient to extinguish the mother's parental rights.

Nor must we lose sight of the overriding consideration of the "best interests of the child"—fondly known in legal circles as "BIC." BIC arises only if the issue of custody is reached, that is, if the courts decide that parental rights reside in both father and mother. This would require a fitness hearing in which the court would try to determine which of the parents was most fit to have custody, and would probably allow visitation rights by the other parent, much as in a divorce case.

More to the point, perhaps, in countering the "a deal is a deal" mentality is the issue of what contracts can legally be written. All states and the federal government have statutes which specifically rule out certain things as subjects of contracts. Thus prostitution, slavery, and baby selling are prohibited in all states. Any contract, for example, to provide sexual services or to sell a baby could indeed be written and signed, but if a party defaulted and was sued, the suit would get nowhere and the plaintiffs might even be open to criminal prosecution.

Can a Father Buy His Baby?

In the various surrogate mother cases around the country that had cropped up, the specific issue of a mother refusing to give up her child had not arisen, so the Baby M case was to set an important precedent. But in anticipation of such cases, and in response to other issues in surrogate mothering being brought to court, many states had given relevant judgments and advanced legal opinions through their attorneys general. One of the most popular opinions was that surrogate mothering violates state "baby selling" statutes. Is this a fair analogy? Is surrogate mothering a form of baby selling?

Legal opinion largely said "yes." At the time, Kentucky provided the best testing ground since the courts at different levels had taken different views and so aired most of the possibilities. The attorney general of Kentucky believed that surrogate mothering constitutes illegal baby selling. A Kentucky court, however, held that surrogate arrangements are very different from adoption arrangements. Kentucky did indeed have strong laws against selling children, but

the court asked how a natural father could be characterized as either adopting or buying his own baby. He pays not for the child per se, but for the *services* of the surrogate in carrying and bearing the child. Since he cannot be buying his own child, the arrangement does not violate baby selling laws. The Kentucky Court of Appeals finally agreed with the attorney general: This *is* an adoption procedure (by the father's wife at least); money changes hands; it does contravene Kentucky laws.

Looking to the Constitution

Thus any such contract must first get over the hurdle of whether or not it is "void as contrary to public policy." Even if it makes it past that test, the issue of "specific performance" is still open. But there is yet another hurdle. Such a contract may still be void if it infringes one or other of the parties' constitutional rights. What relevant constitutional issues might the surrogate mother cases raise? This has been much discussed but boils down essentially to three issues: the constitutional prohibition of slavery (the Thirteenth Amendment and Anti-Peonage Act); the "right to privacy" derived from the Fifth Amendment and applied, for example, to a woman's right to abortion in the famous *Roe v. Wade* case; and the equally derivative "right to procreate" with its corollary the "right to marry." The "right to procreate" is ambiguous insofar as it does not specify whether it extends automatically to custody rights over the results of its exercise. This case was to test just how far a right to procreate went. Then there is the mother's "right to the companionship of her children." And we could go on.

The fact is that often these basic constitutional rights (or basic rights derived from the Constitution) seem to be obscure or in conflict. They only become definitive through court rulings in specific cases. And these rulings can appear to conflict in turn. Much ingenious ink is spilled by eager students in law journal "notes" in attempts to reconcile the varying interpretations of the Constitution. For our purposes it is enough to note that the contract and its enforcement have to face the constitutional hurdles mentioned. Some commentaries, for example, have insisted that since the child is being given up to its father, it is not being enslaved, and therefore the Thirteenth Amendment is not infringed. But this overlooks the issue of whether the contract effectively enslaves the mother. The whole issue is muddied by the fact that family relationships have always been treated by all courts as special cases: Thus children are, according to some ultra-liberal critics, effectively enslaved to their parents with the acquiescence of the courts, and marriage contracts are treated differently from ordinary commercial contracts.

As I have mentioned, one of the most interesting aspects of the surrogate parenting issue is precisely this blurring of what have traditionally been separate areas: family relationships and contractual commercial relationships. The writers of "surrogate parenting" contracts seem to want to have it both ways: They want the contracts upheld as commercial documents, and at the same time they want constitutional protections for the privileged "parental" (i.e., non-commercial) status of the "father."

The combination of unprecedented consequences of non-coital reproductive techniques and the clash of principles in contract versus motherhood, as well as the specifics of the human drama in New Jersey, was what I believe made the Baby M case so intensely interesting to the world. We were not just deciding the fate of one baby, but perhaps getting close to redefining the nature of the family, and even the individual, in a world of Lockean contractual relations gone haywire.

The Court Convenes

I shall not dwell in detail on the trial, since it rapidly became a media circus with the world press corps and all the major television networks in noisy attendance. For three weeks it was the nation's favorite soap opera. The details then are known to the world. And in any case, it is not so much the trial per se as the judge's decision that concerns us here. But we must look briefly at his conduct of the case, because his view reflected closely the majority opinion in the media and the polls. This opinion was of course largely middle-class opinion, and the middle-class commentators, with some notable exceptions, were uncompromisingly on the side of their peers the Sterns, and almost contemptuous of the claims of the feckless, working-class Catholic Whiteheads (who were, of course, never described as such).

For a start, the judge managed to rule out a great deal of testimony that might have been relevant, and to include a great deal that was not. He refused to hear experts who lacked direct knowledge of the parties in the case. Thus the authors of influential books on parent-infant bonding were barred from speaking, while a number of low-level and in some cases grossly incompetent "experts" were allowed to testify because they had interviewed the Whiteheads and/or the Sterns. Evidence about the long-term harm to a mother of losing a child was not allowed, because the purported harm to *this* mother had yet to occur and was therefore "hypothetical."

Mary Beth Whitehead faced other obstacles. A guardian *ad litem*—Lorraine Abrahams—had been appointed to represent Baby M. This meant that a further set of "experts" could be called to testify, without breaking ranks, against Mrs. Whitehead. Their testimony was supposed to be independent— and the guardian swore to this in court—but in fact they met for a total of more than twenty-four hours with the guardian, before and during the trial, and were obviously working in tandem. Together with the experts called by the Sterns they hammered away at Mary Beth's character.

Somewhere in all this the contract issue got lost. The judge initially had ordered two trials: one on the contract, one on custody. The Appeals Court ordered only one trial, so the judge decided, with almost theological finesse, that it should be one trial but in two parts. The first part was heard in a matter of hours, with each counsel arguing the case for and against the legitimacy of the contract. The judge barred any expert testimony on the contractual issue, and insisted that he was not going to get "mired in inquiries dealing with ethics, morality and theology." This meant that the first part of the trial was going to be very brief indeed. As the judge and Skolof wanted, the trial moved quickly into the custody phase, which in turn became a battle over Mrs. Whitehead's character.

Skolof was a custody lawyer, and before the trial he had announced that his tactic was to turn this into a custody battle, which he "knew how to win." First, he delayed the trial as long as possible with numerous requests for more time. The longer Baby M was with the Sterns, the less likely was any court to order her return "in the best interests of the child." This tactic worked perfectly, and it took an order of the Supreme Court of New Jersey to get the trial started on January 5th.

Skolof's next tactic was to present a picture of the Sterns as an upright, middle-class, well-educated professional couple who could give an excellent home to to the baby (including trips to Bloomingdale's), as against the working-class, impoverished, unreliable Whiteheads who could not. In particular, the calm, serious, and capable Mrs. Stern (pediatrician), was to be contrasted with the whimsical, manipulative, dishonest, overprotective, and under-educated Mrs. Whitehead (ex-Go-Go dancer). Harold Cassidy, the Whitehead's *pro bono* lawyer, refused to meet Skolof on his own terms. He would not indulge in "expert" mud-slinging against the Sterns; instead, he tried to build up a good picture of Mrs. Whitehead as a wife, mother, and neighbor, with his experts doing their best to counter the accusations of the Sterns' (and the guardian's) highly paid witnesses. The result of this mismatch was a foregone conclusion, and it is to that result we must now turn.

Parens Patriae Super

Judge Harvey Sorkow rendered his judgment on March 31, 1987, after a three month trial of unprecedented media attention and world-wide publicity. He set the tone from the start:

> The primary issue to be determined by
> this litigation is what are the best interests
> of a child until now called "Baby M." All
> other concerns raised by counsel constitute
> commentary.

This attitude was to determine the whole judgment. Most of the legal issues discussed at length earlier were dismissed by Judge Sorkow as "non-issues." As Skolof had wanted, the trial became a custody battle and the judgment a custody judgment. There can be no equitable justice for the adult parties in the case, said the judge, and in any case it wasn't his place to find it. "The court will seek to achieve justice for the child." It will do this on the basis of the doctrine of *parens patriae*, roughly, "the country as parent."

One must remember that Sorkow was essentially a family court judge, not a contract lawyer or a constitutional expert. He saw his business therefore as the subordination of any other consideration to the "best interests of the child," this being the traditional matter of family court disputes. His dismissal of contract and constitutional issues as "mere commentary" reflected this stance.

> [A]ll should listen again to the plea of the infant as voiced so poignantly by several of the professional witnesses, statements with which this court agrees to such an extent that it will

use its total authority if required to accomplish these ends.

Thus dominated by the notion of *parens patriae,* and clearly of the opinion that the Whiteheads were unsuitable parents while the Sterns were exemplary, he proceeded to validate the contract, terminate Mrs. Whitehead's parental rights, order the adoption by Mrs. Stern of Baby M, and grant sole custody to the Sterns with no rights of visitation for the Whiteheads. Everything was premised on the "best interests of the child." For example, on the issue of "specific performance" the judge ruled:

> This court holds that whether there will be
> specific performance . . . depends on whether
> doing so is in the child's best interest. . . . We
> find by clear and convincing evidence,
> indeed by a measure of evidence reaching
> beyond reasonable doubt, that Melissa's best
> interest will be served by being placed in her
> father's sole custody.

So much for specific performance. On the contract itself, the judge leaned heavily on the fact that there was no New Jersey statute covering surrogacy as such. Laws against baby selling did not apply, he said, because the baby was not sold to her natural father, who only paid for the surrogate's services. The surrogate was indeed a rented uterus. Adoption statutes did not apply, he said, because Mr. Stern did not need to adopt his own child, and, he noted, adoption by Mrs. Stern was not mentioned in the contract. Failing any statutes to govern the case, he argued, the contract should be treated as an ordinary commercial contract, regardless of the peculiar nature of its conditions. Thus, when it came to the issue of Mrs. Whitehead's parental rights, the judge refused to accept that statutory tests, as in adoption cases, applied. There is a presumption, in law, that the biological mother is the fit parent unless a hearing specifically finds her to be unfit, that is, engaged in active, harmful behavior with regard to the child. Mrs. Whitehead was not entitled to such a presumption, said the judge, because in the contract she agreed not to be a "mother." So presumptions about motherhood could not apply to her. She had signed away her rights to maternity.

Constitutional matters got equally short shrift, although the judge was more cautious here. While the best interests of the child should dominate all other concerns *once the child was conceived,* he argued, it was indeed an invasion of privacy and unconstitutional to enforce any of the clauses up to the time of conception. And even after conception, it was clearly unconstitutional to enforce the abortion clause. But all the other clauses, including the all-important termination of parental rights clause, must be "specifically performed."

> The sole legal concepts that control are *parens patriae* and the best interests of the child. To wait for birth, to plan, pray and dream of the joy it will bring and then be told that the child will not come home, that a new set of rules applies and to ask a court to approve such a result deeply offends the conscience of this court.

Nothing is said about the destructive effects on the mother who may wish to keep the child of her body. In fact this is dismissed as another non-issue. She can just go back to where she was, he says. She didn't really want any other children of her own anyway, and her husband had had a vasectomy to this end. Therefore, it was in no way harsh or inequitable to enforce specific performance here. The "right to procreate" issue again is interpreted entirely in favor of the father. In fact, the judge held, any state interference with this right of the father to specific performance would itself be unconstitutional.

The essential provisions of Sorkow's decision were as follows:

1. The surrogate parenting agreement of February 6, 1985, will be specifically enforced.
2. The prior order of the court giving temporary custody to Mr. Stern is herewith made permanent. Prior orders of visitation are vacated.
3. The parental rights of the defendant Mary Beth Whitehead are terminated.
4. Mr. Stern is formally adjudged the father of Melissa Stern.
5. The New Jersey Department of Health [is] directed to amend all records of birth to reflect the paternity and name of the child to be Melissa Stern.
6. The defendants (Whiteheads) . . . must refrain from interfering with the parental and custodial rights of the plaintiff.

Enlightenment in Trenton

Most people, in my experience, stopped following the trial at this point. If they knew anything of the appeal to the New Jersey Supreme Court it was what the media chose to stress: that the Supreme Court confirmed the grant of custody of Baby M to the Sterns. But the court's verdict deserves closer consideration, because on every other point it was a stunning reversal of the lower court's decision. On February 3, 1988, in a unanimous opinion written by Chief Justice C. J. Wilenz, the court:

1. Found the contract to be invalid and contrary to New Jersey law and public policy;
2. Found the *ex parte* order giving temporary custody to the Sterns to have been invalid;
3. Voided the adoption of Baby M by Mrs. Stern;
4. Restored Mrs. Whitehead's parental rights;
5. Affirmed the order giving custody of Baby M to Mr. Stern; and
6. Remanded to the lower court—but with a different judge—the question of the nature and extent of Mrs. Whitehead's future visitation rights.

Note my original argument was that even if the contract were found valid, it should not be enforced. Yet since the court, however, invalidated the contract largely on the basis of its incompatibility with New Jersey law, the question of its enforceability did not arise.

The court was firm in its rejection of surrogacy contracts:

> We invalidate the surrogacy contract because it conflicts with the law and public policy of this State . . . we find the payment of money to a "surrogate" mother illegal, perhaps criminal, and potentially degrading to women. . . . [W]e void both the termination of the surrogate mother's parental rights and the adoption of the child by the wife/stepparent. We thus restore the "surrogate" as the mother of the child.

The illegality of the contract stems from its use of money to procure an adoption through private placement.

> Its use of money for this purpose—and we have no doubt whatsoever that the money is being paid to obtain an adoption and not, as the Sterns argue, for the personal services of Mary Beth Whitehead—is illegal and perhaps criminal.

In addition, the court decided, the contract was in fact "coercive." Prior even to conception, the mother agreed irrevocably to surrender the child to the adoptive couple. She also illegally agreed to surrender her parental rights. The court turned the "best interests of the child" argument—used by the lower court entirely to boost the Stern's case—completely around. The contract itself, the court said, totally ignored the "best interests of the child."

> In this case a termination of parental rights was obtained not by proving the statutory prerequisites but by claiming the benefit of contractual provisions. . . . The contract's basic premise, that the natural parents can decide in advance of birth which one is to have custody of the child, bears no relationship to the settled law that the child's best interests shall determine custody. . . .

In other words, the contract preempted the right to decide custody "in the best interest of the child" that can only lie in the power of the courts. It was not the child's interests that the contract sought to protect, but the father's. The rights of the child were never considered. Indeed: "The surrogacy contract guarantees permanent separation of the child from one of its natural parents," thus running contrary to public policy in the state. "The surrogacy contract violates the policy of this State that the rights of natural parents are equal concerning their child, the father's right no greater than the mother's. . . . The whole purpose of the surrogacy contract was to give the father the exclusive right to the child by destroying the rights of the mother. . . ."

But above all, the court reserved its severest condemnation for the issue mentioned above: the failure of the contract to give any regard for the best interests of the child, which, ironically, as we have seen, was the doctrine central to Judge Sorkow's decision. "There is not the slightest suggestion that any enquiry will be made at any time to determine the fitness of the Sterns as custodial parents, of Mrs. Stern as an adoptive parent, their superiority to Mrs. Whitehead, or the effects on the child of not living with its natural mother."

They conclude severely: "This is the sale of a child, or, at the very least, the sale of a mother's right to her child, the only mitigating factor being that one of the purchasers is the father." So the father here is buying his own child, the court says; he is paying money to obtain exclusive rights to it. He can't do that under the law. The contract is invalid from beginning to end.

On the issue of "informed consent," they found that no potential surrogate could be said to be fully informed in advance of pregnancy and birth:

> Under the contract, the natural mother is irrevocably committed before she knows the strength of her bond with her child. She never makes a totally voluntary, informed decision, for quite clearly any decision prior to the baby's birth is, in the most important sense, uninformed, and any decision after that . . . is less than voluntary.

The justices also recognized the potential harm to the mother otherwise ignored by Judge Sorkow:

> The long-term effects of surrogacy contracts are not known, but feared—the impact on the child who learns she was bought . . . ; the impact on the natural mother as the full weight of her isolation is felt along with the full reality of the sale of her body and her child. . . .

As regards the father's "right to procreate" they insisted that it was "no more than that." It was fulfilled by the artificial insemination and did not extend to the right to custody. This latter right had to be independently established (as in this case they felt it had been).

On the crucial point of the *ex parte* order, which had started the whole thing rolling, they argued as follows:

> When father and mother are separated and disagree, at birth, on custody, only in an extreme, truly rare, case should the child be taken from its mother *pendente lite,* i.e., only in the most unusual case should the child be taken from the mother before the dispute is finally determined by the court on its merits. The probable bond between mother and child, and the child's need, not just the mother's, to strengthen that bond, along with the likelihood, in most cases, of a significantly lesser, if any, bond with the father—all counsel against temporary custody in the father.

It should also be noted that the court went out of its way to repudiate at length the "too harsh" judgment of Mrs. Whitehead's character and even, surprisingly, faced up to the otherwise taboo issue of social class—something that the lower court, the public, and most of the commentators had tried to ignore, treating obvious class differences between the Sterns and Whiteheads as though they were personal merits and defects of the individuals involved.

> We have a further concern regarding the trial court's emphasis on the Sterns' interest in Melissa's education as compared to the Whiteheads'. That this difference is a legitimate factor to be considered we have no doubt. But it should not be overlooked that a best-interests test is designed to create not a new member of the intelligentsia but rather a well-integrated person who might reasonably be expected to be happy with life. "Best interests" does not contain within it any idealized lifestyle; the question boils down to a judgement, consisting of many factors, about the likely future happiness of a human being. Stability, love, family happiness, and, ultimately, support of independence—all rank much higher in predicting future happiness than the likelihood of a college education. . . .

One might have been forgiven at this point for expecting a resounding decision in Mrs. Whitehead's favor on the custody question. But in the end the court ducked from this issue. While Mary Beth might provide love, she might also not provide stability or the possibility of autonomy. The Sterns' experts were against her; her own witnesses were divided; and above all, "most convincingly, the three experts chosen by the court-appointed guardian *ad litem* of Baby M, each clearly free of all bias and interest, unanimously and persuasively recommended custody in the Sterns." This is the only place where this otherwise extraordinarily well-argued judgment falls into absurdity. But it was clear that the members of the court, for all their good sense and sound argument, could not, like most of the rest of middle-class America, find it in their hearts to deprive little Melissa (as she now was) of her trips to Bloomingdale's. Having dumped the major expert—Judge Sorkow—without ceremony, they fell back on the other experts to save them from the consequences of their own logic and enable them to deliver Baby M up to the Sterns in her own "best interest."

At the same time, the court restored fully Mrs. Whitehead's parental rights and hence her rights to visitation. She is the "legal mother," they said, and added somewhat ironically that she should not be "punished one iota because of the [illegal and possibly criminal] surrogacy contract." This was of course only with respect to visitation; she had already been

punished since the illegal and criminal contract was what caused the issuance of the original *ex parte* order, which is what led to Baby M being kept in the primary custody of the Sterns for a year and a half, which in turn became a major argument for leaving her there so as not to disturb her settled situation.

Offspring Without Sex

Our brief on the details of Baby M really ends here. But we have to recognize that "surrogate parenting" is only one of several New Reproductive Technologies (NRTs), all of which raise some similar issues. So-called *in vitro* fertilization, where sperm and egg are brought together in a petri dish, and the resulting fertilized egg implanted in the womb of, say, an infertile woman, has raised hopes for "curing" infertility ever since the technique was developed in Oldham, England, in 1978. But the egg of an infertile woman, together with her husband's sperm, can also be implanted by simple artificial insemination techniques into a surrogate mother.

This raises an interesting conundrum, since the surrogate in this case does not contribute any genetic material to the child she bears. Yet she is still the "genetrix" in our sense, and the *in utero* bonding and bonding at birth will still have taken place. How would her claim stand up in court? There could be no issue of breach of the adoption laws here since the wife of the sperm donor—the equivalent of Elizabeth Stern—would be also the genetic mother of the child. How should the claim of the totally genetic parents here stack up against resistance by the genetically unrelated surrogate? Does the contribution of a bit of the male donor's limitless supply of sperm, and the flushing out of a few ova from the female donor's fallopian tubes match up to nine months gestation and the risks of childbearing and childbirth? Is the surrogate in this case going to feel the child is any the less "hers" because she did not contribute the egg?

Even more bizarre scenarios can be considered. Take the case of an infertile husband with a wife who is fertile but cannot, for some reason, give birth. Her flushed-out ovum could be combined with sperm from a donor and implanted in a surrogate. Here we would have four people involved: a genetic mother married to a prospectively social father plus a genetic father (probably unknown) and an actual genetrix or birth mother. One can run around the possibilities, with the most bizarre being sperm and eggs from unknown donors being externally fused and then implanted in a surrogate who surrenders the eventual child for adoption to two other (possibly infertile) social parents: five people, none of whom had sex with any of the others. In the case of frozen sperm, a child could be that of a dead man; and with frozen embryos a child could be born to long dead parents. With frozen sperm and ova from dead parents being combined, children could technically be orphans at the moment of conception. It will only take a breakthrough in incubator technology to bypass the surrogate mother altogether, and produce offspring not only without sex but without mothers either; then we are truly in Huxley land. For the moment, however, the "rented womb" is still needed and hence will run into all the problems discussed in this chapter should the genetrix lay claim to the child.

Several countries have now introduced legislation to control or outlaw such procedures, so injurious do they seem to accepted notions of love, marriage and the family, and to the "normality" of parent-child relationships. The British Parliament has endorsed embryo research but criminalized surrogacy. The issues evoke deep feelings everywhere, and there is no consensus. On the one side the scientists and doctors, and an increasing number of infertile couples, claim "progress," while the opposition claims everything from "inhumanity" to the gross "unnaturalness" of the whole business. (The Catholic Church is a leading voice in this opposition.) Feminists seem to be divided on this issue. Some see surrogacy as freeing women from the necessity of childbirth to pursue careers and self-fulfillment, others see surrogacy as the apotheosis of sisterhood and cooperation among women, and yet others see it as an attack on the woman in her role as mother and a handing over of even more patriarchal control to males—especially the medical profession, which particularly excites their indignation (and not without reason).

It is scarcely surprising that there should be such passionate debate. This great leap forward in technology leaves us unprepared for what appears to be a total redefinition of the family, of marriage and "lawful procreation," and even of the individual. How much of himself—and in this case certainly herself—does the individual own, for example? If I may sell an ovum to some third party, have I any rights and duties towards the end product? If I donate sperm (actually I would be more likely to sell it) do I have paternal (or even contractual) obliga-

tions to its eventual bawling and gurgling consequences? The majority of us simply find these possibilities too remote from our traditional (and often religiously backed) notions of family and parenthood and love for offspring.

But how can we attack or defend such practices as "unnatural" if we have no established standards of what is "natural" in the first place? And how can we have these standards if relativism informs all our enquiries and tells us that whatever definitions we come up with will be merely social or cultural constructs? I would agree, for example, with those who say that the nuclear family is not a sacrosanct "natural" entity but simply one kind of institutional possibility. I have been saying so for thirty years or more. But as a student of mammalian behavior I would have to disagree that "motherhood" is a similar construct, depending on context for its meaning. A hard look at the mammals (including ourselves) tells us that no matter what the genetic link may be, the genetrix does indeed bond with the child in the womb and at parturition, and hence has a "natural" claim to it. If this is true, it at least gives us somewhere to start.

Thus a woman who has gone through gestation and parturition will be "primed" to bond with her child. If the bond takes, then she is not likely to repudiate it simply because she knows the genes in the child are not her own. The child is already eliciting "mothering" responses, as indeed a non-related adopted infant will do for the parents who take it into their care. Claims of genetic relatedness, then, should not take precedence over those involving powerful proximate—especially bonding—mechanisms.

Other cultures take in stride the idea that a child may not have a father or that children can be born to a dead man. These are not the important things. All these cultures still try to satisfy the basic individual needs for sex, shelter, provisioning, property, dominance, companionship, love, bonding, respect, kinship, children, etc. The various institutional forms by which they do this can vary widely—they are indeed "cultural constructs"—but they are forms which still must answer basic individual needs or risk severe cultural dislocation. This is where relativism fails. Cultural constructs must be rooted in biological reality or they will surely collapse. The NRTs will survive only insofar as they acknowledge these basic realities. We have looked at only one example—if we try to force bonded mothers to give up their children in the name of contract (a cultural construct) we will fail, or at least deserve to fail. But the same principle can be extended to any of the other NRTs. Do they help or hinder the pursuit of those proximate motivations that are programmed into us by evolution to ensure the production of future generations? Here comparative enthnography may help us in showing the limits of human tolerance for variation—which are in fact quite wide. We have to learn how to rewrite the old rules to meet the new circumstances, and to control the new circumstances in the face of timeless realities.

Efforts so far to deal with the issue of NRTs have been largely legislative and restrictive. Surrogacy, for example, simply gets outlawed. Legislators—and social scientists—are happiest as philosopher-kings. But as the Baby M case has shown, we often do not know in advance what the problems will be. Thus a case by case approach may well generate more workable solutions to actual problems than will grand schemes of legislation aiming to solve hypothetical problems all at once. If I may venture an opinion on the surrogacy issue: I do not think surrogacy should be banned, since it has been proven to work in many cases with quite satisfactory results. I do obviously think, however, that a surrogate mother (even if genetically unrelated to her child) should not be required to give up the baby if she does not wish to. That seems to me to be the moral of this case. We can deal with the case of the unfrozen embryo, the product of a long-dead billionaire (and his mistress) whose fortune has already been divided among the other heirs excluding the unstable great-niece in whom the revived embryo has been implanted by an unscrupulous lawyer, when it arises. Michael Crichton is probably already at work on the novel.

An American Dilemma

Thus we come round full circle to the issue that the Baby M case thrust into our unwilling consciousness: How far are we willing to take our insistence on the dominance of the model of contract in social relationships? In a secular society, which is never-theless riddled with sentimental religiosity, are there still some areas that we consider sacred and off-limits to the rules of contract? The advocates of traditional family values seem to think so, and are horrified when children are allowed to sue parents for breaches of implied "family contracts." We are in a socially schizophrenic state. We cling on the one hand to the secular contract model as the only model compatible with our individualist assumptions about how society should work. On the other hand, we seem to want certain areas declared out-of-bounds to the basic rule of contract.

But we simply can't decide where the boundaries are. Even the boundaries of the contracting individual are now becoming fuzzy, and organic products of one's own body (or parts fused with those from other bodies) become commodities subject to contractual agreements. This dilemma cuts across the usual liberal and conservative distinctions. Conservatives are as likely to be confused about the relative weights of contract and status as liberals are. Those who vociferously defend "family values" are equally likely to be those who stoutly defend the sanctity of contracts and the autonomy of the individual. And as we have seen, the issue divides feminists at least three ways.

For the moment, given the New Jersey precedent, it is illegal to write a commercial contract for a baby. But for frozen fertilized ova? The kinds of decisions we are faced with are decisions not just about specific cases, but about the kind of society we want to be. The winning of a revolutionary war provoked us to rethink this problem in the late eighteenth century. The issue of slavery prompted us to rethink it yet again in the late nineteenth century. Perhaps the stubbornness of a New Jersey mother, in her love for her newborn child, will be the catalyst for a new such rethinking in the late twentieth century. We now have the advantage of a profounder understanding of the evolutionary basis of human nature and the limitations of social constructs. But we are very unhappy with the idea of such limitations, particularly when they affect our most cherished ideas. The chances of our getting it right are not good.

SURROGATE MOTHERHOOD AS PRENATAL ADOPTION*

Bonnie Steinbock

The recent case of "Baby M" has brought surrogate motherhood to the forefront of American attention. Ultimately, whether we permit or prohibit surrogacy depends on what we take to be good reasons for preventing people from acting as they wish. A growing number of people want to be, or hire, surrogates; are there legitimate reasons to prevent them? Apart from its intrinsic interest, the issue of surrogate motherhood provides us with an opportunity to examine different justifications for limiting individual freedom.

In the first section of this article, I examine the Baby M case and the lessons it offers. In the second section, I examine claims that surrogacy is ethically unacceptable because it is exploitive, inconsistent with human dignity, or harmful to the children born of such arrangements. I conclude that these reasons justify restrictions on surrogate contracts, rather than an outright ban.

Baby M

Mary Beth Whitehead, a married mother of two, agreed to be inseminated with the sperm of William Stern and to give up the child to him for a fee of $10,000. The baby (whom Ms. Whitehead named Sara, and the Sterns named Melissa) was born on March 27, 1986. Three days later, Ms. Whitehead took her home from the hospital and turned her over to the Sterns.

Then Ms. Whitehead changed her mind. She went to the Sterns' home, distraught, and pleaded to have the baby temporarily. Afraid that she would kill herself, the Sterns agreed. The next week, Ms. Whitehead informed the Sterns that she had decided to keep the child, and threatened to leave the country if court action was taken.

At that point, the situation deteriorated into a cross between the Keystone Kops and Nazi stormtroopers. Accompanied by five policemen, the Sterns went to the Whitehead residence armed with a court order giving them temporary custody of the child. Ms. Whitehead managed to slip the baby out of a window to her husband, and the following morning the Whiteheads fled with the child to Florida, where Ms. Whitehead's parents lived. During the next three months, the Whiteheads lived in roughly twenty different hotels, motels, and homes to avoid apprehension. From time to time, Ms. Whitehead telephoned Mr. Stern to discuss the matter: he taped these conversations on advice of counsel. Ms. Whitehead threatened to kill herself, to kill the child, and to falsely accuse Mr. Stern of sexually molesting her older daughter.

At the end of July 1986, while Ms. Whitehead was hospitalized with a kidney infection, Florida police raided her mother's home, knocking her down, and seized the child. Baby M was placed in the custody of Mr. Stern, and the Whiteheads returned to New Jersey, where they attempted to regain custody. After a long and emotional court battle, Judge Harvey R. Sorkow ruled on March 31, 1987, that the surrogacy contract was valid, and that specific performance was justified in the best interests of the child. Immediately after reading his decision, he called the Sterns into his chambers so that Mr. Stern's wife, Dr. Elizabeth Stern, could legally adopt the child.

This outcome was unexpected and unprecedented. Most commentators had thought that a court would be unlikely to order a reluctant surrogate to give up an infant merely on the basis of a contract.[1] Indeed, if Ms. Whitehead had never surrendered the

---

*From Steinbock, Bonnie. "Surrogate Motherhood as Prenatal Adoption," in *Law, Medicine, and Health Care*, v. 16, no. 1, ('88), pp. 44–50. Reprinted here by permission of American Society of Law, Medicine and Ethics.

child to the Sterns, but had simply taken her home and kept her there, the outcome undoubtedly would have been different. It is also likely that Ms. Whitehead's failure to obey the initial custody order angered Judge Sorkow, and affected his decision.

The decision was appealed to the New Jersey Supreme Court, which issued its decision on February 3, 1988. Writing for a unanimous court, Chief Justice Wilentz reversed the lower court's ruling that the surrogacy contract was valid. The court held that a surrogacy contract that provides money for the surrogate mother, and that includes her irrevocable agreement to surrender her child at birth, is invalid and unenforceable. Since the contract was invalid, Ms. Whitehead did not relinquish, nor were there any other grounds for terminating, her parental rights. Therefore, the adoption of Baby M by Dr. Stern was improperly granted, and Ms. Whitehead remains the child's legal mother.

The court further held that the issue of custody is determined solely by the child's best interests, and it agreed with the lower court that it was in Melissa's best interests to remain with the Sterns. However, Ms. Whitehead, as Baby M's legal as well as natural mother, is entitled to have her own interest in visitation considered. The determination of what kind of visitation rights should be granted to her, and under what conditions, was remanded to the trial court.

The distressing details of this case have led many people to reject surrogacy altogether. Do we really want police officers wrenching infants from their mothers' arms, and prolonged custody battles when surrogates find they are unable to surrender their children, as agreed? Advocates of surrogacy say that to reject the practice wholesale, because of one unfortunate instance, is an example of a "hard case" making bad policy. Opponents reply that it is entirely reasonable to focus on the worst potential outcomes when deciding public policy. Everyone can agree on at least one thing: this particular case seems to have been mismanaged from start to finish, and could serve as a manual of how not to arrange a surrogate birth.

First, it is now clear that Mary Beth Whitehead was not a suitable candidate for surrogate motherhood. Her ambivalence about giving up the child was recognized early on, although this information was not passed on to the Sterns.[2] Second, she had contact with the baby after birth, which is usually avoided in "successful" cases. Typically, the adoptive mother is actively involved in the pregnancy, often serving as the pregnant woman's coach in labor. At birth, the baby is given to the adoptive, not the biological mother. The joy of the adoptive parents in holding their child serves both to promote their bonding and to lessen the pain of separation of the biological mother.

At Ms. Whitehead's request, no one at the hospital was aware of the surrogacy arrangement. She and her husband appeared as the proud parents of "Sara Elizabeth Whitehead," the name on her birth certificate. Ms. Whitehead held her baby, nursed her, and took her home from the hospital—just as she would have done in a normal pregnancy and birth. Not surprisingly, she thought of Sara as her child, and she fought with every weapon at her disposal, honorable and dishonorable, to prevent her being taken away. She can hardly be blamed for doing so.[3]

Why did Dr. Stern, who supposedly had a very good relation with Ms. Whitehead before the birth, not act as her labor coach? One possibility is that Ms. Whitehead, ambivalent about giving up her baby, did not want Dr. Stern involved. At her request, the Sterns' visits to the hospital to see the newborn baby were unobtrusive. It is also possible that Dr. Stern was ambivalent about having a child. The original idea of hiring a surrogate was not hers, but her husband's. It was Mr. Stern who felt a "compelling" need to have a child related to him by blood, having lost all his relatives to the Nazis.

Furthermore, Dr. Stern was not infertile, as was stated in the surrogacy agreement. Rather, in 1979 she was diagnosed by two eye specialists as suffering from optic neuritis, which meant that she "probably" had multiple sclerosis. (This was confirmed by all four experts who testified.) Normal conception was ruled out by the Sterns in late 1982, when a medical colleague told Dr. Stern that his wife, a victim of multiple sclerosis, had suffered a temporary paralysis during pregnancy. "We decided the risk wasn't worth it," Mr. Stern said.[4]

Ms. Whitehead's lawyer, Harold J. Cassidy, dismissed the suggestion that Dr. Stern's "mildest case" of multiple sclerosis determined the Sterns' decision to seek a surrogate. He noted that she was not even treated for multiple sclerosis until after the Baby M dispute had started. "It's almost as though it's an afterthought," he said.[5]

Judge Sorkow deemed the decision to avoid conception "medically reasonable and understandable." The Supreme Court did not go so far, noting that Dr. Stern's "anxiety appears to have exceeded the actual risk, which current medical authorities assess as minimal."[6] Nonetheless, the court acknowledged that her anxiety, including fears that pregnancy might precipitate blindness and paraplegia, was "quite real." Certainly, even a woman who wants a child very much may reasonably wish to avoid becoming blind and paralyzed as a result of pregnancy. Yet is it believable that a woman who really wanted a child would decide against pregnancy *solely* on the basis of *someone else's* medical experience? Would she not consult at least one specialist on her *own* medical condition before deciding it wasn't worth the risk? The conclusion that she was at best ambivalent about bearing a child seems irresistible.

This possibility conjures up many people's worst fears about surrogacy: that prosperous women, who do not want to interrupt their careers, will use poor and educationally disadvantaged women to bear their children. I will return shortly to the question of whether this is exploitive. The issue here is psychological: what kind of mother is Dr. Stern likely to be? If she is unwilling to undergo pregnancy, with its discomforts, inconveniences, and risks, will she be willing to make the considerable sacrifices that good parenting requires? Ms. Whitehead's ability to be a good mother was repeatedly questioned during the trial. She was portrayed as immature, untruthful, hysterical, overly identified with her children, and prone to smothering their independence. Even if all this is true—and I think that Ms. Whitehead's inadequacies were exaggerated—Dr. Stern may not be such a prize either. The choice for Baby M may have been between a highly strung, emotional, overinvolved mother, and a remote, detached, even cold one.[7]

The assessment of Ms. Whitehead's ability to be a good mother was biased by the middle-class prejudices of the judge and of the mental health officials who testified. Ms. Whitehead left school at fifteen, and is not conversant with the latest theories on child rearing: she made the egregious error of giving Sara teddy bears to play with, instead of the more "age-appropriate," expert-approved pans and spoons. She proved to be a total failure at patty-cake. If this is evidence of parental inadequacy, we're all in danger of losing our children.

The Supreme Court felt that Ms. Whitehead was "rather harshly judged" and acknowledged the possibility that the trial court was wrong in its initial award of custody. Nevertheless, it affirmed Judge Sorkow's decision to allow the Sterns to retain custody, as being in Melissa's best interests. George Annas disagrees with the "best interests" approach. He points out that Judge Sorkow awarded temporary custody of Baby M to the Sterns in May 1986, without giving the Whiteheads notice or an opportunity to obtain legal representation. That was a serious wrong and injustice to the Whiteheads. To allow the Sterns to keep the child compounds the original unfairness: "justice requires that reasonable consideration be given to returning Baby M to the permanent custody of the Whiteheads."[8]

But a child is not a possession, to be returned to the rightful owner. It is not fairness to all parties that should determine a child's fate, but what is best for her. As Chief Justice Wilentz rightly stated, "The child's interests come first: we will not punish it for judicial errors, assuming any were made."[9]

Subsequent events have substantiated the claim that giving custody to the Sterns was in Melissa's best interests. After losing custody, Ms. Whitehead, whose husband had undergone a vasectomy, became pregnant by another man. She divorced her husband and married Dean R. Gould last November. These developments indicate that the Whiteheads were not able to offer a stable home, although the argument can be made that their marriage might have survived if not for the strains introduced by the court battle and the loss of Baby M. But even if Judge Sorkow had no reason to prefer the Sterns to the Whiteheads back in May 1986, he was still right to give the Sterns custody in March 1987. To take her away then, at nearly eighteen months of age, from the only parents she had ever known would have been disruptive, cruel, and unfair to her.

Annas' preference for a just solution is premised partly on his belief that there *is* no "best interest" solution to this "tragic custody case." I take it that he means that however custody is resolved, Baby M is the loser. Either way, she will be deprived of one parent. However, a best-interests solution is not a perfect solution. It is simply the solution that is on balance best for the child, given the realities of the situation. Applying this standard, Judge Sorkow was right to give the Sterns custody, and the Supreme Court was right to uphold the decision.

The best-interests argument is based on the assumption that Mr. Stern has at least a *prima facie* claim to Baby M. We certainly would not consider allowing a stranger who kidnapped a baby and managed to elude the police for a year to retain custody on the grounds that he was providing a good home to a child who had known no other parent. However, the Baby M case is not analogous. First, Mr. Stern is Baby M's biological father and, as such, has at least some claim to raise her, which no non-parental kidnapper has. Second, Mary Beth Whitehead *agreed* to give him their baby. Unlike the miller's daughter in

Rumpelstiltskin, the fairy tale to which the Baby M case is sometimes compared, she was not forced into the agreement. Because both Mary Beth Whitehead and Mr. Stern have *prima facie* claims to Baby M, the decision as to who should raise her should be based on her present best interests. Therefore we must, regretfully, tolerate the injustice to Ms. Whitehead, and try to avoid such problems in the future.

It is unfortunate that the court did not decide the issue of visitation on the same basis as custody. By declaring Ms. Whitehead-Gould the legal mother, and maintaining that she is entitled to visitation, the court has prolonged the fight over Baby M. It is hard to see how this can be in her best interests. This is no ordinary divorce case, where the child has a relation with both parents that it is desirable to maintain. As Mr. Stern said at the start of the court hearing to determine visitation, "Melissa has a right to grow and be happy and not be torn between two parents."[10]

The court's decision was well-meaning but internally inconsistent. Out of concern for the best interests of the child, it granted the Sterns custody. At the same time, by holding Ms. Whitehead-Gould to be the legal mother, with visitation rights, it precluded precisely what is most in Melissa's interest, a resolution of the situation. Further, the decision leaves open the distressing possibility that a Baby M situation could happen again. Legislative efforts should be directed toward ensuring that this worst-case scenario never occurs.

Should Surrogacy Be Prohibited?

On June 27, 1988, Michigan became the first state to outlaw commercial contracts for women to bear children for others.[11] Yet making a practice illegal does not necessarily make it go away: witness black-market adoption. The legitimate concerns that support a ban on surrogacy might be better served by careful regulation. However, some practices, such as slavery, are ethically unacceptable, regardless of how carefully regulated they are. Let us consider the arguments that surrogacy is intrinsically unacceptable.

Paternalistic Arguments

These arguments against surrogacy take the form of protecting a potential surrogate from a choice she may later regret. As an argument for banning surro-

gacy, as opposed to providing safeguards to ensure that contracts are freely and knowledgeably undertaken, this is a form of paternalism.

At one time, the characterization of a prohibition as paternalistic was a sufficient reason to reject it. The pendulum has swung back, and many people are willing to accept at least some paternalistic restrictions on freedom. Gerald Dworkin points out that even Mill made one exception to his otherwise absolute rejection of paternalism: he thought that no one should be allowed to sell himself into slavery, because to do so would be to destroy his future autonomy.

This provides a narrow principle to justify some paternalistic interventions. To preserve freedom in the long run, we give up the freedom to make certain choices, those that have results that are "far-reaching, potentially dangerous and irreversible."[12] An example would be a ban on the sale of crack. Virtually everyone who uses crack becomes addicted and, once addicted, a slave to its use. We reasonably and willingly give up our freedom to buy the drug, to protect our ability to make free decisions in the future.

Can a Dworkian argument be made to rule out surrogacy agreements? Admittedly, the decision to give up a child is permanent, and may have disastrous effects on the surrogate mother. However, many decisions may have long-term, disastrous effects (e.g., postponing childbirth for a career, having an abortion, giving a child up for adoption). Clearly we do not want the state to make decisions for us in all these matters. Dworkin's argument is rightly restricted to paternalistic interferences that protect the individual's autonomy or ability to make decisions in the future. Surrogacy does not involve giving up one's autonomy, which distinguishes it from both the crack and selling-oneself-into-slavery examples. Respect for individual freedom requires us to permit people to make choices they may later regret.

Moral Objections

Four main moral objections to surrogacy were outlined in the Warnock Report.[13]

1. It is inconsistent with human dignity that a woman should use her uterus for financial profit.
2. To deliberately become pregnant with the intention of giving up the child distorts the relationship between mother and child.
3. Surrogacy is degrading because it amounts to child-selling.

4. Since there are some risks attached to pregnancy, no woman ought to be asked to undertake pregnancy for another in order to earn money.[14]

We must all agree that a practice that exploits people or violates human dignity is immoral. However, it is not clear that surrogacy is guilty on either count.

Exploitation   The mere fact that pregnancy is *risky* does not make surrogate agreements exploitive, and therefore morally wrong. People often do risky things for money; why should the line be drawn at undergoing pregnancy? The usual response is to compare surrogacy and kidney-selling. The selling of organs is prohibited because of the potential for coercion and exploitation. But why should kidney-selling be viewed as intrinsically coercive? A possible explanation is that no one would do it, unless driven by poverty. The choice is both forced and dangerous, and hence coercive.[15]

The situation is quite different in the case of the race-car driver or stuntman. We do not think that they are *forced* to perform risky activities for money: they freely choose to do so. Unlike selling one's kidneys, these are activities that we can understand (intellectually, anyway) someone choosing to do. Movie stuntmen, for example, often enjoy their work, and derive satisfaction from doing it well. Of course they "do it for the money," in the sense that they would not do it without compensation; few people are willing to work "for free." The element of coercion is missing, however, because they enjoy the job, despite the risks, and could do something else if they chose.

The same is apparently true of most surrogates. "They choose the surrogate role primarily because the fee provides a better economic opportunity than alternative occupations, but also because they enjoy being pregnant and the respect and attention that it draws."[16] Some may derive a feeling of self-worth from an act they regard as highly altruistic: providing a couple with a child they could not otherwise have. If these motives are present, it is far from clear that the surrogate is being exploited. Indeed, it seems objectionally paternalistic to insist that she is.

Human dignity   It may be argued that even if womb-leasing is not necessarily exploitive, it should still be rejected as inconsistent with human dignity. But why? As John Harris points out, hair, blood, and other tissue is often donated or sold; what is so special about the uterus?[17]

Human dignity is more plausibly invoked in the strongest argument against surrogacy, namely, that it is the sale of a child. Children are not property, nor can they be bought or sold.[18] It could be argued that surrogacy is wrong because it is analogous to slavery, and so is inconsistent with human dignity.

However, there are important differences between slavery and a surrogate agreement.[19] The child born of a surrogate is not treated cruelly or deprived of freedom or resold; none of the things that make slavery so awful are part of surrogacy. Still, it may be thought that simply putting a market value on a child is wrong. Human life has intrinsic value; it is literally priceless. Arrangements that ignore this violate our deepest notions of the value of human life. It is profoundly disturbing to hear in a television documentary on surrogacy the boyfriend of a surrogate say, quite candidly, "We're in it for the money."

Judge Sorkow accepted the premise that producing a child for money denigrates human dignity, but he denied that this happens in a surrogate agreement. Ms. Whitehead was not paid for the surrender of the child to the father: she was paid for her willingness to be impregnated and carry Mr. Stern's child to term. The child, once born, is his biological child. "He cannot purchase what is already his."[20]

This is misleading, and not merely because Baby M is as much Ms. Whitehead's child as Mr. Stern's. It is misleading because it glosses over the fact that the surrender of the child was part—indeed, the whole point—of the agreement. If the surrogate were paid merely for being willing to be impregnated and carrying the child to term, then she would fulfill the contract upon giving birth. She could take the money *and* the child. Mr. Stern did not agree to pay Ms. Whitehead merely to *have* his child, but to provide him with a child. The New Jersey Supreme Court held that this violated New Jersey's laws prohibiting the payment or acceptance of money in connection with adoption.

One way to remove the taint of baby-selling would be to limit payment to medical expenses associated with the birth or incurred by the surrogate during pregnancy (as is allowed in many jurisdictions, including New Jersey, in ordinary adoptions).[21] Surrogacy could be seen, not as baby-selling, but as a form of adoption. Nowhere did the Supreme Court find any legal prohibition against surrogacy when there is no payment, and when the surrogate has the right to change her mind and keep the child. However, this solution effectively prohibits surrogacy, since few women would become surrogates solely for self-fulfillment or reasons of altruism.

The question, then, is whether we can reconcile paying the surrogate, beyond her medical expenses, with the idea of surrogacy as prenatal adoption. We can do this by separating the terms of the agreement, which include surrendering the infant at birth to the biological father, from the justification for payment. The payment should be seen as compensation for the risks, sacrifice, and discomfort the surrogate undergoes during pregnancy. This means that if, through no fault on the part of the surrogate, the baby is stillborn, she should still be paid in full, since she has kept her part of the bargain. (By contrast, in the Stern-Whitehead agreement, Ms. Whitehead was to receive only $1,000 for a stillbirth).[22] If, on the other hand, the surrogate changes her mind and decides to keep the child, she would break the agreement, and would not be entitled to any fee or to compensation for expenses incurred during pregnancy.

The Right of Privacy

Most commentators who invoke the right of privacy do so in support of surrogacy.[23] However, George Annas makes the novel argument that the right to rear a child you have borne is also a privacy right, which cannot be prospectively waived. He says:

> [Judge Sorkow] grudgingly concedes that [Ms. Whitehead] could not prospectively give up her right to have an abortion during pregnancy. . . . This would be an intolerable restriction on her liberty and under *Roe v. Wade,* the state has no constitutional authority to enforce a contract that prohibits her from terminating her pregnancy. But why isn't the same logic applicable to the right to rear a child you have given birth to? Her constitutional rights to rear the child she has given birth to are even stronger since they involve even more intimately, and over a lifetime, her privacy rights to reproduce and rear a child in a family setting.[24]

Absent a compelling state interest (such as protecting a child from unfit parents), it certainly would be an intolerable invasion of privacy for the state to take children from their parents. But Baby M has two parents, both of whom now want her. It is not clear why only people who can give birth (i.e., women) should enjoy the right to rear their children.

Moreover, we do allow women to give their children up for adoption after birth. The state enforces those agreements even if the natural mother, after the prescribed waiting period, changes her mind. Why should the right to rear a child be unwaivable before, but not after, birth? Why should the state have the constitutional authority to uphold postnatal, but not prenatal, adoption agreements? It is not clear why birth should affect the waivability of this right or have the constitutional significance that Annas attributes to it.

Nevertheless, there are sound moral and policy, if not constitutional, reasons to provide a postnatal waiting period in surrogate agreements. As the Baby M case makes painfully clear, the surrogate may underestimate the bond created by gestation and the emotional trauma caused by relinquishing the baby. Compassion requires that we acknowledge these findings, and not deprive a woman of the baby she has carried because, before conception, she underestimated the strength of her feelings for it. Providing a waiting period, as in ordinary postnatal adoptions, will help protect women from making irrevocable mistakes, without banning the practice.

Some may object that this gives too little protection to the prospective adoptive parents. They cannot be sure that the baby is theirs until the waiting period is over. While this is hard on them, a similar burden is placed on other adoptive parents. If the absence of a guarantee serves to discourage people from entering surrogacy agreements, that is not necessarily a bad thing, given all the risks inherent in such contracts. In addition, this requirement would make stricter screening and counseling of surrogates essential, a desirable side-effect.

Harm to Others

Paternalistic and moral objections to surrogacy do not seem to justify an outright ban. What about the effect on the offspring of such contracts? We do not yet have solid data on the effects of being a "surrogate child." Any claim that surrogacy creates psychological problems in the children is purely speculative. But what if we did discover that such children have deep feelings of worthlessness from learning that their natural mothers deliberately created them with the intention of giving them away? Might we ban surrogacy as posing an unacceptable risk of psychological harm to the resulting children?

Feelings of worthlessness are harmful. They can prevent people from living happy, fulfilling lives. However, a surrogate child, even one whose life is miserable because of these feelings, cannot claim to have been harmed by the surrogate agreement. Without the agreement, the child would never have existed. Unless she is willing to say that her life is not worth living because of these feelings, that she would be better off never having been born, she cannot claim to have been harmed by being born of a surrogate mother.[25]

Elsewhere I have argued that children can be *wronged* by being brought into existence, even if they are not, strictly speaking, *harmed*.[26] They are wronged if they are deprived of the minimally decent existence to which all citizens are entitled. We owe it to our children to see that they are not born with such serious impairments that their most basic interests will be doomed in advance. If being born to a surrogate is a handicap of this magnitude, comparable to being born blind or deaf or severely mentally retarded, then surrogacy can be seen as wronging the offspring. This would be a strong reason against permitting such contracts. However, it does not seem likely. Probably the problems arising from surrogacy will be like those faced by adopted children and children whose parents divorce. Such problems are not trivial, but neither are they so serious that the child's very existence can be seen as wrongful.

If surrogate children are neither harmed nor wronged by surrogacy, it may seem that the argument for banning surrogacy on grounds of its harmfulness to the offspring evaporates. After all, if the children themselves have no cause for complaint, how can anyone else claim to reject it on their behalf? Yet it seems extremely counter-intuitive to suggest that the risk of emotional damage to the children born of such arrangements is not even relevant to our deliberations. It seems quite reasonable and proper—even morally obligatory—for policymakers to think about the possible detrimental effects of new reproductive technologies, and to reject those likely to create physically or emotionally damaged people. The explanation for this must involve the idea that it is wrong to bring people into

the world in a harmful condition, even if they are not, strictly speaking, harmed by having been brought into existence.[27] Should evidence emerge that surrogacy produces children with serious psychological problems, that would be a strong reason for banning the practice.

There is some evidence on the effect of surrogacy on the other children of the surrogate mother. One woman reported that her daughter, now seventeen, who was eleven at the time of the surrogate birth, "is still having problems with what I did, and as a result she is still angry with me." She explains: "Nobody told me that a child could bond with a baby while you're still pregnant. I didn't realize then that all the times she listened to his heartbeat and felt his legs kick that she was becoming attached to him."[28]

A less sentimental explanation is possible. It seems likely that her daughter, seeing one child given away, was fearful that the same might be done to her. We can expect anxiety and resentment on the part of children whose mothers give away a brother or sister. The psychological harm to these children is clearly relevant to a determination of whether surrogacy is contrary to public policy. At the same time, it should be remembered that many things, including divorce, remarriage, and even moving to a new neighborhood, create anxiety and resentment in children. We should not use the effect on children as an excuse for banning a practice we find bizarre or offensive.

Conclusion

There are many reasons to be extremely cautious of surrogacy. I cannot imagine becoming a surrogate, nor would I advise anyone else to enter into a contract so fraught with peril. But the fact that a practice is risky, foolish, or even morally distasteful is not sufficient reason to outlaw it. It would be better for the state to regulate the practice, and minimize the potential for harm, without infringing on the liberty of citizens.

---

1. See, for example, "Surrogate Motherhood Agreements: Contemporary Legal Aspects of a Biblical Notion," *University of Richmond Law Review,* 16 (1982): 470; "Surrogate Mothers: The Legal Issues," *American Journal of Law & Medicine,* 7 (1981): 338, and Angela Holder, *Legal Issues in Pediatrics and Adolescent Medicine* (New Haven: Yale University Press, 1985), 8: "Where a surrogate mother decides that she does not want to

give the baby up for adoption, as has already happened, *it is clear that no court will enforce a contract entered into before the child was born* in which she agreed to surrender her baby for adoption." Emphasis added.

2. Had the Sterns been informed of the psychologist's concerns as to Ms. Whitehead's suitability to be a surrogate, they might have ended the arrangement, costing the Infertility Center its fee. As

Chief Justice Wilentz said, "It is apparent that the profit motive got the better of the Infertility Center." In the matter of Baby M, Supreme Court of New Jersey, A-39, at 45.

3. "[W]e think it is expecting something well beyond normal human capabilities to suggest that this mother should have parted with her newly born infant without a struggle. . . . We . . . cannot conceive of any other case where a perfectly fit mother was expected to surrender her newly born infant, perhaps forever, and was then told she was a bad mother because she did not." Id.: 79.

4. "Father Recalls Surrogate Was 'Perfect,'" *New York Times*, Jan. 6, 1987, B2.

5. Id.

6. In the matter of Baby M, supra note 2, at 8.

7. This possibility was suggested to me by Susan Vermazen.

8. George Annas, "Baby M: Babies (and Justice) for Sale," Hastings Center Report, 17, no. 3 (1987): 15.

9. In the matter of Baby M, supra note 2, at 75.

10. "Anger and Anguish at Baby M Visitation Hearing," *New York Times*, March 29, 1988, 17.

11. *New York Times,* June 28, 1988, A20.

12. Gerald Dworkin, "Paternalism," in R. A. Wasserstrom, ed., *Morality and the Law* (Belmont, Cal.: Wadsworth, 1971); reprinted in J. Feinberg and H. Gross, eds., *Philosophy of Law,* 3d ed. (Belmont, Cal.: Wadsworth, 1986), 265.

13. M. Warnock, chair, *Report of the Committee of Inquiry into Human Fertilisation and Embryology* (London: Her Majesty's Stationery Office, 1984).

14. As summarized in J. Harris, *The Value of Life* (London: Routledge & Kegan Paul, 1985), 142.

15. For an argument that kidney-selling need not be coercive, see B. A. Brody and H. T. Engelhardt, Jr., *Bioethics: Readings and Cases* (Englewood Cliffs, N.J.: Prentice-Hall, 1987), 331.

16. John Robertson, "Surrogate Mothers: Not So Novel after All," Hastings Center Report, 13, no. 5 (1983): 29; citing P. Parker, "Surrogate Mother's Motivations: Initial Findings," *American Journal of Psychiatry,* 140 (1983): 1.

17. Harris, supra note 14, at 144.

18. Several authors note that it is both illegal and contrary to public policy to buy or sell children, and therefore contracts that contemplate this are unenforceable. See B. Cohen, "Surrogate Mothers: Whose Baby Is It?," *American Journal of Law & Medicine,* 10 (1984): 253; "Surrogate Mother Agreements: Contemporary Legal Aspects of a Biblical Notion," University of Richmond Law Review, 16 (1982): 469.

19. Robertson makes a similar point, supra note 16, at 33.

20. In re Baby "M," 217 N.J. Super. 372, 525 A.2d 1157 (1987).

21. Cohen, supra note 18. See also Angela Holder, "Surrogate Motherhood: Babies for Fun and Profit," *Law, Medicine & Health Care,* 12 (1984): 115.

22. Annas, supra note 8, at 14.

23. See, for example, Robertson, supra note 16, at 32; and S. R. Gersz, "The Contract in Surrogate Motherhood: A Review of the Issues," *Law, Medicine & Health Care,* 12 (1984): 107.

24. Annas, supra note 8.

25. For discussion of these issues, see D. Parfit, "On Doing the Best for Our Children," in M. D. Bayles, ed., *Ethics and Population* (Cambridge, Mass.: Schenkman, 1976); M. D. Bayles, "Harm to the Unconceived," *Philosophy & Public Affairs,* 5 (1976): 292; J. Glover, *Causing Death and Saving Lives* (Harmondsworth, Eng.: Penguin, 1977), 67; John Robertson, "In Vitro Conception and Harm to the Unborn," *Hastings Center Report,* 8 (1978): 13; J. Feinberg, *Harm to Others* (Oxford: Oxford University Press, 1984), 95.

26. Bonnie Steinbock, "The Logical Case for 'Wrongful Life'," *Hastings Center Report,* 16, no. 2 (1986): 15.

27. For the distinction between being harmed and being in a harmful state, see Feinberg, supra note 25, at 99.

28. "Baby M Case Stirs Feelings of Surrogate Mothers," *New York Times,* March 2, 1987, B1.4

Justice, Affirmative Action, and Racial Quotas

EQUAL TREATMENT AND COMPENSATORY DISCRIMINATION*

Thomas Nagel

It is currently easier, or widely thought to be easier, to get certain jobs or to gain admission to certain educational institutions if one is black or a woman than if one is a white man. Whether or not this is true, many people think it should be true, and many others think it should not. The question is: If a black person or a woman is admitted to a law school or medical school, or appointed to a certain academic or administrative post, in preference to a white man who is in other respects better qualified,[1] and if this is done in pursuit of a preferential policy or to fill a quota, is it unjust? Can the white man complain that he has been unjustly treated? It is important to investigate the justice of such practices, because if they are unjust, it is much more difficult to defend them on grounds of social utility. I shall argue that although preferential policies are not required by justice, they are not seriously unjust either—because the system from which they depart is already unjust for reasons having nothing to do with racial or sexual discrimination.

I

In the United States, the following steps seem to have led us to a situation in which these questions arise. First, and not very long ago, it came to be widely accepted that deliberate barriers against the admission of blacks and women to desirable positions should be abolished. Their abolition is by no means complete, and certain educational institutions, for example, may be able to maintain limiting quotas on the admission of women for some time. But deliberate discrimination is widely condemned.

Secondly, it was recognized that even without explicit barriers there could be discrimination, either consciously or unconsciously motivated, and this gave support to self-conscious efforts at impartiality, careful consideration of candidates belonging to the class discriminated against, and attention to the proportions of blacks and women in desirable positions, as evidence that otherwise undetectable bias might be influencing the selections. (Another, related con-

*From Nagel, Thomas. "Equal Treatment and Compensatory Discrimination," in *Philosophy and Public Affairs,* vol. 2, no. 4 (1973), pp. 348–63. Copyright © 1973 by Princeton University Press. Reprinted by permission of Princeton University Press.

sideration is that criteria which were good predictors of performance for one group might turn out to be poor predictors of performance for another group, so that the continued employment of those criteria might introduce a concealed inequity.)

The third step came with the realization that a social system may continue to deny different races or sexes equal opportunity or equal access to desirable positions even after the discriminatory barriers to those positions have been lifted. Socially-caused inequality in the capacity to make use of available opportunities or to compete for available positions may persist, because the society systematically provides to one group more than to another certain educational, social, or economic advantages. Such advantages improve one's competitive position in seeking access to jobs or places in professional schools. Where there has recently been widespread deliberate discrimination in many areas, it will not be surprising if the formerly excluded group experiences relative difficulty in gaining access to newly opened positions, and it is plausible to explain the difficulty at least partly in terms of disadvantages produced by past discrimination. This leads to the adoption of compensatory measures, in the form of special training programs, or financial support, or day-care centers, or apprenticeships, or tutoring. Such measures are designed to qualify those whose reduced qualifications are due to racial or sexual discrimination, either because they have been the direct victims of such discrimination, or because they are deprived as a result of membership in a group or community many of whose other members have been discriminated against. The second of these types of influence covers a great deal, and the importance of the social contribution is not always easy to establish. Nevertheless its effects typically include the loss of such goods as self-esteem, self-confidence, motivation, and ambition—all of which contribute to competitive success and none of which is easily restored by special training programs. Even if social injustice has produced such effects, it may be difficult for society to eradicate them.

This type of justification for compensatory programs raises another question. If it depends on the claim that the disadvantages being compensated for are the product of social injustice, then it becomes important how great the contribution of social injustice actually is, and to what extent the situation is due to social causes not involving injustice, or to causes that are not social, but biological. If one believes that society's responsibility for compensatory measures extends only to those disadvantages due to social in-

justice, one will assign political importance to the degree, if any, to which racial differences in average I.Q. are genetically influenced, or the innate contribution, if any, to the statistical differences, if any, in emotional or intellectual characteristics between men and women. Also, if one believes that among socially-produced inequalities, there is a crucial distinction for the requirement of compensation between those which are produced unjustly and those which are merely the incidental results of just social arrangements, then it will be very important to decide exactly where that line falls: whether, for example, certain intentions must be referred to in arguing that a disadvantage has been unjustly imposed. But let me put those issues aside for the moment.

The fourth stage comes when it is acknowledged that some unjustly caused disadvantages, which create difficulties of access to positions formally open to all, cannot be overcome by special programs of preparatory or remedial training. One is then faced with the alternative of either allowing the effects of social injustice to confer a disadvantage in the access to desirable positions that are filled simply on the basis of qualifications relevant to performance in those positions, or else instituting a system of compensatory discrimination in the selection process to increase access for those whose qualifications are lower at least partly as a result of unjust discrimination in other situations and at other times (and possibly against other persons). This is a difficult choice, and it would certainly be preferable to find a more direct method of rectification, than to balance inequality in one part of the social system by introducing a reverse inequality at a different point. If the society as a whole contains serious injustices with complex effects, there is probably, in any case, no way for a single institution within that society to adjust its criteria for competitive admission or employment so that the effects of injustice are nullified as far as that institution is concerned. There is consequently considerable appeal to the position that places should be filled solely by reference to the criteria relevant to performance, and if this tends to amplify or extend the effects of inequitable treatment elsewhere, the remedy must be found in a more direct attack on those differences in qualifications, rather than in the introduction of irrelevant criteria of appointment or admission which will also sacrifice efficiency, productivity, or effectiveness of the institution in its specific tasks.

At this fourth stage we therefore find a broad division of opinion. There are those who believe that nothing further can legitimately be done in the short run, once the *remediable* unjust inequalities of opportunity between individuals have been dealt with: the irremediable ones are unjust, but any further steps to counterbalance them by reverse discrimination would also be unjust, because they must employ irrelevant criteria. On the other hand, there are those who find it unacceptable in such circumstances to stay with the restricted criteria usually related to successful performance, and who believe that differential admission or hiring standards for worse-off groups are justified because they roughly, though only approximately, compensate for the inequalities of opportunity produced by past injustice.

But at this point there is some temptation to resolve the dilemma and strengthen the argument for preferential standards by proceeding to a fifth stage. One may reflect that if the criteria relevant to the prediction of performance are not inviolable it may not matter whether one violates them to compensate for disadvantages caused by injustice or disadvantages caused in other ways. The fundamental issue is what grounds to use in assigning or admitting people to desirable positions. To settle that issue, one does not have to settle the question of the degree to which racial or sexual discrepancies are socially produced, because the differentials in reward ordinarily correlated with differences in qualifications are not the result of natural justice, but simply the effect of a competitive system trying to fill positions and perform tasks efficiently. Certain abilities may be relevant to filling a job from the point of view of efficiency, but they are not relevant from the point of view of justice, because they provide no indication that one deserves the rewards that go with holding that job. The qualities, experience, and attainments that make success in a certain position likely do not in themselves merit the rewards that happen to attach to occupancy of that position in a competitive economy.

Consequently it might be concluded that if women or black people are less qualified, for *whatever* reason, in the respects that lead to success in the professions that our society rewards most highly, then it would be just to compensate for this disadvantage, within the limits permitted by efficiency, by having suitably different standards for these groups, and thus bringing their access to desirable positions more into line with that of others. Compensatory discrimination would not, on this view, have to be tailored to deal only with the effects of past injustice.

But it is clear that this is not a stable position. For if one abandons the condition that to qualify for compensation an inequity must be socially caused,

then there is no reason to restrict the compensatory measures to well-defined racial or sexual groups. Compensatory selection procedures would have to be applied on an individual basis, within as well as between such groups—each person, regardless of race, sex, or qualifications, being granted equal access to the desirable positions, within limits set by efficiency. This might require randomization of law and medical school admissions, for example, from among all the candidates who were above some minimum standard enabling them to do the work. If we were to act on the principle that different abilities do not merit different rewards, it would result in much more equality than is demanded by proponents of compensatory discrimination.

There is no likelihood that such a radical course will be adopted in the United States, but the fact that it seems to follow naturally from a certain view about how to deal with racial or sexual injustice reveals something important. When we try to deal with the inequality in advantages that results from a disparity in qualifications (however produced) between races or sexes, we are up against a pervasive and fundamental feature of the system, which at every turn exacts costs and presents obstacles in response to attempts to reduce the inequalities. We must face the possibility that the primary injustice with which we have to contend lies in this feature itself, and that some of the worst aspects of what we now perceive as racial or sexual injustice are merely conspicuous manifestations of the great social injustice of differential reward.

II

If differences in the capacity to succeed in the tasks that any society rewards well are visibly correlated, for whatever reason, with other characteristics such as race or religion or social origin, then a system of liberal equality of opportunity will give the appearance of supporting racial or religious or class injustice. Where there is no such correlation, there can be the appearance of justice through equal opportunity. But in reality, there is similar injustice in both cases, and it lies in the schedule of rewards.

The liberal idea of equal treatment demands that people receive equal opportunities if they are equally qualified by talent or education to utilize those opportunities. In requiring the relativization of equal treatment to characteristics in which people are very unequal, it guarantees that the social order will reflect and probably magnify the initial distinctions produced by nature and the past. Liberalism has therefore come under increasing attack in recent years, on the ground that the familiar principle of equal treatment, with its meritocratic conception of relevant differences, seems too weak to combat the inequalities dispensed by nature and the ordinary workings of the social system.

This criticism of the view that people deserve the rewards that accrue to them as a result of their natural talents is not based on the idea that no one can be said to deserve anything.[2] For if no one deserves anything, then no inequalities are contrary to desert, and desert provides no argument for equality. Rather, I am suggesting that for many benefits and disadvantages, certain characteristics of the recipient *are* relevant to what he deserves. If people are equal in the relevant respects, that by itself constitutes a reason to distribute the benefit to them equally.[3]

The relevant features will vary with the benefit or disadvantage, and so will the weight of the resulting considerations of desert. Desert may sometimes, in fact, be a rather unimportant consideration in determining what ought to be done. But I do wish to claim, with reference to a central case, that differential abilities are not usually among the characteristics that determine whether people *deserve* economic and social benefits (though of course they determine whether people *get* such benefits). In fact, I believe that nearly all characteristics are irrelevant to what people deserve in this dimension, and that most people therefore deserve to be treated equally.[4] Perhaps voluntary differences in effort or moral differences in conduct have some bearing on economic and social desert. I do not have a precise view about what features are relevant. I contend only that they are features in which most people do not differ enough to justify very wide differences in reward.[5] (While I realize that these claims are controversial, I shall not try to defend them here, nor to defend the legitimacy of the notion of desert itself. If these things make no sense, neither does the rest of my argument.)

A decision that people are equally or unequally deserving in some respect is not the end of the story. First of all, desert can sometimes be overridden, for example by liberty or even by efficiency. In some cases the presumption of equality is rather weak, and not much is required to depart from it. This will be so if the interest in question is minor or temporally circumscribed, and does not represent an important value in the subject's life.

Secondly, it may be that although an inequality is contrary to desert, no one can benefit from its removal: all that can be done is to worsen the position of those who benefit undeservedly from its presence. Even if one believes that desert is a very important factor in determining just distributions, one need not object to inequalities that are to no one's disadvantage. In other words, it is possible to accept something like Rawls's Difference Principle from the standpoint of an egalitarian view of desert.[6] (I say it is possible. It may not be required. Some may reject the Difference Principle because they regard equality of treatment as a more stringent requirement.)

Thirdly (and most significantly for the present discussion), a determination of relative desert in the distribution of a particular advantage does not even settle the question of *desert* in every case, for there may be other advantages and disadvantages whose distribution is tied to that of the first, and the characteristics relevant to the determination of desert are not necessarily the same from one advantage to another. This bears on the case under consideration in the following way. I have said that people with different talents do not thereby deserve different economic and social rewards. They may, however, deserve different opportunities to exercise and develop those talents.[7] Whenever the distribution of two different types of benefit is connected in this way, through social or economic mechanisms or through natural human reactions, it may be impossible to avoid a distribution contrary to the conditions of desert in respect of at least one of the benefits. Therefore it is likely that a dilemma will arise in which it appears that injustice cannot be entirely avoided. It may then be necessary to decide that justice in the distribution of one advantage has priority over justice in the distribution of another that automatically goes with it.

In the case under discussion, there appears to be a conflict between justice in the distribution of educational and professional opportunities and justice in the distribution of economic and social rewards. I do not deny that there is a presumption, based on something more than efficiency, in favor of giving equal opportunities to those equally likely to succeed. But if the presumption in favor of economic equality is considerably stronger, the justification for departing from it must be stronger too. If this is so, then when "educational" justice and economic justice come into conflict, it will sometimes be necessary to sacrifice the former to the latter.

III

In thinking about racial and sexual discrimination, the view that economic justice has priority may tempt one to proceed to what I have called the fifth stage. One may be inclined to adopt admission quotas, for example, proportional to the representation of a given group in the population, because one senses the injustice of differential rewards per se. Whatever explains the small number of women or blacks in the professions, it has the result that they have less of the financial and social benefits that accrue to members of the professions, and what accounts for those differences cannot justify them. So justice requires that more women and blacks be admitted to the professions.

The trouble with this solution is that it does not locate the injustice accurately, but merely tries to correct the racially or sexually skewed economic distribution which is one of its more conspicuous symptoms. We are enabled to perceive the situation as unjust because we see it, e.g., through its racial manifestations, and race is a subject by now associated in our minds with injustice. However, little is gained by merely transferring the same system of differential rewards, suitably adjusted to achieve comparable proportions, to the class of blacks or the class of women. If it is unjust to reward people differentially for what certain characteristics enable them to do, it is equally unjust whether the distinction is made between a white man and a black man or between two black men, or two white women, or two black women. There is no way of attacking the unjust reward schedules (if indeed they are unjust) of a meritocratic system by attacking their racial or sexual manifestations directly.

In most societies reward is a function of demand, and many of the human characteristics most in demand result largely from *gifts* or *talents*. The greatest injustice in this society, I believe, is neither racial nor sexual but intellectual. I do not mean that it is unjust that some people are more intelligent than others. Nor do I mean that society rewards people differentially simply on the basis of their intelligence: usually it does not. Nevertheless it provides on the average much larger rewards for tasks that require superior intelligence than for those that do not. This is simply the way things work out in a technologically advanced society with a market economy. It does not reflect a social judgment that smart people *deserve* the opportunity to make more money than

dumb people. They may deserve richer educational opportunity, but they do not therefore deserve the material wealth that goes with it. Similar things could be said about society's differential reward of achievements facilitated by other talents or gifts, like beauty, athletic ability, musicality, etc. But intelligence and its development by education provide a particularly significant and pervasive example.

However, a general reform of the current schedule of rewards, even if they are unjust, is beyond the power of individual educational or business institutions, working through their admissions or appointments policies. A competitive economy is bound to reward those with certain training and abilities, and a refusal to do so will put any business enterprise in a poor competitive position. Similarly, those who succeed in medical school or law school will tend to earn more than those who do not—whatever criteria of admission the schools adopt. It is not the procedures of appointment or admission, based on criteria that predict success, that are unjust, but rather what happens as a result of success.

No doubt a completely just solution is not ready to hand. If, as I have claimed, different factors are relevant to what is deserved in the distribution of different benefits and disadvantages, and if the distribution of several distinct advantages is sometimes connected even though the relevant factors are not, then inevitably there will be injustice in some respect, and it may be practically impossible to substitute a principle of distribution which avoids it completely.

Justice may require that we try to reduce the automatic connections between material advantages, cultural opportunity, and institutional authority. But such changes can be brought about, if at all, only by large alterations in the social system, the system of taxation, and the salary structure. They will not be achieved by modifying the admissions or hiring policies of colleges and universities, or even banks, law firms, and businesses.

Compensatory measures in admissions or appointment can be defended on grounds of justice only to the extent that they compensate for specific disadvantages which have themselves been unjustly caused, by factors distinct from the general meritocratic character of the system of distribution of advantageous positions. Such contributions are difficult to verify or estimate; they probably vary among individuals in the oppressed group. Moreover, it is not obvious that where a justification for preferential treatment exists, it is strong enough to create an obligation, since it is doubtful that one element of a pluralistic society is obliged to adopt discriminatory measures to counteract injustice due to another element, or even to the society as a whole.

IV

These considerations suggest that an argument on grounds of justice for the imposition of racial or sexual quotas would be difficult to construct without the aid of premises about the source of unequal qualifications between members of different groups. The more speculative the premises, the weaker the argument. But the question with which I began was not whether compensatory discrimination is *required* by justice, but whether it is *compatible* with justice. To that question I think we can give a different answer. If the reflections about differential reward to which we have been led are correct, then compensatory discrimination need not be seriously unjust, and it may be warranted not by justice but by considerations of social utility. I say not *seriously* unjust, to acknowledge that a departure from the standards relevant to distribution of intellectual opportunities *per se* is itself a kind of injustice. But its seriousness is lessened because the factors relevant to the distribution of intellectual opportunity are irrelevant to the distribution of those material benefits that go with it. This weakens the claim of someone who argues that by virtue of those qualities that make him likely to succeed in a certain position, he deserves to be selected for that position in preference to someone whose qualifications make it likely that he will succeed less well. He cannot claim that justice requires the allocation of positions on the basis of ability, because the result of such allocation, in the present system, is serious injustice of a different kind.

My contention, then, is that where the allocation of one benefit on relevant grounds carries with it the allocation of other, more significant benefits to which those grounds are irrelevant, the departure from those grounds need not be a serious offense against justice. This may be so for two reasons. First, the presumption of equal treatment of relevantly equal persons in respect of the first benefit may not be very strong to begin with. Second, the fairness of abiding by the presumption may be overshadowed by the unfairness of the other distribution correlated with it. Consequently, it may be acceptable to depart from the "relevant" grounds for undramatic reasons of social utility, that would not justify more flagrant

and undiluted examples of unfairness. Naturally a deviation from the usual method will appear unjust to those who are accustomed to regarding ability to succeed as the correct criterion, but this appearance may be an illusion. That depends on how much injustice is involved in the usual method, and whether the reasons for departing from it are good enough, even though they do not correct the injustice.

The problem, of course, is to say what a good reason is. I do not want to produce an argument that will justify not only compensatory discrimination on social grounds, but also ordinary racial or sexual discrimination designed to preserve internal harmony in a business, for instance. Even someone who thought that the system of differential economic rewards for different abilities was unjust would presumably regard it as an *additional* unjustice if standard racial, religious, or sexual discrimination were a factor in the assignment of individuals to highly rewarded positions.

I can offer only a partial account of what makes systematic racial or sexual discrimination so exceptionally unjust. It has no social advantages, and it attaches a sense of reduced worth to a feature with which people are born.[8] A psychological consequence of the systematic attachment of social disadvantages to a certain inborn feature is that both the possessors of the feature and others begin to regard it as an essential and important characteristic, and one which reduces the esteem in which its possessor can be held.[9] Concomitantly, those who do not possess the characteristic gain a certain amount of free esteem by comparison, and the arrangement thus constitutes a gross sacrifice of the most basic personal interests of some for the interests of others, with those sacrificed being on the bottom. (It is because similar things can be said about the social and economic disadvantages that attach to low intelligence that I am inclined to regard that, too, as a major injustice.)

Reverse discrimination need not have these consequences, and it can have social advantages. Suppose, for example, that there is need for a great increase in the number of black doctors, because the health needs of the black community are unlikely to be met otherwise. And suppose that at the present average level of premedical qualifications among black applicants, it would require a huge expansion of total medical school enrollment to supply the desirable absolute number of black doctors without adopting differential admission standards. Such an expansion may be unacceptable either because of its cost or because it would produce a total supply of doctors, black and white, much greater than the society requires. This is a strong argument for accepting reverse discrimination, not on grounds of justice but on grounds of social utility. (In addition, there is the salutary effect on the aspirations and expectations of other blacks, from the visibility of exemplars in formerly inaccessible positions.)

The argument in the other direction, from the point of view of the qualified white applicants who are turned away, is not nearly as strong as the argument against standard racial discrimination. The self-esteem of whites as a group is not endangered by such a practice, since the situation arises only because of their general social dominance, and the aim of the practice is only to benefit blacks, and not to exclude whites. Moreover, although the interests of some are being sacrificed to further the interests of others, it is the better placed who are being sacrificed and the worst placed who are being helped.[10] It is an important feature of the case that the discriminatory measure is designed to favor a group whose social position is exceptionally depressed, with destructive consequences both for the self-esteem of members of the group and for the health and cohesion of the society.[11]

If, therefore, a discriminatory admissions or appointments policy is adopted to mitigate a grave social evil, and it favors a group in a particularly unfortunate social position, and if for these reasons it diverges from a meritocratic system for the assignment of positions which is not itself required by justice, then the discriminatory practice is probably not unjust.[12]

It is not without its costs, however. Not only does it inevitably produce resentment in the better qualified who are passed over because of the policy, but it also allows those in the discriminated-against group who would in fact have failed to gain a desired position in any case on the basis of their qualifications to feel that they may have lost out to someone less qualified because of the discriminatory policy. Similarly, such a practice cannot do much for the self-steem of those who know they have benefited from it, and it may threaten the self-esteem of

those in the favored group who would in fact have gained their positions even in the absence of the discriminatory policy, but who cannot be sure that they are not among its beneficiaries. This is what leads institutions to lie about their policies in this regard, or to hide them behind clouds of obscurantist rhetoric about the discriminatory character of standard admissions criteria. Such concealment is possible and even justified up to a point, but the costs cannot be entirely evaded, and discriminatory practices of this sort will be tolerable only so long as they are clearly contributing to the eradication of great social evils.

V

When racial and sexual injustice have been reduced, we shall still be left with the great injustice of the smart and the dumb, who are so differently rewarded for comparable effort. This would be an injustice even if the system of differential economic and social rewards had no systematic sexual or racial reflection. On the other hand, if the social esteem and economic advantages attaching to different occupations and educational achievements were much more uniform, there would be little cause for concern about racial, ethnic, or sexual patterns in education or work. But of course we do not at present have a method of divorcing professional status from social esteem and economic reward, at least not without a gigantic increase in total social control, on the Chinese model. Perhaps someone will discover a way in which the socially produced inequalities (especially the economic ones) between the intelligent and the unintelligent, the talented and the untalented, or even the beautiful and the ugly, can be reduced without limiting the availability of opportunities, products and services, and without resort to increased coercion or decreased liberty in the choice of work or style of life. In the absence of such a utopian solution, however, the familiar task of balancing liberty against equality will remain with us.[13]

---

1. By saying that the white man is "in other respects better qualified" I mean that if, e.g., a black candidate with similar qualifications had been available for the position, he would have been selected in preference to the black candidate who was in fact selected; or, if the choice had been between two white male candidates of corresponding qualifications, this one would have been selected. Ditto for two white or two black women. (I realize that it may not always be easy to determine similarity of qualifications, and that in some cases similarity of credentials may give evidence of a difference in qualifications—because, e.g., one person had to overcome more severe obstacles to acquire those credentials.)

2. Rawls appears to regard this as the basis of his own view. He believes it makes sense to speak of positive desert only in

the context of distributions by a just system, and not as a pre-institutional conception that can be used to measure the justice of the system. John Rawls, *A Theory of Justice* (Cambridge, Mass., 1971), pp. 310–313.

3. Essentially this view is put forward by Bernard Williams in "The Idea of Equality," in *Philosophy, Politics, and Society* (Second Series), ed. P. Laslett and W. G. Runciman (Oxford, 1964), pp. 110–131.

4. This is distinct from a case in which nothing is relevant because there is no desert in the matter. In that case the fact that people differed in no relevant characteristics would not create a presumption that they be treated equally. It would leave the determination of their treatment entirely to other considerations.

5. It is not my view that we cannot be said to deserve the results of anything which we do not deserve. It is true that a person does not deserve his intelligence, and I have maintained that he does not deserve the rewards that superior intelligence can provide. But neither does he deserve his bad moral character or his above-average willingness to work, yet I believe that he probably does deserve the punishments or rewards that flow from those qualities. For an illuminating discussion of these matters, see Robert Nozick, *Anarchy, State, and Utopia* (New York, Basic Books: forthcoming), chap. 7.

6. Rawls, *op. cit.,* pp. 75–80.

7. Either because differences of ability are relevant to degree of desert in these respects or because people are equally deserving of opportunities proportional to their talents. More likely the latter.

8. For a detailed and penetrating treatment of this and a number of other matters discussed here, see Owen M. Fiss, "A Theory of Fair Employment Laws," *University of Chicago Law Review* 38 (Winter 1971): 235–314.

9. This effect would not be produced by an idiosyncratic discriminatory practice limited to a few eccentrics. If some people decided they would have nothing to do with anyone left-handed, everyone else, including the left-handed, would regard it as a silly objection to an inessential feature. But if everyone shunned the left-handed, left-handedness would become a strong component of their self-image, and those discriminated against would feel they were being despised for their essence. What people regard as their essence is not independent of what they get admired and despised for.

10. This is a preferable direction of sacrifice if one accepts Rawls's egalitarian assumptions about distributive justice. Rawls, *op. cit.,* pp. 100–103.

11. It is therefore not, as some have feared, the first step toward an imposition of minimal or maximal quotas for all racial, religious, and ethnic subgroups of the society.

12. Adam Morton has suggested an interesting alternative, which I shall not try to develop: namely, that the practice is justified not by social utility, but because it will contribute to a more just situation in the future. The practice considered in itself may be unjust, but it is warranted by its greater contribution to justice over the long term, through eradication of a self-perpetuating pattern.

13. I have presented an earlier version of this paper to the New York Group of the Society for Philosophy and Public Affairs, the Princeton Undergraduate Philosophy Club, and the Society for Ethical and Legal Philosophy, and I thank those audiences for their suggestions.

THE MESSAGE OF AFFIRMATIVE ACTION*

Thomas E. Hill, Jr.

Affirmative action programs remain controversial, I suspect, partly because the familiar arguments for and against them start from significantly different moral perspectives. Thus I want to step back for a while from the details of debate about particular programs and give attention to the moral viewpoints presupposed in different *types* of argument. My aim, more specifically, is to compare the "messages" expressed when affirmative action is defended from different moral perspectives. Exclusively forward-looking (for example, utilitarian) arguments, I suggest, tend to express the wrong message, but this is also true of exclusively backward-looking (for example, reparation-based) arguments. However, a moral outlook that focuses on cross-temporal narrative values (such as mutually respectful social relations) suggests a more appropriate account of what affirmative action should try to express. Assessment of the message, admittedly, is only one aspect of a complex issue, but it is a relatively neglected one. My discussion takes for granted some common-sense ideas about the communicative function of action, and so I begin with these.

Actions, as the saying goes, often *speak* louder than words. There are times, too, when only actions

---

*From Hill, Jr., Thomas E. "The Message of Affirmative Action," in *Social Philosophy and Policy,* vol. 8, issue 2, (1991) pp. 108–129. Reprinted by permission of Blackwell Publishers.

can effectively communicate the message we want to convey and times when giving a message is a central part of the purpose of action. What our actions say to others depends largely, though not entirely, upon our avowed reasons for acting; and this is a matter for reflective decision, not something we discover later by looking back at what we did and its effects. The decision is important because "the same act" can have very different consequences, depending upon how we choose to justify it. In a sense, acts done for different reasons are not "the same act" even if they are otherwise similar, and so not merely the consequences but also the moral nature of our acts depends in part on our decisions about the reasons for doing them.

Unfortunately, the message actually conveyed by our actions does not depend only on our intentions and reasons, for our acts may have a meaning for others quite at odds with what we hoped to express. Others may misunderstand our intentions, doubt our sincerity, or discern a subtext that undermines the primary message. Even if sincere, well-intended, and successfully conveyed, the message of an act or policy does not by itself justify the means by which it is conveyed; it is almost always a relevant factor, however, in the moral assessment of an act or policy.

These remarks may strike you as too obvious to be worth mentioning; for, even if we do not usually express the ideas so abstractly, we are all familiar with them in our daily interactions with our friends, families, and colleagues. Who, for example, does not know the importance of the message expressed in offering money to another person, as well as the dangers of misunderstanding? What is superficially the same "act" can be an offer to buy, an admission of guilt, an expression of gratitude, a contribution to a common cause, a condescending display of superiority, or an outrageous insult. Since all this is so familiar, the extent to which these elementary points are ignored in discussions of the pros and cons of social policies such as affirmative action is surprising. The usual presumption is that social policies can be settled entirely by debating the rights involved or by estimating the consequences, narrowly conceived of as separate from the messages that we want to give and those that are likely to be received.

I shall focus attention for a while upon this relatively neglected issue of the message of affirmative action. In particular, I want to consider what message we *should try* to give with affirmative action programs and what messages we should try to avoid.

What is the best way to convey the intended message, and indeed whether it is likely to be heard, are empirical questions that I cannot settle; but the question I propose to consider is nonetheless important, and it is a *prior* question. What do we want to say with our affirmative action programs, and why? Since the message that is received and its consequences are likely to depend to some extent on what we decide, in all sincerity, to be the rationale for such programs, it would be premature and foolish to try to infer or predict these outcomes without adequate reflection on what the message and rationale should be. Also, for those who accept the historical/narrative perspective described in Section IV, there is additional reason to focus first on the desired message; for that perspective treats the message of affirmative action not merely as a minor side effect to be weighed in, for or against, but rather as an important part of the legitimate purpose of affirmative action.

Much useful discussion has been devoted to the constitutionality of affirmative action programs, to the relative moral rights involved, and to the advantages and disadvantages of specific types of programs.[1] By deemphasizing these matters here, I do not mean to suggest that they are unimportant. Even more, my remarks are not meant to convey the message, "It doesn't matter what we do or achieve, all that matters is what we *say*." To the contrary, I believe that mere gestures are insufficient and that universities cannot even communicate what they should by affirmative action policies unless these are sincerely designed to result in increased opportunities for those disadvantaged and insulted by racism and sexism.

I divide my discussion as follows. *First,* I describe briefly two affirmative action programs with which I am acquainted, so that we can have in mind some concrete examples before we turn to controversial principles. *Second,* I summarize why I think that affirmative action programs need not be illegitimate forms of "reverse discrimination" that violate the rights of non-minority males. This is a large issue, well discussed by others, but it must be considered at least briefly in order to open the way for more positive considerations. *Third,* I discuss two familiar strategies for justifying affirmative action and give some reasons for thinking that these should not be considered the whole story. One strategy, the "forward-looking," appeals exclusively to the good results expected from such programs; the other, the "backward-looking," focuses on past injustice and demands reparation. One of my main points is that this very division leads us to overlook some other important considerations. *Fourth,* in a brief philosophical interlude, I sketch a mode of evaluation that seems to provide a helpful alternative or supplement to the traditional sorts of evaluation that have dominated discussions of affirmative action. This suggestion draws from recent work in ethical theory that stresses the importance of historical context, narrative unity, and interpersonal relations. *Fifth,* combining these ideas with my proposal to consider the message of affirmative action, I present some analogies that point to an alternative perspective on the aims of affirmative action programs. Seen from this perspective, programs that stress outreach, encouragement, and development opportunities appear in a more favorable light than those that simply alter standards to meet quotas.

I. Samples of Affirmative Action Programs

Affirmative action programs take various forms and are used in many different contexts. Here, however, I shall concentrate on hiring and admission policies in universities and colleges. Even in this area there are many complexities that must be taken into account in the assessment of particular programs. It may matter, for example, whether the program is voluntary or government-mandated, quota-based or flexible, fixed-term or indefinite, in a formerly segregated institution or not, and so on. Obviously it is impossible to examine all these variations here. It is also unnecessary, for my project is not to defend or criticize specific programs but to raise general questions about how we should approach the issue. Nonetheless, though a full range of cases is not needed for this purpose, it may prove useful to sketch some sample programs that at least illustrate what the more abstract debate is about.

A common feature of affirmative action programs is that they make use of the categories of race and gender (more specifically, blacks and women) in their admissions and hiring policies, and they do so in a way that gives positive weight to being in one or the other of these latter categories. Policies use these classifications in different ways, as is evident in the cases described below.

When I taught at Pomona College in 1966–68, for example, the faculty/student Admissions Committee was blessed, or cursed, with applications numbering several times the number of places for new

students. After a careful study of the correlation between grade-point averages of graduating seniors and data available in their initial application dossiers, a professor had devised a formula for predicting "success" at the college, where success was measured by the student's academic average at graduation from college. The predictive factors included high school grades, national test scores, and a ranking of the high school according to the grades its previous graduates received at the college. All applicants were then ranked according to this formula, which was supposed purely to reflect academic promise. The top ten percent were automatically admitted; a cut-off point was established below which candidates were deemed incapable of handling the college curriculum. Then committee members made a "subjective" evaluation of the remaining (middle) candidates in which the members were supposed to give weight to special talents, high-minded ambition, community service, intriguing personality, and (more generally) the likelihood of contributing to the sort of college community that the evaluators thought desirable. Another cut was made, reflecting both the "pure academic" criteria and the subjective evaluations. Next (as I recall) the football coach, the drama instructor, the orchestra leader, and others were invited to pick a specified number from those above the minimum cut-off if they needed a quarterback, a lead actor, a tuba player, or whatever. Then those identified as minorities but above the minimum cut-off line were admitted, if they had not been already, by a procedure that started with the most qualified academically, moving down the list until the minority applicants to be admitted made up at least a certain percentage of the final number of students to be admitted (10 percent, as I recall). The rest were admitted by their place on the academic list.

Pomona College is a private institution, but some state colleges and universities have adopted policies that are similar in important respects. At the University of California at Los Angeles in the 1970s, I became familiar with a significantly different kind of affirmative action regarding graduate student admissions and faculty hiring and promotion. The emphasis here was on positive efforts to seek out and encourage qualified minority applicants—for example, through recruitment letters, calls, and campus visits. Special funds were allocated to create new faculty positions for qualified minority candidates, and special fellowships were made available to release minority faculty from some teaching duties prior to tenure. Teaching and research interests in race and gender problems were officially recognized as relevant to hiring and promotion decisions in certain departments, provided the usual academic standards were maintained. Guidelines and watchdog committees were established to require departments to prove that, each time they hired a non-minority male, they did so only after a thorough search for and examination of minority and female candidates. Since decisions to hire and promote were still determined by the judgments of diverse individuals, I suspect that some deans, department heads, and voting faculty members carried affirmative action beyond the guidelines, some countered this effect by negative bias, and some simply refused to deviate from what they perceived as "color-blind" and "sex-blind" criteria.

II. Affirmative Action or Reverse Discrimination?

Is affirmative action *necessarily* a morally illegitimate form of "reverse discrimination" that violates the rights of white male applicants?

The question here is not whether some particular affirmative action program is illegitimate, for example, because it uses quotas or causes the deliberate hiring of less qualified teachers; the question, rather, is whether making gender and race a relevant category in university policy is *in itself* unjust. If so, we need not go further with our discussion of the message of affirmative action and its advantages and disadvantages: for however important the need is to communicate and promote social benefits, we should not do so by unjust means.

Some think that the injustice of all affirmative action programs is obvious or easily demonstrated. Two facile but confused arguments seem to have an especially popular appeal. The first goes this way: "Affirmative action, by definition, gives preferential treatment to minorities and women. This is discrimination in their favor and against non-minority males. All discrimination by public institutions is unjust, no matter whether it is the old kind or the newer 'reverse discrimination.' So all affirmative action programs in public institutions are unjust."

This deceptively simple argument, of course, trades on an ambiguity. In one sense, to "discriminate" means to "make a distinction," to pay attention to a difference. In this evaluatively neutral sense, of course, affirmative action programs do discriminate. But public institutions must, and justifiably do, "discriminate"

in this sense—for example, between citizens and non-citizens, freshmen and seniors, the talented and the retarded, and those who pay their bills and those who do not. Whether it is unjust to note and make use of a certain distinction in a given context depends upon many factors: the nature of the institution, the relevant rights of the parties involved, the purposes and effects of making that distinction, and so on.

All this would be obvious except for the fact that the word "discrimination" is also used in a pejorative sense, meaning (roughly) "making use of a distinction in an unjust or illegitimate way." To discriminate in this sense is obviously wrong; but now it remains an open question whether the use of race and gender distinctions in affirmative action programs is really "discrimination" in this sense. The simplistic argument uses the evaluatively neutral sense of "discrimination" to show that affirmative action discriminates; it then shifts to the pejorative sense when it asserts that discrimination is always wrong. Although one may, in the end, *conclude* that all public use of racial and gender distinctions is unjust, to do so requires more of an *argument* than the simple one (just given) that merely exploits an ambiguity of the word "discrimination."

A slightly more sophisticated argument runs as follows: "Affirmative action programs give special benefits to certain individuals 'simply because they are women or blacks.' But one's color and gender are morally irrelevant features of a person. It is unjust for public institutions to give special benefits to individuals solely because they happen to have certain morally irrelevant characteristics. Hence affirmative action programs are always unjust."

A special twist is often added to this argument, as follows: "What was wrong with Jim Crow laws, denial of the vote to women and blacks, and segregation in schools and public facilities was just the fact that such practices treated people differently simply because they happened to have certain morally irrelevant characteristics. Affirmative action programs, however well-intentioned, are doing exactly the same thing. So they are wrong for the same reason."

Now people who argue in this way may well be trying to express something important, which should not be dismissed; but, as it stands, the argument is confused, unfair, and historically inaccurate. The confusion and unfairness lie in the misleading use of the expression "*simply* because they are women or blacks." It is true that typical affirmative action programs, such as those I described earlier, use the categories of "black" (or "minority") and "female" as an instrumental part of a complex policy. This does not mean, however, that the fundamental reason, purpose, or justification of the policy is nothing more than "this individual is black (or female)." To say that someone favors a person *simply because* that person is black (or female)" implies that there is no further reason, purpose, or justification, as if one merely had an utterly arbitrary preference for dark skin as opposed to light or female anatomy over male anatomy. But no serious advocate of affirmative action thinks the program is justified by such personal preferences. On the contrary, advocates argue that, given our historical situation, quite general principles of justice or utility justify the temporary classificatory use of race and gender. That being black or white, male or female, does not in itself make anyone morally better or more deserving is acknowledged on all sides.

Thus even if one should conclude that the attempts to justify affirmative action fail, the fair and clear way to express this would be to say that the grounds that have been offered for using race and gender categories as affirmative action programs do are unconvincing. Unlike the rhetorical claim that they favor individuals "merely because they are black (or female)," this does not insinuate unfairly that the programs were instituted for no reason other than personal taste. And, of course, those of us who believe that there are good reasons for affirmative action policies, with their sorting by gender and race, have even more reason to reject the misleading and insulting description that we advocate special treatment for individuals *merely because* they are blacks or women.

The argument we have been considering is objectionable in another way as well. As Richard Wasserstrom points out, the moral wrongs against blacks and women in the past were not wrong just because people were classified and treated differently according to the morally irrelevant features of gender and color.[2] There was this sort of arbitrary treatment, of course, but the main problem was not that women and blacks were treated differently *somehow* but that they were *treated as no human being should be treated*. Segregation, for example, was in practice not merely a pointless sorting of individuals, like separating people according to the number of letters in their names. It was a way of expressing and perpetuating white contempt for blacks and preserving social structures that kept blacks from taking full advantage of their basic human rights. The mistreatment of women was not

merely that they were arbitrarily selected for the more burdensome but still legitimate social roles. It was, in large part, that the practices expressed an attitude towards women that subtly undermined their chances of making use of even the limited opportunities they had. The proper conclusion, then, is not that any current program that makes use of race and gender categories is simply committing the same old wrongs in reverse. The worst wrongs of the past went far beyond merely the arbitrary use of these categories; moreover, it has yet to be established that the new use of these categories in affirmative action is in fact arbitrary (like the old use). An arbitrary category is one used without good justification; the charge that affirmative action programs use race and gender categories unjustifiably is just what is at issue, not something we can assume at the start.

Another argument to show that affirmative action is unjust is that it violates the rights of white males who apply for admission or jobs in the university. This is a complex issue, discussed at length in journals and before the Supreme Court; rather than review that debate, I will just mention a few of the considerations that lead me to think that, though certain *types* of affirmative action may violate the rights of white males, appropriately designed affirmative action programs do not.

First, no individual, white male or otherwise, has an absolute right to a place in a public university—that is, a right independent of complex considerations of the functions of the university, the reasonable expectations of actual and potential taxpayers and other supporters, the number of places available, the relative merits of other candidates, and so on. What rights does an applicant have? Few would dispute that each individual has a right to "formal justice."[3] That is, one should not be arbitrarily denied a place to which one is entitled under the existing and publicly-declared rules and regulations. Any university must have rules concerning residency, prior education, submission of application forms, taking of entrance tests, and the like, as well as more substantive standards and policies for selecting among those who satisfy these minimal requirements. Formal justice requires that individual administrators do not deviate from the preestablished rules and standards currently in effect, whether from personal preference or high-minded social ideals. But this is not to say that old policies cannot reasonably be changed. One does not, for example, necessarily have a right to be treated by the rules and standards in force when one was born or when one first thought about going to college.

Formal justice is quite limited, however, for it is compatible with substantively unjust rules and standards. In addition to formal justice, each individual citizen has a right that the rules and standards of the university to which he or she applies be made (and, when necessary, changed) only for good reasons, consistent with the purposes of the university and the ideals of justice and basic human equality. This is a more stringent standard; it does establish a *presumption* against using race and gender categories in policies which affect the distribution of opportunities, such as jobs and student status. This is because race and gender, like height and musculature, are not *in themselves* morally relevant chacteristics. Considered in isolation from their connections with other matters, they do not make anyone more, or less, deserving of anything. As the Supreme Court says, they are classifications that are "suspect."[4] But this does not mean that it is always unjust to use them, but only that their use stands in need of justification. What counts as a justification depends crucially upon our assessment of the legitimate purposes of the institution that uses the categories.

No one denies that the education of citizens and the pursuit of knowledge are central among the purposes of public universities. But, when resources are limited, decisions must be made as to what knowledge is to be pursued and who is to be offered education in each institution. Here we must consider the roles that universities play as parts of a complex network of public institutions (of many kinds) in a country committed to democratic ideals and faced with deep social problems. It has never been the practice of universities to disregard their social roles in the name of "purely academic" concerns; given current social problems, few would morally defend such disregard now. The more serious issue is not whether this role should be considered but rather whether the role is better served by affirmative action or by admission and hiring policies that admit only classification by test scores, grades, and past achievements. To decide this, we must look more closely at the purposes that affirmative action is supposed to serve.

III. Strategies of Justification: Consequences and Reparations

Some arguments for affirmative action look exclusively to its future benefits. The idea is that what has happened in the past is not in itself relevant to what we should do; at most, it provides clues as to what acts and policies are likely to bring about the best future. The philosophical tradition associated with this approach is utilitarianism, which declares that the morally right act is whatever produces the best consequences. Traditionally, utilitarianism evaluated consequences in terms of happiness and unhappiness, but the anticipated consequences of affirmative action are often described more specifically. For example, some argue that affirmative action will ease racial tensions, prevent riots, improve services in minority neighborhoods, reduce unemployment, remove inequities in income distribution, eliminate racial and sexual prejudice, and enhance the self-esteem of blacks and women. Some have called attention to the fact that women and minorities provide alternative perspectives on history, literature, philosophy, and politics, and that this has beneficial effects for both education and research.

These are important considerations, not irrelevant to the larger responsibilities of universities. For several reasons, however, I think it is a mistake for advocates of affirmative action to rest their case exclusively on such forward-looking arguments. First, critics raise reasonable doubts about whether affirmative action is necessary to achieve these admirable results. The economist Thomas Sowell argues that a free-market economy can achieve the same results more efficiently; his view is therefore that even if affirmative action has beneficial results (which he denies), it is not necessary for the purpose.[5] Though Sowell's position can be contested, the controversy itself tends to weaken confidence in the entirely forward-looking defense of affirmative action.

An even more obvious reason why affirmative action advocates should explore other avenues for its defense is that the exclusively forward-looking approach must give equal consideration to possible negative consequences of affirmative action. It may be, for example, that affirmative action will temporarily increase racial tensions, especially if its message is misunderstood. Even legitimate use of race and sex categories may encourage others to abuse the categories for unjust purposes. If applied without sensitive regard to the educational and research purposes of the university, affirmative action might severely undermine its efforts to fulfill these primary responsibilities. *If* affirmative action programs were to lower academic standards for blacks and women, they would run the risk of damaging the respect that highly qualified blacks and women have earned by leading others to suspect that these highly qualified people lack the merits of white males in the same positions. This could also be damaging to the self-respect of those who accept affirmative action positions. Even programs that disavow "lower standards" unfortunately arouse the suspicion that they don't really do so, and this by itself can cause problems. Although I believe that well-designed affirmative action programs can minimize these negative effects, the fact that they are a risk is a reason for not resting the case for affirmative action on a delicate balance of costs and benefits.

Reflection on the *message* of affirmative action also leads me to move beyond entirely forward-looking arguments. For if the sole purpose is to bring about a brighter future, then we give the wrong message to both the white males who are rejected and to the women and blacks who are benefited. To the latter what we say, in effect, is this: "Never mind how you have been treated. Forget about the fact that your race or sex has in the past been actively excluded and discouraged, and that you yourself may have had handicaps due to prejudice. Our sole concern is to bring about certain good results in the future, and giving you a break happens to be a useful means for doing this. Don't think this is a recognition of your rights as an individual or your disadvantages as a member of a group. Nor does it mean that we have confidence in your abilities. We would do the same for those who are privileged and academically inferior if it would have the same socially beneficial results."

To the white male who would have had a university position but for affirmative action, the exclusively forward-looking approach says: "We deny you the place you otherwise would have had simply as a means to produce certain socially desirable outcomes. We have not judged that others are more deserving, or have a right, to the place we are giving them instead of you. Past racism and sexism are irrelevant. The point is just that the sacrifice of your concerns is a useful means to the larger end of the future welfare of others."

This, I think, is the wrong message to give. It is also unnecessary. The proper alternative, however, is not to ignore the possible future benefits of affirmative action but rather to take them into account as a part of a larger picture.

A radically different strategy for justifying affirmative action is to rely on backward-looking arguments. Such arguments call our attention to certain events in the past and assert that *because* these past events occurred, we have certain duties now. The modern philosopher who most influentially endorsed such arguments was W. D. Ross.[6] He argued that there are duties of fidelity, justice, gratitude, and reparation that have a moral force independent of any tendency these may have to promote good consequences. The fact that you have made a promise, for example, gives you a strong moral reason to do what you promised, whether or not doing so will on balance have more beneficial consequences. The Rossian principle that is often invoked in affirmative action debates is a principle of reparation. This says that those who wrongfully injure others have a (*prima facie*) duty to apologize and make restitution. Those who have wronged others owe reparation.

James Forman dramatically expressed this idea in New York in 1969 when he presented "The Black Manifesto," which demanded five hundred million dollars in reparation to American blacks from white churches and synagogues.[7] Such organizations, the Manifesto contends, contributed to our history of slavery and racial injustice; as a result, they incurred a debt to the black community that still suffers from its effects. Objections were immediately raised: for example, both slaves and slave-owners are no longer alive; not every American white is guilty of racial oppression; and not every black in America was a victim of slavery and its aftermath.

Bernard Boxill, author of *Blacks and Social Justice,* developed a more sophisticated version of the backward-looking argument with a view to meeting these objections.[8] Let us admit, he says, that both the perpetrators and the primary victims of slavery are gone, and let us not insist that contemporary whites are guilty of perpetrating further injustices. Some do, and some do not, and public administrators cannot be expected to sort out the guilty from the non-guilty. However, reparation, or at least some "compensation,"[9] is still owed, because contemporary whites have reaped the profits of past injustice to blacks. He asks us to consider the analogy with a stolen bicycle. Suppose my parent stole your parent's bicycle some time ago, both have since died, and I "inherited" the bike from my parent, the thief. Though I may be innocent of any wrongdoing (so far), I am in possession of stolen goods rightfully belonging to you, the person who would have inherited the bike if it had not been stolen. For me to keep the bike and declare that I owe you nothing would be wrong, even if I was not the cause of your being deprived. By analogy, present-day whites owe reparations to contemporary blacks, not because they are themselves guilty of causing the disadvantages of blacks, but because they are in possession of advantages that fell to them as a result of the gross injustices of their ancestors. Special advantages continue to fall even to innocent whites because of the ongoing prejudice of their white neighbors.

Although it raises many questions, this line of argument acknowledges some important points missing in most exclusively forward-looking arguments: for example, it stresses the (intrinsic) relevance of past injustice and it calls attention to the rights and current disadvantages of blacks (in contrast with future benefits for others). When developed as an argument for affirmative action, it does not accuse all white males of prejudice and wrongdoing; at the same time, however, it sees the fundamental value as justice. As a result, it avoids giving the message to either rejected white males or reluctant affirmative action applicants that they are "mere means" to a social goal that is largely independent of their rights and interests as individuals.

There are, however, serious problems in trying to justify affirmative action by this backward-looking argument, especially if it is treated as the exclusive or central argument. Degrees of being advantaged and disadvantaged are notoriously hard to measure. New immigrants have not shared our history of past injustices, and so the argument may not apply to them in any straightforward way. The argument appeals to controversial ideas about property rights, inheritance, and group responsibilities. Some argue that affirmative action tends to benefit the least disadvantaged blacks and women; though this does not mean that they are owed nothing, their claims would seem to have lower priority than the needs of the most disadvantaged. Some highly qualified blacks and women object that affirmative action is damaging to their reputations and self-esteem, whereas the reparation argument seems to assume that it is a welcome benefit to all blacks and women.

If we focus on the message that the backward-looking argument sends, there are also some potential problems. Though rightly acknowledging past injustice, the argument (by itself) seems to convey the message that racial and sexual oppression consisted primarily in the loss of tangible goods, or the deprivation of specific rights and opportunities, that can be "paid back" in kind. The background idea, which goes back at least to Aristotle, is that persons wrongfully deprived of their "due" can justly demand an "equivalent" to what they have lost.[10] But, while specific deprivations were an important part

of our racist and sexist past, they are far from the whole story. Among the worst wrongs then, as now, were humiliations and contemptuous treatment of a type that cannot, strictly, be "paid back." The problem was, and is, not just that specific rights and advantages were denied, but that prejudicial attitudes damaged self-esteem, undermined motivations, limited realistic options, and made even "officially open" opportunities seem undesirable. Racism and sexism were (and are) *insults,* not merely tangible *injuries*.[11] These are not the sort of thing that can be adequately measured and repaid with equivalents. The trouble with treating insulting racist and sexist practices on a pure reparation model is not merely the practical difficulty of identifying the offenders, determining the degree of guilt, assessing the amount of payment due, etc. It is also that penalty payments and compensation for lost benefits are not the only, or primary, moral responses that are called for. When affirmative action is defended exclusively by analogy with reparation, it tends to express the misleading message that the evils of racism and sexism are all tangible losses that can be "paid off"; by being silent on the insulting nature of racism and sexism, it tends to add insult to insult.

The message suggested by the reparation argument, by itself, also seems objectionable because it conveys the idea that higher education, teaching, and doing research are mainly benefits awarded in response to self-centered demands. The underlying picture too easily suggested is that applicants are a group of self-interested, bickering people, each grasping for limited "goodies" and insisting on a right to them. When a university grants an opportunity through affirmative action, its message would seem to be this. "We concede that you have a valid claim to this benefit and we yield to your demand, though this is not to suggest that we have confidence in your abilities or any desire to have you here." This invitation seems too concessive, the atmosphere too adversarial, and the emphasis too much on the benefits rather than the responsibilities of being a part of the university.

IV. Philosophical Interlude: An Alternative Perspective

Here I want to digress from the explicit consideration of affirmative action in order to consider more abstract philosophical questions about the ways we evaluate acts and policies. At the risk of oversimplifying, I want to contrast some assumptions that have, until recently, been dominant in ethical theory with alternatives suggested by contemporary philosophers who emphasize historical context, narrative unity, and community values.[12] Although these alternatives, in my opinion, have not yet been adequately developed, there seem to be at least four distinguishable themes worth considering.

First, when we reflect on what we deeply value, we find that we care not merely about the present moment and each future moment in isolation but also about how our past, present, and future cohere or fit together into a life and a piece of history. Some of our values, we might say, are cross-time wholes, with past, present, and future parts united in certain ways. Thus, for example, the commitments I have made, the projects I have begun, what I have shared with those I love, the injuries I have caused, and the hopes I have encouraged importantly affect both whether I am satisfied with my present and how I want the future to go.

Second, in reflecting on stretches of our lives and histories, we frequently use evaluative concepts drawn more from narrative literature than from accounting. Thus, for example, we think of our lives as having significant beginnings, crises, turning points, dramatic tension, character development, climaxes, resolutions, comic interludes, tragic disruptions, and eventually fitting (or unfitting) endings. The value of any moment often depends on what came before and what we anticipate to follow. And since our lives are intertwined with others in a common history, we also care about how our moments cohere with others' life stories. The past is seen as more than a time of accumulated debts and assets, and the future is valued as more than an opportunity for reinvesting and cashing in assets.

Third, evaluation must take into account one's particular historical context, including one's cultural, national, and ethnic traditions, and the actual individuals in one's life. Sometimes this point is exaggerated, I think, to suggest a dubious cultural relativism or "particularism" in ethics: for example, the thesis that what is valuable for a person is defined by the person's culture or that evaluations imply no general reasons beyond particular judgments, such as "That's *our* way" and "John is *my* son."[13] But, construed modestly as a practical or epistemological point, it seems obvious enough, on reflection, that we should take into account the historical context of our acts and that we are often in a better position to judge

what is appropriate in particular cases than we are to articulate universally valid premises supporting the judgment. We can sometimes be reasonably confident about what is right in a particular context without being sure about whether or not there are relevant differences blocking the same judgment in seemingly similar but less familiar contexts. We know, as a truism, that the same judgment applies if there are no relevant differences, but in practice the particular judgment may be more evident than the exact scope of the moral generalizations that hold across many cases. Thus, though giving reasons for our judgments in particular contexts commits us to acknowledging their potential relevance in other contexts, moral judgment cannot be aptly represented simply as deducing specific conclusions from clear and evident general principles.

Fourth, when we evaluate particular acts and policies as parts of lives and histories, what is often most important is the value of the whole, which cannot always be determined by "summing up" the values of the parts. Lives, histories, and interpersonal relations over time are what G. E. Moore called "organic unities"—that is, wholes the value of which is not necessarily the sum of the values of the parts.[14] The point here is not merely the obvious practical limitation that we cannot measure and quantify values in this area. More fundamentally, the idea is that it would be a mistake even to try to evaluate certain unities by assessing different parts in isolation from one another, then adding up all their values. Suppose, for example, a woman with terminal cancer considered two quite different ways of spending her last days. One way, perhaps taking a world cruise, might seem best when evaluated in terms of the quality of each future moment, in isolation from her past and her present ties; but another way, perhaps seeking closure in projects and with estranged family members, might seem more valuable when seen as a part of her whole life.

Taken together, these ideas cast doubt on both the exclusively forward-looking method of assessment and the standard backward-looking alternative. Consequentialism, or the exclusively forward-looking method, attempts to determine what ought to be done at present by fixing attention entirely on future results. To be sure, any sensible consequentialist will consult the past for lessons and clues helpful in predicting future outcomes: for example, recalling that you offended someone yesterday may enable you to predict that the person will be cool to you tomorrow unless you apologize. But beyond this, consequentialists have no concern with the past, for their "bottom line" is always "what happens from now on," evaluated independently of the earlier chapters of our lives and histories. For the consequentialist, assessing a life or history from a narrative perspective becomes impossible or at least bizarre, as what must be evaluated at each shifting moment is "the story from now on" independently of what has already been written.[15]

The standard Rossian alternative to this exclusively forward-looking perspective is to introduce certain (*prima facie*) *duties* to respond to certain past events in specified ways—for example, pay debts, keep promises, pay reparation for injuries. These duties are supposed to be self-evident and universal (though they are *prima facie*), and they do not hold because they tend to promote anything good or valuable. Apart from aspects of the acts mentioned in the principles (for example, fulfilling a promise, returning favors, not injuring, etc.), details of historical and personal context are considered irrelevant.

By contrast, the narrative perspective sketched above considers the past as an integral part of the valued unities that we aim to bring about, not merely as a source of duties. If one has negligently wronged another, Ross regards this past event as generating a duty to pay reparations even if doing so will result in nothing good. But from the narrative perspective, the past becomes relevant in a further way. One may say, for example, that the *whole* consisting of your life and your relationship with that person from the time of the injury into the future will be a better thing if you acknowledge the wrong and make efforts to restore what you have damaged. For Ross, the duty is generated by the past and unrelated to bringing about anything good; from the narrative perspective, however, the requirement is just what is required to bring about a valuable connected whole with past, present, and future parts—the best way to complete a chapter, so to speak, in two intersecting life-stories.

So far, neither the Rossian nor the narrative account has told us much about the ultimate reasons for their evaluations, but they reveal ways to consider the matter. The Rossian asks us to judge particular cases in the light of "self-evident" general principles asserting that certain past events tend to generate present (or future) duties. The alternative perspective calls for examining lives and relationships, over time, in context, as organic unities evaluated (partly) in narrative terms.

To illustrate, consider two persons, John and Mary. John values having Mary's trust and respect, and conversely Mary values having John's; moreover, John values the fact that Mary values being trusted and respected by him, and conversely Mary values the same about John.[16]

Now suppose that other people have been abusive and insulting to Mary, and that John is worried that Mary may take things he had said and done as similarly insulting, even though he does not think that he consciously meant them this way. Though he is worried, Mary does not seem to suspect him; he fears that he may only make matters worse if he raises the issue, creating suspicions she did not have or focusing on doubts that he cannot allay. Perhaps, he thinks, their future relationship would be better served if he just remained silent, hoping that the trouble, if any, will fade in time. If so, consequentialist thinking would recommend silence. Acknowledging this, he might nonetheless feel that duties of friendship and fidelity demand that he raise the issue, regardless of whether or not the result will be worse. Then he would be thinking as a Rossian.

But, instead, he might look at the problem from an alternative perspective, asking himself what response best affirms and contributes to the sort of ongoing relationship he has and wants to continue with Mary. Given their history together, it is important to him to do his part towards restoring the relationship if it indeed has been marred by perceived insults or suspicions. To be sure, he wants *future* relations of mutual trust and respect, but not at any price and not by just any means. Their history together is not irrelevant, for what he values is not merely a future of a certain kind, but that their relationship over time be of the sort he values. He values an ongoing history of mutual trust and respect that *calls for* an explicit response in this current situation, not merely as a means to a brighter future but as a present affirmation of what they value together. Even if unsure which course will be best for the future, he may be reasonably confident that the act that best expresses his respect and trust (and his valuing hers, etc.) is to confront the problem, express his regrets, reaffirm his respect, ask for her trust, be patient with her doubts, and welcome an open dialogue. If the insults were deep and it is not entirely clear whether or not he really associated himself with them, then mere words may not be enough to convey the message or even to assure himself of his own sincerity. Positive efforts, even at considerable cost, may be needed to express appropriately and convincingly what needs to be said. How the next chapter unfolds is not entirely up to him, and he would not be respectful if he presumed otherwise by trying to manipulate the best future unilaterally.

The example concerns only two persons and their personal values, but it illustrates a perspective that one can also take regarding moral problems involving many persons.

V. Mutual Respect, Fair Opportunity, and Affirmative Action

Turning back to our main subject, I suggest that some of the values that give affirmative action its point are best seen as cross-time values that fall outside the exclusively forward-looking and backward-looking perspectives. They include having a history of racial and gender relations governed, so far as possible, by the ideals of mutual respect, trust, and fair opportunity for all.

Our national history provides a context of increasing recognition and broader interpretation of the democratic ideal of the equal dignity of all human beings—an ideal that has been flagrantly abused from the outset, partially affirmed in the bloody Civil War, and increasingly extended in the civil rights movement, but is still far from being fully respected. More specifically, blacks and women were systematically treated in an unfair and demeaning way by public institutions, including universities, until quite recently, and few could confidently claim to have rooted out racism and sexism even now.[17] The historical context is not what grounds or legitimates democratic values, but it is the background of the current problem, the sometimes admirable and often ugly way the chapters up until now have been written.

Consider first the social ideal of mutual respect and trust among citizens. The problem of implementing this in the current context is different from the problem in the two-person example discussed above, for the history of our racial and gender relations is obviously not an idyllic story of mutual respect and trust momentarily interrupted by a crisis. Even so, the question to ask is not merely, "What will promote respectful and trusting racial and gender relations in future generations?", but rather, "Given our checkered past, how can we appropriately express the social value of mutual respect and trust that we want, so far as possible, to characterize our history?" We cannot change our racist and sexist past, but we also cannot express full respect for those present individuals who live in its aftermath if we ignore it. What is called for is not merely repayment of tangible debts incurred by past injuries, but also a message to counter the deep insult inherent in racism and sexism.

Recognizing that problems of this kind are not amenable to easy solutions deduced from self-evident moral generalizations, we may find it helpful instead to reflect on an analogy. Suppose you return to the hometown you left in childhood, remembering with pride its Fourth of July speeches about the values of community, equality, and fairness for all. You discover, however, that the community was never as perfect as you thought. In fact, for years—until quite recently—certain families, who had been disdainfully labeled "the Barefeet," had not only been shunned by most folk but had also been quietly terrorized by a few well-placed citizens. The Barefeet had been arrested on false charges, beaten, raped, and blackmailed into silent submission. The majority, perhaps, would never have done these things, but their contempt for the Barefeet was such that most would have regarded these crimes less important than if they had been done to insiders. Fortunately, the worst offenders have died, and so have the victims of the most outrageous crimes. Majority attitudes have changed somewhat, though often only from open contempt to passive disregard. Some new citizens have come to town, and a few of the Barefeet (now more politely called "Cross-towners") have managed to become successful. Nonetheless, the older Cross-towners are still fearful and resigned, and the younger generation is openly resentful and distrustful when officials proclaim a new commitment to democratic ideals. It is no surprise, then, that few Cross-towners take full advantage of available opportunities and that the two groups tend to isolate themselves from each other.

Now suppose you, as one of the majority, could persuade the rest to give a message to the Cross-towners, a message appropriate to the majority's professed value of being a community committed to mutual respect and trust. What would you propose? And, assuming that doing so would violate no one's rights, what means would you think best to convey that message sincerely and effectively? Some would no doubt suggest simply forgetting about the past and hoping that time will heal the wounds. But, whether effective in the future or not, this plan fails to express full respect for the Cross-towners now. Others might suggest a more legalistic approach, trying to determine exactly who has been the disadvantaged, the degree of loss, which citizens are most responsible, etc., in order to pay off the debt. But this, taken by itself, faces the sorts of disadvantages we have already considered. If, instead, the value of mutual respect and trust is the governing ideal, the appropriate message would be to acknowledge and deplore the past openly, to affirm a commitment to promote mutual respect and trust in the future, to welcome full interchange and participation with the Cross-towners, and to urge them to undertake the risks of overcoming their understandable suspicions by joining in a common effort to work towards fulfilling the ideal. This would address not merely the injury but also the insult implicit in the town's history.

The more difficult question, however, is how we might express such a message effectively and with evident sincerity in an atmosphere already poisoned by the past. Mere words will be taken as mere words; they may in fact turn out to be just that. What is needed is more positive action—concrete steps to prove commitment, to resist backsliding, and to overcome reluctance on both sides. The sort of affirmative action taken in the U.C.L.A. program described in Section I seems especially appropriate for this purpose. Here the emphasis was on outreach, increasing awareness of opportunities, accountability and proof of fairness in procedures, and allocating resources (fellowships, release time, etc.) in a way that showed trust that, if given an adequate chance, those formerly excluded would enrich the university by fully appropriate standards. These seem the most natural way to give force to the message, though arguably other methods may serve the purpose as well.

There is another historical value that is also relevant and seems to favor even more radical steps in affirmative action. The issue is too complex to address adequately here, but it should at least be mentioned. What I have in mind might be called "fair opportunity." That is, implicit in our democratic ideals is the idea that our public institutions should be so arranged that they afford to each person, over time, more or less equal opportunities to develop and make use of his or her natural talents and to participate and contribute to those institutions. The idea is hard to make precise, but it clearly does not mean that all should have equal chances to have a desirable position, regardless of effort and natural aptitude. The physically handicapped and the mentally retarded suffer from natural misfortunes; though society should not ignore them, they cannot expect standards to be rigged to ensure the former equal odds at making the basketball team or the latter equal odds of being appointed to the faculty. Similarly, those who choose not to make the effort to de-

velop their capacities have no right to expect public institutions to include them in a pool from which candidates are selected by lot. But when persons have been disadvantaged by social injustice, having had their initial chances diminished by the network of public institutions themselves, then positive steps are needed to equalize their opportunities over time.

This ideal calls for something more than efforts to ensure that future generations do not suffer from the same disadvantages, for those efforts fail to respond to the unfairness to the present individuals. But, for obvious practical reasons, legal efforts to remedy precisely identifiable disadvantages incurred by individuals are bound to be quite inadequate to address the many subtle losses of opportunity caused by past institutional racism and sexism. Since no perfect solution is possible, we need to choose between this inadequate response and policies that address the problem in a less fine-grained way. Affirmative action programs that employ a working presumption that women and minorities generally have had their opportunities restricted to some degree by institutional racism and sexism will admittedly risk compensating a few who have actually had, on balance, as much opportunity as white males. But the practical alternatives, it seems, are to accept this risk or to refuse to respond at all to the innumerable ways that institutional racism and sexism have undermined opportunities too subtly for the courts to remedy.

Given these options, what would be the message of choosing to limit redress to precisely identifiable losses? This would say, in effect, to women and minorities, "We cannot find a way to ensure *precisely* that each talented and hard-working person has an equal opportunity over time; and, given our options, we count it more important to see that *none* of you women and minorities are overcompensated than to try to see that the *majority* of you have more nearly equal opportunities over your life-time. Your grievances are too subtle and difficult to measure, and your group may be harboring some who were not disadvantaged. We would rather let the majority of white males enjoy the advantages of their unfair head start than risk compensating one of you who does not deserve it."

Now *if* it had been established on antecedent grounds that the affirmative action measures in question would violate the *rights* of white male applicants, then one could argue that these coarse-grained efforts to honor the ideal of fair opportunity are illegitimate. But that premise, I think, has not been established. Affirmative action programs would violate the rights of white males only if, all things considered, their guidelines temporarily favoring women and minorities were arbitrary, not serving the legitimate social role of universities or fulfilling the ideals of fairness and respect for all. The considerations offered here, however, point to the conclusion that some affirmative action programs, even those involving a degree of preferential treatment, are legitimated by ideals of mutual respect, trust, and fair opportunity.

Conclusion

All this, I know, is too brief, loose, and incomplete; I hope it is worth considering nonetheless. The main suggestion is that, ideally, a central purpose of affirmative action would be to communicate a much-needed message, sincerely and effectively. The message is called for not just as a means to future good relations or a dutiful payment of a debt incurred by our past. It is called for by the ideal of being related to other human beings over time, so that our histories and biographies reflect the responses of those who deeply care about fair opportunity, mutual trust, and respect for all.

If so, what should public universities try to say to those offered opportunities through affirmative action? Perhaps something like this: "Whether we individually are among the guilty or not, we acknowledge that you have been wronged—if not by specific injuries which could be named and repaid, at least by the humiliating and debilitating attitudes prevalent in our country and our institutions. We deplore and denounce these attitudes and the wrongs that spring from them. We acknowledge that, so far, most of you have had your opportunities in life diminished by the effects of these attitudes, and we want no one's prospects to be diminished by injustice. We recognize your understandable grounds for suspicion and mistrust when we express these high-minded sentiments, and we want not only to ask respectfully for your trust but also to give concrete evidence of our sincerity. We welcome you respectfully into the university community and ask you to take a full share of the responsibilities as well as the benefits. By creating special opportunities, we recognize the disadvantages you have probably suffered; we show our respect for your talents and our commitment to the ideals of the university, however, by not faking grades and honors for you. Given current attitudes about affirmative action, accepting this position will probably have drawbacks

as well as advantages.[18] It is an opportunity and a responsibility offered neither as charity nor as entitlement, but rather as part of a special effort to welcome and encourage minorities and women to participate more fully in the university at all levels. We believe that this program affirms some of the best ideals implicit in our history without violating the rights of any applicants. We hope that you will choose to accept the position in this spirit as well as for your own benefit."

The appropriate message is no doubt harder to communicate to those who stand to lose some traditional advantages under a legitimate affirmative action program. But if we set aside practical difficulties and suppose that the proper message could be sincerely given and accepted as such, what would it say? Ideally, it would convey an understanding of the moral reasoning for the program; perhaps, in conclusion, it would say something like the following.

"These are the concerns that we felt made necessary the policy under which the university is temporarily giving special attention to women and minorities. We respect your rights to formal justice and to a policy guided by the university's education and research mission as well as its social responsibilities. Our policy in no way implies the view that your opportunities are less important than others', but we estimate (roughly, as we must) that as a white male you have probably had advantages and encouragement that for a long time have been systematically, unfairly, insultingly unavailable to most women and minorities. We deplore invidious race and gender distinctions; we hope that no misunderstanding of our program will prolong them. Unfortunately, nearly all blacks and women have been disadvantaged to some degree by bias against their groups, and it is impractical for universities to undertake the detailed investigations that would be needed to assess how much particular individuals have suffered or gained from racism and sexism. We appeal to you to share the historical values of fair opportunity and mutual respect that underlie this policy; we hope that, even though its effects may be personally disappointing, you can see the policy as an appropriate response to the current situation."

Unfortunately, as interests conflict and tempers rise, it is difficult to convey this idea without giving an unintended message as well. White males unhappy about the immediate effects of affirmative action may read the policy as saying that "justice" is the official word for giving preferential treatment to whatever group one happens to favor. Some may see a subtext insinuating that blacks and women are naturally inferior and "cannot make it on their own." Such cynical readings reveal either misunderstanding or the willful refusal to take the moral reasoning underlying affirmative action seriously. They pose serious obstacles to the success of affirmative action—practical problems that may be more intractable than respectful moral disagreement and counter-argument. But some types of affirmative action invite misunderstanding and suspicion more than others. For this reason, anyone who accepts the general case for affirmative action suggested here would do well to reexamine in detail the means by which they hope to communicate its message.[19]

---

1. See, for example, the following: John Arthur, ed., *Morality and Moral Controversies,* 2nd ed. (Englewood Cliffs: Prentice-Hall, Inc., 1986). ch. 11, pp. 305–47; William T. Blackstone and Robert D. Heslep, eds., *Social Justice and Preferential Treatment* (Athens: The University of Georgia Press, 1977); Bernard Boxill, *Blacks and Social Justice* (Totowa: Rowman and Allanheld, 1984); Marshall Cohen, Thomas Nagel, and Thomas Scanlon, eds., *Equality and Preferential Treatment* (Princeton: Princeton University Press, 1977); Robert K. Fullinwider, *The Reverse Discrimination Controversy* (Totowa: Rowman and Littlefield, 1980); Alan H. Goldman, *Justice and Reverse Discrimination* (Princeton: Princeton University Press, 1979); Kent Greenawalt, *Discrimination and Reverse Discrimination* (New York: Alfred A. Knopf, 1983). Barry R. Gross, ed., *Reverse Discrimination* (Buffalo: Prometheus Press, 1977); Thomas A. Mappes and Jane S. Zembaty, eds., *Social Ethics* (2nd ed.; New York: McGraw-Hill Book Company, 1982), ch. 5, pp. 159–98.

2. See Richard Wasserstrom, "Racism and Sexism," "Preferential Treatment" in his *Philosophy and Social Issues* (Notre Dame: University of Notre Dame Press, 1980).

3. William K. Frankena, "The Concept of Social Justice," in *Social Justice,* ed. Richard B. Brandt (Englewood Cliffs: Prentice-Hall, Inc., 1962), pp. 8–9; Henry Sidgwick, *Methods of Ethics,* 7th ed. (London: Macmillan, 1907), pp. 379, 386ff.; John Rawls, A *Theory of Justice* (Cambridge: Harvard University Press, 1971), pp. 56–60, 180, 235–239, 504ff.

4. *Regents of the University of California v. Allan Bakke,* 98 S.Ct. 2733, 46 L.W. 4896 (1978). Reprinted in Wasserstrom, ed., *Today's Moral Issues,* 2nd ed. (New York: Macmillan Publishing Co., 1975), pp. 149–207, esp. pp. 156–57.

5. Thomas Sowell, *Race and Economics* (New York: David McKay Co., 1975), ch. 6; *Markets and Minorities* (New York: Basic Books, Inc., 1981), pp. 114–15.

6. W.D. Ross, *The Right and the Good* (Oxford: Clarendon Press, 1930).

7. James Forman was at the time director of international affairs for SNCC (Student Nonviolent Coordinating Committee). The "Black Manifesto" stems from an economic development conference sponsored by the Interreligious Foundation for Community Organizations, April 26, 1969, and presented by Forman at the New York Interdenominational Riverside Church on May 4, 1969. Later the demand was raised to three billion dollars. See Robert S. Lecky and H. Elliot Wright, *Black Manifesto* (New York: Sheed and Ward Publishers, 1969), pp. vii, 114–26.

8. Bernard Boxill, "The Morality of Reparation," *Social Theory and Practice,* vol. 2, no. 1 (1972), pp. 113–22, and *Blacks and Social Justice,* ch. 7.

9. In the article cited above, Boxill calls what is owed "reparation," but in the book (above) he calls it "compensation." The latter term, preferred by many, is used more broadly to cover not only restitution for wrongdoing but also "making up" for deficiencies and losses that are not anyone's fault (for example, naturally caused physical handicaps, or damages unavoidably resulting from legitimate and necessary activities). We could describe the backward-looking arguments presented here as demands for "compensation" rather than "reparation," so long as we keep in mind that the compensation is supposed to be due as the morally appropriate response to past wrongdoing.

10. Aristotle, *Nicomachean Ethics,* tr. A. K. Thomson (Baltimore: Penguin Books, Inc., 1955), bk. V, esp. pp. 143–55.

11. See Boxill, *Blacks and Social Justice,* pp. 132ff., and Ronald Dworkin, "Reverse Discrimination," in *Taking Rights Seriously* (Cambridge: Harvard University Press, 1978), pp. 231ff.

12. See, for example, Alasdair MacIntyre, *After Virtue* (Notre Dame: Notre Dame University Press, 1981). Similar themes are found in Carol Gilligan's *In A Different Voice* (Cambridge: Harvard University Press, 1982) and in Lawrence Blum, *Friendship, Altruism, and Morality* (Boston: Routledge and Kegan Paul, 1980).

13. Regarding cultural and moral relativism see, for example, David B. Wong, *Moral Relativity* (Berkeley and Los Angeles: University of California Press, 1984), with an excellent bibliography, and Richard B. Brandt, *Ethical Theory* (Englewood Cliffs: Prentice-Hall, Inc., 1959), ch. 11, pp. 271–94. Versions of particularism are presented in Andrew Oldenquist, "Loyalties," *The Journal of Philosophy,* vol. 79 (1982), pp. 173–93; Lawrence Blum, *Friendship, Altruism, and Morality;* and Bernard Williams, "Persons, Character and Morality" in *Moral Luck* (New York: Cambridge University Press, 1981), pp. 1–19.

14. G. E. Moore, *Principia Ethica* (Cambridge: Cambridge University Press, 1912), pp. 27ff.

15. That is, the evaluation is independent of the past in the sense that the past makes no intrinsic difference to the final judgment and the future is not evaluated as a part of a temporal whole including the past. As noted, however, consequentialists will still look to the past for lessons and clues about how to bring about the best future.

16. For an interesting illustration of reciprocal desires (e.g., A wanting B, B wanting A, A wanting B to want A, B wanting A to want B, A wanting B to want A to want B, etc.), see Thomas Nagel, "Sexual Perversion," *The Journal of Philosophy,* vol. 66 (1969).

17. Racism and sexism present significantly different problems, but I shall not try to analyze the differences here. For the most part (and especially in the analogy to follow) my primary focus is on racism, but the relevance of the general type of moral thinking considered here to the problems of sexism should nonetheless be evident.

18. How severe these drawbacks are will, of course, depend upon the particular means of affirmative action that are selected and how appropriate these are for the situation. For example, if, to meet mandated quotas, highly-ranked colleges and universities offer special admission to students not expected to succeed, then they may well be misleading those students into a wasteful and humiliating experience when those students could have thrived at lower-ranked educational institutions. This practice was explicitly rejected in the policies at Pomona College and at U.C.L.A. described in Section I, but William Allen (a contributor to this volume) suggested to me in discussion that, in his opinion, the practice is quite common. The practice, I think, is unconscionable, and my argument in no way supports it.

Geoffrey Miller . . . described in discussion another possible affirmative action program that would be quite inappropriate to the circumstances but is again not supported by the line of argument I have suggested. He asks us to imagine a "permanent underclass" of immigrants who are "genetically or culturally deficient" and as a result fail to succeed. Since we do not share a common social and cultural history of injustice resulting in their condition, the historical dimension of my case for affirmative action is missing. And since they are a "permanent" underclass, and thus the "genetic or cultural deficiencies" that result in their failure cannot be altered, one cannot argue that universities can help them or even can sincerely give them an encouraging "message" through affirmative action. This does not mean, however, that there are not other reasons for society to extend appropriate help. Also, any suggestion that certain urban populations that are now called a "permanent underclass" are accurately and fairly described by the "fictional" example is politically charged and needs careful examination.

19. Although my aim in this paper has been to survey general types of arguments for thinking that some sort of affirmative action is needed, rather than to argue for any particular program, one cannot reasonably implement the general idea without considering many contextual factors that I have set aside here. Thus, though the moral perspective suggested here seems to favor the second method described in Section I (recruitment, special funds, accountability) over the first method (proportionality, given a fixed lower standard), the need for more detailed discussion is obvious.

CALIFORNIA CONSTITUTION
Article 1 Declaration of Rights

Sec. 31

(a) The State shall not discriminate against, or grant preferential treatment to, any individual or group on the basis of race, sex, color, or ethnicity, or national origin in the operation of public employment, public education, or public contracting.

(b) This section shall apply only to action taken after the section's effective date.

(c) Nothing in this section shall be interpreted in prohibiting bona fide qualifications based on sex which are reasonably necessary to the normal operation of public employment, public education, or public contracting.

(d) Nothing in this section shall be interpreted as invalidating any court order or consent decree which is in force as of the effective date of this section.

(e) Nothing in this section shall be interpreted as prohibiting action which must be taken to establish or maintain eligibility for any federal program, where ineligibility would result in a loss of federal funds to the State.

(f) For the purposes of this section, "State" shall include, but not necessarily be limited to, the State itself, any city, county, city and county, public university system, including the University of California, community college district, school district, special district, or any other political subdivision of governmental instrumentality of or within the State.

(g) The remedies available for violations of this section shall be the same, regardless of the injured party's race, sex, color, ethnicity, or national origin, as are otherwise available for violations of then-existing California antidiscrimination law.

(h) This section shall be self-executing. If any part or parts of this section are found to be in conflict with federal law or the United States Constitution, the section shall be implemented to the maximum extent that federal law and the United States Constitution permit. Any provision held invalid shall be severable from the remaining portions of this section.

Inequality and Gender

THE REASONABLE WOMAN*

Kim Lane Scheppele

In the intense tribalism of our times, empathy seems in short supply, but also in little demand. Newly or partially empowered groups use their small and fragile power to say, "You can't understand me unless you're *like* me," where "like" means of a similar gender or race or other social grouping now acutely aware of its own historical disempowerment. "You can't understand me" sounds like an accusation, and also a warning not to try.

But it is simply not true that people can't understand those whose experiences and values are very different from their own. It isn't easy; it requires work; it takes a certain humility to learn how much of one's own way of seeing the world is dependent on features of oneself that one cannot easily imagine away. But it is possible, with concentrated effort, much willingness to listen to others, and genuine good faith. So perhaps "you can't understand me" shouldn't be understood as a statement about what's possible. Instead it might be heard as a demand that statements about me must be heard in my voice, or at least in the voice of someone who shares my experience and my point of view. "You can't understand me" is a way of saying that you can't flatten my perspective into your perspective on the world. It is a call to stop the effort to find the "view from nowhere" or the apparently point-of-viewless point of view. It is an attack on the conception of objec-

tivity that sees one unitary and coherent point of view as privileged over all the others.

A serious problem for the legitimacy of public institutions occurs when truths become multiple, when stories proliferate in incommensurable versions, when different people with different ways of seeing become empowered to be heard in public debate. The problem is particularly evident in the law. How do courts continue to figure out "what happened" for the purposes of finding a resolution in disputes when the ideal in a multicultural society is no longer a single unassailable truth, but plural and various truths?

We can see the problem of multiple truths most clearly by focusing on consent. Consent is crucial to the legal status of many actions. Consent transforms actions from criminal to legal. For example, a surgical operation is converted from a severe battery to a legitimate procedure by the consent of the patient. Taking someone's car is converted from theft to borrowing by the consent of the owner. Determining whether relevant people have consented is, then, a crucial part of judging actions to be legal. And where disputants diverge over how consent is to be imagined, disputants will also diverge over basic issues of legitimacy.

People with different backgrounds and experiences have different experiences of consent. Consent

*From Kim Lane Scheppele, "The Reasonable Woman," in *The Responsive Community, Rights, and Responsibilities*, vol. I, issue 4, 1991. Reprinted here in abridged form by permission of *The Responsive Community*.

is often associated with choice, but a great deal of the legitimating force of choice depends on how the choices are seen. Most people would agree that the gunman who approaches and says "Your money or your life" is giving you a choice, but it's hard to say that you consented if you hand over your wallet. That's because it is widely recognized that almost everyone would see the "life" option as an unattractive choice. Handing over money feels, understandably, compelled, not chosen. But assume that the choice is between living with someone who beats you or moving out. Moving out sounds like the clear choice—unless you have no money, little chance of supporting yourself, and no independent support system to help you through the transition—and you believe that if you leave, the person you're living with will track you down and beat you worse than before. Men who are self-supporting and physically strong will tend to see that choice differently from women who are not. And if judges are men who assume their partial views represent the only truth, they may see women as having consented to stay, because, after all, the women chose to do so when they could have done otherwise. A judge who decides this way has no empathic imagination. He fails to see the choice as someone else might. He assumes that there is some single right answer in the choice, a right answer whose very claim to universality disguises the partiality of his own perspective. And with this totalizing point of view, his version of consent wins out over the real experience of feeling that one has no choice.

Rape is an area of law in which consent is crucial. If an accused rapist can demonstrate that the victim consented, sex is no longer rape. Many accused rapists use the consent defense at trial, forcing the focus of the trial onto the actions of the victim, who is almost always (and in some states has to be by statute) a woman. Though consent is defense to other crimes as well—theft, for example, or battery—consent poses a particular problem in rape cases, because consent to sex is often thought to be more problematic than consent to being beaten or having one's possessions taken. Sex, after all, is almost always emotionally complicated, and there may well be reasons for appearing to consent at the time and appearing not to have consented later. At least, that's what those who judge often think. This, of course, already tells us something crucial about consent—whether it will be believed in a particular context depends on its plausibility, judged against a set of implicit background standards. But those background standards may not always be shared by all those concerned, particularly the victims. Women have experiences of the world that are not the same as men's, especially when it comes to sex. And given the different perceptions of what is going on, women's views about consent in sex differ systematically from men's.

Let's look at one example. In *Rusk v. State,* a Maryland case, Eddie Rusk was convicted by a jury of raping a woman, referred to in the opinions only as Pat, whom he had met at a singles bar. When she said she was leaving, shortly after meeting him, Rusk asked Pat to drive him home. She agreed, drove him to his apartment in a part of the city that she didn't know, and refused his several invitations to come in. He took the car keys from the ignition and invited her in again. At the trial, Pat said that she was stranded in a strange and dangerous part of Baltimore. She said she believed it was unsafe to try to escape on foot and that she hoped to be able to convince Rusk to give back her car keys and to let her go. She followed him into his room and made no attempt to leave, even when he went down the hall to go to the bathroom. She asked for her car keys back and, when he refused, begged to be able to leave with her car. Rusk repeatedly said she couldn't, but he had no weapon and did not use overwhelming physical force. Rusk pulled her onto the bed and undressed her. Pat started to cry and Rusk put his hands on her throat and "started lightly to choke" her. She then asked, "If I do what you want, will you let me go without killing me?" and he answered yes. She performed oral sex, and then they had sexual intercourse, after which he gave her back the car keys and said she could leave. Charged with rape, Rusk claimed she had consented to sex with him. The appeals courts were called upon to determine whether her actions counted as consent.

This is where the 20 judges who heard the case on appeal (13 in the Court of Special Appeals, the intermediate appeals court in Maryland, and 7 in the Court of Appeals, the state supreme court) split all over the map. In the Court of Special Appeals, in 1979, the vote went 8–5 in favor of reversing the conviction, and in the Court of Appeals, in 1981, the vote was 4–3 in favor of reinstatement. The judges who wanted to overturn the conviction said that Rusk had not used enough force to overcome Pat's resistance if she had really meant not to consent; those who wanted to uphold the conviction said that Pat was afraid enough to make consent implausible.

The judges who found that Pat consented saw her options very differently from the way she reported them. Judge Thompson, for the Court of Special Appeals, noted that she could have sought help or tried to leave without her car. He minimized her reports that she was in a completely strange part of town and was frightened. Justice Cole, dissenting in the Maryland Court of Appeals, stressed that Pat was on an ordinary city street, that she was with a man who did not "grapple with her," and that she *followed* this man (Justice Cole's emphasis) into his apartment knowing what would happen if she did. "She certainly had to realize that they were not going upstairs to play Scrabble," Justice Cole observed.

The judges who found that Pat had *not* consented saw her options at the time more the way Pat said she did. Judge Wilner, dissenting in the Court of Special Appeals, quoted Pat's own words frequently throughout his description of the facts, and emphasized that Rusk's theft of her car keys was equivalent to a threat of force. And Justice Murphy, writing for the Court of Appeals, concluded Pat was "badly frightened . . . unable to think clearly . . . and believ[ed] that she had no other choice in the circumstances."

What these four opinions disagree about is precisely how to see her options and how she might have "reasonably" considered them. But, where the person whose consent is being constructed sees the world very differently from the judges, should judges be using universal (i.e., apparently point-of-viewless) standards that represent how a "reasonable man" would have acted at the time? Or should they consider how Pat herself, or a reasonable person with Pat's background, should have acted?

Good-faith efforts to understand the multiplicity of perspectives and the serious incommensurability of many points of view should make some difference here. Consent matters precisely because the consenter's point of view is crucial to the legitimacy of the actions she takes. To substitute what some hypothetical consenter unlike the particular person whose consent is being sought *would have* done in that circumstance undermines the very idea that makes consent a moral force—respect for the person's self-believed descriptions are checked not against the world that the individual sees but against a world that she does not see because she has a different socially grounded perspective.

In a number of areas of the law, courts already find ways to incorporate the distinctive social knowledge of socially diverse actors. In tort cases, for example, courts adopt some formulation, either explicitly or implicitly, that inquires into what the

reasonable man would have done under the circumstances. As tort doctrine has evolved, the unitary reasonable man has multiplied into the reasonably prudent doctor, the reasonable pilot, and the ordinarily careful horse trainer, among other characters recognizable in law. This multiplication of types of persons shows that existing legal doctrine and considerations of fairness do not require that everyone's perceptions be measured against the same social standard of reasonableness. But the law only incompletely recognizes that special knowledge is acquired not only in occupations but also in other sociological categories that give rise to different ways of seeing the world. The few cases that do mention a reasonable woman in tort law do so only for grammatical consistency, because one of the parties happens to be a woman, not because anything different results from noticing the gender of the parties. The reasonable woman is just like the reasonable man, only with a different pronoun.

But the reasonable woman could be a more sociologically powerful construction if we believed that everyone has "expertise" obtained from living a particular life in a particular social environment. Some of that expertise comes from living as a woman or a person of color. The choices each of us makes, and the degree of consent we express in those choices, depend on how our expertise tells us to evaluate the availability and attractiveness of alternatives. Being female or a person of color in this society is relevant to one's social point of view, and the law would better serve everyone if it recognized that the melting pot no longer melts all points of view into one, if indeed it ever did.

Considering a reasonable woman standard with gender-specific content is, in some ways, nothing new, though it is still controversial. In some areas of legal doctrine, women's unique perspectives have already been taken into account in this way, though only quite recently. In sexual harassment cases, a number of courts have said that the point of view of the reasonable woman should be adopted in determining whether men's behavior in the workplace is disruptive enough to qualify as sexual harassment. In *Ellison v. Brady* (1991), for example, the Ninth Circuit Court of Appeals found that any reasonable woman would have found the persistent and threatening "love letters" from her co-worker objectionable, reasoning:

> We adopt the perspective of a reasonable woman primarily because we believe that a

sex-blind reasonable person standard tends to be male-biased and tends to systematically ignore the experiences of women. The reasonable woman standard does not establish a higher level of protection for women than men. . . . Instead, a gender-conscious examination of sexual harassment enables women to participate in the workplace on an equal footing with men.

The reasonable woman was also decisive in *Robinson v. Jacksonville Shipyards* (Federal District Court, Middle District in Florida, 1991), and in *Yates v. Avco Corp* (6th Circuit, 1987). And it's not only in sexual harassment cases that the reasonable woman makes an appearance. She appears in murder or assault cases where a woman has killed or injured her attacker. In *State v. Wanrow* (1977), the Supreme Court of Washington reversed Yvonne Wanrow's conviction for assault and murder of a man who had allegedly molested her children. The court reversed because the jury had been instructed to consider the woman defendant's actions according to the standard of the reasonable man:

> [The jury instruction] not only establishes an objective standard, but through the persistent use of the masculine gender leaves the jury with the impression the objective standard to be applied is that applicable to an altercation between two men. The impression created— that a 5'4" woman with a cast on her leg and using a crutch must, under the law, somehow repel an assault by a 6'2" intoxicated man without employing weapons in her defense, unless the jury finds her determination of the degree of danger to be objectively reasonable—constitutes a separate and distinct misstatement of the law and, in the context of this case, violates the respondent's right to equal protection of the law. The respondent was entitled to have the jury consider her actions in the light of her own perceptions of the situation, including those perceptions which were the product of our nation's "long and unfortunate history of sex discrimination."

The "reasonable woman," then, has been accepted by some judges (though rejected by others) when the standard would involve importing a substantive judgment into the law that is different from the judgment of the reasonable man. But the places where the reasonable woman has already won some qualified acceptance in legal doctrine present fewer serious challenges to business-as-usual in the law than the rape cases do. In sexual harassment complaints, the relevant law is Title VII of the Civil Rights Act of 1964, whose primary purpose is to remedy past discrimination by stopping present and future discrimination. Seeing the harm from the point of view of the class explicitly protected by the statute is not a radical move, particularly given that the litigated complaints are civil cases. In the criminal cases with women defendants, the *mens rea* ("guilty mind") requirement for almost all crimes already focuses inquiry on the point of view of *this particular defendant*. If this particular defendant happened to be a woman, it would stand to reason that her perspective should be given due consideration without radically challenging existing law. Neither the civil cases involving sexual harassment nor the criminal cases involving women defendants contest the point of view already built into the doctrine for other reasons. But the rape cases are different.

Using the reasonable woman standard in rape cases like *Rusk* means asking the court to see the criminal nature of the defendant's conduct as dependent upon the *victim's* point of view. This is a radical departure for the criminal law, which customarily considers the victim to be just another witness at the trial and which privileges the perspective of the defendant through the *mens rea* requirement. But most crimes have as part of their definitions the lack of consent of the victim. For example, as we have seen, theft becomes borrowing if the owner consents, and battery becomes legitimate surgery with the consent of the patient. Usually consent isn't at issue in criminal trials for battery or theft. But in rape cases, consent is used frequently as a defense, and consent in rape has been taken as consent from men's point of view. Eleven of the 20 judges who heard the *Rusk* case adopted this perspective and the conviction was upheld only because the highest court had a slim majority in Pat's favor. Given the overwhelming focus in criminal cases on the defendant's perceptions of events (even if the defendant is a woman, as we have seen), introducing the perspective of the reasonable woman as a victim represents a major change.

The reasonable woman victim is not in the usual cast of characters of rape cases. Instead, the consent of the rape victim is usually assumed to be a flat fact that can be determined by an outsider's assessment of the evidence: Did she kick and scream? Did she try every avenue of escape? Was her fear the sort of fear I (the judge) would have had under the circumstances? Under these questions, the power of legitimation that consent is supposed to bring evaporates. The consent that is found does not respect the potential consenter's perspective. And if consent is to have the moral force assigned to it in liberal moral theory, the consent must not be imposed by someone who does not attempt to understand the potential consenter's point of view.

Does this mean that a search for consent should always be a quest for what *this* particular person thought at *that* particular time, no matter what the reasonableness of the perception? It would be easy, using the sort of perspective I've been encouraging here, to have as many standards as there are potential consenters and to make the legitimacy of actions requiring consent rest on detailed inquiries in individual instances. And that would be the best possible result for women who are victims of sexual assault. But there are some claims that defendants can make here that need to be considered as well. Criminal law is a vehicle for the expression of the moral standards of the community. The penalties are harsh and the stigma great for criminal conviction. As a result, criminal prosecutions are more serious for the defendants than ordinary civil trials. To base criminal convictions on potentially idiosyncratic perceptions of victims is unfair to those accused. If a woman says yes while meaning no, for example, we cannot expect the accused rapist to figure out what she means. This is why the reasonable woman standard has something to offer here. Adopting the reasonable woman as a social construct in the law allows women's views to have a strong impact on the outcome of rape trials while simultaneously putting men on notice that they must consider how women's perceptions of sexualized situations may be very different from their own. The reasonable woman standard does not require men to guess what is in each woman's mind, but it does require men to respect that women have the right to claim difference. It requires men to see the world through women's eyes.

For women, politically disadvantaged in the construction of sexuality, gender crucially shapes the world. As we saw in the *Rusk* case, Pat, like most women, learned to fear city streets, to count on the men she knew to protect her from lurking dangers. Women don't sexualize situations as quickly as men do, and so they may be slower to recognize danger in the first place. Pat's choice to go into Rusk's room because she was frightened to walk alone at night was an understandable choice, in the same way that the choice to stay in a dreadful living situation is understandable when the alternative is a reasonably seen threat of homelessness. Pat said "no" to sex. Rusk tried to override that "no" by limiting her means of escape. Pat decided it was less dangerous to go with Rusk and not fight him off physically than to risk the streets alone at night. The fact that she chose this option doesn't mean that she consented to sex with him. Her "no" meant no. The reasonable man, who does not fear city streets the way a reasonable woman does and who can fight physically with the expectation of success, may have tried to leave or fight. He would have had other options to reinforce what he meant by "no."

Women, people of color, and other politically disadvantaged groups are ill-served by a standardized concept of a reasonable man or an average person or a point-of-viewless point of view. So, the multiplication of standards against which perception might be judged is crucial to deciding whether women or people of color might have in fact consented to the conditions that the law holds them responsible for. And for starters, women in rape cases will see the world differently than men who face similar choices.

The intense tribalism of our time is a sign that conditions are improving for those whose voices have been silenced in the past. Women and people of color are calling for the recognition of multiple truths and many versions to replace the false unity of totalizing standards. We all owe each other a good-faith attempt to understand how people differently situated in the social order may reasonably see the same set of choices differently. In a pluralistic community, empathy is one of our most crucial resources. Extending the standard of the reasonable woman would be one good way to bring empathy to the law.

STATE V. RUSK *

Court of Appeals of Maryland, 1981

Murphy, C. J. Edward Rusk was found guilty by a jury . . . of second degree rape in violation of Maryland Code Art. 27, § 463(a)(1), which provides in pertinent part:

> A person is guilty of rape in the second degree if the person engages in vaginal intercourse with another person:
> (1) By force or threat of force against the will and without the consent of the other person. . . .

On appeal, the Court of Special Appeals, sitting en banc, reversed the conviction; it concluded by an 8–5 majority that in view of the prevailing law as set forth in *Hazel v. State,* 221 Md. 464, 157 A.2d 922 (1960), insufficient evidence of Rusk's guilt had been adduced at the trial to permit the case to go to the jury. We granted certiorari to consider whether the Court of Special Appeals properly applied the principles of *Hazel.* . . .

At the trial, the 21-year-old prosecuting witness, Pat, testified that on the evening of September 21, 1977, she attended a high school alumnae meeting where she met a girl friend, Terry. After the meeting, Terry and Pat agreed to drive in their respective cars to Fells Point to have a few drinks. . . . They went to a bar where . . . Rusk approached and said "hello" to Terry. Terry, who was then conversing with another individual, momentarily interrupted her conversation and said "Hi, Eddie." Rusk then began talking with Pat and during their conversation both of them acknowledged being separated from their respective spouses and having a child. Pat told Rusk that she had to go home . . . [and] Rusk requested a ride to his apartment. Although Pat did not know Rusk, she thought that Terry knew him. She thereafter agreed to give him a ride. Pat cautioned Rusk on the way to the car that "I'm just giving a ride home, you know, as a friend, not anything to be, you know, thought of other than a ride." . . . After a twenty-minute drive, they arrived at Rusk's apartment. . . . Pat testified that she was totally unfamiliar with the neighborhood. She parked the car at the curb . . . but left the engine running. Rusk asked Pat to come in, but she refused. . . . Pat said that Rusk was fully aware that she did not want to accompany him to his room. Notwithstanding her repeated refusals, Pat testified that Rusk reached over and turned off the ignition to her car and took her car keys. He got out of the car, walked over to her side, opened the door and said, "Now, will you come up?" Pat explained her subsequent actions:

> At that point, because I was scared, because he had my car keys. I didn't know what to do. I was someplace I didn't even know where I was. It was in the city. I didn't know whether to run. I really didn't think at that point, what to do.
> Now, I know that I should have blown the horn. I should have run. There were a million things I could have done. I was scared, at that point, and I didn't do any of them.

Pat testified that at this moment she feared that Rusk would rape her. She said: "[I]t was the way he looked at me, and said 'Come on up, come on up'; and when he took the keys, I knew that was wrong."

It was then about 1 A.M. Pat accompanied Rusk across the street into a totally dark house. . . . Rusk unlocked the door to his one-room apartment, and turned on the light. According to Pat, he told her to sit down. She sat in a chair beside the bed. Rusk sat on the bed. After Rusk talked for a few minutes, he left the room for about one to five minutes. Pat remained seated in the chair. She made no noise and did not attempt to leave. She said that she did not notice a telephone in the room. When Rusk returned, he turned off the light and sat down on the

*289 Md. 230, 424 A.2d 720 (1981). Endnotes omitted.

bed. Pat asked if she could leave; she told him that she wanted to go home and "didn't want to come up." She said, "Now, [that] I came up, can I go?" Rusk, who was still in possession of her car keys, said he wanted her to stay.

Rusk then asked Pat to get on the bed with him. He pulled her by the arms to the bed and began to undress her. . . . Pat removed the rest of her clothing, and then removed Rusk's pants because "he asked me to do it." After they were both undressed Rusk started kissing Pat as she was lying on her back. Pat explained what happened next:

> I was still begging him to please let, you know, let me leave. I said, "you can get alot of other girls down there, for what you want," and he just kept saying, "no"; and then I was really scared, because I can't describe, you know, what was said. It was more the look in his eyes; and I said, at that point—I didn't know what to say; and I said, "If I do what you want, will you let me go without killing me?" Because I didn't know, at that point, what he was going to do; and I started to cry; and when I did, he put his hands on my throat, and started lightly to choke me; and I said, "If I do what you want, will you let me go?" And he said, yes, and at that time, I proceeded to do what he wanted me to.

Pat testified that Rusk made her perform oral sex and then vaginal intercourse.

Immediately after the intercourse, Pat asked if she could leave. She testified that Rusk said, "Yes," after which she got up and got dressed and Rusk returned her car keys. She said that Rusk then

> walked me to my car, and asked if he could see me again; and I said, "Yes"; and he asked me for my telephone number; and I said, "No, I'll see you down Fells Point sometime," just so I could leave.

Pat testified that she "had no intention of meeting him again." She asked him for directions out of the neighborhood and left.

. . . As she sat in her car reflecting on the incident, Pat said she began to

> wonder what would happen if I hadn't of done what he wanted me to do. So I thought the right thing to do was to go report it, and I went from there to Hillendale to find a police car.

She reported the incident to the police at about 3:15 A.M. . . .

Rusk and two of his friends, Michael Trimp and David Carroll, testified on his behalf. According to Trimp, they went in Carroll's car to Buggs' bar to dance, drink and "tr[y] to pick up some ladies." Rusk stayed at the bar, while the others went to get something to eat.

Trimp and Carroll next saw Rusk walking down the street arm-in-arm with a lady whom Trimp was unable to identify. . . .

Carroll's testimony corroborated Trimp's. He saw Rusk walking down the street arm-in-arm with a woman. He said "[s]he was kind of like, you know, snuggling up to him like. . . . She was hanging all over him then." Carroll was fairly certain that Pat was the woman who was with Rusk. . . .

According to Rusk, when they arrived in front of his apartment Pat parked the car and turned the engine off. They sat for several minutes "petting each other." . . . Rusk testified that Pat came willingly to his room and that at no time did he make threatening facial expressions. . . . Rusk explained that after the intercourse, Pat "got uptight."

> Well, she started to cry. She said that—she said, "You guys are all alike," she says, "just out for," you know, "one thing." . . . And she said, that she just wanted to leave; and I said, "Well, okay"; and she walked out to the car. I walked out to the car. She got in the car and left.

Rusk denied placing his hands on Pat's throat or attempting to strangle her. He also denied using force or threats of force to get Pat to have intercourse with him.

In reversing Rusk's second degree rape conviction, the Court of Special Appeals quoting from *Hazel,* noted that:

> Force is an essential element of the crime [of rape] and to justify a conviction, the evidence must warrant a conclusion either that the victim resisted and her resistance was overcome by force or that she was prevented from resisting by threats to her safety.

Writing for the majority, Judge Thompson said:

> In all of the victim's testimony we have been unable to see any resistance on her part to the sex acts and certainly can we see no fear

as would overcome her attempt to resist or escape as required by *Hazel*. Possession of the keys by the accused may have deterred her vehicular escape but hardly a departure seeking help in the rooming house or in the street. We must say that "the way he looked" fails utterly to support the fear required by *Hazel*.

. . . Of course, due process requirements mandate that a criminal conviction not be obtained if the evidence does not reasonably support a finding of guilt beyond a reasonable doubt. However, as the Supreme Court made clear in *Jackson v. Virginia*, 443 U.S. 307 (1979), the reviewing court does not ask itself whether *it* believes that the evidence established guilt beyond a reasonable doubt; rather, the applicable standard is "whether, after viewing the evidence in the light most favorable to the prosecution, *any* rational trier of fact could have found the essential elements of the crime beyond a reasonable doubt." (emphasis in original). . . .

The Court [in *Hazel*] noted that lack of consent is generally established through proof of resistance or by proof that the victim failed to resist because of fear. The degree of fear necessary to obviate the need to prove resistance, and thereby establish lack of consent, was defined in the following manner: "The kind of fear which would render resistance by a woman unnecessary to support a conviction of rape includes, but is not necessarily limited to, a fear of death or serious bodily harm, or a fear so extreme as to preclude resistance, or a fear which would well nigh render her mind incapable of continuing to resist, or a fear that so overpowers her that she does not dare resist."

. . . While *Hazel* made it clear that the victim's fear had to be genuine, it did not pass upon whether a real but unreasonable fear of imminent death or serious bodily harm would suffice. The vast majority of jurisdictions have required that the victim's fear be reasonably grounded in order to obviate the need for either proof of actual force on the part of the assailant or physical resistance on the part of the victim. We think that, generally, this is the correct standard. . . .

We think the reversal of Rusk's conviction by the Court of Special Appeals was in error for the fundamental reason so well expressed in the dissenting opinion by Judge Wilner when he observed that the majority had "trampled upon the first principle of appellate restraint [because it had] substituted [its]

own view of the evidence (and the inferences that may fairly be drawn from it) for that of the judge and jury [and had thereby] improperly invaded the province allotted to those tribunals." In view of the evidence adduced at the trial, the reasonableness of Pat's apprehension of fear was plainly a question of fact for the jury to determine. . . . Quite obviously, the jury disbelieved Rusk and believed Pat's testimony. From her testimony, the jury could have reasonably concluded that the taking of her car keys was intended by Rusk to immobilize her alone, late at night, in a neighborhood with which she was not familiar; that after Pat had repeatedly refused to enter his apartment, Rusk commanded in firm tones that she do so; that Pat was badly frightened and feared that Rusk intended to rape her; . . . that Pat was afraid that Rusk would kill her unless she submitted; that she began to cry and Rusk then put his hands on her throat and began "lightly to choke" her; that Pat asked him if he would let her go without killing her if she complied with his demands; that Rusk gave an affirmative response, after which she finally submitted.

Just where persuasion ends and force begins in cases like the present is essentially a factual issue. . . . Considering all of the evidence in the case, with particular focus upon the actual force applied by Rusk to Pat's neck, we conclude that the jury could rationally find that the essential elements of second degree rape had been established and that Rusk was guilty of that offense beyond a reasonable doubt. . . .

Cole, J., dissenting. [W]hen one of the essential elements of a crime is not sustained by the evidence, the conviction of the defendant cannot stand as a matter of law.

The majority, in applying this standard, concludes that "[i]n view of the evidence adduced at the trial, the reasonableness of Pat's apprehension of fear was plainly a question of fact for the jury to determine." In so concluding, the majority has skipped over the crucial issue. It seems to me that whether the prosecutrix's fear is reasonable becomes a question only after the court determines that the defendant's conduct under the circumstances was reasonably calculated to give rise to a fear on her part to the extent that she was unable to resist. . . .

While courts no longer require a female to resist to the utmost or to resist where resistance would be foolhardy, they do require her acquiescence in the act of intercourse to stem from fear generated by something of substance. She may not simply say, "I was really scared," and thereby transform consent or mere unwillingness into submission by force. These words do not transform a seducer into a rapist. She must follow the natural instinct of every proud female to resist, by more than mere words, the violation of her person by a stranger or an unwelcomed friend. She must make it plain that she regards such sexual acts as abhorrent and repugnant to her natural sense of pride. She must resist unless the defendant has objectively manifested his intent to use physical force to accomplish his purpose. The law regards rape as a crime of violence. The majority today attenuates this proposition. It declares the innocence of an at best distraught young woman. It does not demonstrate the defendant's guilt of the crime of rape.

. . . The majority suggests that "from her testimony the jury could have reasonably concluded that the taking of her keys was intended by Rusk to immobilize her alone, late at night, in a neighborhood with which she was unfamiliar. . . ." But on what facts does the majority so conclude? There is no evidence descriptive of the tone of his voice; her testimony indicates only the bare statement quoted above. . . .

She also testified that she was afraid of "the way he looked," and afraid of his statement, "come on up, come on up." But what can the majority conclude from this statement coupled with a "look" that remained undescribed? There is no evidence whatsoever to suggest that this was anything other than a pattern of conduct consistent with the ordinary seduction of a female acquaintance who at first suggests her disinclination. . . .

The majority relies on the trial court's statement that the defendant responded affirmatively to her question "If I do what you want, will you let me go without killing me?" The majority further suggests that the jury could infer the defendant's affirmative response. The facts belie such inference since by the prosecutrix's own testimony the defendant made *no* response. *He said nothing!*

She then testified that she started to cry and he "started lightly to choke" her, whatever that means. Obviously, the choking was not of any persuasive significance. During this "choking" she was able to talk. She said "If I do what you want will you let me go?" It was at this point that the defendant said yes.

I find it incredible for the majority to conclude that on these facts, without more, a woman was *forced* to commit oral sex upon the defendant and then to engage in vaginal intercourse.

[T]here are no acts or conduct on the part of the defendant to suggest that these fears were created by the defendant or that he made any objective, identifiable threats to her which would give rise to this woman's failure to flee, summon help, scream, or make physical resistance. . . .

In my judgment the State failed to prove the essential element of force beyond a reasonable doubt and, therefore, the judgment of conviction should be reversed. . . .

REGINA V. MORGAN *

House of Lords, 1976

The defendant Morgan and three other defendants were convicted of the forcible rape of Morgan's wife. Morgan's liability rested on his having aided and abetted the three others. The Court of Appeals affirmed all the convictions but certified the following question to the House of Lords:

> Whether in rape the defendant can properly be convicted notwithstanding that he in fact believed that the woman consented, if such a belief was not based on reasonable grounds.

[The applicable statute stated simply: "*Rape*— (1) It is a felony for a man to rape a woman."]

LORD HAILSHAM of St. Marylebone. . . . The question arises in the following way. The appellant Morgan and his three co-appellants, who were all members of the RAF, spent the evening of 15th August 1973 in one another's company. The appellant Morgan was significantly older than the other three, and considerably senior to them in rank. He was . . . married to the alleged victim, but not, it seems, at the time habitually sleeping in the same bed. [B]y the time the appellants arrived at Morgan's house, Mrs. Morgan was already in bed and asleep, until she was awoken by their presence.

According to the version of the facts which she gave in evidence, and which was evidently accepted by the jury, she was aroused from her sleep, . . . held by each of her limbs, . . . while each of the three young appellants in turn had intercourse with her in the presence of the others. . . .

According to Mrs. Morgan she consented to none of this and made her opposition to what was being done very plain indeed. . . .

All four appellants explained in the witness box that they had spent the evening together in Wolverhampton, and by the time of the alleged offences had had a good deal to drink. Their original intention had been to find some women in the town but, when this failed, Morgan made the surprising suggestion to the others that they should all return to his home and have sexual intercourse with his wife. According to the three younger appellants (but not according to Morgan who described this part of their story as "lying") Morgan told them that they must not be surprised if his wife struggled a bit, since she was "kinky" and this was the only way in which she could get "turned on." However this may be, it is clear that Morgan did invite his three companions home in order that they might have sexual intercourse with his wife and, no doubt, he may well have led them in one way or another to believe that she would consent to their doing so. This, however, would only be matter predisposing them to believe that Mrs. Morgan consented, and would not in any way establish that, at the time, they believed she did consent whilst they were having intercourse.

I need not enter into the details of what the appellants said happened after they had arrived at the house. As I have said they admitted that some degree of struggle took place in the wife's bedroom. But all asserted that after she got into the double bedroom she not merely consented to but actively co-operated with and enjoyed what was being done. . . .

The choice before the jury was thus between two stories each wholly incompatible with the other, and in my opinion it would have been quite sufficient for the judge, after suitable warnings about the burden of proof, corroboration, separate verdicts and the admissibility of the statements only against the makers, to tell the jury that they must really choose between the two versions. . . .

The certified question arises because counsel for the appellants raised the question whether, even if the victim [objected], the appellants may . . . have honestly believed that she did [not]. [I]n the summing-up [to the jury] . . . [t]he learned judge said:

---

*[1976] A.C. 182. Endnotes deleted.

[T]he prosecution have to prove that each defendant intended to have sexual intercourse with this woman without her consent. Not merely that he intended to have intercourse with her but that he intended to have intercourse without her consent. Therefore if the defendant believed or may have believed that Mrs. Morgan consented to him having sexual intercourse with her, then there would be no such intent in his mind and he would be not guilty of the offence of rape, but such a belief must be honestly held by the defendant in the first place. He must really believe that. And, secondly, his belief must be a reasonable belief; such a belief as a reasonable man would entertain if he applied his mind and thought about the matter. It is not enough for a defendant to rely upon a belief, even though he honestly held it, if it was completely fanciful; contrary to every indication which could be given which would carry some weight with a reasonable man.

It is on the second proposition about the mental element that the appellants concentrate their criticism. An honest belief in consent, they contend, is enough. It matters not whether it be also reasonable. No doubt a defendant will wish to raise argument or lead evidence to show that this belief was reasonable, since this will support its honesty. No doubt the prosecution will seek to cross-examine or raise arguments or adduce evidence to undermine the contention that the belief is reasonable, because, in the nature of the case, the fact that a belief cannot reasonably be held is a strong ground for saying that it was not in fact held honestly at all. Nonetheless, the appellants contend, the crux of the matter, the factum probandum, or rather the fact to be refuted by the prosecution, is honesty and not honesty plus reasonableness. . . .

The beginning of wisdom in all the "mens rea" cases to which our attention was called is, as was pointed out by Stephen, J., in *R. v. Tolson,* [23 Q.B.D. 168 (1889)], that "mens rea" means a number of quite different things in relation to different crimes. . . .

Once one has accepted, what seems to me abundantly clear, that the prohibited act in rape is non-consensual sexual intercourse, and that the guilty state of mind is an intention to commit it, it seems to me to follow as a matter of inexorable logic that there is no room either for a "defence" of honest belief or mistake, or of a defence of honest and reasonable belief and mistake. Either the prosecution proves that the accused had the requisite intent, or it does not. In the former case it succeeds, and in the latter it fails. Since honest belief clearly negatives intent, the reasonableness or otherwise of that belief can only be evidence for or against the view that the belief and therefore the intent was actually held. . . .

For the above reasons I would answer the question certified in the negative, but would apply the proviso to s. 2(1) of the Criminal Appeal Act 1968 on the ground that no miscarriage of justice has or conceivably could have occurred. In my view, therefore these appeals should be dismissed.

LORD FRASER of Tulleybelton. . . . The argument for the Crown in support of an affirmative answer to the question in this case was not supported by any English decision on rape. It was supported by reference to English decisions in relation to other offences which are more or less analogous to rape . . . . The English case upon which most reliance was placed was *Reg. v. Tolson,* 23 Q.B.D. 168, which was concerned with bigamy, and which decided that a bona fide belief *on reasonable grounds* in the death of the husband at the time of the second marriage afforded a good defence to the indictment for bigamy. The main argument in the case was concerned with the question whether a mistaken belief could be a defence to a charge of bigamy at all, and comparatively little attention was given to the subsidiary point of whether the belief had to be based upon reasonable grounds. The case seems to me therefore of only limited assistance for the present purpose. . . . The difficulty of arguing by analogy from one offence to another is strikingly illustrated by reference to the case of *Reg. v. Prince* (1875) 13 Cox C.C. 138. That case dealt with abduction of a girl under the age of 16, an offence created by section 55 of the Act of 1861. Bramwell, B., with whom five other judges concurred, held that a mistaken and reasonable belief by the defendant that the abducted girl was aged 16 or more was no excuse, because abduction of a young girl was immoral as well as illegal, although a mistaken and reasonable belief by the defendant that he had the consent of the girl's father would have been an excuse. If such differences can exist about mistaken beliefs of different facts in one offence, it is surely dangerous to argue from one offence to another. No doubt a rapist, who mistakenly believes that the woman is consenting to intercourse, must be behaving immorally, by committing fornication or adultery. But those forms of immoral conduct are not intended to be struck at by the law against rape; indeed, they are not now considered appropriate to be visited with penalties of the criminal law at all. There seems therefore to be no reason why they should affect the consequences of the mistaken belief. . . .

For these reasons, I am of the opinion that there is no authority which compels me to answer the question in what I would regard as an illogical way. I would therefore answer the question in the negative—i.e. in favour of the accused. But for the reasons stated by . . . Lord Hailsham . . . I would apply the proviso to the Criminal Appeal Act of 1968 . . . and I would refuse the appeal.

Appeals Dismissed.

STATE V. KELLY*

Supreme Court of New Jersey, 1984

WILENTZ, C. J. . . . On May 24, 1980, defendant, Gladys Kelly, stabbed her husband, Ernest, with a pair of scissors. He died shortly thereafter at a nearby hospital. . . .

Ms. Kelly was indicted for murder. At trial, she did not deny stabbing her husband, but asserted that her action was in self-defense. To establish the requisite state of mind for her self-defense claim, Ms. Kelly called Dr. Lois Veronen as an expert witness to testify about the battered-woman's syndrome. After hearing a lengthy voir dire examination of Dr. Veronen, the trial court ruled that expert testimony concerning the syndrome was inadmissible on the self-defense issue. . . .

Mrs. Kelly was convicted of reckless manslaughter. [We] reverse.

The Kellys had a stormy marriage. Some of the details of their relationship, especially the stabbing, are disputed. The following is Ms. Kelly's version of what happened—a version that the jury could have accepted and, if they had, a version that would make the proffered expert testimony not only relevant, but critical.

The day after the marriage, Mr. Kelly got drunk and knocked Ms. Kelly down. Although a period of calm followed the initial attack, the next seven years were accompanied by periodic and frequent beatings, sometimes as often as once a week. During the attacks, which generally occurred when Mr. Kelly was drunk, he threatened to kill Ms. Kelly and to cut off parts of her body if she tried to leave him. Mr. Kelly often moved out of the house after an attack, later returning with a promise that he would change his ways. Until the day of the homicide, only one of the attacks had taken place in public.

The day before the stabbing, Gladys and Ernest went shopping. They did not have enough money to buy food for the entire week, so Ernest said he would give his wife more money the next day.

The following morning he left for work. Ms. Kelly next saw her husband late that afternoon at a friend's house. She had gone there with her daughter, Annette, to ask Ernest for money to buy food. He told her to wait until they got home, and shortly thereafter the Kellys left. After walking past several houses, Mr. Kelly, who was drunk, angrily asked "What the hell did you come around here for?" He then grabbed the collar of her dress, and the two fell to the ground. He choked her by pushing his fingers against her throat, punched or hit her face, and bit her leg.

A crowd gathered on the street. Two men from the crowd separated them, just as Gladys felt that she was "passing out" from being choked. Fearing that Annette had been pushed around in the crowd, Gladys then left to look for her. . . .

---

*478 A.2d 364 (1984). Endnotes deleted. Text originally appearing as a footnote now appears as an endnote.

After finding her daughter, Ms. Kelly then observed Mr. Kelly running toward her with his hands raised. Within seconds he was right next to her. Unsure of whether he had armed himself while she was looking for their daughter, and thinking that he had come back to kill her, she grabbed a pair of scissors from her pocketbook. She tried to scare him away, but instead stabbed him.[1]

The central question in this case is whether the trial court erred in its exclusion of expert testimony on the battered-woman's syndrome. That testimony was intended to explain defendant's state of mind and bolster her claim of self-defense. We shall first examine the nature of the battered-woman's syndrome and then consider the expert testimony proffered in this case and its relevancy. . . .

As the problem of battered women has begun to receive more attention, sociologists and psychologists have begun to focus on the effects a sustained pattern of physical and psychological abuse can have on a woman. The effects of such abuse are what some scientific observers have termed "the battered-woman's syndrome," a series of common characteristics that appear in women who are abused physically and psychologically over an extended period of time by the dominant male figure in their lives. Dr. Lenore Walker, a prominent writer on the battered-woman's syndrome, defines the battered woman as one

> who is repeatedly subjected to any forceful physical or psychological behavior by a man in order to coerce her to do something he wants her to do without concern for her rights. Battered women include wives or women in any form of intimate relationships with men. Furthermore, in order to be classified as a battered woman, the couple must go through the battering cycle at least twice. Any woman may find herself in an abusive relationship with a man once. If it occurs a second time, and she remains in the situation, she is defined as a battered woman. [L. Walker, *The Battered Woman* (1979) at xv].

According to Dr. Walker, relationships characterized by physical abuse tend to develop battering cycles. Violent behavior directed at the woman occurs in three distinct and repetitive stages that vary both in duration and intensity depending on the individuals involved.

Phase one of the battering cycle is referred to as the "tension-building stage," during which the battering male engages in minor battering incidents and verbal abuse while the woman, beset by fear and tension, attempts to be as placating and passive as possible in order to stave off more serious violence.

Phase two of the battering cycle is the "acute battering incident." At some point during phase one, the tension between the battered woman and the batterer becomes intolerable and more serious violence inevitable. The triggering event that initiates phase two is most often an internal or external event in the life of the battering male, but provocation for more severe violence is sometimes provided by the woman who can no longer tolerate or control her phase-one anger and anxiety.

Phase three of the battering cycle is characterized by extreme contrition and loving behavior on the part of the battering male. During this period the man will often mix his pleas for forgiveness and protestations of devotion with promises to seek professional help, to stop drinking, and to refrain from further violence. For some couples, this period of relative calm may last as long as several months, but in a battering relationship the affection and contrition of the man will eventually fade and phase one of the cycle will start anew.

The cyclical nature of battering behavior helps explain why more women simply do not leave their abusers. The loving behavior demonstrated by the batterer during phase three reinforces whatever hopes these women might have for their mate's reform and keeps them bound to the relationship. R. Langley & R. Levy, Wife Beating: The Silent Crisis 112–14 (1977).

Some women may even perceive the battering cycle as normal, especially if they grew up in a violent household. . . . Other women, however, become so demoralized and degraded by the fact that they cannot predict or control the violence that they sink into a state of psychological paralysis and become unable to take any action at all to improve or alter the situation. There is a tendency in battered women to believe in the omnipotence or strength of their battering husbands and thus to feel that any attempt to resist them is hopeless.

In addition to these psychological impacts, external social and economic factors often make it difficult for some women to extricate themselves from battering relationships. A woman without independent financial resources who wishes to leave her husband often finds it difficult to do so because of a lack of material and social resources. . . . Thus, in a violent confrontation where the first reaction might be to flee, women realize soon that there may be no place to go. Moreover, the stigma that attaches to a woman who leaves the family unit without her children undoubtedly acts as a further deterrent to moving out.

In addition, battered women, when they want to leave the relationship, are typically unwilling to reach out and confide in their friends, family, or the police, either out of shame and humiliation, fear of reprisal by their husband, or the feeling they will not be believed.

Dr. Walker and other commentators have identified several common personality traits of the battered woman: low self-esteem, traditional beliefs about the home, the family, and the female sex role, tremendous feelings of guilt that their marriages are failing, and the tendency to accept responsibility for the batterer's actions.

Finally, battered women are often hesitant to leave a battering relationship because, in addition to their hope of reform on the part of their spouse, they harbor a deep concern about the possible response leaving might provoke in their mates. They literally become trapped by their own fear. Case histories are replete with instances in which a battered wife left her husband only to have him pursue her and subject her to an even more brutal attack.

The combination of all these symptoms—resulting from sustained psychological and physical trauma compounded by aggravating social and economic factors—constitutes the battered-woman's syndrome. Only by understanding these unique pressures that force battered women to remain with their mates, despite their long-standing and reasonable fear of severe bodily harm and the isolation that being a battered woman creates, can a battered woman's state of mind be accurately and fairly understood.

The voir dire testimony of Dr. Veronen, sought to be introduced by defendant Gladys Kelly, conformed essentially to this outline of the battered-woman's syndrome. . . .

In addition, Dr. Veronen was prepared to testify as to how, as a battered woman, Gladys Kelly perceived her situation at the time of the stabbing, and why, in her opinion, defendant did not leave her husband despite the constant beatings she endured.

Whether expert testimony on the battered-woman's syndrome should be admitted in this case depends on whether it is relevant to defendant's claim of self-defense, and, in any event, on whether the proffer meets the standards for admission of expert testimony in this state. We examine first the law of self-defense and consider whether the expert testimony is relevant.

. . . The use of force against another in self-defense is justifiable "when the actor reasonably believes that such force is immediately necessary for the purpose of protecting himself against the use of unlawful force by such other person on the present occasion." N.J.S.A. 2C:3–4(a). Further limitations exist when deadly force is used in self-defense. The use of such deadly force is not justifiable

> unless the actor reasonably believes that such force is necessary to protect himself against death or serious bodily harm. . . . [N.J.S.A. 2C:3–4(b)(2)].

Gladys Kelly claims that she stabbed her husband in self-defense, believing he was about to kill her. The gist of the State's case was that Gladys Kelly was the aggressor, that she consciously intended to kill her husband, and that she certainly was not acting in self-defense.

The credibility of Gladys Kelly is a critical issue in this case. If the jury does not believe Gladys Kelly's account, it cannot find she acted in self-defense. The expert testimony offered was directly relevant to one of the critical elements of that account, namely, what Gladys Kelly believed at the time of the stabbing, and was thus material to establish the honesty of her stated belief that she was in imminent danger of death. . . .

As can be seen from our discussion of the expert testimony, Dr. Veronen would have bolstered Gladys Kelly's credibility. Specifically, by showing that her experience, although concededly difficult to comprehend, was common to that of other women who had been in similarly abusive relationships, Dr. Veronen would have helped the jury understand that Gladys Kelly could have honestly feared that she would suffer serious bodily harm from her husband's attacks, yet still remain with him. This, in turn, would support Ms. Kelly's testimony about her state of mind (that is, that she honestly feared serious bodily harm) at the time of the stabbing. . . .

We also find the expert testimony relevant to the reasonableness of defendant's belief that she was in imminent danger of death or serious injury. We do not mean that the expert's testimony could be used to show that it was understandable that a battered woman might believe that her life was in danger when indeed it was not and when a reasonable person would not have so believed. . . . Expert testimony in that direction would be relevant solely to the honesty of defendant's belief, not its objective reasonableness. Rather, our conclusion is that the expert's testimony, if accepted by the jury, would have aided it in determining whether, under the circumstances, a reasonable person would have believed there was imminent danger to her life.

At the heart of the claim of self-defense was defendant's story that she had been repeatedly subjected to "beatings" over the course of her marriage . . . . When that regular pattern of serious physical abuse is combined with defendant's claim that the decedent sometimes threatened to kill her, defendant's statement that on this occasion she thought she might be killed when she saw Mr. Kelly running toward her could be found to reflect a reasonable fear; that is, it could so be found if the jury believed Gladys Kelly's story of the prior beatings, if it believed her story of the prior threats, and, of course, if it believed her story of the events of that particular day.

The crucial issue of fact on which this expert's testimony would bear is why, given such allegedly severe and constant beatings, combined with threats to kill, defendant had not long ago left decedent. Whether raised by the prosecutor as a factual issue or not, our own common knowledge tells us that most of us, including the ordinary juror, would ask himself or herself just such a question. [O]ne of the common myths, apparently believed by most people, is that battered wives are free to leave. To some, this misconception is followed by the observation that the battered wife is masochistic, proven by her refusal to leave despite the severe beatings; to others, however, the fact that the battered wife stays on unquestionably suggests that the "beatings" could not have been too bad for if they had been, she certainly would have left. The expert could clear up these myths, by explaining that one of the common characteristics of a battered wife is her inability to leave despite such constant beatings; her "learned helplessness"; her lack of anywhere to go; her feeling that if she tried to leave, she would be subjected to even more merciless treatment; her belief in the omnipotence of her battering husband; and sometimes her hope that her husband will change his ways. . . .

The difficulty with the expert's testimony is that it *sounds* as if an expert is giving knowledge to a jury about something the jury knows as well as anyone else, namely, the reasonableness of a person's fear of imminent serious danger. That is not at all, however, what this testimony is *directly* aimed at. It is aimed at an area where the purported common knowledge of the jury may be very much mistaken, an area where jurors' logic, drawn from their

own experience, may lead to a wholly incorrect conclusion. . . . After hearing the expert, instead of saying Gladys Kelly could not have been beaten up so badly for if she had, she certainly would have left, the jury could conclude that her failure to leave was very much part and parcel of her life as a battered wife. The jury could conclude that instead of casting doubt on the accuracy of her testimony about the severity and frequency of prior beatings, her failure to leave actually reinforced her credibility.

Since a retrial is necessary, we think it advisable to indicate the limit of the expert's testimony on this issue of reasonableness. It would not be proper for the expert to express the opinion that defendant's belief on that day was reasonable, not because this is the ultimate issue, but because the area of *expert* knowledge relates, in this regard, to the reasons for defendant's failure to leave her husband. Either the jury accepts or rejects that explanation and, based on that, credits defendant's stories about the beatings she suffered. No expert is needed, however, once the jury has made up its mind on those issues, to tell the jury the logical conclusion, namely, that a person who has in fact been severely and continuously beaten might very well reasonably fear that the imminent beating she was about to suffer could be either life-threatening or pose a risk of serious injury. What the expert could state was that defendant had the battered-woman's syndrome, and could explain that syndrome in detail, relating its characteristics to defendant, but only to enable the jury better to determine the honesty and reasonableness of defendant's belief. Depending on its content, the expert's testimony might also enable the jury to find that the battered wife, because of the prior beatings, numerous beatings, as often as once a week, for seven years, from the day they were married to the day he died, is particularly able to predict accurately the likely extent of violence in any attack on her. That conclusion could significantly affect the jury's evaluation of the reasonableness of defendant's fear for her life.

Having determined that testimony about the battered-woman's syndrome is relevant, we now consider whether Dr. Veronen's testimony satisfies the limitations placed on expert testimony by Evidence Rule 56(2) and by applicable case law. . . . In effect, this Rule imposes three basic requirements for the admission of expert testimony: (1) the intended testimony must concern a subject matter that is beyond the ken of the average juror; (2) the field testified to must be at a state of the art such that an expert's testimony could be sufficiently reliable; and

(3) the witness must have sufficient expertise to offer the intended testimony. . . .

As previously discussed, a battering relationship embodies psychological and societal features that are not well understood by lay observers. . . . It is clear that this subject is beyond the ken of the average juror. . . .

The second requirement that must be met before expert testimony is permitted is a showing that the proposed expert's testimony would be reliable. . .

Dr. Veronen, the proffered expert, testified that the battered-woman's syndrome is acknowledged and accepted by practitioners and professors in the fields of psychology and psychiatry. Dr. Veronen also brought to the court's attention the findings of several researchers who have published reports confirming the presence of the battered-woman's syndrome. . . . Briefs submitted to this Court indicate that there are at least five books and almost seventy scientific articles and papers about the battered-woman's syndrome.

Thus, the record before us reveals that the battered woman's syndrome has a sufficient scientific basis to produce uniform and reasonably reliable results. . . . However, while the record before us could require such a ruling, we refrain from conclusively ruling that Dr. Veronen's proffered testimony about the battered-woman's syndrome would satisfy New Jersey's standard of acceptability for scientific evidence. This is because the State was not given a full opportunity in the trial court to question Dr. Veronen's methodology in studying battered women or her implicit assertion that the battered-woman's syndrome has been accepted by the relevant scientific community. . . .

[Reversed and remanded.]

---

1. This version of the homicide—with a drunk Mr. Kelly as the aggressor both in pushing Ms. Kelly to the ground and again in rushing at her with his hands in a threatening position after the two had been separated—is sharply disputed by the State. The prosecution presented testimony intended to show that the initial scuffle was started by Gladys; that upon disentanglement, while she was restrained by bystanders, she stated that she intended to kill Ernest; that she then chased after him, and upon catching up with him stabbed him with a pair of scissors taken from her pocketbook.

MICHAEL M. V. SUPERIOR COURT OF SONOMA COUNTY*

United States Supreme Court, 1981

Justice REHNQUIST announced the judgment of the Court and delivered an opinion, in which THE CHIEF JUSTICE, Justice STEWART, and Justice POWELL joined.

The question presented in this case is whether California's "statutory rape" law, violates the Equal Protection Clause of the Fourteenth Amendment. Section 261.5 defines unlawful sexual intercourse as "an act of sexual intercourse accomplished with a female not the wife of the perpetrator, where the female is under the age of 18 years." The statute thus makes men alone criminally liable for the act of sexual intercourse.

In July 1978, a complaint was filed in the Municipal Court of Sonoma County, Cal., alleging that petitioner, then a 17½-year-old male, had had unlawful sexual intercourse with a female under the age of 18, in violation of § 261.5. The evidence, adduced at a preliminary hearing showed that at approximately midnight on June 3, 1978, petitioner and two friends approached Sharon, a 16½-year-old female, and her sister as they waited at a bus stop. Petitioner and Sharon, who had already been drinking, moved away from the others and began to kiss. After being struck in the face for rebuffing petitioner's initial advances, Sharon submitted to sexual intercourse with petitioner. Prior to trial, petitioner sought to set aside the information on both state and federal constitutional grounds, asserting that § 261.5 unlawfully discriminated on the basis of gender. The trial court and the California Court of Appeal denied petitioner's request for relief and petitioner sought review in the Supreme Court of California.

The Supreme Court held that "section 261.5 discriminates on the basis of sex because only females may be victims, and only males may violate the section." The court then subjected the classification to "strict scrutiny," stating that it must be justi-

fied by a compelling state interest. It found that the classification was "supported not by mere social convention but by the immutable physiological fact that it is the female exclusively who can become pregnant." Canvassing "the tragic human costs of illegitimate teenage pregnancies," including the large number of teenage abortions, the increased medical risk associated with teenage pregnancies, and the social consequences of teenage childbearing, the court concluded that the State has a compelling interest in preventing such pregnancies. Because males alone can "physiologically cause the result which the law properly seeks to avoid," the court further held that the gender classification was readily justified as a means of identifying offender and victim. For the reasons stated below, we affirm the judgment of the California Supreme Court.

As is evident from our opinions, the Court has had some difficulty in agreeing upon the proper approach and analysis in cases involving challenges to gender-based classifications. The issues posed by such challenges range from issues of standing to the appropriate standard of judicial review for the substantive classification. Unlike the California Supreme Court, we have not held that gender-based classifications are "inherently suspect" and thus we do not apply so-called "strict scrutiny" to those classifications. Our cases have held, however, that the traditional minimum rationality test takes on a somewhat "sharper focus" when gender-based classifications are challenged. In *Reed v. Reed*, for example, the Court stated that a gender-based classification will be upheld if it bears a "fair and substantial relationship" to legitimate state ends, while in *Craig v. Boren*, the Court restated the test to require the classification to bear a "substantial relationship" to "important governmental objectives."

---

*450 *U.S.* 464, 67 *L.Ed.* 2d 437. Citations and endnotes deleted from text.

Underlying these decisions is the principle that a legislature may not "make overbroad generalizations based on sex which are entirely unrelated to any differences between men and women or which demean the ability or social status of the affected class." But because the Equal Protection Clause does not "demand that a statute necessarily apply equally to all persons" or require "'things which are different in fact . . . to be treated in law as though they were the same,'" this Court has consistently upheld statutes where the gender classification is not invidious, but rather realistically reflects the fact that the sexes are not similarly situated in certain circumstances. As the Court has stated, a legislature may "provide for the special problems of women."

Applying those principles to this case, the fact that the California Legislature criminalized the act of illicit sexual intercourse with a minor female is a sure indication of its intent or purpose to discourage that conduct. Precisely why the legislature desired that result is of course somewhat less clear. This Court has long recognized that "[i]nquiries into congressional motives or purposes are a hazardous matter," and the search for the "actual" or "primary" purpose of a statute is likely to be elusive. Here, for example, the individual legislators may have voted for the statute for a variety of reasons. Some legislators may have been concerned about preventing teenage pregnancies, others about protecting young females from physical injury or from the loss of "chastity," and still others about promoting various religious and moral attitudes towards premarital sex.

The justification for the statute offered by the State, and accepted by the Supreme Court of California, is that the legislature sought to prevent illegitimate teenage pregnancies. That finding, of course, is entitled to great deference. And although our cases establish that the State's asserted reason for the enactment of a statute may be rejected, if it "could not have been a goal of the legislation." This is not such a case.

We are satisfied not only that the prevention of illegitimate pregnancy is at least one of the "purposes" of the statute, but also that the State has a strong interest in preventing such pregnancy. At the risk of stating the obvious, teenage pregnancies, which have increased dramatically over the last two decades, have significant social, medical, and economic consequences for both the mother and her child, and the State. Of particular concern to the State is that approximately half of all teenage pregnancies end in abortion. And of those children who are born, their illegitimacy makes them likely candidates to become wards of the State.

We need not be medical doctors to discern that young men and young women are not similarly situated with respect to the problems and the risks of sexual intercourse. Only women may become pregnant, and they suffer disproportionately the profound physical, emotional and psychological consequences of sexual activity. The statute at issue here protects women from sexual intercourse at an age when those consequences are particularly severe.

The question thus boils down to whether a State may attack the problem of sexual intercourse and teenage pregnancy directly by prohibiting a male from having sexual intercourse with a minor female. We hold that such a statute is sufficiently related to the State's objectives to pass constitutional muster.

Because virtually all of the significant harmful and inescapably identifiable consequences of teenage pregnancy fall on the young female, a legislature acts well within its authority when it elects to punish only the participant who, by nature, suffers few of the consequences of his conduct. It is hardly unreasonable for a legislature acting to protect minor females to exclude them from punishment. Moreover, the risk of pregnancy itself constitutes a substantial deterrence to young females. No similar natural sanctions deter males. A criminal sanction imposed solely on males thus serves to roughly "equalize" the deterrents on the sexes.

We are unable to accept petitioner's contention that the statute is impermissibly underinclusive and must, in order to pass judicial scrutiny, be *broadened* so as to hold the female as criminally liable as the male. It is argued that this statute is not *necessary* to deter teenage pregnancy because a gender-neutral statute, where both male and female would be subject to prosecution, would serve that goal equally well. The relevant inquiry, however, is not whether the statute is drawn as precisely as it might have been, but whether the line chosen by the California Legislature is within constitutional limitations.

In any event, we cannot say that a gender-neutral statute would be as effective as the statute California has chosen to enact. The State persuasively contends that a gender-neutral statute would frustrate its interest in effective enforcement. Its view is that a female is surely less likely to report violations of the statute if she herself would be subject to criminal prosecution. In an area already fraught with prosecutorial difficulties, we decline to hold that the Equal Protection Clause requires a legislature to enact a statute so broad that it may well be incapable of enforcement.

We similarly reject petitioner's argument that § 261.5 is impermissibly overbroad because it makes unlawful sexual intercourse with prepubescent females, who are, by definition, incapable of becoming pregnant. Quite apart from the fact that the statute could well be justified on the grounds that very young females are particularly susceptible to physical injury from sexual intercourse, it is ludicrous to suggest that the Constitution requires the California Legislature to limit the scope of its rape statute to older teenagers and exclude young girls.

There remains only petitioner's contention that the statute is unconstitutional as it is applied to him because he, like Sharon, was under 18 at the time of sexual intercourse. Petitioner argues that the statute is flawed because it presumes that as between two persons under 18, the male is the culpable aggressor. We find petitioner's contentions unpersuasive. Contrary to his assertions, the statute does not rest on the assumption that males are generally the aggressors. It is instead an attempt by a legislature to prevent illegitimate teenage pregnancy by providing an additional deterrent for men. The age of the man is irrelevant since young men are as capable as older men of inflicting the harm sought to be prevented.

In upholding the California statute we also recognize that this is not a case where a statute is being challenged on the grounds that it "invidiously discriminates" against females. To the contrary, the statute places a burden on males which is not shared by females. But we find nothing to suggest that men, because of past discrimination or peculiar disadvantages, are in need of the special solicitude of the courts. Nor is this a case where the gender classification is made "solely for . . . administrative convenience," or rests on "the baggage of sexual stereotypes." As we have held, the statute instead reasonably reflects the fact that the consequences of sexual intercourse and pregnancy fall more heavily on the female than on the male.

Accordingly, the judgment of the California Supreme Court is

Affirmed.

Justice STEWART, concurring.

Section 261.5, on its face, classifies on the basis of sex. A male who engages in sexual intercourse with an underage female who is not his wife violates the statute; a female who engages in sexual intercourse with an underage male who is not her husband does not. The petitioner contends that this state law, which punishes only males for the conduct in question, violates his Fourteenth Amendment right to the equal protection of the law. The Court today correctly rejects that contention.

A

At the outset, it should be noted that the statutory discrimination, when viewed as part of the wider scheme of California law, is not as clearcut as might at first appear. Females are not freed from criminal liability in California for engaging in sexual activity that may be harmful. It is unlawful, for example, for any person, of either sex, to molest, annoy, or contribute to the delinquency of anyone under 18 years of age. All persons are prohibited from committing "any lewd or lascivious act," including consensual intercourse, with a child under 14. And members of both sexes may be convicted for engaging in deviant sexual acts with anyone under 18. Finally, females may be brought within the proscription of § 261.5 itself, since a female may be charged with aiding and abetting its violation.

Section 261.5 is thus but one part of a broad statutory scheme that protects all minors from the problems and risks attendant upon adolescent sexual activity. To be sure, § 261.5 creates an additional measure of punishment for males who engage in sexual intercourse with females between the ages of 14 and 17. The question then is whether the Constitution prohibits a state legislature from imposing this *additional* sanction on a gender-specific basis.

B

The Constitution is violated when government, state or federal, invidiously classifies similarly situated people on the basis of the immutable characteristics with which they were born. Thus, detrimental racial classifications by government always violate the Constitution, for the simple reason that, so far as the Constitution is concerned, people of different races are always similarly situated. By contrast, while detrimental gender classifications by government often violate the Constitution, they do not always do so, for the reason that there are differences between males and females that the Constitution necessarily recognizes. In this case we deal with the most basic of these differences: females can become pregnant as the result of sexual intercourse; males cannot.

As was recognized in *Parham v. Hughes,* "a State is not free to make overbroad generalizations based on sex which are entirely unrelated to any differences between men and women or which demean the ability or social status of the affected class." Gender-based classifications may not be based upon administrative convenience, or upon archaic assumptions about the proper roles of the sexes. But we have recognized that in certain narrow circumstances men and women are *not* similarly situated; in these circumstances a gender classification based on clear differences between the sexes is not invidious, and a legislative classification realistically based upon those differences is not unconstitutional. "[G]ender-based classifications are not invariably invalid. When men and women are not in fact similarly situated in the area covered by the legislation in question, the Equal Protection Clause is not violated."

Applying these principles to the classification enacted by the California Legislature, it is readily apparent that § 261.5 does not violate the Equal Protection Clause. Young women and men are not similarly situated with respect to the problems and risk associated with intercourse and pregnancy, and the statute is realistically related to the legitimate state purpose of reducing those problems and risks.

C

As the California Supreme Court's catalog shows, the pregnant unmarried female confronts problems more numerous and more severe than any faced by her male partner. She alone endures the medical risks of pregnancy or abortion. She suffers disproportionately the social, educational, and emotional consequences of pregnancy. Recognizing this disproportion, California has attempted to protect teenage females by prohibiting males from participating in the act necessary for conception.

The fact that males and females are not similarly situated with respect to the risks of sexual intercourse applies with the same force to males under 18 as it does to older males. The risk of pregnancy is a significant deterrent for unwed young females that is not shared by unmarried males, regardless of their age. Experienced observation confirms the commonsense notion that adolescent males disre-

gard the possibility of pregnancy far more than do adolescent females. And to the extent that § 261.5 may punish males for intercourse with prepubescent females, that punishment is justifiable because of the substantial physical risks for prepubescent females that are not shared by their male counterparts.

D

The petitioner argues that the California Legislature could have drafted the statute differently, so that its purpose would be accomplished more precisely. "But the issue, of course, is not whether the statute could have been drafted more wisely, but whether the lines chosen by the . . . [l]egislature are within constitutional limitations." That other States may have decided to attack the same problems more broadly, with gender-neutral statutes, does not mean that every State is constitutionally compelled to do so.

E

In short, the Equal Protection Clause does not mean that the physiological differences between men and women must be disregarded. While those differences must never be permitted to become a pretext for invidious discrimination, no such discrimination is presented by this case. The Constitution surely does not require a State to pretend that demonstrable differences between men and women do not really exist.

Justice BLACKMUN, concurring in the judgment.

It is gratifying that the plurality recognizes that "[a]t the risk of stating the obvious, teenage pregnancies . . . have increased dramatically over the last two decades" and "have significant social, medical, and economic consequences for both the mother and her child, and the State." There have been times when I have wondered whether the Court was capable of this perception, particularly when it has struggled with the different but not unrelated problems that attend abortion issues.

Some might conclude that the two uses of the criminal sanction—here flatly to forbid intercourse in order to forestall teenage pregnancies, and in *Matheson* to prohibit a physician's abortion procedure except upon notice to the parents of the pregnant minor—are vastly different proscriptions. But the basic social and privacy problems are much the same. Both Utah's statute in *Matheson* and California's statute in this case are legislatively created tools intended to achieve similar ends and addressed to the same societal concerns: the control and direction of young people's sexual activities. The plurality opinion impliedly concedes as much when it notes that "approximately half of all teenage pregnancies end in abortion," and that "those children who are born" are "likely candidates to become wards of the State."

I, however, cannot vote to strike down the California statutory rape law, for I think it is a sufficiently reasoned and constitutional effort to control the problem at its inception. For me, there is an important difference between this state action and a State's adamant and rigid refusal to face, or even to recognize, the "significant . . . consequences"—to the woman—of a forced or unwanted conception. I have found it difficult to rule constitutional, for example, state efforts to block, at that later point, a woman's attempt to deal with the enormity of the problem confronting her, just as I have rejected state efforts to prevent women from rationally taking steps to prevent that problem from arising. In contrast, I am persuaded that, although a minor has substantial privacy rights in intimate affairs connected with procreation, California's efforts to prevent teenage pregnancy are to be viewed differently from Utah's efforts to inhibit a woman from dealing with pregnancy once it has become an inevitability.

Craig v. Boren was an opinion which, in large part, I joined. The plurality opinion in the present case points out the Court's respective phrasings of the applicable test in *Reed v. Reed*. I vote to affirm the judgment of the Supreme Court of California and to uphold the State's gender-based classification on that test and as exemplified by those two cases and by *Schlesinger v. Ballard*.

I note, also, that § 261.5 of the California Penal Code is just one of several California statutes intended to protect the juvenile. Justice STEWART, in his concurring opinion, appropriately observes that § 261.5 is "but one part of a broad statutory scheme that protects all minors from the problems and risks attendant upon adolescent sexual activity."

I think, too, that it is only fair, with respect to this particular petitioner, to point out that his partner, Sharon, appears not to have been an unwilling participant in at least the initial stages of the intimacies that took place the night of June 3, 1978. Petitioner's and Sharon's nonacquaintance with each other before the incident; their drinking; their withdrawal from the others of the group; their foreplay, in which she willingly participated and seems to

have encouraged; and the closeness of their ages (a difference of only one year and 18 days) are factors that should make this case an unattractive one to prosecute at all, and especially to prosecute as a felony, rather than as a misdemeanor chargeable under § 261.5. But the State has chosen to prosecute in that manner, and the facts, I reluctantly conclude, may fit the crime.

Justice BRENNAN, with whom Justices WHITE and MARSHALL join, dissenting.

I

It is disturbing to find the Court so splintered on a case that presents such a straightforward issue: Whether the admittedly gender-based classification in Cal. Penal Code Ann. § 261.5 bears a sufficient relationship to the State's asserted goal of preventing teenage pregnancies to survive the "mid-level" constitutional scrutiny mandated by *Craig v. Boren*. Applying the analytical framework provided by our precedents, I am convinced that there is only one proper resolution of this issue: the classification must be declared unconstitutional. I fear that the plurality opinion and Justices STEWART and BLACKMUN reach the opposite result by placing too much emphasis on the desirability of achieving the State's asserted statutory goal—prevention of teenage pregnancy—and not enough emphasis on the fundamental question of whether the sex-based discrimination in the California statute is *substantially* related to the achievement of that goal.

II

After some uncertainty as to the proper framework for analyzing equal protection challenges to statutes containing gender-based classifications, this Court settled upon the proposition that a statute containing a gender-based classification cannot withstand constitutional challenge unless the classification is substantially related to the achievement of an important governmental objective.

The State of California vigorously asserts that the "important governmental objective" to be served by § 261.5 is the prevention of teenage pregnancy. It claims that its statute furthers this goal by deterring sexual activity by males—the class of persons it considers more responsible for causing those pregnancies. But even assuming that prevention of teenage pregnancy is an important governmental objective and that it is in fact an objective of § 261.5, California still has the burden of proving that there are fewer teenage pregnancies under its gender-based statutory rape law than there would be if the law were gender neutral. To meet this burden, the State must show that because its statutory rape law punishes only males, and not females, it more effectively deters minor females from having sexual intercourse. The plurality assumes that a gender-neutral statute would be less effective than § 261.5 in deterring sexual activity because a gender-neutral statute would create significant enforcement problems. The plurality thus accepts the State's assertion that

> a female is surely less likely to report violations of the statute if she herself would be subject to criminal prosecution. In an area already fraught with prosecutorial difficulties, we decline to hold that the Equal Protection Clause requires a legislature to enact a statute so broad that it may well be incapable of enforcement.

However, a State's bare assertion that its gender-based statutory classification substantially furthers an important governmental interest is not enough to meet its burden of proof under *Craig v. Boren.* Rather, the State must produce evidence that will persuade the court that its assertion is true.

The State has not produced such evidence in this case. Moreover, there are at least two serious flaws in the State's assertion that law enforcement problems created by a gender-neutral statutory rape law would make such a statute less effective than a gender-based statute in deterring sexual activity.

First, the experience of other jurisdictions, and California itself, belies the plurality's conclusion that a gender-neutral statutory rape law "may well be incapable of enforcement." There are now at least 37 States that have enacted gender-neutral statutory rape laws. Although most of these laws protect young persons (of either sex) from the sexual exploitation of older individuals, the laws of Arizona, Florida, and Illinois permit prosecution of both minor females and minor males for engaging in mutual sexual conduct. California has introduced no evidence that those States have been handicapped by the enforcement problems the plurality finds so persuasive. Surely, if those States could provide such evidence, we might expect that California would have introduced it.

In addition, the California Legislature in recent years has revised other sections of the Penal Code to make them gender-neutral. For example, Cal. Penal Code Ann. §§ 286(b)(1) and 288a(b)(1), prohibiting sodomy and oral copulation with a "person who is under 18 years of age," could cause two minor homosexuals to be subjected to criminal sanctions for engaging in mutually consensual conduct. Again, the State has introduced no evidence to explain why a gender-neutral statutory rape law would be any more difficult to enforce than those statutes.

The second flaw in the State's assertion is that even assuming that a gender-neutral statute would be more difficult to enforce, the State has still not shown that those enforcement problems would make such a statute less effective than a gender-based statute in deterring minor females from engaging in sexual intercourse. Common sense, however, suggests that a gender-neutral statutory rape law is potentially a *greater* deterrent of sexual activity than a gender-based law, for the simple reason that a gender-neutral law subjects both men and women to criminal sanctions and thus arguably has a deterrent effect on twice as many potential violators. Even if fewer persons were prosecuted under the gender-neutral law, as the State suggests, it would still be true that twice as many persons would be *subject* to arrest. The State's failure to prove that a gender-neutral law would be a less effective deterrent than a gender-based law, like the State's failure to prove that a gender-neutral law would be difficult to enforce, should have led this Court to invalidate § 261.5.

III

Until very recently, no California court or commentator had suggested that the purpose of California's statutory rape law was to protect young women from the risk of pregnancy. Indeed, the historical development of § 261.5 demonstrates that the law was initially enacted on the premise that young women, in contrast to young men, were to be deemed legally incapable of consenting to an act of sexual intercourse. Because their chastity was considered particularly precious, those young women were felt to be uniquely in need of the State's protection. In contrast, young men were assumed to be capable of making such decisions for themselves; the law therefore did not offer them any special protection.

It is perhaps because the gender classification in California's statutory rape law was initially designed to further these outmoded sexual stereotypes, rather than to reduce the incidence of teenage pregnancies, that the State has been unable to demonstrate a substantial relationship between the classification and its newly asserted goal. But whatever the reason, the State has not shown that Cal. Penal Code § 261.5 is any more effective than a gender-neutral law would be in deterring minor females from engaging in sexual intercourse. It has therefore not met its burden of proving that the statutory classification is substantially related to the achievement of its asserted goal.

I would hold that § 261.5 violates the Equal Protection Clause of the Fourteenth Amendment, and I would reverse the judgment of the California Supreme Court.

Justice STEVENS, dissenting.

Local custom and belief—rather than statutory laws of venerable but doubtful ancestry—will determine the volume of sexual activity among unmarried teenagers. The empirical evidence cited by the plurality demonstrates the futility of the notion that a statutory prohibition will significantly affect the volume of that activity or provide a meaningful solution to the problems created by it. Nevertheless, as a matter of constitutional power, unlike my Brother BRENNAN I would have no doubt about the validity of a state law prohibiting all unmarried teenagers from engaging in sexual intercourse. The societal interests in reducing the incidence of venereal disease and teenage pregnancy are sufficient, in my judgment, to justify a prohibition of conduct that increases the risk of those harms.

My conclusion that a nondiscriminatory prohibition would be constitutional does not help me answer the question whether a prohibition applicable to only half of the joint participants in the risk-creating conduct is also valid. It cannot be true that the validity of a total ban is an adequate justification for a selective prohibition; otherwise, the constitutional objection to discriminatory rules would be meaningless. The question in this case is whether the difference between males and females justifies this statutory discrimination based entirely on sex.

The fact that the Court did not immediately acknowledge that the capacity to become pregnant is what primarily differentiates the female from the male does not impeach the validity of the plurality's newly found wisdom. I think the plurality is quite correct in making the assumption that the joint act that this law seeks to prohibit creates a greater risk of harm for the female than for the male. But the plurality surely cannot believe that the risk of pregnancy confronted by the female—any more than the risk of venereal disease confronted by males as well as females—has provided an effective deterrent to voluntary female participation in the risk-creating conduct. Yet the plurality's decision seems to rest on the assumption that the California Legislature acted on the basis of that rather fanciful notion.

In my judgment, the fact that a class of persons is especially vulnerable to a risk that a statute is designed to avoid is a reason for making the statute applicable to that class. The argument that a special need for protection provides a rational explanation for an exemption is one I simply do not comprehend.

In this case, the fact that a female confronts a greater risk of harm than a male is a reason for applying the prohibition to her—not a reason for granting her a license to use her own judgment on whether or not to assume the risk. Surely, if we examine the problem from the point of view of society's interest in preventing the risk-creating conduct from occurring at all, it is irrational to exempt 50% of the potential violators. See dissent of Justice BRENNAN. And, if we view the government's interest as that of a *parens patriae* seeking to protect its subjects from harming themselves, the discrimination is actually perverse. Would a rational parent making rules for the conduct of twin children of opposite sex simultaneously forbid the son and authorize the daughter to engage in conduct that is especially harmful to the daughter? That is the effect of this statutory classification.

If pregnancy or some other special harm is suffered by one of the two participants in the prohibited act, that special harm no doubt would constitute a legitimate mitigating factor in deciding what, if any, punishment might be appropriate in a given case. But from the standpoint of fashioning a general preventive rule—or, indeed, in determining appropriate punishment when neither party in fact has suffered any special harm—I regard a total exemption for the members of the more endangered class as utterly irrational.

In my opinion, the only acceptable justification for a general rule requiring disparate treatment of the two participants in a joint act must be a legislative judgment that one is more guilty than the other. The risk-creating conduct that this statute is designed to prevent requires the participation of two persons—one male and one female. In many situations it is probably true that one is the aggressor and the other is either an unwilling, or at least a less willing, participant in the joint act. If a statute authorized punishment of only one participant and required the prosecutor to prove that that participant had been the aggressor, I assume that the discrimination would be valid. Although the question is less clear, I also assume, for the purpose of deciding this case, that it would be permissible to punish only the male participant, if one element of the offense were proof that he had been the aggressor, or at least in some respects the more responsible participant in the joint act. The statute at issue in this case, however, requires no such proof. The question raised by this statute is whether the State, consistently with the Federal Constitution, may always punish the male and never the female when they are equally responsible or when the female is the more responsible of the two.

It would seem to me that an impartial lawmaker could give only one answer to that question. The fact that the California Legislature has decided to apply its prohibition only to the male may reflect a legislative judgment that in the typical case the male is actually the more guilty party. Any such judgment must, in turn, assume that the decision to engage in the risk-creating conduct is always—or at least typically—a male decision. If that assumption is valid, the statutory classification should also be valid. But what is the support for the assumption? It is not contained in the record of this case or in any legislative history or scholarly study that has been called to our attention. I think it is supported to some extent by traditional attitudes toward male-female relationships. But the possibility that such a habitual attitude may reflect nothing more than an irrational prejudice makes it an insufficient justification for discriminatory treatment that is otherwise blatantly unfair. For, as I read this statute, it requires that one, and only one, of two equally guilty wrongdoers be stigmatized by a criminal conviction.

I cannot accept the State's argument that the constitutionality of the discriminatory rule can be saved by an assumption that prosecutors will commonly invoke this statute only in cases that actually involve a forcible rape, but one that cannot be established by proof beyond a reasonable doubt. That assumption implies that a State has a legitimate interest in convicting a defendant on evidence that is constitutionally insufficient. Of course, the State may create a lesser-included offense that would authorize punishment of the more guilty party, but surely the interest in obtaining convictions on inadequate proof cannot justify a statute that punishes one who is equally or less guilty than his partner.

Nor do I find at all persuasive the suggestion that this discrimination is adequately justified by the desire to encourage females to inform against their male partners. Even if the concept of a wholesale informant's exemption were an acceptable enforcement device, what is the justification for defining the exempt class entirely by reference to sex rather than by reference to a more neutral criterion such as relative innocence? Indeed, if the exempt class is to be composed entirely of members of one sex, what is there to support the view that the statutory purpose will be better served by granting the informing license to females rather than to males? If a discarded male partner informs on a promiscuous female, a timely threat of prosecution might well prevent the precise harm the statute is intended to minimize.

Finally, even if my logic is faulty and there actually is some speculative basis for treating equally guilty males and females differently, I still believe that any such speculative justification would be outweighed by the paramount interest in even-handed enforcement of the law. A rule that authorizes punishment of only one of two equally guilty wrongdoers violates the essence of the constitutional requirement that the sovereign must govern impartially.

I respectfully dissent.

Sexuality, Authenticity, and Modernity*

Leslie Green

1. Borrowed Truths

In his *Journals* for 26 December 1921, André Gide wrote:

> The borrowed truths are the ones to which one clings most tenaciously, and all the more so since they remain foreign to our intimate self. It takes much more precaution to deliver one's own message, much more boldness and prudence, than to sign up with and add one's voice to an already existing party. . . . I believed that it is above all to oneself that it is important to remain faithful.[1]

This celebration of fidelity to oneself gives voice to a central theme of modern consciousness: the search for authenticity. The idea that there is an 'intimate self' whose needs cannot be fulfilled by following 'borrowed truths' is a familiar modern notion and one that contrasts sharply with traditional outlooks. In many pre-modern societies value was believed to be less responsive to the individual: gods, natures, or history were the sort of things that inscribed value on states of affairs, and thus on our lives. Living well was not, therefore, a matter of being true to ourselves, but being true to our creators, natures, or traditions. Moral truths were precisely those things that were borrowed; that was what *made* them true.

That traditional world-view is not very popular now. Epistemological, moral, and political criticisms have done much to undermine it. Modern thinkers[2] ask how we can claim to know such truths. Our knowledge of the requirements of the gods, or of human nature, or even of tradition doesn't seem very secure; if that is what gives value to our lives then we seem to be doomed never to know what makes life worth living. The moral criticism is different. It asks how such external requirements could make our lives better. Lives have to be led from the 'inside', so the relevant sorts of reasons are those which are connected, at least indirectly, with the beliefs and desires we actually hold. And related to this is a political line of criticism. The reputed content of borrowed truths has been dominated by the powerful, and has excluded the marginal. Perhaps religions and what are sometimes called 'traditional'[3] family values made some people's lives more meaningful; but they also ruined many others, and in fairly predictable ways. The publicly available and authoritatively endorsed standards of meaning in our culture have not served everyone well. Indigenous peoples in North America have not been helped by the public conceptions of property that the majority share. Women have not been helped by the popular notions of justice. Sexual minorities have not been helped by the public notions of the family. It is in and around these margins of the polity that people have been readiest to grasp the promise of modernity—that a valuable and authentic life can somehow be constructed from within—not because they are narcissistic, but because public meanings have already failed them.

Modern thinkers tend therefore to be critical of borrowed truths, and insist that each individual (and, in some versions, each group) should pursue a path that is authentically his or her own. This is a mixed blessing. It is exhilarating to be freed from external constraints; but it is also dizzying. In Hannah Arendt's image, we find ourselves thinking 'without bannisters'. This tests our sense of balance, but it doesn't always make the ascent easier. So it is not surprising that in these *fin de siècle* days we find a recrudescence of the hopes and fears that came at the end of the last century.[4] In moral and political theory this is increasingly expressed in a renewed hankering after bannisters. Just when it seemed that gods had died, communities had been atomized, and traditions exhausted, new signs of life are being de-

*From *Canadian Journal of Law and Jurisprudence* Vol. VIII, No. 1 (January 1995).

tected. Whether they can contribute much to our understanding of the modern predicament depends on whether the epistemological, moral and political criticisms can be met.

In this paper, I want to consider the way some of these problems arise around the issue of sexuality. The so-called sexual revolution is a creature of modernity, as is the distinctive notion that there is an inner truth about sexuality.[5] The example is important, not merely because it considers an issue that is too rarely discussed by mainstream philosophy, but because around sexuality the notions of authenticity, being true to oneself, defining one's life with or against traditional meanings, are all right at the surface.

Should we press on with the project of modernity, or go back to pre-modern traditions of argument? But going back would be to abandon the modern ideal of authenticity, of leading one's own life, and that may simply be too late for us. What we need instead, Charles Taylor argues in his Massey Lectures[6], is to retrieve the ideal, to rescue it from its corrupt and corrupting forms. We need to see if we can respect the ideal while rejecting crude forms of relativism, subjectivism, and egoism—hallmarks of what Christopher Lasch called a narcissistic culture. While much of modern thought would endorse Gide's view that we should first strive to be true to ourselves rather than conform to some external standards, Taylor argues that true authenticity depends on leading a life of significance, and that standards of significance must always be external to the agent and grounded in 'horizons' of meaning. And this has profound consequences for the terms on which sexual minorities may demand respect and recognition.

2. The Significance of Difference

The first step, on Taylor's view, is to see how authenticity is bound up with a certain notion of 'significance', of doing and being something that counts. And significance is a public matter; there are no private meanings. So Taylor rejects certain subjectivist, relativist-inclined, theories: 'as though people could determine what is significant, either by decision, or perhaps unwittingly and unwillingly by just feeling that way' (36). This, he thinks, is a delusion. 'Your feeling a certain way can never be sufficient grounds for respecting your position, because your feeling can't *determine* what is significant' (37).

Significance has to do with meaning, and meaning, for lots of well-rehearsed reasons, is a public and not a private matter.

Some philosophers have expressed scepticism about the whole idea that there is anything that *determines* significance; they think meanings are underdetermined by things. Perhaps that is not relevant, for the sense of 'significance' in play is not a purely semantic one, but is related to the idea of 'meaning' as worth that we invoke in phrases like 'the meaning of life'. In any case, we do not need to pursue that here. It will be enough to explore the ways in which Taylor thinks the case for a significant and authentic life may, and may not, be made out.

Taylor objects to a certain, he thinks self-defeating, line of argument about sexual orientation:

> there is a certain discourse of justification of non-standard sexual orientations. People want to argue that heterosexual monogamy is not the only way to achieve sexual fulfilment, that those who are inclined to homosexual relations, for instance, shouldn't feel themselves embarked on a lesser, less worthy path. (37)

But, continues Taylor, at least 'in some forms this discourse slides towards an affirmation of choice itself. All options are equally worthy, because they are freely chosen, and it is choice that confers worth' (37). But this form of subjectivism or 'soft relativism' as he also calls it, ends up being self-defeating.

> But then the choice of sexual orientation loses any special significance. It is on a level with any other preferences, like that for taller or shorter sexual partners, or blonds or brunettes. No one would dream of making discriminating judgements about these preferences, but that's because they are all without importance. They really do just depend on how you feel. Once sexual orientation comes to be assimilated to these, which is what happens when one makes *choice* the crucial justifying reason, the original goal, which was to assert the *equal value* of this orientation, is subtly frustrated. Difference so asserted becomes *insignificant*. (38)

And that's what happens to those moderns whose world view 'implicitly denies the existence of a pre-existing horizon of significance . . .' (38). This denial sets in motion the degeneration of the ideal of authenticity. The notion of being true to oneself becomes shallow, trivial, meaningless. And if difference becomes in this way insignificant, it can hardly demand the kind of respect that minorities claim on its behalf. A politics of identity, as it is sometimes called, would be empty. To seek justice for those identified by such difference would be to celebrate nothing more substantial than minority tastes; it would be to grant 'special rights' as the proponents of anti-gay referenda in Oregon, Colorado, and Idaho warned. To seek recognition of such difference would surely be wrong-headed.[7] But then sexual minorities find themselves in a polemically difficult position. A modern, choice-based view of authenticity fails, and the 'pre-existing horizons of significance' have provided inadequate space for them. Looking inward is self-defeating, but looking outward is oppressive. They have nowhere to turn.

That is why Taylor's is an important argument. His attempt to refute a choice-based conception of authenticity, and his demand that people articulate identities against pre-existing horizons of significance on the pain of incoherence is alarming for the way it represents one familiar defense of the way gay people lead their lives, for the way it seeks to undermine it, and for the alternative it offers. If a modern understanding of authenticity in our sexual lives is not merely unattractive or dizzying, but *self-defeating,* then it just cannot be maintained. No sense of the heroic or tragic is going to sustain us in that. But Taylor's argument is not valid, and its misprision of the issues around sexuality raises more general doubts about his program for retrieval.

3. Sexual Orientations and Life Choices

Arguing about 'authenticity', 'modernity' and 'recognition' as abstract, unsituated terms is rarely fruitful, so let us begin by considering closely Taylor's discussion of a more concrete problem, what he calls the 'justification of non-standard sexual orientations.' This is a difficult notion. I am not just pointing to the import of the presumptions that there is such a thing as a 'standard' orientation (guess which one), or that 'non-standard' orientations need to be justified. Those are unfriendly thoughts. My deeper worry, however, rests with the whole idea of justifying sexual orientations *at all,* and with the relationship between that idea and questions about how to achieve sexual fulfilment or to lead a worthwhile life.

Are sexual orientations *candidates* for 'justification'? If I were asked to justify my sexual orientation, my reaction would be not merely indignation at the presumption of someone who felt entitled to ask such things of me. It would be bafflement. Could I justify my blood-group? My family environment? My place of birth? What sort of considerations would I be expected to adduce? I might express contentment or anxiety about any of those things, and I might give reasons for those attitudes. So it is with sexual orientation. I might discuss the social consequences of having one orientation or another, or speculate on whether or not it pleases the gods. I might decide how to go about living given my orientation. But none of this amounts to anything that can be called a *justification* of my orientation.

People can offer justifications only in certain circumstances: when the state of affairs in question is a product of, or at least responsive to, human action and decision. That is no doubt why Taylor also talks about justifying one's 'choice of sexual orientation' (38). Now this makes more sense, provided that orientations are the kinds of things that are chosen. The etiology of sexual orientation is a matter of great dispute. But there is no evidence to show that orientations are chosen.[8] Nature is not chosen; nurture is not chosen; and although freely chosen actions can sometimes reinforce or repress one's orientation, none of that amounts to anything one could properly call 'choosing a sexual orientation'. Those who talk about 'choice' in the context of sexuality do not deny this at all; they merely focus on those aspects of our sexuality that are partly within the realm of individual control, for example, one's behaviour, social role, and, to a lesser extent, sense of identity. Sexual orientation is anterior to and deeper than all of that. Celibate gay priests are still gay; straight-acting gay men are still gay; and straight-identified men whose predominant erotic interest is in men are still gay. Sexual orientation is a matter of things like one's sexual arousal cues and fantasies, one's primary sources of sexual pleasure and, above all, one's capacity for erotic love. These form the unchosen background to one's erotic life. They are objects neither of choice nor of justification.

What is chosen, let us therefore say, is one's life-path. That is, after all, strongly suggested when Taylor puts the question whether 'heterosexual monogamy' is the 'only way to achieve sexual fulfilment' and (perhaps consequently) whether 'those who are inclined to homosexual relations . . . shouldn't feel themselves embarked on a lesser, less worthy path.' Now, there is no plausible case to be made that heterosexual monogamy is the only way to sexual fulfilment (though there has been endless literary and scientific speculation about whether it is *compatible* with sexual fulfilment for anyone). On a charitable reading, then, the issue must be this: what is it, for a person of a given sexual orientation, that makes his or her choices of behaviour, social role, and personal identity worthy ones? And what makes them authentically his or her own?

Admittedly, Taylor's contrast between 'heterosexual monogamy' and 'homosexual relations' is obscure. It is not clear whether the latter term is a embarrassed euphemism for 'gay sex' or rather a general notion embracing different lifestyles within which a homosexual orientation may find its expression: for instance, homosexual monogamy, homosexual non-monogamy, or heterosexual nonmonogamy—as opposed to heterosexual monogamy or celibacy. (It is hard to avoid the impression that the sloppiness of formulation has a rhetorical function, namely, to associate heterosexuality with monogamy and homosexuality with promiscuity.) So just what is the path that some judge less worthy? In homophobic societies like our own, it is surely *any* of the lives in which gay people act on or even acknowledge their inclinations. Thus, the question is what choices should people of a given orientation make about their lives, and what conditions are necessary in order for those choices to merit respect, at least to the extent that in our public life we would recognize them as no less worthy than others, and that in our private lives we would acknowledge them as being authentic.

When comparing such fundamental and wide-ranging life-choices, how would we know whether one path is less worthy than another? That is a hard question. But Taylor has made the interlocutor's case unfairly difficult. For the interlocutor is trying to argue only that, for example, gay people's giving expression to their desires is *not* a less worthy path than something called 'heterosexual monogamy'. Polemically, that is an important denial, one that is popularly debated. For gay people are often told that their life-paths *are* less worthy than those of others, because, for example, they are unnatural, immoral, or imprudent, dooming them to promiscuity, narcissism, unhappiness, etc. And one's life-path is something that one can reasonably be called on to justify, at least to the extent that it is within one's control. People are called on to justify their paths in a variety of circumstances: when we think they are harmful to others, when we think they betray the potential of the agent leading them, when we think they outrage community values, and so on.

In response, perhaps, to such requests, Taylor imagines his interlocutor trying to defend himself. His path is not less worthy, he says, because it is freely chosen and is thus authentically his own. Now, Taylor sees this, in at least some of its versions, as 'sliding towards' the claim that 'All options are equally worthy, because they are freely chosen, and it is choice that confers worth' (37). We are not given much more of the details of the argument; Taylor's encounter with it is a hit-and-run affair—we have to infer the nature of the collision from the apparent remains. Whatever is said is supposed both to deny any 'pre-existing horizon of significance' and to emphasize the role of choice. So exactly what argument is being imputed here? How does the reference to choice end up being self-defeating?

Consider an analogy. Women sometimes defend the right to choose an abortion on the ground that a free choice, here, is extremely important. But no one—certainly not pro-choice women—takes that argument to mean that whatever is chosen is right. That defense would not assist them, for to appeal to a general propriety of doing whatever one likes will embrace also the contradictory likings of those who oppose abortion. Their argument, however, is clearly intended to exclude those people's choices, and to secure for women a measure of self-determination *even against* the contrary choices of others. Choice therefore figures in a more complex way. It is, in fact, a compressed but comprehensible reference to the ideal of self-determination.

For analogous reasons, that is how we must construe the argument about sexual authenticity. Note that my claim is not simply that Taylor has been unsympathetic to a choice-based view; rather I say that he has not identified the issue correctly. The modern view is that free choice is important because it allows people to be self-determining, to attend to the needs of what Gide called the 'intimate self'. Choice is celebrated by gay people because it permits them to be true to themselves rather than attempt to conform to borrowed truths. This neither presupposes, entails, nor even 'slides towards' the scarcely intelligible idea that all choices are equally worthy. Indeed, it endorses only authenticity-respecting choices as worthy. It condemns, not lack of sexual fulfilment, but dishonesty, self-deception, and the cowardice of clinging to borrowed truths.

It is true that, on this view, sexual orientation is itself simply a matter of having certain feelings and authenticity a matter of living in harmony with those feelings.[9] That too provokes an objection from Taylor: 'as though people could determine what is significant, either by decision, or perhaps unwittingly and unwillingly by just feeling that way' (36). But there is a world of difference between 'decision' and 'feeling'. Decisions are made for reasons, and one possible reason for making a decision is that it accords with one's feelings. So the correct reading of the choice-based view of sexual authenticity is this: 'My path is my own. I have chosen it freely, and I am content with it because and to the extent that it accords with my own inclinations. By choosing this path, I am being true to myself.' That argument, compressed and incomplete though it is, is at least intelligible. Choice is celebrated, not for its own sake, but for its capacity to attend to the needs of the intimate self. Respect for people's choices thus expresses respect for the lives they have made.

Something like this must be the right way to understand the issue, because Taylor wants to argue that a choice-based defense of sexual authenticity is *self-defeating*. Now, 'self-defeating' does not mean 'unintelligible'; it means that the argument undermines its own point. And that is the case he brings: he says that respect for sexual minorities can't be grounded in choice because to do so would fail in its aim, namely, to show that there is some special significance to these choices. Why exactly is this self-defeating? Because now 'the choice of sexual orientation loses any special significance'; it's no different than a preference for blonds over brunettes. And with respect to these, 'No one would dream of making discriminating judgements . . . but that's because they are all without importance. They really do just depend on how you feel' (38). So, by playing up the valorizing power of free choice, sexual orientation gets assimilated to the insignificant and 'the original goal, which was to assert the *equal value* of this orientation, is subtly frustrated.'

This argument is very subtle indeed. For somehow it manages not merely to establish the thesis, but also to change it in the process. The interlocutor started out defending himself against heterosexists, trying to show that his path in life is authentically his own and in that way is *not less worthy* than theirs; but he is now charged with having failed to prove it *of equal value*. This may just be laxity in exposition, but it is significant laxity. There is good reason to think that neither this argument nor any other is going to establish that gay and straight life-paths are of equal value.

Let me explain. To show that two items are of equal value, one must be able to compare them on a common scale. That is often hard to do, particularly with respect to complex things such as life-paths. Life-paths are combinations of elements that define personal and social relations in quite different ways. Consider, for example, gay and straight notions of kinship.[10] Many straight people acknowledge a sharp distinction between family and friends. The core of the straight family is biological, and to it is joined those legally bound by marriage. Friends, however committed and lasting, are thus not family. Gay people (at least in urban North America) do not live this distinction. Biological families often reject their gay children, so mere genetic commonality is not sufficient for kinship. Gay people are refused legally recognized relationships, so those are not necessary. Instead, gay people have what are sometimes called 'families of choice': committed networks of people bound by shared experiences and acknowledging important mutual obligations of support. Now, in seeking to compare and evaluate *just this one aspect* of two life-paths—the sort of family structures one has—one engages an impossible task. How can one say whether life in a gay family or life in a straight family is better? How could one prove them of equal value? Just this one incommensurability suggests that our interlocutor won't be able to show that overall gay and straight life-paths are of equal value. How much less likely still is it that there could be any intelligent overall comparison of gay and straight *lives,* differing not only in kinship structures, but also in attitudes to sexuality, in the sense of personal identity, and, of course, in social and civil status?

Fortunately, one does not need to show that in order to establish that gays are not embarked on a less worthy path. For A is no less worthy than B if *either* A is better than B, A is of equal value to B, or if *A is valuable though incommensurably different from B*. So now we need to know only whether having chosen a life-path can ever valorize it, irrespective of any comparison between it and someone else's life-path. Modern believers in authenticity think that it can, precisely when it matches the needs of the intimate self: so the relevant comparison is not between gay and straight lives, but, for instance, between the kinds of lives open to a particular person—and even here incommensurabilities will be rife. Respect for difference requires, not some net, overall comparison of lives, but just the confidence that each type of life-path is in itself valuable.

4. Options, Issues, and Feelings

So it comes down to this: is choosing to live in harmony with one's deepest inclinations about love something that can valorize that choice and make it a worthy life-path? Perhaps one might reply that if a decision to follow one path rather than another just comes down to inclination, then the matter in question is unimportant. A Kantian, for example, would deny that the shifting, empirical, province of inclination could ever become the kingdom of unshakeable, categorical, moral value. But here, we are primarily concerned with authenticity and non-moral worth, and Taylor's argument is in any case independent of such Kantian premises. His point is simply that, on a choice-emphasizing view, sexual orientation comes off the high-tension wires of significance and is put back down on the ground along with other preferences in sexual partners such as height or hair-colour, etc. Sexuality becomes a matter of trivial difference, and certainly not the locus of urgent, respect-worthy claims. Sexuality in itself is just meaningless.

If that follows, why does it matter?[11] After all, the *interlocutor* does not want sexuality up on the high-tension wire of cosmic significance. He will be content if his object-choice is regarded as no worse than other people's object-choices: they prefer blondes; he prefers blonds.[12] Something has thus gone wrong with this attempt at *reduction*. Remember where we begin: with gay people being challenged to defend their lives, a challenge that notoriously comes in the context of widespread hatred and discrimination. When they say that their life-paths are no less worthy because they authentically accord with their inclinations, Taylor replies that that merely puts it on a par with choice of hair-colour. *But that is an advance.* Gender of object-choice is *not* now treated on a par with hair-colour; it is treated much worse. No one asks those who prefer blondes to justify their life-paths; no one fires them for loving blondes; no jurisdiction refuses to recognize their relationships with blondes, etc. And if social and institutionalized blondphobia did emerge, why would it be a self-defeating argument to point out that those who prefer blonds are merely choosing in accord with their inclinations?

On Taylor's argument it would be self-defeating because it would not attribute the right sort of significance to the choice. Mere inclination undercuts the possibility of the 'discriminating judgements' that we want to make about sexual orientations—

such judgements have no place when we are discussing something that really does have no importance beyond 'how you feel'. There is truth in this. Some choices do seem relatively trivial to us: what to have for lunch, which shoe to put on first, etc. Others seem important: how to vote, how to find love, what work to do. Our moral sentiments are most often engaged over the second kind. Because they are both equally choices, there must be something beyond choice itself that accounts for the significance of the second set. As I argued above, however, all this is conceded by the interlocutor: choice commands respect, because it allows for authentic lives, it gives people the power to be themselves.

Moreover, it is important to take a critical attitude towards the whole idea of making 'discriminating judgements'. Modernity has undercut some of these judgements as illusory and baseless. The modern believes that the world is not as chockfull of significance as his opponent thinks. Can it be denied that this is sometimes an advance? People used to ask, 'Does the size and power of the eagle mean that it is the king of birds?' No one asks that now. But some people do still ask, 'Does the rise of AIDS mean that the gods will punish those who break their rules?' Moderns just think those questions are silly (though perhaps dangerous): eagles and viruses don't mean *anything*. Likewise, they do not ask, 'What is the meaning of the gender of one's object-choice?' These things don't have any significance at all, and much illusion and misery rests on the false supposition that they do. As Gayle Rubin has wisely remarked, in our society 'sexual acts are burdened with an excess of significance.'[13]

But perhaps a different, more political, point is also at stake here. For the debate around sexuality has not just been about personal worth and public recognition, but also—even in the most liberal of countries—about liberty, equality, and justice. While some forward-thinking intellectuals are already limning the post-modern, post-liberal society, gay people throughout much of the "liberal" world still suffer feudal conditions. Liberalism has not yet arrived for people who stand to be imprisoned for offending ancient taboos, who are denied the power to marry, and who are untouchables in a caste system of heterosexual privilege. If sexuality really is meaningless, if it is rooted in nothing grander than fitting lives to inclinations, then why should there be such an *issue* around it? We protect, in our social and legal practices, political views and associations, not because it doesn't matter what people choose, or because opinions are ineffectual or unimportant, but because it does matter and they are important. If sexuality is nothing more than inclination and choice, then perhaps it does not deserve to be in the same category as freedom of expression, association, etc. It is more like the choice between flavours of ice-cream. Perhaps "gay rights" is just the slogan of a special-interest, life-style group who have no better claim to our attention than do coffee-drinkers or pet-owners.

But this political version of the argument also fails, for it relies on a mistaken premise about the way the significance of options is relevant to the permissibility regulating choice among them and attaching social disadvantage to them. It would be intolerable if society were given boundless freedom to interfere in the trivia of life. Of course it is wrong of a government to prohibit the expression of communist views in part because people's views are important to them as individuals and our political life is important to us as a community. And of course the choice whether to tie my left shoe-lace before the right is unimportant. But a government that punished those who tie their left lace first, or allowed them to be subject to private discrimination and abuse, would nonetheless be invading personal liberty. And the reason is not simply that a government that regulates shoe-laces is likely to regulate more significant things, too. It is that pointless interference with personal liberty is wrong and that liberty includes the freedom to choose in line with our inclinations, at least where doing so harms no one.

To appeal to the argument that choosing one's own path is more noble or courageous, as Gide calls it, is indeed to look beyond the individual will, to appeal to standards of nobility or courage. Taylor's position is that such standards get no grip unless one's choice is grounded in something more than feeling:

> [U]nless some options are more significant than others, the very idea of self-choice falls into triviality and hence incoherence. Self-choice as an ideal makes sense only because some *issues* are more significant than others. (39)

But the difficulty with that suggestion is that the second formulation is correct, the first is not, and the pair pivots on an equivocation between 'options' and 'issues'. *Options* are the items up for choice, the things for which one opts. *Issues,* on the other hand, are the kinds of concerns into which the options fall. So, homosexual monogamy is one option a gay man might choose when considering the issue of his life-path.

In the dispute about sexual authenticity, are we talking about options or issues? Plainly, it is options: people are expected to produce arguments to show that the options they have chosen are no less worthy. The issues are not chosen. So there are two different questions: What makes an issue significant? What makes an option valuable? One option does not need to be more significant than another for it to be more valuable (meaning is in an odd index of value). What Taylor evidently has in mind is that the *issue* must be a significant one: one can't take much pride in a self-made life if the only issue one grapples with is what to have for lunch. But the reason that is so is not that a tuna sandwich is no more meaningful than a hamburger, nor that this is the province of brute tastes. It is because the issue— what should I have for lunch?—is trivial; it (normally) engages no important human concerns. In contrast, sexuality matters, not because our sexual orientations involve more than feelings, but because we are embodied creatures, sexual animals with a capacity and need for erotic love. That has nothing to do with the putative significance of the options we may have. To see this, compare our views about interracial marriage. We don't need to prove that there is some special significance to a homoracial as opposed to heteroracial marriage choice in order to think that such choices merit respect and recognition. We need only show that marriage is important. Having established that, we would not go further and ask someone who had decided to pursue a life including a heteroracial marriage to account for the special significance or value of heteroraciality on pain of being silenced or oppressed. Likewise, we do not need to prove there is some special significance to homosexual as opposed to heterosexual partner choice in order to establish the centrality of our sexualities and the importance of authentic choices in expressing them.

Distinguishing in this way between life issues and options is crucial to a clear view of what is at stake. The more significant an issue, the more demanding we are in our normative attitudes towards it. In particular, in public life we tend to be more concerned about the ways in which we respond to the choices people make about important issues than about trivial ones. But even here, there is no tight correlation between the significance of an issue and (say) the permissibility of regulating choice of options with respect to it. As I argued above, it would be quite wrong for a society to regulate the trivial matters of life. It would be wrong to regulate shoe-lace tying pointlessly. Suppose, however, that tying one's left lace first made one more susceptible to chronic back-pain. We might then be more willing to endorse paternalistic regulation here, precisely because shoe-lace-tying is not part of any important form of life; the paternalism would not be an indignity. In contrast, there are other choices we would wish to protect even against paternalistic interference, because the issues in which they are embedded are so important. We would not prohibit inter-racial marriages even if those marriages made the partners more likely targets of abuse. Human sexuality, like choice of marriage partners, is indisputably part of forms of life that are important to people, and it is that rather than the character of the options that engages our attention.

There is thus an unhappy similarity between Taylor's confusion of options and issues and the mistake made by the US Supreme Court in *Bowers v. Hardwick*. The majority upheld Georgia's criminal prohibitions on gay sexuality on the ground that there is no 'fundamental right to engage in homosexual sodomy.' The majority agreed that, quite apart from the long pedigree of legal homophobia, there is no mention of the option of homosexuality in the Constitution, and no good reason to expect one. But as Blackmun J. properly observed in his dissenting judgment, all that is irrelevant: 'The case is no more about a "fundamental right to engage in homosexual sodomy", as the court purports to declare, than *Stanley v. Georgia* was about a fundamental right to watch obscene movies, or *Katz v. United States* was about a fundamental right to place interstate bets from a telephone booth. Rather, this case is about "the most comprehensive of rights and the right of most civilized men", namely, "the right to be let alone." *Olmstead v. United States*.'[14] As a constitutional matter, Michael Hardwick did not have to establish that the option he had chosen in his intimate life was important—indeed, from the law's point of view the option itself is insignificant. He had merely to establish that the issue of sexual intimacy deserved protection.[15] Likewise, to root authenticity in choice one does not have to prove that the options people choose are meaningful, but that they are exercising their powers in important areas.

If we concede, as I have argued, that a homosexual or heterosexual life path is in itself meaningless, and if sexual orientation really is just a matter of feelings, then what is to become of the 'discriminating judgements'—judgements of value and worth—that some people want to make about sexuality?

Some of these judgements we must retain: because authenticity is not the only value in life, we will also need an aesthetics and ethics of sexuality. Many other judgements, however, we should not seek to ground but to abolish. Some 'discriminating judgements' are made by those who plan to discriminate against those whose judgements ignore what they hold to be the external horizons of significance. To show that sexual orientation is an area in which it is appropriate to act according to inclination, according to how one 'just feels', is in this context sufficient to establish that a life path significantly influenced by that consideration *is* one that is no less worthy. Moreover, it is no less worthy in *precisely* the way that a search for tall or dark partners is no less worthy than a search for short or fair ones. And to someone who had the audacity to demand that one justify such a path one might plausibly reply: 'I've chosen it because it accords with my inclinations, so it's no less worthy than yours which accords with your inclinations. It allows me to be myself, to pursue my own good in my own way, to be authentic.'

We should therefore take Gayle Rubin's advice and purge sexuality of its surplus significance; we should not make the discriminating judgements that many insist on. Is it better to be gay or straight? The question is to be refused, not answered. Is it better for gay people to follow gay or straight life-paths? Is it better to respect or degrade sexual minorities? These questions can be discussed. If we came to see sexualities in precisely the way Taylor derides, as matters of brute taste and devoid of deeper significance, would we not be better and more humane people? After all, if there were widespread discrimination, violence, and hatred of those who prefer blondes, it should be a matter of grave concern, even though preferring blondes is, as Taylor says, just a matter of taste. Indeed, we might even think it worse precisely *because* people were getting worked up over, and causing so much human misery over, nothing at all. So to show that the discrimination, violence and hatred that gay people suffer matters, and is wrong, one does *not* need the premise that choice of life-path is *significant* in some cosmic sense.

5. Values and Horizons

At the core of Taylor's doctrine there lies an important and correct thesis: we can appraise choices as better or worse only when they are made on grounds, which grounds must reach beyond choice itself. But no one said that the gay interlocutor in this argument has no grounds. The grounds are obvious: such choices accord with his inclinations. Is it good to serve one's deepest inclinations, or should one instead repress them? And when people are innocently pursuing such inclinations, how should a society respond? Things can be said about this. Instead, Taylor writes:

> Asserting the value of a homosexual orientation has to be done differently, more empirically, one might say, taking into account the actual nature of homo- and heterosexual experience and life. It can't just be assumed a priori, on the grounds that anything we choose is all right. (38)

There are two misguided ideas here. First, we have again the notion that sexual orientations have values and must be defended. Second, the role of choice is again misidentified. No one says that 'anything we choose is all right', for that would commit the interlocutor to endorsing a life of vindictive homophobia provided it is freely chosen. Indeed, the argument Taylor recounts and seeks to refute is inconsistent with the assumption that anything chosen is all right. The person whose deep preference is for blondes chooses *badly* when he chooses a brunette. In Gide's terms, it is *wrong* to follow 'borrowed truths' instead of the needs of the intimate self. Maybe that is an unattractive view—maybe it is too self-centred, or maybe, as some sceptics think, there is no self to centre it. But whatever else it is, it is not self-defeating. What Taylor needs to show is that choosing with our inclinations is not enough to valorize *anything,* but that is hard to endorse. Sexualities are about the capacity for the bodily expression of love, and for that reason sex is precisely the empire of inclination, emotion, and brute feelings. Perhaps nowhere else is it so risky to betray the intimate self in favour of borrowed truths.

I have already expressed my scepticism about the intelligibility of such gross comparisons as are suggested by Taylor's words 'the actual nature of homo- and heterosexual experience and life.' Often, these merely cover the distorted and biassed judgements that circulate in a homophobic society. First, the idea that there is something called 'homosexual life' that we might evaluate on empirical grounds is but crude stereotyping. Second, such commonalities as exist among the diverse life experiences of gay people depend in part on how others treat them. Consider, for example, the epidemic of suicide amongst gay teenagers.[16] That is, I suppose, part of the 'actual nature of homosexual experience and life'. But it establishes nothing about the value of a homosexual orientation, although it is tragically eloquent about the effects of the ridicule and hatred that gay youth suffer at the hands of heterosexual people, especially their parents and peers. What is astonishing in our homophobic societies is thus not that 'the actual nature of homo- and heterosexual experience and life' may differ; it is that in spite of these 'differences' many gay people still choose to live in harmony with their inclinations.

Thus, Taylor's argument in its most general form comes down to this:

1. nothing can be valorized just by the sheer fact that it is freely chosen
2. so if an option has value for the agent it must be in virtue of something about that option other than the fact that it is freely chosen
3. one feature of options is their relation to external horizons of significance, so
4. if an option has value for the agent it must be in virtue of its relation to an external horizon of significance.

The argument fails because (3) specifies a merely sufficient condition for value, while (4) infers a conclusion about its necessary conditions. There are lots of other features of options apart from their standing in relation to external horizons of significance, for example, the extent to which they accord with an agent's deepest inclinations. The central theoretical error thus lies in supposing that if the source of value must be external to the choice, it must also be external to the agent.

Perhaps if there are external horizons of significance they can valorize choices for at least some people. But modernity has done a lot to cloud these horizons. This is an important point; modernist criticism of such horizons is not purely metaphysical or epistemological. It may be true that a naturalistic world-view cannot make room for them and that a naturalistic science cannot get knowledge of them. That is part of our history. But there is another, more significant, part. Criticism of the external horizons has also been political. Marginalized groups have not found much stake in such standards and have found it difficult to control their definition. Certainly that is true of the examples Taylor offers:

Only if I exist in a world in which history, or the demands of nature, or the needs of my fellow human beings, or the duties of citizenship, or the call of God, or something else of this order *matters* crucially, can I define an identity for myself that is not trivial. (40–41)

The supposed demands of history, nature, society, the state, or God haven't been kind to gay people—or for that matter to women, or to the poor, or to people of colour. I'm not saying that this is inevitable; no doubt the possibilities of reconstruction vary from horizon to horizon. But it won't do simply to say that the appropriate relation to the horizons of meaning is not just deference but 'dialogue'. If that only means that we all begin building with the tools we have to hand, it is true but empty. If it means to capture something stronger for our existing traditions of argument, then it is to be rejected. There are horizons of meaning that sexual minorities should simply refuse, dialogues they should simply leave. As Taylor rightly says, meanings are not individual creations; they are public. But there is more, for in some cases they are not merely *socially* constructed; they are *authoritatively* constructed in ways that regulate and limit possible change. It seems to me quite pointless for gay Roman Catholics to keep hoping that the Pope will read John Boswell's books and be persuaded.[17]

Admittedly, Taylor's horizon-list is not a closed one. Maybe there is something else 'of this order' that would skyrocket sexual orientation into the realms of nontriviality. Maybe not. But most gay people would be happy to be allowed to choose according to their inclinations, to identify as it feels comfortable, in the knowledge that in doing so their life-path is no less worthy, and that they have staked out an authentic identity.

How, finally, do we gauge the promise of modernity? There is, Taylor says, not just *misere* but also *grandeur* and that latter can be captured if only we give proper deference to—or at least dialogue with—the preexisting horizons of significance. Those marginalized will, I hope, be forgiven if they feel that they have heard all this before. A theory that emphasises the need to articulate one's identity against standards set externally by nature, or tradition, or gods; one that thinks it appropriate and intelligible that people should justify their sexual orientations; one that discounts the role of inclination in value—these ideas all sound too familiar. Surely to proceed in this way is to give insufficient weight to the moral and political criticisms of the world view in which they once made sense.

A priori arguments in the realm of value are, as Taylor rightly suspects, not too profitable. It is more complicated than that. Value and choice are related in a complex way. But on any credible theory, choosing according to one's inclinations sometimes does serve value, for instance, by allowing one to stake out a life that is authentically one's own. And to remind others that the ground of one's choice is simply that it serves one's inclinations is politically potent, especially when they think the choices are poised miles overhead on high-tension wires. It helps to remind them that there is no cosmic significance here, and that we are all of us just standing with both feet on the ground. Standing here, or, if that proves uncomfortable, over there. That unromantic idea captures one real achievement of modernity: the understanding that even in a disenchanted world it still is possible to lead a life that is both authentic and worthy of respect.

---

1. André Gide, *Journals* ii 282; as cited in Jonathan Dollimore, *Sexual Dissidence: Augustine to Wilde, Freud to Foucault* (Oxford: Clarendon Press, 1991) at 39.
2. The ideas of 'modernity' and 'modern thought' are, of course, unavoidably controversial. For one influential account see Marshall Berman, *All that is Solid Melts into Air: The Experience of Modernity* (New York: Simon and Schuster, 1982). And, although I cannot defend the claim here, it seems to me that the idea of 'post-modern' thought is simply a misnomer. In one version it is but a retreat to a pre-modern irrationalism, in another it is a highly sceptical version of modernism itself.
3. For evidence that, in the American context at least, memories of traditional family life are mostly mythical, see Stephanie Coontz, *The Way We Never Were: American Families and the Nostalgia Trap* (New York: Viking Books, 1992).
4. For some astonishing parallels in the case of sexuality, see Elaine Showalter, *Sexual Anarchy: Gender and Culture at the Fin de Siècle* (New York: Penguin Books, 1990).
5. For some roots of this, see Michel Foucault, *The History of Sexuality* (3 vols.) (New York: Vintage Books, 1978–86).
6. Charles Taylor, *The Malaise of Modernity* (Concord, Ont.: Anansi Press, 1991). Published in the U.S. as *The Ethics of Authenticity* (Cambridge, MA: Harvard University Press, 1991). Page references to this work are included parenthetically in the text.
7. It is important to note that Taylor is himself sympathetic to some forms of a politics of recognition. See C. Taylor et al., *Multiculturalism: Examining the Politics of Recognition* with commentary by A. Gutmann, ed. (Princeton, NJ: Princeton University Press, 1994).

8. An entry into the literature might begin with Alan P. Bell, Martin S. Weinberg, and Sue Kiefer Hammersmith, *Sexual Preference: Its Development in Men and Women* (Bloomington: Indiana University Press, 1981); Michael Ruse, *Homosexuality* (Oxford: Basil Blackwell, 1981); and John C. Gonsiorek & James D. Weinrich, eds, *Homosexuality: Research Implications for Public Policy* (Newbury Park, CA: Sage Publications, 1991).

9. I am not, of course, claiming that the only way to live in harmony with one's feelings is to act on them. There may, for instance, be some celibate gay priests who have made authentic life-choices. They would be cloistered, so to speak, without being closeted. And the same would apply to some cross-orientation relationships: see, e.g., Catherine Whitney, *Uncommon Lives: Gay Men and Straight Women* (New York: New American Library, 1990).

10. See Kath Weston, *Families We Choose: Lesbians, Gays, Kinship* (New York: Columbia University Press, 1991).

11. Skinner remarks of Taylor's philosophy in general that 'what Taylor fears above all is loss of meaning, a fear he appears to experience almost as a phobia.' Q. Skinner, "Who are 'We'? Ambiguities of the Modern Self" (1991) 34 Inquiry 133 at 142.

12. The hair colour example is an interesting one. If a man in our society were gender-indifferent but blond(e)-exclusive in his object choice, he would be classified as a bisexual man who only has sex with blond(e)s. We have no name for blond(e)-sexuals, but not because that sexual orientation does not exist. We do not name it because we do not care about it; our cultural anxieties about sexuality focus on gender almost to the exclusion of anything else.

13. As cited in, Shane Phalen, *Identity Politics: Lesbian Feminism and the Limits of Community* (Philadelphia: Temple University Press, 1989) at 123.

14. 478 U.S. 186 (1986).

15. And, of course, that his choices did not offend other constitutional values; but that was not at issue here. The fact that our sexual choices must respect the rights of others does not show that choice is irrelevant to their value for us. It shows that authenticity, being true to oneself, is not the only thing at stake in sexuality.

16. For discussion of some of the literature, see John C. Gonsiorek, "The Empirical Basis for the Demise of the Illness Model of Homosexuality" in *Homosexuality: Research Implications for Public Policy,* supra note 8 at 133–34.

17. John Boswell, *Christianity, Social Tolerance and Homosexuality: Gay People in Western Europe from the Beginning of the Christian Era to the Fourteenth Century* (Chicago: University of Chicago Press, 1980); and John Boswell, *Same-sex Unions in Premodern Europe* (New York: Villard Books, 1994).

PART FOUR

Responsibility

One convenient way of dividing up the subject matter of law is to begin by distinguishing between private and public law. The function of private law is to provide an authoritative way to resolve disputes between private parties. When one party, the plaintiff, makes a claim against another, the defendant, that the defendant has violated a contractual agreement, or taken possession of land that belongs to the plaintiff, or caused the plaintiff personal injuries by negligent or reckless conduct or, even worse, by deliberately intending such harm, then the apparatus of private law is brought into play to settle the issue. The branches of the private law include the law of torts and the law of contracts. The law of torts decides whether the plaintiff has suffered harms that should be compensated for by payments from the defendant and, if so, how large the compensatory payments should be. The law of contracts can require compensatory monetary payments for breach of contract or in some cases compel specific performance of the action promised but not yet done by the defendant. The aim of public law, on the other hand, is not compensation but rather criminal punishment. In criminal law the party that claims to have been wronged by the defendant is not called the plaintiff but rather the state or the crown or the people. Those wrongful acts that not only injure private parties but also set back widely shared public interests are called crimes.

Whether we are talking about crimes and the issue of punishment or torts and the issue of compensation, we come immediately to an appreciation of the court's role in protecting the rights of the defendant, who is being accused of some kind of wrongful conduct and threatened either with punishment or with legal pressure to make often costly compensation. If the defendant is to have civil liability imposed on him or her or to be convicted of a crime, the defendant must be shown to be responsible for what she did or for the harm suffered by the plaintiff. That means that the defendant's conduct must be shown to have satisfied the definition of the tort or crime she is accused of, that the defendant can be shown to have acted or omitted to act in the appropriately voluntary way, that her conduct was appropriately faulty, and that the faulty action was the cause of a harm or of an unreasonable risk of a harm. Moreover, the defendant must be allowed to cite one or more recognized defenses to the charges. To begin with, she can deny the facts alleged in the accusation or argue that the prosecution (in criminal law) or the plaintiff (in tort law) has unsuccessfully borne the assigned burden of proof (a "failed-proof defense"). The defendant can do this by presenting evidence that tends to undermine the case against her. There is thus something essentially negative about this kind of defense since it aims to negate (or to "negative" as lawyers often put it) the case of the plaintiff (in torts) or the prosecution (in a criminal trial). In contrast, some important defenses are labeled affirmative defenses. The defendant argues in these instances that, even if the other side has successfully shown that the defendant's conduct satisfied the defining elements of the crime or tort charged, there are independent reasons for acquittal (in the case of a crime) or release from civil liability (for harm). At this point, typically, the burden switches to the defendant to plead and prove the affirmative defense (usually with a lighter burden of proof). Defenses of this kind in the criminal law are divided into two subcategories, justifications and excuses. (This terminology is used less frequently in the law of torts than in contract law, and the terms are especially difficult to apply to defenses to negligence, though the terminology fits comfortably enough with various defenses to intentional torts, such as self-defense and consent.)

To justify one's conduct is to show that it was in the circumstances legally right or correct, or at least all right, or permissible—that is, not wrong. Thus a justification, in George Fletcher's words, "renders a nominal violation of the criminal law lawful, and therefore exempt from criminal sanctions."[1] The most common criminal justifications are self-defense, defense of others, defense of property, justified use of force in law enforcement, and necessity (forced choice of the lesser evil). An excuse, on the other hand, does not deny that the defendant has done something prohibited by law and that he did it without justification. The excuse claims only that the defendant could not help doing what he did or didn't know what he was doing—in short, that the defendant was not responsible and therefore is not to blame. Indeed, the criminal action cannot be imputed to the defendant at all, as his doing, without qualification. The most common excuses are infancy (imagine a two-year-old charged with homicide), duress, provocation (a mitigation only), insanity, and intoxication.

Responsibility for Results

That the defendant's action, or perhaps the defendant's faulty action, was the cause of a harm to the plaintiff, is a necessary condition for tort liability.[2] It is also a necessary condition for some, but not all, kinds of criminal liability. One cannot commit murder, for example, unless one's action caused the death of a victim, but one can commit attempted murder, without actually causing a death or any other injury to one's would-be victim. The causal condition is more constant in torts because deciding on compensation is the whole object of a tort proceeding. Unless a harm has been caused, there is nothing to be compensated.

Even when it is clear that the defendant was at fault in acting as she did (for example, that the defendant acted negligently, without due care) and equally clear that the plaintiff was harmed, it may be extremely difficult to know whether that faulty act or omission was the cause of the harm. Sometimes it is not difficult to know that the act was a

necessary condition of the harm or a *conditio sine qua non,* or equivalently a "but for cause." (But for the act, the harm would not have happened.) But that is not enough to warrant pinning the label *cause* on it. But for the actor's father meeting the actor's mother, the harm would not have occurred, because the actor would never have come into existence. And but for the act in this case, the victim would not have gone to the drugstore to buy his newly prescribed medication and would not have met the woman there whom he was eventually to marry. Thus the offspring of that marriage, another human being now in existence, would never have been born, with further consequences on into the infinite future. In order to avoid commitment to the proposition that the liability of a negligent defendant can extend to all those losses that would not have occurred but for the defendant's negligence, legal theorists have urged that legal cause—or proximate cause, as they call it—be understood as a severe restriction of "but for cause," confining it to necessary conditions that are significant and important, or proximate, or near and immediate, or directly traceable, or foreseeable. It is usually acknowledged that whether an act is a "but for cause" of some consequence is a question of fact. Still another common term for causally necessary condition then, is cause-in-fact, and that phrase is often used to contrast "but for cause" with legal cause, the latter being only partly factual and partly decisional—partly a matter of legal policy rather than entirely a matter of fact.

The problem of determining the scope of an individual's liability for the effects of her actions has generated a number of rival theoretical approaches. One is the doctrine of general strict liability in tort, defended by Richard Epstein. If I make a mess on my property, it would be odd for me to ask you to pay for it. If I now move the mess over to your property, that doesn't make my asking you to pay any more reasonable. It is my mess, so I should pay to clean it up. This is true whether or not I intentionally brought it to your property. These intuitions support the idea that liability for loss should be strict. I should be liable for the harms I cause you because by making me liable to you, it is as if the harms I cause injure only myself. In "The Impossibility of General Strict Liability," the first article in Part Four, Stephen Perry convincingly demonstrates the incoherence of this view.

A popular belief in the first half of the twentieth century was that legal, or proximate, cause is simply a blend of cause-in-fact and policy. A court's decision to permit or exclude a given necessary condition as a proximate cause of a plaintiff's harm, it was often said, is a policy decision disguised as a factual discovery. Hart and Honoré, in the work from which their selection is drawn, try to find an alternative to that view. They argue that the common-sense concept of a cause, complex though it may be, provides a framework for determinations of proximate cause that are policy neutral.

Judith Thomson calls our attention to what she calls "the decline of cause" in the law—that is, the weakening, especially in tort law, of the requirement that the defendant's faulty act or omission was the cause of the harm or loss suffered by the plaintiff. In recent times, in some types of cases, it has become sufficient that the faulty act or omission created an unreasonable risk of the kind of harm that actually resulted. It may be that the plaintiff is unable to prove, after the passage of many years, that, say a drug company's proven negligence to persons of a certain class that includes her, was the actual cause of the actual harms she suffered. But more and more persons have begun to ask why that should be necessary at all. (The issue is illustrated in the cases of *Sindell v. Abbot Laboratories* and *Summers v. Tice,* the last two selections in this section.)

Thomson connects this new skepticism about the causal condition for liability to some recent developments in moral theory. Some moral philosophers (Thomson calls them "moral sophisticates") maintain that a negligent actor does no more than create the risk of a harm and is not responsible for the full harm that results. For beyond the risk, the actual results are in large part a matter of luck, for which the actor deserves neither credit nor blame. Suppose we compare two cases in which the blame for wrongful risk creation is equal, harm resulting nevertheless in the one but not in the other case. In these cases only luck, not moral merit or demerit, distinguishes the actors. Thomson notes how contrary this is to the moral responses of the man and woman in the street who make sharply different moral appraisals of the actors, depending on the actual results of their risk creation. In this essay Thomson tries to support their commonsense moral judgments with philosophical argument.

The problem of explaining the moral significance, if any, of actual results also arises in the criminal law. The most familiar example is that of two persons, each intending to kill an enemy. With identical motives and intentions, and in perfectly parallel circumstances, each fires, but only the first succeeds in killing the victim. Unknown to the second assassin, the would-be victim is wearing a bulletproof vest. Thomson offers an argument, not just for continuing our practice of punishing murder more than attempted murder, but also for regarding the successful murderer as more blameworthy. This conclusion is the target of the article by Richard Parker. Parker, concentrating on the criminal law, concludes that the significance of actual harmful results, in both law and morals, is greatly overrated—the man and woman in the street notwithstanding.

In 1928, according to a leading writer on the law of torts, "a bombshell burst upon this field when the New York Court of Appeals, forsaking 'proximate cause,' stated the issue of foreseeability in terms of duty" [the duty of care to someone or other that helps define negligence].[3] The reference is to the case of *Palsgraf v. Long Island Railroad Company,* which has since become "the most discussed and debated of all torts cases."[4] This case is the fifth selection in Part Four. Since 1928 the *Palsgraf* decision has gradually established itself as the prevailing precedent for tort cases with so-called "unforeseeable plaintiffs," but the deep issues in the case are still controversial among theorists, probably because of a vexatious conundrum about justice at the heart of the dispute between the majority and minority opinions in that case. On the one hand, we are inclined to say that a negligent defendant, being the party at fault, ought to compensate wholly innocent people, like Mrs. Palsgraf. To be sure, in cases like *Palsgraf* the negligent party could not have reasonably anticipated any possibility of injury to so remote and unlikely a plaintiff. It is unfair to make them liable to a party who was situated well outside the limits of the genuine risks their negligence had created. On the other hand, we must remember that Mrs. Palsaraf was wholly faultless in this episode and, if there are no alternatives between forcing a negligent railroad company to pay for her injuries or leaving them for her to deal with, justice would seem to favor her claim against the company. Still it must be remembered that the accumulated harm from a minor sort of negligence, if we include harm to those who were well outside the risk created and also those who are not members of the class to whom the risk was created, can be out of all proportion to the defendant's fault. The best rule for cases like this, it might be said, is the one that protects defendants from liability for results beyond their fault and finds a nonarbitrary "place to stop short of infinite liability."[5] Justice Cardozo's majority opinion provides such a place. After all, the railroad did not fulfill its duty of care to the last-minute passenger trying to board, but there was no duty to Mrs. Palsgraf that it left unfulfilled.

Two California Supreme Court decisions conclude this section. Both exemplify what Thomson, in the article discussed above, calls the decline of cause. Suppose two people shoot at a third. One bullet hits the victim in the eye, but it is impossible to determine which bullet was responsible. Should the victim bear the costs simply because he cannot establish who injured him? On the other hand, if both defendants have to pay, then one of them will have to pay though he did not in fact cause the injury. This is the issue addressed in the case of *Summers v. Tice.*

In the case of *Sindell v. Abbot Laboratories,* the daughters of mothers who took the drug DES are stricken with ovarian cancer. No plaintiff can identify which particular pharmaceutical company's version of the drug her mother took. The plaintiffs are, however, able to bring many of the manufacturers together as defendants. A large class of plaintiffs sues the group of manufacturers. If the victims cannot identify whose drug they took may they nonetheless recover damages from the manufacturers? Each drug company has very likely injured many members of the victim class, but there is no way of knowing whose injury was the result of whose pharmaceutical product. What should be done? In *Sindell,* the Supreme Court of California rules that the manufacturers must pay damages proportional to their share of the DES market.

Responsibility for Nonintervention

Both the criminal law and the law of torts in English-speaking countries hold people responsible for certain wrongful interventions in the lives of others. But the Anglo-American law has never helped persons civilly or criminally responsible for their noninterventions in the activities of people to whom they stand in no special legal relation. In this respect English-speaking countries (including 47 of the 50 American states) differ markedly from most of the rest of the world. Most nations have criminal sanctions requiring citizens to attempt "easy rescues" even of total strangers. It is a different matter when the person in a position to rescue an endangered party is related to that person (say, as parent to child) or has special duties to attempt rescue (as, for example, those of a paid lifeguard toward the specific persons who bathe on the guard's assigned stretch of beach), or has contracted with the endangered person to offer constant protection. A morally sensitive person might wonder why there should be duties to rescue *only* in these special cases and not in the case of unrelated parties. Thomas Babington Macaulay, in the very brief selection included here, addresses his remarks primarily to that query. Most British and American legal writers in the last century and a half have agreed that Macaulay satisfactorily defended the Anglo-American practice.

In "The Case for a Duty to Rescue," Ernest J. Weinrib shows how a series of judicial decisions over the past century have moved the common law away from the position articulated by Macaulay. Drawing on these decisions as well as on recent academic work, Weinrib contends that a judicially created duty to effect an easy rescue would lend greater coherence to an already broad pattern of common-law principles. Moreover, he argues that a moral case for such a duty can be made on both utilitarian and Kantian-deontological grounds.

Some Criminal Defenses

The remainder of the selections in Part Four discuss moral or philosophical problems raised by various defenses to criminal liability. The defenses discussed here are not exhaustive, but they are fairly representative. There are two negativing defenses claiming that the prosecution has failed to shoulder the burden of proving beyond a reasonable doubt that all of the definitional elements of the crime have been satisfied. The remainder of the defenses here illustrated, interpreted, and in some cases evaluated, are affirmative defenses; one of these is a justification and two are excuses.

People v. Young is a criminal case involving a very serious mistake of fact. Mr. Young's mistaken belief was that the two ununiformed men he saw beating a third were ordinary thugs; in fact, they were plainclothes policemen trying to make an arrest. His defense involved presenting evidence meant to create a reasonable doubt that all the elements of the crime he had been charged with were satisfied. In particular, he claimed that he lacked *mens rea,* an appropriately guilty mind. He *did* attack policemen and interfere with their legitimate work, but he did not do that act purposely, or knowingly, though it might be argued that he did that act recklessly or possibly even negligently. Another question that arises is whether the court should instruct the jury to use an objective or a subjective standard in appraising Young's false belief. Are they to compare it with the beliefs, whether true or false, of a "reasonable man" in his circumstances? Does the law require his beliefs to be true or only reasonable? Similarly, does the law require his false beliefs to be reasonable or only sincere, honest, and genuine? There are important policy issues behind these questions, as well as the difficult question of fairness to a courageous if quixotic person of good intentions. (Compare this case with *Regina v. Morgan* in Part Three.)

If *Palsgraf* is the most discussed noncriminal real case in our legal history, Lon Fuller's "The Case of the Speluncean Explorers" is certainly the most discussed fictitious criminal case, even though it was composed as recently as 1948. The fictitious defendants in that case might have tried a number of defenses, but the most promising one was necessity (or forced choice of the lesser evil). That is, they could have argued, as some members of the specially appointed judicial panel that heard their case did argue, that they were forced by circumstances beyond their control to choose whether to die of starvation or to select by voluntary lottery a victim to be killed and cannibalized. Following one alternative, four would live and one would die; following the other, all five would die. Their choice of the lesser evil, they could claim, was a justified choice. At least, they might say, that it is not consistent to admit that self-defense can justify homicide while equally threatening impersonal necessity cannot.

The crime at issue in the fictitious tale "The Case of Lady Eldon's French Lace" is attempted smuggling. The attempt was not successful because, unknown to Lady Eldon, the British government had removed French lace from the duty list the day before she tried to smuggle it. It is impossible, so it is said, to commit a crime by doing something that is completely legal. If one is charged with attempt in those circumstances, then one can argue in one's

defense that the *actus reus* (guilty act) specified in the definition of the crime has not been satisfied (a failed proof defense). The *mens rea* condition, however, is sometimes satisfied in spades! There are dozens of exquisitely comical examples in the casebooks of defendants struggling mightily to do something they think is illegal while all the time the act they labor to complete is perfectly legal. Why shouldn't a guilty mind (when it is *that* guilty) be sufficient for criminal liability (as it clearly is for moral guilt)? And is it really impossible to attempt to do something that is impossible?

The remaining selections in Part Four concern the bewildering criminal excuse of insanity. The famous M'Naghten Rules and its leading American rival, the American Law Institute's *Model Penal Code,* are here reprinted. The main issue in *State v. Guido* is "What constitutes a disease?" This question must be answered before a key element in the M'Naghten Rules, that which requires a "disease of the mind," can be considered. Behind these questions, according to Chief Justice Weintraub, lies the assumption that, even if we leave insanity out of the picture, "some wrongdoers are sick and some are bad." How to distinguish between these two classes, if Weintraub's assumption is correct, has proven to be the most difficult—perhaps because the most fundamental—of the puzzles about responsibility.

Alan Dershowitz and others have persuasively argued that mental illness should not be regarded as an independent ground of exculpation but only as a sign that one of the traditional standard grounds—compulsion, ignorance of fact, or excusable ignorance of law—may apply. In "What Is So Special About Mental Illness," Joel Feinberg supports this view but argues that there are nonetheless important moral differences between culpable offenders who are mentally ill and culpable offenders who are not. In cases where mental illness does not exculpate, it should nonetheless affect our attitudes toward the offender, and it may have important implications for the kind of punishment that is appropriate.

1. George Fletcher, "Justification," in *Encyclopedia of Crime and Justice,* p. 941.
2. This bold statement in the text is no longer universally true. See Judith Thomson, "The Decline of Cause."
3. Prosser and Keeton in *The Law of Torts, 5th edition* (St. Paul: West Publishing Co., 1984), p. 284.
4. *Loc. cit.*
5. *Ibid.,* p. 287.

Responsibility for Results

THE IMPOSSIBILITY OF GENERAL STRICT LIABILITY*

Stephen R. Perry

1. Introduction

Both the history of tort law and the recent theoretical literature on the subject suggest that there are two intellectually tenable and more or less equally respectable answers to the question of what should be the general standard of liability in tort, namely fault and strict liability. Each is generally thought to have represented, at one time or another, the dominant approach of the positive common law. Each has its modern theoretical proponents: a fault-based approach has been argued for on grounds of economic efficiency by Richard Posner,[1] for example, and on grounds of individual moral right by, among others, Ronald Dworkin[2] and Ernest Weinrib;[3] strict liability, on the other hand, has received an economic defence in the work of Guido Calabresi,[4] and a rights-based defence in the writings of Richard Epstein.[5] Each of these theorists has felt compelled not only to offer positive arguments in favour of fault or strict liability but also to answer the intellectual case, whether perceived as being founded on a conception of efficiency or of individual rights, for the rival approach.

The present paper has three main objects. The first is to demonstrate that there exists no plausible justification, in terms of individual moral right, for a general standard of strict liability in tort. I shall be focusing upon, and offering a critique of, the arguments presented by Epstein in favour of a corrective justice-type theory of strict liability, but it should be borne in mind that the intention is to defend a general conclusion and not merely to criticize one person's views: where it seems necessary I shall therefore attempt to reformulate or bolster Epstein's position so as to make it as strong a target as possible. It is perhaps worth pointing out in this regard that Epstein is not alone in maintaining that the correct account of moral rights and obligations of reparation demands a standard of strict liability: Robert Nozick, for example, clearly presupposes—although he does not explicitly argue for—an essentially similar view in the development of his libertarian political theory.[6]

The second main object of the paper is to show that, even beyond the question of justification, a general theory of strict liability is in fact not even a possibility: not only are there no valid arguments of moral right for imposing a strict standard in tort, but

---

*I have benefited from the discussions which took place when previous versions of this paper were presented to a faculty seminar at Cornell Law School and to a session of the Law and Policy Workshop at the Faculty of Law, McGill University. I am also grateful to Paul Craig and Frank Buckley for helpful comments on earlier drafts, and to Peter Benson and Ernest Weinrib for many stimulating discussions of tort law. From *Canadian Journal of Law and Jurisprudence* Vol. I, No. 2 (July 1988). Endnotes have been edited and renumbered.

no general theory of truly strict liability, whether defended on economic or on rights-based grounds, is capable in any event of generating determinate results. To put the point in Nozickian terms, there is no determinate conception of a "boundary-crossing" which can be presented independently of a normative notion such as fault. General strict liability is not, therefore, the coherent and well-defined alternative to fault which it has generally been taken to be.

The third object is to make clear that Epstein's own theory of tort liability is not itself a theory of strict liability at all, but rather is best understood as embodying an implicit fault standard. The point here is not simply an exegetical one, nor is it intended merely to underscore the conclusion that a general theory of strict liability is an impossibility. While the conception of fault upon which Epstein's theory can be seen to rely is not deployed by the theory in a consistent way, it is nonetheless consistent in its own terms; it offers, moreover, a distinctive and powerful alternative to the usual modern understanding of the negligence standard, that understanding being that the court must engage in a direct, *ex post* balancing of the respective interests of plaintiff and defendant.[7] Somewhat ironically, the ultimate justification for undertaking a detailed critique of Epstein's theory of tort law thus turns out to be that he points the way towards a more cogent and compelling version of the thesis which he sets out to reject, namely that liability should be determined in accordance with the fault of the actor.

2. Epstein's Defence of Strict Liability

In the case of *Vincent v. Lake Erie Transportation Company*[8] the master of a ship which was owned by the defendant continued to make the ship fast to the plaintiff's dock rather than set out in a dangerously violent storm. The dock was damaged by the battering which resulted from the action of the storm on the ship, and the plaintiff sued for the loss. While stating that the master's action had been reasonable under the circumstances, the court nonetheless held the defendant liable. In the course of discussing this decision Richard Epstein advances the following argument for a general theory of strict liability in tort, where the theory is to be understood as a conception of corrective justice:[9]

Had the Lake Erie Transportation Company owned both the dock and the ship, there could have been no lawsuit as a result of the incident. The Transportation Company, now the sole party involved, would, when faced with the storm, apply some form of cost-benefit analysis in order to decide whether to sacrifice its ship or its dock to the elements. Regardless of the choice made, it would bear the consequences and would have no recourse against anyone else. There is no reason why the company as a defendant in a lawsuit should be able to shift the loss in question because the dock belonged to someone else. The action in tort in effect enables the injured party to require the defendant to treat the loss he has inflicted on another as though it were his own. If the Transportation Company must bear all costs in those cases in which it damages its own property, then it should bear those costs when it damages the property of another. The necessity may justify the decision to cause the damage, but it cannot justify a refusal to make compensation for the damage so caused.

The argument is not limited to the case where the defendant acts with the certain knowledge that his conduct will cause harm to others. It applies with equal force to cases where the defendant acts when he knows that there is only a risk that he will cause harm to others. . . .

If the defendant . . . took the risk of injury to his own person or property, he would bear all the costs and enjoy all the benefits of that decision whether or not it was correct. That same result should apply where a person "only" takes risks with the person or property of other individuals. There is no need to look at the antecedent risk once the harm has come to pass; no need to decide, without guide or reference, which risks are "undue" and which are not. If the defendant harms the plaintiff, then he should pay even if the risk he took was reasonable, just as he should pay in cases of certain harm where the decision to injure was reasonable.

This argument proceeds in a number of stages. At the first stage Epstein argues that if someone has intentionally caused physical harm to another's person or property, even in circumstances where we would not ordinarily regard his action as blameworthy, then the injurer is to be treated as though he had inflicted the loss on himself; he owes reparation to the injured party. At least on first consideration this conclusion seems to be correct, since the injurer has intentionally made use of something which belongs to the plaintiff for his own ends but without the plaintiff's consent, and so in a way which is inconsistent with the latter's entitlement. In *Vincent,* for example, the defendant's servant in effect temporarily appropriated the plaintiff's dock; the defendant therefore had to restore to the plaintiff that which had been "taken" from him, and this involved not simply releasing possession of the dock but also making good the damage which had been caused in the process. The same result should follow even where the defendant has not physically appropriated the plaintiff's person or property for a period of time but has intentionally caused damage nonetheless; the one situation involves a "taking"[10] as much as does the other.

At the second stage of the argument Epstein maintains that there is no difference in principle between acting "with the certain knowledge that [one's] conduct will cause harm to others" (which, in law, amounts to causing the harm intentionally), and acting "when [one] knows that there is only a *risk* that [one] will cause harm to others". This claim is also a plausible one, since the imposition of a known risk, or at least of a known, substantial risk, to someone else's person or property seems to be akin to the "taking" which Epstein says is involved in intentionally causing harm to another for the purpose of furthering one's own ends. There is a difficulty, perhaps, in determining just which risks can plausibly be said to be "takings" in this sense, but I want for the moment to leave that issue aside. At present it will be sufficient to emphasize that Epstein's claim that the two situations are in principle indistinguishable seems to rest on the fact that in both cases the defendant can be said to have in some sense *knowingly* made use of the plaintiff's person or property. As the passages quoted at the beginning of this paragraph make clear, the element of knowledge which is common to both situations seems for Epstein to be crucial.

The third stage in Epstein's overall argument is his conclusion, not stated explicitly in the passages quoted above but affirmed throughout the entire body of his work on tort, that whenever A causes harm to B then A is liable (or at least *prima facie* liable) for B's loss. A general theory of strict liability of this sort obviously presupposes a theory of causation, and this Epstein attempts to provide. I shall consider what he has to say about the nature of causation in the following section, but for the moment I want to focus on the way in which the two preceding stages in Epstein's argument are related to his conclusion that generalized strict liability is the proper regime in tort law. In particular, I want to consider what has happened to the element of knowledge (whether of a certainty or only of a risk of harm) which seems to be a crucial element in the two earlier stages. Has that element perhaps been taken into account in the general theory in some way which is not immediately obvious, or, alternatively, has it simply been omitted from the general theory, both as a requirement of liability and as a factor in the justification of the strict standard, in which case it becomes necessary to inquire more closely into what the justification for that standard is taken to be? I shall label the question which is posed in the previous sentence *A,* and in the remainder of this section I shall consider a number of possible replies which might be made to it. The point of this exercise will be, in the first instance, the interpretive one of trying to determine just what sort of theory of liability Epstein should best be understood as defending. The more fundamental object, however, will be to use the discussion of Epstein's work to ascertain what are the strongest possible arguments that *could* be made for a theory of strict liability, and then to assess both the soundness of the arguments and the viability of the theory.

(i) Action Always Entails Risk

One possible answer to *A*—an answer which would be committed to the first of the two alternatives which the question presents—might be that Epstein is assuming that action always entails risk to others, however small those risks might be, and that a person who chooses to act always knows this, or at least should be taken to know this. The difficulty with this proposed construction of Epstein's general theory is that it makes no distinction between degrees of risk imposed on others; it requires, moreover, only knowledge of the general possibility of harm rather than knowledge of a danger which can be more specifically characterized. When "knowledge of risk" is construed this widely, however, it is no longer clear that the analogy with intentionally making use of what belongs to another in order to further one's own ends still holds good. At the first stage of Epstein's argument it was crucial that the defendant *chose* to impose certain harm on the plaintiff, so that the reasoning at the second stage proceeded by emphasizing the similarity between this situation and that in which the defendant chose to impose only a risk of harm on another. But once the requirement of knowledge is diluted to the extent that awareness of some more or less specific danger is no longer necessary, then it is no longer clear that the defendant can plausibly be said to have *chosen* to have imposed actual or potential costs upon another; as Holmes said, "[a] choice which entails a concealed consequence is as to that consequence no choice".[11] Perhaps the necessary analogy with the first stage of Epstein's argument can still be made out even when the element of knowledge which it presupposes is construed in this very attenuated way, but further argument is necessary to establish this, and it is not immediately clear what form that argument might take.

(ii) No Balancing

A second possible answer to question *A,* and again one which adheres to the first of the two alternatives which the question presents, might take the following form. Perhaps Epstein's general theory of tort liability does continue to take the idea of knowledge of (more or less specific) harm or risk seriously, but simply rejects any *balancing* of the potential harm to the plaintiff against the potential benefits to the defendant of the sort which is required, for example, by Learned Hand's formulation of the standard of care in negligence law.[12] Such an interpretation of Epstein's approach is suggested by the following passage from his paper "Intentional Harms":[13]

> Once a defendant is allowed to excuse himself on the grounds that he acted with due regard for the plaintiff, it follows that he will be able to keep for himself the benefits of his own actions even as he imposes their costs upon a stranger. The crucial question is whether or not the defendant should be allowed to force (and here the words should be taken literally) others to bear his costs *because prior to the accident he made a decision that was rational in the case*. The major premise of the theory of strict liability is that, *prima facie,* he should not be allowed to help himself by taking or destroying the plaintiff's person or property. If in the course of activity conducted for his own gain, the defendant had harmed himself or damaged his own property, he would be required to bear that loss himself *even if the expected gains were worth the risk*

involved, and there is no reason why that result should not be sought by the legal system as well when the initial harm is to the person or property of another.

If this interpretation of Epstein's approach is correct then one would expect the element of knowledge which is present at the first stage of his argument to continue to manifest itself in his generalized theory of tort liability, and the most obvious way in which this might happen would be through the theory of causation which the theory of liability builds upon. I shall consider Epstein's theory of causation in some detail in section 3, and I shall suggest there that at several points the theory does indeed make the truth of causal statements turn on a person's knowledge that he is imposing a danger or risk of harm upon others. For this and other reasons I shall argue that Epstein's putative analysis of causation is best understood as being, at least in part, a theory of personal responsibility rather than a pure account of causation. As we shall see, he would in fact seem to be committed to the view that at least certain kinds of tort actions should be decided in accordance with what is really a variant fault standard; this standard makes liability depend, not on a balancing of the interests of plaintiff and defendant, but simply on whether the defendant knew or should have known that he was creating a certain *level* of risk for persons in the position of the plaintiff. Since this is also the standard of liability which seems most plausibly to be suggested by the second stage of Epstein's argument for strict liability, and since the transition to the third stage is not, as I shall try to show, a move which can legitimately be made, I shall argue that Epstein is, in the end, best regarded as defending a type of fault theory and not a theory of strict liability at all.

It should be emphasized, however, that the conclusion that Epstein is best understood as defending a type of fault theory will only emerge as an interpretation of his work considered as a whole; the commitment to a standard of liability which is framed in terms of whether a defendant knew that he was creating a certain level of risk is made only implicitly, in the theory of causation, and is not in any event consistently adhered to. Epstein himself, moreover, would obviously reject the conclusion that he is really just presenting a type of fault theory, and there are certainly competing currents in his writings which suggest that his conception of liability in tort presupposes quite a different sort of answer to question *A* from that which was just considered. More particularly, there are indications that he would favour an answer to that question which took the second of the two tacks which it holds out, namely the adoption of a theory of truly strict liability, in which the defendant's knowledge of harm that will or might occur to others is simply not relevant. Three possible justifications for such a view, support for all of which can in some greater or lesser degree be found in Epstein's writings, will be considered.

(iii) The Concept of Property Entails Strict Liability

The first of these three possible justifications (and hence the basis of a third possible answer which might be given to question *A*) is suggested by the following passage from an article in which Epstein replies to certain criticisms advanced by Richard Posner:[14]

> In my view the proper conception of ownership compels the adoption of a strict liability principle. . . . [O]wnership is typically defined in terms of inviolability that in turn suggests absolute protection against all invasions. . . . [T]he dominant conception throughout [the case law] is that ownership rights are inviolate.

Epstein is here suggesting that a regime of strict liability in tort is directly entailed by the necessarily absolute nature of private property rights. He also maintains that this is recognized at common law, but that claim is backed up only by references to encroachment cases and to specific performance as being the usual remedy for breach of land-sale contracts. This falls some way short of answering Posner's point that a legal system which for the most part makes tort liability turn on the existence of negligence or of an intention to harm can hardly be said to have acknowledged property rights as absolute. In a more normative vein, after first asking why a plaintiff must "endure the deprivation of rights that can be prevented", Epstein says that "[w]here invasions of the person (or property) are imminent, a defendant should be subject to an injunction, whether the threat is of a deliberate, negligent, or accidental invasion". Stating that injunctions are not universally available only because of the "purely practical" problem that there is often uncertainty as to when an invasion will take place, he concludes that "if the conception of ownership gives injunctive relief without inquiry into

negligence or intention, then the law should award damages on those same principles whenever injunctions cannot be issued because of the danger of overbreadth under conditions of uncertainty".

Epstein's claim about the nature of private property rights does not appear to be necessitated, as a purely conceptual matter, by the ideas of ownership or private property as such, which would seem to be indeterminate so far as the choice among tort regimes is concerned;[15] certainly there is nothing contradictory about the idea of a private property regime in which entitlements are protected by a fault-based liability rule rather than by a rule of strict liability. As for the normative considerations which he discusses, the issue here is precisely what is to count as a "deprivation of [property] rights"; Epstein, however, simply asserts, rather than argues for, the conclusion that any physical interference whatsoever constitutes such a deprivation. He thus fails to consider the possibility that uncertainty about whether a physical interference is going to take place at some time in the future is not just a practical problem but a factor to be taken into account in determining whether any given interference that does occur should be regarded as constituting an infringement of rights (a possibility which, it should be noted, is strongly suggested by the emphasis that Epstein places upon a defendant's *knowledge* of harm or risk at the first two stages of his original argument for strict liability). Furthermore, any normative argument that Epstein might make to the effect that a private property regime necessarily entails a certain standard of liability in tort is very likely to turn out to be an argument that that is the correct liability rule *tout court*. He does not, for example, distinguish between arguments about what the correct standard of liability should be in cases of personal injury on the one hand, and what it should be in cases of damage to material resources on the other, even though it is at best artificial to assert that one has a property interest in one's person.[16] It is thus not at all clear what Epstein's claim about the nature of private property rights is supposed to add to his other arguments for strict liability.

(iv) The Defendant Would Have Borne the Loss Had He Harmed Himself

A second possible justification for a theory of tort liability which is truly strict, in the sense that the defendant's knowledge of certain or potential harm is not taken into account at all, would have us look to that aspect of Epstein's theory which is highlighted by the following sentences, taken from his original argument for strict liability that I quoted more fully earlier:[17]

> Had the Lake Erie Transportation Company owned both the dock and the ship, there could have been no lawsuit as a result of the incident. . . . There is no reason why the company as defendant in a lawsuit should be able to shift the loss in question because the dock belonged to someone else. . . . If the Transportation Company must bear all the costs in those cases in which it damages its own property, then it should bear those costs when it damages the property of another.

The present suggestion, which constitutes the basis for a fourth possible answer to question *A,* is that we are to take the proposed hypothetical seriously: if the defendant had harmed himself rather than another then he would have had to bear the loss, and this fact provides a positive reason for shifting it back to him when it turns out that it is someone else whom he has injured.

There are a number of difficulties with this line of reasoning, however, the most obvious being this: how can a fact of this sort provide any kind of justification, or part of a justification, for shifting a loss? What, for instance, does it add to the first stage of Epstein's original argument to say that the defendant in *Vincent v. Lake Erie* would have had to bear the loss himself if he had owned the plaintiff's dock? The essence of that stage of the argument seemed to be that the defendant had to make reparation because he had intentionally taken the plaintiff's property, without the latter's consent, in order to further his own ends. It is certainly true that the defendant can be said to have dealt with the plaintiff's property *as though* it were his own, a fact which seems to be central to Epstein's conclusion that reparation is called for, but it is not clear how the argument is strengthened by saying that the defendant would have had to bear the loss himself if that property *were* his own. The same point can be made in a slightly different way by asking what relevance the hypothetical consequences of *one* person's actions for himself could possibly have for the moral characterization of a situation that essentially involves *two* persons. By insisting that the answer to a hypothetical question about what one individual might do to himself necessarily bears on the proper reso-

lution of a moral issue that is bilateral in nature, Epstein appears to be committing the cardinal libertarian sin of failing to take seriously the difference between persons.[18]

A related difficulty with the suggested line of argument concerns the fact that a hypothetical which reduces a two-person situation to a one-person situation does not, without more, tell us which of the original two is to bear the loss. For example, if the defendant ship owner and the plaintiff dock owner had been the same person in the *Vincent* case, then it is presumably not only *qua* ship owner but *qua* dock owner that that person would have had to bear the loss himself. Why cannot we conclude from this that Holmes was right in asserting that "[t]he general principle of our law is that loss from accident must lie where it falls"?[19] The answer to this question which Epstein might want to give is that it is the defendant who has chosen to act, not the plaintiff, and that this is the crucial fact which distinguishes between them for the purposes of determining who must bear the loss. A requirement of volition is, moreover, clearly necessary in any event in order to exclude the epileptic who injures someone else in the course of his convulsions, or the person who is carried by others onto the plaintiff's land against his will, from automatically being caught by Epstein's hypothetical.[20] But as soon as one puts the case for strict liability in terms of the defendant's activity as against the plaintiff's passivity, then, once again, it is no longer clear what work is being done by the hypothetical; one need not refer to it in order to state the argument, as is demonstrated by this very simple but powerful formulation by Holmes:[21]

> Every man, it is said, has an absolute right to his person, and so forth, free from detriment at the hands of his neighbours. In the cases put, the plaintiff has done nothing; the defendant, on the other hand, has chosen to act. As between the two, the party whose voluntary conduct has caused the damage should suffer, rather than one who has had no share in producing it.

(v) Activity Versus Passivity

I hope that the discussion in the preceding section makes clear than an answer to Epstein's hypothetical question about the loss that a person would have had to bear if he had injured himself rather than another does not, in and of itself, give rise to a good reason for shifting to him any loss which in fact he did cause to another. The discussion does suggest, however, a third possible justification for a theory of truly strict liability. This line of argument, which also constitutes the fifth and final possible answer to question *A* that will be considered here, looks to the claim that the defendant chose to act whereas the plaintiff did not, so that the latter was merely passively absorbing the effects of the former's conduct. The essence of the argument is that the defendant, while pursuing his own ends, caused injury to the plaintiff, who must be regarded as simply an object of the defendant's activity, so that as between the two of them it is fairer that the defendant rather than the plaintiff bear the loss; otherwise, the defendant will take the benefits of his activity while effectively foisting its costs onto someone else. As Epstein says at one point:[22]

> Once a defendant is allowed to excuse himself
> on the grounds that he acted with due regard
> for the plaintiff, it follows that he will be able
> to keep the benefits of his own actions even
> as he imposes their costs upon a stranger.

To the extent that Epstein is attempting to defend a conception of truly strict liability, and hence one that should not be understood simply as a variant fault theory along the lines which were suggested earlier, I think that this sort of argument —formulated explicitly and then criticized by Holmes—must be regarded as lying at the heart of his position. Not only does it seem to be the most plausible reconstruction of that part of Epstein's discussion which focuses on what the hypothetical consequences of a person's actions for himself would have been, it also appears to be at least implicitly— and sometimes explicitly—presupposed by almost everything which he has to say in favour of a standard of strict liability in tort. He often refers to the unfairness of imposing the costs of one's actions on others,[23] for example, and he places much emphasis on situations in which the defendant had a choice in acting but the plaintiff did not.[24] Occasionally, moreover, he puts the argument for strict liability directly in terms of a distinction between activity and passivity, although when he does this he tends to equate the passivity of the plaintiff, not with doing nothing, but with doing nothing *wrong*[25]. The implications of this way of expressing the argument will be touched upon at the end of this section.

Holmes himself offered two replies to the argument for strict liability that he had formulated in terms of a distinction between the activity of the defendant and the passivity of the plaintiff: one is utilitarian in character, while the other looks to the fact that the argument "offend[s] the sense of justice".[26] The first of these counter-arguments, not having been framed in terms of individual moral right, will not be considered here.[27] The second asserts that it is only the existence of "an opportunity of choice with reference to the consequence complained of" which "distinguishes voluntary acts from spasmodic muscular contractions as a ground of liability", and that "a choice which entails a concealed consequence is as to that consequence no choice".[28] The essence of Holmes' objection is that an unforeseen consequence cannot be said to have been chosen, so that while the defendant may have chosen to act, he did not choose to cause injury or to create a risk of injury; it would therefore be unjust to hold him liable. As it stands, however, this reply does not really answer the argument for strict liability to which Holmes is responding, since the heart of the argument is that the defendant chose to *act,* not that he chose to cause harm. The apparent strength of the argument, and the reason that it emphasizes the defendant's activity as such, is that if the defendant did not have to make reparation then he would be able to retain the benefits of his actions while forcing a passive bystander to bear their costs. This aspect of the argument, which seems, at least on first reflection, to be a very powerful consideration, is independent of whether or not the defendant made a choice to impose those costs (or at least to impose the risk of their occurrence).

There is, however, a straightforward but conclusive objection to the argument for strict liability under scrutiny. Stated in its simplest form, it is that there is no such thing as a passive bystander. Consider, to begin with, a situation in which both the plaintiff and the defendant are active at the moment that the former is injured: an example would be an accident on the highway in which two vehicles collide while both are moving and under the control of their respective drivers. In these circumstances it seems clear not only that no distinction can be drawn between one party's activity and the other's passivity which would permit the justification for strict liability being considered here to take hold, but that in this sort of case it is impossible to apply a pure standard of strict liability in any event. Neither party alone could be said to have "caused" whatever injury might have resulted (whether it had been sustained by the other party, by himself, or by both), so that in the absence of compliance with some sort of fault criterion of liability any shifting of loss would seem, from a purely moral point of view, to be quite arbitrary.[29]

It is interesting to note in this regard that trespass was first displaced by negligence in highway cases, and that even such a staunch defender of strict liability as Baron Bramwell[30] was led to observe that "[w]here two carriages come in collision, if there is no negligence in either it is as much the act of the one driver as of the other that they meet".[31] The general point, that a strict liability standard is impossible to apply where both parties are active, had in fact received at least implicit judicial acknowledgement even in the heyday of trespass. In the well-known case of *Weaver v. Ward*,[32] which involved a shooting incident, the court stated that the defence of inevitable accident would apply "if here the defendant had said, that the plaintiff ran across his piece when it was discharging . . .". Interestingly, this situation is regarded by the court as equivalent to one in which there has been no exercise of volition by the defendant at all, "[a]s if a man by force take my hand and strike you . . .". There is, in fact, something plausible about this asserted equivalence, since in neither situation can it be said, to use Holmes' words, that "the plaintiff has done nothing [while] the defendant . . . has chosen to act".[33] (Of course, the reason that this cannot be said is different in each of the two cases).

Consider next a situation in which, at the time of their interaction, the defendant is engaged in activity but the plaintiff is not. Is there any principled basis for distinguishing between this situation and that in which both parties were simultaneously active at the time the injury occurred? Suppose that the defendant drives into and damages the plaintiff's parked car. I presume it is obvious that it cannot be said without more that the defendant is liable, simply because he was active while the plaintiff was not. The question of who should bear the loss in this situation would seem necessarily to turn on such considerations as whether the defendant was speeding, for example, or whether the plaintiff had parked his car in a dangerous spot (in the middle of the road just beyond a sharp curve, perhaps). The tort inquiry, in other words, must inevitably place under scrutiny actions which were performed by *both* parties—the defendant's act of driving, on the one hand, and the plaintiff's act of parking his car, on the other—even though one of these actions took place prior to the actual occurrence of injury. The plaintiff could only be said to have "done nothing",

to use Holmes' phrase, if we were to impose an artificially narrow time span on the way that we view his interaction with the defendant. Tort law does not, in general, restrict its consideration of the activities of the defendant to those which are near in time or space to the occurrence of the injury, however, and there is no reason in principle why the plaintiff should be treated any differently.

The point that has just been made in connection with the example of the parked car is a general one. Except in unusual circumstances it can be said of any plaintiff that he made a choice to be where he (or his property) was when the harm he suffered occurred, and, just as the defendant was pursuing his own purposes in choosing to act as he did, so in making *his* choice the plaintiff was presumably attempting to further ends of his own. Those anomalous cases of which this cannot be said, as for example where thieves break into the plaintiff's locked car, steal it, and then leave it in a place where the defendant subsequently collides with it, can be set to one side. They are similar to cases in which the defendant is not subject to liability because he did not exercise his volition, for instance because his hand was moved by another, or because he was suffering from an epileptic fit. In general, then, it would seem that, so far as the determination of who is responsible for a loss which has resulted from the interaction of two parties is concerned, there is no principled distinction to be drawn between cases involving an active plaintiff and those in which the plaintiff is supposedly passive. As long as we view the matter in a sufficiently unrestricted time frame, and we have no good reason to do anything else, the interaction between the plaintiff and the defendant which gave rise to injury to the former (and perhaps to the latter as well) is *always,* except in those anomalous cases just discussed, the result of choices to act which were made by both parties. While each was engaged in the pursuit of his own advantage they interacted in such a way that at least one of them was injured, but the determination of which one that was depends simply on empirical considerations: where currently active A trips over currently passive B, for example, either or both or neither might be injured.

There is thus no simple distinction to be drawn between the parties to a tort action such that one can be labelled the "active" injurer, and the other the "passive" victim. This fact gives rise to two related consequences for a theory of strict liability, the first of which has to do with the theory's justification. As I have tried to show, the only plausible argument in moral terms for a standard of strict liability rests upon the very distinction between the activity of the defendant and the passivity of the plaintiff which it does not seem possible to draw. Even the most straightforward sort of case, in which a currently active defendant applies direct force to and injures a currently passive plaintiff—this being what Epstein would call an instance of the paradigm of force—involves an interaction which is in general the result of choices to act that were made by both parties, where each can be assumed to have been engaged in the pursuit of his own individual interest. The simple idea that one party is benefiting from, while the other is bearing at least some of the costs of, a single action (or series of actions) performed by the former is thus a completely misleading picture of the relationship between them. In all but the anomalous cases previously described, we are necessarily dealing in tort law with an intersection of *two* choices to act, not with the effects for one person of a single such choice which has been made by another.[34]

This last point is related to the second of the two consequences for a theory of strict liability which I said were entailed by the impossibility of distinguishing between an active injurer and a passive victim; here what is called into question is not simply the theory's justification but its coherence. The difficulty has already been anticipated in the discussion of two simultaneously active parties, but it is not limited to that situation. If an injury to A is the result of choices to act which were made by both A and B, the most natural and intuitive conclusion is that the actions of both were *causes* of the injury. This also would be the conclusion of the most sophisticated theoretical account of causation in tort law of which I am aware, namely the analysis recently advanced by Richard Wright.[35] Elaborating on an idea of Hart and Honoré's, Wright explicates the concept of a "cause" as a necessary element in a set of conditions that together are jointly sufficient to produce the effect in question, from which it would again follow that the actions of A and B, both being necessary elements in a set of sufficient conditions, were also both causes of the injury to A. If that is so, however, then a general standard of truly strict liability, which requires that A's loss be borne by *the* party who caused it, will fail to generate dispositive results: quite apart from the question of justification, the theory will be incapable of determinate formulation.[36] If this conclusion is correct, then that would

lend some plausibility, based on theoretical considerations, to the claim of many legal historians that at common law liability in trespass never was truly strict.[37] It should be emphasized, however, that the conclusion applies only to a *general* standard of strict liablity. The coherence of what might be called localized standards, in which liability can only be said to be "strict" relative to certan specified preconditions having been met, such as, for example, the defendant's having manufactured a defective product,[38] or his having kept something on his land which would be dangerous if it escaped,[39] is not called into question. It is another matter, and not one that can be dealt with here, whether such localized standards should properly be called strict at all.

Epstein, of course, builds his theory of liability upon the foundation of a theory of causation which is purportedly capable of isolating a specific action as *the* cause of a given injury. This theory will be examined in detail in section 3, where I shall argue that it is, at least in part, really a theory of personal responsibility: it contains implicit normative elements which, while they permit determinate judgments of liability to be made, do so only at the cost of transforming the theory of liability into one that does not adhere to a strict standard. It is, as I have already indicated, best understood as a type of fault theory. Epstein's putative analysis of causation turns out, therefore, not to offer any reason to question the conclusion that a general standard of truly strict liability is an inevitably indeterminate notion, but it is worth emphasizing that even if it or some other account of causation did challenge that conclusion the problem with the *justification* of the standard would remain. . . .

3. Epstein's Theory of Causation

(i) The Theory

Epstein begins his discussion of causation by arguing that a satisfactory account of the concept is not provided by the so-called "but-for" test.[40] A counterfactual proposition which asks whether the plaintiff would not have been injured but for the action of the defendant is not, he says, the "semantic equivalent" of the simple indicative assertion that the defendant caused injury to the plaintiff. There are, moreover, many situations in which we would not even be tempted to say that A was responsible for an injury sustained by B, even though it is true that

B would not have been injured had A not acted as he did. Epstein thinks that this "affinity for absurd hypotheticals" is an argument for abandoning the but-for test "as even a tentative account of the concept of causation". What has happened instead, however, is, he says, that the but-for test has come to be regarded simply as the first, "philosophical" stage of a two-step process, the second stage being the introduction of limitations on liability under the rubric of "proximate cause". But, he notes, the concept of causation is not in fact generally thought to possess any hard content beyond the but-for test, so that these limitations are accordingly regarded as being necessarily grounded in policy and nothing else. Following (as he thinks) Hart and Honoré, Epstein maintains that both this premise and the corresponding conclusion are deeply mistaken.

In his alternative account of causation Epstein says that rather than attempt to offer a general semantic equivalent of the concept he will instead focus on four paradigm cases which all fall under the proposition "A caused B harm".[41] These four paradigms, which are apparently not exhaustive,[42] are: (i) "A hit B" (the paradigm of force); (ii) "A frightened B" (the paradigm of fright or shock); (iii) "A compelled C to hit B" (the paradigm of compulsion); and (iv) "A created a dangerous condition that resulted in B's harm" (the paradigm of dangerous conditions). Each of these paradigms is said to involve a "nonreciprocal causal relation" between A's conduct and some protected interest of B's, which for our purposes will always be the latter's person or property.[43] (Notice that the idea of a non-reciprocal relation is, like the domination metaphor discussed in the preceding section, a hazy surrogate for a more hard-edged distinction between an active injurer and a passive victim; it also resembles the domination notion in possessing no justificatory power of its own.)

The fourth of Epstein's causal paradigms, namely the paradigm of dangerous conditions, he breaks down into three separate classes of cases.[44] The first is that of things which, because they retain a large measure of potential energy that is susceptible to easy release, are inherently dangerous; stored explosives are an example. The second class of dangerous conditions involves the placing of a thing not dangerous in itself in a dangerous position. One sort of instance presupposes the recognition of a right of way, an example of which would be leaving a roller skate in a walkway. Another involves the creation of a condition of instability, such as placing a large rock in a precarious position on top of a hillside. The third

class of dangerous conditions is concerned with products or other things which are dangerous because they are defective. In all such cases "the person who made the product has created a dangerous condition that causes harm when subjected to the stress that it was designed to receive when used in its intended manner".[45] Epstein acknowledges that the paradigm of dangerous conditions gives rise to an appearance of circularity since it defines (a dimension of) causation in terms of the creation of conditions that "result in harm", but says that there is not, in fact, anything circular about this since the expression "result in" is intended to cover only instances of the first three paradigms.

Epstein asserts at one point that "the difficult question is often . . . whether there are in fact any means to distinguish between causation and responsibility, so close is the connection between what a man does and what he is answerable for".[46] He nonetheless regards the four causal paradigms as creating a *prima facie* presumption of liability only. There are three sorts of effective defences which Epstein says can be set up against a *prima facie* causal case, these being causal defences, the defence of assumption of risk, and the defence of plaintiff's trespass.[47] He describes a number of allegations in reply that a plaintiff might then be able to make to a sufficient affirmative defence, and he also sets out various subsequent pleas which one or the other of the parties might be able to rely upon at yet further stages in the sequentially-developed procedural process within which the argument between the two is envisaged as unfolding: the plaintiff might be able to reply to a valid defence that the defendant intentionally harmed him,[48] for example, at which point it might be open to the defendant to plead self-defence or consent.[49] Since our present concern is with Epstein's analysis of causation, the only aspect of his system of pleadings which will be considered here is the category of causal defences.

Epstein states that more than one of the four basic causal paradigms can apply in a single case, and that a relationship of "causal priority" sometimes obtains between paradigms which allows for the possibility of causal defences in these multi-paradigm situations.[50] Suppose, for example, that B compels A to hit B, which is a situation involving two paradigms, namely force and compulsion. Epstein says that the latter constitutes a causal defence to the former because if C compelled A to hit B then A would have an action over against C, and "[t]here is no reason to disturb that judgment as to causal priorities" where B and C are the same person: since compulsion has priority in this sense over force, A has a good causal defence to an action brought against him by B. Epstein maintains that similar reasoning also demonstrates the priority of the paradigm of dangerous conditions over that of force, thereby supporting the conclusion that if A applies force to a dangerous condition created by B, with the result that B is injured, then A again has an effective causal defence. The significance of the priority of the dangerous conditions paradigm is not limited to the establishment of a defence, however, since it also entails that if it was A rather than B who was injured in the situation just described, then A would be entitled to recover his loss from B. Indeed, as Epstein points out in his earliest article on strict liability, if this were not so "then in effect no dangerous conditions could ever rise to causal significance".[51]

(ii) The Theory Analyzed

Epstein's account of causation can be criticized on a number of different grounds, and I shall be focusing here only on those which bear in a fairly direct way on the discussion in section 2 above.[52] His rejection of the but-for test of causation, for example, is vulnerable to several objections, perhaps the most telling of which is that he himself seems to rely on it.[53] The most relevant objection for our present purposes, however, concerns Epstein's argument that the but-for test should be abandoned as an account of causation because it gives rise to absurd hypotheticals. The essence of this argument is that the test is a bad one because it would require us to say that A caused harm to B even in situations where it would be ridiculous to hold A responsible for B's loss. But this is only a criticism of the but-for test as an account of causation if causation and responsibility are taken to be necessarily coterminous concepts. It is of course true, as we saw in section 2, that Epstein presents arguments designed to show that these concepts are indeed coterminous (at least on a first approximation), but, as he himself makes clear, those arguments depend on the assumption that the concept of causation has a content which will permit it to be "explicated and shown to be a suitable basis for the assignment of responsibility".[54] The whole point of Epstein's discussion of causation is to demonstrate that that assumption is justified, however, which means that he must produce an analysis of the concept which is independent of any claims about how responsibility should be assigned; in the context of his overall project it is therefore question-begging to argue against a particular account of causation on the basis of intuitive judgments about who should be responsible for a given type of loss.

The unsoundness of this particular argument which Epstein puts forward in support of the conclusion that the but-for test should be rejected does not, of course, show that his own analysis of causation is defective. But difficulties similar to the one which arises with respect to that argument are also to be found in his own positive account of causation. This can be seen particularly clearly in his discussion of the paradigm of dangerous conditions, which, as Epstein correctly remarks, requires that a distinction be drawn between "dangerous" conditions on the one hand and "mere" conditions on the other. This immediately leads one to ask why it is that only dangerous conditions are to be regarded as causally significant, a question which Epstein addresses in the following terms:[55]

> If all conditions, and not only dangerous ones, were given causal status, then in almost every case the conduct of both the plaintiff and the defendant would both be the "cause" of the harm in question, as a few examples help make plain. H leaves her carving knife in her kitchen drawer. A thief steals the knife and uses it to wound I. Has H caused I harm in any sense of the term? J leaves his car parked on the street. During the night a cyclone picks the car up and carries it along for a half mile until it falls on top of K. Has J caused K harm? The answer to these questions is no. Unlike the cases of dangerous conditions above, neither H nor J could be sued on a theory which alleges that they created a dangerous condition that resulted in harm. It might be possible to show on the strength of other facts not presented that these acts were dangerous when performed. But they are not dangerous as described, for in none of these cases did the prospective defendants make a store of energy which was released by the act of a third party or by natural events.

From the perspective of the discussion in section 2 the distinction between "mere" and "dangerous" conditions is of crucial importance for Epstein's theory, because it constitutes the basis of his analysis in causal terms of interactions between an active party and one who is currently passive—for example,

A driving into B's parked car—of the sort that I contended were problematic for a theory of truly strict liability. Unless it can be said that an action (past or present) of one or the other of the parties was "the" cause of the harm, then it will not be possible to formulate and apply a standard of truly strict liability. Epstein shows a clear awareness in the above-quoted passage of the danger that is posed for a theory of strict liability by the conclusion that "the conduct of both the plaintiff and the defendant [is] the 'cause' of the harm in question", but he thinks he can avoid it in an acceptable way by means of his distinction between dangerous and mere conditions. His motivation is thus clear, but one must still ask what the justification is for "giving" causal status to dangerous conditions alone. In the quoted passage Epstein's answer seems to be that persons who create non-dangerous conditions "could [not] be sued on a theory which alleges that they created a dangerous condition that resulted in harm". This is even more blatantly question-begging than his argument rejecting the but-for test as an account of causation, so let us suppose that what he meant to say is that on no plausible theory of liability could H or J in his examples be held liable for the harm which results to I and K. But this is still just arguing backwards from a conclusion about responsibility to a conclusion about causation, whereas, as was pointed out in the discussion of Epstein's rejection of the but-for test, the general form of his argument requires that the concept of causation receive an independent analysis.

The question-begging nature of Epstein's claim that dangerous conditions have causal status but mere conditions do not becomes clearer if we consider exactly what it is about "dangerous" conditions that warrants our giving them this label. As Warren Seavey correctly pointed out, both "dangerous" and "risky" are concepts which are relative to the information that was or should have been possessed by the actor whose conduct is being evaluated.[56] Consider Epstein's cyclone example in the passage quoted above. If J had no reason to suspect that a cyclone was going to occur, as Epstein is presumably assuming, then of course his act of parking the car on the street could not be considered dangerous. Suppose, however, that the meteorology service has not only managed to predict the cyclone, but knows enough about the factors which influence cyclone movement to be able to say that there is a 70% chance that the cyclone will pass along J's street. Assuming that J has easy access to this infor-

mation, his parking the car on the street might now well be said to be dangerous, even though the physical nature of his act, as well as the objective likelihood of a cyclone picking up the car and dumping it on another person, remain unchanged.[57] The normative questions of whether or not J should have possessed the relevant information, and, if so, of whether the probability of harm was sufficiently great that he should not have left the car on the street (because doing so would be "dangerous"), seem most naturally described as issues of personal responsibility rather than as issues of causation: the causal role in K's injury of J's act of parking the car appears to be the same in both versions of the hypothetical. To ask whether J's act was dangerous is really no different from asking whether, in the usual language of tort law, the car's being picked up by a cyclone and then being dropped on another person was reasonably foreseeable—i.e. whether in all the circumstances J should have foreseen a sufficiently great probability of harm. The answer to this question is not, however, an empirically verifiable matter of the sort that Epstein seems generally to be assuming is involved in causal inquiries.[58]

Epstein recognizes that the term "dangerous" often carries with it connotations of risk and probability of harm, but says that he is using the expression in a restricted sense "with the emphasis upon the 'potential' to cause harm in the narrow sense of that term".[59] It is not at all clear what he means by this, but if the idea is that an act is to be characterized as "dangerous" in objective terms of some sort, independently of the knowledge that was or should have been possessed by the actor, then the term is not only being used in a way that is very much at odds with its usual sense, but also in a way that seems to be inconsistent with Epstein's own understanding of which conditions are dangerous and which are not: if a cyclone picks up a car from a certain spot and drops it on someone, then I presume it was "objectively" dangerous (however that notion is properly to be understood) to have left it at that location. It seems likely, however, that Epstein is not rejecting the relativity of the notion of dangerousness to the knowledge that was or should have been possessed by the actor at the time that he acted, but is simply rejecting a certain conception of which risks or dangers are unacceptable that is framed in terms of a balancing of the plaintiff's and the defendant's interests. This interpretation finds support in the fact that immediately after Epstein says that he is using the term "dangerous" in a restricted sense he goes on to mention the Learned Hand formulation of the negligence standard, and to say that the paradigm of dangerous conditions does not require a cost-benefit analysis to establish the causal connection between the defendant's conduct and the plaintiff's harm.

In section 2(ii) I discussed the possibility that Epstein's theory, or at least certain parts of it, should not be regarded as rejecting the relevance of the defendant's knowledge of risk or probability of harm to his potential liability, but only as rejecting any balancing of the defendant's and the plaintiff's respective interests in the determination of who should bear the loss; his use of the term "dangerous" should, I think, be understood in this light. If that is so, however, then Epstein's theory of causation is better regarded as, at least in part, a theory of responsibility, and his theory of strict liability as a variant fault approach. The conception of fault which emerges here involves not a balancing of interests, but rather a consideration of whether the creator of the condition in question was or should have been aware that its creation imposed a certain *level* of risk upon others. Epstein is, in other words, implicitly envisaging a cut-off point between high, unacceptable risks (those which are associated with dangerous conditions), and low, acceptable risks whose creation will not lead to liability in tort (those associated with mere conditions). The creation of any condition poses some risk, however remote, to somebody, so that if there were no such cut-off point then the distinction between dangerous and mere conditions would collapse. Epstein does not, of course, say anything about the difficult question of how the cut-off point is to be determined, since he does not explicitly acknowledge that it exists.

At one point Epstein says that in the context of the paradigm of dangerous conditions the term "dangerous" does not function as a separate substantive requirement which has been added to a causal element of "conditions" standing alone, in a way that would be analogous to adding it as an extra substantive requirement ("much akin to negligence") to the *prima facie* case which is determined by the paradigm of force.[60] Yet he has distinguished between dangerous and mere conditions, not in terms of an independent analysis of causation, but only in terms of intuitive judgments about who should bear a loss that depend, at least implicitly, on the knowledge of a certain level of risk that was or should have been possessed by the creator of the condition; the unavoidable conclusion would thus seem to be that the term "dangerous" functions in Epstein's theory in ex-

actly the way that he denies. The question that then arises, however, is why this "separate substantive requirement" of fault—to be understood, as I have indicated, in terms of the defendant's (constructive) knowledge of the level of risk which he has imposed upon others—is *not* extended to the paradigm of force. There is no principled basis for limiting this requirement to the paradigm of dangerous conditions,[61] and the only reason why the failure to apply it to the paradigm of force does not result in the sort of indeterminacy to which I said that a general theory of strict liability is inevitably vulnerable is that Epstein applies a kind of implicit closure rule: when A applies force to B, B must bear any loss if he created a dangerous condition, but otherwise A bears the loss. (The basis of this rule is the notion of causal priority, to be further discussed below). Thus while Epstein's theory of causation may in part be a theory of responsibility, it is a theory that contains serious inconsistencies.

The conclusion that Epstein's theory of causation contains an implicit theory of responsibility finds further support in what he has to say about the notion of causal priority. His argument that compulsion constitutes a valid defence to the use of force is, as we have seen, that since a defendant has a cause of action over against a third person who compelled him to hit the plaintiff, he should likewise have a valid defence in the main action where the person who compelled his use of force was the plaintiff himself: the "judgment as to causal priorities" should be the same in both cases. But the argument as so far stated assumes, rather than demonstrates, that compulsion has causal priority over force in the third person case, so it is still necessary to ask why that is so. To the extent that Epstein provides an answer to this question it can be discerned in the following passage:[62]

> [An action over against a third person] is allowed on the strength of the judgment that as between the person who strikes the blow and the one who makes him do it, responsibility should rest with the latter. There is no reason to disturb that judgment as to causal priorities now that it is the plaintiff who induces, but does not deliver, the blow. . . . Force has a causal priority only to the extent that it, unlike compulsion, must be present as a matter of fact in each case in which there is the infliction of physical harm. Yet compulsion, whether by force or fright, has a distinct

priority over force in the sense that it determines responsibility where both are involved in the case, regardless of who is injured.

That an issue which is supposedly causal in nature is being directly determined by an intuitive judgment concerning who should bear responsibility for a loss could not, I think, be clearer. Here, however, it is perhaps less easy than in the case of the paradigm of dangerous conditions to discern what the underlying conception of fault should be taken to be.[63]

At a number of different points Epstein can thus be seen to be presenting intuitive judgments about personal responsibility in the guise of causal judgments. Not only does this have the consequence that his analysis of causation is in part really a theory of responsibility, it also means that that theory, because it is never explicitly acknowledged to be a normative account of personal responsibility, is given neither a systematic development nor a clear moral foundation: Epstein's disguised judgments of responsibility generally do not rise above the level of unconnected intuitions. Furthermore, the hybrid nature of the putative analysis of causation—in part a theory of causation and in part a theory of responsibility, with neither aspect very clearly differentiated—makes it easier for inconsistent elements to work their way into the theory which render it unsatisfactory as an account of either causation or responsibility. We have already seen an example of this in the inconsistency between the paradigms of force and of dangerous conditions regarding the imposition of what amounts to a substantive requirement of fault. Another instance concerns judgments of causal priority between actions. Epstein advances a basic form of argument for the priority of one causal paradigm over another which is, as we have seen, grounded directly in intuitions about personal responsibility. He later introduces another, apparently more causally-oriented notion of "dependence", however, which justifies judgments of priority between individual actions or "forces" rather than between causal paradigms as such (or so one is lead to guess, since he does not explicitly distinguish the two types of priority), and reliance on this notion seems to entail consequences which are somewhat different from those to which the more central aspects of his theory apparently lead.

What Epstein means by "dependence" is not at all clear, since he only gives us examples to go on.[64] An act of hitting is said to be dependent on an act of blocking the hitter's right of way, so that the latter act has priority over the former and the blocker is to be regarded as *prima facie* liable, but no priority can be established between acts of blocking and of speeding "because each proceeded independently of constraints placed upon it by the other".[65] Nor is there any priority between the two acts of hitting which are involved in, for example, an automobile collision, since we are dealing with forces "created independently of one another".[66] To the extent that this notion of dependence can be made sense of,[67] it would seem that an act of hitting is dependent on an act of blocking a right of way, not because there is a right of way involved, but simply because the blocker is wherever he is. An act of hitting a passive party who is not obstructing a right of way would thus still seem to be dependent on an act of blocking: it is true that the passive party is no longer blocking the hitter's right of way but only his path, so that the act of blocking is now a "mere" rather than a "dangerous" condition, but there is no obvious basis for attributing any significance to this difference. Yet Epstein would clearly want to say that the applier of force should be regarded, in the situation where the person who was hit was not obstructing a right of way, as *prima facie* liable for any harm that might result. . . .

5. Conclusion

I have concentrated in this paper on Epstein's own theory of causation, without considering the analyses of the concept which have been put forward by other writers, because he develops it in the specific context of a theory of strict liability. There is, however, no other account of causation in tort law of which I am aware that successfully demonstrates that it is possible to isolate, on non-evaluative or non-normative grounds alone, "the" cause of an injury. Richard Wright has argued very convincingly, for example, that Hart and Honoré's analysis of causation[68] in terms of ordinary language is really best understood as a theory of responsibility.[69] As mentioned in section 2(v), Wright grounds his own theory of causation on their idea that a cause is a necessary element in a set of conditions which together are jointly sufficient to produce the effect in question, concluding that this analysis not only initially explicates the concept of causation but, in effect, exhausts it; from this it follows that so-called proximate causation has nothing to do with causation properly understood. If Wright is correct in this conclusion, as it seems to me that he is, then not only would the act of an "active" party which led to and coincided in time with the occurrence of a given injury, and the preceding act of a "passive" party which led to that person or his property being at the site where the harmful interaction took place, both be causes of the injury, but there would be nothing further to be said about which was the "real" (or the "true" or the "proximate") cause;[70] the determination of who should bear the loss is necessarily an issue to be decided in accordance with a theory of responsibility which, while it will build upon the concept of causation, will not coincide with it. This, however, is just another way of stating that a generalized theory of truly strict liability is impossible.

The theory of tort liability which Epstein develops at some length and which he characterizes as strict in fact implicitly incorporates, as we have seen, a distinctive conception of fault that looks to the level of risk which one person has imposed upon another. It is important to emphasize that this understanding of fault is very different from that which underlies the Learned Hand test, since it does not involve a balancing of the respective interests of plaintiff and defendant or, more generally, of the costs and benefits to society at large. The most fundamental theme of Epstein's work on tort law is, I would suggest, not the defence of strict liability but rather the rejection of this kind of balancing. Consider, for example, the following passage from his recent book *Takings:*[71]

> A negligence rule—at least any patterned on the famous Hand formula of *United States v. Carroll Towing Co.*—states that harm to person or property otherwise tortious shall be excused if the benefits of not preventing the harm are greater than the expected costs of the harm itself. In essence, therefore, the formula allows a defendant to trade the benefits that he (or society at large) receives from his own conduct against the costs inflicted upon the plaintiff.
>
> The objection to this general negligence rule is that it refuses to recognize the moral necessity that the defendant—even if his conduct should not *ex ante* be enjoined—at the very least should be required *prima facie* to pay for the harm his conduct has caused to the person or property of others.

Epstein's argument that the Learned Hand test inappropriately permits one person to impose costs upon others for the sole reason that the personal or social benefits of his activity exceeds those costs is a powerful one. As the discussion in section 2(v) showed, however, it cannot be translated into a defence of general strict liability. From the point of view of individual moral rights the most plausible alternative to the Learned Hand test would instead appear to be the level-of-risk idea which Epstein not only implicitly relies upon at various points but which is also suggested by the second stage of his own original argument for strict liability.[72]

A conception of fault along these lines in fact predominates in the positive law of England and the Commonwealth. The leading English case on the negligence standard is *Bolton v. Stone,*[73] in which a ball hit from the defendants' cricket ground struck the plaintiff in a nearby residential street. The House of Lords held for the defendants, and in the course of his judgment in the case Lord Reid said the following:[74]

> In the crowded conditions of modern life even the most careful person cannot avoid creating some risks and accepting others. What a man must not do, and what I think a careful man tries not to do, is to create a risk which is substantial. . . . In my judgment the test to be applied here is whether the risk of damage to a person on the road was so small that a reasonable man in the position of the appellants, considering the matter from the point of view of safety, would have thought it right to refrain from taking steps to prevent the danger.
>
> In considering that matter I think that it would be right to take into account not only how remote is the chance that a person might be struck but also how serious the consequences are likely to be if a person is struck; but I do not think that it would be right to take account of the difficulty of remedial measures. If cricket cannot be played on a ground without creating a substantial risk, then it should not be played there at all.

Not only does Lord Reid maintain, in common with the other judges in the House of Lords,[75] that liability should turn on a distinction between levels of risk, but he also explicitly denies that the court should take account of the costs which would be incurred in eliminating or decreasing the risk.[76] He thus quite clearly rejects the balancing conception of fault which had been articulated by Learned Hand only several years previously.[77]

The conclusion that Lord Reid's formulation of the negligence standard is, so far as individual moral rights are concerned, the most appropriate one does not, of course, automatically follow from the rejection of the Learned Hand test: an independent justification in positive terms is obviously required. Nor can it be denied that this approach gives rise to certain apparent difficulties, the most obvious being the question of how one is to draw the line between substantial and non-substantial risks. These are not matters which can be considered here; a more thorough explication and defence of Lord Reid's concep- tion of fault—the same conception which is implic- itly adopted by Epstein—will have to await another occasion.[78] For now it must suffice simply to point out that, despite the failure of Epstein's project of developing a general theory of truly strict liability, he may nonetheless have anticipated the correct an- swer to the important question of how the standard of care in negligence law should best be understood. It may yet turn out to be the case, in other words, that once his general theory has been properly in- terpreted and appropriately modified, it can be shown to be fundamentally right.

---

1. See e.g. Richard Posner, "A Theory of Negligence" (1972). 1 *J. Leg. Studies* 29: *The Economic Analysis of Law* (2nd ed., Boston: Little, Brown, 1977).

2. Ronald Dworkin, *Law's Empire* (Cambridge, Mass.: Belknap Press, 1986), ch. 8.

3. See e.g. Ernest Weinrib, "Toward a Moral Theory of Negligence Law" (1983). 2 *Law and Phil* 37: "The Insurance Justification and Private Law" (1985). 14 *J. Leg. Studies* 681.

4. See e.g. Guido Calabresi and Jon T. Hirschoff, "Toward a Test for Strict Liability in Torts" (1972), 81 *Yale L.J.* 1055. In his later work, however, Calabresi is probably best regarded as not de- fending a true theory of strict liability. See n. 36, *infra*.

5. See particularly Richard Epstein, "A Theory of Strict Liability" (1973), 2 *J. Leg. Studies* 151 (hereafter "Strict Liability"); "De- fenses and Subsequent Pleas in a System of Strict Liability" (1974), 3 *J. Leg. Studies* 165 (hereafter "Defenses and Subse- quent Pleas"). These two papers have been reprinted together in Epstein, *A Theory of Strict Liability: Toward a Reformulation of Tort Law* (San Francisco: Cato Institute, 1980). All references in the present article are, however, to the original papers.

6. Robert Nozick, *Anarchy, State, and Utopia* (New York: Basic Books, 1974). See e.g. the reference to unintentional and acci- dental boundary-crossings at 71.

7. This understanding has been adopted not only by Posner, who defends negligence on grounds of economic efficiency, but also by theorists such as Dworkin and Weinrib, who put forward justifications of the fault-based approach which are premised on theories of individual moral right. See references in notes 1–3, *supra*.

8. (1910), 109 Minn. 456, 124 N.W. 221 (S. C. Minn.).

9. Epstein, "Strict Liability", *supra* n. 5 at 158–60.

10. Epstein refers explicitly to tortious acts as "forced takings" in "Causation and Corrective Justice: A Reply to Two Critics" (1979), 8 *J. Leg. Studies* 477 at 501. In his recent book, *Takings: Private Property and the Power of Eminent Domain* (Cam- bridge, Mass.: Harvard University Press, 1985), he emphasizes at 37–41 the similarity, from the point of view of tort law, be- tween conversion and destruction; at 74 he says that "torts themselves are a subclass of takings".

11. Oliver Wendell Holmes, *The Common Law*, Mark DeWolfe Howe, ed. (Boston: Little, Brown, 1963), at 76.

12. In *U.S. v. Carroll Towing Co.* (1947), 159 F. (2d) 169 (2d Cir- cuit), Learned Hand J. said that a person is negligent if the cost of taking adequate precautions is less than what the cost of the injury would be, were it to occur, multiplied by the probability of its occurrence.

13. Richard Epstein, "Intentional Harms" (1975), 4 *J. Leg. Studies* 391 at 398 (emphasis added). There are also many references throughout Epstein's work on tort law to the negligence standard as being defined by the Learned Hand test: see, for example,

14. Epstein, "Causation and Corrective Justice", *supra* n. 10 at 500–501.

15. *Cf.* Weinrib, "Toward a Moral Theory of Negligence Law", *supra* n. 3 at 60–62.

16. *Cf.* A. M. Honoré, "Ownership", in A. G. Guest, ed., *Oxford Es- says in Jurisprudence* (Oxford: University Press, 1961) 107 at 129. It is true that Epstein himself often speaks in terms of own- ing one's own person or body, but when anything might turn on the point he tends to be more circumspect. Thus, in "Causa- tion and Corrective Justice", *supra* n. 10 at 500, he first says that "it by no means contorts the English language to say that each person owns his own body", but then goes on in a footnote to state that "[if] the ownership language does seem artificial, the language of 'personal integrity' can be substituted without change of effect".

17. Epstein, "Strict Liability", *supra* n. 5 at 158; *cf.* "Intentional Harms", *supra* n. 13 at 398.

18. See e.g. Nozick, *supra* n. 6 at 28–35.

19. Holmes, *The Common Law, supra* n. 11 at 76; *cf.* Izhak Engiand, "The System Builders: A Critical Appraisal of Modern American Tort Theory" (1980), 9 *J. Leg. Studies* 27 at 61–62.

20. *Cf.* Epstein, "Strict Liability", *supra* n. 5 at 166; Weinrib, "To- ward a Moral Theory of Negligence Law", *supra* n. 3 at 58–59.

21. Holmes, *The Common Law, supra* n. 11 at 68.

22. "Intentional Harms", *supra* n. 13 at 398; *cf.* Epstein, "Strict Lia- bility", *supra* n. 5 at 159. This aspect of the argument for strict liability was noticed by Baron Bramwell in *Bamford v. Turnley* (1862), 3 B. & S. 66 at 85, 122 E.R. 27 at 33 (Ex. Ch.): "It is for the public benefit that trains should run, but not unless they pay their expences. If one of those expences is the burning down of a wood of such value that the railway owners would not run the train and burn down the wood if it were their own, neither is it for the public benefit they should if the wood is not their own. If, though the wood were their own, they would still find it compensated thus to run trains at the cost of burn- ing the wood, then they obviously ought to compensate the owner of such wood, not being themselves, if they burn it down in making their gains." On the basis of considerations of justice Bramwell thus argues, in effect, for Pareto-superiority over a Kaldor-Hicks conception of economic efficiency. (Notice the similarity to Epstein's argument concerning what the hypo- thetical consequences of a defendant's actions for himself would have been had he, and not the plaintiff, owned the prop- erty affected.) But as Ronald Coase demonstrates in "The Prob- lem of Social Cost" (1960), 3 *J. of L. & Econ.* 1 at 30–34— by means, interestingly enough of a discussion of the same ex- ample employed by Bramwell of a railway burning down neighbouring woods—the economically efficient result will not

necessarily be achieved by always making the railway liable. The criticism which will be offered here of the claim that it is necessarily *just* always to make the railway liable parallels, up to a point, Coase's criticism of the Pigouvian claim that that result is necessarily always *efficient*. See further n. 34, *infra*.

23. See e.g. the quote in the text at n. 22, *supra*.

24. See e.g. Epstein, "Defenses and Subsequent Pleas", *supra* n. 5 at 169, where he rejects private necessity and compulsion by a third party as legitimate defences in tort: "The only proper question for tort law is whether the plaintiff or the defendant will be required to bear the loss. The argument here is only that it is fairer to require the defendant to bear the loss because he had the hard choice of harming or being harmed when, given what is alleged, the plaintiff had no choice at all."

25. See Epstein, "Automobile No-Fault Plans: A Second Look at First Principles" (1980), 3 *Creighton L. Rev.* 769 at 775: "Once, moreover, assumption of risk is confined to narrower grounds, then it is difficult to argue that the plaintiff upon the highway is *never* entitled to the *prima facie* protection that strict liability provides to the landowner. Thus the plaintiff who is injured while sitting in a parked car, or while waiting for the light to change, or while proceeding through an intersection under the protection of a green light, surely has done nothing 'wrong' if struck by some other driver. If the plaintiff owning land is entitled to protection on strict liability principles where (as is almost always the case) his conduct is purely passive, then the same principles should apply as well to passive plaintiffs in the highway case."

26. Holmes, *The Common Law, supra* n. 11 at 75–78.

27. Holmes' utilitarian argument is criticized by Weinrib in "Toward a Moral Theory of Negligence Law", *supra* n. 3 at 42–43.

28. Holmes, *The Common Law, supra* n. 11 at 76.

29. Epstein has a number of techniques for dealing with collision cases; these will be discussed at length in section 4 below.

30. See *Bamford v. Turnley, supra* n. 22.

31. *Fletcher v. Rylands* (1865), 3 H. & C. 774 (Ex.) at 790, per Bramwell B. (dissenting): the majority decision was reversed in (1866), L.R. 1 Ex. 265 (Ex. Ch.): aff'd *sub nom. Rylands v. Fletcher* (1868), L.R. 3 H.L. 330.

32. (1616), Hob. 134.

33. Holmes, *The Common Law, supra* n. 11 at 68.

34. The point being made here was also made by Coase in the course of his critique of the Pigouvian economic tradition of dealing with externalities by distinguishing between the "private" and the "social" product of a single party whose actions were regarded as *the* cause of a given harm. See Coase's discussion in "The Problem of Social Cost", *supra* n. 22 at 12–13, of the case of *Bryant v. Lefever* (1878–79), 4 C.P.D. 172 (C.A.), in which the plaintiff's chimney smoked whenever he lit it because the defendant had build a wall nearby that kept the air from circulating freely: "Who caused the smoke nuisance? . . . [It] was caused both by the man who built the wall *and* by the man who lit the fires . . . Eliminate the wall *or* the fires and the smoke nuisance would disappear. . . . If we are to discuss the problem in terms of causation, both parties cause the damage". Coase's own approach to the economic problem is a global one, requiring the policy-maker "to compare the total product yielded by alternative social arrangements" (*supra* n. 22 at 43). Epstein criticizes Coase on the grounds that he describes harmful interactions "by the use of sentences that differentiate between the role of the *subject* of [a proposition] and the role of the *object*" ("Strict Liability", *supra* n. 5 at 165). Why this grammatical distinction should have any bearing on the analysis of causation is not made clear. It would appear to be nothing more than a metaphor which itself calls for explanation: see further the text accompanying n. 42, *infra*.

35. Richard Wright, "Causation in Tort Law" (1985), 73 *Cul. L. Rev.* 1737.

36. This conclusion should apply, of course, to a general theory of strict liability whose justification is framed in economic terms as well as to one which is defended on grounds of individual

moral right. It is interesting in this regard to consider the development of Guido Calabresi's thought about liability in tort. In an early article, "Some Thoughts on Risk Distribution and the Law of Torts" (1961), 70 *Yale L.J.* 499, Calabresi argued at 533 that "'tort' costs should be borne by *the* activity which causes them . . ." (emphasis added), where the main justification for the resulting general theory of strict liability was a Pigouvian approach to the allocation of resources: "The function of prices is to reflect the actual costs of competing goods, and thus to enable the buyer to cast an informed vote in making his purchases" (*id.* at 502). In subsequent work, however, Calabresi acknowledged that "[t]here is no formula for allocating the cost of an accident among the activities involved", and, in particular, that this problem could not be solved on causal grounds. See "The Decision for Accidents: An Approach to Nonfault Allocation of Costs" (1965), 78 *Harv. L. Rev.* 713 at 725. He also began to recast the concept of allocation of resources in terms of what he eventually came to call general or market deterrence, which "would require allocation of accident costs to those acts or activities . . . which could avoid the accident costs most cheaply". See *The Costs of Accidents* (New Haven: Yale University Press, 1970) at 135. The result is that Calabresi can no longer be regarded as defending a general theory of strict liability, i.e. a theory which would require a given loss to be borne by the actor or enterprise which had *caused* it. More recently, in "Concerning Cause and the Law of Torts" (1975), 43 *U. Chic. L. Rev.* 69 at 85, Calabresi has said that a requirement of causation in the *but for* sense (as opposed to a mere probabilistic linkage between the type of activity and the type of injury in question) is not even necessary in a system of general deterrence.

37. See, for example, Holmes, *The Common Law, supra* n. 11 at 81 ff; P. H. Winfield, "The Myth of Absolute Liability" (1926), 42 *L.Q.R.* 37; S.F.C. Milsom, *Historical Foundations of the Common Law* (2nd ed., London: Butterworths, 1981), at 296–300.

38. In American law, unlike Anglo-Canadian law, liability for defective products is, in some categories of cases, strict in this sense. See generally *Prosser and Keeton on the Law of Torts* (5th ed., St. Paul, Minn.: West Publishing Co., 1984), ch. 17.

39. *Rylands v. Fletcher, supra* n. 31.

40. Epstein, "Strict Liability", *supra* n. 5 at 160–63.

41. *Id.* at 165ff.

42. Epstein, "Defenses and Subsequent Pleas", *supra* n. 5 at 168, n. 10.

43. Epstein, "Intentional Harms", *supra* n. 13 at 432.

44. Epstein, "Strict Liability", *supra* n. 5 at 177–79.

45. *Id.* at 178.

46. *Id.* at 169.

47. Epstein, "Defenses and Subsequent Pleas", *supra* n. 5 at 168.

48. Epstein, "Intentional Harms", *supra* n. 13 at 402.

49. *Id.* at 410–11.

50. "Defenses and Subsequent Pleas", *supra* n. 5 at 174–75.

51. "Strict Liability", *supra,* n. 5 at 180.

52. See I. Englard, "Can Strict Liability be Generalized?" (1982), 2 *Oxford J. Leg. Studies* 245 for a more general critique of Epstein's theory of causation. Richard Wright, *supra* n. 35 at 1750–58, criticizes Epstein's account of causation as really being a theory of responsibility. I shall be arguing in support of a similar conclusion here.

53. I think that he relies on it at a number of different points, one of which is described in n. 71, *infra*.

54. Epstein, "Strict Liability", *supra* n. 5 at 160.

55. *Id.* at 179.

56. Warren Seavey, "Negligence—Subjective or Objective" (1927), 41 *Harv. L. Rev.* 1 at 5–7.

57. Epstein says, in the passage quoted in the text at n. 55, *supra*, that *J*'s act was not dangerous as described because it did not create a store of releasable energy, but that is only one of the categories of dangerous acts which he describes; the act of parking the car, if it could be said to be dangerous, would presumably fall into the category of a thing not dangerous in itself which has been placed in a dangerous position.

58. The non-empirical, normative dimension of Epstein's analysis of causation stands out especially clearly in the case of dangerous conditions which involve rights of way. The status of rights of way in his theory is discussed in section 4 below.

59. Epstein, "Strict Liability", *supra* n. 5 at 185.

60. *Id.* at 186–87.

61. The anomaly here becomes especially clear when it is recalled that the plaintiff's creation of a dangerous condition which is triggered by an application of force by the defendant gives the latter a "causal" defence: Epstein, "Defenses and Subsequent Pleas", *supra* n. 5 at 175–76. In light of what has been said about the meaning of the term "dangerous" in Epstein's theory, the consequence is that the theory contains, despite Epstein's claim to the contrary ("Strict Liability", *supra* n. 5 at 181), what amounts to a defence of contributory fault: the defence is, moreover, a *complete* bar to recovery, even, it would seem, where the defendant's conduct was faulty in the same sense.

62. Epstein, "Defenses and Subsequent Pleas", *supra* n. 5 at 174–75.

63. The intuitive judgment that if a defendant has been compelled by a third party to hit the plaintiff then the defendant should have an action over against the third party seems clearly correct, since the third party has committed what is presumably an intentional, and therefore in the circumstances an obviously wrongful, act. Elsewhere, Epstein tries to justify this conclusion about ultimate responsibility in what are presumably meant to be purely causal terms by saying that the paradigm of compulsion "permits us to link and differentiate the roles of the parties to the suit. A compelled B to hit C: B did not compel A to hit C. Hence it follows that, *prima facie*, B should prevail over A" ("Strict Liability", *supra* n. 5 at 176). The argument is not sound, however, without the addition of further premises concerning the wrongfulness of (intentionally) compelling another to do something against his will, in which case it is not purely causal in character. If Epstein is not assuming the compulsion to be intentional then it is not at all clear to me what he could mean by "compel", but whatever he means by it he needs a premise to the effect that compulsion in that sense is wrongful.

64. Epstein asserts without elaboration ("Defenses and Subsequent Pleas", *supra* n. 5 at 183) that he has borrowed the expression from the *Restatement of Torts* 2d, s. 411, comment c, but while he might have borrowed the expression from there, he has certainly not adopted its sense. Comment *c* distinguishes between different sorts of intervening forces, which are forces that operate to produce harm *after* the act of the person whose conduct is being evaluated has taken place. A dependent force "is one which operates in response to or is a reaction to the stimulus of a situation for which the actor has made himself responsible by his negligent conduct". An independent force "is one the operation of which is not stimulated by a situation created by the actor's conduct". Epstein's examples make it quite clear that whatever he means by dependence, it has nothing to do with these definitions.

65. Epstein, "Defenses and Subsequent Pleas", *supra* n. 5 at 183.

66. *Id.* at 179.

67. Dependence seems in fact to involve a kind of but-for test: the hitting would not have occurred but for the blocking, whereas the speeding would have taken place whether there was an act of blocking or not.

68. H. L. A. Hart and Tony Honoré, *Causation in the Law* (2nd ed., Oxford: Clarendon Press, 1985).

69. Wright, "Causation in Tort Law", *supra* n. 35 at 1745–50. Neil MacCormick makes a similar point, although he seems to imply that Hart and Honoré *intended* to expound a theory of responsibility. See MacCormick, "The Obligation of Reparation", in his *Legal Right and Social Democracy: Essays in Legal and Political Philosophy* (Oxford: Clarendon Press, 1982) 212, at 220. A similar misunderstanding of Hart and Honoré by England ("The System Builders", *supra* n. 19 at 57, n. 135) is criticized by Wright (*supra* n. 35 at 1739, n. 11).

70. See John Fleming, *The Law of Torts* (6th ed., Sydney: Law Book Co., 1983) at 242–44, 250–51 for an analysis of how "the inveterate predilection of the Common Law mind for assigning occurrences to a single responsible cause"—described by Fleming as a "hollow pretence"—led to seriously inconsistent reasoning and the promulgation of highly dubious doctrine in the area of contributory negligence. See also Malcolm MacIntyre, "The Rationale of Last Clear Chance" (1940), 53 *Harv. L. Rev.* 1225 at 1226; MacIntyre, "Last Clear Chance after 30 Years" (1955), 33 *Can. Bar Rev.* 257 at 258–59. Fleming makes an essentially similar point with respect to intervening causes in *The Law of Torts* at 192–93.

71. Epstein, *Takings*, *supra* n. 10 at 40.

72. In "Toward a Moral Theory of Negligence Law", *supra* n. 3 at 52–53, Weinrib argues that the Learned Hand test represents, on a rights-based view, the correct formulation of how the standard of care in negligence law. His argument depends, however, on a counterfactual proposition, concerning what would have transpired had the plaintiff and the defendant been the same person, which resembles the counterfactual relied upon by Epstein in the argument criticized in section 2(iv) above. Weinrib's argument is vulnerable to objections similar to those presented there against Epstein.

73. [1951] A.C. 850 (H.L.). Epstein criticizes the decision in *Bolton v. Stone* in "Strict Liability", *supra* n. 5 at 169–71. As was pointed out in n. 41, *supra*, he also discusses the case in a more recent article. In neither discussion, however, does he recognize that the House of Lords characterizes negligence in a way which is very different from the balancing approach that he seems especially concerned to reject.

74. *Id.* at 867.

75. See *id.* at 858–60 per Lord Porter, 861 per Lord Normand, 863 per Lord Oaksey, and 868–69 per Lord Radcliffe.

76. In the subsequent case of *Overseas Tankship (U.K.) Ltd. v. Miller Steamship Co. Pty. Ltd.* (*The Wagon Mound No. 2*), [1967] A.C. 617 (P.C.), Lord Reid said at 643–44 that the possibility of eliminating the risk could be taken into account so as to justify liability where the degree of risk would ordinarily have been too slight to have led to that result, but only in certain circumstances: a reasonable person would not neglect a "real" risk (i.e. one which is foreseeable but non-substantial) "if action to eliminate it presented no difficulty, involved no disadvantage and required no expense". This is clearly not a balancing test. Lord Reid is simply saying that if the defendant can achieve his own ends by following either of two separate courses of action, where neither is more costly for him and only one is risky for others, then he should opt for the safer alternative. This is just good common sense. On the facts of *The Wagon Mound No. 2* the defendant's servant had discharged bunkering oil from the defendant's ship into Sydney Harbour. The plaintiff's ship was severely damaged when the oil caught fire while floating on the surface of the water, an occurrence which was held to be foreseeable but extremely improbable. Lord Reid stated, at 643, that the defendant's action not only held no advantage for the defendant but was in fact *contrary* to its own interests: "Not only was it an offence to [discharge the oil], but also it involved considerable loss financially. If the ship's engineer had thought about the matter there could have been no question of balancing the advantages and disadvantages. From every point of view it was both his duty and his interest to stop the discharge immediately".

77. See *U.S. v. Carroll Towing Co.*, *supra* n. 12.

78. I shall be presenting such an explication and defence in a forthcoming paper entitled "The Moral Foundations of Tort Law". I have been much assisted in arriving at the conclusion that the negligence standard should be formulated in nonbalancing terms by discussions with Peter Benson.

CAUSATION AND RESPONSIBILITY*

H. L. A. Hart and A. M. Honoré

I. Responsibility in Law and Morals

We have so far traced the outline of a variety of causal concepts the diversity of which is to be seen in such familiar examples of the use of causal language as the following: "The explosion of gas caused the building to collapse," "He made him hand over his money by threatening to shoot," "The consequence of leaving the car unlocked was that it was stolen," "The strike was the cause of the drop in profits."

The main structure of these different forms of causal connection is plain enough, and there are many situations constantly recurring in ordinary life to which they have a clear application; yet it is also true that like many other fundamental notions these have aspects which are vague or indeterminate; they involve the weighing of matters of degree, or the plausibility of hypothetical speculations, for which no exact criteria can be laid down. Hence their application, outside the safe area of simple examples, calls for judgment and is something over which judgments often differ. Even the type of case which is most familiar, and most nearly approximates to Mill's model for "cause and effect," where causal connection between a physical event and some earlier initiating event or human action is traced through a series of physical events, involves an implicit judgment on such imprecise issues as the *normal* condition of the thing concerned and the *abnormality* of what is identified as the cause. Very often, in particular where an omission to take common precautions is asserted to be the cause of some disaster, a speculation as to what *would have* happened had the precaution been taken is involved. Though arguments one way or another over such hypothetical issues may certainly be rational and have more or less "weight," there is a sense in which they cannot be conclusive. When such areas of dispute are reached, the decision whether to describe the facts of a case in the terms of some given form of causal connection will be influenced very much by factors connected with the context and purpose of making the causal statement.

Hitherto we have discussed only one principal purpose for which causal language is used: i.e., when an explanation is sought or provided of some puzzling or unusual occurrence. But as well as this explanatory context, in which we are concerned with what *has* happened, there are many others. Our deliberations about our own conduct often take the form of an inquiry as to the future consequences of alternative actions; here causal connections are *ex hypothesi* bounded by the horizon of the foreseeable. But even if we confine ourselves to causal statements about the past there are still different contexts and purposes to be discriminated. Thus it would be wrong to think of the historian as using causal notions only when he is explaining. The movement of his thought is not always from the later problematic event to something earlier which explains it and in using causal language he is not always engaged in diagnosis. His thought very often takes the contrary direction; for in addition to providing explanations (answers to the question "why?") he is also concerned to trace the outcome, the results, or the consequences of the human actions and omissions which are his usual starting-points, though he may also work out the "effects" of natural events. So he will discuss the consequences of a king's policy or the effects of the Black Death. This is so because the narrative of history is scarcely ever a narrative of brute sequence, but is an account of the roles played by certain factors and especially by human agents. History is written to satisfy not only the need for explanation, but also the desire to identify and assess contributions made by historical figures to changes of importance; to triumphs and disasters, and to human happiness or suffering. This assessment involves tracing "consequences," "effects," or "results," and these are more frequently referred to than "causes" which has a primarily diagnostic or explanatory ring. In one sense of "responsibility" the historian determines the responsibility of human beings for certain types of change; and sometimes he does this with an eye to praising or blaming or passing other forms of moral judgment. But this need not be so; the historian, though concerned to trace the consequences of human action, need not be a moralist.

In the moral judgments of ordinary life, we have occasion to blame people because they have caused harm to others, and also, if less frequently, to insist that morally they are bound to compensate those to whom they have caused harm. These are the moral analogues of more precise legal conceptions; for, in all legal systems, liability to be punished or to make compensation frequently depends on whether actions (or omissions) have caused harm. Moral blame is not of course confined to such cases of causing harm. We blame a man who cheats or lies or breaks promises, even if no one has suffered in the particular case: this has its legal counterpart in the punishment of abortive attempts to commit crimes, and of offences constituted by the unlawful possession of certain kinds of weapons, drugs, or materials, for example, for counterfeiting currency. When the occurrence of harm is an essential part of the ground for blame the connection of the person blamed with the harm may take any of the forms of causal connection we have examined. His action may have initiated a series of physical events dependent on each other and culminating in injury to persons or property, as in wounding and killing. These simple forms are the paradigms for the lawyer's talk of harm "directly" caused. But we blame people also for harm which arises from or is the consequence of their neglect of common precautions; we do this even if harm would not have come about without the intervention of another human being deliberately exploiting the opportunities provided by neglect. The main legal analogue here is liability for "negligence." The wish of many lawyers to talk in this branch of the law of harm being "within the risk of" rather than "caused by" the negligent conduct manifests appreciation of the fact that a different form of relationship is involved in saying that harm is the consequence, on the one hand, of an explosion and, on the other, of a failure to lock the door by which

a thief has entered. Again, we blame people for the harm which we say is the consequence of their influence over others, either exerted by non-rational means or in one of the ways we have designated "interpersonal transactions." To such grounds for responsibility there correspond many important legal conceptions: the instigation of crimes ("commanding" or "procuring") constitutes an important ground of criminal responsibility and the concepts of enticement and of inducement (by threats or misrepresentation) are an element in many civil wrongs as well as in criminal offences.

The law, however, especially in matters of compensation, goes far beyond these causal grounds for responsibility in such doctrines as the vicarious responsibility of a master for his servant's civil wrongs and that of the responsibility of an occupier of property for injuries suffered by passers-by from defects of which the occupier had no knowledge and which he had no opportunity to repair. There is a recognition, perhaps diminishing, of this non-causal ground of responsibility outside the law; responsibility is sometimes admitted by one person or group of persons, even if no precaution has been neglected by them, for harm done by persons related to them in a special way, either by family ties or as members of the same social or political association. Responsibility may be simply "placed" by moral opinion on one person for what others do. The simplest case of such vicarious moral responsibility is that of a parent for damage done by a child; its more complex (and more debatable) form is the moral responsibility of one generation of a nation to make compensation for their predecessors' wrong, such as the Germans admitted in payment of compensation to Israel.

At this point it is necessary to issue a caveat about the meaning of the expression "responsible" if only to avoid prejudicing a question about the character of *legal* determinations of causal connection . . . . Usually in discussion of the law and occasionally in morals, to say that someone is responsible for some harm means that in accordance with legal rules or moral principles it is at least permissible, if not mandatory, to blame or punish or exact compensation from him. In this use[1] the expression "responsible for" does not refer to a factual connection between the person held responsible and the harm but simply to his liability under the rules to be blamed, punished, or made to pay. The expressions "answerable for" or "liable for" are practically synonymous with "responsible for" in *this* use, in which there is no implication that the person held responsible actually *did* or *caused* the harm. In this sense a master is (in English law) responsible for the damage done by his servants acting within the scope of their authority and a parent (in French and German law) for that done by his children; it is in this sense that a guarantor or surety is responsible for the debts or the good behaviour of other persons and an insurer for losses sustained by the insured. Very often, however, especially in discussion of morals, to say that someone is responsible for some harm is to assert (*inter alia*) that he *did* the harm or *caused* it, though such a statement is perhaps rarely confined to this for it usually also carries with it the implication that it is at least permissible to blame or punish him. This double use of the expression no doubt arises from the important fact that doing or causing harm constitutes not only the most usual but the primary type of ground for holding persons responsible in the first sense. We still speak of inanimate or natural causes such as storms, floods, germs, or the failure of electricity supply as "responsible for" disasters; this mode of expression, now taken only to mean that they caused the disasters, no doubt originated in the belief that all that happens is the work of spirits when it is not that of men. Its survival in the modern world is perhaps some testimony to the primacy of causal connection as an element in responsibility and to the intimate connection between the two notions.

We shall consider later an apparent paradox which interprets in a different way the relationship between cause and responsibility. Much modern thought on causation in the law rests on the contention that the statement that someone has caused harm either means no more than that the harm would not have happened without ("but for") his action or where (as in normal legal usage and in all ordinary speech), it apparently means more than this, it is a disguised way of asserting the "normative" judgment that he is responsible in the first sense, i.e. that it is proper or just to blame or punish him or make him pay. On this view to say that a person caused harm is not really, though ostensibly it is, to give a *ground* or *reason* for holding him responsible in the first sense; for we are only in a position to say that he has caused harm when we have decided that he is responsible. Pending consideration of the theories of legal causation which exploit this point of view we shall use the expression "responsible for" only in the first of the two ways explained, i.e. without any implication as to the type

of factual connection between the person held responsible and the harm; and we shall provisionally, though without prejudicing the issue, treat statements that a person caused harm as one sort of nontautologous ground or reason for saying that he is responsible in this sense.

If we may provisionally take what in ordinary life we say and do at its face value, it seems that there coexist in ordinary thought, apart from the law though mirrored in it, several different types of connection between a person's action and eventual harm which render him responsible for it; and in both law and morals the various forms of causal connection between act or omission and harm are the most obvious and least disputable reasons for holding anyone responsible. Yet, in order to understand the extent to which the causal notions of ordinary thought are used in the law, we must bear in mind the many factors which must differentiate moral from legal responsibility in spite of their partial correspondence. The law is not only not bound to follow the moral patterns of attribution of responsibility but, even when it does, it must take into account, in a way which the private moral judgment need not and does not, the general social consequences which are attached to its judgments of responsibility; for they are of a gravity quite different from those attached to moral censure. The use of the legal sanctions of imprisonment, or enforced monetary compensation against individuals, has such formidable repercussions on the general life of society that the fact that individuals have a type of connection with harm which is adequate for moral censure or claims for compensation is only *one* of the factors which the law must consider, in defining the kinds of connection between actions and harm for which it will hold individuals legally responsible. Always to follow the private moral judgment here would be far too expensive for the law: not only in the crude sense that it would entail a vast machinery of courts and officials, but in the more important sense that it would inhibit or discourage too many other valuable activities of society. To limit the *types* of harm which the law will recognize is not enough; even if the types of harm are limited it would still be too much for any society to punish or exact compensation from individuals whenever their connection with harm of such types would justify moral censure. Conversely, social needs may require that compensation should be paid and even (though less obviously) that punishment be inflicted where no such connection between the person held responsible and the harm exists.

So causing harm of a legally recognized sort or being connected with such harm in any of the ways that justify moral blame, though vitally important and perhaps basic in a legal system, is not and should not be either always necessary or always sufficient for legal responsibility. All legal systems in response either to tradition or to social needs both extend responsibility and cut it off in ways which diverge from the simpler principles of moral blame. In England a man is not guilty of murder if the victim of his attack does not die within a year and day. In New York a person who negligently starts a fire is liable to pay only for the first of several houses which it destroys.[2] These limitations imposed by legal policy are *prima facie* distinguishable from limitations due to the frequent requirement of legal rules that responsibility be limited to harm caused by wrongdoing. Yet a whole school of thought maintains that this distinction does not exist or is not worth drawing.

Apart from this, morality can properly leave certain things vague into which a legal system must attempt to import some degree of precision. Outside the law nothing requires us, when we find the case too complex or too strange, to say whether any and, if so, which of the morally significant types of connection between a person's action and harm exists; we can simply say the case is too difficult for us to pass judgment, at least where moral condemnation of others is concerned. No doubt we evade less easily our questions about our own connection with harm, and the great novelists have often described, sometimes in language very like the lawyers, how the conscience may be still tortured by uncertainties as to the *character* of a part in the production of harm, even when all the facts are known.[3] The fact that there is no precise system of punishments or rewards for common sense to administer, and so there are no "forms of action" or "pleadings" to define precise heads of responsibility for harm, means that the principles which guide common-sense attributions of responsibility give precise answers only in relatively simple types of case.

II. Tracing Consequences

"To consequences no limit can be set": "Every event which would not have happened if an earlier event had not happened is the consequence of that earlier event." These two propositions are not equivalent in meaning and are not equally or in the same way at variance with ordinary thought. They have, however, both been urged sometimes in the same breath by the legal theorist[4] and the philosopher: they are indeed sometimes said by lawyers to be "the philosophical doctrine" of causation. It is perhaps not difficult even for the layman to accept the first proposition as a truth about certain physical events; an explosion may cause a flash of light which will be propagated as far as the outer nebulae; its effects or consequences continue indefinitely. It is, however, a different matter to accept the view that whenever a man is murdered with a gun his death was the consequence of (still less an "effect" of or "caused by") the manufacture of the bullet. The first tells a perhaps unfamiliar tale about unfamiliar events; the second introduces an unfamiliar, though, of course, a possible way of speaking about familiar events. It is not that this unrestricted use of "consequence" is unintelligible or never found; it is indeed used to refer to bizarre or fortuitous connections or coincidences: but the point is that the various causal notions employed for the purposes of explanation, attribution of responsibility, or the assessment of contributions to the course of history carry with them implicit limits which are similar in these different employments.

It is, then, the second proposition, defining consequence in terms of "necessary condition," with which theorists are really concerned. This proposition is the corollary of the view that, if we look into the past of any given event, there is an infinite number of events, each of which is a necessary condition of the given event and so, as much as any other, is its cause. This is the "cone"[5] of causation, so called because, since any event has a number of simultaneous conditions, the series fans out as we go back in time. The justification, indeed only partial, for calling this "the philosophical doctrine" of causation is that it resembles Mill's doctrine that "we have no right to give the name of cause to one of the conditions exclusive of the others of them." It differs from Mill's view in taking the essence of causation to be "necessary condition" and not "the sum total"[6] of the sufficient conditions of an event.

Legal theorists have developed this account of cause and consequence to show what is "factual," "objective," or "scientific" in these notions: this they call "cause in fact" and it is usually stressed as a preliminary to the doctrine that any more restricted application of these terms in the law represents nothing in the facts or in the meaning of causation, but expresses fluctuating legal policy or sentiments of what is just or convenient. Moral philosophers have insisted in somewhat similar terms that the consequences of human action are "infinite": this they have urged as an objection against the Utilitarian doctrine that the rightness of a morally right action depends on whether its consequences are better than those of any alternative action in the circumstances. "We should have to trace as far as possible the consequences not only for the persons affected directly but also for those indirectly affected and to these no limit can be set."[7] Hence, so the argument runs, we cannot either inductively establish the Utilitarian doctrine that right acts are "optimific" or use it in particular cases to discover what is right. Yet, however vulnerable at other points Utilitarianism may be as an account of moral judgment, this objection seems to rest on a mistake as to the sense of "consequence." The Utilitarian assertion that the rightness of an action depends on its consequences is not the same as the assertion that it depends on all those later occurrences which would not have happened had the action not been done, to which indeed "no limit can be set." It is important to see that the issue here is not the linguistic one whether the word "consequence" would be understood if used in this way. The point is that, though we could, we do not think in this way in tracing connections between human actions and events. Instead, whenever we are concerned with such connections, whether for the purpose of explaining a puzzling occurrence, assessing responsibility, or giving an intelligible historical narrative, we employ a set of concepts restricting in various ways what counts as a consequence. These restrictions colour *all* our thinking in causal terms; when we find them in the law we are not finding something invented by or peculiar to the law, though of course it is for the law to say when and how far it will use them and, where they are vague, to supplement them.

No short account can be given of the limits thus placed on "consequences" because these limits vary, intelligibly, with the variety of causal connection asserted. Thus we may be tempted by the generalization that consequences must always be something intended or foreseen or at least foreseeable with ordinary care: but counterexamples spring up from many types of context where causal statements are made. If smoking is shown to cause lung cancer this discovery will permit us to describe past as well as future cases of cancer as the effect or consequence of smoking even though no one foresaw or had reasonable grounds to suspect this in the past. What is common and commonly appreciated and hence foreseeable certainly controls the scope of consequences in certain varieties of causal statement but not in all. Again the voluntary intervention of a second person very often constitutes the limit. If a guest sits down at a table laid with knife and fork and plunges the knife into his hostess's breast, her death is not in any context other than a contrived one[8] thought of as caused by, or the effect or result of the waiter's action in laying the table; nor would it be linked with this action as its consequence for any of the purposes, explanatory or attributive, for which we employ causal notions. Yet as we have seen there are many other types of cases where a voluntary action or the harm it does are naturally treated as the consequence of some prior neglect or precaution. Finally, we may think that a simple answer is already supplied by Hume and Mill's doctrine that causal connection rests on general laws asserting regular connection; yet, even in the type of case to which this important doctrine applies, reference to it alone will not solve our problem. For we often trace a causal connection between an antecedent and a consequent which themselves very rarely go together: we do this when the case can be broken down into intermediate stages, which themselves exemplify different generalizations, as when we find that the fall of a tile was the cause of someone's death, rare though this be. Here our problem reappears in the form of the question: When can generalizations be combined in this way?

We shall examine first the central type of case where the problem is of this last-mentioned form. Here the gist of the causal connection lies in the general connection with each other of the successive stages; and is not dependent on the special notions of one person providing another with reasons or exceptional opportunities for actions. This form of causal connection may exist between actions and events, and between purely physical events, and it is in such cases that the words "cause" and "causing" used of the antecedent action or event have their most obvious application. It is convenient to refer to cases of the first type where the consequence is harm as cases of "causing harm," and to refer to cases where harm is the consequence of one person providing another with reasons or opportunities for doing harm as cases of "inducing" or "occasioning" harmful acts.[9] In cases of the first type a voluntary act, or a conjunction of events amounting to a coincidence, operates as a limit in the sense that events subsequent to these are not attributed to the antecedent action or event as its consequence even though they would not have happened without it. Often such a limiting action or coincidence is thought of and described as "intervening": and lawyers speak of them as "superseding" or "extraneous" causes "breaking the chain of causation." To see what these metaphors rest on (and in part obscure) and how such factors operate as a limit we shall consider the detail of three simple cases.

(i) A forest fire breaks out, and later investigation shows that shortly before the outbreak A had flung away a lighted cigarette into the bracken at the edge of the forest, the bracken caught fire, a light breeze got up, and fanned the flames in the direction of the forest. If, on discovering these facts, we hesitate before saying that A's action caused the forest fire this would be to consider the alternative hypothesis that in spite of appearances the fire only succeeded A's action in point of time, that the bracken flickered out harmlessly and the forest fire was caused by something else. To dispose of this it may be necessary to examine in further detail the process of events between the ignition of the bracken and the outbreak of fire in the forest and to show that these exemplified certain types of continuous change. If this is shown, there is no longer any room for doubt: A's action *was* the cause of the fire, whether he intended it or not. This seems and is the simplest of cases. Yet it is important to notice that even in applying our general knowledge to a case as simple as this, indeed in regarding it as simple, we make an implicit use of a distinction between types of factor which constitute a limit in tracing consequences and those which we regard as mere circumstances "through" which we trace them. For the breeze which sprang up after A dropped the cigarette, and without which the fire would not have spread to the forest, was not only subsequent to his action but entirely independent of it: it was, however, a common recurrent feature of the environment, and, as such, it is thought of not as an "intervening" force but as merely part of the circumstances in which the cause "operates." The decision so to regard it is implicitly taken when we combine our knowledge of the successive stages of the process and assert the connection.

It is easy here to be misled by the natural metaphor of a causal "chain," which may lead us to think that the causal process consists of a series of single events each of which is dependent upon (would not have occurred without) its predecessor in the "chain" and so is dependent upon the initiat-

ing action or event. In truth in any causal process we have at each phase not single events but complex sets of conditions, and among these conditions are some which are not only subsequent to, but independent of the initiating action or event. Some of these independent conditions, such as the evening breeze in the example chosen, we classify as mere conditions in or on which the cause operates; others we speak of as "interventions" or "causes." To decide how such independent elements shall be classified is also to decide how we shall combine our knowledge of the different general connections which the successive stages exemplify, and it is important to see that nothing *in* this knowledge itself can resolve this point. We may have to go to science for the relevant general knowledge before we can assert with proper confidence that A's action did cause the fire, but science, though it tells us that an air current was required, is silent on the difference between a current in the form of an evening breeze and one produced by someone who deliberately fanned the flames as they were flickering out in the bracken. Yet an air current in this deliberately induced form is not a "condition" or "mere circumstance" through which we can trace the consequence; its presence would force us to revise the assertion that A caused the fire. Conversely if science helped us to identify as a necessary factor in producing the fire some condition or element of which we had previously been totally ignorant, e.g. the persistence of oxygen, this would leave our original judgment undisturbed if this factor were a common or pervasive feature of the environment or of the thing in question. There is thus indeed an important sense in which it is true that the distinction between cause and conditions is not a "scientific" one. It is not determined by laws or generalizations concerning connections between events.

When we have assembled all our knowledge of the factors involved in the fire, the residual question which we then confront (the attributive question) may be typified as follows: Here is A's action, here is the fire: can the fire be attributed to A's action as its consequence given that there is also this third factor (the breeze or B's intervention) without which the fire would not have happened? It is plain that, both in raising questions of this kind and in answering them, ordinary thought is powerfully influenced by the analogy between the straightforward cases of causal attribution (where the elements required for the production of harm in addition to the initiating action are all "normal" conditions) and even simpler cases of responsibility which we do not ordinarily describe in causal language at all but by the simple transitive verbs of action. These are the cases of the direct manipulation of objects involving changes in them or their position: cases where we say "He pushed it," "He broke it," "He bent it." The cases which we do confidently describe in causal language ("The fire was caused by his carelessness," "He caused a fire") are cases where no other human action or abnormal occurrence is required for the production of the effect, but only normal conditions. Such cases appear as mere long-range or less direct versions or extensions of the most obvious and fundamental case of all for the attribution of responsibility: the case where we can simply say "He did it." Conversely in attaching importance to thus causing harm as a distinct ground of responsibility and in taking certain kinds of factor (whether human interventions or abnormal occurrences), without which the initiating action would not have led to harm, to preclude the description of the case in simple causal terms, common sense is affected by the fact that here, because of the manner in which the harm eventuates, the outcome cannot be represented as a mere extension of the initiating action; the analogy with the fundamental case for responsibility ("He did it") has broken down.

When we understand the power exerted over our ordinary thought by the conception that causing harm is a mere extension of the primary case of doing harm, the interrelated metaphors which seem natural to lawyers and laymen, in describing various aspects of causal connection, fall into place and we can discuss their factual basis. The persistent notion that some kinds of event required in addition to the initiating action for the production of harm "break the chain of causation" is intelligible, if we remember that though such events actually *complete* the *explanation* of the harm (and so *make* rather than *break* the causal explanation) they do, unlike mere normal conditions, break the *analogy* with cases of simple actions. The same analogy accounts for the description of these factors as "new actions" (*novus actus*) or "new causes," "superseding," "extraneous," "intervening forces": and for the description of the initiating action when "the chain of causation" is broken as "no longer operative," "having worn out," *functus officio*.[10] So too when the "chain" is held not to be "broken" the initiating action is said to be still "potent,"[11] "continuing," "contributing," "operative," and the mere conditions held insufficient to break the chain are "part of the background,"[12] "circum-

stances in which the cause operates,"[13] "the stage set," "part of the history."

(ii) *A* throws a lighted cigarette into the bracken which catches fire. Just as the flames are about to flicker out, *B*, who is not acting in concert with *A*, deliberately pours petrol on them. The fire spreads and burns down the forest. *A*'s action, whether or not he intended the forest fire, was not the cause of the fire: *B*'s was.

The voluntary intervention of a second human agent, as in this case, is a paradigm among those factors which preclude the assimilation in causal judgments of the first agent's connection with the eventual harm to the case of simple direct manipulation. Such an intervention displaces the prior action's title to be called the cause and, in the persistent metaphors found in the law, it "reduces" the earlier action and its immediate effects to the level of "mere circumstances" or "part of the history." *B* in this case was not an "instrument" through which *A* worked or a victim of the circumstances *A* has created. He has, on the contrary, freely exploited the circumstances and brought about the fire without the co-operation of any further agent or any chance coincidence. Compared with this the claim of *A*'s action to be ranked the cause of the fire fails. That this and not the moral appraisal of the two actions is the point of comparison seems clear. If *A* and *B* both intended to set the forest on fire, and this destruction is accepted as something wrong or wicked, their moral wickedness, judged by the criterion of intention, is the same. Yet the causal judgment differentiates between them. If their moral guilt is judged by the outcome, this judgment though it would differentiate between them cannot be the source of the causal judgment; for it presupposes it. The difference just is that *B* has caused the harm and *A* has not. Again, if we appraise these actions as good or bad from different points of view, this leaves the causal judgments unchanged. *A* may be a soldier of one side anxious to burn down the enemy's hideout: *B* may be an enemy soldier who has decided that his side is too iniquitous to defend. Whatever is the moral judgment passed on these actions by different speakers it would remain true that *A* had not caused the fire and *B* had.

There are, as we have said, situations in which a voluntary action would not be thought of as an intervention precluding causal connection in this way. These are the cases discussed further below where an opportunity commonly exploited for harmful actions is negligently provided, or one person intentionally provides another with the means, the opportunity, or a certain type of reason for wrongdoing. Except in such cases a voluntary intervention is a limit past which consequences are not traced. By contrast, actions which in any of a variety of different ways are less than fully voluntary are assimilated to the means by which or the circumstances in which the earlier action brings about the consequences. Such actions are not the outcome of an informed choice made without pressure from others, and the different ways in which human action may fall short in this respect range from defective muscular control, through lack of consciousness or knowledge, to the vaguer notions of duress and of predicaments, created by the first agent for the second, in which there is no "fair" choice.

In considering examples of such actions and their bearing on causal judgments there are three dangers to avoid. It would be folly to think that in tracing connections through such actions instead of regarding them, like voluntary interventions, as a limit, ordinary thought has clearly separated out their non-voluntary aspect from others by which they are often accompanied. Thus even in the crude case where A lets off a gun (intentionally or not) and startles B, so that he makes an involuntary movement of his arm which breaks a glass, the commonness of such a reaction as much as its compulsive character may influence the judgment that A's action was the cause of the damage.

Secondly we must not impute to ordinary thought all the fine discriminations that could be made and in fact are to be found in a legal system, or an equal willingness to supply answers to complex questions in causal terms. Where there is no precise system of punishment, compensation or reward to administer, ordinary men will not often have faced such questions as whether the injuries suffered by a motorist who collides with another in swerving to avoid a child are consequences attributable to the neglect of the child's parents in allowing it to wander on to the road. Such questions courts have to answer and in such cases common judgments provide only a general, though still an important indication of what are the relevant factors.

Thirdly, though very frequently non-voluntary actions are assimilated to mere conditions or means by which the first agent brings about the consequences, the assimilation is never quite complete. This is manifested by the general avoidance of many causal locutions which are appropriate when the consequences are traced (as in the first case) through purely physical events. Thus even in the case in which the second agent's role is hardly an "action" at all, e.g. where A hits B, who staggers against a glass window and breaks it, we should say that A's blow made B stagger and break the glass, rather than that A's blow caused the glass to break, though in any explanatory or attributive context the case would be *summarized* by saying that A's action was the cause of the *damage*.

In the last two cases where B's movements are involuntary in the sense that they are not part of any action which he chose or intended to do, their connection with A's action would be described by saying that A's blow *made* B stagger or *caused* him to stagger or that the noise of A's shot *made* him jump. This would be true, whether A intended or expected B to react in this way or not, and the naturalness of treating A's action as the cause of the ultimate damage is due to the causal character of this part of the process involving B's action. The same is, however, true where B's actions are not involuntary movements but A is considered to have made or caused B to do them by less crude means. This is the case if, for example, A uses threats or exploits his authority over B to make B do something, e.g. knock down a door. At least where A's threats are serious harm, or B's act was unquestionably within A's authority to order, he too has made or forced or (in formal quasi-legal parlance) "caused" B to act.

Outside the area of such cases, where B's will would be said either not to be involved at all, or to be overborne by A, are cases where A's act creates a predicament for B *narrowing* the area of choice so that he has either to inflict some harm on himself or others, or sacrifice some important interest or duty. Such cases resemble coercion in that A narrows the area of B's choice but differ from it in that this predicament need not be intentionally created. A sets a house on fire (intentionally or unintentionally): B to save himself has to jump from a height involving certain injury, or to save a child rushes in and is seriously burned. Here, of course, B's movements are not involuntary; the "necessity" of his action is here of a different order. His action is the outcome of a choice between two evils forced on him by A's action. In such cases, when B's injuries are thought of as the consequences of the fire, the implicit judgment is made that his action was the lesser of two evils and in this sense a "reasonable" one which he was obliged to make to avoid the greater evil. This is often paradoxically, though understandably, described by saying that here the agent "had no choice" but to do what he did. Such judgments involve a comparison of the importance of the respective interests sacrificed and preserved, and the final assertion that A's action was the cause of the injuries rests on evaluations about which men may differ.

Finally, the ground for treating some harm which would not have occurred without B's action as the consequence of A's action may be that B acted in ignorance of or under a mistake as to some feature of the situation created by A. Poisoning offers perhaps the simplest example of the bearing on causal judgments of actions which are less than voluntary in this Aristotelian sense. If A intending B's death deliberately poisons B's food and B, knowing this, deliberately takes the poison and dies, A has not, unless he coerced B into eating the poisoned food, caused B's death: if, however, B does not know the food to be poisoned, eats it, and dies, A has caused his death, even if he put the poison in unwittingly. Of course only the roughest judgments are passed in causal terms in such cases outside law courts, where fine degrees of "appreciation" or "reckless shutting of the eyes" may have to be discriminated from "full knowledge." Yet, rough as these are, they indicate clearly enough the controlling principles.

Though in the foregoing cases A's initiating action might often be described as "the cause" of the ultimate harm, this linguistic fact is of subordinate importance to the fact that, for whatever purpose, explanatory, descriptive, or evaluative, consequences of an action are traced, discriminations are made (except in the cases discussed later) between free voluntary interventions and less than voluntary reactions to the first action or the circumstances created by it.

(iii) The analogy with single simple actions which guides the tracing of consequences may be broken by certain kinds of conjunctions of physical events. A hits B who falls to the ground stunned and bruised by the blow; at that moment a tree crashes to the ground and kills B. A has certainly caused B's bruises but not his death: for though the fall of the tree was, like the evening breeze in our earlier example, independent of and subsequent to the initiating action, it would be differentiated from the breeze in any description in causal terms of the connection of B's death with A's action. It is to be noticed that this is not a matter which turns on the intention with which A struck B. Even if A hit B inadvertently or accidentally his blow would still be the cause of B's bruises: he would have caused them, though unintentionally. Conversely even if A had intended his blow to kill, this would have been an attempt to kill but still not the cause of B's death, unless A knew

that the tree was about to fall just at that moment. On this legal and ordinary judgments would be found to agree; and most legal systems would distinguish for the purposes of punishment[14] an attempt with a fatal upshot, issuing by such chance or anomalous events, from "causing death"—the terms in which the offenses of murder and manslaughter are usually defined.

Similarly the causal description of the case does not turn on the moral appraisal of A's action or the wish to punish it. A may be a robber and a murderer and B a saint guarding the place A hoped to plunder. Or B may be a murderer and A a hero who has forced his way into B's retreat. In both cases the causal judgment is the same. A had caused the minor injuries but not B's death, though he tried to kill him. A may indeed be praised or blamed but not for causing B's death. However intimate the connection between responsibility and causation, it does not determine causal judgments in this simple way. Nor does the causal judgment turn on a refusal to attribute grave consequences to actions which normally have less serious results. Had A's blow killed B outright and the tree, falling on his body, merely smashed his watch we should still treat the coincidental character of the fall of the tree as determining the form of causal statement. We should then recognize A's blow as the cause of B's death but not the breaking of the watch.

The connection between A's action and B's death in the first case would naturally be described in the language of *coincidence*. "It was a coincidence: it just happened that, at the very moment when A knocked B down, a tree crashed at the very place where he fell and killed him." The common legal metaphor would describe the fall of the tree as an "extraneous" cause. This, however, is dangerously misleading, as an analysis of the notion of coincidence will show. It suggests merely an event which is subsequent to and independent of some other contingency, and of course the fall of the tree has both these features in relation to A's blow. Yet in these respects the fall of the tree does not differ from the evening breeze in the earlier case where we found no difficulty in tracing causal connection. The full elucidation of the notion of a coincidence is a complex matter for, though it is very important as a limit in tracing consequences, causal questions are not the only ones to which the notion is relevant. The following are its most general characteristics. We speak of a coincidence whenever the conjunction of two or more events in certain spatial or temporal relations (1) is very unlikely by ordinary standards and (2) is for some reason significant or important, provided (3) that they occur without human contrivance and (4) are independent of each other. It is therefore a coincidence if two persons known to each other in London meet without design in Paris on their way to separate independently chosen destinations; or if two persons living in different places independently decide to write a book on the same subject. The first is a coincidence of time and place ("It just happened that we were at the same place at the same time"), and the second a coincidence of time only ("It just happened that they both decided to write on the subject at the same time").

Use of this general notion is made in the special case when the conjunction of two or more events occurs in temporal and/or spatial relationships which are significant, because, as our general knowledge of causal processes shows, this conjunction is required for the production of some given further event. In the language of Mill's idealized model, they form a necessary part of a complex set of jointly sufficient conditions. In the present case the fall of the tree just as B was struck down within its range satisfies the four criteria for a coincidence which we have enumerated. First, though neither event was of a very rare or exceptional kind, their conjunction would be rated very unlikely judged by the standards of ordinary experience. Secondly, this conjunction was causally significant for it was a necessary part of the process terminating in B's death. Thirdly, this conjunction was not consciously designed by $A;$ had he known of the impending fall of the tree and hit B with the intention that he should fall within its range B's death would not have been the result of any coincidence. A would certainly have caused it. The common-sense principle that a contrived conjunction cannot be a coincidence is the element of truth in the legal maxim (too broadly stated even for legal purposes) that an intended consequence cannot be too "remote." Fourthly, each member of the conjunction in this case was independent of the other; whereas if B had fallen against the tree with an impact sufficient to bring it down on him, this sequence of physical events, though freakish in its way, would not be a coincidence and in most contexts of ordinary life, as in the law, the course of events would be summarized by saying that in this case, unlike that of the coincidence, A's act was the cause of B's death, since each stage is the effect of the preceding stage. Thus, the blow forced the victim against the tree, the effect of this was to make the tree fall and the fall of the

tree killed the victim.

One further criterion in addition to these four must be satisfied if a conjunction of events is to rank as a coincidence and as a limit when the consequences of the action are traced. This further criterion again shows the strength of the influence which the analogy with the case of the simple manipulation of things exerts over thought in causal terms. An abnormal *condition* existing at the time of a human intervention is distinguished both by ordinary thought and, with a striking consistency, by most legal systems from an abnormal event or conjunction of events subsequent to that intervention; the former, unlike the latter, are not ranked as coincidences or "extraneous" causes when the consequences of the intervention come to be traced. Thus A innocently gives B a tap over the head of a normally quite harmless character, but because B is then suffering from some rare disease the tap has, as we say, "fatal results." In this case A has caused B's death though unintentionally. The scope of the principle which thus distinguishes contemporaneous abnormal conditions from subsequent events is unclear; but at least where a human being initiates some physical change in a thing, animal, or person, abnormal physical states of the object affected, existing at the time, are ranked as part of the circumstances in which the cause "operates." In the familiar controlling imagery these are part of "the stage already set" before the "intervention."

Judgments about coincidences, though we often agree in making them, depend in two related ways on issues incapable of precise formulation. One of these is patent, the other latent but equally important. Just how unlikely must a conjunction be to rank as a coincidence, and in the light of what knowledge is likelihood to be assessed? The only answer is: "very unlikely in the light of the knowledge available to ordinary men." It is, of course, the indeterminacies of such standards, implicit in causal judgments, that make them inveterately disputable, and call for the exercise of discretion or choice by courts. The second and latent indeterminacy of these judgments depends on the fact that the things or events to which they relate do not have pinned to them some uniquely correct description always to be used in assessing likelihood. It is an important pervasive feature of all our empirical judgments that there is a constant possibility of more or less specific description of any event or thing with which they are concerned. The tree might be described not simply as a "tree" but as a "rotten tree" or as a "fir tree" or a "tree sixty feet tall." So too its fall might be described not as a "fall" but as a fall of a specified distance at a specified velocity. The likelihood of conjunctions framed in these different terms would be differently assessed. The criteria of appropriate description like the standard of likelihood are supplied by consideration of common knowledge. Even if the scientist knew the tree to be rotten and could have predicted its fall with accuracy, this would not change the judgment that its fall at the time when B was struck down within its range was a coincidence; nor would it make the description "rotten tree" appropriate for the assessment of the chances involved in this judgment. There are other controls over the choice of description derived from the degree of specificity of our interests in the final outcome of the causal process. We are concerned with the fall of an object sufficient to cause "death" by impact and the precise force or direction which may account for the detail of the wounds is irrelevant here.

Opportunities and Reasons

Opportunities The discrimination of voluntary interventions as a limit is no longer made when the case, owing to the commonness or appreciable risk of such harmful intervention, can be brought within the scope of the notion of providing an opportunity, known to be commonly exploited for doing harm. Here the limiting principles are different. When A leaves the house unlocked the range of consequences to be attributed to this neglect, as in any other case where precautions are omitted, depends primarily on the way in which such opportunities are commonly exploited. An alternative formulation of this idea is that a subsequent intervention would fall within the scope of consequences if the likelihood of its occurring is one of the reasons for holding A's omission to be negligent.

It is on these lines that we would distinguish between the entry of a thief and of a murderer; the opportunity provided is believed to be sufficiently commonly exploited by thieves to make it usual and often morally or legally obligatory not to provide it. Here, in attributing consequences to prior actions, causal judgments are directly controlled by the notion of the risk created by them. Neglect of such precautions is both unusual and reprehensible. For these reasons it would be hard to separate the two ways in which such neglect deviates from the "norm." Despite this, no simple identification can be made of the notion of responsibility with the causal

connection which is a ground for it. This is so because the provision of an opportunity commonly taken by others is ranked as the cause of the outcome independently of the wish to praise or blame. The causal judgment may be made simply to assess a contribution to some outcome. Thus, whether we think well or ill of the use made of railways, we would still claim that the greater mobility of the population in the nineteenth century was a consequence of their introduction.

It is obvious that the question whether any given intervention is a sufficiently common exploitation of the opportunity provided to come within the risk is again a matter on which judgments may differ, though they often agree. The courts, and perhaps ordinary thought also, often describe those that are sufficiently common as "natural" consequences of the neglect. They have in these terms discriminated the entry of a thief from the entry of a man who burnt the house down, and refused to treat the destruction of the house as a "natural" consequence of the neglect.[15]

We discuss later . . . the argument that this easily intelligible concept of "harm within the risk," overriding as it does the distinctions between voluntary interventions and others, should be used as the general test for determining what subsequent harm should be attributed for legal purposes to prior action. The merits of this proposal to refashion the law along these simple lines are perhaps considerable, yet consequences of actions are in fact often traced both in the law and apart from it in other ways which depend on the discrimination of voluntary interventions from others. We distinguish, after all, as differing though related grounds of responsibility, causing harm by one's own action and providing opportunities for others to do harm, where the guiding analogy with the simple manipulation of things, which underlies causal thought, is less close. When, as in the examples discussed above, we trace consequences through the non-voluntary interventions of others our concern is to show that certain stages of the process have a certain type of connection with the preceding stages, and not, as when the notion of risk is applied, to show that the ultimate outcome is connected in some general way with the initiating action. Thus, when A's shot makes B start and break a glass it is the causal relationship described by the expression "made B start" that we have in mind and not the likelihood that on hearing a shot someone may break a glass. Causal connection may be traced in such cases though the initiating action and the final outcome are not contingencies that commonly go together.

Apart from these conceptual reasons for distinguishing these related grounds for responsibility, it is clear that both in the law . . . and apart from it we constantly treat harm as caused by a person's action though it does not fall "within the risk." If, when *B* broke the glass in the example given above, a splinter flew into *C*'s eye, blinding him, *A*'s action is indeed the cause of *C*'s injury though we may not always blame him for so unusual a consequence.

Reasons   In certain varieties of interpersonal transactions, unlike the case of coercion, the second action is quite voluntary. *A* may not threaten *B* but may bribe or advise or persuade him to do something. Here, *A* does not "cause" or "make" *B* do anything: the strongest words we should use are perhaps that he "induced" or "procured" *B*'s act. Yet the law and

moral principles alike may treat one person as responsible for the harm which another free agent has done "in consequence" of the advice or the inducements which the first has offered. In such cases the limits concern the range of those actions done by *B* which are to rank as the consequence of *A*'s words or deeds. In general this question depends on *A*'s intentions or on the "plan of action" he puts before *B*. If *A* advises or bribes *B* to break in and steal from an empty house and *B* does so, he acts in consequence of *A*'s advice or bribe. If he deliberately burns down the house this would not be treated as the consequence of *A*'s bribe or advice, legally or otherwise, though it may in some sense be true that the burning would not have taken place without the advice or bribe. Nice questions may arise, which the courts have to settle, where *B* diverges from the detail of the plan of action put before him by *A*.

---

1. *Cf. OED* sub tit. Responsible: Answerable, accountable (to another for something); liable to be called to account: "being responsible to the King for what might happen to us," 1662; Hart, "Varieties of Responsibility" (1967) 83 *LQR* 346, reprinted with additions as "Responsibility and Retribution" in Hart, *Punishment and Responsibility* (Oxford, 1968), chap. IX.
2. The rule is defended on the ground that, most houseowners being insured, it promotes efficient loss distribution: Harper and James, *Torts*, s. 20.6 n. 1.
3. See the following passage from *The Golden Bowl* by Henry James. (Mrs. Assingham, whose uncertain self-accusation is described here, had, on the eve of the Prince's marriage, encouraged him to resume an old friendship with Charlotte Stant. The relationship which developed came to threaten the marriage with disaster.) "She had stood for the previous hour in a merciless glare, beaten upon, stared out of countenance, it fairly seemed to her, by intimations of her mistake. For what she was most immediately feeling was that she had in the past been active for these people to ends that were now bearing fruit and that might yet bear a greater crop. She but brooded at first in her corner of the carriage: it was like burying her exposed face, a face too helplessly exposed in the cool lap of the common indifference . . . a world mercifully unconscious and unreproachful. . . . The sense of seeing was strong in her, but she clutched at the comfort of not being sure of what she saw. Not to know what it would represent on a longer view was a help in turn to not making out that her hands were embrued; since

if she had stood in the position of a producing cause she should surely be less vague about what she had produced. This, further, in its way, was a step toward reflecting that when one's connection with any matter was too indirect to be traced, it might be described also as too slight to be deplored" (*The Golden Bowl*, Book 3, chap. 3). We are much indebted to Dame Mary Warnock for this quotation.
4. Lawson, *Negligence in the Civil Law*, p. 53.
5. Glanville Williams, *Joint Torts and Contributory Negligence*, p. 239.
6. Mill, Book III, chap. v, s. 2.
7. Ross, *The Right and the Good*, p. 36.
8. E.g. if the guest was suspected of being a compulsive stabber and the waiter had therefore been told to lay only a plastic knife in his place.
9. In Chaps. VI, VII, XII, XIII of *Causation and the Law* we distinguish these different relationships in the law.
10. *Davies v. Swan Motor Co.* [1947] 2 KB 291, 318.
11. *Minister of Pensions v. Chennell* [1947] KB 250, 256. Lord Wright (1950), 13 *MLR* 3.
12. *Norris v. William Moss & Son Ltd.* [1954] 1 WLR 46, 351.
13. *Minister of Pensions v. Chennel* [1947] KB 250, 256.
14. For the bearing of the principles of punishment on such problems see Chap. XIV of our book, *Causation in the Law*.
15. *Bellows v. Worcester Storage Co.* (1937) 297 Mass. 188, 7 NE 2d 588.

THE DECLINE OF CAUSE[*]

Judith Jarvis Thomson

I

Once upon a time there was a simple way of characterizing tort law. It could in those days be said that the defendant will be declared liable for the plaintiff's loss if and only if the plaintiff proves the following three things: (1) that he suffered a loss, (2) that an act or failure to act on the part of the defendant was proximate cause of the plaintiff's suffering that loss, and (3) that the defendant was at fault in so acting or failing to act. Proximate cause was a messy business, of course, but one thing that was clear was that a person's act or omission was not proximate cause of another person's loss unless it caused the loss.

So much for once upon a time. Fault went first: it began to be possible in certain kinds of cases for a plaintiff to win his suit if he proved (1) that he suffered a loss, and (2) that an act or failure to act on the part of the defendant proximately caused his loss, even though he did not prove (3) that the defendant was at fault in so acting or failing to act. Now cause is going. In a number of cases in recent years the plaintiff has won his suit on proof (1) that he suffered a loss, and (2) that there was a faulty act or omission on the part of the defendant, but without proving (3) that the defendant's faulty act or omission caused the loss. No doubt the plaintiff has to prove *some* connection between his loss and the defendant's faulty act. If I prove I lost my legs this morning, and that you hit your little brother with a brick yesterday, *that* certainly will not suffice for me to win a suit against you for damages for the loss of my legs. The plaintiff has to connect the faulty act with the loss. But in the kind of case I have in mind, the connection he makes need not be causation.

Which kind of case? A good example is *Sindell v. Abbott Laboratories*,[1] which was decided by the California Supreme Court in 1980. The plaintiff alleged she could prove that she developed cancer as a result of the DES taken by her mother while pregnant; she alleged she could prove also that the defendants—eleven drug companies—knew or should have known that DES would cause cancer in the daughters of mothers who took it. In other words, she alleged she could prove (1) that she was harmed, and (2) that the defendant drug companies were at fault. But she was unable to prove, after the passage of so many years, which drug company had marketed the very DES her mother took, so she was unable to prove about any of the drug companies (3) that *its* acts had caused the harm she suffered. All the same, she won the right to get a jury on the fact she alleged she could prove, and the right to win if she could prove them.

An earlier California case—*Summers v. Tice*,[2] decided in 1948—presented the problem that confronted the plaintiff in *Sindell* much more starkly and cleanly. The plaintiff Summers had gone hunting with the two defendants, Tice and Simonson. A quail was flushed, and, as Summers alleged, the defendants fired negligently in Summers' direction; as he also alleged, one of the two wounded him. But he was unable to prove which, since the defendants had fired similar pellets from similar guns. Loss yes, fault yes, but causality could not be proved. However he too won his suit.

My own impression is that cases like *Summers* and *Sindell*—in which loss and fault are clear, but causality cannot be proved—were very rarely won until recently. Why are they being won now? It is an excellent question, with, I am sure, a great many answers. Chief among them is probably a mix of four things: first, the very fact that causality *is* hard to prove in them; together with, second, the felt need to regulate the increasing number of activities which impose risk as a byproduct of technological ad-

[*]From Judith Jarvis Thomson, "The Decline of Cause," in 76 *Georgetown Law Journal* 137. Reprinted with the permission of the publisher, © 1987 The Georgetown Law Journal Association and Georgetown University.

vance; third, an increasing public acceptance of egalitarianism; and fourth, the absence as yet of a mechanism other than the tort suit to regulate those activities and secure a measure of compensation for those who may be being victimized by them.[3]

II

A related phenomenon—at least I think it really must be related—is the increasing dismissiveness about causality that can be seen in legal theorizing. Here are Landes and Posner in an article published in 1983: "causation in the law is an inarticulate groping for economically sound solutions. . . ."[4] In an article published in 1975, Calabresi defends the idea that certain concepts related to causality have a role to play in law, but his defense of that idea would have puzzled many lawyers fifty years ago. He says:

> [I]n law the term "cause" is used in different guises but always to identify those pressure points that are most amenable to the social goals we wish to accomplish. . . . [U]se of such [causal] concepts has great advantages over explicit identification and separation of the goals. Terms with an historical, common law gloss [like "cause"] permit us to consider goals (like spreading) that we do not want to spell out or too obviously assign to judicial institutions.[5]

This dismissiveness about causality is not visible only in those whose legal theorizing is influenced by economics.[6]

III

I am not competent to speak to the question why the law and legal theory have been developing in these ways, or even to the question exactly what forms these developments have taken. What I want to do instead is to mull over one of the sources of the welcome with which these developments have been received by many of the moral philosophers who have taken note of them.

What I have in mind is that there has been a phenomenon equally entitled to be called "The Decline of Cause" in moral theorizing.

The moral sophisticate nowadays is nowhere near as enamored of causality as the ignorant rest of

us. Here is an example. Yesterday, Alfred backed his car out of his driveway without looking. Bad of him!—one ought not do that. Today, Bert backed his car out of his driveway without looking, but lo and behold there was a child at the end of the driveway, and Bert ran over the child and crushed its legs. Horrendous—much worse. Or so many people think.

The moral sophisticate regards that as a vulgar error. "Look," he says, "both Alfred and Bert behaved negligently, indeed equally negligently. Bert crushed a child's legs and Alfred did not, but that was just bad luck for Bert, and good luck for Alfred. After all, it wasn't Bert's fault that there was a child at the foot of his driveway; all Bert was at fault for is exactly what Alfred was at fault for, namely backing his car out of his driveway without looking. So Bert acted no worse than Alfred did, and—other things being equal—Bert is no worse a person than Alfred is."

The moral sophisticate may concede that the law does well to mark a difference between Alfred and Bert in the following two ways: (1) imposing a more severe punishment on Bert than on Alfred, and (2) making Bert, and not Alfred, compensate the child's parents. But if so, he says it is for reasons extraneous to the *moral* valuation proper to them and their acts.

It is clear that the moral sophisticate is going to hold this same view in other pairs of cases too. Murder and attempted murder, of course. Yesterday Charles fired a gun at a man, to kill him; Charles'[s] intended victim was wearing a bullet proof vest, so Charles did not kill him. Today David fired a gun at a man, to kill him; David's intended victim was not wearing a bullet proof anything, so David did kill him. David murdered a man, and Charles only attempted murder, but the moral sophisticate says that David acted no worse than Charles did—for after all, it was just bad luck for Charles that his intended victim was wearing that vest, and thus nothing that Charles can take any credit for.

It seems to me three principles lie behind this moral attitude. The first concerns itself with *acts*. What we do in the world depends on the world as well as on us. If you fire a gun at a man to kill him, then the question whether you do not merely fire a gun at him, but also kill him turns on whether the world cooperates—thus on whether the bullet actually reaches him, as it might not if some third party intervenes, and on whether it enters him when it reaches him, as it might not if he is wearing bullet proof clothes. The first principle I have in mind says that the moral value of what you do in the world turns on and only on that part of it which is *entirely* under your control. When you fire a gun at a man, what is under your control is at most such things as the kind of gun you fire, the time and place at which you fire it, the direction in which you fire it, and the intention with which you fire it—merely to scare your victim, or merely to wound him, or positively to kill him. The rest that happens is up to the world, and is not something that has any bearing on the moral value of your act.

I said "at most." Let us look again at the kind of gun you fire. Is it new? Is it clean? Is it sufficiently powerful to do the work you want it to do? Strictly speaking, that the gun you fire does or does not have these features is not entirely under your control. What is under your control is only that you have made an effort to be sure that you are firing a suitable gun and now think you are: After all, somebody might have secretly replaced your carefully chosen gun with a different one—whether a person did or did not do this is not under your control. Similarly for the time and place at which you fire the gun, and the direction in which you fire it: Somebody might have secretly altered your clocks and roadmaps, and substituted distorting glasses for the glasses you normally wear—whether a person did or did not do this is also not under your control.

Strictly speaking, all that is entirely under your control are your intentions in acting—what you are at any given time setting yourself to be doing. That is not to say that setting yourself to do this or that is all you actually *do;* it is to say that the normal value of what you do *by* setting yourself to act in this or that way turns entirely on the moral value of those settings of yourself to act.

The second of the three principles concerns itself with *failures to act,* or omissions, for short. Consider two switchmen on different railways, Edward and Frank. Both were under a duty to throw a switch at ten this morning, and both failed to do so because they did not want to be bothered. Edward's omission caused a terrible train crash; Frank's omission caused nothing untoward at all, since the train Frank's switch-throwing was to turn had luckily stalled before the fork in the track. If you think murder no worse than attempted murder, you will surely think Edward's omission no worse than Frank's. It was, after all, no credit to Frank, it was merely good luck for him, that his train had stalled. The second principle says that the moral value of an omission—

as of an act—turns on and only on what is entirely under the agent's control. If you could have set yourself to do a thing, and ought to have done so, then your failure to do so is equally bad no matter what your omission does or does not cause.

The cases of Alfred and Bert with which I began are cases to which both principles apply. Alfred and Bert both acted, for they backed their cars down their driveways; and both failed to act, for they failed to look while doing so. Given the two principles, the fact that Bert's acting while failing to act caused a child's legs to be crushed has no bearing at all on the moral value of what he did.

The third of the three principles has to do with the moral value of *persons.* We do think of some people as morally better than others; on what does this judgment turn? Presumably in part on the moral value of what a person does or fails to do. Given the first two principles, however, that is a function only of the moral value of a person's settings of himself to do this or that, and his failures to set himself to do this or that.

But only in part, for there is something else that a friend of these ideas should think bears on a person's moral value. What I have in mind is that if you think that good and bad luck has no bearing on the moral value of an act or omission *or* person, then you should grant that the truth or falsehood of certain counterfactuals is relevant. For example, I do not drive, and a fortiori have never backed a car out of a driveway with *or* without looking. If I had driven, would I on occasion have backed my car out of my driveway without looking? Isn't that relevant to the question how good or bad a person I am?

I am sure that all of us have faced temptations to act badly, and that many of those temptations we have resisted, though some we have not. Most people, however, are lucky enough never to be tempted to do something truly dreadful. For example, I am sure that none of us has ever been in a position of power over prisoners in a concentration camp. I am sure that none of us has been lost at sea in a lifeboat with no provisions other than a plump cabin boy. We have been lucky. How would we behave if we were in such situations? Surely that we would or would not behave in this or that way has a bearing on our moral value as people. One reason why Stanley Milgram's experiments[7] were found so shocking was that they uncovered the fact that a lot of perfectly ordinary people were quite ready to set themselves to cause others a great deal of pain simply on being told by an authority figure in a white coat to do so. Milgram's readers did not think for a moment that the actual absence of pain excused the subjects of the experiments; and they took it that what Milgram had shown was a deep moral failing which may be present in perfectly ordinary people, though without ever in fact showing itself.

How good a person are you? The third principle tells us that to the extent to which you do not know what you would set yourself to do in situations you have been so far lucky as not to have faced, you just do not know how good a person you are.

I described the person who holds these views as the "moral sophisticate," because I think we do think these views more sophisticated than those which tell us to look merely at what happens, more sophisticated even than those which tell us to look *both* at what happens *and* at what is internal to a person—what he sets himself to do, and what he would set himself to do if he were in situations he has never faced. But I might just as well have described the person who holds these views as a Kantian, because it is directly from Kant that they come down to us today. Kant said: "The good will is not good because of what it effects or accomplishes or because of its adequacy to achieve some proposed end; it is good only because of its willing, i.e., it is good of itself. . . . Usefulness or fruitlessness can neither diminish or augment [its] worth."[8] And so similarly for the bad will: it is not bad because of what it causes, but only of itself. We might redescribe the decline of cause in moral philosophy as the triumph of Kant.

That Kant has triumphed seems clear enough. For example, I rather fancy that all of you have at least some inclination to agree with the three principles I drew attention to. I certainly do.

It is of interest to notice that these Kantian ideas are visible even in contemporary defenders of the most un-Kantian moral theory of all. I have Utilitarianism in mind, of course. Classical Utilitarians—such as John Stuart Mill and G.E. Moore—took the view that you have acted wrongly if and only if your act causes there to be less good in the world than you could have caused by choosing some other alternative act which was open to you at the time. Whether you knew it or not. Mill did explicitly grant that a man's intentions in acting do have a bearing on the moral evaluation proper to *him;* but Mill insisted that the morality of a man's *act* turns on, and only on, a comparison between what it does in fact cause, and what his other available alternatives would have caused. But hardly anyone is a Classical

Utilitarian nowadays. Those in favor of its spirit say that the morality of a man's act turns, not on what it in fact causes, but on what he expects it to cause. In short, the morality of action turns, not on actual, but on expected utilities.

Now I think that these Kantian ideas are one source of the welcome with which many moral philosophers have received those developments in law and legal theory that I mentioned at the outset. For example, they think that all of the defendants were at fault in *Sindell* and *Summers*—equally at fault, regardless of whoever in fact caused the harm. So they think that no one can object, on *moral* grounds, to the plaintiffs' winning, and to the defendants' therefore having to share in the plaintiffs' costs.[9]

IV

What should *we* think of all this? It is swimming upstream to try to fight it, but my own feeling is that it smells too much of the study and too little of the open air. Adam Smith said, very plausibly, I think,

> But how well soever we may seem to be persuaded of the truth of [these ideas], when we consider [them] after this manner, in abstract, yet when we come to particular cases, the actual consequences which happen to proceed from any action, have a very great effect upon our sentiments concerning its merit or demerit, and almost always either enhance or diminish our sense of both.[10]

Alfred backed his car out of his driveway without looking, and luckily for him, nothing untoward happened in consequence. Bad of him, we think. But not horrendous. People do that kind of thing often enough. They ought not, but they do, and it seems no great sin. Bert also backed his car out of his driveway without looking, but *he* ran a child down and crushed its legs. As Adam Smith said, we just *do* think that what Bert did was worse than what Alfred did. How can any philosophy be right which tells us we are mistaken in thinking this?

On the other hand, I think that Adam Smith's remark would not have been at all plausible if he had not said "almost always." He said: "the actual consequences which happen to proceed from any action, have a very great effect upon our sentiments concerning its merit or demerit, and *almost always* either enhance or diminish our sense of both."[11] There seem to me to be two kinds of case in which they do not.

To get at the first kind, let me draw your attention to the fact that in every example I have given, right from the outset, the agent whose act did cause a harm was at fault. In the two court cases I began with, all of the defendants were at fault, the drug companies in *Sindell,* the negligent hunters in *Summers.* Alfred and Bert were both careless. Charles and David, each of whom shot at a man to kill him, were both at least attempting murder. And so on. But what of an agent who causes someone to suffer a harm, but not by negligence or intention or by any wrong at all? A child runs out into the street and is run down by a truck driver who is entirely without fault—he has taken all due care to ensure that his truck, and in particular, his brakes, were in good order, and he was driving with all due care. The child simply ran too suddenly, too close, into the path of his truck. Does the very fact that he caused harm to the child diminish our sense of the merit of his actions? I think not. This example comes from Thomas Nagel, and he says about it: "The driver, if he is entirely without fault, will feel terrible about his role in the event, but will not have to reproach himself."[12] Nor will we reproach him. There is nothing to reproach him for. So here is a case of the first kind I had in mind: it is a case in which an agent was not at fault at all in acting, and that a bad consequence happens to flow from his action does not affect our sense of its merit or demerit. In particular, the bad consequence does not make us think worse of his driving than we would have thought had that bad consequence not flowed from it.

Symmetrically, we might imagine someone who does something of no particular merit, and something good just happens to flow from his doing it. For example, suppose a man is standing at a street corner, waiting for a bus. As he waits, he is idly tapping his foot. Through some freak of nature, his tapping his foot causes three lives to be saved. This good consequence does not affect our sense of the merit or demerit of his tapping his foot. In particular, it does not make us think better of his tapping his foot than we would have thought had that good consequence not flowed from it.

Let us go back to that truck driver, whom I will call Unlucky No Fault Driver. His not having been at fault must be the crucial fact about him which makes him an exception to Adam Smith's remarks. For let us now contrast him with two other truck drivers.

Both of them were at fault. They were supposed to check their brakes before leaving the garage, but did not want to be bothered. So both went out with bad brakes. In the case of the first, nothing untoward happened, and I will call him Lucky Fault Driver. I will call the second Unlucky Fault Driver. A child ran in front of Unlucky Fault Driver's truck and he ran it down. I want to have it be clear about Unlucky Fault Driver that he ran the child down not because the child ran too suddenly, too close into the path of his truck, but because his brakes were not in good working order. Had his brakes been in good working order, he would have been able to stop his truck in time; but they were not, so he was not. Lucky Fault Driver acted badly, of course; but I think we do feel that Unlucky Fault Driver acted worse. The fact that a bad consequence flowed from his action does seem to affect our sense of its demerit.

Why? I think the answer is quite simply that Unlucky Fault Driver is to blame for the death he caused. Unlucky No Fault Driver also caused a death; but he is not to blame for it, since he was in no way at fault for causing it. It seems right to say that that is why the bad consequence which flowed from Unlucky No Fault Driver's action does not make us think it worse than we would have thought it had that bad consequence not flowed from it. More generally, it seems right to say that a bad consequence of an action makes that action worse *only* where the agent is to blame for that bad consequence which his action causes.

I am sure that the Kantian moral sophisticate would say at this point, "But surely it was mere bad luck for Unlucky Fault Driver that he caused a child's death. And surely one can't plausibly think a man to blame for something that he caused merely out of bad luck." There is a mistake here, and I think it the main source of the trouble. For it was not *mere* bad luck for Unlucky Fault Driver that he caused a child's death. We need a clearer grip on how bad luck figures in these cases. Unlucky No Fault Driver was in two ways unlucky. It was a piece of bad luck for him that a child ran into his path; and second, it was a piece of bad luck for him that a child ran into his path; but it was not a piece of bad luck for him that he was unable to stop his truck in time. Unlucky Fault Driver was unlucky in only the first of those two ways. It was a piece of bad luck for him that he was unable to stop his truck in time. His being unable to stop his truck in time was due to his bad brakes, and thus to his own negligence. Lucky Fault Driver did not have that first piece of bad luck, so it remains a counterfactual truth about him that *if* he had had it, then he too would have been unable to stop his truck in time. His being unable to stop would not have been a mere piece of bad luck for him, but would, instead, have been due to his negligence.

And it is the very same thing—namely Unlucky Fault Driver's negligence—that makes it not *mere* bad luck for him that he caused the child's death, that also makes him to blame for the child's death. Unlucky No Fault Driver, by contrast, was not at fault; and that is why it was mere bad luck for him that he caused a child's death, and therefore also why he is not to blame for the death of the child he killed.

The Kantian moral sophisticate could of course insist that a man cannot be thought to blame for something if bad luck entered *in any way at all* into the history of his bringing it about. But that seems to me even on its face implausible. Consider, for example, a man who is brought to trial for murder. "Look," his lawyer says to the court, "I grant that the victim's death is not *mere* bad luck for my client, since my client fired a gun at him with the intention of killing him. But the victim's death is in part due to my client's bad luck. For unbeknownst to my client, the victim almost always wore a bullet proof vest, and it was just bad luck for my client that the victim's bullet proof vest happened to be at the cleaners' on the day my client shot at him. So my client cannot be thought to blame for his victim's death." Whatever else will work in a court, *that* won't.

Let us go back now and look again at the first of the three principles that I said lie behind the moral attitude of the Kantian moral sophisticate. The first principle is: the moral value of what you do in the world turns on and only on that part of it which is entirely under your control. That seems to me to be false, and for the reason I have pointed to. Admittedly the two faulty drivers, Lucky Fault Driver and Unlucky Fault Driver, both acted equally negligently, and the difference between them has its source in the fact that one had good luck, the other bad luck. All the same, the difference which has that source is a moral difference, and of a very grave order. For the one is *by* his negligence to blame for a death, and the other is not.

A similar point surely holds of failures to act. Edward and Frank both failed to throw the switch; Edward's (but not Frank's) negligence caused a crash, for which he is therefore to blame. That, I think, is why we think that what he did was worse than what Frank did.

It seems to me, however, that we should be more sympathetic to the third of the three principles I mentioned, which yields that Unlucky Fault Driver is no worse a person than Lucky Fault Driver is, and that Edward is no worse a person than Frank. Counterfactual truths about what people would have done and been to blame for if they had been in circumstances which they were lucky enough to have avoided really are important to us in assessing how good a person is—as important, I think, as truths about what they in fact did and in fact are to blame for.

This difference between our judgments of acts on the one hand and the people who perform them on the other hand may perhaps be due to the fact that different kinds of consequences flow from our arriving at these two different kinds of judgments. When we learn that someone is a bad person—untrustworthy, unreliable, prone to acting without thought for others—what flows from this judgment? Well, our attitude toward him changes, and in consequence we will behave differently toward him in many more or less delicate ways in the future. This reaction is appropriate whether the judgment is provoked by what he actually did *or* by what we have come to learn he would do if he were in circumstances he has not in fact been in. By contrast, some of the consequences of learning that a person has actually acted badly are backward looking. If we learn he is to blame for a dreadful outcome, we do not merely alter our behavior toward him in future, we may also lock him up for what he did, or exact compensation for it from him, or both.[13]

V

Candor, however, compels me to mention a difficulty for what I have been saying. Let us go back to Adam Smith. He said: "the actual consequences which happen to proceed from any action, have a great effect upon our sentiments concerning its merit or demerit, and *almost always* either enhance or diminish our sense of both."[14] I mentioned one class of exceptions. Unlucky No Fault Driver, for example, was merely unlucky. He caused a child's death, but because this was through no fault of his own, we do not think the worse of his actions. Where there is fault, however, I said that consequences do make a difference. We do think worse of Unlucky Fault Driver's actions than of Lucky Fault Driver's actions, and that is because the one is, and the other is not, to blame for a bad outcome.

But there is yet another class of exceptions to Adam Smith's remarks, which makes trouble for any simple treatment of these issues. The simplest example comes from a case I mentioned at the outset, namely *Summers v. Tice*.[15] (That is a wonderful case. If it had not occurred, we would have had to invent it.) The two defendants, Tice and Simonson, both fired negligently in Summers' direction, and one of them shot Summers, but we cannot tell which. Who should pay Summers' bills? Most people feel it right that Tice and Simonson should split the costs. The actual outcome in court was joint and several liability, but arguably that comes to roughly the same thing given the possibility of a suit for contribution, and in any case there are reasons to think that outcome fairer to Summers than a division of the costs. So far so good, nothing puzzling yet.

Now for the source of the puzzlement. Suppose that during the course of the trial evidence came forward which made it as certain as empirical matters ever are that the pellet that caused Summers' injury came from Tice's gun, so that it is Tice who is to blame for Summers' injury. We do, I think, take it to be clear that Simonson should now be dismissed from the suit: no doubt he acted badly, but he is not to blame for the injury, and hence he is not appropriately held liable for its costs.[16] But our *moral* assessment of Tice and Simonson does not shift. We do not think the worse of Tice, or even of Tice's acts, because he, as it turns out, is to blame for the harm; and we do not think the better of Simonson, or of Simonson's acts, because as it turns out, is not to blame for the harm. Our moral attitude does not shift in any way by virtue of the discovery that it is Tice who actually caused the harm. So we really seem to have a second kind of exception to Adam Smith's remarks.

It could of course be said that it is just irrational on our part to fail to distinguish between Tice and Simonson in the way in which we do distinguish between Lucky and Unlucky Fault Drivers. But it does not *feel* irrational. And the moral views of the man and woman in the street are deserving of great respect: they ought not be dismissed as irrational unless it really does turn out that there is no rationale for them.

What bubbles up in us men-and-women-in-the-street is, I think, this: "Simonson nearly caused the very same harm that Tice caused." It is not true of Lucky Fault Driver that he nearly caused the very same harm that Unlucky Fault Driver caused. Or at

least you were not thinking of him as having done so. One driver goes out in one part of town, the other in another; they both have bad brakes; a child runs in front of one, no child runs in front of the other. So far so good. One is to blame for a death and the other is not, and we feel very differently about what they did.

But now let the two drivers set out from the same part of town, down the same street. A child runs in front of both. Both come to a long screeching halt. The child is hit by one truck and not by the other. If the child had been running *ever* so slightly slower, it would have been hit by the other truck. Now the drivers seem to us like Tice and Simonson: we think no worse of what the one did than of what the other did.

This suggests that something else is at work in these cases, possibly two things, in fact.

In the first place, Tice and Simonson did not merely act equally negligently; they each imposed roughly the same risk of harm on a person. Similarly for the two truck drivers who set out from the same part of town, and in front of both of whom one child runs. Not so for two truck drivers who set out from different parts of town. If they both set out with bad brakes, they acted equally negligently; but if a child runs in front of one, and no child so much as gets near the other, they do not in fact impose even roughly the same risk of harm on anyone.

This does make a difference to us. Suppose you back your car out of your driveway without looking, but no child was anywhere near you. Perhaps you will feel bad later on thinking the matter over: after all, it is negligent to back out without looking. But you will not *dwell* on what you did; it would be irrational to lie awake at night shuddering at the thought of what you *might* have caused. But suppose you back your car out of your driveway without looking, and there was a child in the vicinity; indeed, you nearly hit it, and would have hit it but for the child's having noticed a penny up ahead and run faster to get to it. Here the shudder is not out of place. We all know what that terrible, nagging thought is like: it is not merely of what you might have caused, but of what you nearly did cause. You do not feel as bad as you would if you had actually hit the child; but you do feel considerably worse than you would if there had been no child in the vicinity at all.

Adam Smith said that the bad consequences of an act affect our sense of its merit or demerit, and I agreed that this is so if the act was faulty: for the bad things an act causes are things that its agent is to blame for, if his act was faulty. What seems to come out here is that it is not merely the actual bad consequences of an act that affect our sense of its demerit: the higher the risk of bad consequences that the act actually imposes on others, the greater the demerit of the act.

It is puzzling that this should be so, however. Your negligence in backing out of your driveway without looking is no greater or worse if there is a child in the vicinity than if there is not; and since you did not actually hit the child, [you] cannot explain [your] feeling that what you did was worse by appeal to the fact that you are to blame for a harm to the child. *Nobody* was harmed. So there is a gap here, and I hope you will find it as interesting a question as I do just how it is to be filled.

I said it is possible that there are two further things at work in these cases. The second of them is this: Tice and Simonson did not merely act equally negligently, and they did not merely each impose roughly the same risk of harm on *a* person; they each imposed roughly the same risk of harm on one and the same person, namely Summers. Similarly for the two truck drivers who set out from the same part of town, and in front of both of whom one child runs. Does *that* matter to us? I do not find it clear that it does. Dickenson fired his shotgun negligently last Wednesday, and nearly hit someone. He feels awful about what he did, and we think it right that he feel awful about it. Do we think worse of what Simonson did, given he nearly hit someone on Thursday, *and* given also that the person Simonson nearly hit was

in fact hit by Tice? Perhaps so. But it is even harder, I think, to see why that should be so—if it is.

VI

Let me now try to pull this material together just briefly. I began by drawing attention to two phenomena in law—more precisely, one in law itself, the other in legal theory—which seem to warrant saying that as far as tort law is concerned at any rate, there has been a decline of cause. Many people think that if cause declines in law, law to that extent departs from morality. It therefore seemed to me worth drawing attention to the fact that there has been a decline of cause in moral theory too. That decline in part explains why moral theorists who interest themselves in law have welcomed those developments in law and legal theory. But it is of interest for its own sake. As Adam Smith said, when you think about these matters in the abstract, the philosophers seem to be right; but when you come out of the study, they seem to be wrong. Moral theorists must of course ask themselves why that is, and whether there is a rationale for it; that is the job of the moral theorist. But I hope that lawyers will find these questions of interest too. The law certainly is not, and need not be, an exact reflection of the morality of those governed by it; but responsible government tries to be sure it has a sound rationale whenever it departs from that morality, and therefore does well to try to become clear about what that morality is.

---

1. 26 Cal. 3d 88, 163 Cal. Rptr. 132, 607 P.2d 924, cert. denied, 449 U.S. 912 (1980).
2. 33 Cal. 2d 80, 199 P.2d 1 (1948).
3. For an interesting discussion of these and related matters, which brings out their bearing on a particular case, see P. Shuck, *Agent Orange on Trial, Mass Toxic Disasters in the Courts* (1986).
4. Landes & Posner, *Causation in Tort Law: An Economic Approach*, 12 *J.L. Stud.* 109, 131 (1983).
5. Calabresi, *Concerning Cause and the Law of Torts: An Essay for Harry Kalven, Jr.*, 43 *U. Chi. L. Rev.* 69, 106–07 (1975) (emphasis in original).
6. See, e.g., Kelman, *The Necessary Myth of Objective Causation Judgments in Liberal Political Theory*, 63 *Chi-Kent L. Rev* 579 (1987).
7. See S. Milgram, *Obedience to Authority* (1974) (summarizing results of Milgram's experiments).
8. I. Kant, *Foundations of the Metaphysics of Morals* 12–13 (Bobbs-Merill ed. 1969).
9. See, e.g., Fischer & Ennis, *Causation and Liability*, 15 *Phil. & Pub. Affairs* 33 (1986); Kagan, *Causation, Liability, and Internalism*, 15 *Phil. & Pub. Affairs* 41 (1986).
10. A. Smith, *The Theory of Moral Sentiments* 134 (Arlington House ed. 1969).
11. The emphasis is mine.
12. T. Nagel, *Mortal Questions* 28–29 (1979).
13. As I wrote in part III, the moral sophisticate may say that while the law does well to mark a difference between Alfred and Bert (punishing Bert more severely than Alfred, exacting compensation for the injury from Bert), this is for reasons extraneous to the moral valuation proper to them and their acts. I think it is one thing to say the moral valuation proper to them does not warrant differential legal consequences: Bert is surely no worse a person than Alfred is. But it is another thing to say the moral valuation proper to their acts does not warrant differential legal consequences: Bert, after all, is to blame for a harm and Alfred is not, so there really is a moral difference between what Bert did and what Alfred did.
14. A. Smith, *supra* note 10, at 134. The emphasis is mine.
15. 33 Cal. 2d 80, 199 P.2d 1 (1948).
16. Why this should be so is discussed in Thomson, *Remarks on Causation and Liability*, 13 *Phil. & Pub. Affairs* 101 (1984). Criticism of that discussion may be found in Fischer & Ennis, *supra* note 9, and in Kagan, *supra* note 9.

BLAME, PUNISHMENT, AND THE ROLE OF RESULT*

Richard Parker

Rasputin, the story goes, was poisoned with cyanide, shot with pistols, bludgeoned, stabbed, emasculated, then tied with cords, wrapped in cloth and dumped through a hole in the ice in the Neva River. When the body was found, it was discovered that he had worked part way out of his bonds before he succumbed; the cause of death was drowning. Let us suppose for a moment that the object of these horrors had proved, incredibly, to be an even more recalcitrant victim than he was and that he had actually survived his ordeal. Clearly, this supposition has no effect at all with respect to the intentions of Prince Yusupov and his cohorts, the perpetrators of the crime, nor does it affect their conduct in any substantial way—they did everything they could to ensure Rasputin's death, employing means well beyond those ordinarily required. Had he survived, due to his own incredible efforts and constitution, would that diminish the seriousness of the crime committed against him? However we decide to answer this question, it is clear that Rasputin's survival would substantially change the culpability and statutory punishability of Yusupov and company in practically every jurisdiction within the scope of Anglo-American law. It is true, of course, that the parties guilty of such a crime could be punished very severely under existing statutes, but, compared to the penalty for murder, the sanctions attached to aggravated assault, attempted murder, battery, and mayhem—the offenses for which Yusupov is most likely indictable on our supposition—are clearly less forbidding.

I bring up this rather exotic example from the history of homicide to introduce what seems to me to be a serious difficulty in our system of criminal justice. The difficulty, in its most general form, can be put in terms of a question: on what rational grounds can we proportion punishment to the results of an actor's conduct when those results are largely or entirely beyond the actor's control? The distinction between attempts and completed crimes is only the most visible of many which call up this question. Felony-murder, misdemeanor-manslaughter, and reckless or negligent conduct of many kinds involve the same or an analogous problem. In what follows I'll concentrate on a few rather more mundane examples than the Rasputin incident, with particular attention to certain moral aspects of the issues.

I

It is often said that one who engages in criminal wrongdoing thereby incurs a debt to society; the wrongdoer's punishment is conceived as the coin in which the debt is payable. That he owes the debt to *society* rather than to some private individual or collective (who may have suffered a loss at his hands) is often said to be the key to the distinction between criminal law and tort law, or, perhaps better, between criminal harm and tortious harm. Lawrence Becker has discussed this matter[1] with helpful results especially with respect to the analysis of criminal or "social" harm and the role this notion should rightly play in the law of attempts. The position he takes is that it is the *attempt* to accomplish harm, whether the attempt succeed or fail, which is properly the concern of the society and hence the busi-

*Richard Parker, "Blame, Punishment, and the Role of Result," a revision of a paper in *American Philosophical Quarterly,* vol. 21, no. 3 (1984), pp. 1–11. Reprinted by permission of the author and *American Philosophical Quarterly.* A slightly different version of this paper appeared in the *American Philosophical Quarterly*, volume 21, number 3, July 1984. The first draft was written with support from a grant from the National Endowment for the Humanities.

ness of criminal law. Attempts, Becker argues, produce as much justifiable social volatility—his phrase for upset, anxiety, fear, and generally unfavorable reaction—as do successful crimes.[2] Hence the criminal law should make no distinction as regards punishability between a full-fledged attempt and a success, other things being equal.

In a few moments, I shall argue for Becker's conclusion on other, but related, grounds. First, though, I should point out how strongly this conclusion runs counter to both current practice and popular opinion.

In the history of criminal law, the punishment of unsuccessful attempts and other conduct which fails to produce harm is a relatively recent development.[3] Indeed, among the "basic premises which underlie the whole of Anglo-American criminal law" is the statement that, "since the criminal law aims to prevent harm to the public, there can be no crime without harm."[4] Clearly, we do not follow this dictum to the letter, as the law defines many criminal offenses which merely *tend* to have harmful consequences (such as forgery) or which merely produce dangerous situations (such as reckless driving). Still, the emphasis put on actual harm caused is a principal ingredient of the method we use to grade the seriousness of crimes and to determine the severity of punishments.[5] It can also make the difference between criminal and noncriminal conduct.[6]

As is usually the case with the substantive criminal law, there seems to be a connection between the law's emphasis on harm and certain moral intuitions which many people apparently share. It may strike us as gratuitous, for example, to punish a person for an action which in fact caused nobody any harm. What are we punishing him for? one might ask. On the other hand, there is a clear answer to this question if a harmful result is actually produced: he is punished for causing that result. Furthermore, since the criminal law is connected to moral blameworthiness (at least in a way that tort law is not),[7] it is not surprising that most people seem to find it easier to blame one who causes harm more than one who does not. I believe that blameworthiness and punishability should where possible run parallel in the law, but I think it is false that results are generally relevant either to one's blameworthiness or to his punishability.

Consider the following story: you and I attend a party and get roaring drunk. In our host's den we discover a pair of loaded rifles and decide to find out which of us is the better shot by firing out a window at a lamp across the street. Each of us takes several

shots, with no ill effect on the lamp. One of your shots, however, ricochets off the lamppost or by some similar means finds its way into a citizen who, unknown to us, happened to be nearby. The citizen dies as a result of his wound. Now, given the similarity of our conduct, it seems perfectly appropriate to claim equal blameworthiness on our parts. This can be made quite clear, I think, by varying the case a bit. Suppose first that it is not immediately known which of our bullets, yours or mine, that caused the fatal result. It seems strange that we should have to wait to apportion blame until this determination is made, for most people would surely agree that what is necessary to make this apportionment is present in this case before we know whose bullet caused the death. If we *never* discover whose bullet did the fatal damage, is there some hesitancy, some cloudiness of our intuition with respect to how much comparative blame the two of us deserve? I think not. I think most people would be satisfied with equal blame between us, and, importantly, nobody would worry much about a mistake having been made—the mistake of one of us being blamed for something he didn't do or the other for not being blamed for something he did do. If unequal blame is due us, the pain of inconsistency can be avoided only by showing a relevant difference between us. And, if it can be shown that the only difference is that made by the fact that one fired the fatal bullet and one did not, and if it can further be determined that this difference is due to chance (which would be the case if, e.g., only a ballistics test could show whose bullet it was), then there clearly is no *morally* relevant difference between us at all. Hence we are equally blameworthy despite the unequal results of our conduct.

A possible argument on the other side goes this way: one of us is *more blameable* because he is blameable *for more*.[8] I believe that either this argument is question begging, in which case it is valid but has a premise that is false, or else it is a non sequitur. The second alternative is simpler to explain. "Blameable for" is connected in obvious ways to "caused." If you, in our story of a while ago, are said to be blameable for more merely in the sense that you caused more harm, then I have no objection beyond the remark that this way of putting it is misleading. But in this case it simply doesn't follow that you are more blameable in the sense of *morally* blameable. The alternative view of the argument has an individual being blameworthy, in the straightforward moral sense, for the *result* of the action as well as the action itself. The blameworthiness for these *two* items is apparently supposed to "add up" to more blame. Now, there is an obvious distinction between an actor's conduct on one hand and, on the other, that chain of events that begins where his conduct stops and which continues on indefinitely. The view I am urging here is that, properly speaking, only an actor's conduct can be blameworthy. I do not believe that it makes good sense to blame a person for the consequences that in fact flow from his conduct even if they are within the risk of that conduct.[9] I hasten to add that I do not mean that he cannot be held responsible for harm caused that is within the risk of his conduct. I maintain only that such harm is tortious rather than criminal and should be actionable only as such. A burden may rightfully be placed on a person for the harm he causes, but this is conceptually distinct from punishment and does not entail blameworthiness. The individual is blameworthy and punishable, on my view, only for the conduct itself, where conduct is construed as a combination of overt action, state of mind (including intention, knowledge, etc.) and circumstances. Common sense will have to serve here as a guide, and there is good reason to believe that it can.

Consider another example. Imagine that *A* takes a rifle to a place overlooking a stadium where he knows an event is underway and recklessly fires the weapon in the direction of the grandstands. Let us suppose the fortunate consequence of the bullet's striking the bleachers harmlessly after narrowly missing members of the crowd. Compare this with the situation of *B*, who takes his rifle to the same spot on a day when he knows there is no event scheduled and in fact believes the grandstands to be entirely empty. He too fires toward the seats but with unfortunate results: a lone custodian is present policing the stands and he is struck and killed by *B*'s bullet. It takes either a considerable stretch of the imagination or adherence to a bad theory, or both, to want to hold *B* more blameworthy than *A*. Truly, the harm caused by *B*'s conduct far outweighs that caused by *A*'s, the latter being negligible. But it is *A*, on the view I am defending, who is the more blameworthy and whose desert is the greater punishment.

The last example makes it clear what I want to use as a substitute for harm as the device for determining blameworthiness and punishment: the *risk* of harm that the conduct creates.

In the example as described there is another relevant factor: *A*'s *knowingly* creating the risk—he knew there was a crowd in the stands—and *B*'s ignorance of the custodian's presence. In the usual ter-

minology, these circumstances are captured by saying that *A*'s conduct was reckless while *B*'s was negligent. And it is true that we generally find more fault in the former than in the latter. There are at least two things to be said about that. First, I would hold the same view of *A*'s and *B*'s blameworthiness and punishability if *B*'s behavior were reckless instead of merely negligent; if, that is, he had known about the presence of the custodian. In such case, both *A* and *B* knowingly create risks, but *A* creates the greater risk and hence is more punishable. Second, it seems very plausible to believe that one reason why we judge reckless behavior more culpable than negligent behavior is that the former is riskier. A person who will perform an action *knowing* it is likely to cause harm is more apt to actually cause harm than one who would act only if he were ignorant of the likely harm, and this is the case even if the latter *should* have been aware of the harmful prospects (i.e., he is negligent by the standard of the reasonable man).

In cases of recklessness and negligence, it is fair and accurate to speak of the person who causes harm and, on current practice, is punished for it beyond what he would have been had no harm resulted, as being punished for his bad luck. (And it is his bad luck that he is being punished!) Seen this way, I think it is plain that the "extra" punishment is impossible to justify morally. In fact, if there is *something* wrong with punishing for harm caused in cases like these, then there is *everything* wrong with it. Let me borrow a statement of the relevant principle from Hyman Gross—the principle that liability ought to match culpability, a "general principle of proportion between crime and punishment,"

> is a principle of just desert that serves as the foundation of every criminal sentence that is justifiable. . . . Indeed, the requirement that punishment not be disproportionately great, which is a corollary of just desert, is dictated by the same principle that does not allow punishment of the innocent, for any punishment in excess of what is deserved for the criminal conduct is punishment without guilt.[10]

I need to add only that nobody is ever guilty of having bad luck, at least not in any relevant sense of "guilty."

In the recent examples, the person causing the harm in each case might indeed be said to be guilty by misfortune. The other side of this coin are those who are innocent by good fortune. Attempters, among others, fall into this category, and the position I advocate in such cases is in principle the same as that regarding negligently and recklessly caused harm. Whether we are talking about intentional or unintentional creation of risk, that is to say, has nothing to do with the point at issue: a person who performs a last step attempt—that is, one who does everything within his power that he believes necessary to complete a crime—and whose failure is due to a chance event not within his control, is no less blameworthy and ought to be no less punishable than one who is successful in bringing his intended result about. The reason is exactly analogous to those in the earlier cases: there are no grounds for punishing the attempter and the successful offender differently aside from the already criticized grounds of punishing for whatever good or bad luck attends one's activities. Punishment on these grounds is no less immoral than unequal punishment for unequal results in cases of negligence. For, if a given punishment is the just desert for a completed crime, then no less a punishment is the just desert of at least some attempts to commit that crime.[11] On the other hand, if we punish the attempter less than the successful offender, we punish the latter "in excess of what is deserved for the criminal conduct." Indeed, the punishment we visit on the successful criminal beyond that which we visit on the attempter is nothing less than "punishment without guilt."

II

The conclusion just reached may seem strange at first. If it does it is probably because of an underlying conceptual shift entailed by the present view. The shift is as follows. I've said that it is the risk-creating aspect of conduct that makes it punishable and not the results of that conduct. Implicit in that claim is a change in the very notion of a crime. For anything that counts as a *result* of conduct rather than a *part of* that conduct ought not strictly speaking be a part of a crime; only conduct can be criminal. This produces some admittedly strange results. For example, on the view I present, there can be no such crime as murder, at least as it is currently conceived, because on the current view the production of a corpse is, in a crucial sense, an irrelevant feature. (The sense in which it *is* relevant will be noted in a moment.) What is crucially relevant is the *likelihood* of a death resulting from the conduct in question. Consider the case of A, who produces a water pistol and begins squirt-

ing water at B, confident in his belief that he can kill B by eroding him to death.[12] We are not quick to find A guilty of a serious crime because, despite his intention and his action, he has done little that is likely to produce serious harm to B. Possibly more serious is the case of C, who puts a harmless drug in D's drink, thinking it is strychnine. The kind of conduct of which C is guilty may be dangerous indeed; exactly how dangerous it is depends largely upon what measures he took to ensure that the drug was strychnine. If it was incompetence that produced the mistake—he was suffering from the delusion that strychnine was contained in the sugar bowl on D's dinner table, for example—then the seriousness, and the likelihood of his harming D, is minimal. If it was chance—e.g., he happened to pick up an unlabeled bottle of saccharin that was next to his unlabeled strychnine bottle—then the seriousness and the dangerousness of the conduct escalate dramatically.

Gross provides a notion of harmful conduct that helps clarify matters. Harmful conduct is conduct that may or may not cause actual harm, but, if it does not, this fortunate consequence is due merely to chance.[13] This notion allows a concise statement of the primary claim I seek to defend: conduct is blameworthy and may create liability for punishment because and to the extent that it is harmful. There is also the corollary that an act may be deemed a crime to the extent that it is harmful.[14]

This principle (or these principles) may, with luck, capture the intuitions of those who were persuaded by the earlier claim that we ought not to punish those whose actions produce harm as the result of chance any more than those whose similar actions produce no harm. But it is important to notice that an action performed with evil intent is as well included under this principle as one performed negligently; we are talking about the entire array of criminal activity because we are talking about the very notion of a crime.

I indicated that the harm actually produced by conduct is not always irrelevant to an evaluation of the culpability attributable to that conduct, even on the theory proposed here. The relevance of a harmful result is in the form of evidence that the conduct in question was indeed harmful. In the case of the drunken shooting match that you and I held a few pages back, there is a claim that I can make that you cannot, i.e., that I *knew* that my bullets would not strike anybody. Under the circumstances described I would hardly be able to give any grounds for it, but it might, with corroborating evidence, provide a defense under circumstances where my conduct was not *ex hypothesi* as risky as that which actually produced the fatal harm. In general, the production of a harmful result is *prima facie* evidence that the conduct that produced it was likely to produce it. Such a result, or lack of one, would ordinarily help to locate properly a burden of proof on the defense or the prosecution, respectively. This, it seems to me, is the proper function of result. If it actually played this role, the conceptual scheme in many criminal cases would be substantially different from what it is currently. For example, the crime of involuntary manslaughter—a felony in most states—would be stricken from the books. A person who, on current practice, is indictable for such a crime would stand trial, on my view, for an offense of negligence or recklessness, and the death he caused would be offered as evidence of the negligence or recklessness of his conduct.

III

Let's next take a brief look at what seems to be behind most of the opposition to the view I have presented. There are two items that bear scrutiny in the accepted opinion. First, there is the view that, when an individual does something that might cause harm, he is taking a gamble of a sort, and when one gambles there are times when he wins and times when he loses. If one wins, so much the better; there is no harm done and nothing to pay for. If he loses, then he should be prepared to pay for it. After all, one hears, life itself is a gamble. This view has very little to recommend it. While it is true that we all take risks whether we get out of bed in the morning or not, surely we do not want to increase the amount of risk to which we are subject by building them into our system of criminal justice. We ought not to gear punishment to actual harm caused for exactly the same reason that we ought not to determine whether a person should be punished by flipping a coin or casting dice. Fortune may make us healthy, wealthy, or wise, but it ought not determine whether we go to prison.

A second point has to do with an explanation of why, in the common view, we fixate so readily on result when we consider the enormity or triviality of a crime. The result, when it is produced, provides a focus for our attention—it provides something tangible for us to get upset about. We do take the business of punishment seriously, and, given the

kind of creatures we are, we are hesitant about punishing a person when we do not *feel* an actual loss of some sort. Take the person who drunkenly drives his automobile at a high rate of speed, jumps a curb, and careens down a sidewalk. We may think of the harm he *might* have caused, but that brings only a kind of "abstract" loss to mind. If he actually strikes and kills a child, however, there is a particular harm caused, and this gives our attention—our fears, our sense of outrage—a focal point: it was *this* child's life that was lost. And this is something that operates more powerfully in us, something that sets off our "retributive urge."[15] The point is confirmed, I think, by what we ordinarily do in the case of a near miss. Should the drunkenly driven automobile narrowly miss a child walking down the sidewalk, we are apt to be more outraged by the driver's conduct than if no child had been present. In such a case we have something more than an abstraction (an imagined child that might have been on the sidewalk when in fact none was nearby) on which to focus—the details of what might have happened are more clear. "You might have killed *that* child," we want to say, whereas we have nobody to refer to if there is no near miss. But, if we carefully consider what is operating here, I think we will conclude that what the presence of the child who is narrowly missed really furnishes us is *evidence* that the driver was in no position to avoid hitting whomever might have been in the way. The evidence is simply greater when a death or injury actually occurs. If ample evidence can be given that the driver would have killed a person on the sidewalk, had there been one there, then we have as much *right* to be upset—and to punish—as if there actually had been a victim, even if in fact we are less inclined to be upset—and to punish—in such a case. But the proper conclusion is stronger than this; we are bound by the principle of justice that like cases be treated alike to punish the same whether there is a child struck, a child narrowly missed, or nobody on the sidewalk at all, provided the evidence is sufficient to show that the driver would have done what he did regardless of anyone's presence in his path. So the difference in emotional response is understandable but not really relevant to the culpability of the offender.

The fact that we respond emotionally to results of offenses has sometimes been offered as a reason for grading and creating offenses on the basis of their results. J.F. Stephen criticized (and managed to get amended) the Indian Penal Code for the omission of the crime of negligent manslaughter. The omission failed to recognize "the effect which an offense produces on the feelings and imagination of mankind."[16] Stephen admitted that result might be due purely to fortune and that it had nothing to do with the punishment one might deserve. But still, in a case where two negligent actors produce different results, "it gratifies a natural public feeling to choose out for punishment that one who actually has caused great harm, and the effect in the way of preventing a repetition of the offense is much the same as if both were punished."[17] Stephen's first point hardly requires rebuttal; it might gratify a public feeling to stage gladiatorial contests on television but it is not therefore the business of the government to produce them. True, public sentiment must be taken into some account in the structure of the system, but it is as much the business of that system to lead and to mold public opinion as it is to gratify public feelings. Deterrence does not help the other side either. Let's distinguish between special deterrence (deterring *this* offender from repeating his offense) and general deterrence (deterring other members of the society). With respect to the first, unequal punishment appears to accomplish nothing; a lighter penalty for an attempt or nonharmful result could hardly discourage an offender from repeating his conduct, and, other things being equal, it is not at all clear that he is less apt to commit the offense again than one who actually causes harm—my suspicion is that quite the contrary is true. Other factors than result are almost certainly more relevant to determining the likelihood of repetition: the offender's personality, background, etc. In the case of general deterrence a number of problems arise, many of them speculative or empirical in nature and too complex to be dealt with here.[18] From a moral point of view, however, we might note that a general deterrence justification of unequal treatment has the criminal justice system *using* an individual to accomplish a general social end not directly connected with his own culpability.[19] The situation is no different from unusually harsh "exemplary" sentences and no less unjust.

To close, let me sum up. I take the principle that like cases should be treated alike to be a main part of the notion of justice that operates in our treatment of criminal offenders as well as in society at large. It is a person's conduct, I contend, for which we may properly blame him and hold him liable for punishment. Harm that results from a person's conduct is not strictly speaking a part of that conduct and does not provide grounds for distinguishing between culpability and nonculpability, nor does it form a basis for grading offensive conduct with respect to liability for punishment. This becomes especially clear when we notice how much the results of conduct are susceptible to the intervention of chance—factors not a part of the actor's conduct and not within his direct control. The extent to which a given offense, consequences aside, is culpable and merits punishment depends, among other factors, upon the likelihood that harm will result from it. Whatever harm is actually produced should serve only as the basis for a rebuttable claim about the likelihood of such harm.

When result is allowed to form the basis for unequal punishment in otherwise similar cases, I have argued, the effect is to punish one whose action produces harm beyond what is that person's just desert. And this provides a moral ground for ruling out result as a factor in determining the severity of punishment.

Implicit in this view is a conceptual change in the notion of a crime. In principle, this notion should not include reference to harm actually caused but be restricted solely to conduct. The problem of determining more or less exactly what the scope and limits of conduct are looms large, but it is present already in many regions of the criminal law and common sense, properly directed, will serve sufficiently as a reliable guide.

The principle of liability for risk-creating or harmful conduct (in the sense of "harmful" described above) should serve as a guiding principle in the definitions of crimes and in the determination of appropriate sentences. At a bare minimum, it requires the elimination of certain current statutory provisions that mandate unequal punishment for offenses that are otherwise distinguished only by fortune. Otherwise we must simply face the rude fact that one of the most crucial elements of our system—indeed, our *notion*—of criminal justice is blind luck.

---

1. In "Criminal Attempt and the Theory of the Law of Crimes," *Philosophy and Public Affairs*, vol. 3 (1974), pp. 262–94.

2. *Ibid.*, pp. 271–75.

3. See W. LaFave and A. Scott, *Criminal Law* (St. Paul, 1972), p. 423.

4. *Ibid.*, p. 7.
5. Attempt is punishable in California by a maximum of one-half the maximum term for the completed crime. The Model Penal Code of the American Law Institute makes a misdemeanor of reckless conduct which creates a risk of injury if no harm or even bodily injury occurs; but if death occurs, the offense is manslaughter, a second degree felony. §§ 211.1 (1)(a), 211.2, 210.3 (Official Draft, 1962).
6. "Negligent conduct, not criminal in the absence of harm, becomes a misdemeanor if bodily injury occurs under some limited circumstances, and a felony of the third degree if death results." J. Schulhofer, discussing the Model Penal Code in "Harm and Punishment," *University of Pennsylvania Law Review*, vol. 122 (1974), p. 1499.
7. LaFave and Scott, *op. cit.*, pp. 9ff. Hart argues that the criminal law must not be permitted to create crimes out of conduct that lacks the blameworthiness deserving of moral condemnation. See H. M. Hart, Jr., "The Aims of the Criminal Law," in *Law and Contemporary Problems*, vol. 23 (1958), pp. 401, 404–6.
8. This argument was once suggested to me, not very enthusiastically, by the late F. A. Siegler.
9. A harm is "within the risk" of an action if, under the circumstances, it is a reasonably expectable or foreseeable (some say "natural") consequence of that action.
10. *A Theory of Criminal Justice* (Oxford, 1978), p. 436.
11. For some attempts it would not be the just desert, or we could not know that it was, because of an evidentiary point that is discussed later.
12. The example is cribbed from Richard Wasserstrom, whom I thank for discussions on this topic.
13. Gross, *op. cit.*, pp. 428ff.
14. It may not be a crime simply because it may not be against the law.
15. The phrase is due to John Junker, who is also responsible for stimulating my initial interest in this topic.
16. *History of the Criminal Law*, vol. III (London, 1883), pp. 311ff.
17. *Ibid.*
18. A treatment of several aspects of the problem is available in Schulhofer, *op. cit.*, pp. 1572–77.
19. See Gross, *op. cit.*, pp. 390ff.

PALSGRAF V. THE LONG ISLAND RAILROAD CO.*

New York Court of Appeals, 1928

CARDOZO, Ch. J. Plaintiff was standing on a platform of defendant's railroad after buying a ticket to go to Rockaway Beach. A train stopped at the station, bound for another place. Two men ran forward to catch it. One of the men reached the platform of the car without mishap, though the train was already moving. The other man, carrying a package, jumped aboard the car, but seemed unsteady as if about to fall. A guard on the car, who had held the door open, reached forward to help him in, and another guard on the platform pushed him from behind. In this act, the package was dislodged, and fell upon the rails. It was a package of small size, about fifteen inches long, and was covered by a newspaper. In fact it contained fireworks, but there was nothing in its appearance to give notice of its contents. The fireworks when they fell exploded. The shock of the explosion threw down some scales at the other end of the platform, many feet away. The scales struck the plaintiff, causing injuries for which she sues.

The conduct of the defendant's guard, if a wrong in its relation to the holder of the package, was not a wrong in its relation to the plaintiff, standing far away. Relatively to her it was not negligence at all. Nothing in the situation gave notice that the falling package had in it the potency of peril to persons thus removed. Negligence is not actionable unless it involves in the invasion of a legally protected interest, the violation of a right. "Proof of negligence in the air, so to speak, will not do." "Negligence is the absence of care, according to the circumstances." The plaintiff as she stood upon the platform of the station might claim to be protected against intentional invasion of her bodily security. Such invasion

*248 N.Y. 339 (1928). Citations omitted.

is not charged. She might claim to be protected against unintentional invasion by conduct involving in the thought of reasonable men an unreasonable hazard that such invasion would ensue. These, from the point of view of the law, were the bounds of her immunity, with perhaps some rare exceptions, survivals for the most part of ancient forms of liability, where conduct is held to be at the peril of the actor (*Sullivan v. Dunham,* 161 N.Y. 290). If no hazard was apparent to the eye of ordinary vigilance, an act innocent and harmless, at least to outward seeming, with reference to her, did not take to itself the quality of a tort because it happened to be a wrong, though apparently not one involving the risk of bodily insecurity, with reference to someone else. "In every instance, before negligence can be predicated of a given act, back of the act must be sought and found a duty to the individual complaining, the observance of which would have averted or avoided the injury." "The ideas of negligence and duty are strictly correlative." (BOWEN, L. J., in *Thomas v. Quartermaine,* 18 *Q.B.D.* 685, 694.) The plaintiff sues in her own right for a wrong personal to her, and not as the vicarious beneficiary of a breach of duty to another.

A different conclusion will involve us, and swiftly too, in a maze of contradictions. A guard stumbles over a package which has been left upon a platform. It seems to be a bundle of newspapers. It turns out to be a can of dynamite. To the eye of ordinary vigilance, the bundle is abandoned waste, which may be kicked or trod on with impunity. Is a passenger at the other end of the platform protected by the law against the unsuspected hazard concealed beneath the waste? If not, is the result to be any different, so far as the distant passenger is concerned, when the guard stumbles over a valise which a truckman or a porter has left upon the walk? The passenger far away, if the victim of a wrong at all, has a cause of action, not derivative, but original and primary. His claim to be protected against invasion of his bodily security is neither greater nor less because the act resulting in the invasion is a wrong to another far removed. In this case, the rights that are said to have been violated, the interests said to have been invaded, are not even of the same order. The man was not injured in his person nor even put in danger. The purpose of the act, as well as its effect, was to make his person safe. If there was a wrong to him at all, which may very well be doubted, it was a wrong to a property interest only, the safety of his package. Out of this wrong to property, which threatened injury to nothing else, there has passed, we are told, to the plaintiff by derivation or succession a right of action for the invasion of an interest of another order, the right to bodily security. The diversity of interests emphasizes the futility of the effort to build the plaintiff's right upon the basis of a wrong to someone else. The gain is one of emphasis, for a like result would follow if the interests were the same. Even then, the orbit of the danger as disclosed to the eye of reasonable vigilance would be the orbit of the duty. One who jostles one's neighbor in a crowd does not invade the rights of others standing at the outer fringe when the unintended contact casts a bomb upon the ground. The wrongdoer, as to them is the man who carries the bomb, not the one who explodes it without suspicion of the danger. Life will have to be made over, and human nature transformed, before prevision so extravagant can be accepted as the norm of conduct, the customary standard to which behavior must conform.

The argument for the plaintiff is built upon the shifting meanings of such words as "wrong" and "wrongful," and shares their instability. What the plaintiff must show is "a wrong" to herself, *i.e.,* a violation of her own right, and not merely a wrong to someone else, nor conduct "wrongful" because unsocial, but not "a wrong" to anyone. We are told that one who drives at reckless speed through a crowded city street is guilty of a negligent act and, therefore, of a wrongful one irrespective of the consequences. Negligent the act is, and wrongful in the sense that it is unsocial, but wrongful and unsocial in relation to other travelers, only because the eye of vigilance perceives the risk of damage. If the same act were to be committed on a speedway or a race course, it would lose its wrongful quality. The risk reasonably to be perceived defines the duty to be obeyed, and risk imports relation; it is risk to another or to others within the range of apprehension (Seavey, Negligence, Subjective or Objective, 41 *H. L. Rv.* 6; *Boronkay v. Robinson & Carpenter,* 247 *N.Y.* 365). This does not mean, of course, that one who launches a destructive force is always relieved of liability if the force, though known to be destructive, pursues an unexpected path. It was not necessary that the defendant should have had notice of the particular method in which an accident would occur, if the possibility of an accident was clear to the ordinarily prudent eye. Some acts, such as shooting, are so imminently dangerous to any one who may come within reach of the missile, however unexpectedly, as to impose a duty of prevision not far

from that of an insurer. Even today, and much oftener in earlier stages of the law, one acts sometimes
at one's peril. Under this head, it may be, fall certain
cases of what is known as transferred intent, an act
willfully dangerous to A resulting by misadventure
in injury to B. These cases aside, wrong is defined
in terms of the natural or probable, at least when unintentional. The range of reasonable apprehension
is at times a question for the court, and at times, if
varying inferences are possible, a question for the
jury. Here, by concession, there was nothing in the
situation to suggest to the most cautious mind that
the parcel wrapped in newspaper would spread
wreckage through the station. If the guard had
thrown it down knowingly and willfully, he would
not have threatened the plaintiff's safety, so far as
appearances could warn him. His conduct would
not have involved, even then, an unreasonable
probability of invasion of her bodily security. Liability can be no greater where the act is inadvertent.

Negligence, like risk, is thus a term of relation.
Negligence in the abstract, apart from things related,
is surely not a tort, if indeed it is understandable at
all. Negligence is not a tort unless it results in the
commission of a wrong, and the commission of a
wrong imports the violation of a right, in this case,
we are told, the right to be protected against interference with one's bodily security. But bodily security is protected, not against all forms of interference
or aggression, but only against some. One who
seeks redress at law does not make out a cause of
action by showing without more that there has been
damage to his person. If the harm was not willful,
he must show that the act as to him had possibilities
of danger so many and apparent as to entitle him to
be protected against the doing of it though the harm
was unintended. Affront to personality is still the
keynote of the wrong. Confirmation of this view will
be found in the history and development of the action on the case. Negligence as a basis of civil liability was unknown to medieval law. For damage to
the person, the sole remedy was trespass, and trespass did not lie in the absence of aggression, and
that direct and personal. Liability for other damage,
as where a servant without orders from the master
does or omits something to the damage of another,
is a plant of later growth. When it emerged out of
the legal soil, it was thought of as a variant of trespass, an offshoot of the parent stock. This appears
in the form of action, which was known as trespass
on the case. The victim does not sue derivatively, or
by right of subrogation, to vindicate an interest invaded in the person of another. Thus to view his
cause of action is to ignore the fundamental difference between tort and crime. He sues for breach of
a duty owing to himself.

The law of causation, remote or proximate, is
thus foreign to the case before us. The question of
liability is always anterior to the question of the measure of the consequences that go with liability. If
there is no tort to be redressed, there is no occasion
to consider what damage might be recovered if there
were a finding of a tort. We may assume, without
deciding, that negligence, not at large or in the abstract, but in relation to the plaintiff, would entail liability for any and all consequences, however novel
or extraordinary. There is room for argument that a
distinction is to be drawn according to the diversity
of interests invaded by the act, as where conduct
negligent in that it threatens an insignificant invasion of an interest in property results in an unforeseeable invasion of an interest of another order, as
e.g., one of bodily security. Perhaps other distinctions may be necessary. We do not go into the question now. The consequences to be followed must
first be rooted in a wrong.

The judgment of the Appellate Division and
that of the Trial Term should be reversed, and the
complaint dismissed, with costs in all courts.

ANDREWS, J. (dissenting). Assisting a passenger
to board a train, the defendant's servant negligently
knocked a package from his arms. It fell between the
platform and the cars. Of its contents the servant
knew and could know nothing. A violent explosion
followed. The concussion broke some scales standing a considerable distance away. In falling they injured the plaintiff, an intending passenger.

Upon these facts may she recover the damages she has suffered in an action brought against
the master? The result we shall reach depends upon
our theory as to the nature of negligence. Is it a relative concept—the breach of some duty owing to a
particular person or to particular persons? Or where
there is an act which unreasonably threatens the
safety of others, is the doer liable for all its proximate consequences, even where they result in injury
to one who would generally be thought to be outside the radius of danger? This is not a mere dispute
as to words. We might not believe that to the average mind the dropping of the bundle would seem
to involve the probability of harm to the plaintiff
standing many feet away whatever might be the case
as to the owner or to one so near as to be likely to
be struck by its fall. If, however, we adopt the sec-

ond hypothesis we have to inquire only as the relation between cause and effect. We deal in terms of proximate cause, not of negligence.

Negligence may be defined roughly as an act or omission which unreasonably does or may affect the rights of others, or which unreasonably fails to protect oneself from the dangers resulting from such acts. Here I confine myself to the first branch of the definition. Nor do I comment on the word "unreasonable." For present purposes it sufficiently describes that average of conduct that society requires of its members.

There must be both the act or the omission, and the right. It is the act itself, not the intent of the actor, that is important. In criminal law both the intent and the result are to be considered. Intent again is material in tort actions, where punitive damages are sought, dependent on actual malice—not on merely reckless conduct. But here neither insanity nor infancy lessens responsibility.

As has been said, except in cases of contributory negligence, there must be rights which are or may be affected. Often though injury has occurred, no rights of him who suffers have been touched. A licensee or trespasser upon my land has no claim to affirmative care on my part that the land be made safe. Where a railroad is required to fence its tracks against cattle, no man's rights are injured should he wander upon the road because such fence is absent. An unborn child may not demand immunity from personal harm.

But we are told that "there is no negligence unless there is in the particular case a legal duty to take care, and this duty must be one which is owed to the plaintiff himself and not merely to others." This, I think too narrow a conception. Where there is the unreasonable act, and some right that may be affected there is negligence whether damage does or does not result. That is immaterial. Should we drive down Broadway at a reckless speed, we are negligent whether we strike an approaching car or miss it by an inch. The act itself is wrongful. It is a wrong not only to those who happen to be within the radius of danger but to all who might have been there—a wrong to the public at large. Such is the language of the street. Such the language of the courts when speaking of contributory negligence. Such again and again their language in speaking of the duty of some defendant and discussing proximate cause in cases where such a discussion is wholly irrelevant on any other theory. As was said by Mr. Justice HOLMES many years ago, "the measure

of the defendant's duty in determining whether a wrong has been committed is one thing, the measure of liability when a wrong has been committed is another." Due care is a duty imposed on each one of us to protect society from unnecessary danger not to protect *A, B* or *C* alone.

It may well be that there is no such thing as negligence in the abstract. "Proof of negligence in the air, so to speak, will not do." In an empty world negligence would not exist. It does involve a relationship between man and his fellows. But not merely a relationship between man and those whom he might reasonably expect his act would injure. Rather, a relationship between him and those whom he does in fact injure. If his act has a tendency to harm some one, it harms him a mile away as surely as it does those on the scene. We now permit children to recover for the negligent killing of the father. It was never prevented on the theory that no duty was owing to them. A husband may be compensated for the loss of his wife's services. To say that the wrongdoer was negligent as to the husband as well as to the wife is merely an attempt to fit facts to theory. An insurance company paying a fire loss recovers its payment of the negligent incendiary. We speak of subrogation—of suing in the right of the insured. Behind the cloud of words is the fact they hide, that the act, wrongful as to the insured, has also injured the company. Even if it be true that the fault of father, wife or insured will prevent recovery, it is because we consider the original negligence not the proximate cause of the injury.

In the well-known *Polemis Case* (1921, 3 *K.B.* 560), SCRUTTON, L. J., said that the dropping of a plank was negligent for it might injure "workman or cargo or ship." Because of either possibility the owner of the vessel was to be made good for his loss. The act being wrongful the doer was liable for its proximate results. Criticized and explained as this statement may have been, I think it states the law as it should be and as it is.

The proposition is this. Every one owes to the world at large the duty of refraining from those acts that may unreasonably threaten the safety of others. Such an act occurs. Not only is he wronged to whom harm might reasonably be expected to result, but he also who is in fact injured, even if he be outside what would generally be thought the danger zone. There needs be duty due the one complaining but this is not a duty to a particular individual because as to him harm might be expected. Harm to someone being the natural result of the act, not only that one alone, but all those in fact injured may complain. We have never, I think, held otherwise. Indeed in the *Di Caprio* case we said that a breach of a general ordinance defining the degree of care to be exercised in one's calling is evidence of negligence as to every one. We did not limit this statement to those who might be expected to be exposed to danger. Unreasonable risk being taken, its consequences are not confined to those who might probably be hurt.

If this be so, we do not have a plaintiff suing by "derivation or succession." Her action is original and primary. Her claim is for a breach of duty to herself—not that she is subrogated to any right of action of the owner of the parcel or of a passenger standing at the scene of the explosion.

The right to recover damages rests on additional considerations. The plaintiff's rights must be injured, and this injury must be caused by the negligence. We build a dam, but are negligent as to its foundations. Breaking, it injures property down stream. We are not liable if all this happened because of some reason other than the insecure foundation. But when injuries do result from our unlawful act we are liable for the consequences. It does not matter that they are unusual, unexpected, unforeseen and unforeseeable. But there is one limitation. The damages must be so connected with the negligence that the latter may be said to be the proximate cause of the former.

These two words have never been given an inclusive definition. What is a cause in a legal sense, still more what is a proximate cause, depend in each case upon many considerations, as does the existence of negligence itself. Any philosophical doctrine of causation does not help us. A boy throws a stone into a pond. The ripples spread. The water level rises. The history of that pond is altered to all eternity. It will be altered by other causes also. Yet it will be forever the resultant of all causes combined. Each one will have an influence. How great only omniscience can say. You may speak of a chain, or if you please, a net. An analogy is of little aid. Each cause brings about future events. Without each the future would not be the same. Each is proximate in the sense it is essential. But that is not what we mean by the word. Nor on the other hand do we mean sole cause. There is no such thing.

Should analogy be thought helpful, however, I prefer that of a stream. The spring, starting on its journey, is joined by tributary after tributary. The river, reaching the ocean, comes from a hundred sources. No man may say whence any drop of water

is derived. Yet for a time distinction may be possible. Into the clear creek, brown swamp water flows from the left. Later, from the right comes water stained by its clay bed. The three may remain for a space, sharply divided. But at last, inevitably no trace of separation remains. They are so commingled that all distinction is lost.

As we have said, we cannot trace the effect of an act to the end, if end there is. Again, however, we may trace it part of the way. A murder at Sarajevo may be the necessary antecedent to an assassination in London twenty years hence. An overturned lantern may burn all Chicago. We may follow the fire from the shed to the last building. We rightly say the fire started by the lantern caused its destruction.

A cause, but not the proximate cause. What we do mean by the word "proximate" is, that because of convenience, of public policy, of a rough sense of justice, the law arbitrarily declines to trace a series of events beyond a certain point. This is not logic, it is practical politics. Take our rule as to fires. Sparks from my burning haystack set on fire my house and my neighbor's. I may recover from a negligent railroad. He may not. Yet the wrongful act as directly harmed the one as the other. We may regret that the line was drawn just where it was, but drawn somewhere it had to be. We said the act of the railroad was not the proximate cause of our neighbor's fire. Cause it surely was. The words we used were simply indicative of our notions of public policy. Other courts think differently. But somewhere they reach the point where they cannot say the stream comes from any one source.

Take the illustration given in an unpublished manuscript by a distinguished and helpful writer on the law of torts. A chauffeur negligently collides with another car which is filled with dynamite, although he could not know it. An explosion follows. *A*, walking on the sidewalk nearby, is killed. *B*, sitting in a window of a building opposite, is cut by flying glass. *C*, likewise sitting in a window a block away, is similarly injured. And a further illustration. A nursemaid, ten blocks away, startled by the noise, involuntarily drops a baby from her arms to the walk. We are told that *C* may not recover while *A* may. As to *B* it is a question for court or jury. We will all agree that the baby might not. Because, we are again told, the chauffeur had no reason to believe his conduct involved any risk of injuring either *C* or the baby. As to them he was not negligent.

But the chauffeur, being negligent in risking the collision, his belief that the scope of the harm he might do would be limited is immaterial. His act unreasonably jeopardized the safety of anyone who might be affected by it. *C's* injury and that of the baby were directly traceable to the collision. Without that, the injury would not have happened. *C* had the right to sit in his office, secure from such dangers. The baby was entitled to use the sidewalk with reasonable safety.

The true theory is, it seems to me, that the injury to *C*, if in truth he is to be denied recovery, and the injury to the baby is that their several injuries were not the proximate result of the negligence. And here not what the chauffeur had reason to believe would be the result of his conduct, but what the prudent would foresee, may have a bearing. May have some bearing, for the problem of proximate cause is not to be solved by any one consideration.

It is all a question of expediency. There are no fixed rules to govern our judgment. There are simply matters of which we may take account. We have in somewhat different connection spoken of "the stream of events." We have asked whether that stream was deflected—whether it was forced into new and unexpected channels. This is rather rhetoric than law. There is in truth little to guide us other than common sense.

There are some hints that may help us. The proximate cause, involved as it may be with many other causes, must be, at the least, something without which the event would not happen. The court must ask itself whether there was a natural and continuous sequence between cause and effect. Was the one a substantial factor in producing the other? Was there a direct connection between them, without too many intervening causes? Is the effect of cause on result not too attenuated? Is the cause likely, in the usual judgment of mankind, to produce the result? Or by the exercise of prudent foresight could the result be foreseen? Is the result too remote from the cause, and here we consider remoteness in time and space, where we passed upon the construction of a contract—but something was also said on this subject. Clearly we must so consider, for the greater the distance either in time or space, the more surely do other causes intervene to affect the result. When a lantern is overturned the firing of a shed is a fairly direct consequence. Many things contribute to the spread of the conflagration—the force of the wind, the direction and width of street, the character of intervening structures, other factors. We draw an uncertain and wavering line, but draw it we must as best we can.

Once again, it is all a question of fair judgment, always keeping in mind the fact that we endeavor to make a rule in each case that will be practical and in keeping with the general understanding of mankind.

Here another question must be answered. In the case supposed it is said, and said correctly, that the chauffeur is liable for the direct effect of the explosion although he had no reason to suppose it would follow a collision. "The fact that the injury occurred in a different manner than that which might have been expected does not prevent the chauffeur's negligence from being in law the cause of the injury." But the natural results of a negligent act—the results which a prudent man would or should foresee—do have a bearing upon the decision as to proximate cause. We have said so repeatedly. What should be foreseen? No human foresight would suggest that a collision itself might injure one a block away. On the contrary, given an explosion, such a possibility might be reasonably expected. I think the direct connection, the foresight of which the courts speak, assumes prevision of the explosion, for the immediate results of which, at least, the chauffeur is responsible.

It may be said this is unjust. Why? In fairness he should make good every injury flowing from his negligence. Not because of tenderness toward him we say he need not answer for all that follows his wrong. We look back to the catastrophe, the fire kindled by the spark, or the explosion. We trace the consequences—not indefinitely, but to a certain point. And to aid us in fixing that point we ask what might ordinarily be expected to follow the fire or the explosion.

This last suggestion is the factor which must determine the case before us. The act upon which defendant's liability rests is knocking an apparently harmless package onto the platform. The act was negligent. For its proximate consequences the defendant is liable. If its contents were broken, to the owner; if it fell upon and crushed a passenger's foot, then to him. If it exploded and injured one in the immediate vicinity, to him also as to *A* in the illustration. Mrs. Palsgraf was standing some distance away. How far cannot be told from the record—apparently twenty-five or thirty feet. Perhaps less. Except for the explosion, she would not have been injured. We are told by the appellant in his brief "it cannot be denied that the explosion was the direct cause of the plaintiff's injuries." So it was a substantial factor in producing the result—there was here a natural and continuous sequence—direct connection. The only intervening cause was that instead of blowing her to the ground the concussion smashed the weighing machine which in turn fell upon her. There was no remoteness in time, little in space. And surely, given such an explosion as here it needed no great foresight to predict that the natural result would be to injure one on the platform at no greater distance from its scene than was the plaintiff. Just how no one might be able to predict. Whether by flying fragments, by broken glass, by wreckage of machines or structures no one could say. But injury in some form was most probable.

Under these circumstances I cannot say as a matter of law that the plaintiff's injuries were not the proximate result of the negligence. That is all we have before us. The court refused to so charge. No request was made to submit the matter to the jury as a question of fact, even would that have been proper upon the record before us.

The judgment appealed from should be affirmed, with costs.

POUND, LEHMAN and KELLOGG, J J., concur with CARDOZO, CH. J.; ANDREWS, J., dissents in opinion in which CRANE and O'BRIEN, J J., concur.

Judgment reversed, etc.

·

SUMMERS V. TICE*

Supreme Court of California, in Bank, 1948

CARTER, Justice.

Each of the two defendants appeals from a judgment against them in an action for personal injuries. Pursuant to stipulation the appeals have been consolidated.

Plaintiff's action was against both defendants for an injury to his right eye and face as the result of being struck by bird shot discharged from a shotgun. The case was tried by the court without a jury and the court found that on November 20, 1945, plaintiff and the two defendants were hunting quail on the open range. Each of the defendants was armed with a 12 gauge shotgun loaded with shells containing $7\frac{1}{2}$ size shot. Prior to going hunting plaintiff discussed the hunting procedure with defendants, indicating that they were to exercise care when shooting and to "keep in line." In the course of hunting plaintiff proceeded up a hill, thus placing the hunters at the points of a triangle. The view of defendants with reference to plaintiff was unobstructed and they knew his location. Defendant Tice flushed a quail which rose in flight to a ten foot elevation and flew between plaintiff and defendants. Both defendants shot at the quail, shooting in plaintiff's direction. At that time defendants were 75 yards from plaintiff. One shot struck plaintiff in his eye and another in his upper lip. Finally it was found by the court that as the direct result of the shooting by defendants the shots struck plaintiff as above mentioned and that defendants were negligent in so shooting and plaintiff was not contributorily negligent.

[1] First, on the subject of negligence, defendant Simonson contends that the evidence is insufficient to sustain the finding on that score, but he does not point out wherein it is lacking. There is evidence that both defendants, at about the same time or one immediately after the other, shot at a quail and in so doing shot toward plaintiff who was uphill from them, and that they knew his location. That is sufficient from which the trial court could conclude that they acted with respect to plaintiff other than as persons of ordinary prudence. The issue was one of fact for the trial court. (See, *Rudd v. Byrnes,* 156 Cal. 636, 105 P. 957, 26 *L.R.A.,* N.S., 134, 20 Ann. Cas. 124.)

*199 *Pacific Reporter* 2d 1.

Defendant Tice states in his opening brief, "we have decided not to argue the insufficiency of negligence on the part of defendant Tice." It is true he states in his answer to plaintiff's petition for a hearing in this court that he did not concede this point but he does not argue it. Nothing more need be said on the subject.

[2, 3] Defendant Simonson urges that plaintiff was guilty of contributory negligence and assumed the risk as a matter of law. He cites no authority for the proposition that by going on a hunting party the various hunters assume the risk of negligence on the part of their companions. Such a tenet is not reasonable. It is true that plaintiff suggested that they all "stay in line," presumably abreast, while hunting; and he went uphill at somewhat of a right angle to the hunting line, but he also cautioned that they use care, and defendants knew plaintiff's position. We hold, therefore, that the trial court was justified in finding that he did not assume the risk or act other than as a person of ordinary prudence under the circumstances. (See, *Anthony v. Hobbie,* 25 Cal.2d 814, 818, 155 P. 2d 826; *Rudd v. Byrnes,* supra.) None of the cases cited by Simonson are in point.

The problem presented in this case is whether the judgment against both defendants may stand. It is argued by defendants that they are not joint tort feasors, and thus jointly and severally liable, as they were not acting in concert, and that there is not sufficient evidence to show which defendant was guilty of the negligence which caused the injuries—the shooting by Tice or that by Simonson. Tice argues that there is evidence to show that the shot which struck plaintiff came from Simonson's gun because of admissions allegedly made by him to third persons and no evidence that they came from his gun. Further in connection with the latter contention, the court failed to find on plaintiff's allegation in his complaint that he did not know which one was at fault—did not find which defendant was guilty of the negligence which caused the injuries to plaintiff.

[4] Considering the last argument first, we believe it is clear that the court sufficiently found on the issue that defendants were jointly liable and that thus the negligence of both was the cause of the injury or to that legal effect. It found that both defendants were negligent and "That as a direct and proximate result of the shots fired by *defendants, and each of them,* a birdshot pellet was caused to and did lodge in plaintiff's right eye and that another birdshot pellet was caused to and did lodge in plaintiff's upper lip." In so doing the court evidently did not give credence to the admissions of Simonson to third persons that he fired the shots, which it was justified in doing. It thus determined that the negligence of both defendants was the legal cause of the injury—or that both were responsible. Implicit in such finding is the assumption that the court was unable to ascertain whether the shots were from the gun of one defendant or the other or one shot from each of them. The one shot that entered plaintiff's eye was the major factor in assessing damages and that shot could not have come from the gun of both defendants. It was from one or the other only.

It has been held that where a group of persons are on a hunting party, or otherwise engaged in the use of firearms, and two of them are negligent in firing in the direction of a third person who is injured thereby, both of those so firing are liable for the injury suffered by the third person, although the negligence of only one of them could have caused the injury. (*Moore v. Foster,* Miss., 180 So. 73; *Oliver v. Miles,* Miss., 110 So. 666, 50 *A.L.R.* 357; *Reyher v. Mayne,* 90 *Colo.* 856, 10 *P.2d* 1109; *Benson v. Ross,* 143 *Mich.* 452, 106 *N.W.* 1120, 114 *Am.St.Rep.* 675.) The same rule has been applied in criminal cases (*State v. Newberg,* 129 Or. 564, 278 P. 568, 63 *A.L.R.* 1225), and both drivers have been held liable for the negligence of one where they engaged in a racing contest causing an injury to a third person. (*Saisa v. Lilja,* 1 *Cir.,* 76 F.2d 380.) These cases speak of the action of defendants as being in concert as the ground of decision, yet it would seem they are straining that concept and the more reasonable basis appears in *Oliver v. Miles,* supra. There two persons were hunting together. Both shot at some partridges and in so doing shot across the highway injuring plaintiff who was traveling on it. The court stated they were acting in concert and thus both were liable. The court then stated [110 *So.* 668]: "We think that . . . each is liable for the resulting injury to the boy, although no one can say definitely who actually shot him. *To hold otherwise would be to exonerate both from liability, although each was negligent, and the injury resulted from such negligence.*" [Emphasis added.] 110 So. p. 668. It is said in the Restatement: "For harm resulting to a third person from the tortious conduct of another, a person is liable if he . . . (b) knows that the other's conduct constitutes a breach of duty and gives substantial assistance or encouragement to the other so to conduct himself, or (c) gives substantial assistance to the other in accomplishing a tortious result and his own conduct, separately considered, constitutes a breach of duty to the third person." (Rest., *Torts,* sec. 876(b) (c).) Under subsection (b) the example is given: "A and B are members of a hunting party. Each of them in the presence of the other shoots across a public road at an animal, this being negligent as to persons on the road. A hits the animal. B's bullet strikes C, a traveler on the road. A is liable to C." (Rest., *Torts,* Sec. 876(b), Com., Illus. 3.) An illustration given under subsection (c) is the same as above except the factor of both defendants shooting is missing and joint liability is not imposed. It is further said that: "If two forces are actively operating, one because of the actor's negligence, the other not because of any misconduct on his part, and each of itself is sufficient to bring about harm to another, the actor's negligence may be held by the jury to be a substantial factor in bringing it about." (Rest., *Torts,* sec. 432.) Dean Wigmore has this to say: "When two or more persons by their acts are possibly the sole cause of a harm, or when two or more acts of the same person are possibly the sole cause, and the plaintiff has introduced evidence that the one of the two persons, or the one of the same person's two acts, is culpable, then the defendant has the burden of proving that the other person, or his other act, was the sole cause of the harm. (b) . . . The real reason for the rule that each joint tortfeasor is responsible for the whole damage is the practical unfairness of denying the injured person redress simply because he cannot prove how much damage each did, when it is certain that between them they did all; let them be the ones to apportion it among themselves. Since, then, the difficulty of proof is the reason, the rule should apply whenever the harm has plural causes, and not merely when they acted in conscious concert. . . ." (Wigmore, *Select Cases on the Law of Torts,* sec. 153.) Similarly Professor Carpenter has said: "[Suppose] the case where A and B independently shoot at C and but one bullet touches C's body. In such case, such proof as is ordinarily required that either A or B shot C, of course fails. It is suggested that there should be a relaxation of the proof required of the plaintiff . . . where the injury occurs as the result of one where more than one independent force is operating, and it is impossible to determine that the force set in operation by defendant did not in fact constitute a cause of the damage, and where it may have caused the damage, but the plaintiff is unable to establish that it was a cause." (20 *Cal.L.Rev.* 406.)

[5] When we consider the relative position of the parties and the results that would flow if plaintiff was required to pin the injury on one of the defendants only, a requirement that the burden of proof on that subject be shifted to defendants becomes manifest. They are both wrongdoers—both negligent toward plaintiff. They brought about a situation where the negligence of one of them injured the plaintiff, hence it should rest with them each to absolve himself if he can. The injured party has been placed by defendants in the unfair position of pointing to which defendant caused the harm. If one can escape the other may also and plaintiff is remediless. Ordinarily defendants are in a far better position to offer evidence to determine which one caused the injury. This reasoning has recently found favor in this Court. In a quite analogous situation this Court held that a patient injured while unconscious on an operating table in a hospital could hold all or any of the persons who had any connection with the operation even though he could not select the particular acts by the particular person which led to his disability. (*Ybarra v. Spangard,* 25 *Cal. 2d* 486, 154 *P.2d* 687, 162 *A.L.R.* 1258.) There the Court was considering whether the patient could avail himself of *res ipsa loquitur,* rather than where the burden of proof lay, yet the effect of the decision is that plaintiff has made out a case when he has produced evidence which gives rise to an inference of negligence which was the proximate cause of the injury. It is up to defendants to explain the cause of the injury. It was there said: "If the doctrine is to continue to serve a useful purpose, we should not forget that 'the particular force and justice of the rule, regarded as a presumption throwing upon the party charged the duty of producing evidence, consists in the circumstance that the chief evidence of the true cause, whether culpable or innocent, is practically accessible to him but inaccessible to the injured person.'" (25 *Cal. 2d* at page 490, 154 *P. 2d* at page 689, 162 *A.L.R.* 1258.) Similarly in the instant case plaintiff is not able to establish which of defendants caused his injury.

The foregoing discussion disposes of the authorities cited by defendants such as *Kraft v. Smith,* 24 *Cal. 2d* 124, 148 *P. 2d* 23, and *Hernandez v. Southern California Gas Co.,* 213 *Cal.* 384, 2 *P. 2d* 360, stating the general rule that one defendant is not liable for the independent tort of the other defendant, or that ordinarily the plaintiff must show a causal connection between the negligence and the injury. There was an entire lack of such connection in the Hernandez case and there were not several negligent defendants, one of whom must have caused the injury.

Defendants rely upon *Christensen v. Los Angeles Electrical Supply Co.,* 112 *Cal.App.* 629, 297 *P.* 614, holding that a defendant is not liable where he negligently knocked down with his car a pedestrian and a third person then ran over the prostrate person. That involves the question of intervening cause which we do not have here. Moreover it is out of harmony with the current rule on that subject and was properly questioned in *Hill v. Peres,* 136 *Cal. App.* 132, 28 *P. 2d* 946 (hearing in this Court denied), and must be deemed disapproved. (See *Mosley v. Arden Farms Co.,* 26 *Cal. 2d* 213, 157 *P. 2d* 372, 158 *A.L.R.* 872; *Sawyer v. Southern California Gas Co.,* 206 *Cal.* 366, 274 *P.* 544; 6 *Cal. Jur. Ten Yr.Supp., Automobiles,* sec. 349; 19 *Cal. Jur.* 570–72.)

Cases are cited for the proposition that where two or more tort feasors acting independently of each other cause an injury to plaintiff, they are not joint tort feasors and plaintiff must establish the portion of the damage caused by each, even though it is impossible to prove the portion of the injury caused by each. See *Slater v. Pacific American Oil Co.,* 212 *Cal.* 648, 300 *P.* 31; *Miller v. Highland Ditch Co.,* 87 *Cal.* 430, 25 *P.* 550, 22 *Am. St. Rep.* 254; *People v. Gold Run D. & M. Co.,* 66 *Cal.* 138, 4 *P.* 1152, 56 *Am. Rep.* 80; *Wade v. Thorsen,* 5 *Cal. App. 2d* 706, 43 *P. 2d* 592; *California Orange Co. v. Riverside P. C. Co.,* 50 *Cal. App.* 522, 195 *P.* 694; *City of Oakland v. Pacific Gas & E. Co.,* 47 *Cal. App. 2d* 444, 118 *P. 2d* 328. In view of the foregoing discussion it is apparent that defendants in cases like the present one may be treated as liable on the same basis as joint tort feasors, and hence the last cited cases are distinguishable inasmuch as they involve independent tort feasors.

[6] In addition to that, however, it should be pointed out that the same reasons of policy and justice shift the burden to each of defendants to absolve himself if he can—relieving the wronged person of the duty of apportioning the injury to a particular defendant, apply here where we are concerned with whether plaintiff is required to supply evidence for the apportionment of damages. If defendants are independent tort feasors and thus each liable for the damage caused by him alone, and, at least, where the matter of apportionment is incapable of proof, the innocent wronged party should not be deprived of his right to redress. The wrongdoers should be left to work out between themselves any apportionment. (See *Colonial Ins. Co. v. Industrial Acc. Com.,* 29 *Cal. 2d* 79, 172 *P. 2d* 884.) Some of the cited cases refer to the difficulty of apportioning the burden of damages between the independent tort feasors, and say that where factually a correct division cannot be made, the trier of fact may make it the best it can, which would be more or less a guess, stressing the factor that the wrongdoers are not in a position to complain of uncertainty. (*California Orange Co. v. Riverside P. C. Co.,* supra.)

[7] It is urged that plaintiff now has changed the theory of his case in claiming a concert of action; that he did not plead or prove such concert. From what has been said it is clear that there has been no change in theory. The joint liability, as well as the lack of knowledge as to which defendant was liable, was pleaded and the proof developed the case under either theory. We have seen that for the reasons of policy discussed herein, the case is based upon the legal proposition that, under the circumstances here presented, each defendant is liable for the whole damage whether they are deemed to be acting in concert or independently.

The judgment is affirmed.

GIBSON, C. J., and SHENK, EDMONDS, TRAYNOR, SCHAUER, and SPENCE, J J., concur.

SINDELL V. ABBOTT LABORATORIES*

Supreme Court of California, 1980

MOSK, Justice.

This case involves a complex problem both timely and significant: may a plaintiff, injured as the result of a drug administered to her mother during pregnancy, who knows the type of drug involved but cannot identify the manufacturer of the precise product, hold liable for her injuries a maker of a drug produced from an identical formula?

Plaintiff Judith Sindell brought an action against eleven drug companies and Does 1 through 100, on behalf of herself and other women similarly situated. The complaint alleges as follows:

Between 1941 and 1971, defendants were engaged in the business of manufacturing, promoting, and marketing diethylstilbesterol (DES), a drug which is a synthetic compound of the female hormone estrogen. The drug was administered to plaintiff's mother and the mothers of the class she represents,[1] for the purpose of preventing miscarriage. In 1947, the Food and Drug Administration authorized the marketing of DES as a miscarriage preventative, but only on an experimental basis, with a requirement that the drug contain a warning label to that effect.

DES may cause cancerous vaginal and cervical growths in the daughters exposed to it before birth, because their mothers took the drug during pregnancy. The form of cancer from which these daughters suffer is known as adenocarcinoma, and it manifests itself after a minimum latent period of 10 or 12 years. It is a fast-spreading and deadly disease, and radical surgery is required to prevent it from spreading. DES also causes adenosis, precancerous vaginal and cervical growths which may spread to other areas of the body. The treatment for adenosis is cauterization, surgery, or cryosurgery. Women who suffer from this condition must be monitored by biopsy or colposcopic examination twice a year, a painful and expensive procedure. Thousands of women whose mothers received DES during pregnancy are unaware of the effects of the drug.

In 1971, the Food and Drug Administration ordered defendants to cease marketing and promoting DES for the purpose of preventing miscarriages, and to warn physicians and the public that the drug should not be used by pregnant women because of the danger to their unborn children.

During the period defendants marketed DES, they knew or should have known that it was a carcinogenic substance, that there was a grave danger after varying periods of latency it would cause cancerous and precancerous growths in the daughters of the mothers who took it, and that it was ineffective to prevent miscarriage. Nevertheless, defendants continued to advertise and market the drug as a miscarriage preventative. They failed to test DES for efficacy and safety; the tests performed by others, upon which they relied, indicated that it was not safe or effective. In violation of the authorization of the Food and Drug Administration, defendants marketed DES on an unlimited basis rather than as an experimental drug, and they failed to warn of its potential danger.[2]

Because of defendants' advertised assurances that DES was safe and effective to prevent miscarriage, plaintiff was exposed to the drug prior to her birth. She became aware of the danger from such exposure within one year of the time she filed her complaint. As a result of the DES ingested by her mother, plaintiff developed a malignant bladder tumor which was removed by surgery. She suffers from adenosis and must constantly be monitored by biopsy or colposcopy to insure early warning of further malignancy.

The first cause of action alleges that defendants were jointly and individually negligent in that they manufactured, marketed and promoted DES as a safe and efficacious drug to prevent miscarriage, without adequate testing or warning, and without monitoring or reporting its effects.

*Sup., 163 *California Reporter* 132.

A separate cause of action alleges that defendants are jointly liable regardless of which particular brand of DES was ingested by plaintiff's mother because defendants collaborated in marketing, promoting and testing the drug, relied upon each other's tests, and adhered to an industry-wide safety standard. DES was produced from a common and mutually agreed upon formula as a fungible drug interchangeable with other brands of the same product; defendants knew or should have known that it was customary for doctors to prescribe the drug by its generic rather than its brand name and that pharmacists filled prescriptions from whatever brand of the drug happened to be in stock.

Other causes of action are based upon theories of strict liability, violation of express and implied warranties, false and fraudulent representations, misbranding of drugs in violation of federal law, conspiracy and "lack of consent."

Each cause of action alleges that defendants are jointly liable because they acted in concert, on the basis of express and implied agreements, and in reliance upon and ratification and exploitation of each other's testing and marketing methods.

Plaintiff seeks compensatory damages of $1 million and punitive damages of $10 million for herself. For the members of her class, she prays for equitable relief in the form of an order that defendants warn physicians and others of the danger of DES and the necessity of performing certain tests to determine the presence of disease caused by the drug, and that they establish free clinics in California to perform such tests.

Defendants demurred to the complaint. While the complaint did not expressly allege that plaintiff could not identify the manufacturer of the precise drug ingested by her mother, she stated in her points and authorities in opposition to the demurrers filed by some of the defendants that she was unable to make the identification, and the trial court sustained the demurrers of these defendants without leave to amend on the ground that plaintiff did not and stated she could not identify which defendant had manufactured the drug responsible for her injuries. Thereupon, the court dismissed the action.[3] This appeal involves only five of ten defendants named in the complaint.[4]

Plaintiff Maureen Rogers filed a complaint containing allegations generally similar to those made by Sindell. She seeks compensatory and punitive damages on her own behalf, and on behalf of a class described in substantially the same terms as in Sindell's complaint, as well as equitable relief comparable to that sought by Sindell. The trial court sustained demurrers of E. R. Squibb & Sons, The Upjohn Company, and Rexall Drug Company.[5] Subsequent to the dismissal of her action against these defendants, Rogers amended the complaint to allege that Eli Lilly and Company, one of the defendants named in her complaint, had manufactured the drug used by her mother. Although Sindell's action and the present case have been consolidated on appeal, much of the discussion which follows will apply to Rogers only if she does not succeed in establishing that Eli Lilly and Company manufactured the DES taken by her mother. "Plaintiff" as used in this opinion refers to Sindell, and we discuss only the allegations of Sindell's complaint.

This case is but one of a number filed throughout the country seeking to hold drug manufacturers liable for injuries allegedly resulting from DES prescribed to the plaintiffs' mothers since 1947.[6] According to a note in the *Fordham Law Review,* estimates of the number of women who took the drug during pregnancy range from 1½ million to 3 million. Hundreds, perhaps thousands, of the daughters of these women suffer from adenocarcinoma, and the incidence of vaginal adenosis among them is 30 to 90 percent. (Comment, *DES and a Proposed Theory of Enterprise Liability* (1978) 46 *Fordham L. Rev.* 963, 964–67 [hereafter Fordham Comment].) Most of the cases are still pending. With two exceptions,[7] those that have been decided resulted in judgments in favor of the drug company defendants because of the failure of the plaintiffs to identify the manufacturer of the DES prescribed to their mothers.[8] The same result was reached in a recent California case. (*McCreery v. Eli Lilly & Co.* (1978) 87 *Cal. App. 3d* 77, 82–84, 150 *Cal. Rptr.* 730.) The present action is another attempt to overcome this obstacle to recovery.

[1] We begin with the proposition that, as a general rule, the imposition of liability depends upon a showing by the plaintiff that his or her injuries were caused by the act of the defendant or by an instrumentality under the defendant's control. The rule applies whether the injury resulted from an accidental event (e.g., *Shunk v. Bosworth* (6th *Cir.* 1964) 334 *F. 2d* 309) or from the use of a defective product. (E. g., *Wetzel v. Eaton Corporation* (*D. Minn.* 1973) 62 *F.R.D.* 22, 29–30; *Garcia v. Joseph Vince Co.* (1978) 84 *Cal. App. 3d* 868, 873–75, 148 *Cal. Rptr.* 843; and see annot. collection of cases in 51 *A.L.R. 3d* 1344, 1351; 1 *Hursh and Bailey, American Law of Products Liability 2d* [1974] p. 125.)

There are, however, exceptions to this rule. Plaintiff's complaint suggests several bases upon which defendants may be held liable for her injuries even though she cannot demonstrate the name of the manufacturer which produced the DES actually taken by her mother. The first of these theories, classically illustrated by *Summers v. Tice* (1948) 33 *Cal. 2d* 80, 199 *P. 2d* 1, places the burden of proof of causation upon tortious defendants in certain circumstances. The second basis of liability emerging from the complaint is that defendants acted in concert to cause injury to plaintiff. There is a third and novel approach to the problem, sometimes called the theory of "enterprise liability," but which we prefer to designate by the more accurate term of "industry-wide" liability,[9] which might obviate the necessity for identifying the manufacturer of the injury-causing drug. We shall conclude that these doctrines, as previously interpreted, may not be applied to hold defendants liable under the allegations of this complaint. However, we shall propose and adopt a fourth basis for permitting the action to be tried, grounded upon an extension of the *Summers* doctrine.

I

Plaintiff places primary reliance upon cases which hold that if a party cannot identify which of two or more defendants caused an injury, the burden of proof may shift to the defendants to show that they were not responsible for the harm. This principle is sometimes referred to as the "alternative liability" theory.

The celebrated case of *Summers v. Tice,* supra, 33 Cal.2d 80, 199 P.2d 1, a unanimous opinion of this court, best exemplifies the rule. In *Summers,* the plaintiff was injured when two hunters negligently shot in his direction. It could not be determined which of them had fired the shot which actually caused the injury to the plaintiff's eye, but both defendants were nevertheless held jointly and severally liable for the whole of the damages. We reasoned that both were wrongdoers, both were negligent toward the plaintiff, and that it would be unfair to require plaintiff to isolate the defendant responsible, because if the one pointed out were to escape liability, the other might also, and the plaintiff-victim would be shorn of any remedy. In these circumstances, we held, the burden of proof shifted to the defendants, "each to absolve himself if he can." (*Id.,* p. 86, 199 *P. 2d* p. 4.) We stated that

under these or similar circumstances a defendant is ordinarily in a "far better position" to offer evidence to determine whether he or another defendant caused the injury.

In *Summers,* we relied upon *Ybarra v. Spangard* (1944) 25 *Cal. 2d* 486, 154 *P. 2d* 687. There, the plaintiff was injured while he was unconscious during the course of surgery. He sought damages against several doctors and a nurse who attended him while he was unconscious. We held that it would be unreasonable to require him to identify the particular defendant who had performed the alleged negligent act because he was unconscious at the time of the injury and the defendants exercised control over the instrumentalities which caused the harm. Therefore, under the doctrine of res ipsa loquitur, an inference of negligence arose that defendants were required to meet by explaining their conduct.[10]

The rule developed in *Summers* has been embodied in the Restatement of Torts. (*Rest. 2d* Torts, § 433B, subsec. (3).)[11] Indeed, the *Summers* facts are used as an illustration (p. 447).

Defendants assert that these principles are inapplicable here. First, they insist that a predicate to shifting the burden of proof under *Summers-Ybarra* is that the defendants must have greater access to information regarding the cause of the injuries than the plaintiff, whereas in the present case the reverse appears.

Plaintiff does not claim that defendants are in a better position than she to identify the manufacturer of the drug taken by her mother or, indeed, that they have the ability to do so at all, but argues, rather, that *Summers* does not impose such a requirement as a condition to the shifting of the burden of proof. In this respect we believe plaintiff is correct.

In *Summers,* the circumstances of the accident themselves precluded an explanation of its cause. To be sure, *Summers* states that defendants are "[o]rdinarily . . . in a far better position to offer evidence to determine which one caused the injury" than a plaintiff (33 *Cal. 2d* 80, at p. 86, 199 *P. 2d* 1 at p. 4), but the decision does not determine that this "ordinary" situation was present. Neither the facts nor the language of the opinion indicate that the two defendants, simultaneously shooting in the same direction, were in a better position than the plaintiff to ascertain whose shot caused the injury. As the opinion acknowledges, it was impossible for the trial court to determine whether the shot which entered the plaintiff's eye came from the gun of one defendant or the other. Nevertheless, burden of proof was shifted to the defendants.

Here, as in *Summers,* the circumstances of the injury appear to render identification of the manufacturer of the drug ingested by plaintiff's mother impossible by either plaintiff or defendants, and it cannot reasonably be said that one is in a better position than the other to make the identification. Because many years elapsed between the time the drug was taken and the manifestation of plaintiff's injuries she, and many other daughters of mothers who took DES, are unable to make such identification.[12] Certainly there can be no implication that plaintiff is at fault in failing to do so—the event occurred while plaintiff was *in utero,* a generation ago.[13]

On the other hand, it cannot be said with assurance that defendants have the means to make the identification. In this connection, they point out that drug manufacturers ordinarily have no direct contact with the patients who take a drug prescribed by their doctors. Defendants sell to wholesalers, who in turn supply the product to physicians and pharmacies. Manufacturers do not maintain records of the persons who take the drugs they produce, and the selection of the medication is made by the physician rather than the manufacturer. Nor do we conclude that the absence of evidence on this subject is due to the fault of defendants. While it is alleged that they produced a defective product with delayed effects and without adequate warnings, the difficulty or impossibility of identification results primarily from the passage of time rather than from their allegedly negligent acts of failing to provide adequate warnings. Thus *Haft v. Lone Palm Hotel* (1970) 3 *Cal. 3d* 756, 91 *Cal. Rptr.* 745, 478 *P. 2d* 465, upon which plaintiff relies, is distinguishable.[14]

It is important to observe, however, that while defendants do not have means superior to plaintiff to identify the maker of the precise drug taken by her mother, they may in some instances be able to prove that they did not manufacture the injury-causing substance. In the present case, for example, one of the original defendants was dismissed from the action upon proof that it did not manufacture DES until after plaintiff was born.

Thus we conclude that the fact defendants do not have greater access to information which might establish the identity of the manufacturer of the DES which injured plaintiff does not per se prevent application of the *Summers* rule.

[2] Nevertheless, plaintiff may not prevail in her claim that the *Summers* rationale should be em-

ployed to fix the whole liability for her injuries upon defendants, at least as those principles have previously been applied.[15] There is an important difference between the situation involved in *Summers* and the present case. There, all the parties who were or could have been responsible for the harm to the plaintiff were joined as defendants. Here, by contrast, there are approximately 200 drug companies which made DES, any of which might have manufactured the injury-producing drug.[16]

Defendants maintain that, while in *Summers* there was a 50 percent chance that one of the two defendants was responsible for the plaintiff's injuries, here since any one of 200 companies which manufactured DES might have made the product which harmed plaintiff, there is no rational basis upon which to infer that any defendant in this action caused plaintiff's injuries, nor even a reasonable possibility that they were responsible.[17]

These arguments are persuasive if we measure the chance that any one of the defendants supplied the injury-causing drug by the number of possible tortfeasors. In such a context, the possibility that any of the five defendants supplied the DES to plaintiff's mother is so remote that it would be unfair to require each defendant to exonerate itself. There may be a substantial likelihood that none of the five defendants joined in the action made the DES which caused the injury, and that the offending producer not named would escape liability altogether. While we propose, *infra,* an adaptation of the rule in *Summers* which will substantially overcome these difficulties, defendants appear to be correct that the rule, as previously applied, cannot relieve plaintiff of the burden of proving the identity of the manufacturer which made the drug causing her injuries.[18]

II

The second principle upon which plaintiff relies is the so-called "concert of action" theory. Preliminarily, we briefly describe the procedure a drug manufacturer must follow before placing a drug on the market. Under federal law as it read prior to 1962, a new drug was defined as one "not generally recognized as . . . safe." (§ 102, 76 *Stat.* 781 (Oct. 10, 1962).) Such a substance could be marketed only if a new drug application had been filed with the Food and Drug Administration and had become "effective."[19] If the agency determined that a product was no longer a "new drug," i.e., that it was "generally recognized as . . . safe," (21 *U.S.C.A.* § 321, subd. (p) (1)) it could be manufactured by any drug company without submitting an application to the agency. According to defendants, 123 new drug applications for DES had been approved by 1952, and in that year DES was declared not to be a "new drug," thus allowing any manufacturer to produce it without prior testing and without submitting a new drug application to the Food and Drug Administration.

With this background we consider whether the complaint states a claim based upon "concert of action" among defendants. The elements of this doctrine are prescribed in section 876 of the Restatement of Torts. The section provides, "For harm resulting to a third person from the tortious conduct of another, one is subject to liability if he (a) does a tortious act in concert with the other or pursuant to a common design with him, or (b) knows that the other's conduct constitutes a breach of duty and gives substantial assistance or encouragement to the other so to conduct himself, or (c) gives substantial assistance to the other in accomplishing a tortious result and his own conduct, separately considered, constitutes a breach of duty to the third person." With respect to this doctrine, Prosser states that "those who, in pursuance of a common plan or design to commit a tortious act, actively take part in it, or further it by cooperation or request, or who lend aid or encouragement to the wrongdoer, or ratify and adopt his acts done for their benefit, are equally liable with him. [¶] Express agreement is not necessary, and all that is required is that there be a tacit understanding . . ." (Prosser, *Law of Torts* (4th ed. 1971), sec. 46, p. 292.)

Plaintiff contends that her complaint states a cause of action under these principles. She alleges that defendants' wrongful conduct "is the result of planned and concerted action, express and implied agreements, collaboration in, reliance upon, acquiescence in and ratification, exploitation and adoption of each other's testing, marketing methods, lack of warnings . . . and other acts or omissions . . ." and that "acting individually and in concert, [defendants] promoted, approved, authorized, acquiesced in, and reaped profits from sales" of DES. These allegations, plaintiff claims, state a "tacit understanding" among defendants to commit a tortious act against her.

[3] In our view, this litany of charges is insufficient to allege a cause of action under the rules stated above. The gravamen of the charge of concert is that defendants failed to adequately test the drug or to give sufficient warning of its dangers and

that they relied upon the tests performed by one another and took advantage of each others' promotional and marketing techniques. These allegations do not amount to a charge that there was a tacit understanding or a common plan among defendants to fail to conduct adequate tests or give sufficient warnings, and that they substantially aided and encouraged one another in these omissions.

The complaint charges also that defendants produced DES from a "common and mutually agreed upon formula," allowing pharmacists to treat the drug as a "fungible commodity" and to fill prescriptions from whatever brand of DES they had on hand at the time. It is difficult to understand how these allegations can form the basis of a cause of action for wrongful conduct by defendants, acting in concert. The formula for DES is a scientific constant. It is set forth in the United States Pharmacopoeia, and any manufacturer producing that drug must, with exceptions not relevant here, utilize the formula set forth in that compendium. (21 *U.S.C.A.* § 351, subd. [b].)

What the complaint appears to charge is defendants' parallel or imitative conduct in that they relied upon each others' testing and promotion methods. But such conduct describes a common practice in industry: a producer avails himself of the experience and methods of others making the same or similar products. Application of the concept of concert of action to this situation would expand the doctrine far beyond its intended scope and would render virtually any manufacturer liable for the defective products of an entire industry, even if it could be demonstrated that the product which caused the injury was not made by the defendant.

None of the cases cited by plaintiff supports a conclusion that defendants may be held liable for concerted tortious acts. They involve conduct by a small number of individuals whose actions resulted in a tort against a single plaintiff, usually over a short span of time, and the defendant held liable was either a direct participant in the acts which caused damage,[20] or encouraged and assisted the person who directly caused the injuries by participating in a joint activity.[21]

Orser v. George (1967) 252 *Cal. App. 2d* 660, 60 *Cal. Rptr.* 708 upon which plaintiff primarily relies, is also distinguishable. There, three hunters negligently shot at a mudhen in decedent's direction. Two of them shot alternately with the gun which released the bullet resulting in the fatal wound, and the third, using a different gun, fired alternately at the same target, shooting in the same line of fire, perhaps acting tortiously. It was held that there was a possibility the third hunter knew the conduct of the others was tortious toward the decedent and gave them substantial assistance and encouragement, and that it was also possible his conduct, separately considered, was a breach of duty toward decedent. Thus, the granting of summary judgment was reversed as to the third hunter.

The situation in *Orser* is similar to *Agovino v. Kunze,* supra, 181 *Cal. App. 2d* 591, 5 Cal.Rptr. 534, in which liability was imposed upon a participant in a drag race, rather than to the facts alleged in the present case. There is no allegation here that each defendant knew the other defendants' conduct was tortious toward plaintiff, and that they assisted and encouraged one another to inadequately test DES and to provide inadequate warnings. Indeed, it seems dubious whether liability on the concert of action theory can be predicated upon substantial assistance and encouragement given by one alleged tortfeasor to another pursuant to a tacit understanding to fail to perform an act. Thus, there was no concert of action among defendants within the meaning of that doctrine.

III

A third theory upon which plaintiff relies is the concept of industry-wide liability, or according to the terminology of the parties, "enterprise liability." This theory was suggested in *Hall v. E. I. Du Pont de Nemours & Co., Inc.* (*E.D.N.Y.* 1972) 345 *F. Supp.* 353. In that case, plaintiffs were 34 children injured by the explosion of blasting caps in 12 separate incidents which occurred in 10 different states between 1955 and 1959. The defendants were six blasting cap manufacturers, comprising virtually the entire blasting cap industry in the United States, and their trade association. There were, however, a number of Canadian blasting cap manufacturers which could have supplied the caps. The gravamen of the complaint was that the practice of the industry of omitting a warning on individual blasting caps and of failing to take other safety measures created an unreasonable risk of harm, resulting in the plaintiffs' injuries. The complaint did not identify a particular manufacturer of a cap which caused a particular injury.[22]

The court reasoned as follows: there was evidence that defendants, acting independently, had adhered to an industry-wide standard with regard to the safety features of blasting caps, that they had in effect delegated some functions of safety investigation and design, such as labelling, to their trade association, and that there was industry-wide cooperation in the manufacture and design of blasting caps. In these circumstances, the evidence supported a conclusion that all the defendants jointly controlled the risk. Thus, if plaintiffs could establish by a preponderance of the evidence that the caps were manufactured by one of the defendants, the burden of proof as to causation would shift to all the defendants. The court noted that this theory of liability applied to industries composed of a small number of units, and that what would be fair and reasonable with regard to an industry of five or ten producers might be manifestly unreasonable if applied to a decentralized industry composed of countless small producers.[23]

Plaintiff attempts to state a cause of action under the rationale of *Hall.* She alleges joint enterprise and collaboration among defendants in the production, marketing, promotion and testing of DES, and "concerted promulgation and adherence to industry-wide testing, safety, warning and efficacy standards" for the drug. We have concluded above that allegations that defendants relied upon one another's testing and promotion methods do not state a cause of action for concerted conduct to commit a tortious act. Under the theory of industry-wide liability, however, each manufacturer could be liable for all injuries caused by DES by virtue of adherence to an industry-wide standard of safety.

In the Fordham Comment, the industry-wide theory of liability is discussed and refined in the context of its applicability to actions alleging injuries resulting from DES. The author explains causation under that theory as follows,". . . [T]he industrywide standard becomes itself the cause of plaintiff's injury, just as defendants' joint plan is the cause of injury in the traditional concert of action plea. Each defendant's adherence perpetuates this standard, which results in the manufacture of the particular, unidentifiable injury-producing product. Therefore, each industry member has contributed to plaintiff's injury." (Fordham Comment, supra, at p. 997.)

The Comment proposes seven requirements for a cause of action based upon industry-wide liability,[24] and suggests that if a plaintiff proves these elements, the burden of proof of causation should be shifted to the defendants, who may exonerate themselves only by showing that their product could not have caused the injury.[25]

[4] We decline to apply this theory in the present case. At least 200 manufacturers produced DES;

Hall, which involved 6 manufacturers representing the entire blasting cap industry in the United States, cautioned against application of the doctrine espoused therein to a large number of producers. (345 *F. Supp.* at p. 378.) Moreover, in *Hall,* the conclusion that the defendants jointly controlled the risk was based upon allegations that they had delegated some functions relating to safety to a trade association. There are no such allegations here, and we have concluded above that plaintiff has failed to allege liability on a concert of action theory.

Equally important, the drug industry is closely regulated by the Food and Drug Administration, which actively controls the testing and manufacture of drugs and the method by which they are marketed, including the contents of warning labels.[26] To a considerable degree, therefore, the standards followed by drug manufacturers are suggested or compelled by the government. Adherence to those standards cannot, of course, absolve a manufacturer of liability to which it would otherwise be subject. (*Stevens v. Parke, Davis & Co.* (1973) 9 *Cal. 3d* 51, 65, 107 *Cal. Rptr.* 45, 507 *P. 2d* 653.) But since the government plays such a pervasive role in formulating the criteria for the testing and marketing of drugs, it would be unfair to impose upon a manufacturer liability for injuries resulting from the use of a drug which it did not supply simply because it followed the standards of the industry.[27]

IV

If we were confined to the theories of *Summers* and *Hall,* we would be constrained to hold that the judgment must be sustained. Should we require that plaintiff identify the manufacturer which supplied the DES used by her mother or that all DES manufacturers be joined in the action, she would effectively be precluded from any recovery. As defendants candidly admit, there is little likelihood that all the manufacturers who made DES at the time in question are still in business or that they are subject to the jurisdiction of the California courts. There are, however, forceful arguments in favor of holding that plaintiff has a cause of action.

In our contemporary complex industrialized society, advances in science and technology create fungible goods which may harm consumers and which cannot be traced to any specific producer. The response of the courts can be either to adhere rigidly to prior doctrine, denying recovery to those injured by such products, or to fashion remedies to meet these changing needs. Just as Justice Traynor in his landmark concurring opinion in *Escola v. Coca Cola Bottling Company* (1944) 24 *Cal. 2d* 453, 467–68, 150 *P.2d* 436, recognized that in an era of mass production and complex marketing methods the traditional standard of negligence was insufficient to govern the obligations of manufacturer to consumer, so should we acknowledge that some adaptation of the rules of causation and liability may be appropriate in these recurring circumstances. The Restatement comments that modification of the *Summers* rule may be necessary in a situation like that before us. (See fn. 16, *ante.*)

The most persuasive reason for finding plaintiff states a cause of action is that advanced in *Summers:* as between an innocent plaintiff and negligent defendants, the latter should bear the cost of the injury. Here, as in *Summers,* plaintiff is not at fault in failing to provide evidence of causation, and although the absence of such evidence is not attributable to the defendants either, their conduct in marketing a drug the effects of which are delayed for many years played a significant role in creating the unavailability of proof.

From a broader policy standpoint, defendants are better able to bear the cost of injury resulting from the manufacture of a defective product. As was said by Justice Traynor in *Escola,* "[t]he cost of an injury and the loss of time or health may be an overwhelming misfortune to the person injured, and a needless one, for the risk of injury can be insured by the manufacturer and distributed among the public as a cost of doing business." (24 *Cal. 2d* p. 462, 150 *P. 2d* p. 441; see also *Rest. 2d Torts,* § 402A, com. c, pp. 349–50.) The manufacturer is in the best position to discover and guard against defects in its products and to warn of harmful effects; thus, holding it liable for defects and failure to warn of harmful effects will provide an incentive to product safety. (*Cronin v. J.B.E. Olson Corp.* (1972) 8 *Cal. 3d* 121, 129, 104 *Cal. Rptr.* 433, 501 *P. 2d* 1153; *Beech Aircraft Corp. v. Superior Court* (1976) 61 *Cal. App. 3d* 501, 522–23, 132 *Cal. Rptr.* 541.) These considerations are particularly significant where medication is involved, for the consumer is virtually helpless to protect himself from serious, sometimes permanent, sometimes fatal, injuries caused by deleterious drugs.

[5] Where, as here, all defendants produced a drug from an identical formula and the manufacturer of the DES which caused plaintiff's injuries cannot

be identified through no fault of plaintiff, a modification of the rule of *Summers* is warranted. As we have seen, an undiluted *Summers* rationale is inappropriate to shift the burden of proof of causation to defendants because if we measure the chance that any particular manufacturer supplied the injury-causing product by the number of producers of DES, there is a possibility that none of the five defendants in this case produced the offending substance and that the responsible manufacturer, not named in the action, will escape liability.

But we approach the issue of causation from a different perspective: we hold it to be reasonable in the present context to measure the likelihood that any of the defendants supplied the product which allegedly injured plaintiff by the percentage which the DES sold by each of them for the purpose of preventing miscarriage bears to the entire production of the drug sold by all for that purpose. Plaintiff asserts in her briefs that Eli Lilly and Company and 5 or 6 other companies produced 90 percent of the DES marketed. If at trial this is established to be the fact, then there is a corresponding likelihood that this comparative handful of producers manufactured the DES which caused plaintiff's injuries, and only a 10 percent likelihood that the offending producer would escape liability.[28]

If plaintiff joins in the action the manufacturers of a substantial share of the DES which her mother might have taken, the injustice of shifting the burden of proof to defendants to demonstrate that they could not have made the substance which injured plaintiff is significantly diminished. While 75 to 80 percent of the market is suggested as the requirement by the Fordham Comment (at p. 996), we hold only that a substantial percentage is required.

The presence in the action of a substantial share of the appropriate market also provides a ready means to apportion damages among the defendants. Each defendant will be held liable for the proportion of the judgment represented by its share of that market unless it demonstrates that it could not have made the product which caused plaintiff's injuries. In the present case, as we have seen, one DES manufacturer was dismissed from the action upon filing a declaration that it had not manufactured DES until after plaintiff was born. Once plaintiff has met her burden of joining the required defendants, they in turn may cross-complaint against other DES manufacturers, not joined in the action, which they can allege might have supplied the injury-causing product.

Under this approach, each manufacturer's liability would approximate its responsibility for the injuries caused by its own products. Some minor discrepancy in the correlation between market share and liability is inevitable; therefore, a defendant may be held liable for a somewhat different percentage of the damage than its share of the appropriate market would justify. It is probably impossible, with the passage of time, to determine market share with mathematical exactitude. But just as a jury cannot be expected to determine the precise relationship between fault and liability in applying the doctrine of comparative fault (*Li v. Yellow Cab Co.* [1975] 13 *Cal. 3d* 804, 119 *Cal. Rptr.* 858, 532 *P. 2d* 1226) or partial indemnity (*American Motorcycle Ass'n v. Superior Court* (1978) 20 *Cal. 3d* 578, 146 *Cal. Rptr.* 182, 578 *P. 2d* 899), the difficulty of apportioning damages among the defendant producers in exact relation to their market share does not seriously militate against the rule we adopt. As we said in *Summers* with regard to the liability of independent tortfeasors, where a correct division of liability cannot be made "the trier of fact may make it the best it can." (33 *Cal. 2d* at p. 88, 199 *P. 2d* at p. 5.)

We are not unmindful of the practical problems involved in defining the market and determining market share,[29] but these are largely matters of proof which properly cannot be determined at the pleading stage of these proceedings. Defendants urge that it would be both unfair and contrary to public policy to hold them liable for plaintiff's injuries in the absence of proof that one of them supplied the drug responsible for the damage. Most of their arguments, however, are based upon the assumption that one manufacturer would be held responsible for the products of another or for those of all other manufacturers if plaintiff ultimately prevails. But under the rule we adopt, each manufacturer's liability for an injury would be approximately equivalent to the damages caused by the DES it manufactured.[30]

The judgments are reversed.

BIRD, C. J., and NEWMAN and WHITE,* J J., concur.

RICHARDSON, Justice, dissenting.

I respectfully dissent. In these consolidated cases the majority adopts a wholly new theory which contains these ingredients: The plaintiffs were not alive at the time of the commission of the tortious acts. They sue a generation later. They are permitted to receive substantial damages from multiple defendants without any proof that any defendant caused or even probably caused plaintiffs' injuries.

Although the majority purports to change only the required burden of proof by shifting it from plaintiffs to defendants, the effect of its holding is to guarantee that plaintiffs will prevail on the causation issue because defendants are no more capable of disproving factual causation than plaintiffs are of proving it. "Market share" liability thus represents a new high water mark in tort law. The ramifications seem almost limitless, a fact which prompted one recent commentator, in criticizing a substantially identical theory, to conclude that "Elimination of the burden of proof as to identification [of the manufacturer whose drug injured plaintiff] would impose a liability which would exceed absolute liability." (Coggins, *Industry-Wide Liability* [1979] 13 *Suffolk L. Rev.* 980, 998, fn. omitted; see also, pp. 1000–1001.) In my view, the majority's departure from traditional tort doctrine is unwise.

The applicable principles of causation are very well established. A leading torts scholar, Dean Prosser, has authoritatively put it this way: "An *essential* element of the plaintiff's cause of action for negligence, *or for that matter for any other tort,* is that there be some reasonable connection between the act or omission of the defendant and the damage which the plaintiff has suffered." (Prosser, *Torts* [4th ed. 1971] § 41, p. 236, italics added.) With particular reference to the matter before us, and in the context of products liability, the requirement of a causation element has been recognized as equally fundamental. "It is clear that any holding that a producer, manufacturer, seller, or a person in a similar position, is liable for injury caused by a particular product, must necessarily be predicated upon proof that the product in question was one for whose condition the defendant was in some way responsible. Thus, for example, if recovery is sought from a manufacturer, *it must be shown that he actually was the manufacturer of the product which caused the injury; . . .*" (1 Hursh & Bailey, *American Law of Products Liability* [2d ed. 1974] § 1:41, p. 125, italics added; accord, *Prosser,* supra, § 103, at pp. 671–72; 2 Dooley, *Modern Tort Law* [1977] § 32.03, p. 243.) Indeed, an inability to prove this causal link between defendant's conduct and plaintiff's injury has proven fatal in prior cases brought against manufacturers of DES by persons who were situated in positions identical to those of plaintiffs herein. (See *McCreery v. Eli Lilly & Co.* [1978] 87 *Cal. App. 3d* 77, 82, 150 *Cal. Rptr.* 730; *Gray v. United States* [*D. Tex.* 1978] 445 *F. Supp.* 337, 338.)

The majority now expressly abandons the foregoing traditional requirement of some causal connection between defendants' act and plaintiffs' injury in the creation of its new modified industry-wide tort. Conceptually, the doctrine of absolute liability which heretofore in negligence law has substituted only for the requirement of a breach of defendant's duty of care, under the majority's hand now subsumes the additional necessity of a causal relationship.

According to the majority, in the present case plaintiffs have openly conceded that they are unable to identify the particular entity which manufactured the drug consumed by their mothers. In fact, plaintiffs have joined only *five* of the approximately *two hundred* drug companies which manufactured DES. Thus, the case constitutes far more than a mere factual variant upon the theme composed in *Summers v. Tice* (1948) 33 *Cal. 2d* 80, 199 *P. 2d* 1, wherein plaintiff joined as codefendants the *only* two persons who could have injured him. As the majority must acknowledge, our *Summers* rule applies only to cases in which ". . . it is proved that harm has been caused to the plaintiff by . . . one of [the named defendants], but there is uncertainty as to which one has caused it, . . ." (*Rest. 2d Torts,* § 433B, subd. [3].) In the present case, in stark contrast, it remains wholly speculative and conjectural whether *any* of the five named defendants actually caused plaintiffs' injuries.

The fact that plaintiffs cannot tie defendants to the injury-producing drug does not trouble the majority for it declares that the *Summers* requirement of proof of actual causation by a named defendant is satisfied by a joinder of those defendants who have *together* manufactured "*a substantial percentage*" of the DES which has been marketed. Notably lacking from the majority's expression of its new rule, unfortunately, is any definition or guidance as to what should constitute a "substantial" share of the relevant market. The issue is entirely open-ended and the answer, presumably, is anyone's guess.

Much more significant, however, is the consequence of this unprecedented extension of liability. Recovery is permitted from a handful of defendants *each* of whom *individually* may account for a comparatively small share of the relevant market, so long as the *aggregate* business of those who have been sued is deemed "substantial." In other words, a particular defendant may be held proportionately liable *even though mathematically it is much more likely than not that it played no role whatever in causing plaintiffs' injuries.* Plaintiffs have strikingly capsulated their reasoning by insisting ". . . that while one manufacturer's product may not have injured a particular plaintiff, we can assume that it injured a different plaintiff and all we are talking about is a mere matching of plaintiffs and defendants." (Counsel's letter [Oct. 16, 1979] p. 3.) In adopting the foregoing rationale the majority rejects over 100 years of tort law which required that before tort liability was imposed a "matching" of defendant's conduct and plaintiff's injury was absolutely essential. Furthermore, in bestowing on plaintiffs this new largess the majority sprinkles the rain of liability upon all the joined defendants alike—those who may be tortfeasors and those who may have had nothing at all to do with plaintiffs' injury—and an added bonus is conferred. Plaintiffs are free to pick and choose their targets.

The "market share" thesis may be paraphrased. Plaintiffs have been hurt by *someone* who made DES. Because of the lapse of time no one can prove who made it. Perhaps it was not the named defendants who made it, but they did make some. Although DES was apparently safe at the time it was used, it was subsequently proven unsafe as to some daughters of some users. Plaintiffs have suffered injury and defendants are wealthy. There should be a remedy. Strict products liability is unavailable because the element of causation is lacking. Strike that requirement and label what remains "alternative" liability, "industry-wide" liability, or "market share" liability, proving thereby that if you hit the square peg hard and often enough the round holes will really become square, although you may splinter the board in the process.

The foregoing result is directly contrary to long established tort principles. Once again, in the words of Dean Prosser, the applicable rule is: "[Plaintiff] must introduce evidence which affords a reasonable basis for the conclusion that it is more likely than not that the conduct of the defendant was a substantial factor in bringing about the result. *A mere possibility of such causation is not enough;* and when the matter remains one of pure speculation or conjecture, or the probabilities are at best evenly balanced, it becomes the duty of the court to direct a verdict for the defendant." (*Prosser,* supra, § 41, at p. 241, italics added, fns. omitted.) Under the majority's new reasoning, however, a defendant is fair game if it happens to be engaged in a similar business and causation is *possible,* even though remote.

In passing, I note the majority's dubious use of market share data. It is perfectly proper to use such information to assist in proving, circumstantially, that a particular defendant probably caused plaintiffs' injuries. Circumstantial evidence may be used as a basis for proving the requisite probable causation. (*Id.,* at p. 242.) The majority, however, authorizes the use of such evidence for an entirely different purpose, namely, to impose and allocate liability among multiple defendants only one of whom *may* have produced the drug which injured plaintiffs. Because this use of market share evidence does not implicate *any* particular defendant, I believe such data are entirely irrelevant and inadmissible, and that the majority errs in such use. In the absence of some statutory authority there is no legal basis for such use.

Although seeming to acknowledge that imposition of liability upon defendants who probably did not cause plaintiffs' injuries is unfair, the majority justifies this inequity on the ground that "each manufacturer's liability for an injury would be approximately equivalent to the damages caused by the DES it manufactured." (*Ante,* p. 146 of 163 *Cal. Rptr.,* p. 938 of 607 *P. 2d.*) In other words, because each defendant's liability is proportionate to its market share, supposedly "each manufacturer's liability would approximate its responsibility for the injuries caused by his own products." (*Ante,* p. 145 of 163 *Cal. Rptr.,* p. 937 of 607 *P. 2d.*) The majority dodges the "practical problems" thereby presented, choosing to describe them as "matters of proof." However, the difficulties, in my view, are not so easily ducked, for they relate not to evidentiary matters but to the fundamental question of liability itself.

Additionally, it is readily apparent that "market share" liability will fall unevenly and disproportionately upon those manufacturers who are amenable to suit in California. On the assumption that no other state will adopt so radical a departure from traditional tort principles, it may be concluded that under the majority's reasoning those defendants who are brought to trial in this state will bear effective joint responsibility for 100 percent of plaintiffs' injuries despite the fact that their "substantial" aggregate market share may be considerably less. This undeniable fact forces the majority to concede that, "a defendant may be held liable for a somewhat different percentage of the damage than its share of the appropriate market would justify." (*Ante,* p. 145 of 163 *Cal. Rptr.,* p. 937 of 607 *P. 2d.*) With due deference, I suggest that the complete unfairness of such a result in a case involving only five of two hundred manufacturers is readily manifest.

Furthermore, several other important policy considerations persuade me that the majority holding is both inequitable and improper. The injustice inherent in the majority's new theory of liability is compounded by the fact that plaintiffs who use it are treated far more favorably than are the plaintiffs in routine tort actions. In most tort cases plaintiff knows the identity of the person who has caused his injuries. In such a case, plaintiff, of course, has no option to seek recovery from an entire industry or a "substantial" segment thereof, but in the usual instance can recover, if at all, only from the particular defendant causing injury. Such a defendant may or may not be either solvent or amenable to process. Plaintiff in the ordinary tort case must take a chance that defendant can be reached and can respond financially. On what principle should those plaintiffs who wholly fail to prove any causation, an essential element of the traditional tort cause of action, be rewarded by being offered both a wider selection of potential defendants and a greater opportunity for recovery?

The majority attempts to justify its new liability on the ground that defendants herein are "better able to bear the cost of injury resulting from the manufacture of a defective product." (*Ante,* p. 144 of 163 *Cal. Rptr.,* p. 936 of 607 *P. 2d.*) This "deep pocket" theory of liability, fastening liability on defendants presumably because they are rich, has understandable popular appeal and might be tolerable in a case disclosing substantially stronger evidence of causation than herein appears. But as a general proposition, a defendant's wealth is an unreliable indicator of fault, and should play no part, at least consciously, in the legal analysis of the problem. In the absence of proof that a particular defendant caused or at least probably caused plaintiff's injuries, a defendant's ability to bear the cost thereof is no more pertinent to the underlying issue of liability than its "substantial" share of the relevant market. A system priding itself on "*equal* justice under law" does not flower when the *liability* as well as the *damage* aspect of a tort action is determined by a defendant's wealth. The inevitable consequence of such a result is to create and perpetuate two rules of law—one applicable to wealthy defendants, and another standard pertaining to defendants who are poor or who have modest means. Moreover, considerable doubts have been expressed regarding the ability of the drug industry, and especially its smaller members, to bear the substantial economic costs (from both damage awards and high insurance premiums) inherent in imposing an industry-wide liability. (See *Coggins,* supra, 13 Suffolk L.Rev. at pp. 1003–6, 1010–11.)

An important and substantial countervailing public policy in defendants' favor was very recently expressed in a similar DES case, *McCreery v. Eli Lilly & Co.,* supra, 87 *Cal. App. 3d* 77, 86–87, 150 *Cal. Rptr.* 730. Although the majority herein impliedly rejects the appellate court's holding, in my opinion pertinent language of the *McCreery* court, based upon the Restatement of Torts and bearing on the majority's "market share" theory, is well worth repeating: "Application of the comments to the Restatement Second of Torts, section 402A, to this situation compels a rejection of the imposition of liability. As the comment states, '. . . It is also true in particular of many new or experimental drugs as to which, because of lack of time and opportunity for sufficient medical experience, there can be no assurance of safety, or perhaps even of purity of ingredients, but such experience as there is justifies the marketing and use of the drug notwithstanding a medically recognizable risk. The seller of such products, again, with the qualification that they are properly prepared and marketed, and proper warning is given, where the situation calls for it, is not to be held to strict liability for unfortunate consequences attending their use, merely because he has undertaken to supply the public with an apparently useful and desirable product, attended with a known but apparently reasonable risk.' (*Rest. 2d Torts,* § 402A, comment k.) *This section implicitly recognizes the social policy behind the development of new pharmaceutical preparations.* As one commentator states, '[t]he social and economic benefits from mobilizing the industry's resources in the war against disease and in reducing the costs of medical care are potentially enormous. The development of new drugs in the last three decades has already resulted in great social benefits. The potential gains from further advances remain large. To risk such gains is unwise. Our major objective should be to encourage a continued high level of industry investment in pharmaceutical R & D [research and development].' (Schwartzman, *The Expected Return from Pharmaceutical Research: Sources of New Drugs and the Profitability of R & D Investment* [1975] p. 54.)" *McCreery v. Eli Lilly & Co.,* supra, 87 *Cal. App. 3d* 77, 86–87, 150 *Cal. Rptr.* 730, 736, italics added; see also *Coggins,* supra, 13 *Suffolk L. Rev.* at p. 1004.)

In the present case the majority imposes liability more than 20 years after ingestion of drugs which at the time they were used, after careful testing, had the full approval of the United States Food and Drug Administration. It seems to me that liability in the manner created by the majority must inevitably inhibit, if not the research or development, at least the dissemination of new pharmaceutical drugs. Such a result, as explained by the Restatement, is wholly inconsistent with traditional tort theory.

I also suggest that imposition of so sweeping a liability may well prove to be extremely shortsighted from the standpoint of broad social policy. Who is to say whether, and at what time and in what form, the drug industry upon which the majority now fastens this blanket liability, may develop a miracle drug critical to the diagnosis, treatment, or, indeed, cure of the very disease in question? It is counterproductive to inflict civil damages upon *all* manufacturers for the side effects and medical complications which surface in the children of the users a generation after ingestion of the drugs, particularly when, at the time of their use, the drugs met every fair test and medical standard then available and applicable. Such a result requires of the pharmaceutical industry a foresight, prescience and anticipation far beyond the most exacting standards of the relevant scientific disciplines. In effect, the majority requires the pharmaceutical research laboratory to install a piece of new equipment—the psychic's crystal ball.

I am not unmindful of the serious medical consequences of plaintiffs' injuries, and the equally serious implications to the class which she purports to represent. In balancing the various policy considerations, however, I also observe that the incidence of vaginal cancer among "DES daughters" has been variously estimated at one-tenth of 1 percent to four-tenths of 1 percent. (13 *Suffolk L. Rev.*, supra, p. 999, fn. 92.) These facts raise some penetrating questions. Ninety-nine plus percent of "DES daughters" have never developed cancer. Must a drug manufacturer to escape this blanket liability wait for a generation of testing before it may disseminate drugs? If a drug has beneficial purposes for the majority of users but harmful side effects are later revealed for a small fraction of consumers, will the manufacturer be absolutely liable? If adverse medical consequences, wholly unknown to the most careful and meticulous of present scientists, surface in *two* or *three* generations, will similar liability be imposed? In my opinion, common sense and reality combine to warn that a "market share" theory goes too far. Legally, it expects too much.

I believe that the scales of justice tip against imposition of this new liability because of the foregoing elements of unfairness to some defendants who may have had nothing whatever to do with causing any injury, the unwarranted preference created for this particular class of plaintiffs, the violence done to traditional tort principles by the drastic expansion of liability proposed, the injury threatened to the public interest in continued unrestricted basic medical research as stressed by the Restatement, and the other reasons heretofore expressed.

The majority's decision effectively makes the entire drug industry (or at least its California members) an insurer of all injuries attributable to defective drugs of uncertain or unprovable origin, including those injuries manifesting themselves a generation later, and regardless of whether particular defendants had any part whatever in causing the claimed injury. Respectfully, I think this is unreasonable overreaction for the purpose of achieving what is perceived to be a socially satisfying result.

Finally, I am disturbed by the broad and ominous ramifications of the majority's holding. The law review comment, which is the wellspring of the majority's new theory, conceding the widespread consequences of industry-wide liability, openly acknowledges that "The DES cases are only the tip of an iceberg." (Comment, *DES and a Proposed Theory of Enterprise Liability* [1978] 46 *Fordham L. Rev.* 963, 1007.) Although the pharmaceutical drug industry may be the first target of this new sanction, the majority's reasoning has equally threatening application to many other areas of business and commercial activities.

Given the grave and sweeping economic, social, and medical effects of "market share" liability, the policy decision to introduce and define it should rest not with us, but with the Legislature which is currently considering not only major statutory reform of California product liability law in general, but the DES problem in particular. (See Sen. Bill No. 1392 [1979–80 *Reg. Sess.*], which would establish and appropriate funds for the education, identification, and screening of persons exposed to DES, and would prohibit health care and hospital service plans from excluding or limiting coverage to persons exposed to DES.) An alternative proposal for administrative compensation, described as "a limited version of no-fault products liability" has been suggested by one commentator. (*Coggins,* supra, 13 *Suffolk L. Rev.* at pp. 1019–21.) Compensation under such a plan would be awarded by an administrative tribunal from funds collected "via a tax paid by all manufacturers." (P. 1020, fn. omitted.) In any event, the problem invites a legislative rather than an attempted judicial solution.

I would affirm the judgments of dismissal.

CLARK and MANUEL, J J., concur.

Rehearing denied; CLARK, RICHARDSON and MANUEL, J J., dissenting.

1. The plaintiff class alleged consists of "girls and women who are residents of California and who have been exposed to DES before birth and who may or may not know that fact or the dangers" to which they were exposed. Defendants are also sued as representatives of a class of drug manufacturers which sold DES after 1941.

2. It is alleged also that defendants failed to determine if there was any means to avoid or treat the effects of DES upon the daughters of women exposed to it during pregnancy, and failed to monitor the carcinogenic effects of the drug.

3. There are minor variations in the procedures employed as to the various defendants. Thus, for example, Eli Lilly and Company filed a motion for summary judgment, or alternatively judgment on the pleadings, rather than a demurrer; the court treated the motion as a demurrer.

    The demurrer of Abbott Laboratories, the first defendant to file a demurrer and the first to secure a dismissal, was sustained with leave to amend on the ground that plaintiff had failed to allege that a product manufactured by Abbott had caused her injuries (as opposed to the reason given by the trial court for sustaining the demurrers of the other defendants that plaintiff expressly stated that she could not identify a particular manufacturer). Upon plaintiff's failure to amend the complaint, the action was dismissed as to Abbott. A few days after the dismissal, plaintiff stated in a brief in opposition to the demurrers filed by defendants other than Abbott that she could not make the identification.

    Abbott asserts that as to it the issue we consider on the appeal is not properly raised because plaintiff's statement that she could not identify the manufacturer was not made until after the action had been dismissed as to Abbott. This contention is without merit. Plaintiff's failure to amend her complaint after Abbott's demurrer was sustained with leave to amend was based upon her inability to identify a specific manufacturer. Clearly, Abbott interpreted the complaint in this fashion, for it moved for dismissal on the ground that the complaint alleges that plaintiff "does not know the identity of the drug . . . ingested" by her mother. Thus, Abbott may not now claim that the complaint is insufficient to raise the issue involved in this appeal.

    The trial court did not determine other issues raised by the complaint, such as whether the case was properly brought as a class action.

4. Abbott Laboratories, Eli Lilly and Company, E. R. Squibb and Sons, The Upjohn Company, and Rexall Drug Company are respondents. The action was dismissed or the appeal abandoned on various grounds as to other defendants named in the complaint; e.g., one defendant demonstrated it had not manufactured DES during the period plaintiff's mother took the drug.

5. While the trial court did not specify the ground upon which the demurrers were sustained, the points and authorities filed by the parties emphasized the failure of Rogers to identify a particular manufacturer as the source of her injuries, and we may assume for the purpose of this appeal that this was the basis of the court's order.

6. DES was marketed under many different trade names.

7. In a recent New York case a jury found in the plaintiff's favor in spite of her inability to identify a specific manufacturer of DES. An appeal is pending. (*Bichler v. Eli Lilly and Co.* [Sup. Ct.N.Y.1979].) A Michigan appellate court recently held that plaintiffs had stated a cause of action against several manufacturers of DES even though identification could not be made. (*Abel v. Eli Lilly and Co.* [decided Dec. 5, 1979] Docket No. 60497.] That decision is on appeal to the Supreme Court of Michigan.

8. E. g., *Gray v. United States* (S. D. Tex. 1978) 445 *F. Supp.* 337. In their briefs, defendants refer to a number of other cases in which trial courts have dismissed actions in DES cases on the ground stated above.

9. The term "enterprise liability" is sometimes used broadly to mean that losses caused by an enterprise should be borne by it. (Klemme Enterprise Liability [1976] 47 *Colo. L. Rev.* 153, 158.)

10. Other cases cited by plaintiff for the proposition stated in *Summers* are only peripherally relevant. For example, in *Ray v. Alad Corporation* (1977) 19 *Cal. 3d* 22, 136 *Cal. Rptr.* 574, 560 *P. 2d* 3, the plaintiff brought an action in strict liability for personal injuries sustained when he fell from a defective ladder manufactured by the defendant's predecessor corporation. We held that, although under the general rule governing corporate succession the defendant could not be held responsible, nevertheless a "special departure" from that rule was justified in the particular circumstances. The defendant had succeeded to the good will of the manufacturer of the ladder, and it could obtain insurance against the risk of liability, whereas the plaintiff would be left without redress if he could not hold the defendant liable. The question whether one corporation should, for policy reasons, be answerable for the products manufactured by its predecessor is a different issue than that we describe above.

11. Section 433B, subsection (3) of the Restatement provides: "Where the conduct of two or more actors is tortious, and it is proved that harm has been caused to the plaintiff by only one of them, but there is uncertainty as to which one has caused it, the burden is upon each such actor to prove that he has not caused the harm." The reason underlying the rule is "the injustice of permitting proved wrongdoers, who among them have inflicted an injury upon the entirely innocent plaintiff, to escape liability merely because the nature of their conduct and the resulting harm has made it difficult or impossible to prove which of them has caused the harm." (*Rest. 2d Torts*, § 433B, com. f, p. 446.)

12. The trial court was not required to determine whether plaintiff had made sufficient efforts to establish identification since it concluded that her failure to do so was fatal to her claim. The court accepted at face value plaintiff's assertion that she could not make the identification, and for purposes of this appeal we make the same assumption.

13. Defendants maintain that plaintiff is in a better position than they are to identify the manufacturer because her mother might recall the name of the prescribing physician or the hospital or pharmacy where the drug originated, and might know the brand and strength of dosage, the appearance of the medication, or other details from which the manufacturer might be identified, whereas they possess none of this information. As we point out in footnote 12, we assume for purposes of this appeal that plaintiff cannot point to any particular manufacturer as the producer of the DES taken by her mother.

14. In *Haft*, a father and his young son drowned in defendants' swimming pool. There were no witnesses to the accident. Defendants were negligent in failing to provide a lifeguard, as required by law. We held that the absence of evidence of causation was a direct and foreseeable result of the defendants' negligence, and that, therefore, the burden of proof on the issue of causation was upon defendants. Plaintiff attempts to bring herself within this holding. She asserts that defendants' failure to discover or warn of the dangers of DES and to label the drug as experimental caused her mother to fail to keep records or remember the brand name of the drug prescribed to her "since she was unaware of any reason to do so for a period of 10 to 20 years." There is no proper analogy to *Haft* here. While in *Haft* the presence of a lifeguard on the scene would have provided a witness to the accident and probably prevented it, plaintiff asks us to speculate that if the DES taken by her mother had been labelled as an experimental drug, she would have recalled or recorded the name of the manufacturer and passed this information on to her daughter. It cannot be said here that the absence of evidence of causation was a "direct and foreseeable result" of defendants' failure to provide a warning label.

15. Plaintiff relies upon three older cases for the proposition that the burden of proof may be shifted to defendants to explain the cause of an accident even if less than all of them are before the court. (*Benson v. Ross* [1906] 143 *Mich.* 452, 106 *N.W.* 1120; *Moore v. Foster* (1938) 182 *Miss.* 15, 180 *So.* 73; *Oliver v. Miles* (1927) 144 *Miss.* 852, 110 *So.* 666.) These cases do not relate to

the shifting of the burden of proof; rather, they imposed liability upon one of two or more joint tortfeasors on the ground that they acted in concert in committing a negligent act. This theory of concerted action as a basis for defendants' liability will be discussed *infra*. In *Summers*, we stated that these cases were "straining" the concept of concerted action and that the "more reasonable" basis for holding defendants jointly liable when more than one of them had committed a tort and plaintiff could not establish the identity of the party who had caused the damage was the danger that otherwise two negligent parties might be exonerated. (*Summers, 33 Cal. 2d* 80, at pp. 84–85, 199 *P. 2d* 1.)

16. According to the Restatement, the burden of proof shifts to the defendants only if the plaintiff can demonstrate that all defendants acted tortiously and that the harm resulted from the conduct of one of them. (*Rest. 2d Torts,* § 433B, com. g, p. 446.) It goes on to state that the rule thus far has been applied only where all the actors involved are joined as defendants and where the conduct of all is simultaneous in time, but cases might arise in which some modification of the rule would be necessary if one of the actors is or cannot be joined, or because of the effects of lapse of time, or other circumstances. (*Id.,* com. h, p. 446.)

17. Defendants claim further that the effect of shifting the burden of proof to them to demonstrate that they did not manufacture the DES which caused the injury would create a rebuttable presumption that one of them made the drug taken by plaintiff's mother, and that this presumption would deny them due process because there is no rational basis for the inference.

18. *Garcia v. Joseph Vince Co.*, supra, 84 *Cal. App. 3d* 868, 148 *Cal. Rptr.* 843, relied upon by defendants, presents a distinguishable factual situation. The plaintiff in *Garcia* was injured by a defective saber. He was unable to identify which of two manufacturers had produced the weapon because it was commingled with other sabers after the accident. In a suit against both manufacturers, the court refused to apply the *Summers* rationale on the ground that the plaintiff had not shown that either defendant had violated a duty to him. Thus in *Garcia,* only one of the two defendants was alleged to have manufactured a defective product, and the plaintiff's inability to identify which of the two was negligent resulted in a judgment for both defendants. (See also *Wetzel v. Eaton,* supra, 62 *F.R.D.* 22.) Here, by contrast, the DES manufactured by all defendants is alleged to be defective, but plaintiff is unable to demonstrate which of the defendants supplied the precise DES which caused her injuries.

19. A new drug application became "effective" automatically if the Secretary of Health, Education and Welfare failed within a certain period of time to disapprove the application. If the agency had insufficient information to decide whether the drug was safe or had information that it was unsafe, the application was denied. (§ 505, 52 *Stat.* 1052 [June 25, 1938].) Since 1962, affirmative approval of an application has been required before a new drug may be marketed. (21 *U.S.C.A.* § 355, subd. [c].)

20. *Weinberg Co. v. Bixby* (1921) 185 *Cal.* 87, 103, 196 *P. 25*, involved a husband who was held liable with his wife for wrongful diversion of flood waters although he had given his wife title to the land upon which the outlet causing the diversion was constructed. He not only owned land affected by the flood waters, but he was his wife's agent for the purpose of reopening the outlet which caused the damage. In *Meyer v. Thomas* (1936) 18 *Cal. App. 2d* 299, 305–306, 63 *P.2d* 1176, both defendants participated in the conversion of a note and deed of trust.

21. In *Agovino v. Kunze* (1960) 181 *Cal. App.* 2d 591, 599, 5 *Cal. Rptr.* 534, a participant in a drag race was held liable for injuries to a plaintiff who collided with the car of another racer. In *Loeb v. Kimmerie* (1932) 215 *Cal.* 143, 151, 9 *P. 2d* 199, a defendant who encouraged another defendant to commit an assault was held jointly liable for the plaintiff's injuries. Also see *Weirum v. RKO General, Inc.* (1975) 15 *Cal. 3d* 40, 123 *Cal. Rptr.* 468, 539 *P. 2d* 36.

22. We deliberately employ the term "suggested" to describe the effect of the *Hall* opinion because of the uncertain posture of the decision as authority. The defendants moved to dismiss the action on the ground that the plaintiffs had not stated a claim, and they also sought to sever the claims of the various plaintiffs and transfer them to the district court in the place where each accident occurred. The opinion discusses various possible bases of liability, including industry-wide liability, upon the assumption that there existed a national body of state tort law. (345 *F. Supp.* at p. 360.) At the conclusion of its opinion, the court called for briefs on the choice-of-law issues involved in the case. In a subsequent opinion, the same court decided, after briefs had been filed on the choice-of-law question, that the plaintiffs' claims should be severed, and it transferred each one to the federal court sitting in the district where the accident occurred. (*Chance v. E. I. Du Pont de Nemours & Co., Inc.* (E.D.N.Y. 1974) 371 *F. Supp.* 439.) Thereafter, the transferred cases resulted in judgments for defendants upon various grounds unrelated to the theory of industry-wide liability. (*Lehtonen v. E. I. Du Pont de Nemours & Co., Inc.* (D. Mont. 1975) 389 *F. Supp.* 633 [failure to amend complaint within 30 days]; *Davis v. E. I. Du Pont de Nemours & Co., Inc.* (W.D.N.C. 1974) 400 *F. Supp.* 1347 [statute of limitations]; *Ball v. E. I. Du Pont de Nemours & Co., Inc.* (6th Cir. 1975) 519 *F. 2d* 715 [jury verdict in favor of defendant after plaintiff identified the manufacturer of the blasting cap which caused his injuries].) The parties have not indicated the status of the remaining cases transferred.

23. In discussing strict liability, the *Hall* court mentioned the drug industry, stating, "In cases where manufacturers have more experience, more information, and more control over the risky properties of their products than do drug manufacturers, courts have applied a broader concept of foreseeability which approaches the enterprise liability rationale." (345 *F. Supp.* 353 at p. 370.)

24. The suggested requirements are as follows:

1. There existed an insufficient, industry-wide standard of safety as to the manufacture of the product.

2. Plaintiff is not at fault for the absence of evidence identifying the causative agent but, rather, this absence of proof is due to defendant's conduct.

3. A generically similar defective product was manufactured by all the defendants.

4. Plaintiff's injury was caused by this defect.

5. Defendants owed a duty to the class of which plaintiff was a member.

6. There is clear and convincing evidence that plaintiff's injury was caused by a product made by one of the defendants. For example, the joined defendants accounted for a high percentage of such defective products on the market at the time of plaintiff's injury.

7. All defendants were tortfeasors.

25. The Fordham Comment takes exception to one aspect of the theory of industry-wide liability as set forth in *Hall,* i. e., the conclusion that a plaintiff is only required to show by a preponderance of the evidence that one of the defendants manufactured the product which caused her injury. The Comment suggests that a plaintiff be required to prove by clear and convincing evidence that one of the defendants before the court was responsible and that this standard of proof would require that the plaintiff join in the action the producers of 75 or 80 percent of the DES prescribed for prevention of miscarriage. It is also suggested that the damages be apportioned among the defendants according to their share of the market for DES. (Fordham Comment, supra, 999–1000.)

26. Federal regulations may specify the type of tests a manufacturer must perform for certain drugs (21 *C.F.R.* § 436.206 et seq.), the type of packaging used (§ 429.10), the warnings which appear on labels (§ 369.20), and the standards to be followed in the manufacture of a drug (§ 211.22 et seq.).

27. *Abel v. Eli Lilly and Company*, the Michigan case referred to above which held that the plaintiffs had stated a cause of action against several manufacturers of DES even though they could not identify a particular manufacturer as the source of a particular injury (see fn.7, *ante*), relied upon the theories of concerted action and alternative liability.

28. The Fordham Comment explains the connection between percentage of market share and liability as follows: "[I]f X Manufacturer sold one-fifth of all the DES prescribed for pregnancy and identification could be made in all cases, X would be the sole defendant in approximately one-fifth of all cases and liable for all the damages in those cases. Under alternative liability, X would be joined in all cases in which identification could not be made, but liable for only one-fifth of the total damages in these cases. X would pay the same amount either way. Although the correlation is not, in practice, perfect [footnote omitted], it is close enough so that defendants' objections on the ground of fairness lose their value." (Fordham Comment, supra, at p. 94.)

29. Defendants assert that there are no figures available to determine market share, that DES was provided for a number of uses other than to prevent miscarriage and it would be difficult to ascertain what proportion of the drug was used as a miscarriage preventative, and that the establishment of a time frame and area for market share would pose problems.

30. The dissent concludes by implying the problem will disappear if the Legislature appropriates funds "for the education, identification, and screening of persons exposed to DES." While such a measure may arguably be helpful in the abstract, it does not address the issue involved here: damages for injuries which have been or will be suffered. Nor, as a principle, do we see any justification for shifting the financial burden for such damages from drug manufacturers to the taxpayers of California.
*Assigned by the Chairman of the Judicial Council.

Responsibility for Nonintervention

Notes on the Indian Penal Code[*]

Thomas Babington Macaulay

Early in the progress of the Code it became necessary for us to consider the following question: When acts are made punishable on the ground that those acts produce, or are intended to produce, or are known to be likely to produce, certain evil effects, to what extent ought omissions which produce, which are intended to produce, or which are known to be likely to produce, the same evil effects to be made punishable?

Two things we take to be evident; first, that some of these omissions ought to be punished in exactly the same manner in which acts are punished; secondly, that not all these omissions ought to be punished. It will hardly be disputed that a jailer who voluntarily causes the death of a prisoner by omitting to supply that prisoner with food, or a nurse who voluntarily causes the death of an infant entrusted to her care by omitting to take it out of a tub of water into which it has fallen, ought to be treated as guilty of murder. On the other hand, it will hardly be maintained that a man should be punished as a murderer because he omitted to relieve a beggar, even though there might be the clearest proof that the death of the beggar was the effect of this omission, and that the man who omitted to give the alms knew that the death of the beggar was likely to be

the effect of the omission. It will hardly be maintained that a surgeon ought to be treated as a murderer for refusing to go from Calcutta to Meerut to perform an operation, although it should be absolutely certain that this surgeon was the only person in India who could perform it, and that if it were not performed, the person who required it would die. It is difficult to say whether a penal code which should put no omissions on the same footing with acts, or a penal code which should put all omissions on the same footing with acts, would produce consequences more absurd and revolting. There is no country in which either of these principles is adopted. Indeed, it is hard to conceive how, if either were adopted, society could be held together.

It is plain, therefore, that a middle course must be taken; but it is not easy to determine what that middle course ought to be. The absurdity of the two extremes is obvious. But there are innumerable intermediate points; and wherever the line of demarcation may be drawn it will, we fear, include some cases which we might wish to exempt, and will exempt some which we might wish to include. . . .

What we propose is this, that where acts are made punishable on the ground that they have caused, or have been intended to cause, or have

---

[*]From *Works of Lord Macaulay*, Trevelyan, ed., vol. 7 (1866), pp. 493–97.

been known to be likely to cause, a certain evil effect, omissions which have caused, which have been intended to cause, or which have been known to be likely to cause the same effect, shall be punishable in the same manner, provided that such omissions were, on other grounds, illegal. An omission is illegal . . . if it be an offense, if it be a breach of some direction of law, or if it be such a wrong as would be a good ground for a civil action.

We cannot defend this rule better than by giving a few illustrations of the way in which it will operate. *A* omits to give *Z* food, and by that omission voluntarily causes *Z's* death. Is this murder? Under our rule it is murder if *A* was *Z's* gaoler, directed by the law to furnish *Z* with food. It is murder if *Z* was the infant child of and had, therefore, a legal right to sustenance, which right a Civil Court would enforce against *A*. It is murder if *Z* was a bedridden invalid, and *A* a nurse hired to feed *Z*. It is murder if *A* was detaining *Z* in unlawful confinement, and had thus contracted . . . a legal obligation to furnish during the continuance of the confinement, with necessaries. It is not murder if *Z* is a beggar, who has no other claim on *A* than that of humanity.

A omits to tell *Z* that a river is swollen so high that *Z* cannot safely attempt to ford it, and by this omission voluntarily causes *Z's* death. This is murder, if *A* is a peon stationed by authority to warn travellers from attempting to ford the river. It is a murder if *A* is a guide who had contracted to conduct *Z*. It is not murder if *A* is a person on whom *Z* has no other claim than that of humanity.

A savage dog fastens on *Z*. *A* omits to call off the dog, knowing that if the dog not be called off, it is likely that *Z* will be killed. *Z* is killed. This is murder in *A,* if the dog belonged to *A,* inasmuch as his omission to take proper order with the dog is illegal. But if *A* be a mere passerby, it is not murder.

We are sensible that in some of the cases which we have put, our rule may appear too lenient; but we do not think that it can be made more severe without disturbing the whole order of society. It is true that the man who, having abundance of wealth, suffers a fellow creature to die of hunger at his feet, is a bad man, a worse man, probably, than many of those for whom we have provided very severe punishment. But we are unable to see where, if we make such a man legally punishable, we can draw the line. If the rich man who refuses to save a beggar's life at the cost of a little copper is a murderer, is the poor man just one degree above beggary also to be a murderer if he omits to invite the beggar to

partake his hard-earned rice? Again, if the rich man is a murderer for refusing to save the beggar's life at the cost of a little copper, is he also to be a murderer if he refuses to save the beggar's life at the cost of a thousand rupees? Suppose *A* to be fully convinced that nothing can save *Z's* life unless *Z* leave Bengal and reside a year at the Cape; is *A,* however wealthy he may be, to be punished as a murderer because he will not, at his own expense, send *Z* to the Cape? Surely not. Yet it will be difficult to say on what principle we can punish *A* for not spending an anna to save *Z's* life, and leave him unpunished for not spending a thousand rupees to save *Z's* life. The distinction between a legal and an illegal omission is perfectly plain and intelligible; but the distinction between a large and a small sum of money is very far from being so, not to say that a sum which is small to one man is large to another.

The same argument holds good in the case of the ford. It is true that none but a very depraved man would suffer another to be drowned when he might prevent it by a word. But if we punish such a man, where are we to stop? How much exertion are we to require? Is a person to be a murderer if he does not go fifty yards through the sun of Bengal at noon in May in order to caution a traveller against a swollen river? Is he to be a murderer if he does not go a hundred yards?—if he does not go a mile?—if he does not go ten? What is the precise amount of trouble and inconvenience which he is to endure? The distinction between the guide who is bound to conduct the traveller as safely as he can, and a mere stranger is a clear distinction. But the distinction between a stranger who will not give a halloo to save a man's life, and a stranger who will not run a mile to save a man's life, is very far from being equally clear.

It is, indeed, most highly desirable that men should not merely abstain from doing harm to their neighbours, but should render active services to their neighbours. In general, however, the penal law must content itself with keeping men from doing positive harm, and must leave to public opinion, and to the teachers of morality and religion, the office of furnishing men with motives for doing positive good. It is evident that to attempt to punish men by law for not rendering to others all the service which it is their duty to render to others would be preposterous. We must grant impunity to the vast majority of those omissions which a benevolent morality would pronounce reprehensible, and must content ourselves with punishing such omissions only when they are distinguished from the rest by some circumstance which marks them out as peculiarly fit objects of penal legislation. Now, no circumstance appears to us so well fitted to be the mark as the circumstance which we have selected. It will generally be found in the most atrocious cases of omission; it will scarcely ever be found in a venial case of omission; and it is more clear and certain than any other mark that has occurred to us. That there are objections to the line which we propose to draw, we have admitted. But there are objections to every line which can be drawn, and some lines must be drawn. . . .

THE CASE FOR A DUTY TO RESCUE*

Ernest J. Weinrib

No observer would have any difficulty outlining the current state of the law throughout the common-law world regarding the duty to rescue. Except when the person endangered and the potential rescuer are linked in a special relationship, there is no such duty.[1] This general rule rests on the law's distinction between the infliction of harm and the failure to prevent it. The distinction between misfeasance and nonfeasance in turn reflects deeply rooted intuitions about causation, and it has played a critical role in the development of the common-law notions of contract and tort and of the boundary between them. In large part because this distinction is so fundamental to the common law, the courts have uniformly refused to enunciate a general duty to rescue,[2] even in the face of repeated criticisms that the absence of such a duty is callous.[3] Nonetheless, recent developments, both judicial and academic, justify a reconsideration of the common-law position.

On the judicial side, many of the outposts of the doctrine that there is no general duty to rescue have fallen. Recognizing the meritoriousness of rescue and the desirability of encouraging it, the courts have increasingly accorded favorable treatment to injured rescuers. When a rescuer sues for compensation for his injuries, voluntary assumption of risk cannot be interposed as a defense,[4] contributory negligence comes into play only if the plaintiff has been reckless,[5] and a broad range of rescue attempts are deemed reasonably foreseeable by the defendant.[6] Moreover, the courts have increased the number of special relationships that require one person to aid another in peril.[7] These developments have made the general absence of a duty to rescue seem more eccentric and isolated.[8] They have also raised the possibility that the general rule is in the process of being consumed and supplanted by the widening ambit of the exceptions[9] and that the relationship between the general rule and the exceptions may be fundamentally incoherent.

On the academic side, recent writing has given new life to the debate on rescue. Professor Coase's approach, for example, implies that, from an economic point of view, the distinction between misfeasance and nonfeasance that supports the common-law rule is without significance. For Coase, the real issue is whether the alleged tortfeasor is to be allowed to impose the cost of his physical activity on the plaintiff, or whether the plaintiff, by his invocation of the legal process, will be allowed to harm the alleged tortfeasor.[10] For this approach, only the resulting distribution of costs matters; whether this result is accomplished by the defendant's operations in the physical world or by the plaintiff's operations in the legal world is not itself important. The refusal to accord a special recognition to the role of the court, and

*I would like to thank Professor Charles Fried of Harvard University and my colleagues Professor A. S. Weinrib and Professor S. A. Schiff for commenting on earlier drafts of this article. Ernest Weinrib is Professor, Faculty of Law, University of Toronto. 90 *Yale Law Journal* 247 (1980). Endnotes have been edited and renumbered.

the assimilation of the court to an agency for the distribution of costs, has implications for the position of a person seeking judicial intervention. Because distinctions based on causation are obliterated in Coase's model of reciprocal harm, a plaintiff can claim no special consideration as the victim of another's action, and a defendant does not necessarily escape liability because the harm complained of was not caused by any of his actions. The causal nihilism of Coase's world,[11] which has its roots in utilitarian thought extending back to Bentham,[12] thus subverts the misfeasance-nonfeasance distinction and changes the terms on which the rescue problem is discussed.[13]

The most important critics of the economic approach to law have all in their various ways been concerned with rehabilitating causation as a central feature of law and morals.[14] It is the work of Professor Epstein,[15] among this group of scholars, that is of particular importance in connection with rescue. For Professor Epstein, causation is so pivotal a notion in a legal system that values liberty that it is not only *a* basis of liability in tort, but the *only* basis of liability in tort. This emphasis on causation has its roots in ethical thought leading back not to Bentham's utilitarianism but to Kant's injunction against treating other persons as means rather than as ends,[16] a principle that seems to presuppose an idea of acting upon others that does not encompass nonfeasance. Relying on this tradition for his critique of the economic approach, Epstein has argued that the absence of a general duty to rescue is not an unfortunate fossil of a more barbaric age but is a morally defensible thread in the overall fabric of the common law.

Critics of the common-law position have generally proposed that the courts ought to recognize a duty to effect what might be termed an easy rescue, that is, a duty that would arise whenever one person is caught in a dangerous situation that another can alleviate at no significant cost to himself.[17] The requirements of emergency and lack of prejudice distinguish the proposed obligation to rescue from the usual tort duties connected with misfeasance: the latter duties can be present in routine situations and can impose considerable costs on those who are subject to them. The recent judicial and academic developments bear upon this proposal in diverse ways. The tort decisions that recognize the distinctive merit of the rescuer stand in easy harmony with the proposed duty. The academic writings, on the other hand, seem incompatible with a duty of easy rescue. The Coasian framework would reject the restrictions on

the duty because these restrictions acknowledge the fundamental character of the distinction between misfeasance and nonfeasance. For Epstein, by contrast, the difference between nonfeasance and misfeasance is fundamental, but the chasm between these two concepts is so deep that only duties respecting misfeasance can be accommodated within the common law of torts. The proposed duty to rescue thus seems to be unacceptable both from an instrumentalist and from a Kantian point of view.

This article sets forth an argument in favor of a judicially created duty to effect an easy rescue. Because any special principle about rescue presupposes the distinction between misfeasance and nonfeasance, section I delineates this distinction and shows how it informs the policies behind the general common-law rule on rescue and some of the special-relationship exceptions. Section II sets forth and analyzes the arguments that have been offered, especially by Professor Epstein, against a generalized legal duty to rescue. This analysis, having highlighted the legal and ethical issues central to the argument against such a duty, clears the ground for the argument for the recognition by the common law of a duty of easy rescue. Section III argues that our moral intuitions are reflected in a coherent and growing pattern in the common law, a pattern indicating that the understanding of liberty in a market society does not preclude a legal obligation to rescue. Finally, section IV turns to the philosophic aspects of this pattern; it argues that a general duty of easy rescue can find support either on Benthamite-utilitarian or Kantian-deontological grounds. The article argues, in sum, that a duty of easy rescue would strengthen an already-broad pattern of common-law principles and that such a duty can plausibly be justified within both of the ethical traditions that inform the common-law system.

I. The Distinction Between Misfeasance and Nonfeasance

In his classic essay of 1908, Professor Francis H. Bohlen pointed out that "misfeasance differs from nonfeasance in two respects; in the character of the conduct complained of, and second, in the nature of the detriment suffered in consequence thereof."[18] With respect to the first difference, Bohlen asserted that the distinction between active and passive misconduct is, though in practice difficult to draw, in theory obvious. About the second difference Bohlen was more specific. In cases of misfeasance, the victim's position is changed for the worse through the creation of a negative quantity in the form of a positive loss or new harm. In cases of nonfeasance, on the other hand, there is merely a failure to benefit the victim, which is a loss only in the sense that a positive quantity is not added.

Bohlen stated these distinctions in skeletal form only, without providing the elaboration they require. For instance, the use of positive and negative quantities to explain the difference in the nature of the detriment presupposes not only a computational ledger but also a baseline with reference to which the computation is performed. Bohlen seems to have assumed that the baseline was the victim's position immediately prior to the incident that gives rise to the litigation, as when the victim of an automobile accident complains of the loss of a previously healthy limb. Since Bohlen's time, however, tort law has come to permit the imposition of liability for injuries that are not most naturally described as the loss of something actually possessed at an earlier time. A plaintiff, for example, can recover for economic injury not only when he has lost funds that he previously had,[19] but also when the loss represents a potential profit that he had not yet realized.[20] Similarly, when an infant sues for prenatal injuries, recovery does not depend on whether the injury was inflicted on a limb that was already formed or whether the injury prevented the formation of a limb.[21]

Bohlen's other distinction, that concerned with the character of the misconduct, also needs elaboration. Bohlen himself acknowledged one of the problems when he pointed to the practical difficulties of characterizing behavior having elements of both active and passive misconduct. An illustration of this borderland situation is the old case of *Newton v. Ellis*,[22] in which the plaintiff sued for injuries received at night when passing his carriage by a hole in the highway that the defendant had excavated but had failed to light. The court viewed the digging of the hole and the failure to light it as one complex act rather than as two separate events, one an act, the other a failure to act. Bohlen would have agreed,[23] but his distinction does not explain why one should prefer one characterization of the situation to the other. For principled use by courts, the unelaborated distinction between active and passive conduct is inadequate.[24]

To begin elucidating the distinction between misfeasance and nonfeasance, consider the following fairly clear and extreme paradigmatic situations:

A. An automobile driver (defendant) fails to apply his brakes in time, and a pedestrian (plaintiff) is thereby hurt.
B. One person (defendant) sees another (plaintiff) drowning in a pool of water and refuses to toss him an easily available rope.

In both cases there has been a failure to act: in A, a failure to press the brakes; in B, a failure to toss the rope. Yet A and B are not both instances of nonfeasance.[25] On an intuitive understanding of causation, the defendant in A caused the injury, whereas the defendant in B did not. On one of tort law's prime understandings of causation, however, that conclusion is problematic. In both A and B, the defendants are but-for causes of injury: neither the injury in A nor the drowning in B would have happened had the defendants not failed to act in the specified ways.

The but-for test of factual causation first focuses on the time at which the defendant failed to act to prevent harm to the plaintiff, then compares the actual course of events after that time with a hypothetical course of events for the same subsequent period. Within that temporal framework, the structures of A and B are identical. What differentiates A from B is the course of events prior to the starting point. In B, there was no significant interaction between the plaintiff and the defendant in that earlier period: when encountered by the defendant, the plaintiff was already exposed to danger. In A, by contrast, the defendant, in the antecedent period, played a part in the creation of the very danger that he subsequently failed to abate. To treat A as identical to B is thus to start *in medias res*. Situations like A, in which misfeasance masquerades as nonfeasance, have aptly been categorized as "pseudo-nonfeasance."[26]

Action can be variously described, and pseudo-nonfeasance is one instance of the technique of distorting the description by focusing on only one of the phases of an action.[27] This technique was presented in *Newton v. Ellis*,[28] where the defendant argued that the gravamen of the suit was the failure to put up a light rather than the digging of the hole in the highway. This argument would have equated the excavator of the hole with the rest of the world by confining judicial attention to a phase subsequent to that in which the defendant established a unique relationship with the particular hole and thereby with all passing drivers. Although not all courts are sensitive to the dynamics of pseudo-nonfeasance,[29] the court in this case was alert to the distorting technique and insisted upon looking at the excavator's behavior in its entirety.[30]

The difference between real nonfeasance and pseudo-nonfeasance can be formulated by transforming the but-for test so that it attends not to the actual injury but to the risk of injury. In this view, situation B is a case of real nonfeasance because the risk of drowning existed independent of the defendant's presence or absence; the defendant's part in the materialization of the risk has no bearing on this fact. Situation A, by contrast, is a case of pseudo-nonfeasance because the defendant's driving of his car was a factual cause of the plaintiff's exposure to the risk of the injury that he suffered. In *Newton v. Ellis,* for example, the danger of falling into the excavator's hole would not have existed but for the defendant's having dug it.

Distinguishing misfeasance from nonfeasance on the basis of the defendant's participation in the creation of the risk is adequate not only for the extreme situations of A and B but also for more complicated situations. In particular, because this formulation of the distinction focuses on the defendant's having had some role in the creation of the risk, and not on the quality of that role, the defendant's fault in creating the risk is irrelevant to the decision whether a case is one of nonfeasance or not. Fault, of course, is relevant to the decision whether the defendant is liable, but the fault need not attach in the phase of risk creation; rather, it might be found in the subsequent phase, when the defendant failed to abate the risk. Consider the following situations, in which the faulty conduct at issue is intentional:

C. An automobile driver (defendant) intentionally drives onto another's (plaintiff's) foot and leaves the car there.

D. An automobile driver (defendant) without fault drives onto another's (plaintiff's) foot, but when he becomes aware of his action, he refuses to remove his car.[31]

In D, the defendant might argue that the court should assess his conduct only from the time of his refusal to move the car, and that from that perspective, the car's position on the plaintiff's foot was an unfortunate happenstance for which he was not at fault. This argument, like the one put forward in situation A, equates the defendant with all bystanders by ignoring the distinctive role of the defendant in bringing about the tortious contact between car and foot. The defendants in both C and D participated in the creation of the plaintiff's peril and intended the consequent harm to the plaintiffs. The only difference is one of sequence: in D the intent followed, whereas in C it preceded, the arrival of the automobile on the plaintiff's foot. The law recognizes this difference by refusing in D to impose liability on the defendant for harm caused during the period between the initial contact and the formation of his intention to continue it.

The same analysis can be applied to cases of negligence. In *Oke v. Weide Transport Ltd. and Carra,*[32] the defendant driver, without fault, knocked down a traffic sign, embedding the metal post in the ground. The next day, another driver drove over the post and was impaled. The plaintiff alleged that the defendant was negligent in failing to report the dangerous road condition to the police. On the analysis of nonfeasance under consideration, this case is essentially similar to *Newton v. Ellis,* which also concerned a failure by the defendant to abate a dangerous highway condition that he had created. The only difference is that in *Newton,* the defendant intentionally created the condition requiring abatement, whereas in *Oke* the defendant created the peril without fault. The defendant in *Oke* is exempt from liability for damage to the sign, of course, but with respect to liability to the injured driver, his position is identical to that of the defendant in *Newton:* each was negligent in failing to alleviate a danger that he himself had created. To ignore the defendant's role in creating the peril would be to equate the position of the defendant with that of any other motorist who happened to pass by and notice the danger. Those members of the court in *Oke* who considered the nonfeasance issue explicitly refused to make this equation.[33]

Participation by the defendant in the creation of the risk, even if such participation is innocent, is thus the crucial factor in distinguishing misfeasance from nonfeasance.[34] The law's acknowledgement of the importance of this factor is clear in some contexts, oblique in others. For instance, some statutes require a driver who is involved in an accident to offer assistance to its victims regardless of his fault in causing the accident.[35] Courts also frequently hold occupiers of land liable for failure to abate the dangers to which their use of the land has innocently exposed others, at least where the injured party is an invitee.[36] In addition, the common law now imposes a duty on the captain of a vessel to rescue a sailor or passenger who falls overboard. For many years, the law exonerated the captain who neglected to rescue as long as the need to rescue arose without his fault.[37] Recently, however, courts have recognized that the very act of taking a person out in one's boat constitutes participation in the creation of the danger of drowning.[38] The resulting duty to rescue is imposed only on the owner or operator of the boat because of this participation and because of the passenger's necessary dependence on him.[39] The duty does not extend to other parties who might be in a position to rescue a person from a danger that arose independently of them: to impose such a duty would be to cross the line from misfeasance to nonfeasance.

The analysis of nonfeasance in terms of risk creation also explains why, even though a risk may have arisen independently of a defendant, he is responsible for aggravation of the danger, that is, for substantially increasing the likelihood that it will materialize in harm. By diminishing the ability of the victim or of others to abate the danger, the defendant, though innocent of the original danger, must account for the increased risk. Indeed, the defendant's action can occur before the original risk even begins to materialize, as when an insurance agent neglects to arrange for the negotiated coverage.[40] Although the inducing of reliance is the most usual example of aggravating an independent risk,[41] it does not exhaust the category. Cutting off the victim from the aid that third parties might naturally be inclined to give is as much misfeasance as lulling the victim into a false sense of security and decreasing his ability to remove himself from peril. Although it may be nonfeasance to refuse to rescue a drowning person whose predicament arose independently, it is misfeasance to hide the rope that others might toss out to him.[42]

II. Arguments Against a Duty to Rescue

Both courts and commentators generally consider it morally outrageous that the defense of nonfeasance can deny endangered persons a legal right to easy rescue.[43] Yet the defense is taken to be so basic to the law and so compelling that it overrides the moral perceptions of the judges and the shared attitudes of the community. This in itself is a tribute to the power of the idea of nonfeasance. Few legal concepts, however, are applied in an absolute or monolithic manner. The purpose of this section is to explore the justifications that can be offered in support of the common-law position, and thus to discover the limits of the nonfeasance idea.

The most explicit and elaborate justification of the absence of a duty to rescue—almost the only such attempt in the legal literature[44]—appears in an important and ambitious article by Professor Richard Epstein.[45] Epstein's work challenges the conception of tort law as a body of law embodying utilitarian and economic assumptions and seeks to develop "a normative theory of torts that takes into account common sense notions of individual responsibility."[46] In his view, the idea that one is responsible for whatever harm one causes is the fundamental moral principle in the law of torts: unless one of a few specified excuses can be invoked, liability should follow from a finding of causation of harm. Thus strict liability should replace negligence as the dominant notion in tort law. More importantly for the rescue situation, absence of causation renders one immune from liability; in particular, there should be no duty to abate a danger one did not cause.

Epstein's conception of responsibility purports to reflect common morality in its attention both to the effects on other persons of an individual's conduct and to the motive with which actions are performed.

> [M]ost systems of conventional morality try to distinguish between those circumstances in which a person should be compelled to act for the benefit of his fellow man, and those cases where he should be allowed to do so only if prompted by the appropriate motives. To put the point in other terms, the distinction is taken between that conduct which is required and that which, so to speak is beyond the call of duty. If that distinction is accepted as part of a common morality, then the argument in favor of the good Samaritan rule is that it, better than any possible alternatives, serves to mark off the first class of activities from the second. Compensation for harm caused can be demanded in accordance with the principles of strict liability. Failure to aid those in need can invoke at most moral censure on the ground that the person so accused did not voluntarily conform his conduct to some "universal" principle of justice. The rules of causation, which create liability in the first case, deny it in the second. It may well be that the conduct of individuals who do not aid fellow men is under some circumstances outrageous, but it does not follow that a legal system that does not enforce a duty to aid is outrageous as well.[47]

This passage is problematic in a number of ways. First, the conclusion that there is no obligation to rescue under any circumstances seems to conflict with Epstein's general purpose to develop a normative theory corresponding to common-sense morality. Criticism of the common-law position on rescue, after all, rests on the perception that, as a matter of inarticulate common sense, it is wrong for one person to stand by as another suffers an injury that could easily be prevented.[48] Moreover, Epstein concedes that the behavior of such defendants is "under some circumstances outrageous." There is a paradox in concluding, as Epstein does, that the legal doctrine in question, reprobated though it is, is actually in accord with common-sense notions of morality.

Second, as a defense of the common-law position on rescue, Epstein's single-minded concern with causation may prove too much. Although there is no general requirement of rescue at common law, rescue is required if any of several special relationships exists between the parties.[49] Epstein's defense of the common-law position on rescue poses the dilemma of abandoning that part of the position requiring rescue in special circumstances or acknowledging that tort liability is not based solely on causation.

These criticisms of Epstein's argument point to a lack of coherence among the argument's premises, actual conclusions, and purported conclusion. The argument, however, is also somewhat obscure. Epstein's argument that the absence of a duty to rescue at common law is consistent with moral principles is open to any of several interpretations. It might be a denial that there is a moral obligation to rescue, even though failure to rescue arouses "moral censure" and outrage, because rescue falls in the class of conduct that is "beyond the call of duty." Alternatively, the argument might be conceding that there is a moral obligation to rescue but denying that the creation of a parallel legal duty is justified. Moreover, this second interpretation might suppose either that, as a matter of principle, a chasm exists between the ethical and the legal realms, or that the transformation of this particular ethical duty into a legal one is inappropriate. An assessment of Epstein's argument must begin by examining the far-reaching issues raised by these various interpretations.

Epstein seeks to justify the absence of a common-law duty to rescue by invoking the distinction in common morality between acts that are required and acts that are beyond the call of duty.[50] This distinction has been the subject of much attention in moral and legal philosophy—for example, in Lon

Fuller's development of a contrast between the morality of duty and the morality of aspiration.[51] Acts that are beyond the call of duty demand of the agent extraordinary heroism or sacrifice, and "while we praise their performance, we do not condemn their non-performance."[52] The very fact that a failure to rescue may evoke moral censure, as Epstein concedes, is a strong indication that the rescue was obligatory and not supererogatory. The distinction that Epstein endorses therefore should not lead him to a simple denial of any duty to rescue; rather it should lead to efforts to structure the duty to avoid requiring of the rescuer the heroism or sacrifice that characterizes the morality of aspiration. In fact, all the proposals of the last two centuries for a legal duty to rescue have been structured in this way.[53]

Epstein thus cannot sustain the position that failure to effect an easy rescue is not immoral.[54] His remarks can alternatively be interpreted as conceding that rescue is a moral requirement but denying that it should be a legal one. That he probably intends this view is indicated by his comment that although failure to aid a person may be outrageous, "it does not follow that a legal system that does not enforce a duty to aid is outrageous as well."[55] This attempt to separate morality and legality may in turn reflect any of the following three notions: that transforming this particular moral duty into a legal duty is administratively difficult, that legal duties are generally disjoint from moral ones, or that there is some reason of principle that disqualifies this particular moral duty from being a legal duty.[56]

The first of these alternatives is frequently invoked.[57] The adherents of this position point to the difficulty of determining who among the many potential rescuers should be held liable. This point can also be made in terms of fairness: singling out one from a group of equally culpable non-rescuers is unfairly to differentiate among like cases.[58] Why these difficulties should be of decisive weight, however, is hard to see. Even if there are many possible rescuers, the difficulties are no less surmountable than are those in cases of negligence involving many tortfeasors. Though potentially more complicated on average, the rules could be the same: the victim has a right to only one recovery, and all tortfeasors are liable to the victim, but they are entitled to contribution among themselves. The device of contribution, moreover, might be invoked by the defendant to prevent his being unfairly singled out: because the purpose of contribution is to prevent the unjust enrichment that would otherwise accrue when one party is forced by law to discharge an obligation to which others are also subject,[59] a defendant would be able to claim contribution from other potential rescuers.

The second interpretation of Epstein's argument, that moral and legal duties are in principle separate, is the most comprehensive of the three. Under this approach, the immorality of not rescuing has no bearing on whether the omission should be legally condemned.[60] Although this proposition seems to raise basic and longstanding jurisprudential questions, it does not raise the ancient dispute between natural-law theory and positive-law theory. An adherent of natural-law theory can more readily pass between the moral and the legal domains, but the positivist too, though perhaps more skeptical about the feasibility of discovering moral duties, can approve the creation of a legal duty to parallel a moral one. For the legal positivist, law may have any content, moral or immoral,[61] and particular moral duties can be made into legal ones.[62]

More affirmatively, the role of the common-law judge centrally involves making moral duties into legal ones. The disqualification of moral considerations from the judge's decision would leave him with very sparse resources. Formalist reasoning from preexisting rules is indeterminate in many cases.[63] Moreover, if the system is consistent, no rules, including the premises for such formalist reasoning, could have moral dimensions. The first case in any new line of development could not be justified on legal grounds alone; yet it would be decisive for all posterity. Indeed, it is difficult to imagine how a judge in a case of first impression would proceed. Conversely, moral duties not only provide a basis for judicial justification; they also provide a minimal standard for legal legitimacy. If any legal obligations are legitimate, legal obligations that duplicate preexisting moral ones must be. The only grounds for opposing the imposition of such a legal duty would be the general one that law should not coerce.[64]

The third interpretation of Epstein's position postulates a disjunction in principle not between moral and legal duties generally, but between the particular moral duty to effect an easy rescue and its proposed legal analogue. Such a position combines an admission that rescue is morally required, a recognition that legal duties may justifiably be created to parallel moral ones, and a principled argument that the moral duty to rescue is beyond the justifiable scope of state action. . . .

In his defense of the common-law position, Epstein argues that confining the duty to rescue to situations of emergency and lack of inconvenience would not be feasible. . . . If the proposed duty is admitted, he argues, no principled basis could be found to prevent unacceptable infringements of individual liberty. Charitable contributions in amounts dependent on the donor's wealth would become compulsory if it were substantially certain that without them someone would die. Moreover, because the inconvenience to the reluctant rescuer could be eliminated by the victim's offer of objectively suitable reimbursement, the rescuer would find himself coerced to exchange the means of salvation for compensation. Once such forced exchanges are required, says Epstein, there will be no way to distinguish liberty from obligation or contract from tort.[65]

This argument is the most powerful objection that can be made to the judicial creation and enforcement of a duty to effect an easy rescue. The argument does not merely assert the priority of liberty: the rescue proposal's emergency and convenience limitations, which are absent in misfeasance situations, reflect that priority. Rather, Epstein's argument is that no principles that respect the priority of liberty can distinguish between rescue and beneficence. The next two sections of this article explore and respond to this argument.

III. Common-Law Foundations for a Duty of Easy Rescue

To the extent that an issue of interpersonal action is not made the subject of a tort or criminal duty, it is remitted to the operation of the law of contract. If neither tort law nor criminal law imposes a duty to rescue, the relations between rescuer and victim are left entirely to the contractual arrangements between them. Absent any duty, a victim cannot conscript a rescuer's services; he must purchase them under the usual contractual mechanisms.[66]

Contract law gives practical application to a market society's reliance on consensual private ordering, and thus provides the principal embodiment in the law of the ideal of individual liberty.[67] It both gives individuals the means to exercise their liberty and restricts liberty where, for either practical or ideological reasons, the circumstances are not appropriate for its exercise. In particular, the law of contract presupposes a certain social equality of those who engage in the bargaining process.[68] In thus giving shape to the ideal of liberty in its application to specific circumstances, contract law can be looked to for evidence of the extent to which, and the situations in which, the law prizes individual liberty.

To the extent that contract law reveals principles that distinguish a duty to rescue from a more thoroughgoing duty of beneficence, it provides a response to Professor Epstein's challenge to find a principled basis for imposing a duty to rescue that respects the law's ideal of liberty. The object of this section of the article is to demonstrate that such principles exist. More generally, this section shows that there is a pattern in the common law that the creation of a duty of easy rescue would extend in a coherent manner.

The common-law position on nonfeasance generally relies on contract law, and hence on the market, to regulate the provision of aid to others for independently existing dangers.[69] There are exceptions, however, that require a person to abate a risk to another even though he had no part in creating the risk. These exceptions exemplify the relationship between the existence of a tort obligation and the absence of any social value in the liberty to contract.

A recent case illustrates the relationship. In *O'Rourke v. Schacht*,[70] a police officer was held liable in tort for failing to warn automobile drivers of a dangerous highway condition that he had not created.[71] In the course of his duties, he had come across a section of road where a sign warning of highway excavation had been knocked down. The court's holding required the policeman to confer a benefit on other drivers without permitting him to bargain for compensation. Because society's interest in upholding freedom to contract, if present at all, is very attenuated, however, this coercion and the concomitant deprivation of the opportunity to contract are not serious. The transaction costs of negotiating with successive drivers are so high, and the form of negotiation is so unmanageable, that contracting would be highly inefficient if not completely unfeasible.[72] More importantly, a policeman's contract to sell information about road conditions would be undesirable and perhaps unenforceable.[73] The police officer is already under a public duty, reinforced by statute, to promote highway safety; his liberty not to further this goal is not prized by the legal system.[74]

The court in *O'Rourke* laid particular stress on the police officer's statutory obligation to maintain a traffic patrol, and it is especially important to clarify the role of the statute.[75] As read in the light of the legislative intent, the statute did not create a civil cause of action, but it did supply authoritative evidence of a public policy signaling the weakness of contract values in this context, and it is therefore relevant to the judicial decision.[76] The framework of individual liberty embodied in the law of contract, and reflected in the statute, is thus seen not to be violated by the imposition of a duty in tort.

The pattern of a tort obligation existing when the values of contractual liberty are absent is also illustrated by the duty that family members owe to each other.[77] Despite its intuitive clarity, this duty has proved difficult to analyze. Bohlen, for instance, could do no better than to classify it among a miscellany of situations, and to assert that it derived broadly from "the ability of the one upon whom the duty is alleged to rest to afford the necessary protection and the dependence and helplessness of him who claims that the duty is owing to him."[78] This justification for a duty to rescue goes far beyond anything the common law or its critics supported. The contract-values analysis provides a much better justification for the family category. The common law has traditionally held that, absent express evidence of intention to the contrary, family agreements are "outside the realm of contracts" and that "each house is a domain into which the King's writ does not seek to run."[79] Moreover, statutory requirements that certain family members supply certain necessities of life to those within their charge are common.[80] The law thus deems some family relations never appropriate for market regulation, and others regulable only when natural affection is clearly inadequate to support or account for the relations.[81]

The conceptual pattern revealed by special-relationship exceptions casts light on the reach of the main rule. The thread that runs through the apparently diverse cases of police officer and family member is the law's refusal to recognize persons in these roles as market agents and its consequent tolerance for the deprivation of liberty involved in coercing them to act. When an endangered stranger can be rescued with ease, elements of the same pattern are present. If a potential rescuer struck a bargain with a drowning person before tossing him a rope, the agreement reached would be unenforceable as unconscionable or made under duress. Thus, in *Post v. Jones*,[82] the United States Supreme Court held unforceable a contract imposed by rescuers on whalers who had been marooned in the Arctic. Noting the passivity and helplessness of the defendant and the absence of market conditions for competition, the Court declared the agreement "a transaction which has no characteristic of a valid contract."[83] In this sort of emergency, there are no liberty-of-contract values to be vindicated by the absence of a tort duty. It therefore seems that the imposition of a duty to effect an easy rescue in an emergency would form a coherent part of a growing pattern[84] in those doctrines that most fully embody the common law's notion of individual liberty.

The relationship between tort obligation and contract values also provides a way of circumscribing the duty to rescue and thus of answering the formidable objections to recognizing such a duty. The responses depend in part on the fact that the duty is to be created and enforced by the judiciary, not by another branch of government. One of Professor Epstein's objections, it will be recalled, was that the imposition of a duty of easy rescue would be impossible to confine within acceptable limits: the wealthy, for example, would be compelled to make charitable contributions to alleviate hardships in emergencies.[85] This result would be unacceptable in our legal system because it would make the wealth of the parties a consideration in the litigation and would thus confound corrective and distributive justice; it would transform the system of adjudicating private claims into an administrative agency of the welfare state. The duty of easy rescue, however, can be distinguished from the broader duty of beneficence. In the rescue context, the resource to be expended (time and effort directed at aiding the victim) cannot be traded on the market, and no administrative scheme could be established to ensure the socially desirable level of benefits. In the charity context, by contrast, the resource to be expended (money) can be traded on the market, and an administrative scheme could be established not only to ensure the socially desirable level of benefits but to do so at a lower social cost than could a judicially enforced duty in tort, or so the welfare state assumes. In other words, in Epstein's example of charitable contributions, but not in the rescue situation, there is a societal interest in preserving contractual liberty, and an administrative solution is preferable to a judicial one. There is thus a principled reason why a duty of easy rescue need not lead to a general duty of charity or beneficence.

This seemingly exotic but important point was at stake in *London Borough of Southwark v. Williams*.[86] The plaintiff borough had left some houses unoccupied pending redevelopment, and squatters seeking shelter in London's severe housing shortage occupied them. In the borough's suit to regain possession, the defendants interposed the defense of necessity; in fact, it does appear that without

this housing the squatters' plight would have been appalling. The issue in the case—whether the private-necessity defense is good—closely resembles the issue in the rescue situation. In both situations, a person who had no part in the creation of another's peril has the power to abate the danger. The issues raised by the two cases are different only in the means of transferring the resources of salvation. In the rescue context, the law asks whether the person having the resources is obliged to make them available to the person in need. In the necessity context, the law asks whether the person needing the resources may simply appropriate them. The fundamental question raised by both legal issues is under what circumstances involuntary transfers are legitimate.

All members of the *Southwark* court held that, although the law recognized a defense of necessity, the defense did not apply in this case. The court divided, however, on the rationale for the result. Lord Justice Megaw focused on the process aspects of the problem. Because the court had no criteria to allocate housing, and because the court could not be certain that all potential claimants were before it, the borough's policy regarding the distribution of scarce accommodation was for political, not judicial, processes to set. Moreover, judicial approval of the squatter's occupation, he thought, would both undermine the orderly administrative procedures for housing distribution and give an unfair preference to the squatters over others seeking public housing. The necessity defense, whatever its scope, must stop short of transforming the courts into an agency for the general redistribution of wealth.[87]

Lord Denning and Lord Justice Edmund Davies concentrated on substantive counterparts to the procedural concerns of Lord Justice Megaw. "[I]f homelessness were once admitted as a defense to trespass," Lord Denning feared, "no one's house could be safe;"[88] anarchy and disorder would result. As in Epstein's example of coerced charity, the commodity involved could legitimately be traded for gain on the market, whose orderly processes would be disrupted by recognition of the necessity defense in these circumstances. Yet both judges assumed that a plea of necessity would be upheld in other circumstances. In language reminiscent of suggested formulations of the duty to rescue, Lord Justice Edmund Davies restricted the operation of the necessity defense to "an urgent situation of imminent peril,"[89] a situation one of whose distinguishing characteristics is the suspension of values associated with liberty to contract. Because of the close relation between the necessity and nonfeasance arguments, this restriction can be transferred to the nonfeasance context, so that even if a duty of easy rescue were adopted, a claim by homeless persons that a house owner was obligated to admit them to his property could rationally be dismissed, even though the claimants needed shelter and the house was otherwise unoccupied.[90]

Using the absence of contract values as a point of reference for creating a duty to rescue raises several important questions. One is whether such an approach to justifying the adoption of a common-law rule is circular. To say that the scarce resource in the *Southwark* case can be traded on the market, one might object, is to say only that the law permits such trading; one cannot in turn justify this legal treatment by pointing back to the market. The legal argument for a duty to rescue in emergencies, however, is not one of deduction but one of coherence. Recognizing that the central concepts are those of obligation and liberty, the argument looks for the common law's concrete manifestation of society's general intuitions about these concepts. Examining instances of the operation of these concepts, the argument extracts general features from the instances, searching for and shaping a coherent pattern that fits as much of the law as possible while respecting the underlying ethical intuitions.[91]

A second question raised by the contract-values approach to the rescue problem is whether the approach helps to define the precise contours of the duty. How urgent must the emergency be? Even if the absence of inconvenience to the rescuer is regarded objectively in terms of market values, is there not a large gray area between the extremes of tossing a rope and donating to charity? It is these problems of demarcation, "the difficulties of setting any standards of unselfish service to fellow men,"[92] that have traditionally been seen as insurmountable obstacles to a general requirement of rescue; Kant's view of beneficence as an ethical but not a legal duty, for example, depends on this indeterminacy. However, the issue is not whether the imposition of a duty to rescue will create an area of indeterminacy. Because legal language is very often "open textured,"[93] the vagueness of a legal principle cannot be a sufficient ground for repudiating it, especially in a tort system that enshrines the concept of reasonableness as a fundamental notion. The correct question is whether the indeterminacy in a rescue principle will be legally manageable.

The contract-values approach to defining a duty of easy rescue answers this question by refer-

ence to contract law and the necessity defense, where the common-law experience has contradicted Kant's insistence on precision in legal norms. The line between abuse of unequal bargaining position and the legitimate exercise of market power is notoriously difficult to draw;[94] yet few would say that the rescue agreement imposed upon marooned whalers that was at issue in *Post v. Jones*[95] should have been enforceable. Similarly, the possibility of overextending the necessity defense in *London Borough of Southwark v. Williams* entails not the repudiation of the defense, but only care in its application. Both duress and necessity are vague but manageable concepts; a duty of easy rescue defined to extend the pattern created by the law's use of these concepts should be equally manageable. . . .[96]

A legal duty to rescue would involve the recognition of an obligation to confer a benefit on a person whose plight is not the result of one's own actions. The traditional objection to the judicial enunciation of such a duty has been that coerced service for another interferes with personal liberty. The burden of this section has been to show that, to the extent that the notion of personal liberty is reflected in the values associated with liberty of contract, the imposition of a duty to effect an easy rescue in situations where such values are absent does not significantly violate personal liberty. Such a legal requirement of rescue would correspond to existing restrictions on the power to contract. It remains for the final section of this article to argue that the two principal philosophical traditions in our legal culture both provide affirmative arguments for the creation of the duty. Together with the observations that the special-relationship exceptions seem to be eroding the general rule and that even the defenders of the general rule admit the existence of a moral duty of easy rescue, this argument suggests that the refusal of the common law to impose a duty of easy rescue is an anomaly that can and should be corrected.

IV. Philosophical Foundations for a Duty of Easy Rescue

This article has been concerned with the interplay between our moral intuitions and various aspects of the legal structure. The distinction between misfeasance and nonfeasance was accepted as a suitable starting point that required elucidation rather than justification. Also accepted was the intuition that failure to effect an easy rescue was morally reprehensible. From these premises, the article criticized arguments supporting the legal order's refusal to reflect the moral intuition about rescue, and argued that a legal duty of easy rescue would fit into a coherent pattern formed by a miscellany of doctrines in the common law of contract and of tort.

Having eliminated objections to a legal duty of easy rescue, and shown its compatibility with existing doctrines, the final section of the article puts forth arguments for the adoption of such a duty. To this end, the section attempts to give philosophical specificity to the moral sentiment that condemns a failure to effect an easy rescue. Attention is devoted to the two traditions of moral philosophy represented by Kant and by Bentham, for those traditions have dominated efforts of the last two centuries to explicate and systematize our moral notions. If the law is to be "the witness and external deposit of our moral life,"[97] the demonstration that both traditions provide support for a duty of easy rescue implies that the absence of a duty to rescue at common law is an aberration that should be corrected.

Consideration of the utilitarian approach towards rescue must begin with Jeremy Bentham's thought on the problem. "[I]n cases where the person is in danger," he asked, "why should it not be made the duty of every man to save another from mischief, when it can be done without prejudicing himself . . . ?"[98] Bentham supported the implicit answer to this question with several illustrations: using water at hand to quench a fire in a woman's headdress; moving a sleeping drunk whose face is in a puddle; warning a person about to carry a lighted candle into a room strewn with gunpowder. Bentham clearly had in mind a legal duty that would be triggered by the combination of the victim's emergency and the absence of inconvenience to the rescuer— that is, by the features of most of the proposed reforms requiring rescue.[99] Unfortunately, the rhetorical question was the whole of Bentham's argument for his position. With this question, Bentham appealed directly to his reader's moral intuition; he did not show how his proposed duty can be derived through his distinctive felicific calculus.[100]

Can one supply the Benthamite justification that Bentham himself omitted? Because the avoidance of injury or death[101] obviously contributes to the greatest happiness of the greatest number, the difficulties revolve not around the basic requirement of rescue but around the limitations placed upon that requirement by the notions of emergency and absence of inconvenience. Those limitations have no parallel with respect to participation in putting others at risk; they apply only in cases of nonfeasance. Indeed, Bentham's comments come in a section of his *Introduction to the Principles of Morals and Legislation* that distinguishes beneficence (increasing another's happiness) from probity (forbearing to diminish another's happiness). Yet Bentham had earlier contended that the distinction between acts of omission and acts of commission was of no significance.[102] The utilitarian's only concern is that an individual bring about a situation that results in a higher surplus of pleasure over pain than would any of the alternative situations that his actions could produce. Consequences are important; how they are reached is not. The distinction between nonfeasance and misfeasance has no place in this theory, and neither would the rescue duty's emergency or convenience limitations, which apply only after that distinction is made.

One solution to the apparent inconsistency between the rescue limitations and Benthamite theory's regard only for consequences is to drop the conditions of emergency and convenience as limitations on the duty to rescue. The position could be taken that there is an obligation to rescue whenever rescuing would result in greater net happiness than not rescuing. This principle, it is important to observe, cannot really be a principle about rescuing as that concept is generally understood. As a matter of common usage, a rescue presupposes the existence of an emergency, of a predicament that poses danger of greater magnitude and imminence than one ordinarily encounters. The proposed principle, however, requires no emergency to trigger a duty to act. The principle, in fact, is one of beneficence, not rescue, and should be formulated more generally to require providing aid whenever it will yield greater net happiness than not providing aid.

Eliminating the limitations regarding emergency and convenience might transform a requirement of rescue conceived along utilitarian lines into a requirement of perfect and general altruism. This demand of perfect altruism would be undesirable for several reasons. First, it would encourage the obnoxious character known to the law as the officious intermeddler. Also, its imposition of a duty of continual saintliness and heroism is unrealistic. Moreover, it would overwhelm the relationships founded on friendship and love as well as the distinction between the praiseworthy and the required; it would thereby obscure some efficient ways, in the utilitarian's eyes, of organizing and stimulating beneficence.[103] Finally, and most fundamentally, it would be self-defeating. The requirement of aid assumes that there is some other person who has at least a minimal core of personhood as well as projects of his own that the altruist can further. In a society of perfect and general altruism, however, any potential recipient of aid would himself be an altruist, who must, accordingly, subordinate the pursuit of his own projects to the rendering of aid to others. No one could claim for his own projects the priority that would provide others with a stable object of their altruistic ministrations. Each person would continually find himself obligated to attempt to embrace a phantom.[104]

Although the utilitarian principle that requires the provision of aid whenever it will result in greater net happiness than failure to aid easily slips into the pure-altruism duty, it need not lead to so extreme a position. The obvious alternative interpretation of the principle is that aid is not obligatory whenever the costs to one's own projects outweigh the benefits to the recipient's. This interpretation avoids the embracing-of-phantoms objection to pure altruism, but it is subject to all the other criticisms of the purer theory. Because the cost-benefit calculus is so difficult to perform in particular instances, the duty would remain ill-defined. In many cases, therefore, it would encourage the officious intermeddler, seem unrealistically to require saintliness, overwhelm friendship and love, and obliterate the distinction between the praiseworthy and the required. Moreover, the vagueness of the duty would lead many individuals unhappily and inefficiently to drop their own projects in preference for those of others.

A different formulation of the rescue duty is needed to harness and temper the utilitarian impulses toward altruism and to direct them more precisely toward an intelligible goal. One important weakness of a too-generally beneficent utilitarianism is that it tempts one to consider only the immediate consequences of particular acts, and not the longer term consequences, the most important of which are the expectations generated that such acts will continue. If, as the classical utilitarians believed,[105] the general happiness is advanced when people engage in productive activities that are of value to others, the harm done by a duty of general beneficence, in either version discussed above, would override its specific benefits. The deadening of industry resulting from both reliance on beneficence and devotion to beneficence would in the long run be an evil greater than the countenancing of individual in-

stances of unfulfilled needs or wants. "In all cases of helping," wrote John Stuart Mill, in a passage concerned only with the reliance costs,

> there are two sets of consequences to be considered: the consequences of the assistance and the consequences of relying on the assistance. The former are generally beneficial, but the latter, for the most part, injurious. . . . There are few things for which it is more mischievous that people should rely on the habitual aid of others than for the means of subsistence, and unhappily there is no lesson which they more easily learn.[106]

Utilitarianism can use the notion of reliance to restrict the requirement of beneficence. If an act of beneficence would tend to induce reliance on similar acts, it should be avoided. If the act of beneficence does not have this tendency, it should be performed as long as the benefit produced is greater than the cost of performance. In the latter case, there are no harmful effects on industry flowing from excessive reliance to outweigh the specific benefits. This rule can account for Bentham's restriction of the duty to rescue to situations of emergency. People do not regularly expose themselves to extraordinary dangers in reliance on the relief that may be available if the emergency materializes, and only a fool would deliberately court a peril because he or others had previously been rescued from a similar one. As Sidgwick put it, an emergency rescue "will have no bad effect on the receiver, from the exceptional nature of the emergency."[107] Furthermore, an emergency is not only a desperate situation; it is also a situation that deviates from society's usual pattern. The relief of an emergency is therefore unlikely to induce reliance on the assistance of others in normal conditions. The abnormality of emergencies also means that rescuers can confidently pursue their own projects under normal circumstances. The motive for industry that Bentham located in each person's needs is not undermined by extraordinary and isolated events.

The role of emergency in the utilitarian obligation to rescue corresponds to, and illuminates, the definition of a legal duty to rescue by reference to the absence of contract values, as set out in the previous section. Utilitarian philosophy and the concept of the market are closely related.[108] Both regard individuals as maximizers of their own happiness, and both see the use of contracts to acquire and to exchange property as conducive to the public good. Contract law's refusal to enforce certain transactions sets them apart from the usual structure of relationships, in which the satisfaction of the parties' needs and desires can legitimately serve as a stimulus to exchange. The person who sees a member of his own family in difficulty and the police officer who notices a hazard on the highway may not act as ordinary members of the market with respect to those endangered. Those pockets of contractual non-enforcement are sufficiently isolated that they are unlikely to be generalized: they will not generate a widespread reliance on assistance or sense of obligation to assist in settings where market exchanges are permitted and common.

An emergency is similar. Contract values are absent in such a situation because the assistance required is of such a kind that it cannot be purchased on ordinary commercial terms. Suspension of contract values in an emergency will not result in a general deadening of individual industry; the utilitarian can therefore confine his calculus to the specific consequences of the rescue. The denial of relief to the Southwark squatters[109] is a case in point. The desperate situation there was a consequence of poverty and not an extraordinary condition that deviated from the ordinary pattern of contemporary existence. The utilitarian must be concerned in that situation that judicially coercing individual assistance to the poor will generate a reliance whose harmful effects will, in the long run and across society as a whole, outweigh the benefits of the specific assistance.

Bentham's intuitive restriction of beneficence to situations of emergency can thus be supported on utilitarian grounds. Is the same true of the inconvenience limitation? As with the emergency restriction, finding utilitarian support requires looking behind the specific action to its social and legal context. For the utilitarian, the enforcement of a duty through legal sanctions is always an evil, which can be justified only to avoid a greater evil. If the sanction is applied, the offender suffers the pain of punishment. If the prospect of the sanction is sufficient to deter conduct, those deterred suffer the detriment of frustrated preferences. Moreover, the apparatus of enforcement siphons off social resources from other projects promoting the general happiness.

Accordingly, a utilitarian will be restrained and circumspect in the elaboration of legal duties. In particular, he will not pitch a standard of behavior at too high a level: the higher the standard, the more onerous it will be to the person subjected to it, the greater the pleasure that he must forego in adhering to it, and the greater his resistance to its demands. A high standard entails both more severe punishment and a more elaborate apparatus of detection and enforcement. Applied to the rescue situation, this reasoning implies that some convenience restriction should be adopted as part of the duty. Compelling the rescuer to place himself in physical danger, for instance, would be inefficacious, to use Bentham's terminology, because such coercion cannot influence the will: "the evil, which he sees himself about to undergo . . . is so great that the evil denounced by the penal clause . . . cannot appear greater."[110] Limiting the duty of rescue to emergency situations where the rescue will not inconvenience the rescuer—as judicial decisions would elaborate that limitation and thus give direction to individuals—minimizes both the interference with the rescuer's own preferences and the difficulties of enforcement that would result from recalcitrance. Bentham's second limitation can thus also be supported on a utilitarian basis.

The utilitarian arguments for the duty to rescue and for the limitations on that duty rest primarily on administrative considerations. The arguments focus not so much on the parties and their duties as persons as on the difficulties that might be created throughout the whole range of societal interactions. The elements of the duty are evaluated in terms of their likely consequences, no matter how remote. In the convenience limitation, for instance, whether the rescuer *ought* to feel aggrieved at the requirements of a high standard is of no concern. The likelihood that he *will* feel aggrieved is all that matters: for the Benthamite utilitarian, general happiness is the criterion of evaluation and not itself an object of evaluation.[111] Moreover, recalcitrance necessitates more costly enforcement, and that consequence must also enter the calculus. The same is true for the emergency limitation. The argument for that limitation focused on the possibility that a particular instance of assistance would, by example, induce socially detrimental general reliance or beneficence. This use of example does not explore either the fairness of singling out particular persons for particular treatment or the consistency and scope of certain principles. Rather, the argument examines the cumulative consequences of repetition, and decides whether a particular person should perform a particular act on the basis of the act's implications for the entire society's market arrangements.

At least one philosopher has argued that administrative considerations of this sort are not moral ones at all, or that they are moral only in a derivative sense.[112] In this view, the administrative and enforcement considerations on which the utilitarian account of rescue rests are irrelevant to the individual's obligations as a moral agent. The individual should ask what he ought to do, not how others can compel him to fulfill his duty.[113] The merit of this view is its observation that any utilitarian version of a duty to rescue has nuances that do not ring true to the moral contours of the situation. The person in need of rescue stands in danger of serious physical injury or loss of life, harms not quite comparable by any quantitative measure to other losses of happiness. Health and life are not merely components of the aggregate of goods that an individual enjoys. Rather, they are constitutive of the individual, who partakes of them in a unique and intimate way; they are the preconditions for the enjoyment of other goods.[114] Moreover, there is something false in viewing an act of rescue as a contribution to the greatest happiness of the greatest number.[115] If there is an obligation to rescue, it is owed to particular persons rather than to the greatest number. Any such duty would require the rescuing not only of the eminent heart surgeon but also of the hermit bachelor; and even the duty to rescue the heart surgeon would be owed primarily to him, not to his present or prospective patients.

Because the utilitarian account of rescue thus appears to lack an important moral ingredient, and because utilitarianism is not the law's only important philosophical tradition, it is worth attempting to outline a non-utilitarian version of the obligation to rescue. Although the two approaches support the same conclusion, the arguments are different in texture.[116] In particular, the non-utilitarian argument recognizes the distinctive importance of avoiding physical injury or death; it resists the assimilation of health and life to other goods. This attention to the centrality of the person avoids the utilitarian dilemma of either demanding excessive beneficence or having recourse to administrative considerations, which shifts the focus away from the rescuer's obligation to a particular endangered individual. In the non-utilitarian argument, of course, administrative considerations are not ignored; to do so would be impossible in elaborating an argument that attempts to provide an ethical foundation for a judicially enforced duty to rescue. Nonetheless, the non-utilitarian's use of administrative considerations differs from the utilitarian's. The utilitarian weaves the fabric of the duty to rescue out of administrative strands; the cost of administration and enforcement are relevant to the very existence of the duty. The non-utilitarian, by contrast, justifies a legal duty to rescue independently of the

administrative costs; the mechanisms of enforcement are invoked only to structure and to coordinate the operation of the duty.

The deontological argument begins with the observation that the idea of an individual's being under a moral duty is intimately related to the notion that health and life are of distinctive importance. The concept of duty applies only to an individual endowed with the capacity to make choices and to set ends for himself.[117] Further, the person, as a purposive and choosing entity, does not merely set physical integrity as one of his ends; he requires it as a precondition to the accomplishment of the purposes that his freedom gives him the power to set. As Kant put it, physical integrity is "the basic *stuff* (the matter) in man without which he could not realize his ends."[118]

A person contemplating the ethical exercise of his freedom of action must impose certain restrictions on that freedom. Because morality is something he shares with all humanity,[119] he cannot claim a preferred moral position for himself. Any moral claim he makes must, by its very nature as a moral claim, be one to which he is subject when others can assert it. Acting on the basis of his own personhood therefore demands recognition of the personhood of others. This recognition, however, cannot be elaborated in the first instance in terms of the enjoyment of ordinary material goods. Because no conception of happiness is shared by everyone and is constant throughout any individual's life, the universal concept of personhood cannot be reflected in a system of moral duties directed at the satisfaction of unstable desires for such goods.[120] Physical integrity, by contrast, is necessary for the accomplishment of any human aim, and so is an appropriate subject for a system of mutually restraining duties.

An individual contemplating his actions from a moral point of view must recognize that all others form their projects on a substratum of physical integrity. If he claims the freedom to pursue his projects as a moral right, he cannot as a rational and moral agent deny to others the same freedom. Because his claim to that freedom implies a right to the physical integrity that is necessary to its exercise, he must concede to others the right to physical integrity that he implicitly and inevitably claims for himself.[121]

This conception of the right to life and health derives from the notion of personhood that is presupposed by the concept of moral action. So too do the right's natural limitations. The duty of beneficence exacted by this right need not collapse into a comprehensive and self-defeating altruism. Respect for another's physical security does not entail fore-going one's own.[122] The right to life and health, seen to give content to the universal concept of personhood, must be ascribed not only to others, but also to oneself. As Kant put it,

> since all *other* men with the exception of myself would not be *all* men, and the maxim would then not have the universality of a law, as it must have in order to be obligatory, the law prescribing the duty of benevolence will include myself, as the object of benevolence, in the command of practical reason.[123]

Moreover, the universalizing process radiates outward from the actor: it is only one's desire to act that makes necessary the exploration of the action's implicit claims and thus of the rights that he must rationally concede to others.[124] The priority of the actor is thus embedded in the structure of the argument and should be reflected in the concrete duties that the argument yields.

This outline of deontological analysis can be applied to examine the standard suggestion that the common law should recognize a duty to effect an easy rescue. Such a duty would be the judicial analogue of the moral obligation to respect the person of another and to safeguard his physical integrity, which is necessary for whatever aims he chooses to pursue. The emergency and convenience limitations also fit quite readily into the analysis. An emergency is a particularly imminent threat to physical security, and the convenience limitation reflects the rescuer's entitlement to the priority of his own physical security over that of the endangered person. Although the proposed legal duty fits comfortably within the deontological moral duty of beneficence, however, the two are not coextensive. Emergencies are not the only circumstances in which life and health are threatened; disease, starvation, and poverty can affect the physical substratum of personhood on a routine basis. If legal duties must reflect moral ones, should not a legal duty to rescue be supplemented by a legal duty to alleviate those less isolated abridgments of physical security?

The convenience limitation on the rescue duty might similarly be loosened in a deontological analysis. One tempting extension would be very far-reaching: if the physical substratum is the "basic *stuff* (the matter) in man without which he could not realize his ends,"[125] and if we are under a duty to safeguard that substratum in others as in ourselves, the priority that the rescuer can legitimately grant to

himself can be only with respect to his physical integrity. Under this extension, a rescuer could—indeed would be obligated to—abstain from acting only if the act would place him in physical danger; if it would not put him in danger, he would be required to attempt a rescue, no matter what the disruption of his life. In Macaulay's famous example,[126] the surgeon would have to travel from Calcutta to Meerut to perform an operation that only he could perform, because the journey, though inconvenient, would not be dangerous. Indeed, he would have to make the trip even if he were about to leave for Europe or to greet members of his family arriving on an incoming ship. The patient's right to physical security would rank ahead of the satisfaction of the surgeon's contingent desires.

The deontological approach to rescue does not compel such a drastic extension. Although every moral person must value physical integrity, its protection is not an end in itself. Rather, physical security is valued because it allows individuals to realize their own projects and purposes. Whatever the reach of the right to physical integrity, therefore, it must allow the rescuer to satisfy his purposes in a reasonably coherent way.[127] Still, though the extension of the moral duty cannot be so drastic as to require the sacrifice of all of a person's projects, it can be substantial. It can require the rescuer to undergo considerable inconvenience short of fundamental changes in the fabric of his life. The deontological duty relaxes both the emergency and convenience limitations of the duty of easy rescue in emergencies: it applies not only in emergencies but whenever physical integrity is threatened, and it applies even when the rescuer might have to undergo considerable inconveniences. The duty might, after all, obligate Macaulay's surgeon to travel from Calcutta to Meerut. Would it also require the wealthy to use at least some of their resources to alleviate the plight of the starving and the afflicted? For those concerned about the possibility of setting principled limits to a duty of rescue,[128] the question is critical.

The objection to an affirmative answer to the question rests on the premises that even the wealthy are under no obligation to be charitable and that the afflicted have no right to receive charity. Under the deontological theory, those premises are incorrect. The duty of beneficence derives from the concept of personhood; it is therefore not properly called charity, for the benefactor's performance of this duty is no reason for self-congratulation.[129] Although the duty is an imperfect one—"since no determinate limits can be assigned to what should be done, the duty has in it a play-room for doing more or less,"[130] as Kant said—it is nonetheless a duty to the performance of which the recipient is entitled.

The extent of the duty of beneficence, of course, can still be troubling. It is the indeterminateness of the duty, the "play-room," that is particularly relevant to this problem. Kant meant by this expression that the form and the amount of the benefaction would vary, depending on the resources of the benefactor, the identity of the recipient, and the recipient's own conception of happiness.[131] The indeterminateness, however, applies not only to the form of the benefaction but also to the linking of particular benefactors to particular beneficiaries. Why should any particular person be singled out of the whole group of potential benefactors, and why should the benefit be conferred on one rather than another person in need? If a duty "may be *exacted* from a person, as one exacts a debt,"[132] it is a debt that leaves unclear the precise terms of discharge as well as the identities of obligor and obligee.

The proper response to this indeterminacy is not to deny that there is a duty. What is required is to set up social institutions to perform the necessary tasks of coordination and determination. Those institutions would ensure that no person is singled out unfairly either for burdens or for benefits, and that the forms of benefaction correlate both with the resources of those who give and with the needs of those who receive. In fact, all Western democracies undertake to perform this task through programs for social assistance. The institutions they establish, however, are primarily legislative and administrative; precisely because a general duty of beneficence is imperfect, it cannot be judicially enforced. The traditional claim-settling function of courts does not permit the transfer of a resource from one person to another solely because the former has it and the latter needs it. Such judicial action would unfairly prefer one needy person over others[133] and unfairly burden one resourceful person over others. Because the duty of beneficence is general and indeterminate, it does not, in the absence of legislative action that specifies and coordinates, yield judicially enforceable moral claims by individuals against others.

The significant characteristic of the emergency and convenience limitations is that, in combination, they eliminate the "play-room" inherent in the duty of beneficence, thus providing a principled response to Kant and to Epstein and rendering the narrower duty to rescue appropriate for judicial enforcement.

An emergency marks a particular person as physically endangered in a way that is not general or routine throughout the society. An imminent peril cannot await assistance from the appropriate social institutions. The provision of aid to an emergency victim does not deplete the social resources committed to the alleviation of more routine threats to physical integrity. Moreover, aid in such circumstances presents no unfairness problems in singling out a particular person to receive the aid. Similarly, emergency aid does not unfairly single out one of a class of routinely advantaged persons; the rescuer just happens to find himself for a short period in a position, which few if any others share, to render a service to some specific person. In addition, when a rescue can be accomplished without a significant disruption of his own projects, the rescuer's freedom to realize his own ends is not abridged by the duty to preserve the physical security of another.[134] In sum, when there is an emergency that the rescuer can alleviate with no inconvenience to himself, the general duty of beneficence that is suspended over society like a floating charge is temporarily revealed to identify a particular obligor and obligee, and to define obligations that are specific enough for judicial enforcement.

Conclusion

The problem of rescue is a central issue in the controversies about the relationships between law and morality, between contract and tort, and between utilitarian and deontological ethics. The argument of this article has been that tort law's adoption of a duty of easy rescue in emergencies would fit a common-law pattern, found principally in contract law, that gives expression to the law's understanding of liberty. This pattern reveals that the common law is already instinct with the attitude of benevolence on which a duty to rescue is grounded. The attitude of benevolence is accepted by many legal commentators as a basic moral intuition, yet the particular duty proposed in this article can be systematically elaborated in both the utilitarian and deontological traditions. For those who believe that law should attempt to render concrete the notion of ethical dealing between persons, as well as for those concerned about the method of common-law evolution or about the social costs of legal rules, the article provides an argument for changing the common-law rule on rescue.

1. *See* W. Prosser, *The Law of Torts* § 56, at 338–43 (4th ed. 1971) (special relationships include husband-wife, shipmaster-crew, proprietor-customer, carrier-passenger, educator-pupil, and employer-employee); Note, *The Duty to Rescue,* 47 *Ind. L. J.* 321, 321 & n.3 (1972) (same).

For the law in non-common-law jurisdictions, see Feldbrugge, *Good and Bad Samaritans: A Comparative Survey of Criminal Law Provisions Concerning Failure to Rescue,* 14 *Am. J. Comp. L.* 630 (1966); Rudzinski, *The Duty to Rescue: A Comparative Analysis,* in *The Good Samaritan and the Law* 91 (J. Ratcliffe ed. 1966); Note, *Stalking the Good Samaritan: Communists, Capitalists and the Duty to Rescue,* 1976 *Utah L. Rev.* 529.

Cases from Canadian and British jurisdictions serve as the principal illustrations in this article, but the relevant American case law is noted throughout.

2. *See, e.g., Buch v. Amory Mfg. Co.,* 69 N.H. 257, 44 A. 809 (1897); *Home Office v. Dorset Yacht Co.,* [1970] A.C. 1004, 1029–30 (H.L.) (Lord Reid).

3. For several of the criticisms of the common-law rule, see note 17 *infra* (citing sources).

4. *See Haynes v. Harwood,* [1935] 1 K.B. 146 (C.A.); *cf. Perpich v. Leetonia Mining Co.,* 118 *Minn.* 508, 512, 137 *N.W.* 12, 14 (1912) (rescuer may recover from imperiled person for injuries sustained in rescue attempt, unless rescuer acted with extreme recklessness); *Echert v. Long Island R.R.,* 43 *N.Y.* 502 (1871) (same).

5. *See Horsley v. MacLaren,* 22 D.L.R. *3d* 545, 558 (Can. 1971) (no contributory negligence of rescuer absent recklessness); J. Fleming, *The Law of Torts* 159 (4th ed. 1971) (contributory negligence not good defense unless rescue foolhardy).

6. *See Hammonds v. Haven,* 280 *S.W.* 2d 814 (Mo. 1955) (jury question whether pedestrian's assumption of dangerous position on road to warn drivers of hazard was reasonable); *Guca v. Pittsburgh Rys.,* 367 *Pa.* 579, 583, 80 *A.* 2d 779, 781 (1951) (reasonable to stand on railroad tracks to warn of car stuck in tracks); H. Hart & A. Honoré, *Causation in the Law* 239 (1959) (rescuer may recover where there is little practical foreseeability of his injury); Fleming, *Remoteness and Duty; The Control Devices in Liability for Negligence,* 31 *Can. B. Rev.* 471, 486 (1953) (limits of foreseeability have been stretched to encourage rescue attempts); Linden, *Down with Foreseeability: Of Thin Skulls and Rescuers,* 47 *Can. B. Rev.* 544 (1969) (same).

7. There are several recent examples. *See, e.g., Anderson v. Atchison, T. & S.F. Ry.,* 333 U.S. 821, 823 (1948) (employer-employee); *Devlin v. Safeway Stores, Inc.,* 235 *F. Supp.* 882, 887 (S.D.N.Y. 1964) (proprietor-customer); *Pridgen v. Boston Hous. Auth.,* 364 *Mass.* 696, 308 *N.E.* 2d 467 (1974) (landlord-trespasser); *Farwell v. Keaton,* 396 *Mich.* 281, 290–91, 240 *N.W.2d* 217, 221–22 (1976) (companion-companion); *O'Rourke v. Schacht,* 1 *Can. S. Ct.* 53 (1976) (police officer-driver); *Horsley v. MacLaren,* 22 D.L.R. *3d* 545, 552 (Can. 1971) (boat operator-passenger).

8. *See Horsley v. MacLaren,* 22 D.L.R. *3d* 545, 557 (Can. 1971) (Laskin, J.) ("The evolution of the law on this subject [the compensation of injured rescuers], originating in the moral approbation of assistance to a person in peril, involved a break with the 'mind your own business' philosophy.")

9. *See Caldwell v. Bechtel,* 631 *F.* 2d 989, 1000 (D.D.C. 1980) (recent holdings "suggest that courts have been eroding the general rule that there is no duty to act to help another in distress, by creating exceptions based upon a relationship between the actors") (footnotes omitted).

10. *See* Coase, *The Problem of Social Cost,* 3 *J. L. & Econ.* 1, 2 (1960).

11. *See* G. Fletcher, *Rethinking Criminal Law* 592 (1978).

12. *See* J. Bentham, *An Introduction to the Principles of Morals and Legislation* 74–83 (J. Burns & H. Hart eds. 1970).

13. For an example of consequentialist analysis in the economic mode, see R. Posner, *Economic Analysis of Law* § 4.8, at 76–77 (1972). The relationship between utilitarianism and Posner's

principle of wealth-maximization, as well as the normative validity of Posner's approach, are currently the subject of controversy. *See* Coleman, *Efficiency, Exchange, and Auction: Philosophic Aspects of the Economic Approach to Law,* 68 *Calif. L. Rev.* 221 (1980); Posner, *The Ethical and Political Basis of the Efficiency Norm in Common Law Adjudication,* 8 *Hofstra L. Rev.* 487 (1980); Posner, *Utilitarianism, Economics, and Legal Theory,* 8 *J. Legal Stud.* 103 (1979); Weinrib, *Utilitarianism, Economics, and Legal Theory,* 30 *U. Toronto L. J.* 307 (1980); *Symposium—Change in the Common Law: Legal and Economic Perspectives,* 9 *J. Legal Stud.* 189 (1980).

14. *E.g.,* G. Fletcher, *supra* note 11; C. Fried, *Right and Wrong* (1978); Epstein, *Defences and Subsequent Pleas in a System of Strict Liability,* 3 *J. Legal Stud.* 165, 167 (1974); Epstein, *A Theory of Strict Liability,* 2 *J. Legal Stud.* 151, 160–89 (1973) [hereinafter cited as *Epstein Theory*]; Fletcher, *Fairness and Utility in Tort Theory,* 85 *Harv. L. Rev.* 537 (1972).

15. *Epstein Theory, supra* note 14, at 189–204.

16. I. Kant, *Fundamental Principles of the Metaphysic of Ethics* 62 (10th ed. T. Abbott trans. 1955).

17. *E.g.,* J. Bentham, *supra* note 12, at 292–93 ("The limits of the law on this head seem . . . to be capable of being extended a good deal farther than they seem to have been extended hitherto. In particular, in cases where the person is in danger, why should it not be made the duty of every man to save another from mischief, when it can be done without prejudicing himself, as well as to abstain from bringing it on him?"); *see* M. Shapo, *The Duty to Act: Tort Law, Power and Public Policy* at xii, 64–68 (1978); Ames, *Law and Morals,* 22 *Harv. L. Rev.* 92, 113 (1908); Franklin, *Vermont Requires Rescue,* 25 *Stan. L. Rev.* 51 (1972); Rudolf, *The Duty to Act: A Proposed Rule,* 44 *Neb. L. Rev.* 499, 509 (1965). For recent legislation in the province of Quebec, see Barakett & Jobin, *Une Modeste Loi du Bon Samaritain pour le Québéc,* 54 *Can. B. Rev.* 290 (1976).

18. Bohlen, *The Moral Duty to Aid Others as a Basis of Tort Liability,* 56 *U. Pa. L. Rev.* 217, 220 (1908).

19. *See Giuliano Constr. Co. v. Simmons,* 147 *Conn.* 441, 162 *A.* 2d 511 (1960); *Bankston v. Dumont,* 205 *Miss.* 272, 38 *So.* 2d 721 (1949); *Hedley Byrne & Co. v. Heller & Partners,* [1964] A.C. 465 (H.L.).

20. *See Sorenson v. Chevrolet Motor Co.,* 171 *Minn.* 260, 214 *N.W.* 754 (1927); *Rivtow Marine v. Washington Iron Works,* 40 D.L.R. *3d* 530 (Can. 1973); *Spartan Steel & Alloys v. Martin & Co.,* [1972] 3 *All E.R.* 557 (C.A.).

21. *See Watt v. Rama,* [1972] *Vict.* 353 (S. Ct.); *Duval v. Seguin,* 40 D.L.R. *3d* 666 (Ont. C.A. 1973). For recovery for injuries that are not only pre-natal but pre-conceptional, see *Renslow v. Mennonite Hospital,* 40 *Ill. App. 3d* 234, 351 *N.E.* 2d 870 (1976).

22. 119 *Eng. Rep.* 424 (K.B. 1855).

23. Bohlen, *supra* note 18, at 220 n.6.

24. Nonfeasance is not equivalent to the nonperformance of an act in one recognized sense of the word "act." Tort theory defines an "act" as a voluntary muscular contraction or as an external manifestation of the will. *See* O. Holmes, *The Common Law* 54 (1881); *Restatement (Second) of Torts* § 2 (1965). Though primitive, *see* G. Ryle, *The Concept of Mind* 62 (1949); Fitzgerald, *Voluntary and Involuntary Acts,* in *Oxford Essays in Jurisprudence* 1 (A. Guest ed. 1961), these definitions capture a basic feature of our notions of responsibility by setting as a minimal condition of liability the defendant's ability to avoid inflicting the harm that his behavior has caused. Thus, no liability attaches to a person who has been carried forcibly onto another's land, *Smith v. Stone,* 82 *Eng. Rep.* 533 (K.B. 1647), or has injured another while unconscious, *Stokes v. Carlson,* 362 *Mo.* 93, 240 *S.W.* 2d 132 (1951); *Slattery v. Haley,* [1923] 3 *D.L.R.* 156 (Ont. App. Div.). A defendant who is pleading nonfeasance, however, has performed an act in this narrow sense. Indeed his act may have

been quite callously deliberate, as when an employer vindictively refuses to make an elevator available to employees who wish to emerge from a mine. *Herd v. Weardale Steel, Coal, & Coke Co.,* [1913] 3 *K.B.* 771 (*C.A.*), *aff'd,* [1915] *A.C.* 67 (*H.L.*). A defendant in a nonfeasance case, then, can concede that in one sense he has acted and yet argue that in a second sense he has not acted.

25. *But see Kelly v. Metropolitan Ry.,* [1895] 1 *Q.B.* 944 (negligence may be by action or by inaction).

26. McNeice & Thornton, *Affirmative Duties in Tort,* 58 *Yale L. J.* 1272, 1272–73 (1949).

27. The philosopher J. L. Austin described the various ways of dividing an action as follows:

[W]hat is *an* or *one* or *the* action? For we can generally split up what might be named as one action in several distinct ways, into different *stretches* or *phases* or *stages.* Stages have already been mentioned: we can dismantle the machinery of the act, and describe (and excuse) separately the intelligence, the appreciation, the planning, the decision, the execution and so forth. Phases are rather different: we can say that he painted a picture or fought a campaign, or else we can say that first he laid on this stroke of paint and then then that, first he fought this action and then that. Stretches are different again: a single term descriptive of what he did may be made to cover either a smaller or a larger stretch of events, those excluded by the narrower description being then called 'consequences' or 'results' or 'effects' or the like of his act.

J. Austin, *A Plea for Excuses,* in *Philosophical Papers* 123, 149 (1961).

28. 119 *Eng. Rep.* 424 (K.B. 1855).

29. *See, e.g., Miller & Brown Ltd. v. City of Vancouver,* 59 *D.L.R. 2d* 640 (*B.C.C.A.* 1966) (failure of defendant to lop off bough of tree he planted held to be nonfeasance).

30. *Newton v. Ellis,* 119 *Eng. Rep.* 424, 428 (*K.B.* 1855) (Erle, J.) ("Here the cause of action is the making of the hole, compounded with a not putting up a light. When these are blended, the result is no more than if two positive acts were committed, such as digging the hole and throwing out the dirt: the two would make up one act."); *cf. id.* at 427–28 (Coleridge, J.) (actions constitute one complex act).

31. A similar situation was presented in *Fagan v. Commissioner of Metropolitan Police,* [1969] 1 *Q.B.* 439.

32. 41 *D.L.R. 2d* 53 (*Man. C.A.* 1963). For comparable cases, see *Simonsen v. Thorin,* 120 *Neb.* 684, 234 *N.W.* 628 (1931); *Montgomery v. National Convoy & Trucking Co.,* 186 *S.C.* 167, 195 *S.E.* 247 (1937).

33. *Oke v. Weide Transport Ltd. & Carra,* 41 *D.L.R. 2d* 53, 62–63 (*Man. C.A.* 1963) (Freedman, J. A., dissenting). The majority held that there was no negligence in failing to report because the victim's death happened under such extraordinary circumstances that it was not reasonably foreseeable. This holding eliminated the need to decide whether there was a duty to report the condition of the sign. The validity of the dissenting opinion's approach to the nonfeasance issue has been supported by *Rivtow Marine v. Washington Iron Works,* 40 *D.L.R. 3d* 530 (*Can.* 1973), where the Supreme Court of Canada held that the manufacturer of a defective item that causes economic loss is beyond the reach of liability for negligence in manufacturing it, but that he is under a duty to abate the danger thus created by warning of the defect when he becomes aware of it.

34. In cases that focus on the materialization of risk, the "but-for" test must be supplemented by consideration of substantiality and remoteness. Similarly, where the creation of risk is at issue, supplementary factors are also needed. Otherwise, a worker whose labor contributed to the manufacture of an automobile will have his behavior placed within the category of misfeasance if he fails to aid a person injured by that automobile. Considerations of remoteness and substantiality are currently of no practical importance, however, because the courts have erred on the side of an excessively restrictive view of misfeasance, *see* notes 31 & 33 *supra,* rather than an excessively expansive one.

35. *E.g., Cal. Veh. Code* § 20001 (*West* 1971); *Criminal Code, Can. Rev. Stat.* ch. C-34, s. 232 (1970); *Highway Traffic Act, Ont. Rev. Stat.* ch. 202, s. 140 (1970).

36. *E.g., Jordan House Ltd. v. Menow & Honsberger,* 38 *D.L.R. 3d* 105 (Can. 1973); *cf. Tubbs v. Argus,* 140 *Ind. App.* 695, 225 *N.E. 2d* 841 (1967) (invitee in automobile).

To the extent that tort law's function is to shape the behavior of the defendant, the status of the plaintiff in such circumstances should not be crucial: in many cases, that status is unknown to the defendant at the moment when action is required. Some courts have recognized the primary importance of the defendant's control over the instrumentality causing injury. *E.g., L. S. Ayres & Co. v. Hicks,* 220 *Ind.* 86, 40 *N.E. 2d* 334 (1942); *Tubbs v. Argus,* 140 *Ind. App.* 695, 225 *N.E. 2d* 841 (1967). Moreover, several recent cases have held that liability for failure to abate a danger may be imposed on an occupier of property even when the persons injured are licensees or trespassers. *E.g., Smith v. Arbaugh's Restaurant,* 469 *F. 2d* 97 (*D.C. Cir.* 1972); *Pridgen v. Boston Hous. Auth.,* 364 *Mass.* 696, 308 *N.E. 2d* 467 (1974).

37. *Vanvalkenburg v. Northern Navigation Co.,* 19 *D.L.R.* 649 (*Ont. S. Ct.* 1913).

38. Most courts now hold that a captain must make reasonable attempts to rescue crew members. *E.g., Harris v. Pennsylvania R.R.,* 50 *F. 2d* 866, 868 (4th Cir. 1931).

39. *See Hutchinson v. Dickie,* 162 *F. 2d* 103, 106 (6th Cir.), *cert. denied,* 332 *U.S.* 830 (1947) (yacht captain has duty to use reasonable care to rescue social guest on yacht for pleasure cruise); *Horsley v. MacLaren,* 22 *D.L.R. 3d* 545, 546 (*Can.* 1971) (same).

40. *Fine's Flowers Ltd. v. General Accident Assur. Co. of Can.,* 81 *D.L.R. 3d* 139 (*Ont. C.A.* 1977) (insurance agent liable for failure to obtain requested full coverage for plaintiff's greenhouses); *Baxter v. Jones,* 6 *Ont. L.R.* 360 (*C.A.* 1903) (general insurance agent liable for failure to notify plaintiff's other insurers of additional insurance). *Baxter* can be seen either as a case of misplaced reliance or, because the placing of the subsequent insurance without notice to the other insurers deprived the insured of coverage he previously had, as a case in which the agent participated in the creation of a risk.

41. This type of misfeasance is therefore usually viewed as in the legal borderland between tort and contract. *See* Seavey, *Reliance Upon Gratuitous Promises or Other Conduct,* 64 *Harv. L. Rev.* 913, 914 (1951); Wright, *Negligent "Acts or Omissions,"* 19 *Can. B. Rev.* 465, 471 n.14 (1941).

42. *See Zelenko v. Gimbel Bros.,* 158 *Misc.* 904, 287 *N.Y.S.* 134 (Sup. Ct. 1935) (department store assumed duty towards ailing customer when it moved her to isolated infirmary, where other aid could not reach her).

43. *See* note 17 *supra;* note 48 *infra.*

44. For another recent defense of the common-law rule, see Note, *supra* note 1. In R. Posner, *supra* note 13, Richard Posner suggests that a duty to rescue might be inefficient, but in Landes & Posner, *Salvors, Finders, Good Samaritans and Other Rescuers: An Economic Study of Law and Altruism,* 7 *J. Legal Stud.* 83, 126 (1978), the conclusion is much more qualified. D'Amato, *The "Bad Samaritan" Paradigm,* 70 *Nw. U.L. Rev.* 798, 802 (1975), accepts Epstein's argument that there should be no tort liability for failure to rescue, but proposes that there should be criminal liability. Epstein himself has reiterated his position on rescue. *See* Epstein, *Causation and Corrective Justice,* 8 *J. Legal Stud.* 477, 491–93 (1979).

45. *Epstein Theory, supra* note 14, at 189–204.

46. *Id.* at 151.

47. *Id.* at 200–01.

48. Even judges who have dismissed claims by victims against callous non-rescuers have indicated the moral revulsion with which they regard the defendant's inaction. *E.g., Union Pacific Ry. v. Cappier,* 66 *Kan.* 649, 653, 72 *P.* 281, 282 (1903); *Buch v. Amory Mfg. Co.,* 69 *N.H.* 257, 260, 44 *A.* 809, 810 (1898); *Yania v. Bigan,* 397 *Pa.* 316, 332, 155 *A. 2d* 343, 346 (1959).

49. *See* note 1 *supra.*

50. The Epstein paragraph quoted above says many things in a small compass, and interpretation is difficult. Epstein seems to regard cases in which conduct is beyond the call of duty as equivalent to cases in which a person should be "allowed" to benefit his fellow man only if prompted by the appropriate motives. I have no idea what Epstein means by this. The issue is whether rescue is obligatory, not whether it is permitted. John Stuart Mill mentioned the problem of whether it is right to rescue a person if one's motive is to preserve him for torture, J. S. Mill, *Utilitarianism* 26 n.* (1888), which may be the problem that Epstein had in mind, but such a tiny problem cannot be relevant to the issue of a general duty to rescue.

51. L. Fuller, *The Morality of Law* 3, 30–32 (1964). In recent moral philosophy, the seminal essay is Urmson, *Saints and Heroes,* in *Essays in Moral Philosophy* 198–216 (A. Melden ed. 1958); *cf.* R. Flathman, *Political Obligation* 34–38 (1972) (distinguishing obligation from aspiration towards ideal).

52. H. Sidgwick, *The Methods of Ethics* 219 (7th ed. 1907); *see* R. Flathman, *supra* note 51, at 155–56. Flathman points out that to think that obligation implies praise bespeaks either misapprehension or an unsettled moral environment. But there may be exceptional circumstances where praise is in order. If the jewelry in Guy de Maupassant's story, *La Parure,* had been real, would not the enormous sacrifices undergone by the borrowers have been praiseworthy, even though they were endured solely for the purpose of repaying a debt? Similarly, would not the soldier be praiseworthy who undertakes an exceptionally dangerous, though obligatory, mission in wartime?

53. The various proposals in *The Good Samaritan and the Law, supra* note 1, are so structured.

54. The discussion to this point does not, of course, show that rescue is morally required. It has been concerned only with critically exploring the implications of Epstein's defense of the common-law position. Section IV of this article considers rescue as a moral requirement.

55. *See* p. 259 *supra.*

56. The first and third propositions address the specific character of the rescue duty; the second addresses, in general, the relationship of law and morality. *See* pp. 260–61 *supra.*

57. *E.g., Home Office v. Dorset Yacht Co.,* [1970] A.C. 1004, 1027 (*H.L.*) (Lord Reid) ("And when a person has done nothing to put himself in any relationship with another person in distress or with his property mere accidental propinquity does not require him to go to that person's assistance. There may be a moral duty to do so, but it is not practicable to make it a legal duty."); *see Tarasoff v. Regents of Univ. of Cal.,* 17 *Cal. 3d* 425, 435 n.5, 551 *P. 2d* 334, 343 n.5, 131 *Cal. Rptr.* 14, 23 n.5 (1976) (common law rule is "[m]orally questionable" but "owes its survival to 'the difficulties of setting any workable standards of unselfish service to fellow men, and of making any workable rule to cover possible situations where fifty people might fail to rescue . . .' (Prosser, *Torts* (4th ed. 1971) § 56, p. 341).")

58. *See* Fried, *Right and Wrong—Preliminary Considerations,* 5 *J. Legal Stud.* 165, 181–82 (1976).

59. *See* Weinrib, *Contribution in a Contractual Setting,* 54 *Can. B. Rev.* 338, 342 (1976).

60. *Cf. Union Pacific Ry. v. Cappier,* 66 *Kan.* 649, 653, 72 *P.* 281, 282 (1903) ("With the humane side of the question courts are not concerned. It is the omission or negligent discharge of legal duties only which come within the sphere of judicial cognizance.") A more extreme version of this position is implied in *Schacht v. The Queen,* 30 *D.L.R. 3d* 641, 651 (Ont. C.A. 1972) ("Much as the humanitarian spirit which motivated the conduct of the good Samaritan has been lauded, it was rooted in moral philosophy, hence from the legal standpoint the *laissez-faire* attitude of the priest and the Levite was condoned.") For this view, the existence of a moral duty to rescue is not only irrelevant to the judgment but precludes the construction of a parallel legal duty.

61. Thus, it is not surprising that the sort of content that Dworkin finds in the common law is consistent with the formal analysis

of the positivists. *See* Weinreb, *Law As Order,* 91 *Harv. L. Rev.* 909 (1978).

62. The writings of John Austin illustrate how legal positivism can be combined with legal reform. Austin, who said that "the existence of law is one thing, its merit or demerit is another," J. Austin, *The Province of Jurisprudence Determined* 184 (H. Hart ed. 1954), derived several consequences from this statement: an immoral law may be valid; when conscience counsels disobedience to law, it is only out of ignorance or self-interest; and because moral judgments are always in dispute, judicial attention to morality as a basis for decision may result in arbitrariness. Austin, however, did not assert that the existence of a moral obligation is irrelevant to the construction of a parallel legal obligation. On the contrary, his distinction between the law as it is and as it ought to be was borrowed from Bentham, J. Bentham, *A Fragment on Government,* in *A Comment on the Commentaries and a Fragment on Government* 393, 397 (J. Burns & H. Hart eds. 1977), who used it as a tool for criticizing Blackstone's complacent description of the common law and for proposing reform of the law on utilitarian principles. *See* Hart, *Positivism and the Separation of Law and Morals,* 71 *Harv. L. Rev.* 593, 597 (1958). Even Austin believed that there is no general reason for not translating a rationally justifiable moral view into a legal obligation.

A utilitarian positivist like Austin would hold, at most, that particular moral duties should not be enforced as legal duties if the process of enforcement would be too costly. The classical utilitarians, however, did not consider this objection fatal to a duty to effect an easy rescue. *See* pp. 279–86 *infra.*

63. *See* B. Cardozo, *The Nature of the Judicial Process* 14–24 (1921).

64. This notion of legal obligation is embodied in the concept of *malum in se,* which was seized upon by critics of Hobbes centuries ago to specify the minimum content of political obligation, and thus to reject pure political contractarianism. *See* S. Clarke, *A Discourse of Natural Religion* 228 (1706), *reprinted in* 1 D. Raphael, *British Moralists 1650–1800,* at 191, 196 (1969); R. Cudworth, *A Treatise Concerning Eternal and Immutable Morality* 122 (1731), *reprinted in* 1 D. Raphael, *supra,* at 105; *cf.* 1 W. Blackstone, *Commentaries* *54–55 (positive law has no force with regard to naturally wrong actions). The concept cannot embody a complete theory of political obligation because it ignores *mala prohibita* and the political element of obligations; but it does provide a minimum content.

65. *Epstein Theory, supra* note 14, at 199.

66. *See* Hale, *Prima Facie Torts, Combination and Non-Feasance,* 46 *Colum. L. Rev.* 196, 214 (1946).

67. *See* Dworkin, *Liberalism,* in *Public and Private Morality* 113, 128 (S. Hampshire ed. 1978).

68. *See* C. Fried, *supra* note 14, at 100.

69. *See* W. Prosser, *supra* note 1, § 92, at 613–16.

70. 1 *Can. S. Ct.* 53 (1976).

71. In *Newton v. Ellis,* 119 *Eng. Rep.* 424 (*K.B.* 1855), and *Oke v. Weide Transport Ltd. & Carra,* 41 *D.L.R. 2d* 53 (Man. C.A. 1963), the defendants had created the danger on the highway.

72. Economists found one of this justification for having an issue dealt with by tort rather than by contract. *E.g.,* Calabresi & Melamed, *Property Rules, Liability Rules, and Inalienability: One View of the Cathedral,* 85 *Harv. L. Rev.* 1089, 1106 (1972); Posner, *Strict Liability: A Comment,* 2 *J. Legal Stud.* 205, 219 (1973).

73. *Cf. Gray v. Martino,* 19 *N.J.L.* 462, 103 *A.* 24 (1918) (police officer may not receive reward for recovery of stolen property); English Law Revision Committee, *The Statute of Frauds and the Doctrine of Consideration,* 15 *Can. B. Rev.* 585, 605 (1937) (reprinting *Law Revision Committee, Sixth Interim Report,* Cmd. 5449).

In *England v. Davidson,* 113 *Eng. Rep.* 640 (*Q.B.* 1840), the court held enforceable a promise to give a reward for information regarding the commission of a crime, even though the claimant of the reward was a police constable. Two circumstances should be noted. First, the court considered the policeman not bound by duty to reveal the information, thus implying that if he had been so bound, the contract would not have been enforceable. Second, the offer was made to the whole world, not specifically to police constables; thus, it does not follow from the case that the constable would have been able to initiate or to engage in negotiations for the divulging of particular information.

74. These remarks on liberty deal only with the market position of a police officer when contract values are manifest. Of course, there is also an administrative justification for not forcing the officer to act: he should be free to allocate his scarce resources of time and attention to the problems that seem most urgent to him or to his superiors. But this consideration concerns only the adequacy of particular conduct as an attempt to fulfill the duty to act; it does not concern the existence of the duty. The problem it raises is not the interaction of tort law with contract, but the interaction of tort law with the discretion of administrative agents. Here the courts have evinced a reasonably limited respect for the exercise of bona fide discretion by public authorities. *See, e.g., American Exch. Bank v. United States,* 257 *F. 2d* 938 (7th Cir. 1958) (Federal Tort Claims Act not violated by discretionary decision not to install handrails on public staircase); *City of Freeport v. Isbell,* 83 *Ill.* 440 (1877) (misfeasance-nonfeasance distinction applied to find no liability for city inaction); *Anns v. London Borough of Merton,* [1978] *A.C.* 728, 754 (*H.L.*) (Lord Wilberforce) (public agency not liable if act or omission within statutorily defined discretion); *Home Office v. Dorset Yacht Co.,* [1970] *A.C.* 1004, 1068 (*H.L.*) (Lord Diplock) (same). In *O'Rourke v. Schacht,* 1 *Can. S. Ct.* 53 (1976), *aff'g Schacht v. The Queen,* 30 *D.L.R. 3d* 641 (Ont. C.A. 1972), there was apparently no police business of competing urgency. *See* 30 *D.L.R. 3d* at 644.

75. A dissenting opinion reasoned that if the police officer were liable, the liability must flow either from the legislation or from the common law. The statute was excluded because there was no indication that the legislature intended to create civil liability. The common law was excluded because the danger in question existed independently of the defendant, whose behavior was therefore an instance of pure nonfeasance. Because liability could be based on neither statute nor common law, there could be no liability. *O'Rourke v. Schacht,* 1 *Can. S. Ct.* 53, 74–87 (1976) (Martland, J., dissenting). This argument, contrary to the familiar common-law practice, *see* note 89 *infra,* views statutes and the common law as watertight compartments.

76. The use of statutes as sources of public policy is common practice in common-law adjudication. *See* Landis, *Statutes and the Sources of the Law,* in *Harvard Legal Essays* 213 (1934), *reprinted in* 2 *Harv. J. Legis.* 7 (1965); Traynor, *Statutes Revolving in Common-Law Orbits,* 17 *Cath. U.L. Rev.* 401 (1968); *cf. Jordan House Ltd. v. Menow,* 38 *D.L.R. 3d* 105, 110 (Can. 1973) (statute described as "crystallizing a relevant fact situation which, because of its authoritative source, the Court was entitled to consider in determining, on common law principles, whether a duty of care should be raised"). The legislative-intent approach has often been criticized. *E.g.,* C. Wright, *Cases on the Law of Torts* 284 (4th ed. 1967); Alexander, *Legislation and the Standard of Care in Negligence,* 42 *Can. B. Rev.* 243 (1964); Morris, *The Role of Criminal Statutes in Negligence Actions,* 49 *Colum. L. Rev.* 21 (1949).

77. *See People v. Beardsley,* 150 *Mich.* 206, 113 *N.W.* 1128 (1907); *Territory v. Manton,* 8 *Mont.* 95, 19 *P.* 387 (1888); *R. v. Russell,* [1933] *Vict.* 59.

78. Bohlen, *supra* note 18, at 227.

79. *Balfour v. Balfour,* [1919] 2 *K.B.* 571, 579 (C.A.).

80. For example, in *Sommers v. Putnam Bd. of Educ.,* 113 *Ohio St.* 177, 148 *N.E.* 682 (1925), a statute requiring a man to see that his children attend school formed one ground for holding the school board liable for the costs that the man incurred in transporting his children to school when the school board failed to perform its statutory duty to provide transportation.

81. In placing value and reliance on natural affection, the law exhibits its commitment to the ethical priority of certain human ties. The argument given below for a duty of easy rescue that rests on Kantian principles.

82. 60 *U.S.* (19 How.) 150 (1857).

83. I*d.* at 159; *see United States v. Bethlehem Steel Corp.,* 315 *U.S.* 289, *327–30* (1942) (Frankfurter, J., dissenting) (fundamental principle of law that courts will not enforce bargains in which one party has unconscionably taken advantage of necessities and distress of other party).

84. *See* note 9 *supra.*

85. A similar point was made by T. Macaulay, *A Penal Code Prepared by the Indian Law Commissioners,* note M (1837), *reprinted in* M. Friedland, *Cases and Materials on Criminal Law and Procedure* 265–68 (5th ed. 1978):

> On the other hand, it will hardly be maintained that a man should be punished as a murderer because he omitted to relieve a beggar even though there might be the clearest proof that the death of the beggar was the effect of this omission, and that the man who omitted to give the alms knew that the death of the beggar was likely to be the effect of the omission.

86. [1971] 2 *All E.R.* 175 (C.A.).

87. For a discussion of the necessity defense in American law, see W. Prosser, *supra* note 1, § 24, at 124–27.

88. *London Borough of Southwark v. Williams,* [1971] 2 *All E.R.* 175, 179 (C.A.) (Lord Denning, M.R.).

89. *Id.* at 181; *cf. Depue v. Flateau,* 100 *Minn.* 299, 111 *N.W.* 1 (1907) (jury question whether dinner host negligent in refusing request of ill guest to spend the night). Prosser noted that "the privilege of necessity resembles those of self-defense and defense of property," but he also deemed it unwise to confine this privilege "within too narrow limits." W. Prosser, *supra* note 1, § 24, at 127 & n.18.

90. It is sufficient for purposes of this article if the *Southwark* case shows the attitude of the common law to involuntary exchanges between individuals of a commodity that has market value. This theory does not, however, completely justify the holding of the case. The owner in *Southwark* was not an individual but a public authority, and the house in question was not being used at all but had been boarded up by the municipality and then rendered habitable by the efforts of the squatters. Evicting the squatters and restoring the property to its unoccupied status might be an example of wasting the resource. It might be in accord with a liberal theory of law to allow a waste of property by *individuals,* because it is illegitimate to interfere with the individual's satisfaction of his self-regarding desires, and wasting his own resources might provide him with satisfaction. *Cf.* J. Rawls, *A Theory of Justice* 432–33 (1971) (definition of individual satisfaction in moral theory must accommodate highly idiosyncratic preferences). *But see Brown v. Burdett,* 21 *Ch. D.* 667 (1882) (restricting satisfaction from posthumous waste). By contrast, a public authority must always act in the public interest and not for the satisfaction of its desires; allowing waste should therefore be beyond the bounds of its discretion. Thus, Lord Justice Megaw's concern for the integrity of the queue would be misplaced if there were no queue for this property. Similarly, Lord Denning's generalization from this case to property in general confounds the roles of a private individual and a public authority.

I am grateful to my colleague Professor Arnold Weinrib for discussion of these points. They merit more attention, and we hope to deal with them elsewhere.

91. Rawls' notion of "reflective equilibrium" is similar. *See* J. Rawls, *supra* note 104, at 20, 48. For the relationship between this notion and legal reasoning, see Dworkin, *The Original Position,* 40 *U. Chi. L. Rev.* 500, 511 (1973).

92. W. Prosser, *supra* note 1, § 56, at 341.

93. *See* H. L. A. Hart, *The Concept of Law* 120 (1961).

94. Some commentators have argued that the law now excessively restricts market freedom. *E.g.,* Trebilocock, *The Doctrine of Inequality of Bargaining Powers: Post-Benthamite Economics in the House of Lords,* 26 *U. Toronto L.J.* 359 (1976).

95. 60 *U.S.* (19 How.) 150 (1856).

96. *[1971] 2 All E.R.* 175 (C.A.).

97. Holmes, *The Path of the Law,* 10 *Harv. L. Rev.* 457, 459 (1897).

98. J. Bentham, *supra* note 12, at 293; *see* 1 J. Bentham, *The Principles of Legislation* 85–86 (R. Hildreth ed. 1840).

99. *See* note 17 *supra.*

100. *See* J. Bentham, *supra* note 12, at 38–41. That something is askew in Bentham's analysis is indicated by his statement that for many beneficent acts, "the beneficial quality of the act depends essentially upon the disposition of the agent; that is, upon the motives by which he appears to have been prompted to perform it." *Id.* at 322. In utilitarian theory, however, there is no such thing as a good or bad motive, only motives that cause good or bad acts. *See id.* at 97–130.

101. On the controversy over the significance of death for classical utilitarianism, see Henson, *Utilitarianism and the Wrongness of Killing,* 80 *Phil. Rev.* 320 (1971); Sumner, *A Matter of Life and Death,* 10 *Nous* 145 (1976).

102. *See* J. Bentham, *supra* note 12, at 74–83.

103. *See* H. Sidgwick, *supra* note 52, at 492–93.

104. J. Rawls, *supra* note 90, at 189; *cf.* C. Fried, *supra* note 14, at 15 (crude consequentialist position can lead to paralysis, obsession, and contradiction).

105. *E.g.,* J. Bentham, *Principles of the Civil Code,* in 1 *Works* 303–04 (J. Bowring ed. 1843).

116. J. S. Mill, *The Principles of Political Economy* 967 (W. Ashley ed. 1923).

107. H. Sidgwick, *supra* note 52, at 437.

108. The relationship has been noticed by critics of both. *See, e.g.,* C. Macpherson, *Democratic Theory: Essays in Retrieval* 4 (1973); Marx & Engels, *The German Ideology,* in *Karl Marx: Selected Writings* 185 (D. McLellan ed. 1977).

109. *London Borough of Southwark v. Williams,* [1971] 2 *All E.R.* 175 (C.A.).

110. J. Bentham, *supra* note 12, at 162 (footnote omitted).

111. *Id.* at 13. For Bentham, the pleasures of good will count equally with the pleasures of malevolence. *See id.* at 44. Bentham wrote:

Let a man's motive be ill-will; call it even malice, envy, cruelty; it is still a kind of pleasure that is his motive: the pleasure he takes at the thought of the pain which he sees, or expects to see, his adversary undergo. Now even this wretched pleasure taken by itself, is good: it may be faint; it may be short: it must at any rate be impure: yet while it lasts, and before any bad consequences arrive, it is as good as any other that is not more intense.

Id. at 100 n.e. Mill's attempt to modify this position is notorious. *See* J. S. Mill, *supra* note 50, at 26–31.

112. *See* Fried, *supra* note 58, at 182.

113. Fried traces this view back to Kant. *Id.* Bentham, however, also comes close to this view in his distinction between private ethics and the art of government. *See* J. Bentham, *supra* note 12, at 285. But a utilitarian justification of rescue that ignores administrative considerations merely leads back to excessive beneficence.

114. *See* C. Fried, *Medical Experimentation: Personal Integrity and Social Policy* 95–96 (1974); I. Kant, *supra* note 76, at 112. The distinctive quality of physical integrity relative to the goods of property also lies at the root of Hume's account of justice. *See* D. Hume, *A Treatise of Human Nature* 489 (2d ed. L. Selby-Bigge 1978).

115. A. Gewirth, *Reason and Morality* 218 (1978); Dworkin, *Hard Cases,* 88 *Harv. L. Rev.* 1057, 1076 (1975).

116. *See* Fried, *supra* note 58, at 182–84.

117. The concept of duty does not apply to creatures that act out of necessity. I. Kant, *Critique of Practical Reason* 28 (L. Beck trans. 1956); I. Kant, *supra* note 16, at 78–102.

118. I. Kant, *The Metaphysical Principles of Virtue* (M. Gregor, trans. 1964) at 112.

119. The parable of the Good Samaritan, *Luke* 10:30, itself emphasizes in its opening formulation that the only relevant quality of the man who fell among the robbers was that he was a human being. *See* E. Cahn, *The Moral Decision* 195 (1955).

120. *See* I. Kant, *supra* note 117, at 27.

121. The argument leans heavily on the work of Professor Alan Gewirth. *See* A. Gewirth, *supra* note 115; Gewirth, *The 'Is-Ought' Problem Resolved,* 47 *Proc. & Addresses Amer. Phil. Ass'n* 34 (1974); Gewirth, *The Normative Structure of Action,* 25 *Rev. Metaphysics* 238 (1971). My purpose is more modest than his in one crucial respect: it is enough for my purpose that a person who assumes a moral point of view would elaborate a deontological justification of rescue, whereas Gewirth argues that a rational actor must assume the moral point of view. For discussion of this wider claim, see Grunebaum, *Gewirth and a Reluctant Protagonist,* 86 *Ethics* 274 (1976); Veatch, *Paying Heed to Gewirth's Principle of Categorial Consistency,* 86 *Ethics* 278 (1976); Gewirth, *Action and Rights: A Reply,* 86 *Ethics* 288 (1976).

122. *See* I. Kant, *supra* note 118, at 53, 122.

123. *Id.* at 118.

124. Kant wrote:

[*R*]*ational nature exists as an end in itself.* Man necessarily conceives his own existence as being so: so far then this is a *subjective* principle of human actions. But every other rational being regards its existence similarly, just on the same principle that holds for me; so that it is at the same time an objective principle, from which as a supreme practical law all laws of the will must be capable of being deduced.

I. Kant, *supra* note 16, at 46 (footnote omitted). For the problems of interpretation in this passage, see H. Jones, *Kant's Principle of Personality* 20–26 (1971); Haezrahi, *The Concept of Man as an End-in-Himself,* in I. Kant, *Foundations of the Metaphysics of Morals with Critical Essays* 292 (L. Beck trans. R. Wolff ed. 1969). On the priority of the self, see I. Kant, *supra* note 76, at 119; Fried, *The Lawyer as Friend: The Moral Foundations of the Lawyer-Client Relation,* 85 *Yale L.J.* 1060, 1070 (1976).

125. I. Kant, *supra* note 118, at 112.

126. *See* p. 272 *supra.*

127. A similar point is made by Professor Fried in C. Fried, *supra* note 14, at 123.

128. *E.g., Epstein Theory, supra* note 14, at 198–99.

129. I. Kant, *supra* note 118, at 54; *see* J. S. Mill, *supra* note 50, at 74–75.

130. *See* I. Kant, *supra* note 118, at 121.

131. *See* M. Gregor, *Laws of Freedom* 95–112, 194–96 (1963).

132. J. S. Mill, *supra* note 50, at 232–33.

133. The unfairness of preferring the squatters to other homeless persons was adverted to by Lord Justice Megaw in *London Borough of Southwark v. Williams,* [1971] 2 *All E.R.* 175, 182 (C.A.) (Megaw, L.J.).

134. In I. Kant, *supra* note 118, at 49, Kant writes: "Imperfect duties, accordingly, are only *duties of virtue.* To fulfill them is *merit* (*meritum* = +a); but to transgress them is not so much *guilt* (*demeritum* = −a) as rather mere *lack of* moral *worth* (= 0), unless the agent makes it his principle not to submit to these duties." Is not a person who refuses to rescue another at no cost to himself "making it his principle not to submit to these duties?"

Some Criminal Defenses

PEOPLE V. YOUNG*

New York Court of Appeals, 1962

Per Curiam. Whether one, who in good faith aggressively intervenes in a struggle between another person and a police officer in civilian dress attempting to effect the lawful arrest of the third person, may be properly convicted of assault in the third degree is a question of law of first impression here.

The opinions in the court below in the absence of precedents in this State carefully expound the opposing views found in other jurisdictions. The majority in the Appellate Division have adopted the minority rule in the other States that one who intervenes in a struggle between strangers under the mistaken but reasonable belief that he is protecting another who he assumes is being unlawfully beaten is thereby exonerated from criminal liability. The weight of authority holds with the dissenters below that one who goes to the aid of a third person does so at his peril.

While the doctrine espoused by the majority of the court below may have support in some States, we feel that such a policy would not be conducive to an orderly society. We agree with the settled policy of law in most jurisdictions that the right of a person to defend another ordinarily should not be greater than such person's right to defend himself. Subdivision 3 of section 246 of the Penal Law does not apply as no offense was being committed on the person of the one resisting the lawful arrest. Whatever may be the public policy where the felony charged requires proof of a specific intent and the issue is justifiable homicide, it is not relevant in a prosecution for assault in the third degree where it is only necessary to show that the defendant knowingly struck a blow.

In this case there can be no doubt that the defendant intended to assault the police officer in civilian dress. The resulting assault was forceful. Hence motive or mistake of fact is of no significance as the defendant was not charged with a crime requiring such intent or knowledge. To be guilty of third degree assault "It is sufficient that the defendant voluntarily intended to commit the unlawful act of touching" (1 *Wharton's Criminal Law and Procedure* [1957], § 338, p. 685). Since in these circumstances the aggression was inexcusable the defendant was properly convicted.

Accordingly, the order of the Appellate Division should be reversed and the information reinstated.

Froessel, J. (dissenting). The law is clear that one may kill in defense of another when there is reasonable, though mistaken, ground for believing that the person slain is about to commit a felony or to do some great personal injury to the apparent victim (Penal Law, § 1055); yet the majority now hold, for the first time, that in the event of a simple assault under similar circumstances, the mistaken belief, no matter how reasonable, is no defense.

Briefly, the relevant facts are these: On a Friday afternoon at about 3:40, Detectives Driscoll and Murphy, not in uniform, observed an argument tak-

*11 *N.Y.S. 2d* 274 (1962). Citations omitted.

ing place between a motorist and one McGriff in the street in front of premises 64 West 54th Street, in midtown Manhattan. Driscoll attempted to chase Mc-Griff out of the roadway in order to allow traffic to pass, but McGriff refused to move back; his actions caused a crowd to collect. After identifying himself to McGriff, Driscoll placed him under arrest. As Mc-Griff resisted, defendant "came out of the crowd" from Driscoll's rear and struck Murphy about the head with his fist. In the ensuing struggle Driscoll's right kneecap was injured when defendant fell on top of him. At the station house, defendant said he had not known or thought Driscoll and Murphy were police officers.

Defendant testified that while he was proceeding on 54th Street he observed two white men, who appeared to be 45 or 50 years old, pulling on a "colored boy" (McGriff), who appeared to be a lad about 18, whom he did not know. The men had nearly pulled McGriff's pants off, and he was crying. Defendant admitted he knew nothing of what had transpired between the officers and McGriff, and made no inquiry of anyone; he just came there and pulled the officer away from McGriff.

Defendant was convicted of assault third degree. In reversing upon the law and dismissing the information, the Appellate Division held that one is not "criminally liable for assault in the third degree if he goes to the aid of another whom he mistakenly, but *reasonably,* believes is being unlawfully beaten, and thereby injures one of the apparent assaulters" (emphasis supplied). While in my opinion the majority below correctly stated the law, I would reverse here and remit so that the Appellate Division may pass on the question of whether or not defendant's conduct was reasonable in light of the circumstances presented at the trial (*Code Crim. Pro.,* §§ 543-a, 543-b).

As the majority below pointed out, assault is a crime derived from the common law (*People v. Katz,* 290 *N.Y.* 361, 365). Basic to the imposition of criminal liability both at common law and under our statutory law is the existence in the one who committed the prohibited act of what has been variously termed a guilty mind, a *mens rea* or a criminal intent.

Criminal intent requires an awareness of wrongdoing. When conduct is based upon mistake of fact reasonably entertained, there can be no such awareness and, therefore, no criminal culpability. In *People ex rel. Hegeman v. Corrigan* (195 *N.Y.* 1, 12) we stated: "it is very apparent that the innocence or criminality of the intent in a particular act generally depends on the knowledge or belief of the actor at

the time. An honest and *reasonable* belief in the existence of circumstances which, if true, would make the act for which the defendant is prosecuted innocent, would be a good defense." (Emphasis supplied.)

It is undisputed that defendant did not know that Driscoll and Murphy were detectives in plain clothes engaged in lawfully apprehending an alleged disorderly person. If, therefore, defendant *reasonably* believed he was lawfully assisting another, he would not have been guilty of a crime. Subdivision 3 of section 246 of the Penal Law provides that it is not unlawful to use force "When committed either by the party about to be injured or *by another person in his aid or defense, in preventing or attempting to prevent an offense against his person,* if the force or violence used is not more than sufficient to prevent such offense" (emphasis supplied). The law is thus clear that if defendant entertained an "honest and reasonable belief" (*People ex rel. Hegeman v. Corrigan,* 195 *N.Y.* 1, 12 *supra*) that the facts were as he perceived them to be, he would be exonerated from criminal liability.

By ignoring one of the most basic principles of criminal law—that crimes *mala in se* require proof of at least general criminal intent—the majority now hold that the defense of mistake of fact is "of no significance." We are not here dealing with one of "a narrow class of exceptions" (*People v. Katz,* 290 *N.Y.* 361, 365, *supra*) where the Legislature has created crimes which do not depend on *criminal* intent but which are complete on the mere intentional doing of an act *malum prohibitum.* (9 *N. Y. 2d* 51, 58; *People v. Werner,* 174 *N.Y.* 132, *supra*).

There is no need, in my opinion, to consider the law of other States, for New York policy clearly supports the view that one may act on appearances reasonably ascertained, as does New Jersey. Our Penal Law (§ 1055), to which I have already alluded, is a statement of that policy. The same policy was expressed by this court in *People v. Maine* (166 *N.Y.* 50). There, the defendant observed his brother fighting in the street with two other men; he stepped in and stabbed to death one of the latter. The defense was justifiable homicide under the predecessor of section 1055. The court held it reversible error to admit into evidence the declarations of the defendant's brother, made before defendant happened upon the scene, which tended to show that the brother was the aggressor. We said (p. 52): "Of course the acts and conduct of the defendant must be judged solely with reference to the situation as it was when he first and afterwards saw it." Mistake of relevant fact, reasonably entertained, is thus a defense to homicide under section 1055 (*People v. Governale,* 193 *N.Y.* 581, 588), and one who kills in defense of another and proffers this defense of justification is to be judged according to the circumstances as they appeared to him.

The mistaken belief, however, must be one which is reasonably entertained, and the question of reasonableness is for the trier of the facts. "The question is not merely what did the accused believe, but also, what did he have the right to believe?" (*People v. Rodawald,* 177 *N.Y.* 408, 427.) Without passing on the facts of the instant case, the Appellate Division had no right to assume that defendant's conduct was reasonable, and to dismiss the information as a matter of law. Nor do we have the right to reinstate the verdict without giving the Appellate Division the opportunity to pass upon the facts (*Code Crim. Pro.,* § 543-b).

Although the majority of our court are now purporting to fashion a policy "conducive to an orderly society," by their decision they have defeated their avowed purpose. What public interest is promoted by a principle which would deter one from coming to the aid of a fellow citizen who he has reasonable ground to apprehend is in imminent danger of personal injury at the hands of assailants? Is it reasonable to denominate, as justifiable homicide, a slaying committed under a mistaken but reasonably held belief, and deny this same defense of justification to one using less force? Logic, as well as historical background and related precedent, dictates that the rule and policy expressed by our Legislature in the case of homicide, which is an assault resulting in death, should likewise be applicable to a much less serious assault not resulting in death.

I would reverse the order appealed from and remit the case to the Appellate Division pursuant to section 543-b of the Code of Criminal Procedure "for determination upon the questions of fact raised in that court."

Chief Judge Desmond and Judges Dye, Fuld, Burke and Foster concur in *Per Curiam* opinion; Judge Froessel dissents in an opinion in which Judge Van Voorhis concurs.

Order reversed, etc.

THE CASE OF THE SPELUNCEAN EXPLORERS*

Lon L. Fuller

The defendants, having been indicted for the crime of murder, were convicted and sentenced to be hanged by the Court of General Instances of the County of Stowfield. They bring a petition of error before this Court. The facts sufficiently appear in the opinion of the Chief Justice.

TRUEPENNY, C. J. The four defendants are members of the Speluncean Society, an organization of amateurs interested in the exploration of caves. Early in May of 4299 they, in the company of Roger Whetmore, then also a member of the Society, penetrated into the interior of a limestone cavern of the type found in the Central Plateau of this Commonwealth. While they were in a position remote from the entrance to the cave, a landslide occurred. Heavy boulders fell in such a manner as to block completely the only known opening to the cave. When the men discovered their predicament they settled themselves near the obstructed entrance to wait until a rescue party should remove the detritus that prevented them from leaving their underground prison. On the failure of Whetmore and the defendants to return to their homes, the Secretary of the Society was notified by their families. It appears that the explorers had left in-

*Lon L. Fuller, "The Case of the Speluncean Explorers," *Harvard Law Review*, vol. 62 (1949), pp. 616–45. Reprinted by permission of the *Harvard Law Review* and Mr. John N. Roche.

dications at the headquarters of the Society concerning the location of the cave they proposed to visit. A rescue party was promptly dispatched to the spot.

The task of rescue proved one of overwhelming difficulty. It was necessary to supplement the forces of the original party by repeated increments of men and machines, which had to be conveyed at great expense to the remote and isolated region in which the cave was located. A huge temporary camp of workmen, engineers, geologists, and other experts was established. The work of removing the obstruction was several times frustrated by fresh landslides. In one of these, ten of the workmen engaged in clearing the entrance were killed. The treasury of the Speluncean Society was soon exhausted in the rescue effort, and the sum of eight hundred thousand frelars, raised partly by popular subscription and partly by legislative grant, was expended before the imprisoned men were rescued. Success was finally achieved on the thirty-second day after the men entered the cave.

Since it was known that the explorers had carried with them only scant provisions, and since it was also known that there was no animal or vegetable matter within the cave on which they might subsist, anxiety was early felt that they might meet death by starvation before access to them could be obtained. On the twentieth day of their imprisonment it was learned for the first time that they had taken with them into the cave a portable wireless machine capable of both sending and receiving messages. A similar machine was promptly installed in the rescue camp and oral communication established with the unfortunate men within the mountain. They asked to be informed how long a time would be required to release them. The engineers in charge of the project answered that at least ten days would be required even if no new landslides occurred. The explorers then asked if any physicians were present, and were placed in communication with a committee of medical experts. The imprisoned men described their condition and the rations they had taken with them, and asked for a medical opinion whether they would be likely to live without food for ten days longer. The chairman of the committee of physicians told them that there was little possibility of this. The wireless machine within the cave then remained silent for eight hours. When communication was reestablished the men asked to speak again with the physicians. The chairman of the physicians' committee was placed before the apparatus, and Whetmore, speaking on behalf of himself and the defendants, asked

whether they would be able to survive for ten days longer if they consumed the flesh of one of their number. The physicians' chairman reluctantly answered this question in the affirmative. Whetmore asked whether it would be advisable for them to cast lots to determine which of them should be eaten. None of the physicians present was willing to answer the question. Whetmore then asked if there were among the party a judge or other official of the government who would answer this question. None of these attached to the rescue camp was willing to assume the role of advisor in this matter. He then asked if any minister or priest would answer their question, and none was found who would do so. Thereafter no further messages were received from within the cave, and it was assumed (erroneously, it later appeared) that the electric batteries of the explorers' wireless machine had become exhausted. When the imprisoned men were finally released it was learned that on the twenty-third day after their entrance into the cave Whetmore had been killed and eaten by his companions.

From the testimony of the defendants, which was accepted by the jury, it appears that it was Whetmore who first proposed that they might find the nutriment without which survival was impossible in the flesh of one of their own number. It was also Whetmore who first proposed the use of some method of casting lots, calling the attention of the defendants to a pair of dice he happened to have with him. The defendants were at first reluctant to adopt so desperate a procedure, but after the conversations by wireless related above, they finally agreed on the plan proposed by Whetmore. After much discussion of the mathematical problems involved, agreement was finally reached on a method of determining the issue by the use of the dice.

Before the dice were cast, however, Whetmore declared that he withdrew from the arrangement, as he had decided on reflection to wait for another week before embracing an expedient so frightful and odious. The others charged him with a breach of faith and proceeded to cast the dice. When it came Whetmore's turn, the dice were cast for him by one of the defendants, and he was asked to declare any objections he might have to the fairness of the throw. He stated that he had no such objections. The throw went against him, and he was then put to death and eaten by his companions.

After the rescue of the defendants, and after they had completed a stay in a hospital where they underwent a course of treatment for malnutrition and shock, they were indicted for the murder of Roger Whetmore. At the trial, after the testimony had been concluded, the foreman of the jury (a lawyer by profession) inquired of the court whether the jury might not find a special verdict, leaving it to the court to say whether on the facts as found the defendants were guilty. After some discussion, both the Prosecutor and counsel for the defendants indicated their acceptance of this procedure, and it was adopted by the court. In a lengthy special verdict the jury found the facts as I have related them above, and found further that if on these facts the defendants were guilty of the crime charged against them, then they found the defendants guilty. On the basis of this verdict, the trial judge ruled that the defendants were guilty of murdering Roger Whetmore. The judge then sentenced them to be hanged, the law of our Commonwealth permitting him no discretion with respect to the penalty to be imposed. After the release of the jury, its members joined in a communication to the Chief Executive asking that the sentence be commuted to an imprisonment of six months. The trial judge addressed a similar communication to the Chief Executive. As yet no action with respect to these pleas has been taken, as the Chief Executive is apparently awaiting our disposition of this petition of error.

It seems to me that in dealing with this extraordinary case the jury and the trial judge followed a course that was not only fair and wise, but the only course that was open to them under the law. The language of our statute is well known: "Whoever shall willfully take the life of another shall be punished by death." *N.C.S.A.* (N.S.) § 12-A. This statute permits of no exception applicable to this case, however our sympathies may incline us to make allowance for the tragic situation in which these men found themselves.

In a case like this the principle of executive clemency seems admirably suited to mitigate the rigors of the law, and I propose to my colleagues that we follow the example of the jury and the trial judge by joining in the communications they have addressed to the Chief Executive. There is every reason to believe that these requests for clemency will be heeded, coming as they do from those who have studied the case and had an opportunity to become thoroughly acquainted with all its circumstances. It is highly improbable that the Chief Executive would deny these requests unless he were himself to hold hearings at least as extensive as those involved in the trial below, which lasted for three months. The holding of such hearings (which would virtually amount to a retrial of the case) would scarcely be compatible with the function of the Executive as it is usually conceived. I think we may therefore assume that some form of clemency will be extended to these defendants. If this is done, then justice will be accomplished without impairing either the letter or spirit of our statutes and without offering any encouragement for the disregard of law.

FOSTER, J. I am shocked that the Chief Justice, in an effort to escape the embarrassments of this tragic case, should have adopted, and should have proposed to his colleagues, an expedient at once so sordid and so obvious. I believe something more is on trial in this case than the fate of these unfortunate explorers; that is the law of our Commonwealth. If this Court declares that under our law these men have committed a crime, then our law is itself convicted in the tribunal of common sense, no matter what happens to the individuals involved in this petition of error. For us to assert that the law we uphold and expound compels us to a conclusion we are ashamed of, and from which we can only escape by appealing to a dispensation resting within the personal whim of the Executive, seems to me to amount to an admission that the law of this Commonwealth no longer pretends to incorporate justice.

For myself, I do not believe that our law compels the monstrous conclusion that these men are murderers. I believe, on the contrary, that it declares them to be innocent of any crime. I rest this conclusion on two independent grounds, either of which is of itself sufficient to justify the acquittal of these defendants.

The first of these grounds rests on a premise that may arouse opposition until it has been examined candidly. I take the view that the enacted or positive law of this Commonwealth, including all of its statutes and precedents, is inapplicable to this case, and that the case is governed instead by what ancient writers in Europe and America called "the law of nature."

This conclusion rests on the proposition that our positive law is predicated on the possibility of men's coexistence in society. When a situation arises in which the coexistence of men becomes impossible, then a condition that underlies all of our precedents and statutes has ceased to exist. When that condition disappears, then it is my opinion that the force of our positive law disappears with it. We are not accustomed to applying the maxim *cessante ratione legis, cessat et ipsa lex* to the whole of our enacted law, but I believe that this is a case where the maxim should be so applied.

The proposition that all positive law is based on the possibility of men's coexistence has a strange sound, not because the truth it contains is strange, but simply because it is a truth so obvious and pervasive that we seldom have occasion to give words to it. Like the air we breathe, it so pervades our environment that we forget that it exists until we are suddenly deprived of it. Whatever particular objects may be sought by the various branches of our law, it is apparent on reflection that all of them are directed toward facilitating and improving men's coexistence and regulating with fairness and equity the relations of their life in common. When the assumption that men may live together loses its truth, as it obviously did in this extraordinary situation where life only became possible by the taking of life, then the basic premises underlying our whole legal order have lost their meaning and force.

Had the tragic events of this case taken place a mile beyond the territorial limits of our Commonwealth, no one would pretend that our law was applicable to them. We recognize that jurisdiction rests on a territorial basis. The grounds of this principle are by no means obvious and are seldom examined. I take it that this principle is supported by an assumption that it is feasible to impose a single legal order upon a group of men only if they live together within the confines of a given area of the earth's surface. The premise that men shall coexist in a group underlies, then, the territorial principle, as it does all of law. Now I contend that a case may be removed morally from the force of a legal order, as well as geographically. If we look to the purposes of law and government, and to the premises underlying our positive law, these men when they made their fateful decision were as remote from our legal order as if they had been a thousand miles beyond our boundaries. Even in a physical sense, their underground prison was separated from our courts and writ-servers by a solid curtain of rock that could be removed only after the most extraordinary expenditures of time and effort.

I conclude, therefore, that at the time Roger Whetmore's life was ended by these defendants, they were, to use the quaint language of the nineteenth-century writers, not in a "state of civil society" but in a "state of nature." This has the consequence that the law applicable to them is not the enacted and established law of this Commonwealth, but the law derived from those principles that were appropriate to their condition. I have no hesitancy in saying that under those principles they were guiltless of any crime.

What these men did was done in pursuance of an agreement accepted by all of them and first proposed by Whetmore himself. Since it was apparent that their extraordinary predicament made inapplicable the usual principles that regulate men's relations with one another, it was necessary for them to draw, as it were, a new charter of government appropriate to the situation in which they found themselves.

It has from antiquity been recognized that the most basic principle of law or government is to be found in the notion of contract or agreement. Ancient thinkers, especially during the period from 1600 to 1900, used to base government itself on a supposed original social compact. Skeptics pointed out that this theory contradicted the known facts of history, and that there was no scientific evidence to support the notion that any government was ever founded in the manner supposed by the theory. Moralists replied that, if the compact was a fiction from a historical point of view, the notion of compact or agreement furnished the only ethical justification on which the powers of government, which include that of taking life, could be rested. The powers of government can only be justified morally on the ground that these are powers that reasonable men would agree upon and accept if they were faced with the necessity of constructing anew some order to make their life in common possible.

Fortunately, our Commonwealth is not bothered by the perplexities that beset the ancients. We know as a matter of historical truth that our government was founded upon a contract or free accord of men. The archaeological proof is conclusive that in the first period following the Great Spiral the survivors of that holocaust voluntarily came together and drew up a charter of government. Sophistical writers have raised questions as to the power of those remote contractors to bind future generations, but the fact remains that our government traces itself back in an unbroken line to that original charter.

If, therefore, our hangmen have the power to end men's lives, if our sheriffs have the power to put delinquent tenants in the street, if our police have the power to incarcerate the inebriated reveler, these powers find their moral justification in that original compact of our forefathers. If we can find no higher source for our legal order, what higher source should we expect these starving unfortunates to find for the order they adopted for themselves?

I believe that the line of argument I have just expounded permits of no rational answer. I realize that it will probably be received with a certain discomfort by many who read this opinion, who will be inclined to suspect that some hidden sophistry must underlie a demonstration that leads to so many unfamiliar conclusions. The source of this discomfort is, however, easy to identify. The usual conditions of human existence incline us to think of human life as an absolute value, not to be sacrificed under any circumstances. There is much that is fictitious about this conception even when it is applied to the ordinary relations of society. We have an illustration of this truth in the very case before us. Ten workmen were killed in the process of removing the rocks from the opening to the cave. Did not the engineers and government officials who directed the rescue effort know that the operations they were undertaking were dangerous and involved a serious risk to the lives of the workmen executing them? If it was proper that these ten lives should be sacrificed to save the lives of five imprisoned explorers, why then are we told it was wrong for these explorers to carry out an arrangement which would save four lives at the cost of one?

Every highway, every tunnel, every building we project involves a risk to human life. Taking these projects in the aggregate, we can calculate with some precision how many deaths the construction of them will require; statisticians can tell you the average cost in human lives of a thousand miles of a four-lane concrete highway. Yet we deliberately and knowingly incur and pay this cost on the assumption that the values obtained for those who survive outweigh the loss. If these things can be said of a society functioning above ground in a normal and ordinary manner, what shall we say of the supposed absolute value of a human life in the desperate situation in which these defendants and their companion Whetmore found themselves?

This concludes the exposition of the first ground of my decision. My second ground proceeds by rejecting hypothetically all the premises on which I have so far proceeded. I concede for purposes of argument that I am wrong in saying that the situation of these men removed them from the effect of our positive law, and I assume that the Consolidated Statutes have the power to penetrate five hundred feet of rock and to impose themselves upon these starving men huddled in their underground prison.

Now it is, of course, perfectly clear that these men did an act that violates the literal wording of the statute which declares that he who "shall willfully take the life of another" is a murderer. But one of the most ancient bits of legal wisdom is the saying that a man may break the letter of the law without breaking the law itself. Every proposition of positive law, whether contained in a statute or a judicial precedent, is to be interpreted reasonably, in the light of its evident purpose. This is a truth so elementary that it is hardly necessary to expatiate on it. Illustrations of its application are numberless and are to be found in every branch of the law. In *Commonwealth v. Staymore* the defendant was convicted under a statute making it a crime to leave one's car parked in certain areas for a period longer than two hours. The defendant had attempted to remove his car, but was prevented from doing so because the streets were obstructed by a political demonstration in which he took no part and which he had no reason to anticipate. His conviction was set aside by this Court, although his case fell squarely within the wording of the statute. Again, in *Fehler v. Neegas* there was before this Court for construction a statute in which the word "not" had plainly been transposed from its intended position in the final and most crucial section of the act. This transposition was contained in all the successive drafts of the act, where it was apparently overlooked by the draftsmen and sponsors of the legislation. No one was able to prove how the error came about, yet it was apparent that, taking account of the contents of the statute as a whole, an error had been made, since a literal reading of the final clause rendered it inconsistent with everything that had gone before and with the object of the enactment as stated in its preamble. This Court refused to accept a literal interpretation of the statute, and in effect rectified its language by reading the word "not" into the place where it was evidently intended to go.

The statute before us for interpretation has never been applied literally. Centuries ago it was established that a killing in self-defense is excused. There is nothing in the wording of the statute that suggests this exception. Various attempts have been made to reconcile the legal treatment of self-defense with the words of the statute, but in my opinion these are all merely ingenious sophistries. The truth is that the exception in favor of self-defense cannot be reconciled with the *words* of the statute, but only with its *purpose*.

The true reconciliation of the excuse of self-defense with the statute making it a crime to kill another is to be found in the following line of reasoning. One of the principal objects underlying any criminal legislation is that of deterring men from crime. Now it is apparent that if it were declared to be the law that a killing in self-defense is murder such a rule could not operate in a deterrent manner.

A man whose life is threatened will repel his aggressor, whatever the law may say. Looking therefore to the broad purposes of criminal legislation, we may safely declare that this statute was not intended to apply to cases of self-defense.

When the rationale of the excuse of self-defense is thus explained, it becomes apparent that precisely the same reasoning is applicable to the case at bar. If in the future any group of men ever find themselves in the tragic predicament of these defendants, we may be sure that their decision whether to live or die will not be controlled by the contents of our criminal code. Accordingly, if we read this statute intelligently it is apparent that it does not apply to this case. The withdrawal of this situation from the effect of the statute is justified by precisely the same considerations that were applied by our predecessors in office centuries ago to the case of self-defense.

There are those who raise the cry of judicial usurpation whenever a court, after analyzing the purpose of a statute, gives to its words a meaning that is not at once apparent to the casual reader who has not studied the statute closely or examined the objectives it seeks to attain. Let me say emphatically that I accept without reservation the proposition that this Court is bound by the statutes of our Commonwealth and that it exercises its powers in subservience to the duly expressed will of the Chamber of Representatives. The line of reasoning I have applied above raises no question of fidelity to enacted law, though it may possibly raise a question of the distinction between intelligent and unintelligent fidelity. No superior wants a servant who lacks the capacity to read between the lines. The stupidest housemaid knows that when she is told "to peel the soup and skim the potatoes" her mistress does not mean what she says. She also knows that when her master tells her to "drop everything and come running" he has overlooked the possibility that she is at the moment in the act of rescuing the baby from the rain barrel. Surely we have a right to expect the same modicum of intelligence from the judiciary. The correction of obvious legislative errors or oversights is not to supplant the legislative will, but to make that will effective.

I therefore conclude that on any aspect under which this case may be viewed these defendants are innocent of the crime of murdering Roger Whetmore, and that the conviction should be set aside.

TATTING, J. In the discharge of my duties as a justice of this Court, I am usually able to dissociate the emotional and intellectual sides of my reactions, and to decide the case before me entirely on the basis of the latter. In passing on this tragic case I find that my usual resources fail me. On the emotional side I find myself torn between sympathy for these men and a feeling of abhorrence and disgust at the monstrous act they committed. I had hoped that I would be able to put these contradictory emotions to one side as irrelevant, and to decide the case on the basis of a convincing and logical demonstration of the result demanded by our law. Unfortunately, this deliverance has not been vouchsafed for me.

As I analyze the opinion just rendered by my brother Foster, I find that it is shot through with contradictions and fallacies. Let us begin with his first proposition: these men were not subject to our law because they were not in a "state of civil society" but in a "state of nature." I am not clear why this is so, whether it is because of the thickness of the rock that imprisoned them, or because they were hungry, or because they had set up a "new charter of government" by which the usual rules of law were to be supplanted by a throw of the dice. Other difficulties intrude themselves. If these men passed from the jurisdiction of our law to that of "the law of nature," at what moment did this occur? Was it when the entrance to the cave was blocked, or when the threat of starvation reached a certain undefined degree of intensity, or when the agreement for the throwing of the dice was made? These uncertainties in the doctrine proposed by my brother are capable of producing real difficulties. Suppose, for example, one of these men had had his twenty-first birthday while he was imprisoned within the mountain. On what date would we have to consider that he had attained his majority—when he reached the age of twenty-one, at which time he was, by hypothesis, removed from the effects of our law, or only when he was released from the cave and became again subject to what my brother calls our "positive law"? These difficulties may seem fanciful, yet they only serve to reveal the fanciful nature of the doctrine that is capable of giving rise to them.

But it is not necessary to explore these niceties further to demonstrate the absurdity of my brother's position. Mr. Justice Foster and I are the appointed judges of a court of the Commonwealth of Newgarth, sworn and empowered to administer the laws of that Commonwealth. By what authority do we resolve ourselves into a Court of Nature? If these men were indeed under the law of nature, whence comes our authority to expound and apply that law. Certainly *we* are not in a state of nature.

Let us look at the contents of this code of nature that my brother proposes we adopt as our own and apply to this case. What a topsy-turvy and odious code it is! It is a code in which the law of contracts is more fundamental than the law of murder. It is a code under which a man may make a valid agreement empowering his fellows to eat his own body. Under the provisions of this code, furthermore, such an agreement once made is irrevocable, and if one of the parties attempts to withdraw, the others may take the law into their own hands and enforce the contract by violence—for though my brother passes over in convenient silence the effect of Whetmore's withdrawal, this is the necessary implication of his argument.

The principles my brother expounds contain other implications that cannot be tolerated. He argues that when the defendants set upon Whetmore and killed him (we know not how, perhaps by pounding him with stones) they were only exercising the rights conferred upon them by their bargain. Suppose, however, that Whetmore had had concealed upon his person a revolver, and that when he saw the defendants about to slaughter him he had shot them to death in order to save his own life. My brother's reasoning applied to these facts would make Whetmore out to be a murderer, since the excuse of self-defense would have to be denied to him. If his assailants were acting rightfully in seeking to bring about his death, then of course he could no more plead the excuse that he was defending his own life than could a condemned prisoner who struck down the executioner lawfully attempting to place the noose about his neck.

All of these considerations make it impossible for me to accept the first part of my brother's argument. I can neither accept his notion that these men were under a code of nature which this Court was bound to apply to them, nor can I accept the odious and perverted rules that he would read into that code. I come now to the second part of my brother's opinion, in which he seeks to show that the defendants did not violate the provisions of *N.C.S.A.* (N.S.) § 12-A. Here the way, instead of being clear, becomes for me misty and ambiguous, though my brother seems unaware of the difficulties that inhere in his demonstrations.

The gist of my brother's argument may be stated in the following terms: No statute, whatever its language, should be applied in a way that contradicts its purpose. One of the purposes of any criminal statute is to deter. The application of the statute making it a crime to kill another to the peculiar facts of this case would contradict this purpose, for it is impossible to believe that the contents of the criminal code could operate in a deterrent manner on men faced with the alternative of life or death. The reasoning by which this exception is read into the statute is, my brother observes, the same as that which is applied in order to provide the excuse of self-defense.

On the face of things this demonstration seems very convincing indeed. My brother's interpretation of the rationale of the excuse of self-defense is in fact supported by a decision of this court, *Commonwealth v. Parry,* a precedent I happened to encounter in my research on this case. Though *Commonwealth v. Parry* seems generally to have been overlooked in the texts and subsequent decisions, it supports unambiguously the interpretation my brother has put upon the excuse of self-defense.

Now let me outline briefly, however, the perplexities that assail me when I examine my brother's demonstration more closely. It is true that a statute should be applied in the light of its purpose and that *one* of the purposes of criminal legislation is recognized to be deterrence. The difficulty is that other purposes are also ascribed to the law of crimes. It has been said that one of its objects is to provide an orderly outlet for the instinctive human demand for retribution. *Commonwealth v. Scape.* It has also been said that its object is the rehabilitation of the wrongdoer. *Commonwealth v. Makeover.* Other theories have been propounded. Assuming that we must interpret a statute in the light of its purpose, what are we to do when it has many purposes or when its purposes are disputed?

A similar difficulty is presented by the fact that although there is authority for my brother's interpretation of the excuse of self-defense, there is other authority which assigns to that excuse a different rationale. Indeed, until I happened on *Commonwealth v. Parry* I had never heard of the explanation given by my brother. The taught doctrine of our law schools, memorized by generations of law students, runs in the following terms: The statute concerning murder requires a "willful" act. The man who acts to repel an aggressive threat to his own life does not act "willfully," but in response to an impulse deeply ingrained in human nature. I suspect that there is hardly a lawyer in this Commonwealth who is not familiar with this line of reasoning, especially since the point is a great favorite of the bar examiners.

Now the familiar explanation for the excuse of self-defense just expounded obviously cannot be applied by analogy to the facts of this case. These men acted not only "willfully" but with great deliberation and after hours of discussing what they should do. Again we encounter a forked path, with one line of reasoning leading us in one direction and another in a direction that is exactly the opposite. This perplexity is in this case compounded, as it were, for we have to set off one explanation, incorporated in a virtually unknown precedent of this Court, against another explanation, which forms a part of the taught legal tradition of our law schools, but which, so far as I know, has never been adopted in any judicial decision.

I recognize the relevance of the precedents cited by my brother concerning the displaced "not" and the defendant who parked overtime. But what are we to do with one of the landmarks of our jurisprudence, which again my brother passes over in silence? This is *Commonwealth v. Valjean.* Though the case is somewhat obscurely reported, it appears that the defendant was indicted for the larceny of a loaf of bread, and offered as a defense that he was in a condition approaching starvation. The court refused to accept this defense. If hunger cannot justify the theft of wholesome and natural food, how can it justify the killing and eating of a man? Again, if we look at the thing in terms of deterrence, is it likely that a man will starve to death to avoid a jail sentence for the theft of a loaf of bread? My brother's demonstrations would compel us to overrule *Commonwealth v. Valjean,* and many other precedents that have been built on that case.

Again, I have difficulty in saying that no deterrent effect whatever could be attributed to a decision that these men were guilty of murder. The stigma of the word "murderer" is such that it is quite likely, I believe, that if these men had known that their act was deemed by the law to be murder they would have waited for a few days at least before carrying out their plan. During that time some unexpected relief might have come. I realize that this observation only reduces the distinction to a matter of degree, and does not destroy it altogether. It is certainly true that the element of deterrence would be less in this case than is normally involved in the application of the criminal law.

There is still a further difficulty in my brother Foster's proposal to read an exception into the statute to favor this case, though again a difficulty not even intimated in his opinion. What shall be the scope of this exception? Here the men cast lots and the victim was himself originally a party to the agreement. What would we have to decide if Whetmore had refused from the beginning to participate in the plan? Would

a majority be permitted to overrule him? Or, suppose that no plan were adopted at all and the others simply conspired to bring about Whetmore's death, justifying their act by saying that he was in the weakest condition. Or again, that a plan of selection was followed but one based on a different justification than the one adopted here, as if the others were atheists and insisted that Whetmore should die because he was the only one who believed in an afterlife. These illustrations could be multiplied, but enough have been suggested to reveal what a quagmire of hidden difficulties my brother's reasoning contains.

Of course I realize on reflection that I may be concerning myself with a problem that will never arise, since it is unlikely that any group of men will ever again be brought to commit the dread act that was involved here. Yet, on still further reflection, even if we are certain that no similar case will arise again, do not the illustrations I have given show the lack of any coherent and rational principle in the rule my brother proposes? Should not the soundness of a principle be tested by the conclusions it entails, without reference to the accidents of later litigational history? Still, if this is so, why is it that we of this Court so often discuss the question whether we are likely to have later occasion to apply a principle urged for the solution of the case before us? Is this a situation where a line of reasoning not originally proper has become sanctioned by precedent, so that we are permitted to apply it and may even be under an obligation to do so?

The more I examine this case and think about it, the more deeply I become involved. My mind becomes entangled in the meshes of the very nets I throw out for my own rescue. I find that almost every consideration that bears on the decision of the case is counterbalanced by an opposing consideration leading in the opposite direction. My brother Foster has not furnished to me, nor can I discover for myself, any formula capable of resolving the equivocations that beset me on all sides.

I have given this case the best thought of which I am capable. I have scarcely slept since it was argued before us. When I feel myself inclined to accept the view of my brother Foster, I am repelled by a feeling that his arguments are intellectually unsound and approach mere rationalization. On the other hand, when I incline toward upholding the conviction, I am struck by the absurdity of directing that these men be put to death when their lives have been saved at the cost of the lives of ten heroic workmen. It is to me a matter of regret that the Prosecutor saw fit to ask for an indictment for murder. If we had a provision in our statutes making it a crime to eat human flesh, that would have been a more appropriate charge. If no other charge suited to the facts of this case could be brought against the defendants, it would have been wiser, I think, not to have indicted them at all. Unfortunately, however, the men have been indicted and tried, and we have therefore been drawn into this unfortunate affair.

Since I have been wholly unable to resolve the doubts that beset me about the law of this case, I am with regret announcing a step that is, I believe, unprecedented in the history of this tribunal. I declare my withdrawal from the decision of this case.

KEEN, J. I should like to begin by setting to one side two questions which are not before this Court.

The first of these is whether executive clemency should be extended to these defendants if the conviction is affirmed. Under our system of government, that is a question for the Chief Executive, not for us. I therefore disapprove of that passage in the opinion of the Chief Justice in which he in effect gives instructions to the Chief Executive as to what he should do in this case and suggests that some impropriety will attach if these instructions are not heeded. This is a confusion of governmental functions—a confusion of which the judiciary should be the last to be guilty. I wish to state that if I were the Chief Executive I would go farther in the direction of clemency than the pleas addressed to him propose. I would pardon these men altogether, since I believe that they have already suffered enough to pay for any offense they may have committed. I want it to be understood that this remark is made in my capacity as a private citizen who by the accident of his office happens to have acquired an intimate acquaintance with the facts of this case. In the discharge of my duties as judge, it is neither my function to address directions to the Chief Executive, nor to take into account what he may or may not do, in reaching my own decision, which must be controlled entirely by the law of this Commonwealth.

The second question that I wish to put to one side is that of deciding whether what these men did was "right" or "wrong," "wicked" or "good." That is also a question that is irrelevant to the discharge of my office as a judge sworn to apply, not my conceptions of morality, but the law of the land. In putting this question to one side I think I can also safely dismiss without comment the first and more poetic portion of my brother Foster's opinion. The element of

fantasy contained in the arguments developed there has been sufficiently revealed in my brother Tatting's somewhat solemn attempt to take those arguments seriously.

The sole question before us for decision is whether these defendants did, within the meaning of *N.C.S.A.* (N.S.) § 12-A, willfully take the life of Roger Whetmore. The exact language of the statute is as follows: "Whoever shall willfully take the life of another shall be punished by death." Now I should suppose that any candid observer, content to extract from these words their natural meaning, would concede at once that these defendants did "willfully take the life" of Roger Whetmore.

Whence arise all the difficulties of the case, then, and the necessity for so many pages of discussion about what ought to be so obvious? The difficulties, in whatever tortured form they may present themselves, all trace back to a single source, and that is a failure to distinguish the legal from the moral aspects of this case. To put it bluntly, my brothers do not like the fact that the written law requires the conviction of these defendants. Neither do I, but unlike my brothers I respect the obligations of an office that requires me to put my personal predilections out of my mind when I come to interpret and apply the law of this Commonwealth.

Now, of course, my brother Foster does not admit that he is actuated by a personal dislike of the written law. Instead he develops a familiar line of argument according to which the court may disregard the express language of a statute when something not contained in the statute itself, called its "purpose," can be employed to justify the result the court considers proper. Because this is an old issue between myself and my colleague, I should like, before discussing his particular application of the argument to the facts of this case, to say something about the historical background of this issue and its implications for law and government generally.

There was a time in this Commonwealth when judges did in fact legislate very freely, and all of us know that during that period some of our statutes were rather thoroughly made over by the judiciary. That was a time when the accepted principles of political science did not designate with any certainty the rank and function of the various arms of the state. We all know the tragic issue of that uncertainty in the brief civil war that arose out of the conflict between the judiciary, on the one hand, and the executive and the legislature, on the other. There is no need to recount here the factors that contributed to that unseemly struggle for power, though they included the unrepresentative character of the Chamber, resulting from a division of the country into election districts that no longer accorded with the actual distribution of the population, and the forceful personality and wide popular following of the then Chief Justice. It is enough to observe that those days are behind us, and that in place of the uncertainty that then reigned we now have a clear-cut principle, which is the supremacy of the legislative branch of our government. From that principle flows the obligation of the judiciary to enforce faithfully the written law, and to interpret that law in accordance with its plain meaning without reference to our personal desires or our individual conceptions of justice. I am not concerned with the question whether the principle that forbids the judicial revision of statutes is right or wrong, desirable or undesirable; I observe merely that this principle has become a tacit premise underlying the whole of the legal and governmental order I am sworn to administer.

Yet though the principle of the supremacy of the legislature has been accepted in theory for centuries, such is the tenacity of professional tradition and the force of fixed habits of thought that many of the judiciary have still not accommodated themselves to the restricted role which the new order imposes on them. My brother Foster is one of that group; his way of dealing with statutes is exactly that of a judge living in the 3900's.

We are all familiar with the process by which the judicial reform of disfavored legislative enactments is accomplished. Anyone who has followed the written opinions of Mr. Justice Foster will have had an opportunity to see it at work in every branch of the law. I am personally so familiar with the process that in the event of my brother's incapacity I am sure I could write a satisfactory opinion for him without any prompting whatever, beyond being informed whether he liked the effect of the terms of the statute as applied to the case before him.

The process of judicial reform requires three steps. The first of these is to divine some single "purpose" which the statute serves. This is done although not one statute in a hundred has any such single purpose, and although the objectives of nearly every statute are differently interpreted by the different classes of its sponsors. The second step is to discover that a mythical being called "the legislator," in the pursuit of this imagined "purpose,"

overlooked something or left some gap or imperfection in his work. Then comes the final and most refreshing part of the task, which is, of course, to fill in the blank thus created. . . .

My brother Foster's penchant for finding holes in statutes reminds one of the story told by an ancient author about the man who ate a pair of shoes. Asked how he liked them, he replied that the part he liked best was the holes. That is the way my brother feels about statutes; the more holes they have in them the better he likes them. In short, he doesn't like statutes.

One could not wish for a better case to illustrate the specious nature of this gap-filling process than the one before us. My brother thinks he knows exactly what was sought when men made murder a crime, and that was something he calls "deterrence." My brother Tatting has already shown how much is passed over in that interpretation. But I think the trouble goes deeper. I doubt very much whether our statute making murder a crime really has a "purpose" in any ordinary sense of the term. Primarily, such a statute reflects a deeply-felt human conviction that murder is wrong and that something should be done to the man who commits it. If we were forced to be more articulate about the matter, we would probably take refuge in the more sophisticated theories of the criminologists, which, of course, were certainly not in the minds of those who drafted our statute. We might also observe that men will do their own work more effectively and live happier lives if they are protected against the threat of violent assault. Bearing in mind that the victims of murders are often unpleasant people, we might add some suggestion that the matter of disposing of undesirables is not a function suited to private enterprise, but should be a state monopoly. All of which reminds me of the attorney who once argued before us that a statute licensing physicians was a good thing because it would lead to lower life insurance rates by lifting the level of general health. There is such a thing as overexplaining the obvious.

If we do not know the purpose of § 12-A, how can we possibly say there is a "gap" in it? How can we know what its draftsmen thought about the question of killing men in order to eat them? My brother Tatting has revealed an understandable, though perhaps slightly exaggerated revulsion to cannibalism. How do we know that his remote ancestors did not feel the same revulsion to an even higher degree? Anthropologists say that the dread felt for a forbidden act may be increased by the fact that the conditions of a tribe's life create special temptations toward it, as incest is most severely condemned among those whose village relations make it most likely to occur. Certainly the period following the Great Spiral was one that had implicit in it temptations to anthropophagy. Perhaps it was for that very reason that our ancestors expressed their prohibition in so broad and unqualified a form. All of this is conjecture, of course, but it remains abundantly clear that neither I nor my brother Foster knows what the "purpose" of § 12-A is.

Considerations similar to those I have just outlined are also applicable to the exception in favor of self-defense, which plays so large a role in the reasoning of my brothers Foster and Tatting. It is of course true that in *Commonwealth v. Parry* an obiter dictum justified this exception on the assumption that the purpose of criminal legislation is to deter. It may well also be true that generations of law students have been taught that the true explanation of the exception lies in the fact that a man who acts in self-defense does not act "willfully," and that the same students have passed their bar examinations by repeating what their professors told them. These last observations I could dismiss, of course, as irrelevant for the simple reason that professors and bar examiners have not as yet any commission to make our laws for us. But again the real trouble lies deeper. As in dealing with the statute, so in dealing with the exception, the question is not the conjectural *purpose* of the rule, but its *scope*. Now the scope of the exception in favor of self-defense as it has been applied by this Court is plain: it applies to cases of resisting an aggressive threat to the party's own life. It is therefore too clear for argument that this case does not fall within the scope of the exception, since it is plain that Whetmore made no threat against the lives of these defendants.

The essential shabbiness of my brother Foster's attempt to cloak his remaking of the written law with an air of legitimacy comes tragically to the surface in my brother Tatting's opinion. In that opinion Justice Tatting struggles manfully to combine his colleague's loose moralisms with his own sense of fidelity to the written law. The issue of this struggle could only be that which occurred, a complete default in the discharge of the judicial function. You simply cannot apply a statute as it is written and remake it to meet your own wishes at the same time.

Now I know that the line of reasoning I have developed in this opinion will not be acceptable to those who look only to the immediate effects of a decision and ignore the long-run implications of an assumption by the judiciary of a power of dispensation. A hard decision is never a popular decision. Judges have been celebrated in literature for their sly prowess in devising some quibble by which a litigant could be deprived of his rights where the public thought it was wrong for him to assert those rights. But I believe that judicial dispensation does more harm in the long run than hard decisions. Hard cases may even have a certain moral value by bringing home to the people their own responsibilities toward the law that is ultimately their creation, and by reminding them that there is no principle of personal grace that can relieve the mistakes of their representatives.

Indeed, I will go farther and say that not only are the principles I have been expounding those *which are soundest for our present conditions,* but that we would have inherited a better legal system from our forefathers if those principles had been observed from the beginning. For example, with respect to the excuse of self-defense, if our courts had stood steadfast on the language of the statute the result would undoubtedly have been a legislative revision of it. Such a revision would have drawn on the assistance of natural philosophers and psychologists, and the resulting regulation of the matter would have had an understandable and rational basis, instead of the hodgepodge of verbalisms and metaphysical distinctions that have emerged from the judicial and professorial treatment.

These concluding remarks are, of course, beyond any duties that I have to discharge with relation to this case, but I include them here because I feel deeply that my colleagues are insufficiently aware of the dangers implicit in the conceptions of the judicial office advocated by my brother Foster.

I conclude that the conviction should be affirmed.

HANDY, J. I have listened with amazement to the tortured ratiocinations to which this simple case has given rise. I never cease to wonder at my colleagues' ability to throw an obscuring curtain of legalisms about every issue presented to them for decision. We have heard this afternoon learned disquisitions on the distinction between positive law and the law of nature, the language of the statute and the purpose of the statute, judicial functions and executive functions, judicial legislation and legislative legislation. My only disappointment was that someone did not raise the question of the legal nature of the bargain struck in the cave—whether it was unilateral or bilateral, and whether Whetmore could not be considered as having revoked an offer prior to action taken thereunder.

What have all these things to do with the case? The problem before us is what we, as officers of the government, ought to do with these defendants. That is a question of practical wisdom, to be exercised in a context, not of abstract theory, but of human realities. When the case is approached in this light, it becomes, I think, one of the easiest to decide that has ever been argued before this Court.

Before stating my own conclusions about the merits of the case, I should like to discuss briefly some of the more fundamental issues involved—issues on which my colleagues and I have been divided ever since I have been on the bench.

I have never been able to make my brothers see that government is a human affair, and that men are ruled, not by words on paper or by abstract theories, but by other men. They are ruled well when their rules understand the feelings and conceptions of the masses. They are ruled badly when that understanding is lacking.

Of all branches of the government, the judiciary is the most likely to lose its contact with the common man. The reasons for this are, of course, fairly obvious. Where the masses react to a situation in terms of a few salient features, we pick into little pieces every situation presented to us. Lawyers are hired by both sides to analyze and dissect. Judges and attorneys vie with one another to see who can discover the greatest number of difficulties and distinctions in a single set of facts. Each side tries to find cases, real or imagined, that will embarrass the demonstrations of the other side. To escape this embarrassment, still further distinctions are invented and imported into the situation. When a set of facts has been subjected to this kind of treatment for a sufficient time, all the life and juice have gone out of it and we have left a handful of dust.

Now I realize that wherever you have rules and abstract principles lawyers are going to be able to make distinctions. To some extent the sort of thing I have been describing is a necessary evil attaching to any formal regulation of human affairs. But I think that the area which really stands in need of such regulation is greatly overestimated. There are, of course, a few fundamental rules of the game that must be accepted if the game is to go on at all. I would include among these the rules relating to the conduct of elections, the appointment of public officials, and the term during which an office is held. Here some re-

straint on discretion and dispensation, some adherence to form, some scruple for what does and what does not fall within the rule, is, I concede, essential. Perhaps the area of basic principle should be expanded to include certain other rules, such as those designed to preserve the free civilmoign system.

But outside of these fields I believe that all government officials, including judges, will do their jobs best if they treat forms and abstract concepts as instruments. We should take as our model, I think, the good administrator, who accommodates procedures and principles to the case at hand, selecting from among the available forms those most suited to reach the proper result.

The most obvious advantage of this method of government is that it permits us to go about our daily tasks with efficiency and common sense. My adherence to this philosophy has, however, deeper roots. I believe that it is only with the insight this philosophy gives that we can preserve the flexibility essential if we are to keep our actions in reasonable accord with the sentiments of those subject to our rule. More governments have been wrecked, and more human misery caused, by the lack of this accord between ruler and ruled than by any other factor that can be discerned in history. Once we drive a sufficient wedge between the mass of people and those who direct their legal, political, and economic life, our society is ruined. Then neither Foster's law of nature nor Keen's fidelity to written law will avail us anything.

Now when these conceptions are applied to the case before us, its decision becomes, as I have said, perfectly easy. In order to demonstrate this I shall have to introduce certain realities that my brothers in their coy decorum have seen fit to pass over in silence, although they are just as acutely aware of them as I am.

The first of these is that this case has aroused an enormous public interest, both here and abroad. Almost every newspaper and magazine has carried articles about it; columnists have shared with their readers confidential information as to the next governmental move; hundreds of letters-to-the-editor have been printed. One of the great newspaper chains made a poll of public opinion on the question, "What do you think the Supreme Court should do with the Speluncean explorers?" About ninety percent expressed a belief that the defendants should be pardoned or let off with a kind of token punishment. It is perfectly clear, then, how the public feels about the case. We could have known this without the poll, of course, on the basis of common sense, or even by observing that on this Court there are apparently four-and-a-half men, or ninety percent, who share the common opinion.

This makes it obvious, not only what we should do, but what we must do if we are to preserve between ourselves and public opinion a reasonable and decent accord. Declaring these men innocent need not involve us in any undignified quibble or trick. No principle of statutory construction is required that is not consistent with the past practices of this Court. Certainly no layman would think that in letting these men off we had stretched the statute any more than our ancestors did when they created the excuse of self-defense. If a more detailed demonstration of the method of reconciling our decision with the statute is required, I should be content to rest on the arguments developed in the second and less visionary part of my brother Foster's opinion.

Now I know that my brothers will be horrified by my suggestion that this Court should take account of public opinion. They will tell you that public opinion is emotional and capricious, that it is based on half-truths and listens to witnesses who are not subject to cross-examination. They will tell you that the law surrounds the trial of a case like this with elaborate safeguards, designed to insure that the truth will be known and that every rational consideration bearing on the issues of the case has been taken into account. They will warn you that all of these safeguards go for naught if a mass opinion formed outside this framework is allowed to have any influence on our decision.

But let us look candidly at some of the realities of the administration of our criminal law. When a man is accused of crime, there are, speaking generally, four ways in which he may escape punishment. One of these is a determination by a judge that under the applicable law he has committed no crime. This is, of course, a determination that takes place in a rather formal and abstract atmosphere. But look at the other three ways in which he may escape punishment. These are: (1) a decision by the Prosecutor not to ask for an indictment; (2) an acquittal by the jury; (3) a pardon or commutation of sentence by the executive. Can anyone pretend that these decisions are held within a rigid and formal framework of rules that prevents factual error, excludes emotional and personal factors, and guarantees that all the forms of the law will be observed?

In the case of the jury we do, to be sure, attempt to cabin their deliberations within the area of the legally relevant, but there is no need to deceive ourselves into believing that this attempt is really successful. In the normal course of events the case now before us would have gone on all of its issues directly to the jury. Had this occurred we can be confident that there would have been an acquittal or at least a division that would have prevented a conviction. If the jury had been instructed that the men's hunger and their agreement were no defense to the charge of murder, their verdict would in all likelihood have ignored this instruction and would have involved a good deal more twisting of the letter of the law than any that is likely to tempt us. Of course the only reason that didn't occur in this case was the fortuitous circumstance that the foreman of the jury happened to be a lawyer. His learning enabled him to devise a form of words that would allow the jury to dodge its usual responsibilities.

My brother Tatting expresses annoyance that the Prosecutor did not, in effect, decide the case for him by not asking for an indictment. Strict as he is himself in complying with the demands of legal theory, he is quite content to have the fate of these men decided out of court by the Prosecutor on the basis of common sense. The Chief Justice, on the other hand, wants the application of common sense postponed to the very end, though like Tatting, he wants no personal part in it.

This brings me to the concluding portion of my remarks, which has to do with executive clemency. Before discussing that topic directly, I want to make a related observation about the poll of public opinion. As I have said, ninety percent of the people wanted the Supreme Court to let the men off entirely or with a more or less nominal punishment. The ten percent constituted a very oddly assorted group, with the most curious and divergent opinions. One of our university experts has made a study of this group and has found that its members fall into certain patterns. A substantial portion of them are subscribers to "crank" newspapers of limited circulation that gave their readers a distorted version of the facts of the case. Some thought that "Speluncean" means "cannibal" and that anthropophagy is a tenet of the Society. But the point I want to make, however, is this: although almost every conceivable variety and shade of opinion was represented in this group, there was, so far as I know, not one of them, nor a single member of the majority of ninety percent, who said, "I think it would be a fine thing to have the courts sentence these men to be hanged, and then to have another branch of the government come along and pardon them." Yet this is a solution that has more or less dominated our discussions and which our Chief Justice proposes as a way by which we can avoid doing an injustice and at the same time preserve respect for law. He can be assured that if he is preserving anybody's morale, it is his own, and not the public's, which knows nothing of his distinctions. I mention this matter because I wish to emphasize once more the danger that we may get lost in the patterns of our own thought and forget that these patterns often cast not the slightest shadow on the outside world.

I come now to the most crucial fact in this case, a fact known to all of us on this Court, though one that my brothers have seen fit to keep under the cover of their judicial robes. This is the frightening likelihood that if the issue is left to him, the Chief Executive will refuse to pardon these men or commute their sentence. As we all know, our Chief Executive is a man now well advanced in years, of very stiff notions. Public clamor usually operates on him with the reverse of the effect intended. As I have told my brothers, it happens that my wife's niece is an intimate friend of his secretary. I have learned in this indirect, but, I think, wholly reliable way, that he is firmly determined not to commute the sentence if these men are found to have violated the law.

No one regrets more than I the necessity for relying in so important a matter on information that could be characterized as gossip. If I had my way this would not happen, for I would adopt the sensible course of sitting down with the Executive, going over the case with him, finding out what his views are, and perhaps working out with him a common program for handling the situation. But of course my brothers would never hear of such a thing.

Their scruple about acquiring accurate information directly does not prevent them from being very perturbed about what they have learned indirectly. Their acquaintance with the facts I have just related explains why the Chief Justice, ordinarily a model of decorum, saw fit in his opinion to flap his judicial robes in the face of the Executive and threaten him with excommunication if he failed to commute the sentence. It explains, I suspect, my brother Foster's feat of levitation by which a whole library of law books was lifted from the shoulders of these defendants. It explains also why even my legalistic brother Keen emulated Pooh-Bah in the ancient comedy by stepping to the other side of the stage to address a few remarks to the Executive "in my capacity as a private citizen." (I may remark, incidentally, that the advice of Private Citizen Keen will appear in the reports of this court printed at taxpayer's expense.)

I must confess that as I grow older I become more and more perplexed at men's refusal to apply their common sense to problems of law and government, and this truly tragic case has deepened my sense of discouragement and dismay. I only wish that I could convince my brothers of the wisdom of the principles I have applied to the judicial office since I first assumed it. As a matter of fact, by a kind of sad rounding of the circle, I encountered issues like those involved here in the very first case I tried as Judge of the Court of General Instances in Fanleigh County.

A religious sect had unfrocked a minister who, they said, had gone over to the views and practices of a rival sect. The minister circulated a handbill making charges against the authorities who had expelled him. Certain lay members of the church announced a public meeting at which they proposed to explain the position of the church. The minister attended this meeting. Some said he slipped in unobserved in a disguise; his own testimony was that he had walked in openly as a member of the public. At any rate, when the speeches began he interrupted with certain questions about the affairs of the church and made some statements in defense of his own views. He was set upon by members of the audience and given a pretty thorough pommeling, receiving among other injuries a broken jaw. He brought a suit for damages against the association that sponsored the meeting and against ten named individuals who he alleged were his assailants.

When we came to the trial, the case at first seemed very complicated to me. The attorneys raised a host of legal issues. There were nice questions on the admissibility of evidence, and, in connection with the suit against the association, some difficult problems turning on the question whether the minister was a trespasser or a licensee. As a novice on the bench I was eager to apply my law school learning and I began studying these questions closely, reading all the authorities and preparing well-documented rulings. As I studied the case I became more and more involved in its legal intricacies and I began to get into a state approaching that of my brother Tatting in this case. Suddenly, however, it dawned on me that all these perplexing issues really had nothing to do with the case, and I began examining it in the light of common sense. The case at once gained a new perspective, and I saw that the only thing for me to do was to direct a verdict for the defendants for lack of evidence.

I was led to this conclusion by the following considerations. The melee in which the plaintiff was injured had been a very confused affair, with some people trying to get to the center of the disturbance, while others were trying to get away from it; some striking at the plaintiff, while others were apparently trying to protect him. It would have taken weeks to find out the truth of the matter. I decided that nobody's broken jaw was worth that much to the Commonwealth. (The minister's injuries, incidentally, had meanwhile healed without disfigurement and without any impairment of normal faculties.) Furthermore, I felt very strongly that the plaintiff had to a large extent brought the thing on himself. He knew how inflamed passions were about the affair, and could easily have found another forum for the expression of his views. My decision was widely approved by the press and public opinion, neither of which could tolerate the views and practices that the expelled minister was attempting to defend.

Now, thirty years later, thanks to an ambitious Prosecutor and a legalistic jury foreman, I am faced with a case that raises issues which are at bottom much like those involved in that case. The world does not seem to change much, except that this time it is not a question of a judgment for five or six hundred frelars, but of the life or death of four men who have already suffered more torment and humiliation than most of us would endure in a thousand years. I conclude that the defendants are innocent of the crime charged, and that the conviction and sentence should be set aside.

TATTING, J. I have been asked by the Chief Justice whether, after listening to the two opinions just rendered, I desire to re-examine the position previously taken by me. I wish to state that after hearing these opinions I am greatly strengthened in my conviction that I ought not to participate in the decision of this case.

The Supreme Court being evenly divided, the conviction and sentence of the Court of General Instances is *affirmed*. It is ordered that the execution of the sentence shall occur at 6 A.M., Friday, April 2, 4300, at which time the Public Executioner is directed to proceed with all convenient dispatch to hang each of the defendants by the neck until he is dead.

Postscript

Now that the court has spoken, the reader puzzled by the choice of date may wish to be reminded that the centuries which separate us from the year 4300 are roughly equal to those that have passed since the Age of Pericles. There is probably no need to observe that the *Speluncean Case* itself is intended neither as a work of satire nor as a prediction in any ordinary sense of the term. As for the judges who make up Chief Justice Truepenny's court, they are, of course, as mythical as the facts and precedents with which they deal. The reader who refuses to accept this view, and who seeks to trace out contemporary resemblances where none is intended or contemplated, should be warned that he is engaged in a frolic of his own, which may possibly lead him to miss whatever modest truths are contained in the opinions delivered by the Supreme Court of Newgarth. The case was constructed for the sole purpose of bringing into a common focus certain divergent philosophies of law and government. These philosophies presented men with live questions of choice in the days of Plato and Aristotle. Perhaps they will continue to do so when our era has had its say about them. If there is any element of prediction in the case, it does not go beyond a suggestion that the questions involved are among the permanent problems of the human race.

THE CASE OF LADY ELDON'S FRENCH LACE
A Hypothetical Decision on a
Hypothetical State of Facts[*]

Sanford H. Kadish and Stephen J. Schulhofer

A perennial in the crop of attempt hypotheticals was suggested by Dr. Wharton.[1] "Lady Eldon, when traveling with her husband on the Continent, bought what she supposed to be a quantity of French lace, which she hid, concealing it from Lord Eldon in one of the pockets of the coach. The package was brought to light by a customs officer at Dover. The lace turned out to be an English manufactured article, of little value, and of course, not subject to duty. Lady Eldon had bought it at a price vastly above its value, believing it to be genuine, intending to smuggle it into England." Dr. Wharton, supra, and Professor Sayre[2] conclude that she could be found guilty of an attempt since she intended to smuggle dutiable lace into England. Professor Keedy disagrees, finding the fallacy of the argument in the failure to recognize "that the particular lace which Lady Eldon intended to bring into England was not subject to duty and therefore, although there was the wish to smuggle, there was not the intent to do so."[3]

Keedy was employing the distinction he has advanced between intent, on the one hand, and motive, desire, and expectation, on the other,[4] a distinction that served as the linchpin of the decision in *People v. Jaffe* . . . and *United States v. Berrigan.* . . . As he sees it, what people intend to do on a particular occasion is to be determined by what they do in fact, rather than by what they thought they were doing. The lace was in fact not dutiable; thus, there was no intent on the part of Lady Eldon to smuggle dutiable French lace into the country, and there could be no conviction of the crime of attempt to do so, since what she intended to do on this view was

not a crime—a straightforward case of legal impossibility. Professor Perkins has not, so far as we can tell, addressed himself to this particular case. But from what he has written it is clear that he would concur with Keedy. Presumably his analysis would rest on his distinction between primary and secondary intent.[5] Only the former may be considered in determining the existence of the necessary intent to establish an attempt. It, like Keedy's term *intent,* is determined by what the actor objectively and in fact did. What the actor believed he was doing, on the level of the facts as the actor took them to be, constitutes secondary intent. Apparently the latter is basically the same in description and function as what Keedy refers to as the motive, desire, or expectation.

We concur with Wharton and Sayre.

We submit, with respect, that Keedy and Perkins, and the courts that follow their reasoning, have been guilty of some plain silliness in supporting their position. Their conclusion that Lady Eldon must be acquitted rests on the premise that what a person intends to do is what he actually does, even if that was the furthest thing from the person's mind:

"You're eating my salad."

"Sorry, I didn't mean to; I thought it was mine."

"You might have *thought* it was yours. But in fact it was mine. Therefore you intended to eat mine. You should be ashamed!"

Surely this is an extraordinary way of regarding what a person intended, quite at odds with common sense and common language. Where a circumstance

---

[*]From Sanford H. Kadish and Stephen J. Schulhofer, "The Case of Lady Eldon's French Lace," in *Criminal Law and Its Processes,* by Sanford Kadish and Stephen Schulhofer, (Boston: Little, Brown and Co., 1989), pp. 669–75. Reprinted by permission of Little, Brown and Company.

is not known to the actor, there is no way consistent with straight thought that his act can be regarded as intentional as to that circumstance.

But, of course, it is hardly unknown for courts to adopt strained and artificial reasoning in support of a sound result otherwise thought beyond their reach. Is that the case here? Is it sound to conclude that the type of conduct engaged in by Lady Eldon should not be made criminal? Let us consider if it is.

Suppose Lady Eldon believed she had purchased an inexpensive English lace but in fact had purchased an expensive French lace. Certainly she could not be found guilty of smuggling if she got past the customs inspector or of an attempt if she failed. The reason is that the intent to smuggle French lace, necessary to establish either offense, does not exist. (We are assuming this is not a crime of absolute liability.) And it does not exist because her intent is judged by what she believed she was doing and not by what she in fact did. Now why should it make any more difference in Wharton's hypothetical that her act was objectively lawful than it does in our variation that her act was objectively unlawful? Why in both cases should not the intent be judged by the same standard, what she believed she was doing, rather than what she did in fact?

It may be answered that while an innocent mind can exculpate, a criminal mind simpliciter cannot implicate. The reasoning might be as follows: There is no legitimate purpose to be served by punishing those who mean to act blamelessly; and while a purpose could be served by punishing a person who decides to commit a crime (to the extent that all must first decide to commit an intentional crime before actually committing it, some will thereby be prevented from committing it, at this or another occasion) other considerations make it inexpedient and undesirable to do so. What are those considerations? They are those, presumably, which underlie the principle which forbids punishing a man for his thoughts alone; i.e., that thinking evil is not a reliable indication that a man will do evil and the criminal law may properly concern itself only with acts. . . .

But can this be said of Lady Eldon? Has she merely *thought* to smuggle French lace? Or rather has she *done* everything in her power and all she thought necessary to smuggle French lace? Has she shown herself to be less eligible for the imposition of criminal sanctions because, through no fault of her own, she failed? Surely not.

From the basic postulate that the law concerns itself with acts and not thoughts, it may be argued that the law is concerned not with what a person *may* do but with what he in fact *does*. This, however, is quite erroneous. There are many crimes that may be established without proof that acts have occurred that have invaded the interest sought to be protected. The law of attempts and conspiracy are prime examples. It is what is apprehended that the actor would subsequently do and not what he has done that constitutes the basis of criminality. As Holmes has pointed out, even larceny may be viewed in this way, since there is no requirement that the possessor be permanently deprived of his property, only that the actor intend to deprive him of it.[6] Looked at objectively, apart from intent, the acts done may be wholly innocuous—like striking a match or having a quiet conversation. The innocuous acts are made criminal because, combined with the requisite intent of the actor, they demonstrate him to be sufficiently likely to commit the injury that the law seeks to prevent, to justify the application of criminal sanctions.

Perhaps it may be argued that there is a different policy consideration supporting exculpation in cases like Lady Eldon's—namely, that in real cases, as opposed to hypotheticals, intention must be proved rather than supposed, and it is too dangerous to the innocent to permit juries to speculate on a defendant's intent in the absence of actions that strongly evidence that intent. One may fully agree with this, however, without concluding that Lady Eldon should be acquitted. Of course it would be evidentiary of Lady Eldon's intent to smuggle if she had been found with dutiable French lace at the border. (But only evidentiary—after all, she might have thought it was English lace, or it might have been put with her things by her maid without her knowledge.) But why should it be held, as it was in *United States v. Oviedo* . . . that, since the lace was nondutiable in fact, a finding of intent will necessarily be suspect, regardless of the strength of the evidence? Is it not perfectly possible that a reasonable jury could find this intent beyond a reasonable doubt even if the lace was nondutiable? Suppose, for example, that the lace were carefully secreted in a specially tailored, concealed pocket of the coach; that the coachman testified to incriminating statements Lady Eldon made to Lord Eldon; that a letter from her to her sister, which described her newly bought "French lace" in exquisite and appreciative detail, had been introduced; that her receipt showed she paid a price appropriate for French lace rather than for the vastly less expensive English lace. There would seem little danger to the innocent in allowing a jury to find an attempt to smuggle French lace on these facts. Indeed, in cases like *Jaffe* and *Berrigan,* "attempt" is charged only because of the involvement of an undercover agent, whose participation prevents completion of the intended crime. Whatever else one may say about such investigatory tactics, they do not necessarily render suspect the evidence of the defendant's intent; indeed, in practice, they usually render that evidence far *less* speculative than it otherwise would be. The proper remedy for speculative and unreliable jury findings of intent is a court alert to preclude such findings in particular cases where the evidence is insufficient.

In the end, then, the arguments in favor of Lady Eldon (and those which have been used to reverse conviction in cases like *Jaffe, Oviedo,* and *Berrigan*) are founded on unpersuasive policy considerations rationalized by a peculiar and Pickwickian interpretation of what it means to intend to do an act, one that is utterly at odds both with the common usage of our language and its usage elsewhere in the criminal law.[7] *We conclude that the innocuous character of the action actually done (innocuous in the sense that it could not constitute a crime under the actual circumstances) will not save her from an attempt conviction if she believed that the circumstances were otherwise, and, had her belief been correct, what she set out to do would constitute a crime.* This is the principle that has found favor in virtually every serious statutory effort to deal with the problem, and in numerous decisions reached without benefit of a specific statute to tell the court that a person intends to do what he thinks he intends to do.

We must say a few words more about the final qualification to the principle just asserted; namely, that "had her belief (in the circumstances) been correct, what she set out to do would constitute a crime." The point can best be made by altering the hypothetical. Suppose the lace that Lady Eldon had purchased was in fact the expensive French lace she meant to buy. The customs officer at Dover brings it to light. He then says to Lady Eldon: "Lucky for you you returned to England today rather than yesterday. I just received word this morning that the government has removed French lace from the duty list." Could Lady Eldon be held for attempt to smuggle in these circumstances?[8] Certainly what she did and what she intended to do were not different simply because she acted one day later, when French lace was removed from the duty list. But there is this important difference: that at the time she acted, *what* she intended to do (always judged, of course, from her own perspective) was not a violation of the criminal law, even though she

thought it was. Of course, in doing what she did she showed that she was a person who would break a law. But what law? The law against smuggling French lace? There no longer was such a law. The criminal laws generally? Fortunately our law has not gone so far in accepting that *any* possibility for social protection is sufficient to justify criminal punishment. A mere disposition to engage in conduct thought to be criminal is much too speculative a basis for inferring that the actor will engage in some other kind of conduct that *is* illegal. At least for purposes of criminal liability (as opposed to sentencing) we are not prepared to generalize proclivities beyond the proclivity to commit the specific crime charged.[9] And, as Professor Williams has pointed out, "if the legislature has not seen fit to prohibit the consummated act, a mere approach to consummation should a fortiori be guiltless. Any other view would offend against the principle of legality; in effect the law of attempt would be used to manufacture a new crime, when the legislature has left the situation outside the ambit of the law." Glanville Williams, *Criminal Law: The General Part* 633–34 (2d ed. 1961). Had the criminal law been changed as supposed in our variation of the Lady Eldon hypothetical, therefore, it would be just as wrong to convict her as to convict an abortionist of attempted abortion where the abortion was committed, unknown to the defendant, after the abortion law was repealed or held invalid. These are the true cases of legal impossibility.

But, it should be noted, these situations are totally different from cases like *Jaffe* and *Berrigan,* even though the courts in each case made it seem otherwise, by asserting that what the defendants intended to do could not have constituted a crime. What the abortionist intended to do (and did) could not constitute a crime because there was no such crime. What Jaffe and Berrigan intended to do (and thought they did) was indeed a crime. It is only through a perverse use of intent that we can say that Jaffe intended to receive honestly obtained property or that Berrigan intended to send out a letter the warden knew about, and that therefore they intended to do what was no crime at all.

Lady Eldon, in the actual hypothetical, in contrast to the hypothetical hypothetical, presents no more a case of genuine legal impossibility than do *Jaffe* and *Berrigan.* She will be convicted of attempt to smuggle French lace.

COMMENT, 5 *Hypothetical L. Rev.* 1, 3–4 (1962–1989): The hypothetical *Lady Eldon* decision is a good effort, but it doesn't quite work.

First: Consider the case of a voodoo practitioner who practices his art upon a doll firmly intending to kill his victim and believing he will succeed. Or consider a safecracker who tries to open a safe with magic incantations. Under the formulation of *Lady Eldon,* each of these defendants, more pathetic than dangerous, would be guilty of attempt. Conviction of the defendants in these cases would be no less absurd than their own actions.

The Model Penal Code, in recognition of this problem, gives a court the power to dismiss a prosecution or decrease the penalty if "the particular conduct charged to constitute a criminal attempt . . . is so inherently unlikely to result or culminate in the commission of a crime that neither such conduct nor the actor presents a public danger." Section 5.05(2). But this is to commend the matter to the discretion of the judge; it is not a statement of a rule of law. A better approach is that taken by the revised Minnesota Criminal Code which states an exception to its rule that impossibility is no defense where the "impossibility would have been clearly evident to a person of normal understanding." *Minn. Stat. Ann.* § 609.17.2. A similar solution has been developed by Professor Robbins, who proposes that a person be guilty of attempt only when "he purposely does or omits to do anything that, *under the circumstances as a reasonable person would believe them to be,*" is a substantial step in a course of conduct planned to culminate in commission of the crime.[10]

Second: The effort to deal with the so-called "true legal impossibility" problem comes off more smoothly than convincingly. Consider the following case. Two friends, Mr. Fact and Mr. Law, go hunting in the morning of October 15 in the fields of the state of Dakota, whose law makes it a misdemeanor to hunt any time other than from October 1 to November 30. Both kill deer on the first day out, October 15. Mr. Fact, however, was under the erroneous belief that the date was September 15, and Mr. Law was under the erroneous belief that the hunting season was confined to the month of November, as it was the previous year. Under the *Lady Eldon* formulation, Mr. Fact could be convicted of an attempt to hunt out of season, but Mr. Law could not be. We fail to see how any rational system of criminal law could justify convicting one and acquitting the other on so fragile and unpersuasive a distinction that one was suffering under a mistake of fact, and the other under a mistake of law. Certainly if the ultimate test is the dangerousness of the actor (i.e., readiness to violate the law), as *Lady Eldon* would have it, no distinction is warranted—Mr. Law has indicated himself to be no less "dangerous" than Mr. Fact.

Third: In formulating a rule that would eliminate the defense of factual impossibility in all cases, the opinion overlooks the strong case for retaining the defense in one class of cases. These are the cases in which the acts done by the defendant are as consistent with an innocent as with a culpable state of mind. Take for example the old saw about the professor who takes his own umbrella thinking it belongs to his colleague. The act is utterly neutral. A man taking his own umbrella conveys no evidence of guilt. Now of course the matter changes if it can be *proven* that he believed it was his colleague's umbrella. But proof of state of mind where there are only ambiguous acts to support the inference is inherently unreliable.

Consider how the Model Penal Code deals with this very concern when it addresses itself to a different problem, i.e., drawing the line between preparation and attempt. This is typically the situation in which the actor has not yet completed all he set out to do. In Section 5.01, the Model Penal Code not only reflects existing law in requiring some substantial step toward commission of the crime. It also requires that the step at the same time be "strongly corroborative of the actor's criminal purpose." Why is this required? It may be supposed that the primary function of this requirement is to avoid the risk of false convictions; the animating idea is that where the evidence of intent falls below a certain level we are not willing to allow the jury to speculate.

Now both the *Lady Eldon* opinion and the Model Penal Code are shortsighted for not seeing that the same concern may exist in the class of impossibility cases under discussion. In this respect the court in *Oviedo* . . . and cases that have followed its lead,[11] are on very solid ground. If apprehension of false convictions calls for the requirement that the acts strongly corroborate the intent in those cases where the acts fall short of what was intended by the actor, then the same concern calls for the same requirement where the actor has done all he meant to do. If it is answered that in the latter cases the completed pattern of conduct carries the criminal intent on its face, the response must be that while this is generally so, it need not be so. The professor taking his own umbrella surely is such a case.

To put the suggestion in statutory form, we suggest the following amendment to the Model Penal Code's Section 5.01:

"A person is guilty of an attempt to commit a crime if, acting with the kind of culpability otherwise required for commission of the crime, he: (a) purposely engages in conduct that *strongly corrobo-* *rates the required culpability and* would constitute the crime if the attendant circumstances were as he believes them to be. . . ."

---

1. Criminal Law 304 n. 9 (12th ed. 1932).
2. Criminal Attempts, 41 *Harv. L. Rev.* 821, 852 (1928).
3. Criminal Attempts at Common Law, 102 *U. Pa. L. Rev.* 464, 477 n. 85 (1954).
4. *Id.* at 466–68.
5. Rollin M. Perkins, Criminal Attempt and Related Problems, 2 *U.C.L.A.L. Rev.* 319, 330–32 (1955).
6. Consider the Missouri court's justification for reversing the conviction of a hunter for attempting to take a deer out of season where the evidence showed that he shot a stuffed deer, placed in the woods by a game warden, believing it to be alive: "If the state's evidence showed an attempt to take the dummy, it fell far short of proving an attempt to take a deer." *State v. Guffey*, 262 *S.W. 2d* 152 (Mo. App. 1953).
7. For an actual prosecution presenting just this problem, see *Regina v. Taaffe*, page 270 supra. Consider also a news story that appeared during the 1974 sugar shortage in England: "Travellers trying to beat Britain's sugar shortage are smuggling more and more of it into this country. They do not know that importing sugar is legal. A woman filled a shoebox with sugar and wrapped it like a gift, with fancy ribbons and bright paper. Another woman had sugar in a can marked 'face powder.' Customs officials chuckled at the reaction of sugar smugglers when they found out there was nothing wrong in what they were doing." *N.Y. Herald Tribune*, Oct. 22, 1974, reprinted in Glanville Williams, *Textbook of Criminal Law* 398 (1978).
8. See the discussion in Chapter 1, pages 26–36 supra, concerning the use of evidence of other crimes committed by the defendant.
9. Ira P. Robbins, Attempting the Impossible: The Emerging Consensus, 23 *Harv. J. Legisl.* 377, 441 (1986) (emphasis added). See also *N.J. Stat. Ann.* §; 2C:5-1a(1). . . .
10. E.g., *United States v. Bagnariol*, 665 *F. 2d* 877 (9th Cir. 1981).
11. On the issues raised by this statutory proposal, see Robbins, footnote 1 supra at 400–12:. . . Thomas Weigend, Why Lady Eldon Should Be Acquitted: The Social Harm in Attempting the Impossible, 27 *De Paul L. Rev.* 231 (1979). A related proposal has been developed by Professor Fletcher, who suggests that attempts be punishable only when two conditions are satisfied: "the actor must attempt an act punishable under the law, and, further, this attempt must be dangerous on its face." George P. Fletcher, Constructing a Theory of Impossible Attempts, 5 *Crim. J. Ethics* 53, 67 (1986) (emphasis added). Professor Fletcher locates his proposal in "a theory that stresses the individual's right to an autonomous sphere free of state intrusion. Being suspected of dangerous propensities does not in itself justify the state's incursions into our private sphere. The minimal demand is that the actor's dangerousness express itself in an objectively dangerous act that treads upon the rights of others." *Id.*

THE M'NAGHTEN RULES*

House of Lords, 1843

(Q.I.) "What is the law respecting alleged crimes committed by persons afflicted with insane delusion in respect of one or more particular subjects or persons: as for instance, where, at the time of the commission of the alleged crime, the accused knew he was acting contrary to law, but did the act complained of with a view, under the influence of insane delusion, of redressing or revenging some supposed grievance or injury, or of producing some supposed public benefit?"

(A.I.) "Assuming that your lordships' inquiries are confined to those persons who labor under such partial delusions only, and are not in other respects insane, we are of opinion that notwithstanding the accused did the act complained of with a view, under the influence of insane delusion, of redressing or avenging some supposed grievance or injury, or of producing some public benefit, he is nevertheless punishable, according to the nature of the crime committed, if he knew at the time of committing such crime that he was acting contrary to law, by which expression we understand your lordships to mean the law of the land."

(Q.II.) "What are the proper questions to be submitted to the jury where a person alleged to be afflicted with insane delusion respecting one or more particular subjects or persons is charged with the commission of a crime (murder, for example), and insanity is set up as a defence?"

(Q.III.) "In what terms ought the question to be left to the jury as to the prisoner's state of mind at the time when the act was committed?"

(A.II and A.III.) "As these two questions appear to us to be more conveniently answered together, we submit our opinion to be that the jury ought to be told in all cases that every man is presumed to be sane, and to possess a sufficient degree of reason to be responsible for his crimes, until the contrary be proved to their satisfaction; and that to establish a defence on the ground of insanity it must be clearly proved that, at the time of committing the act, the accused was labouring under such a defect of reason, from disease of the mind, as not to know the nature and quality of the act he was doing, or, if he did know it, that he did not know he was doing what was wrong. The mode of putting the latter part of the question to the jury on these occasions has generally been whether the accused at the time of doing the act knew the difference between right and wrong: which mode, though rarely, if ever, leading to any mistake with the jury, is not, as we conceive, so accurate when put generally and in the abstract as when put with reference to the party's knowledge of right and wrong, in respect to the very act with which he is charged. If the question were to be put as to the knowledge of the accused solely and exclusively with reference to the law of the land, it might tend to confound the jury, by inducing them to believe that an actual knowledge of the law of the land was essential in order to lead to conviction: whereas, the law is administered upon the principle that everyone must be taken conclusively to know it, without proof that he does know it. If the accused was conscious that the act was one that he ought not to do, and if that act was at the same time contrary to the law of the land, he is punishable; and the usual course, therefore, has been to leave the question to the jury, whether the accused had a sufficient degree of reason to know that he was doing an act that was wrong; and this course we think is correct, accompanied with such observations and explanations as the circumstances of each particular case may require."

(Q.IV.) "If a person under an insane delusion as to existing facts commits an offence in consequence thereof, is he thereby excused?"

(A.IV.) "The answer must, of course, depend on the nature of the delusion; but making the same assumption as we did before, namely, that he labors under such partial delusion only, and is not in other

---

*10 *Cl. 2nd F.* 200 at p. 209.

respects insane, we think he must be considered in the same situation as to responsibility as if the facts with respect to which the delusion exists were real. For example, if under the influence of his delusion he supposes another man to be in the act of attempting to take away his life, and he kills that man, as he supposes in self-defence, he would be exempt from punishment. If his delusion was that the deceased had inflicted a serious injury to his character and fortune, and he killed him in revenge for such supposed injury, he would be liable to punishment."

THE INSANITY DEFENSE*

The American Law Institute

Article 4. Responsibility

Section 4.01. Mental Disease or Defect Excluding Responsibility

(1) A person is not responsible for criminal conduct if at the time of such conduct as a result of mental disease or defect he lacks substantial capacity either to appreciate the criminality of his conduct or to coform his conduct to the requirements of law.

(2) The terms "mental disease or defect" do not include an abnormality manifested only by repeated criminal or otherwise antisocial conduct.

Alternative formulations of paragraph (1)

(a) A person is not responsible for criminal conduct if at the time of such conduct as a result of mental disease or defect his capacity either to appreciate the criminality of his conduct or to conform his conduct to the requirements of law is so substantially impaired that he cannot justly be held responsible.

(b) A person is not responsible for criminal conduct if at the time of such conduct as a result of mental disease or defect he lacks substantial capacity to appreciate the criminality of his conduct or is in such state that the prospect of conviction and punishment cannot constitute a significant restraining influence upon him.

Comments § 4.01.
Article 4. Responsibility

Section 4.01. Mental Disease or Defect Excluding Responsibility

The Problem of Defining the Criteria of Irresponsibility
1. No problem in the drafting of a penal code presents larger intrinsic difficulty than that of determining when individuals whose conduct would otherwise be criminal ought to be exculpated on the ground that they were suffering from mental disease or defect when they acted as they did. What is involved specifically is the drawing of a line between the use of public agencies and public force to condemn the offender by conviction, with resultant sanctions in which there is inescapably a punitive ingredient (however constructive we may attempt to make the process of correction) and modes of disposition in which that ingredient is absent, even though restraint may be involved. To put the matter differently, the problem is to discriminate between the cases where a punitive-correctional disposition is

appropriate and those in which a medical-custodial disposition is the only kind the law should allow.

2. The traditional M'Naghten rule resolves the problem solely in regard to the capacity of the individual to know what he was doing and to know that it was wrong. Absent these minimal elements of rationality, condemnation and punishment are obviously both unjust and futile. They are unjust because the individual could not, by hypothesis, have employed reason to restrain the act; he did not and he could not know the facts essential to bring reason into play. On the same ground, they are futile. A madman who believes that he is squeezing lemons when he chokes his wife or thinks that homicide is the command of God is plainly beyond reach of the restraining influence of law; he needs restraint but condemnation is entirely meaningless and ineffective. Thus the attacks on the M'Naghten rule as an inept definition of insanity or as an arbitrary definition in terms of special symptoms are entirely misconceived. The *rationale* of the position is that these are cases in which reason cannot operate and in which it is totally impossible for individuals to be deterred. Moreover, the category defined by the rule is so extreme that to the ordinary man the exculpation of the persons it encompasses bespeaks no weakness in the law. He does not identify such persons and himself; they are a world apart.

Jurisdictions in which the M'Naghten test has been expanded to include the case where mental disease produces an "irresistible impulse" proceed on the same *rationale*. They recognize, however, that cognitive factors are not the only ones that preclude inhibition; that even though cognition still obtains, mental disorder may produce a total incapacity for self-control. The same result is sometimes reached under M'Naghten proper, in the view, strongly put forth by Stephen, that "knowledge" requires more than the capacity to verbalize right answers to a question, it implies capacity to function in the light of knowledge. Stephen, *History of English Criminal Law*, Vol. 2, p. 171. . . . In modern psychiatric terms, the "fundamental difference between verbal or purely intellectual knowledge and the mysterious other kind of knowledge is familiar to every clinical psychiatrist; it is the difference between knowledge divorced from affect and knowledge so fused with affect that it becomes a human reality." Zilboorg, "Misconceptions of Legal Insanity," 9 *Am. J. Orthopsychiatry,* pp. 540, 552. . . .

3. The draft accepts the view that any effort to exclude the nondeterrables from strictly penal sanctions must take account of the impairment of volitional capacity no less than of impairment of cognition; and that this result should be achieved directly in the formulation of the test, rather than left to mitigation in the application of M'Naghten. It also accepts the criticism of the "irresistible impulse" formulation as inept in so far as it may be impliedly restricted to sudden, spontaneous acts as distinguished from insane propulsions that are accompanied by brooding or reflection. . . .

Both the main formulation recommended and alternative (a) deem the proper question on this branch of the inquiry to be whether the defendant is without capacity to conform his conduct to the requirements of law. . . .

Alternative (b) states the issue differently. Instead of asking whether the defendant had capacity to conform his conduct to the requirements of law, it asks whether, in consequence of mental disease or defect, the threat of punishment could not exercise a significant restraining influence upon him. To some extent, of course, these are the same inquiries. To the extent that they diverge, the latter asks a narrower and harder question, involving the assessment of capacity to respond to a single influence, the threat of punishment. Both Dr. Guttmacher and Dr. Overholser considered the assessment of responsiveness to this one influence too difficult for psychiatric judgment. Hence, though the issue framed by the alternative may well be thought to state the question that is most precisely relevant for legal purposes, the Reporter and the Council deemed the inquiry impolitic upon this ground. In so far as nondeterrability is the determination that is sought, it must be reached by probing general capacity to conform to the requirements of law. The validity of this conclusion is submitted, however, to the judgment of the Institute.

4. One further problem must be faced. In addressing itself to impairment of the cognitive capacity, M'Naghten demands that impairment be complete: the actor must *not* know. So, too, the irresistible impulse criterion presupposes a complete impairment of capacity for self-control. The extremity of these conceptions is, we think, the point that poses largest difficulty to psychiatrists when called upon to aid in their administration. The schizophrenic, for example, is disoriented from reality; the disorientation is extreme; but it is rarely total. Most psychotics will respond to a command of someone in authority within the mental hospital; they thus have some capacity to conform to a norm. But this is very different from the question whether they have

the capacity to conform to requirements that are not thus immediately symbolized by an attendant or policeman at the elbow. Nothing makes the inquiry into responsibility more unreal for the psychiatrist than limitation of the issue to some ultimate extreme of total incapacity, when clinical experience reveals only a graded scale with marks along the way. . . .

We think this difficulty can and must be met. The law must recognize that when there is no black and white it must content itself with different shades of gray. The draft, accordingly, does not demand *complete* impairment of capacity. It asks instead for *substantial* impairment. This is all, we think, that candid witnesses, called on to infer the nature of the situation at a time that they did not observe, can ever confidently say, even when they know that a disorder was extreme.

If substantial impairment of capacity is to suffice, there remains the question whether this alone should be the test or whether the criterion should state the principle that measures how substantial it must be. To identify the degree of impairment with precision is, of course, impossible both verbally and logically. The recommended formulation is content to rest upon the term "substantial" to support the weight of judgment; if capacity is greatly impaired, that presumably should be sufficient. Alternative (a) proposes to submit the issue squarely to the jury's sense of justice, asking expressly whether the capacity of the defendant "was so substantially impaired that he cannot justly be held responsible." Some members of the Council deemed it unwise to present questions of justice to the jury, preferring a submission that in form, at least, confines the inquiry to fact. The proponents of the alternative contend that since the jury normally will feel that it is only just to exculpate if the disorder was extreme, that otherwise conviction is demanded, it is safer to invoke the jury's sense of justice than to rest entirely on the single word "substantial," imputing no specific measure of degree. The issue is an important one and it is submitted for consideration by the Institute.

5. The draft rejects the formulation warmly supported by psychiatrists and recently adopted by the Court of Appeals for the District of Columbia in *Durham v. United States,* 214, *F. 2d* 862 (1954), namely, "that an accused is not criminally responsible if his unlawful act was the product of mental disease or defect." . . .

The difficulty with this formulation inheres in the ambiguity of "product." If interpreted to lead to irresponsibility unless the defendant would have engaged in the criminal conduct even if he had not suffered from the disease or defect, it is too broad: an answer that he would have done so can be given very rarely; this is intrinsic to the concept of the singleness of personality and unity of mental processes that psychiatry regards as fundamental. If interpreted to call for a standard of causality less relaxed than but-for cause, there are but two alternatives to be considered: (1) a mode of causality involving total incapacity or (2) a mode of causality which involves substantial incapacity. See Wechsler, "The Criteria of Criminal Responsibility," 22 *U. of Chi. L. Rev.* (1955), p. 367. But if either of these causal concepts is intended, the formulation ought to set it forth.

The draft also rejects the proposal of the majority of the recent Royal Commission on Capital Punishment, namely, "to leave to the jury to determine whether at the time of the act the accused was suffering from disease of the mind (or mental deficiency) to such a degree that he ought not to be held responsible." *Report* (1953), par. 333, p. 116. While we agree, as we have indicated, that mental disease or defect involves gradations of degree that should be recognized, we think the legal standard ought to focus on the *consequences* of disease or defect that have a bearing on the justice of conviction and of punishment. The Royal Commission proposal fails in this respect.

6. Paragraph (2) of section 4.01 is designed to exclude from the concept of "mental disease or defect" the case of so-called "psychopathic personality." The reason for the exclusion is that, as the Royal Commission put it, psychopathy "is a statistical abnormality; that is to say, the psychopath differs from a normal person only quantitatively or in degree, not qualitatively; and the diagnosis of psychopathic personality does not carry with it any explanation of the causes of the abnormality." While it may not be feasible to formulate a definition of "disease," there is much to be said for excluding a condition that is manifested only by the behavior phenomena that must, by hypothesis, be the result of disease for irresponsibility to be established. Although British psychiatrists have agreed, on the whole, that psychopathy should not be called "disease," there is considerable difference of opinion on the point in the United States. Yet it does not seem useful to contemplate the litigation of what is essentially a matter of terminology; nor is it right to have the legal result rest upon the resolution of a dispute of this kind.

STATE V. GUIDO*

New Jersey Supreme Court, 1963

WEINTRAUB, C. J. Adele Guido was convicted of murder in the second degree and sentenced to imprisonment for a minimum of 24 years and a maximum of 27 years. She appeals directly to this Court. . . .

The victim was defendant's husband. When they first met, she was a young girl and he a professional fighter of some success. . . .

All the details of the marital discord need not be stated. [Defendant] wanted a divorce, while decedent insisted upon holding on to her notwithstanding he would not or could not end his extra marital romance and assume the role of a responsible husband and parent. . . . In the early morning of April 17, 1961, after deceased fell asleep on a couch in the living room while watching television, defendant, according to her testimony, took the gun and went into her room, intending to end her life. Deciding that suicide would be no solution, she returned to the living room to put the weapon back in the suitcase, but when her eyes fell upon Guido, she raised the weapon and fired until it was empty.

With respect to physical abuse, the jury could find that although there were only a few incidents of actual injury, there was the constant threat of it from a man who had to have his way and who would not let go of a woman who had had her fill. It appears that on several occasions shortly before the homicide defendant called the local police to express her fear of harm. . . .

Defendant claimed "temporary" insanity. She was examined by two court-appointed psychiatrists. [Their] report contained sundry medical findings and ultimately the opinion that defendant was "legally" sane at the time of the shooting. Mr. Saltzman [defense counsel] met with the psychiatrists, and after some three hours of debate the psychiatrists changed their opinion as to "legal" insanity although their underlying medical findings remained the same. They then retyped the last page of their report.

On cross-examination of the first defense psychiatrist, it was developed that the original report had been revised. We do not know how the prosecutor learned of the change. The record shows that on its own initiative the court immediately directed that "Counsel shall produce the original report to the prosecutor." . . . What followed was some high drama that the occasion did not warrant.

Mr. Saltzman . . . returned from his office with the original report. The court undertook to interrogate him [out of the presence of the jury] with respect to the receipt of the changed last page. . . . With much formality the trial court . . . elicited step by step the receipt and transmittal of the papers. . . . The trial then resumed before the jury. . . .

Defense counsel and defense psychiatrists were thus subjected to a humiliating experience. Later the prosecutor berated them in his summation. He said "the defense in this case—I am sorry to say this—has been concocted"; . . . that Mr. Saltzman was "in cahoots with Doctors Galen and Chodosh and perpetrated a fraud on this Court"; and "how, how can you believe a woman who lends herself to the deception that was practiced on the Court, on this Court by the doctors and her attorney? Certainly she knew about it."

The trial judge did not stop this unjustifiable attack. On the contrary he intervened in a way that tended to sustain it. . . .

When the basis of the change in the experts' opinion was explored, it quickly appeared that the change was thoroughly consistent with honesty however mistaken it might be. In the minds of the witnesses the change involved no alteration whatever in their medical findings. Rather it stemmed from an altered understanding of the law's concept of insanity. Specifically, the doctors originally understood that the "disease of the mind" required by the *M'Naghten* concept of legal insanity to which we adhere, means

*40 *N.J.* 191, 191 A.2d 45 (1963).

a *psychosis* and not some lesser illness or functional aberration. As the result of their pretrial debate with Mr. Saltzman, the doctors concluded they had had too narrow a view of M'Naghten and that the "anxiety neurosis" they had found did qualify as a "disease" within the legal rule, and hence when the anxiety reached a "panic" state, "meaning simply a severe disorganizing degree of anxiety," defendant did not know right from wrong and she did not know what she was doing was wrong because of that "disease." . . .

The change in the opinions of the defense psychiatrists simply focuses attention upon an area of undeniable obscurity. As we have said, the *M'Naghten* rule requires a "disease of the mind." The competing concepts of legal insanity also require a disease (or defect) of the mind. . . . But the hard question under any concept of legal insanity is, What constitutes a "disease"? . . . The postulate is that some wrongdoers are sick while others are bad, and that it is against good morals to stigmatize the sick. Who then are the sick whose illness shows they are free of moral blame? We cannot turn to the psychiatrist for a list of illnesses which have that quality because, for all his insight into the dynamics of behavior, he has not solved the riddle of blame. The question remains an ethical one, the answer to which lies beyond scientific truth.

The *M'Naghten* rule does not identify the disease which will excuse, but rather stresses a specific effect of disease, i.e., that at the time of the committing of the act the accused was laboring under a defect of reason such as not to know the nature and quality of the act he was doing, or, if he did know it, that he did not know what he was doing was wrong. But although emphasis is thus upon a state of mind, it is nonetheless required that that state be due to "disease" and not something else. So our cases contrast that concept of insanity with "emotional insanity" or "moral insanity" which, upon the dichotomy mentioned above, is attributed to moral depravity or weakness and hence will not excuse the offender even if his rage was so blinding that he did not really appreciate what he was doing or that it was wrong. . . . Yet the traditional charge of the *M'Naghten* rule to the jury does not attempt to say what is meant by "disease," and [there is a] rather universal reluctance to assay a definition. . . .

Our cases seem not to have explored the question. . . . And so here, . . . we should not finally decide whether the testimony of the psychiatrists revealed a disease. . . . We have described the problem, not to resolve it, but simply to reveal the room for disputation, to the end of demonstrating the unfairness of charging defendant, her attorney, and her witnesses with a fraud when the change in the experts' opinion, however frivolous it may be in law, involved no departure from prior medical findings but rather a change in the witnesses' understanding of what the law means by "disease." . . .

The judgment is reversed. . . .

WHAT IS SO SPECIAL ABOUT MENTAL ILLNESS?*

Joel Feinberg

Professor Dershowitz has very effectively put psychiatry in its proper place.[1] As far as the law and public policy are concerned, a psychiatrist is an expert on the diagnosis and treatment of mental illness. His testimony becomes relevant to questions of responsibility only when mental illness itself is relevant to such questions, and that is only when it deprives a person of the capacity to conform his conduct to the requirements of law. Mental illness should not itself be an independent ground of exculpation, but only a sign that one of the traditional standard grounds—compulsion, ignorance of fact, or excusable ignorance of law—may apply. Mental illness, then, while often relevant to questions of responsibility, is no more significant—and significant in no different way—than other sources of compulsion and misapprehension.

Now although I am almost completely convinced that this is the correct account of the matter, I am nevertheless going to air my few lingering doubts as if they were potent objections, just to see what will happen to them. I shall suggest, then, in what follows, that mental illness has an independent significance for questions of responsibility not fully accounted for by reference to its power to deprive one of the capacity to be law-abiding.

I

At the outset we must distinguish two questions about the relation of mental illness to criminal punishment. (There are two parallel questions about the bearing of mental illness on civil commitment.)

1. How are mentally sick persons to be distinguished from normal persons?

2. When should we accept mental illness as an excuse?

The first appears to be a medical question that requires the expertise of the psychiatrist to answer; the second appears to be an essentially controversial question of public policy that cannot be answered by referring to the special expertise of any particular group.

Some psychiatrists may wish to deny this rigid separation between the two questions. They might hold it self-evident that sick people are not to be treated as responsible people; hence the criteria of illness are themselves criteria of nonresponsibility. But, obviously, this won't do. First of all, the fact of illness itself, even greatly incapacitating illness, does not automatically lead us to withhold ascription of responsibility, or else we would treat *physical* illness as an automatic excuse. But in fact we would not change our judgments of Bonnie and Clyde one jot if we discovered that they both had had 103-degree fevers during one of their bank robberies, or of Al Capone if we learned that he had ordered one of his gangland assassinations while suffering from an advanced case of chicken pox. Secondly, there are various crimes that can be committed by persons suffering from mental illnesses that can have no relevant bearing on their motivation. We may take exhibitionism to be an excuse for indecent exposure, or pedophilia for child molestation, but neither would be a plausible defense to the charge of income-tax evasion or price-fixing conspiracy. These examples show, I think, that the mere fact of mental illness, no more than the mere fact of physical illness, automatically excuses. We need some further criterion, then, for distinguishing cases of mental illness that do excuse from those that do not, and this further ques-

*From *Doing and Deserving* (Princeton: Princeton University Press, 1970) 272–92.

tion is not an exclusively psychiatric one. What we want to know is this: what is it about mental illness that makes it an excuse when it is an excuse?

So much, I think, is clear. But now there are two types of moves open to us. The first is preferred by most legal writers, and it is the one to which I am most favorably disposed. According to this view, there is nothing very special about mental disease as such. Mental illness is only one of numerous possible causes of *incapacity,* and it is incapacity—or, more precisely, the incapability to conform to law—that is incompatible with responsibility. Ultimately, there is only one kind of consideration that should lead us to exempt a person from responsibility for his wrongful deeds, and that is that he *couldn't help it.* Sometimes a mental illness compels a man to do wrong, or at least makes it unreasonably difficult for him to abstain, and in these cases we say that, because he was ill, he couldn't help what he did and, therefore, is not to be held responsible for his deviant conduct. But in other cases, as we have seen, mental illness no more compels a given wrongful act than the chicken pox does, or may be totally irrelevant to the explanation of the wrongdoing, in that the wrongdoer would have done his wrong even if he had been perfectly healthy. What counts, then, for questions of responsibility is whether the accused could have helped himself, not whether he was mentally well or ill.

Aristotle put much the same point in somewhat different but equally familiar language. A man is responsible, said Aristotle, for all and only those of his actions that were voluntary; to whatever extent we think a given action less than voluntary, to that extent we are inclined to exempt the actor from responsibility for it. There are, according to Aristotle, two primary ways in which an action can fail to be voluntary: it can be the result of *compulsion,* or it can be done in *ignorance.* Thus if a hurricane wind blows you twenty yards across a street, you cannot be said to have crossed the street voluntarily, since you were compelled to do it and given no choice at all in the matter. And if you put arsenic in your wife's coffee honestly but mistakenly believing it to be sugar, you cannot be said to have poisoned her voluntarily, since you acted in genuine ignorance of what you were doing.

Now if we take just a few slight liberties with Aristotle, we can interpret most of the traditionally recognized legal excuses in terms of his categories. Acting under duress or necessity, or in self-defense, or defense of others, or defense of property, and so

on, can all be treated as cases of acting under compulsion, whereas ignorance or mistake of fact, ignorance or mistake of law, and perhaps even what used to be called "moral idiocy" or ignorance of the "difference between right and wrong" can all be treated as cases of acting in responsibility-cancelling ignorance. On the view I am considering (a view which has gained much favor among lawyers, and to which Professor Dershowitz, I feel sure, is friendly), the mental illness of an actor is not still a third way in which his actions might fail to be voluntary; rather, it is a factor which may or may not compel him to act in certain ways, or which may or may not delude, or mislead, or misinform him in ways that would lead him to act in ignorance. Indeed, on this view, mental illness ought not even to be an independent category of exculpation on a level with, say, self-defense or mistake of fact. Self-defense and relevant blameless mistakes of fact always excuse, whereas mental illness excuses only when it compels or deludes. We now know of the existence of inner compulsions unsuspected by Aristotle: obsessive ideas, hysterical reactions, neurotic compulsion, phobias, and addictions. Other mental illnesses characteristically produce delusions and hallucinations. But not all neurotic and psychotic disorders by any means produce compulsive or delusionary symptoms, and even those that do are not always sufficient to explain the criminal conduct of the person suffering from them.

The nineteenth-century judges who formulated the famous McNaghten Rules were presumably quite sympathetic with the view I have been describing, that there really is nothing very special about mental illness. These rules are not at all concerned with neurotically compulsive behavior—a category which simply was not before their minds at the time. Rather, they were concerned with those dramatic and conspicuous disorders that involve what we call today "paranoid delusions" and "psychotic hallucinations." The interesting thing about the rules is that they treat these aberrations precisely the same as any other innocent "mistakes of fact"; in effect the main point of this part of the McNaghten Rules is to acknowledge that mistakes of fact resulting from "disease of the mind" really are genuine and innocent and, therefore, have the same exculpatory force as more commonplace errors and false beliefs. The rules state that, "when a man acts under an insane delusion, then he is excused only when it is the case that *if* the facts were as he supposed them his act would be innocent. . . ." Thus if a man suffers the insane delusion that a passerby on the street is an enemy agent about to launch a mortal attack on him and kills him in what he thinks is "self-defense," he is excused, since if the facts were as he falsely supposed them to be, his act would have been innocent. But if (in James Vorenberg's example) he shoots his wife because, in his insane delusion, he thinks her hair has turned gray, he will be convicted, since even if her hair had turned gray, that would not have been an allowable defense. Note that the mental disease that leads to the insane delusion in these instances is given no special significance except insofar as it mediates the application of another kind of defense that can be used by mentally healthy as well as mentally ill defendants.

The McNaghten Rules do, however, make one important concession to the peculiarity of mental illness. Mentally normal persons, for the most part, are not permitted to plead *ignorance of the law* as a defense, especially for crimes that are "malum *in se*." No normal person, for example, can plead in the state of Arizona that "he didn't know that murder is prohibited in Arizona." *That* kind of ignorance could hardly ever occur in a normal person, and even if it did, it would be negligent rather than innocent ignorance. (One should at least take the trouble to find out whether a state prohibits murder before killing someone in that state!) If a person, however, is so grossly ignorant of what is permitted that he would murder even (as the saying goes) with "a policeman at his elbow," then if his ignorance is attributable to a diseased mind and therefore innocent, he is excused. One can conceive (just barely) of such a case. Imagine a man standing on a street corner chatting with a policeman. A third person saunters up, calmly shoots and kills the man, turns to the astonished policeman and says "Good morning, officer," and starts to walk away. When the policeman apprehends him, then *he* is the astonished one. "Why, what have I done wrong?" he asks in genuine puzzlement.

In accepting this kind of ignorance when it stems from disease as an excuse, the McNaghten Rules do not really make *much* of a concession to the uniqueness of mental illness. Ignorance of law does not excuse in the normal case because the law imposes a duty on all normal persons to find out what is prohibited at their own peril. When a statute has been duly promulgated, every normal person is presumed to know about it. If any given normal person fails to be informed, his ignorance is the consequence of his own negligence, and he is to blame

for it. But when the ignorance is the consequence of illness, it is involuntary or faultless ignorance and may therefore be accepted as an excuse. Again, it is not the mental illness as such which excuses, but rather the ignorance which is its indirect byproduct. The ultimate rationale of the exculpation is that the actor "couldn't help it." We hardly need the separate insanity defense at all if we accept the propositions that mentally ill people may be subject to internal compulsions, that mental illness can cause innocent ignorance, and that both compulsion and innocent ignorance are themselves excuses.

Suppose a mentally ill defendant is acquitted on the ground that his illness has rendered his unlawful conduct involuntary in one of these traditional ways. He may still be a menace to himself or others, even though he is perfectly innocent of any crime. Hence the state reserves to itself or to others the right to initiate civil commitment proceedings. Now whether it follows acquittal or is quite independent of any prior criminal proceedings, civil commitment can have one or both of two different purposes, and for each of these purposes the mere fact of mental illness is not a sufficient condition. The two purposes are (1) forcible detention of a dangerous person to prevent him from committing a crime and (2) compulsory therapeutic confinement of a mentally ill person "for his own good." For the purpose of preventive detention, mental illness is neither a necessary nor a sufficient condition: not necessary because mentally normal persons too can be very dangerous in certain circumstances,[2] and not sufficient because some mentally ill people, unhappy or withdrawn as they may be, are still quite harmless. Hence psychiatric testimony that a person is mentally ill is hardly sufficient to justify detaining him without a further showing of dangerousness. What is needed are very high standards of due process at detention hearings analogous to those governing criminal trials and, as Professor Dershowitz points out, clear and precise legal definitions of "harmfulness" and "danger."

The other possible purpose of civil commitment—compulsory therapy—does of course require mental illness as a necessary condition, and here psychiatric testimony is crucial. But if civil liberty has any appeal to us and if state paternalism is repugnant, we can hardly regard the simple fact of mental illness as sufficient warrant for imposing therapeutic confinement on a person against his will. To force a person to submit to our benevolence is a fearsome and ugly kind of tyranny. The traditional doctrine of *Parens Patriae* to which Professor Dershowitz refers, however, authorizes such coercion only in very special and, I think, unobjectionable circumstances. Some mental illnesses so affect the cognitive processes that a victim is unable to make inferences or decisions—a severe disablement indeed. According to the *Parens Patriae* doctrine, the state has the duty to exercise its "sovereign power of guardianship" over these intellectually defective and disordered persons who are unable to realize their needs on their own. But even on occasions where this doctrine applies, the state presumes to "decide for a man as . . . he would decide for himself if he were of sound mind."[3] By no means all mentally ill persons, however, suffer from defects of reason. Many or most of them suffer from emotional or volitional disorders that leave their cognitive faculties quite unimpaired. To impose compulsory therapy on such persons would be as objectionably paternalistic as imposing involuntary cures for warts or headaches or tooth decay.

To summarize the view I have been considering: a mere finding of mental illness is not itself a sufficient ground for exempting a person from responsibility for a given action; nor is it a sufficient ground for finding him not to be a responsible or competent person generally, with the loss of civil rights such a finding necessarily entails. At most, in criminal proceedings mental illness may be evidence that one of the traditional grounds for moral exculpation—compulsion or ignorance—applies to the case at hand, and in civil commitment hearings it may be evidence of dangerousness or of cognitive impairment. But it has no independent moral or legal significance in itself either as an excuse or as a ground for commitment.

II

I fully accept this account of the relation of mental illness to civil commitment. Preventive detention of a person who has committed no crime is a desperate move that should be made only when a person's continued liberty would constitute a clear and present danger of substantial harm to others. We should require proof of a very great danger indeed before resorting to such measures if only because people are inclined generally to overestimate threats to safety and to underestimate the social value of indi-

vidual liberty. Mere evidence of mental illness by itself does not provide such proof. Nor does it by itself provide proof of that mental derangement or incompetence to grant or withhold consent that is required if compulsory therapeutic confinement is to be justified. But, for all of that, I have a lingering doubt that the above account does full justice to the moral significance of mental illness as it bears on blame and punishment. I shall devote the remainder of my remarks to a statement of that doubt.

Let me turn immediately to the kind of case that troubles me. I have in mind cases of criminal conduct which appear to be both voluntary (by the usual Aristotelian tests) and sick. Let me give some examples and then contrast them with normal voluntary criminal acts.

First consider a nonviolent child molester. He is sexually attracted to five- and six-year-old boys and girls. His rational faculties are perfectly normal. He knows that sexual contacts with children are forbidden by the criminal law, and he takes no unnecessary risks of detection. For the most part, he manages to do without sex altogether. When he does molest a child he characteristically feels guilt, if not remorse, afterward. He has no understanding of his own motivation and often regrets that his tastes are so odd.

Next in our rogues' gallery is a repetitive exhibitionist. He has been arrested numerous times for exposing his genitalia in public. He does this not to solicit or threaten, but simply to derive satisfaction from the act itself: exposure for exposure's sake. For some reason he cannot understand, he finds such exposure immensely gratifying. Still, he knows that it is offensive to others, that it is in a way publicly humiliating, that it is prohibited by law, and that the chances of being caught and punished are always very great. These things trouble him much and often, but not always, lead him to restrain himself when the impulse to self-exposure arises.

My third example is drawn from a landmark case in the criminal law, one of the first in which kleptomania was accepted as an excuse: *State v. McCullough,* 114 Iowa 532 (1901). The defendant, a high school student, was charged with stealing a school book worth seventy-five cents. It was discovered that stolen property in his possession included "14 silverine watches, 2 old brass watches, 2 old clocks, 24 razors, 21 pairs of cuff buttons, 15 watch chains, 6 pistols, 7 combs, 34 jack knives, 9 bicycle wrenches, 4 padlocks, 7 pair of clippers, 3 bicycle saddles, 1 box of old keys, 4 pairs of scissors,

5 pocket mirrors, 6 mouth organs, rulers, bolts, calipers, oil cans, washers, punches, pulleys, spoons, penholders, ramrods, violin strings, etc." ["etc."!]. One can barely imagine the great price in anxiety this boy must have paid for his vast accumulation of worthless junk.

Finally, consider a well-off man who shoplifts only one kind of item, women's brassieres. He could easily afford to pay for these items and, indeed, often does when there is no other way of getting them, or when he is in danger of being caught. He does not enjoy stealing them and suffers great anxiety in worrying about being found out. Yet his storerooms are overflowing with brassieres. He burgles homes only to steal them; he assaults women only to rip off their brassieres and flee. And if you ask him for an explanation of his bizarre conduct, he will confess himself as puzzled by it as any observer.

Now, for contrast, consider some typical voluntary normal crimes. A respectable middle-aged bank teller, after weighing the risks carefully, embezzles bank funds and runs off to Mexico with his expensive lady friend. A homeowner in desperate need of cash sets his own house on fire to defraud an insurance company. A teenager steals a parked car and drives to a nearby city for a thrill. An angry man consumed with jealousy, or indignation, or vengefulness, or spite commits criminal battery on a person he hates. A revolutionary throws a bomb at the king's carriage during an insurrection. These criminals act from a great variety of unmysterious motives—avarice, gain, lust, hate, ideological zeal; they are all rationally capable of calculating risks; they all act voluntarily.

How do the "sick" criminals in my earlier list differ from these normal ones? We might be tempted to answer that the pedophiliac, the exhibitionist, the kleptomaniac, and the fetishist are all "compulsives" and that their criminal conduct is therefore not entirely voluntary after all; but I believe it is important to understand that this answer is unsatisfactory. There is no *a priori* reason why the desires, impulses, and motives that lead a person to do bizarre things need necessarily be more powerful or compulsive than the desires that lead normal men to do perfectly ordinary things. It is by no means self-evident, for example, that the sex drives of a pedophiliac or an exhibitionist must always be stronger than the sexual desires normal men and women may feel for one another.

There is much obscurity in the notion of the "strength of a desire," but I think several points are clear and relevant to our purposes. The first is that, strictly speaking, no impulse is "irresistible." For every case of giving in to a desire, I would argue, it will be true that, if the person had tried harder, he would have resisted it successfully. The psychological situation is never—or hardly ever—like that of the man who hangs from a windowsill by his fingernails until the sheer physical force of gravity rips his nails off and sends him plummeting to the ground, or like that of the man who dives from a sinking ship in the middle of the ocean and swims until he is exhausted and then drowns. Human endurance puts a severe limit on how long one can stay afloat in an ocean; but there is no comparable limit to our ability to resist temptation. Nevertheless, it does make sense to say that some desires are stronger than others and that some have an intensity and power that are felt as overwhelming. Some desires, in fact, may be so difficult to resist for a given person in a given state at a given time that it would be unreasonable to expect him to resist. A dieting man with a strong sweet tooth may find it difficult to resist eating an ice cream sundae for dessert; but a man who has not eaten for a week will have a much harder time still resisting the desire to eat a loaf of bread, which just happens to belong to his neighbor. Any person in a weakened condition, whether the cause be hunger or depression, fatigue or gripping emotion, will be less able to resist any given anti-social impulse than a person in a normal condition. But, again, there is no reason to suppose that bizarre appetites and odd tastes are always connected with a "weakened condition," so that they are necessarily more difficult to resist than ordinary desires. And thus there is no reason to suppose that so-called sick desires must always be compulsive or unreasonably difficult to resist.

It might seem to follow that there is *no* morally significant difference between normal and mentally ill offenders, that the one class is just as responsible as the other, provided only that their criminal actions are voluntary in the usual sense. But if this is the proper conclusion, then I am at a loss to see what difference there can be between mental illness and plain wickedness. As an ordinary citizen, before I begin to get confused by philosophy, I sometimes permit myself to feel anger and outrage at normal criminals, whereas I cannot help feeling some pity (mixed, perhaps, with repugnance) toward those whose conduct appears bizarre and unnatural. But unless I can find some morally telling difference between the two classes of criminals, then these natural attitudes must be radically reshaped, so that the fetish thief, for example, be thought as wicked as the professional burglar.

There do seem to be some striking differences between the two classes, however, and perhaps some of these can rescue my prephilosophical attitudes. Most of them have to do not with the criminal's intentions, but with his underlying motivation—the basis of the appeal in his immediate goals or objectives. The first such difference is that the sick criminal's motives appear quite *unintelligible* to us. We sometimes express our puzzlement by saying that his crimes have no apparent motive at all. We cannot see any better than the criminal himself "what he gets out of it," and it overburdens our imaginative faculties to put ourselves in his shoes. We understand the avaricious, irascible, or jealous man's motives all too well, and we resent him for them. But where crimes resist explanation in terms of ordinary motives, we hardly know what to resent. Here the old maxim "to understand all is to forgive all" seems to be turned on its ear. It is closer to the truth to say of mentally ill wrongdoers that to forgive is to despair of understanding.

Yet mere unintelligibility of motive is not likely to advance our search for the moral significance of mental illness very far, especially if we take the criterion of unintelligibility in turn to be the frustration of our "imaginative capacities" to put ourselves in the criminal's shoes and understand what he gets out of his crimes. This test of imaginability is far too elastic and variable. On the one hand, it seems too loose, since it permits the classification as unintelligible (or even sick) of *any* particular passion or taste, provided only that it is sufficiently different from those of the person making the judgment. Some nonsmokers cannot understand what smokers get out of their noxious habit, and males can hardly understand what it is like to enjoy bearing children. On the other hand, once we begin tightening up the test of imaginability, there is likely to be no stopping place short of the point at which *all* motives become intelligible to anyone with a moderately good imagination and sense of analogy. The important thing is not that the sick criminal's motives may seem unintelligible, but rather that they are unintelligible in a certain respect or for a certain reason.

We get closer to the heart of the matter, I think, if we say that the mentally ill criminal's motives are unintelligible because they are irrational—not just unreasonable, but *irrational*. All voluntary wrongdoing, of course, is unreasonable. It is always unreasonable conduct to promote one's own good at another's expense, to be cruel, deceitful, or unfair. But in a proper sense of "rational," made familiar by economists and lawyers, wrongdoing, though unreasonable, can be perfectly rational. A wrongdoer might well calculate his own interests, and gains and risks thereto, and decide to advance them at another's expense, without making a single intellectual mistake. A rational motive, in the present sense, is simply a *self-interested* motive, or perhaps an intelligently self-interested one. The motives of mentally ill criminals are not usually very self-interested. The Supreme Court of Iowa, in overturning the conviction of young McCullough, held that the question for the jury should have been: did the accused steal because of a mental disease driving him by "an insane and irresistible impulse" to steal, or did he commit said acts "through excessive greed or avarice?" The Court's alternatives are not exhaustive. Very likely McCullough's impulses were neither irresistible nor "greedy and avaricious." Greed and avarice are forms of selfishness, excessive desires for material goods and riches for oneself. As motives they are preeminently self-interested and "rational." McCullough's sick desires, however, were not for his own good, material or otherwise. He stole objects that could do him no good at all and assumed irrational risks in the process. The desire to steal and hoard these useless trinkets was a genuine enough desire, and it was *his* desire; but it does not follow that it was a desire to promote his own good.

This point too, however, can be overstated. It may well be true that none of the mentally ill crimes we are considering is done from a self-interested motive, but this feature hardly distinguishes them (yet) from a wide variety of voluntary crimes of great blameworthiness committed by perfectly normal criminals. By no means all voluntary crimes by normal criminals are done from the motive of gain. Some are done to advance or retard a cause, to help a loved one, or to hurt an enemy, often at great cost to the criminal's self-interest. What distinguishes the sick crimes we have been considering is not that they are unself-interested, but rather that they are *not interested at all*. They do not further *any* of the actor's interests, self *or* other-regarding, benevolent or malevolent. The fetishist's shoplifting is not rational and self-serving; he attains no economic objective by it. But neither does it hurt anyone he hates nor help anyone he loves; it neither gains him good will and prestige, nor satisfies his conscience, nor fulfills his ideals. It is, in short, not interested behavior.

But even this distinction does not quite get to the very core of the matter. The fetishist's behavior not only fails to be interested; it fails even to appear interested to him. To be sure, it is designed to fulfill the desire which is its immediate motive; but fulfillment of desire is not necessarily the same thing as abiding satisfaction. He may be gratified or relieved for an instant, but this kind of fulfillment of desire leaves only the taste of ashes in one's mouth. The important point is that his behavior tends to be *contrary to interest,* as *senseless* almost as the repetitive beating of one's head against an unyielding stone wall. Bishop Butler was one of the first to point out how profoundly misleading it is to call such behavior "self-indulgent" simply because it appears voluntary, fulfills the actor's own desire, and leads to an instant's satisfaction before a torrent of guilt and anxiety. One might as well call the thirsty marooned sailor "self-indulgent" when he drinks deeply of the sea water that will surely dry him out further, as he well knows.

I believe there is a tendency in human nature, quite opposite to the one I have already mentioned, to consider the senselessness of a crime a kind of moral aggravation. That a cruel crime seemed pointless or senseless, a source of no gain to anyone, makes the harm it caused seem in the most absolute sense *unnecessary,* and that rubs salt in our psychic wounds. The harm was *all for nothing,* we lament, as if an intelligible motive would make our wounds any less injurious or the wounder less blameable. What happens, I think, is that the senselessness of a crime, particularly when it seems contrary to the criminal's interest, is profoundly frustrating. We are naturally disposed to be angry at the selfishly cruel, the ruthlessly self-aggrandizing man; but that anger is frustrated when we learn that the criminal, for no reason *he* could understand, was hurting *himself* as well as his victim. That is simply not the way properly self-respecting wicked persons are supposed to behave! But then we become angry at him precisely because we cannot be angry in the usual ways. We blame him now for our own frustration—not only for the harm he has caused, but for his not getting anything out of it. Indignation will always out.

Still, in a calmer reflective moment, punishment of the pitiably odd is likely to seem a kind of "pouring it on." Indeed, we might well say of such people what the more forgiving Epictetus said of all wrongdoers, that they are sufficiently punished simply to be the sorts of persons they are. Their crimes are obviously profitless to themselves and serve no apparent other-regarding interest, either malevolent or benevolent. Thus if the point of punishment is to

take the profit out of crime, it is superfluous to impose it upon them.

Not only are the motives of some mentally ill but noncompulsive wrongdoers *senseless,* they are senseless in the special way that permits us to speak of them as *incoherent.* Their motives do not fit together and make a coherent whole because one kind of desire, conspicuous as a sore thumb, keeps getting in the way. These desires serve ill the rest of their important interests, including their overriding interest in personal integration and internal harmony. They "gum up the works," as we would say of machinery, and throw the person out of "proper working order." The reason they do is that, insofar as these desires are fulfilled, barriers are put in the paths of the others. They are inconsistent with the others in that it is impossible for all to be jointly satisfied, even though it is possible that the others could, in principle, be satisfied together. Moreover, the "senseless" desires, because they do not cohere, are likely to seem alien, not fully expressive of their owner's essential character.[4] When a person acts to satisfy them, it is as if he were acting on somebody else's desires. And, indeed, the alien desires may have a distinct kind of unifying character of their own, as if a new person were grafted on to the old one.

The final and perhaps most important feature common to the examples of voluntary crimes by mentally ill persons is the actor's *lack of insight into his own motives.* The normal person, in rehearsing the possibilities open to him, finds some prospects appealing and others repugnant, and he usually (but not always) knows what it is about a given prospect that makes it appealing or repugnant. If robbing a bank appeals to him, the reason may be that the excitement, the romance, or (far more likely) the money attracts him; and if having more money appeals to him, he usually knows *why* it does too. Normal persons, to be sure, can be mistaken. A criminal may think it is the adventure that is attracting him, instead of the money, or vice versa. It is easy enough to be confused about these things. Often enough we can test our understanding of our own motives by experimental methods. I may think that prospect *X,* which has characteristics *a, b,* and *c,* appeals to me solely because of *a;* but then, to my surprise, prospect *Y,* which has characteristics *a* and *b,* but not *c, repels* me. Hence I conclude that it was not simply the *a*-ness of *X* after all that attracted me. Moreover, even a person who is a model of mental health will be often ignorant or mistaken about the *ultimate* basis of appeal in the things that appeal to him.

The mentally ill person, however, will be radically and fundamentally benighted about the source of the appeal in his immediate objectives, and the truth will be hid from his view by an internal iron curtain. He may think that he is constructed in such a way that little children arouse him sexually, and that is the end of the matter, hardly suspecting that it is the playful, exploratory, irresponsible, and non-threatening character of his recollected childhood experiences that moves him; or he may think that "exposure for exposure's sake" is what appeals to him in the idea of public undress, whereas really what appeals to him is the public "affirmation of masculinity, a cry of 'Look, here is proof I am a man.'"[5] The true basis of appeal in the criminal's motivation may be, or become, obvious to an outsider, but his illness keeps him blind to it, often, I think, because this blindness is a necessary condition of the appeal itself. At any rate, his lack of self-awareness is no merely contingent thing, like the ignorance that can be charged to absentmindedness, unperceptiveness, objective ambiguities, or the garden varieties of self-deception. The ignorance is the necessary consequence, perhaps even a constituent, of the mental illness, which, taken as a collection of interconnected symptoms, is an alien condition involuntarily suffered.

III

We come back to our original question, then, in a new guise: why should the incoherent and self-concealed character of the mentally ill man's motives be a ground for special consideration when he has voluntarily committed a crime? Perhaps we should enlarge our conception of *compulsion* so that senseless, misunderstood motives automatically count as compulsive. If Jones's chronic desire to do something harmful is as powerful as, but no more powerful than, normal people's desires to do socially acceptable things, then we might think of Jones's desire as a kind of unfair burden. It is no harder for him to restrain on individual occasions, but he must be restraining it *always;* one slip and he is undone. He is really quite unlucky to have this greater burden and danger. The ordinary person is excused when he is made to do what he does not want to

do; but the mentally ill man, the argument might go, is excused because of the compulsive weight of his profitless *wants* themselves.

There may be some justice in this argument, but there is little logic. When we begin to tamper this profoundly with the concept of compulsion, it is likely to come completely apart. If men can be said to be compelled by their own quite resistible desires, then what is there left to contrast compulsion with?

A more plausible move is to enlarge our conception of what it is to act "in ignorance"—the other category in the Aristotelian formula. The kleptomaniac and the fetishist have no conception of what it is that drives them to their bizarre actions. As we have seen, their conduct may well seem as puzzling to themselves as to any observer. So there is a sense in which they do not know, or realize, what it is they are really doing, and perhaps we should make this ignorance a ground for exculpation; but if we do, we shall be in danger of providing a defense for almost all criminals, normal and ill alike. The bank robber, who is deceived into thinking that it is the adventure that appeals to him when it really is the money, has this excuse available to him, as well as the bully who thinks he inflicts beatings in self-defense when it really is the sight of blood that appeals to him. Lack of insight by itself, then, can hardly be a workable extension of the ignorance defense in courts of law.

It is plain, I think, why the penal law requires rather strict interpretations of compulsion and ignorance. One of its major aims is to deter wrongdoers by providing them with a motive, namely, fear of punishment, which they would not otherwise have for refraining from crime. In close cases involving competent calculators, this new motive might be sufficient to tip the motivational scales toward self-restraint. Mentally ill but rationally competent offenders of the sort I have been discussing, provided only that they *can* restrain themselves, are eminently suited for responsibility because the fear of punishment might make some difference in their behavior. But if they truly cannot help what they do, then the fear of punishment is totally useless and might as well not be induced in them in the first place.

Thus, from the point of view of what punishment can achieve for others, it is a perfectly appropriate mode of treatment for rationally competent, noncompulsive, mentally ill persons. But from the point of view of what can be achieved for the offender himself, I still think it is altogether inappropriate. Some of the aims of an enlightened criminal law, after all, do concern the offender himself. Sometimes punishment is supposed to "reform" him by intimidation. This no doubt works once in a while for normally prudent and self-interested offenders. For others, greater claims still are made for punishment, which is expected to achieve not merely effective intimidation but also moral regeneration of the offender. But if we treat the mentally ill criminal in precisely the same way as we treat the normal one, we can only bring him to the point of hopeless despair. The prisoner, still devoid of insight into his own motives, will naturally come to wonder how his so-called illness differs from plain wickedness. His bizarre desires will be taken as simply "given," as evil impulses with no point and no reward, simply "there," an integral and irreducible part of himself; and there is no one more pitiably incorrigible than the man convinced of his own intrinsic wickedness and simply resigned to it.

I agree with Professor Dershowitz that it is outrageous to impose compulsory therapeutic treatment on an unwilling, mentally competent subject. I submit, however, that punishment imposed on the mentally ill, even though it might produce a small social gain in deterrence, is an equally odious measure. I admit that, insofar as the sick offender has voluntarily committed a crime he could have avoided, the state has a perfect right to deprive him of his liberty for a limited period; but, instead of using that time to have him break up rocks with the convicted embezzlers and burglars, we should be making every sympathetic effort to enable him to understand himself, in the hope that self-revelation will permit him to become a responsible citizen.[6] There is no easy way to avoid the problems that come from the institutional mixture of compulsion and therapy. I am afraid I must leave them for my legal and psychiatric friends. My aim in this paper has been the very limited one of showing that mental illness, even without compulsion and general cognitive impairment, is a good deal more pertinent to our moral concerns than the mumps or chicken pox.

---

1. Alan M. Dershowitz, "The Psychiatrist's Power in Civil Commitment: A Knife that Cuts Both Ways." An abridged version of this talk was published in *Psychology Today*, 2/9 (Feb. 1969), 43–47.
2. Consider Professor Dershowitz's example of Dallas Williams, "who at age thirty-nine had spent half his life in jail for seven convictions of assault with a deadly weapon and one conviction of manslaughter. Just before his scheduled release from jail, the government petitioned for his civil commitment. Two psychiatrists testified that although 'at the present time [he] shows no evidence of active mental illness . . . his is potentially dangerous to others and if released is likely to repeat his patterns of criminal behavior, and might commit homicide.' The judge, in denying the government's petition and ordering Williams' release, observed that: 'the courts have no legal basis for ordering confinement on mere apprehension of future unlawful acts. They must wait until another crime is committed or the person is found insane.' Within months of his release, Williams lived up to the prediction of the psychiatrists and shot two men to death in an unprovoked attack." *Ibid.*, 44.
3. Note on "Civil Restraint, Mental Illness, and the Right to Treatment," *Yale Law Review*, 77/1 (1967), 87.
4. Hence the point of the ancient metaphor of "possession."
5. Paul H. Gebhard et al., *Report on Sex Offenders* (New York: Harper & Row, and Paul B. Hoeber, 1965), 399.
6. I.e., he is clutchable, but not necessarily punishable.

PART FIVE

Punishment

What distinguishes criminal law from the various branches of private law is that criminal law's assigned function is to determine whether or not an accused person is properly to be *punished* for prior conduct. Tort law, in contrast—except in hybrid judgments of punitive damages—is unconcerned with punishment. Its assigned function is to determine which of two contending parties is to pay the bill for damages produced when the one party's flawed conduct seemed to be the cause of the other party's loss or injury. The philosophy of criminal law, then, must commence with an analysis of the concept of punishment, just as tort theory must begin by coming to terms with the idea of compensation. Punishment is what defines and distinguishes criminal law; it is what that branch of the law is for, "the name of its game," its "bottom line."

For that reason the concept of legal punishment, in its own right, is of central theoretical importance to a philosopher of law. In addition, solutions to the puzzles it poses for the philosopher are also presupposed by problems, both theoretical and practical, throughout the substantive criminal law. Questions about the necessary conditions of criminal liability, for example, are often answered in different ways by philosophers with differing conceptions of the nature and moral grounding of punishment. That these two types of disagreement should appear together is no mere coincidence. Differing views about the conditions of criminal responsibility can derive specifically from prior disagreements over the nature of punishment. Even in the practical contexts in which law cases are adjudicated, decisions often hinge upon which definition of *punishment* a judge's argument endorses.

What Is Legal Punishment?

In the 1950s there seemed for a time to be promise of a resolution of the traditional impasse in the philosophy of punishment. The promising new developments were primarily due to more careful definitions of the term *legal punishment*. Largely through the examples of Anthony Flew, Stanley Berm, Herbert Hart, and John Rawls, philosophers began to distinguish between defining and justifying punishment, between particular instances of punishment and punishment as a general practice within an institutional structure, and between moral and legal guilt, among other things. The hope was that the new distinctions and more accurate definitions would permit reformulations of ancient unitary questions now seen to be separable. No one view carried the day, but people were especially excited by the idea that the general practice of punishment is something retributive in its defining operations and utilitarian in its justifying aims. The influential definition from Flew had five conditions. To paraphrase, one party's treatment of another can properly be called legal punishment only if (1) it is hard treatment (2) inflicted for a violation of legal rules (3) on the actual or supposed violator (4) imposed and administered by human beings other than the supposed violator himself (5) who have the authority to do so under the rules of the governing legal system. If the sense of punishment captured by Flew's definition is the "general practice" sense, then the practice it analyzes seems clearly justifiable by its likely deterrence of would-be violators. But, unlike other utilitarian theories, it does not define a practice whose internal or constitutive rules could ever permit the knowing punishment of the innocent. That kind of barbarism, in fact, is explicitly ruled out by condition (3) of the definition.

Joel Feinberg, in his 1964 article, "The Expressive Function of Punishment," had no quarrel with the basic Flew strategy. Feinberg argued, however, that Flew's definition was inadequate—though not in a way directly relating to Flew's main purpose. Feinberg argued that the five-pronged Flew definition was too broad. Although all the legal practices we would normally call punishment are indeed punishment according to Flew's definition, some of the practices we would not call punishment ("in the strict and narrow sense of special interest to the moralist") also fall within the scope of the definition. Feinberg had in mind as properly excludable the sanctions he called "mere penalties," such as parking tickets, taxes, and football penalties. To exclude them from the class of dealings properly called punishments, he proposed that a sixth condition be added to Flew's definition: namely, that proper punishments, unlike mere penalties, express (often through their conventional symbolism) resentment, disapproval, condemnation, or reprobation. Now the definition seemed neither too broad nor too narrow.

Once this expressive function of punishment is recognized, however, new questions arise. To what extent, and by what methods, should criminal punishment express to the community and to the offender messages about what is shameful or disgusting? If official expression of condemnation is an aim of punishment, does this justify public shaming of offenders? Toni Massaro takes up these questions in "Shame, Culture and American Criminal Law." Massaro concludes that there is not adequate justification for the recent trend toward public shaming in the sentencing practices of some American courts.

What, If Anything, Justifies Legal Punishment?

We have already mentioned the impasse over the justification of legal punishment, but we have failed to mention the three-sided nature of the disagreement. As "The Classic Debate" by Feinberg describes, more and more writers have come to regard both the pure retributivist theory and the pure utilitarian theory as too extreme to be credible. They have opted instead for a mixed theory.[1] According to that theory, since moral guilt is said to be a necessary condition for an act of legal punishment to be justified, then social util-

ity cannot, by itself, be sufficient; and since social utility is deemed necessary, it follows that moral guilt, all by itself, cannot be sufficient. Since the pure retributivist holds that moral guilt is sufficient to justify punishment, even in the absence of expected good consequences for *anybody,* then that theory is false. And since the pure utilitarian holds that social utility is sufficient, even without moral guilt, to justify legal punishment, then this theory is false too. Thus, both pure theories would have to give up their claims that their favorite justifying factors (moral guilt in the one case, social utility in the other) are sufficient for successful justification. The mixed theory would then hold that (1) moral guilt is necessary, but not alone sufficient; (2) social utility is necessary, but not alone sufficient; (3) moral guilt and social utility are severally necessary and jointly sufficient.

The adherent of the mixed theory is then relieved of the burden of defending two of the most difficult claims customarily made by philosophers of punishment. The first is the claim of Immanuel Kant (1724–1804) that, even if a desert island community were to disband and scatter throughout the world, they have a right, indeed a *duty,* to execute all the convicted murderers in their custody, their moral guilt being sufficient warrant. The second possibly embarrassing claim is that which must be defended by the pure utilitarian, at least according to the opponents of that theory. The utilitarian must either justify the occasional knowing punishment of the innocent, it is commonly alleged, or rebut the accusation that pure utilitarian theory logically implies that the innocent may, in certain rare circumstances, properly be punished. The circumstances described in the "embarrassing example" put forth by the opponents of pure utilitarianism sometimes go beyond being rare. They sometimes are so incredibly unlikely that they appear "fantastic," in the manner of sloppily contrived science fiction. So long as these fictitious descriptions are not logically contradictory or violative of laws of nature and hence impossible on their face, philosophers have shown little hesitation in using counterexamples against one another. C. L. Ten, in his selection here, considers precisely this question: Do fantastic counterexamples, despite their being fantastic, undermine or discredit somehow the philosophical theses they are aimed at? Ten concludes his sensitive discussion by offering a set of fantastic counterexamples of his own against utilitarianism.

The mixed theory of punishment has more difficulty dealing with the third question distinguished by Feinberg in his "Classic Debate" article: "How should we determine how much punishment is the correct amount?" or put differently, "How should we interpret the requirement that 'the punishment must fit the crime?'" Insofar as the mixed theory is committed *both* to retributive and to utilitarian considerations, it must find a way to blend those normally irreconcilable factors in deciding how much punishment to dish out. And that is not easy to do.

Until recently the only important representatives of pure moralistic retributivism were the nineteenth-century German philosophers Immanuel Kant and Friedrich Hegel and their followers. But their writings are typically so obscure that they perplex rather than stimulate students. But in Michael Moore's article on the subject, included here, we have a work marked not only by profundity and subtlety but also clarity. This work, we think, even if it is not totally convincing, deserves to become a classic. (It is quite long, however, and should be read in at least two installments.) Moore's essay is all the more valuable in being uncompromising. He knows very well what rehabilitation theory is, and he rejects it. He knows what vengeance is, and he rejects it. He knows what mixed theories are, and he rejects them. He is the pure retributivist of Feinberg's "Classic Debate" article, a person who will not back away from the sufficiency thesis.

Moore's article is especially important for the way it responds to arguments against retributivism. He deals with one of these arguments, in particular, in detail—the argument whose first prominent spokesman was the German writer Friedrich Nietzsche (1844–1900). Retributive punishments have been associated with some of the most unsavory of human emotions. Not only do these emotions produce the attitudes and judgments that are then embodied in retributivist punishments, but they are themselves strengthened by the retributive practices and made even more disreputable. Nietzsche is a marvelously insightful literary psychologist who can be quite convincing even as he explains and exposes the typical mechanism by which people acquire the emotional dispositions that he lumps under the French term *ressentiment:* "resentment, fear, anger, cowardice, hostility, aggression, cruelty, sadism, envy, jealousy, guilt, self-loathing, hypocrisy, and [especially] self-deception."

Moore could have taken the quick way with the Nietzschean argument and simply convicted its proponents of committing "the genetic fallacy"—inferring the falsity of a proposition from some truths about how people come to acquire a belief in that proposi-

tion. No matter how unsavory the emotions that lead one to believe some proposition, that proposition might yet be true. It is a fallacy to affirm its falsehood on the sole basis of the way people come to acquire a belief in it, just as it is a fallacy to infer its falsity from the unsavoriness of the emotions it may come in time to encourage. Moore, however, doesn't leave it at that. He treats the Nietzschean argument with great respect and devotes many pages of his own to an account of the moral and immoral emotions, the epistemic and psychological import of emotions in general, and particularly in relation to our moral judgments. One of his most effective devices is to turn the argument back on his opponents by showing how antiretributive judgments can be motivated by some of the most unsavory human emotions. Very likely no conclusive proofs are given on either side of the debate about the morality of punishment, if only because of confusion about where the initial burden of proof belongs in this kind of debate. But at least two great benefits result from Moore's treatment of the issues. First, he identifies pivotal issues and clarifies arguments on both sides. Second, he treats us to one of the most thorough and sensitive discussions of the relations between moral judgment and emotion since Aristotle proclaimed that the realm of moral philosophy concerns not only our dispositions to act in certain ways in certain kinds of circumstances, but also our dispositions to have the *feelings* that are appropriate to the various situations in which we may find ourselves.

As is to be expected, Moore's skillful defense of pure retributivism leaves many challenges unmet. Advancing the argument against pure retributivism, Russ Shafer-Landau argues that it cannot answer any of the three questions that a comprehensive theory of punishment must answer. What is punishment's general justifying aim? Which actions warrant punishment and which do not? And what is the proper degree or amount of punishment for a given offense? Shafer-Landau considers and rejects a variety of recent retributivist attempts to answer these questions.

Victims' Rights: Restitution or Vengeance?

The "vindictive theory of punishment," as Feinberg called it in "The Classic Debate," has never been popular with philosophers because it gives a major role in the justification of legal punishment to vengeance, a response that most philosophers regard as primitive, superstitious, and irrational. Retributivists especially have taken great pains to distance themselves from any theory that even tolerates vengeance, much less to one that enshrines it near the top of the hierarchy of justificatory aims for punishment. Retributivists have been constantly challenged to answer the utilitarian accusation that retribution is merely vengeance in disguise, a charge that does not always go away when the retributivist rejoins by indicting his or her critic for committing the "genetic fallacy." In recent years, perhaps under the growing influence of the victims' rights movement, there has been something of a change in this scenario. Formerly, retributivists unanimously abhorred vengeance; now some of them, instead of denying the connection between retribution and vengeance, suggest that vengeance need not be as disreputable as philosophers have long believed. In particular, *victims* of crimes are in a position to demand vengeance, since nonvictims—though they can demand that there be a return of the criminal's wrongdoing back on him "out of principle," or to "restore a moral equilibrium," or for some similarly impersonal moral reason—cannot themselves be the ones to enjoy retaliating or getting even. Also, if vengeance is thought to be a way of coping with such barely tolerable intense emotions as wrath and hatred, it belongs uniquely to a victim, if to anyone.

The selections from J. L. Mackie and Jeffrie G. Murphy both deal with some aspect of the rights we can ascribe to the victims of crimes as such. Mackie, who as an ethical subjectivist denies that there are objective moral truths, discusses the evolutionary advantages of retributive sentiments. Murphy deals more directly with the current demands of the politically active victims' rights movement and the point of the metaphor of "getting even." It seems almost as if every major issue in this text regarding criminal law is involved in the debate in *Payne v. Tennessee*. This case involves the admissibility of victim-impact statements and Justice Scalia's insistence that "the harm caused by criminal acts must be considered in assessing responsibility," even when the occurrence or nonoccurrence of the harm is such that some would call a "matter of luck." (See in Part Four, for example, the contributions of Richard Parker and Judith Thompson.)

The Death Penalty

The final section in this part concerns one specific criminal punishment—the death penalty. It deserves

its own section because the disagreements it inspires between abolitionists and defenders of death as a punishment are among the most intractable in our public life, not to mention the halls of academe. Almost all the abstract philosophical principles of the criminal law, those debated in the chapters on justice and responsibility as well as this chapter on punishment, are here applied to one specific problem, and difficult as the abstract issues are, the concrete issue in which they collide is more difficult still. (This is evident in the two cases that begin this subsection, *Furman v. Georgia* and *Woodson v. North Carolina*.) That, no doubt, is partly because "death is different." The sentence of death is irrevocable and its errors are uncorrectable. Also contributing to the difficulty is an argument that cuts both ways. On the one hand, killing a person seems to be a uniquely inappropriate way of imparting the moral teaching that killing people is morally wrong (a consideration that tells against the death penalty). Yet our failure to reserve the most extreme of all the morally acceptable punishments in our system for the most serious crime is a poor way of registering the extreme seriousness with which we regard this most horrifying of crimes. We give appropriate symbolism to that seriousness when we solemnly exact the greatest penalty for its commission. Anything less would misrepresent our feelings by trivializing them (relatively speaking).

Still another reason why the capital punishment debate seems so difficult to resolve is that on both sides can be found such gifted philosophers as Ernest van den Haag (in favor of capital punishment) and Stephen Nathanson (opposed). We cannot run away from a problem, however, even when it is, like this one, philosophical at its roots, just because disagreements among the learned seem to be intractable. In any event, the Supreme Court keeps returning to the problem, so it is hardly ever likely to drop from public view.

Many opponents of capital punishment during the 1960s, following the lead of Professor Charles Black of the Yale Law School,[2] argued that the selection by our system of only a small handful of convicted murderers (and at that time occasional rapists and traitors) strongly suggested that such selection was in large part a process characterized by "arbitrariness and caprice." Justice would require that morally relevant differences among the particular criminal acts being punished should be treated in proportionately different ways and that the death penalty be reserved for the most egregious ("morally aggravated") crimes. But in fact the differential treatment accorded the prisoners seemed to have no relation whatever to any "morally relevant differences" among their actions. They appeared as a group almost as if they had been selected randomly, by a process no more related to justice than a lottery is.

The North Carolina legislature evaded judicial efforts to reform its sentencing procedures by passing a bill making mandatory the sentence of death for *all* first-degree murders. No one could accuse *them* of arbitrariness, the legislators thought, since they treated all their murderers exactly alike: they executed all of them. But in the case of *Woodson v. North Carolina,* the Supreme Court gave its reasons for holding mandatory death penalties unconstitutional, apart from a reason that suggests itself immediately: to treat all murderers exactly alike is to imply that there are no morally relevant differences among them, a proposition that will amaze all students of moral philosophy.

Furman v. Georgia, decided by the Court in 1972, gave some moderate encouragement to the abolitionists, but not great excitement, for there were nine separate opinions delivered! Two justices of the five endorsing the majority opinion argued that all capital punishment is "cruel and unusual" and therefore forbidden by the Eighth Amendment. The remaining three members of the majority argued, with minor variations among them, that it is only the way capital punishment is currently administered that makes it unconstitutional, in effect citing arbitrariness rather than cruelty as the ground of unconstitutionality. The Court's rejection of capital punishment was really only temporary and provisional. The death penalty is unconstitutional basically because "out of a large number of persons 'eligible' in law for the punishment of death a few were selected as if at random, by no stated (or perhaps statable) criteria, while all the rest suffered the lesser penalty of imprisonment."[3]

The remaining four justices, those in the minority, argued that there were no sufficient reasons, at least not now, for finding the death penalty unconstitutional. That gave abolitionists very little to cheer about.

Almost immediately various state legislatures tried to get around *Furman v. Georgia* by revising the sentencing provisions in their penal codes. Two tactics were used. Some, like North Carolina, tried to make death sentences nonarbitrary by making them mandatory for some crimes. That evasive path was soon closed. The other method was to change their sentencing provisions so that they accorded more closely with the reasoning in *Furman.* Separate trials allowing juries to decide sentences after the regular trial at which the defendant was convicted was another new idea. In some states bills were passed containing lists of aggravating and mitigating circumstances and requirements that some score tallied up from those lists must lead juries either to the death penalty or imprisonment, whichever is most appropriate given the score. Such criteria of nonarbitrariness were refined in many judicial test cases and legislative debates throughout the country. These eventually received the stamp of approval from the Supreme Court. Soon the number of court-approved sentencing procedures was large. Eventually the worst criminals (according to the plan) or the unluckiest ones (not according to the plan) began once more to be hanged, gassed, and electrocuted. And we are back to where we were before 1962. There is probably less arbitrariness in the system now, but very little less cruelty. Whether the death penalty is never, sometimes, or always cruel, in itself or in its context, and whether it is cruel enough in any case to be unconstitutional is a problem for the Supreme Court. But that does not mean that philosophers may not second-guess.

---

1. In regard to Feinberg's terminology in "The Classic Debate": Some minor revision is necessary in this discussion of Feinberg's terminology if the mixed theory is to be coherent.

2. Charles L. Black, *Capital Punishment: The Inevitability of Caprice and Mistake* (New York: W. W. Norton & Co., 1974).
3. *Ibid.,* p. 12.

What is Legal Punishment?

THE EXPRESSIVE FUNCTION OF PUNISHMENT*

Joel Feinberg

It might well appear to a moral philosopher absorbed in the classical literature of his discipline, or to a moralist sensitive to injustice and suffering, that recent philosophical discussions of the problem of punishment have somehow missed the point of his interest. Recent influential articles[1] have quite sensibly distinguished between questions of definition and justification, between justifying general rules and particular decisions, between moral and legal guilt. So much is all to the good. When these articles go on to *define* "punishment," however, it seems to many that they leave out of their ken altogether the very element that makes punishment theoretically puzzling and morally disquieting. Punishment is defined, in effect, as the infliction of hard treatment by an authority on a person for his prior failing in some respect (usually an infraction of a rule or command).[2] There may be a very general sense of the word "punishment" which is well expressed by this definition; but even if that is so, we can distinguish a narrower, more emphatic sense that slips through its meshes. Imprisonment at hard labor for committing a felony is a clear case of punishment in the emphatic sense; but I think we would be less willing to apply that term to parking tickets, offside penalties, sackings, flunkings, and disqualifications. Examples of the latter sort that I propose to call *penalties* (merely), so

that I may inquire further what distinguishes punishment, in the strict and narrow sense that interests the moralist, from other kinds of penalties.[3]

One method of answering this question is to focus one's attention on the class of nonpunitive penalties in an effort to discover some clearly identifiable characteristic common to them all, and absent from all punishments, on which the distinction between the two might be grounded. The hypotheses yielded by this approach, however, are not likely to survive close scrutiny. One might conclude, for example, that mere penalties are less severe than punishments, but although this is generally true, it is not necessarily and universally so. Again we might be tempted to interpret penalties as mere "price-tags" attached to certain types of behavior that are generally undesirable, so that only those with especially strong motivation will be willing to pay the price.[4] So, for example, deliberate efforts on the part of some western states to keep roads from urban centers to wilderness areas few in number and poor in quality are essentially no different from various parking fines and football penalties. In each case a certain kind of conduct is discouraged without being absolutely prohibited: Anyone who desires strongly enough to get to the wilderness (or park overtime, or interfere with a pass) may do so provided he is willing to pay the

---

*From Joel Feinberg, *Doing and Deserving* (Princeton, N.J.: Princeton University Press, 1970), pp. 95–118.

penalty (price). On this view penalties are, in effect, licensing fees, different from other purchased permits in that the price is often paid afterward rather than in advance. Since a similar interpretation of punishments seems implausible, it might be alleged that this is the basis of the distinction between penalties and punishments. However, while a great number of penalties can, no doubt, plausibly be treated as retroactive license fees, this is hardly true of all of them. It is certainly not true, for example, of most demotions, firings, and flunkings, that they are "prices" paid for some already consumed benefit; and even parking fines are sanctions for rules "meant to be taken seriously as . . . standard[s] of behavior,"[5] and thus are more than mere public parking fees.

Rather than look for a characteristic common and peculiar to the penalties on which to ground the distinction between penalties and punishments, we would be better advised, I think, to cast our attention to the examples of punishments. Both penalties and punishments are authoritative deprivations for failures; but apart from these common features, penalties have a miscellaneous character, whereas punishments have an important additional characteristic in common. That characteristic, or specific difference, I shall argue, is a certain expressive function: Punishment is a conventional device for the expression of attitudes of resentment and indignation, and of judgments of disapproval and reprobation, either on the part of the punishing authority himself or of those "in whose name" the punishment is inflicted. Punishment, in short, has a *symbolic significance* largely missing from other kinds of penalties.

The reprobative symbolism of punishment and its character as "hard treatment," while never separate in reality, must be carefully distinguished for purposes of analysis. Reprobation is itself painful, whether or not it is accompanied by further "hard treatment"; and hard treatment, such as fine of imprisonment, because of its conventional symbolism, can itself be reprobatory; but still we can conceive of ritualistic condemnation unaccompanied by any *further* hard treatment, and of inflictions and deprivations which, because of different symbolic conventions, have no reprobative force. It will be my thesis in this essay that (1) both the hard treatment aspect of punishment and its reprobative function must be part of the *definition* of legal punishment; and (2) each of these aspects raises its own kind of question about the *justification* of legal punishment as a general practice. I shall argue that some of the jobs punishment does, and some of the conceptual

problems it raises, cannot be intelligibly described unless (1) is true; and that the incoherence of a familiar form of the retributive theory results from failure to appreciate the force of (2).

I. Punishment As Condemnation

That the expression of the community's condemnation is an essential ingredient in legal punishment is widely acknowledged by legal writers. Henry M. Hart, for example, gives eloquent emphasis to the point:

> What distinguishes a criminal from a civil sanction and all that distinguishes it, it is ventured, is the judgment of community condemnation which accompanies . . . its imposition. As Professor Gardner wrote not long ago, in a distinct but cognate connection:
>
> "The essence of punishment for moral delinquency lies in the criminal conviction itself. One may lose more money on the stock market than in a courtroom; a prisoner of war camp may well provide a harsher environment than a state prison; death on the field of battle has the same physical characteristics as death by sentence of law. It is the expression of the community's hatred, fear, or contempt for the convict which alone characterizes physical hardship as punishment."
>
> If this is what a "criminal" penalty is, then we can say readily enough what a "crime" is . . . . It is conduct which, if duly shown to have taken place, will incur a formal and solemn pronouncement of the moral condemnation of the community. . . . Indeed the condemnation plus the added [unpleasant physical] consequences may well be considered, compendiously, as constituting the punishment.[6]

Professor Hart's compendious definition needs qualification in one respect. The moral condemnation and the "unpleasant consequences" that he rightly identifies as essential elements of punishment are not as distinct and separate as he suggests. It is not always the case that the convicted prisoner is first solemnly condemned and then subjected to unpleasant physical treatment. It would be more accurate in many cases to say that the unpleasant treatment itself expresses the condemnation, and that this expressive aspect of his incarceration is precisely the element by reason of which it is properly characterized as punishment and not mere penalty. The administrator who regretfully suspends the license of a conscientious but accident-prone driver can inflict a deprivation without any scolding, express or implied; but the reckless motorist who is sent to prison for six months is thereby inevitably subject to shame and ignominy—the very walls of his cell condemn him and his record becomes a stigma.

To say that the very physical treatment itself expresses condemnation is to say simply that certain forms of hard treatment have become the conventional symbols of public reprobation. This is neither more nor less paradoxical than to say that certain words have become conventional vehicles in our language for the expression of certain attitudes, or that champagne is the alcoholic beverage traditionally used in celebration of great events, or that black is the color of mourning. Moreover, particular kinds of punishment are often used to express quite specific attitudes (loosely speaking, this is part of their "meaning"); note the differences, for example, between beheading a nobleman and hanging a yeoman, burning a heretic and hanging a traitor, hanging an enemy soldier and executing him by firing squad.

It is much easier to show that punishment has a symbolic significance than to say exactly what it is that punishment expresses. At its best, in civilized and democratic countries, punishment surely expresses the community's strong *disapproval* of what the criminal did. Indeed it can be said that punishment expresses the *judgment* (as distinct from any emotion) of the community that what the criminal did was wrong. I think it is fair to say of our community, however, that punishment generally expresses more than judgments of disapproval; it is also a symbolic way of getting back at the criminal, of expressing a kind of vindictive resentment. To any reader who has in fact spent time in a prison, I venture to say, even Professor Gardner's strong terms—"hatred, fear, or contempt for the convict"—will not seem too strong an account of what imprisonment is universally taken to express. Not only does the criminal feel the naked hostility of his guards and the outside world—that would be fierce enough—but that hostility is self-righteous as well. His punishment bears the aspect of legitimized vengefulness; hence there is much truth in J. F. Stephen's celebrated remark that "The criminal law stands to the passion of revenge in much the same relation as marriage to the sexual appetite."[7]

If we reserve the less dramatic term "resentment" for the various vengeful attitudes, and the term "reprobation" for the stern judgment of disapproval, then perhaps we can characterize *condemnation* (or denunciation) as a kind of fusing of resentment and reprobation. That these two elements are generally to be found in legal punishment was well understood by the authors of the Report of the Royal Commission on Capital Punishment:

> Discussion of the principle of retribution is apt to be confused because the word is not always used in the same sense. Sometimes it is intended to mean vengeance, sometimes reprobation. In the first sense the idea is that of satisfaction by the State of a wronged individual's desire to be avenged; in the second it is that of the State's *marking* its disapproval of the breaking of its laws by a punishment proportionate to the gravity of the offense [my italics].[8]

II. Some Derivative Symbolic Functions of Punishment

The relation of the expressive function of punishment to its various central purposes is not always easy to trace. Symbolic public condemnation added to deprivation may help or hinder deterrence, reform, and rehabilitation—the evidence is not clear. On the other hand, there are other functions of punishment, often lost sight of in the preoccupation with deterrence and reform, that presuppose the expressive function and would be impossible without it.

1. Authoritative disavowal

Consider the standard international practice of demanding that a nation whose agent has unlawfully violated the complaining nation's rights should punish the offending agent. For example, suppose that an airplane of nation *A* fires on an airplane of nation *B* while the latter is flying over international waters. Very likely high authorities in nation *B* will send a note of protest to their counterparts in nation *A* demanding, among other things, that the transgressive pilot be punished. Punishing the pilot is an emphatic, dramatic, and well-understood way of *condemning* and thereby *disavowing* his act. It tells the world that the pilot had no right to do what he did, that he was on his own in doing it, that his government does not condone that sort of thing. It testifies thereby to government *A*'s recognition of the violated rights of government *B* in the affected area, and therefore to the wrongfulness of the pilot's act. Failure to punish the pilot tells the world that government *A* does not consider him to have been personally at fault. That in turn is to claim responsibility for the act, which in effect labels that act as an "instrument of deliberate national policy," and therefore an act of war. In that case either formal hostilities or humiliating loss of face by one side or the other almost certainly follows. None of this makes any sense without the well understood reprobative symbolism of punishment. In quite parallel ways punishment enables employers to disavow the acts of their employees (though not civil liability for those acts), and fathers the destructive acts of their sons.

2. Symbolic nonacquiescence: "Speaking in the name of the people"

The symbolic function of punishment also explains why even those sophisticated persons who abjure resentment of criminals and look with small favor generally on the penal law are likely to demand that certain kinds of conduct be punished when or if the law lets them go by. In the state of Texas, so-called "paramour killings" are regarded by the law as not merely mitigated, but completely justifiable.[9] Many humanitarians, I believe, will feel quite spontaneously that a great injustice is done when such killings are left unpunished. The sense of violated justice, moreover, might be distinct and unaccompanied by any frustrated *schadenfreude* toward the killer, lust for blood or vengeance, or metaphysical concern lest the universe stay "out of joint." The demand for punishment in cases of this sort may instead represent the feeling that paramour killings deserve to be *condemned*, that the law in condoning, even approving of them, speaks for all citizens in expressing a wholly inappropriate attitude toward them. For, in effect, the law expresses the judgment of the "people of Texas," in whose name it speaks, that the vindictive satisfaction in the mind of the cuckolded husband is a thing of greater value than the very life of his wife's lover. The demand that paramour killings be punished may simply be the demand that this lopsided value judgment be withdrawn and that the state *go on record* against paramour killings, and the law *testify to the recognition* that such killings are wrongful. Punishment no doubt would also help deter killers. This too is a desid-

eratum and a closely related one, but it is not to be identified with reprobation; for deterrence might be achieved by a dozen other techniques, from simple penalties and forfeitures to exhortation and propaganda; but effective public denunciation and, through it, symbolic nonacquiescence in the crime, seem virtually to require punishment.

This symbolic function of punishment was given great emphasis by Kant, who, characteristically, proceeded to exaggerate its importance. Even if a desert island community were to disband, Kant argued, its members should first execute the last murderer left in its jails, "for otherwise they might all be regarded as participators in the [unpunished] murder. . . ."[10] This Kantian idea that in failing to punish wicked acts society endorses them and thus becomes *particeps criminis* does seem to reflect, however dimly, something embedded in common sense. A similar notion underlies whatever is intelligible in the widespread notion that all citizens share the responsibility for political atrocities. Insofar as there is a coherent argument behind the extravagant distributions of guilt made by existentialists and other literary figures, it can be reconstructed in some such way as this: To whatever extent a political act is done "in one's name," to that extent one is responsible for it. A citizen can avoid responsibility in advance by explicitly disowning the government as his spokesman, or after the fact through open protest, resistance, and so on. Otherwise, by "acquiescing" in what is done in one's name, one incurs the responsibility for it. The root notion here is a kind of "power of attorney" a government has for its citizens.

3. Vindication of the law

Sometimes the state goes on record through its statutes, in a way that might well please a conscientious citizen in whose name it speaks, but then through official evasion and unreliable enforcement, gives rise to doubts that the law really means what it says. It is murder in Mississippi, as elsewhere, for a white man intentionally to kill a Negro; but if grand juries refuse to issue indictments or if trial juries refuse to convict, and this is well understood by most citizens, then it is in a purely formal and empty sense indeed that killings of Negroes by whites are illegal in Mississippi. Yet the law stays on the books, to give ever-less-convincing lip service to a noble moral judgment. A statute honored mainly in the breach begins to lose its character as law, unless, as we say, it is *vindicated* (emphatically reaffirmed); and clearly the way to do this (indeed the only way) is to punish those who violate it.

Similarly, *punitive damages*, so-called, are sometimes awarded the plaintiff in a civil action, as a supplement to compensation for his injuries. What more dramatic way of vindicating his violated right can be imagined than to have a court thus forcibly condemn its violation through the symbolic machinery of punishment?

4. Absolution of others

When something scandalous has occurred and it is clear that the wrongdoer must be one of a small number of suspects, then the state, by punishing one of these parties, thereby relieves the others of suspicion, and informally absolves them of blame. Moreover, quite often the absolution of an accuser hangs as much in the balance at a criminal trial as the inculpation of the accused. A good example of this can be found in James Gould Cozzen's novel, *By Love Possessed*. A young girl, after an evening of illicit sexual activity with her boyfriend, is found out by her bullying mother, who then insists that she clear her name by bringing criminal charges against the boy. He used physical force, the girl charges; she freely consented, he replies. If the jury finds him guilty of rape, it will by the same token absolve her from (moral) guilt; and her reputation as well as his rides on the outcome. Could not the state do this job without punishment? Perhaps, but when it speaks by punishing, its message is loud, and sure of getting across.

III. The Constitutional Problem of Defining Legal Punishment

A philosophical theory of punishment that, through inadequate definition, leaves out the condemnatory function, not only will disappoint the moralist and the traditional moral philosopher; it will seem offensively irrelevant as well to the constitutional lawyer, whose vital concern with punishment is both conceptual, and therefore genuinely philosophical, and practically urgent. The distinction between punishment and mere penalties is a familiar one in the criminal law, where theorists have long engaged in what Jerome Hall calls "dubious dogmatics distinguishing 'civil penalties' from punitive sanctions, and

'public wrongs' from crimes."[11] Our courts now regard it as true (by definition) that all criminal statutes are punitive (merely labeling an act a crime does not make it one unless sanctions are specified); but to the converse question whether all statutes specifying sanctions are *criminal* statutes, the courts are reluctant to give an affirmative reply. There are now a great number of statutes that permit "unpleasant consequences" to be inflicted on persons and yet are surely not criminal statutes—tax bills, for example, are aimed at regulating, not forbidding, certain types of activity. How to classify borderline cases as either "regulative" or "punitive" is not merely an idle conceptual riddle; it very quickly draws the courts into questions of great constitutional import. There are elaborate constitutional safeguards for persons faced with the prospect of punishment; but these do not, or need not, apply when the threatened hard treatment merely "regulates an activity."

The 1960 Supreme Court case of *Flemming v. Nestor*[12] is a dramatic (and shocking) example of how a man's fate can depend on whether a government-inflicted deprivation is interpreted as a "regulative" or "punitive" sanction. Nestor had immigrated to the United States from Bulgaria in 1913, and in 1955 became eligible for old-age benefits under the Social Security Act. In 1956, however, he was deported in accordance with the Immigration and Nationality Act, for having been a member of the Communist Party from 1933 to 1939. This was a hard fate for a man who had been in America for forty-three years and who was no longer a Communist; but at least he would have his social security benefits to support him in his exiled old age. Or so he thought. Section 202 of the amended Social Security Act, however,

> provides for the termination of old-age, survivor, and disability insurance benefits payable to . . . an alien individual who, after September 1, 1954 (the date of enactment of the section) is deported under the Immigration and Nationality Act on any one of certain specified grounds, including past membership in the Communist Party.[13]

Accordingly, Nestor was informed that his benefits would cease.

Nestor then brought suit in a District Court for a reversal of the administrative decision. The court found in his favor and held § 202 of the Social Security Act unconstitutional, on the grounds that termination of [Nestor's] benefits amounts to punishing him without a judicial trial, that [it] constitutes the imposition of punishment by legislative act rendering § 202 a bill of attainder; and that the punishment exacted is imposed for past conduct not unlawful when engaged in, thereby violating the constitutional prohibition on ex post facto laws.[14]

The Secretary of Health, Education, and Welfare, Mr. Flemming, then appealed this decision to the Supreme Court.

It was essential to the argument of the District Court that the termination of old-age benefits under § 202 was in fact punishment, for if it were properly classified as nonpunitive deprivation, then none of the cited constitutional guarantees was relevant. The constitution, for example, does not forbid all retroactive laws, but only those providing punishment. (Retroactive tax laws may also be hard and unfair, but they are not unconstitutional.) The question before the Supreme Court then was whether the hardship imposed by § 202 was punishment. Did this not bring the Court face to face with the properly philosophical question "What is punishment?" and is it not clear that under the usual definition that fails to distinguish punishment from mere penalties, this particular judicial problem could not even arise?

The fate of the appellee Nestor can be recounted briefly. The five man majority of the court held that he had not been punished—this despite Mr. Justice Brennan's eloquent characterization of him in a dissenting opinion as "an aging man deprived of the means with which to live after being separated from his family and exiled to live among strangers in a land he quit forty-seven years ago."[15] Mr. Justice Harlan, writing for the majority, argued that the termination of benefits, like the deportation itself, was the exercise of the plenary power of Congress incident to the regulation of an activity.

Similarly, the setting by a State of qualifications for the practice of medicine, and their modification from time to time, is an incident of the State's power to protect the health and safety of its citizens, and its decision to bar from practice persons who commit or have committed a felony is taken as evidencing an intent to exercise that regulatory power, and not a purpose to add to the punishment of ex-felons.[16]

Mr. Justice Brennan, on the other hand, argued that it is impossible to think of any purpose the provision in question could possibly serve except to "strike" at "aliens deported for conduct displeasing to the lawmakers."[17]

Surely Justice Brennan seems right in finding in the sanction the expression of Congressional reprobation, and therefore "punitive intent"; but the sanction itself (in Justice Harlan's words, "the mere denial of a noncontractual governmental benefit"[18]) was not a conventional vehicle for the expression of censure, being wholly outside the apparatus of the criminal law. It therefore lacked the reprobative symbolism essential to punishment generally, and was thus, in its hybrid character, able to generate confusion and judicial disagreement. It was as if Congress had "condemned" a certain class of persons privately in stage whispers, rather than by pinning the infamous label of criminal on them and letting that symbol do the condemning in an open and public way. Congress without question "intended" to punish a certain class of aliens and did indeed select sanctions of appropriate severity for that use; but the deprivation they selected was not of an appropriate kind to perform the function of public condemnation. A father who "punishes" his son for a displeasing act the father had not thought to forbid in advance, by sneaking up on him from behind and then throwing him bodily across the room against the wall, would be in much the same position as the legislators of the amended Social Security Act, especially if he then denied to the son that his physical assault on him had had any "punitive intent," asserting that it was a mere exercise of his parental prerogative to rearrange the household furnishings and other objects in his own living room. This would be to tarnish the paternal authority and infect all later genuine punishments with hollow hypocrisy. This also happens when legislators go outside the criminal law to do the criminal law's job.

In 1961 the New York State Legislature passed the so-called "Subversive Drivers Act" requiring "suspension and revocation of the driver's license of anyone who has been convicted, under the Smith Act, of advocating the overthrow of the Federal government." *The Reporter* magazine[19] quoted the sponsor of the bill as admitting that it was aimed primarily at one person, Communist Benjamin Davis, who had only recently won a court fight to regain his driver's license after his five year term in prison. *The Reporter* estimated that at most a "few dozen"

people would be kept from driving by the new legislation. Was this punishment? Not at all, said the bill's
sponsor, Assemblyman Paul Taylor. The legislature
was simply exercising its right to regulate automobile
traffic in the interest of public safety:

> Driving licenses, Assemblyman Taylor
> explained . . . are not a "right" but a "valuable
> privilege." The Smith Act Communists, after
> all, were convicted of advocating the
> overthrow of the government by force, vio-
> lence, or assassination. ("They always leave
> out the assassination," he remarked. "I like to
> put it in.") Anyone who was convicted under
> such an act had to be "a person pretty well
> dedicated to a certain point of view," the as-
> semblyman continued, and anyone with that
> particular point of view "can't be concerned
> about the rights of others." Being concerned
> about the rights of others, he concluded, "is a
> prerequisite of being a good driver."[20]

This shows how transparent can be the effort to mask
punitive intent. The Smith Act ex-convicts were
treated with such severity and in such circumstances
that no nonpunitive legislative purpose could *plausibly* be maintained; yet that *kind* of treatment (quite
apart from its severity) lacks the reprobative symbolism essential to clear public denunciation. After all,
aged, crippled, and blind persons are also deprived
of their licenses, so it is not *necessarily* the case that
reprobation attaches to that kind of sanction. And so
victims of a cruel law understandably claim that they
have been punished, and retroactively at that. Yet
strictly speaking they have not been *punished*; they
have been treated much worse.

IV. The Problem of Strict Criminal Liability

The distinction between punishments and mere
penalties, and the essentially reprobative function of
the former, can also help clarify the controversy
among writers on the criminal law about the propriety of so-called "strict liability offenses"—offenses for
the conviction of which there need be no showing
of "fault" or "culpability" on the part of the accused.
If it can be shown that he committed an act proscribed by statute then he is guilty irrespective of
whether he had justification or excuse for what he
did. Perhaps the most familiar examples come from

the traffic laws: Leaving a car parked beyond the permitted time in a restricted zone is automatically to violate the law, and penalties will be imposed however
good the excuse. Many strict liability statutes do not
even require an overt act; these proscribe not certain
conduct but certain *results*. Some make mere unconscious possession of contraband, firearms, or narcotics a crime, others the sale of misbranded articles
or impure foods. The liability for so-called "public
welfare offenses" may seem especially severe:

> . . . with rare exceptions, it became definitely
> established that *mens rea* is not essential in
> the public welfare offenses, indeed that even
> a very high degree of care is irrelevant. Thus
> a seller of cattle feed was convicted of violat-
> ing a statute forbidding misrepresentation of
> the percentage of oil in the product, despite
> the fact that he had employed a reputable
> chemist to make the analysis and had even
> understated the chemist's findings.[21]

The rationale of strict liability in public welfare
statutes is that violation of the public interest is more
likely to be prevented by unconditional liability than
by liability that can be defeated by some kind of excuse; that even though liability without "fault" is severe, it is one of the known risks incurred by
businessmen; and that besides, the sanctions are *only
fines*, hence not really "punitive" in character. On the
other hand, strict liability to *imprisonment* (or "punishment proper") "has been held by many to be incompatible with the basic requirements of our
Anglo-American, and indeed, any civilized jurisprudence."[22] Why should this be? In both kinds of case,
defendants may have sanctions inflicted upon them
even though they are acknowledged to be without
fault; and the difference cannot be simply that imprisonment is always and necessarily a greater hurt
than fine, for this is not always so. Rather, the reason
why strict liability to imprisonment (punishment) is
so much more repugnant to our sense of justice than
is strict liability to fine (penalty) is simply that imprisonment in modern times has taken on the symbolism of public reprobation. In the words of Justice
Brandeis, "It is . . . imprisonment in a penitentiary,
which now renders a crime infamous."[23] We are familiar with the practice of penalizing persons for "offenses" they could not help. It happens every day in
football games, business firms, traffic courts, and the
like. But there is something very odd and offensive
in *punishing* people for admittedly faultless conduct;
for not only is it arbitrary and cruel to *condemn*

someone for something he did (admittedly) without fault, it is also self-defeating and irrational.

Though their abundant proliferation[24] is a relatively recent phenomenon, statutory offenses with nonpunitive sanctions have long been familiar to legal commentators, and long a source of uneasiness to them. This is "indicated by the persistent search for an appropriate label, such as "public torts," "public welfare offenses," "prohibitory laws," "prohibited acts," "regulatory offenses," "police regulations," "administrative misdemeanors," "quasi-crimes," or "civil offences."" [25] These represent alternatives to the unacceptable categorization of traffic infractions, inadvertent violations of commercial regulations, and the like, as *crimes*, their perpetrators as *criminals,* and their penalties as *punishments*. The drafters of the new Model Penal Code have defined a class of infractions of penal law forming no part of the substantive criminal law. These they call "violations," and their sanctions "civil penalties."

Section 1.04. Classes of Crimes: Violations

(1) An offense defined by this code or by any other statute of this State, for which a sentence of [death or of] imprisonment is authorized, constitutes a crime. Crimes are classified as felonies, misdemeanors, or petty misdemeanors.

[(2), (3), (4) define felonies, misdemeanors, and petty misdemeanors.]

(5) An offense defined by this Code or by any other statute of this State constitutes a violation if it is so designated in this Code or in the law defining the offense or if no other sentence than a fine, or fine and forfeiture or other civil penalty is authorized upon conviction or if it is defined by a statute other than this Code which now provides that the offense shall not constitute a crime. A violation does not constitute a crime and conviction of a violation shall not give rise to any disability or legal disadvantage based on conviction of a criminal offense.[26]

Since violations, unlike crimes, carry no social stigma, it is often argued that there is no serious injustice if, in the interest of quick and effective law enforcement, violators are held unconditionally liable. This line of argument is persuasive when we consider only parking and minor traffic violations, illegal sales of various kinds, and violations of health and safety codes, where the penalties serve as warnings and the fines are light. But the argument loses all cogency when the "civil penalties" are severe—heavy fines, forfeitures of property, removal from office, suspension of a license, withholding of an important "benefit," and the like. The condemnation of the faultless may be the most flagrant injustice, but the good natured, noncondemnatory infliction of severe hardship on the innocent is little better. It is useful to distinguish violations and civil penalties from crimes and punishments; but it does not follow that the safeguards of culpability requirements and due process which justice demands for the latter are always irrelevant encumbrances to the former. Two things are morally wrong: (1) to condemn a faultless man while inflicting pain or deprivation on him however slight (unjust punishment); and (2) to inflict unnecessary and severe suffering on a faultless man even in the absence of condemnation (unjust civil penalty). To exact a two dollar fine from a hapless violator for overtime parking, however, even though he could not possibly have helped it, is to do neither of these things.

V. Justifying Legal Punishment; Letting the Punishment Fit the Crime

Public condemnation, whether avowed through the stigmatizing symbolism of punishment or unavowed but clearly discernible (mere "punitive intent"), can greatly magnify the suffering caused by its attendant mode of hard treatment. Samuel Butler keenly appreciated the difference between reprobative hard treatment (punishment) and the same treatment sans reprobation:

. . . we should hate a single flogging given in the way of mere punishment more than the amputation of a limb, if it were kindly and courteously performed from a wish to help us out of our difficulty, and with the full consciousness on the part of the doctor that it was only by an accident of constitution that he was not in the like plight himself. So the Erewhonians take a flogging once a week, and a diet of bread and water for two or three months together, whenever their straightener recommends it.[27]

Even floggings and imposed fastings do not constitute punishments, then, where social conventions are such that they do not express public censure (what Butler called "scouting"); and as therapeutic treatments simply, rather than punishments, they are easier to take.

Yet floggings and fastings do hurt, and far more than is justified by their Erewhonian (therapeutic) objectives. The same is true of our own State Mental Hospitals where criminal psychopaths are often sent for "rehabilitation": Solitary confinement may not hurt *quite* so much when called "the quiet room," or the forced support of heavy fire extinguishers when called "hydrotherapy";[28] but their infliction on patients can be so cruel (whether or not their quasi-medical names mask punitive intent) as to demand justification.

Hard treatment and symbolic condemnation, then, are not only both necessary to an adequate definition of "punishment"; each also poses a special problem for the justification of punishment. The reprobative symbolism of punishment is subject to attack not only as an independent source of suffering but as the vehicle of undeserved responsive attitudes and unfair judgments of blame. One kind of skeptic, granting that penalties are needed if legal rules are to be enforced, and also that society would be impossible without general and predictable obedience to such rules, might nevertheless question the need to add condemnation to the penalizing of violators. Hard treatment of violators, he might grant, is an unhappy necessity, but reprobation of the offender is offensively self-righteous and cruel; adding gratuitous insult to necessary injury can serve no useful purpose. A partial answer to this kind of skeptic has already been given. The condemnatory aspect of punishment does serve a socially useful purpose: It is precisely the element in punishment that makes possible the performance of such symbolic functions as disavowal, nonacquiescence, vindication, and absolution.

Another kind of skeptic might readily grant that the reprobative symbolism of punishment is necessary to and justified by these various derivative functions. Indeed, he may even add deterrence to the list, for condemnation is likely to make it clear where it would not otherwise be so that a penalty is not a mere price-tag. Granting that point, however, this kind of skeptic would have us consider whether the ends that justify public condemnation of criminal conduct might not be achieved equally well by means of less painful symbolic machinery. There was a time, after all, when the gallows and the rack were the leading clear symbols of shame and ignominy. Now we condemn felons to penal servitude

as the way of rendering their crimes infamous. Could not the job be done still more economically? Isn't there a way to stigmatize without inflicting any further (pointless) pain to the body, to family, to creative capacity?

One can imagine an elaborate public ritual, exploiting the trustiest devices of religion and mystery, music and drama, to express in the most solemn way the community's condemnation of a criminal for his dastardly deed. Such a ritual might condemn so very emphatically that there could be no doubt of its genuineness, thus rendering symbolically superfluous any further hard physical treatment. Such a device would preserve the condemnatory function of punishment while dispensing with its usual physical forms—incarceration and corporal mistreatment. Perhaps this is only idle fantasy; perhaps there is more to it. The question is surely open. The only point I wish to make here is one about the nature of the question. The problem of justifying punishment, when it takes this form, may really be that of justifying our particular symbols of infamy.

Whatever the form of skeptical challenge to the institution of punishment, however, there is one traditional answer to it that seems to me to be incoherent. I refer to that form of the Retributive Theory which mentions neither condemnation nor vengeance, but insists instead that the ultimate justifying purpose of punishment is to match off moral gravity and pain, to give each offender exactly that amount of pain the evil of his offense calls for, on the alleged principle of justice that the wicked should suffer pain in exact proportion to their turpitude.

I will only mention in passing the familiar and potent objections to this view.[29] The innocent presumably deserve not to suffer just as the guilty are supposed to deserve to suffer; yet it is impossible to hurt an evil man without imposing suffering on those who love or depend on him. Deciding the right amount of suffering to inflict in a given case would require an assessment of the character of the offender as manifested through his whole life, and also his total lifelong balance of pleasure and pain, an obvious impossibility. Moreover, justice would probably demand the abandonment of general rules in the interests of individuation of punishment since there will inevitably be inequalities of moral guilt in the commission of the same crime, and inequalities of suffering from the same punishment. If not dispensed with, however, general rules must list all crimes in the order of their moral gravity, all punishments in the order of their severity, and the match-ings between the two scales. But the moral gravity scale would have to list motives and purposes, not simply types of overt acts, for a given crime can be committed from any kind of "mental state," and its "moral gravity" in a given case surely must depend in part on its accompanying motive. Condign punishment then would have to match suffering to motive (desire, belief, etc.), not to dangerousness or to amount of harm done. Hence some petty larcenies would be punished more severely than some murders. It is not likely we should wish to give power to judges and juries to make such difficult moral judgments. Worse than this, the judgments required are not merely "difficult," they are in principle impossible. It may seem "self-evident" to some moralists that the passionate impulsive killer, for example, deserves less suffering for his wickedness than the scheming deliberate killer; but if the question of comparative *dangerousness* is left out of mind, reasonable men not only can but will disagree in their appraisals of comparative blameworthiness, and there appears no rational way of resolving the issue.[30] Certainly, there is no rational way of demonstrating that one deserves exactly twice or three-eighths or twelve-ninths as much suffering as the other; yet on some forms, at least, of this theory, the amount of suffering inflicted for any two crimes should stand in exact proportion to the "amounts" of wickedness in the criminals.

For all that, however, the pain-fitting-wickedness version of the retributive theory does erect its edifice of moral superstition on a foundation in moral common sense, for justice *does* require that in some (other) sense "the punishment fit the crime." What justice requires is that the *condemnatory aspect* of the punishment suit the crime, that the crime be of a kind that is truly worthy of reprobation. Further, the degree of disapproval expressed by the punishment should "fit" the crime only in the unproblematic sense that the more serious crimes should receive stronger disapproval than the less serious ones, the seriousness of the crime being determined by the amount of harm it generally causes and the degree to which people are disposed to commit it. That is quite another thing than requiring that the hard treatment component, considered apart from its symbolic function, should "fit" the moral quality of a specific criminal act, assessed quite independently of its relation to social harm. Given our conventions, of course, condemnation is expressed by hard treatment, and the degree of harshness of the latter expresses the degree of reprobation of the former; still this should not blind us to the fact that it is social disapproval and its appropriate expression that should fit the crime, and not hard treatment (pain) as such. Pain should match guilt only insofar as its infliction is the symbolic vehicle of public condemnation.

---

1. See especially the following: A. Flew, "The Justification of Punishment," *Philosophy,* 29 (1954), 291–307; S. I. Benn, "An Approach to the Problems of Punishment," *Philosophy,* 33 (1958), 325–341; and H. L. A. Hart, "Prolegomenon to the Principles of Punishment," *Proceedings of the Aristotelian Society,* 60 (1959–60), 1–26.

2. Hart and Benn both borrow Flew's definition. In Hart's paraphrase, punishment "(i) . . . must involve pain or other consequences normally considered unpleasant. (ii) It must be for an offense against legal rules. (iii) It must be of an actual or supposed offender for his offense. (iv) It must be intentionally administered by human beings other than the offender. (v) It must be imposed and administered by an authority constituted by a legal system against which the offense is committed." (*op. cit.,* p. 4.)

3. The distinction between punishments and penalties was first called to my attention by Dr. Anita Fritz of the University of Connecticut. Similar distinctions in different terminologies have been made by many. Pollock and Maitland speak of "true afflictive punishments" as opposed to outlawry, private vengeance, fine, and emendation. (*History of English Law,* 2d ed., II, pp. 451 ff.) The phrase "afflictive punishment" was invented by Bentham (*Rationale of Punishment,* London, 1830): "These [corporal] punishments are almost always attended with a portion of ignominy, and this does not always increase with the organic pain, but principally depends upon the condition [social class] of the offender." (p. 83). James Stephen says of legal punishment that it "should always connote . . . moral infamy." (*History of the Criminal Law,* II, p. 171.) Lasswell and Donnelly distinguish "condemnation sanctions" and "other deprivations." ("The Continuing Debate over Responsibility: An Introduction to Isolating the Condemnation Sanction," *Yale Law Journal,* 68, 1959.) The traditional common law distinction is between "infamous" and "noninfamous" crimes and punishments. Conviction of an "infamous crime" rendered a person liable to such postpunitive civil disabilities as incompetence to be a witness.

4. That even punishments proper are to be interpreted as taxes on certain kinds of conduct is a view often associated with O. W. Holmes, Jr. For an excellent discussion of Holmes's fluctuations on this question see Mark De Wolfe Howe, *Justice Holmes, The Proving Years* (Cambridge, Mass., 1963), pp. 74–80. See also Lon Fuller, *The Morality of Law* (New Haven, 1964), Chap. II, part 7, and H. L. A. Hart, *The Concept of Law* (Oxford, 1961), p. 39, for illuminating comparisons and contrasts of punishment and taxation.

5. H. L. A. Hart, *loc. cit.*

6. Henry M. Hart, "The Aims of the Criminal Law," *Law and Contemporary Problems,* 23 (1958), II, A, 4.

7. *General View of the Criminal Law of England,* First ed. (London, 1863), p. 99.

8. (London, 1953), pp. 17–18.

9. The Texas Penal Code (Art. 1220) states: "Homicide is justifiable when committed by the husband upon one taken in the act of

adultery with the wife, provided the killing takes place before the parties to the act have separated. Such circumstances cannot justify a homicide when it appears that there has been on the part of the husband, any connivance in or assent to the adulterous connection." New Mexico and Utah have similar statutes. For some striking descriptions of perfectly legal paramour killings in Texas, see John Bainbridge, *The Super-Americans* (Garden City, 1961), pp. 238 ff.

10. *The Philosophy of Law*, trans. W. Hastie (Edinburgh, 1887), p. 198.

11. *General Principles of Criminal Law*, 2d ed. (Indianapolis, 1960), p. 328, hereafter cited as GPCL.

12. *Flemming v. Nestor* 80 S. Ct. 1367 (1960).

13. *Ibid.*, p. 1370.

14. *Ibid.*, p. 1374 (interspersed citations omitted).

15. *Ibid.*, p. 1385.

16. *Ibid.*, pp. 1375–76.

17. *Ibid.*, p. 1387.

18. *Ibid.*, p. 1376.

19. *The Reporter* (May 11, 1961), p. 14.

20. *Loc. cit.*

21. Jerome Hall, *GPCL*, p. 329.

22. Richard A. Wasserstrom, "Strict Liability in the Criminal Law," *Stanford Law Review*, 12 (1960), p. 730.

23. *United States v. Moreland*, 258 *U.S.* 433, 447–48. Quoted in Hall, *GPCL*, p. 327.

24. "A depth study of Wisconsin statutes in 1956 revealed that of 1113 statutes creating criminal offenses [punishable by fine, imprisonment, or both] which were in force in 1953, no less than 660 used language in the definitions of the offenses which omitted all reference to a mental element, and which therefore, under the canons of construction which have come to govern these matters, left it open to the courts to impose strict liability if they saw fit." Colin Howard, "Not Proven," *Adelaide Law Review*, 1 (1962), 274. The study cited is: Remington, Robinson and Zick, "Liability Without Fault Criminal Statutes," *Wisconsin Law Review* (1956), 625, 636.

25. Rollin M. Perkins, *Criminal Law* (Brooklyn, 1957), pp. 701–2.

26. American Law Institute, *Model Penal Code, Proposed Official Draft* (Philadelphia, 1962).

27. Erewhon (London, 1901), Chapter 10.

28. These two examples are cited by Francis A. Allen in "Criminal Justice, Legal Values and the Rehabilitative Ideal," *Journal of Criminal Law, Criminology and Police Science*, 50 (1959), 229.

29. For more convincing statements of these arguments, see *iter alia*: W. D. Ross, *The Right and the Good* (Oxford, 1930), pp. 56–65; J. D. Mabbott, "Punishment," *Mind*, 49 (1939); A. C. Ewing, *The Morality of Punishment* (London, 1929), Chap. 1; and F. Dostoevsky, *The House of the Dead*.

30. Cf. Jerome Michael and Herbert Wechsler, *Criminal Law and Its Administration* (Chicago, 1940), "Note on Deliberation and Character," pp. 170–72.

SHAME, CULTURE, AND AMERICAN CRIMINAL LAW*

Toni M. Massaro

The most unhappy hours in our lives are those in which we recollect times past to our own blushing—If we are immortal that must be the Hell.

—*Keats*

I. Introduction

On October 26, 1989, a Rhode Island Superior Court judge ordered Stephen J. Germershausen to place the following four-by-six-inch ad with his picture in the *Providence Journal-Bulletin:* "'I am Stephen Germershausen. I am 29 years old. . . . I was convicted of child molestation. . . . If you are a child molester, get professional help immediately, or you may find your picture and name in the paper, and your life under control of the state.'"[1] Purchasing this ad was a condition of his probation.[2]

In another era, Germershausen might have been put on a wheel and had all of the bones in his body cracked, one at a time.[3] During the late 1600s, he might have been nailed by both ears to a pillory, then whipped twenty times,[4] or branded with an "*M*" for molester.[5] He might have been banished or exiled from the United States.[6] Or, he might have been placed in public stocks[7] and forced to apologize and make financial restitution to the families of his three victims.[8] Electing an alternative not unlike some of these penalties, the Rhode Island judge imposed on Germershausen a thirty-five-year suspended sentence, with thirty-five years' probation, and compelled him to publicize his conviction with this newspaper ad.[9]

Germershausen's publicity sentence is part of a modest trend in criminal law. In a smattering of recent cases, several judges have required defendants to apologize publicly to their victims[10] or to wear signs listing their offenses.[11] An Oregon judge makes some offenders buy newspaper ads to apologize for their misdeeds.[12] And the State of Nevada now allows convicted drunk drivers to elect between imprisonment or performing community service while dressed in clothing that identifies them as drunk drivers.[13]

These throwbacks to colonial-type penalties spring from frustration with the conventional options of prison and parole.[14] Prison overcrowding, as well as recurring doubts about the appropriateness and the effectiveness of incarceration, make imprisonment seem infeasible, unduly harsh, or otherwise unacceptable in some cases. Yet, many judges believe that to parole the convicted individual is too lenient.[15] In an attempt to fill this gap, reformers have proposed a host of alternative, creative sentencing strategies, which have begun to reshape criminal justice in the United States.[16]

The resort to formal shaming as a criminal sanction is only one of several attempts to expand the sentencer's arsenal in an effective, inexpensive manner. Formal shaming, however, is perhaps the most sensational of these new penalties. It also exploits, in a particularly dramatic and explicit fashion, the assumed link between people's sense of shame and their tendency to observe legal norms. The purpose of this Article is to analyze whether this link is one that American criminal court judges can, or should, exploit.

*Toni Massaro is Professor of Law, University of Arizona. B.S. 1977, Northwestern University; J.D. 1980, William & Mary.— Ed. I am grateful to Barbara Babcock, Tom Grey, Ted Schneyer, David Wexler, Walter Weyrauch, and Rob Williams for their instructive critiques of an earlier version of the manuscript. Copyright 1990 by Toni M. Massaro. 89 *Michigan Law Review* 1880 (1991). Endnotes have been edited and renumbered. I also am indebted to the following people for their exceptional research assistance: Fred Diaz, Day Williams, David Alavezos, and Raymond Van Dyke.

I begin with a description of the new shaming sanctions and the possible justifications for this type of penalty.[17] I then identify both psychological and anthropological aspects of the phenomenon of shame, or "losing face."[18] I describe several cultures in which shaming practices are, or were, significant means of sanctioning behavior, and outline the shared features of these cultures.[19]

These psychological and anthropological materials, taken together, suggest that shaming practices are most effective and meaningful when five conditions are satisfied. First, the potential offenders must be members of an identifiable group, such as a close-knit religious or ethnic community. Second, the legal sanctions must actually compromise potential offenders' group social standing.[20] That is, the affected group must concur with the legal decision-maker's estimation of what is, or should be, humiliating to group members. Third, the shaming must be communicated to the group and the group must withdraw from the offender—shun her—physically, emotionally, financially, or otherwise.[21] Fourth, the shamed person must fear withdrawal by the group.[22] Finally, the shamed person must be afforded some means of regaining community esteem, unless the misdeed is so grave that the offender must be permanently exiled or demoted.[23]

I apply these five characteristics to modern American communities, and speculate about whether formal shaming by contemporary American criminal courts within their communities makes practical sense.[24] I argue that the dominant social and cultural traditions in the United States do not reflect the level of interdependence, strong norm cohesion, and robust communitarianism that tends to characterize cultures in which shaming is prevalent and effective. Moreover, federal and state law enforcement includes no public ritual or ceremony for reintegrating or "forgiving" a shamed offender. Given these circumstances, I conclude that public shaming by a criminal court judge will be, at most, a retributive spectacle that is devoid of other positive community-expressive or community-reinforcing content. Additionally, I hypothesize that these judicial shamings will not significantly deter crime in most urban, and likely many nonurban American settings.[25]

Finally, I consider whether shaming is a reasonably humane method of punishing criminals, regardless of its practical effectiveness. In particular, I address the limiting concerns of proportionality,[26] equality,[27] and cruelty.[28] I maintain that these three concerns, which are raised by all forms of punish-

ment, are particularly strong with shaming punishments and point against use of these penalties.[29] These conclusions are relevant to all publicly imposed criminal sanctions to the extent that all methods of public punishment attempt to exploit the target community's shared sense of revulsion and shame.

II. The Revival

A. Introduction

The revival of shaming springs from profound and widespread dissatisfaction with existing methods of punishment. In particular, many people, including judges, doubt the effectiveness and humanity of prison.[30] Yet, the main alternative to prison—parole—is equally unattractive, both because the community fears the often unmonitored return of the offender to its neighborhoods, and because most people believe criminals should not go unpunished.[31]

This dissatisfaction with the primary punishment options has led to experimental, creative sanctions and probation conditions, which include the "shaming and shunning" practices. The full range of these experimental alternatives includes furlough programs,[32] community service sentences,[33] home surveillance systems,[34] so-called "shock probation,"[35] forced charitable contributions,[36] chemical therapy,[37] forced birth control,[38] and even one recent case of court-ordered castration.[39] Shaming penalties thus are one strand of a larger movement to expand the sentencer's arsenal of penalties.

Unlike these other punishment innovations, however, the shaming sanctions are explicitly designed to make a public spectacle of the offender's conviction and punishment, and to trigger a negative, downward change in the offender's self-concept.[40] Embarrassment and consequent social isolation may result from any punishment; but with most other sanctions shame and shunning are incidental and, some would argue, undesirable consequences of the penalty. With shaming penalties, in contrast, embarrassment is the principal purpose of the punishment. In the following sections I describe several modern instances of formal attempts to shame offenders.

B. Signs

The most obvious illustrations of shaming are the sign sanctions. Well-publicized[41] examples of sign punishments are the convicted drunk driver bumper sticker[42] and distinctive license plate.[43] The convicted driver may continue to exercise driving privileges only if she affixes the identifying sign to her vehicle.

Judge Titus, the Sarasota County Florida judge who initiated the bumper sticker penalty in 1985, claims that after the program began, drunk driving incidents dropped one third in the county.[44] In explaining why she imposed the glow-in-the-dark sticker penalty, Judge Titus said that tougher fines had failed to curb drunk driving. She noted that "many people who are convicted of DUI as first offenders are well adjusted in society. They hold good jobs and value their social standing. . . . The DUI sticker capitalized on [their] fear of public notice," by bringing "shame, disgrace and a ruined reputation."[45]

The state of Nevada recently adopted a statute that allows the judge to order a defendant to perform forty-eight hours of work for the community while dressed in clothing that identifies her as a DUI offender.[46] In a decision involving a defendant convicted under this statute, the U.S. Supreme Court speculated that this penalty was "less embarrassing and less onerous than six months in jail."[47]

Identifying signs have also been part of sentences imposed on sex offenders. In one case, a repeat offender was required, as a condition of probation, to post signs with letters at least three inches high on his residence and vehicle doors that read: DANGEROUS SEX OFFENDER—NO CHILDREN ALLOWED.[48] Other courts have required sex offenders to place ads in the local newspaper publicizing their offenses, as in the Rhode Island case described above.[49]

C. Apologies

A second type of shame sanction is the public apology or "confession." Judge Elaine Crane of Willoughby Municipal Court in Ohio orders some first-time offenders to write a "confessional" letter to the local newspaper.[50] In Tennessee, a judge ordered a defendant convicted of aiding in the sale of a stolen vehicle to confess his crime before a church congregation.[51] In Newport, Oregon, a town of 8500 people, a convicted criminal may be ordered to write and pay for a newspaper ad in which she announces the subject of her conviction and apologizes to the community.[52] One man who opted for the public apology in lieu of a prison sentence stated that the cost of the social embarrassment paled when compared to the cost of six months in prison.[53]

Another sanction closely related to the apology is compelled interaction between the defendant and her victims. For example, a defendant convicted of drunk driving may have to meet with people whose lives have been adversely affected by drunk drivers.[54] The sentencer who orders these face-to-face encounters may be motivated more by the desire to promote consciousness-raising in the defendant or retributive satisfaction for the victims, however, than by the desire to shame the offender. Still, the opportunity for victims to confront the defendant and to describe how her deed has injured them may well trigger shame or guilt in the defendant, as well as satisfy the victims' expressive needs in some instances.[55]

These modern penalties bear a strong resemblance to the pillory, and other humiliatory sanctions of the American colonial period. The obvious question is whether these sanctions make as much sense today, given our alternatives, as they arguably made in the seventeenth century. In other words, does shaming deter crime, rehabilitate offenders, or serve any other legitimate punishment objective, given contemporary cultural conditions? If it is not likely to effect these ends, then should the new sanctions be condemned as misguided spasms of judicial and legislative pique?

III. Theoretical Justifications

> [T]heories of punishment are not theories in any normal sense. They are not, as scientific theories are, assertions or contentions as to what is or what is not the case. . . . On the contrary, those major positions concerning punishment which are called deterrent or retributive or reformative "theories" of punishment are moral *claims* as to what justifies the practice of punishment—claims as to why, morally, it *should* or *may* be used.[56]

A. Introduction

In any sensible and humane legal order, punishment should be reasonably related to legitimate government ends. Thus, a preliminary question is whether shaming may promote a valid government end. A second, related concern is whether shaming is a humane and fair means of achieving that end.

Classical penology identifies four ends of punishment of criminal offenders: retribution, rehabilitation, deterrence, and incapacitation.[57] Some authors have posited supplementary reasons for government-imposed punishment, such as that it satisfies and controls passion and thereby promotes efficiency in norm enforcement,[58] or that it promotes a moral education.[59] Nevertheless, the classical justifications still dominate philosophical debates about punishment. In the following sections, I describe briefly these classical justifications, and apply them to modern shaming sanctions. I conclude that as a theoretical matter, shaming may be justifiable under any of the classical theories of punishment. I further conclude, however, that these four general theories, taken together, offer abstract, theoretical justifications for nearly any negative response to criminal behavior. Thus, the more critical inquiries are whether the shaming penalties in fact will promote any of these theoretical ends, and whether shaming is a humane way to achieve these ends.

B. Retribution

Retributivists argue that punishment is justified by the desire to counteract or "compensate" for the harm inflicted by the wrongdoer. It is, in short, retaliation against someone who "deserves it." "An eye for an eye" is proper redress for a crime, in order to set right the moral balance.[60] This focus is retrospective, and weighs only the value that the offender has denied society.

Modern law construes crime as an offense against the state.[61] As such, the harm to be redressed is the injury to society, and is measured through its eyes. The damage to the victim is relevant only to the extent that she is part of the larger society. Retribution thus is not satisfied by victim compensation per se. Likewise, an individual victim's assessment of the harm inflicted is not dispositive.

Retributive justice is nonconsequentialist in that it is uninterested in influencing the offender's future behavior or the behavior of other community members. It presupposes free will by the criminal actor and demands a "proportional" negative response to her willful wrongdoing.[62] As such, the theory tends to ignore contextual or individual complexities in favor of the criminal act itself. Retributive punishment thus is both an emotional expression of disgust and an exacting of commensurate revenge that is meant to satisfy moral notions about just deserts. Retributivists believe that what goes around *should* come

around (though they may disagree about why); the aim of punishment is to see that it *does* come around.

The primary attraction of retributivism is that it has ancient roots, and satisfies deep emotional, intuitive instincts. Moreover, its ends are simply stated and seem fairly easy to secure. We punish in order to avenge the harm, not to deter, rehabilitate, or contain. Revenge is easier to accomplish than these other objectives.

In recent decades retributivists have gained adherents,[63] in part because of widespread skepticism about the rehabilitative or deterrence effects of contemporary sanctions,[64] and also because some people fear the potential for abuse and the disproportionality of rehabilitation-based punishment schemes. Retribution has become an appealing alternative to these other less favored theories[65] because it justifies punishment even when no deterrence or rehabilitation results.

Pure retributivist principles can justify the new shaming practices. If, for example, a driver kills a young child in the course of operating a motor vehicle while intoxicated, forcing the driver to wear a sign in public does promote retribution ends in a simple sense. The penalty need not, under retribution theory, deter others or convince the defendant not to drive while drunk again. Its justification lies in the fact that the defendant broke the law, and so "deserves" to be punished regardless of any future effects of the punishment. If wearing a sign exacts pain, then it is justified by the offender's past pain-inflicting acts. Community outrage is expressed, and the moral calculus is set right.

Of course, pure retributivism, and thus any retributivist-based attempt to justify signs, rests on fairly shallow reasoning,[66] namely, that the law has to punish crime, however it can. Major objections to pure retributivism,[67] which apply equally to retributivist justifications for shaming, are that it does not prevent the abuses of unequal, disproportional, or inhumane punishment.[68]

Even for a pure retributivist, however, the question remains whether, in a particular community, wearing a sign or apologizing would be perceived as a negative sanction, and thus would satisfy the community's interest in revenge. I address this issue in a later section.

C. Rehabilitation

A second, also controversial, justification for punishment is rehabilitation of offenders. This theory is easily stated and understood: the government punishes offenders in order to change their norm-violating ways.[69] Punishment therefore should promote specific deterrence ends, that is, deterrence of this particular offender. It may do so through negative stimuli, so that the offender fears being punished again and so avoids the behavior, or through training and opportunities for reflection that actually change the defendant's attitude as well as her behavior.[70]

Rehabilitation theory gained popularity in the United States during the late 1800s, and dominated penal philosophy during most of the 1900s.[71] Despite the initial promise of rehabilitation as a humane and sensible organizing principle of punishment, however, its appeal waned.[72] The central reason for this decline was that the practical complexity, coupled with the extreme moral complexity, of refashioning human character to cabin or obliterate criminal instincts overwhelmed reformers.[73]

Indeed, the rising doubts about whether rehabilitation is a convincing justification for punishment go deeper than skepticism about whether prisons reform offenders. Some observers question whether any feasible, humane punishment method can reform criminals. They argue that the people most in need of "character reform" are most impervious to it. Environmental, economic, biogenetic, psychological, and other external and internal factors in place before and after the rehabilitative intervention are, they claim, far more influential on offender character and behavior than any state-imposed intervention can ever be.

Moreover, some critics observe, successful rehabilitation may be difficult to assess. An offender can beguile her therapists, the parole board, or others into believing that she has "really changed" this time, and has powerful incentives to engage in such a charade. Measuring rehabilitation of a human being thus can be as difficult as predicting her future dangerousness, which is difficult indeed.[74]

Despite these and other criticisms of rehabilitation theory, a confirmed rehabilitationist could argue that experience proves only that our past methods do not reform offenders, not that rehabilitation cannot ever work. Absent proof to the contrary, she might add, shaming sanctions can be justified under rehabilitation theory. If, for example, a particular offender were sufficiently pained by wearing a sign that announced her status as a convicted felon, then she might be "scared straight," and refrain from committing that offense in the future. More obviously, if an offender is compelled to apologize to, or interact with victims, then she might become sensitized to the human consequences of criminal acts. The experience might cause her to realize more fully her responsibility to others and thus to avoid conduct that could imperil them. Shaming therefore can be justified under rehabilitation theory, provided that the evidence, which is not yet available, bears out that this "rehabilitation" in fact influences behavior.[75]

In sum, rehabilitation theory arguably offers an analytically sound defense of shaming practices. Because, however, rehabilitation theory anticipates offender reform, the rehabilitation-based justification for shaming ultimately depends on whether a particular shame sanction in fact will effect this consequence.[76]

D. Deterrence

According to deterrence theory, the primary goal of punishment is not to reform the offender or to cancel the moral debt of her crime; it is to prevent future crimes.[77] Deterrence theory holds that society inflicts punishment on wrongdoers in order to deter the commission of similar delicts by the same offender (specific deterrence) or by others (general deterrence). Indeed, a significant number of philosophers insist that deterrence is the *only* legitimate end of punishment,[78] provided that the punishment is not unreasonably harsh. Certainly, deterrence figures prominently in most Western theories of punishment.[79]

The primary objections to deterrence theory are practical ones, though theoretical objections surely can be, and have been, made.[80] The common practical complaints are, first, that deterrence effects are virtually impossible to gauge accurately,[81] and second, that the theory wrongly presupposes that criminal acts are motivated by rational, cost-benefit analyses by wrongdoers.[82] The theory also assumes that sanctions can inspire fear in some, or most, onlookers. Different people, however, experience fear differently. The punishment thus must be one that scares a significant number of would-be perpetrators.[83]

The assumed causal link between threat and deterrence cannot be verified without better knowledge than we currently possess, both about the specific causes of norm-violating behavior, and about the relation between deterrence and personality. In a well-known study of deterrence, Zimring and Hawkins illustrate the byzantine complexity of tracing the effect of legal threats[84] on human behavior. For example, intuition probably suggests that a legal sanction would decrease the attractiveness of the sanctioned conduct. In fact, however, a sanction can actually *enhance* the attractiveness of the proscribed conduct, though this reaction may not be sustained.[85] That is, a sanction can place *both* positive and negative value on an activity, and "no general statement can be made about which pull will be stronger."[86] Empirical proof of the assumptions on which deterrence theory rests therefore depends on extremely complex assessments of human motivation and behavior. Given these complexities, the deterrence literature is equivocal and not at all susceptible to simple summaries.

Deterrence theorists do agree, however, that strong socialization is a significant predictor of law-abiding behavior. As Zimring and Hawkins observe, "social disapproval, which is an important part of most threatened consequences, will be carefully avoided by the strongly socialized individual."[87] Thus, legal threats are most likely to be effective in constraining the behavior of strongly socialized people, who already tend not to engage in criminal behavior. Many deterrence theorists also believe, despite the lack of absolute empirical proof, both that legal threats impose at least some constraint on deviant behavior, and that legal threats' best justification lies in this desirable effect.[88]

A deterrence theorist likely would conclude that, as a theoretical matter, shaming sanctions probably are justifiable. Signs and apologies—like any other negative consequence of a criminal conviction—might deter the specific offender or other would-be offenders from committing similar acts.[89] And, like all penalties, shaming sanctions should deter most effectively those people who are most strongly socialized. This means, of course, that the population most vulnerable to humiliatory punishments probably includes mainly, if not only, those people who least *need* them as an incentive to avoid wrongdoing. But a deterrence theorist might respond that this merely indicates that shaming sanctions may be redundant deterrence tools; it does not mean that deterrence ends cannot justify these sanctions.

Deterrence of future wrongdoing thus may be an adequate justification for the new shaming sanctions. Indeed, the judges and legislators who have proposed shaming sanctions probably believe quite strongly that the threat of social ostracism will deter people from committing similar crimes. As was true of rehabilitation theory, however, deterrence theory is consequentialist; as such, a complete justification of shaming based on deterrence theory must consider whether the assumed deterrence consequences

of these new sanctions actually occur. The critical inquiry for deterrence theorists thus becomes whether shaming in fact will prevent future crimes.[90]

E. Incapacitation

The final classical justification for shaming sanctions is incapacitation. Incapacitation theory holds that punishment should protect the community from the offender, either by confining her physically, or otherwise disabling her from committing future crimes.[91] An incapacitationist favors external controls on an offender with demonstrated criminal propensities, rather than relying on the offender's capacity for self-control. Imprisonment, banishment, home electronic surveillance, branding, mutilation, chemical treatment, and castration all are examples of incapacitive punishments.[92] Each seeks either to physically remove the offender from society, or to make criminal acts substantially more difficult to perform.

Incapacitation theory has at least two significant weaknesses. The first is that it assumes that we can predict which criminals pose an ongoing risk of harm. Incapacitationists often rely on past criminal activity, demographic factors, or other variables as strong predictors of future criminal activity. If these variables do not yield accurate predictions, however, then some offenders will be punished who do not, in an incapacitationist's sense, "deserve" it. The second weakness, according to some observers, is that the theory is too forgiving of some offenders. Incapacitationists believe that offenders who pose no future risk to the community should not be punished, though they may have committed quite serious criminal acts. For example, "heat of passion" murderers, or other criminals who act on situation-specific or person-specific impulses and are unlikely to commit future transgressions, can be released if they pose little or no danger to others. To retributivists in particular, this is an unacceptable response to a serious injury.

Despite these potential shortcomings, incapacitation theory offers support to the shaming sanctions. Public apologies, confessions, or signs may well be incapacitative, in that they might make future criminal acts more difficult for the offender to perform. Publicizing the offender's identity may alert community members of her criminal past and cause them to isolate her socially or professionally. People might, for example, refuse a convicted embezzler a position that gives her access to funds. A known child molester may be denied contact with children. And a convicted drunk driver may be refused alcohol or a job that involves use of a vehicle. As such, the shaming sanctions may have a disabling effect on the offenders, and thus may claim to serve incapacitation-type ends.

F. Conclusion

The traditional theories of punishment suggest that all of the new shaming sanctions can be justified under one or several of the basic theories. Indeed, any and all forms of punishment that our contemporary legal order might concoct likely would be consistent with at least one of these four capacious and controversial theories.

In the United States, no one theory clearly dominates all criminal punishment practices in a coherent, comprehensive way. Rather, justifications that courts and legislatures offer for punishment practices seem to reflect a pluralistic theory of punishment. As such, the political acceptability of any punishment technique, including shame sanctions, will depend on whether the evidence indicates that it actually promotes *any* of the four classical ends of punishment, rather than on whether it promotes a particular end. That is, does the new shaming in fact deter, rehabilitate, or incapacitate criminals, *or* exact proportional revenge for crime? And, if it does promote any of these ends in fact, is this shaming a reasonably humane way to further these ends? In the remaining sections, I explore both the likely practical effectiveness and the humaneness of shaming.

IV. The Emotion of "Shame"

Were they ashamed when they had committed abomination? Nay, they were not at all ashamed, neither could they blush.[93]

In order to evaluate both the practical effectiveness and the humaneness of a shaming sanction, one first must define the phenomenon of shame and identify the conditions under which it occurs. The key sources of this definition and the conditions of shame are psychological and anthropological materials.

Psychological studies demonstrate the complexity and gravity of the shame emotion, and the extreme difficulty that judges are likely to experience if they attempt to craft sanctions that match offender-specific definitions of shame. Psychologists describe shame[94] as a highly individual experience that strikes at the center of human personality. The emotion evoked is a feeling, a "kind of fear of dishonor . . . [that] produces an effect similar to that produced by fear of danger."[95] This feeling is triggered by tension between an individual's ego ideal and her conscious or unconscious awareness of the ego's actual potential.[96]

Shame forces a downward redefinition of oneself, and causes the shamed person to feel transformed into something less than her prior, idealized image.[97] Wurmser describes the reaction as follows:

> In shame one feels frozen, immovable, paralyzed, even turned into stone or into another creature, such as an ass or a pig (not only in jokes, but in dreams, delusions, and myths as well); contempt by another has succeeded in changing the human partner into a mere thing, into a nothing. . . . The loss of love in shame can be described as a radical decrease of respect for the subject as a person with his own dignity; it is a disregard for his having a self in its own right and with its own prestige. . . . The thrust of this aggression is to *dehumanize*.[98]

This dehumanization and social demotion typically occur only when a shameful trait or act becomes visible, and is exposed to others.[99] Thus, one condition of the shame emotion is an audience. As one writer has said, "Shame is essentially public; if no one else knows, there is no basis for shame. And if your action is seen, you can diminish shame only by running from the group."[100] Shaming requires witnesses who will learn of the shameful act and who will condemn it.

The audience to a shaming must include people who are important to the offender,[101] or she will not be "ashamed." The anxiety that shaming exploits is a fear of abandonment or isolation, usually from a social group or other community that is necessary or valuable to the individual.[102] The individual fears that, given the revelation of her shameful act and transformation into a lesser self, people will disregard or abandon her. Abandonment or isolation from a group is anxiety-producing only for an individual who shares the values of the community or at least fears exposure before them. To be effective, the public rebuke therefore must threaten a significant relationship.[103]

Goffman describes shame as a dynamic social exchange in which an individual "loses face" or becomes "shamefaced."[104] As he defines it, face is "the positive social value a person effectively claims for

himself by the line others assume he has taken during a particular contact."[105] Face is lost

> when information is brought forth in some
> way about his social worth which cannot be
> integrated . . . into the line that is being sus-
> tained for him. . . . [He is] *out of face* when he
> participates in a contact with others without
> having ready a line of the kind participants in
> such situations are expected to take.[106]

In other words, shame requires a social encounter, an
interaction between an individual and the group that
exposes weaknesses or deficiencies in the individual
and that reduces her post-shaming social standing or
compromises her own idealized prior image.

Other psychologists likewise stress the social
dynamics of shaming. John Braithwaite, who has written extensively on shame and punishment, has noted
that "[w]hereas an actual punishment will only be administered by one person or a limited number of
criminal justice officials, the shaming associated with
punishment may involve almost all of the members
of a community."[107] This means that the relevant audience must experience and must communicate a
roughly common sense of outrage at, or contempt for,
the sanctioned member's actions. If all or most of
them ignore the spectacle, it loses its sting. This audience participation often includes withdrawal from the
offender. Public shaming in many instances is followed by community shunning. Indeed, shaming exploits one's fear of shunning by others, or banishment
from the community.[108]

V. Cultural Context

The modern cry in Western countries for
community alternatives to the established systems of crime control is a belated need for
simpler solutions to crime than repression by
helicopters, electronics, computerization of
records, and armed policemen. Unfortunately,
the "communities" referred to are often not in
existence so that despite the awareness, such
lessons are difficult to learn from the
advanced urban complexes.[109]

A. Introduction

In addition to the individual-specific psychological
meaning of shame is a culture-specific[110] or anthro-

pological meaning that influences the effectiveness of
a shaming sanction. Because shaming involves audience participation or shunning of the offender or
both, cultural patterns and norms of behavior partly
determine whether the audience will participate in
the ritual. Also, to the extent that social conformity is
achieved through a shared sense of shame and
guilt,[111] these emotions necessarily have community-
or culture-dependent meanings. There is, in other
words, a "cultural ego ideal."[112] For example, if a
culture idealizes work as a means of accomplishment, then a beggar in that culture "'ought to be
ashamed.'"[113] Indeed, these cultural meanings may
be inescapable.[114] Finally, if the purpose of official
shaming is to deter members of the community from
committing similar acts, then the judge must be able
to ascertain and exploit this shared sense of shame. . . .

D. Shaming in White Colonial America

The white colonists of the United States inflicted on
wrongdoers a host of punishments that bear a striking resemblance to the new shaming tools. In a turn
of the century account,[115] A. M. Earle describes the
colonists as "vastly touchy and resentful about being
called opprobrious or bantering names; often running
petulantly to the court about it and seeking redress
by prosecution of the offender."[116] This ultra-
sensitivity, she remarks, enhanced the effectiveness
of the shaming sanctions.[117] Moreover, the social intimacy of colonial communities meant that criminal offenders typically were known members of the group,
not transient outsiders.[118] Thus, the fear of disgrace
before the community was considerable.[119]

One colonial shaming sanction, the admonition, was administered as follows:

> Faced with a community member who had
> committed a serious offense, the magistrates
> or clergymen would lecture him privately to
> elicit his repentance and a resolution to re-
> form. The offender would then be brought
> into open court for a formal admonition by
> the magistrate, a public confession of wrong-
> doing, and a pronouncement of sentence,
> wholly or partially suspended to symbolize
> the community's forgiveness.[120]

The admonition was a "go and sin no more" lecture,
which was followed by a public apology or confession. The practice has been documented in seventeenth-century Virginia, where it involved both
church and state. The offender often was forced to

confess publicly to her congregation,[121] sometimes dressed in a white cloth,[122] and beg their forgiveness.[123] This forgiveness, or redemption, effectively drew the offender back into the fold and further reinforced the moral order.

The forced wearing of signs or letters that listed one's offense also occurred throughout the colonies.[124] In early Maryland, offenders were compelled to stand in the pillory wearing a sign listing their crimes.[125] Permanent labeling, through branding the offender, was another colonial method of punishing criminals.[126]

The victims of permanent labeling practices in the colonies included a vast range of offenders.[127] The temporary forms of labeling—wearing signs or initials—differed from the permanent labeling of branding or maiming in that the former punishment was intended to elicit shame but in a reintegrative fashion. Branding and maiming, in contrast, were permanent stigmas, which in effect cast the person out of the community, though they did not involve physical banishment.[128] Branding and maiming also were designed in part to prevent the offender from committing future similar acts,[129] either by warning future victims of their criminal propensities or by disabling the offender.

Other colonial forms of humiliation punishment included the "bilbo"—a bar of iron with two sliding shackles, like handcuffs, into which the prisoner's legs were locked.[130] Earle describes the use of the bilbo sentence in seventeenth-century Massachusetts, where, for example, one "Jams Woodward" was sentenced to be "'sett [sic] in the bilbowes for being drunk at Newetowne.'"[131] And, of course, there was the pillory, the humiliating character of which was sometimes compounded by forcing the offender not only to be sent there, but to go with dough on his head[132] or with cabbages on his head,[133] or with other symbols of his particular offense. The crowd then might seal the prisoner's mortification by throwing stale eggs at him.[134]

The ducking stool, which was used in particular for "scolding women,"[135] the stocks,[136] and the pillory all were customary features of the colonial county courthouses. Jails were uncommon before the late 1600s.[137]

The white colonists thus earned their reputation for severity in dealing with offenders.[138] Puritan culture, especially the belief in the doctrine of predestination, may help to explain the seemingly unfeeling tone, and the specific methods, of Puritan punishment.[139] The Puritans understood deviant be-

havior to be a mark of a person whose fixed, evil nature was becoming manifest. Their deep fear of evil and desire to reinforce the strict moral order of the community led them to emphasize formal public apologies and confessions because they believed that these public expressions of guilt and remorse would reinforce the moral order. Moreover, even if the criminal were condemned to death, the officials sought her confession before the execution. The condemned person in effect would stand aside from her own life and misdeeds, pronounce them the work of the devil, and join, figuratively speaking, the crowd that affirmed the correctness of her execution.[140] This cooperation in, or "consent" to, the penalty may have relieved somewhat the Puritans' underlying discomfort, however buried, in punishing an offender whose sins were believed to be beyond her power to prevent.

Puritans' indoctrination into the will of God and the laws of nature, as the Puritans perceived them, began in childhood.[141] During the early months of life, the infant was treated indulgently. Shortly thereafter, a radical shift occurred toward a harsh, disciplined life.[142] The object was to curb or beat down the child's wilfulness as soon as possible in a direct confrontation with "original sin."[143] The effect, in psychological terms, was to deprive the child of a confident sense of autonomy.[144] As psychologists have observed, "the reverse of autonomy is the distress created by deep inner trends of shame and doubt."[145] Thus, the Puritan child became an adult who was extremely sensitive to public exposure and shame.[146]

E. Conclusion

The effectiveness of shaming sanctions, whether formal or informal, hinges on a variety of cultural conditions. Informal sanctions appear to work best within relatively bounded, close-knit communities, whose members "don't mind their own business" and who rely on each other.[147] These cultures have widely shared moral or behavioral expectations of their citizens, which are publicly expressed.[148] High expectations of social responsibility, coupled with close social bonding, a deemphasis of personal autonomy, and strong family attachment, produce conditions that are conducive to reintegrative shaming.[149] Effective shaming also entails a strong identification between the shamed offender and other members of the community.[150]

These cultural factors help to explain why shaming as a form of social control occurs more often within small societies that are characterized by intimate face-to-face associations, interdependence, and cooperation.[151] Close relations of this type often are missing from modern urban settings.[152] The gravity of humiliatory punishments to an individual also will hinge on her relative power and resources. If she must depend greatly on the group for social, economic, or political support, or cannot leave the group easily, then a social sanction will have a tremendous impact.[153] Thus, those people who are most likely to defy social norms and risk shaming sanctions, even within close-knit societies, are the very rich and the very poor. The rich can afford to defy the norms because they are insulated by their wealth. The poor may defy the norms simply because they cannot afford to conform, and because they have less "social standing" to lose.[154]

The final factor that seems to contribute to effective shaming is the culture's capacity and instinct for reinforcement of socially *correct* behavior. In intimate societies, the organs of authority often deliver both praise and rebuke. They also have established rituals for reclaiming the shamed one, should she prove herself worthy.

VI. Application

A. Introduction

In the following sections, I apply the foregoing psychological and anthropological materials to modern American criminal law enforcement, and speculate about whether shaming is likely to yield positive social benefits. I focus in particular on whether shaming will deter crime, insofar as I regard this as the main objective of those who favor shame sanctions.

First, I raise doubts about a court's ability to identify the individual meaning of shame, as is necessary to effect specific deterrence or rehabilitation ends. The complex nature of shame, and the practical limitations on a judge's time and inclination to make accurate estimations about an offender's ego ideal, suggest that customized shame sanctions are an impractical objective.

Second, I note that in most criminal court contexts, especially those in large urban centers, the cultural conditions of effective, humane shaming seem absent. Unlike the intimate face-to-face cultures that rely heavily on shaming, cities in the United States typically are not characterized by high interdepen-

dence among citizens, strong norm cohesiveness, or robust communitarianism. Moreover, the primary conditions to effective shaming—audience awareness and participation, a cohesive body of would-be offenders who perceive and are sensitive to the same shame, judicial personnel and procedures that can tailor sanctions to the target audience sensitivities, and a formal means of reintegrating shamed offenders—seem only weakly present in these settings. This suggests that even sanctions that are intended to exploit a community-specific, versus offender-specific, definition of shame likewise are unlikely to effect significant deterrence.

Third, I list several institutional, administrative, and other practical problems with shaming that may make it unworkable. Fourth, I invoke the historical decline of shaming as a warning against its revival. Finally, I describe a context in which many people imagine that shaming would prove exceptionally effective—middle-class crime. I suggest that even as applied to this status sensitive population, shaming may not add measurably to the deterrence value of existing sanctions.

These conclusions are subject to an obvious and important caveat. No empirical work currently is available with which to test the practical impact of shaming sanctions. What follow, therefore, are provisional hypotheses.

B. Shaming and Offender-Specific Factors

The signal insight from the psychological studies of shame is that the experience is personal. People are reared differently and exposed to different peer relationships and other personality shaping influences; as such, they experience shame differently.[155] Psychologists offer general statements about one's ego ideal, but these merely describe how life experiences tend to shape the ego ideal, rather than what, precisely, those events include. For example, they believe shame hinges on the extent to which a person has a confident sense of her autonomy. They do not know, however, how to assure this confidence or how to ascertain which adults lack this training and hence are exceptionally prone to shame. For a judge in a criminal case to take into account the multiple, individual meanings of shame thus would be difficult indeed.[156]

A second, practical implication of the psychological work on shame likewise suggests that shaming may not have impressive specific deterrence or rehabilitative effects. The people who are most vulnerable to shaming are the ones who are most strongly socialized.[157] This means that the people most likely to respond to public shaming sanctions are nonoffender members of the audience, not potential offenders. An offender has demonstrated her imperviousness to the relative cost of public shaming by committing the act in question. Unless she is the first person to suffer the public humiliation, or otherwise has no warning that her actions might trigger public shame, she apparently was not deterred, for whatever reasons, by the prospect of shaming. Of course, she may have imagined, unreasonably or not, that she would evade detection. In any event, the threat of a possible conviction and shaming best deters the people who most fear social disapproval, who usually are not offenders.[158]

On the contrary, public degradation ceremonies may reduce inhibitions that tend to cabin criminal instincts, according to some theorists. The anticipated effect of public shaming is a downward change in status, coupled with symbolic and actual shunning of the offender by others.[159] Indeed, this shunning of convicted offenders may occur even when public officials try to contain it.[160] Once the offender's status is changed, though, she may have a reduced incentive to avoid the behaviors that triggered the demotion.[161] This is especially true when, as is the case in modern American criminal courts, there is no public ritual, ceremony, or other procedure for *reestablishing* or regaining the lost status. Modern shaming, like modern punishment in general, is not "reintegrative." The stigmatized offender thus may "drift" toward subcultures that are more accepting of her particular norm violations.[162] Association with the subculture in turn may facilitate future crime, especially for crimes that require multiple actors or hard-to-obtain materials, tools, or connections.

Labeling theorists believe that these potential negative consequences of stigmatizing offenders outweigh any benefits. Specifically, they argue that by labeling an offender "deviant"—which shaming sanctions clearly try to do—the state may produce "secondary deviance," or criminal acts that are a result of the labeling.[163] Critics of labeling theory, such as Walter Gove, quite sensibly have responded that no empirical data prove that the secondary deviance is a result of the labeling, versus whatever conditions or instincts prompted the primary offense.[164] These critics further maintain that good results can flow from labeling, such as isolating the offender and thereby preventing corruption of others (incapacitation), deterring other potential deviants (general deterrence), forcing the offender out of a criminal lifestyle, and, perhaps, channeling her toward appropriate rehabilitative services (specific deterrence and rehabilitation).[165]

The strength of these last claims I will address below. The evidence on the first claim, that labeling or stigmatizing an offender may increase the chances of subsequent delinquent behavior, is inconclusive. The most accurate statement is that we do not know, for certain, whether labeling produces secondary deviance. If the labeling theorists are correct, however, then shaming not only may not promote specific deterrence or rehabilitative ends, it may defeat them. Moreover, the more effective the shaming, the more counterproductive it may become. The judge thus would need to predict both the offender's individual susceptibility to shame and her likely post-shaming behavior. Each factor in turn might vary with the nature of the offense, the nature of the shaming sanction, and pre- and post-conviction environmental, and other offender-specific conditions. With some crimes, there is little doubt that some offenders feel sincere shame, but do not stop their behavior. Some spouse abusers, for example, may experience acute remorse after a beating episode, yet repeat the beatings.[166]

A final implication of the psychological aspects of shame, which raises both practical and fairness concerns, is the nature of the wound that shaming seeks to inflict. When it works, it redefines a person in a negative, often irreversible, way. Effective shame sanctions strike at an offender's psychological core. To allow government officials to search for and manipulate this vulnerable core is worrisome, to say the least. Moreover, nothing in the psychological materials on shame, or in the available literature on the stigmatic aspect of punishment, indicates that a judge or any other person can reconstruct that core after the defendant has "done her time" in the "public stocks." Certainly, nothing in contemporary criminal punishment practices suggests that judges have adopted procedures for rebuilding this core.

C. Shaming and Modern Cultural Patterns

Anthropological and historical materials are especially pertinent to estimations of the general deterrence effects of shunning and shame. The signal insight of these materials is that for shaming to be an effective method of controlling community behavior, the community in question must be receptive to these methods. This receptivity depends on whether the community satisfies the several cultural

and institutional conditions that have been identified as characteristics of so-called shame cultures.

The cultural conditions of effective shaming
seem weakly present, at best, in many contemporary
American cities. Indeed, shaming sanctions run
counter to the pattern of existing methods of norm
enforcement in the United States. First, most law enforcement is conducted outside of public view. Private security officers, employers, or other nonpublic
agents play a significant, nonpublic role in norm enforcement.[167] Even when public agents do enforce
punishment, however, it rarely comes to the attention
of the rest of the community in any systematic, high-
profile manner.[168] Millions of people are arrested and
convicted each year, but only a handful excite significant national or local interest or attention.

Formal shaming thus would constitute a significant change in law enforcement: it would attempt
to bring to public attention a wide spectrum of criminal case dispositions. This shift, however, would require a dramatic restructuring of existing practice
and procedure and a reversal of the strong trend toward privatization of criminal punishment. The
question is whether such a reversal is likely to produce substantial public benefits.

The most thoughtful argument in favor of de-
privatizing criminal law has come from John Braithwaite. Braithwaite insists that public shaming would
improve the effectiveness of criminal law enforcement because it would help to create a shared,
moral conception of order. He maintains that the
"uncoupling" of shame and punishment in the
United States has been a mistake that partly explains
our rising crime rates, as compared to the low crime
rates of Japan.[169] He argues, therefore, that we
should reestablish the cultural tradition of shaming
wrongdoers, and explicitly link shame and punishment. That is, shaming not only can work, it is an
essential aspect of a sound and effective legal order
and thus must be revived in the United States.

The main problem with Braithwaite's suggestion, however, and with the contemporary revival of
shaming sanctions, is that our tradition of shaming
cannot be "reestablished" if the cultural conditions
to this tradition have eroded. Population increases
and geographical expanse confound such efforts in
the United States, and may help to explain why
Japan, as well as certain island or tribal cultures,
have continued to couple shame and punishment
more effectively than the United States has.

Other factors likewise play a role, and point
against the likelihood that shaming will deter offenders in most contemporary American settings. First,
the United States as a nation is not known for the
highly developed sense of social interdependency
that characterizes the Japanese[170] and that appears
to be an integral condition of effective shaming.

Second, the official agents of norm enforcement often are viewed with suspicion or hostility.
Most people in the United States, especially those in
large urban centers, do not see police officers or
judges as members of their "family,"[171] or otherwise
part of a benign network of interconnected social
actors. Impersonal, authoritarian, and detached law
enforcement agents likely cannot easily substitute
for the collaborative, private, interdependent networks of social control that tend to exist in small societies, or in morally cohesive larger societies.
Moreover, the social unit that is mainly responsible
for inculcating cultural shame values, the family,
often is missing, culturally isolated, or dysfunctional.

A third significant distinction between the
United States and most shame cultures is its cultural
complexity. A federal or state judge's jurisdiction
typically extends over several subcultures, even
when the geographical region is relatively small.
These subcultural variations can give rise to different definitions of shame, which may confound official efforts to deter crime through shaming.

This is not to say, however, that Americans
have no commonly shared instincts about crime or
about shame. A majority of Americans likely agree
that most of the acts we now call crimes should
be.[172] For example, few American subcultures condone murder, child abuse, or theft, though some may
tolerate deviant acts more readily than others,[173] and
may construe differently the adequate justifications
or mitigating factors for these crimes. Likewise, some
fairly large subcultures likely exist whose members
are in substantial agreement about certain aspects of
right and wrong. Nevertheless, American subculturalism, or cultural pluralism, is pronounced enough to
make broad conclusions about our moral coherence
suspect, and thus to undermine the likely effectiveness of widespread government attempts to shame
offenders, absent significant decentralization of criminal law authority and the delivery of formal norm
enforcement power to the local subcultures. . . .

Finally, the anthropological studies further
suggest that the effectiveness of shaming as a
method of norm enforcement depends partly on
whether a culture shames *reintegratively*. If the community has rituals to redeem and reclaim the chas-
tened offender afterwards, and shaming is based in

part on optimism about her responsiveness to this grooming, then the shaming is reintegrative. The earmarks of reintegrative shame cultures include social cohesiveness, a strong family system, high communitarianism, and social control mechanisms that aim to control by reintegration into the cohesive networks, rather than by formal restraint.[174]

These conditions, however, are not currently dominant in the United States.[175] Our legal institutions and national personality tend to reflect the dominant American philosophical emphasis on individuality, independence, and autonomy, rather than on interdependence, community, or shared values. Liberal values are significantly more pronounced in American legal culture than in any of the cultures that rely most effectively and notoriously on shame sanctions. For example, the Japanese concepts of shame to one's name and "honor," as defined by fulfillment of social roles, fit awkwardly at best into prevailing American visions of individual personality and self-reliance. As such, the notion that the government in criminal cases not only should exploit cultural definitions of shame, but should attempt to *forge* these definitions, would offend many Americans. Again, this strong aversion to government encroachment on individual autonomy is not our only national tradition, nor is it the dominant one within all American subcultures. Competing and supplemental traditions, such as the community-oriented traditions of North American Indian tribes, clearly exist and challenge the dominant cultural stress on "individuality." Nevertheless, the national, state and even most local cultures lack a profound sense of mutual obligation and community.[176]

Braithwaite acknowledges this relative absence of optimal cultural conditions for shaming in the United States. He nevertheless believes that even in highly individualistic cultures such as the United States, shaming still will reduce crime more effectively than punishment that is unaccompanied by moralizing and denunciation.[177] But Braithwaite's theory is based entirely on conditions that he admits are not met in the dominant, contemporary American culture. To take one striking example, he observes that "the way we respond to deviance, particularly crime, in the West, gives free play to degradation ceremonies of both a formal and informal kind to certify deviance, while providing almost no place in the culture for ceremonies to decertify deviance."[178] Despite this important admission, he adheres to his optimistic vision of the favorable possibilities of devising shame ceremonies that are "rein-

tegrative," not disintegrative. Moreover, his optimism extends to the favorable possibilities of significant revisions of ideology; he rejects a strong embrace of individualism as too dated and outmoded.[179] He would direct the focus of norm enforcement away from the state, and toward alternative, intermediate communities of interest—such as the workplace, schools, or other association contexts.[180]

This is a comprehensive and utopian agenda indeed, the fulfillment of which might well enhance the favorable possibilities of effective shaming sanctions. But it demands root-down readjustment of the dominant contemporary consciousness about personal responsibility for crime control and norm observation. Short of such a profound ideological shift, coupled with significant structural and procedural changes to facilitate that shift, our modern state-imposed shame sanctions will lack the cultural foundations that Braithwaite himself deems essential. . . .

In sum, the anthropological materials suggest that for shaming to be an effective and humane punishment technique, the culture must match reformers' expectations. If reintegrative shaming is the goal, as it is under Braithwaite's model, then the existing culture must be characterized by social interconnection, mutual dependency, and social cohesion. If the culture lacks these qualities, as our dominant culture seems to, then shaming may prove as counterproductive and harsh as spanking a child does in a family governed by authoritarianism, nonnurturance, and impersonal control. . . .

E. Institutional Constraints and Other Practical Concerns

Finally, even if the foregoing objections to shaming could be overcome, the sanction might still prove impractical for several reasons. First, if the penalty were to become a common sanction, it may produce a shaming overload, which could reduce public interest in these displays and thereby lessen the deterrence impact. This decline in public interest could prove expensive to monitor. At least three million people pass through the state and federal corrections systems each year.[181] Approximately two thirds of the offenders who are under correctional supervision are on probation or parole, and thus have been returned to the community.[182] If only one half of this two thirds was sentenced to shame sanctions, this still might involve one million shamings per year for the government to publish and for the public to consume.

Daily announcements of criminal incidents, which appear in many local newspapers, thus would expand considerably. At first glance, though, this may seem a workable and relatively inexpensive alternative to prison, despite the high number of shamings. Government might exploit television, radio, newspapers, billboards, as well as other communication vehicles to announce criminal conduct. All of these methods—except perhaps televised shaming—probably would cost far less than incarceration, supervised probation, or rehabilitative therapy.

These penalties would soon be ignored, however. The main reason that most of the modern shaming sanctions described in this Article have garnered media attention is that they are curiosities, and hence newsworthy. This interest surely would wane if shaming became commonplace. That is, shaming is an inherently short-fused sanction.

The primary problem with a dramatic increase in the number of shamings thus would not be the initial cost of implementing or monitoring shaming punishments, but the practical problem of how to measure *and* respond to changes in public reactions to the shaming of one million offenders a year. For example, the court would need to assess whether and when the public would begin to ignore this flood of information. Public curiosity at first might be high, but likely would not endure. Moreover, in major metropolitan areas the shaming ads might occupy enough space to warrant addition of a pull-out section of the newspaper, which might easily be tossed aside, unread, along with other newspaper inserts. To avoid this, courts might adopt different types of shaming. For example, a judge may instead impose home-centered shamings, such as lawn signs or bumper stickers. These more localized shamings, however, would entail more localized, "customized" shaming impact assessments.

Evaluations of public responses to various types of shaming might resemble the public opinion surveys, market research, or other assessments of popular opinion that businesses or politicians commonly must make to sell or promote their products or themselves. Sophisticated work in this area likely costs more, and involves more specialized expertise, than reformers may imagine. Yet if states fail to undertake this kind of analysis, then shaming sanctions are unlikely to maintain the deterrence impact that is their primary justification.[183]

Even if shamings were well-publicized and did continue to command significant public attention, however, they might affect the public's reaction to crimes and criminals in ways that the shame sanction advocates may not have anticipated, and may not desire. As I have indicated, most punishment now tends to take place out of public view.[184] This is especially true in densely populated urban settings, where anonymity and disinterest in others' lives often are governing rules of public interpersonal relations. Accordingly, the community can distance itself psychologically from the process and results of punishment.[185] This distancing is reinforced by the fact that the few criminals who are personalized and who do come to popular attention are the particularly grotesque, bizarre, or flamboyant offenders.[186]

Public shaming, by definition, would mean wider public exposure to punishment, and hence to a greater number of less sensational defendants. Assuming that the criminal sanctions were imposed evenly, then at least for offenses that touch a cross-section of the population—such as drunk driving, shoplifting, spouse and child abuse, or tax fraud—the public would directly confront the impact of legal sanctions on the lives of people with whom more people can empathize.

Several practical effects, some adverse, might flow from this "deprivatization" of criminal law. It would of course bring the gravity of these offenses home to more people. This, in fact, is what the sanctioners hope will occur. The stronger our identification with the offender the greater our sense that we could end up in her same predicament. This certainly might deter others from committing similar crimes, which likely is the principal aim of the shame sentence. On the other hand, however, public discomfort and strong identification with offenders[187] might also result in public resistance to the sanction, and thus a softening of the criminal laws, or even a call for reprivatization,[188] as is evidenced by the demise of public spectacles in seventeenth- and eighteenth-century Europe. These consequences, of course, may not seem undesirable to all observers. My point here is that I doubt that reformers have taken them into account.

Public reactions to public shaming sanctions thus likely would be variable and complex. They would hinge on the nature of the sanction, the identity of the offenders, the character of the crime, and the perceived identification of the target audience with the offender. Audience acceptance of and cooperation in this "ritual" may be far more unpredictable and various than the judges and legislators who favor shaming sanctions suppose. Public sanctioning may even, in some cases, lead to an increase in violation of laws. The superficial appeal of this revival, upon closer inspection, thus begins to erode when one looks deeper at the nature of shame, the cultural context in which shaming has been "revived," and the multiple practical, institutional, and situational problems that may emerge.

F. Middle-Class Offenders: Windows of Shaming Opportunity?

Despite the foregoing arguments against shaming, some readers likely remain persuaded that a good public spanking will "work" for some offenders. One population of lawbreakers in particular—strongly socialized, middle-class offenders—may seem especially vulnerable to shaming because it tends to satisfy most of the cultural, psychological, and other conditions of shaming. Thus, some people would argue, shaming may make sense as a means of controlling bad behavior in this pocket of moral cohesion.

The argument that middle-class offenders will respond to shame sanctions has some force. Middle-class members likely most fear loss of social status, both because they have such status to lose and because it is precariously balanced. The members of this group have not attained, and most likely never will attain, the immunity from shunning and ostracism that exceptional wealth or high social standing affords. Acquisition of exceptional wealth, enough to elevate one to upper-class status, seldom occurs in one lifetime. Movement of this sort usually involves high risk behavior, entrepreneurial genius, or exceptional good luck—all low frequency occurrences. High social standing is even harder to obtain. Typically, it is inherited and immutable. Although marriage can enhance one's social standing, the elevation is less authentic, less stable, and not always generally acknowledged. Thus, elevation to a demonstrably higher social class is simply not possible for the vast majority of middle-class or lower middle-class people.

Demotion to a lower social class, in contrast, is always a distinct possibility. Middle-class status typically hinges on steady income and observation of middle-class rules of behavior. Loss of one's job, major illness, divorce, or notorious violation of middle-class norms, without more, can precipitate a slide into the lower class. Middle-class offenders thus may seem to be "ideal" targets for shaming sanctions. They are the people most likely to worry about public appearances, to be vulnerable to moralistic or judgmental social groups, to defer to authority, and

to be relatively conventional in attitudes toward "law and order." Thus, for crimes that are likely to be committed by middle-class people, the shaming sanctions may work best, if they work anywhere. These crimes would include, among others, drinking offenses, driving offenses, embezzlement, drug offenses, spouse abuse, child abuse, and tax fraud.

Even here, though, the many practical limitations of the sort I already have named may surface and undermine the effectiveness of the shaming tactics. The middle class is subject to the same range of intraclass personality deviations, individualized meanings of shame, and unpredictable responses to shame sanctions as are other subcultures. Childrearing practices, to name one of many variables that influence the shame phenomenon, vary widely among members of the middle class. Also, even middle-class offenders likely are not as conventional or susceptible to shame as we imagine. For example, in *State v. Rosenberger*,[189] the defendant had held a respectable position with American Telephone and Telegraph (AT&T). Rosenberger stole two AT&T checks, totaling $375,000, and deposited them into his personal checking account. The defendant argued that his "shame and disgrace" in being convicted was sufficient punishment. Judge Imbriani rejected this argument for the following pertinent reasons:

> [The defendant] had minimal roots anywhere and lived in Bound Brook for only two years prior to this offense. After being fired by AT & T he moved to California and quickly obtained a new and equally lucrative position. There is no evidence that he is now shunned socially, financially or otherwise. He still earns as much as he did at AT & T and it is probable that his new neighbors are totally unaware of his criminal conduct. So where is the shame? With whom has he been disgraced? How has he been punished? It is apparent that he simply moved his employment and residence 3,000 miles and continued his same life style without so much as a hitch.[190]

That is, even some members of the middle class, especially in large cities, may not care enough about what "society" thinks to make shaming a demonstrably more effective tool than mere conviction and customary punishments. Residential and occupational mobility, coupled with a generally eroded sense of community, can undermine the effectiveness of stigma punishments, even for the social groups traditionally most sensitive to stigma.

C. Conclusion

The meaning of any punishment is partly contextual. The penitentiary, to the Quakers, was a benign invention, meant to redeem the prisoner, not torture her.[191] Given modern cultural conditions, the meaning of shame sanctions is not benign. Rather, the message of modern shaming is predominantly harsh and disintegrative, not reintegrative. It is likely to be construed by the viewers, and experienced by the offender, as purely retributive—not rehabilitative or redemptive. And if it does deter anyone, it likely will deter most effectively those people for whom conviction and conventional punishments are threatening enough.

Braithwaite probably is correct when he says that "[y]ou cannot take the moral content out of social control and expect social control to work. If there is no morality about the law, if it is just a game of rational economic tradeoffs, cheating will be rife."[192] But his assumption that a society that replaces conventional punishment with reintegrative shaming will have less crime[193] seems unduly optimistic. It also ignores the extent to which a "punitive" practice in one context may be "reintegrative" in another and vice versa. The more promising sequence for his brand of reform is for informal, nongovernment institutions first to reconstitute a consensus about moral behavior and next to establish mechanisms for effective negative and positive reinforcement of behavior. Decentralization of authority, revitalization of family bonds and communal bonds, and a more robust sense of interdependence and responsibility to others thus should precede, or at least accompany, any legislative or judicial attempt to shame people into norm observation. Absent these preliminary and formidable steps, a formal shaming sanction is unlikely to convey the moral content Braithwaite desires. Rather, it will represent a purely retributive slap by an unforgiving and impersonal authority, and a feeble form of criminal justice.

VII. Humaneness Factors

> The combination of stigma and loss of liberty that inheres in criminal punishment represents a net loss in human dignity and autonomy. It is tempting to contemplate avoidance of that loss. . . . [O]ther things being equal, we should prefer punishments that do not entail stigma and loss of liberty to those that do.[194]

A. Introduction

In the preceding sections, I explored whether shaming is likely to promote valid punishment ends, in theory and in practice. In this final section, I consider whether the shaming sanctions are reasonably humane. The humaneness of a penalty depends on a host of factors, including whether it is proportional to the crime, is administered in an even-handed manner across offenders, and is not exceptionally degrading or cruel.[195]

All existing forms of punishment violate these principles to some degree, insofar as state-imposed punishment is an inexact, unevenly experienced, and often highly coercive response to norm violations. Nevertheless, the elusiveness of shame, the unreflective way in which the new shaming sanctions have been developed, and the serious harm to human dignity that truly effective shaming can cause, all suggest that the fairness objections to official shunning and shame are particularly compelling.

B. Proportionality

Proportionality of a penalty can be assessed in at least two ways: the punishment can be matched to the crime, ignoring offender-specific variations, or the punishment can be matched to the crime, taking into account offender-specific mitigating factors, such as remorse.

For a punishment under either account to "match" the crime, though, it must be a measurable sanction. With shaming, the harm to the offender is almost wholly intangible and cannot be assessed. Psychological studies of shame indicate that the same stimulus may produce deep shame in some offenders and no shame in others. Thus, to the extent that punishment is justified both as a negative and a *proportional* reaction to crime, shaming may offend both qualities: it may not, for some offenders, be "negative" at all, and the same stimulus may not be experienced equally by equally culpable actors.

This latter objection, of course, is hardly unique to shaming penalties; the impact of money fines, incarceration or any other penalty is felt unevenly as well. Likewise, shame is a potential, often likely, consequence of all forms of public punishment. The question, however, is not whether peripheral and disproportional stigmatizing already is part of the criminal process, but whether it is a desirable part that should be augmented and exploited. That other penalties may produce similar untoward consequences does not make these objections pointless when applied to shaming. Also, most conventional punishments involve at least some measurable, transsituational factors, such as the hours of community service, the months spent in prison, or the dollars assessed as a fine. Judges thus can be reasonably confident both about whether a penalty has been imposed, and whether the dosage of the penalty is increasing, regardless of the offender's personality or social circumstances. Money and time, at least, are susceptible to numerical estimations; embarrassment, ego strength, and social standing defy quantitative assessment.

Another proportionality concern is that the stigma of shaming may be irreversible. This possibility presumably would have to be taken into account in the court's or legislature's proportionality assessment. Fear of the peripheral and long-lasting effects of stigma associated with all punishments has convinced some penologists that officials should try to contain, not enhance, the publicity and labeling aspect of a criminal sanction.[196] With new shaming sanctions, however, judicial efforts to confine the shame to a discrete time period are unlikely to work. On the contrary, such efforts seem inconsistent with the effort to publicize the punishment. Once an offense becomes notorious, the public will do as it chooses with the information, regardless of official admonitions. This would be especially true in work and social relationships, where shunning might be acute for some offenders.

Officials also must consider the potential unfairness of stigma spillover. Whenever a person is sanctioned, the negative impact may extend to her family or other associates. This spillover effect is augmented when the offense is widely publicized or sensationalized. For example, one study of prisoners' wives' feelings of shame indicates that the wives were particularly embarrassed when their spouse's behavior and conviction were publicized in the local news media.[197] Expanded use of public shaming surely would deliver more convincing blows to these innocent others' reputations than conventional punishment methods already tend to. Although this could enhance the deterrence impact of a shaming sentence, at least to the extent that would-be offenders care about bringing disgrace to their intimate associates and kin, this does not necessarily entitle lawmakers or judges to exploit this apprehension.

One likely response to all of these proportionality objections is that they rely on individual-specific factors. Proportionality might instead be defined as matching the sanction to the offense, not to the offender.[198] The "eye for an eye" might be estimated not on the basis of actual shame experienced by the offender and her family, but on how much shame an average member of the community might or should feel if she were ordered to wear the same sign. Thus, proportionality inquiries would become less complex, at least insofar as the limitless range of individual shades of shame would not need to be consulted or reckoned.

The problem with this alternative is that these shaming schedules still would need to identify and grade an intensely slippery variable. The "cultural meaning of shame" within the United States is exceedingly amorphous, if indeed one national meaning exists. Neither legislators nor judges are likely to be able to define this variable accurately, let alone determine the precise spectacle that will match both the culture's definitions of shame and the gravity of the offense.[199] For example, on what possible basis might a sentencing reform commission decide that holding a sign in public was a proportional punishment for child molestation? Or, if a trial judge were to devise this sentence, how might the appellate court handle the defendant's argument that this sanction was not proportional to the crime? A coherent, articulable argument that a sign sanction is, or is not, "proportional" to this offense is difficult to imagine.

Equally difficult to express would be reasons for distinguishing more severe shaming sanctions from less harsh ones. Certainly, holding a sign in public for one week seems worse than a one-day sentence, but this is for reasons distinct from the shaming aspect of the sanction; for example, the deprivation of liberty would be greater. If everyone in town, or at least everyone significant to the offender, saw her during the first hour, then the subsequent hours would be irrelevant to the sanction's stigmatic impact, though liberty interests would become a stronger factor. Even if only one person saw the offender during the first hour, the stigma effect may be spread by that witness' relating the incident to others. In any event, the full measure of the stigma probably would be met at a certain threshold, after which "more shaming," "longer shaming," or wider publication would not matter much to the offender's reputation or sense of shame. Widespread, effective publication of the shaming probably would cause that shame threshold to be reached more *quickly* than ineffective publication, but it may not influence the final impact of disclosure.

Thus, for those observers who regard proportionality as a crucial and tight limitation on punishment, the stigma consequences of any punishment are undesirable because they are beyond our ability to control, measure, or justify rationally. Either we must take the varying contextual aspects of stigma into account, which demands a degree of sophistication that we currently lack, or we must try to minimize or contain it despite any potential sacrifice of deterrent efficacy.[200]

C. Equality

Erving Goffman once wrote that "the more power and prestige the others have, the more a person is likely to show considerations for their feelings."[201] To the extent that shame sanctions are "custom designed" to the offender, and not part of any sentencing guidelines, they thus are subject to the abuse of unequal application. If judges have discretion to fashion creative sentences, they may be inclined to deliver harsher sentences to some defendants than to others.[202]

The modern revivals of shaming are not part of comprehensive shame schedules, but seem instead to be episodic, almost whimsical bursts of judicial, legislative, or prosecutorial inspiration. One significant danger in such an ad hoc approach is that the "test group" for shaming will be the offenders with the least political or other means of objecting or retaliating. More powerful offenders may receive alternative sanctions like "community service," or fines.

The risk of unequal application of shame sanctions might be controlled by requiring that legislatures adopt mandatory sentencing guidelines, applied evenly to all offenders. But, as the current debates about mandatory sentencing in the federal system show, this form of equality can compromise equality in other senses.[203] For example, the legislature could insist that every person who steals $200 worth of goods be compelled to stand for one hour in the town square with a sign that reads "I am a thief." This would satisfy one rather static definition of equality. The only factor relevant to the punishment decision would be whether the same offense had been committed. But if one offender stole $200 worth of groceries for her family, and the other stole a $200 stereo, then a different sense of equality would be offended. Similarly, if one offender, who had never before stolen anything in her life and enjoyed widespread public respect, were facing her first criminal charge, whereas the other had a string of prior property offenses and had a reputation as a thief, then the hour in the square for the first would

not be the same as the hour in the square for the second. One could, of course, simply define equality as "same offense—same sign." But to do so would compromise other important meanings of equality.

This problem, of course, is pervasive. Individualized approaches to criminal law enforcement will always both promote *and* defeat equality objectives, no matter what sanction we impose. No plausible sentencing schedule can anticipate the entire range of the individual factors that may determine the impact of a sanction. This aspect of the equality dilemma may be especially profound with shaming sanctions, however, because "shame" is elusive and intensely offender-specific. Also, if judges did take the individualized meaning of a shame sanction into account, this could lead to the "unfair" result that prominent, white collar or upper-class offenders, who have more social status to lose, would receive milder sentences than less prominent lower-class offenders.[204] Yet if this individualized meaning is ignored, this could lead to unduly punitive sentences for some offenders, beyond any plausible specific or even general deterrence needs.

At present, the modern shame sanctions violate both senses of equality. They are neither part of a general, equally administered sentencing scheme, nor the product of reflective, individualized estimations of the offender's sense of shame. We do not know, for example, why the Rhode Island judge ordered Stephen Germershausen, but not other sex offenders, to place an ad in the newspaper for his offense. Nothing in the reported account of his sentence suggests that the judge selected Germershausen for this sentence because he was unusually likely to respond to this type of sentence, or because he deserved it more than other offenders. Rather, the judge simply wanted to set an example; equality concerns were not part of her stated sentencing calculus. This is a serious omission, however, and raises the strong concern that the revival of shaming may violate the principle of even-handed punishments.

D. Cruelty

The final fairness concern is the most difficult to define, though it makes immediate intuitive sense and may best capture the potential offense of an effective shaming sanction. When a shame sanction hits home, it is a direct assault on a basic need of all people,[205] the esteem of others. The troublesome inquiry is whether we should approve of government punishment that is principally designed to withdraw this esteem. In other words, is this type of dehumanizing punishment too "cruel" to be an acceptable sanction?

A common response to this concern is that the criminal has bargained away, or sacrificed involuntarily, her social standing in exchange for the projected fruits of her criminal activity. Social stability demands that public officials impose the burden of shame and guilt on those who defy basic, shared rules of civility and order. Some people thus argue that if some individuals' self-esteem is lost through the criminal process, then their loss is justified by our collective interest in our mutual protection, freedom, and well-being. Some may even argue that the offender's dignity is affirmed by holding her accountable for her actions, because this implies a belief that she is a rational, autonomous person.

As far as it goes, and as general as it is, the argument makes considerable sense. The argument depends, of course, on one's views about the etiology of crime, the effectiveness of degradation in curbing future behavior, and the danger of state-imposed punishments aimed directly at wounding offender's self-esteem and social standing. But even if we accept that government-imposed self-esteem losses are justifiable under some punishment circumstances, we still must determine whether a *particular* method of withdrawing that esteem produces adequate public good to justify these individual harms.

This resolution turns on several factors. First, it hinges on the nature of the wound that punishment inflicts. Psychological studies of shame are important to this inquiry because they disclose how serious the harm of effective shaming may be. The likely practical consequences of shaming also are important because they determine whether the competing societal interest warrants this potential assault on human dignity. Taken together, the likely practical advantages of shaming seem to be far less than its proponents imagine. Indeed, they may be negligible. This suggests that the balance of community versus individual offender concerns may tip decidedly in favor of the offender in the case of shame sanctions.

One could reach this same conclusion simply by arguing that it is always immoral to intentionally degrade a human being. This argument, though, would render any punishment scheme "immoral," a result I regard as senseless, in both practical and moral terms. When we wound others—by robbing, assaulting, driving recklessly, cheating, or otherwise—we can expect and in some sense deserve rebuke. This rebuke may well lower our social

standing, and hence compromise our self-image. If we deny states the power to injure one's social standing, we deny them the power to convict and punish criminals. I would oppose such a result, as would most people. Nonetheless, whenever we place the power to rebuke in the hands of the government, liberalism reminds us to be extremely wary of that authority, and to demand that the power be exercised minimally, uniformly, and subject to constant reexamination and supervision.

State-enforced shaming authorizes public officials to search for and destroy or damage an offender's dignity. Aggressive use of such authority may be an Orwellian prospect, particularly when reintegration is not part of the punishment process. Absent far more compelling evidence than we currently possess that shaming would produce demonstrably better results than conventional punishments, then, shaming should not become part of the sentencer's arsenal.

VIII. Conclusion

Jurists and legislators have good reason to be frustrated by the failures of past attempts to find effective, humane, and economic punishment techniques. But shaming sanctions are not the solution. We cannot wish away the absence of cultural conditions that might make shaming a meaningful cultural ritual. We likewise cannot ignore the profound harm that effective shaming, where it can be achieved, may cause.

The historical demise of public shaming in dominant Western culture was prompted by rationalistic and humanistic instincts. The experiences that gave rise to those instincts should inform modern attempts to fashion rational, humane criminal punishment. They caution against widespread revival of the pillory and stocks in the United States. Absent thoroughgoing changes in the nature of the modern state, in criminal court procedures and personnel, and in the dominant culture's conception of the relationship between the individual and her community, the modern shaming sanctions will not work. At best, they are likely to prove futile, even silly, responses to crime. At worst, they may become highly destructive, state-imposed assaults on human personality.

---

1. Hulick, *Molester's Sentence: Photo Ad in Paper,* Ariz. Republic, Nov. 9, 1989, at A1, col. 1 (state ed.).

2. *Id.*

3. *See, e.g.,* L. Berkson, *The Concept of Cruel and Unusual Punishment* 4 (1975) (describing various punitive practices of England and colonial America).

4. *See* R. Semmes, *Crime and Punishment in Early Maryland* 30 (1938) (describing punishment given to a witness who was found guilty of perjury).

5. *See id.* at 35 (reporting that in 1663, Maryland laws provided that county justices should be given irons for burning "malefactors"—perhaps "*H*" for "hog stealer," "*R*" for "runaway slave," "*M*" for "murderer," or "*T*" for "thief").

6. *See id.* at 38 (noting that banishment from the province was a penalty in Maryland during the late 1600s).

7. *Id.* at 39 (noting that to set a man in stocks was a usual form of punishment in Maryland during the late 1600s).

8. In fact, the judge also ordered him to contribute $1000 to a program financed by a rape crisis center for child victims of sexual assault. *See* Hulick, *supra* note 1. The remedy of forcing a defendant to make financial restitution to the victim of a crime has a long history in the United States. Semmes describes an early Maryland case in which a convicted forger was ordered "'set on the pillory and loose one of her ears,'" after which she was to be "imprisoned for twelve months and to pay double costs and damages" to the victim of the forgery. R. Semmes, *supra* note 4, at 32. Money fines, of course, have a far longer history than the American experience, as the ancient concept of the "wergeld" proves. *See* P. Spierenburg, *The Spectacle of Suffering* 3 (1984).

9. *See* Hulick, *supra* note 1.

10. *See infra* text accompanying notes 50–55.

11. *See infra* text accompanying notes 41–49.

12. *With Jails Overcrowded, Judges Look for Innovative Sentences to Fit Crimes,* Chicago Daily L. Bull., Feb. 24, 1988, at 1, col. 5. In another recent example, a New Hampshire judge ordered a man convicted of raping a 10-year-old boy "to buy ads in two local newspapers apologizing for his crime." *Flogging?, Newsweek,* Apr. 22, 1991, at 6.

13. *See Blanton v. City of North Las Vegas,* 489 *U.S.* 538 (1989) (referring to *Nev. Rev. Stat.* 484.3792 (1)(a)(2)) (1987).

14. *See infra* notes 30–31 and accompanying text.

15. Money fines likewise do not fill the judges' sanctions gap for several reasons. First, many defendants cannot pay the fines. Second, those who can afford them may pass the cost on to their "customers." *See, e.g.,* Fisse, *Sanctions Against Corporations: The Limitations of Fines and the Enterprise of Creating Alternatives,* in *Corrigible Corporations and Unruly Law* 137, 140 (B. Fisse & P. French eds. 1985). Moreover, even when fines might be an effective deterrent, popular opinion may demand that the defendant pay for her misdeeds with more than cash. *See* French, *Publicity and the Control of Corporate Conduct: Hester Prynne's New Image,* in *Corrigible Corporations and Unruly Law, supra,* at 159–60.

16. Malcolm, *New Strategies to Fight Crime Go Far Beyond Stiffer Terms and More Cells, N.Y. Times,* Oct. 10, 1990, at A16, col. 1.

17. *See infra* Part II.B.

18. *See infra* Part IV.

19. *See infra* Part V.A.

20. *See infra* Part V.E.

21. *See infra* Part IV.

22. *See infra* Part V.E.

23. *See infra* Part V.B.

24. *See infra* Part VI.B.

25. *See infra* Part VI.C.

26. *See infra* Part VII.B.

27. *See infra* Part VII.C.

28. *See infra* Part VII.D.

29. *Id.*

30. American prisons are terribly overcrowded and expensive to run. *See, e.g.,* Finn, *Judicial Responses to Prison Crowding,* 67 *Judicature* 318, 319 (1984) (noting that state prison populations increased 54% between 1973 and 1982); *Prison Overcrowding Project Update, Crim. J. Newsletter,* Mar. 28, 1983, at 6; Silas, *Homebodies A.B.A.J.* May 1, 1986, at 28, 29 (reporting that Oklahoma's prison population doubled between 1979 and 1984, prompting the state legislature to expand home detention as an alternative to incarceration); *With Jails Overcrowded, Judges Look for Innovative Sentences to Fit Crimes, Chicago Daily L. Bull.,* Feb. 24, 1988, at 1, col. 4 (quoting a district court judge who says he imposes novel sentences because the prisons and detention centers are overcrowded); *see generally* Farrington & Nuttall, *Prison Size, Overcrowding, Prison Violence, and Recidivism,* 8 *J. Crim. Just.* 221 (1980); Holbert & Call, *The Perspective of State Correctional Officials on Prison Overcrowding: Causes, Court Orders, and Solutions, Fed. Probation,* Mar. 1989, at 25; *The Prison Overcrowding Crisis,* 12 *N.Y.U. Rev. L. & Soc. Change* 1 (1983–84); Robbins & Buser, *Punitive Conditions of Prison Confinement: An Analysis of* Pugh v. Locke *and Federal Court Supervision of State Penal Administration Under the Eighth Amendment,* 29 *Stan. L. Rev.* 893 (1977).

Prisons also can be dangerous and deplorable places, as evidenced by the prisoners' rights decisions of the 1960s–1980s. *See, e.g., Rhodes v. Chapman,* 452 *U.S.* 337 (1981); *Bell v. Wolfish,* 441 *U.S.* 520 (1979); *Estelle v. Gamble,* 429 *U.S.* 97 (1976); *Procunier v. Martinez,* 416 *U.S.* 396 (1974); *Tousaint v. McCarthy,* 801 *F. 2d* 1080 (9th Cir. 1986); *Badgley v. Santacroce,* 800 *F. 2d* 33 (2d Cir. 1986); *Martinez v. Mancusi,* 443 *F. 2d* 921 (2d Cir. 1970), *cert. denied,* 401 *U.S.* 983 (1971); *Hamilton v. Covington,* 445 *F. Supp.* 195 (W.D. Ark. 1978). Finn reports that "[b]y 1976, over 19,000 petitions for relief had been filed in federal courts, representing over 15 percent of the entire civil filings. . . . By the end of 1982, 31 states were under court order to remedy crowded conditions alone, and another nine were facing similar court challenges." Finn, *supra,* at 264.

31. Objections to lenient sentences and to uneven enforcement of the criminal penalties led to the adoption of mandatory sentencing guidelines in the federal system. *See U.S. Sentencing Commn., Federal Sentencing Guidelines Manual* (1988). The guidelines were upheld as constitutional in *Mistretta v. United States,* 488 *U.S.* 361 (1989). Nevertheless, the guidelines continue to be extremely controversial. *See, e.g.,* Bishop, *Mandatory Sentences in Drug Cases: Is the Law Defeating Its Purpose?, N.Y. Times,* June 8, 1990, at B16, col. 3. The nature and tenor of these debates reveal how divided and confused attitudes about proper punishment ends remain in the United States, even among the "experts."

32. *See, e.g.,* R. Steggerda & P. Venezia, *Community-Based Alternatives to Traditional Corrections* 9–12 (1974) (research conducted by the Research Center of the National Council on Crime and Delinquency describing community-based alternatives to incarceration, including work-release, residential facilities, fines, and probation with support services); Unger, *Private Pomona Company Has an Alternative to Jail, L.A. Daily J.,* May 19, 1986, § II, at 1, col. 3 (describing California's experimentation with privately run work furlough programs, in lieu of incarceration).

33. *See, e.g., Doctor Sentenced to Heal in India, Natl. L.J.,* Aug. 25, 1980, at 3, col. 1 (psychiatrist convicted of Medicare fraud ordered to give medical services in India); *With Jails Overcrowded, Judges Look for Innovative Sentences to Fit Crimes, Chicago Daily L. Bull.,* Feb. 24, 1988, at 1, col. 4 (describing Chicago judge's sentencing of a defendant who harassed blacks to 200 hours of community service with the NAACP); Wise, *Was the Judge's "Sentence" Off Base?, Natl. L.J.,* Mar. 5, 1984, at 43, col. 1 (baseball player Al Bumbry sentenced to 20 minutes of signing autographs for speeding); *Sentenced to Happy Hours,*

Natl. L.J., Apr. 12, 1982, at 39, col. 3 (cocktail lounge owner ordered to provide liquor to geriatric ward of local hospital after lounge was cited for overcrowding; pizza parlor owner ordered to provide pizzas to hospital patients; and music student convicted of drunk driving ordered to play concerts for patients). For a critical reaction to community service penalties, both as an insufficiently harsh penalty and as a perversion of the concept of public service as activity inspired by public spiritedness, not a court order, see Gordon, *Community Service, Mark of Disgrace, N.Y. Times,* Mar. 12, 1990, at A17, col. 3.

34. "Home detention" is the pretrial or post-conviction, full- or part-time restriction of a defendant to her own home. *See, e.g.,* Silas, *supra* note 30, at 28 (describing sentences of home confinement, used by a majority of the states as alternatives to prison); Gombossy, *Florist Placed Under 'House Arrest' in Credit Card Scam, Natl. L.J.,* Aug. 11, 1986, at 6, col. 1 (discussing house arrest as response to prison overcrowding in a Connecticut case, and in other jurisdictions); *A Prisoner in His Own Home, Natl. L.J.,* Feb. 15, 1982, at 35, col. 3 (describing sentence confining burglar to his mother's property for two years); Berg, *Home Detention Gaining Support, Crim. Justice Newsletter,* Nov. 21, 1983, at 3, col. 1; Berg, *Electronic Leashes Popular—But Effective?, L.A. Daily J.,* Aug. 14, 1987, at 5, col. 1; *Federal Judge, Citing Costs of Prison, Imposes "House Arrest," Crim. Justice Newsletter,* Oct. 1, 1985, at 2, col. 2; *see generally* Rush, *Deinstitutional Incapacitation: Home Detention in Pre-Trial and Post-Conviction Contexts,* 13 *N. Ky. L. Rev.* 375, 378 (1987). Home detention can be monitored by intensive human supervision or by electronic surveillance through electronic monitors secured to the defendant's ankle or wrist. *Id.* at 378.

35. Shock probation is the short-term incarceration of a first offender, intended to "scare her straight" by showing her the harsh reality of penitentiary life. *See generally* Note, *Shock Probation: An Alternative to Traditional Forms of Sentencing,* 12 *Texas Tech. L. Rev.* 697 (1981).

36. *See, e.g.,* Liss, *A Fine Way to Give to Charity, Natl. L.J.,* Nov. 26, 1984, at 47, col. 1. *See generally* Note, *Charitable Contributions as a Condition of Federal Probation for Corporate Defendants: A Controversial Sanction Under New Law,* 60 *Notre Dame L. Rev.* 530 (1985).

37. *See, e.g.,* Demsky, *The Use of Depo-Provera in the Treatment of Sex Offenders,* 5 *J. Legal Med.* 295 (1984) (discussing the compelled use of chemical hormone regulation with convicted sex offenders).

38. *See A Misconceived Ruling, L.A. Daily J.,* June 7, 1988, at 4, col. 1 (editorial).

39. *See* Goldfarb, *Practice of Using Castration as Sentence Being Questioned, Crim. Justice Newsletter,* Feb. 15, 1984, at 3, col. 2 (reporting choice between castration or a 30-year sentence that a South Carolina judge gave to three rapists). *But see Mickle v. Henrichs,* 262 *F. Supp.* 687 (D. Nev. 1918) (declaring unconstitutional a Nevada statute that authorized vasectomies for certain sex offenders); *Davis v. Berry,* 216 *F.* 413 (S.D. Iowa 1914), *revd. on other grounds,* 242 *U.S.* 468 (1917) (invalidating similar legislation in Iowa).

40. *See infra* notes 94–99 and accompanying text.

41. *See* Nordheimer, *In-House Dispute: Drunken Driver Bumper Sticker, N.Y. Times,* June 6, 1985, at A22, col. 3; *Scarlet Bumper: Humiliating Drunk Drivers, Time,* June 17, 1985, at 52.

42. *See, e.g., Goldschmitt v. State,* 490 *So. 2d* 123 (Fla. Dist. Ct. App. 1986) (per curiam), *appeal denied,* 496 *So. 2d* 142 (Fla. 1986). *See generally* Note, *The Bumper Sticker: The Innovation That Failed,* 22 *New Eng. L. Rev.* 643 (1988) (discussing the legality and impact of the bumper sticker penalty); Ohle & Wise, *Stick Goes the Bumper, Natl. L.J.,* Dec. 28, 1981, at 35, col. 2 (describing bumper sticker sanctions imposed by Washington state court judge).

43. *See Ohio Rev. Code Ann.* § 4503.231 (Page's 1988). The Ohio statute, which took effect in 1986, reads as follows:

> No motor vehicle registered in the name of a person whose certificate of registration and identification license plates have

been impounded . . . shall be operated or driven on any highway in this state unless it displays identification license plates which are a different color from those regularly issued and carry a special serial number that may be readily identified by law enforcement officers.

The statute was applied in *State v. Barbone,* No. 3653, slip. op. (Ohio Ct. App. June 26, 1987) (requiring convicted drunk driver to display the different color plates pursuant to § 4503.231).

44. Titus, *"Scarlet Letter" a Just Punishment* (Council of State Governments publication) (on file with author). Judge Titus reports that Sarasota County's DUI arrest rate dropped 33% during January–June 1986 over the same period in 1985. She says nothing indicated that the decline was due to decreased police patrols. *Id.*

45. *Id.* Judge Titus added that the sentence might also force alcoholics to acknowledge their illness, and that the glow-in-the-dark sticker might aid law enforcement officers in apprehending drivers who violated their driving restrictions. *Id.*

46. *Nev. Rev. Stat.* § 484.3792 (1)(a)(2) (1987).

47. *Blanton v. City of North Las Vegas,* 489 *U.S.* 544 (1989). Justice Marshall wrote the opinion. The issue before the Court was whether the defendant had a sixth amendment right to trial by jury under the Nevada statute. The right does not attach for "petty offenses," which usually means offenses for which the maximum imprisonment is six months or less. In observing that the distinctive attire was less offensive than a six-month jail sentence, though, the Court noted that the record failed to describe the clothing or where and when it had to be worn. *Blanton,* 489 *U.S.* at 544 n. 10.

The case raises an interesting question for "innovative sentencing" reforms: when is the alternative sanction penalty grave enough to trigger the jury trial right?

48. *State v. Bateman,* 95 *Or. App.* 456, 771 *P. 2d* 314 (en banc), *cert denied,* 308 *Or.* 197, 777 *P. 2d* 410 (1989); *see also "Scarlet Letter" Sentence OK'd by Ore. Court, Natl. L.J.,* Nov. 23, 1987, at 9, col. 4.

49. Hulick, *supra* note 1. The judge, Corinne P. Grande, reportedly imposed the sentence as a condition of the offender's probation because "these cases aren't publicized" and "[t]here doesn't appear to be sufficient social response to people like [the defendant]." *Id.* at A14. She added, "It seemed to me that [the defendant] ought to be made a public example." *Id; see also Better than Prison, Peninsula Times Tribune,* Jan. 4, 1990, at A9, col. 2 (picture of defendant who agreed to wear for one year a T-shirt that read "My Record and Two Six Packs Equal Four Years" on the front, and "I'm on Felony Probation" on the back instead of returning to prison); Mintz, *Judge Turns Confessing into a Religious Experience, Natl. L.J.,* Feb. 6, 1984, at 47, col. 2 (describing sanction requiring car thief to post five-by-four-foot sign in his yard announcing that he was a thief).

50. *See Enforcing the "Law" of the Letter, Natl. L.J.,* May 3, 1982, at 55, at col. 2. The judge stated that the purpose of the sentence is to ask the defendant what she has learned and to apologize to her victim. *Id.*

51. *See* Mintz, *supra* note 49, at 47; *cf. Woman Ordered to Apologize to Man Falsely Accused of Rape, Gainsville Sun,* July 3, 1990, at 4A, col. 3 (describing an order of a Nebraska judge that a woman who falsely accused a man of rape run radio and newspaper advertisements apologizing to him).

52. *See* Mathews, *Freedom Means Having to Say You're Sorry, Wash. Post,* Nov. 9, 1986, at A3, col. 1. In this report, the district attorney and probation officer who initiated the program explain that the idea "'grew out of pure, sheer frustration.'" *Id.* They add that in a small town, the publication would at least warn other citizens of the dangerousness of some offenders. A local judge is reported to have said that he saw no problem with apology ads, as long as they were part of a plea bargain and not an imposed sentence. *Id.*

53. *Id.* Some more recent media accounts have criticized the shaming punishment, however. For example, a recent *Newsweek* article characterized apology advertisements as "a scarlet letter

for the 1990s" and noted opponents' comparison of the practice to "public flogging." *See Flogging?, supra* note 12.

54. *See, e.g.,* Egan, *Pain Relived in War on Drunk Driving, N.Y. Times,* Mar. 16, 1989, at A16, col. 2 (describing a Redmond, Washington, program under which anyone convicted of drunk driving must spend an hour with a victim's panel composed of people whose lives have been changed adversely by drunk drivers). Forced interaction is also used as a sanction for racially insensitive or abusive conduct on some college campuses. For example, the University of Michigan adopted a controversial Policy on Discrimination and Discriminatory Harassment by Students in the University Environment, under which some students had been sentenced to write apologies to the campus newspaper and to attend counseling or small group discussions. *See* Hentoff, *Watching What You Say on Campus, Wash. Post,* Sept. 14, 1989, at A23, col. 3. The policy was struck down as unconstitutional. *Doe v. University of Michigan,* 721 *F. Supp.* 852 (E.D. Mich. 1989).

    A different approach to victim satisfaction in a drunk driving case was fashioned by the parties in a civil case in Virginia. The parents of a teenage girl killed by a drunk driver agreed to settle the lawsuit for $936, but demanded that the teen defendant pay the amount $1 per week. The parents insisted on the $1 weekly payments in order to remind the defendant weekly of what he had done to their daughter. *See* Campbell, *Parent Won't Let DUI Driver Forget, Gainesville Sun,* Mar. 31, 1990, at 2A, col. 5.

55. An apology is a sophisticated social gesture, as Goffman has observed. *See* E. Goffman, *Relations in Public* 113 (1971). He has described the apology as a device "through which an individual splits himself into two parts, the part that is guilty of an offense and the part that dissociates itself from the delict and affirms a belief in the offended rule." *Id.* According to Goffman, an apology is a form of "ritual work," that may not compensate for the loss, but that expresses a pious attitude toward the rule. Thus it is "*a matter of indicating a relationship, not compensating a loss.*" *Id.* at 118.

> As Goffman has put it:
> In its fullest form, the apology has several elements: expression of embarrassment and chagrin; clarification that one knows what conduct has been expected and sympathizes with the application of negative sanction; verbal rejection, repudiation, and disavowal of the wrong way of behaving along with vilification of the self that so behaved; espousal of the right way and an avowal henceforth to pursue that course; performance of penance and the volunteering of restitution.

Id. at 113. Given this characteristic, apologies have a "one-time" effectiveness: if the offender repeats the crime, then his apology is revealed to be insincere, and he has proven himself to be more the self that committed the misdeed than the self that was originally embarrassed. *Id.* at 165–66. The "relationship" indicated by the apology thus is shown to be false.

    The apology sanction seems to rest on the mistaken assumption that all victims will react favorably to the offender's contribution. Different victims, though, will experience a crime differently. Not all victims want or need offender remorse, explanations, or confessions. *See generally* Henderson, *The Wrongs of Victim's Rights,* 37 *Stan. L. Rev.* 937, 964–66 (1985) (discussing the ways in which one-dimensional assumptions about victims' experiences can distort discussions of criminal procedures designed to protect "victims' rights").

    A victim's satisfaction in an apology often may be meager or none, depending on the crime and on the victim. For example, a robbery victim may be far more satisfied if she reclaims the loot from unrepentant criminals than if she receives an apology, but not money, from a truly contrite one. E. Goffman, *supra,* at 116. The effectiveness of an apology sanction, like that of shaming sanctions in general, thus hinges on a number of psychological and social variables, which may vary among crimes, victims, and perpetrators.

56. H. L. A. Hart, *Punishment and Responsibility* 72 (1968).

57. *See generally* M. Frankel, *Criminal Sentences—Law Without Order* 106 (1972) (defining retribution, rehabilitation, incapacitation, and deterrence).

58. *See, e.g.,* Ingber, *A Dialectic: The Fulfillment and Decrease of Passion in Criminal Law,* 28 *Rutgers L. Rev.* 861 (1975).

59. *See, e.g.,* Hampton, *The Moral Education Theory of Punishment,* 13 *Phil. & Pub. Aff.* 208 (1984); *Introduction to Contemporary Punishment: Views, Explanations and Justifications* 5 (R. Gerber & P. McAnary eds. 1972). The moral education theory seems to be one form of rehabilitation, to the extent that it seeks to reform the criminal and encourage right-thinking as a path to right-acting. It is also a form of deterrence, to the extent that the moral "education" inherent in public punishment is directed both at the offender *and* the onlookers. The hope, I assume, is that they all will "learn something" and avoid breaching these moral lessons in the future. Punishment as "homily" might also satisfy retributivist ends if its delivery makes victims feel more "whole." Thus the moral education theory is not a *distinct* justification or theory of punishment. Rather, it is one tool for promoting norm enforcement. *Cf.* E. Durkheim, *The Division of Labor in Society* 108–9 (G. Simpson trans. 1933) (describing the goal of punishment as the affirmation of a common morality by expressing outrage at the breach of the legal/social order).

60. *See, e.g.,* H. L. A. Hart, *supra* note 56, at 233–35. But Hart also acknowledged that different justifications for punishment become relevant at different points in a "morally acceptable account of punishment." *Id.* at 3. His definition of retributivism takes into account the voluntary nature of the wrongful act and whether the return of suffering to the offender is itself just as good. *Id.* at 231.

    Kant and Hegel are among the most prominent adherents to the view that the main justification of punishment is retribution, and that this is an end in and of itself. Some theology comports with this view, though the reconciliation there is between a deity and man; it is not an earthbound exchange. *See* W. Tsao, *Rational Approach to Crime and Punishment* 7–8 (1955). For example, retributive principles are expressed in Judeo-Christian writings. *Leviticus* 24:17–22.

61. This construction has been the subject of mounting criticism, which has been described as the "victim's rights" movement. For a description and critique of this movement, see Henderson, *supra* note 55, at 942–53.

62. Montesquieu, writing in the eighteenth century, emphasized proportionality as a necessary element of just punishment. Beccaria, writing in the same century, likewise stressed proportionality. *See* W. Tsao, *supra* note 60, at 29–30.

63. *See* Berns, *Retribution as a Ground for Punishment,* in *Crime and Punishment: Issues in Criminal Justice* 1 (F. Baumann & K. Jensen eds. 1989); Gardner, *The Renaissance of Retribution—An Examination of Doing Justice,* 1976 *Wis. L. Rev.* 781; Henderson, *supra* note 55, at 945–48; Robinson, *Moral Science, Social Science, and The Idea of Justice,* in *Crime and Punishment: Issues in Criminal Justice, supra,* at 15; Rush, *supra* note 34, at 396 n.5. A different, perhaps related approach—which emphasizes the victim as the focus of criminal law—is the "restitutionary approach." This approach argues that restitution to victims, other injured parties, and society should be the purpose of punishment. *See, e.g.,* C. Abel & F. Marsh, *Punishment and Restitution* 12 (1984). Still another contemporary turn on retribution theory is a recent article that develops a moral-emotive theory of punishment based on retributivist assumptions. *See* Pillsbury, *Emotional Justice: Moralizing the Passions of Criminal Punishment,* 74 *Cornell L. Rev.* 655 (1989).

64. Henderson, *supra* note 55, at 945–48.

65. The only other alternative to deterrence and rehabilitation is incapacitation, which poses its own practical and moral difficulties. *See infra* section III.E.

66. "Retributivism" does not necessarily tell us when, or which, criminals "deserve it." Is punishment triggered by a conviction? Only an "accurate" conviction? Only an accurate conviction for

violation of a "good" law? Also, as Packer has explained, some retributivists believe that the punishment is for the *criminal's* own good. It is a means by which she realizes her moral character. *See* H. Packer, *The Limits of the Criminal Sanction* 38 (1968). Others argue that it is for society's sake. *Id.* at 37–38. Pure retributivists, however, can argue it is for neither the criminal nor society's sake, and ignore consequences altogether.

67. *See, e.g.,* O. W. Holmes, *The Common Law* 45 (1881) (describing retribution as "only vengeance in disguise"); J. Bentham, *The Principles of Morals and Legislation* 179–89 (1907) (implicitly rejecting retribution in favor of deterrence theory).

68. For example, retributivism presupposes that commensurability is a workable guidepost for punishment. But what precisely does "an eye for an eye" mean? In what way, if at all, can the sentencer ascertain the "proportionality" of a punishment for drunk driving or child molestation? "An eye for an eye" is one thing; a "sign for a molestation or human life" quite another. The sign sanction may be too much, too different, or, too little, depending on one's perspective, a perspective one can justify only by entirely subjective, intuitive assessments of "equal harm."

A second problem lies in the pure retributivists' questionable assumption of free will. For example, if a drunk driver is an alcoholic, is her moral culpability the same as a DUI offender unafflicted by this disease? Unless the preliminary, and highly problematic, assumption of free will is irrebuttable, then individual factors like alcoholism pose tough complicating factors for retribution theory in general and thus also for retributivist justifications of shaming. To ignore these factors may result in disproportionate, unequal, and inhumane punishment. Yet, if one admits some individual factors into the inquiry, then it becomes difficult to justify blanket exclusion of others, such as environmental or situational pressures that may make drinking and driving more or less the product of "free will." Problems of determinism and free will are inescapable, unless one ignores them completely, which only pure retributivists are willing to do.

69. *See* F. Allen, *The Decline of the Rehabilitative Ideal* 2–4 (1981).

70. I include both reactions as evidence of rehabilitation, though pure rehabilitation anticipates the latter, complete character metamorphosis, whereas specific deterrence does not. Professor Blecker describes the distinction between pure rehabilitation and specific deterrence as follows:

Specific deterrence and rehabilitation do overlap. Perhaps specific deterrence is a threat of repeating a bad time inside [prison], whereas rehabilitation is a promise of a better time outside. . . .

Rehabilitation—or reformation—essentially consists in the acquisition of attitudes, values, habits and skills by which an "enlightened" criminal comes to value himself as a valid member of a society in which he can function productively and lawfully.

Blecker, *Haven or Hell? Inside Lorton Central Prison: Experiences of Punishment Justified,* 42 *Stan. L. Rev.* 1149, 1197 (1990).

71. *See* F. Allen, *supra* note 69, at 5–7. Allen marks the decline of the rehabilitative ideal as occurring in 1970s. *Id.*

72. *See id.* at 24–25 (describing critiques of rehabilitation theory).

73. *See* H. Packer, *supra* note 66, at 55–58. For example, incarceration does not seem to reform criminals, as its early advocates hoped it would. On the contrary, prison may congeal criminal characters and teach inmates new norm-breaking skills; *see, e.g.,* Blecker, *supra* note 70, at 1192–202, or may even be an attractive setting to some few prisoners. *See, e.g.,* Duncan, *"Cradled on the Sea:" Positive Images of Prison and Theories of Punishment,* 76 *Calif. L. Rev.* 1201, 1219–30 (1988). Current recidivism rates also suggest that a rehabilitation justification for imprisonment is implausible. Ex-prisoners simply are not forswearing crime in large numbers.

74. *See, e.g.,* Slobogin, *Dangerousness and Expertise,* 133 *U. Pa. L. Rev.* 97, 110 (1984) (discussing the inaccuracy of clinical estimations of future dangerousness).

75. Less clear is whether exile-type sanctions would promote rehabilitation ends. The message of banishment seems quite the opposite: you are *beyond* reform, and so must be expelled. For example, Aristotle wrote that "punishments and penalties should be imposed on those who disobey and are of inferior nature, while the *incurably bad* should be completely banished." *The Nicomachean Ethics of Aristotle* 271 (D. Ross trans. 1966) (emphasis added). The only conceivable rehabilitation-based justification for permanent exile would be that the loss of social identity in one community might hurt enough to discourage the offender from risking banishment from another. Thus banishment might be an attempt at "transcommunity" rehabilitation. It seems very unlikely, however—at least to me—that those who banish offenders are acting out of rehabilitation instincts, or that banishment has reforming effects. Absent the opportunity to and the formal means of rejoining the community post-banishment, the more compelling justification for banishment is containment—that is, an attempt to protect the community from the offender by keeping her removed from them. For shaming sanctions, in contrast, rehabilitation-type justifications do make sense and may well be the reason that some modern reformers favor these methods.

76. *See infra* section VI.C.

77. *See generally* J. Andenaes, *Punishment and Deterrence* 1 (1974); *Panel on Research on Deterrent and Incapacitative Effects, Natl. Academy of Sci., Deterrence and Incapacitation: Estimating the Effects of Criminal Sanctions on Crime Rates* 4 (1978) [hereinafter *Deterrence and Incapacitation*] (deterrent effects indicated by an inverse relationship between sanction levels and crime rates). The philosophical foundation traditionally invoked in support of deterrence theory is utilitarianism. Punishment is regarded as an evil that contributes to the greatest good for the greatest number by preventing a greater evil. *See* J. Bentham, *supra* note 67, at 171; H. Packer, *supra* note 66, at 39.

78. C. Beccaria, *On Crimes and Punishments* 75 (1953); J. Bentham, *supra* note 67, at 179–89.

79. Blecker, *supra* note 70, at 1173 (pointing out the roots of deterrence theory in Plato's writings).

80. For example, some philosophers point out that if deterrence is one's sole theory of punishment, then one would not object to the punishment of an innocent person in order to deter others. Also, if general deterrence is the only end, then we need not actually punish offenders; apparent threats are sufficient. To a utilitarian, then, "real justice" is irrelevant, as long as others are deterred.

81. For a discussion of the difficulties of assessing the deterrent effects of punishment, *see Deterrence and Incapacitation, supra* note 77, at 61–63.

82. *See, e.g.,* J. Andenaes, *supra* note 77, at 42–44 (describing critiques of deterrence theory that question the assumption of rational behavior by potential offenders). In his historical account of capital punishment, G. R. Scott suggests that public punishments may not deter crime. G. Scott, *The History of Capital Punishment* (1950). The following interview is of a convict whose death sentence had been remitted, though he had been "within an ace of being hanged for coining." *Id.* at 63.

Q: "Have you often seen an execution?"
A: "Yes, often."
Q: "Did not it frighten you?"
A: "No—why should it?
Q: "Did it not make you think that the same would happen to yourself?"
A: "Not a bit."
Q: "What did you think then?"
A: "Think? Why, I thought it was a—shame."
Q: "Now when you have been going to run a great risk of being caught and hanged, did the thought never come into your head, that it would be as well to avoid the risk?"
A: "Never."
Q: "Not when you remembered having seen men hanged for the same thing?"

A: "Oh! I never remembered anything about it; and if I had, what difference would that make. We must all take our chance. I never thought it would fall on me, and I don't think it ever will." *Id.*

Such anecdotes fuel our worst nightmares about crime. We prefer to think that most people can, and do, imagine themselves "on the gallows," and that this possible scenario curbs lawbreaking instincts. That is, shame sanctions, like legal threats in general, presuppose a positive correlation between negative penalties for a behavior and avoidance of it. But the prospect of shame may not necessarily provide avoidance. Whether and to what extent it does hinge on multiple, contradictory theories about criminal personality and about subcultures of deviance.

Sigmund Freud, for one, believed that criminals committed bad acts in order to be caught and punished. He theorized that unresolved, unconscious guilt and anxiety lead offenders to commit the acts and be punished. S. Freud, *The Ego and the Id* (1961). That is, whatever motivates nondeviant members of society to conform to established norms may not motivate deviants. If Freud was correct, then adding to or "piling on" more stigma to conviction penalties may not deter a larger population than already is deterred by the prospect of conviction and punishment. Those who *are* susceptible to this sort of legal threat tend to obey the laws anyway. Those who do *not* obey laws are unlikely to be deterred more by the additional stigmatizing effect of public shame than by conviction and conventional punishments. The key to controlling this group might be increasing their perceived chances of getting caught—though according to Freud, even certain apprehension would not deter some offenders, because they may *want* to be caught.

Other commentators likewise present a psychological portrait of criminal subcultures that undermines strong deterrence claims for shame sanctions. Reporting on this work, one article notes that some theorists describe the offender as someone who "does not experience real guilt or shame concerning his crimes. . . . Indeed, the successful offender is described as triumphant. . . . [The] criminal is always self-confident and never thinks of his actions as being morally wrong." Frazier & Meisenhelder, *Exploratory Notes on Criminality and Emotional Ambivalence,* 8 *Qualitative Soc.* 266, 268 (1985) (describing the work of Yochelson and Samenow).

Likely a *more* accurate profile, however, is that most criminals believe not that their acts are morally correct, but that they are in some way emotionally satisfying, justified, or "thrilling." *Id.* at 271. To most offenders, then, doing wrong is not intrinsically good, but it may seem worth it.

83. *See* W. Tsao, *supra* note 60, at 58–59; F. Zimring & G. Hawkins, *Deterrence* 245–48 (1973).

84. Zimring and Hawkins coined the phrase "legal threat." *See* F. Zimring & G. Hawkins, *supra* note 83, at 91–92.

85. *See* F. Zimring & G. Hawkins, *supra* note 83, at 94–96; *see also* J. Katz, *Seductions of Crime: The Moral and Sensual Attraction of Doing Evil* (1988).

86. F. Zimring & G. Hawkins, *supra* note 83, at 96.

87. *Id.* at 120. Gerber and McAnary have made a similar point, concluding as follows:

> The prevention of crime as a goal of society is not ultimately achieved by either crass fear or huge detention centers but by a successful communication of disapproval. It is a moral process which depends for its success on a widely accepted system of law which reflect[s] a consensus of values and embod[ies] a fairness in procedure that guarantees equality of enforcement. (*Introduction* to *Contemporary Punishment: Views, Explanations and Justifications, supra* note 59, at 5).

88. *See* F. Zimring & G. Hawkins, *supra* note 83, at 93; *see also* J. Andenaes, *supra* note 77, at 16–29; Cramton, *Driver Behavior and Legal Sanctions,* 67 *Mich. L. Rev.* 421, 452–53 (1969). This belief is weakened by data that tend to show that existing sanctions, especially incarceration, are not significant deterrents of criminal behavior. *See, e.g., Deterrence and Incapacitation, supra* note 77, at 37–42, 59–63.

89. Whether banishment is meant to serve even general deterrence ends, however, is questionable. Again, the more likely purpose is containment, not deterrence. But the threat of expulsion surely would frighten community members who value community acceptance. See Liggio, *The Transportation of Criminals: A Brief Political-Economic History,* in *Assessing the Criminal: Restitution, Retribution, and the Legal Process* 273, 281–83 (R. Barnett & J. Hagel eds. 1977).

90. *See infra* section VI.B.

91. *See, e.g.,* H. Packer, *supra* note 66, at 48–53.

92. *See supra* notes 32–39 and accompanying text.

93. *Jeremiah* 6:15.

94. The dictionary defines shame as "a painful emotion caused by consciousness of guilt, shortcoming, or impropriety in one's own behavior or in the behavior or position of [another]." *Webster's Third New International Dictionary* 2086 (1986).

95. *The Nicomachean Ethics of Aristotle, supra* note 75, at 104–5.

96. *See, e.g.,* G. Piers & M. Singer, *Shame and Guilt* 28–29 (1971). The psychological theories that elaborate on shame are fairly recent. Freud and Jung dealt only briefly with the emotion of shame in their celebrated works. *See generally* Hultberg, *Shame—A Hidden Emotion,* 33 *J. Analytical Psychology* 109, 111–13 (1988) (offering a brief historical survey on the treatment of shame in in-depth psychology). Anthropologists, not psychologists, have emphasized the role of shame in their studies. *See id.* at 113–15.

97. G. Piers & M. Singer, *supra* note 96, at 26–27.

98. L. Wurmser, *The Mask of Shame* 81 (1981) (emphasis added); *see also* Hultberg, *supra* note 96, at 116.

99. C. Schneider, *Shame, Exposure and Privacy* 34–35 (1977); *see also* E. Erikson, *Childhood and Society* 252 (2d ed. 1963) (describing the exposure and visibility inherent in shame).

Psychologists have attempted to distinguish "guilt" from "shame." *See, e.g.,* A. Buss, *Self-Consciousness and Social Anxiety* 157, 159–61 (1980) ("*Shame* is a fear of abandonment; guilt is a fear of castration"); H. Lynd, *On Shame and the Search for Identity* 34–36, 50, 64 (1958); S. Miller, *The Shame Experience* 140–43 (1985) (distinguishing shame from guilt on the basis that shame involves attention to a defect in a specific self-image, whereas guilt involves attention to one's actions, not one's self-image); L. Wurmser, *supra* note 98, at 80–82 (concluding that shame sanctions use contempt as the punishment; guilt sanctions use anger and hatred); Frazier & Meisenhelder, *supra* note 82, at 274–80 (contrasting guilt and shame on the basis of whether the emotion is based on internal (guilt) or external (shame) controls).

Some anthropologists have relied on these distinctions to categorize certain cultures as "shame" or "guilt" cultures, depending on whether they rely on external or internal sanctions. *See* G. Piers & M. Singer, *supra* note 96 at 59–61 (describing and reformulating these distinctions).

In legal discourse, happily, these fine-tuned psychological distinctions between guilt (internal) and shame (external) may be overlooked. As other commentators have observed, criminal law theorists need only concern themselves with whether public opinion plays some role in character formation and behavior. *See* J. Braithwaite, *Crime, Shame, and Reintegration* 57 (1989); Note, *A Perspective on Non-Legal Social Controls: The Sanctions of Shame and Guilt in Representative Cultural Settings,* 35 *Ind. L.J.* 196, 199–204, 206 (1959). They need not decide whether negative public opinion evokes "shame" versus the closely related phenomenon of "guilt." Consequently, I use the term "shame" throughout, but mean it to include the guilt emotion wherever guilt would likewise be produced by public shaming.

100. A. Buss, *supra* note 99, at 159; *cf.* H. Lynd, *supra* note 99, at 27–28 (concluding that "[t]he exposure may be to others but, whether others are or are not involved, it is always . . .exposure to one's own eyes"); G. Piers & M. Singer, *supra* note 96, at 66–68 (observing that the audience need not be actual for a person to experience shame; it can be fantasized).

101. A. Buss, *supra* note 99, at 160.
102. *See, e.g.,* G. Piers & M. Singer, *supra* note 96, at 29 ("Behind the feeling of shame stands not the fear of hatred, but the fear of *contempt* which, on an even deeper level of the unconscious, spells fear of *abandonment,* the death by emotional starvation."); H. Lynd, *supra* note 99, at 67; Hultberg, *supra* note 96, at 115–16 (Shame "is the fear of being excluded from human society. Shame implies fear of total abandonment. It is not a fear of physical death, but of psychic extinction."). As Goffman has observed, an individual may violate some social expectation or norm, yet be "untouched by this failure," when the individual is sufficiently alienated from the censuring group. He is "protected by identity beliefs of his own, he feels that he is a full-fledged normal human being, and that we are the ones who are not 'quite' human." E. Goffman, *Stigma* 6 (1963).
103. C. Schneider, *supra* note 99, at 36.
104. E. Goffman, *On Face-Work,* in *Interaction Ritual* 5, 8–9 (1967).
105. *Id.* at 5.
106. *Id.* at 8; *see also* E. Erikson, *supra* note 99, at 406 (describing the infantile roots of shame and the fear of "loss of face before all-surrounding, mocking audiences").
107. J. Braithwaite, *supra* note 99, at 73.
108. Exile of an offender may occur in one of two ways. The community may be ordered to, or elect to, avoid the offender socially or otherwise; or, the court or other community official may take steps to secure her physical or other isolation from the community even absent community cooperation. The first type of exile is shunning; the second is banishment. Banishment typically is reserved for the most egregious cases, where the offender must be expelled altogether from the community or some part thereof. The banishment may be temporary, like a limited-term sentence, or permanent, like lawyer disbarment.

    Banishment represents the ultimate downward manipulation of social identity of an offender. In effect, the local identity is erased, eradicated. The shunning is complete and permanent. The defendant must effect new contacts elsewhere, and begin a job and life in another community. Shunning is a less severe punishment, at least to the extent that the individual remains in the community and may have the opportunity to regain her neighbor's approval.

    Shunning and banishment of an offender can serve several functions. First (and likely foremost) is the protection of the community from the exiled one. Second is the deterrence of similar acts by other remaining members of the community. A third possible function is to prevent retaliation by some members of the community toward the offender, and divisive factionalization of the group.

    Effective shunning practices, like effective shaming, require audience participation. The audience must be willing to assume not only the role of approving spectator, but also that of active disciplinarian. The penalty's effectiveness depends upon the community's willingness to endorse the sentence by avoiding the wrongdoer. Audience complicity of this sort may be secured in several ways. Community withdrawal from a wrongdoer is particularly likely to occur in a community with powerful social and normative cohesion, like the Amish or the gypsies. But it may also occur in a community that punishes its members, formally or informally, if they fail to cooperate in shunning the offender. This may occur in authoritarian regimes that can inspire sufficient fear in its people to secure their cooperation.

    Of course, the members of all communities may shun an offender because they fear harm from the offender. For example, an employer may be disinclined to hire a convicted thief out of fear of her propensity to commit similar bad acts, such as embezzlement. Formalized shunning and banishment rituals nevertheless are more characteristic of close-bound, distinctive communities, than of impersonal, less distinctive cultures.

109. W. Clifford, *Crime Control in Japan* 175 (1976).
110. Words like "culture," "community," or "society" have elusive meanings. Goffman captures this slipperiness in the following passage:

    To say that a particular practice is formed *in* a given place (or a given class of places) leaves a great deal unspecified even when systematically collected data are available. For it is often unclear whether it is claimed that the practice occurs throughout the place or only somewhere in it, and if throughout, whether this is the only place it occurs. Furthermore, [some] social arrangements and small behaviors . . . have the awkward property of pertaining not to a set of individuals that can be bounded nicely, like the citizens of a particular nation state, but to groupings whose boundaries we know very little about. . . . In any case, the reference unit "American Society" (which I use throughout), is something of a conceptual scandal, very nearly a contradiction in terms; the social unit "civilization" (whatever that might mean) is as relevant as that of nation state. (E. Goffman, *supra* note 55, at xiv–xv).

    The dangers of obscuring contextual complexities by invoking broad-brush terms like "culture" are massive. Everything that ethnographers say in general about a people or social group may be wrong in practical, particular applications. These errors may be compounded when cultural generalizations are plucked from their original anthropological context and applied to new, foreign settings, like criminal law theory. Nevertheless, generalizations may offer useful organizing outlines of significant tendencies in human relations. Goffman himself assumes this, insofar as he relies on the reference units of "society" and "Western society" despite his misgivings about these words.

111. *See* G. Piers & M. Singer, *supra* note 96, at 53–55 (describing the role of shame and guilt in socialization of the individual).
112. *Cf. id.* at 91 (calling it a cultural "super ego" in reliance on Sigmund Freud's works); H. Lynd, *supra* note 99, at 28 ("The particular aspects of the self especially vulnerable to exposure differ in different cultures.").
113. G. Piers & M. Singer, *supra* note 96, at 54–55; *see also* Kaufman & Raphael, *Shame: A Perspective on Jewish Identity, J. Psychology & Judaism,* Spring 1987, at 30, 34 (describing sources of shame in contemporary American society, such as failure to succeed, unpopularity, and failure to be independent); Myers, *Emotions and the Self: A Theory of Personhood and Political Order Among Pintupi Aborigines,* 7 *Ethos* 343, 349 (1979) (describing the cultural understandings that may give rise to an emotion—such as shame—or to a sense of its appropriateness).
114. As Piers has observed, "[m]any a Utopian writer has tried to project a society which is cohesive without fear of guilt-creating punishment and without shame-producing competition. No attempt at realization has succeeded so far." G. Piers & M. Singer, *supra* note 96, at 55.
115. A. Earle, *Curious Punishments of Bygone Days* (1896).
116. *Id.* at 1.
117. *Id.* at 2.
118. Hirsch, *From Pillory to Penitentiary: The Rise of Criminal Incarceration in Early Massachusetts,* 80 *Mich. L. Rev.* 1179, 1223–24 (1982).
119. At least one historian reports, however, that the humiliatory punishments were rarely imposed on social elites. Instead, these offenders were ordered to pay a fine. *See* E. Powers, *Crime and Punishment in Early Massachusetts* 195 (1966).
120. Hirsch, *supra* note 118 at 1224; *see also* E. Powers, *supra* note 119 at 197, 202–4 (describing public confessions).
121. A. Earle, *supra* note 115, at 20, 35–36.
122. *Id.* at 111–13.
123. One account of punishment methods in Maryland during the late 1600s reports that a man "was forced to stand in open court 'with a paper on his breast declaring his offence [sic].'" R. Semmes, *supra* note 4, at 39. In another case, a husband

and wife were required to kneel before the county justices and ask for forgiveness. The justices in the case explained that they required the married couple to kneel before them because the couple had no other way to make satisfaction. *Id.* at 39.

124. A prominent literary example of the role of such shaming appears in N. Hawthorne, *The Scarlet Letter* (1850).

125. R. Semmes, *supra* note 4, at 32; *see also* E. Powers, *supra* note 161, at 198–201 (describing signs and symbols of early Massachusetts); Hirsch, *supra* note 160, at 1226 (describing wearing of signs as punishment in early Massachusetts).

126. R. Semmes, *supra* note 4, at 35. The colonists, however, were not the originators of the labeling custom. The practice dates at least from the twelfth century. *See* A. Earle, *supra* note 157, at 94.

127. Some Quakers were branded or maimed for practicing their faith. A. Earle, *supra* note 157, at 138–42. Other offenders who were marked with signs or initials were drunkards; *see id.* at 88, cheats, *see id.* at 53–54, slanderers, *see* R. Semmes, *supra* note 4, at 40, hog stealers, murderers, thieves, and runaway slaves, *see id.* at 35.

128. Hirsch, *supra* note 118, at 1228.

129. *Id.*

130. A. Earle, *supra* note 115, at 3–4.

131. *Id.* at 5.

132. *Id.* at 51 (describing the punishment of a dishonest baker).

133. *Id.* (describing the punishment of a person who had stolen cabbages).

134. *Id.* at 52.

135. *Id.* at 11, 17 (noting that the sentence was designed to "silence idle tongues").

136. *Id.* at 29. The stocks were regarded as low class, so that gentlemen were not sentenced to the stocks. The pillory was "aristocratic in comparison. . . ." *Id.* at 35.

137. R. Semmes, *supra* note 4, at 34–35. The absence of formal prisons, however, did not mean that defendants were never physically confined. For example, Cuthbert Fenwik, "a prominent Maryland colonist," once was confined to a house that became the "prison" of St. Mary's County, but was allowed to venture to within one-half mile of the house. *Id.* at 32.

Public whippings also were a common form of punishment, and were often shockingly brutal. K. Erikson, *Wayward Puritans* 188 (1966). Like the stocks, however, this punishment was not inflicted on "gentlemen." R. Semmes, *supra* note 4, at 38–39; *see supra* note 178.

138. Still, punishment elsewhere in the world—then and now—was and is in many ways more severe. One commentator speculates that the reason the Puritans' methods nevertheless seem exceptionally harsh is that they were delivered in "cold righteousness," with a "relentless kind of certainty" that paid scant attention to offender motives, victim grief, community anger or any other emotion. K. Erikson, *supra* note 179, at 189. Erikson reasons that Puritan justice had a "flat, mechanical tone because it dealt with the laws of nature rather than the decisions of men." *Id.*

139. *See id.* at 194–95.

140. *Id.* at 195 ("The victim [was] asked to endorse the action of the court and to share in the judgment against him, to move back into the community as a witness to his own execution."); *see also supra* text accompanying note 55. This emphasis on cooperation by the criminal was not unique to the Puritans. During the 1700s in Amsterdam, the authorities likewise encouraged penitence of criminals, such that "[t]he execution of a disbeliever was not a perfect one." P. Spierenburg, *supra* note 8, at 59.

141. *See, e.g.,* Demos, *Developmental Perspectives on the History of Childhood,* 2 *J. Interdisciplinary, Hist.* 315, 320–21 (1971).

142. *Id.* at 321.

143. *Id.* at 320–21.

144. *Id.* at 321.

145. *Id.* at 323.

146. *Id.* at 324. The Puritans' sensitivity to public shame is reflected in the large number of defamation actions they filed, as well as in the range of humilitiatory punishments they employed. *Id.* at 325.

147. J. Braithwaite, *supra* note 99, at 8.

148. *Id.* at 10; *see also* Schwartz, *Social Factors in the Development of Legal Control: A Case Study of Two Israeli Settlements,* 63 *Yale L.J.* 471, 483 (1954).

149. J. Braithwaite, *supra* note 99, at 30.

150. Schwartz, *supra* note 190, at 483.

151. *Id.* at 477 (quoting C. Cooley, *Social Organization* 23 (1909)); *see also* Merry, *Rethinking Gossip and Scandal,* in 1 *Toward a General Theory of Social Control: Fundamentals* 271, (D. Black ed. 1984).

152. When, however, urban conditions create tight-knit social pockets or neighborhoods with equivalent "economic and social interdependence and barriers to mobility outside the community," then informal social sanctions in the form of gossip may be powerful curbs on social behavior. *See* Merry, *supra* note 193, at 289–90. The potential adverse consequences of shaming within these pockets are the same as in other small-scale societies, including ostracism, shunning, ridicule, and banishment. *Id.* at 284–86.

153. *Id.* at 282, 286; *see also* Grimes & Turk, *Labeling in Context,* in *Crime, Law, and Sanctions: Theoretical Perspectives* 34, 55 (M. Krohn & R. Akers eds. 1978) (noting that "[t]he effect of labeling upon self-definition depends upon the relative power of each involved individual, as each impinges upon the others in the course of the highly personal enterprise of self-definition"); *cf.* Jensen & Erikson, *The Social Meaning of Sanctions,* in *id.* at 119, 133 (concluding that "those subjects who attribute stigmatic consequences to official labels are least likely to engage in behavior which is liable to labeling. Those most likely to deviate are those for whom official labeling may be socially meaningless.").

154. Merry, *supra* note 193, at 283–84.

155. *See supra* Part IV.

156. *See infra* Part VII.

157. *See supra* text accompanying note 103; *cf.* Jensen & Erikson, *supra* note 153, at 133. Lawrence Friedman once ironically remarked that, "Criminals, it was commonly observed, did not blush." L. Friedman, *A History of American Law* 601 (2d ed. 1985). In fact, however, psychological studies on shame suggest otherwise, though offenders may blush at *different things* than nonoffenders.

158. *See* Jensen & Erickson, *supra* note 153, at 133. The authors conclude that

those subjects who attribute stigmatic consequences to official labels are least likely to engage in behavior which is liable to labeling. Those most likely to deviate are those for whom official labeling may be socially meaningless. Thus, those most likely to be labeled may be the least likely to be affected by labeling. . . . To understand the variable consequences of labeling requires an understanding of the social meaning of sanctions. (*Id.*)

159. *See* F. Zimring & G. Hawkins, *supra* note 83, at 191; J. Braithwaite, *supra* note 99, at 60.

160. F. Zimring & G. Hawkins, *supra* note 83, at 191.

161. *Id.* at 193. If, however, the stigmatized offender cannot locate or gain the acceptance of a subculture that tolerates her stigma, then she may adopt a life of solitary deviance, or try to regain admission into the dominant culture. J. Braithwaite, *supra* note 99, at 68. For some crimes, such as drug offenses, solitary deviance may be impossible. A drug offender needs, at the least, a supplier or a buyer. *Id.* at 67.

162. *See* D. Matza, *Delinquency and Drift* (1964).

163. *See generally* R. Trojanowicz & M. Morash, *Juvenile Delinquency: Concepts and Control* 59–61 (4th ed. 1987); Gove, *The Labelling Perspective: An Overview,* in *The Labelling of Deviance* 9 (W. Gove 2d ed. 1980); Mahoney, *The Effect of Labeling Upon Youths in the Juvenile Justice System: A Review*

of the Evidence, 8 *Law & Socy. Rev.* 583, 584–85 (1974); *see also* J. Freedman & A. Doob, *Deviancy: The Psychology of Being Different* (1968) (describing influence on experimental groups of public disclosure of their "deviance" from "average" scores on a "personality" test. Those identified as deviants first sought to conceal their deviancy. Once it was disclosed, however, they chose to associate with other "deviant" subjects).

164. Gove, *supra* note 205, at 13–15 (collecting empirical work); *see also* Mahoney, *supra* note 205, at 588–89; Wellford, *Labeling Theory and Criminology: An Assessment*, 22 *Soc. Probs.* 332 (1975).

165. Gove, *supra* note 163, at 18.

166. *See, e.g.,* L. Walker, *The Battered Woman* 65–66 (1979). *But see* J. Fleming, *Stopping Wife Abuse* 289 (1979) (noting that not all men express regret after a beating episode).

167. *See* J. Braithwaite, *supra* note 99, at 60–61.

168. In fact, most criminal cases do not reach the trial stage. The overwhelming majority are plea bargained and thus escape public scrutiny. *See generally* Alschuler, *The Defense Attorney's Role in Plea Bargaining*, 84 *Yale L.J.* 1179 (1975); Alschuler, *The Prosecutor's Role in Plea Bargaining*, 36 *U. Chi. L. Rev.* 50 (1968); Alschuler, *The Trial Judge's Role in Plea Bargaining*, 76 *Colum. L. Rev.* 1059 (1976); Vorenburg, *Decent Restraint of Prosecutorial Power*, 94 *Harv. L. Rev.* 1521 (1981).

169. J. Braithwaite, *supra* note 99, at 61.

170. *Id.* at 62, 84 (emphasizing the highly developed communitarianism in Japanese society).

171. *Id.* at 62–63 (contrasting the Japanese view of authority with the North American view).

172. *Id.* at 39 (noting that "extreme versions of subculturalism which posit wholesale rejection of the criminal law by substantial sections of the community simply do not wash").

173. *Id.* at 66.

174. J. Braithwaite, *supra* note 99, at 84–85.

175. *Id.* at 86.

176. *Id.* (noting that most Western societies are characterized more by individualism than communitarianism).

177. *Id.*

178. *Id.* at 163. A more optimistic account of our criminal law process is that of James Boyd White, who describes the criminal law as a system of meaning in which we "blame" the defendant and thereby preserve her dignity and our communal claims as well. White sees this system of meaning as one that, even when the defendant is punished, still recognizes her as a member of the community. J. B. White, *Heracles' Bow: Essays on the Rhetoric and Poetics of the Law* 209 (1985). This forgiving notion of blaming corresponds with Braithwaite's "reintegrative" concept of shaming. As a normative account of just punishment, I find it attractive. As a descriptive account of modern criminal law, I am unpersuaded. Robert Cover's account seems more compelling. *See* Cover, *Violence and the Word*, 95 *Yale L.J.* 1601, 1601 (1986) (concluding that "[l]egal interpretation takes place in a field of pain and death").

179. *See* J. Braithwaite, *supra* note 99, at 169–70.

180. *Id.* at 172–73. Braithwaite remarks that a shift to communitarianism eventually may occur because it would serve the interests of American capital. *Id.* at 174.

181. *See* R. Carter, R. McGee & E. Nelson, *Corrections in America* 1 (1975). The current figures likely are much higher than these 1975 figures reflect.

182. *Id.* at 11.

183. Other practical and fairness problems also may emerge. For example, if courts resorted to home-centered shamings, such as lawn signs, neighboring property owners likely would object. They first might attempt to drive the offender from the neighborhood. If she refused to move, however, the property owners likely would resent the judge who imposed the sentence and could complain about, if not sue over, the stigma spillover onto these innocent neighbors. Cabining the effects of these customized shame sanctions thus could be quite complicated. Assuring that all shame sanctions had *some* effect,

and *continued* to do so, however, would be more complicated. At present, courts have no mechanisms for conducting such inquiries. These mechanisms, though, would need to be explored before widespread use of shaming could proceed.

184. *See supra* note 168.

185. For a discussion of the psychological works that describe the role of identification with another person and empathy for her, see Henderson, *Legality and Empathy*, 85 *Mich. L. Rev.* 1574 (1987).

186. Occasionally, a sympathetic figure will capture public attention. A devoted elderly husband will end a spouse's misery, or a wrongly accused person will be vindicated and released. More often, however, the offenders who receive concentrated mainstream or tabloid attention are people like Richard Ramirez, who murdered 13 people in southern California and who, we are told, on one occasion "gouged out the eyes of the victim." *See Court in Los Angeles Gives 'Night Stalker' Death in 13 Killings*. *N.Y. Times*, Nov. 8, 1989, at A18, col. 5. The news account reported that shortly before he was sentenced to die in the gas chamber he made a statement that included remarks like "Lucifer dwells within us all," and "I am beyond evil." *Id.* Such selective accounts of criminal court business enable the public to see criminals as alien "others" and to favor quite strict crime-control measures.

187. Increased identification with offenders contributed to the demise of public executions in Europe. Pieter Spierenburg states, in his study of public executions and other public punishments in the seventeenth- and eighteenth-century Amsterdam, that "[b]y the end of the eighteenth century some of the audience could feel the pain of delinquents on the scaffold.... [I]nterhuman identification had increased." P. Spierenburg, *supra* note 8, at 184.

188. The public resistance to spectacle punishment in Europe led to the decline of *public* punishment, not of punishment in general; that is, it led to privatization. *See id.*

189. 207 *N.J. Super.* 350, 504 *A. 2d* 160 (1985).

190. 207 *N.J. Super.* at 356–58, 504 *A. 2d* at 164.

191. *See* T. Dumm, *Democracy and Punishment* 65 (1987).

192. J. Braithwaite, *supra* note 99, at 142

193. *Id.* at 80.

194. H. Packer, *supra* note 66, at 255.

195. I do not address the constitutional arguments against such sanctions, which of course are particularized fairness arguments, because other writers already have done so. *See, e.g.,* Note, *supra* note 42, at 658–60; Note, *The Modern Day Scarlet Letter: A Critical Analysis of Modern Probation Conditions*, 1989 *Duke L.J.* 1357, 1376–78, 1381–84; Note, "*Scarlet Letter*" *Punishment: Yesterday's Outlawed Penalty Is Today's Probation Condition*, 36 *Clev. St. L. Rev.* 613, 624–34 (1988); Note, *Sentenced to Wear the Scarlet Letter: Judicial Innovations in Sentencing—Are They Constitutional?*, 93 *Dickinson L. Rev.* 759 (1989).

One of the principal constitutional objections is based on the eighth amendment's proscription against cruel and unusual punishment. Constitutional arguments also might be based on the due process and equal protection clauses, on the first amendment, and on the right to privacy. Resolution of these constitutional points should depend, to a large degree, on how courts resolve the proportionality, equality, and dignity concerns raised in the following sections. As the Court in *Hutto v. Finney* explained: "The Eighth Amendment's ban on inflicting cruel and unusual punishments . . . 'proscribe[s] more than physically barbarous punishments'. . . . It prohibits penalties that are grossly disproportionate to the offense, . . . as well as those that transgress today's 'broad and idealistic concepts of dignity, civilized standards, humanity, and decency.'" 437 *U.S.* 678, 685 (1978) (quoting *Estelle v. Gamble*, 429 *U.S.* 97, 102 [1976]).

196. *See* N. Walker, *Punishment, Danger and Stigma: The Morality of Criminal Justice* 147 (1980) (noting that many countries

today have laws designed to limit the stigma of a conviction, by allowing for official expurgation of the record).

197. Fishman, *Stigmatization and Prisoners' Wives' Feelings of Shame* 9 *Deviant Behav.* 169, 174 (1988).

198. The recently adopted Federal Sentencing Guidelines take this approach in part, by deeming offender-specific characteristics such as education and vocational skills, family ties and responsibilities, and community ties as "not ordinarily relevant" in sentencing. *U.S. Sentencing Commn., Federal Sentencing Guidelines Manual* §§ 5H1.2, 5H1.6, at 240–41 (1988). The guidelines do regard as relevant the defendant's "acceptance of responsibility" for her criminal conduct. *Id.* at § 3E1.1, at 197. They list as evidence of this acceptance specific conduct, not mere verbal expressions of regret or responsibility. *Id.* More to the point of this Article, a federal commission that in the 1970s debated reforms of federal criminal law expressly considered and rejected the "publicity" sanctions "as inappropriate with respect either to organizations or to individuals, despite its possible deterrent effect, since it came too close to the adoption of a policy approving social ridicule as a sanction." *Natl. Commn. on Reform of Fed. Crim. Laws, Final Report,* § 3007, Comment (1971).

199. Again, however, I am not arguing that we have no shared consensus of "right or wrong," but that "shame" is a particularly elusive phenomenon. For example, the "cultural meaning" of other wrong conduct—such as race discrimination—may be susceptible to judicial interpretation in ways that the cultural meaning of shame is not. *Cf.* Lawrence, *The Id, the Ego, and Equal Protection: Reckoning with Unconscious Racism,* 39 *Stan. L. Rev.* 317, 355–62 (1987) (arguing that racially discriminatory acts have a cultural meaning that courts are capable of construing).

200. *See* N. Walker, *supra* note 196, at 161. Walker suggests a third alternative, but it would not apply to shame punishments.

This alternative would be for the punisher to simply ignore the unofficial stigma effect of the punishment, and demand only that the official punishment be proportional, *Id.* With shame punishments, of course, the official punishment *is* the stigma.

201. E. Goffman, *supra* note 104, at 10 n.3.

202. *See* E. Powers, *supra* note 119, at 195–96 (noting that it was the poorer thieves, drunkards, and liars who were suitable candidates for the stocks; respected citizens were more likely to be fined).

203. The deeper equality issues at stake with shaming sanctions, like those at stake with sanctions generally, are virtually insoluble. In another context, Jencks has explored the elusive meaning of "equal treatment" in terms that demonstrate several potential "inequalities" in delivering equal punishments to all offenders. He demonstrates, through a concrete example, the extent to which the meaning of equality depends on one's theory of justice. For example, a utilitarian will demand a different sort of equality than someone who embraces a moralistic theory of justice. As applied to punishment generally, and to shaming in particular, Jencks' discussion shows that the "equality" of punishment depends on whether we focus principally on the offender or on society as a whole. Jencks, *Whom Must We Treat Equally for Educational Opportunity to be Equal?,* 98 *Ethics* 518 (1988).

204. See *State v. Rosenberger,* 207 *N.J. Super.* 350, 358, 504 *A. 2d* 160, 165 (1985) (noting that white-collar criminals stand a significantly lower chance of serving a long sentence if convicted than do bank robbers); Bramwell, *Alternative Sentencing or Part-Time Imprisonment Is Discriminatory,* 26 *How. L.J.* 1265, 1268 (1983) (arguing that "[a]lternative sentencing creates a two-tier system of justice and is indicative of basic unfairness and favoritism").

205. *See* J. Rawls, *A Theory of Justice* 440 (1971).

What, If Anything, Justifies Legal Punishment?

THE CLASSIC DEBATE*

Joel Feinberg

The traditional debate among philosophers over the justification of legal punishment has been between partisans of the "retributive" and "utilitarian" theories. Neither the term "retributive" nor the term "utilitarian" has been used with perfect uniformity and precision, but, by and large, those who have been called utilitarians have insisted that punishment of the guilty is at best a necessary evil justified only as a means to the prevention of evils even greater than itself. "Retributivism," on the other hand, has labeled a large miscellany of theories united only in their opposition to the utilitarian theory. It may best serve clarity, therefore, to define the utilitarian theory with relative precision (as above) and then define retributivism as its logical contradictory, so that the two theories are not only mutually exclusive but also jointly exhaustive. Discussion of the various varieties of retributivism can then proceed.

Perhaps the leading form of the retributive theory includes major elements identifiable in the following formulations:

> It is an end in itself that the guilty should suffer pain. . . . The primary justification of punishment is always to be found in the fact that an offense has been committed which

deserves the punishment, not in any future advantage to be gained by its infliction.[1]

> Punishment is justified only on the ground that wrongdoing merits punishment. It is morally fitting that a person who does wrong should suffer in proportion to his wrongdoing. That a criminal should be punished follows from his guilt, and the severity of the appropriate punishment depends on the depravity of the act. The state of affairs where a wrongdoer suffers punishment is morally better than one where he does not, and is so irrespective of consequences.[2]

Justification, according to these accounts, must look backward in time to guilt rather than forward to "advantages"; the formulations are rich in moral terminology ("merits," "morally fitting," "wrongdoing," "morally better"); there is great emphasis on *desert*. For those reasons, we might well refer to this as a "moralistic" version of the retributive theory. As such it can be contrasted with a "legalistic" version, according to which punishment is for lawbreaking, not (necessarily) for wrongdoing. Legalistic retributivism holds that the justification of punishment is always to be found in the fact that a rule has been broken

---

*Published in previous editions as part of the introduction to this section.

for the violation of which a certain penalty is specified, whether or not the offender incurs any moral guilt. The offender, properly apprised in advance of the penalty, voluntarily assumes the risk of punishment, and when he or she receives comeuppance, he or she can have no complaint. As one recent legalistic retributivist put it,

> Punishment is a corollary not of law but of lawbreaking. Legislators do not choose to punish. They hope no punishment will be needed. Their laws would succeed even if no punishment occurred. The criminal makes the essential choice: he "brings it on himself."[3]

Both moralistic and legalistic retributivism have "pure" and "impure" variants. In their pure formulations, they are totally free of utilitarian admixture. Moral or legal guilt (as the case may be) is not only a necessary condition for justified punishment, it is quite sufficient "irrespective of consequences." In the impure formulation, both guilt (moral or legal) and conducibility to good consequences are necessary for justified punishment, but neither is sufficient without the other. This mixed theory could with some propriety be called "impure utilitarianism" as well as "impure retributivism." Since we have stipulated, however, that a retributive theory is one which is not wholly utilitarian, we are committed to the latter usage.

A complete theory of punishment will not only specify the conditions under which punishment should and should not be administered, it will also provide a general criterion for determining the amount or degree of punishment. It is not only unjust to be punished undeservedly and to be let off although meriting punishment, it is also unfair to be punished severely for a minor offense or lightly for a heinous one. What is the right amount of punishment? There is one kind of answer especially distinctive of retributivism in all of its forms: an answer in terms of fittingness or proportion. The punishment must *fit* the crime; its degree must be *proportionate* to the seriousness or moral gravity of the offense. Retributivists are often understandably vague about the practical interpretations of the key notions of fittingness, proportion, and moral gravity. Sometimes aesthetic analogies are employed (such as matching and clashing colors, or harmonious and dissonant chords). Some retributivists, including Immanuel Kant, attempt to apply the ancient principle of *lex talionis* (the law of retaliation): The punishment should match the crime not only in the degree of harm inflicted on its victim, but also in the mode and manner of the infliction: fines for larceny, physical beatings for battery, capital punishment for murder. Other retributivists, however, explicitly reject the doctrine of retaliation in kind; hence, that doctrine is better treated as a logically independent thesis commonly associated with retributivism rather than as an essential component of the theory.

Defined as the exhaustive class of alternatives to the utilitarian theory, retributivism of course is subject to no simple summary. It will be useful to subsequent discussions, however, to summarize that popular variant of the theory which can be called *pure moralistic retributivism* as consistent (at least) of the following propositions:

1. Moral guilt is a necessary condition for justified punishment.
2. Moral guilt is a sufficient condition ("irrespective of consequences") for justified punishment.
3. The proper amount of punishment to be inflicted upon the morally guilty offender is that amount which fits, matches, or is proportionate to the moral gravity of the offense.

That it is never justified to punish a morally blameless person for his or her "offense" (thesis 1) may not be quite self-evident, but it does find strong support in moral common sense. Thesis 2, however, is likely to prove an embarrassment for the pure retributivist, for it would have him or her approve the infliction of suffering on a person (albeit a *guilty* person) even when no good to the offender, the victim, or society at large is likely to result. "How can two wrongs make a right, or two evils a good?" he or she will be asked by the utilitarian, and in this case it is the utilitarian who will claim to speak for "moral common sense." In reply, the pure retributivist is likely to concede that inflicting suffering on an offender is not "good in itself," but will also point out that single acts cannot be judged simply "in themselves" with no concern for the context in which they fit and the events preceding them which are their occasion. Personal sadness is not a "good in itself" either, and yet when it is a response to the perceived sufferings of another it has a unique appropriateness. Glee, considered "in itself," looks much more like an intrinsically good mental state, but glee does not morally fit the perception of another's pain any more than an orange shirt aesthetically fits shocking pink trousers. Similarly, it may be true (the analogy is admittedly imperfect) that "while the moral evil in the offender and the pain of the punishment are each considered separately evils, it is intrinsically good that a certain relation exist or be established between them."[4] In this way the pure retributivist, relying on moral intuitions, can deny that a deliberate imposition of suffering on a human being is either good in itself or good as a means, and yet find it justified, nevertheless, as an essential component of an intrinsically good relation. Perhaps that is to put the point too strongly. All the retributivist needs to establish is that the complex situation preceding the infliction of punishment can be made better than it otherwise would be by the addition to it of the offender's suffering.

The utilitarian is not only unconvinced by arguments of this kind, he or she is also likely to find a "suspicious connection" between philosophical retributivism and the primitive lust for vengeance. The moralistic retributivist protests that he or she eschews anger or any other passion and seeks not revenge, but justice and the satisfaction of desert. Punishment, after all, is not the only kind of treatment we bestow upon persons simply because we think they deserve it. Teachers give students the grades they have earned with no thought of "future advantage," and with eyes firmly fixed on past performance. There is no necessary jubilation at good performance or vindictive pleasure in assigning low grades. And much the same is true of the assignments of rewards, prizes, grants, compensation, civil liability, and so on. Justice requires assignment on the basis of desert alone. To be sure, there is

> a great danger of revengeful and sadistic tendencies finding vent under the unconscious disguise of a righteous indignation calling for just punishment, since the evil desire for revenge, if not identical with the latter, bears a resemblance to it sufficiently close to deceive those who want an excuse.[5]

Indeed, it is commonly thought that our modern notions of retributive justice have grown out of earlier practices, like the vendetta and the law of deodand, that were through and through expressions of the urge to vengeance.[6] Still, the retributivist replies, it is unfair to *identify* a belief with one of its corruptions, or a modern practice with its historical antecedents. The latter mistake is an instance of the "genetic fallacy" which is committed whenever one confuses an account of how something came to be the way it is with an analysis of what it has become.

The third thesis of the pure moralistic retributivist has also been subject to heavy attack. Can it really be the business of the state to ensure that happiness and unhappiness are distributed among citizens in proportion to their moral deserts? Think of the practical difficulties involved in the attempt simply to apportion pain to moral guilt in a given case, with no help from utilitarian considerations. First of all, it is usually impossible to punish an offender without inflicting suffering on those who love or depend upon him and may themselves be entirely innocent, morally speaking. In that way, punishing the guilty is self-defeating from the moralistic retributive point of view. It will do more to increase than to diminish the disproportion between unhappiness and desert throughout society. Secondly, the aim of apportioning pain to guilt would in some cases require punishing "trivial" moral offenses, like rudeness, as heavily as more socially harmful crimes, since there can be as much genuine wickedness in the former as the latter. Thirdly, there is the problem of accumulation. Deciding the right amount of suffering to inflict in a given case would entail an assessment of the character of the offender as manifested throughout his or her whole life (and not simply at one weak moment) and also an assessment of his or her total lifelong balance of pleasure and pain. Moreover, there are inevitably inequalities of moral guilt in the commission of the same crime by different offenders, as well as inequalities of suffering from the same punishment. Application of the pure retributive theory then would require the abandonment of fixed penalties for various crimes and the substitution of individuated penalties selected in each case by an authority to fit the offender's uniquely personal guilt and vulnerability.

The utilitarian theory of punishment holds that punishment is never good in itself, but is (like bad-tasting medicine) justified when, and only when, it is a means to such future goods as *correction* (reform) of the offender, *protection* of society against other offenses from the same offender, and *deterrence* of other would-be offenders. (The list is not exhaustive.) Giving the offender the pain he deserves because of his wickedness is either not a coherent notion, on this theory, or else not a morally respectable independent reason for punishing. In fact, the utilitarian theory arose in the eighteenth century as part of a conscious reaction to cruel and uneconomical social institutions (including prisons) that were normally defended, if at all, in righteously moralistic terms.

For purposes of clarity, the utilitarian theory of punishment should be distinguished from utilitarianism as a general moral theory. The standard of right conduct generally, according to the latter, is conducibility to good consequences. Any act at all, whether that of a private citizen, a legislator, or a judge, is morally right if and only if it is likely, on the best evidence, to do more good or less harm all around than any alternative conduct open to the actor. (The standard for judging the goodness of consequences, in turn, for Jeremy Bentham and the early utilitarians was the amount of human happiness they contained, but many later utilitarians had more complicated conceptions of intrinsic value.) All proponents of general utilitarianism, of course, are also supporters of the utilitarian theory of punishment, but there is no logical necessity that in respect to punishment a utilitarian be a general utilitarian across the board.

The utilitarian theory of punishment can be summarized in three propositions parallel to those used above to summarize pure moralistic retributivism. According to this theory:

1. Social utility (correction, prevention, deterrence, et cetera) is a necessary condition for justified punishment.
2. Social utility is a sufficient condition for justified punishment.
3. The proper amount of punishment to be inflicted upon the offender is that amount which will do the most good or the least harm to all those who will be affected by it.

The first thesis enjoys the strongest support from common sense, though not so strong as to preclude controversy. For the retributivist, as has been seen, punishing the guilty is an end in itself quite apart from any gain in social utility. The utilitarian is apt to reply that if reform of the criminal could be secured with no loss of deterrence by simply giving him or her a pill that would have the same effect, then nothing would be lost by not punishing him or her, and the substitute treatment would be "sheer gain."

Thesis 2, however, is the utilitarian's greatest embarrassment. The retributivist opponent argues forcefully against it that in certain easily imaginable circumstances it would justify punishment of the (legally) innocent, a consequence which all would regard as a moral abomination. Some utilitarians deny that punishment of the innocent could *ever* be the alternative that has the best consequences in social utility, but this reply seems arbitrary and dogmatic. Other utilitarians claim that "punishment of the innocent" is a self-contradiction. The concept of punishment, they argue,[7] itself implies hard treatment imposed upon

the guilty as a conscious and deliberate response to their guilt. That guilt is part of the very definition of punishment, these writers claim, is shown by the absurdity of saying "I am punishing you for something you have not done," which sounds very much like "I am curing you even though you are not sick." Since all punishment is understood to be for guilt, they conclude, they can hardly be interpreted as advocating punishing without guilt. H. L. A. Hart[8] calls this move a "definitional stop," and charges that it is an "abuse of definition," and indeed it is, if put forward by a proponent of the general utilitarian theory. If the right act in all contexts is the one which is likely to have the best consequences, then conceivably the act of framing an innocent man could sometimes be right; and the question of whether such mistreatment of the innocent party could properly be called "punishment" is a mere question of words having no bearing on the utilitarian's embarrassment. If, on the other hand, the definitional stop is employed by a defender of the utilitarian theory of the justification of punishment who is not a utilitarian across the board, then it seems to be a legitimate argumentative move. Such a utilitarian is defending official infliction of hard treatment (deprivation of liberty, suffering, et cetera) on *those who are legally guilty*, a practice to which he or she refers by using the word "punishment," as justified when and only when there is probably social utility in it.

No kind of utilitarian, however, will have plausible recourse to the definitional stop in defending thesis 3 from the retributivist charge that it would, in certain easily imaginable circumstances, justify excessive and/or insufficient penalties. The appeal again is to moral common sense: It would be manifestly unfair to inflict a mere two dollar fine on a convicted murderer or life imprisonment, under a balance of terror policy, for parking offenses. In either case, the punishment imposed would violate the retributivist's thesis 3, that the punishment be proportional to the moral gravity of the offense. And yet, if these were the penalties likely to have the best effects generally, the utilitarian in the theory of punishment would be committed to their support. He or she could not argue that excessive or deficient penalties are not "really" punishments. Instead he would have to argue, as does Jeremy Bentham, that the proper employment of the utilitarian method simply could not lead to penalties so far out of line with our moral intuitions as the retributivist charges.

So far vengeance has not been mentioned except in the context of charge and countercharge between theorists who have no use for it. There are writers, however, who have kind words for vengeance and give it a central role in their theories of the justification of punishment. We can call these approaches the Vindictive Theory of Punishment (to distinguish them from legalistic and moralistic forms of retributivism) and then subsume its leading varieties under either the utilitarian or the retributive rubrics. Vindictive theories are of three different kinds: (1) The *escape-valve version*, commonly associated with the names of James Fitzjames Stephen and Oliver Wendell Holmes, Jr., and currently in favor with some psychoanalytic writers, holds that legal punishment is an orderly outlet for aggressive feelings, which would otherwise demand satisfaction in socially disruptive ways. The prevention of private vendettas through a state monopoly on vengeance is one of the chief ways in which legal punishment has social utility. The escape-valve theory is thus easily assimilated by the utilitarian theory of punishment. (2) The *hedonistic version* of the vindictive theory finds the justification of punishment in the pleasure it gives people (particularly the victim of the crime and his or her loved ones) to see the criminal suffer for the crime. For most utilitarians, and certainly for Bentham, any kind of pleasure—even spiteful, sadistic, or vindictive pleasure, just insofar as it *is* pleasure—counts as a good in the computation of social utility, just as pain—any kind of pain—counts as an evil. (This is sufficient to discredit hedonistic utilitarianism thoroughly, according to its retributivist critics.) The hedonistic version of the vindictive theory, then, is also subsumable under the utilitarian rubric. Finally, (3) the *romantic version* of the vindictive theory, very popular among the uneducated, holds that the justification of punishment is to be found in the emotions of hate and anger it expresses, these emotions being those allegedly felt by all normal or right-thinking people. I call this theory "romantic," despite certain misleading associations of that word, because, like any philosophical theory so labeled, it holds that certain emotions and the actions they inspire are self-certifying, needing no further justification. It is therefore not a kind of utilitarian theory and must be classified as a variety of retributivism, although in its emphasis on feeling it is in marked contrast to more typical retributive theories that eschew emotion and emphasize proportion and desert.

Some anthropologists have traced vindictive feelings and judgments to an origin in the "tribal morality" which universally prevails in primitive cultures, and which presumably governed the tribal life of our own prehistoric ancestors. If an anthropologist turned his attention to our modern criminal codes, he would discover evidence that tribalism has never entirely vacated its position in the criminal law. There are some provisions for which the vindictive theory (in any of its forms) would provide a ready rationale, but for which the utilitarian and moralistic retributivist theories are hard put to discover a plausible defense. Completed crimes, for example, are punished more severely than attempted crimes that fail for accidental reasons. This should not be surprising since the more harm caused the victim, his or her loved ones, and those of the public who can identify imaginatively with them, the more anger there will be at the criminal. If the purpose of punishment is to satisfy that anger, then we should expect that those who succeed in harming will be punished more than the bunglers who fail, even if the motives and intentions of the bunglers were every bit as wicked.

---

1. A. C. Ewing, *The Morality of Punishment* (London: Kegan Paul, 1929), p. 13.
2. John Rawls, "Concepts of Rules," *The Philosophical Review*, LXIV (1955), pp. 4, 5.
3. J. D. Mabbott, "Punishment," *Mind*, LXVIII (1939), p. 161.
4. A. C. Ewing, *Ethics* (New York: Macmillan, 1953), pp. 169–70.
5. Ewing, *Morality of Punishment*, p. 27.
6. See O. W. Holmes, Jr., *The Common Law* (Boston: Little, Brown, 1881) and Henry Maine, *Ancient Law*. 1861 Reprint. (Boston: Beacon Press, 1963).
7. See, for example, Anthony Quinton, "On Punishment," *Analysis*, XIV (1954), pp. 1933–42.
8. H. L. A. Hart, *Punishment and Responsibility* (New York and Oxford: Oxford University Press, 1968), pp. 5, 6.

FANTASTIC COUNTEREXAMPLES AND THE UTILITARIAN THEORY*

C. L. Ten

2.1. The Effects of Punishment

The utilitarian theory justifies punishment solely in terms of the good consequences produced. There are disagreements among utilitarians about the nature of the good consequences which punishment is supposed to produce. Some utilitarians may even believe that the harm done by punishment outweighs the good, and hence punishment is not justified. But many utilitarians see the main beneficial effects of punishment in terms of the reduction of crime, and believe that punishing offenders will have at least some, if not all, of the following good effects. First, punishment acts as a deterrent to crime. The deterrent effects can be both individual and general. Punishment deters the offender who is punished from committing similar offences in future, and it also deters potential offenders. The offender who is punished is supposed to be deterred by his experience of punishment and the threat of being punished again if he re-offends and is convicted. This is the individual deterrent effect. The general deterrent effect of punishment on potential offenders works through the threat of their being subjected to the same kind of punishment that was meted out to the convicted offender.

Secondly, punishment is supposed to have reformative or rehabilitative effects.[1] This is confined to the offender who is punished. He is reformed in the sense that the effect of punishment is to change his values so that he will not commit similar offences in future because he believes such offences to be wrong. But if he abstains from criminal acts simply because he is afraid of being caught and punished again, then he is deterred rather than reformed and rehabilitated by punishment. So the effects of individual deterrence and rehabilitation are the same. What distinguishes them is the difference in motivation.

The third good consequence of punishment is its incapacitative effect. When an offender is serving his sentence in prison, he is taken out of general social circulation and is therefore prevented from committing a variety of offences, even though he may neither be deterred nor reformed by punishment. Of course punishment would not have an overall incapacitative effect if the offender would not have re-offended even if he were free, or if his incarceration led someone else, who would not otherwise have done so, to engage in criminal activity, perhaps as his replacement in a gang. While in prison, the offender might still commit certain offences: he might assault a fellow prisoner or a prison guard. But his opportunities are generally reduced. In some cases, however, his contacts with other prisoners would create opportunities for further involvement in crime when he is released. The incapacitative effect, though perhaps most likely in the case of imprisonment, may also be present in other forms of punishment. For example, parole may have some incapacitative effect in that although the offender is free, the fact that he is under supervision may restrict his opportunities for criminal activities.

The empirical evidence of the effects of punishment is very complex, but a brief survey will be of some use.

It looks as if the present state of our knowledge provides no basis for claiming that punishment by imprisonment reforms or rehabilitates the criminal, or that it is an individual deterrent. The position is well summed up by the Report of the Panel of the National Research Council in the United States on

---

*From C. L. Ten, *Crime, Guilt, and Punishment* (1987), pp. 7–37. Reprinted by permission of Oxford University Press.

Research on Deterrent and Incapacitative Effects, hereafter referred to as the Panel:

> The available research on the impact of various treatment strategies both in and out of prison seems to indicate that, after controlling for initial selection differences, there are generally no statistically significant differences between the subsequent recidivism of offenders, regardless of the form of "treatment." This suggests that neither rehabilitative nor criminogenic effects operate very strongly. Therefore, at an aggregate level, these confounding effects are probably safely ignored.[2]

By "criminogenic effects" the Panel refers to the undesirable effects of imprisonment in either increasing the criminal's propensity to commit crimes or to extend the duration of his criminal career. Such effects are the opposite of the rehabilitative effects. So the present evidence seems to suggest that in general the effect of imprisonment, or of the various programmes for rehabilitation which accompany imprisonment, is neither to make the criminal a better nor a worse person with respect to the standards of behaviour set by the criminal law.

The evidence also suggests that in general punishment has no individual deterrent effect. Daniel Nagin points out that at the observational level it is difficult to distinguish between individual (or what he calls special) deterrence and rehabilitation. He concludes that, "The figures suggest that recidivism rates cannot be affected by varying the severity of the punishment, at least within acceptable limits."[3] But Nagin cautiously adds that the evidence is only preliminary.

In a few specific cases there is indeed some evidence of the individual deterrent effect of punishment. Thus Johannes Andenaes draws attention to a study of amateur shoplifters which shows that detection and arrest, even without prosecution, produces serious shock. There is little or no recidivism among those who are apprehended and interrogated by the store police and then set free without being formally charged.[4] A study of drunk driving in Sweden also shows that those drivers who had been arrested estimated the risk of being arrested as many times higher than other drivers.[5]

There is disagreement about the general deterrent effects of punishment. Johannes Andenaes believes that, "In general terms it can only be stated that general deterrence works well in some fields and works poorly or not at all in other fields."[6] But in 1974 Gordon Tullock published an article, "Does

Punishment Deter Crime?," in which he surveyed the work done by economists and sociologists.[7] Tullock points out that economists began their work under the impression that punishment would deter crime because demand curves slope downwards showing that if the cost of a good is increased then less of it will be consumed. So if the cost of committing crime is increased by more severe punishment, then there will be fewer crimes. Sociologists, on the other hand, started out with the intention of confirming what was then the accepted view in their discipline that punishment would not deter crime. But Tullock argues that, although their starting points and assumptions were radically different, both economists and sociologists, after analysing the evidence, came to the same conclusion that punishment did indeed deter crime. After surveying their studies Tullock himself is convinced that "the empirical evidence is clear," and he states his conclusion unequivocally: "Even granting the fact that most potential criminals have only a rough idea as to the frequency and severity of punishment, multiple regression studies show that increasing the frequency or severity of the punishment does reduce the likelihood that a given crime will be committed."[8]

However, Tullock's confidence about the clarity of the empirical evidence is not shared by the Panel. The Panel argues that although the evidence consistently establishes a negative association between crime rates and sanctions (as measured by the risks of apprehension, conviction, or imprisonment), that is higher crime rates are associated with lower sanctions and vice versa, this does not necessarily show the general deterrent effect of sanctions. The negative association may be partly or wholly explained in terms of lower sanctions being the effect rather than the cause of higher crime rates. Higher crime rates may so overburden the resources of the criminal justice system that they reduce its ability to deal with new offenders. Overburdened judges and prosecuters may use their discretion to dismiss or reduce charges, or to offer attractive plea bargains.[9] Overcrowding of prisons may lead to a reduction in the time served in prison as more prisoners are released early on parole. The sanctions imposed on certain crimes may be reduced. So unless one can separate out the effect of higher crime rates on sanctions from the deterrent effect of sanctions on crime, one cannot interpret the evidence as establishing the presence of the general deterrent effect of punishment. The Panel's cautious assessment of the evidence is summed up in its remark that "we cannot yet assert that the evidence warrants an affirmative conclusion regarding deterrence," but the Panel adds that "the evidence certainly favours a proposition supporting deterrence more than it favours one asserting that deterrence is absent."[10] On the other hand, the Panel believes that the evidence does not even show a significant negative association between crime rates and the severity of punishment as measured by the time served in prison, but suggests that this may partly be accounted for in terms of various distortions.[11]

Moving from the analysis of statistics to the experimental evidence, the Panel identifies three studies which are not methodologically flawed. Of these, two show that the level of crime decreased significantly with increases in the level of sanctions, while one showed that the removal of criminal sanctions for abortions in Hawaii did not affect the incidence of abortions.[12] So it looks as if the present experimental evidence does not permit the drawing of general conclusions. But much of the experimental evidence is consistent with the operation of deterrence, as has been noted by Nigel Walker.[13]

Finally, we turn to the incapacitative effect of punishment. In her review of the literature for the Panel, Jacqueline Cohen suggests that disagreements about the magnitude of that effect can be attributed almost entirely to the different estimates of the average crime rate of prisoners.[14] The estimate of the increase in crime if current prison use were reduced or eliminated has been as low as five per cent.[15] Estimating the incapacitative effect of present prison policies is one thing. There is also the different question as to what we can expect the incapacitative effect to be if present policies are changed. Here one estimate is of a five fold decrease in crime, but Cohen points out that this can only be achieved by increasing the prison population by between 355 per cent and 567 per cent.[16] The incapacitative effect will not be the same for all crimes. Cohen points out that using the assumptions made by the available models, the increase in prison population required to reduce violent crimes is much less than the increases needed for similar reductions in other crimes. Violent crimes can be reduced by 10 per cent with less than 30 per cent increase in prison population.[17] This kind of consideration has led to an increasing interest in the use of selective incapacitation in which the focus of imprisonment is on certain types of offenders who are identified as having a high rate of committing crimes.[18]

We see that the evidence is perhaps more hospitable to the claim that punishment has some general deterrent effect and some incapacitative effect than it is to the claim that it has individual deterrent effect or that it rehabilitates offenders. This will no doubt be puzzling to some, but it provides a basis for caution in responding to a high rate of recidivism. Where there is such a high rate, it shows that punishment does not deter those who are punished. But it does not show that potential offenders are not in fact deterred by punishment, or that punishment does not incapacitate.

2.2. Punishing the Innocent

Let us now assume that the beneficial consequences of punishment outweigh the suffering that it inflicts on offenders. Critics of the utilitarian theory argue that if punishment is to be justified solely in terms of its good consequences, then punishment cannot be confined to offenders. There might be situations in which punishing an innocent person would produce better consequences than alternative courses of action. The utilitarian is therefore committed to punishing the innocent person. This objection has played an important role in the rejection of the utilitarian theory.

Let us consider an example made famous in the literature by H. J. McCloskey.[19] Suppose that in a particular town with a mixed population a man from one racial group rapes a woman from the other group. Because of existing racial tensions the crime is likely to produce racial violence with many people being injured, unless the guilty man is apprehended quickly. Suppose further that the sheriff of the town can prevent the violence by framing an innocent man who was near the scene of the crime, and who will be accepted by the community as the guilty person. Surely, it is argued, the best consequences will be produced by the sheriff's fabrication of evidence against him which will result in his conviction and severe punishment. But the critics maintain that the sheriff's act and the subsequent punishment of the innocent man are both wrong.

There are many ways in which utilitarians, or those sympathetic to them, can respond to this objection, and I shall consider some of their main arguments. First, it is argued that "punishing the innocent" is a logical contradiction because punishment implies guilt. Secondly, the premises of the objection are challenged. It is suggested that punishing the innocent man will not in fact produce the best consequences if we take into account all the consequences of such punishment including the long-term and less obvious consequences. Thirdly, it is claimed that the only situations in which punishing the innocent is optimific are hypothetical and "fantastic" situations rather than situations which arise, or are likely to occur, in the real world. It is then argued that for a variety of reasons, utilitarians should not be worried by what they are committed to in such fantastic situations. In discussing this third response, I shall also consider the views of those utilitarians who maintain that the punishment of the innocent would indeed be justified in situations where it produces the best consequences. If "commonsense morality" or our intuitions disagree, so much the worse for them.

2.3. Punishment and Guilt

In his well-known paper, "On Punishment," Anthony Quinton argues that the notion of "punishment" implies guilt in the sense that "punishment" is defined in part as the infliction of suffering on the guilty.[20] So when suffering is inflicted on innocent people, this cannot be properly described as punishment but as something else—judicial terrorism or social surgery. If we inflict suffering on an innocent man and try to pass it off as punishment, we are guilty of lying since we make a lying imputation that he is guilty and responsible for an offence. Part of Quinton's argument seems to rest on the importance of distinguishing between, for example, typhoid carriers and criminals even though both may sometimes be treated in rather similar ways. Thus a typhoid carrier, or a person with an infectious disease, will be quarantined. He will lose his freedom in much the same way that a criminal is deprived of his freedom when he is jailed. And yet we do not call quarantine a form of punishment precisely because the disease carrier is not guilty of an offence.

It is certainly true that in the typical cases of punishment it is inflicted on a person guilty of an offence. But the crucial issue is whether we can extend the notion of punishment to the infliction of suffering on the innocent without at the same time losing the distinction between punishment and various activities like the quarantine of disease carriers and certain kinds of medical or dental treatment which are painful.

In all these cases there is the infliction of some unpleasantness or suffering, but it is only in the case of punishment that the unpleasantness is essential to what is to be done. As Wasserstrom puts it "the point of the imposition of a deprivation when it is unmistakably a punishment is that it is being imposed because it is a deprivation, because the person upon whom it is being imposed should thereby be made to suffer and in that respect be worse off than before."[21] On the other hand, the unpleasantness experienced by those who are quarantined, or by those undergoing medical treatment, is only incidental, and not essential to what needs to be done. Advances in medical technology may lead to the replacement of painful forms of treatment by pleasant, but still effective, treatment. Medical treatment does not have to be painful at all: a sweet pill is as much a medicine as a bitter pill. Similarly, quarantine implies a degree of isolation to prevent the spread of the infection, and that in itself will be unpleasant. But it can, if resources permit, be greatly outweighed by the pleasures of the surroundings in which one is put. But punishment implies at least an overall degree of unpleasantness. So we can distinguish between punishment and quarantine without falling back on the notion that the person who is punished must be guilty, or must at least be supposed to be guilty, of an offence.

However, the truth of the matter seems to be a bit more complex than we have so far acknowledged, and Quinton's argument, though mistaken, is interesting because it gestures towards that truth. Consider the difference between a monetary fine, which is a form of punishment, and a tax which is not. Arguably both are essentially unpleasant although both may be accepted or approved of as fully justified. What then is the difference between them? In *The Concept of Law* H. L. A. Hart points out that punishment involves "an offence or breach of duty in the form of violation of a rule set up to guide the conduct of ordinary citizens."[22] When someone is punished, he has violated a standard of conduct to which he is supposed to conform. But when he pays a tax, he has not breached any such standard of conduct. The main purpose of taxes is to raise revenue and not to set up a standard of correct conduct. Indeed the revenue-raising function of a tax would be defeated if people generally reacted to income tax by not working, or to Value Added Tax by not eating in restaurants. On the other hand, the purpose of punishment is not defeated if, as a result of it, people cease to breach the relevant standard of conduct. On the contrary, the threat of punishment is most effective when it is unnecessary to carry it out. This important difference between punishment and a tax can be blurred, as Hart acknowledges, when, for example, those running a business simply assimilate the relatively small fines for breaches of rules into the costs of the goods they produce, and pass them on to their consumers. It is also blurred in the other direction when a government imposes a tax on luxury goods partly in order to discourage their use.

A related difference between punishment and other forms of deprivation or unpleasant treatment is that punishment expresses condemnation or disapproval of the conduct punished.[23] The person punished is blamed for what he did, and this explains the peculiar unfairness of punishing the innocent who are of course blameless.

But now, if we accept the idea that punishment involves the breach of a standard of conduct, how is this different from Quinton's point that punishment is always for an offence? The element of truth in Quinton's position is that there must be some wrongdoing or some offence for there to be punishment. But this is not to say that the person punished must be the offender. An innocent person can be punished for an offence committed by someone else. This can happen not only when the legal authority makes a mistake and punishes the wrong person, but also when it deliberately frames an innocent person.

But suppose now that my arguments fail, and Quinton's analysis of the concept of punishment is correct. It certainly does not follow that it is wrong to imprison innocent people or even to execute them. What follows is merely that we cannot *describe* these acts as *punishing* the innocent. But the real issue is a moral issue as to whether we are justified in inflicting suffering on innocent persons. Admittedly this is not exactly the same issue as whether we should *punish* the innocent which raises the additional problem of whether we may unjustly blame the blameless, but none the less it is a serious moral issue. Quinton argues that "the suffering associated with punishment *may* not be inflicted on them, firstly, as brutal and secondly, if it is represented as punishment, as involving a lie."[24] The second objection does not hold if we do not represent the infliction of suffering on the innocent as a form of punishment. And the first objection is not one of which utilitarians can avail themselves if the brutal treatment of the innocent will in fact produce the best consequences. So the argument against the utilitarian can now be reformulated as follows: why should we confine ourselves to punishment in those cases where the infliction of suffering on the innocent will produce the best consequences?

The objection to the utilitarian position is clearly moral, and hence it cannot be evaded by appealing even to a correct definition of the notion of punishment. A proper regard for the way in which terms are used will enable us to describe correctly the moral problem which confronts us, but it cannot solve that problem for us.

2.4. The Disutility of Punishing the Innocent

The second utilitarian response to the charge that utilitarians are committed to punishing the innocent draws our attention to the less obvious bad consequences of punishing innocent persons, and argues that on balance the punishment of the innocent will always produce worse consequences than the failure to do so. For example, it is claimed that the fact that an innocent man has been punished will soon leak out, and when that happens, there will be a loss of confidence in the sheriff and widespread fear among the population that any one of them might be the next innocent victim of the sheriff's attempt to prevent similar violence in future. Furthermore, the sheriff himself will have his sensibilities blunted once the barrier against framing and punishing the innocent has been removed. He is more likely to adopt a similar policy the next time he faces a problem of maintaining order, and on that occasion, there may be no strong utilitarian case for punishing an innocent person. It is also not certain that there will in fact be racial violence if an innocent person is not punished. On the other hand, the suffering of the innocent person who is punished is very real. The suffering of the innocent man is likely to be greater than that of the guilty. The punishment will come as a big shock to the innocent man, and he will be angered and distressed in a way that the guilty person will not be.[25]

But at each point of this utilitarian response, the critic can counter by tightening up the description of the example under consideration. Thus the sheriff suffers from a sudden fatal illness soon after the punishment of the innocent man, and he makes no death-bed confessions. No one else knows about the fabrication of evidence and the secret is buried with the sheriff. The innocent man who is punished has no relatives or close friends, and he himself is well endowed with an unusual temperament which faces unexpected disaster with calm resignation. We must not forget the unconvicted real offender who is still free and conceivably could give the whole show away. So he dies unexpectedly when he is run over by a bus on his way to the sheriff's funeral. Now we are back where we started with an example in which the punishment of an innocent person produces the best consequences and so should be accepted by the utilitarian.

2.5. Fantastic Examples and Moral Principles

But at this stage of the debate, the utilitarian will introduce a new, and by far the most complex and exciting, argument. He or she will argue that the nearer the critic gets to producing a water-tight example in which it is certain that punishing an innocent person will be optimific, the more fantastic the example becomes. The utilitarian moral theory cannot be defeated by the production of fantastic examples which are irrelevant to everyday moral argument in the real world.

It is strange that the rejection of fantastic examples has come to play such an important part in the writings of some utilitarian writers. In a radio talk "Does Oxford Moral Philosophy Corrupt Youth?" Anscombe attacked the use of such examples by utilitarian-minded philosophers. She parodied their method of argument with an example in which you have to decide what you ought to do when you have to move forward but "stepping with your right foot means killing twenty-five fine young men while stepping with your left foot would kill fifty drooling old ones."[26] Rising to the occasion, Anscombe gives the answer: "Obviously the right thing to do would be to jump and polish off the lot."[27] Today the attacks on the use of fantastic examples in moral argument are much more likely to come from utilitarians, irritated by attempts to undermine their moral principles which proceed by way of showing that in some conceivable, but very unlikely, situations, they are committed to all sorts of monstrous and outrageous acts—the punishment and killing of innocent people, torture, racial and religious persecutions, etc.

I want to argue that there is an important role for fantastic examples in moral argument. I shall, for the time being at least, assume that it is only in fantastic situations that the punishment of the innocent will produce the best consequences.

Suppose that you make a moral judgement: "It's wrong to stick knives into people."[28] A philosopher replies: "But suppose that human beings are so constructed that whenever you stick knives into their bodies you trigger off a mechanism which stimulates the pleasure-centres of their brains such that they experience very pleasurable sensations. Now surely it would then not be wrong to stick knives into them. Indeed mightn't it sometimes be obligatory to do so?" Is the philosopher just a smart Alec? Not necessarily. He or she may be trying to draw a distinction between, on the one hand, a subordinate or secondary moral principle, and on the other hand, a fundamental or ultimate moral principle. Sticking knives into people is only a subordinate moral principle: it is wrong only because it harms them. In the fantastic world imagined by the philosopher it would therefore not be wrong to stick knives into people. On the other hand the principle that we should not harm people may be a fundamental moral principle, and if it is, then, unlike a subordinate moral principle, it still holds good even in the fantastic world. In that world, it would not be wrong to stick knives into people, but it would still be wrong to harm them. Suppose that in the fantastic world, shaking hands would cause enormous pain. We would then have a new subordinate principle, applicable to that world, but not to our real world, that one ought not to shake hands unless both parties were masochists.

A subordinate moral principle is one which has to be justified in terms of another moral principle, whereas a fundamental moral principle is not justified by appealing to another moral principle. For the utilitarian, there is only one fundamental moral principle and that is the principle that one should always produce the best consequences. Thus from the utilitarian point of view the wrongness of punishing innocent people is only subordinate. It derives its justification from the fundamental utilitarian principle. It is wrong to punish the innocent only in so far as such punishment produces worse consequences than an alternative course of action. But for some non-utilitarians punishing the innocent is itself a fundamental moral principle. Our discussion of the philosopher's example suggests that fundamental moral principles apply even to fantastic situations. If this is correct, then we have a good reason for using fantastic examples to test the fundamental utilitarian principle. Utilitarians cannot therefore claim that their principle is only applicable to the real world and thereby refuse to consider the implications of the principle in fantastic situations. They can only fall back on this argument if the principle is subordinate, but it is not.

Furthermore, since subordinate principles do not apply to all situations whereas fundamental principles do, we can use fantastic situations to help us decide whether a particular principle is subordinate or fundamental. The principle that we are presently interested in is about the wrongness of punishing the innocent. We want to decide whether this principle is derivable from the utilitarian principle. If it is, then it is a subordinate principle. But if it is wrong to punish the innocent even when such punishment will produce the best consequences, then the utilitarian principle cannot be the only fundamental moral principle. We will not have shown that the wrongness of punishing the innocent is itself fundamental, for it may be based on a non-utilitarian fundamental moral principle. But even showing that much is enough to refute the utilitarian theory of punishment as providing the only basis for the justification of punishment.

In an interesting defence of consequentialism against moral absolutism, Kai Nielsen argues: "What is brutal or vile, for example, throwing a knife at a human being just for the fun of it, would not be so, if human beings were invulnerable to harm from such a direction because they had a metallic exoskeleton. Similarly, what is, as things are, morally intolerable, for example, the judicial killing of the innocent, need not be morally intolerable in all conceivable circumstances."[29] The two cases are however different in that the wrongness of throwing a knife at a human being just for the fun of it is clearly subordinate to some fundamental principle like that of not harming innocent human beings. On the other hand, for some non-utilitarians, the injunction against the judicial killing of the innocent is not a subordinate principle but an instance of a fundamental non-utilitarian moral principle against the killing of the innocent. Even if Nielsen is right that such a non-utilitarian principle may be violated in some conceivable circumstances, this does not show that the principle derives its force from consequentialist considerations. A non-utilitarian fundamental moral principle need not be absolutist in the sense that it must never be violated no matter what the consequences. It may sometimes be overridden by utilitarian considerations. But even when it is overridden, it "applies" or "holds good" in the sense that it embodies a morally relevant consideration which has to be taken into account in deciding what to do.

(It has "the dimension of weight" that Ronald Dworkin attributes to legal principles as opposed to legal rules, so that even when a legal principle does not determine or necessitate a particular decision, it still states a reason that argues in one direction rather than another.)[30]

Thus some moderate non-utilitarians will side with utilitarian against the absolutist when for example the failure to punish or to harm an innocent person produces very much worse consequences to others than the harm caused to the innocent. In such a case although moderate non-utilitarians give a negative moral weight to punishing or harming the innocent, which is independent of utilitarian considerations, the weight may not be good enough to outweigh the positive weight which both they and the utilitarian give to avoidance of a great deal of suffering to others. But sometimes the consequences of punishing or harming the innocent can be *clearly better* than the consequences of not punishing or harming even though they are not *much better,* and in such situations whereas the utilitarian would still punish or harm the innocent, the moderate non-utilitarian would not. This difference has not been sufficiently appreciated because of the ambiguity in the claim that the consequences of one act are clearly better than those of all alternative acts. Sometimes what we mean is that the consequences are much better. But sometimes the difference is clearly better when it is only slightly better, but it is clear that it is slightly better. The clarity here refers not to the size of the difference but to the vividness of our perception of the difference. Thus under appropriate conditions, a person who is 5'8" tall can be clearly taller than a person who is 5'7" because, although the difference in height is small, it is clear that it is a small difference. The relevance of this to our discussion is that in situations where the consequences of punishing or harming the innocent, relative to all other alternative courses of action, are clearly, even though only slightly, better in this sense, the utilitarian would regard such punishment or harm as justifiably inflicted. But now moderate non-utilitarians would disagree because the independent negative weight they give to punishing or harming the innocent is enough to override the slightly better consequences.

If, as we are now assuming to be true, there are no actual situations in which the punishment of the innocent will produce the best consequences, then we have a good reason for appealing to fantastic situations. In the real world both the utilitarian and the non-utilitarian will, for different reasons, believe it wrong to punish the innocent. We need therefore a fantastic situation in which the utilitarian and nonutilitarian responses will diverge to discover which is more plausible. In this context the role played by fantastic examples is rather like that of controlled experiments in science. Suppose that when two factors, A and B are present together we get an effect E. But suppose further that in the natural world A and B are inseparable. Scientists may wish to find out whether it is A or B singly, or the combination of them, which causes the effect E. To do this they will artificially create in the laboratory situations in which A and B are isolated from each other and then see whether E will still be produced. To object to the scientists' work on the ground that in the natural world A and B are inseparable is to show a considerable misunderstanding of what is going on. Of course the analogy is appropriate only up to a point. The fantastic example is supposed to separate what in the real world is inseparable, namely, the very bad consequences of punishing the innocent and the injustice of such punishment. But the fantastic example cannot provide a conclusive argument against the utilitarian principle because it is always open to the utilitarian to reject the view that punishing the innocent is still wrong when it produces the best consequences, in the way that it is not open for someone to claim that A alone causes E when it is shown that B singly can also cause E. But confronting utilitarians with a situation that they will not face in the real world helps them, and others who may be attracted by their view, to appreciate more clearly its implications. It is one thing to know in the abstract that we are committed to all sorts of actions which promote the best consequences. But it is quite another thing to know in vivid detail some of the numerous implications that our principle has in various circumstances. Well chosen fantastic examples will help us to understand the nature of our fundamental moral principles and their underlying assumptions.

But I have said enough to explain why I think that there is a place for fantastic examples in moral argument. I cannot therefore accept the vigorous attack on fantastic examples put forward by Sprigge, who argues: "A utilitarian will see no point in trying to imagine oneself looking with approval on the imaginary situation, since this is likely to weaken the feelings while not serving as a preparation for any actual situation."[31] His point is that if in the real world the punishment of the innocent will never produce the best consequences, then the utilitarian will develop strong feelings of aversion towards such punishment. They cause unnecessary harm. But if we now confront the utilitarian with a fantastic situation in which the punishment of the innocent is justified on utilitarian grounds, then the utilitarian will acknowledge this fact. But he will be uneasy because he has an aversion towards punishing the innocent which was built up through his experience in the real world. He does not wish to dwell on fantastic examples because they will weaken his strong feelings against punishing the innocent. He has every reason to sustain these feelings since he is not ever going to be confronted with a situation in the real world in which he would endorse the punishment of the innocent.

But Sprigge's argument seems to miss the point about the use of fantastic example. He *assumes* that the utilitarian principle is the correct fundamental principle and uses it to decide what disposition he should cultivate. If one takes for granted that utilitarianism is correct, then one would have utilitarian reasons for doing or abstaining from many actions. For example one might decide not even to argue with non-utilitarians for fear that this might weaken one's utilitarian dispositions. But the issue with which we are concerned is whether utilitarianism is a correct moral doctrine. Fantastic examples will help us decide by illuminating the assumptions and implications of utilitarianism and of alternative principles. Even though a fantastic situation will never occur in the real world, it can, by presenting us with relatively simple and sharp alternatives, help us to understand the nature and strength of our commitment to various values. Even a person already inclined towards utilitarianism cannot afford to allow dispositions based on the acceptance of subordinate moral principles to develop into prejudices with a life of their own, and cut off from the fundamental utilitarian principle which is for him their ultimate justification. As situations in the world change, new subordinate moral principles are necessary to replace old ones or to supplement them. But fundamental principles do not change and hence it is important that we decide the status of various principles.

But Sprigge has another argument against the use of fantastic examples. He points out that we may not be able to focus properly on a fantastic example. Certain features of the real world are absent in the fantastic example, but because we are used to these features, we may unwittingly smuggle them into the fantastic example. Thus in the real world punishing an innocent person will produce very bad consequences. However, in a fantastic example, such bad consequences are explicitly ruled out and it is, on the other hand, stipulated that there will be some very good consequences. But Sprigge points out, "If one finds oneself still half-inclined to call such punishment wrong, it may well be because one does not really succeed in envisaging the situation just as described, but surrounds it with those circumstances of real life which would in fact create a greater probability of unhappiness in its consequences than happiness."[32]

There is certainly some truth in Sprigge's comments and we can bring this out more clearly by considering the details of a type of fantastic example which is sometimes used against the hedonistic utilitarian. The hedonistic utilitarian believes that pleasure is the only thing intrinsically good, or good in itself, and pain is the only thing intrinsically bad, and that we should always act to maximize the total amount of pleasure. Imagine a world in which there are nurses and doctors who are dedicated to their patients, but who secretly get a peculiar form of sadistic pleasure out of the patients' suffering. This sadism is peculiar because it does not affect the conduct of the nurses and doctors towards their patients. They never allow their patients to suffer one moment longer than is necessary. Nor do they display their enjoyment of their patients' suffering in any way that will distress others. So perhaps we are to imagine them having their tea-breaks in some remote corner of the hospital and rejoicing at their patients' suffering, but then returning with renewed vigour to attend to the patients. If the hedonistic utilitarian had a choice between creating two worlds, one in which there are these doctors and nurses, and another in which there are these doctors and nurses, and another in which everything else is exactly the same except that the doctors and nurses are not sadistic, then he or she would create the first world. But the critic points out that this is surely wrong in spite of the fact that there will be more pleasure in the first world. If we agree with the critic, can we be sure that our preference for the second world is not based on our failure to envisage the first world exactly as it has been presented to us? Perhaps we tend to smuggle into the first world the wide-ranging effects that sadism normally has. We might therefore find it difficult to come to terms with the innocent sadism of the doctors and nurses. Perhaps we do not fully appreciate that their innocent sadism is good only for a few harmless laughs, and there is no danger of the doctors and nurses prolonging the suffering of their patients when no one else is around. And if we clearly confront the fantastic example as it is described then perhaps we may well agree with the hedonistic utilitarian that we ought to create the first world in preference to the second. Sprigge's argument does appear to be quite powerful when applied to this kind of fantastic example. But it is not an argument which shows that fantastic examples as such have no place in moral reasoning. What the argument does is to warn us of the dangers of not considering fantastic examples as they are described, and of using fantastic examples which involve too radical a change in human nature or in the world in which we live. Thus although it is logically possible for there to be "innocent sadists," it is difficult to imagine why they will not prolong the suffering of their patients if they gain so much pleasure from the suffering. But this difficulty may in the end be purely subjective, and the example may still be usefully employed in arguing with some people. In any case, examples can be fantastic in the sense of being very unlikely to occur in the real world even though they do not involve radical distortions of human nature or the world in which we live. An unusual combination of individually familiar circumstances may be most unlikely, but there is normally no difficulty in imagining its occurrence. Cases in real life may involve too complex assessments of the consequences of our actions, and those with different views will be bogged down in purely factual disagreements. So there is sometimes an advantage in using a fantastic example in which we can stipulate the consequences of certain actions so that discussion can then focus on the fundamental moral issues at stake.

Another attack on the use of fantastic examples is made by R. M. Hare in his stimulating defence of utilitarianism particularly in his book *Moral Thinking: Its Levels, Method and Point.*[33] Hare makes an important and illuminating distinction between two levels of moral thinking—the intuitive level and the critical level. We need relatively simple moral principles to help us decide what to do in everyday life when we are faced with new situations which resemble past situations in some important respects. Without such principles we will have to face each new situation from scratch and decide what to do without the benefit of useful dispositions developed through the adoption and application of such principles. These principles will also protect us from the temptation to special pleading which leads us to think in a manner which suits our own interests at the expense of the interests of others. Thus if we do not adopt the principle that lying is wrong, we are likely to persuade ourselves that in a particular situation the benefit of a lie to us is enormous and the harm to others only slight when in fact, if we view the situation impartially, we will discover that the lie causes much greater harm than good. So far we are operating at the intuitive level where our thinking is constrained by limitations of time and knowledge. But moral thinking cannot end at this level for there may be conflicts in the moral principles which we adopt at the intuitive level and these have to be resolved at another level, the critical level, where we are not subject to the limitations present at the intuitive level. Critical thinking is also necessary to determine whether a principle at the intuitive level is applicable to a new situation which differs from the cases covered by the principle in some important respects, and more generally to decide on the right course of action in unusual situations. Hare thinks that at the critical level the principle to be adopted is one which calls for the maximization of the satisfaction of preferences or desires, and this is a version of utilitarianism that is sometimes called preference utilitarianism. I shall not be concerned here with his argument for utilitarianism. But in the light of his distinction between the two levels of moral thinking, Hare would relegate the principle that it is wrong to punish the innocent to the intuitive level.[34]

Principles at the intuitive level are selected by critical thinking. We select those principles whose acceptance will produce actions which will best approximate to those actions which an archangel with superhuman qualities and no human weaknesses will recommend when he engages in critical thinking. For Hare, this means that the principles to be accepted at the intuitive level are those which will best promote the utilitarian end of maximizing the satisfaction of desires in the actual world.

Hare points out that the opponents of utilitarianism use fantastic examples in order to show that in such cases the utilitarian answers as to how we should act conflict with our common intuitions grounded on the acceptance of principles at the intuitive level.[35] But such conflicts do not undermine utilitarianism because our common intuitions about, for example, the wrongness of punishing the innocent, are designed for the actual world, and might not be appropriate to fantastic situations which do not occur in the actual world. So if, in fantastic situations, utilitarianism recommends the punishment of the innocent, then this does not show that utilitarianism is in any way defective. Hare challenges the critic of utilitarianism to specify the level at which his fantastic examples are to be considered. If they are brought in at the intuitive level then they are irrelevant since they do not refer to situations which will occur in the actual world. Hare maintains that fantastic examples are admissible at the critical level, but argues that at this level no appeal can be made to moral intuitions which cannot cope with such unusual cases.[36]

Hare's insistence that the discussion should be conducted *either* at the intuitive level *or* at the critical level is a little unfair. This is because a principle about the wrongness of punishing innocent people is simple enough to be used at the intuitive level, but at the same time it might also embody moral considerations which have an irreducible role to play at the critical level. At the critical level, it might well be, as we shall see later, that the intuitive principle, couched in exceptionless terms, would need to be qualified. But this does not mean that the moral consideration embodied in the principle is only derivative from other considerations and does not itself make an independent moral claim on us. As a utilitarian, Hare has a critical principle which specifies only one type of moral consideration as relevant, the maximization of the satisfaction of desires. This is the utilitarian end, and the intuitive principles are selected on the basis of their relative superiority in promoting this end in the actual world. These intuitive principles can be specified independently of the utilitarian end. The formulations of the principles do not *require* any reference to the maximization of desires. The relation between them and utilitarianism is simply that of means to end. The intuitive principles therefore cannot be chosen on the basis of the critical principle alone, but must be sensitive to the social situations in the actual world in which intuitive principles are to be applied. It is likely that in different societies different intuitive principles will be selected. But those non-utilitarians who believe that certain actions are intrinsically right or wrong, and that punishing the innocent is one such type of intrinsically wrong act, will view the relation between critical and intuitive principles differently. At least some of their intuitive principles will be relatively constant across cultural and social differences, and they will represent a more generalized version of their critical principles. They are not means to the realization of the non-utilitarian critical principles but rather imperfect exemplifications of those principles. They are imperfect because at the critical level the intuitive principles would have to be qualified since there are situations in which two such principles may conflict. Thus at the critical level we might discover that we are prepared to override the unqualified wrongness of punishing the innocent if large enough harms are avoided by such punishment. But this does not mean that the wrongness of punishing the innocent is simply dependent on the badness of the consequences it produces. Both the utilitarian and the non-utilitarian might agree at the intuitive level without also agreeing at the critical level. Hare allows the appeal to fantastic examples at the critical level, and such appeals may be necessary to clarify the nature of the principles that we are prepared to accept at that level. Thus a fundamental issue to be settled at that level is whether critical moral thinking is controlled by one principle, as Hare and other utilitarians suggest, or whether it has to find room for an irreducible plurality of moral principles as many non-utilitarians believe.[37]

But now once the discussion shifts to the critical level, are we not caught in the grips of Hare's argument that even though fantastic examples are permissible, the appeal to moral intuitions is not? So the fact that utilitarianism conflicts with our moral intuitions cannot be used as an argument against utilitarianism. Hare sometimes refers disparagingly to these antiutilitarian moral intuitions as "the received opinion" and argues that they have no probative force.[38] Thus he points out that as recently as the early twentieth century the received opinion was against "mixed bathing" even though "mixed bathing" had a utilitarian justification.[39] The example is well chosen for at a time when nude bathing is the issue, and when some energy-conscious bodies are urging us to have "mixed showers," it is unlikely that anyone today would share the previously received opinion that there was something wrong with men and women, amply clothed, enjoying the same beaches together. The example shows that received opinion can embody prejudices, and therefore moral intuitions of this kind should not be used at the critical level. Indeed, Hare argues that moral intuitions should be modified by critical thinking which will inculcate the *right* intuitions whether or not these coincide with the received opinions.[40]

Hare's argument is successful against those who use moral intuitions as bed-rock considerations round which critical thinking must be constructed. But that is not the way that fantastic examples have featured in our discussion so far. I have pointed out that we appeal to fantastic examples to better appreciate the implications of our fundamental moral

commitments. If we cannot accept some of these implications then we have to give up or modify our fundamental moral values. Thus utilitarians would have to accept all the implications of utilitarianism in actual and hypothetical situations, and if they want us to accept utilitarianism, then they must also persuade us that none of these implications is unacceptable to us. Fantastic examples have an honourable role to play even within the framework of Hare's moral theory. For in his theory to accept a moral judgement is to accept a universal prescription, and to accept a prescription is to act on it. The utilitarian principle that one ought always to produce the best consequences is itself a generalized moral judgement which identifies only one feature of actions as being relevant, namely the consequences produced. This being the case, anyone who accepts that principle must be prepared to act in all situations, actual or fantastic, in which the action will produce the best consequences. Fantastic examples help to test the genuineness and the strength of a person's commitment to utilitarianism. It is inadequate for a utilitarian to respond, in advance of a consideration of specific examples, that he or she is prepared to accept all the implications of utilitarianism. The utilitarian can of course be sure that whenever utilitarianism is inconsistent with a particular moral judgement others are inclined to accept, then that particular moral judgement will involve the acceptance of a course of action which will not produce the best consequences. But it is one thing to know this in general terms; it is quite another thing to repudiate all such particular judgements in the vast variety of situations in which they involve the non-production of the best consequences. Utilitarians may well find that in a particular case their insufficiently tested faith in their ability to resist recalcitrant counter-examples is in fact misplaced. Their moral beliefs may be more complex than they suppose, and utilitarianism may not be able to impose an order on their thinking.[41] What is true of the professed utilitarian will also be true of any person engaged in moral thinking. Fantastic examples probe the depths of our thinking. In using such examples, we are not appealing to the received opinion, but to the reflective judgement of each party to a moral argument as to how he or she would respond to particular situations. No matter how moral agents arrive at their critical moral principles, they still have to be sure that they know and can accept the implications of these principles.

2.6. Moral Dilemmas and Complexities

I have so far only been concerned to explain and justify the use of fantastic examples in moral argument. But we cannot assume that once fantastic examples are introduced, utilitarianism rather than non-utilitarian moral beliefs will be in difficulties. The conclusion that it is sometimes right to punish the innocent is one to which utilitarians are committed, but this may well be the correct conclusion. I have already mentioned this possibility earlier in our discussion. There are different ways of reaching the same moral conclusion in a particular case, and I shall now argue that even if the utilitarian's answer in a particular case, fantastic or otherwise, is correct, his or her reasoning to that answer may not be as illuminating as a non-utilitarian approach.

Let us consider a different example in which some non-utilitarians will also agree with the utilitarian that the normally strong moral injunction against torturing human beings may have to be violated. Anthony Quinton gives the example of "a man planting a bomb in a large hospital, which no one but he knows how to defuse and no one dare touch for fear of setting it off."[42] Quinton thinks that torturing the man could be justifiable given that it is an emergency situation with no time to resort to other methods, and there is no doubt about the bomb-planter's responsibility for, or capacity to produce, the violent act. The bomb-planter's responsibility for the act, and the fact that a much greater degree of suffering will be experienced by the innocent patients and staff of the hospital if the bomb were not defused in time, are certainly morally relevant features of the situation. But it is unclear whether these features can best be accounted for within the utilitarian framework of thinking. The example suggests that utilitarianism can mount a powerful attack on at least some forms of moral absolutism which share the view that there are certain kinds of acts, of which torture is one, which are always wrong, irrespective of the consequences.

But suppose now that the bomb-planter shows a considerable capacity for withstanding or evading torture (perhaps he conveniently faints whenever he is about to be tortured). There is very little time left, but it is discovered that the bomb-planter has a wife to whom he is very attached. If a moderate amount of physical pain were inflicted on her, the bomb-planter will defuse the bomb. Would it be wrong to harm his wife? This is in some ways like a case in which the punishment of an innocent person will prevent very bad consequences from occurring. If the pain to be inflicted on the innocent wife is very much less than the suffering of the people in the hospital, then both utilitarians and some non-utilitarians will agree that the act is justifiable. But does it follow that, other things being equal, we would be prepared to inflict the same amount of physical suffering on the wife as we would on the bomb-planter himself? Suppose we had a choice between torturing the bomb-planter and inflicting slightly less suffering on his innocent wife to achieve the same result. The fact that he is responsible for planting the bomb whereas she is innocent should be sufficient for us to choose him rather than her. This shows that we attach some weight, independent of utilitarian considerations, to not using innocent people unjustly for the benefit of others. On the other hand, there is no similar injustice in making the bomb-planter suffer if it is through his own act that we are confronted with the situation in which his suffering is the lesser of two evils. We would of course regret that we had to choose between two evils, and some might also regard torture as an evil requiring a special justification. Utilitarianism cannot adequately capture the injustice of using innocent people as means towards desirable ends because it treats the difference between torturing the bomb-planter and torturing his innocent wife as merely a difference in the consequences of the respective acts.

Let us pursue further the claim that utilitarianism does not do justice to the complexity of moral thinking. Suppose now that our notorious bomb-planter has placed a peculiar bomb in a large children's hospital such that if the bomb exploded it will release a gas which will cause all those in the hospital to experience an unpleasant itch for just a couple of minutes. But the side effects are that all future direct descendants of the inhabitants of the hospital will also, once in a lifetime, each experience a two-minute unpleasant itch. There is no possibility of a cure, but there are no bad consequences. In a few generations, the total undesirable consequences of the bomb's explosion is that thousands of people will have each experienced such two-minute itches. Let us assume that the only way to prevent the explosion of the bomb is to torture the innocent child of the bomb-planter. In such a situation it would be wrong to torture the innocent child no matter how many other people would each suffer two-minute itches if we did not torture. But this is precisely the conclusion that the utilitarian cannot accept because although each person suffers only a little, if there are many such sufferers, the bad consequences when added together, will sooner or later exceed the great suffering of the tortured child. As the well-known rhymes go:

> Little drops of water,
>   Little grains of sand,
> Make the mighty ocean
>   And the pleasant land.

So too, little two-minute itches can add up to one mighty pain.

If pleasures and pains can be aggregated, as utilitarians believe, then the lesser pains of many people can exceed the much greater pain of one person. No matter how great the suffering of being tortured, it is still a finite amount that can be exceeded. No matter how slight the unpleasantness of an itch may be, if there are enough people experiencing it, then the aggregate will exceed the agony of one person being tortured. The only way in which utilitarians can get round this is by introducing certain discontinuities of scale in which, for example, no aggregate of the much lesser pains of many persons can outweigh the great suffering caused by the torture of one person. But this would be an *ad hoc* device which can find no motivation within utilitarianism itself, and will destroy some of its distinctive features. It is irrelevant from the utilitarian point of view that in the case of the tortured child all the great suffering is experienced by one person, whereas in the case of the little itches the unpleasantness is spread out very thinly over many people, and no single person experiences the total suffering.[43] Utilitarians are only interested in the distribution of good and bad consequences when this affects the total. An equal distribution of benefits and burdens is not in itself better than a very unequal one if the two distributions yield the same total happiness or welfare. In the actual world, differences in distribution will of course often affect the total welfare, but the fantastic example helps to bring out the point that in certain situations utilitarians are committed to sacrificing the major interest of one person in order to promote the minor interests of many persons. In practice this commitment would lead to the justification of the exemplary punishment of an offender for a relatively trivial offence if this would deter many others from committing similar offences. This is an issue to which we will return.

Let me summarize my objections to the utilitarian theory because these objections have to be taken into account in constructing a more acceptable theory of punishment. The first objection is that the utilitarian theory does not give any independent weight to the injustice of punishing the innocent. If the theory regards such punishment as wrong, then it is wrong simply in virtue of the fact that it produces bad consequences. Secondly, there are situations in which the utilitarian theory permits and even requires us to inflict great suffering on one person in order to prevent many other persons from each experiencing a very much smaller amount of suffering.

2.7. A Return to the Real World

I have so far assumed, for the sake of argument, that it is only in fantastic situations that utilitarians are committed to punishing the innocent. But it is now time to say something about this assumption. Most utilitarians seem to make the assumption. Thus Hare writes: "The retributivists are right at the intuitive level, and the utilitarians at the critical level."[44] But contrast this with David Richards's claim in *The Moral Criticism of Law* that the utilitarian theory of punishment "clearly seems to allow and even require the punishment of the innocent, since it is very plausible that a higher degree of criminal deterrence would be achieved by punishing the children or relatives or friends or lovers of criminals in addition to or even in place of the criminal. Primitive systems of law often do exactly this, . . ."[45] In the face of these conflicting claims, two remarks are appropriate. First, no one can claim with confidence that, on the balance of probabilities, there are no actual cases in which punishing the innocent will produce the best consequences. But secondly, the strength of our conviction, which is shared by many utilitarians, that punishing the innocent in the real world is unjustified, cannot be accounted for simply on the basis of utilitarian considerations. If we were guided by purely utilitarian considerations, we would not be entitled to be as confident as we in fact are that such punishment in the real world is wrong, and we should indeed be prepared to experiment with limited proposals for the punishment of the innocent.

Indeed we can go further and argue that in the present state of our knowledge, surveyed earlier, the evidence of the desirable effects of punishment is not always as firmly based as is often assumed, and this presents some difficulties for a purely utilitarian justification of punishment. From the utilitarian point of view punishing offenders produces bad consequences which are certain and not speculative, namely the suffering inflicted directly by punishment on offenders and indirectly on their friends and relatives. Against this, there is no equally firm evidence, in all cases where punishment is thought to be justified, of its countervailing good effects. There is some evidence of incapacitative effects although the extent of these effects varies with different types of offences, and the evidence is also consistent with there being some general deterrent effect. Again, there is good reason to think that the total abandonment of the practice of punishment would have unfortunate results. But there are specific crimes in which the utilitarian case for punishment, while not ruled out, is not particularly strong. It is then unclear what we should do in the present state of our knowledge if we were guided by purely utilitarian considerations. In fact our thinking on these matters is also guided by non-utilitarian considerations. Other things being equal, we think it better that the guilty should suffer through punishment than that there should be similar suffering by the innocent victims of crime. Again, given that the practice of punishment has some utilitarian justification, there will also be offenders who may justifiably be punished by appealing to non-utilitarian considerations. For example, if the punishment for some offences can be justified on utilitarian grounds in terms of the general deterrent effect and the incapacitative effect of such punishment, then it is unfair to allow those who have committed more serious offences to go unpunished even if in these latter cases the existing evidence is inadequate to show that punishment has similar good effects.

I do not believe that the practice of punishment would be justified if there were a decisive utilitarian case against it, or if it did not at least have some utilitarian support. But this is not to say that all desirable aspects of that practice can be justified in purely utilitarian terms.

---

1. Jack P. Gibbs distinguishes between "rehabilitation" and "reformation." An offender is "rehabilitated" if he ceases to violate the law as a result of non-punitive means, whereas he is "reformed" if he ceases to violate the law as a result of punishment, but for reasons independent of the fear of punishment. See *Crime, Punishment, and Deterrence* (New York, 1975), p. 72. I use the two terms interchangeably and broadly to refer to cases in which the offender, after serving a sentence, no longer commits crimes because he believes that criminal behaviour is wrong and not because he fears punishment. His changed values can be brought about by punishment itself or by non-punitive means. Jean Hampton develops a sophisticated version of the moral education view of punishment according to which punishment communicates a moral message aimed at educating both the wrongdoer and the rest of society about the immorality of the offence. She is eager to distinguish her view from rehabilitative theories of punishment both in terms of the different ends to be achieved and the methods used to attain those ends. According to her, the aim of rehabilitation is to make the offender accept society's mores and operate successfully in society, and the pursuit of these goals is not constrained by respect for the autonomy of the wrongdoer. See "The Moral Education Theory of Punishment," *Philosophy & Public Affairs*, 13 (1984).
2. Alfred Blumstein, Jacqueline Cohen, and Daniel Nagin (eds.), *Deterrence and Incapacitation: Estimating the Effects of Criminal Sanctions on Crime Rates*, National Academy of Sciences, Panel on Research on Deterrent and Incapacitative Effects (Washington, 1978), p. 66. Hereafter this book will be referred to as The Panel.
3. Daniel Nagin, "General Deterrence: A Review of the Empirical Evidence," in *The Panel*, p. 96.
4. Johannes Andenaes, "Does Punishment Deter Crime?" in Gertrude Ezorsky (ed.), *Philosophical Perspectives on Punishment* (Albany, 1972), p. 354.
5. *Ibid.*, p. 354.
6. *Ibid.*, p. 346.
7. Gordon Tullcock, "Does Punishment Deter Crime?" *The Public Interest* (1974), pp. 103–11.
8. *Ibid.*, p. 109.
9. *The Panel*, p. 39.
10. *Ibid.*, p. 7.
11. *Ibid.*, pp. 37–8.
12. *Ibid.*, p. 55.
13. Nigel Walker, *Punishment, Danger and Stigma* (Oxford, 1980), pp. 77–80.
14. Jacqueline Cohen, "The Incapacitative Effect of Imprisonment: A Critical Review of the Literature," in *The Panel*, p. 209.
15. *Ibid.*, p. 188.
16. *Ibid.*, p. 218.
17. *Ibid.*, p. 227.
18. See Mark H. Moore, Susan R. Estrich, Daniel McGillis, and William Spelman, *Dangerous Offenders: The Elusive Target of Justice* (Cambridge, 1984). I discuss the problem of dangerous offenders in Ch. 6.
19. See H. J. McCloskey, "A Non-utilitarian Approach to Punishment," in Michael D. Bayles (ed.), *Contemporary Utilitarianism* (New York, 1968). Some of the details of my example in the text differ from McCloskey's examples.
20. Anthony M. Quinton, "On Punishment," in H. B. Acton (ed.), *The Philosophy of Punishment* (London, 1969), pp. 58–9.
21. Richard A. Wasserstrom, "Capital Punishment as Punishment: Some Theoretical Issues and Objections," *Midwest Studies in Philosophy*, 7 (1982), p. 476. See also H. J. McCloskey, "The Complexity of the Concepts of Punishment," *Philosophy*, 37 (1962), p. 323.
22. H. L. A. Hart, *The Concept of Law* (Oxford, 1961), p. 39.
23. For an excellent discussion of this feature of punishment, see Joel Feinberg, "The Expressive Function of Punishment," in Hyman Gross and Andrew von Hirsch (eds.), *Sentencing* (New York & Oxford, 1981).
24. "On Punishment," p. 59.
25. Some of these utilitarian objections to punishing the innocent are voiced by T. L. S. Sprigge, "A Utilitarian Reply to Dr. McCloskey," in Michael D. Bayles (ed.), *Contemporary Utilitarianism* (New York, 1968), pp. 278–82.
26. G. E. M. Anscombe, "Does Oxford Moral Philosophy Corrupt Youth?" *The Listener* (14 February 1957), p. 267.

27. *Ibid.*, p. 267.
28. See the interesting discussion in Kai Nielsen, "Against Moral Conservatism," in Karsten J. Struhl and Paula Rothenberg Struhl (eds.), *Ethics in Perspective* (New York, 1975), especially pp. 119–20. This article is reprinted from *Ethics,* 82 (1971–72), pp. 219–31.
29. *Ibid.*, p. 120.
30. Ronald Dworkin, *Taking Rights Seriously* (London, 1978), pp. 26–27.
31. T. L. S. Sprigge, "A Utilitarian Reply to Dr. McCloskey," p. 275.
32. *Ibid.*, p. 276.
33. R. M. Hare, *Moral Thinking: Its Levels, Method and Point* (Oxford, 1981), esp. Chs. 1–3 and 8–9.
34. *Ibid.*, pp. 162–63. Hare's argument for utilitarianism is critically discussed by Bernard Williams, *Ethics and the Limits of Philosophy* (London, 1985), pp. 82–92.
35. *Ibid.*, pp. 48–49.
36. *Ibid.*, pp. 131–32.
37. See Stuart Hampshire, *Two Theories of Morality* (Oxford, 1977).
38. *Moral Thinking: Its Levels, Method and Point, op. cit.,* p. 12. See also "The Argument from Received Opinion," in R. M. Hare, *Essays on Philosophical Method* (London, 1971), p. 122.
39. "The Argument from Received Opinion," p. 127.
40. *Moral Thinking: Its Levels, Method and Point,* p. 142. A different view of the relation between intuitions and general moral principles or ethical theories is given by Bernard Williams, *Ethics and the Limits of Philosophy*, Ch. 6.
41. See Stuart Hampshire, *Two Theories of Morality*, pp. 26–27.
42. Anthony M. Quinton, "Views," *The Listener* (2 December 1971), p. 758.
43. Some critics have accused utilitarianism of ignoring "the separateness of persons." For an illuminating discussion, see H. L. A. Hart, "Between Utility and Rights," in H. L. A. Hart, *Essays in Jurisprudence and Philosophy* (Oxford, 1983).
44. *Moral Thinking: Its Levels, Method and Point,* p. 163.
45. David A. J. Richards, *The Moral Criticism of Law* (Encino & Belmont, 1977), pp. 232–33.

THE MORAL WORTH OF RETRIBUTION*

Michael S. Moore

Retributivism and the Possible Modes of its Justification

Since I will in this chapter seek to justify the retributive theory of punishment, I will first say what such a theory is. *Retributivism* is the view that punishment is justified by the moral culpability of those who receive it. A retributivist punishes because, and only because, the offender deserves it. Retributivism thus stands in stark contrast to utilitarian views that justify punishment of past offenses by the greater good of preventing future offenses. It also contrasts sharply with rehabilitative views, according to which punishment is justified by the reforming good it does the criminal.

Less clearly, retributivism also differs from a variety of views that are often paraded as retributivist, but that in fact are not. Such views are typically put forward by people who cannot understand how anyone could think that moral desert by itself could justify punishment. Such persons scramble about for other goods that punishment achieves and label

these, quite misleadingly, "retributivism." The leading confusions seem to me to be seven in number.

1. First, retributivism is sometimes identified with a particular measure of punishment such as *lex talionis,* an eye for an eye (e.g., Wilson and Herrnstein, 1985, p. 496), or with a kind of punishment such as the death penalty. Yet retributivism answers a question prior to the questions to which these could be answers. True enough, retributivists at some point have to answer the "how much" and "what type" questions for specific offenses, and they are committed to the principle that punishment should be graded in proportion to desert; but they are not committed to any particular penalty scheme nor to any particular penalty as being deserved. Separate argument is needed to answer these "how much" and "what type" questions, *after* one has described why one is punishing at all. It is quite possible to be a retributivist and to be against both the death penalty and *lex talionis,* the idea that crimes should be punished by like acts being done to the criminal.

*From Michael Moore, "The Moral Worth of Retribution," in *Responsibility, Character, and the Emotions,* ed. Ferdinand Schoeman. Copyright © Cambridge University Press, 1987. Reprinted with the permission of Cambridge University Press.

2. Contrary to Anthony Quinton (1954) and others (see Hart, 1968), retributivism is *not* "the view that only the guilty are to be punished." A retributivist will subscribe to such a view, but that is not what is distinctive about retributivism. The distinctive aspect of retributivism is that the moral desert of an offender is a *sufficient* reason to punish him or her; the principle Quinton advocates make such moral desert only a *necessary* condition of punishment. Other reasons—typically, crime prevention reasons—must be added to moral desert, in this view, for punishment to be justified. Retributivism has no room for such additional reasons. That future crime might also be prevented by punishment is a happy surplus for a retributivist, but no part of the justification for punishing.

3. Retributivism is not the view that punishment of offenders satisfies the desires for vengeance of their victims. The harm that is punishment can be justified by the good it does psychologically to the victims of crime, whose suffering is thought to have a special claim on the structuring of the criminal justice system (see Honderich, 1969, p. 30). To me, this is not retributivism. A retributivist can justify punishment as deserved even if the criminal's victims are indifferent (or even opposed) to punishing the one who hurt them. Indeed, a retributivist should urge punishment on all offenders who deserve it, even if *no* victims wanted it.

4. Relatedly, retributivism is not the view that the preferences of all citizens (not just crime victims) should be satisfied. A preference utilitarian might well believe, as did Sir James Fitzjames Stephen (1967 at p. 152), that punishment should be exacted "for the sake of gratifying the feeling of hatred—call it revenge, resentment, or what you will—which the contemplation of such [criminal] conduct excites in healthily constituted minds . . . ," or that "the feeling of hatred and the desire of vengeance . . . are important elements of human nature which ought . . . to be satisfied in a regular public and legal manner." Yet a retributivist need not believe such things, but only that morally culpable persons should be punished, irrespective of what other citizens feel, desire, or prefer.

5. Relatedly, retributivism is not the view that punishment is justified because without it vengeful citizens would take the law into their own hands. Usually it is those who are hostile to retributivism, such as Justice Marshall (1976), who link it to this indefensible idea. Punishment for a retributivist is not justified by the need to prevent private violence, which is an essentially utilitarian justification. Even in the most well-mannered state, those criminals who deserve punishment should get it, according to retributivism.

6. Nor is retributivism to be confused with denunciatory theories of punishment (Feinberg, 1971). In this latter view punishment is justified because punishment is the vehicle through which society can express its condemnation of the criminal's behavior. This is a utilitarian theory, not a retributive one, for punishment is in this view to be justified by the good consequences it achieves—either the psychological satisfactions denunciation achieves, or the prevention of private violence, or the prevention of future crimes through the education benefits of such denunciation. A retributivist justifies punishment by none of these supposed good consequences of punishing.

7. Finally, retributivism should not be confused with a theory of formal justice (the treating of like cases alike). Retributivism is not, as McCloskey (1965) has urged, "a particular application of a general principle of justice, namely, that equals should be treated equally and unequals unequally." True, a retributivist who also subscribes to the principle of formal justice is committed to punishing equally those persons who are equally deserving. However, the principle of formal justice says nothing about punishing anybody for anything; such a principle only dictates that, *if* we punish anyone, we must do so equally. Why we should punish anyone is the question retributivism purports to answer, a question not answered by the distinct principle of formal justice.

Retributivism is a very straightforward theory of punishment: We are justified in punishing because and only because offenders deserve it. Moral culpability ("desert")[1] is in such a view both a sufficient as well as a necessary condition of liability to punitive sanctions. Such justification gives society more than merely a right to punish culpable offenders. It does this, making it not unfair to punish them, but retributivism justifies more than this. For a retributivist, the moral culpability of an offender also gives society the *duty* to punish. Retributivism, in other words, is truly a theory of justice such that, if it is true, we have an obligation to set up institutions so that retribution is achieved.

Retributivism, so construed, joins corrective justice theories of torts, natural right theories of property, and promissory theories of contract as deontological alternatives to utilitarian justifications; in each case, the institutions of punishment, tort compensation, property, and contract are justified by the rightness or fairness of the institution in question, not by the good consequences such institution may generate. Further, for each of these theories, moral desert plays the crucial justificatory role: Tort sanctions are justified whenever the plaintiff does not deserve to suffer the harm uncompensated and the defendant by his or her conduct has created an unjust situation that permits corrective action; property rights are justified whenever one party, by his or her labor, first possession, or intrinsic ownership of his or her own body, has come by such actions or status morally to deserve such entitlements; and contractual liability is justified by the fairness of imposing it on one who deserves it (because of his or her voluntary undertaking, but subsequent and unexcused breach).

Once the deontological nature of retributivism is fully appreciated, it is often concluded that such a view cannot be justified. You either believe punishment to be inherently right, or you do not, and that is all there is to be said about it. As Hugo Bedau (1978) once put it:

> Either he [the retributivist] appeals to something else—some good end—that is accomplished by the practice of punishment, in which case he is open to the criticism that he has a nonretributivist, consequentialist justification for the practice of punishment. Or his justification does not appeal to something else, in which case it is open to the criticism that it is circular and futile.

Such a restricted view of the justifications open to a retributivist leads theorists in one of two directions: Either they hang on to retributivism, urging that it is to be justified "logically" (i.e., nonmorally), as inherent in the ideas of punishment (Quinton, 1954) or of law (Fingarette, 1977); or they give up retributivism as an inherently unjustifiable view (Benn and Peters, 1959). In either case, retributivism is unfairly treated, since the first alternative trivializes it and the second eliminates it.

Bedau's dilemma is surely overstated. Retributivism is no worse off in the modes of its possible justification than any other deontological theory. In the first place, one might become (like Bedau himself, apparently) a kind of "reluctant retributivist." A reluctant retributivist is someone who is somewhat repelled by retributivism but who nonetheless believes: (1) that there should be punishment; (2) that the only theories of punishment possible are utilitarian, rehabilitative, retributive, or some mixture of these; and (3) that

there are decisive objections to utilitarian and rehabilitative theories of punishment, as well as to any mixed theory that uses either of these views in any combination. Such a person, as I have argued elsewhere (Moore, 1982b; also Moore, 1984, chap. 6), becomes, however reluctantly, a retributivist by default.

In the second place, positive arguments can be given for retributivism that do not appeal to some good consequences of punishing. It simply is not true that "appeals to authority apart, we can justify rules and institutions only by showing that they yield advantages" or that "to justify is to provide reasons in terms of something else accepted as valuable" (Benn and Peters, 1959, pp. 175–76). Coherence theories of justification in ethics allow two nonconsequentialist possibilities here:

1. We might justify a principle such as retributivism by showing how it follows from some yet more general principle of justice that we think to be true.
2. Alternatively, we can justify a moral principle by showing that it best accounts for those of our more particular judgments that we also believe to be true.

In a perfectly coherent moral system, the retributive principle would be justified in both these ways, by being part of the best theory of our moral sentiments, considered as a whole.

The first of these deontological argument strategies is made familiar to us by arguments such as that of Herbert Morris (1976), who urges that retributivism follows from some general ideas about reciprocal advantage in social relations. Without assessing the merits of these proposals one way or another, I wish to pursue the other strategy. I examine the more particular judgments that seem to be best accounted for in terms of a principle of punishment for just deserts.

These more particular judgments are quite familiar. I suspect that almost everyone at least has a tendency—one that he may correct as soon as he detects it himself, but at least a tendency—to judge culpable wrongdoers as deserving of punishment. Consider some examples Mike Royko has used to get the blood to the eyes of readers of his newspaper column:

> The small crowd that gathered outside the prison to protest the execution of Steven Judy softly sang "We Shall Overcome.". . .
>
> But it didn't seem quite the same hearing it sung out of concern for someone who, on

finding a woman with a flat tire, raped and murdered her and drowned her three small children, then said that he hadn't been "losing any sleep" over his crimes. . . .

I remember the grocer's wife. She was a plump, happy woman who enjoyed the long workday she shared with her husband in their ma-and-pa store. One evening, two young men came in and showed guns, and the grocer gave them everything in the cash register.

For no reason, almost as an afterthought, one of the men shot the grocer in the face. The woman stood only a few feet from her husband when he was turned into a dead, bloody mess.

She was about 50 when it happened. In a few years her mind was almost gone, and she looked 80. They might as well have killed her too.

Then there was the woman I got to know after her daughter was killed by a wolfpack gang during a motoring trip. The mother called me occasionally, but nothing that I said could ease her torment. It ended when she took her own life.

A couple of years ago I spent a long evening with the husband, sister and parents of a fine young woman who had been forced into the trunk of a car in a hospital parking lot. The degenerate who kidnapped her kept her in the trunk, like an ant in a jar, until he got tired of the game. Then he killed her.

[Reprinted by permission: Tribune Media Services]

Most people react to such atrocities with an intuitive judgment that punishment (at least of some kind and to some degree) is warranted. Many will quickly add, however, that what accounts for their intuitive judgment is the need for deterrence, or the need to incapacitate such a dangerous person, or the need to reform the person. My own view is that these addenda are just "bad reasons for what we believe on instinct anyway," to paraphrase Bradley's general view of justification in ethics.

To see whether this is so, construct a thought experiment of the kind Kant (1965, p. 102) originated. Imagine that these same crimes are being done, but that there is no utilitarian or rehabilitative reason to punish. The murderer has truly found Christ, for example, so that he or she does not need to be reformed; he or she is not dangerous for the same

reason; and the crime can go undetected so that general deterrence does not demand punishment (alternatively, we can pretend to punish and pay the person the money the punishment would have cost us to keep his or her mouth shut, which will also serve the ends of general deterrence). In such a situation, should the criminal still be punished? My hypothesis is that most of us still feel some inclination, no matter how tentative, to punish. That is the particular judgment I wish to examine. (For those persons—saints or moral lepers, we shall see which—who do not have even a tentative inclination to punish, I argue that the reason for affirming such inclinations are also reasons to feel such inclinations.)

The Case Against Retributive Judgments

The puzzle I put about particular retributive judgments is this: Why are these particular judgments so suspect—"primitive," "barbarous," "a throwback"—when other judgments in terms of moral desert are accorded places of honor in widely accepted moral arguments? Very generally, there seem to me to be five explanations (and supposed justifications) for this discriminatory treatment of retributive judgments about deserved punishment.

1. First and foremost there is the popularly accepted belief that punishment for its own sake does no good. "By punishing the offender you cannot undo the crime," might be the slogan for this point of view. I mention this view only to put it aside, for it is but a reiteration of the consequentialist idea that only further good consequences achieved by punishment could possibly justify the practice. Unnoticed by those who hold this position is that they abandon such consequentialism when it comes to other areas of morals. It is a sufficient justification not to scapegoat innocent individuals, that they do not deserve to be punished; the injustice of punishing those who do not deserve it seems to stand perfectly well by itself as a justification of our practices, without need for further good consequences we might achieve. Why do not we similarly say that the injustice of the guilty going unpunished can equally stand by itself as a justification for punishment, without need of a showing of further good consequences? It simply is not the case that justification always requires the showing of further good consequences.

Those who oppose retributivism often protest at this point that punishment is a clear harm to the one punished, and the intentional causing of this harm requires some good thereby achieved to justify it; whereas *not* punishing the innocent is not a harm and thus does not stand in need of justification by good consequences. Yet this response simply begs the question against retributivism. Retributivism purports to be a theory of justice, and as such claims that punishing the guilty achieves something good—namely, justice—and that therefore reference to any other good consequences is simply beside the point. One cannot defeat the central retributivist claim—that justice is achieved by punishing the guilty—simply by assuming that it is false.

The question-begging character of this response can be seen by imagining a like response in areas of tort, property, or contract law. Forcing another to pay tort or contract damages, or to forgo use and possession of some thing, is a clear harm that corrective justice theories of tort, promissory theories of contract, or natural right theories of property are willing to impose on defendants. Suppose no one gains anything of economic significance by certain classes of such impositions—as, for example, in cases where the plaintiff has died without heirs after his cause of action accrued. "It does no good to force the defendant to pay," interposed as an objection to corrective justice theories of tort, promissory theories of contract, or natural right theories of property simply denies what these theories assert: that something good *is* achieved by imposing liability in such cases—namely, that justice is done.

This "harm requires justification" objection thus leaves untouched the question of whether the rendering of justice cannot in all such cases be the good that justifies the harm all such theories impose on defendants. I accordingly put aside this initial objection to retributivism, relying as it does either on an unjustifiable discrimination between retributivism and other deontological theories, or upon a blunderbuss assault on deontological theories as such.

2. A second and very popular suspicion about retributive judgments is that they presuppose an indefensible objectivism about morals. Sometimes this objection is put metaphysically: There is no such thing as desert or culpability (J. Mackie, 1982). More often the point is put as a more cautious epistemological modesty: "Even if there is such a thing as desert, we can never know who is deserving." For religious people, this last variation usually contrasts us to God, who alone can know what people truly deserve. As Beccaria (1964, pp. 17–18) put it centuries ago:

> [W]hat insect will dare take the place of divine justice . . . ? The gravity of sin depends upon the inscrutable wickedness of the heart. No finite being can know it without revelation. How then can it furnish a standard for the punishment of crimes?

We might call this the "don't play God" objection.

One way to deal with this objection is to show that moral judgments generally (and judgments about culpability particularly) are both objectively true and knowable by persons. Showing both is a complicated business, and since I have attempted such a showing elsewhere (Moore, 1982a), let me try a different tack. A striking feature of the "don't play God" objection is how inconsistently it is applied. Let us revert to our use of desert as a limiting condition on punishment: We certainly seem confident both that it is true and that we can know that it is true, that we should not punish the morally innocent because they do not deserve it. Neither metaphysical skepticism nor epistemological modesty gets in our way when we use lack of moral desert as a reason not to punish. Why should it be different when we use presence of desert as a reason to punish? If we can know when someone does *not* deserve punishment, mustn't we know when someone *does* deserve punishment? Consider the illogic in the following passages from Karl Menninger (1968):

> The very word *justice* irritates scientists. No surgeon expects to be asked if an operation for cancer is just or not. No doctor will be reproached on the grounds that the dose of penicillin he has prescribed is less or more than *justice* would stipulate. (p. 17)
>
> It does not advance a solution to use the word justice. It is a subjective emotional word. . . . The concept is so vague, so distorted in its applications, so hypocritical, and usually so irrelevant that it offers no help in the solution of the crime problem which it exists to combat but results in its exact opposite—injustice, injustice to everybody. (pp. 10–11)

Apparently Dr. Karl knows injustice when he sees it, even if justice is a useless concept.

Analogously, consider our reliance on moral desert when we allocate initial property entitlements. We think that the person who works hard to produce a novel deserves the right to determine when and under what conditions the novel will be copied for others to read. The novelist's labor gives him or her the moral right. How can we know this—how can it be true—if desert can be judged only by those with Godlike omniscience, or worse, does not even exist? Such skepticism about just deserts would throw out a great deal that we will not throw out. To me, this shows that no one really believes that moral desert does not exist or that we could not know it if it did. Something else makes us suspect our retributive judgments than supposed moral skepticism or epistemological modesty.

3. One particular form of moral skepticism merits separate attention in this context: This is the skepticism that asserts that no one is really responsible for anything because everything we do is caused by factors over which we have no control, and therefore none of us is really guilty or deserving of punishment. "Tout comprendre c'est tout pardonner," as the folk wisdom has it.

The main problem with this bit of folk wisdom is that it is false. To understand all (the causes of behavior) is not to forgive all. To match proverb for proverb: "Everybody has a story," as many convicts well know, realizing that such stories hardly excuse (Morse, 1984, p. 1499).

To do more than match proverbs against this objection to retributivism requires an extended excursion into compatibilist moral psychology. Having done that recently (Moore, 1985a), I will not recapitulate the argument defending the view that most people are responsible for what they do irrespective of the truth of determinism. In any case, if retributivism is to be rejected on hard determinist grounds, all justice theories in property, contract, and torts would have to be rejected as well, since no one could act in a way (viz., freely) so as to deserve anything.

4. A fourth popular suspicion about using moral desert as a justification to punish takes the opposite tack from the last objection. Here the thought is not that *none* of us are guilty, but rather that *all* of us are guilty—so that if we each got what we truly deserved, we would all be punished. How, then, can such a ubiquitous human condition be used to single out some but not all for punishment? Christ, of course, is the most famous purveyor of this argument when he dissuades the Pharisees from stoning an adulteress with an explicit appeal to their own guilt: "He that is without sin among you, let him first cast a stone at her" (John 8:3–11).

If we take this literally (I will give it a more charitable interpretation later), this is pretty clumsy

moral philosophy. It is true that all of us are guilty of some immoralities, probably on a daily basis. Yet for most people reading this essay, the immoralities in question are things like manipulating others unfairly; not caring deeply enough about another's suffering; not being charitable for the limitations of others; convenient lies; and so forth (Shklar, 1984). Few of us have raped and murdered a woman, drowned her three small children, and felt no remorse about it afterward, to revert to one of Royko's examples. It is simply false—and obviously so—to equate guilt at the subtle immoralities of personal relationships with the gross violations of persons that violent crime represents. We do not all deserve the punishment of a murderer for the simple and sufficient reason that we are not all murderers, or anything like murderers in culpability.

One can of course quote more scripture here—"He that lusts after a woman has already committed adultery with her"—but that also is to miss some obvious and basic moral distinctions. Freud is surely to be preferred to scripture here, when he urged that we must give credit where credit is due: If our conscience is such that we do not allow ourselves to act on our admittedly wicked fantasies, that makes us a better person than one who not only dreams of such atrocities, but brings them about (see Moore, 1980, p. 1629, n. 198; compare Fingarette, 1955; Morris, 1976, p. 124).

The short of it is that desert is not such an ubiquitous feature of human personality that it cannot be a marker of punishment. To think otherwise is to gloss over obvious moral distinctions, a glossing that to me is so obviously wrong that it can only be a cover for a judgment made on other grounds.

5. It is often said that retributive judgments are "irrational." They are irrational, it is said, because they are based on "emotion rather than reason." Such irrational emotion cannot be the basis for justifying a legal institution such as punishment. Legal institutions can be justified only by reason, not by yielding to irrational emotions, whether ours or others'. Henry Weihofen (1956, pp. 130–31) once stated this objection forthrightly:

> It is not only criminals who are motivated by
> irrational and emotional impulses. The
> same is true also of lawyers and judges,
> butchers and bakers. And it is especially true
> on such a subject as punishment of criminals.
> This is a matter on which we are all inclined
> to have deep feelings. When a reprehensible

crime is committed, strong emotional reactions take place in all of us. Some people will be impelled to go out at once and work off their tensions in a lynching orgy. Even the calmest, most law-abiding of us is likely to be deeply stirred. . . . It is one of the marks of a civilized culture that it has devised legal procedures that minimize the impact of emotional reactions and strive for calm and rational disposition. But lawyers, judges and jurors are still human, and objective, rational inquiry is made difficult by the very irrationality of the human mind itself. . . . Consciously we want to be rational. We prefer to think of ourselves as governed by reason rather than as creatures swept by irrational emotions. . . .[2]

This objection, as stated, proves far too much for its own good. Think for a moment about the intimate connection between our emotions and morality, a matter we explore later in this chapter. Although Kantian beings who could know morality without relying upon their emotions are perhaps conceivable—just barely—that surely is not us. We need our emotions to know about the injustice of racial discrimination, the unfairness of depriving another of a favorite possession, the immorality of punishing the innocent. Our emotions are our main heuristic guide to finding out what is morally right.

We do both of them and morality a strong disservice when we accept the old shibboleth that emotions are opposed to rationality. There is, as I have argued elsewhere (Moore, 1982a, 1984; see also de Sousa, 1980; Scruton, 1980), a rationality of emotions that can make them trustworthy guides to moral insight. Emotions are rational when they are intelligibly proportionate in their intensity to their objects, when they are not inherently conflicted, when they are coherently orderable, and instantiate over time an intelligible character. We also judge when emotions are appropriate to their objects; that is, when they are *correct*.

The upshot is that unless one severs any connection of our legal institutions to morals, one cannot condemn an institution because it is based on "emotion." Some emotions generate moral insights our legal system could hardly do without, such as the insight that it is outrageously unfair to punish an innocent person. Imagine condemning the legal ban on punishing the innocent because it is based on emotion and not on reason.

To be sure, there is also a sense of rationality opposed to emotionality (Moore, 1984, pp. 107–8). This is the sense in which we view rationality as reason and will and see these faculties as "unhinged" by powerful emotional storms. It is this sense of emotionality we use when we partially excuse a killer because the act was the product of extreme passion, not cool rationality. It is also this sense of rationality versus emotionality that is sometimes played upon by those making this objection to retributivism. The picture is one in which the retributivist emotions unhinge our reason by their power.

Karen Horney's assumption that vindictiveness is always neurotic (and thus always undesirable) is based upon this kind of characterization:

> Often there is no more holding back a person driven toward revenge than an alcoholic determined to go on a binge. Any reasoning meets with cold disdain. Logic no longer prevails. Whether or not the situation is appropriate does not matter. It overrides prudence. Consequences for himself and others are brushed aside. He is as inaccessible as anybody who is in the grip of a blind passion. (Horney, 1948, p. 5).

There is more than a little truth to this conception of the emotional base of retributivism. Literature is rich in faithful depictions of otherwise rational and moral people being unhinged by an urge to punish another for a wrong. Susan Jacoby (1984) recounts the tale of Michael Kohlhaas, written into a novel in 1806 by Heinrich von Kleist. Kohlhaas is depicted as a benevolent man, a horse dealer, friendly, kind, loyal to those around him, but one whose life is altered by the dominating passion of revenge. Kohlhaas's animals are maltreated by his neighbor—a man of higher social position—and Kohlhaas, in his unbending quest to make the offending squire pay, "eventually destroys his business and his marriage (his wife is killed by the enemies he has made); burns down the squire's house; murders innocent inhabitants of the castle; and incites a revolt that lays waste to much of the surrounding countryside" (pp. 51–52).

This is pathological and is fairly described as reason being overcome by a domineering, obsessive emotion. Yet it is surely not the case that the retributive urge always operates like this. Pathological cases can be found for any emotions, including benevolent ones. We should not judge the moral worth of an emotion by cases where it dominates reason, unless we are willing to say that such an emotion typically leads to such pathology; and the retributive intuition described here does not. One can have the intuition that the guilty deserve punishment, and one can have emotional outrage when they do not get it, without having one's reason dominated by an emotional storm. We may feel morally outraged at some guilty criminal going unpunished, but that need be no more unhinging of our reason than our outrage at the innocent being punished. In both cases, intense emotions may generate firm moral convictions; in each case, the emotions can get out of hand and dominate reason—but that is not reason to discount the moral judgments such emotions support when they do *not* get out of hand.

Despite the foregoing, I think that the most serious objection to retributivism as a theory of punishment lies in the emotional base of retributive judgments. As thus far construed, the objection is, as we have seen, ill-fated. If stated as an objection to there being an emotional base at all to judgments about deserved punishment, the objection is far too broad to be acceptable. All moral judgments would lose to such a charge if it were well founded. If stated as an objection to the unhinging quality of retributive emotions, the objection is psychologically implausible. Any emotion in pathological cases can unhinge reason, and there is nothing about retributive emotions that make it at all plausible that they always unhinge our reason when we experience them. The objection thus needs a third construction, which is this: The emotions that give rise to retributive judgments are always pathological—not in their intensity or their ability to unhinge our reason, but in their very nature. Some emotions, such as racial prejudice, have no moral worth even if typically experienced in a not very intense way. The true objection here is that the retributive urge is one such emotion.

In discussing this version of the objection to the emotional base of retributivism, I shall by and large rely on Nietzsche, who to my mind remains one of the most penetrating psychologists of the unsavory side of our emotional life. He is also one of the few thinkers to have delved deeply into the psychology of revenge. There is surprisingly little written on revenge in modern psychiatry, in large part because psychiatrists regard revenge "like sex before Freud . . . , condemned as immature and undesirable and thus unworthy of serious scientific investigation" (Harvey Lomas, quoted in Jacoby, 1984, p. 169).

"Mistrust," Nietzsche's Zarathustra advises us, "all in whom the impulse to punish is powerful" (*Zarathustra,* p. 212). Nietzsche clearly believes that the retributive emotions can get in the way of that celebration of life that makes us better—I would say virtuous—human beings. As he said in *The Gay Science:* "I do not want to wage war against what is ugly. I do not want to accuse; I do not even want to accuse those who accuse. *Looking away* shall be my only negation" (p. 223). And as he repeated later: "Let us not become darker ourselves on their [criminals'] account, like all those who punish others and feel dissatisfied. Let us sooner step aside. Let us look away" (p. 254).

What is the awful vision from which we should avert our gaze? If Nietzsche is right, truly a witch's brew: resentment, fear, anger, cowardice, hostility, aggression, cruelty, sadism, envy, jealousy, guilt, self-loathing, hypocrisy and self-deception—those "reactive affects" that Nietzsche sometimes lumped under the French term *ressentiment* (*Genealogy,* p. 74). All this, Nietzsche believed, lies behind our judgments of retributive justice.

Consider first resentment. One of Nietzsche's deepest insights into moral genealogy (Danto, 1965) is how much the retributive urge is based on resentment. As Max Scheler (1961, p. 46), once explained Nietzsche's insight here: "Revenge . . . , based as it is upon an experience of impotence, is always primarily a matter of those who are 'weak' in some respect." If we feel physically, psychologically, or politically weak, we will feel threatened by those we perceive to be stronger, such as those willing and able to use physical violence. Moreover, if we are actually or vicariously injured by such stronger persons, our weakness may prevent us from venting in the most direct way the anger such violation generates. Rather than either venting such anger directly through our own action (of retaliation), or at least feeling able to do so but choosing to refrain, our real or perceived helplessness transforms the anger into the brooding resentment of those who lack power. Such resentment, Nietzsche rightly thinks, can poison the soul, with its unstable equilibrium of repressed anger and repressing fear. A resentful person is burdened with an emotional conflict that is both ugly and harmful. It is better for us, because of this, to "look away" rather than to brood about revenge.

Our weakness and its accompanying emotions of fear and resentment can also make our retributive inclination seem cowardly, herdlike, and weak. As Nietzsche observed at one point: "'Punishment' . . .

is simply a copy . . . of the normal attitude toward a hated, disarmed, prostrated enemy, who has lost not only every right and protection, but all hope of quarter as well . . ." (*Genealogy,* pp. 72–73). Yet unlike the victor in a fight who has won and who can afford to be merciful to a vanquished foe, those who wish to punish may feel that this is their first opportunity to get back, an opportunity they cannot afford to pass up. When Christ talks about throwing stones, it is not because we are all equally guilty that we should not throw the stones; rather, there is something cowardly in a group of persons throwing stones at one who is now helpless. Such cowardice can be exhibited by the need of such persons for group reinforcement (which is why avengers may refuse to throw the *first* stone—it would set one apart from the group). It is no accident that the retributive urge calls up images of mobs, groups who together finally find the strength to strike back at an only now helpless foe. Our fear and our resentment of criminals can make us look small and cowardly in our retaliation in a way that immediate retaliation by one without fear or resentment does not.

Our fear of criminals need not always be due to our sense of their power to hurt; sometimes we may feel such fears just because they are different. For some people, there is a link between fear of strangers and fear of criminals, a link partly reflected by the extraordinary group reinforcement they receive when their retributive urges are shared. Such a link is also reflected in the we-they attitude many adopt about criminals, an attitude suggesting that criminals are fundamentally different and outside the group about whom we need be concerned. This is the criminal as outlaw, an attitude that, although neither causing nor caused by prejudice and bigotries of various kinds, nonetheless invites such other fears of differences to get expressed in retributive judgments.

Even when we do not feel weak and threatened by criminals, we may find other emotions underlying our retributive judgments that are not very pretty. Surely one of the uglier spectacles of our times are the parties by fraternity boys outside the gates of prisons when an execution is taking place. What makes such spectacles so ugly is the cruelty and sadistic pleasure at the suffering of others that they express. Such people feel entitled to let go of the normal constraints on expressing such unsavory emotions because the legitimacy of retribution licenses it. It is all right to enjoy the suffering of criminals, because it is deserved suffering. Deserved punishment, as Nietzsche perceived, can be "a warrant for and title to cruelty" (*Genealogy,* p. 65). It can give us "the pleasure of being allowed to vent [our] power freely upon one who is powerless, the voluptuous pleasure of doing evil for the pleasure of doing it, the enjoyment of violation" (p. 65). Our retributive judgments, in such a case, look like a rationalization of, and excuse for, venting emotions we would be better off without.

There are admittedly other avenues in this society for people to vent sadistic enjoyment of another's suffering. One that comes to mind are such films as *The Texas Chainsaw Massacre.* Reported audience reaction to a scene depicting a helpless female about to be dismembered by a chainsaw included cries of "Cut the bitch." The unrestrained sadism in such reactions is a deep sickness of the soul. To the extent that our inclinations to punish are based on a like emotion, it too, as Menninger says (1968, p. 201), lines us "up with the Marquis de Sade, who believed in pleasure, especially the pleasure derived from making someone else feel displeasure."

There is also envy and jealousy sometimes to be found lying at the emotional base of our retributive inclinations (*Zarathustra,* p. 213). We seem to have some admiration for criminals, an admiration reflected in the attention we give them in the media and the arts. We may admire their strength and courage; criminals, as Herbert Morris (1976, p. 132) aptly describes it, may manifest "what we too often do not, power and daring, a willingness to risk oneself for the satisfaction of strong desires." Thackeray had the same insight, writing *Vanity Fair* in large part to show us how much more we admire strength (Becky) than we do more conventional moral virtues (Amelia). Moreover, within the breasts of most of us beat some criminal desires. Not only may we admire the strength of will criminals may exhibit, but we may also be excited by the desires they allow themselves to satisfy. We thus may suffer a double dose of envy, both of the desires acted on and the strength that is exhibited in acting on them. Such envy and jealousy fuels the retributive urge, because punishment will tear down the object of such feelings.

Guilt has an interesting relationship to envy here. If criminals sometimes do what we might like to do but restrain ourselves from doing by our guilt, crime may excite a particularly virulent kind of envy. We may be envious not only of the power and the satisfaction of desires represented by criminal behavior, but even more of the freedom from guilt we may attribute to the criminal. Our own guilt in such a case may be challenged by apparent examples of such guiltless freedom to act on forbidden desires; if so, our defense is to transform the envy into the desire to destroy that which so challenges our own precarious balance between good and evil.

Guilt can give rise to our retributive judgments about others without the "good offices" of the emotions of envy and jealousy. Such retributivist judgments may simply project our own guilt onto the criminal and by doing so, lessen our guilt feelings because we are better than he. Henry Weihofen (1956, p. 138) aptly describes this Freudian insight about retribution:

> No one is more ferocious in demanding that the murderer or the rapist "pay" for his crime than the man who has felt strong impulses in the same direction. No one is more bitter in condemning the "loose" woman that the "good" women who have on occasion guiltily enjoyed some purple dreams themselves. It is never he who is without sin who casts the first stone.
>
> Along with the stone, we cast our own sins onto the criminal. In this way we relieve our own sense of guilt without actually having to suffer the punishment—a convenient and even pleasant device for it not only relieves us of sin, but makes us feel actually virtuous.

The retributive urge often seems to be accompanied by the additional nonvirtues of self-deception and hypocrisy. Few people like to think of themselves as weak and resentful, fearful, cowardly, cruel and sadistic, envious, jealous, and guilt-ridden. Accordingly, if they possess such emotions and traits when they make retributive judgments, they have every reason to deceive themselves about it. Such self-deception Nietzsche thought to be "the masterpiece of these black magicians, who make whiteness, milk, and innocence of every blackness . . ." (*Genealogy,* p. 47; see also Horney, 1948, p. 4). "These cellar rodents full of vengefulness and hatred" have reconceived their black emotions into an abstract virtue:

> "We good men—*we are the just*"—what they desire they call, not retaliation, but "the triumph of *justice*"; what they hate is not their enemy, no! They hate "injustice," they hate "godlessness"; what they believe in and hope for is not the hope of revenge . . . but the victory of God, of the *just* God, over the godless. . . . (*Genealogy,* p. 48)

Self-deception and hypocrisy themselves are vices, and to the extent that our retributive judgments encourage them—because we cannot affirm the emotional base of such judgments—we would be better without them.

To this basically Nietzschean indictment of the emotions on which retributive judgments seem to be based, we may add the insight of some feminists that the urge to retaliate is an instance of a male and macho stereotype that is itself no virtue. As Susan Jacoby (1984, chap. 6) points out, there are actually two not entirely consistent stereotypes that operate here. One is that revenge is a male prerogative because it is the manly thing to do. The other is that women are the greatest avengers because (harking back to Nietzsche) their physical and political weakness demands subtler, more repressed, and thus more intense modes of retaliation. Such views are compliments neither to men nor to women. Such stereotypes, like racial prejudice and other differences mentioned earlier, do not cause our retributive judgments so much as they find in such judgments a vehicle for their expression.

Finally, consider the kind of "scoring mentality" that accompanies retributive judgments. As Scheler (1961, p. 46) noted: "It is of the essence of revenge that it always contains the *consciousness* of 'tit for tat,' so that it is never a mere emotional reaction." Nietzsche too scorned the "shopkeeper's scales and the desire to balance guilt and punishment" (*Dawn,* p. 86) as a part of the retributive urge. Retributivism requires a kind of keeping track of another's moral ledger that seems distasteful. Retributive judgments seem legalistic, a standing on one's rights or a satisfaction with "doing one's duty" that psychologically crowds out more virtuous modes of relating to others. "Bother justice," E. M. Forster has his protagonist exclaim in *Howards End.* Margaret later goes on to say that she will have "none of this absurd screaming about justice. . . . Nor am I concerned with duty. I'm concerned with the character of various people whom we know, and how, things being as they are, things may be made a little better" (p. 228). Aristotle (Book VII) understood the same point in his familiar thought that "between friends there is no need of justice." Relate to others in a way that does not concern itself with giving them their just deserts, positive or negative. Those who keep track of favors owed, debts due, or punishments deserved cut themselves off from modes of relating to others that can be both more virtuous (because supererogatory) and also more rewarding than demanding rights or acting on duties.

There is no question, I think, that insofar as the retributive urge is based on such emotions as these, or causes us to instantiate traits such as self-deception, the urge is bad for us. It makes us less well formed, less virtuous human beings to experience such emotions—or, more accurately, to be the sort of person who has such emotions. This insight about what are and what are not virtuous emotions to have persuades many people that they ought not to make retributive judgments. For it is natural to feel that such judgments are contaminated by their black emotional sources. Defense lawyers have long recognized our tendency to withdraw or soften our retributive demands once we see the emotional base for them. Consider Clarence Darrow's appeals to Judge Caverly's virtue in Darrow's famous closing argument in the Loeb and Leopold sentencing hearing:

> I have heard in the last six weeks nothing but the cry for blood. I have heard from the office of the State's Attorney only ugly hate. I have heard precedents quoted which would be a disgrace to a savage race. . .
>
> [Y]our Honor stands between the future and past. I know the future is with me. . . . I am pleading for life, understanding, charity, kindness, and the infinite mercy that considers all. I am pleading that we overcome cruelty with kindness and hatred with love. . . . I am pleading for a time when hatred and cruelty will not control the hearts of men. When we can learn by reason and judgment and understanding and faith that . . . mercy is the highest attribute of man. . . . If I can succeed . . . I have done something to help human understanding, to temper justice with mercy, to overcome hate with love. I was reading last night of the aspiration of the old Persian poet, Omar Khayyam. It appealed to me as the highest that I can vision. I wish it was in my heart, and I wish it was in the hearts of all. "So I be written in the Book of Love, I do not care that Book above, erase my name or write it as you will, so I be written in the Book of Love." (Hicks, 1925, pp. 995, 1084)

Persuasive words. For who does not want to be written in the Book of Love? Who wants to be written in the books of hate, cruelty, cowardice, envy, resentment, and the like? Judge Caverly certainly did not, and decided against a death sentence for Loeb or Leopold.

Yet the more one looks at this argument, the more questionable it becomes. What does the virtue of the holder of a judgment have to do with the truth (or lack of it) of that judgment? Why should we think that Judge Caverly's damaging his virtue by deciding against Loeb and Leopold—increasing his virtue if he decides the other way—has anything to do with the truth of the judgment "Loeb and Leopold deserve to die"? How can a judge expect to reach sound moral conclusions about Loeb and Leopold by focusing on which decision will most enhance *his* (the judge's) virtue? This seems to be a form of ad hominem argument, and a rather selfish version to boot, given its narcissistic preoccupation with one's own virtue.

The most persuasive case against retributivism is thus in danger of complete collapse. The charge is this: Even if it makes us morally worse to make retributive judgments—because of the emotions that give rise to such judgments—that lack of virtue on our part is simply irrelevant to the assessment of whether retributive judgments are true. To assess this issue requires that we look in greater detail at the connections between our emotions and our moral judgments, which I propose to do next.

Morality and the Emotions

The charge laid at the end of the last section is a form of the "genetic fallacy" objection. Such an objection urges that it is fallacious to infer the falsity of a proposition from some truths (no matter how unsavory) about the genesis of people's belief in that proposition. A common example is to infer the falsity of our moral beliefs from the fact that they are caused by an education that could easily have been otherwise (see Moore, 1982a, pp. 1097–101). The ad hominem argument presented in the last section is like this, because it infers the falsity of retributivism from the unnice emotional origins of people's belief in retributivism.

To respond adequately to this genetic fallacy objection, the antiretributivist must establish that the emotional base of a moral judgment is relevant to that judgment's truth. If we leave ethics for a moment, one can see that sometimes it is no fallacy to infer the falsity of a judgment from the truth of some explanation of why people come to such judgment. Suppose the proposition in question was: "Sticks become bent when immersed in water, straight again when removed." Suppose the common explanation for why people believe this proposition to be true is in terms of their perceptual experience with sticks partly immersed in water—namely, they look bent to them. If we have grounds to believe that these perceptual experiences as a class are unreliable—an "illusion"—then it is no fallacy to infer the falsity of the proposition from an explanation of people's beliefs showing such beliefs to be the product of an illusion. Knowing what we do about the unreliability of perceptual experience when light is refracted in mediums of different density, we are entitled to disbelieve those who rely on such experiences in coming to their beliefs about sticks in liquid.

The antiretributivist would make a similar construction of the Nietzschean case against retributivism, likening Nietzsche's explanation of people's beliefs in retributivism (as due to the emotions of *ressentiment*) to an explanation of a perceptual belief in terms of a known illusion or hallucination. Whether there can be such a thing as a moral hallucination or illusion, and if so, whether the emotions of *ressentiment* should be seen as such hallucinating experiences, depends upon an affirmative answer to two questions:

1. Are any emotions epistemically relevant to the truth of moral judgments?
2. If so, is it the virtuous nature of an emotion that tells us whether it has epistemic import?

I shall consider these questions in order.

With respect to the first question, we should distinguish four different views on how the emotions are relevant either to the discovery or to the justification of moral judgments.

1. One is suggested by Kant's famous remarks in the *Groundwork* (1964, pp. 65–67) to the effect that moral worth is found in actions motivated only by reverence for the moral law, not in actions motivated by the inclinations, no matter how benevolent or virtuous. Such a view would make the emotions that generate a moral belief irrelevant to the truth of that belief. Good emotions could as easily generate false beliefs as true ones, and bad emotions could as easily generate true beliefs as false ones. The truth of a moral proposition would be governed solely by reasoning from the categorical imperative or other supreme principle of morality itself discoverable by reason alone, not from any emotional experience.

In this view there is no analogy between the relation of the emotions and moral truth, on the one hand, and the relation of perceptual experiences and scientific truth, on the other. Accordingly, a Kantian about this should find the genetic fallacy objection conclusive when applied to Nietzsche; the lack of virtue of the emotions that generate retributivism has nothing to do with the truth of retributivism because the emotions generally have no epistemic import for the truth of moral judgments. In this view the emotions are relevant neither to justifying a moral judgment as true nor to discovering it to be true.

2. An opposite conclusion about the force of the genetic fallacy objection in this context should be drawn by those who think that the emotions have everything to do with moral truth. This second view about the connection of the emotions to moral truth is the view of the conventionalist (or relativist) about morals. Lord Devlin's writings (1971) on the morality of homosexual behavior provide a convenient example. According to Devlin, homosexual behavior is immoral (and may be legally prohibited) whenever enough people feel deeply enough that it is bad. "It is not nearly enough," Devlin reminds us, "to say that a majority dislike a practice, there must be a real feeling of reprobation. . . . No society can do without intolerance, indignation, and disgust; they are the forces behind the moral law. . ." (p. 40).

In this view, the emotions of a people constitute moral truth. If most people feel deeply enough that a practice is immoral, then it is immoral, in this conventionalist view. This means that if the emotional base for some moral belief is undermined, then necessarily the belief cannot be true. If Nietzsche, for example, can show that the emotions that generate retributivist beliefs are contaminated, then necessarily retributivism is not morally right.

How could Devlin admit the possibility of this kind of undermining of the emotional base of retributivism, given the total absence of reason checking emotion in his conventionalist view of morals? For someone like Devlin, after all, morals just *are* feelings shared by a majority. Yet such majority feelings can be changed if that majority can be emotionally repelled by a subset of its own emotions. And if enough people are repelled enough by the Nietzschean case against *ressentiment,* then the retributive urge must be excluded from those conventions of shared feelings that constitute morality.

This conventionalist view about morality results in there being no genetic fallacy objection to be interposed against Nietzsche. To attack the emotional base of retributivism would be to attack retributivism itself.

Yet such a strong epistemic connection of the emotions to moral truth cannot be sustained. That a large percentage of Americans, perhaps a majority, have feelings of disgust, fear, and hatred of gays does not end a moral inquiry into the truth or falsity of the proposition that gays may be discriminated against, in housing, employment, or elsewhere. A person seeking to arrive at the truth about just treatment for minorities cannot accept his or her own emotional reactions as settling the issue (nor, more obviously, can the person accept the emotional reactions of others). Each must judge for himself or herself whether those emotions are harbingers of moral insight or whether they are the "hallucinations" of the emotional life that must be discarded in our search for the truth. The same, of course, is true for our sense perceptions vis-à-vis scientific truths. Sticks may look bent when partly immersed in water, but that does not mean that they really are bent. Our sense perception is not veridical, and there is no reason to suppose that our emotions are any better guarantors of knowledge.

3. This analogy of the emotions to sensory perception suggests a third way of thinking of the epistemic connection of the emotions to morality, a conception that is also, unfortunately, misleading. This is the route of intuitionism. An intuitionist, as I am here using the word, believes that the emotions stand to moral judgment in a relation exactly analogous to the relation between perceptual experience and scientific judgment. For an intuitionist, the analogy is only an analogy, however, for such a person sees morals and science as distinct realms of knowledge, each with their own distinct experiential base. Such an intuitionist will usually be a metaphysical dualist, believing that such distinct modes of knowing must imply that there are distinct modes of being. (An example of this is how introspectionism goes hand in hand with dualism in the philosophy of mind.)

In any case, the intuitionist will regard emotions as crucial to morals, for they are the data from which moral theory is constructed. Without the emotions generating intuitions, there could be no moral insight, for this kind of intuitionist. An intuitionist is not committed to the emotions being veridical; indeed, to maintain the parallel to sensory perception, the intuitionist should say that the felt justice of punishing for its own sake is *good evidence* that it is just to punish for its own sake, but allow that the inference could be mistaken.

4. I must confess there is much in the intuitionist's account that I find tempting. Still, the dead ends of dualistic metaphysics and the lumpy epistemology of discrete cognitive realms is sufficient reason to avoid intuitionism and nonnaturalism in ethics, as it is to avoid introspectionism and dualism in psychology (Moore, 1985, 1987). We can avoid this metaphysical and epistemological lumpiness by thinking of the emotions as heuristic guides to moral insight, but not as the experience out of which moral theory is constructed. In this view, moral knowledge does not rest on its own unique experiential base, the emotions. Such a view could even concede the empiricist idea that all knowledge (moral knowledge included) rests on sensory experience and the inferences drawable from it.

Consider a judgment that another is morally culpable for some harm. An intuitionist would view culpability as a special kind of property not observable by the senses (a "nonnatural" property), and known only by that special faculty of intuition provided by our emotional life. I think, on the contrary, that culpability is not a property in some special realm. True, we cannot see it but must infer its existence from other properties, such as voluntariness of action, accountability, intention, causation, lack of excuse or justification. But then we cannot see those properties either. We infer the existence of an intention in another from behavioral clues; we do not see causal relations, but infer their existence as well. Culpability is no less a natural property of persons than is intentionality, voluntariness, and so on; none are visible properties, all must be inferred from other evidence. Yet these facts do not demand a special mode of existence, and a special mode of knowing, for any of such properties (see my response to Mackie's well-known "queerness" objection in Moore, 1982a).

If we think of (moral) properties such as culpability in this way, then the emotions are not strictly necessary for there to be moral knowledge. We can imagine a being who could make correct inferences about culpability, as about other things such as intentionality, even if he or she were devoid of any relevant emotional life. True, the being would not *feel* about, for example, justice as we feel about it; yet he or she could know injustice, in the sense of being able to pick it out, as well as we.

The emotions are thus heuristic guides for us, an extra source of insight into moral truths beyond the knowledge we can gain from sensory and inferential capacities alone. One might think of them as I would think of conscious experience vis-à-vis knowledge of mind: My conscious experience of deciding to get a haircut is one way I can come to know that I intend to get a haircut; yet I or others can come to know that I intend to get a haircut in a variety of other ways, including perhaps someday by physiological measurements. My introspective, "privileged access" is only a heuristic guide to learning about my sensations, intentions, and so on that others do not possess. It is not essential to an intention that I be conscious of it, any more than it is essential to the injustice of an institution that I or others feel negatively toward it. The usual judgments I make about my intentions may be judgments reached by reflection on my conscious deliberative processes, just as my usual judgments about justice may be reached via some strong feelings; but the usual route to knowledge—of minds or morals—is not to be confused with what mental states or moral qualities *are*.

The upshot of this is that our emotions are important but not essential in our reaching moral truths. Contra Kant, there is an epistemic connection between our emotions and morality, but it is neither of the strong connections that conventionalism or intuitionism would posit. In the present context, the payoff of seeing this latter point lies in seeing when we may find some emotions wanting as epistemic indicators of moral truth. It is possible, in this last view, for there to be emotions that are "moral hallucinations," and it is therefore open to a Nietzschean to claim that our retributive inclinations are of this kind.

We come, then, to the second question—is the virtue of possessing an emotion relevant to that emotion's epistemic import? We should begin by being clear about the two different ways in which the emotions may be connected to morality before we inquire into the relation between them. We have hitherto been discussing what I would call the epistemic connection of the emotions to morality, distinguishing strong views of this connection (like Devlin's) from weaker views, such as my own or Kant's. Yet there is another possible way in which morality is related to our emotional life. This is where the emotions are themselves the objects of moral judgment. I call this the substantive connection of morality to the emotions.

The substantive connection can be grasped by reflecting on the judgments we make when we are not concerned with ascribing legal liability. The part of morality that is incorporated into our criminal law is by and large the morality of will and reason, by virtue of which we make the crudest of responsibility ascriptions. Voluntariness of action, accountability, intentionality, causation, justification, and excuse are the primary categories in terms of which we

judge someone as morally culpable and thus legally punishable (Moore, 1984, chap. 2). Compare the less legalistic moral judgments we make in daily life: We often think of ourselves or others as more or less virtuous, depending on what emotions we feel on what occasions (Lyons, 1980; Dent, 1984). We make judgments, in other words, not just about the wrong actions a bad person wills, but also about the evil emotions a bad person feels. As Bernard Williams (1973, p. 207) has noted, there is a morality

> . . . about what a man ought or ought not to feel in certain circumstances, or, more broadly, about the ways in which various emotions may be considered as distinctive, mean or hateful, while others appear as creative, generous, admirable, or—merely —such as one would hope for from a decent human being. Considerations like these certainly play a large part in moral thought, except perhaps in that of the most restricted and legalistic kind. . . .

Consider a person who feels little or no compassion for others less fortunate. This person's behavior need not be that of a scrooge—he may do all the morally acceptable things, such as donate to charities, help blind persons across the street, not inflict needless suffering, and so on. Yet he does such things out of a priggish concern for propriety, including the propriety he attains by having a good opinion of himself. He does not feel any compassion for the objects of his charity; indeed, he regards them as inferior beings who exist for him mainly to be the objects of his virtue. Such a person is morally inferior to—less virtuous than—another whose actions may be no better but whose emotional life includes compassion (Blum, 1980).

Contrast this collection of the emotions and morality with the epistemic connection. Staying with the example of compassion: We may take our feelings of compassion for some disadvantaged persons to be the harbingers of a moral insight about what that group deserves. Suppose you travel to India and find the poverty of many Indians to be distressing. You might take that feeling of compassion to be the originator of a moral insight about the nature of distributive justice—namely, that the geographic limits you had previously observed in applying some ideal of distributive justice seem arbitrary, a matter of political expediency at best. In such a case, the emotional experience of compassion may generate a firm moral conviction that distributive justice knows no political boundaries or geographical limits, but extends to all persons.

The epistemic connection of the emotions to morality is quite different from the substantive connection. With the latter, we judge the emotions as virtuous or not; the emotions in such a case are the object of moral evaluation. With the former, we are not seeking to judge the moral worth of an emotion as a virtue; rather, we seek to learn from such emotions the correct moral judgments to make about some other institution, practice, act, or agent.

Having distinguished the two connections of morality to the emotions, it remains to inquire whether there is not some relation between them. One wishing to use Nietzsche's kind of insights to attack retributivism, and yet escape the genetic fallacy objection, must assert that there is some such relation. The idea is that we use our own virtue in possessing an emotion as the touchstone of whether that emotion is "hallucinatory" or not: If the possession of an emotion makes us more virtuous, then that emotion is a good heuristic for coming to moral judgments that are true; if the possession of an emotion makes us less virtuous, then that emotion is a good heuristic for coming to moral judgments that are false. This possibility, of course, would complete the antiretributivist's answer to the genetic fallacy charge. For then the vice of possessing the emotions of *ressentiment* gives us good reason to suppose that the moral judgments to which those emotions give rise—namely, retributive judgments—are false.

This is possible, but what reason do we have to think that such a connection—between the judge's virtue, and the truth of the judgment he or she is making—holds? Counterexamples certainly spring to mind; consider two of them.

1. As Herbert Morris has examined . . . there is such a thing as nonmoral guilt. Think, for example, of the guilt one might feel at having made a tragic choice: There were only two options, neither happy ones, and one chose to do the lesser evil. Using Philippa Foot's much-discussed example: A railroad switchman can only turn a moving trolley car onto one line or another, but he cannot stop it; he chooses to turn the car onto the line where only one trapped workman will be killed; on the other line, five workmen were trapped and would have been killed had the trolley car gone their way. The switchman is not morally culpable in directing the trolley on the line where only one workman would be killed. The alternative being even worse, the switchman was justified in doing what he did. Still

the switchman should feel regret, remorse, and even guilt at killing the one workman. The switchman who experiences such emotions is a more virtuous person than one who has a "don't cry over what can't be helped" attitude toward the whole affair.

If both moral judgments are right—the switchman is not culpable (guilty), but his feeling guilty is virtuous—then we cannot say that the emotions that make us virtuous are necessarily the emotions that are good heuristic guides to moral truth. For if the latter were true, this switchman's (virtuous) feeling guilty should mean that the associated judgment, "I am guilty," is true; but it is not.

2. Just as some emotions are virtuous even though their associated judgments are not true, so some emotions that are not virtuous to possess may nonetheless spawn judgments that are true. Think of the institution of private property and its Lockean justifications in terms of the exercised liberty of one who mixes her labor with a thing. I think that the Lockean judgment, "she deserves the property right because she created the thing in the first place," to be true when applied to a novelist seeking copyright protections for a novel. Yet I also think that the emotions that are my heuristic guide to that judgment are suspect, at the least, in their enhancement of my virtue.

For are not the emotions that call to mind Lockean intuitions about deserved property entitlements essentially selfish emotions that make us worse for possessing them? (See E.M. Forster, 1936, pp. 22–26; Becker, 1977, p. 96). We are entitled, from what we have done, to exclude others from the enjoyment of the products of our labor. My intuition is that this is true, but I am not proud of the selfish emotions that generate this intuition. They seem to consist too much of pride and self-congratulation to be virtues. To me at least, the nonvirtuous nature of the emotional base of Lockean property theories does not make me doubt their truth; it would be unfair to deprive another of the products of his or her labor, however much it would be better if we (and the other) did not beat our chests so much about our own accomplishments.

These examples are perhaps controversial, but I doubt that the point they illustrate is. The virtue (or lack of it) in the possession of our emotion is not an infallible guide to the epistemic import such as emotion may possess.

Is the first even a *fallible* guide to the second? A defender of retributivism might well think not. Such a person might compare the situation in science: What is the relevance, he or she might ask, of the virtue of a perceptual experience (say one induced by drugs) to the epistemic import of such an experience? What possible reason is there to think that the moral worth of a visual experience will correlate with its epistemic import? Tripping on LSD and looking at pornography may be equally lacking in virtue, but only one of them is likely to produce untrue beliefs about, for example, anatomical features of human beings.

Yet what if we substituted an example where the virtue in question is not so obviously removed from the truth of any scientific judgments? Suppose we focused on what might be called the "virtues of a scientist," traits such as analytical capacity, creativity, curiosity, being careful, and ambition. It is not nearly so implausible to think that beliefs produced through the exercise of these traits are more likely true, and that those produced by the analytically dull, the plodding, the mechanical, the careless or the lazy are more likely false.

Similarly, in ethics we should recognize that the virtue of (or vice) of an emotion may often, but not always, be taken as an indication of the truth (or falsity) of the judgment to which it leads. Indeed, would it not be remarkable to think that one could arrive at the judgments about science or morals only through emotions or traits that made one morally odious? Although not contradictory, it would surely be an oddly cohering morality that valued, say, equal treatment and also extolled the virtue of those prejudiced attitudes that typically produce discriminating judgments. We value moral and scientific truth too highly to think that there could be any virtues so counterproductive to the attainment of truth.

In any case, what other criterion could there be for the epistemic reliability of the emotions? If such reliability had nothing to do with the virtue of such emotions, what would be our test? Rawls (1971, p. 48) suggests that we look to those "conditions favorable for deliberation and judgment in general" when we seek to isolate those "considered judgments" that in reflective equilibrium justify his two principles of justice. Which conditions are these?

[We] can discard those judgments made with hesitation, or in which we have little confidence. Similarly, those given when we are upset or frightened, or when we stand to gain one way or the other can be left aside. All these judgments are likely to be erroneous or to be influenced by an excessive attention to our own interests. (p. 47; see also Copp, 1984)

Yet this test is too dispassionate, too judicial. Rawls's test for *judgments* that have epistemic import cannot be turned into a test for *emotions* because Rawls, like Kant, pretty much ignores the emotional base of moral judgment.

If we look in this way for a purely cognitive test for when emotions are epistemically reliable, my suspicion is that we will always end up slighting the role of the emotions in generating moral insight. We will do this because a purely cognitive test will inevitably seek to derive a criterion of epistemic warrant that is independent of any theory generated from the emotions themselves. It is like attempting to set up a criterion of epistemic warrant for perceptual experiences without using any theory derived from such experiences. Yet surely in science we do not expect to have to come up with some prescientific test for the epistemic import of sensory experience *before* we meld those experiences into a scientific theory. Rather, we rely on the body of scientific theory itself to justify exclusions of experience from the data. It is because we know what we do about optics that leads us to discount the illusion that a stick partly immersed in water looks bent; it is because we know what we do about drugs, mental disease, sensory deprivation, and the like, that we discount hallucinatory perceptual experiences. In science we quite literally explain such experiences away by using the very theories of which such experiences are part of the data. We are entitled to make the parallel move in ethics, so that our substantive moral theories—not some pale, preliminary, judicial, nonmoral litmus test—give us the criteria for weeding out emotions with misleading epistemic import. Those substantive theories of what justice is, for example, make it very unlikely that prejudice could be a virtue, or that compassion could not.

The upshot of all of this is that the genetic fallacy objection with which we began this section is inconclusive when interposed by the retributivist against the Nietzschean analysis of the retributive urge. If Nietzsche is right in asserting that our retributive beliefs are always motivated by the emotions of *ressentiment,* and right that the possession of those emotions makes us less virtuous, then we have grounds to reject retributivism as a philosophy of punishment. True, such a Nietzschean argument could not be a knockdown winner—from what has been said, it is possible that the nonvirtuous emotions of *ressentiment* nonetheless generate true moral judgments about what wrongdoers deserve. Yet this would have to be established by justifying the retributive principle in some way other than by showing it to be the best expression of our more particular judgments about criminals. Without such independent justification of retributivism, Nietzsche gives us reason to believe the retributive principle to be false when he shows us how lacking in virtue are the emotions that generate retributive judgments. For without such an independent justification, here as elsewhere we are entitled to rely on the connection that generally (but not inevitably) holds between the virtue in possessing an emotion and the truth of the judgment that that emotion generates.

The Correctness of Retributive Judgments

As previewed in the first part of this chapter, there are two justificatory routes a coherentist might use in justifying retributivism. First, because of the Nietzschean attack on the retributive urge, a retributivist might abandon the justificatory route that begins with our particular judgments about punishment in individual cases, and instead focus on how retributivism is justified because of its coherence with other, more general moral beliefs we are prepared to accept. He or she might show how there is an odd lacunae in our moral judgments about desert if the retributive principle is not accepted. That is, when passing out rewards, the desert of those whose labor produced them is (for Lockeans) both a necessary and a sufficient condition for allocating a property entitlement in them. The presence of such desert justifies giving the reward to them; the absence of such desert justifies withholding it from them. Similarly, when passing out legal duties to pay for harms caused, the culpability of he or she who caused the harm and the lack of culpability of he or she who suffers the harm, is (in standard corrective justice theories) both necessary and sufficient to justify tort liability. It is only with punishment that we have an asymmetry; namely (as even most nonretributivists will assert), that desert is a necessary condition of punishment, but not sufficient by itself to justify punishment.

Such an asymmetry does not by itself render a deontologist's social theory incoherent if he or she rejects retributivism (although it might if one isolated a general principle of just deserts common to corrective justice, property allocations, and retributive justice). My only point here is that if there were such incoherence without retributivism, the latter would be justified even if the retributive urge is unworthy

of us. Nothing in the Nietzschean case against retributivism could prevent this. Still, since my approach is to justify retributivism by using our more particular judgments about punishment, I need to take seriously the Nietzschean case against those judgments.

The problem with the Nietzschean case against retributivism does not lie, as we have seen, in its presupposition that generally there is a strong connection between virtuous emotions and true moral judgments, vices and false moral judgments. The real problem for the Nietzschean critic is to show that retributive judgments are *inevitably* motivated by the black emotions of *ressentiment*. For if the critic cannot show this, then much of the contamination of those particular judgments is lifted. It is lifted because the retributive judgment would then not arise out of the kind of moral hallucination nonvirtuous emotions typically represent; rather, the retributive judgment would be only the vehicle for the expression of the emotions of *ressentiment*—dangerous for that reason, but not lacking in epistemic import for that reason.

Consider an analogy in meta ethics. The position I have defended elsewhere (Moore, 1982a), moral realism, is an admittedly dangerous view about which to proselytize. It is dangerous because many people use moral realism as a vehicle to express intolerance and contempt for autonomy. Many people may even accept moral realism because it seems to them to have this potential for intolerant imperialism against the differing moral beliefs of others. Yet these psychological facts, to my mind, constitute no argument against the truth of moral realism. They do not because I am able to separate moral realism from intolerance: logically I see that a moral realist can defend tolerance, pluralism, and autonomy as much (more?) as anyone, and psychologically I do not see any inevitability in my moral realist views being motivated by intolerance. Making these separations, the fact that many people use moral realism to express their intolerance—or even are motivated to moral realist beliefs by their intolerance—loses any epistemic sting. It makes me cautious about holding forth about moral realism with intolerant audiences, but it does not give me reason to be cautious about the truth of moral realism.

As much seems to me to be true about retributivism. I shall make the argument in three steps: First, that the inevitability of linking *ressentiment* emotions to retributive judgments is weakened when one notes, as Nietzsche himself did, that *anti-*retributive judgments are also often motivated by some of those same nonvirtuous emotions; second, that in our own individual cases we can imagine being motivated to make retributive judgments by the virtuous emotions of guilt and fellow feeling; and third, that because punishment is a social institution, unlike private vengeance, it can help us to control the emotions retributive punishment expresses by controlling the aspects of punishment that all too easily allow it to express *ressentiment*.

1. A paraphrase of Zarathustra, of which Nietzsche no doubt would have approved, would be that we should beware all those in whom the urge to punish is either actually, or claimed to be, nonexistent. As Nietzsche does tell us:

> if you are cursed, I do not like it that you want to bless. Rather, join a little in the cursing. And if you have been done a great wrong, then quickly add five little ones: a gruesome sight is a person single-mindedly obsessed by a wrong. . . . A wrong shared is half right. . . . A little revenge is more human than no revenge. (*Zarathrustra, p. 180*)

Everyone gets angry when their bodily integrity or other important interests are violated by another. If they care about other human beings, they are vicariously injured when someone close to them—or distant, depending on the reach of their empathy—is wronged. It is human to feel such anger at wrongful violation, and Nietzsche's thought is that not to express the anger in some retaliation is a recipe for *ressentiment* itself.

One might of course think that retaliation is a second best solution; better not to feel the anger at all so that the choice of expressing it in action, or of repressing it into the subtle revenge of pity, is not necessary (see Horney, 1948, p. 3). Leaving aside whether such willing away of anger is possible, is it desirable? While it has a saintly ring to it to turn the other cheek so long as it is one's own cheek that has just been slapped, is it virtuous to feel nothing stronger than sympathy for the suffering of others at the hands of wrongdoers? Where is that compassionate concern for others that is outraged because another person could have so unnecessarily caused such suffering?

Karen Horney concluded that "[t]he vindictive person thus is egocentric . . . because he has more or less severed his emotional relations to other human beings" (1948, p. 12). Yet isn't this even more often true of one who feels anger only when he himself suffers at the hands of a wrongdoer, not when others

suffer? An egocentric lack of compassion for others may explain the antiretributivist, forgiving attitude as easily as it may explain the desire for vengeance.

Sometimes the compassion for victims is not absent, but gets transferred to the person who is now about to suffer; namely, the wrongdoer. Such a transfer of compassion is not justified by the relative merits of the two classes of persons, unless we are to think that there is some reason to prefer wrongdoers to victims as the appropriate objects of compassion. "Out of sight, out of mind" is the reason that suggests itself, but this psychological tendency can hardly justify forgetting those who have suffered at the hands of others. My own view is that such a transfer of concern from victim to criminal occurs in large part because of our unwillingness to face our own revulsion at what was done (Gaylin, 1983, p. 123). It allows us to look away from the horror that another person was willing to cause.

We almost cannot bear the sight. We invent for the wrongdoers a set of excusing conditions that we would not tolerate for a moment in ourselves. When they transgress, virtuous people know how ill it lies to "excuse" themselves by pointing to their own childhood or past, their lack of parental love, their need for esteem, and other causes (Moore, 1985a). Virtuous people do not use the childish "something made me do it" because they know that that denies their essential freedom in bringing about some harm. They know that they did it, chose to do it, caused though that choice surely was by factors themselves unchosen. Yet we cannot stand to apply to criminals the same standard of responsibility that we apply to ourselves because we cannot stand to acknowledge that there is such a thing as evil in the world—and, worst of all, that it is not "inhuman" but a part of creatures not so different from ourselves. Lack of anger at criminals, if it does not represent simple indifference to the sufferings of others, may represent our self-deception about the potential for evil in humanity.

Such lack of anger may also represent the same fear of criminals that can motivate retributive judgments. Nietzsche:

> There is a point in the history of society when it becomes so pathologically soft and tender that among other things it sides even with those who harm it, criminals, and does this quite seriously and honestly. Punishing somehow seems unfair to it, and it is certain that imagining "punishment" and "being supposed to punish" hurts it, arouses fear in it.

"It is not enough to render him *undangerous*?
Why still punish? Punishing itself is terrible."
With this question, herd morality, the morality
of timidity, draws its ultimate consequence.
. . . The imperative of herd timidity: "We want
that some day there should be *nothing any-
more to be afraid of!*" (*Beyond Good and
Evil*, p. 114)

By repressing anger at wrongful violation, we may
be attempting to deny that we live in a society in
which there really are fearful and awful people.

Yet again, our transfer of fellow-feeling from
victim to criminal, and its accompanying elimination
of anger, may represent something other than indifference or inability to face evil or our own fears. It
may represent a narcissism that is itself no virtue. A
criminal, after all, represents an opportunity to exercise (and display, a separate point) one's virtue. The
virtue in question is compassion for someone now
threatened with harm. Yet such egoistic compassion
becomes something other than compassion. It becomes just what Nietzsche said it becomes, the elevation of self by pity. Remarkably, one can lose
compassionate concern for another by the self-
conscious egoistic caricature of compassion we distinguish as pity. In pity we do not care about the
other any more for his own sake, but only insofar as
he allows *us* to become, in our own and others' eyes,
better. We should beware, to adopt yet another paraphrase of Nietzsche, this one by Philippa Foot (1973,
p. 168), all those who find others best when they find
them most in need. We should beware of them because such people lack precisely the ability to feel
that compassion whose outward form they ape.

2. Resentment, indifference to others, self-
deception, fear, cowardice, and pity are not virtues.
They do not perhaps add up to the witches' brew of
a full batch of the *ressentiment* emotions, but to the
extent they motivate antiretributive judgments, they
make such judgments suspect. If one accepts, as
Nietzsche did, that both retributive and antiretributive judgments are often motivated by, or at least expressions of, nonvirtuous emotions, where does that
leave us? It should leave us asking whether we cannot make our judgments about punishment in such
a way that they are not motivated by either set of
unworthy emotions.

When we make a retributive judgment—such
as that Stephen Judy deserved the death penalty for
his rape-murder of a young mother and his murder
of her three children—we need not be motivated by

the *ressentiment* emotions. Nor is the alternative some
abstract, Kantian concern for justice, derived by reason alone and unsullied by any strong emotional origin. Our concern for retributive justice might be
motivated by very deep emotions that are nonetheless of a wholly virtuous nature. These are the feelings of guilt we would have if we did the kinds of
acts that fill the criminal appellate reports of any state.

The psychiatrist Willard Gaylin interviewed a
number of people closely connected to the brutal
hammering death of Bonnie Garland by her jilted
boyfriend, Richard Herrin. He asked a number of
those in a Christian order that had been particularly
forgiving of Richard whether they could imagine
themselves performing such an act under any set of
circumstances. Their answer was uniformly "Yes."
All of us can at least find it conceivable that there
might be circumstances under which we could perform an act like Herrin's—not exactly the same, perhaps, but something pretty horrible. All of us do
share this much of our common nature with the
worst of criminals. (For those with a greater we–they
attitude toward criminals, the thought experiment
that follows must be run with a somewhat less horrible act than Richard's.)

Then ask yourself: What would you feel like if
it was you who had intentionally smashed open the
skull of a 23-year-old woman with a claw hammer
while she was asleep, a woman whose fatal defect
was a desire to free herself from your too clinging
embrace? My own response, I hope, would be that I
would feel guilty unto death. I couldn't imagine any
suffering that could be imposed upon me that would
be unfair because it exceeded what I deserved.

Is that virtuous? Such deep feelings of guilt
seem to me to be the only tolerable response of a
moral being. "Virtue" is perhaps an odd word in the
context of extreme culpability, but such guilt seems,
at the least, very appropriate. One ought to feel so
guilty one wants to die. Such sickness unto death is
to my mind more virtuous than the nonguilty state to
which Richard Herrin brought himself, with some
help from Christian counseling about the need for
self-forgiveness. After three years of prison on an
eight- to twenty-five-year sentence for "heat of passion" manslaughter, Richard thought he had suffered
quite enough for the killing of Bonnie:

HERRIN: I feel the sentence was excessive.
 Gaylin: Let's talk about that a little.
HERRIN: Well, I feel that way now and after the first
           years. The judge had gone overboard. . . .

Considering all the factors that I feel the judge should have considered: prior history of arrest, my personality background, my capacity for a productive life in society—you know, those kinds of things—I don't think he took those into consideration. He looked at the crime itself and responded to a lot of public pressure or maybe his own personal feelings, I don't know. I'm not going to accuse him of anything, but I was given the maximum sentence. This being my first arrest and considering the circumstances, I don't think I should have been given eight to twenty-five years.

GAYLIN: What do you think would have been a fair sentence?

HERRIN: Well, after a year or two in prison, I felt that was enough. . . .

GAYLIN: How would you answer the kind of person who says, for Bonnie, it's her whole life; for you it's eight years. What's eight years compared to the more years she might have had?

HERRIN: I can't deny that it's grossly unfair to Bonnie but there's nothing I can do about it. . . .

She's gone—I can't bring her back. I would rather that she had survived as a complete person, but she didn't. I'm not, again . . . I'm not saying that I shouldn't have been punished, but the punishment I feel is excessive. I feel I have five more years to go, and I feel that's just too much. There's no . . . I don't see any purpose in it. It's sad what happened, but it's even sadder to waste another life. I feel I'm being wasted in here.

GAYLIN: But what about the people who say, Look, if you got two years, then someone who robs should get only two days. You know, the idea of commensurate punishment. If it is a very serious crime it has to be a very serious punishment. Are you saying two years of prison is a very serious punishment considering what you did?

HERRIN: For me, yes.[3]

Compared to such shallow, easily obtained self-absolution for a horrible violation of another, a deep sense of guilt looks very virtuous indeed.

To be sure, there is an entire tradition that regards guilt as a useless passion (see Kaufmann, 1973). For one thing, it is always backward-looking rather than allowing one to get on with life. For another, it betrays an indecision that Nietzsche among others found unattractive: "The bite of conscience is indecent," Nietzsche thought (*Twilight,* p. 467), because it betrays the earlier decision about which one feels guilty. Yet Nietzsche and his followers are simply wrong here. Guilt feelings are often a virtue precisely because they do look to the past. As Herbert Morris (1976, p. 108) has argued, morality itself—including the morality of good character—has to take the past seriously. The alternative, of not crying over spilt milk (or blood), is truly indecent. A moral being *feels* guilty when he or she *is* guilty of past wrongs.

The virtue of feeling guilty is not raised so that punishment can be justified by its capacity to induce guilt. That is a possible retributive theory of punishment—a kind of moral rehabilitative theory—but it is not mine (see Morris, 1981). Rather, the virtue of our own imagined guilt is relevant because of the general connection between the virtue of an emotion and its epistemic import. We should trust what our imagined guilt feelings tell us; for acts like those of Richard Herrin, that if we did them we would be so guilty that some extraordinarily severe punishment would be deserved. We should trust the judgments such imagined guilt feelings spawn because nonneurotic guilt, unlike *ressentiment,* comes with good epistemic credentials.

Next, we need to be clear just what judgments it is that our guilt feelings validate in this way. First and foremost, to *feel* guilty causes the judgment that we *are* guilty, in the sense that we are morally culpable. Second, such guilt feelings typically engender the judgment that we deserve punishment. I mean this not only in the weak sense of desert—that it would not be unfair to be punished—but also and more important in the strong sense that we *ought* to be punished.

One might think that this second judgment of desert (in either its weak or its strong sense) is uncalled for by our feelings of guilt, that the judgment to which our guilt feelings lead is the judgment that we ought to repair as best we can the damage we have done. Such a view would justify corrective justice theories of punishment, but not retributive theories. Yet I think that this puts too nice a face on our guilt feelings. They do not generate only a judgment that we ought to make amends in this compensatory way. Rather—and this is what troubles many critics of guilt as an emotion—to feel guilty is to judge that we must suffer. We can see this plainly if we imagine ourselves having made provisions for Bonnie's family, comforting them in any way possible, and then feeling that our debt for killing her has been paid. It is so clear that such corrective actions do *not* satisfy guilt that to feel that they do is not to have felt guilty to begin with.

Our feelings of guilt thus generate a judgment that we deserve the suffering that is punishment. If the feelings of guilt are virtuous to possess, we have reason to believe that this last judgment is correct, generated as it is by emotions whose epistemic import is not in question.

Last, we should ask whether there is any reason not to make the same judgment about Richard Herrin's actual deserts as we are willing to make about our own hypothetical deserts. If we experience any reluctance to transfer the guilt and desert *we* would possess, had we done what Richard Herrin did, to Herrin himself, we should examine that reluctance carefully. Doesn't it come from feeling more of a person than Richard? We are probably not persons who grew up in the barrio of East Los Angeles, or who found Yale an alien and disorienting culture. In any case, we certainly have never been subject to the exact same stresses and motivations as Richard Herrin. Therefore, it may be tempting to withhold from Richard the benefit each of us gives himself or herself: the benefit of being the subjective seat of a will that, although caused, is nonetheless capable of both choice and responsibility (Moore, 1985a).

Such discrimination is a temptation to be resisted, because it is no virtue. It is elitist and condescending toward others not to grant them the same responsibility and desert you grant to yourself. Admittedly, there are excuses the benefit of which others as well as yourself may avail themselves. Yet that is not the distinction invoked here. Herrin had no excuse the rest of us could not come up with in terms of various causes for our choices. To refuse to grant him the same responsibility and desert as you would grant yourself is thus an instance of what Sartre called bad faith, the treating of a free, subjective will as an object (see also Strawson, 1968). It is a refusal to admit that the rest of humanity shares with us that which makes us most distinctively human, our capacity to will and reason—and thus to be and do evil. Far from evincing fellow feeling and the allowing of others to participate in our moral life, it excludes them as less than persons.

Rather than succumbing to this elitism masquerading as egalitarianism, we should ask ourselves what Herrin deserves by asking what *we* would de-

serve had we done such an act. In answering this question we should listen to our guilt feelings, feelings whose epistemic import is not in question in the same way as are those of *ressentiment*. Such guilt feelings should tell us that to do an act like Herrin's is to forfeit forever any lighthearted idea of going on as before. One should feel so awful that the idea of again leading a life unchanged from before, with the same goals and hopes and happiness, should appear revoltingly incomprehensible.[4]

3. It is admittedly not an easy task to separate the emotions one feels, and then in addition, discriminate which of them is the cause of one's retributive judgments. We can no more choose which emotion it will be that causes our judgments or actions than we can choose the reason for which we act. We can choose whether to act or not and whether to judge one way or another, but we cannot make it be true that some particular reason or emotion caused our action or our judgment. We must look inward as best we can to detect, but not to will, which emotions bring about our judgments; and here there is plenty of room for error and self-deception.

When we move from our judgments about the justice of retribution in the abstract, however, to the justice of a social institution that exists to exact retribution, perhaps we can gain some greater clarity. For if we recognize the dangers retributive punishment presents for the expression of resentment, sadism, and so on, we have every reason to design our punishment institutions to minimize the opportunity for such feelings to be expressed. There is no contradiction in attempting to make a retributive punishment system humane; doing so allows penitentiaries to be faithful to their names—places for penance, not excuses for sadism, prejudice, hatred, and the like.

Even the old biblical injunction—"Vengeance is mine, saith the Lord"—has something of this insight behind it. Retributive punishment is dangerous for individual persons to carry out, dangerous to their virtue and, because of that, unclear in its justification. But implicit in the biblical injunction is a promise that retribution will be exacted. For those like myself who are not theists, that cleansing function must be performed by the state, not God. If the state can perform such a function, it removes from retributive punishment, not the guilt, as Nietzsche (*Genealogy,* p. 95) and Sartre (1955) have it, but the ressentiment.

1. "Moral culpability" as I am here using the phrase does not presuppose that the act done is morally bad, only that it is legally prohibited. An actor is culpable in this conception when, in doing an action violating some criminal prohibition, he or she satisfies those conditions of fair fault ascription. On this, see Moore (1985b), pp. 14–15. Usually, of course, most serious crimes are also serious moral breaches.

2. Excerpt from *The Urge to Punish* by Henry Weihofen. Copyright © 1956 by Henry Weihofen. Reprinted by permission of Farrar, Straus and Giroux, Inc.

3. From W. Gaylin, *The Killing of Bonnie Garland*, pp. 325–27. Copyright © 1982 by Pip Enterprises, Inc. Reprinted by permission of Simon & Schuster, Inc.

4. One may have noticed that the thought experiment just concluded has six steps to it. It is perhaps helpful to separate them explicitly: (1) The psychological presupposition that it is possible to engage in the thought experiment at all—that we can imagine we could do an act like Richard Herrin's. (2) The psychological question of what we would feel if we did such an action—guilty and deserving of punishment. (3) The moral question of the virtue of that feeling—that guilt is a virtuous emotion to feel when we have done such a wrongful act. (4) The psychological question of what judgments are typically caused by the emotions of guilt—the judgments that we are guilty (culpable) and that we deserve to be punished. (5) The moral question of the correctness of the first person judgment that we deserve to be punished—as an inference drawn from the virtue of the emotion of guilt that spawns such a judgment. (6) The moral question of the correctness of the third person judgment that Richard Herrin deserves to be punished—as an inference drawn from the fact that we would deserve to be punished if we had done the act that Herrin did. One might believe that the thought experiment requires a seventh step—namely, that the state ought to punish those who deserve it. And in terms of a complete justification of a retributive theory of punishment, this last step is a necessary one. My aim throughout this paper has been more limited: to validate particular judgments, such as that Stephen Judy deserved the death penalty. The thought experiment is designed to get us only this far, leaving for further argument (hinted at in the text that closes this section) that the state has the right and the duty to set up institutions which give persons their just deserts.

References

Beccaria

1964: *On Crimes and Punishments* (J. Grigson, trans.), in A. Manzoni (ed.), *The Column of Infamy* (Oxford: Oxford University Press.)

Becker, L.

1977: *Property Rights* (London: Routledge and Kegan Paul).

Bedau, H.

1978: "Retribution and the Theory of Punishment," *Journal of Philosophy,* Vol. 75: 601–20.

Benn, S. I. and Peters, R. S.

1959: *Social Principles and the Democratic State* (London: Allen and Unwin).

Blum, L.

1980: "Compassion," in A. Rorty (ed.), *Explaining Emotions* (Berkeley and Los Angeles: University of California Press).

Calhoun, C.

1984: Cognitive Emotions?" in C. Calhoun and R. Soloman (eds.), *What Is an Emotion?* (Oxford: Oxford University Press).

Copp, D.

1984: "Considered Judgments and Moral Justification: Conservatism in Moral Theory," in D. Copp and D. Zimmerman (eds.), *Morality, Reason and Truth* (Totowa, NJ: Rowman and Allenheld).

Danto, A.

1965: *Nietzsche as Philosopher* (New York: Macmillan).

Dent, M.

1984: *The Moral Psychology of the Virtues* (Cambridge: Cambridge University Press).

Devlin, P.

1971: "Morals and the Criminal Law," in R. Wasserstrom (ed.), *Morality and the Law* (Belmont, CA: Wadsworth).

Feinberg, J.

1971: "The Expressive Function of Punishment," in his *Doing and Deserving* (Princeton, NJ: Princeton University Press).

Fingarette, H.

1977: "Punishment and Suffering," *Proc. Amer. Phil. Assoc.,* Vol. 50: 499–525.

1955: "Psychoanalytic Perspectives on Moral Guilt and Responsibility: A Re-evaluation," *Philos. and Phenomenological Research,* Vol. 16: 18–36.

Foot, P.

1973: "Nietzsche: The Revaluation of Values," in R. Solomon (ed.), *Nietzsche: A Collection of Critical Essays* (Garden City, NY: Doubleday Anchor Books).

Forster, E. M.

1921: *Howards End* (New York: Knopf).

1936:
"My Woods," in his *Abinger Harvest* (New York: Harcourt, Brace and World).

Gaylin, W.

1983: *The Killing of Bonnie Garland* (New York: Penguin Books).

Hart, H. L. A.

1968: *Punishment and Responsibility* (Oxford: Oxford University Press).

Hicks, C. E. (ed.)

1925: *Famous American Jury Speeches* (St. Paul, MN: West Publishing).

Honderich, T.

1969: *Punishment: The Supposed Justifications* (London: Hutchinson).

Horney, K.

1948: "The Value of Vindictiveness," *Amer. Journal of Psychoanalysis,* Vol. 8: 3–12.

Jacoby, S.

1984: *Wild Justice: The Evolution of Revenge* (New York: Harper and Row).

Kant, I.

1964: *Groundwork of the Metaphysics of Morals* (Paton trans.) (New York: Harper).

1965: *The Metaphysical Elements of Justice* (J. Ladd trans.) (Indianapolis: Bobbs-Merrill).

Kaufmann, W.

1973: *Without Guilt and Justice* (New York: Dell).

Lyons, W.

1980: *Emotion* (Cambridge: Cambridge University Press).

McCloskey, H. J.

1965: "A Non-Utilitarian Approach to Punishment," *Inquiry,* Vol. 8: 249–63.

Mackie, J.

1982: "Morality and the Retributive Emotions," *Criminal Justice Ethics,* Vol. 1: 3–10.

Marshall, T.

1976: Concurring in *Gregg v. Georgia,* 428 U.S. 153.

Menninger, K.

1968: *The Crime of Punishment* (New York: Viking Press).

Moore, M.

1980: "Responsibility and the Unconscious," *Southern California Law Review,* Vol. 53: 1563–675.

1982a: "Moral Reality," *Wisconsin Law Review,* Vol. [1982]: 1061–1156.

1982b: "Closet Retributivism," *USC Cites,* Vol. [Spring–Summer 1982]: 9–16.

1984: *Law and Psychiatry: Rethinking the Relationship* (Cambridge: Cambridge University Press).

1985a: "Causation and the Excuses," *California Law Review,* Vol. 73: 201–59.

1985b: "The Moral and Metaphysical Sources of the Criminal Law," in J. R. Pennock and J. Chapman (eds.), *Nomos XXVII: Criminal Justice* (New York: New York University Press).

1987: "Mind, Brain, and Unconscious," in C. Wright and P. Clark (eds.), *Mind, Psychoanalysis, and Science* (Oxford: Blackwell).

Morris, H.

1976: *On Guilt and Innocence* (Berkeley and Los Angeles: University of California Press).
"Nonmoral Guilt," this volume," Chapter 9.

1981: "A Paternalistic Theory of Punishment," *Amer. Phil. Quarterly,* Vol. 18: 263–71.

Morse, S.

1984: "Justice, Mercy, and Craziness," *Stanford Law Review,* Vol. 36: 1485–1515.

Nietzsche, F.

1966: *Beyond Good and Evil* (Kaufmann, trans.) (New York: Vintage).

1954: *Thus Spoke Zarathustra,* in W. Kaufmann (ed.), *The Portable Nietzsche* (New York: Viking).

1954: *The Dawn,* in W. Kaufmann (ed.), *The Portable Nietzsche* (New York: Viking).

1974: *The Gay Science* (Kaufmann, trans.) (New York: Vintage).

1969: *On the Genealogy of Morals* (Kaufmann, trans.) (New York: Vintage).

1954: *Twilight of the Idols,* in W. Kaufmann (ed.), *The Portable Nietzsche* (New York: Viking).

Quinton, A.

1954: "On Punishment," *Analysis,* Vol. 14: 1933–42.

Rawls, J.

1971: *A Theory of Justice* (Cambridge, MA: Harvard University Press).

Royko, M.

1981: "Nothing Gained by Killing a Killer? Oh Yes, There Is," *Los Angeles Times,* March 13, Sec. II, p. 7.

Sartre, J.-P.

1955: *The Flies,* in *No Exit and Three Other Plays* (New York: Vintage).

Scheler, M.

1961: *Ressentiment* (Holdheim trans.) (New York: Free Press).

Scruton, R.

1980: "Emotion, Practical Knowledge, and Common Culture," in A. Rorty (ed.), *Explaining Emotions* (Berkeley and Los Angeles: University of California Press).

Shklar, J.

1984: *Ordinary Vices* (Cambridge, MA: Harvard University Press).

de Sousa, R.

1980: "The Rationality of the Emotions," in A. Rorty (ed.), *Explaining Emotions* (Berkeley and Los Angeles: University of California Press).

Stephen, Sir James

1967: *Liberty, Equality, Fraternity* (Cambridge: Cambridge University Press).

Strawson, P. F.

1968: "Freedom and Resentment," in his *Studies in the Philosophy of Thought and Action* (Oxford: Oxford University Press).

Weihofen, H.

1956: *The Urge to Punish* (New York: Farrar, Straus and Cudahy).

Williams, B.

1973: "Morality and the Emotions," in his *Problems of Self* (Cambridge: Cambridge University Press).

Wilson, J. and Herrnstein, R.

1985: *Crime and Human Nature* (New York: Simon and Schuster).

THE FAILURE OF RETRIBUTIVISM*

Russ Shafer-Landau

Three concerns lie at the heart of any justification of punishment. The first is one of general justifying aim: why license punishment as the appropriate response to wrongdoing, as opposed to (say) restitution, therapy or exile? This question is properly distinguished from questions of amount (how much to punish) and liability (which kinds of behavior we ought to sanction). A comprehensive theory would be able to supply a single moral principle or a small set of such principles as the basis for providing an integrated response to these three questions. I believe that retributivism must fail as a comprehensive theory, because it cannot satisfactorily answer any one of them.

I. Liability

Standardly, retributivists have begun their account of penal liability by insisting that legal guilt should be predicated on moral guilt. However, retributivists have had difficulty moving beyond this limiting condition and fleshing out a full account of criminal liability. Things would be economical if retributivists could defend the claim that commission of a moral wrong is both necessary and sufficient for criminal proscription. But it might not even be necessary.[1] And it's certainly not sufficient; not even die-hard legal moralists claim that every immorality should be criminalizable.

Thus retributivists need to supply us with an account of why only certain immoralities merit legal punishment. This means that retributivists hoping to construct a complete theory of penal justice cannot be satisfied with asserting that the point of punishment is simply to annul wrongdoing, mete out just deserts, or treat people as their rational wills would allow. Such basic accounts are insufficient to direct the creation of liability guidelines, since they offer

*From *Philosophical Studies* 82(3): 289–316, June 1996. © Kluwer Academic Publishers. Printed in the Netherlands. Endnotes have been edited and renumbered.

no basis for singling out just a subset of moral wrongs for punishment.

In order to provide such a basis, retributivists must rely on their conception of why we should have a system of penal responses at all. Sophisticated retributivists must cite as punishment's general justifying aim the redress of some *specific kind(s) of* moral wrong. Recent retributivist accounts have done just this, and so offer promise of satisfactorily addressing the liability question.

There are two basic sorts of moral wrong that have been identified as penal liability triggers. The first involves the imposition of certain kinds of harms; the second involves the accrual of unfair advantages. Regarding the first, different retributivist theories can be spun out depending on which sorts of harm one is centrally concerned to redress. Jean Hampton, for instance, justifies punishment by citing the need to combat the harmful messages of inferiority sent by certain sorts of morally offensive behavior.[2] Though Hampton does not explicitly discuss questions of criminal liability, it seems a fair extension of her theory to say that behavior is properly criminalizable if and only if it demeans its victim. Since some moral wrongs lack victims, and others fail to demean, we have a ready way of showing that only a subclass of wrongs is properly subject to criminal liability.

Other retributivists, including Herbert Morris,[3] Jeffrie Murphy,[4] Wojciech Sadurski,[5] George Sher,[6] and Michael Davis,[7] justify punishment on the basis of rectifying an unfair advantage obtained through wrongdoing. Since some moral wrongdoing presumably fails to create such an advantage, it follows that there is no basis for criminalizing such behavior. So again we have a way of demarcating the class of moral wrongs properly subject to criminalization. Immorality per se will not be a sufficient condition for criminal liability.

Hampton's retributivism seems unable to adequately solve the liability question, since many sorts of criminal conduct do not demean anybody, e.g., tax evasion, drunk driving, criminal trespass or conspiracy. So long as we can justifiably punish such behavior through the criminal law, we cannot insist that demeaning behavior is necessary for criminal liability. Nor is it sufficient, since a parent's demeaning of his child, while ugly and regrettable, need not be criminalized.

Hampton's theory is nevertheless instructive because it squarely addresses a problem few retributivists have tackled. A complete retributive theory will explain why certain behaviors should be dealt with through the criminal law, rather than through the mechanisms of private law. One explanation, implied by Hampton's theory, is that certain classes of harms are more morally serious than others, and these more serious offenses require the extra severity of criminal sanctions. This is a promising approach, but it comes at the cost of entirely undoing the settled classes of criminal and civil offenses. For many civil offenses (e.g., battery, wrongful death) are morally graver than many criminal ones (narcotics possession, flag desecration).

Such an approach is also in tension with another desideratum of penal theory, *viz.,* an explanation of why the state should occupy the plaintiff's role in criminal cases. One element in traditional explanations is that criminal prosecution can justifiably proceed even in the absence of determinate injury to private citizens. But this very absence calls into question whether crimes must be more serious than torts or contract violations; which latter are predicated on real harm suffered by real people.

The tidiest way to resolve these apparent conflicts is to argue that criminal liability should extend to all and only harms against the state. This resolves the argumentative puzzle of the previous paragraph, because it promises to explain how an action can be seriously immoral even without a determinate personal victim. And the state's role as plaintiff is also explained, because it is the state that is harmed. But the ready metaphor of state harm must be cashed out, and this has yet to be successfully accomplished. One obvious way is to view state harm as that conduct which harms a state's citizens. But private law can and does proscribe and remedy such harms. Another reading is that a state is harmed by its laws being broken. But this would yield state harm every time an administrative, contract or tort law is violated. A third view sees state harm as that conduct that undermines the allegiance or cohesion of the citizenry, or its confidence in a state's ability to provide security. But many, possibly most activities we hope to see punished fail to have such an undermining effect. Until retributivists offer a plausible conception of state harm, this approach to liability triggers will remain unsatisfactory. . . .

The retributive accounts based on correction of a maldistribution of benefits and burdens have also failed to circumscribe the class of immoralities in determining liability. Each theorist has understood the relevant liability-triggering immorality as that unfair advantage gained by violating a morally justified legal prohibition. The relevant unfair advantage is not viewed as consisting of or measured by the amount of material or psychological benefit gained by the criminal, or that amount of impoverishment the criminal inflicts on any determinate individual. Rather, the unfair advantage consists in the extra measure of freedom gained through criminal behavior, and is gotten at the expense of *all* law-abiders. The relevant unfairness is often explained by citing the frustration of the reliance interests of others in one's law-abiding behavior. These interests are justifiably protected because the state has duly promulgated the criminal statutes and hence provided would-be offenders with fair warning of the treatment they can expect if they violate the code.

Regardless of the merits of such theories, they cannot help us here, since they mislocate the relevant sort of wrongdoing that can serve as a liability trigger. These views *presuppose* the existence of a criminal code, rather than providing assistance in constructing one. They do not tell us which behavior to criminalize, but instead tell us that whatever the content of the criminal code, violators may be punished so long as citizens have received fair warning and the laws are morally justified. But this leaves the original question unanswered. The criminal law must proscribe some but not all immoralities. Where to draw the boundaries is precisely the question of how to circumscribe criminal liability.

We can see that unfair advantage views fail to answer that question by constructing a dilemma. On the first horn, violation of any duly promulgated law will confer unfairly gained freedom, and so properly warrant punishment. In this case, fair warning justifies punishment even of violators of very unjust laws. That is hardly consonant with the retributive aim of doing justice. On the second horn, punishment is warranted if and only if the offender violates a law that is both duly promulgated and morally justified. This avoids the problem of the first horn, but requires a theory that demarcates those immoralities properly deserving of punishment. Unfair advantage theorists have failed to supply such a theory. Until they do, their versions of retributivism will remain seriously incomplete.

II. General Justifying Aim

Punishment is presumptively unjustified because it involves the deliberate infliction of coercive, sometimes painful treatment. Retributivism seeks to over-ride that presumption by citing the moral requirement to mete out just deserts for wrongdoers. This response has attracted widespread criticism that usually proceeds in the following way: either this moral requirement is self-justifying or it isn't. If it isn't self-justifying, then appeal must be made to some ulterior good obtained through punishment (e.g., deterrence). In that case, the resulting general justifying aim isn't retributive at all. To the possibility that the retributivist moral requirement might be self-justifying, opponents simply disagree and charge that such manoeuvres are question-begging.[8]

The standard charges do not cut too deeply. In the first place, they presuppose a foundationalist moral epistemology. The successful development of a coherentist method of ethical justification[9] would allow the retributivist the possibility of slipping through the horns of the dilemma. To do this, the retributivist would have to show that various beliefs can be made sense of by the penal aim of doing justice, and show that the coherence that emerges would be broader and deeper than that which emerges by incorporating competing consequentialist principles into one's belief network.[10]

Even if foundationalism is correct, however, the standard criticisms fall short. Consequentialists too must leave some assumptions about value undefended, and there's no reason to think that their appeal to deterrence or reformation will be any more self-justifying than an appeal to meting out just deserts. Further, retributivists about general justifying aim need not claim that their moral requirement is self-justifying. Their view about how best to respond to certain offenses may derive from yet more fundamental moral views, including those of the person, of human dignity, rights theory and (perhaps) of rationality. A subsidiary moral principle could represent the general penal justifying aim, without being either self-justifying or foundational.

Still, deflating the standard criticisms does not get retributivists all they need. They must provide positive arguments for two conclusions: first, that there should be a system of criminal law at all, and second, that such a system should be structured by the ultimate rationale of giving wrongdoers what they deserve.

A citizenry enamored of its liberty will naturally want to restrict state power. Since the criminal law issues penalties that restrict liberty more than the demands of compensation or restitution imposed by private law, we need special justification for criminal sanctions. Imagine a society whose legal system was wholly private. What kinds of worries would push its citizens to embrace a criminal law?[11]

The retributivist must answer that the citizenry should be first and foremost concerned with giving legal violators their just deserts, where doing this requires forcing offenders to do more than pay compensation or restitution. The focus must be on making offenders worse off than they were status quo ante, rather than restoring a victim to previous levels. Doing this would not be costless. Because criminal sanctions are typically more severe than civil ones, procedural safeguards will have to be heightened. A broader policing network will be required. Penal institutions must be erected, and the judiciary augmented. Taxes must greatly increase to pay for these expenditures. And the inevitable miscarriages of justice will be more injurious and less reparable. These costs must be incurred no matter the justification for a criminal law. But is it reasonable to incur them for the sole aim of ensuring that wrongdoers suffer commensurately to their misdeeds?

If the answer is "No", then retributivism cannot be the proper rationale for a system of punishment. And there is good reason to think that a negative response is the appropriate one. Imagine a society that incurred these extra costs, improved its ability to mete out just deserts, and (improbably) saw their crime rate increase.[12] It seems unlikely that morality could be so demanding as to require the additional costs when doing so diminished the security of those who had to bear them. That such a scenario is unlikely is beside the point. The imagined scenario reveals our deep belief in the importance of crime-reduction as a goal of the criminal law. Such reduction isn't, as retributivists would claim, merely a contingent, ancillary benefit, playing no justificatory role in the assumption of the deep costs associated with instituting a system of criminal justice. We can allow that meting out justice is intrinsically valuable. We can even allow that retributivists have a plausible conception of the content of penal justice. But we need an argument to show that such justice is more valuable than diminishing crime and enhancing personal security. Retributivists have not been able to deliver that argument.

Their best effort consists in trying to show that deterrence rationales will license disastrous policies, such as punishing the innocent. Such arguments are faulty, however, quite apart from the likelihood that such "punishment" would be inefficacious. That we aim to prevent crime does not mean that we license any and every means to that goal. Various rights-respecting constraints can be introduced, either as a complementary element at the level of general justifying aim, or at the determination of what sort of behavior will count as criminal. We could, for instance, make the aim of the criminal law the reduction of rights violations,[13] or we could insist that no behavior will be criminalized unless it violates rights, or we could insist on a number of procedural safeguards designed to prevent innocents from being punished. In any event, much of this worry is generated by the thought that the deterrence theorist must cite the elimination or minimization of crime as punishment's general justifying aim. But no sensible theorist would do that, as this would lead to a police state. Once we see that the relevant aim should be specified only as the *reduction* of crime, it becomes clear that we can seek a greater or lesser amount of such reduction by comparing its admitted benefits with its attendant costs. Deterrence theorists needn't argue that the benefits of crime reduction must be purchased at any cost whatever.

Rather than trying to show that a deterrence aim leads to horrific consequences, theorists might try to establish the priority of retributive aims by showing that they alone can be derived from very deep moral principles. This is a more promising strategy, but I don't think it yields a determinate victor. The requirement that we respect rights may be satisfied by meting out harsh treatment to offenders, but it is also satisfied by structuring criminal sanctions so as to reduce rights violations. The injunction to respect human dignity is possibly fulfilled by meting out retribution, but it is surely fulfilled by purposely reducing offenses to human dignity. Promoting justice may be attained by giving offenders what they deserve, but it is also attained by ensuring that fewer people violate the rights of their fellow citizens. The demands of equality can be met by ensuring that similar offenders receive similar punishments, but this demand is consonant with a deterrence rationale as well as a retributive one.

Our deep attachment to the goal of crime reduction, combined with retributivism's inability to defend the priority of meting out just deserts, implies that the state aim of enhancing individual security is at least as important as that of righting wrongs. It is reasonable for citizens in a private law system to insist that the great costs of creating and enforcing a criminal law be borne only if they yield an important reduction in harmful conduct. That is all one has to show in order to undermine the claim that retributivism is the sole general justifying aim of punishment. Nor is it probable that retribution and deterrence could be coordinate general aims, since these distinct rationales will likely enjoin the creation of conflicting liability triggers and sentencing statutes, yielding an incoherent body of law.

If the priority of retributive aims cannot be defended, and coordinate justifying aims are implausible, then we have a presumptive case against retributivism as a general penal justifying aim. This case can be strengthened once we recall that the relevant issue is not whether, from a moral point of view, deterrence is as great a value as retribution. The question is rather what the appropriate role of the state should be. Instituting a criminal law greatly enhances the powers of the state over its citizens. That requires justification. If it is true that significant liberties can justifiably be curtailed by the state only if such restrictions redound to the interest of those who may suffer from them, then the prima facie case against retributivism and for deterrence is strengthened. A penal institution successfully regulated by a deterrence aim will yield a more secure citizenry. Each will recover some benefit. A retributive scheme, on the other hand, needn't confer additional security, and views any such benefit as a welcome but inessential part of its aim. Its concern is with making criminals suffer, not with reducing crime or making victims whole. Ensuring just deserts *may* be intrinsically valuable, but it needn't promote anyone's interests. Thus retributivism is inconsistent with the condition that state power be enhanced only if this promotes the interests of those who may suffer from it.

This condition is a hallmark of liberal political theory, and it reinforces a familiar, if usually ill-defined feeling, that a retributivist justifying aim must be an illiberal one. To greatly increase state control over citizens, in order to annul wrongdoing, is to allow for the diminution of citizen liberty in the name of securing the "free-floating good" of meting out deserved punishment. Goods are free-floating just in case they do not promote any particular person's interests.[14] Just as liberals reject criminal statutes that prevent merely free-floating evils, so too they should reject those incursions on personal liberty justified solely in the name of securing free-floating goods. The correction of the "cosmic injustice" that results from failing to punish wrongdoers commensurately with their crimes is one such good (if a good at all). But no one with an inkling of liberal sympathies ought to endorse the promotion of this good as the aim for structuring a penal system.

This is hardly a refutation of retributivism, of course, since I haven't argued for any version of po-

litical liberalism. Nor can I here. But even those who find liberalisms unattractive should concede the weakness of standard retributive arguments against deterrence, and should agree that the values and principles supporting retributivism support deterrence aims equally well. Even if we grant the intrinsic value of doing retributive justice, we have yet to receive a good argument for the priority of retributive aims in structuring a system of criminal law.

III. Amount

Many of those who have abandoned retributive accounts of liability and rationale have nonetheless maintained that we must incorporate a retributive principle of distribution to determine how much offenders ought to be punished. They cite a lack of confidence in the judicial system and attendant social disutilities if the state were to abandon retributive sentencing policies. Interestingly, it seems that most philosophers have reached something of an "overlapping consensus" on sentencing guidelines, if on nothing else. And this consensus is strongly retributivist.

I want to challenge this consensus in three ways. I begin by criticizing specific retributivist proposals for apportioning punishment. I then examine the merits of strong retributivism—the thesis that all the guilty must be punished. I conclude by criticizing the notion of moral desert that must underlie any retributive theory of determining the severity of punishment.

A. Specific Retributive Proposals

The classic accompaniment to retributivism is lex talionis. Lex requires imposing a harm on a criminal identical to the one he imposed on his victim. Lex is just the kind of principle a retributivist needs—one that can offer determinate advice about what an offender morally deserves for his wrongdoing. But there are four well-known difficulties with this principle. First, it would require the state to undertake morally pernicious activities in response to heinous offenses. Second, it can give no guidance as to how to punish certain crimes, e.g., counterfeiting, hijacking, or kidnapping if offenders have no children of their own. Third, meting out punishment in proportion to harm leaves out differences in *mens rea* entirely—the same harm done negligently, recklessly or intentionally will be punished identically. And fourth, lex will allow some crimes to be punished too little—attempts that cause no harm, or any number of criminal free-riding offenses (like tax fraud) where the harm is spread out among so many participants that it becomes negligible or nonexistent for each "victim".

Friends of lex talionis have tried to avoid these problems by modifying it in the following way. Rather than being forced to experience the very same kind of treatment as they imposed on their victims, criminals should instead be made to undergo the same amount of suffering as they imposed on their victim. But this too is inadequate, since it fails to address the third and fourth problems above. It also creates a fifth problem: it fails to yield determinate advice about how much to punish, owing to theoretical and epistemological difficulties associated with measuring a victim's experiences of pain and making interpersonal comparisons of suffering. Amending lex yet again so as to vary the amount of punishment depending on both suffering and mental culpability[15] solves the third problem, but not the fourth or fifth. And it creates another new problem: how to meld the suffering and culpability indices so as to yield a determinate amount of punishment. . . .

Partly as a response to the problems of lex talionis, most retributivists have withdrawn their focus on the harms suffered by victims, and instead moved toward a view of deserved punishment as based on an unfair distribution of benefits and burdens that criminals create by their illegal behavior.

Different versions of such theories can be developed depending on how one understands the unfair advantage whose redress is required by punishment. Morris' early work hinted at the idea that the relevant burden assumed by law-abiding citizens was the frustration of one's criminal impulses, and the corresponding advantage the indulgence of such impulses. But this was probably not Morris' considered view,[16] and anyway fails because it presupposes a desire to violate the law that most law-abiding citizens do not have.

Sadurski has rightly criticized a different view, one that identifies the relevant unfair benefit as that amount of material gain or psychological satisfaction gotten through criminal conduct. Many crimes confer no benefit of either sort. Absent such benefits, there is no basis for punishment on such views. Further, in many cases where such benefits are accrued, the accumulation of these benefits is a contingent matter and plays no role in the justifying reasons for

making such conduct criminal in the first place.[17] In any event, such a view implies that the unfair advantage whose correction determines the proper sentence is that advantage gained over the one who directly suffers from one's criminal conduct. But any such view presumably reduces to a harm-based approach, where the focus is on redressing the harm suffered by the victim of a crime. Views that concentrate on unfair distributions of benefits and burdens relocate the criminal's unfair advantage to that benefit gained over all other law-abiding citizens.

This focus explains Sadurski's own contention that the relevant advantage gained by criminal conduct is the benefit of non-restraint. All other law-abiding citizens assume this burden, and the taking of such a benefit calls for correction. The relevant benefits are measured by the extra liberty a criminal has arrogated to himself, eschewing self-restraint and taking advantage of options others refrain from. The crucial failure of such an account is its inability to explain why a criminal's extra liberty increases in proportion to the wrongness of his conduct. Such an increase must occur if the point of punishment is to correct the unfair advantage that consists in disregarding limitations on one's liberty. According to this theory, if we hope to justly punish a murderer more than a shoplifter, the murderer must have gained a far greater amount of liberty from his violation. But there does not seem to be any sense of "liberty" according to which this is true. Sadurski's central thesis—that the relevant benefit (enhanced liberty) increases with the moral seriousness of one's criminal conduct—appears implausible on any natural understanding of benefits, liberty or restraint.[18]

George Sher's account[19] is strikingly similar to Sadurski's. Sher agrees with Sadurski in identifying the unfair advantage gained by criminals as some extra amount of freedom. He also agrees that this amount of freedom is best measured by the moral gravity of the prohibition violated. When it comes to defending this claim, however, Sher does no better than Sadurski. Sher's defense comes in a discussion comparing the extra freedom gained by a murderer and by a tax cheat. But the defense amounts to just a single sentence: "Because the murderer evades a prohibition of far greater force—because he thus 'gets away with more'—his net gain in freedom remains greater.[20] This seems more a restatement than a justification of the position requiring defense.

Even if these challenges can be successfully dealt with, the problem of commensurability remains. Murder is a more serious offense than tax fraud. But even if there were some sort of scale by which we could measure the difference, we would still need to know how severely to punish the tax cheat. Neither the moral prohibition on tax evasion nor the values protected by it can tell us just how much punishment such a crime deserves. A moral prohibition's relative stringency can tell us how much an offender deserves for its violation only if we already have a noncomparative assessment of the moral deserts for at least one offense. But such assessments cannot be provided by a theory that makes only ordinal measurements of seriousness. If unfair advantage is a function of the immorality of one's conduct, then we need a means of correlating the degree of immorality with a determinate amount of suffering or suspended liberties. Once we have one such correlation, we might be able to increase or decrease the severity of punishment with the gravity of the offense.[21] But unfair advantage theorists have offered no advice about how we might produce this first correlation. And, as I shall argue in section C, they *cannot* supply any such theory to do so. This inability to assign determinate sentences will persist so long as retributivists proportion unfair advantage to the immorality of criminal conduct. . . .

B. Weak and Strong Retributivism

Retributivism has standardly been divided into strong and weak versions: Strong retributivism is the thesis that all the guilty must be punished, and weak retributivism the thesis that only the guilty may be punished. Consistent retributivists should demand the stronger version. Weak retributivism allows sentencing policies that fail to give offenders what they deserve. It does not insist that all the guilty be punished commensurately with their deserts, or even that all the guilty be punished. If the point of punishment is to ensure that justice is done, and justice is cashed out in terms of giving people what they deserve, then retributivists must opt for strong retributivism.

Strong retributivism itself has a weaker and a stronger version:

[1] the guilty must be punished, but no more than they deserve to be;
[2] the guilty must be punished just as much as they deserve to be.

Again, if the general justifying aim of punishment is to ensure justice by meting out punishment commensurate with desert, then the retributivist must endorse the stronger version [2]. Accepting [1] alone allows an offender to be punished in a disproportionately mild way that will fail to repay harm for harm or to fully correct an unfair distribution of benefits and burdens.

I think that there are problems with both versions of the strong retributivist thesis, though I will only tentatively question thesis [1]. My objection to it rests on two claims: that increased penalties for recidivists are justified, and that such penalties exceed what offenders deserve. After all, their behavior and mental state may be effectively identical to that of a first-time offender, so this would appear to argue for the claim that recidivists in such cases deserve no more than first-time offenders. Providing the arguments necessary to substantiate these claims would take us too far afield, however, so I leave this only as a tentative criticism.

Even if [1] is ultimately vindicated, retributivists about the general justifying aim need to defend [2] as well, and here I think more serious problems arise.[22] First, such a requirement forbids extending pardons, suspended sentences or amnesties that grant clemency to justly convicted offenders. Second, it also disallows any form of plea bargaining, since such "bargains" invariably allow jurisdictions to save on litigation expenses in exchange for an agreement that defendants plead guilty to fewer or lesser charges than they in fact deserve. And third, the requirement that all be punished in accordance with full deserts forbids judges from exercising the virtue of mercy when sentencing. Mercy "tempers" justice by justifying the imposition of a penalty less harsh than is deserved by an offender. [2] would disallow such treatment.[23]

A yet more serious worry is that [2] may actually undermine justice. As Joel Feinberg has shown,[24] desert claims do not exhaust considerations of justice. This creates the possibility that giving offenders what they deserve may violate a distinct principle of justice. And that in fact is what happens. Determinations of moral desert constitute a kind of noncomparative justice; we needn't make reference to the conduct or deserts of similar offenders to determine what any particular offender deserves.[25] Giving offenders what they deserve is ultimately a matter of making a punishment commensurate with a crime. One can't establish commensurability simply by examining how similar offenders are treated. One first requires a noncomparative assessment. I will later give reasons for thinking that the commensurability requirement cannot be satisfied. But even if we assume that it can, conflicts of justice may arise.

That is because justice is also concerned with ensuring that similar conduct be treated similarly. It is a failure of comparative justice when those who have committed like crimes are treated dissimilarly, especially if the bases of the dissimilar treatment are morally arbitrary. In societies today, comparative injustice is widespread, as the selection of charges and the stiffness of sentences very often depends on morally irrelevant features (e.g., affluence or skin color). In one sense, then, it is unjust to give some people what they deserve, because they are being treated, relative to others morally like them, as inferiors because of morally irrelevant considerations.[26] Insisting that thesis [2] guide penal law is to insist that the demands of noncomparative justice trump those of comparative justice. Retributivists have offered no reason to support such a policy.[27] In any event, the retributive appeal to doing justice in the general justifying aim provides no reason for favoring application of noncomparative over comparative justice. So, while there might be reasons for giving offenders what they deserve, other principles of justice provide at least equally compelling reasons for refraining from doing so.

A final problem with thesis [2] is that it forbids any cost-benefit calculations in the creation or application of sentencing guidelines. Education, poverty reduction, health care and other essential services must compete with penal institutions for the limited amount of available governmental resources. There is no reason to think that the costs of giving all offenders their just deserts must be borne, regardless of how seriously this impinges on a government's ability to provide these other services.[28]

Interestingly, fulfilling [2] is effectively to demand something even stronger than that required by retributivism's general justifying aim. Retributivism's underlying rationale—meting out just deserts—represents the claim that of all available justifications for penal institutions, justice-based ones are the best. It is, we might say, an intra-institutional justification. But [2] goes farther, and says that priority in the funding of social institutions must go to penal ones, if hard choices must be made. [2] presupposes a comparative, inter-institutional assessment. The general justifying aim is to this extent more modest, since it makes no claims about prioritizing the values embedded in different social institutions.

C. Moral Desert

Given the many problems with strong retributivism, friends of retributivism might hope to retain their emphasis on just deserts while abandoning the requirement that all guilty parties be punished as much as they deserve. They might try to find a position intermediate between weak and strong retributivism, or somewhere between theses [1] and [2] of strong retributivism. I don't think that any such salvage operation can be successful, however, because the ultimate basis on which retributivists must proportion punishment—moral desert—cannot do the work required of it.

Imagine trying to determine just what punishment a criminal deserves. The obvious first response is to look at the relevant sentencing statute. But matters surely cannot rest here for the retributivist, because some actual laws will unjustly prohibit conduct that is morally innocuous, and others will enjoin behavior that is morally condemnable. People who violate such laws don't deserve their punishment in the sense necessary for retributivism, since meting out such "desert" will be a failure of justice, not its vindication. What retributivists must insist on is that the legal punishment people deserve be accurately tailored to redress the moral wrong they have committed.

A retributivist requires that punishment be both proportional and commensurate with the offense. Proportionality is satisfied by ensuring that morally graver offenses receive harsher punishments. But satisfying proportionality requirements does nothing to ensure that punishments are commensurate with their crimes. If our criminal code includes fifty offenses, ranked according to severity, and fifty punishments, ranging by one-year increments from a ten-year to a sixty-year incarceration, proportionality can readily be satisfied. But few will think that the mildest criminal offense should be met with a ten year deprivation.

The problem for retributivists is that the notion of moral desert cannot supply any index for satisfying the commensurability requirement. This is because desert-based considerations can specify determinate punishments or rewards only if they operate within rule-based contexts. Where the rules for receiving an 'A' on a paper or a checkmate in chess are clear, we can readily speak of a recipient's desert determining how she ought to be treated. But there are no correlative rules in the moral domain that can link the gravity of a moral offense with a determinate imposition of suffering or suspension of liberty.

Having abandoned lex talionis, so that punishment is no longer a matter of imposing the same kinds of harms or suffering as those imposed by an offender, determining moral desert becomes a matter of correlating punishment, typically incarceration, with something that is usually very different from it. There is little that incarceration shares with embezzlement, auto theft, rape or defamation. The drastic differences in kind between punishment and offense should make us suspicious about moral desert's ability to do what retributivists require of it.

Since the state is engaged in deliberately harming the criminal, retributivists must be able to cite good reasons to suppose that any particular sentence being meted out is commensurate with the offender's desert. This requires a theory that can supply reasons for thinking that other more or less severe punishments are inappropriate. But once we abandon lex, and bracket considerations of how like offenders are treated (which we are entitled to do, since we still need to know whether the punishments of these similar offenders are commensurate with their crimes), the moral resources for correlating moral wrongs with incarceration run out. Moral desert offers us no way of knowing that a punishment is too great or too small, and so no way of knowing whether it is commensurate with the crime. In short, there are no determinate moral criteria that can translate the gravity of an offense into even a roughly correlative measure of deserved punishment. What reason can be given for thinking that an auto theft is equivalent to sixty days or one year or eleven years of incarceration? Judgments of noncomparative punitive justice must be made more or less arbitrarily within a retributivist system of basing legal desert on moral desert.

It will not do for retributivists to insist that this is simply a variation on a familiar problem of moral vagueness.[29] Claims of desert, they might say, are admittedly vague, but so too are most moral claims. Since this doesn't prevent us from constructive investigation elsewhere in the moral (or nonmoral) domain, it shouldn't be seen as an insuperable problem in justifying a theory of just deserts.

A predicate may be vague either because it allows for borderline cases (e.g., "adolescent", "red", "dusk"), or because it is overgeneral/underspecific (e.g., "few", "largish", "in the future").[30] I am not claiming that moral desert is inefficacious in setting punishments because it generates a penumbral range of borderline cases where we are uncertain about appropriate deserts. Vagueness of this first sort is innocuous.[31] But moral desert is not vague in this way. To generate a borderline case, properties or predicates must have fairly determinate criteria of application. Moral desert lacks anything resembling this. It offers us *no* concrete guidance about where to set punishments. If it is vague at all, its vagueness is a kind of radical underspecificity. To claim that desert can determine the amount of morally justified punishment is equivalent to saying simply that an offender should receive neither too much nor too little punishment. Moral desert offers no determinate criteria for identifying what's to count as too much or too little. That kind of underspecity is fatal to a moral principle.

Conclusion

The three sets of concerns I have focused on in this paper must form the core of any theory of justified punishment. If I am right, retributivism lacks the resources to adequately address any one of them.

Retributive theories fail to offer guidance in circumscribing criminal liability. Harm-based theories have yet to offer a plausible candidate harm whose perpetration will be necessary and sufficient to trigger criminal sanctions. Unfair advantage theorists presuppose the existence of a settled body of criminal statutes, and so presuppose an answer to the question of liability, rather than providing one.

When it comes to punishment's general justifying aim, retributivists have failed to demonstrate the inferiority of crime-reduction as at least a coordinate fundamental aim in structuring penal systems. Further, retributivists must abandon any prospect of allying their penal theory with a political theory that justifies (a system of) criminal sanctions only if such sanctions redound to the interests of those who might suffer from them. Retributivism's insistence on the correction of "cosmic injustice", even if the suffering of the guilty promotes no one's interests, entails an allegiance to illiberal political theories that has yet to receive any adequate defense.

Retributive theories have failed to offer a plausible account of how to structure a determinate sentencing policy. Lex talionis, the natural candidate for supplying such a policy for harm-based theorists, is inadequate in any of its many guises. And the unfair-advantage proposals collapse on their own terms, since they fail to give any adequate measure of the unfair advantage conferred by criminal conduct. Further, all retributive theories are pushed by their general justifying aim to endorse the thesis that all the guilty must be punished just as much as they deserve to be. This is problematic because it disallows judicial mercy, plea bargains and executive clemency, requires that we disregard the costs of meting out just deserts, and prioritizes noncomparative over comparative justice without any argument for doing so. Even if retributivists had adequate replies to these concerns, their reliance on an intolerably vague conception of moral desert undermines any hope of satisfying the commensurability requirement, a fundamental component of any retributive theory.

There are two ways of assessing theories of punishment. One might first take the view that sufficiently strong criticisms of a theory are enough to knock it out of philosophical competition as a candidate penal justification. Or one might say that no matter how damaging the criticisms, we cannot exclude a theory from eligibility without first looking at the depths of the problems faced by its competitors. My aim in this paper has been to convince adherents of the first view that the problems associated with retributivism are grave enough to disqualify it from philosophical eligibility. With regard to the second approach, one must concede that within the short compass of an article it is impossible to make the kinds of inter-theoretic comparisons required to properly assess retributivism. Still, those who remain tempted by retributivism—those who see it as the least worst justificatory option—must, if I am right, see its competitors as remarkably implausible. This may be an accurate assessment of the field. But if it is, I would sooner withdraw my conviction that punishment is justified than allow the deliberate infliction of suffering to proceed under a retributive banner so riddled with holes.

---

1. It won't be necessary if strict or vicarious liability statutes can occupy a place in a justified system of criminal law, or if we are ever justified in assigning liability on the basis of objective standards (i.e., what a reasonable person would do or believe in similar circumstances) that particular offenders cannot meet. For a good discussion see Richard Wasserstrom, "Strict Criminal Liability", *Stanford Law Review* 12 (1960), pp. 730–45.

2. Hampton, "A New Theory of Retribution", in C. Morris and R. Frey, *Liability and Responsibility* (New York: Cambridge University Press, 1991), pp. 377–414. This is a revision of her earlier views expressed in J. Hampton and J. Murphy, *Forgiveness and Mercy* (New York: Cambridge University Press, 1989).

3. Morris, "Persons and Punishment", *Monist* 52 (1968), pp. 475–501. Morris' article has importantly influenced all of the subsequent retributive accounts that focus on the redress of unfair distributions of burdens and benefits created by criminal conduct. Morris has since abandoned his retributive theory; see "A Paternalistic Theory of Punishment", *American Philosophical Quarterly* 18 (1981), pp. 263–71.

4. Murphy, *Retribution, Justice and Therapy* (Boston: Reidel, 1979), pp. 77–115 and 223–49.

5. Sadurski, *Giving Desert its Due* (Boston: Reidel, 1985), pp. 221–60.

6. Sher, *Desert* (Princeton: Princeton University Press, 1987), pp. 69–90.

7. Davis, "How to Make the Punishment Fit the Crime", *Ethics* 93 (1983), pp. 726–52; "Criminal Desert and Unfair Advantage: What's the Connection?", *Law and Philosophy* 12 (1993), pp. 133–56.

8. Examples of these criticisms include S. Benn and R. S. Peters, *Social Principles and the Democratic State* (London: Allen and Unwin), pp. 175–176; H. L. A. Hart, *Punishment and Responsibility* (New York: Oxford University Press, 1968), pp. 234–35; H. Bedau, "Retribution and the Theory of Punishment", *Journal of Philosophy* 75 (1978), pp. 601–21, at 615–17; P. Pettit and R. Braithwaite, *Not Just Deserts* (New York: Oxford University Press, 1990), p. 165.

9. See Norman Daniels, "Wide Reflective Equilibrium and Theory Acceptance in Ethics", *Journal of Philosophy* 76 (1979), pp. 256–82, and David Brink, *Moral Realism and the Foundations of Ethics* (New York: Cambridge University Press, 1989), pp. 100–43 for detailed accounts of how this sort of view should be elaborated and justified.

10. This is Michael Moore's strategy of defending retributivism. See Moore, "The Moral Worth of Retribution", in F. Schoeman, ed., *Responsibility, Character and the Emotions* (New York: Cambridge University Press, 1987), pp. 179–219. Moore's view is ably criticized by David Dolinko, "Some Thoughts about Retributivism", *Ethics* 101 (1991), pp. 535–57.

11. This question is a variant on a thought experiment proposed by Jeffrie Murphy in his very useful discussion, "Why Have a Criminal Law at all?", pp. 110–17 of Murphy and J. Coleman, *Philosophy of Law* (Totowa, N.J.: Rowman and Littlefield, 1987). See also Murphy, "Retribution, Moral Education and the Liberal State", *Criminal Justice Ethics* 4 (1985), pp. 3–10.

12. Douglas Husak explores this possibility in his fine article "Why Punish the Deserving?", *NOUS* 26 (1993), pp. 447–64.

13. See, e.g., Rex Martin's *A System of Rights* (New York: Oxford University Press, 1993), ch. 10.

14. I take this notion from Joel Feinberg, *Harmless Wrongdoing* (New York: Oxford University Press, 1988), pp. 18–20.

15. See, e.g., Igor Primoratz, *Justifying Legal Punishment* (Atlantic Highlands, N.J.: Humanities Press, 1989), pp. 79–82, 85–94; Robert Nozick, *Philosophical Explanations* (Cambridge: Harvard University Press, 1981), pp. 363–66, 388–90.

16. I think Richard Burgh has provided a fine reconstruction of Morris' views on this matter. He rightly interprets Morris as viewing the relevant unfair benefit gotten by criminality as that sphere of noninterference gained from general obedience to a particular law. I also think that the criticisms Burgh makes of Morris' view are sound, and so will not recapitulate them here. See Burgh, "Do the Guilty Deserve Punishment", *Journal of Philosophy* 79 (1982), pp. 193–210, and 203–5. Burgh's criticisms of Jeffrie Murphy's early views are also relevant here, and also, to my mind, conclusive in refuting the view that identifies the relevant unfair advantage as that benefit gotten by everyone else's obedience to the entire system of law. See Burgh, *op. cit.,* pp. 207–9.

17. See Sadurski, *op. cit.,* p. 228.

18. Sadurski claims that "it is a mere tautology to say that a more serious crime brings about more benefits of non-self-restraint to the perpetrator: the 'seriousness' of the crime is actually measured by the degree of intrusion by the offender into the protected sphere of autonomy of another person" [229]. The problem here is that the statement following the colon is supposed to be a gloss on the one preceding it. But we can allow that the seriousness of a crime is measured as Sadurski says, without agreeing that one's benefit of non-restraint is correlated with the seriousness of one's offense. It is this last claim that Sadurski needs to, but does not, defend. It seems anything but tautologous to me.

19. Sher, *op. cit.,* n. 6.

20. *Ibid.,* p. 82.

21. Even this is unlikely, however, since the ordinal gradations will almost certainly not align along interval or ratio scales. That makes it impossible to tell just how much graver one offense is than another. Short of such knowledge, sentencing codes have no way justifiably to align the second-least-serious offence with the second-least-serious punishment.

22. For interesting complementary criticisms of strong retributivism see Pettit and Braithwaite, *op. cit.,* pp. 167–74. Pettit and Braithwaite distinguish weak from strong retributivism as I do, but view strong retributivism as identical to thesis [2]. They don't consider thesis [1].

23. On one reading of desert, this is not so. According to H. Scott Hestevold ("Disjunctive Desert", *American Philosophical Quarterly* 20 [1983], pp. 357–62), an offender's desert consists in a disjunctive aggregate of penalties. There is rarely (if ever) just a single treatment a person's conduct deserves. The various penalties an offender may deserve can be ranked as to severity; mercy consists in apportioning one of the less severe penalties. Thus putative conflicts between justice and mercy dissolve; merciful conduct is a subset of deserved treatment.

The merits of this view cannot be fully tested without a substantive conception of desert for some moral or legal domain. Still, I have some preliminary doubts. Many examples of merciful treatment seem to be ones that are so lenient as to undermine the claim that a wrongdoer deserves it. Just think of cases where victims gain control over their cruel oppressors, only to let them go free while renouncing vengeance. This seems the epitome of mercy, though it is treatment the oppressors can hardly be said to deserve.

24. Feinberg, "Justice and Personal Desert", in *Doing and Deserving* (Princeton: Princeton University Press, 1970), pp. 55–94.

25. Though this understanding of noncomparative desert will suffice for our purposes, much subtler accounts are available. See J. Feinberg, "Noncomparative Justice", *Philosophical Review* 83 (1974), pp. 297–338; P. Montague, "Comparative and Noncomparative Justice", *Philosophical Quarterly* (1980), pp. 131–40; J. Hoffman, "A New Theory of Comparative and Noncomparative Justice", *Philosophical Studies* 70 (1993), pp. 165–83.

26. This sort of argument, applied to capital punishment, is given by Stephen Nathanson, "Does it Matter whether the Death Penalty is Arbitrarily Administered?" *Philosophy and Public Affairs* 14 (1985), pp. 149–64.

27. The closest anyone comes is Ernest van den Haag. See, e.g., van den Haag's contribution to his collaborative book with John Conrad, *The Death Penalty: A Debate* (New York: Plenum Press, 1983); "The Collapse of the Case against Capital Punishment", *National Review* March 31, 1978; "Refuting Reiman and Nathanson", *Philosophy and Public Affairs* 14 (1985), pp. 165–76. Van den Haag insists that what justice requires is not to give minority or poor defendants less than what they deserve, but to give the privileged their full deserts. But his argument for this always presupposes the very premise that needs establishing—*viz.,* that all things considered, justice requires giving offenders what they deserve, that the demands of noncomparative justice always take priority over those of comparative justice.

28. This thesis is ably developed in Husak's recent article, *op. cit.*

29. Igor Primoratz suggests something very close to this in *Justifying Legal Punishment*, p. 81.

30. See Roy Sorenson, "The Ambiguity of Vagueness and Precision", *Pacific Philosophical Quarterly* 70 (1989), pp. 174–83.

31. I defend this claim in "Vagueness, Borderline Cases and Moral Realism", *American Philosophical Quarterly* (forthcoming).

Victims' Rights:
Restitution or Vengeance?

RETRIBUTIVISM:
A Test Case for Ethical Objectivity*

J. L. Mackie

I

In my *Ethics: Inventing Right and Wrong* I have argued that there is a real issue about the objectivity or subjectivity of moral principles and values, and I have tried to clarify this issue, which is often treated in a confused way, and to say what I take the central problem to be. I have also argued that neither objectivism nor subjectivism can be dismissed as incoherent, and neither view can be established merely by conceptual or linguistic analysis, or indeed by any other sort of *a priori* argument. To decide whether moral principles and values are objective or subjective in the important sense, we have to consider which view can be developed so as to provide the best overall explanation of all the relevant phenomena or data, all the moral (or related) "appearances" with which we are confronted. I would relate this question to what Hume, for example, says in Book III of the *Treatise*. I do not think that he has *shown* in any conclusive way by the end of Book III Part i that moral distinctions are not derived from "reason" and that they are derived from a "moral sense" or

from "sentiment." Hume's case for these theses is still incomplete at this point. It is completed only when he has shown, by the end of Book III Part iii, how on a "sentimentalist" foundation he can develop a sociological and psychological explanation of both the "artificial" and the "natural" virtues, that is, can explain why these various dispositions occur and why they are cultivated and approved of in human society, fairly uniformly though with some variations.

An examination of retributivism will, I suggest, contribute usefully to this discussion. Many people seem to have moral intuitions of a retributivist sort. But are these genuine intuitions which reveal objectively valid moral principles or requirements, or are they rather expressions of sentiments for which we should seek, and can find, psychological or sociological or even biological explanations? I shall argue that purportedly objective retributivist *principles* cannot be defended, but that retributivist *sentiments*— deeply ingrained, highly developed and organized— can be readily understood.

It is becoming more common for philosophers to declare their adherence to the retributive theory of punishment. This may be understood as an offshoot of the widespread tendency to reject utilitarianism in favor of some view which takes as central such concepts as those of justice and rights. However, this adherence may go along with a very broad or loose account of what the retributive theory is. Thus Jeffrie G. Murphy says that "A retributive theory of punishment is one which characterizes punishment primarily in terms of the concepts of justice, rights, and desert—i.e. is concerned with the just punishment, the punishment the criminal deserves, the punishment society has the right to inflict (and the criminal has the right to expect)."[1] J. G. Cottingham, in an admirable recent article, finds among views which have been called retributivist at least nine distinct approaches, and almost as many distinct strategies for justifying punishment, not all of which would fall under Murphy's description, broad though it is.[2]

Cottingham's headings are as follows: Repayment Theory (that by being punished the criminal repays a debt to society); Desert Theory (which seems to reduce to the bald assertion that crime deserves punishment, that it simply is just that the offender should be punished); Penalty Theory and Minimalism (I shall say more about these two later); Satisfaction Theory (that punishment is justified by the satisfaction that it gives to the victim of the crime or to others who have been injured or outraged by it); Fair Play Theory (that failure to punish would be unfair to those who, unlike the criminal, have obeyed the rules, and so have forgone satisfactions or advantages that the criminal has gained by breaking them); Placation Theory (that a god who has been angered by, say, a murder must be placated by the execution of the murderer, or else he will go on being angry with the whole nation); Annulment Theory (that the punishment somehow cancels or annuls the crime); and Denunciation Theory (that punishment is justified as an emphatic denunciation of a crime).

These are certainly a mixed bag. Cottingham takes the notion of repayment of a debt as what is central in retributivism, and rightly complains that several of the approaches he has listed have little to do with this. But let me suggest a way of bringing some sort of order into this mass of ideas.

It is true that *retribuo* in Latin means "I pay back." But surely the central notion is not that the criminal repays a debt, pays something back to society, but that someone else pays the criminal back for what he has done. Punitive retribution is the repaying of harm with harm, as reward is the repaying of benefit with benefit. We can class as an essentially retributivist approach any that sees at least some *prima facie* rightness in the repaying of evil with evil, especially a proportionate evil, but returning no evil where no evil has been done. This entails that justifications of punishment are retributive in so far as they are retrospective. On the other hand, suggestions (which Cottingham mentions under Penalty Theory and Minimalism) that a previous wrong act is a merely logical or definitional requirement for something to count as punishment, not in any way a moral justification, would be better not counted as retributivist.

Approaches that count as retributivist in this sense of involving retrospective justification must, however, be further subdivided. One important division is between what I would call *positive* and *negative* retributivism. Positive retributivism sees the previous wrong act as in itself a reason for inflicting a penalty. The crime at least tends positively to justify a penalty; but it may or may not be held that the wrong act is in itself morally *sufficient* for the penalty, or that it absolutely requires the penalty, irrespective of all other considerations. Negative retributivism (for which "minimalism" may be another name) holds that those who are not guilty must not (that is, morally must not, not *logically cannot*) be punished, that the absence of a crime morally requires the non-infliction of a penalty. There is also a quantitative variant of negative retributivism, that even if someone is guilty of a crime it is wrong to punish him more severely than is proportional to the crime. And of course there is an analogous quantitative variant of positive retributivism, that a crime of a certain degree of wrongness positively calls for a proportionate penalty.

This distinction is important for at least two reasons. One is that once they are distinguished negative retributivism will be found to have a greater measure of general acceptance than positive retributivism. Many thinking people who hold firmly that it is morally wrong in itself to punish the innocent —not merely definitionally impossible—and also wrong in itself to punish the guilty beyond the degree of their guilt, are far less confident that a previous wrong act in itself, if considerations of deterrence and the like are clearly set aside, even tends to provide a positive justification of a penalty. People are often negative but not positive retributivists. The other reason is that if we try to develop and explain these various retributivist theses, the positive and negative ones seem to call for or to fit in with quite different lines of thought. For example, very general and obviously attractive principles about the rights of individuals or human rights provide immediate backing for the thesis that it is wrong to punish the innocent; but these take us no distance at all towards a positive reason for punishing the guilty just because they are guilty.

Even negative retributivism, however, is not without its problems, particularly if it is taken to include permissive clauses: you must not punish the innocent, but *you may punish the guilty;* you must not punish excessively, but *you may punish up to a proportionate degree.* These permissive clauses still do not assert positive retributivism, they do not say that wrong acts are positively a reason *for* imposing penalties; but they do say that wrong acts somehow cancel the basic reason for not imposing penalties; the guilty person loses his immunity in proportion to his guilt. Strictly, then, we should recognize permissive retributivism as a third variety, intermediate between negative and positive. The three principles can be stated briefly as follows:

Negative retributivism: One who is not guilty must not be punished.

Permissive retributivism: One who is guilty may be punished.

Positive retributivism: One who is guilty ought to be punished. (This "ought" may vary in strength between indicating only a weak *prima facie* reason and asserting an absolute requirement.)

The "must not," "may," and "ought" in each of these is moral. Also, these are to be considered as principles, morally valid in their own right. Obviously, the same statements could occur as derived rules in, for example, a utilitarian theory, where they would be explained and justified by their beneficial consequences, but they would not then constitute any sort of retributivism. For completeness, we should add quantitative variants of each of these three principles. Once these complications have been introduced, some further explanation is certainly needed both for the quantitative version of negative retributivism and for both versions of the permissive view. However, I leave these problems aside; they are as nothing compared with the difficulties in positive retributivism.

So far I have been drawing mainly formal distinctions, and have thus isolated the general form of a positive retributivist thesis, that a wrong act in itself positively calls for the imposition of a (proportionate) penalty. But this is a very dark saying. *Why* should it be so? Is there any way in which we can

make sense of this curious principle, at least by relating it to some network of other moral ideas?

It is here, as developments or explanations or further justifications of the positive retributivist thesis, that several of the approaches listed by Cottingham come in: repayment, satisfaction, fair play, placation, annulment, denunciation. "Desert" is not such a further explanation, but is just the general, as yet unexplained, notion of positive retributivism itself. But these (and one or two more that have been suggested, which Cottingham does not list) are a remarkably unimpressive collection. They are, indeed, the philosophical analogues of the sort of opponents that a chessplayer would like to have if he were going to play, blindfold, a dozen or so opponents at once. Each of them can be despatched, with ease, in a very few moves.

Satisfaction: What this might justify, if it justified anything, would seldom be proportional to the wrongness of the crime. It would entail severer penalties where the surviving victims of the crime were of a vindictive nature, but lighter ones where the victims were forgiving or "Christian" in spirit. It would entail the punishment of any behavior in proportion to its unpopularity, whether it was criminal or not. In any case, this is obviously a consequentialist justification: the penalty is being justified by the satisfaction it is likely to produce. Its connection with retributivism is merely that widespread satisfaction, felt by others besides the surviving victims of the crime, will be produced by the punishment of criminals only if many members of the society are already retributivists. But that does not make this itself a retributivist justification, and it has no power to explain any strictly retributivist principle.

Placation: This, too, is obviously consequentialist. The reason it offers for punishing rests upon the supposed bad consequences of failing to punish—the god will still be angry. But these consequences themselves depend upon the supposed retributivist opinions of the god in question. Far from explaining retributivism, this account requires that there should be some *other* morally adequate explanation of retributivism, if it is to be ascribed to a morally respectable god.

Denunciation: This also seems to be consequentialist. It has sometimes been called the "educative" theory of punishment. It tries to justify punishment by way of its tendency to produce in the public an attitude of greater hostility to the crime. This also, therefore, has no tendency to explain the retributivist principle, though, like satisfaction and placation, it may presuppose retributivist views. A public which already sees punishment as being deserved by the wrongness of the previous act is more likely to interpret a punishment as a dramatic assertion that the act punished was wrong.

These three approaches, then, are not really retributivist, though in one way or another they ride on the back of retributivism. Three others of the approaches listed, repayment, annulment, and fair play, do a little better in that they are genuinely retributivist in our sense. They are retrospective, non-consequentialist, because in each case the alleged justification is complete once the penalty has been inflicted; no further results of this are relied upon. But otherwise these approaches are equally unsatisfactory.

Repayment: How does the criminal's suffering or deprivation pay anything to society? No doubt repaying a debt often hurts the person who pays it, but it does not follow that anything that hurts someone amounts to his repaying a debt. If Jones owes Smith $10, it will hurt Jones just as much if he has to throw $10 away as if he has to give it to Smith, but throwing it away will not repay the debt. If the criminal's suffering or deprivation or incarceration doesn't do any good to society, it cannot be the payment of a debt to society. So this account is simply incoherent unless it is transformed into a theory of reparations, which are not punishment, or into the satisfaction theory which, as we saw, is consequentialist and will not explain retributivism.

Annulment: This notion, as Cottingham says, goes back at least to Hegel. But the remark he quotes (". . . das Aufheben des Verbrechens, das sonst gelten würde, und die Wiederherstellung des Rechts") would be better translated as referring to "the annulment of the crime, which would otherwise *remain in force,* and the restoration of right." Hegel's idea seems to be that as long as a criminal goes scot-free, the crime itself still exists, still flourishes, but when the criminal is adequately punished the crime itself is somehow wiped out. It is not, therefore, by any sort of repayment or restitution that "right is restored," but just by trampling on the previously flourishing crime. But this notion is simply incoherent: there is no comprehensible way in which a penalty wipes out an otherwise still-existing crime. What makes this suggestion plausible is a confusion with deterrence and prevention. A penalty may help, by deterrence, to wipe out, not the past crime, but other similar crimes which, but for the deterrence, would be committed either by this same criminal or by others; that is, it may help to wipe out

a criminal tradition or practice. Similarly, the locking up or killing of a criminal will put a temporary or a permanent stop to his criminal career. But in neither case is it the past crime that is annulled or wiped out, and deterrence and prevention are plainly consequentialist justifications, not retributivist ones.

Kant's remark that if the "last murderer" is not executed blood-guilt will adhere to the people, which Cottingham takes as an appeal to the placation theory, might be better understood as something like an anticipation of Hegel's notion of annulment. The guilt, the badness, of the crime is still floating around as long as the criminal is unpunished, and by letting him go free the people would share in this guilt as accessories after the act. But to suppose that this guilt is extinguished by the carrying out of the penalty requires the incomprehensible Hegelian notion of annulment, and to say that the people would be accessories if they did not punish the criminal presupposes, and therefore cannot explain, the principle that the crime in itself morally requires the penalty.

Fair play: Here the suggestion is that the various members of society are all in competition with one another, a competition governed by rules. The criminal has gained an unfair advantage by breaking the rules; to restore fairness this advantage must be taken away from him. Unlike our last two approaches, this one is not incoherent; it makes perfectly good sense in certain contexts. It has its clearest exemplification in the award of a penalty in football (soccer) when there has been a foul in the penalty area, that is, when a player or his shot has been illegally stopped in the neighborhood of the other side's goal. It is also retributivist in our basic sense of being retrospective; the justification is complete when the penalty has been imposed; fairness has then (roughly at least) been restored, irrespective of whether there are or are not any further desirable consequences. The trouble with this approach, however, is that it has little relation to most cases of punishment. Any serious attempt to apply it would lead to bizarre results, not at all well correlated with what is thought of as desert or degree of wrongness or guilt. It implies that penalties should as far as possible be proportional to the advantage that the criminal has gained, in the social competition, by breaking the rules, just as a foul near the opponents' goal is penalized much more than one elsewhere. Thus if a businessman has secured a contract worth $100,000, but has exceeded the speed limit in order to get to the relevant appointment on time, he should presumably be fined $100,000, whereas a fine of $1 would be enough for someone who murders a blind cripple to rob him of $1. And so on. Unsuccessful attempts at murder (or anything else) should not be punished at all. There should be an advantage rule, as there is in football, where the referee will not penalize an infringement if the innocent side still has the advantage anyway. So while there are things that this fair play principle can plausibly be used to justify, it has little bearing on most legal penalties and will not serve as an expansion or explanation of the basic principle of retribution or desert, of the idea that a wrong act in itself calls for a penalty proportionate to its degree of wrongness.

But perhaps it will be said that what matters is not the loot but the self-indulgence. Someone who commits a crime, even if he gets very little out of it, has still let himself go in a way that law-abiding people do not, and his punishment only brings him back into balance with their self-restraint. But when we switch to this topic of self-indulgence the analogy of a competitive game becomes even less apt. The ideal of equality in self-indulgence is so remote that we hardly even think of it. If it were unusual self-indulgence that we objected to and wanted to counterbalance, it would be the rich, the owners of yachts and racehorses, and businessmen with elastic expense accounts, that we should be getting after, not thieves and murderers. Again many murders arise out of domestic conflicts, and most of these only from long-standing problems. When people eventually kill their husbands or wives or lovers, they have probably already shown far more self-restraint, in not having so earlier, than those who are more happily or more placidly situated, and on the score of equality in restraint and indulgence would be entitled to let their hair down and kill someone once in a while.

What is basically wrong with the fair play approach, as these rather fantastic examples bring out, is that it focuses on the advantage that may have been gained by the criminal in some sort of social competition, whereas the point of punishment surely lies not in this but in wrongness of his act and the harm that he has done or tried to do. We can agree that he has acted unfairly, and that this implies that he cannot say that it is unfair if he suffers some proportionate penalty, if someone acts against him in a way that would otherwise have been similarly wrong. But this takes us only to a defence of permissive retributivism. It is still quite unclear how fair-

ness *to the law abiding* is secured by the punishing of the law-breaker in itself, that is, unless this punishment secures some benefit for the law-abiding. So the fair play theory still fails to yield any defence of the principle of positive retributivism.

A suggestion not on Cottingham's list, which is often used to support retributivism, is that it peculiarly respects the dignity of persons on whom penalties may or may not be imposed. We can see the force of this as a support for negative retributivism, though it is an understatement to say only that someone's dignity has been invaded if, while innocent, he is made to suffer for the sake of some benefit to others. Again, it may help to explain permissive retributivism: someone's dignity is perhaps being respected if it is his own choice that cancels his immunity. Penalties which accord with negative and permissive retributivism do not invade anyone's basic area of freedom. But these considerations give no support whatever to positive retributivism once it has been clearly distinguished from the other two views. It is quite incomprehensible how punishing a person because he has done wrong respects or enhances his dignity. Even as an argument against retributivism's traditional rivals as positive justifications of punishment, deterrence and utilitarianism generally, this has force. At most it shows that there should be restrictions on the deterrent (etc.) use of punishment, and this is commonly agreed by utilitarians although they hold that deterrence and the like are the only positive reasons for punishing. The utilitarian view can be and usually is developed in a way that introduces the negative and permissive theses as derived rules. Positive retributivism cannot gain even a comparative advantage by this appeal to dignity.

An even stranger suggestion on the retributivist side is that the criminal has a right to be punished. In general a right is something that the right-holder can either exercise or waive as he chooses, and most criminals would gladly waive this alleged right. If one of them would not, it could only be either because he actually wanted the penalty for itself, and then it would not be a punishment, or because he was himself a very keen retributivist—but then this, as a moral explanation of retributivism, would be circular, like the theories of satisfaction and placation we considered earlier. An associated view is that the criminal wills his own punishment. This may be just the point already noted, that it is by his own choice that he has lost his immunity; but this supports only the negative and permissive theses, not the positive one. Alternatively, what is invoked here may be Rousseau's general will: the criminal, *qua* citizen, subscribes to and helps to make the universal law by an application of which he is punished. Where this is true, it will help to justify punishment, and may indeed justify positive retributivist theses as derived rules about the imposition of penalties. Once the validity of the universal law attaching a penalty to a crime is established, the only further justification needed to provide *some* positive reason for imposing the penalty in a particular case is the retrospective one that a crime of the relevant sort has been committed. But this—which is, perhaps, the core of what Cottingham calls the penalty theory—explains positive retributivism only as a working rule, not as a justifying principle in its own right. Everything depends on the prior validity of the universal law, and this, on the present approach, depends on the two questions, whether the general will has actually made the universal law that is being applied and whether it was reasonable for it to do so. Since all the arguments for the positive retributivist *principle* are so weak, an affirmative answer to the second of these questions would have either to invoke non-retributivist considerations, or to move to some non-objectivist point of view, or both.

II

And that, it seems, is that. Every one of these approaches fails completely to supply any coherent expansion or explanation of the retributivist principle, and, as far as I know, there are no others on offer. On the other hand it is plain that a considerable number of people have what would be called an intuition that a wrong action in itself calls for the infliction of suffering or deprivation on the agent. In fact we might go further than this. Many people, perhaps most people, find unsatisfactory what I might call the standard compromise position about punishment.

What I mean by the compromise position is this. Negative retributivism is explained as a consequence of the rights of innocent persons, and permissive retributivism on the ground that a non-innocent person has to some extent lost those rights: rights make sense within a system of reciprocal rights, so that someone who has violated the rights of others cannot fairly claim the corresponding rights for himself. This system of reciprocal rights may in turn be explained within, say, some kind of utilitarian theory, or again it may be put forward on its own. In either case, this line of thought brings us to

the point that someone who has done wrong *may* be punished, though someone who has done no wrong must not. But—the compromise runs—the positive decision to punish is justified, if at all, by the benefits that are likely to result from so doing, for example, by way of the deterrence of crime. So we combine negative and permissive retributivism (themselves explained immediately in terms of rights, though *perhaps* also, more indirectly, in terms of utility) with a positive justification of penalties that appeals directly to utility.

This compromise looks neat, and has therefore commended itself to some philosophers. But I think that most people will, on reflection, find it unsatisfactory. They will not feel happy about imposing a penalty on someone for the sake of benefits to others, even if he has lost his right to immunity, unless they can say further that he positively deserves this penalty. Strange though this may be, we want to be able to appeal to a positive retributivist principle as well as to whatever utilitarian or in general consequentialist justifications there may be. Also, positive retributivism is not a completely isolated moral principle: it has a counterpart in the view that gratitude and reward are morally appropriate. We feel that someone who has helped another person deserves gratitude, and that someone who has done good generally, especially something outstanding good, deserves some reward. And he deserves a reward simply because of what he has done, not because rewarding him will bring about this or that good further consequence.

Indeed, we could go further still: our basic moral concepts themselves of good and bad, right and wrong, cannot be adequately analyzed unless we include a retributive element, the notion of returning benefit for benefit and harm for harm. What is bad or wrong, for example, is not simply what is harmful or what is forbidden: it is thought of also as what deserves condemnation, where condemnation is some kind of hostile and unpleasant reaction. Equally, what is good or right is not simply what is beneficial or what is recommended: it is thought of also as what deserves praise and commendation, what calls for a friendly and pleasant response.

Have we, then, been engaged in a vain and unnecessary task of trying to explain and justify positive retributivism? It is rather true merely by definition that what is wrong or bad deserves punishment and that what is right or good deserves reward? Is it part of the very concepts of wrong, bad, right, and good that they carry such deserts with them?

It would be a mistake thus to dismiss the problem. For even if it is part of these concepts that good and bad deserve reward and punishment, there is still the question whether and how those concepts themselves are to be justified or explained. For example, if the concept of something's being bad combines the notions of its being *harmful* and *forbidden* and *deserving a hostile response,* we still have the question why these three notions should go together, in particular why what is harmful and forbidden deserves a hostile response. That these elements go together is a synthetic judgment, even though the combination of them emerges from the analysis of *bad*.

Now as allegedly objective moral principles, this combination, and the corresponding combination of being *beneficial, recommended,* and *deserving of a favorable response,* are still quite obscure, though they are undoubtedly deeply entrenched in our thought. But as soon as we make the Humean move of saying that moral distinctions are founded on sentiment, not on reason, the obscurity disappears. If we ask, not, "Why do wrong actions deserve penalties and good actions deserve reward?" but rather "Why do we have an ingrained tendency to see wrong actions as calling for penalties and good actions as calling for reward?" then it is not difficult to outline an answer.

First let us consider the tendency to feel and show gratitude for benefits, and its hostile counterpart, the tendency to feel and express resentment of injuries. There is no doubt that these are very widespread human dispositions, and what look like the same or similar tendencies are not difficult to detect in some non-human animals. Nor is there the slightest difficulty in understanding how such instinctive patterns of behavior, and feelings that harmonize with that behavior, could have developed by an evolutionary process of biological natural selection. Since gratitude will reward the benefactor, and since tendencies that are rewarded are thereby psychologically reinforced, gratitude will tend to encourage further similar benefactions, and so will benefit the creature that feels and displays gratitude. We are not, of course, saying (as Hobbes did) that what looks like gratitude is really egoistically calculated behavior aimed at encouraging future benefits. The feeling of gratitude may be and normally is straightforward, sincere, and noncalculating; it is, so to speak, the natural selection process that does the calculating, not the grateful agent himself. Thus uncalculating gratitude will be produced *because* of the benefits it is

likely to bring, but the agent himself does not act gratefully *for the sake of* or *in anticipation of* those benefits. Similarly resentment of injuries is likely to discourage similar injuries, and so again will benefit the creature that feels and displays resentment, and thus there will be natural selection in favor of resentment, though again the resentment in the agent himself will normally be spontaneous, not calculated.

Gratitude, however, is a favorable reaction by a particular agent to actions that have benefited *him,* and resentment similarly is a hostile reaction by a particular agent to actions that have harmed *him*. Reward and punishment are more generalized forms of retribution: they are responses to actions that are seen as good or bad in general, not as good or bad to some particular agent, and the retributive attitudes which we have to explain are those of seeing the good or bad actions as calling for reward or punishment as such, not as calling for favorable or hostile reactions *from* particular agents. The attitudes to be explained, therefore, are generalizations of gratitude and resentment in these two respects: specific reference to those to whom good or harm has been done is eliminated, and the attitudes arise in persons generally who know about the good or harm, not only in those who are themselves benefited or harmed.

However, once we have explained gratitude and resentment, it is easy to understand these generalizations of them. Hume would say that such generalization arises from sympathy; but a sociological explanation would be better than this purely psychological one. Within a social group, people tend to feel and show gratitude and resentment on behalf of one another, in some respects at least, because they are reciprocally benefited by doing so. Cooperation in resentment and gratitude grows up for the same reason that gratitude itself does, that it tends to be beneficial to each of the cooperators. This may be either an instinctive tendency, to be explained by biological natural selection, or a cultural trait or "meme," to be explained by a process of social evolution that is an analogue of biological selection. In saying this, we must guard against three errors. First, we are not saying that this cooperation is calculating from the point of view of the cooperators themselves: they feel genuine sympathy, righteous indignation, and the like. But they have come to feel in these ways as a result of some biological or social selective process in which the benefits of such cooperation has played a key role. But, secondly, we are not saying that this cooperation in gratitude and resentment has arisen because of its general utility, because the social group as a whole has been benefited by it. No doubt the group is benefited, but that would not in itself be a good explanation. A practice which *would* be socially useful may fail to arise; it is unlikely to arise unless it produces results which favor its own spreading and surviving, unless it works so as to propagate the genes or "memes" on which it depends; and in general this requires that it should benefit the individuals who engage in that practice. But cooperation in gratitude and resentment meets this requirement: it can grow up as a convention which in fact benefits all parties, even without being deliberately adopted for that purpose. However, thirdly, it is just not the case that all sorts of gratitude and resentment are generalized equally. Only some kinds of harm are socially, cooperatively, resented, and cooperation in gratitude is even more restricted. Again we must seek and can find sociological reasons for these differences: only with particular kinds of harm are the conditions favorable for the growth of a convention of cooperative hostility to them, so only some kinds of harm are

seen as wrong and as calling for general resentment and punishment. For example, theft is cooperatively resented, but commercial competition is not.

In conclusion, therefore, I maintain that it is easy to understand why we have a deeply ingrained tendency to see wrong actions as calling for penalties and some sorts of good actions as calling for reward. Though retributive principles cannot be defended, with any plausibility, as allegedly objective moral truths, retributive attitudes can be readily understood and explained as sentiments that have grown up and are sustained partly through biological processes, and partly through analogous sociological ones.

That is why I have, in the title of this paper, called retributivism a test case for ethical objectivity. On objectivist assumptions, its force and its persistence are incomprehensible, but on a subjectivist or (in Hume's sense) sentimentalist approach they are easily understood.

---

1. Jeffrie G. Murphy, in "Cruel and Unusual Punishments," to appear in the proceedings of the 1979 Conference of the Royal Institute of Philosophy on Law and Morality.

2. J. G. Cottingham, "Varieties of Retribution," *Philosophical Quarterly*, July 1979.

GETTING EVEN:
The Role of the Victim*

Jeffrie G. Murphy

Not if his gifts outnumbered the sea sands
or all the dust grains in the world could
Agamemnon ever appease me—not till he
pays me back full measure, pain for pain,
dishonor for dishonor.

—*Iliad* (IX. 383–86)

I. Introduction[1]

Achilles is vindictive; he wants to get even with
Agamemnon. Being so disposed, he sounds rather
like many current crime victims who angrily complain that the American system of criminal justice
will not allow them the satisfactions they rightfully
seek. These victims often feel that their particular injuries are ignored while the system addresses itself
to some abstract injury to the state or to the rule of
law itself—a focus that appears to result in wrongdoers being treated with much greater solicitation
and respect than their victims receive. If the actual
victims are noticed at all (other than to alert the state
to a violation of *its* interests), they will likely be told
that there is another branch of law—tort law—that
has the job of dealing with private injuries and grievances and that, if they pursue this route at their own
expense, they might ultimately get some financial
compensation for the wrongs done to them. However, just as Achilles felt that mere compensation
was inadequate to the kind of injury done to him by
Agamemnon, many of these victims will often claim
that the injuries they have suffered (brutal rape, perhaps) do not admit of financial compensation. How,
they might ask, can a dollar value be set on the humiliation and degradation they have experienced?
They might also note that those who injure them
tend, unlike Agamemnon, to be judgment-proof—so

lacking in resources as to be unable to make any
meaningful contribution to any compensation package that the victim may win. From such a perspective and from such feelings has the "victims' rights
movement" in part been born.[2]

In this essay I will address simply *one* of the
many issues raised by this movement—namely, the
issue of the legitimacy of hatred and desires for revenge as operative values in a system of criminal
law. It is widely assumed—as a part of liberal culture, particularly Christian liberal culture—that such
psychological states are either unambiguously evil
or unambiguously sick and that, in either case, they
deserve no place in the moral and legal outlook of
civilized people. Thus opponents of the victims'
rights movement will often characterize it as simply
the institutionalization of vindictiveness—where
such a characterization is supposed to serve as a *re-
ductio ad absurdum* of the movement. Proponents
of the movement will then generally take great pains
attempting to show that the movement is *not* based
on these admittedly evil feelings but on something
else—social utility or justice, perhaps. Thus, both
sides seem to agree that if the movement is indeed
based on these feelings and the desire to institutionalize them, then the movement is a mistake.

Since I am skeptical that this agreement is justified, I will in this essay attempt to do two things:
(1) I will suggest that the burden of proof should be
placed on those who in principle *oppose* hatred, vindictiveness and revenge—that someone other than
the champions of these responses should be put on
the defensive for a change; and (2) I will suggest that
this burden might not be as easy to bear as some
might initially think. My purpose is neither to celebrate hatred and its close cousins nor to argue posi-

*From Jeffrie G. Murphy, "Getting Even: The Role of the Victim," in *Social Philosophy and Policy,* vol. 7, issue 2 (1990), pp.
209–25. Reprinted by permission of Blackwell Publishers.

tively that this feeling and its associated practices should be built into the criminal law. I rather seek to expose some bad arguments against it and its institutionalization (but also to highlight some important arguments against it) in the hope that its possible role—and indeed the whole victims' rights movement—can be seen in a clearer and fairer light.

II. Who Has the Burden of Proof?

As a starting point in inquiry, I am inclined to accept what might be called a bias or presumption in favor of common sense—namely, that absent some good argument to make us withdraw our common-sense beliefs and attitudes, we should regard them as reasonable. We should not always feel obligated to defend our ordinary views, but should rather impose the burden of challenge on others—being honestly willing, of course, to abandon the comfort of the received wisdom if we are indeed provided with good arguments for so doing. The underlying assumption behind this bias or presumption can, I think, partly be understood in (loosely) evolutionary terms. Our ordinary views and attitudes must, at least at one time, have had *something* going for them—some useful and adaptive contact with our social world or with the world of nature. Otherwise, it would be hard to see why these beliefs and attitudes would survive and be so deeply entrenched in our psyches. Of course, some beliefs and attitudes that might have been adaptive at some distant time in our evolutionary history (e.g., racist beliefs and attitudes, perhaps) can properly be seen in present circumstances as maladaptive, irrational, and evil. But we come to see this, I assume, not because this was always obviously so (it clearly was *not*), but because we have listened to and been persuaded by overwhelming practical and moral arguments for a change in these beliefs and attitudes. Such an example, however, does not demonstrate the unreasonableness of a presumption in favor of common sense any more than the confident conviction of some guilty people demonstrates the unreasonableness of the presumption of innocence in criminal procedure.

In my role as armchair, anecdotal social scientist, I have come to the conclusion that most of us *do* accept, as a matter of common sense, the appropriateness of hatred and revenge in some circumstances—specifically, when these responses are exhibited by victims of serious wrongdoing and are directed against those who have wronged them. (In *Forgiveness and Mercy,* I call this "retributive hatred."[3]) Although most people pay a kind of general Sunday school lip service to the idea that even these hatreds are evil, their more casual conversations and practices will often fly in the face of these pious clich;aaes. Give them the right criminal (e.g., John Mitchell for Watergate era liberals) and they will warm to shared fantasies of giving that criminal his "pain for pain, dishonor for dishonor." This also comes out rather clearly in people's entertainment preferences. For example, I recently resaw (with some equally civilized and equally liberal friends) the movie *Silverado.* In this classy Western, we are presented with four honest and decent men (and their friends and families) being subjected to unspeakable injuries by thugs of unspeakable evil. When, in the closing moments of the movie, these men take—and, indeed, *gleefully* take—their violent revenge on those who have wronged them, all who watched cheered them on and found this outcome not only aesthetically pleasing but morally satisfying. And I think that the vast majority of other normal people would have experienced a comparable reaction—otherwise, how could we explain the great popularity of revenge entertainment? We like to see the portrayal of evil people getting their painful but just deserts, and we particularly enjoy it when these deserts are administered by their victims. Portrayals are, of course, fiction and fantasy—and many of those who approve of the fictional portrayal of revenge might still have deep and even final objections to having it occur in the real world. (Perhaps, for example, they believe that we are never actually able to know that we confront the kind of genuine evil that is simply a given in the world of fiction—that, unlike The Shadow, we are unable to know what evil lurks in the hearts of men.) But this is a practical objection; it makes no contribution to establishing that all feelings of hatred and revenge are intrinsically, or inherently, or in principle irrational or immoral. Feelings that we genuinely regard as inherently depraved (e.g., racial hatred) we would not even welcome as fantasy or fiction; thus, I think, we would have great doubts about a person who applauded the fictionally portrayed successes of a Nazi deathcamp commandant—even if he followed up his entertainment by saying "But, of course, I would hate to see this happen in the real world." Thus I think that most typical, decent, mentally healthy people have a kind of commonsense approval of some righteous hatred and revenge (but not of simply unprovoked malicious hatred or racial hatred) and are in some sense willing publicly to admit this, at least symbolically—e.g., they will stand without shame in line to see such revenge movies as *Silverado,* but not to see a film that glorifies racial hatred.

So perhaps we can grant that those who are willing to take the trouble to present a case in favor of some hatreds and acts of revenge are really seeking not to challenge but simply to reinforce common sense—that most people, even if unwilling to provide verbal endorsement of such a view, do in fact find it acceptable in principle for victims to resent and hate those who wrong them and to seek revenge against those who victimize them.[4] (Perhaps Christianity's victory over pagan common sense here is largely verbal.) But, if this is so, then it looks as though we have the beginnings of an argument for the institutionalization of these feelings—an argument from *democracy.* For what is a democracy except a form of government in which the majority gets to have its dominant preferences enacted into law—even if those preferences are condemned by a refined and condescending elite? Thus, if most people want to create a system of criminal law that institutionalizes and expresses the hatreds and desires for revenge that crime victims feel toward those who have wronged them, what principle would allow anyone to say nay to the will of the people thus expressed?

This principle, perhaps: that the fundamental rights of citizens may not be abridged even when the majority so desires. Such a principle defines a *constitutionally constrained* democracy (as opposed to a pure democracy) and characterizes the kind of democracy at least theoretically present in the United States. Thus, since one of the presupposed principles of this society is that the government may not treat people (even criminals) in brutally inhuman ways, the United States Constitution imposes (in the Eighth Amendment) an absolute ban on such "cruel and unusual" punishments as torture.[5] This ban is not to be seen as an expression of the will of the people; it is rather a principled check, an absolute side-constraint, on what the people will be *allowed* to will.

I think that this constitutional excursion dramatically reinforces the point I want to make about burden of proof here. We may, I think, regard American society as one in which the majority may do whatever it jolly well feels like *unless* one can demonstrate that what it feels like doing is *fundamentally wrong in principle.* (I take it that the Bill of Rights seeks to provide an initial—but not a final—analysis of what it means to say that a governmental act is fundamen-

tally wrong in principle.) To use my earlier language: the presumption is that the will of the majority should determine policy, and thus the burden of proof lies upon those who—for any majoritarian outcome—would seek to prevent it. My question, then, is this: can it be shown to be fundamentally wrong in principle for the suffering that criminals receive from the state to be contingent to any degree on hatreds and desires for revenge felt by their victims? Do criminals have a fundamental right to be shielded from the consequences of such feelings? Since I think I have shown that it is not obvious that they do (and that, in fact, people, tend to believe quite the contrary), those who would argue for the irrelevance or injustice of those feelings and their institutionalization should do just that—namely, *argue.* They have the burden of proof. I will thus now begin to explore what these arguments might be and the degree to which, if at all, they are successful.

III. Making the Case Against Hatred and Revenge

Those who condemn hatred and revenge can avail themselves of two different strategies of argument. They can argue (1) that the emotions involved in these responses are inherently irrational (like phobias) or inherently evil (like sadism or unprovoked malice). Or they can argue (2) that, whatever the merits of the emotions themselves (even assuming they are intrinsically splendid), it would either be unwise or wrong in principle for these emotions to have any effect on the administration of criminal punishment. (Some—e.g., Kant—have reasoned this way about compassion and mercy—suggesting that compassion, though a splendid and admirable emotion in itself and often productive of wonderful results in other contexts, may produce excessive acts of mercy—and thus undermine justice—if too influential on judges or those with the power of pardon.[6]) While (1) is my primary interest in this paper, it is so frequently tied in with (2) that I think it will be worthwhile to discuss and evaluate them both in the present context.

IV. The Rational Case Against Hatred

Surely hatred cannot be regarded as irrational simply because it is an emotion. Emotions (e.g., guilt, shame, fear, envy, jealousy, hatred, love, and com-passion) are not like mere sensations (e.g., head-aches): one sign of this is that we can speak sensibly of irrational emotions but not of irrational headaches or other sensations. (What is a phobia except an irra-tional fear? And what would it mean to call some fears irrational unless it makes sense to refer to oth-ers as rational?) Of course we sometimes speak of people themselves as being irrational if they allow emotions to dominate their personalities to an exces-sive degree—e.g. Spinoza's point about a rational person being one who is not *led* by a fear of death.[7] But is there any good reason to assume that hatred and desires for revenge are uniquely able to domi-nate or lead in a way that other emotions are not? Consider the character of Michael Kohlhaas in von Kleist's famous story.[8] Why will so many people say of a character such as Kohlhaas that he was over-come, or dominated by, or in the thrall of vindictive-ness—but would not tend to describe (for example) Mother Teresa as overcome, or dominated by, or in the thrall of compassion? (Is this anything more than a misleading way of noting that one likes compas-sion and does not like vindictiveness? Is a moral point masquerading as a psychological point and a question thereby being begged?) The literature of ha-tred and revenge does, of course, tend to portray these responses carried to a pathological extreme, but this may tell us more about what makes litera-ture interesting than anything basic about human psychology. (What a boring story it would have been had Kohlhaas simply beaten up a couple of people and taken his horses back.) Surely *any* emotion can be carried to a pathological extreme; does not the fact that we can identify pathological extensions of retributive hatred (e.g., Michael Kohlhaas's) suggest that there must be non-pathological instances of this emotion? And must this emotion have an inevitable tendency to provoke excessive behavior—as it did for Kohlhaas? What if the person is provoked by this emotion to seek only a level of revenge that we, on other grounds (utility or justice), would find accept-able? Are there no such people? Are all people who seek revenge really after consequences so extreme and socially disruptive that we must regard them as crazed? (It is, of course, question-begging to say that these feelings are irrational simply because they often prompt people such as Kohlhaas to act outside the law. For perhaps these feelings prompt people to il-legality only because we, not learning the lesson of Athena and the Furies, have refused to make a proper home for them and institutionalize them into

the legal system.) And consider Nietzche's famous ar-gument against *ressentiment* (a kind of hatred)—namely, that it tends to poison a person from within.[9] But why, according to Nietzsche, does it so poison? It is because it is *repressed;* thus, Nietzsche's point argues equally for getting rid of the emotion *or for expressing it*—e.g., through getting even.

We might, of course, regard an emotion as ir-rational if it lacks any point or purpose that we can understand or with which we can sympathize. John Rawls argues in this way, for example, about the emotion of (malicious) envy. For what is the point, Rawls asks, of simply desiring that another lose some benefit when that benefit was not wrongfully acquired and when the benefit, when lost, will not transfer to the malicious envier?[10] Although I think that Rawls's position is not without problems, I will for present purposes grant it. Analogous arguments will not obviously condemn retributive hatred as ir-rational, however, since this emotion (with which, I have already argued, most of us sympathize) often has as its point the desire to annul (perceived) wrongful gains and to give people their (perceived) just deserts—in short, to "get even" through revenge. That, and not something further, is its point. Unless the desire to bring about these states of affairs is it-self always wrong or irrational, then surely the emo-tion of retributive hatred—as a desire to bring them about—cannot be condemned as pointless and thus as irrational. (One would surely not want to give as one's argument against retributive hatred an appeal to some notion of pointlessness that would, if ac-cepted, refute all deontological considerations in ethics.) But is revenge acceptable? I will explore this question in the final section of the paper, but it would, of course, beg the question simply to assume at this point that it is not.

The above considerations suggest to me that it is going to be very difficult to make a case that ha-tred (as a desire for revenge) is inherently irrational—the moral equivalent of a phobia. Though obviously (because by definition) pathological extensions of this emotion will not be present in a rational person, a lesser degree might well play some roles in the psy-ches of rational and healthy people—e.g., prompting them to seek restitution for injuries, liberating them from the bondage of resentment (through getting even), maintaining their self-respect, and even (by making themselves known as disposed to revenge) warding off some aggressors who might otherwise challenge their security and invade their "moral space." Thus if a case is to be made against the emotion of retributive hatred itself, the case will have to be *moral*—a case that the emotion, however rational it may be in some prudential or therapeutic sense for the person who experiences it, is still evil and would not be present in a truly virtuous person. It is to this moral case that I will now turn.

V. The Moral Case Against Hatred

The idea that hatred and desires for revenge are evil dispositions of character is linked, in our Christian culture, to the idea that these dispositions are *sinful.* God, through Jesus Christ, commands that we love and forgive our enemies rather than seek from them the "eye for an eye" that was characteristic of the older law.[11] If somebody embraces the Christian religion (so interpreted), then such a person does have—in my view—a sufficient moral reason to regard hatred as a vice and all acts based upon it as evils. All argument on the issue could thus stop here, as arguments have a way of doing when they collide with total faith.

My present inquiry, however, is this: does the moral case against retributive hatred essentially depend upon such faith or can a case that does not depend upon religious belief—a purely secular case—be made? I think that such a case may be possible and, indeed, that it might be possible even to draw a large part of the case from a secular interpretation of some Christian parables. This should not be surprising, since many Christians wish to regard their God as a supremely rational being. If so, He presumably did not command love and forgiveness of enemies capriciously (e.g., He did not flip a coin to get this command) but rather knew that such dispositions were of some benefit to us, His creatures. But if God had good reasons for issuing these commands, it is not impossible that we—with our reason—could discover at least part of the case that prompted Him and see its good moral sense for ourselves.

Consider, with this in mind, the story of Jesus at the stoning of the adulteress (there cautioning the crowd to "Let him who is without sin cast the first stone").[12] Think of this story in conjunction with the famous passage, "*Vengeance is mine; I will repay, saith the Lord.*"[13] Consider also the parable of the unforgiving servant.[14]

The fact that God reserves vengeance for Himself suggests that, in His view, the desire for vengeance is not an inherently irrational (or even in-

herently evil) disposition of character. (Otherwise, God would be condemning Himself.) It is rather that He has reasons for claiming that the disposition to vengeance is a uniquely divine prerogative. What might these reasons be? Presumably they are that only God *knows enough* and only God is *good enough* to seek vengeance reliably and without hypocrisy. His creatures lack these epistemological and moral qualifications; they must therefore wait and depend upon God to get the job done.[15] Thus these scriptural passages can be interpreted to mean that human beings, given their radical limitations, always manifest vices— specifically, the vices of *presumption* and *hypocrisy*—if they have and indulge feelings of retributive hatred.

Is this claim plausible? Are we too ignorant to be reliable retributive haters? Are we ourselves too morally flawed to hate, without hypocrisy, those who wrong us? Let us consider each of these questions separately.

What is it that we are unable to know about wrongdoers that poses no problem for God? We surely know what *acts* are unacceptable, and thus perhaps the problem is supposed to lie in some lack of ability we have in knowing the *mental states* and *dispositions of the will* present in wrongdoers. Kant, for example, claims that only God can "know the heart"; given his view that moral condemnation is addressed to the inner disposition of will, he argues (in his *Religion,* but not elsewhere) that human ignorance of such matters precludes the acceptability of the kind of harsh condemnation of others that legitimately hating them would involve.[16]

I think that this argument is important—one that should make us (as I stress in great detail in the book) *very cautious* of what we do in this area—but I am not convinced that it makes a fatal case against the moral legitimacy of all retributive hatred. For Kant is well known as being (to put it mildly) in favor of punishment; given his commitments to justice, he would want to condemn strenuously a system of punishment that employed only strict liability. This means, of course, that he would (like us) want a system of criminal liability that involves *mens rea,* excuse, and justification. But such a system can be administered only if, *in some sense,* we *can* "read the heart." Thus those who would make flip arguments against retributive hatred based upon some supposed inability to determine the appropriate inner dispositions should note the massive (and certainly unwelcome) reforms in the criminal law—and perhaps in our whole moral conception of personal responsibility—that would flow from the literal acceptance of such a slogan.

So too, I think, for those who would make an overly ambitious use of the important insight that each one of us is morally flawed ("Let him who is without sin. . .") and often stands in need of some gentle response, such as forgiveness from others (a point of the parable of the unforgiving servant). For such things are in fact, of course, matters of degree. That I have certain vices (a certain lack of generosity, perhaps) does not mean that I ever have or ever would even contemplate treating another human being in the way that Michael Kohlhaas was treated by those who wronged him, or in the way that some rape victims are brutalized by their attackers. Thus it seems that although I may not be utterly without sin, I may well be without sin *in the relevant sense* in some cases. And why may I not, without hypocrisy, indulge retributive hatred in these cases? John Rawls has taught us the useful device in ethics of imagining ourselves in all possible roles that will be affected by the moral rules we adopt. As one who may sometimes need the love and forgiveness of others, I will of course want a world where retributive hatred does not reign unchecked. But as someone who may sometimes want to get even for terrible wrongs done to me, I might not want to create a social world wherein desires for revenge are utterly condemned—regarded as, in themselves, signs of irrationality or vice.

Finally, there is the argument from moral equality. According to this argument (often appealed to by Christians), all human beings are of equal moral worth—perhaps even absolute moral worth—and are to be equally loved, because it is both irrational and immoral for any one of these creatures to rule any of his equals outside the domain of benevolent concern—as hatred certainly does. (In religious terms, this Kantian point might be made by saying that we are all children of God and equally beloved in His sight; that God's perspective should then be adopted in our own dealings with our fellow humans.) To this argument I have the following response: that all human beings (no matter how morally vile) are to be loved strikes me as a claim whose *intrinsic implausibility* is staggering. Thus, I can imagine no reason for taking such a claim seriously unless one views it as a command of God—i.e., one therefore has an *extrinsic* reason for taking it seriously. Here, then, we perhaps have a good example of an ethical issue where a secular world view leads us in one direction and the Christian world view leads us in quite another—perhaps dashing any hasty optimism (present, I think, in some strands of liberal Christianity) about the ultimate compatibility or reconciliation of the two.[17]

I conclude from the above that the case against the rationality and morality of the emotion I have labeled retributive hatred has not been made. Thus, I think that we may properly retain our common-sense belief that this feeling is sometimes acceptable—and sometimes even laudable. Those of us who want to retain the concept of genuine evil—in discussing the Holocaust perhaps—the perpetrators of which merit hatred are not yet defeated. As noted earlier, however, this does not establish that it is ever permissible for us to *act* on such feelings or that the law should ever assist us in so acting. Desires for revenge are one thing; acts of revenge are quite another. Thus I shall now move to a consideration of the permissibility of revenge itself.

VI. The General Case Against Revenge and Its Role in Criminal Law (Especially Sentencing)

By "revenge," I will mean any injury inflicted on a wrongdoer that satisfies the retributive hatred felt by that wrongdoer's victim and that is justified because of that satisfaction.[18] I here assume again (for the reasons earlier noted) that the burden of argument lies on those who would oppose the legitimacy of revenge, and I assume that the arguments given will (like all arguments in ethics) be either consequentialist arguments or arguments of principle.[19] I also believe that the really impressive and important arguments will be those of the latter sort.

Why might revenge be disutilitarian—wrong on consequentialist grounds? The most common thing said against it is that it is socially disruptive—it is likely to provoke an unpredictable and destabilizing level of conflict. But this argument, of course, seems most impressive as an argument against *private* revenge—vigilante activity—and, if this is the only argument, really supports rather than undermines the claim that revenge ought to be institutionalized by the state: that is, that the state, taking on the personae of crime victims, should elevate (at least some of) the private grievances of individuals to the status of public grievances. If revenge is not intrinsically evil or wrong in principle, why should its public expression not be justified by these two consequences: (1) the satisfaction given to victims and (2) the resulting tendency to defuse the potentiality for private revenge and its resulting social turmoil?[20] (This does not mean that the state should take on all desires for revenge—some are excessive—but it does suggest reasons why the state might take on some of them.) And consider the standard utilitarian value of deterrence: might not potential criminals be given an extra incentive to remain law-abiding if they know that they live in a system where victim outrage (or, in murder cases, survivor outrage) might have a bearing on their level of punishment?[21]

The above considerations suggest that the purely utilitarian or consequentialist case against the institutionalization of revenge is going to be fragile. Some utilitarian arguments will tell against the practice, and others will tell in its favor; an impartial observer might well conclude that the latter arguments, on balance, win the day. This is, of course, often the case with utilitarian arguments on complex issues; we often, after all, lack the kind of hard empirical evidence that would be needed really to establish the probability of the claimed consequences. We thus often run the risk of lapsing into anecdotes and hunches that are often tailored to the outcome we want to justify. For this reason, those who want a *fatal* argument to block the institutionalization of revenge had better attempt an argument from principle, for one great virtue of such arguments is that they are invulnerable to the shifting winds of empirical guesswork.

Are there good arguments that institutionalized revenge is wrong in principle? I think that there are two that must be taken very seriously:

1. *The argument from retributive justice.* "All criminals have a fundamental right not to be punished in excess of their just deserts. A person is punished in excess of his just deserts if he is punished with greater severity than the blameworthy character of his conduct would justify. A person cannot coherently be held blameworthy for the degree to which he is hated by those he wrongs (very blameworthy for injuring thin-skinned victims and minimally blameworthy for injuring stoic victims?), and thus any criminal sentencing that takes account of victim hatred (as any revenge system would have to do) violates a fundamental right, is unjust, and is thus wrong in principle."

2. *The argument from equal protection and due process.* "All criminals have a fundamental right to be protected against sentencing procedures that are inherently arbitrary and capricious. Sentencing systems based on victim hatred will inevitably have this feature and are thus wrong in principle."

These are very important arguments. (They were also the essential arguments at issue in the 1987 United States Supreme Court case of *Booth v. Maryland*—a case, regarded by many as a major setback to the victims' rights movement, holding that victim impact statements may not influence sentencing in capital cases.[22]) I take these arguments seriously, and I would like to consider them with some care. I will consider them in reverse order.

VII. The Argument from Equal Protection and Due Process

The best argument that revenge systems are inherently arbitrary and capricious lies in the fact that retributive hatred—the basis for such systems—is essentially a *subjective* response to being wronged; as such, it can vary enormously from one victim to the next. Thus, the very same injury that will be brushed off as trivial by those with a stoic disposition will generate anguish and deep hatred in the highly sensitive. Also, the level of hatred involved might well be a function of factors about the criminal that any reasonable person would regard as clearly irrelevant to culpability—e.g., the white rape victim who feels more deeply wronged if raped by a black person than if raped by a white person. If fairness requires that potential criminals receive accurate notice of the exact nature of the proscribed conduct and its attached penalties, it is hard to see how such notice could be given in a system where sentencing might actually depend upon factors that admit of such wide and subjective variation.[23] And if criminals have a right to be protected against mere prejudice (e.g., racial hatred), it might seem difficult if not impossible to give them this protection in a hate-based system, since hatreds often are a function of prejudices. I am by no means sure that it would not be possible to design procedures that would keep arbitrary and capricious sentencing at an acceptable level—i.e., at a level no greater than that already present and accepted at other points in the system—but we have at last found a principled objection to revenge that cannot simply be summarily dismissed. Those who look fondly upon revenge have an obligation to take this objection very seriously—i.e., seriously enough to recognize that the burden of argument may now have been properly shifted back to them and to take on the burden of formulating procedures to control these potential abuses. Of course, if it can be shown that criminals have a fundamental right to be sentenced in proportion to personal blameworthiness and that revenge is inconsistent with such a right, then we have the basis for an absolute ban on revenge (an absolute ban on its institutionalization) regardless of procedure. The procedural argument is thus secondary to what I have called "the argument from retributive justice," and it is to this most important argument that I shall now turn.[24]

VIII. The Argument from Retributive Justice

In *Booth v. Maryland* Justice Powell, writing for the majority, held that victim impact statements (VISs) are constitutionally imper~missible in capital sentencing. Such statements—or actual testimony by victims if they are allowed to attend and speak at sentencing hearings—are very likely, according to Powell, to influence judges (or juries in states where juries have a sentencing role) to inflict cruel and unusual punishments. Their use and influence thus violates the Eighth Amendment.[25]

Powell essentially gives two arguments to support this view. One argument (a procedural one of the kind explored above) is that emotional appeals from attractive and articulate victims are likely to focus the judge's attention away from the legally relevant issues and produce arbitrary and capricious sentencing.[26] More fundamental than this procedural argument, however, is Powell's articulation of the principle that, in his view, defines what *is* legally relevant. Speaking essentially as a retributivist, Powell claims that criminal defendants in capital cases have a right that their sentence be solely a function of their personal *blameworthiness*—i.e., factors solely based on "the character of the individual and the circumstances of the crime" or on the defendant's "personal responsibility and moral guilt." Since VIS

information may be, according to Powell, wholly unrelated to the blameworthiness of a particular defendant, and may cause the sentencing decision to turn on irrelevant factors such as the degree to which the victim's family is able to articulate grief and defend the victim's worth, such evidence will inevitably and improperly shift the focus away from the defendant and what he deserves. The essence of the argument, then, is this: sentencing should be based on what is morally blameworthy about the defendant; one is blameworthy only for that which is one's fault or which one brings about under one's own control; the degree to which a victim will be upset or outraged by what is done to him or will be able to articulate feelings is subjective and variable; it is thus not within the defendant's control; therefore, it would be wrong in principle to let sentencing depend to any degree on such matters.

Given the wide variety of penal purposes that are often articulated by judges in sentencing (see, for example, Judge Frankel's well-known sentencing opinion in *U.S. v. Bergman*[27]), it is odd that Powell should only emphasize the one retributive purpose of making suffering proportional to blameworthiness. (I will, for present purposes, ignore the special problems posed by the fact that *Booth* is a capital case, since I am interested in victim revenge and VISs in general.) We know that judges—both in sentencing and in approving plea-bargain agreements—typically weigh such factors as jail crowding, likelihood of recidivism, impact on the defendant's family, the defendant's age and health, possible service the defendant might perform for the community, the need for special and general deterrence, the need for incapacitation, and the possibility of reform; none of these having any obvious connection with moral blameworthiness or any other valid retributive purpose. It is hard to see, if this long laundry list of (perhaps laudable) social and personal goals properly gets to play a role in sentencing, why it would be wrong in principle to find room for VISs as well.

Consider also the major (and, no doubt, quite unwelcome) reforms in the criminal law that a literal application of the moral blamewor~thiness principle would entail. As Justices Scalia and White noted in their dissents in *Booth,* we currently feel comfortable with making the penalty for successful murder more severe than that for an attempted murder that fails through a fortuity; yet it is obvious that the moral blameworthiness in the two cases is identical. We also punish reckless driving that kills much more severely than reckless driving *simpliciter;* yet, as Thomas Nagel would say, it is surely differences in "moral luck" rather than any differences in moral blamewor~thiness that distinguish the two cases.[28] Thus a decision to endorse some strong blameworthiness principle will not be cost-free; for it will force us to ignore other important factors—e.g., *harm* caused—that have typically been thought to be central to criminal liability. And with respect to the other factors, it is by no means obvious that VISs will be utterly irrelevant to them. For example: can the victim's personal response to the person who violated him tell us *nothing* about the degree of harm suffered? Is the revenge interest present in the victim worthy of no attention in a world where (for example) the community's supposed interest in service that the defendant might perform is regarded as relevant? All of this needs to be thought about much more deeply.[29]

But perhaps blameworthiness should be viewed simply as a *negative* retributive constraint on permissible punishment—a factor that sets an upper bound on the degree to which the state may legitimately pursue its other interests in punishing (e.g., crime deterrence). This might solve, for example, the puzzle about attempts. For even if attempters and succeeders have the same degree of blameworthiness, the state might have good reasons for punishing attempters less severely; no wrong will be done in such a system so long as the succeeders are not punished in excess of their just deserts understood as a function of their moral blameworthiness.

If we accept this weakened notion of retributivism, however, it is hard to see how this will form a principled objection to the institutionalization of victim revenge and the use of VISs. For, on this view, why not simply allow these factors to have influence—perhaps to counter sentimental tendencies to show mercy or make plans for community service—so long as their influence is capped off at the point when maximum just deserts for the offense is reached? This would, of course, simply be to restate Stephen's point: respect victim hatred and revenge, but institutionalize them so that their excesses can be constrained by other values equally worthy of respect in a system of criminal law.

IX. Conclusion

Let me close these ruminations on hatred and revenge by considering one final challenge to them. I

can imagine a critic now arguing as follows: your case for hatred and revenge within the limits set by blameworthiness and desert has saved hatred and revenge at a very high price—namely, you have made them *redundant.* If these responses must operate within a context defined by retributive just deserts, then how does the account of punishment you call hatred-based revenge differ from what Kant, and Herbert Morris, your own previous self, and others have simply called retributivism?

My short response to this is the following: I have elsewhere argued that, given a traditional liberal-libertarian conception of the state (as modelled in social contract terms), it is hard to see why there is any important state interest served in securing retributive values—in seeing that wrongdoers get their just deserts—for the sake of these values themselves.[30] If rational contractors were forming a state, it is easy to see why they might give up some liberty and resources to protect themselves against assault (a basic human desire) by adopting a deterrence scheme of criminal law. It is very hard, however, to see why they would do this simply to achieve a state of affairs that seems of merely abstract worth—namely, one where wrongdoers get their just deserts. In short: given the rarity of an intense sense of abstract justice, classical retributivism seems unmotivated within liberal theory.

If desires for revenge are basic and important to many people, however, this would provide some motivational grounds—in victim hatred—for those schemes of criminal justice we tend to call retributive; securing the revenge interests involved might, even in traditional liberal terms, prompt social contractors to be willing to make the sacrifices necessary to maintain a (constrained) system of revenge. Abstract concern for justice might explain the blameworthiness cap on punishment, but garden variety desires for revenge may gener~ate—and quite properly generate—some of the values that drive the system up to that point.[31]

I will not, however, press this argument. If a consequence of my view is that it will ultimately be impossible to draw a sharp distinction between the desire for retributive justice and the desire for revenge, then this in itself will put revenge in better philosophical company than it normally enjoys. Perhaps it will achieve the kind of impartial re-hearing for hatred and revenge that it has been the primary purpose of this essay to provoke.[32]

Let me now close by summarizing the main thrust of my argument. Crime victims often want to influence sentencing, and their motives for this are often vindictive. Perhaps such motives are dishonorable; perhaps giving a legal role to victims so motivated would indeed produce deep harm to our system of criminal justice. I have attempted to show that this has simply been assumed and not demonstrated, however, and that—in fairness to those victims—it should be demonstrated before the state simply dismisses as irrational or evil the passionate claims of those whom it has failed to protect from criminal violence.

---

1. The present essay builds on some ideas initially developed in ch. 3 ("Hatred: A Qualified Defense") of *Forgiveness and Mercy*, by Jeffrie G. Murphy (Chapters 1, 3 and 5) and Jean Hampton (Chapters 2 and 4), (Cambridge: Cambridge University Press, 1988).

2. The phrase "victims' rights movement" refers to those who advocate changes in criminal law and procedure that will (at least in their view) make crime victims more satisfied with the system. Rules of evidence that make it harder for defense attorneys to probe a claimed rape victim's sexual past, finding ways to allow claimed victims of child abuse to testify with less embarrassment or fear (e.g., on video or behind a screen), and allowing crime victims to influence criminal sentencing (e.g., by presenting victim impact statements to the sentencing judge) are examples of developments that may be viewed as victories for the victims' rights movement. The 1987 United States Supreme Court case of *Booth v. Maryland*, where victim impact statements were ruled unconstitutional in capital cases, may be viewed as a setback for the victims' rights movement. (This case will be discussed below.) It should be noted that the phrase "victims' rights" is importantly misleading as a characterization of some of the practices noted above. Since the use of a victim impact statement occurs after a criminal conviction (though prior to sentencing), the word "victim" here is appropriate. Prior to a conviction, however, we do not know for sure that we actually have a victim; all we know for sure is that we have an accuser. Thus it would be better if those who favor such things as shield laws to prevent unnecessary probing of an alleged rape victim's sexual past would refer to these practices as a matter of "accusers' rights." Also, is it correct to refer to these practices as rights at all, or should they simply be characterized (by those who favor them) as good policy?

3. Although I tend to support the legitimacy of what I call retributive hatred, I am inclined to agree with Willard Gaylin's claim that much anger and hatred in contemporary culture is—though understandable—irrational and maladaptive. See his *The Rage Within: Anger in Modern Life* (New York: Penguin Books, 1989).

4. Those who have come out in support of some instances of hatred and revenge include God ("Vengeance is mine . . . etc."), Aristotle (*Nicomachean Ethics*, 1125b ff.), Adam Smith (*The Theory of Moral Sentiments*, Indianapolis: Liberty Press, 1982, p. 38), James Fitzjames Stephen (*A History of the Criminal Law of England*, London, 1883, Vol. II, pp. 81 ff.), Ernest van den Haag ("In Defense of the Death Penalty," *Criminal Law Bulletin*, Vol. 14, No. 1, Jan.–Feb. 1978), Walter Berns (*For Capital Punishment*, New York: Basic Books, 1979), and Robert Axelrod (indirectly—as an endorsement of the strategy of "tit for tat" in iterated prisoner's dilemmas—in his *The Evolution of Cooperation*, New York: Basic Books, 1984). I also present a supportive case for these responses in *Forgiveness and Mercy*. In this book I suggest that, in addition to the social usefulness of these responses in some contexts, some considerations of vice and virtue also offer relevant support—namely, that a person's failure to resent wrongs done to him and to manifest retributive hatred toward the wrongdoer may be a sign that he has the vice of servility (a lack of proper self-respect and a lack of proper tendencies for self-defense). I would hate to have readers unfamiliar with the book conclude from the present paper that I see no moral and social problems with retributive hatred, however, so let me note that the book contains numerous qualifications and cautions with respect to my defense of this emotion—qualifications and cautions that considerably constrain the domain of its legitimacy. No doubt the reader will want to check this out, and I recommend that he do so by purchasing—preferably in the hardcover edition—a copy of the book.

5. Amendment VIII of the United States Constitution reads as follows: "Excessive bail shall not be required, nor excessive fines imposed, nor cruel and unusual punishments inflicted." This has been interpreted by the United States Supreme Court to rule out such inherently barbaric punishments as torture, punishments that are radically disproportionate to the gravity of the offense, and the punishment of death when administered in an arbitrary and capricious fashion.

6. Might not hatred and compassion stand or fall together with respect to criminal punishment? If it is wrong to increase a criminal sentence out of hatred, will it not also be wrong to decrease a criminal sentence out of compassion? Can one consistently be meticulous and strict about justice only in one direction? Perhaps we tend to be more lax about mercy because we think that the compassion on which it is based is, unlike hatred, an acceptable or even admirable emotion. But this, of course, needs to be shown. For Kant's discussion, see his *The Metaphysical Elements of Justice* (Indianapolis: Bobbs-Merrill, 1965), p. 107.

7. *Ethics*, Four, LXVII.

8. Heinrich von Kleist's 1810 story Michael Kohlhaas portrays a man who, when he fails to receive legal justice over a comparatively small injury done to him (theft and abuse of his horses), takes matters into his own hands. In his pursuit of revenge, he forms an army, kills large numbers of people, and nearly topples the government under which he lives. This story was retold by E. L. Doctorow in his 1975 novel *Ragtime*—wherein Michael Kohlhaas becomes Coalhouse Walker.

9. *On the Genealogy of Morals*, Essay I, Section 10.

10. *A Theory of Justice* (Cambridge: Harvard University Press, 1971, secs. 80 and 81).

11. Matthew 5:38–48. The older law is well represented in Psalms 58:10–11: "The righteous shall rejoice when he seeth the vengeance: he shall wash his feet in the blood of the wicked. So that a man shall say, Verily there is a reward for the righteous." In Aeschylus's Oresteia, the Furies represent sentiments of this kind. Athena refuses to banish them, however, because she respects the impulses they represent and believes that, by institutionalizing them under due process of law, she can make them such valuable forces in support of community morality that they will become known as "the kindly ones."

12. John 8:7.

13. Romans 12:19.

14. Matthew 18:21–35.

15. God seems to promise that the job of vengeance will get done. Is this to reassure His creatures that their hated enemies may not go eternally unpunished? But why should He pander to His creatures' desires for vengeance, unless these desires are in some sense both rationally and morally legitimate on their part? May these creatures not even look forward with delight to the coming divine retribution on their enemies? May they not even

have pleasing fantasies of it? When it happens, may they not look down from heaven with delight at the torments of their enemies below? Is God here in some sense promising (like Athena) to "institutionalize" (in His divine law) these legitimate feelings and thereby make their personal expression unnecessary? I raise these questions not to be impious, but simply to make the point that the "Vengeance is mine" passage can be read simply as a command that humans not act on retributive hatre~d—leaving open the possibility that feeling retributive hatred is neither an evil nor a vice. I do not believe that the simple command to love and forgive one's enemies is comparably ambiguous, however, for here feelings themselves are clearly the object of the command.

16. For a discussion of those aspects of Kant's moral philosophy that appear to be in tension with his commitments to retributivism, see my "Does Kant Have a Theory of Punishment?" in *Columbia Law Review*, Volume 87, No. 3 (April 1987).

17. Suppose I am willing to grant that hatred would properly be addressed toward me if I performed (with full responsibility) certain evil acts. Perhaps I would even resent it and regard it as an insult (because it would challenge my status as a responsible moral agent) if such hatred was not directed toward me in these circumstances. If I then address such hatred to others when they (with full respon~sibility) perform such acts, it is not clear that I violate any important equality demand. Saint Augustine tells us that we should "hate the sin but not the sinner." But if it is permissible to hate the act because it is bad, why is it wrong to hate the actor because he is bad? Of course, if the wrongdoer sincerely repents, this may block the legitimacy of hating or even resenting him—a theme I pursue in Ch. 1 of *Forgiveness and Mercy*.

18. Revenge is not to be identified with vigilante activity, and indeed I will assume for purposes of this paper that anyone who seeks revenge in ways that are illegal acts wrongly (not to mention uncreatively). The issue that I mainly want to explore, of course, is if the law itself should find a way of institutionalizing some of this revenge and thereby perhaps eliminate some temptations to self-help. I will also be assuming throughout that we are dealing with cases where the victims are not fantasizing the wrongdoing but have accurate beliefs that they have been wronged, accurate beliefs about the nature and degree of the wrong done to them, and accurate beliefs that the wrongdoer is as fully responsible for that wrongdoing as any human being ever is for any wrongdoing.

19. Some people might also suggest virtue arguments, but I am suspicious of their use in this context. For example: it is often suggested, as an argument against capital punishment, that it is wrong because of what it does to the characters of those who favor and inflict it—namely, it degrades and debases and dehumanizes them. But this is by no means obvious. In my view, a person is debased by the doing of X only if X is wrong (unjust, say), and thus—absent an independent showing that X is wrong—the character de~basement argument will not get off the ground. Similarly, engaging in revenge will debase people only if it can be shown, on independent grounds, that revenge is wrong. So too for the common "two wrongs do not make a right" clich;aae that is often trotted out here. Obviously, those who regard revenge as justified will not see it as a wrong; they will thus quite properly fail to see the relevance of the cliché to their claim.

20. This, I take it, is the point of James Fitzjames Stephen's famous analogy between the criminal law and the law of marriage (see note 4). He argued that we deal in each case with a passion that is legitimate (the desire for revenge in the one case and sexual desire in the other), but we have also learned that the passion in question has high potential to provoke disruptive behavior. Thus, the way to honor the passion without risking serious social disruption is for the law to regulate that passion—to provide it with a proper channel for expression. Taking victim hatred seriously in this way (by building it into legal practice) may thus benefit both the community and the victims

themselves, for the practice recognizes the validity of the hatred while placing important constraints on its excess. Such institutionalization might even help to educate persons on the legitimate bounds of hatred.

21. One might, of course, argue that such a deterrent system is unpredictable—an acceptable consequence from the point of view of deterrence, perhaps, but a disutilitarian consequence from many other points of view (e.g., liberty). I think that this is an important argument. However, since I think that unpredictability is an evil essentially because of its unfairness rather than because of its potentially disruptive social consequences, I will treat this as an objection of principle in the next section.

22. 482 U.S. 496 (1987). A victim impact statement is a statement from the crime victim or some representative of the victim that seeks to influence sentencing by stressing the impact of the crime on the victim and the victim's desires (or perhaps the survivor's desires in a murder case) with respect to the sentence.

23. Expressions of hatred might, of course, be evidence that something of assumed relevance to criminal liability—e.g., the existence of a certain level of harm—is present. I will explore this idea a bit later in the paper. As Ellen Paul has pointed out to me, one could argue that if criminals knew that they would face varying degrees of punishment based on the degree of hatred felt by their victims, they would factor this into their calculations of advantage/disadvantage before committing the crime. A rational criminal might then presume that his victim might be one with great capacity for hatred, and this might augment the deterrent value of the law. The criminal, by committing an illegal act, puts himself willingly and knowingly (but within limits, of course) in a kind of punishment lottery with respect to the harm that actually results from what he does. So why not a comparable lottery (again within limits) with respect to hatred and desires for revenge that might be felt by his victim?

24. Had the United States Supreme Court held that capital punishment is, like torture, inherently cruel and unusual punishment, consid~eration of the procedural problems surrounding the administration of that punishment would never have achieved their current prominence. The reason why *Furman v. Georgia* (408 U.S. 238 (1972)) and most later death penalty cases have dealt primarily with procedural matters—the desire to avoid arbitrary and capricious capital sentences—is that the Court has held that the penalty of death is not inherently cruel and unusual—at least with respect to some crimes of murder. Thus, it is not surprising that, in America, most principled legal objections to the death penalty now take a procedural form.

25. The Court did not clearly indicate what it will rule on VISs in non-capital cases. In capital cases, of course, the VISs are not primary victim impact statements (the primary victim being dead) but rather statements from concerned survivors—e.g., family members con~sidered as secondary victims.

26. It is not made clear why this poses any greater problem than that posed when the same victim appears as a witness during trial. Freedom from cross-examination, perhaps? Might it not be possible to allow such cross-examination at a sentencing hearing?

27. *United States v. Bergman*, United States District Court, S.D.N.Y., 416 F. Supp. 496 (1976). Rabbi Bergman, owner of several nursing homes, had been part of a scheme to defraud the United States government with respect to Medicaid payments. In his sentencing opinion, Judge Frankel explores a variety of punitive purposes that he believes must be weighed: retribution, community outrage, community support for the Rabbi because of his many philanthropic ventures, special and general deterrence, etc.

28. Thomas Nagel, "Moral Luck," in his *Mortal Questions* (Cambridge: Cambridge University Press, 1979).

29. The problem being noted here is that of the inconsistency of insisting on a blameworthiness basis for punishment in a system that gives the same weight to harm that most systems of criminal law currently do. This does not entail abandonment of a blameworthiness basis, of course, for one might instead avoid the inconsistency by arguing on retributivist grounds for the abandonment (or considerable qualification) of the relevance

of harm. For an exploration of this issue, see Stephen J. Schul-
hofer, "Harm and Punishment: A Critique of Emphasis on the
Results of Conduct in the Criminal Law," 122 University of
Pennsylvania Law Review 1497 (1974).

30. See my "Retributivism, Moral Education, and the Liberal State"
in *Criminal Justice Ethics,* Vol. 4, no. 1 (Winter/Spring, 1985).
For a skeptical attack on the common idea that there is a sharp
distinction in principle between criminal law (with the state as
injured party) and tort law (with individual victims as injured
parties), see my "Why Have the Criminal Law at All?" in ch. 3
of The Philosophy of Law: An Introduction to Jurisprudence,
by Jeffrie G. Murphy (Chapters 1, 2 and 3) and Jules L. Coleman (Chapters 4 and 5) (Totowa: Rowman and Allanheld,
1984). (A revised edition of this book will appear from Westview Press in late 1989.)

31. Even Herbert Morris's very abstract notion of criminal punishment as annulment of wrongful gains or unfair advantages (in

his "Persons and Punishment," *The Monist,* Volume 52, Number
4, October 1968) may ultimately depend not upon some abstract sense of justice (the desire to see justice done for its own
sake) but on something very like victim revenge. What, on Morris's theory, motivates me to want the criminal (as free-rider)
punished? That he has taken an unfair advantage of those who
have been law-abiding. But that means, given that I am one of
those who has been law-abiding, he has taken unfair advantage of me—he has derived a wrongful gain at my expense. If
this is what is most vivid in my mind (as it surely will be), then
in what sense is my desire to see him punished impersonal and
not a kind of victim revenge?

32. Most philosophical defenses of retributivism (including some of
my own previous essays) take great pains to distinguish retribution (which is taken to be just) from vengeance (which is
taken to be unjust or evil in some other way). Perhaps such attempts at drawing a sharp distinction have been misdirected.

---

*PAYNE V. TENNESSEE**

United States Supreme Court, 1991

Chief Justice REHNQUIST delivered the opinion of the
court.

In this case we reconsider our holdings in
Booth v. Maryland, and *South Carolina v. Gathers,*
that the Eighth Amendment bars the admission of
victim impact evidence during the penalty phase of
a capital trial.

The petitioner, Pervis Tyrone Payne, was convicted by a jury on two counts of first-degree murder and one count of assault with intent to commit
murder in the first degree. He was sentenced to
death for each of the murders, and to 30 years in
prison for the assault.

The victims of Payne's offenses were 28-year-
old Charisse Christopher, her 2-year-old daughter
Lacie, and her 3-year-old son Nicholas. The three
lived together in an apartment in Millington, Tennessee, across the hall from Payne's girlfriend, Bobbie Thomas. On Saturday, June 27, 1987, Payne
visited Thomas' apartment several times in expectation of her return from her mother's house in
Arkansas, but found no one at home. On one visit,

he left his overnight bag, containing clothes and other
items for his weekend stay, in the hallway outside
Thomas' apartment. With the bag were three cans of
malt liquor.

Payne passed the morning and early afternoon
injecting cocaine and drinking beer. Later, he drove
around the town with a friend in the friend's car,
each of them taking turns reading a pornographic
magazine. Sometime around 3 P.M., Payne returned
to the apartment complex, entered the Christophers'
apartment, and began making sexual advances towards Charisse. Charisse resisted and Payne became
violent. A neighbor who resided in the apartment directly beneath the Christophers, heard Charisse
screaming, "'Get out, get out,' as if she were telling
the children to leave." The noise briefly subsided and
then began, "'horribly loud.'" The neighbor called the
police after she heard a "blood curdling scream" from
the Christopher apartment. Brief for Respondent.

When the first police officer arrived at the
scene, he immediately encountered Payne who was
leaving the apartment building, so covered with

---

*No. 90-5721. Argued April 24, 1991. Decided June 27, 1991. Not all deletions are noted in this edited text.

blood that he appeared to be "'sweating blood.'" The officer confronted Payne, who responded, "'I'm the complainant.'" When the officer asked, "'What's going on up there?'" Payne struck the officer with the overnight bag, dropped his tennis shoes, and fled.

Inside the apartment, the police encountered a horrifying scene. Blood covered the walls and floor throughout the unit. Charisse and her children were lying on the floor in the kitchen. Nicholas, despite several wounds inflicted by a butcher knife that completely penetrated his body from front to back, was still breathing. Miraculously, he survived, but not until after undergoing seven hours of surgery and a transfusion of 1700 cc's of blood—400 to 500 cc's more than his estimated normal blood volume. Charisse and Lacie were dead.

Charisse's body was found on the kitchen floor on her back, her legs fully extended. She had sustained 42 direct knife wounds and 42 defensive wounds on her arms and hands. The wounds were caused by 41 separate thrusts of a butcher knife. None of the 84 wounds inflicted by Payne were individually fatal; rather, the cause of death was most likely bleeding from all of the wounds.

Lacie's body was on the kitchen floor near her mother. She had suffered stab wounds to the chest, abdomen, back, and head. The murder weapon, a butcher knife, was found at her feet. Payne's baseball cap was snapped on her arm near her elbow. Three cans of malt liquor bearing Payne's fingerprints were found on a table near her body, and a fourth empty one was on the landing outside the apartment door.

Payne was apprehended later that day hiding in the attic of the home of a former girlfriend. As he descended the stairs of the attic, he stated to the arresting officers, "Man, I ain't killed no woman." According to one of the officers, Payne had "a wild look about him. His pupils were contracted. He was foaming at the mouth, saliva. He appeared to be very nervous. He was breathing real rapid." He had blood on his body and clothes and several scratches across his chest. It was later determined that the blood stains matched the victims' blood types. A search of his pockets revealed a packet containing cocaine residue, a hypodermic syringe wrapper, and a cap from a hypodermic syringe. His overnight bag, containing a bloody white shirt, was found in a nearby dumpster.

At trial, Payne took the stand and, despite the overwhelming and relatively uncontroverted evidence against him, testified that he had not harmed any of the Christophers. Rather, he asserted that another man had raced by him as he was walking up the stairs to the floor where the Christophers lived. He stated that he had gotten blood on himself when, after hearing moans from the Christophers' apartment, he had tried to help the victims. According to his testimony, he panicked and fled when he heard police sirens and noticed the blood on his clothes. The jury returned guilty verdicts against Payne on all counts.

During the sentencing phase of the trial, Payne presented the testimony of four witnesses: his mother and father, Bobbie Thomas, and Dr. John T. Huston, a clinical psychologist specializing in criminal court evaluation work. Bobbie Thomas testified that she met Payne at church, during a time when she was being abused by her husband. She stated that Payne was a very caring person, and that he devoted much time and attention to her three children, who were being affected by her marital difficulties. She said that the children had come to love him very much and would miss him, and that he "behaved just like a father that loved his kids." She asserted that he did not drink, nor did he use drugs, and that it was generally inconsistent with Payne's character to have committed these crimes.

Dr. Huston testified that based on Payne's low score on an IQ test, Payne was "mentally handicapped." Huston also said that Payne was neither psychotic nor schizophrenic, and that Payne was the most polite prisoner he had ever met. Payne's parents testified that their son had no prior criminal record and had never been arrested. They also stated that Payne had no history of alcohol or drug abuse, he worked with his father as a painter, he was good with children, and that he was a good son.

The State presented the testimony of Charisse's mother, Mary Zvolanek. When asked how Nicholas had been affected by the murders of his mother and sister, she responded:

> He cries for his mom. He doesn't seem to understand why she doesn't come home. And he cries for his sister Lacie. He comes to me many times during the week and asks me, "Grandmama, do you miss my Lacie." And I tell him yes. He says, "I'm worried about my Lacie." (App. 30.)

In arguing for the death penalty during closing argument, the prosecutor commented on the continuing effects of Nicholas' experience, stating:

> But we do know that Nicholas was alive. And Nicholas was in the same room. Nicholas was

still conscious. His eyes were open. He responded to the paramedics. He was able to follow their directions. He was able to hold his intestines in as he was carried to the ambulance. So he knew what happened to his mother and baby sister.

There is nothing you can do to ease the pain of any of the families involved in this case. There is nothing you can do to ease the pain of Bernice or Carl Payne, and that's a tragedy. There is nothing you can do basically to ease the pain of Mr. and Mrs. Zvolanek, and that's a tragedy. They will have to live with it the rest of their lives. There is obviously nothing you can do for Charisse and Lacie Jo. But there is something that you can do for Nicholas.

Somewhere down the road Nicholas is going to grow up, hopefully. He's going to want to know what happened. And he is going to know what happened to his baby sister and his mother. He is going to want to know what type of justice was done. He is going to want to know what happened. With your verdict, you will provide the answer.

In the rebuttal to Payne's closing argument, the prosecutor stated:

You saw the videotape this morning. You saw what Nicholas Christopher will carry in his mind forever. When you talk about cruel, when you talk about atrocious, and when you talk about heinous, that picture will always come into your mind, probably throughout the rest of your lives.

. . . No one will ever know about Lacie Jo because she never had the chance to grow up. Her life was taken from her at the age of two years old. So, no there won't be a high school principal to talk about Lacie Jo Christopher, and there won't be anybody to take her to her high school prom. And there won't be anybody there—there won't be her mother there or Nicholas' mother there to kiss him at night. His mother will never kiss him good night or pat him as he goes off to bed, or hold him and sing him a lullaby. . . .

[Petitioner's attorney] wants you to think about a good reputation, people who love the defendant and things about him. He doesn't want you to think about the people who love Charisse Christopher, her mother and daddy who loved her. The people who loved little Lacie Jo, the grandparents who are still here. The brother who mourns for her every single day and wants to know where his best little playmate is. He doesn't have anybody to watch cartoons with him, a little one. These are the things that go into why it is especially cruel, heinous, and atrocious, the burden that that child will carry forever."

The jury sentenced Payne to death on each of the murder counts.

The Supreme Court of Tennessee affirmed the conviction and sentence. The court rejected Payne's contention that the admission of the grandmother's testimony and the State's closing argument constituted prejudicial violations of his rights under the Eighth Amendment as applied in *Booth v. Maryland,* and *South Carolina v. Gathers.* The court characterized the grandmother's testimony as "technically irrelevant," but concluded that it "did not create a constitutionally unacceptable risk of an arbitrary imposition of the death penalty and was harmless beyond a reasonable doubt."

The court determined that the prosecutor's comments during closing argument were "relevant to [Payne's] personal responsibility and moral guilt." The court explained that "[w]hen a person deliberately picks a butcher knife out of a kitchen drawer and proceeds to stab to death a twenty-eight-year-old mother, her two-and-one-half-year-old daughter and her three-and-one-half-year-old son, in the same room, the physical and mental condition of the boy he left for dead is surely relevant in determining his 'blameworthiness.'" The court concluded that any violation of Payne's rights under *Booth* and *Gathers* "was harmless beyond a reasonable doubt."

We granted certiorari to reconsider our holdings in *Booth* and *Gathers* that the Eighth Amendment prohibits a capital sentencing jury from considering "victim impact" evidence relating to the personal characteristics of the victim and the emotional impact of the crimes on the victim's family.

In *Booth,* the defendant robbed and murdered an elderly couple. As required by a state statute, a victim impact statement was prepared based on interviews with the victims' son, daughter, son-in-law, and granddaughter. The statement, which described the personal characteristics of the victims, the emotional impact of the crimes on the family, and set forth the family members' opinions and characterizations of the crimes and the defendant, was submitted to the jury at sentencing. The jury imposed the death penalty. The conviction and sentence were affirmed on appeal by the State's highest court.

This Court held by a 5-to-4 vote that the Eighth Amendment prohibits a jury from considering a victim impact statement at the sentencing phase of a capital trial. The Court made clear that the admissibility of victim impact evidence was not to be determined on a case-by-case basis, but that such evidence was *per se* inadmissible in the sentencing phase of a capital case except to the extent that it "relate[d] directly to the circumstances of the crime." In *Gathers,* decided two years later, the Court extended the rule announced in *Booth* to statements made by a prosecutor to the sentencing jury regarding the personal qualities of the victim.

The *Booth* Court began its analysis with the observation that the capital defendant must be treated as a "'uniquely individual human bein[g],'" and therefore the Constitution requires the jury to make an individualized determination as to whether the defendant should be executed based on the "'character of the individual and the circumstances of the crime.'" The Court concluded that while no prior decision of this Court had mandated that only the defendant's character and immediate characteristics of the crime may constitutionally be considered, other factors are irrelevant to the capital sentencing decision unless they have "some bearing on the defendant's 'personal responsibility and moral guilt.'" To the extent that victim impact evidence presents "factors about which the defendant was unaware, and that were irrelevant to the decision to kill," the Court concluded, it has nothing to do with the "blameworthiness of a particular defendant." Evidence of the victim's character, the Court observed, "could well distract the sentencing jury from its constitutionally required task [of] determining whether the death penalty is appropriate in light of the background and record of the accused and the particular circumstances of the crime." The Court concluded that, except to the extent that victim impact evidence relates "directly to the circumstances of the crime," the prosecution may not introduce such evidence at a capital sentencing hearing because "it creates an impermissible risk that the capital sentencing decision will be made in an arbitrary manner."

Booth and *Gathers* were based on two premises: that evidence relating to a particular victim or to the harm that a capital defendant causes a victim's family do not in general reflect on the defendant's "blameworthiness," and that only evidence relating to "blameworthiness" is relevant to the capital sentencing decision. However, the assessment of harm caused by the defendant as a result of the crime charged has understandably been an important concern of the criminal law, both in determining the elements of the offense and in determining the appropriate punishment. Thus, two equally blameworthy criminal defendants may be guilty of different offenses solely because their acts cause differing amounts of harm. "If a bank robber aims his gun at a guard, pulls the trigger, and kills his target, he may be put to death. If the gun unexpectedly misfires, he may not. His moral guilt in both cases is identical, but his responsibility in the former is greater." The same is true with respect to two defendants, each of whom participates in a robbery, and each of whom acts with reckless disregard for human life; if the robbery in which the first defendant participated results in the death of a victim, he may be subjected to the death penalty, but if the robbery in which the second defendant participates does not result in the death of a victim, the death penalty may not be imposed.

The principles which have guided criminal sentencing—as opposed to criminal liability—have varied with the times. The book of Exodus prescribes the *Lex talionis,* "An eye for an eye, a tooth for a tooth." Exodus 21:22–23. In England and on the continent of Europe, as recently as the 18th century crimes which would be regarded as quite minor today were capital offenses. Writing in the 18th century, the Italian criminologist Cesare Beccaria advocated the idea that "the punishment should fit the crime." He said that "[w]e have seen that the true measure of crimes is the injury done to society."

Gradually the list of crimes punishable by death diminished, and legislatures began grading the severity of crimes in accordance with the harm done by the criminal. The sentence for a given offense, rather than being precisely fixed by the legislature, was prescribed in terms of a minimum and a maximum, with the actual sentence to be decided by the judge. With the increasing importance of probation, as opposed to imprisonment, as a part of the penological process, some States such as California developed the "indeterminate sentence," where the time of incarceration was left almost entirely to the penological authorities rather than to the courts. But more recently the pendulum has swung back. The Federal Sentencing Guidelines, which went into effect in 1987, provided for very precise calibration of sentences, depending upon a number of factors.

These factors relate both to the subjective guilt of the defendant and to the harm caused by his acts.

Wherever judges in recent years have had discretion to impose sentence, the consideration of the harm caused by the crime has been an important factor in the exercise of that discretion:

> The first significance of harm in Anglo-American jurisprudence is, then, as a prerequisite to the criminal sanction. The second significance of harm—one no less important to judges—is as a measure of the seriousness of the offense and therefore as a standard for determining the severity of the sentence that will be meted out.

Whatever the prevailing sentencing philosophy, the sentencing authority has always been free to consider a wide range of relevant material. In the federal system, we observed that "a judge may appropriately conduct an inquiry broad in scope, largely unlimited as to the kind of information he may consider, or the source from which it may come." Even in the context of capital sentencing, prior to *Booth* the joint opinion of Justices Stewart, Powell, and STEVENS in *Gregg v. Georgia* had rejected petitioner's attack on the Georgia statute because of the "wide scope of evidence and argument allowed at presentence hearings." The joint opinion stated:

> We think that the Georgia court wisely has chosen not to impose unnecessary restrictions on the evidence that can be offered at such a hearing and to approve open and far-ranging argument. . . . So long as the evidence introduced and the arguments made at the presentence hearing do not prejudice a defendant, it is preferable not to impose restrictions. We think it desirable for the jury to have as much information before it as possible when it makes the sentencing decision.

The Maryland statute involved in *Booth* required that the presentence report in all felony cases include a "victim impact statement" which would describe the effect of the crime on the victim and his family. Congress and most of the States have, in recent years, enacted similar legislation to enable the sentencing authority to consider information about the harm caused by the crime committed by the defendant. The evidence involved in the present case was not admitted pursuant to any such enactment, but its purpose and effect was much the same as if it had been. While the admission of this particular kind of evidence—designed to portray for the sentencing authority the actual harm caused by a particular crime—is of recent origin, this fact hardly renders it unconstitutional.

"We have held that a State cannot preclude the sentencer from considering 'any relevant mitigating evidence' that the defendant proffers in support of a sentence less than death." Thus we have, as the Court observed in *Booth*, required that the capital defendant be treated as a "'uniquely individual human bein[g].'" But it was never held or even suggested in any of our cases preceding *Booth* that the defendant, entitled as he was to individualized consideration, was to receive that consideration wholly apart from the crime which he had committed. The language quoted from *Woodson* in the *Booth* opinion was not intended to describe a class of evidence that *could not* be received, but a class of evidence which *must* be received. Any doubt on the matter is dispelled by comparing the language in *Woodson* with the language from *Gregg v. Georgia,* quoted above, which was handed down the same day as *Woodson*. This misreading of precedent in *Booth* has, we think, unfairly weighted the scales in a capital trial; while virtually no limits are placed on the relevant mitigating evidence a capital defendant may introduce concerning his own circumstances, the State is barred from either offering "a glimpse of the life" which a defendant "chose to extinguish," or demonstrating the loss to the victim's family and to society which have resulted from the defendant's homicide.

Booth reasoned that victim impact evidence must be excluded because it would be difficult, if not impossible, for the defendant to rebut such evidence without shifting the focus of the sentencing hearing away from the defendant, thus creating a "'mini-trial' on the victim's character." In many cases the evidence relating to the victim is already before the jury at least in part because of its relevance at the guilt phase of the trial. But even as to additional evidence admitted at the sentencing phase, the mere fact that for tactical reasons it might not be prudent for the defense to rebut victim impact evidence makes the case no different than others in which a party is faced with this sort of a dilemma. As we explained in rejecting the contention that expert testimony on future dangerousness should be excluded from capital trials, "the rules of evidence generally extant at the federal and state levels anticipate that relevant, unprivileged evidence should be admitted and its weight left to the factfinder, who would have the benefit of cross examination and contrary evidence by the opposing party."

Payne echoes the concern voiced in *Booth*'s case that the admission of victim impact evidence permits a jury to find that defendants whose victims were assets to their community are more deserving of punishment than those whose victims are perceived to be less worthy. As a general matter, however, victim impact evidence is not offered to encourage comparative judgments of this kind—for instance, that the killer of a hardworking, devoted parent deserves the death penalty, but that the murderer of a reprobate does not. It is designed to show instead *each* victim's "uniqueness as an individual human being," whatever the jury might think the loss to the community resulting from his death might be. The facts of *Gathers* are an excellent illustration of this: the evidence showed that the victim was an out of work, mentally handicapped individual, perhaps not, in the eyes of most, a significant contributor to society, but nonetheless a murdered human being.

Under our constitutional system, the primary responsibility for defining crimes against state law, fixing punishments for the commission of these crimes, and establishing procedures for criminal trials rests with the States. The state laws respecting crimes, punishments, and criminal procedure are of course subject to the overriding provisions of the United States Constitution. Where the State imposes the death penalty for a particular crime, we have held that the Eighth Amendment imposes special limitations upon that process.

> First, there is a required threshold below which the death penalty cannot be imposed. In this context, the State must establish rational criteria that narrow the decisionmaker's judgment as to whether the circumstances of a particular defendant's case meet the threshold. Moreover, a societal consensus that the death penalty is disproportionate to a particular offense prevents a State from imposing the death penalty for that offense. Second, States cannot limit the sentencer's consideration of any relevant circumstance that could cause it to decline to impose the penalty. In this respect, the State cannot challenge the sentencer's discretion, but must allow it to consider any relevant information offered by the defendant.

But, as we noted in *California v. Ramos,* "[b]eyond these limitations . . . the Court has deferred to the State's choice of substantive factors relevant to the penalty determination."

"Within the constitutional limitations defined by our cases, the States enjoy their traditional latitude to prescribe the method by which those who commit murder should be punished." The States remain free, in capital cases, as well as others, to devise new procedures and new remedies to meet felt needs. Victim impact evidence is simply another form or method of informing the sentencing authority about the specific harm caused by the crime in question, evidence of a general type long considered by sentencing authorities. We think the *Booth* Court was wrong in stating that this kind of evidence leads to the arbitrary imposition of the death penalty. In the majority of cases, and in this case, victim impact evidence serves entirely legitimate purposes. In the event that evidence is introduced that is so unduly prejudicial that it renders the trial fundamentally unfair, the Due Process Clause of the Fourteenth Amendment provides a mechanism for relief. Courts have always taken into consideration the harm done by the defendant in imposing sentence, and the evidence adduced in this case was illustrative of the harm caused by Payne's double murder.

We are now of the view that a State may properly conclude that for the jury to assess meaningfully the defendant's moral culpability and blameworthiness, it should have before it at the sentencing phase evidence of the specific harm caused by the defendant. "[T]he State has a legitimate interest in counteracting the mitigating evidence which the defendant is entitled to put in, by reminding the sentencer that just as the murderer should be considered as an individual, so too the victim is an individual whose death represents a unique loss to society and in particular to his family." By turning the victim into a "faceless stranger at the penalty phase of a capital trial," *Gathers*. *Booth* deprives the State of the full moral force of its evidence and may prevent the jury from having before it all the information necessary to determine the proper punishment for a first-degree murder.

The present case is an example of the potential for such unfairness. The capital sentencing jury heard testimony from Payne's girlfriend that they met at church, that he was affectionate, caring, kind to her children, that he was not an abuser of drugs or alcohol, and that it was inconsistent with his character to have committed the murders. Payne's parents testified that he was a good son, and a clinical psychologist testified that Payne was an extremely polite prisoner and suffered from a low IQ. None of this testimony was related to the circumstances of

Payne's brutal crimes. In contrast, the only evidence of the impact of Payne's offenses during the sentencing phase was Nicholas' grandmother's description—in response to a single question—that the child misses his mother and baby sister. Payne argues that the Eighth Amendment commands that the jury's death sentence must be set aside because the jury heard this testimony. But the testimony illustrated quite poignantly some of the harm that Payne's killing had caused; there is nothing unfair about allowing the jury to bear in mind that harm at the same time as it considers the mitigating evidence introduced by the defendant. The Supreme Court of Tennessee in this case obviously felt the unfairness of the rule pronounced by *Booth* when it said "[i]t is an affront to the civilized members of the human race to say that at sentencing in a capital case, a parade of witnesses may praise the background, character and good deeds of Defendant (as was done in this case), without limitation as to relevancy, but nothing may be said that bears upon the character of, or the harm imposed, upon the victims."

In *Gathers,* as indicated above, we extended the holding of *Booth* barring victim impact evidence to the prosecutor's argument to the jury. Human nature being what it is, capable lawyers trying cases to juries try to convey to the jurors that the people involved in the underlying events are, or were, living human beings, with something to be gained or lost from the jury's verdict. Under the aegis of the Eighth Amendment, we have given the broadest latitude to the defendant to introduce relevant mitigating evidence reflecting on his individual personality, and the defendant's attorney may argue that evidence to the jury. Petitioner's attorney in this case did just that. For the reasons discussed above, we now reject the view—expressed in *Gathers*—that a State may not permit the prosecutor to similarly argue to the jury the human cost of the crime of which the defendant stands convicted. We reaffirm the view expressed by Justice Cardozo in *Snyder v. Massachusetts:* "justice, though due to the accused, is due to the accuser also. The concept of fairness must not be strained till it is narrowed to a filament. We are to keep the balance true."

We thus hold that if the State chooses to permit the admission of victim impact evidence and prosecutorial argument on that subject, the Eighth Amendment erects no *per se* bar. A State may legitimately conclude that evidence about the victim and about the impact of the murder on the victim's family is relevant to the jury's decision as to whether or not the death penalty should be imposed. There is no reason to treat such evidence differently than other relevant evidence is treated.

Payne and his *amicus* argue that despite these numerous infirmities in the rule created by *Booth* and *Gathers,* we should adhere to the doctrine of *stare decisis* and stop short of overruling those cases. *Stare decisis* is the preferred course because it promotes the evenhanded, predictable, and consistent development of legal principles, fosters reliance on judicial decisions, and contributes to the actual and perceived integrity of the judicial process. Adhering to precedent "is usually the wise policy, because in most matters it is more important that the applicable rule of law be settled than it be settled right." Nevertheless, when governing decisions are unworkable or are badly reasoned, "this Court has never felt constrained to follow precedent." *Stare decisis* is not an inexorable command; rather, it "is a principle of policy and not a mechanical formula of adherence to the latest decision." This is particularly true in constitutional cases, because in such cases "correction through legislative action is practically impossible." Considerations in favor of *stare decisis* are at their acme in cases involving property and contract rights, where reliance interests are involved, the opposite is true in cases such as the present one involving procedural and evidentiary rules.

Applying these general principles, the Court has during the past 20 Terms overruled in whole or in part 33 of its previous constitutional decisions. *Booth* and *Gathers* were decided by the narrowest of margins, over spirited dissents challenging the basic underpinnings of those decisions. They have been questioned by members of the Court in later decisions, and have defied consistent application by the lower courts. Reconsidering these decisions now, we conclude for the reasons heretofore stated, that they were wrongly decided and should be, and now are, overruled. We accordingly affirm the judgment of the Supreme Court of Tennessee.

Affirmed.

Justice O'CONNOR, with whom Justice WHITE and Justice KENNEDY join, concurring.

In my view, a State may legitimately determine that victim impact evidence is relevant to a capital sentencing proceeding. A State may decide that the jury, before determining whether a convicted murderer should receive the death penalty, should know the full extent of the harm caused by the crime, including its impact on the victim's family and community.

A State may decide also that the jury should see "a quick glimpse of the life petitioner chose to extinguish," to remind the jury that the person whose life was taken was a unique human being.

Given that victim impact evidence is potentially relevant, nothing in the Eighth Amendment commands that States treat it differently than other kinds of relevant evidence. "The Eighth Amendment stands as a shield against those practices and punishments which are either inherently cruel or which so offend the moral consensus of this society as to be deemed cruel and unusual." Certainly there is no strong societal consensus that a jury may not take into account the loss suffered by a victim's family or that a murder victim must remain a faceless stranger at the penalty phase of a capital trial. Just the opposite is true. Most States have enacted legislation enabling judges and juries to consider victim impact evidence. The possibility that this evidence may in some cases be unduly inflammatory does not justify a prophylactic, constitutionally based rule that this evidence may never be admitted. Trial courts routinely exclude evidence that is unduly inflammatory; where inflammatory evidence is improperly admitted, appellate courts carefully review the record to determine whether the error was prejudicial.

We do not hold today that victim impact evidence must be admitted, or even that it should be admitted. We hold merely that if a State decides to permit consideration of this evidence, "the Eighth Amendment erects no *per se* bar." If, in a particular case, a witness' testimony or a prosecutor's remark so infects the sentencing proceeding as to render it fundamentally unfair, the defendant may seek appropriate relief under the Due Process Clause of the Fourteenth Amendment.

That line was not crossed in this case. The State called as a witness Mary Zvolanek, Nicholas' grandmother. Her testimony was brief. She explained that Nicholas cried for his mother and baby sister and could not understand why they didn't come home. I do not doubt that the jurors were moved by this testimony—who would not have been? But surely this brief statement did not inflame their passions more than did the facts of the crime: Charisse Christopher was stabbed 41 times with a butcher knife and bled to death; her 2-year-old daughter Lacie was killed by repeated thrusts of that same knife; and 3-year-old Nicholas, despite stab wounds that penetrated completely through his body from front to back, survived—only to witness the brutal murders of his mother and baby sister. In light of the jury's unavoid-

able familiarity with the facts of Payne's vicious attack, I cannot conclude that the additional information provided by Mary Zvolanek's testimony deprived petitioner of due process.

Nor did the prosecutor's comments about Charisse and Lacie in the closing argument violate the Constitution. The jury had earlier seen a videotape of the murder scene that included the slashed and bloody corpses of Charisse and Lacie. In arguing that Payne deserved the death penalty, the prosecutor sought to remind the jury that Charisse and Lacie were more than just lifeless bodies on a videotape, that they were unique human beings. The prosecutor remarked that Charisse would never again sing a lullaby to her son and that Lacie would never attend a high school prom. In my view, these statements were permissible. "Murder is the ultimate act of depersonalization." It transforms a living person with hopes, dreams, and fears into a corpse, thereby taking away all that is special and unique about the person. The Constitution does not preclude a State from deciding to give some of that back.

I agree with the Court that *Booth v. Maryland,* and *Gathers,* were wrongly decided. The Eighth Amendment does not prohibit a State from choosing to admit evidence concerning a murder victim's personal characteristics or the impact of the crime on the victim's family and community. *Booth* also addressed another kind of victim impact evidence— opinions of the victim's family about the crime, the defendant, and the appropriate sentence. As the Court notes in today's decision, we do not reach this issue as no evidence of this kind was introduced at petitioner's trial. Nor do we express an opinion as to other aspects of the prosecutor's conduct. As to the victim impact evidence that was introduced, its admission did not violate the Constitution. Accordingly, I join the Court's opinion.

Justice SCALIA, with whom Justice O'CONNOR and Justice KENNEDY join as to Part II, concurring.

I

The Court correctly observes the injustice of requiring the exclusion of relevant aggravating evidence during capital sentencing, while requiring the admission of all relevant mitigating evidence. I have previously expressed my belief that the latter requirement is both wrong and, when combined with the remainder of our capital sentencing jurisprudence, unworkable. Even if it were abandoned, however, I would still affirm the judgment here. True enough, the Eighth Amendment permits parity between mitigating and aggravating factors. But more broadly and fundamentally still, it permits the People to decide (within the limits of other constitutional guarantees) what is a crime and what constitutes aggravation and mitigation of a crime.

II

The response to Justice MARSHALL's strenuous defense of the virtues of *stare decisis* can be found in the writings of Justice MARSHALL himself. That doctrine, he has reminded us, "is not 'an imprisonment of reason.'" If there was ever a case that defied reason, it was *Booth v. Maryland,* imposing a constitutional rule that had absolutely no basis in constitutional text, in historical practice, or in logic. Justice MARSHALL has also explained that "[t]he jurist concerned with public confidence in, and acceptance of the judicial system might well consider that, however admirable its resolute adherence to the law as it was, a decision contrary to the public sense of justice as it is, operates, so far as it is known, to diminish respect for the courts and for law itself." *Booth's* stunning *ipse dixit,* that a crime's unanticipated consequences must be deemed "irrelevant" to the sentence, conflicts with a public sense of justice keen enough that it has found voice in a nationwide "victim's rights" movement.

Today, however, Justice MARSHALL demands of us some "special justification"—*beyond* the mere conviction that the rule of *Booth* significantly harms our criminal justice system and is egregiously wrong—before we can be absolved of exercising "[p]ower, not reason." I do not think that is fair. In fact, quite to the contrary, what would enshrine power as the governing principle of this Court is the notion that an important constitutional decision with plainly inadequate rational support *must* be left in place for the sole reason that it once attracted five votes.

It seems to me difficult for those who were in the majority in *Booth* to hold themselves forth as ardent apostles of *stare decisis.* That doctrine, to the extent it rests upon anything more than administrative convenience, is merely the application to judicial precedents of a more general principle that the settled practices and expectations of a democratic

society should generally not be disturbed by the courts. It is hard to have a genuine regard for *stare decisis* without honoring that more general principle as well. A decision of this Court which, while not overruling a prior holding, nonetheless announces a novel rule, contrary to long and unchallenged practice, and pronounces it to be the Law of the Land— such a decision, no less than an explicit overruling, should be approached with great caution. It was, I suggest, *Booth,* and not today's decision, that compromised the fundamental values underlying the doctrine of *stare decisis.*

Justice SOUTER, with whom Justice KENNEDY joins, concurring.

I join the Court's opinion addressing two categories of facts excluded from consideration at capital sentencing proceedings by *Booth v. Maryland* and *South Carolina v. Gathers,* information revealing the individuality of the victim and the impact of the crime on the victim's survivors. As to these two categories, I believe *Booth* and *Gathers* were wrongly decided.

To my knowledge, our legal tradition has never included a general rule that evidence of a crime's effects on the victim and others is, standing alone, irrelevant to a sentencing determination of the defendant's culpability. Indeed, as the Court's opinion today, and dissents in *Booth* and *Gathers* make clear, criminal conduct has traditionally been categorized and penalized differently according to consequences not specifically intended, but determined in part by conditions unknown to a defendant when he acted. The majority opinion in *Booth* nonetheless characterized the consideration in a capital sentencing proceeding of a victim's individuality and the consequences of his death on his survivors as "irrelevant" and productive of "arbitrary and capricious" results, insofar as that would allow the sentencing authority to take account of information not specifically contemplated by the defendant prior to his ultimate criminal decision. This condemnation comprehends two quite separate elements. As to one such element the condemnation is merited but insufficient to justify the rule in *Booth,* and as to the other it is mistaken.

Evidence about the victim and survivors, and any jury argument predicated on it, can of course be so inflammatory as to risk a verdict impermissibly based on passion, not deliberation. But this is just as true when the defendant knew of the specific facts as when he was ignorant of their details, and in each case there is a traditional guard against the inflammatory risk, in the trial judge's authority and responsibility to control the proceedings consistently with due process, on which ground defendants may object and, if necessary, appeal. With the command of due process before us, this Court and the other courts of the state and federal systems will perform the "duty to search for constitutional error with painstaking care," an obligation "never more exacting than it is in a capital case."

Booth, supra, nonetheless goes further and imposes a blanket prohibition on consideration of evidence of the victim's individuality and the consequential harm to survivors as irrelevant to the choice between imprisonment and execution, except when such evidence goes to the "circumstances of the crime," *id.,* 482 U.S., at 502, 107 S.Ct., at 2532, and probably then only when the facts in question were known to the defendant and relevant to his decision to kill, *id.,* at 505, 107 S.Ct., at 2534. This prohibition rests on the belief that consideration of such details about the victim and survivors as may have been outside the defendant's knowledge is inconsistent with the sentencing jury's Eighth Amendment duty "in the unique circumstance of a capital sentencing hearing . . . to focus on the defendant as a uniquely individual human bein[g]." The assumption made is that the obligation to consider the defendant's uniqueness limits the data about a crime's impact, on which a defendant's moral guilt may be calculated, to the facts he specifically knew and presumably considered. His uniqueness, in other words, is defined by the specifics of his knowledge and the reasoning that is thought to follow from it.

To hold, however, that in setting the appropriate sentence a defendant must be considered in his uniqueness is not to require that only unique qualities be considered. While a defendant's anticipation of specific consequences to the victims of his intended act is relevant to sentencing, such detailed foreknowledge does not exhaust the category of morally relevant fact. One such fact that is known to all murderers and relevant to the blameworthiness of each one was identified by the *Booth* majority itself when it barred the sentencing authority in capital cases from considering "the full range of foreseeable consequences of a defendant's actions." Murder has foreseeable consequences. When it happens, it is always to distinct individuals, and after it happens other victims are left behind. Every defendant knows, if endowed with the mental competence for criminal responsibility, that the life he will

take by his homicidal behavior is that of a unique person, like himself, and that the person to be killed probably has close associates, "survivors," who will suffer harms and deprivations from the victim's death. Just as defendants know that they are not faceless human ciphers, they know that their victims are not valueless fungibles, and just as defendants appreciate the web of relationships and dependencies in which they live, they know that their victims are not human islands, but individuals with parents or children, spouses or friends or dependents. Thus, when a defendant chooses to kill, or to raise the risk of a victim's death, this choice necessarily relates to a whole human being and threatens an association of others, who may be distinctly hurt. The fact that the defendant may not know the details of a victim's life and characteristics, or the exact identities and needs of those who may survive, should not in any way obscure the further facts that death is always to a "unique" individual, and harm to some group of survivors is a consequence of a successful homicidal act so foreseeable as to be virtually inevitable.

That foreseeability of the killing's consequences imbues them with direct moral relevance, cf. *Penry v. Lynaugh, supra,* 492 U.S., at 328, 109 S.Ct., at 2952 (death penalty should be "'reasoned moral response'"), and evidence of the specific harm caused when a homicidal risk is realized is nothing more than evidence of the risk that the defendant originally chose to run despite the kinds of consequences that were obviously foreseeable. It is morally both defensible and appropriate to consider such evidence when penalizing a murderer, like other criminals, in light of common knowledge and the moral responsibility that such knowledge entails. Any failure to take account of a victim's individuality and the effects of his death upon close survivors would thus more appropriately be called an act of lenity than their consideration an invitation to arbitrary sentencing. Indeed, given a defendant's option to introduce relevant evidence in mitigation, sentencing without such evidence of victim impact may be seen as a significantly imbalanced process.

I so view the relevance of the two categories of victim impact evidence at issue here, and I fully agree with the majority's conclusion, and the opinions expressed by the dissenters in *Booth* and *Gathers,* that nothing in the Eighth Amendment's condemnation of cruel and unusual punishment would require that evidence to be excluded.

I do not, however, rest my decision to overrule wholly on the constitutional error that I see in the cases in question. I must rely as well on my further view that *Booth* sets an unworkable standard of constitutional relevance that threatens, on its own terms, to produce such arbitrary consequences and uncertainty of application as virtually to guarantee a result far diminished from the case's promise of appropriately individualized sentencing for capital defendants. These conclusions will be seen to result from the interaction of three facts. First, although *Booth* was prompted by the introduction of a systematically prepared "victim impact statement" at the sentencing phase of the trial, *Booth's* restriction of relevant facts to what the defendant knew and considered in deciding to kill applies to any evidence, however derived or presented. Second, details of which the defendant was unaware, about the victim and survivors, will customarily be disclosed by the evidence introduced at the guilt phase of the trial. Third, the jury that determines guilt will usually determine, or make recommendations about, the imposition of capital punishment.

A hypothetical case will illustrate these facts and raise what I view as the serious practical problems with application of the *Booth* standard. Assume that a minister, unidentified as such and wearing no clerical collar, walks down a street to his church office on a brief errand, while his wife and adolescent daughter wait for him in a parked car. He is robbed and killed by a stranger, and his survivors witness his death. What are the circumstances of the crime that can be considered at the sentencing phase under *Booth?* The defendant did not know his victim was a minister, or that he had a wife and child, let alone that they were watching. Under *Booth,* these facts were irrelevant to his decision to kill, and they should be barred from consideration at sentencing. Yet evidence of them will surely be admitted at the guilt phase of the trial. The widow will testify to what she saw, and in so doing she will not be asked to pretend that she was a mere bystander. She could not succeed at that if she tried. The daughter may well testify too. The jury will not be kept from knowing that the victim was a minister, with a wife and child, on an errand to his church. This is so not only because the widow will not try to deceive the jury about her relationship, but also because the usual standards of trial relevance afford factfinders enough information about surrounding circumstances to let them make sense of the narrowly material facts of the crime itself. No one claims that jurors in a capital case should be deprived of such common contextual evidence, even though the defendant knew

nothing about the errand, the victim's occupation or his family. And yet, if these facts are not kept from the jury at the guilt stage, they will be in the jurors' minds at the sentencing stage.

Booth thus raises a dilemma with very practical consequences. If we were to require the rules of guilt-phase evidence to be changed to guarantee the full effect of *Booth's* promise to exclude consideration of specific facts unknown to the defendant and thus supposedly without significance in morally evaluating his decision to kill, we would seriously reduce the comprehensibility of most trials by depriving jurors of those details of context that allow them to understand what is being described. If, on the other hand, we are to leave the rules of trial evidence alone, *Booth's* objective will not be attained without requiring a separate sentencing jury to be empaneled. This would be a major imposition on the States, however, and I suppose that no one would seriously consider adding such a further requirement.

But, even if *Booth* were extended one way or the other to exclude completely from the sentencing proceeding all facts about the crime's victims not known by the defendant, the case would be vulnerable to the further charge that it would lead to arbitrary sentencing results. In the preceding hypothetical, *Booth* would require that all evidence about the victim's family, including its very existence, be excluded from sentencing consideration because the defendant did not know of it when he killed the victim. Yet, if the victim's daughter had screamed "Daddy, look out," as the defendant approached the victim with drawn gun, then the evidence of at least the daughter's survivorship would be admissible even under a strict reading of *Booth,* because the defendant, prior to killing, had been made aware of the daughter's existence, which therefore became relevant in evaluating the defendant's decision to kill. Resting a decision about the admission of impact evidence on such a fortuity is arbitrary.

Thus, the status quo is unsatisfactory and the question is whether the case that has produced it should be overruled. In this instance, as in any other, overruling a precedent of this Court is a matter of no small import, for "the doctrine of *stare decisis* is of fundamental importance to the rule of law." But, even in constitutional cases, the doctrine carries such persuasive force that we have always required a departure from precedent to be supported by some "special justification."

The Court has a special justification in this case. *Booth* promises more than it can deliver, given the unresolved tension between common evidentiary standards at the guilt phase and *Booth's* promise of a sentencing determination free from the consideration of facts unknown to the defendant and irrelevant to his decision to kill. An extension of the case to guarantee a sentencing authority free from the influence of information extraneous under *Booth* would be either an unworkable or a costly extension of an erroneous principle and would itself create a risk of arbitrary results. There is only one other course open to us. We can recede from the erroneous holding that created the tension and extended the false promise, and there is precedent in our *stare decisis* jurisprudence for doing just this. In prior cases, when this Court has confronted a wrongly decided, unworkable precedent calling for some further action by the Court, we have chosen not to compound the original error, but to overrule the precedent. Following this course here not only has itself the support of precedent but of practical sense as well. Therefore, I join the Court in its partial overruling of *Booth* and *Gathers.*

Justice MARSHALL, with whom Justice BLACKMUN joins, dissenting.

Power, not reason, is the new currency of this Court's decisionmaking. Four Terms ago, a five-Justice majority of this Court held that "victim impact" evidence of the type at issue in this case could not constitutionally be introduced during the penalty phase of a capital trial. By another 5-4 vote, a majority of this Court rebuffed an attack upon this ruling just two Terms ago. Nevertheless, having expressly invited respondent to renew the attack, today's majority overrules *Booth* and *Gathers* and credits the dissenting views expressed in those cases. Neither the law nor the facts supporting *Booth* and *Gathers* underwent any change in the last four years. Only the personnel of this Court did.

In dispatching *Booth* and *Gathers* to their graves, today's majority ominously suggests that an even more extensive upheaval of this Court's precedents may be in store. Renouncing this Court's historical commitment to a conception of "the judiciary as a source of impersonal and reasoned judgments," the majority declares itself free to discard any principle of constitutional liberty which was recognized or reaffirmed over the dissenting votes of four Justices and with which five or more Justices *now* disagree. The implications of this radical new exception to the doctrine of *stare decisis* are staggering. The majority today sends a clear signal that scores of established constitutional liberties are now ripe for reconsideration, thereby inviting the very type of open defiance of our precedents that the majority rewards in this case. Because I believe that this Court owes more to its constitutional precedents in general and to *Booth* and *Gathers* in particular, I dissent.

I

Speaking for the Court as then constituted, Justice Powell and Justice Brennan set out the rationale for excluding victim-impact evidence from the sentencing proceedings in a capital case. As the majorities in *Booth* and *Gathers* recognized, the core principle of this Court's capital jurisprudence is that the sentence of death must reflect an "'*individualized* determination'" of the defendant's "'personal responsibility and moral guilt'" and must be based upon factors that channel the jury's discretion "'so as to minimize the risk of wholly arbitrary and capricious action.'" The State's introduction of victim-impact evidence, Justice Powell and Justice Brennan explained, violates this fundamental principle. Where, as is ordinarily the case, the defendant was unaware of the personal circumstances of his victim, admitting evidence of the victim's character and the impact of the murder upon the victim's family predicates the sentencing determination on "factors . . . wholly unrelated to the blameworthiness of [the] particular defendant." And even where the defendant *was* in a position to foresee the likely impact of his conduct, admission of victim impact evidence creates an unacceptable risk of sentencing arbitrariness. As Justice Powell explained in *Booth,* the probative value of such evidence is always outweighed by its prejudicial effect because of its inherent capacity to draw the jury's attention away from the character of the defendant and the circumstances of the crime to such illicit considerations as the eloquence with which family members express their grief and the status of the victim in the community. I continue to find these considerations wholly persuasive, and I see no purpose in trying to improve upon Justice Powell's and Justice Brennan's exposition of them.

There is nothing new in the majority's discussion of the supposed deficiencies in *Booth* and *Gathers.* Every one of the arguments made by the majority can be found in the dissenting opinions filed in those two cases, and . . . each argument was convincingly answered by Justice Powell and Justice Brennan.

But contrary to the impression that one might receive from reading the majority's lengthy rehearsing of the issues addressed in *Booth* and *Gathers,* the outcome of this case does not turn simply on who—the *Booth* and *Gathers* majorities or the *Booth* and *Gathers* dissenters—had the better of the argument. Justice Powell and Justice Brennan's position carried the day in those cases and became the law of the land. The real question, then, is whether today's majority has come forward with the type of extraordinary showing that this Court has historically demanded before overruling one of its precedents. In my view, the majority clearly has not made any such showing. Indeed, the striking feature of the majority's opinion is its radical assertion that it need not even try.

II

The overruling of one of this Court's precedents ought to be a matter of great moment and consequence. Although the doctrine of *stare decisis* is not an "inexorable command," this Court has repeatedly stressed that fidelity to precedent is fundamental to "a society governed by the rule of law."

Consequently, this Court has never departed from precedent without "special justification." Such justifications include the advent of "subsequent changes or development in the law" that undermine a decision's rationale, *Patterson v. McLean Credit Union,* the need "to bring [a decision] into agreement with experience and with facts newly ascertained," and a showing that a particular precedent has become a "detriment to coherence and consistency in the law."

The majority cannot seriously claim that *any* of these traditional bases for overruling a precedent applies to *Booth* or *Gathers.* The majority does not suggest that the legal rationale of these decisions has been undercut by changes or developments in doctrine during the last two years. Nor does the majority claim that experience over that period of time has discredited the principle that "any decision to impose the death sentence be, and appear to be, based on reason rather than caprice or emotion."

The majority does assert that *Booth* and *Gathers* "have defied consistent application by the lower courts," *ante,* at 2610, but the evidence that the majority proffers is so feeble that the majority cannot sincerely expect anyone to believe this claim. To support its contention, the majority points to Justice

O'CONNOR's dissent in *Gathers,* which noted a division among lower courts over whether *Booth* prohibited prosecutorial arguments relating to the victim's personal characteristics. That, of course, was the issue expressly considered and resolved in *Gathers.* The majority also cites THE CHIEF JUSTICE's dissent in *Mills v. Maryland.* That opinion does not contain a *single word* about any supposed "[in]consistent application" of *Booth* in the lower courts. Finally, the majority refers to a divided Ohio Supreme Court decision disposing of an issue concerning victim-impact evidence. Obviously, if a division among the members of a single lower court in a single case were sufficient to demonstrate that a particular precedent was a "detriment to coherence and consistency in the law," there would hardly be a decision in United States Reports that we would not be obliged to reconsider.

It takes little real detective work to discern just what *has* changed since this Court decided *Booth* and *Gathers:* this Court's own personnel. Indeed, the majority candidly explains why this particular contingency, which until now has been almost universally understood *not* to be sufficient to warrant overruling a precedent, *is* sufficient to justify overruling *Booth* and *Gathers.* "Considerations in favor of *stare decisis* are at their acme," the majority explains, "in cases involving property and contract rights, where reliance interests are involved[;] the opposite is true in cases such as the present one involving procedural and evidentiary rules." In addition, the majority points out, "*Booth* and *Gathers* were decided by the narrowest of margins, over spirited dissents" and thereafter were "questioned by members of the Court." Taken together, these considerations make it legitimate, in the majority's view, to elevate the position of the *Booth* and *Gathers* dissenters into the law of the land.

This truncation of the Court's duty to stand by its own precedents is astonishing. By limiting full protection of the doctrine of *stare decisis* to "cases involving property and contract rights," the majority sends a clear signal that essentially *all* decisions implementing the personal liberties protected by the Bill of Rights and the Fourteenth Amendment are open to reexamination. Taking into account the majority's additional criterion for overruling—that a case either was decided or reaffirmed by a 5–4 margin "over spirited dissen[t]," the continued vitality of literally scores of decisions must be understood to depend on nothing more than the proclivities of the individuals who *now* comprise a majority of this Court.

In my view, this impoverished conception of *stare decisis* cannot possibly be reconciled with the values that inform the proper judicial function. Contrary to what the majority suggests, *stare decisis* is important not merely because individuals rely on precedent to structure their commercial activity but because fidelity to precedent is part and parcel of a conception of "the judiciary as a source of impersonal and reasoned judgments." Indeed, this function of *stare decisis* is in many respects even *more* critical in adjudication involving constitutional liberties than in adjudication involving commercial entitlements. Because enforcement of the Bill of Rights and the Fourteenth Amendment frequently requires this Court to rein in the forces of democratic politics, this Court can legitimately lay claim to compliance with its directives only if the public understands the Court to be implementing "principles . . . founded in the law rather than in the proclivities of individuals." Thus, as Justice STEVENS has explained, the "stron[g] presumption of validity" to which "recently decided cases" are entitled "is an essential thread in the mantle of protection that the law affords the individual. . . . It is the unpopular or beleaguered individual— not the man in power—who has the greatest stake in the integrity of the law."

Carried to its logical conclusion, the majority's debilitated conception of *stare decisis* would destroy the Court's very capacity to resolve authoritatively the abiding conflicts between those with power and those without. If this Court shows so little respect for its own precedents, it can hardly expect them to be treated more respectfully by the state actors whom these decisions are supposed to bind. By signaling its willingness to give fresh consideration to any constitutional liberty recognized by a 5–4 vote "over spirited dissen[t]," the majority invites state actors to renew the very policies deemed unconstitutional in the hope that this Court may now reverse course, even if it has only recently reaffirmed the constitutional liberty in question.

Indeed, the majority's disposition of this case nicely illustrates the rewards of such a strategy of defiance. The Tennessee Supreme Court did nothing in this case to disguise its contempt for this Court's decisions in *Booth* and *Gathers*. Summing up its reaction to those cases, it concluded:

> It is an affront to the civilized members of the human race to say that at sentencing in a capital case, a parade of witnesses may praise the background, character and good deeds of Defendant (as was done in this case), without limitation as to relevancy, but nothing may be said that bears upon the character of, or harm imposed, upon the victims.

Offering no explanation for how this case could possibly be distinguished from *Booth* and *Gathers*—for obviously, there is none to offer—the court perfunctorily declared that the victim-impact evidence and the prosecutor's argument based on this evidence "did not violate either [of those decisions]." It cannot be clearer that the court simply declined to be bound by this Court's precedents.

Far from condemning this blatant disregard for the rule of law, the majority applauds it. In the Tennessee Supreme Court's denigration of *Booth* and *Gathers* as "an affront to the civilized members of the human race," the majority finds only confirmation of "the unfairness of the rule pronounced by" the majorities in those cases. It is hard to imagine a more complete abdication of this Court's historic commitment to defending the supremacy of its own pronouncements on issues of constitutional liberty. In light of the cost that such abdication exacts on the authoritativeness of *all* of this Court's pronouncements, it is also hard to imagine a more short-sighted strategy for effecting change in our constitutional order.

III

Today's decision charts an unmistakable course. If the majority's radical reconstruction of the rules for overturning this Court's decisions is to be taken at face value—and the majority offers us no reason why it should not—then the overruling of *Booth* and *Gathers* is but a preview of an even broader and more far-reaching assault upon this Court's precedents. Cast aside today are those condemned to face society's ultimate penalty. Tomorrow's victims may be minorities, women, or the indigent. Inevitably, this campaign to resurrect yesterday's "spirited dissents" will squander the authority and the legitimacy of this Court as a protector of the powerless.
I dissent.

Justice STEVENS, with whom Justice BLACKMUN joins, dissenting.

The novel rule that the Court announces today represents a dramatic departure from the principles that have governed our capital sentencing jurisprudence for decades. Justice MARSHALL is properly concerned about the majority's trivialization of the doctrine of *stare decisis*. But even if *Booth* and *Gathers* had not been decided, today's decision would represent a sharp break with past decisions. Our cases provide no support whatsoever for the majority's conclusion that the prosecutor may introduce evidence that sheds no light on the defendant's guilt or moral culpability, and thus serves no purpose other than to encourage jurors to decide in favor of death rather than life on the basis of their emotions rather than their reason.

Until today our capital punishment jurisprudence has required that any decision to impose the death penalty be based solely on evidence that tends to inform the jury about the character of the offense and the character of the defendant. Evidence that serves no purpose other than to appeal to the sympathies or emotions of the jurors has never been considered admissible. Thus, if a defendant, who had murdered a convenience store clerk in cold blood in the course of an armed robbery, offered evidence unknown to him at the time of the crime about the immoral character of his victim, all would recognize immediately that the evidence was irrelevant and inadmissible. Evenhanded justice requires that the same constraint be imposed on the advocate of the death penalty.

I

In *Williams v. New York,* this Court considered the scope of the inquiry that should precede the imposition of a death sentence. Relying on practices that had developed "both before and since the American colonies became a nation," Justice Black described the wide latitude that had been accorded judges in considering the source and type of evidence that is relevant to the sentencing determination. Notably, that opinion refers not only to the relevance of evidence establishing the defendant's guilt, but also to the relevance of "the fullest information possible concerning the defendant's life and characteristics." "Victim impact" evidence, however, was unheard of when *Williams* was decided. The relevant evidence of harm to society consisted of proof that the defendant was guilty of the offense charged in the indictment.

Almost 30 years after our decision in *Williams* the Court reviewed the scope of evidence relevant in capital sentencing. In his plurality opinion, Chief Justice Burger concluded that in a capital case, the sentencer must not be prevented "from considering, as a mitigating factor, any aspect of a defendant's character or record and any of the circumstances of the offense that the defendant proffers as a basis for a sentence less than death." As in *Williams,* the character of the offense and the character of the offender constituted the entire category of relevant evidence. "Victim impact" evidence was still unheard of when *Lockett* was decided.

As the Court acknowledges today, the use of victim impact evidence "is of recent origin." Insofar as the Court's jurisprudence is concerned, this type of evidence made its first appearance in 1987 in *Booth v. Maryland.* In his opinion for the Court, Justice Powell noted that our prior cases had stated that the question whether an individual defendant should be executed is to be determined on the basis of "'the character of the individual and the circumstances of the crime.'" Relying on those cases and on *Enmund v. Florida,* the Court concluded that unless evidence has some bearing on the defendant's personal responsibility and moral guilt, its admission would create a risk that a death sentence might be based on considerations that are constitutionally impermissible or totally irrelevant to the sentencing process. Evidence that served no purpose except to describe the personal characteristics of the victim and the emotional impact of the crime on the victim's family was therefore constitutionally irrelevant.

Our decision in *Booth* was entirely consistent with the practices that had been followed "both before and since the American colonies became a nation." Our holding was mandated by our capital punishment jurisprudence, which requires any decision to impose the death penalty to be based on reason rather than caprice or emotion. The dissenting opinions in *Booth* and in *Gathers* can be searched in vain for any judicial precedent sanctioning the use of evidence unrelated to the character of the offense or the character of the offender in the sentencing process. Today, however, relying on nothing more than those dissenting opinions, the Court abandons rules of relevance that are older than the Nation itself, and ventures into uncharted seas of irrelevance.

II

Today's majority has obviously been moved by an argument that has strong political appeal but no proper place in a reasoned judicial opinion. Because our decision in *Lockett* recognizes the defendant's right to introduce all mitigating evidence that may inform the jury about his character, the Court suggests that fairness requires that the State be allowed to respond with similar evidence about the *victim*. This argument is a classic *non sequitur*. The victim is not on trial; her character, whether good or bad, cannot therefore constitute either an aggravating or mitigating circumstance.

Even if introduction of evidence about the victim could be equated with introduction of evidence about the defendant, the argument would remain flawed in both its premise and its conclusion. The conclusion that exclusion of victim impact evidence results in a significantly imbalanced sentencing procedure is simply inaccurate. Just as the defendant is entitled to introduce any relevant mitigating evidence, so the State may rebut that evidence and may designate any relevant conduct to be an aggravating factor provided that the factor is sufficiently well defined and consistently applied to cabin the sentencer's discretion.

The premise that a criminal prosecution requires an even-handed balance between the State and the defendant is also incorrect. The Constitution grants certain rights to the criminal defendant and imposes special limitations on the State designed to protect the individual from overreaching by the disproportionately powerful State. Thus, the State must prove a defendant's guilt beyond a reasonable doubt. Rules of evidence are also weighted in the defendant's favor. For example, the prosecution generally cannot introduce evidence of the defendant's character to prove his propensity to commit a crime, but the defendant can introduce such reputation evidence to show his law-abiding nature. Even if balance were required or desirable, today's decision, by permitting both the defendant and the State to introduce irrelevant evidence for the sentencer's consideration without any guidance, surely does nothing to enhance parity in the sentencing process.

III

Victim impact evidence, as used in this case, has two flaws, both related to the Eighth Amendment's command that the punishment of death may not be meted out arbitrarily or capriciously. First, aspects of the character of the victim unforeseeable to the defendant at the time of his crime are irrelevant to the defendant's "personal responsibility and moral guilt" and therefore cannot justify a death sentence.

Second, the quantity and quality of victim impact evidence sufficient to turn a verdict of life in prison into a verdict of death is not defined until after the crime has been committed and therefore cannot possibly be applied consistently in different cases. The sentencer's unguided consideration of victim impact evidence thus conflicts with the principle central to our capital punishment jurisprudence that, "where discretion is afforded a sentencing body on a matter so grave as the determination of whether a human life should be taken or spared, that discretion must be suitably directed and limited so as to minimize the risk of wholly arbitrary and capricious action." Open-ended reliance by a capital sentencer on victim impact evidence simply does not provide a "principled way to distinguish [cases], in which the death penalty [i]s imposed, from the many cases in which it [i]s not."

The majority attempts to justify the admission of victim impact evidence by arguing that "consideration of the harm caused by the crime has been an important factor in the exercise of [sentencing] discretion." This statement is misleading and inaccurate. It is misleading because it is not limited to harm that is foreseeable. It is inaccurate because it fails to differentiate between legislative determinations and judicial sentencing. It is true that an evaluation of the harm caused by different kinds of wrongful conduct is a critical aspect in legislative definitions of offenses and determinations concerning sentencing guidelines. There is a rational correlation between moral culpability and the foreseeable harm caused by criminal conduct. Moreover, in the capital sentencing area, legislative identification of the special aggravating factors that may justify the imposition of the death penalty is entirely appropriate. But the majority cites no authority for the suggestion that unforeseeable and indirect harms to a victim's family are properly considered as aggravating evidence on a case-by-case basis.

The dissents in *Booth* and *Gathers* and the majority today offer only the recent decision in *Tison v. Arizona* and two legislative examples to support their contention that harm to the victim has traditionally influenced sentencing discretion. *Tison* held that the death penalty may be imposed on a felon who acts with reckless disregard for human life if a death occurs in the course of the felony, even though capital punishment cannot be imposed if no one dies as a result of the crime. The first legislative example is that attempted murder and murder are classified as two different offenses subject to different punishments. The second legislative example is that a person who drives while intoxicated is guilty of vehicular homicide if his actions result in a death but is not guilty of this offense if he has the good fortune to make it home without killing anyone.

These three scenarios, however, are fully consistent with the Eighth Amendment jurisprudence reflected in *Booth* and *Gathers* and do not demonstrate that harm to the victim may be considered by a capital sentencer in the ad hoc and post hoc manner authorized by today's majority. The majority's examples demonstrate only that harm to the victim may justify enhanced punishment if the harm is both foreseeable to the defendant and clearly identified in advance of the crime by the legislature as a class of harm that should in every case result in more severe punishment.

In each scenario, the defendants could reasonably foresee that their acts might result in loss of human life. In addition, in each, the decision that the defendants should be treated differently was made prior to the crime by the legislature, the decision of which is subject to scrutiny for basic rationality. Finally, in each scenario, every defendant who causes the well-defined harm of destroying a human life will be subject to the determination that his conduct should be punished more severely. The majority's scenarios therefore provide no support for its holding, which permits a jury to sentence a defendant to death because of harm to the victim and his family that the defendant could not foresee, which was not even identified until after the crime had been committed, and which may be deemed by the jury, without any rational explanation, to justify a death sentence in one case but not in another. Unlike the rule elucidated by the scenarios on which the majority relies, the majority's holding offends the Eighth Amendment because it permits the sentencer to rely on irrelevant evidence in an arbitrary and capricious manner.

The majority's argument that "the sentencing authority has always been free to consider a wide range of *relevant* material," thus cannot justify consideration of victim impact evidence that is *irrelevant* because it details harms that the defendant could not have foreseen. Nor does the majority's citation of *Gregg v. Georgia* concerning the "wide scope of evidence and argument allowed at presentence hearings," support today's holding. The *Gregg*

plurality endorsed the sentencer's consideration of a wide range of evidence "[s]o long as the evidence introduced and the arguments made at the presentence hearing do not prejudice a defendant." Irrelevant victim impact evidence that distracts the sentencer from the proper focus of sentencing and encourages reliance on emotion and other arbitrary factors necessarily prejudices the defendant.

The majority's apparent inability to understand this fact is highlighted by its misunderstanding of Justice Powell's argument in *Booth* that admission of victim impact evidence is undesirable because it risks shifting the focus of the sentencing hearing away from the defendant and the circumstances of the crime and creating a "'mini-trial' on the victim's character." *Booth* found this risk insupportable not, as today's majority suggests, because it creates a "tactical" "dilemma" for the defendant, but because it allows the possibility that the jury will be so distracted by prejudicial and irrelevant considerations that it will base its life-or-death decision on whim or caprice.

IV

The majority thus does far more than validate a State's judgment that "the jury should see 'a quick glimpse of the life petitioner chose to extinguish.'" Instead, it allows a jury to hold a defendant responsible for a whole array of harms that he could not foresee and for which he is therefore not blameworthy. Justice SOUTER argues that these harms are sufficiently foreseeable to hold the defendant accountable because "[e]very defendant knows, if endowed with the mental competence for criminal responsibility, that the life he will take by his homicidal behavior is that of a unique person, like himself, and that the person who will be killed probably has close associates, 'survivors,' who will suffer harms and deprivations from the victim's death." But every juror and trial judge knows this much as well. Evidence about who those survivors are and what harms and deprivations they have suffered is therefore not necessary to apprise the sentencer of any information that was actually foreseeable to the defendant. Its only function can be to "divert the jury's attention away from the defendant's background and record, and the circumstances of the crime."

Arguing in the alternative, Justice SOUTER correctly points out that victim impact evidence will sometimes come to the attention of the jury during the guilt phase of the trial. He reasons that the ideal of basing sentencing determinations entirely on the moral culpability of the defendant is therefore unattainable unless a different jury is empaneled for the sentencing hearing. Thus, to justify overruling *Booth,* he assumes that the decision must otherwise be extended far beyond its actual holding.

Justice SOUTER'S assumption is entirely unwarranted. For as long as the contours of relevance at sentencing hearings have been limited to evidence concerning the character of the offense and the character of the offender, the law has also recognized that evidence that is admissible for a proper purpose may not be excluded because it is inadmissible for other purposes and may indirectly prejudice the jury. In the case before us today, much of what might be characterized as victim impact evidence was properly admitted during the guilt phase of the trial and, given the horrible character of this crime, may have been sufficient to justify the Tennessee Supreme Court's conclusion that the error was harmless because the jury would necessarily have imposed the death sentence even absent the error. The fact that a good deal of such evidence is routinely and properly brought to the attention of the jury merely indicates that the rule of *Booth* may not affect the outcome of many cases.

In reaching our decision today, however, we should not be concerned with the cases in which victim impact evidence will not make a difference. We should be concerned instead with the cases in which it will make a difference. In those cases, defendants will be sentenced arbitrarily to death on the basis of evidence that would not otherwise be admissible because it is irrelevant to the defendants' moral culpability. The Constitution's proscription against the arbitrary imposition of the death penalty must necessarily proscribe the admission of evidence that serves no purpose other than to result in such arbitrary sentences.

V

The notion that the inability to produce an ideal system of justice in which every punishment is precisely married to the defendant's blameworthiness somehow justifies a rule that completely divorces some capital sentencing determinations from moral culpability is incomprehensible to me. Also incomprehensible is the argument that such a rule is required for the jury to take into account that each murder victim is a "unique" human being. The fact that each of us is unique is a proposition so obvious that it surely requires no evidentiary support. What is not obvious, however, is the way in which the character or reputation in one case may differ from that of other possible victims. Evidence offered to prove such differences can only be intended to identify some victims as more worthy of protection than others. Such proof risks decisions based on the same invidious motives as a prosecutor's decision to seek the death penalty if a victim is white but to accept a plea bargain if the victim is black.

Given the current popularity of capital punishment in a crime-ridden society, the political appeal of arguments that assume that increasing the severity of sentences is the best cure for the cancer of crime, and the political strength of the "victims' rights" movement, I recognize that today's decision will be greeted with enthusiasm by a large number of concerned and thoughtful citizens. The great tragedy of the decision, however, is the danger that the "hydraulic pressure" of public opinion that Justice Holmes once described—and that properly influences the deliberations of democratic legislatures—has played a role not only in the Court's decision to hear this case, and in its decision to reach the constitutional question without pausing to consider affirming on the basis of the Tennessee Supreme Court's rationale, but even in its resolution of the constitutional issue involved. Today is a sad day for a great institution.

The Death Penalty

FURMAN V. GEORGIA[*]

United States Supreme Court, 1972

Mr. Justice DOUGLAS, concurring.

In these three cases the death penalty was imposed, one of them for murder, and two for rape.[1] In each the determination of whether the penalty should be death or a lighter punishment was left by the State to the discretion of the judge or of the jury. In each of the three cases the trial was to a jury. They are here on petitions for certiorari which we granted limited to the question whether the imposition and execution of the death penalty constitutes "cruel and unusual punishment" within the meaning of the Eighth Amendment as applied to the States by the Fourteenth. I vote to vacate each judgment, believing that the exaction of the death penalty does violate the Eighth and Fourteenth Amendments.

. . . We cannot say from facts disclosed in these records that these defendants were sentenced to death because they were black. Yet our task is not restricted to an effort to divine what motives impelled these death penalties. Rather, we deal with a system of law and of justice that leaves to the uncontrolled discretion of judges or juries the determination whether defendants committing these crimes should die or be imprisoned. Under these laws no standards govern the selection of the penalty. People live or die, dependent on the whim of one man or of 12.

. . . In a Nation committed to equal protection of the laws there is no permissible "caste" aspect[2] of law enforcement. Yet we know that the discretion of judges and juries in imposing the death penalty enables the penalty to be selectively applied, feeding prejudices against the accused if he is poor and despised, and lacking political clout, or if he is a member of a suspect or unpopular minority, and saving those who by social position may be in a more protected position. In ancient Hindu law a Brahman was exempt from capital punishment,[3] and in those days, "[g]enerally, in the law books, punishment increased in severity as social status diminished."[4] We have, I fear, taken in practice the same position, partially as a result of making the death penalty discretionary and partially as a result of the ability of the rich to purchase the services of the most respected and most resourceful legal talent in the Nation.

The high service rendered by the "cruel and unusual" punishment clause of the Eighth Amendment is to require legislatures to write penal laws that are evenhanded, nonselective, and nonarbitrary, and to require judges to see to it that general laws are not applied sparsely, selectively, and spottily to unpopular groups.

A law that stated that anyone making more than $50,000 would be exempt from the death penalty would plainly fall, as would a law that in terms said that blacks, those who never went beyond the fifth grade in school, those who made less than $3,000 a year, or those who were unpopular or unstable should be the only people executed. A law

[*]408 U.S. 238 (1972). Excerpts only. Footnotes numbered as in the original. Two cases from Georgia and one from Texas were considered and decided together by the Supreme Court. Endnotes have been renumbered.

which in the overall view reaches that result in practice[5] has no more sanctity than a law which in terms provides the same.

Thus, these discretionary statutes are unconstitutional in their operation. They are pregnant with discrimination and discrimination is an ingredient not compatible with the idea of equal protection of the laws that is implicit in the ban on "cruel and unusual" punishments.

Any law which is nondiscriminatory on its face may be applied in such a way as to violate the Equal Protection Clause of the Fourteenth Amendment. *Yick Wo v. Hopkins,* 118 U.S. 356. Such conceivably might be the fate of a mandatory death penalty, where equal or lesser sentences were imposed on the elite, a harsher one or the minorities or members of the lower castes. Whether a mandatory death penalty would otherwise be constitutional is a question I do not reach.

I concur in the judgments of the Court.

Mr. Justice BRENNAN, concurring.

. . . There are, then, four principles by which we may determine whether a particular punishment is "cruel and unusual." The primary principle, which I believe supplies the essential predicate for the application of the others, is that a punishment must not by its severity be degrading to human dignity. The paradigm violation of this principle would be the infliction of a torturous punishment of the type that the Clause has always prohibited. Yet "[i]t is unlikely that any State at this moment in history," *Robinson v. California,* 370 U.S., at 666, would pass a law providing for the infliction of such a punishment. Indeed, no such punishment has ever been before this Court. The same may be said of the other principles. It is unlikely that this Court will confront a severe punishment that is obviously inflicted in wholly arbitrary fashion; no State would engage in a reign of blind terror. Nor is it likely that this Court will be called upon to review a severe punishment that is clearly and totally rejected throughout society; no legislature would be able even to authorize the infliction of such a punishment. Nor, finally, is it likely that this Court will have to consider a severe punishment that is patently unnecessary; no State today would inflict a severe punishment knowing that there was no reason whatever for doing so. In short, we are unlikely to have occasion to determine that a punishment is fatally offensive under any one principle.

Since the Bill of Rights was adopted, this Court has adjudged only three punishments to be within the prohibition of the Clause. See *Weems v. United States,* 217 U.S. 349 (1910) (12 years in chains at hard and painful labor); *Trop v. Dulles,* 356 U.S. 86 (1958) (expatriation); *Robinson v. California,* 370 U.S. 660 (1962) (imprisonment for narcotics addiction). Each punishment, of course, was degrading to human dignity, but of none could it be said conclusively that it was fatally offensive under one or the other of the principles. Rather, these "cruel and unusual punishments" seriously implicated several of the principles, and it was the application of the principles in combination that supported the judgment. That, indeed, is not surprising. The function of these principles, after all, is simply to provide means by which a court can determine whether a challenged punishment comports with human dignity. They are, therefore, interrelated, and in most cases it will be their convergence that will justify the conclusion that a punishment is "cruel and unusual." The test, then, will ordinarily be a cumulative one: If a punishment is unusually severe, if there is a strong probability that it is inflicted arbitrarily, if it is substantially rejected by contemporary society, and if there is no reason to believe that it serves any penal purpose more effectively than some less severe punishment, then the continued infliction of that punishment violates the command of the Clause that the State may not inflict inhuman and uncivilized punishments upon those convicted of crimes.

. . . The question, then, is whether the deliberate infliction of death is today consistent with the command of the Clause that the State may not inflict punishments that do not comport with human dignity. I will analyze the punishment of death in terms of the principles set out above and the cumulative test to which they lead: It is a denial of human dignity for the State arbitrarily to subject a person to an unusually severe punishment that society has indicated it does not regard as acceptable, and that cannot be shown to serve any penal purpose more effectively than a significantly less drastic punishment. Under these principles and this test, death is today a "cruel and unusual" punishment.

Death is a unique punishment in the United States. In a society that so strongly affirms the sanctity of life, not surprisingly the common view is that death is the ultimate sanction. This natural human feeling appears all about us. There has been no national debate about punishment, in general or by imprisonment, comparable to the debate about the punishment of death. No other punishment has been so continuously restricted, see *infra,* at 296–298, nor has any State yet abolished prisons, as some have abolished this punishment. And those States that still inflict death reserve it for the most heinous crimes. Juries, of course, have always treated death cases differently, as have governors exercising their communication powers. Criminal defendants are of the same view. "As all practicing lawyers know, who have defended persons charged with capital offenses, often the only goal possible is to avoid the death penalty." *Griffin v. Illinois,* 351 U.S. 12, 28 (1956) (Burton and Minton, JJ., dissenting). Some legislatures have required particular procedures, such as two-stage trials and automatic appeals, applicable only in death cases. "It is the universal experience in the administration of criminal justice that those charged with capital offenses are granted special considerations." *Ibid.* See *Williams v. Florida,* 399 U.S. 78, 103 (1970) (all States require juries of 12 in death cases). This Court, too, almost always treats death cases as a class apart.[6] And the unfortunate effect of this punishment upon the functioning of the judicial process is well known; no other punishment has a similar effect.

The only explanation for the uniqueness of death is its extreme severity. Death is today an unusually severe punishment, unusual in its pain, in its finality, and in its enormity. No other existing punishment is comparable to death in terms of physical and mental suffering. Although our information is not conclusive, it appears that there is no method available that guarantees an immediate and painless death.[7] Since the discontinuance of flogging as a constitutionally permissible punishment, *Jackson v. Bishop,* 404 F. 2d 571 (CA8 1968), death remains as the only punishment that may involve the conscious infliction of physical pain. In addition, we know that mental pain is an inseparable part of our practice of punishing criminals by death for the prospect of pending execution exacts a frightful toll during the inevitable long wait between the imposition of sentence and the actual infliction of death. Cf *Ex parte Medley,* 134 U.S. 160, 172 (1890). As the California Supreme Court pointed out, "the process of carrying out a verdict of death is often so degrading and brutalizing to the human spirit as to constitute psychological torture." *People v. Anderson,* 6 Cal. 3d 628, 649, 493 P. 2d 880, 894 (1972).[8] Indeed, as Mr. Justice Frankfurter noted, "the onset of insanity while awaiting execution of a death sentence is not a rare phenomenon." *Solesbee v. Balkcom,* 339 U.S. 9, 14 (1950) (dissenting opinion). The "fate of ever-increasing fear and distress" to which the expatriate is subjected, *Trop v. Dulles,* 356 U.S., at 102, can only

exist to a greater degree for a person confined in prison awaiting death.[9]

The unusual severity of death is manifested most clearly in its finality and enormity. Death, in these respects, is in a class by itself. Expatriation, for example, is a punishment that "destroys for the individual the political existence that was centuries in the development," that "strips the citizen of his status in the national and international political community," and that puts "[h]is very existence" in jeopardy. Expatriation thus inherently entails "the total destruction of the individual's status in organized society." *Id.,* at 101. "In short, the expatriate has lost the right to have rights." *Id.,* at 102. Yet, demonstrably, expatriation is not "a fate worse than death." *Id.,* at 125 (Frankfurther, J., dissenting).[10] Although death, like expatriation, destroys the individual's "political existence" and his "status in organized society," it does more, for, unlike expatriation, death also destroys "[h]is very existence." There is, too at least the possibility that the expatriate will in the future regain "the right to have rights." Death forecloses even that possibility.

Death is truly an awesome punishment. The calculated killing of a human being by the State involves, by its very nature, a denial of the executed person's humanity. The contrast with the plight of a person punished by imprisonment is evident. An individual in prison does not lose "the right to have rights." A prisoner retains, for example, the constitutional rights to the free exercise of religion, to be free of cruel and unusual punishments, and to treatment as a "person" for purposes of due process of law and the equal protection of the laws. A prisoner remains a member of the human family. Moreover, he retains the right of access to the courts. His punishment is not irrevocable. Apart from the common charge, grounded upon the recognition of human fallibility, that the punishment of death must inevitably be inflicted upon innocent men, we know that death has been the lot of men whose convictions were unconstitutionally secured in view of later, retroactively applied, holdings of this Court. The punishment itself may have been unconstitutionally inflicted, see *Witherspoon v. Illinois,* 391 U.S. 510 (1968), yet the finality of death precludes relief. An executed person has indeed "lost the right to have rights." As one 19th century proponent of punishing criminals by death declared, "When a man is hung, there is an end of our relations with him. His execution is a way of saying, 'You are not fit for this world, take your chance elsewhere.'"[11]

In comparison to all other punishments today, then, the deliberate extinguishment of human life by the State is uniquely degrading to human dignity. I would not hesitate to hold, on that ground alone, that death is today a "cruel and unusual" punishment, were it not that death is a punishment of longstanding usage and acceptance in this country. I therefore turn to the second principle—that the State may not arbitrarily inflict an unusually severe punishment.

. . . When the punishment of death is inflicted in a trivial number of the cases in which it is legally available, the conclusion is virtually inescapable that it is being inflicted arbitrarily. Indeed, it smacks of little more than a lottery system. The States claim, however, that this rarity is evidence not of arbitrariness, but of informed selectivity: Death is inflicted, they say, only in "extreme" cases.

Informed selectivity, of course, is a value not to be denigrated. Yet presumably the States could make precisely the same claim if there were 10 executions per year, or five, or even if there were but one. That there may be as many as 50 per year does not strengthen the claim. When the rate of infliction is at this low level, it is highly implausible that only the worst criminals or the criminals who commit the worst crimes are selected for this punishment. No one has yet suggested a rational basis that could differentiate in those terms the few who die from the many who go to prison. Crimes and criminals simply do not admit of a distinction that can be drawn so finely as to explain, on that ground, the execution of such a tiny sample of those eligible. Certainly the laws that provide for this punishment do not attempt to draw that distinction; all cases to which the laws apply are necessarily "extreme." Nor is the distinction credible in fact. If, for example, petitioner Furman or his crime illustrates the "extreme," then nearly all murderers and their murders are also "extreme."[12] Furthermore, our procedures in death cases, rather than resulting in the selection of "extreme" cases for this punishment, actually sanction an arbitrary selection. For this Court has held that juries may, as they do, make the decision whether to impose a death sentence wholly unguided by standards governing that decision. *McGautha v. California,* 402 U.S. 183, 196–208 (1971). In other words, our procedures are not constructed to guard against the totally capricious selection of criminals for the punishment of death.

Although it is difficult to imagine what further facts would be necessary in order to prove that death is, as my Brother Stewart puts it, "wantonly and . . .

freakishly" inflicted, I need not conclude that arbitrary infliction is patently obvious. I am not considering this punishment by the isolated light of one principle. The probability of arbitrariness is sufficiently substantial that it can be relied upon, in combination with the other principles, in reaching a judgment on the constitutionality of this punishment.

When there is a strong probability that an unusually severe and degrading punishment is being inflicted arbitrarily, we may well expect that society will disapprove of its infliction. I turn, therefore, to the third principle. An examination of the history and present operation of the American practice of punishing criminals by death reveals that this punishment has been almost totally rejected by contemporary society.

. . . The progressive decline in, and the current rarity of, the infliction of death demonstrate that our society seriously questions the appropriateness of this punishment today. The States point out that many legislatures authorize death as the punishment for certain crimes and that substantial segments of the public, as reflected in opinion polls and referendum votes, continue to support it. Yet the availability of this punishment through statutory authorization, as well as the polls and referenda, which amount simply to approval of that authorization, simply underscores the extent to which our society has in fact rejected this punishment. When an unusually severe punishment is authorized for wide-scale application but not, because of society's refusal, inflicted save in a few instances, the inference is compelling that there is a deep-seated reluctance to inflict it. Indeed, the likelihood is great that the punishment is tolerated only because of its disuse. The objective indicator of society's view of an unusually severe punishment is what society does with it, and today society will inflict death upon only a small sample of the eligible criminals. Rejection could hardly be more complete without becoming absolute. At the very least, I must conclude that contemporary society views this punishment with substantial doubt.

The final principle to be considered is that an unusually severe and degrading punishment may not be excessive in view of the purposes for which it is inflicted. This principle, too, is related to the others. When there is a strong probability that the State is arbitrarily inflicting an unusually severe punishment that is subject to grave societal doubts, it is likely also that the punishment cannot be shown to be serving any penal purpose that could not be served equally well by some less severe punishment.

The States' primary claim is that death is a necessary punishment because it prevents the commission of capital crimes more effectively than any less severe punishment. The first part of this claim is that the infliction of death is necessary to stop the individuals executed from committing further crimes. The sufficient answer to this is that if a criminal convicted of a capital crime poses a danger to society, effective administration of the State's pardon and parole laws can delay or deny his release from prison, and techniques of isolation can eliminate or minimize the danger while he remains confined.

The more significant argument is that the threat of death prevents the commission of capital crimes because it deters potential criminals who would not be deterred by the threat of imprisonment. The argument is not based upon evidence that the threat of death is a superior deterrent. Indeed, as my Brother Marshall establishes, the available evidence uniformly indicates, although it does not conclusively prove, that the threat of death has no greater deterrent effect than the threat of imprisonment. The States argue, however, that they are entitled to rely upon common human experience, and that experience, they say, supports the conclusion that death must be a more effective deterrent than any less severe punishment. Because people fear death the most, the argument runs, the threat of death must be the greatest deterrent.

It is important to focus upon the precise import of this argument. It is not denied that many, and probably most, capital crimes cannot be deterred by the threat of punishment. Thus the argument can apply only to those who think rationally about the commission of capital crimes. Particularly is that true when the potential criminal, under this argument, must not only consider the risk of punishment, but also distinguish between two possible punishments. The concern, then, is with a particular type of potential criminal, the rational person who will commit a capital crime knowing that the punishment is long-term imprisonment, which may well be for the rest of his life, but will not commit the crime knowing that the punishment is death. On the face of it, the assumption that such persons exist is implausible.

In any event, this argument cannot be appraised in the abstract. We are not presented with the theoretical question whether under any imaginable circumstances the threat of death might be a greater deterrent to the commission of capital crimes than the threat of imprisonment. We are concerned with the practice of punishing criminals by death as it exists in the United States today. Proponents of this argument necessarily admit that its validity depends upon the existence of a system in which the punishment of death is invariably and swiftly imposed. Our system, of course, satisfies neither condition. A rational person contemplating a murder or rape is confronted, not with the certainty of a speedy death, but with the slightest possibility that he will be executed in the distant future. The risk of death is remote and improbable; in contrast, the risk of long-term imprisonment is near and great. In short, whatever the speculative validity of the assumption that the threat of death is a superior deterrent, there is no reason to believe that as currently administered the punishment of death is necessary to deter the commission of capital crimes. Whatever might be the case were all or substantially all eligible criminals quickly put to death, unverifiable possibilities are an insufficient basis upon which to conclude that the threat of death today has any greater deterrent efficacy than the threat of imprisonment.[13]

There is, however, another aspect to the argument that the punishment of death is necessary for the protection of society. The infliction of death, the States urge, serves to manifest the community's outrage at the commission of the crime. It is, they say, a concrete public expression of moral indignation that inculcates respect for the law and helps assure a more peaceful community. Moreover, we are told, not only does the punishment of death exert this widespread moralizing influence upon community values, it also satisfies the popular demand for grievous condemnation of abhorrent crimes and thus prevents disorder, lynching, and attempts by private citizens to take the law into their own hands.

The question, however, is not whether death serves these supposed purposes of punishment, but whether death serves them more effectively than imprisonment. There is no evidence whatever that utilization of imprisonment rather than death encourages private blood feuds and other disorders. Surely if there were such a danger, the execution of a handful of criminals each year would not prevent it. The assertion that death alone is a sufficiently emphatic denunciation for capital crimes suffers from the same defect. If capital crimes require the punishment of death in order to provide moral reinforcement for the basic values of the community, those values can only be undermined when death is so rarely inflicted upon the criminals who commit the crimes. Furthermore, it is certainly doubtful that the infliction of death by the State does in fact strengthen the community's moral code; if the deliberate extinguishment of human life has any effect at all, it more likely tends to lower our respect for life and brutalize our values. That, after all, is why we no longer carry out public executions. In any event, this claim simply means that one purpose of punishment is to indicate social disapproval of crime. To serve that purpose our laws distribute punishments according to the gravity of crimes and punish more severely the crimes society regards as more serious. That purpose cannot justify any particular punishment as the upper limit of severity.

Mr. Justice WHITE, concurring.

. . . Most important, a major goal of the criminal law—to deter others by punishing the convicted criminal—would not be substantially served where the penalty is so seldom invoked that it ceases to be the credible threat essential to influence the conduct of others. For present purposes I accept the morality and utility of punishing one person to influence another. I accept also the effectiveness of punishment generally and need not reject the death penalty as a more effective deterrent than a lesser punishment. But common sense and experience tell us that seldom-enforced laws become ineffective measures for controlling human conduct and that the death penalty, unless imposed with sufficient frequency, will make little contribution to deterring those crimes for which it may be exacted.

The imposition and execution of the death penalty are obviously cruel in the dictionary sense. But the penalty has not been considered cruel and unusual punishment in the constitutional sense because it was thought justified by the social ends it was deemed to serve. At the moment that it ceases realistically to further these purposes, however, the emerging question is whether its imposition in such circumstances would violate the Eighth Amendment. It is my view that it would, for its imposition would then be the pointless and needless extinction of life with only marginal contributions to any discernible social or public purposes. A penalty with such negligible returns to the State would be patently excessive and cruel and unusual punishment violative of the Eighth Amendment.

It is also my judgment that this point has been reached with respect to capital punishment as it is presently administered under the statutes involved in these cases. Concededly, it is difficult to prove as a general proposition that capital punishment, however administered, more effectively serves the ends of the criminal law than does imprisonment. But however that may be, I cannot avoid the conclusion that as the statutes before us are now administered,

the penalty is so infrequently imposed that the threat of execution is too attenuated to be of substantial service to criminal justice.

I need not restate the facts and figures that appear in the opinions of my Brethren. Nor can I "prove" my conclusion from these data. But, like my Brethren, I must arrive at judgment; and I can do no more than state a conclusion based on 10 years of almost daily exposure to the facts and circumstances of hundreds and hundreds of federal and state criminal cases involving crimes for which death is the authorized penalty. That conclusion, as I have said, is that the death penalty is exacted with great infrequency even for the most atrocious crimes and that there is no meaningful basis for distinguishing the few cases in which it is imposed from the many cases in which it is not. The short of it is that the policy of vesting sentencing authority primarily in juries—a decision largely motivated by the desire to mitigate the harshness of the law and to bring community judgment to bear on the sentence as well as guilt or innocence—has so effectively achieved its aims that capital punishment within the confines of the statutes now before us has for all practical purposes run its course.

Mr. Chief Justice BURGER, with whom Mr. Justice BLACKMUN, Mr. Justice POWELL, and Mr. Justice REHNQUIST join, dissenting.

. . . There are no obvious indications that capital punishment offends the conscience of society to such a degree that our traditional deference to the legislative judgment must be abandoned. It is not a punishment such as burning at the stake that everyone would ineffably find to be repugnant to all civilized standards. Nor is it a punishment so roundly condemned that only a few aberrant legislatures have retained it on the statute books. Capital punishment is authorized by statute in 40 States, the District of Columbia, and in the federal courts for the commission of certain crimes.[14] On four occasions in the last 11 years Congress has added to the list of federal crimes punishable by death.[15] In looking for reliable indicia of contemporary attitude, none more trustworthy has been advanced.

One conceivable source of evidence that legislatures have abdicated their essentially barometric role with respect to community values would be public opinion polls, of which there have been many in the past decade addressed to the question of capital punishment. Without assessing the reliability of such polls, or intimating that any judicial reliance could ever be placed on them, it need only be noted that the reported results have shown nothing approximating the universal condemnation of capital punishment that might lead us to suspect that the legislatures in general have lost touch with current social values.[16]

Counsel for petitioners rely on a different body of empirical evidence. They argue, in effect, that the number of cases in which the death penalty is imposed, as compared with the number of cases in which it is statutorily available, reflects a general revulsion toward the penalty that would lead to its repeal if only it were more generally and widely enforced. It cannot be gainsaid that by the choice of juries—and sometimes judges[17]—the death penalty is imposed in far fewer than half the cases in which it is available.[18] To go further and characterize the rate of imposition as "freakishly rare," as petitioners insist, is unwarranted hyperbole. And regardless of its characterization, the rate of imposition does not impel the conclusion that capital punishment is now regarded as intolerably cruel or uncivilized.

It is argued that in those capital cases where juries have recommended mercy, they have given expression to civilized values and effectively renounced the legislative authorization for capital punishment. At the same time it is argued that where juries have made the awesome decision to send men to their deaths, they have acted arbitrarily and without sensitivity to prevailing standards of decency. This explanation for the infrequency of imposition of capital punishment is unsupported by known facts, and is inconsistent in principle with everything this Court has ever said about the functioning of juries in capital cases.

In *McGautha v. California,* decided only one year ago, the Court held that there was no mandate in the Due Process Clause of the Fourteenth Amendment that juries be given instructions as to when the death penalty should be imposed. After reviewing the autonomy that juries have traditionally exercised in capital cases and noting the practical difficulties of framing manageable instructions, this Court concluded that judicially articulated standards were not needed to insure a responsible decision as to penalty. Nothing in *McGautha* licenses capital juries to act arbitrarily or assumes that they have so acted in the past. On the contrary, the assumption underlying the *McGautha* ruling is that juries "will act with due regard for the consequences of their decision." 402 U.S., at 208.

The responsibility of juries deciding capital cases in our system of justice was nowhere better described than in *Witherspoon v. Illinois, supra:*

[A] jury that must choose between life imprisonment and capital punishment can do little more—and must do nothing less—than express *the conscience of the community* on the ultimate question of life or death.

And one of the most important functions any jury can perform in making such a selection is to maintain a link between contemporary community values and the penal system—a link without which the determination of punishment could hardly reflect "the evolving standards of decency that mark the progress of a maturing society." (391 U.S., at 519 and n. 15 emphasis added).

The selectivity of juries in imposing the punishment of death is properly viewed as a refinement on rather than a repudiation of, the statutory authorization for that penalty. Legislatures prescribe the categories of crimes for which the death penalty should be available, and, acting as "the conscience of the community," juries are entrusted to determine in individual cases that the ultimate punishment is warranted. Juries are undoubtedly influenced in this judgment by myriad factors. The motive or lack of motive of the perpetrator, the degree of injury or suffering of the victim or victims, and the degree of brutality in the commission of the crime would seem to be prominent among these factors. Given the general awareness that death is no longer a routine punishment for the crimes for which it is made available, it is hardly surprising that juries have been increasingly meticulous in their imposition of the penalty. But to assume from the mere fact of relative infrequency that only a random assortment of pariahs are sentenced to death, is to cast grave doubt on the basic integrity of our jury system.

It would, of course, be unrealistic to assume that juries have been perfectly consistent in choosing the cases where the death penalty is to be imposed, for no human institution performs with perfect consistency. There are doubtless prisoners on death row who would not be there had they been tried before a different jury or in a different State. In this sense their fate has been controlled by a fortuitous circumstance. However, this element of fortuity does not stand as an indictment either of the general functioning of juries in capital cases or of the integrity of jury decisions in individual cases. There is no empirical basis for concluding that juries have generally failed to discharge in good faith the responsibility described in *Witherspoon*—that of choosing between life and death in individual cases according to the dictates of community values.[19]

. . . It seems remarkable to me that with our basic trust in lay jurors as the keystone in our system of criminal justice, it should now be suggested that we take the most sensitive and important of all decisions away from them. I could more easily be persuaded that mandatory sentences of death, without the intervening and ameliorating impact of lay jurors, are so arbitrary and doctrinaire that they violate the Constitution. The very infrequency of death penalties imposed by jurors attests their cautious and discriminating reservation of that penalty for the most extreme cases. I had thought that nothing was clearer in history, as we noted in *McGautha* one year ago, than the American abhorrence of "the common-law rule imposing a mandatory death sentence on all convicted murderers." 402 U.S., at 198. As the concurring opinion of Mr. Justice Marshall shows, *ante,* at 339, the 19th century movement away from mandatory death sentences marked an enlightened introduction of flexibility into the sentencing process. It recognized that individual culpability is not always measured by the category of the crime committed. This change in sentencing practice was greeted by the Court as a humanizing development. See *Win-ston v. United States,* 172 *U.S.* 303 (1899); cf. *Calton v. Utah,* 130 *U.S.* 83 (1889). See also *Andres v. United States,* 333 *U.S.* 740, 753 (1948) (Frankfurter, J., concurring). I do not see how this history can be ignored and how it can be suggested that the Eighth Amendment demands the elimination of the most sensitive feature of the sentencing system.

As a general matter, the evolution of penal concepts in this country has not been marked by great progress, nor have the results up to now been crowned with significant success. If anywhere in the whole spectrum of criminal justice fresh ideas deserve sober analysis, the sentencing and correctional area ranks high on the list. But it has been widely accepted that mandatory sentences for crimes do not best serve the ends of the criminal justice system. Now, after the long process of drawing away from the blind imposition of uniform sentences for every person convicted of a particular offense, we are confronted with an argument perhaps implying that only the legislatures may determine that a sentence of death is appropriate, without the intervening evaluation of jurors or judges. This approach threatens to turn back the progress of penal reform, which has moved until recently at too slow a rate to absorb significant setbacks.

---

1. The opinion of the Supreme Court of Georgia affirming Furman's conviction of murder and sentence of death is reported in 225 *Ga.* 253, 167 *S.E.* 2d 628, and its opinion affirming Jackson's conviction of rape and sentence of death is reported in 225 *Ga.* 790, 171 *S.E.* 2d 501. The conviction of Branch of rape and the sentence of death were affirmed by the Court of Criminal Appeals of Texas and reported in 447 *S.W.* 2d 932.
2. See Johnson, *The Negro and Crime*, 217 Annals Amer. Acad. Pol. & Soc. Sci. 93 (1941).
3. See J. Spellman, Political *Theory of Ancient India* 112 (1964).
4. C. Drekmeier, Kingship and Community in Early India 233 (1962).
5. Cf. B. Prettyman, Jr., Death and The Supreme Court 296–97 (1961). "The disparity of representation in capital cases raises doubt about capital punishment itself, which has been abolished in only nine states. If a James Avery [345 U.S. 559] can be saved from electrocution because his attorney made timely objection to the selection of a jury by the use of yellow and white tickets, while an Aubry Williams [349 U.S. 375] can be sent to his death by a jury selected in precisely the same manner, we are imposing our most extreme penalty in an uneven fashion.

   The problem of proper representation is not a problem of money, as some have claimed, but of a lawyer's ability, and it is not true that only the rich have able lawyers. Both the rich and the poor usually are well represented—the poor because more often than not the best attorneys are appointed to defend them. It is the middle-class defendant, who can afford to hire an attorney but not a very good one, who is at a disadvantage. Certainly William Fikes [352 U.S. 191], despite the anomalous position in which he finds himself today, received as effective and intelligent a de-fense from his court-appointed attorneys as he would have received from an attorney his family had scraped together enough money to hire.

   And it is not only a matter of ability. An attorney must be found who is prepared to spend precious hours—the basic commodity he has to sell—on a case that seldom fully compensates him and often brings him no fee at all. The public has no conception of the time and effort devoted by attorneys to indigent cases. And in a first-degree case, the added responsibility of having a man's life depend upon the outcome exacts a heavy toll.

6. "That life is at stake is of course another important factor in creating the extraordinary situation. The difference between capital and non-capital offenses is the basis of differentiation in law in diverse ways in which the distinction becomes relevant." *Williams v. Georgia,* 349 *U.S.* 375, 391 (1955) (Frankfurter, J.). "When the penalty is death, we, like state court judges, are tempted to strain the evidence and even, in close cases, the law in order to give a doubtfully condemned man another chance." *Stein v. New York,* 346 *U.S.* 156 (1953) (Jackson, J.). "In death cases doubts such as those presented here should be resolved in favor of the accused." *Andres v. United States,* 333 *U.S.* 740, 752 (1948) (Reed, J.). Mr. Justice Harlan expressed the point strongly: "I do not concede that whatever process is 'due' an offender faced with a fine or a prison sentence necessarily satisfies the requirements of the Constitution in a capital case. The distinction is by no means novel, . . . nor is it negligible, being literally that between life and death." *Reid v. Covert,* 354 *U.S.* 1, 77 (1957) (concurring in result). And, of course, for many years this Court distinguished death cases from all others for purposes of the con-

stitutional right to counsel. See *Powell v. Alabama*, 287 *U.S.* 45 (1932); *Betts v. Brady*, 316 *U.S.* 455 (1942); *Bute v. Illinois*, 333 *U.S.* 640 (1948).

7. See Report of Royal Commission on Capital Punishment 1949–53, ¶¶ 700–789, pp. 246–73 (1953); Hearings on S. 1760 before the Subcommittee on Criminal Laws and Procedures of the Senate Committee on the Judiciary, 90th Cong., 2d Sess., 19–21 (1968) (testimony of Clinton Duffy); H. Barnes & N. Teeters, New Horizons in Criminology 306–309 (3d ed. 1959); C. Chessman, Trial by Ordeal 195–202 (1955); M. DiSalle, The Power of Life and Death 84–85 (1965); C. Duffy, 88 Men and 2 Women 13–14 (1962); B. Eshelman, Death Row Chaplain 26–29, 101–4, 159–64 (1962); R. Hammer, Between Life and Death 208–12 (1969); K. Lamott, Chronicles of San Quentin 228–31 (1961); L. Lawes, Life and Death in Sing Sing 170–71 (1928); Rubin, The Supreme Court, Cruel and Unusual Punishment, and the Death Penalty, 15 Crime & Delin. 121, 128–29 (1969); Comment, The Death Penalty Cases, 56 Calif. L. Rev. 1268, 1338–41 (1968); Brief *amici curiae* filed by James V. Bennett, Clinton T. Duffy, Robert G. Sarver, Harry C. Tinsley, and Lawrence E. Wilson 12–14.

8. See H. Barnes & N. Teeters, New Horizons in Criminology 309–11 (2d ed. 1959); Camus, Reflections on the Guillotine, in A. Camus, Resistance, Rebellion, and Death 131, 151–56 (1960); C. Duffy, 88 Men and 2 Women 68–70, 254 (1962); R. Hammer, *Between Life and Death* 222–35, 244–50, 269–72 (1969); S. Rubin, The Law of Criminal Correction 340 (1963); Bluestone & McGahee, Reaction to Extreme Stress: Impending Death by Execution, 119 Amer. J. Psychiatry 393 (1962); Gottlieb, Capital Punishment, 15 Crime & Delin. 1, 8–10 (1969); West, Medicine and Capital Punishment, in Hearings on S. 1760 before the Subcommittee on Criminal Laws and Procedures of the Senate Committee on the Judiciary, 90th Cong., 2d Sess., 124 (1968); Ziferstein, Crime and Punishment, The Center Magazine 84 (Jan. 1968); Comment, The Death Penalty Cases, 56 Calif. L. Rev. 1268, 1342 (1968); Note, Mental Suffering under Sentence of Death: A Cruel and Unusual Punishment, 57 Iowa L. Rev. 814 (1972).

9. The State, of course, does not purposely impose the lengthy waiting period in order to inflict further suffering. The impact upon the individual is not the less severe on that account. It is no answer to assert that long delays exist only because condemned criminals avail themselves of their full panoply of legal rights. The right not to be subjected to inhuman treatment cannot, of course, be played off against the right to pursue due process of law, but, apart from that, the plain truth is that it is society that demands, even against the wishes of the criminal, that all legal avenues be explored before the execution is finally carried out.

10. It was recognized in *Trop* itself that expatriation is a "punishment short of death." 356 U.S., at 99. Death, however, was distinguished on the ground that it was "still widely accepted." *Ibid.*

11. Stephen, Capital Punishments, 69 Fraser's Magazine 753, 763 (1864).

12. The victim surprised Furman in the act of burglarizing the victim's home in the middle of the night. While escaping, Furman killed the victim with one pistol shot fired through the closed kitchen door from the outside. At the trial, Furman gave his version of the killing:

> They got me charged with murder and I admit, I admit going to these folks' home and they did caught me in there and I was coming back out, backing up and there was a wire down there on the floor. I was coming out backwards and fell back and I didn't intend to kill nobody. I didn't know they was behind the door. The gun went off and I didn't know nothing about no murder until they arrested me, and when the gun went off I was down on the floor and I got up and ran. That's all to it. (App. 54–55.)

The Georgia Supreme Court accepted that version:

> The admission in open court by the accused . . . that during the period in which he was involved in the commission of a criminal act at the home of the deceased, he accidentally tripped over a wire in leaving the premises

causing the gun to go off, together with other facts and circumstances surrounding the death of the deceased by violent means, was sufficient to support the verdict of guilty of murder. . . . (*Furman v. State*, 225 *Ga.* 253, 254, 167 S.E. 2d 628, 629 (1969).)

About Furman himself, the jury knew only that he was black and that, according to his statement at trial, he was 26 years old and worked at "Superior Upholstery." App. 54. It took the jury one hour and 35 minutes to return a verdict of guilt and a sentence of death. *Id.*, at 64–65.

13. There is also the more limited argument that death is a necessary punishment when criminals are already serving or subject to a sentence of life imprisonment. If the only punishment available is further imprisonment, it is said, those criminals will have nothing to lose by committing further crimes, and accordingly the threat of death is the sole deterrent. But "life" imprisonment is a misnomer today. Rarely, if ever, do crimes carry a mandatory life sentence without possibility of parole. That possibility ensures that criminals do not reach the point where further crimes are free of consequences. Moreover, if this argument is simply an assertion that the threat, of death is a more effective deterrent than the threat of increased imprisonment by denial of release on parole, then, as noted above, there is simply no evidence to support it.

14. See Department of Justice, National Prisoner Statistics No. 46, Capital Punishment 1930–1970, p. 50 (Aug. 1971). Since the publication of the Department of Justice report, capital punishment has been judicially abolished in California, People v. Anderson, 6 Cal. 3d 628, 493 P. 2d 880, cert. denied, 406 U.S. 813 (1972). The States where capital punishment is no longer authorized are Alaska, California, Hawaii, Iowa, Maine, Michigan, Minnesota, Oregon, West Virginia, and Wisconsin.

15. See Act of Jan. 2, 1971, Pub. L. 91–644, Tit. IV, § 15, 84 Stat. 1891, 18 U.S.C. § 351; see Act of Oct. 15, 1970, Pub. L. 91–452, Tit. XI, § 1102 (a), 84 Stat. 956, 18 U.S.C. § 844 (f) (i); Act of Aug. 28, 1965, 79 Stat. 580, 18 U.S.C. § 1751; Act of Sept. 5, 1961, § 1, 75 Stat. 466, 49 U.S.C. § 1472 (i). See also opinion of Mr. Justice Blackmun, post, at 412–13.

16. A 1966 poll indicated that 42% of those polled favored capital punishment while 47% opposed it, and 11% had no opinion. A 1969 poll found 51% in favor, 40% opposed, and 9% with no opinion. See Erskine, The Polls: Capital Punishment, 34 Public Opinion Quarterly 290 (1970).

17. The jury plays the predominant role in sentencing in capital cases in this country. Available evidence indicates that where the judge determines the sentence, the death penalty is imposed with a slightly greater frequency than where the jury makes the determination. H. Kalven & H. Zeisel, The American Jury 436 (1966).

18. In the decade from 1961–70, an average of 106 persons per year received the death sentence in the United States, ranging from a low of 85 in 1967 to a high of 140 in 1961; 127 persons received the death sentence in 1970. Department of Justice, National Prisoner Statistics No. 46, Capital Punishment 1930–70, p. 9. See also Bedau, The Death Penalty in America, 35 Fed. Prob., No. 2, p. 32 (1971). Although accurate figures are difficult to obtain, it is thought that from 15% to 20% of those convicted of murder are sentenced to death in States where it is authorized. See, for example, McGee, Capital Punishment as Seen by a Correctional Administrator, 28 Fed. Prob., No. 2, pp. 11, 12 (1964); Bedau, Death Sentences in New Jersey 1907–60, 19 *Rutgers L. Rev.* 1, 30 (1964); Florida Division of Corrections, Seventh Biennial Report (July 1, 1968, to June 30, 1970) 82 and the few other crimes made punishable by death in certain States is considerably lower. See, for example, Florida Division of Corrections, Seventh Biennial Report, supra, at 83; Partington, The Incidence of the Death Penalty for Rape in Virginia, 22 *Wash. & Lee L. Rev.* 43–44, 71–73 (1965).

19. Counsel for petitioners make the conclusory statement that "[t]hose who are selected to die are the poor and powerless, personally ugly and socially unacceptable." Brief for Petitioner in No. 68-5027, p. 51. However, the sources cited contain no empirical findings to undermine the general premise that juries

impose the death penalty in the most extreme cases. One study has discerned a statistically noticeable difference between the rate of imposition on blue collar and white collar defendants; the study otherwise concludes that juries do follow rational patterns in imposing the sentence of death. Note, A Study of the California Penalty Jury in First-Degree-Murder Cases, 21 *Stan. L. Rev.* 1297 (1969). See also H. Kalven & H. Zeisel, The American Jury 434–49 (1966).

Statistics are also cited to show that the death penalty has been imposed in a racially discriminatory manner. Such statistics suggest, at least as a historical matter, that Negroes have been sentenced to death with greater frequency than whites in several States, particularly for the crime of interracial rape. See, for example, Koeninger, Capital Punishment in Texas, 1924–1968, 15 Crime & Delin. 132 (1969).

WOODSON V. NORTH CAROLINA*

United States Supreme Court, 1976

Judgment of the Court, and opinion of Mr. Justice STEWART, Mr. Justice POWELL, and Mr. Justice STEVENS, announced by Mr. Justice STEWART.

The question in this case is whether the imposition of a death sentence for the crime of first-degree murder under the law of North Carolina violates the Eighth and Fourteenth Amendments.

I

The petitioners were convicted of first-degree murder as the result of their participation in an armed robbery of a convenience food store, in the course of which the cashier was killed and a customer was seriously wounded. There were four participants in the robbery: the petitioners James Tyrone Woodson and Luby Waxton and two others, Leonard Tucker and Johnnie Lee Carroll. At the petitioners' trial Tucker and Carroll testified for the prosecution after having been permitted to plead guilty to lesser offenses; the petitioners testified in their own defense.

The evidence for the prosecution established that the four men had been discussing a possible robbery for some time. On the fatal day Woodson had been drinking heavily. About 9:30 P.M., Waxton and Tucker came to the trailer where Woodson was staying. When Woodson came out of the trailer, Waxton struck him in the face and threatened to kill him in an effort to make him sober up and come along on the robbery. The three proceeded to Waxton's trailer where they met Carroll. Waxton armed himself with a nickel-plated derringer, and Tucker handed Woodson a rifle. The four then set out by automobile to rob the store. Upon arriving at their destination Tucker and Waxton went into the store while Carroll and Woodson remained in the car as lookouts. Once inside the store, Tucker purchased a package of cigarettes from the woman cashier. Waxton then also asked for a package of cigarettes, but as the cashier approached him he pulled the derringer out of his hip pocket and fatally shot her at point-blank range. Waxton then took the money tray from the cash register and gave it to Tucker, who carried it out of the store, pushing past an entering customer as he reached the door. After he was outside, Tucker heard a second shot from inside the store, and shortly thereafter Waxton emerged, carrying a handful of paper money. Tucker and Waxton got in the car and the four drove away.

The petitioners' testimony agreed in large part with this version of the circumstances of the robbery. It differed diametrically in one important respect: Waxton claimed that he never had a gun, and that Tucker had shot both the cashier and the customer.

---

*428 *U.S.* 280, 49 *L. Ed. 2d* 944. No. 75–5491. Argued March 31, 1976. Decided July 2, 1976.

During the trial Waxton asked to be allowed to plead guilty to the same lesser offenses to which Tucker had pleaded guilty, but the solicitor refused to accept the pleas. Woodson, by contrast, maintained throughout the trial that he had been coerced by Waxton, that he was therefore innocent, and that he would not consider pleading guilty to any offense.

The petitioners were found guilty on all charges, and, as was required by statute, sentenced to death. The Supreme Court of North Carolina affirmed. We granted certiorari, to consider whether the imposition of the death penalties in this case comports with the Eighth and Fourteenth Amendments to the United States Constitution.

II

The petitioners argue that the imposition of the death penalty under any circumstances is cruel and unusual punishment in violation of the Eighth and Fourteenth Amendments. We reject this argument for the reasons stated today in *Gregg v. Georgia.*

III

At the time of this Court's decision in *Furman v. Georgia*, North Carolina law provided that in cases of first-degree murder, the jury in its unbridled discretion could choose whether the convicted defendant should be sentenced to death or to life imprisonment. After the *Furman* decision the Supreme Court of North Carolina in *State v. Waddell*, held unconstitutional the provision of the death penalty statute that gave the jury the option of returning a verdict of guilty without capital punishment, but held further that this provision was severable so that the statute survived as a mandatory death penalty law.

The North Carolina General Assembly in 1974 followed the court's lead and enacted a new statute that was essentially unchanged from the old one except that it made the death penalty mandatory. The statute now reads as follows:

Murder in the first and second degree defined; punishment.—A murder which shall be perpetrated by means of poison, lying in wait, imprisonment, starving, torture, or by any other kind of willful, deliberate and premeditated killing, or which shall be committed in the perpetration or attempt to perpetrate any arson, rape, robbery, kidnapping, burglary or other felony, shall be deemed to be murder in the first degree and shall be punished with death. All other kinds of murder shall be deemed murder in the second degree, and shall be punished by imprisonment for a term of not less than two years nor more than life imprisonment in the State's prison.

It was under this statute that the petitioners, who committed their crime on June 3, 1974, were tried, convicted, and sentenced to death.

North Carolina, unlike Florida, Georgia, and Texas, has thus responded to the *Furman* decision by making death the mandatory sentence for all persons convicted of first-degree murder. In ruling on the constitutionality of the sentences imposed on the petitioners under this North Carolina statute, the Court now addresses for the first time the question whether a death sentence returned pursuant to a law imposing a mandatory death penalty for a broad category of homicidal offenses constitutes cruel and unusual punishment within the meaning of the Eighth and Fourteenth Amendments. The issue, like that explored in *Furman*, involves the procedure employed by the State to select persons for the unique and irreversible penalty of death.

A

The Eighth Amendment stands to assure that the State's power to punish is "exercised within the limits of civilized standards." Central to the application of the Amendment is a determination of contemporary standards regarding the infliction of punishment. As discussed in *Gregg v. Georgia*, indicia of societal values identified in prior opinions include history and traditional usage, legislative enactments, and jury determinations.

In order to provide a frame for assessing the relevancy of these factors in this case we begin by sketching the history of mandatory death penalty statutes in the United States. At the time the Eighth Amendment was adopted in 1791, the States uniformly followed the common-law practice of making death the exclusive and mandatory sentence for certain specified offenses. Although the range of capital offenses in the American Colonies was quite limited in comparison to the more than 200 offenses then punishable by death in England, the Colonies at the time of the Revolution imposed death sentences on all persons convicted of any of a considerable number of crimes, typically including at a minimum, murder, treason, piracy, arson, rape, robbery, burglary, and sodomy. As at common law, all homicides that were not involuntary, provoked, justified, or excused constituted murder and were automatically punished by death. Almost from the outset jurors reacted unfavorably to the harshness of mandatory death sentences. The States initially responded to this expression of public dissatisfaction with mandatory statutes by limiting the classes of capital offenses.

This reform, however, left unresolved the problem posed by the not infrequent refusal of juries to convict murderers rather than subject them to automatic death sentences. In 1794, Pennsylvania attempted to alleviate the undue severity of the law by confining the mandatory death penalty to "murder of the first degree" encompassing all "willful, deliberate and premeditated" killings. Other jurisdictions, including Virginia and Ohio, soon enacted similar measures, and within a generation the practice spread to most of the States.

Despite the broad acceptance of the division of murder into degrees, the reform proved to be an unsatisfactory means of identifying persons appropriately punishable by death. Although its failure was due in part to the amorphous nature of the controlling concepts of willfulness, deliberateness, and premeditation, a more fundamental weakness of the reform soon became apparent. Juries continued to find the death penalty inappropriate in a significant number of first-degree murder cases and refused to return guilty verdicts for that crime.

The inadequacy of distinguishing between murderers solely on the basis of legislative criteria narrowing the definition of the capital offense led the States to grant juries sentencing discretion in capital cases. Tennessee in 1838, followed by Alabama in 1841, and Louisiana in 1846, were the first States to abandon mandatory death sentences in favor of discretionary death penalty statutes. This flexibility remedied the harshness of mandatory statutes by permitting the jury to respond to mitigating factors by withholding the death penalty. By the turn of the century, 23 States and the Federal Government had made death sentences discretionary for first-degree murder and other capital offenses. During the next two decades 14 additional States replaced their mandatory death penalty statutes. Thus,

by the end of World War I, all but eight States, Hawaii, and the District of Columbia either had adopted discretionary death penalty schemes or abolished the death penalty altogether. By 1963, all of these remaining jurisdictions had replaced their automatic death penalty statutes with discretionary jury sentencing.

The history of mandatory death penalty statutes in the United States thus reveals that the practice of sentencing to death all persons convicted of a particular offense has been rejected as unduly harsh and unworkably rigid. The two crucial indicators of evolving standards of decency respecting the imposition of punishment in our society—jury determinations and legislative enactments—both point conclusively to the repudiation of automatic death sentences. At least since the Revolution, American jurors have, with some regularity, disregarded their oaths and refused to convict defendants where a death sentence was the automatic consequence of a guilty verdict. As we have seen, the initial movement to reduce the number of capital offenses and to separate murder into degrees was prompted in part by the reaction of jurors as well as by reformers who objected to the imposition of death as the penalty for any crime. Nineteenth century journalists, statesmen, and jurists repeatedly observed that jurors were often deterred from convicting palpably guilty men of first-degree murder under mandatory statutes. Thereafter, continuing evidence of jury reluctance to convict persons of capital offenses in mandatory death penalty jurisdictions resulted in legislative authorization of discretionary jury sentencing—by Congress for federal crimes in 1897, by North Carolina in 1949, and by Congress for the District of Columbia in 1962.

As we have noted today in *Gregg v. Georgia*, legislative measures adopted by the people's chosen representatives weigh heavily in ascertaining contemporary standards of decency. The consistent course charted by the state legislatures and by Congress since the middle of the past century demonstrates that the aversion of jurors to mandatory death penalty statutes is shared by society at large.

Still further evidence of the incompatibility of mandatory death penalties with contemporary values is provided by the results of jury sentencing under discretionary statutes. In *Witherspoon v. Illinois*, the Court observed that "one of the most important functions any jury can perform" in exercising its discretion to choose "between life imprisonment and capital punishment" is "to maintain a link between contemporary community values and the penal system." Various studies indicate that even in first-degree murder cases juries with sentencing discretion do not impose the death penalty "with any great frequency." The actions of sentencing juries suggest that under contemporary standards of decency death is viewed as an inappropriate punishment for a substantial portion of convicted first-degree murderers.

Although the Court has never ruled on the constitutionality of mandatory death penalty statutes, on several occasions dating back to 1899 it has commented upon our society's aversion to automatic death sentences. In *Winston v. United States*, the Court noted that the "hardship of punishing with death every crime coming within the definition of murder at common law, and the reluctance of jurors to concur in a capital conviction, have induced American legislatures, in modern times, to allow some cases of murder to be punished by imprisonment, instead of by death." Fifty years after *Winston*, the Court underscored the marked transformation in our attitudes toward mandatory sentences: "The belief no longer prevails that every offense in a like legal category calls for an identical punishment without regard to the past life and habits of a particular offender. This whole country has traveled far from the period in which the death sentence was an automatic and commonplace result of convictions. . . ."

More recently, the Court in *McGautha v. California*, detailed the evolution of discretionary imposition of death sentences in this country, prompted by what it termed the American "rebellion against the common-law rule imposing a mandatory death sentence on all convicted murderers." Perhaps the one important factor about evolving social values regarding capital punishment upon which the Members of the *Furman* Court agreed was the accuracy of *McGautha*'s assessment of our Nation's rejection of mandatory death sentences. Mr. Justice Blackmun, for example, emphasized that legislation requiring an automatic death sentence for specified crimes would be "regressive and of an antique mold" and would mark a return to a "point in our criminology [passed beyond] long ago." The Chief Justice, speaking for the four dissenting Justices in *Furman*, discussed the question of mandatory death sentences at some length:

> I had thought that nothing was clearer in history, as we noted in *McGautha* one year ago, than the American abhorrence of "the common-law rule imposing a mandatory death sentence on all convicted murderers." As the concurring opinion of Mr. Justice Marshall

shows, the 19th century movement away from mandatory death sentences marked an enlightened introduction of flexibility into the sentencing process. It recognized that individual culpability is not always measured by the category of the crime committed. This change in sentencing practice was greeted by the Court as a humanizing development.

Although it seems beyond dispute that, at the time of the *Furman* decision in 1972, mandatory death penalty statutes had been renounced by American juries and legislatures, there remains the question whether the mandatory statutes adopted by North Carolina and a number of other States following *Furman* evince a sudden reversal of societal values regarding the imposition of capital punishment. In view of the persistent and unswerving legislative rejection of mandatory death penalty statutes beginning in 1838 and continuing for more than 130 years until *Furman*, it seems evident that the post-*Furman* enactments reflect attempts by the States to retain the death penalty in a form consistent with the Constitution, rather than a renewed societal acceptance of mandatory death sentencing. The fact that some States have adopted mandatory measures following *Furman* while others have legislated standards to guide jury discretion appears attributable to diverse readings of this Court's multi-opinioned decision in that case.

A brief examination of the background of the current North Carolina statute serves to reaffirm our assessment of its limited utility as an indicator of contemporary values regarding mandatory death sentences. Before 1949, North Carolina imposed a mandatory death sentence on any person convicted of rape or first-degree murder. That year, a study commission created by the state legislature recommended that juries be granted discretion to recommend life sentences in all capital cases:

> We propose that a recommendation of mercy by the jury in capital cases automatically carry with it a life sentence. Only three other states now have the mandatory death penalty and we believe its retention will be definitely harmful. Quite frequently, juries refuse to convict for rape or first degree murder because, from all the circumstances, they do not believe the defendant, although guilty, should suffer death. The result is that verdicts are returned hardly in harmony with evidence. Our proposal is already in effect in respect to the crimes of burglary and arson. There is

much testimony that it has proved beneficial in such cases. We think the law can now be broadened to include all capital crimes.

The 1949 session of the General Assembly of North Carolina adopted the proposed modifications of its rape and murder statutes. Although in subsequent years numerous bills were introduced in the legislature to limit further or abolish the death penalty in North Carolina, they were rejected as were two 1969 proposals to return to mandatory death sentences for all capital offenses.

As noted, when the Supreme Court of North Carolina analyzed the constitutionality of the State's death penalty statute following this Court's decision in *Furman*, it severed the 1949 proviso authorizing jury sentencing discretion and held that "the remainder of the statute with death as the mandatory punishment . . . remains in full force and effect." The North Carolina General Assembly then followed the course found constitutional in *Waddell* and enacted a first-degree murder provision identical to the mandatory statute in operation prior to the authorization of jury discretion. The State's brief in this case relates that the legislature sought to remove "*all* sentencing discretion [so that] there could be no successful *Furman* based attack on the North Carolina statute."

It is now well established that the Eighth Amendment draws much of its meaning from "the evolving standards of decency that mark the progress of a maturing society." As the above discussion makes clear, one of the most significant developments in our society's treatment of capital punishment has been the rejection of the common-law practice of inexorably imposing a death sentence upon every person convicted of a specified offense. North Carolina's mandatory death penalty statute for first-degree murder departs markedly from contemporary standards respecting the imposition of the punishment of death and thus cannot be applied consistently with the Eighth and Fourteenth Amendments' requirement that the State's power to punish "be exercised within the limits of civilized standards."

B

A separate deficiency of North Carolina's mandatory death sentence statute is its failure to provide a constitutionally tolerable response to *Furman*'s rejection of unbridled jury discretion in the imposition of capital sentences. Central to the limited holding in *Furman* was the conviction that the vesting of stan-

dardless sentencing power in the jury violated the Eighth and Fourteenth Amendments. It is argued that North Carolina has remedied the inadequacies of the death penalty statutes held unconstitutional in *Furman* by withdrawing all sentencing discretion from juries in capital cases. But when one considers the long and consistent American experience with the death penalty in first-degree murder cases, it becomes evident that mandatory statutes enacted in response to *Furman* have simply papered over the problem of unguided and unchecked jury discretion.

As we have noted in Part III-A, *supra*, there is general agreement that American juries have persistently refused to convict a significant portion of persons charged with first-degree murder of that offense under mandatory death penalty statutes. The North Carolina study commission, reported that juries in that State "[q]uite frequently" were deterred from rendering guilty verdicts of first-degree murder because of the enormity of the sentence automatically imposed. Moreover, as a matter of historic fact, juries operating under discretionary sentencing statutes have consistently returned death sentences in only a minority of first-degree murder cases. In view of the historic record, it is only reasonable to assume that many juries under mandatory statutes will continue to consider the grave consequences of a conviction in reaching a verdict. North Carolina's mandatory death penalty statute provides no standards to guide the jury in its inevitable exercise of the power to determine which first-degree murderers shall live and which shall die. And there is no way under the North Carolina law for the judiciary to check arbitrary and capricious exercise of that power through a review of death sentences. Instead of rationalizing the sentencing process, a mandatory scheme may well exacerbate the problem identified in *Furman* by resting the penalty determination on the particular jury's willingness to act lawlessly. While a mandatory death penalty statute may reasonably be expected to increase the number of persons sentenced to death, it does not fulfill *Furman*'s basic requirement by replacing arbitrary and wanton jury discretion with objective standards to guide, regularize, and make rationally reviewable the process for imposing a sentence of death.

C

A third constitutional shortcoming of the North Carolina statute is its failure to allow the particularized consideration of relevant aspects of the character and record of each convicted defendant before the imposition upon him of a sentence of death. In *Furman,* members of the Court acknowledge what cannot fairly be denied—that death is a punishment different from all other sanctions in kind rather than degree. A process that accords no significance to relevant facets of the character and record of the individual offender or the circumstances of the particular offense excludes from consideration in fixing the ultimate punishment of death the possibility of compassionate or mitigating factors stemming from the diverse frailties of humankind. It treats all persons convicted of a designated offense not as uniquely individual human beings, but as members of a faceless, undifferentiated mass to be subjected to the blind infliction of the penalty of death.

This Court has previously recognized that "[f]or the determination of sentences, justice generally requires consideration of more than the particular acts by which the crime was committed and that there be taken into account the circumstances of the offense together with the character and propensities of the offender." Consideration of both the offender and the offense in order to arrive at a just and appropriate sentence has been viewed as a progressive and humanizing development. While the prevailing practice of individualizing sentencing determinations generally reflects simply enlightened policy rather than a constitutional imperative, we believe that in capital cases the fundamental respect for humanity underlying the Eighth Amendment requires consideration of the character and record of the individual offender and the circumstances of the particular offense as a constitutionally indispensable part of the process of inflicting the penalty of death.

This conclusion rests squarely on the predicate that the penalty of death is qualitatively different from a sentence of imprisonment, however long. Death, in its finality, differs more from life imprisonment than a 100-year prison term differs from one of only a year or two. Because of that qualitative difference, there is a corresponding difference in the need for reliability in the determination that death is the appropriate punishment in a specific case.

For the reasons stated, we conclude that the death sentences imposed upon the petitioners under North Carolina's mandatory death sentence statute violated the Eighth and Fourteenth Amendments and therefore must be set aside. The judgment of the Supreme Court of North Carolina is reversed insofar as it upheld the death sentences imposed upon the petitioners, and the case is remanded for further proceedings not inconsistent with this opinion.

It is so ordered.

Mr. Justice BRENNAN, concurring in the judgment.

For the reasons stated in my dissenting opinion in *Gregg v. Georgia*, I concur in the judgment that sets aside the death sentences imposed under the North Carolina death sentence statute as violative of the Eighth and Fourteenth Amendments.

Mr. Justice MARSHALL, concurring in the judgment.

For the reasons stated in my dissenting opinion in *Gregg v. Georgia*, I am of the view that the death penalty is a cruel and unusual punishment forbidden by the Eighth and Fourteenth Amendments. I therefore concur in the Court's judgment.

Mr. Justice WHITE, with whom THE CHIEF JUSTICE and Mr. Justice REHNQUIST join, dissenting.

Following *Furman v. Georgia*, the North Carolina Supreme Court considered the effect of that case on the North Carolina criminal statutes which imposed the death penalty for first-degree murder and other crimes but which provided that "if at the time of rendering its verdict in open court, the jury shall so recommend, the punishment shall be imprisonment for life in the State's prison, and the court shall so instruct the jury." *State v. Waddell*, determined that *Furman v. Georgia* invalidated only the proviso giving the jury the power to limit the penalty to life imprisonment and that thenceforward death was the mandatory penalty for the specified capital crimes. Thereafter N.C.Gen.Stat. § 14–17 was amended to eliminate the express dispensing power of the jury and to add kidnapping to the underlying felonies for which death is the specified penalty. As amended in 1974, the section reads as follows:

A murder which shall be perpetrated by means of poison, lying in wait, imprisonment, starving, torture, or by any other kind of willful, deliberate and premeditated killing, or which shall be committed in the perpetration or attempt to perpetrate any arson, rape, robbery, kidnapping, burglary or other felony, shall be deemed to be murder in the first degree and shall be punished with death. All other kinds of murder shall be deemed murder in the second degree, and shall be punished by imprisonment for a term of not less than two years nor more than life imprisonment in the State's prison.

It was under this statute that the petitioners in this case were convicted of first-degree murder and the mandatory death sentences imposed.

The facts of record and the proceedings in this case leading to petitioners' convictions for first-degree murder and their death sentences appear in the opinion of Mr. Justice STEWART, Mr. Justice POWELL, and Mr. Justice STEVENS. The issues in the case are very similar, if not identical, to those in *Roberts v. Louisiana*. For the reasons stated in my dissenting opinion in that case, I reject petitioners' arguments that the death penalty in any circumstances is a violation of the Eighth Amendment and that the North Carolina statute, although making the imposition of the death penalty mandatory upon proof of guilt and a verdict of first-degree murder, will nevertheless result in the death penalty being imposed so seldom and arbitrarily that it is void under *Furman v. Georgia*. As is also apparent from my dissenting opinion in *Roberts v. Louisiana*, I also disagree with the two additional grounds which the plurality *sua sponte* offers for invalidating the North Carolina statute. I would affirm the judgment of the North Carolina Supreme Court.

Mr. Justice BLACKMUN, dissenting.

I dissent for the reasons set forth in my dissent in *Furman v. Georgia*, and in the other dissenting opinions I joined in that case.

Mr. Justice REHNQUIST, dissenting.

I

The difficulties which attend the plurality's explanation for the result it reaches tend at first to obscure difficulties at least as significant which inhere in the unarticulated premises necessarily underlying that explanation. I advert to the latter only briefly, in order to devote the major and following portion of this dissent to those issues which the plurality actually considers.

As an original proposition, it is by no means clear that the prohibition against cruel and unusual punishments embodied in the Eighth Amendment, and made applicable to the States by the Fourteenth Amendment, *Robinson v. California*, was not limited to those punishments deemed cruel and unusual at the time of the adoption of the Bill of Rights. *McGautha v. California*. If *Weems v. United States*, dealing not with the Eighth Amendment but with an identical provision contained in the Philippine Constitution, and the plurality opinion in *Trop v. Dulles*,

are to be taken as indicating the contrary, they should surely be weighed against statements in cases such as *Wilkerson v. Utah, In re Kemmler, Louisiana ex rel. Francis v. Resweber*, and the plurality opinion in *Trop* itself, that the infliction of capital punishment is not in itself violative of the Cruel and Unusual Punishments Clause. Thus for the plurality to begin its analysis with the assumption that it need only demonstrate that "evolving standards of decency" show that contemporary "society" has rejected such provisions is itself a somewhat shaky point of departure. But even if the assumption be conceded, the plurality opinion's analysis nonetheless founders.

The plurality relies first upon its conclusion that society has turned away from the mandatory imposition of death sentences, and second upon its conclusion that the North Carolina system has "simply papered over" the problem of unbridled jury discretion which two of the separate opinions in *Furman v. Georgia* identified as the basis for the judgment rendering the death sentences there reviewed unconstitutional. The third "constitutional shortcoming" of the North Carolina statute is said to be "its failure to allow the particularized consideration of relevant aspects of the character and record of each convicted defendant before the imposition upon him of a sentence of death."

I do not believe that any one of these reasons singly, or all of them together, can withstand careful analysis. Contrary to the plurality's assertions, they would import into the Cruel and Unusual Punishments Clause procedural requirements which find no support in our cases. Their application will result in the invalidation of a death sentence imposed upon a defendant convicted of first-degree murder under the North Carolina system, and the upholding of the same sentence imposed on an identical defendant convicted on identical evidence of first-degree murder under the Florida, Georgia, or Texas systems—a result surely as "freakish" as that condemned in the separate opinions in *Furman*.

II

The plurality is simply mistaken in its assertion that "[t]he history of mandatory death penalty statutes in the United States thus reveals that the practice of sentencing to death all persons convicted of a particular offense has been rejected as unduly harsh and unworkably rigid." This conclusion is purportedly based on two historic developments: the first a series of legislative decisions during the 19th century narrowing the class of offenses punishable by death; the second a series of legislative decisions during both the 19th and 20th centuries, through which mandatory imposition of the death penalty largely gave way to jury discretion in deciding whether or not to impose this ultimate sanction. The first development may have some relevance to the plurality's argument in general but has no bearing at all upon this case. The second development, properly analyzed, has virtually no relevance even to the plurality's argument.

There can be no question that the legislative and other materials discussed in the plurality's opinion show a widespread conclusion on the part of state legislatures during the 19th century that the penalty of death was being required for too broad a range of crimes, and that these legislatures proceeded to narrow the range of crimes for which such penalty could be imposed. If this case involved the imposition of the death penalty for an offense such as burglary or sodomy, the virtually unanimous trend in the legislatures of the States to exclude such offenders from liability for capital punishment might bear on the plurality's Eighth Amendment argument. But petitioners were convicted of first-degree murder, and there is not the slightest suggestion in the material relied upon by the plurality that there had been any turning away at all, much less any such unanimous turning away, from the death penalty as a punishment for those guilty of first-degree murder. The legislative narrowing of the spectrum of capital crimes, therefore, while very arguably representing a general societal judgment since the trend was so widespread, simply never reached far enough to exclude the sort of aggravated homicide of which petitioners stand convicted.

The second string to the plurality's analytical bow is that legislative change from mandatory to discretionary imposition of the death sentence likewise evidences societal rejection of mandatory death penalties. The plurality simply does not make out this part of its case, however, in large part because it treats as being of equal dignity with legislative judgments the judgments of particular juries and of individual jurors.

There was undoubted dissatisfaction, from more than one sector of 19th century society, with the operation of mandatory death sentences. One segment of that society was totally opposed to capital punishment, and was apparently willing to accept the substitution of discretionary imposition of that penalty for its mandatory imposition as a halfway house on the road to total abolition. Another segment was equally unhappy with the operation of the mandatory system, but for an entirely different reason. As the plurality recognizes, this second segment of society was unhappy with the operation of the mandatory system, not because of the death sentences imposed under it, but because people obviously guilty of criminal offenses were not being convicted under it. Change to a discretionary system was accepted by these persons not because they thought mandatory imposition of the death penalty was cruel and unusual, but because they thought that if jurors were permitted to return a sentence other than death upon the conviction of a capital crime, fewer guilty defendants would be acquitted.

So far as the action of juries is concerned, the fact that in some cases juries operating under the mandatory system refused to convict obviously guilty defendants does not reflect any "turning away" from the death penalty, or the mandatory death penalty, supporting the proposition that it is "cruel and unusual." Given the requirement of unanimity with respect to jury verdicts in capital cases, a requirement which prevails today in States which accept a nonunanimous verdict in the case of other crimes, it is apparent that a single juror could prevent a jury from returning a verdict of conviction. Occasional refusals to convict, therefore, may just as easily have represented the intransigence of only a small minority of 12 jurors as well as the unanimous judgment of all 12. The fact that the presence of such jurors could prevent conviction in a given case, even though the majority of society, speaking through legislatures, had decreed that it should be imposed, certainly does not indicate that society as a whole rejected mandatory punishment for such offenders; it does not even indicate that those few members of society who serve on juries, as a whole, had done so.

The introduction of discretionary sentencing likewise creates no inference that contemporary society had rejected the mandatory system as unduly severe. Legislatures enacting discretionary sentencing statutes had no reason to think that there would not be roughly the same number of capital convictions under the new system as under the old. The same subjective juror responses which resulted in juror nullification under the old system were legitimized, but in the absence of those subjective responses to a particular set of facts, a capital sentence could as likely be anticipated under the discretionary system as under the mandatory. And at least some of those who would have been acquitted under the mandatory system would be subjected to at least *some* punishment under the discretionary system, rather than escaping altogether a penalty for the crime of which they were guilty. That society was unwilling to accept the paradox presented to it by the actions of some maverick juries or jurors—the acquittal of palpably guilty defendants—hardly reflects the sort of an "evolving standard of decency" to which the plurality professes obeisance.

Nor do the opinions in *Furman* which indicate a preference for discretionary sentencing in capital cases suggest in the slightest that a mandatory sentencing procedure would be cruel and unusual. The plurality concedes, as it must, that following *Furman* 10 States enacted laws providing for mandatory capital punishment. See State Capital Punishment Statutes Enacted Subsequent to *Furman v. Georgia*. These enactments the plurality seeks to explain as due to a wrong-headed reading of the holding in *Furman*. But this explanation simply does not wash. While those States may be presumed to have preferred their prior systems reposing sentencing discretion in juries or judges, they indisputably preferred mandatory capital punishment to no capital punishment at all. Their willingness to enact statutes providing that penalty is utterly inconsistent with the notion that they regarded mandatory capital sentencing as beyond "evolving standards of decency." The plurality's glib rejection of *these* legislative decisions as having little weight on the scale which it finds in the Eighth Amendment seems to me more an instance of its desire to save the people from themselves than a conscientious effort to ascertain the content of any "evolving standard of decency."

III

The second constitutional flaw which the plurality finds in North Carolina's mandatory system is that it has simply "papered over" the problem of unchecked jury discretion. The plurality states that "there is general agreement that American juries have persistently refused to convict a significant portion of persons charged with first-degree murder of that offense under mandatory death penalty statutes." The plurality also states that "as a matter of historic fact, juries operating under discretionary sentencing statutes have consistently returned death sentences in only a minority of first-degree murder cases." The basic factual assumption of the plurality seems to be that for any given number of first-degree murder defendants subject to capital punishment, there will be a certain number of jurors who will be unwilling to impose the death penalty even though they are entirely satisfied that the necessary elements of the substantive offense are made out.

In North Carolina jurors unwilling to impose the death penalty may simply hang a jury or they may so assert themselves that a verdict of not guilty is brought in; in Louisiana they will have a similar effect in causing some juries to bring in a verdict of guilty of a lesser included offense even though all the jurors are satisfied that the elements of the greater offense are made out. Such jurors, of course, are violating their oath, but such violation is not only consistent with the majority's hypothesis; the majority's hypothesis is bottomed on its occurrence.

For purposes of argument, I accept the plurality's hypothesis; but it seems to me impossible to conclude from it that a mandatory death sentence statute such as North Carolina enacted is any less sound constitutionally than are the systems enacted by Georgia, Florida, and Texas which the Court upholds.

In Georgia juries are entitled to return a sentence of life, rather than death, for no reason whatever, simply based upon their own subjective notions of what is right and what is wrong. In Florida the judge and jury are required to weigh legislatively enacted aggravating factors against legislatively enacted mitigating factors, and then base their choice between life or death on an estimate of the result of that weighing. Substantial discretion exists here, too, though it is somewhat more canalized than it is in Georgia. Why these types of discretion are regarded by the plurality as constitutionally permissible, while that which may occur in the North Carolina system is not, is not readily apparent. The freakish and arbitrary nature of the death penalty described in the separate concurring opinions of Justices Stewart, and White in *Furman* arose not from the perception that so *many* capital sentences were being imposed but from the perception that so *few* were bring imposed. To conclude that the North Carolina system is bad because juror nullification may permit jury discretion while concluding that the Georgia and Florida systems are sound because they *require* this same discretion, is, as the plurality opinion demonstrates, inexplicable.

The Texas system much more closely approximates the mandatory North Carolina system which is struck down today. The jury is required to answer three statutory questions. If the questions are unanimously answered in the affirmative, the death penalty *must* be imposed. It is extremely difficult to see how this system can be any less subject to the infirmities caused by juror nullification which the plurality concludes are fatal to North Carolina's statute. Justices STEWART, POWELL, and STEVENS apparently think they can sidestep this inconsistency because of their belief that one of the three questions will permit consideration of mitigating factors justifying imposition of a life sentence. It is, however, as those Justices recognize, far from clear that the statute is to be read in such a fashion. In any event, while the imposition of such unlimited consideration of mitigating factors may conform to the plurality's novel constitutional doctrine that "[a] jury must be allowed to consider on the basis of all relevant evidence not only why a death sentence should be imposed, but also why it should not be imposed," the resulting system seems as likely as any to produce the unbridled discretion which was condemned by the separate opinions in *Furman*.

The plurality seems to believe that provision for appellate review will afford a check upon the instances of juror arbitrariness in a discretionary system. But it is not at all apparent that appellate review of death sentences, through a process of comparing the facts of one case in which a death sentence was imposed with the facts of another in which such a sentence was imposed, will afford any meaningful protection against whatever arbitrariness results from jury discretion. All that such review of death sentences can provide is a comparison of fact situations which must in their nature be highly particularized if not unique, and the only relief which it can afford is to single out the occasional death sentence which in the view of the reviewing court does not conform to the standards established by the legislature.

It is established, of course, that there is no right to appellate review of a criminal sentence. *McKane v. Durston*. That question is not at issue here, since North Carolina, along with the other four States whose systems the petitioners are challenging in these cases, provides appellate review for a death sentence imposed in one of its trial courts.

By definition, of course, there can be no separate appellate review of the factual basis for the sentencing decision in a mandatory system. If it is once established in a fairly conducted trial that the defendant has in fact committed the crime in question, the only question as to the sentence which can be raised on appeal is whether a legislative determination that such a crime should be punished by death violates the Cruel and Unusual Punishments Clause of the Eighth Amendment. Here both peti-

tioners were convicted of first-degree murder, and there is no serious question raised by the plurality that death is not a constitutionally permissible penalty for such a crime.

But the plurality sees another role for appellate review in its description of the reasons why the Georgia, Texas, and Florida systems are upheld, and the North Carolina system struck down. And it is doubtless true that Georgia in particular has made a substantial effort to respond to the concerns expressed in *Furman*, not an easy task considering the glossolalial manner in which those concerns were expressed. The Georgia Supreme Court has indicated that the Georgia death penalty statute requires it to review death sentences imposed by juries on the basis of rough "proportionality." It has announced that it will not sustain, at least at the present time, death penalties imposed for armed robbery because that penalty is so seldom imposed by juries for that offense. It has also indicated that it will not sustain death penalties imposed for rape in certain fact situations, because the death penalty has been so seldom imposed on facts similar to those situations.

But while the Georgia response may be an admirable one as a matter of policy, it has imperfections, if a failure to conform completely to the dictates of the separate opinions in *Furman* be deemed imperfections, which the opinion of Justices STEWART, POWELL, and STEVENS does not point out. Although there may be some disagreement between that opinion, and the opinion of my Brother White in *Gregg v. Georgia*, which I have joined, as to whether the proportionality review conducted by the Supreme Court of Georgia is based solely upon capital sentences imposed, or upon all sentences imposed in cases where a capital sentence could have been imposed by law, I shall assume for the purposes of this discussion that the system contemplates the latter. But this is still far from a guarantee of any equality in sentencing, and is likewise no guarantee against juror nullification. Under the Georgia system, the jury is free to recommend life imprisonment, as opposed to death, for no stated reason whatever. The Georgia Supreme Court cannot know, therefore, when it is reviewing jury sentences for life in capital cases, whether the jurors found aggravating circumstances present, but nonetheless decided to recommend mercy, or instead found no aggravating circumstances at all and opted for mercy. So the "proportionality" type of review, while it would perhaps achieve its objective if there were no possible factual lacunae in the jury verdicts, will not achieve its objective because there are necessarily such lacunae.

IN DEFENSE OF THE DEATH PENALTY:
A Practical and Moral Analysis*

Ernest van den Haag

Three questions about the death penalty so overlap that they must each be answered. I shall ask seriatim: Is the death penalty constitutional? Is it useful? Is the death penalty morally justifiable? . . .

Regardless of constitutional interpretation, the morality and legitimacy of the abolitionist argument regarding capriciousness, discretion, or discrimination, would be more persuasive if it were alleged that those selectively executed are not guilty. But the argument merely maintains that some guilty, but favored, persons or groups escape the death penalty. This is hardly sufficient for letting others escape it. On the contrary, that some guilty persons or groups elude it argues for *extending* the death penalty to them.[1]

Justice requires punishing the guilty—as many of the guilty as possible—even if only some can be punished, and sparing the innocent—as many of the innocent as possible, even if not all are spared. Morally, justice must always be preferred to equality. It would surely be wrong to treat everybody with equal injustice in preference to meting out justice to some. Justice cannot ever permit sparing some guilty persons, or punishing some innocent ones, for the sake of equality—because others have been unjustly spared or punished. In practice, penalties never could be applied if we insisted that they cannot be inflicted on any guilty persons unless we are able to make sure that they are equally applied to all other guilty persons. Anyone familiar with law enforcement knows that punishments can be inflicted only on an unavoidably capricious selection of the guilty.

Although it does not warrant serious discussion, the argument from capriciousness looms large in briefs and decisions. For the last seventy years, courts have tried—lamentably and unproductively—to prevent errors of procedure, or of evidence collection, or of decision-making, by the paradoxical method of letting defendants go free as a punishment, or warning, to errant law enforcers. Yet the strategy admittedly never has prevented the errors it was designed to prevent—although it has released countless guilty persons.[2] There is no more merit in the attempt to persuade the courts to let all capital crime defendants go free of capital punishment because some have wrongly escaped it, than in attempting to persuade the courts to let all burglars go, because some have wrongly escaped detection or imprisonment.

Is the death penalty morally just and/or useful? This is the essential moral, as distinguished from the constitutional, question. Discrimination is irrelevant to this moral question. If the death penalty were distributed equally and uncapriciously and with superhuman perfection to all the guilty, but were morally unjust, it would be unjust in each case. Contrariwise, if the death penalty is morally just, however discriminatorily applied to only some of the guilty, it remains just in each case in which it is applied.

The utilitarian (political) effects of unequal justice may well be detrimental to the social fabric because they outrage our passion for equality before the law. Unequal justice also is morally repellent. Nonetheless unequal justice is still justice. The guilty do not become innocent or less deserving of punishment because others escaped it. Nor does any innocent deserve punishment because others suffer it. Justice remains just, however unequal, while injustice remains unjust, however equal. While both are desired, justice and equality are not identical. Equality before the law should be extended and enforced—but not at the expense of justice.

Capriciousness, at any rate, is used as a sham argument against capital punishment by abolition-

*From Ernest van den Haag, "In Defense of the Death Penalty: A Political and Moral Analysis," in *Criminal Bulletin*, vol. 14, no. 1 (1978), pp. 51–68. Reprinted here by permission of Warren, Gorham and Lamont, Inc.

ists. They would oppose the death penalty if it could be meted out without any discretion. They would oppose the death penalty in a homogeneous country without racial discrimination. And they would oppose the death penalty if the incomes of those executed and of those spared were the same. Actually, abolitionists oppose the death penalty, not its possible maldistribution.

What about persons executed in error? The objection here is not that some of the guilty escape, but that some of the innocent do not—a matter far more serious than discrimination among the guilty. Yet, when urged by abolitionists, this, along with all distributional arguments, is a sham. Why? Abolitionists are opposed to the death penalty for the guilty as much as for the innocent. Hence, the question of guilt, if at all relevant to their position, cannot be decisive for them. Guilt is decisive only to those who urge the death penalty for the guilty. They must worry about distribution—part of the justice they seek.

The execution of innocents believed guilty is a miscarriage of justice that must be opposed whenever detected. But such miscarriages of justice do not warrant abolition of the death penalty. Unless the moral drawbacks of an activity or practice, which include the possible death of innocent bystanders, outweigh the moral advantages, which include the innocent lives that might be saved by it, the activity is warranted. Most human activities—medicine, manufacturing, automobile and air traffic, sports, not to speak of wars and revolutions—cause the death of innocent bystanders. Nevertheless, if the advantages sufficiently outweigh the disadvantages, human activities, including those of the penal system with all its punishments, are morally justified.

Is there evidence supporting the usefulness of the death penalty in securing the life of the citizens? Researchers in the past found no statistical evidence for the effects sought, marginal deterrent effects, or deterrent effects over and above those of alternative sanctions. However, in the last few years new and more sophisticated studies have led Professor Isaac Ehrlich to conclude that over the period 1933–1969, "an additional execution per year . . . may have resulted (on the average) in 7 or 8 fewer murders."[3] Other investigators have confirmed Ehrlich's tentative results. Not surprisingly, refutations have been attempted, and Professor Ehrlich has offered his rebuttals.[4] The matter will remain controversial for some time. However, two tentative conclusions can be drawn with some confidence. First, Ehrlich has shown that previous investigations, that did not find

deterrent effects of the death penalty, suffered from fatal defects. Second, there is now some likelihood—much more than hitherto—of statistically demonstrating marginal deterrent effects.

Thus, with respect to deterrence, we must now choose:

1. To trade the certain shortening of the life of a convicted murderer against the survival of between seven and eight innocent victims whose future murder by others becomes more probable, unless the convicted murderer is executed;
2. To trade the certain survival of the convicted murderer against the loss of the lives of between seven and eight innocent victims, who are more likely to be murdered by others if the convicted murderer is allowed to survive.

Prudence as well as morality command us to choose the first alternative.[5]

If executions had a zero marginal effect, they could not be justified in deterrent terms. But even the pre-Ehrlich investigations did not demonstrate this. They merely found that an above-zero effect could not be demonstrated statistically. While we do not know at present the degree of confidence with which we can assign an above marginal deterrent effect to executions, we can be more confident than in the past. I should now regard it as irresponsible not to shorten the lives of convicted murderers simply because we cannot be altogether sure that their execution will lengthen the lives of innocent victims: It seems immoral to let convicted murderers survive at the probable—or even at the merely possible—expense of the lives of innocent victims who might have been spared had the murderers been executed.

In principle, one could experiment to test the hypothesis of zero marginal effect. The most direct way would be to legislate the death penalty for certain kinds of murder if committed, say, on weekdays, but never on Sunday. Or, on Monday, Wednesday, and Friday, and not on other days. (The days could be changed around every few years to avoid possible bias.) I am convinced there would be fewer murders on death-penalty than on life-imprisonment days. Unfortunately, the experiment faces formidable obstacles.[6]

Our penal system rests on the proposition that more severe penalties are more deterrent than less severe penalties. We assume, rightly, I believe, that a $5 fine deters rape less than a $500 fine, and that the threat of five years in prison will deter more than either fine.[7] This assumption of the penal system rests on the common experience that, once aware of them, people learn to avoid natural dangers the more likely these are to be injurious and the more severe the likely injuries. People endowed with ordinary common sense (a class which includes some sociologists) have found no reason why behavior with respect to legal dangers should differ from behavior with respect to natural dangers. Indeed, it does not. Hence, the legal system proportions threatened penalties to the gravity of crimes, both to do justice and to achieve deterrence in proportion to that gravity.

Thus, if it is true that the more severe the penalty the greater the deterrent effect, then the most severe penalty—the death penalty—would have the greatest deterrent effect. Arguments to the contrary assume either that capital crimes never are deterrable (sometimes merely because not all capital crimes have been deterred), or that, beyond some point, the deterrent effect of added severity is necessarily zero. Perhaps. But the burden of proof must be borne by those who presume to have located the point of zero marginal returns before the death penalty.

As an additional commonsense observation, I should add that without the death penalty, we necessarily confer immunity on just those persons most likely to be in need of deterrent threats. Thus, prisoners serving life sentences can kill fellow prisoners or guards with impunity. Prison wardens are unlikely to prevent violence in prisons as long as they give humane treatment to inmates and have no threats of additional punishment available for the murderers among them who are already serving life sentences. I cannot see the moral or utilitarian reasons for giving permanent immunity to homicidal life prisoners, thereby endangering the other prisoners and the guards, and in effect preferring the life prisoners to their victims.

Outside the prison context, an offender who expects a life sentence for his offense may murder his victim, or witnesses, or the arresting officer, to improve his chances of escaping. He could not be threatened with an additional penalty for his additional crime—an open invitation. Only the death penalty could deter in such cases. If there is but a possibility—and I believe there is a probability—that it will, we should retain it.

However, deterrence requires that the threat of the ultimate penalty be reserved for the ultimate crime. It may be prevented by that threat. Hence, the extreme punishment should never be prescribed when the offender, because already threatened by it, might add to his crimes with impunity. Thus, rape, or

kidnapping, should not incur the death penalty, while killing the victim of either crime should. This may not stop an Eichmann after his first murder, but it will stop most people before. The range of punishments is not infinite; it is necessarily more restricted than the range of crimes. Since death is the ultimate penalty, it must be reserved for the ultimate crime.

Consider now some popular arguments against capital punishment.

According to Beccaria, with the death penalty the "laws which punish homicide . . . themselves commit it," thus giving "an example of barbarity." Those who speak of "legalized murder" use an oxymoronic phrase to echo this allegation. Legally imposed punishments such as fines, incarcerations, or executions, although often physically identical to the crimes punished, are not crimes or their moral equivalent. The difference between crimes and lawful acts is not physical, but legal. Driving a stolen car is a crime, although not physically different from driving a car you own. Unlawful imprisonment and kidnapping need not differ physically from the lawful arrest and incarceration used to punish unlawful imprisonment and kidnapping. Finally, whether a lawful punishment gives an "example of barbarity" depends on how the moral difference between crime and punishment is perceived. To suggest that its physical quality, ipso facto, morally disqualifies the punishment, is to assume what is to be shown.

It is possible that all displays of violence, criminal or punitive, influence people to engage in unlawful imitations. This seems one good reason not to have public executions. But it does not argue against executions. Objections to displaying on television the process of violently subduing a resistant offender do not argue against actually engaging in the process.[8] Arguments against the public display of vivisections, or the painful medications, do not argue against either. Arguments against the public display of sexual activity do not argue against sexual activity. Arguments against public executions, then, do not argue against executions.[9] While the deterrent effect of punishments depends on their being known, the deterrent effect does not depend on punishments being carried out publicly. For example, the threat of imprisonment deters, but incarcerated persons are not on public display.

Abolitionists often maintain that most capital crimes are "acts of passion" that (1) could not be restrained by the threat of the death penalty, and (2) do not deserve it morally even if other crimes might. It is not clear to me why a crime motivated by, say, sexual passion, is morally less deserving of punishment than one motivated by passion for money. Is the sexual passion morally more respectable than others? More gripping? More popular? Generally, is violence in personal conflicts morally more excusable than violence among people who do not know each other? A precarious case might be made for such a view, but I shall not attempt to make it.

Perhaps it is true, however, that many murders are irrational "acts of passion" that cannot be deterred by the threat of the death penalty. Either for this reason or because "crimes of passion" are thought less blameworthy than other homicides, most "crimes of passion" are not punishable by death now.[10]

But if most murders are irrational acts, it would seem that the traditional threat of the death penalty has succeeded in deterring most rational people, or most people when rational, from committing the threatened act, and that the fear of the penalty continues to deter all but those who cannot be deterred by any penalty. Hardly a reason for abolishing the death penalty. Indeed, that capital crimes are committed mostly by irrational persons and only by some rational ones would suggest that more might commit these crimes if the penalty were lower. This hardly argues against capital punishment. Else, we would have to abolish penalties whenever they succeed in deterring people. Yet, abolitionists urge that capital punishment be abolished because capital crimes are often committed by the irrational—as though deterring the rational is not quite enough.

Finally, some observations on an anecdote reported by Boswell and repeated ad nauseam. Dr. Johnson found pickpockets active in a crowd assembled to see one of their number hanged. He concluded that executions do not deter. His conclusion does not follow from his observation.

1. Since the penalty Johnson witnessed was what pickpockets had expected all along, they had no reason to reduce their activities. Deterrence is expected to increase only when penalties do.
2. At most, a public execution could have had the deterrent effect Dr. Johnson expected because of its visibility. But it may have had a contrary effect: The spectacle of execution was probably more fascinating to the crowd than other spectacles; public executions thus might distract attention from the activities of pickpockets and thereby increase their opportunities more than other spectacles would. Hence, an execution crowd might have been more inviting to pickpockets than other crowds. (As mentioned before, deterrence depends on knowledge, but does not require visibility.)
3. Even when the penalty is greatly increased, let alone when it is unchanged, the deterrent effect of penalties is usually slight with respect to those already committed to criminal activities.[11] Deterrence is effective by restraining people as yet not committed to criminal occupation from entering it.

The risk of a penalty is the cost of crime offenders must expect. When this cost is high enough, relative to the expected benefit, it will deter a considerable number of people who would have entered an occupation—criminal or otherwise—had the cost been lower. In this respect, the effects of the costs of crime are not different from the effects of the cost of automobiles or movie tickets, or from the effects of the cost of any occupation relative to its benefits. When (comparative) net benefits decrease because of cost increases, the flow of new entrants does. But those already in the occupation usually continue.
4. Finally, Dr. Johnson did not actually address the question of the deterrent effect of execution in any respect whatever. To do so, he would have had to compare the number of pocket-picking episodes in the crowd assembled to witness the execution with the number of such episodes in a similar crowd assembled for some other purpose. He did not do so, probably because he thought that a deterrent effect occurs only if the crime is altogether eliminated. That is a common misunderstanding. Crime can only be reduced, not eliminated. However harsh the penalties, there are always nondeterrables. Thus, most people can be deterred, but never all.

One popular moral objection to capital punishment is that it gratifies the desire for revenge, regarded as unworthy. The Bible quotes the Lord declaring: "Vengeance is mine" (Romans 12:19). He thus legitimized vengeance and reserved it to Himself. However, the Bible also enjoins, "the murderer shall surely be put to death" (Numbers 35:16–18), recognizing that the death penalty can be warranted—whatever the motive. Religious tradition certainly suggests no less.[12]

The motives for the death penalty may indeed include vengeance. Vengeance as a compensatory and psychologically reparatory satisfaction for an injured party, group, or society, may be a legitimate human motive—despite the biblical injunction. I do not see wherein that motive is morally blameworthy. When regulated and directed by law, vengeance also is socially useful: Legal vengeance solidifies social solidarity against lawbreakers and is the alternative to the private revenge of those who feel harmed.

However, vengeance is irrelevant to the death penalty, which must be justified by its purpose, whatever the motive. An action, or rule, or penalty, is neither justified nor discredited by the motive for it. No rule should be discarded or regarded as morally wrong because of the motive of those who support it. Actions, or rules, or penalties, are justified by their intent and by their effectiveness in achieving it, not by the motives of supporters.[13] Capital punishment is warranted if it achieves its purpose: doing justice and deterring crime, regardless of whether it gratifies vengeful feelings.

We must examine now the specific characteristics of capital punishment before turning to its purely moral aspects. Capital punishment is feared above all punishments because (1) it is not merely irreversible as most other penalties are, but also irrevocable; (2) it hastens an event, which unlike pain, deprivation, or injury, is unique in every life and never has been reported on by anyone. Death is an experience that cannot actually be experienced and ends all experience.[14] Because it is as unknown as it is certain, death is universally feared. The fear of death is often attached to the penalty that hastens it—as though, without the penalty, death would not come. (3) When death is imposed as a deliberate punishment by one's fellow men, it signifies a complete severing of human solidarity. The convict is rejected by human society, found unworthy of sharing life with it. This total rejection exacerbates the natural separation anxiety and fear of annihilation. The marginal deterrent effect of executions depends on these characteristics, and the moral justification of the death penalty, above and beyond the deterrent effect, does no less.

Hitherto I have relied on logic and fact. Without relinquishing either, I must appeal to plausibility as well, as I turn to questions of morality unalloyed to other issues. For, whatever ancillary service facts and logic can render, what one is persuaded to accept as morally right or wrong ultimately depends on what seems to be plausible.

If there is nothing for the sake of which one may be put to death, can there be anything worth dying for? If there is nothing worth dying for, is there any moral value worth living for? Is a life that cannot be transcended by anything beyond itself more valu-

able than one that can be transcended? Is existence, life, itself a moral value never to be given up for the sake of anything? Does a value system in which any life, however it is lived, becomes the highest of goods, enhance the value of human life or cheapen it? I shall content myself here with raising the questions.[15]

"The life of each man should be sacred to each other man," the ancients tell us. They unflinchingly executed murderers.[16] They realized it is not enough to proclaim the sacredness and inviolability of human life. It must be secured as well, by threatening with the loss of their own life those who violate what has been proclaimed as inviolable—the right of innocents to live. Else, the inviolability of human life is neither credibly proclaimed nor actually protected. No society can profess that the lives of its members are secure if those who did not allow innocent others to continue living are themselves allowed to continue living—at the expense of the community. Does it not cheapen human life to punish the murderer by incarcerating him as one does a pickpocket? Murder differs in quality from other crimes and deserves, therefore, a punishment that differs in quality from other punishments.

If it were shown that no punishment is more deterrent than a trivial fine, capital punishment for murder would remain just, even if not useful. For murder is not a trifling offense. Punishment must be proportioned to the gravity of the crime, if only to denounce it and to vindicate the importance of the norm violated. Thus, all penal systems proportion punishments to crimes. The worse the crime the higher the penalty deserved. Why not the highest penalty—death—for the worst crime—wanton murder? Those rejecting the death penalty have the burden of showing that no crime deserves capital punishment[17]—a burden which they have not so far been willing to bear.

Abolitionists are wrong when they insist that we all have an equally inalienable right to live to our natural term—that if the victim deserved to live, so does the murderer. That takes egalitarianism too far for my taste: The crime sets victim and murderer apart; if the victim died, the murderer does not deserve to live. The thought that there are some who think that murderers have as much right to live as their victims oppresses me. So does the thought that a Stalin or a Hitler should have the right to go on living.

Never to execute a wrongdoer, regardless of how depraved his acts, is to proclaim that no act can be so irredeemably vicious as to deserve death—that no human being can be wicked enough to be deprived of life. Who actually believes that? I find it easier to believe that those who affect such a view do so because of a failure of nerve. They do not think themselves—and therefore anyone else—competent to decide questions of life and death. Aware of human frailty they shudder at the gravity of the decision and refuse to make it. The irrevocability of a verdict of death is contrary to the modern spirit that likes to pretend that nothing ever is definitive, that everything is open-ended, that doubts must always be entertained and revisions made. Such an attitude may be proper for inquiring philosophers and scientists. But not for courts. They can evade decisions on life and death only by giving up their paramount duties: to do justice, to secure the lives of the citizens, and to vindicate the norms society holds inviolable.

One may object that the death penalty either cannot actually achieve the vindication of violated norms, or is not needed for it. If so, failure to inflict death does not belittle the crime, nor imply that the life of the criminal is of greater importance than the moral value he violated, or the harm he did to his victim. But it is not so. In all societies, the degree of social disapproval of wicked acts is expressed in the degree of punishment threatened.[18] Thus, punishments both proclaim and enforce social values according to the importance given to them. There is no other way for society to affirm its value. To refuse to punish any crime with death, then, is to avow that the negative weight of a crime can never exceed the positive value of the life of the person who committed it. I find that proposition implausible.

---

1. Nor do I read the Constitution to command us to prefer equality to justice. Surely, "due process of law" is meant to do justice; and "the equal protection of the law" is meant to extend justice equally to all.
2. It seems odd that the courts, which have been willing to take a managerial role to remedy discrimination in schooling, should find no better remedy for discrimination or other errors in the distribution of penalties by the courts than to abolish the penalty distributed.
3. Ehrlich, "The Deterrent Effect of Capital Punishment: A Question of Life and Death," Amer. Econ. Rev. (June 1975). In the period studied, capital punishment was already infrequent and uncertain. Its deterrent effect might be greater when more frequently imposed for capital crimes, so that a prospective offender would feel more certain of it.
4. See *Journal of Legal Studies* (Jan. 1977); *Journal of Political Economy* (June 1977); and *American Economic Review* (June 1977).
5. I thought so even when I believed that the probability of deterrent effects might remain unknown. (See van den Haag, "On Deterrence and the Death Penalty," *J. Crim. I.C. & P.S.* (June 1969).) That probability is now more likely to become known and to be greater than was apparent a few years ago.
6. It would, however, isolate deterrent effects of the punishment from incapacitating ones, and also from the effect of Durkheimian "normative validation" where it does not depend on threats.
7. As indicated before, demonstrations are not available for the exact addition to deterrence of each added degree of severity in various circumstances, and with respect to various acts. We have so far coasted on a sea of plausible assumptions.
8. There is a good argument against unnecessary public displays of violence here. (See van den Haag, "What to Do About TV Violence," *The Alternative* (Aug./Sept. 1976).)
9. It may be noted that in Beccaria's time, executions were regarded as public entertainments. *Tempora mutantur, et nos mutamur in illis.*
10. I have reservations on both these counts, being convinced that many crimes among relatives and friends are as blameworthy and as deterrable as crimes among strangers. Thus, major heroin dealers in New York are threatened with life imprisonment. In the absence of the death penalty, they find it advantageous to have witnesses killed. Such murders surely are not acts of passion in the classical sense, although they occur among associates. They are in practice encouraged by the penal law.
11. The high degree of uncertainty and arbitrariness of penalization in Johnson's time may also have weakened deterrent effects. Witnessing an execution cannot correct this defect.
12. Since religion expects both justice and vengeance in the world to come, the faithful may dispense with either in this world, and with any particular penalties, although they seldom have. But a secular state must do justice here and now, it cannot assume that another power, elsewhere, will do justice where its courts did not.

     For that matter, Romans 12:19 barely precedes Romans 13:4, which tells us [the ruler] "beareth not the sword in vain for he is the minister of God, a revenger to execute wrath upon him that doeth evil." It is not unreasonable to interpret Romans 12:19 to mean that revenge is to be delegated by the injured to the authorities.
13. Different motives (the reasons why something is done) may generate the same action (what is done), purpose, or intent, just as the same motive may lead to different actions.
14. Actually, being dead is no different from not being born, a (non)experience we all had before being born. But death is not so perceived. The process of dying, a quite different matter, is confused with it. In turn, dying is feared mainly because death is anticipated, even though death is feared because it is confused with dying.
15. Insofar as these questions are psychological, empirical evidence would not be irrelevant. But it is likely to be evaluated in terms depending on moral views.
16. Not always. On the disastrous consequences of periodic failure to do so, Sir Henry Maine waxes with eloquent sorrow in his *Ancient Law* 408–9.
17. One may argue that some crimes deserve more than execution, and that on the above reasoning, torture may be justified. But penalties have already been reduced to a few kinds—fines, confinement, and execution—so the issue is academic. Unlike the death penalty, torture also have become repulsive to us. (Some reasons for this public revulsion are listed in Chapter X [of] van den Haag, *Punishing Criminals: Concerning a Very Old and Painful Question* (1975).)
18. Social approval is usually less unanimous, and the system of rewards reflects it less.

SHOULD WE EXECUTE THOSE WHO DESERVE TO DIE?*

Stephen Nathanson

Many people believe that murderers deserve to die and therefore that the state ought to execute them. I will call this reasoning the "argument from desert."

The argument from desert has very broad appeal, and death penalty opponents need to show that it is mistaken if their position is to be taken seriously. In order to show this, death penalty opponents must make a convincing case for the truth of at least one of the following statements:

1. People who commit murder do not deserve to die.
2. Even if people who commit murder deserve to die, it is wrong for the state to execute them.

If either one of these statements can be established, then the argument from desert fails.

I will try to show that both of these statements are true and therefore that the argument from desert does not provide a morally sound justification for the death penalty.

Giving People What They Deserve

In beginning our consideration of the argument from desert, let us assume that death penalty advocates are correct in asserting that murderers deserve to die. While it may appear that if we assume this, then the argument for the death penalty is unstoppable, this impression is mistaken. There is no inconsistency in conceding that murderers deserve to die and still opposing the death penalty. These two beliefs are consistent because there may be quite good reasons in particular cases why people should not get what they deserve. This is especially true when the body that is to give someone his just deserts is the government.

One reason for not giving a person what he deserves is that doing so conflicts with other obligations that one has. In chapter 2, I mentioned the brutalization hypothesis, according to which executions actually cause homicides. If this hypothesis is true, it provides the government with a powerful reason not to execute convicted murderers, even if they deserve to die. The reason is that the government's policy of giving murderers their just deserts would be carried out at the cost of having innocent people lose their lives. Faced with a choice between giving murderers what they deserve and protecting innocent lives, the government ought to choose protection of the innocent over execution of the guilty. It is more important to save innocent lives than to terminate guilty ones, and it is a more central function of government that it protect people's well-being than that it carry out the distribution of just deserts.

This example is somewhat hypothetical because the brutalization effect remains controversial and has not yet influenced governmental policy. In any case, there are many ways in which our legal system currently departs from a policy of giving people what they deserve. One such case is the prohibition of double jeopardy. Our system does not permit a person to be tried more than once for a particular crime. If he is tried and acquitted, that is the end of it.

Now imagine a case of a person who has been accused of murder. He is tried and acquitted, and as he leaves the courthouse, he tells reporters, "I did it, and I got away with it." If this person did commit the murder and if murderers deserve to die, then he deserves to die. Nonetheless, the government may not prosecute him again for this charge and may not punish him, even though, from a moral point of view, he deserves to die. In this case, the prohibition on double jeopardy outweighs whatever obligation there might be to give this person what he deserves.

Considering this situation, one could claim, of course, that it shows that the legal system is defective and that we ought to abolish the double jeopardy rule. There are good reasons, however, for retaining the prohibition of double jeopardy. It protects all citizens from continued threats and harassment by government officials. If we could always be brought back for retrial even though we had been acquitted of the crime in question, then we would be continually exposed to threats by unscrupulous officials. The double jeopardy rule provides a significant protection for all citizens, and it is wise to keep the rule, even if this means sometimes failing to give the guilty what they deserve.

If giving people what they deserve were the only function of the legal system, these problems would not arise. The design of our legal system incorporates other aims, however. We have already seen this in discussing the costs of capital punishment and the necessity for procedural safeguards surrounding its use. The effect of these multiple aims is that we must sometimes sacrifice the goal of giving people what they deserve in order to satisfy other goals of greater importance. So, even if one concedes that murderers deserve to die, one need not grant that the government ought to execute them. This is because executing them may conflict with other important goals or ideals.

Death penalty supporters might concede this point in principle but deny that any such conflicts arise with respect to the death penalty. The question we must answer, then, is whether there are significant legal or moral goals and ideals which conflict with the imposition of the death penalty.

Furman v. Georgia

The Eighth Amendment to the United States Constitution prohibits the use of cruel and unusual punishments, and in 1972, the Supreme Court decided that the death penalty, *as it was then administered*, was cruel and unusual.

While each justice wrote a separate opinion in *Furman v. Georgia,* the most significant argument that emerged against the death penalty was based on the view that the death penalty was imposed in an arbitrary manner. In a widely accepted analysis of the Court's action, Charles Black has written:

The decisive ground of the 1972 Furman case anti-capital punishment ruling—the ground persuasive to the marginal justices needed for a majority—was that, out of a large number of persons "eligible" in law for the punishment, a few were selected as if at random, by no stated (or perhaps statable) criteria, while all the rest suffered the lesser penalty of imprisonment.[1]

In focusing, then, on how the death penalty was administered, the Court was not concerned with whether the actual executions were performed in a cruel and unusual manner. Rather, the justices were concerned with the procedures under which death penalty sentences were being determined, and they judged the punishment to be unacceptable because life and death decisions were being made in an arbitrary way.

In understanding the Court's reasoning, it is important to recall that current laws do not embody the judgment that all people guilty of homicide deserve to die. Some killings are not even called "murder," but are classified as manslaughter, usually because there was no intention to kill. Even among murders, the laws of many states distinguish between first and second degrees of murder. Only those guilty of first degree murder are eligible for the death penalty, and even among these, judges or juries may decide that their crimes were not sufficiently terrible to merit death. The aim of this system of classifications is to select those killings which are the very worst and to impose the death penalty only in these cases. Underlying this system, then, is the judgment that only those guilty of the worst murders deserve to die. Some people who murder deserve a lesser punishment.

The Court's complaint with the administration of the death penalty was that this system of grading punishments according to the crime was not working. Decisions concerning executions were being made arbitrarily and not on the basis of facts about the crime. This was happening because the law contained no clear criteria that juries could apply when deciding which murderers ought to be executed and which ought to be imprisoned. In the absence of clear criteria, these judgments were determined by legally irrelevant factors.

In explaining their positions, different justices on the Court emphasized different forms of arbitrariness. Justice Stewart objected to the random aspects of the sentencing process, explaining his objection as follows:

> These death sentences are cruel and unusual in the same way that being struck by lightning is cruel and unusual. For of all the people convicted of rapes and murders in 1967 and 1968, *many just as reprehensible as these*, the petitioners are among *a capriciously selected random handful* upon whom the sentence has in fact been imposed.[2]

In other words, there was no reasonable basis for the execution of these people and the imprisonment of others. Many were equally reprehensible, and so it was "cruel and unusual" to single out only a few for the severest punishment.

Other justices stressed a fact that had long been emphasized by death penalty opponents, its discriminatory application. According to them, the application of the death penalty was arbitrary but not entirely random. Rather, racial bias created a situation in which blacks were more likely to be executed than whites. In fact, prejudice had a significant double effect on sentencing, since blacks who killed whites were among those most likely to be executed, while whites who killed blacks were the least likely to be sentenced to die.[3] Similarly, economic and social status influenced these judgments in illegitimate ways. These were the arbitrary features stressed by Justice Douglas. As he wrote,

> In a Nation committed to equal protection of the laws there is no permissible "caste" aspect of law enforcement. Yet we know that the discretion of judges and juries in imposing the death penalty enables the penalty to be selectively applied, feeding prejudices against the accused if he is poor and despised, and lacking political clout, or if he is a member of a suspect or unpopular minority, and saving those who by social position may be in a more protected position.[4]

Douglas argued, then, that the death penalty was cruel and unusual because it was applied to people (or not applied to them) for reasons that were legally irrelevant and impermissible. It would violate the Constitution to have a law that permitted the execution only of poor people or members of racial minorities. Since this was how the death penalty was operating in fact, its use under those conditions was unconstitutional.

The Moral Basis of the *Furman* Decision

In considering these issues, the Supreme Court was treating them as matters of constitutional law. The question facing the Court was whether the arbitrary imposition of the death penalty made it unconstitutional. Nonetheless, the issues involved in the *Furman* case are not solely matters of constitutional law. For opponents of the death penalty, the pattern of arbitrary and discriminatory sentencing is itself a deplorable moral injustice. Even if these practices were permissible under the Constitution, they would still be morally unjust.

I believe that this moral condemnation is appropriate and that the Court's reasoning has moral as well as legal force. The *Furman* argument illuminates the true but paradoxical judgment that it can be morally unjust to punish someone for a crime even if he morally deserves to be punished.

In order to see that it can actually be unjust to give someone what he deserves, imagine a group of fifty people, all of whom have committed dreadful murders. Suppose that each one's act is so horrible that we would have no trouble concluding that each one deserved to die. In spite of this, however, only those with red hair are sentenced to die, while all others are given lesser sentences. In this situation, the red-headed murderers would certainly feel that they were being treated unjustly, and I think that they would be correct.

Even if a person deserves to die, that is not enough to make his execution just. In addition, it is necessary that he be executed *because* he deserves to die. In the case I have described, we cannot explain why the red-headed murderers were sentenced to die by saying that they deserved it. This explanation is insufficient because others who were equally deserving were not sentenced to die. So, if we try to explain the decision to execute some but not others, the explanation would be that they were people with red hair who had committed heinous murders. Yet, it is surely unjust to execute someone *because* he is a red-headed murderer rather than a blond or black-haired murderer. This would be cruel and unusual in the sense stressed by Douglas, since it would involve basing the degree of punishment on features of a person which are irrelevant. It is especially unjust if the punishment is determined by features of a person over which he has little or no control.

Even if we grant, then, that only those who deserve to die are ever sentenced to die, we would be forced to see the death penalty as unjust if its actual imposition depended on such factors as race, economic status, ability to acquire adequate legal representation, or other facts which have nothing to do with a person's culpability. That is the underlying moral argument of the *Furman* decision, and it is a powerful, important moral argument, even apart from its constitutional significance.

Eliminating Arbitrariness

The problem of arbitrariness has been addressed by death penalty supporters in two ways. After the *Furman* decision, state legis~latures passed new laws that were designed to eliminate the influence of arbitrary features from death penalty impositions. Two strategies were pursued. In some states, the death penalty was made mandatory for certain types of crimes. Anyone convicted of them would be executed so that both randomness and discrimination could play no role. This strategy was rejected by the Supreme Court. In *Woodson v. North Carolina,* it ruled that mandatory death sentences were unconstitutional, since they failed to permit consideration of individual differences among defendants.[5]

The second legislative strategy was to leave room for judgment but to eliminate arbitrariness by providing specific guidelines for juries to follow in deciding on the appropriate sentence. This is the strategy of "guided discretion," under which the law leaves the final judgment to juries but specifies what kinds of reasons may be used in determining whether a particular murderer ought to be executed or imprisoned. Typically, these guidelines consist of lists of aggravating and mitigating circumstances, features of the crimes or persons that may make the crime worse or less bad. The new laws also included other procedural safeguards, such as automatic appeals or reviews of death sentences and separate sentencing hearings, which allow defendants to present additional factors on their behalf.

In its 1976 decision in *Gregg v. Georgia,* the Supreme Court ruled that statutes incorporating "guided discretion" and other safeguards were constitutional because they made arbitrariness sufficiently unlikely. In making this ruling, the Court did not reject the *Furman* argument that arbitrarily imposed executions are cruel and unusual. Rather, it claimed that arbitrariness had been sufficiently eliminated so as to guarantee fair proceedings and controlled, unbiased sentencing.

The Gregg decision has prompted death penalty opponents to argue that "guided discretion" is an illusion and that even under the new laws, sentences in capital cases continue to be arbitrary and discriminatory. I do not at this point want to consider the evidence for these claims. Instead, I simply want to point out that if these claims are correct, then the Court would be bound to return to its earlier judgment that the death penalty was unconstitutional. This is because the Court did not reject the argument that *if* the death penalty is arbitrarily administered, then it violates the Constitution. Instead, it decided that under the new laws, the death penalty would no longer be administered arbitrarily.

Against the Argument from Arbitrariness

Although death penalty supporters have tried to make death sentencing less arbitrary, some of them explicitly reject the use of the argument from arbitrariness as a criticism of the death penalty. While favoring fairer sentencing, they think that the Court was wrong to accept the argument from arbitrariness in the first place. They think that the death penalty can be just even if it is administered in an arbitrary and discriminatory way. For those who hold this position, evidence showing the continued influence of arbitrary and discriminatory factors would have no force because, in their view, it never was legally or morally relevant to the question of whether death is a just punishment.

This rejection of the argument from arbitrariness has been stated forcefully by Ernest van den Haag, a longtime defender of the death penalty. According to van den Haag,

> the abolitionist argument from capriciousness, or discretion, or discrimination, would be more persuasive if it were alleged that those selectively executed are not guilty. But the argument merely maintains that some other guilty but more favored persons, or groups, escape the death penalty. This is hardly sufficient for letting anyone else found guilty

escape the penalty. On the contrary, that some guilty persons or groups elude it argues for extending the death penalty to them.[6]

For van den Haag, the only injustice that occurs here is that some people who deserve death are not executed. In his opinion, however, the failure to execute these fortunate people does not show that it is unjust to execute others who are no more deserving of death but are simply less fortunate.

From van den Haag's point of view, the justice of punishments is entirely a matter of individual desert. As he writes:

> Justice requires punishing the guilty—as many of the guilty as possible, even if only some can be punished—and sparing the innocent—as many of the innocent as possible, even if not all are spared. It would surely be wrong to treat everybody with equal injustice in preference to meting out justice at least to some. . . . [If] the death penalty is morally just, *however discriminatorily applied to only some of the guilty*, it does remain just *in each case* in which it is applied.[7]

According to van den Haag, then, the justice of individual punishments depends on individual guilt alone and not on whether punishments are equally distributed among the class of guilty people.

Van den Haag's argument is important because it threatens to undermine the moral basis of the *Furman* decision. It dismisses as irrelevant the abolitionist argument that the death penalty is unjust because its use in the United States has been inextricably bound up with patterns of racial discrimination. Even if we find this history abhorrent, we may yet think that van den Haag's argument is plausible. Its plausibility derives from the fact that we believe that it is often legitimate to punish or reward people, even though we know that others who are equally deserving will not be punished or rewarded. Here are two cases where common sense appears to support van den Haag's view about the requirements of justice.

A. A driver is caught speeding, ticketed, and required to pay a fine. Although we know that the percentage of speeders who are actually punished is extremely small, we would probably regard it as a joke if the driver protested that he was being treated unjustly or if someone argued that no one

should be fined for speeding unless all speeders were fined.

B. A person performs a heroic act and receives a substantial reward, in addition to the respect and admiration of his fellow citizens. Because he deserves the reward, we think it just that he receive it, even though many equally heroic persons are not treated similarly. That most heroes are unsung is no reason to avoid rewarding this particular heroic individual.

Both of these cases appear to support van den Haag's view that we should do justice in individual cases whenever we can and that our failure to treat people as they deserve in all cases provides no reason to withhold deserved punishment or reward from particular individuals. If this is correct, then we must give up the argument from arbitrariness and accept van den Haag's view that "unequal justice is justice still."

Arbitrary Decisions About Who Deserves What

In order to evaluate this objection to the argument from arbitrariness, we need to look at the original argument more closely. What a closer look reveals is that there is in fact more than one problem of arbitrariness. Van den Haag fails to take note of this, and for this reason, his discussion leaves untouched many of the central issues raised by the argument.

We need to distinguish two different arguments, which I will call the argument from arbitrary judgment and the argument from arbitrary imposition. In making this distinction, I do not mean to contrast two stages in the actual legal process. Rather, the contrast is meant to help us focus on two different grounds for the claim that the death penalty is unjust because arbitrary.

Van den Haag assumes that judges and juries can and do make nonarbitrary judgments about what people deserve and that the problem of arbitrariness arises only in the imposition of punishments. For him, the arbitrariness arises when we try to determine who among those who deserve to die will actually be executed. This is what I want to call the argument from arbitrary imposition. It assumes that we know who deserves to die, and it objects to the fact that only some of those who deserve to die are executed. This version of the argument is expressed by Justice Stewart in the passage which I quoted earlier, and it is this argument which van den Haag addresses.

In doing so, however, he completely neglects the argument from arbitrary judgment. According to this argument, the determination of *who* deserves to die is itself arbitrary. It is not simply that arbitrary factors determine who among the deserving will be condemned to die. Rather, the problem is that the judgment concerning who deserves to die is itself a product of arbitrary factors. In other words, van den Haag assumes that we know who the deserving are, but this is just the assumption that the second form of the argument challenges.

Charles Black is clearly drawing our attention to the problem of arbitrary judgment when he writes that

> the official choices—by prosecutors, judges, juries, and governors—that divide those who are to die from those who are to live are on the whole not made, and cannot be made, under standards that are consistently meaningful and clear, but . . . they are often made, and in the foreseeable future will continue to be made, under no standards at all or under pseudo-standards without discoverable meaning.[8]

If Black is correct, judgments about who deserves a particular punishment are arbitrary because the law does not contain meaningful standards for distinguishing those who deserve death from those who deserve imprisonment. Given this lack of standards, factors that should have no influence will in fact be the primary bases of decision.

This important argument is completely neglected by van den Haag. In order to defend the death penalty against this criticism, he would have to show that our laws contain adequate criteria for deciding whether people deserve death or imprisonment and that judges and juries have made judgments of desert in a nonarbitrary way. Van den Haag makes no effort to do this. He simply assumes that the legal system does a good job of distinguishing those who deserve to die from those who do not. This, however, is just what the argument from arbitrary judgment challenges.

Van den Haag's assumption may gain plausibility from his tendency to oversimplify the kinds of judgments that need to be made. In contrast with Black, who stresses the complexity of the law of homicide and the many steps in the legal process leading toward punishment, van den Haag is content with the abstract maxim that "justice requires punishing the guilty . . . and sparing the innocent." This maxim makes it look as if officials and jurors are faced with the simple choice of dividing people into two neat categories, the guilty and the innocent. And if we think of these as *factual* rather than *legal* categories, it makes it look as if the only judgment that they must make is whether one person did or did not kill another.

In fact, of course, the judgments that must be made are much more complicated than this. To be guilty of a murder that merits the death penalty is not the same as having killed another person. While the basic factual judgment that one person has caused the death of another is itself not always easy to make, the legal judgments involved are more complex still. Of those who kill, some may have committed no crime at all if their action is judged to be justifiable homicide. For those guilty of some form of homicide, we need to decide how to classify their act within the degrees of homicide. What did the killer intend to do? Was he under duress? Was he provoked by the victim? Did he act with malice? Had the act been planned or was it spontaneous? These are among the factual issues that arise when juries try to determine the legal status of the action. Beyond these are legal questions. Was the act murder or manslaughter? And if it was murder, was it first or second degree murder? And if it was first degree murder, did any of the mitigating or aggravating circumstances characterize the act? These are the sorts of issues that actually confront prosecutors, juries, and judges, and they go well beyond the more familiar "whodunit" types of questions.[9]

If prosecutors, juries, and judges do not have clear criteria by which to sort out these issues or if the criteria can be neglected in practice, then judgments about who deserves to face death rather than imprisonment will be arbitrary. This would undermine van den Haag's optimistic assumption that it is only those who genuinely deserve execution who are sentenced to die.

In stressing the complexities of the judgments involved, I have tried to show why it is plausible to believe that the resulting judgments could well be influenced by arbitrary factors. Further, I assume that if we are not confident that the death penalty is imposed on those who truly deserve it, then we would reject the punishment as unjust. This is the moral force of the argument from arbitrary judgment. Even if those who deserve to die ought to be executed, we ought not to allow the state to execute them if the procedures adopted by the state are unlikely to separate the deserving from the undeserving in a rational and just manner. History supports the view that the death penalty has been imposed on those who are less favored for reasons which have nothing to do with their crimes. The judgment that they deserved to die has often been the result of prejudice, and their executions were unjust for this reason.[10]

Is the System Still Arbitrary?

One may wonder, however, whether this sort of arbitrary judgment is still occurring in the administration of the death penalty. Is there any evidence for the continued presence of this form of arbitrariness? Didn't the Supreme Court's Gregg decision show that this sort of arbitrariness is no longer a problem?

To decide whether the problem of arbitrariness remains, one could either examine the new laws themselves to see whether the criteria for selecting those who deserve death are clear and adequate, or one could study the actual legal process and its results to see what factors play a role in leading to actual sentences. Both types of investigations have been carried out, and the case for continuing arbitrariness and discrimination is quite strong. Since my primary purpose here is to show that the existence of arbitrariness is morally relevant to our assessment of the death penalty, I will mention only a few points that indicate that the system remains flawed by arbitrariness. Others have made the case for the persistence of arbitrariness with force and in great detail.[11]

In his book *Capital Punishment: The Inevitability of Caprice and Mistake,* Charles Black shows how unclear are the lists of mitigating and aggravating circumstances which are supposed to guide juries in their sentencing decisions. His purely legal analysis is strongly supported by evidence about the actual workings of the system. In a study of sentencing under the new post-*Furman* laws, William Bowers and Glen Pierce found strong evidence of continued and systematic racial discrimination in the process leading to a sentence of death. I will mention just a few items from their study.

Under the new laws, as they were applied between 1972 and 1977, the highest probability of a death sentence was found to occur in those cases where the killer was black and the victim white. The lowest probability of execution was found where the victim was black and the killer white. This same pattern emerged in a study by William Bowers and Glen Pierce of sentencing in Florida, Georgia, Texas, and Ohio. In Ohio and Florida during this period, there were 127 cases of whites killing blacks, and not one of these murderers was sentenced to death. At the same time, blacks who killed whites in these states had about a 25 percent chance of receiving a death sentence.[12]

The following chart, taken from the Bowers and Pierce study, shows the relationship between the races of victims and killers and the probability of a death sentence as this was exhibited in Ohio between 1974 and 1977.

Racial Grouping	Total	Death Sentences	Death Sentence Probability
Black kills white	173	44	.254
White kills white	803	37	.046
Black kills black	1170	20	.017
White kills black	47	0	.000

These findings strongly suggest that judgments about the seriousness of crimes and the amount of blameworthiness attaching to criminals are strongly influenced by deep-seated racial prejudices. It appears that judges and juries regard the killing of a white by a black as a more serious crime than the killing of a black by a white. Thus, they judge that blacks killing whites deserve more severe punishments than whites killing blacks. Given the bluntness of our ordinary moral judgments and the deep roots of racial prejudice in our society, it is perhaps not surprising that these results occur. But it is clear that no law which embodied these criteria, grading crimes by the race of victims and offenders, would be constitutional. Yet the administration of our laws reveals the de facto operation of just these discriminatory criteria.

Whatever role the criteria for assessing murders play, they do not effectively prevent the operation of discriminatory influences, and so they fail to eliminate the arbitrariness which the *Furman* ruling condemned. Rather than genuinely guiding judgments, the lists of mitigating and aggravating circumstances seem only to provide the language by which juries can justify judgments made on other grounds. This view is further supported by other data in the Bowers and Pierce study. If one compares the Florida and Georgia death penalty statutes, the following difference emerges. In Georgia, the law lists ten aggravating circumstances. If a jury finds one of these circumstances characterizing a particular murder, it can recommend death, and the judge *must* accept their recommendation. In Florida, eight aggravating circumstances are listed, and the jury must determine that aggravating circumstances outweigh mitigating ones. On this basis, they can recommend death, but the judge need not accept their judgment.

As a result of these differences, Florida juries must find more aggravating circumstances to support a recommendation of death than do Georgia juries. It is plausible to suppose that murders in Florida and Georgia do not themselves differ in systematic ways. If jury judgments about aggravating circumstances differ systematically, that would suggest that judgments about whether the defendant ought to be executed are made independently of the criteria and then fitted to the criteria in order to provide a legal rationalization for the decision. In particular, while it is implausible to suppose that murders committed in Florida are objectively worse than those committed in Georgia, we might expect to find that juries discover more aggravating circumstances in Florida so as to justify their independent conviction that a particular individual deserves to die.

This is just what Bowers and Pierce found. While juries in Georgia found 46 percent of the murders they considered to be especially vile or heinous, Florida juries found these features in 89 percent of the murders they judged. Likewise, while Georgia juries found the factor of "risk to others" in only 1 percent of the cases facing them, Florida juries found that 28 percent of their murders involved a risk to the lives of others beyond the victim. Similar results are found in all but one of the categories compared, further confirming the judgment that "guided discretion" remains a rather unguided and arbitrary process. The criteria function more as rationalizations of sentencing decisions than as determinants of them.

Finally, while there are many stages in the legal process leading to an execution, the Supreme Court's decision in Gregg focused only on the question of whether juries were provided with adequate guidelines in capital cases. It is important to recall, however, that important decisions are made by prosecutors, judges, governors, and clemency boards as well. The case of prosecutors is especially important and instructive. Prosecutors must decide what charges to file, whether to try to convict a person of manslaughter or murder and whether to press for the death penalty. In making these decisions, they often consider how good a chance they have of winning a case. This does not seem unreasonable, but it is easy to see how this could perpetuate and play upon racial and other prejudices. The black defendant or killer of a white victim may be more likely to be charged with first degree murder in the first place because the prosecutor expects to find a jury that is less sympathetic to these defendants.[13] In many cases, those who are already disadvantaged in society have a greater chance of being charged with more serious crimes, while others more fortunate never face a life or death judgment from a jury because their killing has been classified as manslaughter by the prosecutor. The process is unjustly discriminatory and is arbitrary as well because the judgment is not based on a notion of what the defendant deserves. It is based on a calculation of success or failure in court, which is itself influenced by factors which ought to play no role in the legal process.

Conclusions

In this chapter, we have seen that the system of capital punishment does not operate so as to execute people only on the basis of what they deserve. Other arbitrary factors play a significant role in determining who is to die for killing another human being. In *Furman v. Georgia,* the Supreme Court recognized that an injustice could occur even in cases where a person who is condemned to die actually deserves that punishment. I have tried to explain the moral basis for considering this an injustice.

I have also considered the objection that arbitrariness is irrelevant because justice requires only that those who are punished deserve it. How others are treated is irrelevant. In replying to this objection, I noted the importance of distinguishing two forms of the argument from arbitrariness—the argument from arbitrary judgment and the argument from arbitrary imposition. What I have tried to show is that van den Haag neglects the argument from arbitrary judgment and assumes that all those who are sentenced to die deserve this treatment. This optimistic assumption is unfounded, however, and I have cited some of the evidence that death sentences remain arbitrary and discriminatory in spite of the guided discretion system which the Supreme Court approved in *Gregg v. Georgia* and has upheld in subsequent decisions.

I should note that although much of the arbitrariness I have discussed arises from patterns of racial prejudice in the United States, this argument is not only relevant to the death penalty in our society. There is nothing unique about the situation in which societies contain both favored and unfavored groups. The groups may be identified by race, religion, class, political orientation, or other features. Wherever these divisions exist, arbitrariness and discrimination will be obstacles to the just administration of the law.

---

1. *Capital Punishment: The Inevitability of Caprice and Mistake*, 2d ed. (New York: Norton, 1981), 20.
2. From *Furman v. Georgia*, 408 U.S. 239 (1972); reprinted in H. Bedau, *The Death Penalty in America*, 3d ed. (New York: Oxford University Press, 1982), 263–64; emphasis added.
3. For extensive evidence of racial discrimination in the imposition of the death penalty, see W. Bowers, *Legal Homicide* (Boston: Northeastern University Press, 1984), chs. 3 and 7.
4. Reprinted in Bedau, 3d ed., 255.
5. 428 U.S. 280–324 (1976); excerpted in Bedau, 3d ed., 288–293.
6. "The Collapse of the Case Against Capital Punishment," *National Review*, March 31, 1978, 397. A briefer version of this paper appeared in the *Criminal Law Bulletin* 14 (1978): 51–68 and is reprinted in Bedau, 3d ed., 323–33.
7. *Ibid.*, emphasis added.
8. Black, 29.
9. For an interesting account of a case in which classification problems emerge quite vividly, see Steven Phillips, *No Heroes, No Villains* (New York: Random House, 1977).
10. For historical material about the United States, see William Bowers, *Legal Homicide*, part I.
11. For this evidence, see Charles Black, *Capital Punishment,* passim; William Bowers and Glen Pierce, "Racial Discrimination and Criminal Homicide under Post-*Furman* Statutes," in W. Bowers, *Legal Homicide*, ch. 7, and reprinted in Bedau, 3d ed., 206–23; Ursula Bentele, "The Death Penalty in Georgia: Still Arbitrary," *Washington University Law Quarterly* 62 (1985): 573–646; and Samuel Gross and Robert Mauro, "Patterns of Death: An Analysis of Racial Disparities in Capital Sentencing and Homicide Victimization," *Stanford Law Review* 37 (1984): 27–153.
12. For a chart showing these figures in full, see Bowers, 225; reprinted in Bedau, 3d ed., 213.
13. On this point, see Bentele, 615.